# BRIEF CONTENTS

# CONTENTS

## PART I POLITICS

*The study of politics is the study of influence and the influential. . . .
The influential are those who get the most of what there is to get.
Those who get the most are elite; the rest are mass.*

Harold Lasswell

### 1 POLITICS: WHO GETS WHAT, WHEN, AND HOW 1

### 2 POLITICAL CULTURE: IDEAS IN CONFLICT 27

# PART II CONSTITUTION

*The ascendancy of any elite depends upon the success of the practices it adopts. . . . The Constitution, written and unwritten, embodies the practices which are deemed most fundamental to the governmental and social order.*

Harold Lasswell

## 3 THE CONSTITUTION: LIMITING GOVERNMENTAL POWER 61

## 4 FEDERALISM: DIVIDING GOVERNMENTAL POWER 97

# PART III    PARTICIPANTS

*People strive for power—to get the most of what there is to get.*
Harold Lasswell

## 9 INTEREST GROUPS: GETTING THEIR SHARE AND MORE  287

## PART IV    INSTITUTIONS

*Authority is the expected and legitimate possession of power.*
Harold Lasswell

## 10 CONGRESS: POLITICS ON CAPITOL HILL  327

# Part V  Outcomes

*That political science concentrates upon the influential does not imply the
neglect of the total distribution of values throughout the community. . . .
The emphasis upon the probability that the few (elite) will get the most does not
imply that the many (mass) do not profit from some political changes.*

Harold Lasswell

## 14  POLITICS AND PERSONAL LIBERTY  515

## 15  POLITICS AND CIVIL RIGHTS  555

## APPENDIX 698

# PREFACE

## PERSPECTIVE

This second edition of *Politics in America,* although much changed in appearance and substantially revised to reflect the current political landscape, retains the organization and perspective of the first edition. It is about "who gets what, when, and how." It relies on Harold Lasswell's classic definition of politics to present a clear, concise, and stimulating introduction to the American political system.

The *who* are the participants in politics: voters, interest groups, parties, television and the press, corporations and labor unions, lawyers and lobbyists, foundations and think tanks, and elected and appointed government officials, including members of Congress, the president, judges, and bureaucrats. The *what* of politics are public policies: the decisions that governments make concerning social welfare, health care, national defense, law enforcement, the environment, and thousands of other issues that come before them. The *when* and *how* are the political process: campaigns and elections, political news reporting, television debates, fund raising, lobbying and logrolling in Congress, policy making in the White House and executive agencies, and decision making in the courts.

Politics is an activity by which people try to get more of whatever there is to get. It is the struggle over the allocation of values in society. There would be no politics if everyone agreed on who should govern, who should get what, what government should do, and who should pay for it. But conflicts arise from disagreement over these questions. Politics consists of all of the activities—reasonable discussion, impassioned oratory, campaigning, balloting, fund raising, advertising, lobbying, demonstrating, rioting, street fighting, and waging war—by which conflict is carried on. Managing conflict is the principle function of the political system.

Power is the goal of political activity—power to decide who gets what, when, and how. Power is an instrumental value. It allows its holders to decide about the distribution of other values, such as wealth, celebrity, respect, deference, safety, and well-being. But it is also an end value itself; to many, power is its own reward.

*Politics in America,* Second Edition, introduces students to the American political system by examining the struggle for power—the participants, the stakes, the processes, and the institutional arenas.

## ORGANIZATION

**Part I, "Politics,"** begins with Laswell's classic definition of politics and proceeds to describe the nature and functions of government and the meaning of democracy. It poses the question: How democratic is the American political system? It describes the American political culture: its contradictions between liberty and conformity, political equality and economic inequality, equality of opportunity and equality of results, cherished beliefs and actual conditions. It examines cultural conflict, immigration, and social mobility. It describes ideological conflict in American politics, laying the groundwork for understanding the struggle over who gets what.

**Part II, "Constitution,"** describes the politics of constitution making—deciding how to decide. It describes how the struggle over the U.S. Constitution reflected the distribution of power in the new nation. It focuses on the classic arguments of the Founders for limiting and dividing governmental power ("Ambition must be made to counteract ambition") and the structural arrangements designed to accomplish this end. It describes the accumulation of power in Washington over two centuries and the efforts to "devolve" power to the states.

**Part III, "Participants,"** begins by examining individual participation in politics—the way people acquire and hold political opinions and act on them through voting and protest activity. It examines the influences of family, school, gender, and race in shaping political opinion. It describes the power of the mass media, particularly television, in setting the agenda for politics and policy making. It describes how organization concentrates power—to win public office in the case of party organizations, and to influence policy in the case of interest groups. It assesses the role of personal ambition in politics: in the decision to run for office, in the organization and conduct of political campaigns, and in the retention of office. And it focuses on the role of money in politics.

**Part IV, "Institutions,"** describes the various governmental arenas in which the struggle for power takes place—the Congress, the presidency, the bureaucracy, the courts. More important, it evaluates the power that comes with control of each of these institutions.

**Part V, "Outcomes,"** deals with public policies—the result of the struggle over the allocation of values. It is especially concerned with the two fundamental values of American society—liberty and equality. Each is examined in separate chapters, as are economic policies, welfare policies, and national security policies.

## INSTRUCTIONAL FEATURES

*Politics in America,* Second Edition, is written to be lively and absorbing, reflecting the teaching philosophy that stimulating students' interest in politics and public affairs is the most important goal of an introductory course. The struggle for power in society is not a dull topic, and textbooks should not make it so.

Each chapter opens with a brief poll, called "Ask Yourself About Politics," that alerts students to the crucial issues the chapter covers and the impact of those issues on their lives. The body of each chapter is divided into *text* and *features*. The text provides the framework for understanding American politics. In each chapter it begins with a brief discussion of power in relation to the subject matter of the chapter; for example: limiting governmental power (Chapter 3, "The Constitution"), dividing governmental power (Chapter 4, "Federalism"), the power of the media (Chapter 6, "Mass Media"), the power of organizations (Chapter 7, "Political Parties"), the power of Congress (Chapter 10, "Congress"), presidential power (Chapter 11, "The President"), bureaucratic power (Chapter 12, "The Bureaucracy"), judicial power (Chapter 13, "Courts"), power and individual liberty (Chapter 14, "Politics and Personal Liberty"), and power among nations (Chapter 18, "Politics and National Security"). It then proceeds to discuss the central participants, institutions, and outcomes in the American political system. It concludes with a concise summary and suggestions for further reading. A *running glossary* in the margin helps students master important concepts.

The *features* in each chapter parallel the text material and provide timeliness, relevance, stimulation, and perspective. They are designed to capture student interest and attention.

- **"What Do You Think?"** These features pose controversial questions to students and provide national opinion survey data on them. They cover a wide range of interests. Examples include: "Can You Trust the Government?" "Is Government Run by a Few Big Interests Looking Out for Themselves?" "Are You a Liberal or a Conservative?" "Should We Amend the Constitution to Balance the Budget?" "What Forms of Protest Are Acceptable?" "Should the Media Report on the Private Lives of Public Officials?" "Should We Mix Politics and Religion?" "Term Limits for Elected Officials?" "How Would You Rate the President?" "Do Bureaucrats in Washington Have Too Much Power?" "What Constitutes Sexual Harassment?" "Are the Police and Courts Tough Enough?" "Should We Enact a Flat Tax?"

- **"A Conflicting View"** These features challenge students to rethink conventional notions about American politics. They are designed to be controversial. "Politics as Violence," for example, briefly summarizes the view that much of American political development has been accompanied by violence. Other "Conflicting View" features include: "An Economic Interpretation of the Constitution," "Objections to the Constitution by an Anti-Federalist," "The Dark Side of Federalism," "Muzzle the Media and Win the War," "Trash the Two-Party System," "The War on Drugs as a Threat to Liberty," "Bureaucratic Rules Are Suffocating America," "Government Programs as a Cause of Poverty," and "Legalize Drugs to Reduce Crime."

- **"Compared to What?"** These features provide some perspective on the United States by comparing it with other nations; for example, "Freedom and Democracy in the World" and "Authoritarianism and Totalitarianism." Others compare nations on such characteristics as political culture, written constitutions, federal unions, voter turnout, television culture, political parties, women in power, the size of government, crime and punishment, tax burdens, and health care.

- **"People in Politics"** These features are designed to personalize politics for students, to convince them that the participants in the struggle for power are real people. They discuss where prominent people in politics went to school, how they got started in politics, how their careers developed, and how much power they came to possess. Some of these features focus on important historical figures; for example Thomas Hobbes, John Locke, James Madison, George Washington, and Martin Luther King, Jr. Others focus on contemporary political figures; for example, Bill Clinton, Bob Dole, Newt Gingrich, Sonny Bono, Larry King, Rush Limbaugh, Ron Brown, Ross Perot, Ralph Nader, Henry Cisneros, Sandra Day O'Connor, Hillary Rodham Clinton, Christine Todd Whitman, Carol Moseley Braun, and Colin Powell. Some of these features deliberately focus on people whose political influence is significant, yet less visible; for example, William Rehnquist, P. J. O'Rourke, Alan Greenspan, and Marian Wright Edelman.

- **"Up Close"** These features illustrate the struggle over who gets what. They range over a wide variety of current political conflicts, such as: "Ideology on Campus: Students versus Professors," "Think Tanks: The Battle of Ideas," "ERA—Three States Short," "Abortion: The Hot-Button Issue," "Television: The Dominant Medium," "The Hollywood Liberals," "Popular Images of the Democratic and Republican Parties," "EMILY's List," "Dirty Politics," "AARP—The Nation's Most Powerful Interest Group," "The Christian Coalition: Organizing the Faithful," "The Keating Five: Service to Constituents for a Price," "Iran-Contra and the White House Staff," "Al Gore, Reinventing Government," "The Confirmation of Clarence Thomas," "Privacy, Abortion, and the Constitution," "Black and White Opinion on Affirmative Action," "Entitlements Drive Government Spending," "Homelessness in America," and "The Use of Force: Operation Desert Storm."

- **"Across the USA"** These features provide maps that summarize important statistical and demographic information relevant to American politics.

*Politics in America,* Second Edition, is designed for courses that reserve classroom time to discuss politics—to spark interest in public affairs, to argue and debate issues, to take exception to public opinion or to the conflicting views set forth in the features. Students can be asked to come to class prepared to set forth their own views about the features. Classroom time can be used to ensure student understanding of text material and, perhaps more important, to stimulate student interest in politics and public affairs.

## UP-TO-DATE ELECTION COVERAGE

*Politics in America,* Second Edition, focuses attention on the 1996 presidential election. It sets the scene by reporting on the surprising Republican victory in the 1994 congressional election, the battles over the "Contract with America," and the struggles between Congress and the president over the budget. It describes the political milieu—the nation's distrust of government and cynicism toward politics, the disaffection toward parties, the influence of Christian conservatives, the role of organized interest groups, the chase for money, and the appeal of independents and Washington "outsiders." It tracks opinion polls during the campaign, assesses the strategies of the Clinton and Dole campaigns, and analyzes the election outcome. Special attention is given to the media-centered nature of the campaign, including the influence of TV talk shows, talk radio, "horse-race" news coverage, negative advertising, "dirty politics," and the all-important presidential debates.

## BIAS

*Politics in America,* Second Edition, strives for a balanced presentation, but "balanced" does not mean dull. It does *not* mean the avoidance of controversy; it does *not* mean that every sentence is laden with modifying clauses and softening adjectives, or that every paragraph is laced with tedious platitudes. Liberal and conservative arguments are set forth clearly and forcefully. Race and gender are given particular attention, not because it is currently fashionable to do so, but because American politics has long been driven by these factors. Features on controversial topics—for example, violence, civil disobedience, free speech, abortion, the confirmation of Clarence Thomas, the right to bear arms, affirmative action, spending and deficits, poverty and homelessness, the use of military force—are designed to stimulate argument, not to soothe feelings. All political institutions come under very critical scrutiny—the mass media, political parties, interest groups, Congress, the presidency, the bureaucracy, and the courts. And government policies—on civil liberty and civil rights issues, on the economy and social welfare, and on international affairs—are subject to critical review. Indeed, if there is a bias in *Politics in America,* Second Edition, it is against the uncritical acceptance of prevailing political culture and the unthinking approval of institutional power.

## SUPPLEMENTS AVAILABLE FOR THE INSTRUCTOR

- **Instructor's Manual** (0-13-258310-0) For each chapter, a summary, review of concepts, lecture suggestions and topic outlines, and additional resource materials—including a guide to media resources—are provided.

- **Strategies for Teaching American Government: A Guide for the New Instructor** (0-13-339003-9) This unique guide offers a wealth of practical advice and information to help new instructors face the challenges of teaching American government. It addresses a wide range of issues, including setting course goals, conducting the class, constructing and evaluating tests or written assignments, and advising students.

- **Test Item File** (0-13-258351-8) Thoroughly reviewed and revised to ensure the highest level of quality and accuracy, this file offers over 1800 questions in multiple choice, true/false, and essay format with page references to the text.

- **Prentice Hall Custom Test** A computerized test bank contains the items from the Test Item File. The program allows full editing of questions and the addition of instructor-generated items. Other special features include random generation, scrambling question order, and test preview before printing. Available in DOS and Macintosh versions.

- **Telephone Test Preparation Service** With one call to our toll-free 800 number, you can have Prentice Hall prepare tests with up to 200 questions chosen from the Test Item File, on bond paper or ditto master. Within 48 hours of your request, you will receive a personalized exam with answer key.

- **American Government Transparencies, Series III and Series IV** These sets of 75 to 100 four-color transparency acetates reproduce illustrations, charts, and maps from the text as well as from additional sources.

- **Instructor's Guide to American Government Transparencies, Series III and IV** This brief guide provides descriptions, teaching suggestions, and discussion questions for each transparency. There is a separate guide for each set of transparencies.

-  **ABC News/Prentice Hall Video Library** Images in American Government (0-13-364498-7); Issues in American Government (0-13-304023-2); Election '96 (0-13-258393-3). Prentice Hall and ABC News bring this innovative video collection to your American government classroom. This video library brings chapter concepts to life by illustrating them with newsworthy topics and pressing issues. The library consists of feature segments from such award-winning programs as *Nightline, 20/20, World News Tonight/The American Agenda,* and *This Week with David Brinkley.*

- **Instructor's Guide to ABC News/Prentice Hall Video Library** (0-13-364696-3) Available for use with the ABC News/Prentice Hall Video Library, this guide provides a brief synopsis and discussion questions for each segment in the library.

- **Prentice Hall Laserdisk** Images in American Government (0-13-075565-6) The story of American government is vividly illustrated with this exciting technology. This disk contains approximately 200 still images and over one hour of moving images to support the concepts in the text. Accompanying manuals are provided.

## SUPPLEMENTS AVAILABLE FOR THE STUDENT

- **Study Guide** (0-13-258369-0) Includes chapter outlines, study notes, a glossary, and practice tests designed to reinforce information in the text and help students develop a greater understanding of American government and politics.

- **A Guide to Civic Literacy** (0-13-304015-1) Written by James Chesney and Otto Feinstein, both at Wayne State University, this brief booklet provides ideas and suggestions for students to get involved in politics. It includes nine political activities on topics such as agenda building, coalition building, registering, educating and mobilizing voters, and increasing accountability.

- **Prentice Hall Critical Thinking Audio Cassette** (0-13-678335-X) A 60-minute cassette teaches students how to develop their critical thinking and study skills. The first 50 minutes concentrate on critical thinking skills, specifically on how to ask the right questions. The final 10 minutes offer helpful tips on how to study, take notes, and be a more active, effective learner.

-  **The New York Times/ Prentice Hall** *Themes of the Times* Prentice Hall joins forces with the premier news publication, *The New York Times,* to provide a student newspaper supplement containing recent articles pertinent to American government. These articles augment the text material and provide real-world examples. Updated twice a year.

- **American Government Simulation Games, Series III** 3.5" DOS (0-13-566282-6); Windows (0-13-566308-3); Macintosh (0-13-566332-6). Seven simulations engage students in various role-playing situations: Bill of Rights; House of Representatives; Presidential Budget; Secretary of State; Supreme Court; Washington Ethics; and Crime and Social Policy. Developed by G. David Garson, North Carolina State University.

- **Multimedia Guide to American Government** Windows (0-13-340456-0). This unique student resource provides text, video, simulations, quizzes, timelines, and study guide tools in CD-ROM format to engage students in the study of government and politics. Developed by G. David Garson, North Carolina State University.

- **Web Site** Students and professors can now take full advantage of the World Wide Web to enrich the study of American Government through the *Politics in America* Web site. This resource correlates the text with material available on the Internet. Featured on the Web site are chapter objectives, study questions, and news updates, as well as links to information from other sites on the Web that reinforce the content of each chapter. Address: http://www.prenhall.com/dye

- **Political Science on the Internet** (0-13-266594-8) This brief guide introduces students to the origin and innovations behind the Internet and provides clear strategies for navigating the complexity of the Internet and World Wide Web. Exercises within and at the end of the chapters allow students to practice searching for the myriad of resources available to the student of political science. This 48-page supplementary book is free to students when purchased as a package with *Politics in America,* Second Edition.

# ACKNOWLEDGMENTS

*Politics in America,* Second Edition, reflects the influence of many splendid teachers, students, and colleagues who have helped me over the years. I am grateful for the early guidance of Frank Sorauf, my undergraduate student adviser at Pennsylvania State College, and James G. Coke, my Ph.D. dissertation director at the University of Pennsylvania. Georgia Parthenos at the University of Georgia and Malcolm Parsons at Florida State University gave me my first teaching posts. But my students over the years contributed most to my education—notably Susan MacManus, Kent Penney, Ed Benton, James Ammons, and especially John Robey. Several of my colleagues gave advice on various parts of this book: Glen Parker (on Congress), Suzanne Parker (on public opinion), James Gwartney (on economics), Robert Lichter (on the mass media), Charles Barrioux (on Bureaucracy), and especially Harmon Zeigler, whose knowledge of politics is unbounded.

At Florida State University, I am indebted to the timely research assistance provided by R. Thomas Dye, Ph.D. candidate in History, and Christopher Stream, Ph.D. candidate in Public Administration. And I am deeply grateful to Harriet Crawford of the Policy Sciences Center, who turned my scratchings into a manuscript.

At Prentice Hall I am indebted to Mike Bickerstaff, Nancy Roberts, and Charlyce Jones Owen for their confidence in the project, and to Theresa Cooksey for her inspiration. Jean Smith of Jean Smith Associates and David Chodoff at Prentice Hall provided invaluable editorial guidance, and Serena Hoffman guided the book smoothly through production with professional competence.

Finally, I would like to thank the many reviewers who evaluated the text and contributed invaluable advice:

Danny Adkinson, *Oklahoma State University*
Weston Agor, *University of Texas at El Paso*
Angela Burger, *UWC-Marathon Company*
Frank Colon, *Lehigh University*
Roy Dawes, *University of Southwestern Louisiana*
John Ellis, *San Antonio College*
Larry Elowitz, *University of Southwestern Louisiana*
Edward Fox, *Eastern Washington University*
Marilyn A. W. Garr, *Johnson County Community College*
Henry Glick, *Florida State University*
John Green, *University of Akron*
Dale Herspring, *Kansas State University*

Fred Kramer, *University of Massachusetts at Amherst*
Dale Krane, *University of Nebraska at Omaha*
Nancy McGlen, *Niagara University*
John McGlennon, *College of William and Mary*
James Meader, *Augustana College*
Jo Anne Myers, *Marist College*
Max Neiman, *University of California-Riverside*
Christopher Petras, *Central Michigan University*
Bruce Rogers, *American River College*
Bill Rutherford, *Odessa University*
John Shea, *West Chester University*
Robert Small, *Massosoit County College*
Henry Steck, *SUNY-Cortland*
Gerald Strom, *University of Illinois at Chicago*
Morris M. Wilhelm, *Indiana University Southeast*
Al Waite, *Central Texas College*

# ABOUT THE AUTHOR

Thomas R. Dye is McKenzie Professor of Government and Policy Sciences at Florida State University. He regularly teaches a large introductory class in American politics and was University Teacher of the Year in 1987. He received his B.A. and M.A. degrees from Pennsylvania State University and his Ph.D. degree from the University of Pennsylvania. He is the author of numerous books and articles in American government and public policy, including *The Irony of Democracy, Politics in States and Communities, Understanding Public Policy, Who's Running America, American Politics in the Media Age, Power in Society, Politics, Economics, and the Public,* and *American Federalism: Competition Among Governments.* His books have been translated into many languages, including Russian and Chinese, and published abroad. He has served as president of the Southern Political Science Association, president of the Policy Studies Organization, and secretary of the American Political Science Association. He has taught at the University of Pennsylvania, the University of Wisconsin, and the University of Georgia, and served as a visiting scholar at Bar-Ilan University, Israel, the Brookings Institution, Washington, and elsewhere. He is a member of Phi Beta Kappa, Omicron Delta Kappa, and Phi Kappa Phi, and is listed in most major biographical directories.

*Florida State University Teacher of the Year, 1987*

chapter

1

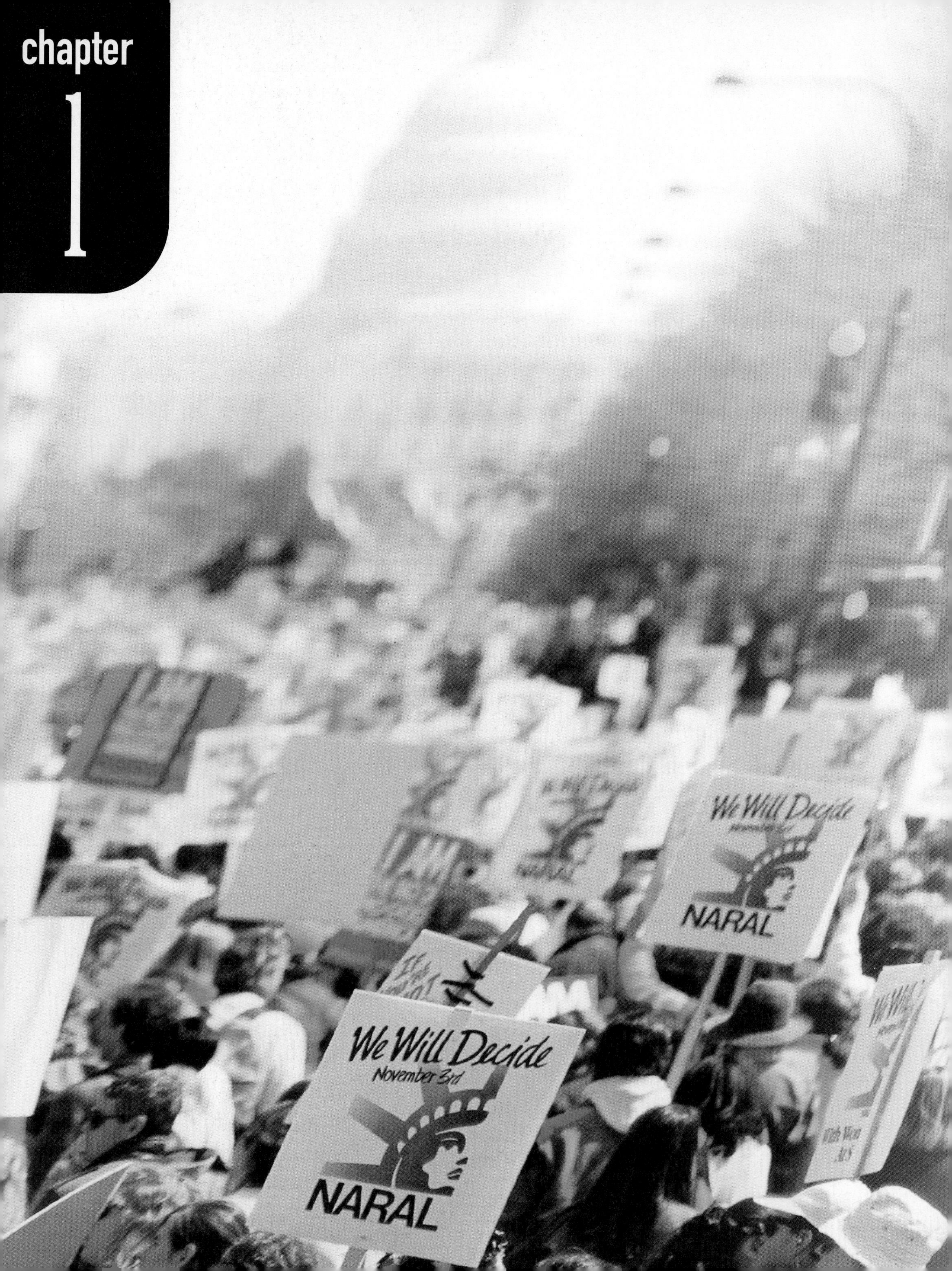

# POLITICS
# WHO GETS WHAT, WHEN, AND HOW

## ASK YOURSELF ABOUT POLITICS

**1** Can you trust the government to do what is right most of the time?
Yes ☐   No ☐

**2** Should any group other than the government have the right to use force?
Yes ☐   No ☐

**3** Is it ever right to disobey the law?
Yes ☐   No ☐

**4** Should important decisions in a democracy be submitted to voters rather than decided by Congress?
Yes ☐   No ☐

**5** Has government in the United States grown too big?
Yes ☐   No ☐

**6** In a democracy should "majority rule" be able to limit the rights of members of an unpopular or dangerous minority?
Yes ☐   No ☐

**7** Is government pretty much run by a few big interests looking out for themselves?
Yes ☐   No ☐

Who has power and how they use it are the basis of all these questions. Issues of power underlie everything we call politics and the study of political science.

## POLITICS AND POLITICAL SCIENCE

**Politics** is deciding "who gets what, when, and how." It is an activity by which people try to get more of whatever there is to get—money, prestige, jobs, respect, sex, even power itself. Politics occurs in many different settings. We talk about office politics, student politics, union politics, church politics, and so forth. But political science usually limits its attention to *politics in government.*

   **Political science** is the study of politics, or the study of who gets what, when, and how. The *who* are the participants in politics—voters, interest groups, parties, television and the press, corporations and labor unions, lawyers and lobbyists, foundations and think tanks, and elected and appointed government officials, including members of Congress, the presi-

FIGURE 1-1 **Who Gets What, When, and How**

*Political science is the study of politics. The study of politics includes the question of "Who governs?" (that is, who are the participants in politics, both within and outside of government); the question of when and how political decisions are made (that is, how the institutions and processes of politics function); and the question of what outcomes are produced (that is, what public policies are adopted). Shown here are some of the topics of concern to political science.*

## Who Governs: Participants

### Governmental

President and White House staff
Executive Office of the President, including Office of Management and Budget
Cabinet officers and executive agency heads
Bureaucrats

Congress members
Congressional staff

Supreme Court justices
Federal appellate and district judges

### Nongovernmental

Voters
Campaign contributors
Interest group leaders and members
Party leaders and party identifiers in the electorate
Corporate and union leaders
Media leaders, including press and television anchors and reporters
Lawyers and lobbyists
Think tanks and foundation personnel

## When and How: Institutions and Processes

### Institutions

Constitution
   Separation of powers
   Checks and balances
   Federalism
   Judicial review
   Amendment procedures
   Electoral system

Presidency
Congress
   Senate
   House of Representatives

Courts
   Supreme Court
   Appellate Court
   District Court

Parties
   National Committees
   Conventions
   State and local organizations

Press and television

### Processes

Socialization and learning
Opinion formation
Party identification
Voting
Contributing
Joining organizations
Talking politics

Running for office
Campaigning
Polling
Fund raising
Parading and demonstrating
Nonviolent direct action
Violence

Agenda setting
Lobbying
Logrolling
Deciding
Budgeting
Implementing and evaluating
Adjudicating

## What Outcomes: Public Policies

Civil liberties
Civil rights
Equality
Criminal justice
Welfare
Social Security
Health
Education

Energy
Environmental protection
Economic development
Economic stability
Taxation
Government spending and deficits
National defense
Foreign affairs

**Politics:** Deciding who gets what, when, and how.

**Political science:** The study of politics: who governs, for what ends, and by what means.

dent, judges, and bureaucrats. The *what* of politics are public policies—the decisions that governments make concerning social welfare, health care, national defense, law enforcement, the environment, and thousands of other issues that come before governments. The *when* and *how* are the political process—campaigns and elections, political news reporting, television debates, fund raising, lobbying,

*Conflict exists in all political activities as participants struggle over who gets what, when, and how. From the streets to the Congress to the White House, participants in the political process compete to further their goals and ambitions.*

decision making in the White House and executive agencies, and decision making in the courts.

Political science is generally concerned with three questions: *Who governs? For what ends? By what means?* Throughout this book, we will be concerned with who participates in politics, who benefits most from government decisions, who bears the greatest costs, and how these decisions are made (see Figure 1-1).

Politics would be simple if everyone agreed on who should govern, who should get what, who should pay for it, and how and when it should be done. But conflict arises from disagreements over these questions, and sometimes the question of confidence in the government itself underlies the conflict (see *What Do You Think?* "Can You Trust the Government?"). Politics arises out of conflict, and it consists of all the activities—reasonable discussion, impassioned oratory, balloting, campaigning, lobbying, parading, rioting, street fighting, and waging war—by which conflict is carried on.

## POLITICS AND GOVERNMENT

What distinguishes governmental politics from politics in other institutions in society? After all, parents, teachers, unions, banks, corporations, and many other organizations make decisions about who gets what in society. The answer is that only **government** decisions can *extend to the whole society,* and only government

**Government:** An organization extending to the whole society that can legitimately use force to carry out its decisions.

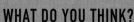

## Can You Trust the Government?

Americans are suspicious of big government. Many do not trust the government in Washington "to do what is right." While commentators often bemoan Americans' lack of confidence in government, this attitude may be a blessing in disguise. After all, if people are too trusting of government, always ready to believe that what the government does is right, they are vulnerable to bad government. A little suspicion of government may be good protection for a free people.

Confidence in government has varied over the years, as measured by polls asking, "How much of the time do you think you can trust the government in Washington to do what is right? Just about always? Most of the time? Some of the time? None of the time?" During the early years of the Johnson Administration (and even earlier, during the Kennedy and Eisenhower presidencies), public confidence in government was high. But defeat and humiliation in Vietnam appeared to diminish public confidence. On the heels of the Vietnam experience came the Watergate scandal and President Richard Nixon's forced resignation—the first resignation of a president in U.S. history—which caused public confidence in government to fall further. Presidents Gerald Ford and Jimmy Carter were unable to halt the downward

slump, and the Iranian hostage crisis in 1980 caused public confidence in government to slide even lower.

Throughout the long years of decline in public confidence in government, television has broadcast many negative images of government and public policy. Television producers seldom consider good news as "news" but instead focus on violence, scandal, corruption, and incompetence. Bad news drives out the good on television. People heavily exposed to negative television reporting gradually lose their trust in government. So the explanation for the decline in public confidence in government in the past three decades may be a product of: (1) a series of disturbing events (the Vietnam War, the Watergate scandal, and the Iranian hostage crisis); and/or (2) television reporting of these events and negative television reporting in general.

Public confidence in government grew during the Reagan presidency. Ronald Reagan himself, paradoxically, was publicly critical of government. In his Inaugural Address in 1981, he said: "Government is not the solution to our problem. Government is the problem." Perhaps President Reagan's personal popularity was part of the reason that popular confidence in government rose.

Economic recessions erode public confidence in government. People expect the president and Congress to lead them out of "hard times." The recession of 1990–92 was not particularly deep by historical standards, but it was one of the nation's longest

can *legitimately use force.* Other institutions encompass only a part of society: for example, students and faculty in a college, members of a church or union, employees or customers of a corporation. And individuals have a legal right to voluntarily withdraw from nongovernmental organizations. But governments make decisions affecting everyone, and no one can voluntarily withdraw from government's authority (without leaving the country, and thus becoming subject to some other government's authority). Some individuals and organizations— muggers, gangs, crime families—occasionally use physical force to get what they want. In fact, the history of the United States has been punctuated by examples of physical force used for political ends (see *A Conflicting View:* "American Politics as Violence"). But only governments can use force legitimately; that is, people generally accept the necessity for the government to act forcefully.

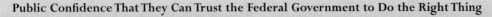

**Public Confidence That They Can Trust the Federal Government to Do the Right Thing**

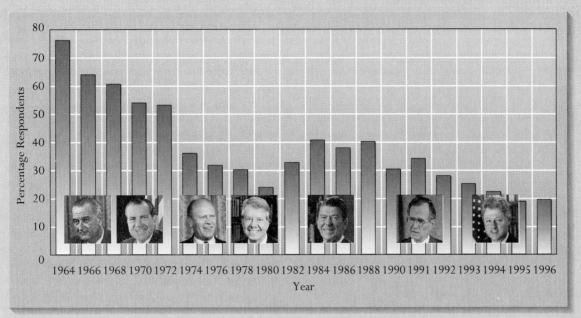

*Source:* Gallup Opinion Polls; Arthur H. Miller, "Confidence in Government during the 1980's," *American Politics Quarterly,* 19 (April 1991):147–73.

periods of slowed economic progress. George Bush's Gulf War success raised public confidence only temporarily; the perceived failure of his administration to act decisively to restore the nation's economic health helped to send public confidence in government back down to historic lows. Public trust in government fell to a new low during the Clinton presidency. Indeed, Clinton attributed failure of Congress to enact a national health care program to popular distrust of government.

Most people would say that they obey the law in order to avoid fines and stay out of prison. But if large numbers of people all decided to disobey the law at the same time, the government would not have enough police or jails to hold them all. The government can rely on force only against relatively small numbers of offenders. Most of us, most of the time, obey laws out of habit—the habit of compliance. We have been taught to believe that law and order are necessary and that government is right to punish those who disobey its laws.

Government thus enjoys **legitimacy,** or rightfulness, in its use of force.[1] A democratic government has a special claim to legitimacy, because it is based on the consent of its people, who participate in the selection of its leaders and the making of its laws. Those who disagree with a law have the option of working for its change by speaking out, petitioning, demonstrating, forming interest groups or

**Legitimacy:** Widespread acceptance of something as necessary, rightful, and legally binding.

# American Politics as Violence

We think of one of the central functions of government, especially democratic government, as the peaceful management of conflict in society and the protection of individual safety. Yet political violence has played a prominent role in American history. The United States was founded in armed revolution, and violence has been both a source of power and a stimulus to social change ever since. Despite their pious pronouncements against it, Americans have frequently employed violence, even in their most idealistic endeavors.

The longest and most brutal violence in American history—that between whites and Native Americans—began when the first settlers arrived in 1607. The "Indian Wars" continued with only temporary truces for nearly 300 years, until the final battle at Wounded Knee, South Dakota, in 1890. Early colonial experience in a rugged frontier country gave rise to the tradition of an armed civilian militia, which was used successfully in the Revolutionary War against British rule.

After the Revolutionary War, many armed farmers and debtors resorted to violence to assert their economic interests. The most serious rebellion broke out in 1786 in Massachusetts, when a band of insurgents, composed of farmers and laborers and led by Bunker Hill veteran Daniel Shays, captured several courthouses. Shays's Rebellion was put down by a small mercenary army paid for by well-to-do citizens who feared that a wholesale attack on property rights was imminent. The growing violence in the states contributed to the momentum leading to the Constitutional Convention of 1787, where a new central government was established with the power to "insure domestic Tranquility," guarantee a "Republican Form of Government," and protect against violence within the new nation. Thus the Constitution reflects the concern of the Founders about violence.

Ratification of the Constitution did not stop violence, however. Vigilantism (taking the law into one's own hands) arose in response to a perennial American problem: the absence of effective law and order in the frontier region. Practically every state and territory west of the Appalachians had at one time or another a well-organized vigilante movement, frequently backed by prominent citizens.

The ultimate turning of citizen on citizen—the Civil War—was the bloodiest war Americans ever fought. Total battle deaths of the northern and southern armies almost equaled American battle deaths in World War II, even though the United States population at the time of the Civil War was only one-quarter that of the World War II period.

Violence was also a prime ingredient of the early labor movement in the United States. Both management and workers resorted to violence in the struggles accompanying the Industrial Revolution. The last great spasm of violence in the history of American labor came in the 1930s, with the strikes and plant takeovers that accompanied the successful drive to unionize the automobile, steel, and other mass-production industries.

A long history of racial violence continues to plague the United States. Slavery itself was accompanied by untold violence. It is estimated that one-third to one-half of the Africans captured in slave raids never survived the ordeal of initiation into slavery. A slave insurrection in 1831, led by Nat Turner, resulted in the deaths of fifty-seven white persons and the later execution of Turner and more than forty of his followers. After the Civil War, racial strife and Ku Klux Klan activity became routine in the old Confederacy, and the white supremacy movement employed violence to reestablish white rule in the southern social system. Racial violence directed against blacks—whipping, torture, and lynching—was fairly common from the 1870s to the 1930s. During World War II, serious racial violence erupted in Detroit, where black and white mobs battled each other in 1943. More than 150 major riots involving race were reported in American cities from 1965 to 1968, and the rioting, burning, and looting in south-central Los Angeles in 1992 reminded the nation that violence—and the conditions that foment it—are continuing threats to society.

Americans think of democratic politics as stable, with the authority to govern transferred peacefully from one administration to the next according to the preferences of the electorate. Yet political assassinations have taken the lives of four presidents: Abraham Lincoln in 1865, James A. Garfield in 1881, William McKinley in 1901, and John F. Kennedy in 1963. Several other presidents have been the targets of assassination attempts, and the assassination of Dr. Martin Luther King, Jr., in 1968 ended an era of progress in civil rights in America.

parties, voting against unpopular leaders, or running for office themselves. Since people living in a democracy can effect change by "working within the system," they have a greater moral obligation to obey the law than people living under regimes in which they have no voice. However, there may be some occasions when "civil disobedience" even in a democracy may be morally justified (see *A Conflicting View:* "Sometimes It's Right to Disobey the Law").

## THE PURPOSES OF GOVERNMENT

All governments tax, penalize, punish, restrict, and regulate their people. Governments in the United States—the federal government in Washington, the 50 state governments, and the more than 86,000 local governments—take nearly 40 cents out of every dollar Americans earn. Each year, the Congress enacts about 500 laws; federal bureaucracies publish about 19,000 rules and regulations; the state legislatures enact about 25,000 laws; and cities, counties, school districts, and other local governments enact countless local ordinances. Each of these laws restricts our freedom in some way. Each dollar taken out of our wages or profits reduces our freedom to choose what to do with our money.

Why do people put up with governments? An answer to this question can be found in the words of the Preamble to the Constitution of the United States:

> We the people of the United States, in Order to form a more perfect Union, establish Justice, insure domestic Tranquility, provide for the common defense, promote the general Welfare, and secure the Blessings of Liberty to ourselves and our Posterity, do ordain and establish this Constitution for the United States of America.

*To Establish Justice and Insure Domestic Tranquility*   Government manages conflict and maintains order. We might think of government as a **social contract** among people who agree to allow themselves to be regulated and taxed in exchange for protection of their lives and property. No society can allow individuals or groups to settle their conflicts by street fighting, murder, kidnapping, rioting, bombing, or terrorism. Whenever government fails to control such violence, we say that there has been "a breakdown in law and order." Indeed, when government loses control consistently, the government itself often breaks down. Without the protection of government, human lives and property are endangered, and only those skilled with fists and weapons have much of a chance of survival. The seventeenth-century English political philosopher Thomas Hobbes described life without government as "a war where every man is enemy to every

**Social contract:** The idea that government originates as an implied contract among individuals who agree to obey laws in exchange for protection of their rights.

*PEANUTS reprinted by permission of UFS, Inc.*

# Sometimes It's Right to Disobey the Law

Civil disobedience is the nonviolent violation of laws that people believe to be unjust. Civil disobedience denies the *legitimacy,* or rightfulness, of a law and implies that a higher moral authority takes precedence over unjust laws. It is frequently a political tactic of minorities. (Majorities can more easily change laws through conventional political activity.) It is also an attractive tactic for groups who wish to change the status quo.

Why resort to civil disobedience in a democracy? Why not work within the democratic system to change unjust laws? In 1963, a group of Alabama clergy posed these questions to Martin Luther King, Jr., and asked him to call off mass demonstrations in Birmingham, Alabama. King, who had been arrested in the demonstrations, replied in his now-famous "Letter from Birmingham City Jail":

*Dr. Martin Luther King, Jr., shown here marching in Missis-sippi with his wife Coretta Scott King and others, used civil disobedience to advance the rights of African Americans during the 1950s and 1960s.*

> You may well ask, "Why direct action? Why sit-ins, marches, etc.?" . . . Nonviolent direct action seeks to create such a crisis and establish such creative tension that a community that has constantly refused to negotiate is forced to confront the issue. It seeks to so dramatize the issue that it can no longer be ignored. . . . One may well ask, "How can you advocate breaking some laws and obeying others?" The answer is found in the fact that there are unjust laws. I would be the first to advocate obeying just laws. One has not only a legal but a moral responsibility to obey just laws. Conversely, one has a moral responsibility to disobey unjust laws.

King argued that *nonviolent direct action* was a vital aspect of democratic politics. The political purpose of civil disobedience is to call attention or "to bear witness" to the existence of injustices. Only laws regarded as unjust are broken, and they are broken openly, without hatred or violence. Punishment is actively sought rather than avoided, since punishment will further emphasize the injustice of the laws.

The objective of nonviolent civil disobedience is to stir the conscience of an apathetic majority and to win support for measures that will eliminate the

injustices. By accepting punishment for the violation of an unjust law, persons practicing civil disobedience demonstrate their sincerity. They hope to shame the majority and to make it ask itself how far it is willing to go to protect the status quo. Thus, according to King's teachings, civil disobedience is clearly differentiated from hatred and violence:

> In no sense do I advocate evading or defying the law as the rabid segregationist would do. This would lead to anarchy. One who breaks an unjust law must do it openly, lovingly (not hatefully as the white mothers did in New Orleans when they were seen on television screaming "nigger, nigger, nigger") and with a willingness to accept the penalty. I submit that an individual who breaks a law that conscience tells him is unjust, and willingly accepts the penalty by staying in jail to arouse the conscience of the community over its injustice, is in reality expressing the very highest respect for law.

In 1964, Martin Luther King, Jr., received the Nobel Peace Prize in recognition of his extraordinary contributions to the development of nonviolent methods of social change.

*Source:* Martin Luther King, Jr., "Letter from Birmingham City Jail," April 16, 1963.

## Thomas Hobbes and the Need for Leviathan

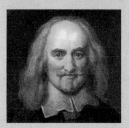

The notion of life without government holds a certain romantic appeal, since all governments restrict personal freedom. *Anarchism* is a term describing opposition to government in any form. But what would life really be like without any government at all?

The English political philosopher Thomas Hobbes (1588–1679) warned that the true state of nature (without any government or social organization at all) would be a "war of everyone against everyone" in which life would be "solitary, poor, nasty, brutish, and short." Hobbes's beliefs about the cruelty and violence of human nature led him to conclude that a strong and powerful government, which he called Leviathan after a biblical sea monster, was essential to the preservation of life, property, justice, and freedom. "Where there is no common power, there is no law; where no law, no justice. Force and fraud [become] the two cardinal virtues."

Hobbes fled England during that nation's civil war, whose violence, brutality, and waste of life and property inspired his most important work, *Leviathan* (1651). In it, Hobbes argued that government derived its power from the consent of the people. But Hobbes's view of the social contract was a one-sided bargain; fear drove people to agree to surrender their liberty in exchange for protection from others. The government's power had to be absolute, Hobbes believed, because only such a Leviathan government could successfully control the violent propensities of mankind.

The Hobbesian view of human nature and life without government is very pessimistic. Yet today, when we observe the total breakdown of law and order in societies from Somalia to Bosnia to riot-torn cities at home, we are reminded of the aptness of Hobbes's warnings.

man," where people live in "continual fear and danger of violent death"[2] (see *People in Politics:* "Thomas Hobbes and the Need for Leviathan").

*To Provide for the Common Defense*　Many anthropologists link the origins of government to warfare—to the need of early communities to protect themselves from raids by outsiders and to organize raids against others. Since the Revolutionary War, the United States government has been responsible for the country's defense, but today, with a diminished threat to national security from the states of the former Soviet Union, national defense absorbs less than 16 percent of the *federal* government's budget and less than 10 percent of *all* government spending—federal, state, and local combined. Nevertheless, national defense remains a primary responsibility of the U.S. government.

*To Promote the General Welfare*　Government promotes the general welfare in a number of ways. It provides **public goods**—goods and services that private markets cannot readily furnish either because they are too expensive for individuals to buy for themselves (for example, a national park, a highway, or a sewage disposal plant) or because if one person bought them, everyone else would "free-ride," or use them without paying (for example, clean air, police protection, or national defense). Nevertheless, Americans acquire most of their goods and services on the **free market**, through voluntary exchange among indi-

**Public goods:** Goods and services that cannot readily be provided by markets, either because they are too expensive for a single individual to buy, or because if one person bought them, everyone else would use them without paying.

**Free market:** Free competition for voluntary exchange among individuals, firms, and corporations.

## How Big Is Government and What Does It Do?

Government in the United States has grown enormously throughout the twentieth century, both in absolute terms and in relation to the size of the national economy. The size of the economy is usually measured by the gross domestic product (GDP), the sum of all the goods and services produced in the United States in a year. Governments accounted for only about 8 percent of the GDP at the beginning of the century, and most governmental activities were carried out by state and local governments. Two world wars, the New Deal programs devised during the Great Depression of the 1930s, and the growth of the Great Society programs of the 1960s and 1970s all greatly expanded the size of government, particularly the federal government. The rise in government growth relative to the economy leveled off during the Reagan presidency (1981–89). Today, federal expenditures amount to about 23 percent of GDP, and total governmental expenditures are about 35 percent of GDP (see Graph A).

Not everything that government does is reflected in governmental expenditures. *Regulatory activity,* for example, especially environmental regulations, imposes significant costs on individuals and businesses; these costs are *not* shown in government budgets. Nevertheless, government spending is a common indicator of governmental functions and priorities. For example, Graph B indicates that the

**(A) What Government Spends**

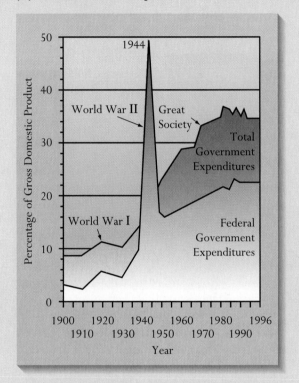

*Source: Budget of the United States Government, 1996.*

*federal government* spends more on senior citizens—in Social Security and Medicare outlays—than on any *other* function, including national defense. The national debt is now so large that interest payments

---

viduals, firms, and corporations. The **gross domestic product (GDP)**—the dollar sum of all the goods and services produced in the United States in a year—amounts to nearly $7 trillion. Government spending in the United States—federal, state, and local governments combined—amounts to nearly $2.5 trillion, or about 35 percent of the gross domestic product (see *Up Close:* "How Big Is the Government and What Does It Do?").

Governments also regulate society. Free markets cannot function effectively if individuals and firms engage in fraud, deception, or unfair competition, or if contracts cannot be enforced. Moreover, many economic activities impose costs on persons who are not direct participants in these activities. Economists refer to such costs as **externalities.** A factory that produces air pollution or waste water

**Gross domestic product (GDP):** The dollar sum of all the goods and services produced in a nation in a year.

**Externalities:** Costs imposed upon people who are not direct participants in an activity.

## (B) What the Federal Government Does

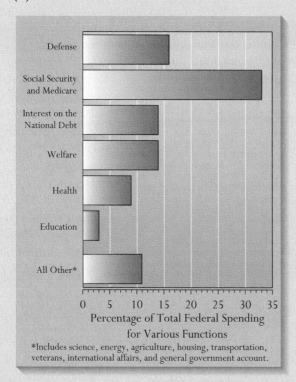

Percentage of Total Federal Spending
for Various Functions
*Includes science, energy, agriculture, housing, transportation,
veterans, international affairs, and general government account.

*Source: Budget of the United States Government, 1996.*

## (C) What State and Local Governments Do

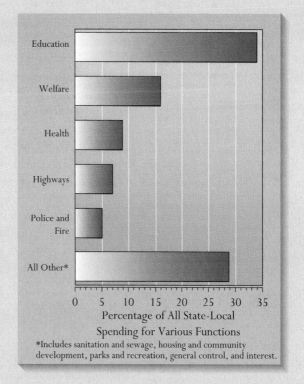

Percentage of All State-Local
Spending for Various Functions
*Includes sanitation and sewage, housing and community
development, parks and recreation, general control, and interest.

*Source: Statistical Abstract of the United States, 1995.*

on it consume 14 percent of all federal spending. Federal welfare and health programs account for substantial budget outlays, but federal financial support of education is very modest.

*State and local governments* in the United States bear the major burden of public education. Welfare and health functions consume larger shares of their budgets than highways and law enforcement do (see Graph C).

imposes external costs on community residents who would otherwise enjoy cleaner air or water. A junkyard that creates an eyesore makes life less pleasant for neighbors and passersby. Many government regulations are designed to reduce these external costs.

To promote general welfare, governments also use **income transfers** from taxpayers to people who are regarded as deserving. Government agencies and programs provide support and care for individuals who cannot supply these things for themselves through the private job market; for example, ill, elderly, and disabled people and dependent children cannot usually be expected to find productive employment. However, it is important to realize that payments to the poor are less than one-fifth of all government transfer payments to individuals. The

**Income transfers:**

Government transfers of income from taxpayers to persons regarded as deserving.

largest income transfer programs are Social Security and Medicare, which are paid to the elderly regardless of their personal wealth. Other large transfer payments go to farmers, veterans, and the unemployed, as well as to a wide variety of businesses. As we shall see, the struggle of individuals and groups to obtain direct government payments is a major motivator of political activity.

*To Secure the Blessings of Liberty*    All governments must maintain order, protect national security, provide public goods, regulate society, and care for those unable to fend for themselves. But *democratic* governments have a special added responsibility—to protect individual liberty by ensuring that all people are treated equally before the law. No one is above the law. The president must obey the Constitution and laws of the United States, and so must members of Congress, governors, judges, and the police. A democratic government must protect people's freedom to speak and write what they please, to practice their religion, to petition, to form groups or parties, to enjoy personal privacy, and to exercise their rights if accused of a crime.

The concentration of government power can be a threat to freedom. If a democratic government acquires great power in order to maintain order, protect national security, or provide many collective goods and services, it runs the risk of becoming too powerful for the preservation of freedom. The question is how to keep government from becoming so big that it threatens the individual liberty it was established to protect.

## THE MEANING OF DEMOCRACY

Throughout the centuries, thinkers in many different cultures contributed to the development of democratic government. Early Greek philosophers contributed the word **democracy,** which means "rule by the many." But there is no single definition of *democracy,* nor is there a tightly organized system of democratic thought. It is better, perhaps, to speak of democratic traditions than of a single democratic ideology.

Unfortunately, the looseness of the term *democracy* allows it to be perverted by *anti*democratic governments. There is hardly a nation in the world that does not *claim* to be "democratic." Governments that outlaw political opposition, suppress dissent, discourage religion, and deny fundamental freedoms of speech and press still claim to be "democracies," "democratic republics," or "people's republics" (for example, the Democratic People's Republic of Korea is the official name of Communist North Korea). These governments defend their use of the term *democracy* by claiming that their policies reflect the true interests of their people. But they are unwilling to allow political freedoms or to hold free elections in order to find out whether their people really agree with their policies. In effect, they use the term as a political slogan rather than a true description of their government.[3]

The actual existence of **democratic ideals** varies considerably from country to country, regardless of their names (see *Compared to What?* "Freedom and Democracy in the World"). A meaningful definition of democracy must include the following ideals: recognition of the dignity of every individual, equal protection of the laws for every individual, opportunity for everyone to participate in public decisions, and decision making by majority rule, with one person having one vote.

**Democracy:** A governing system in which the people govern themselves; from the Greek term meaning "rule by the many."

**Democratic ideals:** Individual dignity, equality before the law, widespread participation in public decisions, and public decisions by majority rule, with one person having one vote.

# Freedom and Democracy in the World

Worldwide progress toward freedom and democracy has been evident over the past decade, not only in the collapse of communism in Eastern Europe and the Soviet Union but also in the movements toward democracy in such nations as South Africa, South Korea, Taiwan, and Nicaragua. Nevertheless, more than half the world's people live under governments that can hardly be called democracies.

One way to assess the degree of democracy in a governmental system is to consider its record in ensuring political freedoms—enabling citizens to participate meaningfully in government—and individual liberties. A checklist for political freedoms might include whether the chief executive and national legislature are elected; whether elections are generally fair, with open campaigning and honest tabulation of votes; and whether multiple candidates and parties participate. A checklist for individual liberties might include whether the press and broadcasting are free and independent of the government; whether people are free to assemble and protest and form opposition parties; whether religious institutions, labor unions, business organizations, and other groups are free and independent of the government; and whether individuals are free to own property, travel, and move their residence.

The Freedom House, a New York–based think tank that regularly surveys political conditions around the world, ranks nations according to the amount of political freedom and individual liberty they allow. The categories are "Free," "Partly Free," and "Not Free," based on each nation's combined average score on political freedom and individual liberty.

**The Map of Freedom**

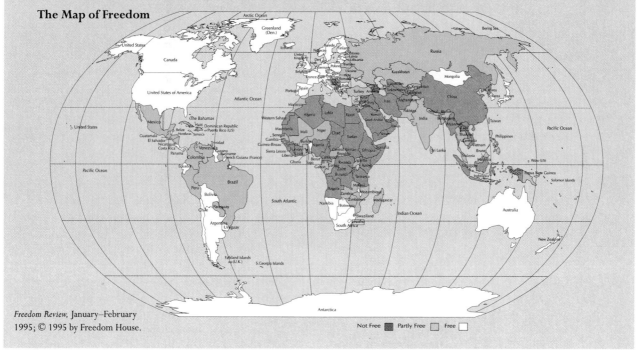

Freedom Review, January–February 1995; © 1995 by Freedom House.

*Individual Dignity*   The underlying value of democracy is the dignity of the individual. Human beings are entitled to life and liberty, personal property, and equal protection under the law. These liberties are *not* granted by governments; they belong to every person born into the world. The English political philosopher John Locke (1632–1704) argued that a higher "natural law" guaranteed liberty to every person and that this natural law was morally superior to all human

# John Locke and the Justification of Revolution

The most important single voice influencing the thought of the nation's Founders was that of John Locke (1632–1704). Locke's writings, especially his *Second Treatise on Government* (1690), inspired the American Revolution, the Declaration of Independence, and the Constitution of the United States.

Like Thomas Hobbes, Locke was an aristocrat who was forced to flee during England's civil war. Yet despite living in fear of political persecution, he never adopted Hobbes's pessimistic view of human nature. Rather, he held that people are basically decent, orderly, social-minded, and capable of self-government.

In his *Treatise on Civil Government* (1688), Locke argued that "all men are by nature free, equal, and independent" and all enjoy "the rights to life, liberty, and property." These laws of nature are "self-evident" to those who "make use of reason." People "consent" to enter into a social contract and "accept the bonds of government" in order to better protect their rights. People "unite in a commonwealth" especially for "the preservation of their property." Government is based upon the consent of the people. An "absolute monarch" is "inconsistent with civil society" because people retain the ability to judge for themselves whether their rights are truly being protected by government. The only justification for government is its ability to protect life, liberty, and property.

It follows that any government that "transgresses" on these rights, "either by ambition, fear, folly, or corruption," breaches the social contract and "forfeits the power the people had put into its hands."

The people then have the right to "resume their original liberty," dissolve their bonds with the government, and create a new government "such as they think fit." Thus Locke endorsed the right of revolution—the moral right of a people to dissolve a government that violates their fundamental rights. But he advised that people should not undertake such an action unless confronted with a long list of serious grievances and many "fruitless attempts" to redress them. And he reassured rulers that a good government has nothing to fear from acceptance of his theory of the right of revolution.

In writing the Declaration of Independence in 1776, Thomas Jefferson borrowed heavily from Locke (perhaps even to the point of plagiarism) in his eloquent defense of the American Revolution:

> We hold these Truths to be self-evident, that all Men are created equal, that they are endowed by their Creator with certain unalienable Rights, that among these are Life, Liberty, and the Pursuit of Happiness—That to secure these Rights, Governments are instituted among Men, deriving their just Powers from the Consent of the Governed, that whenever any Form of Government becomes destructive of these Ends, it is the Right of the People to alter or to abolish it, . . . when a long Train of Abuses and Usurpations, pursuing invariably the same Object, evinces a Design to reduce them under absolute Despotism, it is their Right, it is their Duty, to throw off such Government. . . . The History of the present King of Great Britain is a History of repeated Injuries and Usurpations, all having in direct Object the Establishment of an absolute Tyranny over these States. . . .
>
> We, therefore, the Representatives of the UNITED STATES OF AMERICA, in General Congress, Assembled, appealing to the Supreme Judge of the World for the Rectitude of our Intentions, do, in the Name, and by Authority of the good People of these Colonies, solemnly Publish and Declare, That these United Colonies are, and of Right ought to be, Free and Independent States.

laws and governments. Each individual possesses "certain inalienable Rights, among these are Life, Liberty, and Property"[4] (see *People in Politics:* "John Locke and the Justification of Revolution").

Individual dignity requires personal freedom. People who are directed by governments in every aspect of their lives, people who are "collectivized" and made into workers for the state, people who are enslaved—all are denied the personal dignity to which all human beings are entitled. Democratic governments try to minimize the role of government in the lives of citizens.

*Equality*    True democracy requires equal protection of the law for every individual. Democratic governments cannot discriminate between blacks and whites, or men and women, or rich and poor, or any groups of people in applying the law. Not only must a democratic government refrain from discrimination itself, but it must also work to prevent discrimination in society generally. Today our notion of equality extends to equality of opportunity—the obligation of government to ensure that all Americans have an opportunity to develop their full potential.

*Participation in Decision Making*    Democracy means individual participation in the decisions that affect individuals' lives. People should be free to choose for themselves how they want to live. Individual participation in government is necessary for individual dignity. People in a democracy should not have decisions made *for* them but *by* them. Even if they make mistakes, it is better that they be permitted to do so than to take away their rights to make their own decisions. The true democrat would reject even a wise and benevolent dictatorship because it would threaten the individual's character, self-reliance, and dignity. The argument for democracy is *not* that the people will always choose wise policies for themselves but that people who cannot choose for themselves are not really free.

*Majority Rule: One Person, One Vote*    Collective decision making in democracies must be by majority rule with each person having one vote. That is, each person's vote must be equal to every other person's, regardless of status, money, or fame. Whenever any individual is denied political equality because of race, sex, or wealth, then the government is not truly democratic. Majorities are not always right. But majority *rule* means that all persons have an equal say in decisions that affect them. If people are truly equal, their votes must count equally, and a majority vote must decide the issue, even if the majority decides foolishly.

## THE PARADOX OF DEMOCRACY

What if a *majority* of the people decide to attack the rights of some unpopular individuals or minority groups? What if hate, prejudice, or racism infects a majority of people and they vote for leaders who promise to "get rid of the Jews" or "put blacks in their place" or "bash a few gays"? What if a majority of people vote to take away the property of wealthy people and distribute it among themselves? Do we abide by the principle of majority rule and allow the majority to do what it wants? Or do we defend the principle of individual liberty and limit the majority's power? If we enshrine the principle of majority rule, we are

*The paradox of democracy balances the principle of majority rule against the principle of individual liberty. When the German people voted Adolf Hitler and the Nazi Party into power, did majority rule give the Nazis free rein to restrict the individual liberties of the people? Or did those who abhorred the trespasses of their government have the right to fight against its power?*

placing all our confidence in the wisdom and righteousness of the majority of the people. Yet we know that democracy means more than majority rule, that it also means freedom and dignity for the individual. How do we resolve this **paradox of democracy**—the potential for conflict between majority rule and individual freedom?

The Founders of the American nation were not sure that freedom would be safe in the hands of the majority. In *The Federalist Papers* in 1787, James Madison warned *against* a direct democracy: "Pure democracy . . . can admit of no cure for the mischiefs of faction. . . . There is nothing to check the inducements to sacrifice the weaker party, or an obnoxious individual."[5] So the Constitution (see "The Structure of the Government" in Chapter 3 for more detail) provides a number of arrangements designed to *limit the power of majorities,* including:

1. *Representative democracy* (which the Founders called **republican government**), in which elected leaders rather than the people themselves decide public issues.

2. *A separation of powers* system, in which each decision-making body—the Congress, the president, and the Supreme Court—is selected by different means for different terms, so that a majority cannot change the nation's leadership easily or quickly.

3. A system of *checks and balances,* so that each branch of government can restrain actions of other branches.

**Paradox of democracy:** The potential for conflict between individual freedom and majority rule.

**Republican government:** A system in which elected leaders decide public issues.

CHAPTER 1 • POLITICS: WHO GETS WHAT, WHEN, AND HOW

4. *Federalism,* in which the national government shares power with state governments.

5. *Judicial review,* by which courts can declare laws and government actions that violate constitutional rights to be null and void. This arrangement is not made explicit in the Constitution but is implied from Article VI, declaring the Constitution to be "the supreme Law of the Land."

More important than these structural arrangements for protecting individuals and groups from majorities is the principle of **limited government** itself. Limited government means that the power that government exercises over individuals is clearly limited, that there are some personal liberties that even majorities cannot regulate, and that government itself is restrained by law.

No government can be truly democratic if it directs every aspect of its citizens' lives. Individuals must be free to shape their own lives, free from the dictates of governments or even majorities of their fellow citizens. Indeed, we call a government with *un*limited power over its citizens totalitarian. Under **totalitarianism,** the individual possesses no personal liberty. Totalitarian governments decide what people can say or write; what unions, churches, or parties they can join, if any; where people must live; what work they must do; what goods they can find in stores and what they will be allowed to buy and sell; whether citizens will be allowed to travel outside of their country; and so on. Under a totalitarian government, the total life of the individual is subject to government control (see *Compared to What?* "Authoritarianism and Totalitarianism").

Limited government places individual liberty beyond the reach of majorities. Under a limited government, even if a majority of voters wanted to, they could not prohibit communists or atheists or racists from speaking or writing. Nor could they ban certain religions, set aside the rights of criminal defendants to a fair trial, or prohibit people from moving or quitting their jobs. These rights belong to individuals, not to majorities or governments.

**Constitutions,** written or unwritten, are the principal means by which governmental powers are limited. Constitutions set forth the liberties of individuals and restrain governments from interfering with these liberties. Consider, for example, the opening words of the First Amendment to the U.S. Constitution: "Congress shall make no law respecting an establishment of religion, or prohibiting the free exercise thereof." This amendment places religious belief beyond the reach of the government. The government itself is restrained by law. It cannot, even by majority vote, interfere with the personal liberty to worship as one wishes. In addition, the courts, armed with the power of judicial review, can declare laws passed by majority vote of Congress or state legislatures unconstitutional (see "Judicial Power" in Chapter 13).

Throughout this book we will be examining how well limited constitutional government succeeds in preserving individual liberty in the United States. We will examine free speech and press, the mass media, religious freedom, the freedom to protest and demonstrate, and the freedom to support political candidates and interest groups of all kinds. We will examine how well the U.S. Constitution protects individuals from discrimination and inequality. And we will examine how far government can go in regulating work, homes, business, and the marketplace without destroying individual liberty.

**Limited government:** The principle that government power over the individual is limited, that there are some personal liberties that even a majority cannot regulate, and that government itself is restrained by law.

**Totalitarianism:** Rule by an elite that exercises unlimited power over individuals in all aspects of life.

**Constitution:** Written or unwritten rules by which government operates, including limits on governmental power.

# Authoritarianism and Totalitarianism

*Authoritarianism* is a form of government in which the rulers tolerate no public opposition and there are no legal means to remove these rulers from power. Some authoritarian regimes are *dictatorships* in which power is held by a single individual; others are *juntas* in which power is held by a small group of military officers. While authoritarian governments permit no challenges to their political rule, they generally allow people to go about their religious, social, business, and recreational activities relatively undisturbed. *Totalitarianism* is a form of authoritarian government in which the rulers recognize no limits to their authority and try to regulate virtually all aspects of social and economic life. The term *totalitarian* derives from the "totality" of the rulers' ambitions; they tolerate no opposition in any sphere of life and aim for complete control of the society and its future.

Totalitarian governments are characterized by an elaborate ideology that covers every phase of the individual's life: a single political party that is identical with the government; widespread use of intimidation; complete control of mass media; monopoly control of weaponry and armed forces; and direction of the economy by the state bureaucracy. The most notable examples of totalitarian government are the three that were responsible for perhaps the most grotesque acts of genocide in history: Nazi Germany, Stalinist Russia, and Cambodia under the Khmer Rouge. In each case, terror was used as an instrument of policy, and millions of people were slaughtered at the whim of a regime that was utterly convinced of its own righteousness.

*Political sociologists have observed that the military in authoritarian societies have a distinct body language. Soldiers in Nazi Germany and, as seen here, the former Soviet Union used a "goose step" when on parade—a march in which the knee is unbent and the foot, encased in a heavy boot, is stamped on the ground, providing a powerful image of authority and force. In democratic societies, the goose step is not employed; indeed, it is regarded as somewhat ridiculous.*

## DIRECT VERSUS REPRESENTATIVE DEMOCRACY

In the Gettysburg Address, Abraham Lincoln spoke about "a government of the people, by the people, for the people," and his ringing phrase remains an American ideal. But can we take this phrase literally? There are more than 250 million Americans spread over 4 million square miles. If we brought everyone together, standing shoulder to shoulder, they would occupy 66 square miles. One round of five-minute speeches by everyone would take 5,000 years. "People could be born, grow old, and die while they waited for the assembly to make one decision."[6]

**Direct democracy** (also called pure or participatory democracy), where everyone actively participates in every decision, is rare. The closest approximation to direct democracy in American government may be the traditional New England town meeting, where all of the citizens come together face-to-face to decide about town affairs. But today most New England towns vest authority in a board of officials elected by the townspeople to make policy decisions between town meetings, and professional administrators are appointed to supervise the day-to-day town services. The town meeting is rapidly vanishing because citizens cannot spend so much of their time and energy in community decision making.

**Representative democracy** recognizes that it is impossible to expect millions of people to come together and decide every issue. Instead, representatives of the people are elected by the people to decide issues on behalf of the people. Elections must be open to competition so that the people can choose representatives who reflect their own views. And elections must take place in an environment of free speech and press, so that both candidates and voters can freely express their views. Finally, elections must be held periodically so that representatives can be thrown out of office if they no longer reflect the views of the majority of the people.

No government can claim to be a representative democracy, then, unless:

1.  Representatives are selected by vote of all the people.
2.  Elections are open to competition.
3.  Candidates and voters can freely express themselves.
4.  Representatives are selected periodically.

So when we hear of "elections" in which only one party is permitted to run candidates, candidates are not free to express their views, or leaders are elected "for life," then we know that these governments are *not* really democracies, regardless of what they may call themselves.

Throughout this book, as we examine how well representative democracy works in the United States, we will consider such questions as participation in elections and why some people do not vote, whether parties and candidates offer the voters real alternatives, whether modern political campaigning informs voters or only confuses them, and whether elected representatives are responsive to the wishes of voters—the kinds of questions that concern political science.

## WHO REALLY GOVERNS?

Democracy is an inspiring ideal. But is democratic government really possible? Is it possible for millions of people to govern themselves, with every voice having equal influence? Or will a small number of people inevitably acquire more power than others? To what extent is democracy attainable in *any* society, and how democratic is the American political system? That is, who really governs (see *What Do*

*Direct democracy still lives in many New England towns, where citizens come together periodically to pass laws, elect officials, and make decisions about such matters as taxation and land use.*

**Direct democracy:** A governing system in which every person participates actively in every public decision, rather than delegating decision making to representatives.

**Representative democracy:** The governing system in which public decision making is delegated to representatives of the people chosen by popular vote in free, open, and periodic election.

## Is Government Run by a Few Big Interests Looking Out for Themselves?

The public's perception of government has become increasingly cynical over the years. This cynicism is reflected in responses to the question: "Would you say that government is pretty much run by a few big interests looking out for themselves or that it is run for the benefit of all the people?" This perception parallels the *elitist* view of government insofar as it sees a few big interests as running the government. (However, some elite theorists would argue that, in general, elites govern in the public interest—that is, "for the benefit of all.")

The view that the government is run by a few big interests gained rapid acceptance during the administrations of Lyndon Johnson (1963–68) and, especially, Richard Nixon (1969–74). These were the years of the Vietnam War (1965–73) and the Watergate scandal (1972–74). Neither of our next two presidents, Gerald Ford and Jimmy Carter, could convince the public that government was run "for the benefit of all." In contrast, President Ronald Reagan seemed to create a more favorable public perception of government in his first term, 1981–84. But in his second term, the Iran-Contra scandal again increased popular skepticism about government. And during the administrations of President George Bush (1989–93) and Bill Clinton (beginning 1993) public belief that the government is run by a few big interests looking out for themselves rose to an all-time high.

**Public Perception of Government**

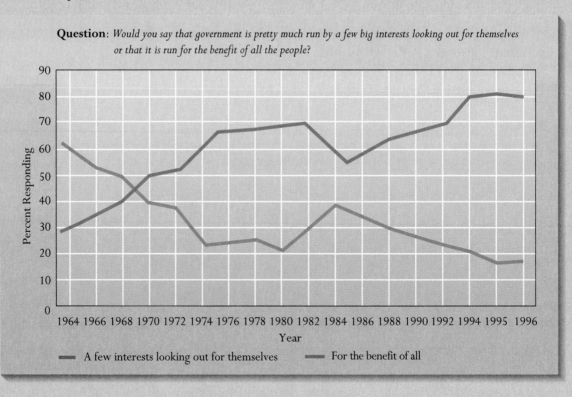

**Question**: *Would you say that government is pretty much run by a few big interests looking out for themselves or that it is run for the benefit of all the people?*

— A few interests looking out for themselves    — For the benefit of all

*Source:* Gallup opinion polls.

*The Elitist Perspective*    "Government is always government by the few, whether in the name of the few, the one, or the many."[7] This quotation from political scientist Harold Lasswell expresses the basic idea of **elitism.** All societies, including democracies, divide themselves into the few who have power and the many who do not. In every society, there is a division of labor. Only a few people are directly involved in governing a nation; most people are content to let others undertake the tasks of government. The *elite* are the few who have power; the *masses* are the many who do not. This theory holds that an elite is inevitable in *any* social organization. We cannot form a club, a church, a business, or a government without selecting some people to provide leadership. And leaders will always have a perspective on the organization different from that of its members.

In any large, complex society, then, whether or not it is a democracy, decisions are made by tiny minorities. Out of more than 250 million Americans, only a few thousand individuals at most participate directly in decisions about war and peace, wages and prices, employment and production, law and justice, taxes and benefits, health and welfare.

Elitism does *not* mean that leaders always exploit or oppress members. On the contrary, elites may be very concerned for the welfare of the masses. Elite status may be open to ambitious, talented, or educated individuals from the masses or may be closed to all except the wealthy. Elites may be very responsive to public opinion, or they may ignore the usually apathetic and ill-informed masses. But whether elites are self-seeking or public-spirited, open or closed, responsive or unresponsive, it is they and not the masses who actually make the decisions.

Contemporary elite theory argues that power in America is concentrated in a small *institutional* elite. Sociologist C. Wright Mills popularized the term *power elite* in arguing that leaders of corporations, the military establishment, and the national government come together at the top of a giant pyramid of power.[8] Other social scientists have found that more than half of the nation's total assets are concentrated in the one hundred largest corporations and fifty largest banks; that the officers and directors of these corporations and banks interact frequently with leaders of government, the mass media, foundations, and universities; and that these leaders are drawn disproportionately from wealthy, educated, upper-class, white, male, Anglo-Saxon Protestant groups in American society.[9]

Most people do not regularly concern themselves with decision making in Washington. They are more concerned with their jobs, family, sports, and recreation than they are with politics. They are not well informed about tax laws, foreign policy, or even who represents them in Congress. Since the "masses" are largely apathetic and ill-informed about policy questions, their views are likely to be influenced more by what they see and hear on television than by their own experience. Most communication flows downward from elites to masses. Elitism argues that the masses have at best only an indirect influence on the decisions of elites.

*The Pluralist Perspective*    No one seriously argues that all Americans participate in *all* of the decisions that shape their lives; that majority preferences *always* prevail; that the values of life, liberty, and property are *never* sacrificed; or that *every* American enjoys equality of opportunity. Nevertheless, most American

**Elitism:** The theory that all societies, even democracies, are divided into the few who govern and the many who do not.

## Sources of Facts about American Government

***America Votes*** Richard M. Scammon and Alice V. McGillivray, eds. Published biennially by Congressional Quarterly, Inc., 1414 22d St., NW, Washington, D.C., 20037 and available in most university libraries.

This work contains statistics on voting for president, governor, senator, and Congress member by state, congressional district, and county for primary and general elections.

***Statistical Abstract of the United States*** Published by U.S. Department of Commerce. Available in most libraries and through the Government Printing Office, Washington, D.C., 20402.

Published annually, this volume presents summary statistics on the political, social, and economic organization of the United States. It serves not only as a source for statistics of national importance but also as a guide to further information, since references are given to the sources of all tables.

***Budget of the United States Government*** Office of Management and Budget, Executive Office of the President. Available in government document libraries and through the Government Printing Office, Washington, D.C., 20402.

In addition to the annual budget message of the president, it contains a detailed department-by-department account of proposed budget items, giving the previous year's actual figures, the present year's estimated expenditures, and the coming year's proposed amounts. It also contains tables of estimates for trust funds and supplemental figures, including historical comparisons of budget receipts and expenditures.

***Congressional Quarterly Weekly Report*** Available in most university libraries and from Congressional Quarterly, Inc., 1414 22d St. NW, Washington, D.C., 20037.

A reliable, useful, and timely news service, offering weekly summary sections: Nation Report, Political Report, Executive Branch, and Lobby Report, as well as congressional activity in committees and on the floor. Includes all the key votes taken each week in the House and Senate.

***Congressional Quarterly Almanac*** Available in most university libraries and from Congressional Quarterly, Inc., 1414 22d St. NW, Washington, D.C., 20037.

Each volume offers a survey of legislation for each session of Congress. Major congressional action is summarized in sections dealing with categories of legislation (e.g., agriculture, labor, appropriations, crime) subdivided according to specific topics. Includes voting information on individual measures.

political scientists argue that the American system of government, which they describe as "pluralist," is the best possible approximation of the democratic ideal in a large, complex society. Pluralism is designed to make the theory of democracy "more realistic."[10]

**Pluralism** is the belief that democracy can be achieved in a large, complex society by competition, bargaining, and compromise among organized groups and that individuals can participate in decision making through membership in these groups and by choosing among parties and candidates in elections.

Pluralists recognize that the individual acting alone is no match for giant government bureaucracies, big corporations and banks, the television networks, labor unions, or other powerful interest groups. Instead, pluralists rely on *competition* among these organizations to protect the interests of individuals. They hope that countervailing centers of power—big business, big labor, big government—

**Pluralism:** The theory that democracy can be achieved through competition among multiple organized groups and that individuals can participate in politics through group memberships and elections.

**United States Government Organizational Manual** Published by the National Archives and Records Administration. Available in most university libraries and from the Government Printing Office, Washington, D.C., 20037.

The official organization handbook of the federal government, giving information on the organization, activities, and current officials of the various departments, bureaus, offices, commissions, and so forth, with descriptions of quasi-official agencies and selected international organizations; includes organizational charts.

**Congressional Directory** Published by the Office of Congressional Directory, U.S. Congress, and available in most libraries and from the Government Printing Office, Washington, D.C., 20037.

Lists members of Congress, committee assignments, telephone numbers, and maps of congressional districts.

**Congressional Record** Published by the U.S. Congress and available in research libraries and from the Government Printing Office, Washington, D.C., 20037.

Issued daily while Congress is in session. Contains the president's messages, congressional speeches, debates in full, and a record of votes.

**United States Statutes at Large** Published by the National Archives and Records Administration. Available in most university libraries and from the Government Printing Office, Washington, D.C., 20037.

Laws passed by Congress and signed by the president organized chronologically.

**United States Code** Available in law libraries and many university libraries and published by the Government Printing Office, Washington, D.C., 20037.

All general and permanent laws of the United States, arranged under titles—that is, by subject matter.

**United States Reports** Available in law libraries and many university libraries and published by the Government Printing Office, Washington, D.C., 20037.

Official text of all opinions of the Supreme Court in bound form plus comprehensive tables of cases reported, cases cited, statutes cited, and subject index. Approximately two to five volumes per term.

**Federal Register** Published by the National Archives and Records Administration. Available in most university libraries and from the Government Printing Office, Washington, D.C., 20037.

Official text of presidential documents, executive agency regulations (with their legal effects), and proposed rules and regulations and legal notices.

will check one another and prevent any single group from abusing its power and oppressing individual Americans.

Individuals in a pluralist democracy may not participate directly in decision making, but they can join and support *interest groups* whose leaders bargain on their behalf in the political arena. People are more effective in organized groups—for example, the Sierra Club for environmentalists, the American Civil Liberties Union (ACLU) for civil rights advocates, the National Association for the Advancement of Colored People (NAACP) or the Urban League for African Americans, the American Legion or Veterans of Foreign Wars for veterans, and the National Rifle Association (NRA) for opponents of gun control.

According to the pluralist view, the Democratic and Republican parties are really coalitions of groups: the national Democratic Party is a coalition of union members, big-city residents, blacks, Catholics, Jews, and, until recently, southerners; the national Republican Party is a coalition of business and professional people, suburbanites, farmers, and white Protestants. When voters choose candidates and parties, they are helping to determine which interest groups will enjoy a better reception in government.

Pluralists contend that there are multiple leadership groups in society (hence the term *pluralism*). They contend that power is widely dispersed among these groups; that no one group, not even the wealthy upper class, dominates decision making; and that groups that are influential in one area of decision making are not necessarily the same groups that are influential in other areas of decision making. Different groups of leaders make decisions in different issue areas.

Pluralism recognizes that public policy does not always coincide with majority preferences. Instead, public policy is the "equilibrium" reached in the conflict among group interests. It is the balance of competing interest groups, and therefore, say the pluralists, it is a reasonable approximation of society's preferences.

## DEMOCRACY IN AMERICA

Is democracy alive and well in America today? *Elitism* raises serious questions about the possibility of achieving true democracy in any large, complex society. *Pluralism* is more comforting; it offers a way of reaffirming democratic values and providing some practical solutions to the problem of individual participation in a modern society.

There is no doubt about the strength of democratic *ideals* in American society. These ideals—individual dignity, equality, popular participation in government, and majority rule—are the standards by which we judge the performance of the American political system. But we are still faced with the task of describing the *reality* of American politics.

This book will explore who gets what, when, and how in the American political system; who participates in politics; what policies are decided upon; and when and how these decisions are made (see also *Up Close:* "Sources of Facts about American Government"). In so doing, it will raise many questions about democracy, elitism, and pluralism in American life. But you will have to provide your own answers. At the end of your studies, you will have to decide for yourself whether the American political system is truly democratic. Your studies will help inform your judgment, but you yourself must make that judgment. That is the burden of freedom.

## SUMMARY NOTES

Politics is deciding who gets what, when, and how. It occurs in many different settings, but political science focuses on politics in government.

- Political science focuses on three central questions:
  Who governs?
  For what ends?
  By what means?

- Government is distinguished from other social organizations in that it:
  Extends to the whole society.
  Can legitimately use force.
- The purposes of government are to:
  Maintain order in society.
  Provide for national defense.

Provide "public goods."

Regulate society.

Transfer income.

Protect individual liberty.

- The ideals of democracy include:

Recognition of individual dignity and personal freedom.

Equality before the law.

Widespread participation in decision making.

Majority rule, with one person equaling one vote.

- The principles of democracy pose a paradox: How can we resolve conflicts between our belief in majority rule and our belief in individual freedom?

- Limited government places individual liberty beyond the reach of majorities. Constitutions are the principal means of limiting government power.

- Direct democracy, in which everyone participates in every public decision, is very rare. Representative democracy means that public decisions are made by representatives elected by the people, in elections held periodically and open to competition, in which candidates and voters freely express themselves.

- Who really governs? The elitist perspective on American democracy focuses on the small number of leaders who actually decide national issues, compared to the mass of citizens who are apathetic and ill-informed about politics. A pluralist perspective focuses on competition among organized groups in society, with individuals participating through group membership and voting for parties and candidates in elections.

- How democratic is American government today? Democratic ideals are widely shared in our society. But you must make your own informed judgment about the realities of American politics.

## SELECTED READINGS

CRONIN, THOMAS J. *Direct Democracy*. Cambridge, Mass.: Harvard University Press, 1989. A thoughtful discussion of direct versus representative democracy, as well as a review of initiative, referendum, and recall devices.

DAHL, ROBERT A. *Democracy and Its Critics*. New Haven, Conn.: Yale University Press, 1989. A defense of modern democracy from the pluralist perspective.

DYE, THOMAS R., and HARMON ZEIGLER. *The Irony of Democracy*. 10th ed. Belmont, Calif.: Wadsworth Publishing, 1996. An interpretation of American politics from the elitist perspective.

FUKUYAMA, FRANCIS. *Trust*. New York: Free Press, 1995. Argues that the breakdown of trust in America—not only in the government but at a person-to-person level—is burdening the nation with formal rules and regulations, lengthy contracts, bureaucracy, lawyers, and lawsuits.

LASSWELL, HAROLD. *Politics: Who Gets What, When, and How*. New York: McGraw-Hill, 1936. Classic description of the nature of politics and the study of political science by America's foremost political scientist of the twentieth century.

MILLS, C. WRIGHT. *The Power Elite*. New York: Oxford University Press, 1956. Classic Marxist critique of elitism in American society, setting forth the argument that "corporate chieftains," "military warlords," and a "political directorate" come together to form the nation's power elite.

O'ROURKE, P. J. *Parliament of Whores*. New York: Atlantic Monthly Press, 1991. A humorist undertakes to explain American government as not only "huge, stupid, greedy" and making "nosy, officious, and dangerous intrusions into the smallest corners of life," but, worse, "boring."

PAGE, BENJAMIN I., and ROBERT Y. SHAPIRO. *The Rational Public*. Chicago: University of Chicago Press, 1992. An examination of fifty years of public opinion polls convinces these authors that American government is generally responsive to the views of the majority.

# POLITICAL CULTURE
# IDEAS IN CONFLICT

## CHAPTER OUTLINE

## FEATURES

## POLITICAL CULTURE

Ideas have power. We are all influenced by ideas—beliefs, values, symbols—more than we realize. Ideas provide us with rationalizations for ways of life, with guides for determining right and wrong, and with emotional impulses to action. Political institutions are shaped by ideas, and political leaders are constrained by them.

The term **political culture** refers to widely shared ideas—powerful indeed—about who should govern, for what ends, and by what means. **Values** are shared ideas about what is good and desirable. Values provide standards for judging what is right or wrong. **Beliefs** are shared ideas about what is true. Values and beliefs are often related. For example, if we believe

## ASK YOURSELF ABOUT POLITICS

**1** Do you consider yourself politically conservative, moderate, or liberal?
Conservative ☐  Moderate ☐
Liberal ☐

**2** Should racists be allowed to speak on college campuses?
Yes ☐  No ☐

**3** Is it the government's responsibility to reduce income differences between people?
Yes ☐  No ☐

**4** If incomes were made more equal, would people still be motivated to work hard?
Yes ☐  No ☐

**5** Do Americans today still have the opportunity to significantly improve their condition in life?
Yes ☐  No ☐

**6** Should the U.S. government curtail immigration to America?
Yes ☐  No ☐

**7** Should illegal immigrants be denied welfare benefits?
Yes ☐  No ☐

**8** Is American culture racist and sexist?
Yes ☐  No ☐

Ask yourself if your answers to these question are widely shared by most citizens of the United States. Your answers probably reflect not only your own beliefs and values but also those of the political culture to which you belong.

27

*Students at Augustana College react to the verdict in the O.J. Simpson case. The verdict focused national attention on the great differences between the beliefs of whites and African Americans about the basic American value of justice and the role of racism in the criminal justice system.*

that human beings are endowed by God with rights to life, liberty, and property, then we will value the protection of these rights. Thus beliefs can justify values.

Cultural descriptions are *generalizations* about the values and beliefs of many people in society, but these generalizations do not apply to everyone. There may be important variations in values and beliefs within a society; these variations are frequently referred to as *subcultures* and may arise from such diverse bases as religion or ethnic identity or political group membership.

Because *conflict* is dramatic, it tends to capture our attention and lead us to overlook the many shared values and beliefs that constitute the American political culture. The media often focus on controversy, confrontation, and violence as more "newsworthy" than broad agreement on fundamental values. Yet there is broad agreement. In America, for example, no one expects that officeholders defeated in elections will try to retain power by calling out the military. No one believes it is right for public officials to accept bribes, or sell government offices, or inherit their positions. Yet in many political cultures, past and present, such conditions have been widely accepted.

*Contradictions*    Agreement over values in a political culture is no guarantee that there will not be contradictions between these values and actual conditions. People in and out of politics frequently act contrary to their professed values. No doubt the most grievous contradiction between professed national beliefs and actual conditions in America is found in the long history of slavery, segregation, and racial discrimination. The contradiction between the words of the Declaration of Independence that "all men are created equal" and the practices of slavery and segregation became the "American dilemma."[1] But this contradiction does not mean that professed values are worthless; the very existence of the gap between values and behavior becomes a motivation for change. The history of the civil

**Political culture:** Widely shared views about who should govern, for what ends, and by what means.

**Values:** Shared ideas as to what is good and desirable.

**Beliefs:** Shared ideas as to what is true.

CHAPTER 2 • POLITICAL CULTURE: IDEAS IN CONFLICT

rights movement might be viewed as an effort to "bear witness" to the contradiction between the belief in equality and the existence of segregation and discrimination.[2] Whatever the obstacles to racial equality in America, these obstacles would be even greater if the nation's political culture did *not* include a professed belief in equality.

A political culture does not mean that shared principles are always applied in every circumstance. For example, people may truly believe in the principle of "free speech for all, no matter what their views might be," and yet when asked whether racists should be allowed to speak on a college campus, many people will say no. Thus general agreement with abstract principles of freedom of speech, freedom of the press, and academic freedom does not always ensure their application to specific individuals or groups[3] (see *Up Close:* "Freedom Yes, But for Whom to Say What?").

*Conflict*   The idea of political culture does not mean an absence of conflict over values and beliefs. Indeed, much of politics involves conflict over very fundamental values. The American nation has experienced a bloody civil war, political assassinations, rioting and burning of cities, the forced resignation of a president, and other direct challenges to our political foundations. Indeed, much of this book will deal with serious political conflict. Yet Americans do share many common ways of thinking about politics.

## THE LIBERAL TRADITION IN AMERICA

No political value has been more widely held in the United States than individual *liberty.* The very beginnings of our history as a nation were shaped by **classical liberalism,** which asserted the worth and dignity of the individual. This political philosophy emphasized the rational ability of human beings to determine their own destinies, and it rejected ideas, practices, and institutions that submerged individuals into a larger whole and thus deprived them of their dignity. The only restriction on the individual was not to interfere with the liberties of others.

*Political Liberty*   Classical liberalism grew out of the eighteenth-century Enlightenment, the Age of Reason in which great philosophers such as Voltaire, John Locke, Jean-Jacques Rousseau, Adam Smith, and Thomas Jefferson affirmed their faith in reason, virtue, and common sense. Classical liberalism originated as an attack on the hereditary prerogatives and distinctions of a feudal society, the monarchy, the privileged aristocracy, and the state-established church.

Classical liberalism motivated America's Founders to declare their independence from England, to write the U.S. Constitution, and to establish the Republic. It rationalized their actions and provided ideological legitimacy for the new nation. Locke, as we saw in Chapter 1, argued that a natural law, or moral principle, guaranteed every person "certain inalienable Rights," among them "Life, Liberty, and Property," and that human beings form a social contract with one another to establish a government to help protect their rights. Implicit in the social contract and the liberal notion of freedom is the belief that governmental activity and restrictions on the individual should be kept to a minimum.

**Classical liberalism:** A philosophy asserting the worth and dignity of the individual.

# Freedom Yes, But for Whom to Say What?

American political culture places great value on personal liberty, yet Americans frequently fail to apply general principles to specific circumstances. Americans overwhelmingly support the general principles of free speech and press, but they are ambivalent about specific applications of these freedoms to individuals, groups, or books that "criticize," "denounce," or "preach the overthrow" of the government.

Americans are frequently willing to restrict the freedoms of particularly obnoxious groups. A generation ago it was "communists" and "atheists" who were unpopular and whose freedoms were questioned.

One interpretation of the increase over time in willingness of Americans to allow communists and atheists to speak in their communities and to have their books in public libraries is that Americans are growing more tolerant of dissenting opinion because of increased exposure to democratic norms through education and the mass media. A more cynical interpretation is that there has been little change in "real" tolerance for unpopular groups but rather a change in *which* groups are considered particularly obnoxious. Over time, communists and atheists have become less threatening. But people are still willing to restrict the liberties of those they dislike; for example, racists, pro-abortion or anti-abortion groups, homosexuals, and neo-Nazis. In other words, some people who would defend the liberties of communists and atheists may be willing to deny the same liberties to racists or Nazis. "Liberty" may depend on who says what.

Indeed, "content-controlled" questions in which respondents were first given a list of groups and asked which they liked least, and then asked whether they would restrict the liberties of their "least-liked" group, revealed surprising levels of intolerance.

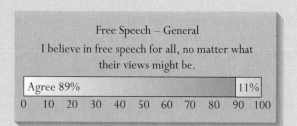

Free Speech – General

I believe in free speech for all, no matter what their views might be.

Agree 89%    11%

Free Speech – Specific

If a group asks to use a public building to hold a meeting denouncing the government, their request should be granted.

Agree 23%    Disagree 57%    NR 20%

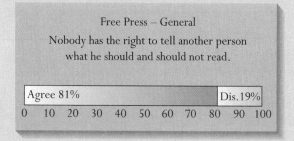

Free Press – General

Nobody has the right to tell another person what he should and should not read.

Agree 81%    Dis. 19%

Free Press – Specific

Books that preach the overthrow of the government should be made available by the library, just like any other book.

Agree 32%    Disagree 50%    18%

*Source:* Based on Herbert McClosky and Alida Brill, *Dimensions of Tolerance: What Americans Believe about Civil Liberties* (New York: Russell Sage Foundation, 1983).

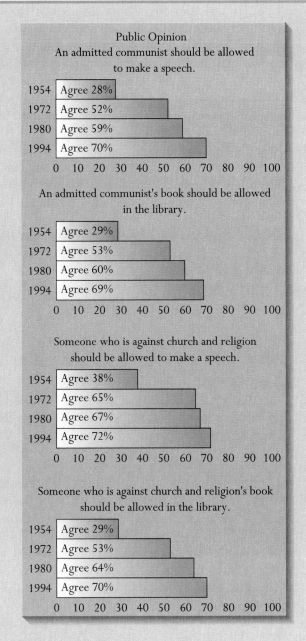

Public Opinion

An admitted communist should be allowed to make a speech.

| | |
|---|---|
| 1954 | Agree 28% |
| 1972 | Agree 52% |
| 1980 | Agree 59% |
| 1994 | Agree 70% |

0 10 20 30 40 50 60 70 80 90 100

An admitted communist's book should be allowed in the library.

| | |
|---|---|
| 1954 | Agree 29% |
| 1972 | Agree 53% |
| 1980 | Agree 60% |
| 1994 | Agree 69% |

0 10 20 30 40 50 60 70 80 90 100

Someone who is against church and religion should be allowed to make a speech.

| | |
|---|---|
| 1954 | Agree 38% |
| 1972 | Agree 65% |
| 1980 | Agree 67% |
| 1994 | Agree 72% |

0 10 20 30 40 50 60 70 80 90 100

Someone who is against church and religion's book should be allowed in the library.

| | |
|---|---|
| 1954 | Agree 29% |
| 1972 | Agree 53% |
| 1980 | Agree 64% |
| 1994 | Agree 70% |

0 10 20 30 40 50 60 70 80 90 100

*Source: General Social Survey.*

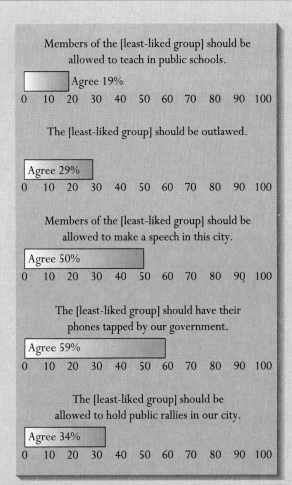

Members of the [least-liked group] should be allowed to teach in public schools.

Agree 19%

0 10 20 30 40 50 60 70 80 90 100

The [least-liked group] should be outlawed.

Agree 29%

0 10 20 30 40 50 60 70 80 90 100

Members of the [least-liked group] should be allowed to make a speech in this city.

Agree 50%

0 10 20 30 40 50 60 70 80 90 100

The [least-liked group] should have their phones tapped by our government.

Agree 59%

0 10 20 30 40 50 60 70 80 90 100

The [least-liked group] should be allowed to hold public rallies in our city.

Agree 34%

0 10 20 30 40 50 60 70 80 90 100

*Source:* John L. Sullivan, James Piereson, and George Marcus, *Political Tolerance and American Democracy* (Chicago: University of Chicago Press, 1982), p. 67.

*Economic Freedom*    Classical liberalism as a *political* idea is closely related to capitalism as an *economic* idea. **Capitalism** asserts the individual's right to own private property and to buy, sell, rent, and trade that property in a free market. The economic version of freedom is the freedom to make contracts, to bargain for one's services, to move from job to job, to join labor unions, to start one's own business. Capitalism stresses individual rationality in economic matters—freedom of choice in working, producing, buying, and selling—and limited governmental intervention in economic affairs. Classical liberalism emphasizes individual rationality in voter choice—freedom of speech, press, and political activity—and limitations on governmental power over individual liberty. In classical liberal politics, individuals are free to speak out, to form political parties, and to vote as they please—to pursue their political interests as they think best. In classical liberal economics, individuals are free to find work, to start businesses, and to spend their money as they please—to pursue their economic interests as they think best. The role of government is restricted to protecting private property, enforcing contracts, and performing only those functions and services that cannot be performed by the private market.

The value of liberty in these political and economic spheres has been paramount throughout our history. Only equality competes with liberty as the most honored value in the American political culture.

## DILEMMAS OF EQUALITY

Since the bold assertion of the Declaration of Independence that "all men are created equal," Americans have generally believed that no person has greater worth than any other person. The principle of equal worth and dignity was a radical idea in 1776, when much of the world was dominated by hereditary monarchies, titled nobilities, and rigid caste and class systems. Belief in equality drove the expansion of voting rights in the early 1800s and ultimately destroyed the institution of slavery. Abraham Lincoln understood that equality was not so much a description of reality as an ideal to be aspired to: "a standard maxim for a free society which should be familiar to all, and revered by all; constantly looked to, constantly labored for, and even though never perfectly attained, constantly approximated and thereby augmenting the happiness and value of life to all people of all colors everywhere."[4] The millions who immigrated to the United States viewed this country as a land not only of opportunity but of *equal* opportunity, where everyone, regardless of birth, could rise in wealth and status based upon hard work, natural talents, and perhaps good luck.

Today, most Americans agree that no one is intrinsically "better" than anyone else. This belief in equality, then, is fundamental to Americans, but a closer examination shows that throughout our history it has been tested, as beliefs and values so often are, by political realities.

*Political Equality*    The nation's Founders shared the belief that the law should apply equally to all—that birth, status, or wealth do not justify differential application of the laws. But *legal equality* did not necessarily mean **political equality,** at least not in 1787 when the U.S. Constitution was written. The Constitution left the issue of voter qualification to the states to decide for themselves. At that time, all states imposed either property or taxpayer qualifications for voting. Neither

**Capitalism:** An economic system asserting the individual's right to own private property and to buy, sell, rent, and trade that property in a free market.

**Political equality:** A belief that the law should apply equally to all and that every person's vote counts equally.

CHAPTER 2 • POLITICAL CULTURE: IDEAS IN CONFLICT

women nor slaves could vote anywhere. The expansion of voting rights to universal suffrage required many bitter battles over the course of two centuries. The long history of the struggle over voting rights illustrates the contradictions between values and practices (see "Securing the Right to Vote" in Chapter 5). Yet in the absence of the *value* of equality, voting rights might have remained restricted.

*Equality of Opportunity*    The American ideal of equality extends to **equality of opportunity**—the elimination of artificial barriers to success in life. The term *equality of opportunity* refers to the ability to make of oneself what one can, to develop one's talents and abilities, and to be rewarded for one's work, initiative, and achievement. Equality of opportunity means that everyone comes to the same starting line in life, with the same chance of success, and that whatever differences develop over time do so as a result of abilities, talents, initiative, hard work, and perhaps good luck.

Americans do not generally resent the fact that physicians, engineers, airline pilots, and others who have spent time and energy acquiring particular skills make more money than those whose jobs require fewer skills and less training. Neither do most Americans resent the fact that people who risk their own time and money to build a business, bring new or better products to market, and create jobs for others make more money than their employees. Nor do many Americans begrudge multimillion-dollar incomes to sports figures, rock singers, and movie stars whose talents entertain the public. And few Americans object when someone wins a million-dollar lottery, as long as everyone who entered the lottery had an equal chance at winning. Americans are generally willing to have government act to ensure equality of opportunity—to ensure that everyone has an equal chance at getting an education, landing a job, and buying a home, and that no barriers of race, sex, religion, or ethnicity bar individual advancement. Differences arise over whether special efforts such as *affirmative action* should be undertaken to overcome the effects of past discriminatory barriers (see "Affirmative Action in the Courts" and "Affirmative Action in the Congress" in Chapter 15). But the ideal of equality of opportunity is widely shared.

*Equality of Results*    **Equality of results** refers to the equal sharing of income and material rewards. Equality of results means that everyone starts *and finishes* the race together, regardless of ability, talent, initiative, or work. Those who argue on behalf of this notion of equality say that if individuals are truly equal, then everyone should enjoy generally equal conditions in life. According to this belief, we should appreciate an individual's skills, work, knowledge, and contributions to society without creating inequalities of wealth and income. Government should act to *transfer* wealth and income from the rich to the poor to increase the total happiness of society.

But equality of results, or absolute equality, is *not* a widely shared value in the United States. This notion of equality was referred to as "leveling" by Thomas Jefferson and generally has been denounced by the nation's political leadership—and by most Americans—then and now:

> To take from one, because it is thought his own industry and that of his fathers has acquired too much, in order to spare to others who have not exercised equal industry and skill, is to violate arbitrarily . . . the guarantee to everyone the free exercise of his industry and the fruits acquired by it.[5]

**Equality of opportunity:** The elimination of artificial barriers to success in life and the opportunity for everyone to strive for success.

**Equality of results:** The equal sharing of income and material goods regardless of one's efforts in life.

The taking of private property from those who acquired it legitimately, for no other reason than to equalize wealth or income, is widely viewed as morally wrong. Moreover, many people believe that society generally would suffer if incomes were equalized. Absolute equality among people would remove incentives to work, save, or produce. Everyone would slack off, production would decline, goods would be in short supply, and everyone would end up poorer than ever. So some inequality may be essential for the well-being of society.

Thus, Americans believe strongly in equality of opportunity but not necessarily equality of results (see Figure 2-1). Americans seek fairness rather than equality of incomes.

**FIGURE 2-1**

**Beliefs about Equality**

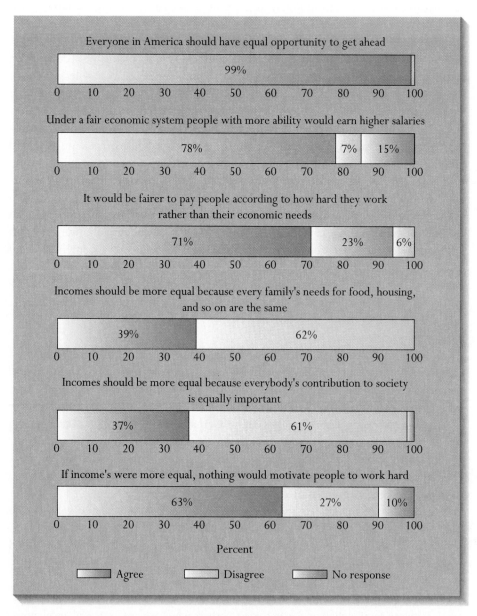

*Source:* Questions 1–3 based on Herbert McClosky and John Zaller, *The American Ethos: Public Attitudes toward Capitalism and Democracy* (Cambridge, Mass.: Harvard University Press, 1984), pp. 83–84; questions 4–6 based on James R. Kluegel and Eliot R. Smith, *Beliefs about Inequality: Americans' Views of What Is and What Ought to Be* (New York: Aldine de Gruyter, 1986).

CHAPTER 2 • POLITICAL CULTURE: IDEAS IN CONFLICT

*Fairness* Americans value "fairness" even though they do not always agree on what is fair. Most Americans support a "floor" on income and material well-being—a level that no one, regardless of his or her condition, should be permitted to fall below—even though they differ over how high that floor should be. Indeed, the belief in a floor is consistent with the belief in equality of opportunity; extreme poverty would deny people, especially children, the opportunity to compete in life.[6] But very few Americans want to place a "ceiling" on income or wealth. This unwillingness to limit top income extends to nearly all groups in the United States, the poor as well as the rich. Generally, Americans want people who cannot provide for themselves to be well cared for, especially children, the elderly, the ill, and the disabled. They are often willing to "soak the rich" when searching for new tax sources, believing that the rich can easily afford to bear the burdens of government. But, unlike citizens in other Western democracies, Americans generally do *not* believe that government should equalize incomes (see *Compared to What?* "Should Government Equalize Incomes?").

## COMPARED TO WHAT?

## Should Government Equalize Incomes?

While American political culture emphasizes equality of *opportunity*, the political culture in the Western Europe democracies is much more inclined toward equality of *results*. Americans generally believe that government should provide a "floor," or safety net, to protect people against true hardship; but they are generally unwilling to place a "ceiling" on incomes, or to give government the task of equalizing income differences between people. In contrast, majorities in most other Western democracies agree with the statement: "It is government's responsibility to reduce income differences between people."

*Source: U.S. News and World Report,* August 7, 1989, p. 25, reporting data gathered by Gallup International Research Institute, International Research Associates, National Opinion Research Center, and International Social Survey Program, 1987–88.

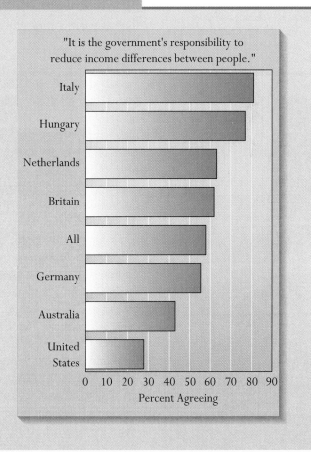

"It is the government's responsibility to reduce income differences between people."

*Equality in Politics versus Economics*   Americans make a clear distinction between the *private economic* sphere of life and the *public political* sphere.[7] In the private economic sphere, they value the principle of "earned deserts," meaning that individuals are entitled to what they achieve through hard work, skill, talent, risk, and even good luck. They are willing to tolerate inequalities of result in economics. Self-interested behavior in the marketplace is seen as appropriate and even beneficial, if properly constrained by rules that apply equally to everyone. But in the public political sphere, Americans value absolute equality—one person, one vote. They condemn disparities of power and influence among individuals. Self-interested behavior in politics is seen as corrupt.

As long as the economic and political spheres of life are perceived as separate, then economic inequalities and political equalities can exist side by side in a society.

## INEQUALITY OF INCOME AND WEALTH

Conflict in society is generated more often by inequalities among people than by hardship or deprivation. Material well-being and standards of living are usually expressed in aggregate measures for a whole society—for example, gross domestic product per capita, income per capita, average life expectancy, infant mortality rate. These measures of societal well-being are vitally important to a nation and its people, but *political* conflict is more likely to occur over the *distribution* of well-being *within* a society. Unequal distributions can generate conflict even in a very affluent society with high levels of income and a high standard of living.

*As income differences between the "haves" and the "have-nots" increased in America during the 1980s and the early 1990s, more of its citizens fell through the cracks in the system and joined the ranks of the impoverished and homeless.*

*Inequality of Income*   Let us examine inequality of income in the United States systematically. Figure 2-2 divides all American families into five groups, or *quintiles*—from the lowest one-fifth in personal income to the highest one-fifth—and shows the percentage of total family personal income received by each of these groups over the years. (If perfect income equality existed, each fifth of American families would receive 20 percent of all family personal income.) The poorest one-fifth received only 3.5 percent of all family personal income in 1929; today, this group does a little better, at 4.2 percent of family personal income. The highest one-fifth received 54.4 percent of all family personal income in 1929; today, its percentage has declined to 46.2. This was the only income group to lose in relation to other income groups. Notice that the middle classes (second, third, and fourth quintiles) improved their relative income positions more than the poor. Another measure of income equalization over time is the decline in the percentage of income received by the top 5 percent of American families. This group received 30 percent of all family income in 1929, but only 19.1 percent today.

While income differences in the United States have declined over the long run, inequality has actually *increased* in recent years. The income of the poorest quintile declined from 5.4 to 4.2 percent of total income between 1970 and 1993; the income of the highest quintile rose from 40.9 to 46.2 percent of total income. This reversal of historical trends has generated both political rhetoric and serious scholarly inquiry about its causes.

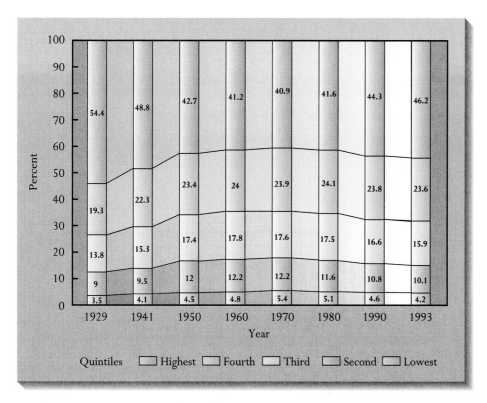

Source: *Statistical Abstract of the United States, 1995,* p. 475.

**FIGURE 2-2** The Distribution of Income in the United States (Percentage Distribution of Family Personal Income)

*Assessing Blame*   The political argument that income inequality increased because of reduced federal social welfare payments in the 1980s is untrue. Aggregate government social welfare transfer payments did not decline, either in real dollars or as a percentage of gross domestic product. It is true that the *rate of increase* in social welfare spending declined in the 1980s, but total social welfare spending by governments remained at approximately 18.5 percent of gross domestic product (GDP) throughout the 1980s.

Recent increases in inequality in the United States are a product of several social and economic trends: (1) the decline of the manufacturing sector of the economy (with its relatively high-paying blue-collar jobs) and the ascendancy of the communications, information, and service sectors of the economy (with a combination of high-paying and low-paying jobs); (2) the rise in the number of two-wage families, making single-wage, female-headed households relatively less affluent; (3) demographic trends, which include larger proportions of aged and larger proportions of female-headed families; and (4) global competition, which restrains wages in unskilled and semiskilled jobs while rewarding people in high-technology, high-productivity occupations.

*Inequality of Wealth*   Inequalities of wealth in the United States are even greater than inequalities of income. *Wealth* is the total value of a family's assets—bank accounts, stocks, bonds, mutual funds, business equity, houses, cars, and major appliances—minus outstanding debts, such as credit card balances, mortgages, and other loans. The top 1 percent of families in the United States owns almost 40 percent of all family wealth (see Figure 2-3). Inequality of wealth appeared to be diminishing until the mid-1970s, but in recent years it has surged

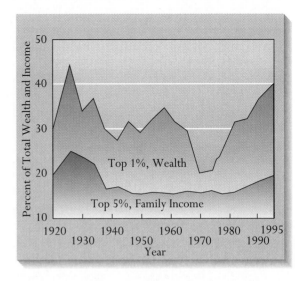

FIGURE 2-3   Inequality of
Wealth and Income

Source: U.S. Bureau of the Census, *Current Population Reports, 1995;* see also
Edward N. Wolff, *Top Heavy* (New York: Twentieth Century Fund, 1995),
p. 28.

sharply. Not surprisingly, age is the key determinant of family wealth; persons age
fifty to sixty-five are by far the wealthiest, with persons over sixty-five close
behind; young families generally have less than one-third of the assets of retirees.

## SOCIAL MOBILITY

Political conflict over inequality might be greater in the United States if it were
not for the prospect of social mobility. All societies are stratified, or layered, but
societies differ greatly in **social mobility**—that is, in the extent to which people move upward or downward in income and status over a lifetime or over generations. Fairly steep inequalities may be tolerated politically if people have a reasonable expectation of moving up in income or status over time, or at least of
seeing their children do so. Mobility and the expectation of mobility, over a lifetime or over generations, may be the key to understanding why **class conflict** in
America is not as widespread or as intense as it is in many other nations.

The United States describes itself as the land of opportunity. The really important political question may be how much real opportunity exists for individual
Americans to improve their conditions in life relative to others. The impression
given by Figure 2-2 is one of a static distribution system, with families permanently placed in upper or lower fifths of income earners. But there is considerable
evidence of both upward and downward movement by people among income
groupings.[8] About a third of the families in the poorest one-fifth will move
upward within a decade, and about a third of families in the richest one-fifth will
fall out of this top category (see Figure 2-4). However, there appears to have been
some slowing of this mobility during the 1980s; one's chances of escaping the
bottom have diminished somewhat. Thus, the nation is currently experiencing not
only an increase in equality but also a slowing of social mobility.

The *belief* in social mobility—that people have a good opportunity to get ahead
if they study or work long and hard, save and invest wisely, display initiative and

**Social mobility:** The extent to
which people move upward or
downward in income and status
over a lifetime or generations.

**Class conflict:** Conflict
between upper and lower social
classes over wealth and power.

CHAPTER 2 • POLITICAL CULTURE: IDEAS IN CONFLICT

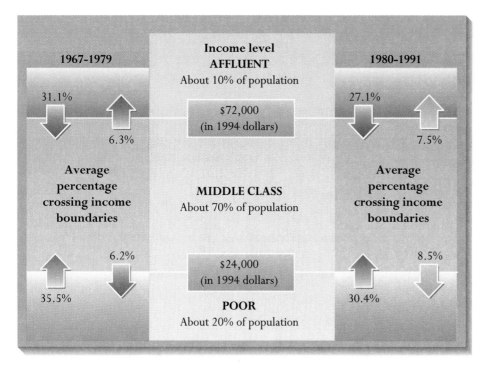

FIGURE 2-4  Social Mobility over Time

*Source:* Greg J. Duncan, Northwestern University, from data from Panel Study of Income Dynamics, as reported in *New York Times,* June 4, 1995, p. E4.

enterprise in business affairs—reduces the potential for conflict among classes. Social mobility diminishes **class consciousness,** which is the awareness of one's class position and the feeling of political solidarity with others in the same class in opposition to other classes. If class lines were impermeable and no one had any reasonable expectation of moving up or seeing his or her children move up, then class consciousness would rise and political conflict among classes would intensify.

Historically, most of the people who came to settle in this country did so because of their belief that their lives would be better here, and the political culture of our country today has been greatly affected by the beliefs and values they brought with them.

## A NATION OF IMMIGRANTS

The United States is a nation of immigrants, from the first "boat people" (Pilgrims) to the latest Cuban *balseros* ("rafters"). Americans are proud of their immigrant heritage and the freedom and opportunity the nation has extended to generations of "huddled masses yearning to be free"—words emblazoned upon the Statue of Liberty in New York's harbor. Today about 8 percent of the U.S. population is foreign-born.

The United States accepts more immigrants than all other nations of the world combined. The vast majority of immigrants in recent years come from less-developed nations of Asia and Latin America (see Figure 2-5). Most immigrants come to the United States for economic opportunity. Most personify the traits we typically think of as American: opportunism, ambition, perseverance, initiative,

**Class consciousness:** An awareness of one's class position and a feeling of political solidarity with others within the same class in opposition to other classes.

POLITICAL CULTURE: IDEAS IN CONFLICT • CHAPTER 2

*Cuban balseros ("rafters") setting off in a flimsy craft hoping to reach Miami. The Clinton administration has recently discouraged the kind of massive exodus of Cubans that occurred in the early 1980s during the Mariel boatlift.*

and a willingness to work hard. As immigrants have always done, they frequently take dirty, low-paying, thankless jobs that other Americans shun. When they open their own businesses, they often do so in blighted, crime-ridden neighborhoods long since abandoned by other entrepreneurs.

*National Immigration Policy*    Immigration policy is a responsibility of the national government. It was not until 1882 that Congress passed the first legislation restricting entry into the United States of persons alleged to be "undesirable" and virtually all Asians. Following the end of World War I, Congress passed the comprehensive Immigration Act of 1921, which established maximum numbers of new immigrants each year and set a quota for each foreign country at 3 percent of the number of that nation's foreign-born living in the United States in 1910,

**FIGURE 2-5**    **Origins of Legal Immigrants, 1981–90**

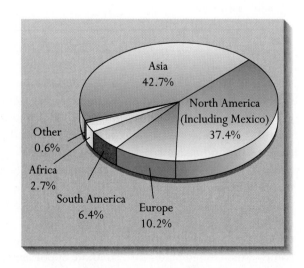

Asia
42.7%

North America
(Including Mexico)
37.4%

Other
0.6%

Africa
2.7%

South America
6.4%

Europe
10.2%

*Source: Statistical Abstract of the United States, 1995, p. 11.*

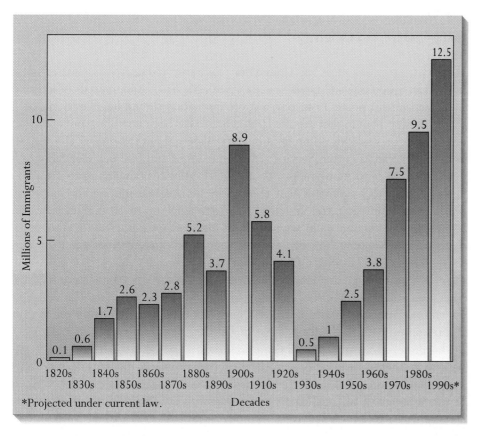

FIGURE 2-6 Immigration to the United States by Decades

*Projected under current law.

Decades

*Source: Statistical Abstract of the United States, 1995, p. 10.*

later reduced to 2 percent of the number in 1890. These restrictions reflected anti-immigration feelings that were generally directed at the large wave of Southern and Eastern European Catholic and Jewish immigrants (Poland, Russia, Hungary, Italy, Greece) entering the United States prior to World War I (see Figure 2-6). The law did *not* set any quotas for immigrants from the Western Hemisphere, and immigration from Mexico sharply increased. It was not until the Immigration and Nationality Act of 1965 that national origin quotas were abolished, replaced by preference categories for relatives and family members and professional and highly skilled persons.

Immigration "reform" was the announced goal of Congress in the Immigration Reform and Control Act of 1986, also known as the Simpson-Mazzoli Act. It sought to control immigration by placing principal responsibility on employers; it set fines for knowingly hiring an illegal alien, with prison terms for repeat offenders. However, it allowed employers to accept many different forms of easily forged documentation and at the same time subjected them to penalties for discriminating against legal foreign-born residents. To win political support, the act granted amnesty to illegal aliens who had lived in the United States since 1982. But the act failed to reduce the flow of either legal or illegal immigrants.

Today, roughly a million people per year are admitted *legally* to the United States as "lawful permanent residents" (persons who have needed job skills or who have relatives who are U.S. citizens); or as "refugees," or "asylees" (persons with "a well-founded fear of persecution" in their country of origin). In addition, more than 20 million people are awarded visas each year to enter the United States for study, pleasure, or business.

*Illegal Immigration*    The United States is a free and prosperous society with more than 5,000 miles of borders (2,000 with Mexico) and hundreds of international air and sea ports. In theory, a sovereign nation should be able to maintain secure borders, but in practice the United States has been unwilling and unable to do so. Estimates of illegal immigration vary widely, from the official U.S. Immigration and Naturalization Service (INS) estimate of 400,000 per year (about 45 percent of the legal immigration) to unofficial estimates ranging up to 3 million per year. The INS estimates that about 4 million illegal immigrants currently reside in the United States; unofficial estimates range up to 10 million or more. Many illegal immigrants slip across U.S. borders or enter ports with false documentation, while many more overstay tourist or student visas (and are not counted by the INS as illegal immigrants).[9]

As a free society, the United States is not prepared to undertake massive roundups and summary deportations of millions of illegal residents. The Fifth and Fourteenth Amendments to the U.S. Constitution require that every *person* (not just citizen) be afforded "due process of law." The INS may turn back persons at the border or even hold them in detention camps. The Coast Guard may intercept boats at sea and return persons to their country of origin.[10] Aliens have no constitutional right to come to the United States. However, once in the United States, whether legally or illegally, every person is entitled to due process of law and equal protection of the laws. People are thus entitled to a fair hearing prior to any government attempt to deport them. Aliens are entitled to apply for asylum and present evidence at a hearing of their "well-founded fear of prosecution" if returned to their country. Experience has shown that the only way to reduce the flow of illegal immigration is to control it at the border, an expensive and difficult but not impossible task. Localized experiments in border enforcement have indicated that, with significant increases in INS personnel and technology, illegal immigration can be reduced by half or more.

*Cultural Conflict*    The politics of immigration centers on both cultural and economic conflicts. While most Americans are themselves the descendants of immigrants (Native Americans constitute about 1 percent of the population), there is a widespread belief that today's immigrants are different from earlier waves. Population projections based on current immigration and fertility (birth) rates suggest that the ethnic character of the nation will shift dramatically over time because so many immigrants today are from Asia and Latin America rather than Europe.

The United States has always been an ethnically pluralist society, but all immigrants were expected to adopt American political culture—including liberty, economic freedom, political equality, and equality of opportunity—and to learn American history and traditions, as well as the English language. The nation's motto has been "E Pluribus Unum" (From Many, One) since 1782, but opponents of large-scale immigration fear that immigration currently represents a threat to cultural and political unity.[11] There have long been Italian, Irish, Polish, Chinese, and other ethnic neighborhoods in big cities, but the children of immigrants, if not the immigrants themselves, quickly became "Americanized." In contrast, today policy makers are divided over whether to protect and preserve language and cultural differences, for example through bilingual education, bilingual language ballots, and "language minority" voting districts (all currently required by amendments and interpretations of the Civil Rights Act of 1964 and the Voting Rights Act of 1965; see Chapter 14).

Economists differ over the economic impact of immigration—whether it creates jobs and new business or creates a surplus of labor and reduces wages. It is not clear whether the taxes paid by immigrants add more to the revenues of governments than the services they use or vice versa.[12] Currently neither the states nor the federal government accurately tracks the immigration status of welfare recipients or public school pupils, two subjects of widespread debate in this country (see *What Do You Think?* "Should Illegal Immigrants Be Denied Welfare Benefits?"). It is believed, however, that immigrant families are generally younger and more likely to have school-age children.

## WHAT DO YOU THINK?

# Should Illegal Immigrants Be Denied Welfare Benefits?

California's Proposition 187 in 1994 set off a national debate over immigration. Placed on the ballot by citizen initiative, Proposition 187 denies public education, nonemergency health care, and social service benefits to illegal aliens in that state. The initiative was supported by Republican Governor Pete Wilson, who claimed that the state spent more than $2 billion per year providing public support for more than 2 million illegal aliens living in California. The denial of education and health care to children was branded by opponents as especially mean-spirited and cruel.

Following a highly spirited and well-publicized contest over the initiative, California voters approved it by a solid 59 to 41 percent. The constitutionality of the measure is questionable—the Fourteenth Amendment declares that no state shall "deny to any person within its jurisdiction the equal protection of the laws"—and its implementation has been halted by federal courts. But the vote sent a loud message to Washington that Californians resented the national government's mandating state funding of benefits for illegal immigration that the national government itself failed to control.

National surveys report that the denial of public services to illegal immigrants has widespread support. When asked, "Do you favor or oppose having a law in your state—similar to Proposition 187 in California—that requires state and local government

agencies to stop providing health benefits and public education to illegal immigrants including children?" such a law was favored overall by 58 percent (67 percent among Republicans, 55 percent among Democrats, and 56 percent among Independents) and was opposed by 36 percent.

Popular support for legal immigration appears to have declined over the years:

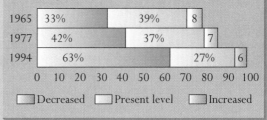

**Question**: *In your view should immigration be kept at its present level, increased, or decreased?*

| | Decreased | Present level | Increased |
|---|---|---|---|
| 1965 | 33% | 39% | 8 |
| 1977 | 42% | 37% | 7 |
| 1994 | 63% | 27% | 6 |

Most Americans agree that immigrants make valued contributions: that they "are productive citizens once they get their feet on the ground" (63 percent), "are hardworking" (58 percent), "are basically good honest people" (55 percent). However, majorities also believe that immigrants "are a burden on taxpayers" (66 percent), "take jobs from Americans" (58 percent), and "add to the crime problem" (56 percent).

*Source:* Gallup and Yankelovich polls, reported in *American Enterprise* 6 (March/April 1995): 105.

**Ideology:** A consistent and integrated system of ideas, values, and beliefs.

Political opposition to increased border enforcement and reduced immigration comes from a variety of sources. Large numbers of Americans identify with the aspirations of people striving to come to the United States, whether legally or illegally. Many Americans still have family and relatives living abroad who may wish to immigrate. Hispanic groups have been especially concerned about immigration enforcement efforts that may lead to discrimination against all Hispanic Americans. Powerful industry groups that benefit from the availability of illegal immigrants—such as agriculture, restaurants, clothing, and hospitals—lobby in Washington to weaken enforcement efforts. Some employers prefer hiring illegal immigrants because they are willing to work at hard jobs for low pay and few if any benefits. Foreign governments, especially Mexico, have also protested U.S. enforcement policies.

## IDEOLOGIES: LIBERALISM AND CONSERVATISM

An **ideology** is a consistent and integrated system of ideas, values, and beliefs. A political ideology tells us who *should* get what, when, and how; that is, it tells us who *ought* to govern and what goals they *ought* to pursue. When we use ideological terms such as *liberalism* and *conservatism,* we imply reasonably integrated sets of values and beliefs. And when we pin ideological labels on people, we imply that they are fairly consistent in the application of these values and beliefs in public affairs. In reality, neither political leaders nor citizens always display integrated or consistent opinions; many hold conservative views on some issues and liberal views on others.[13] Most Americans avoid ideological labeling, either by describing themselves as "moderate" or "middle-of-the-road" or by simply declining to

( FIGURE 2-7 )   **Americans: Liberal, Moderate, Conservative**

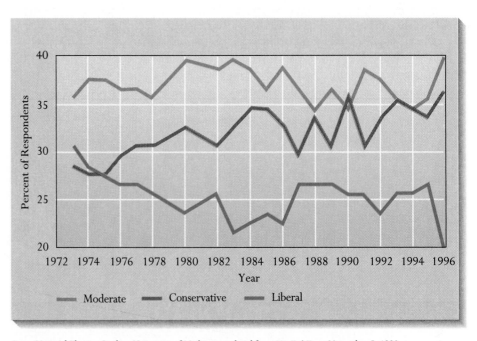

Source: National Election Studies, University of Michigan, updated from *New York Times,* November 5, 1992.

CHAPTER 2 • POLITICAL CULTURE: IDEAS IN CONFLICT

place themselves on an ideological scale. (Over the years, between 25 and 33 percent of respondents in national polls say they "don't know" or "haven't thought about it" when asked about their liberal or conservative sentiments.) But as Figure 2-7 shows, among those who choose an ideological label to describe their politics, conservatives consistently outnumber liberals.

Despite inconsistencies in opinion and avoidance of labeling, ideology plays an important role in American politics. People do have political beliefs about who *should* get what in society, even when they do not use ideological terms to describe these beliefs (see *Across the USA:* "Liberalism and Conservatism"). More important, perhaps, political *elites*—elected and appointed officeholders, media reporters and commentators, party officials and interest-group leaders, and others active in politics—are generally more consistent in their political views than nonelites and are more likely to use ideological terms in describing politics.[14]

*Modern Conservatism: Individualism plus Traditional Values*   Modern **conservatism** combines a belief in free markets, limited government, and individual self-reliance in economic affairs with a belief in the value of tradition, law,

**Conservatism:** A belief in the value of free markets, limited government, and individual self-reliance in economic affairs, combined with a belief in the value of tradition, law, and morality in social affairs.

## ACROSS THE USA

# Liberalism and Conservatism

*States might be classified in terms of their voters' self-identification in opinion surveys as liberal, moderate, or conservative. The most conservative state was Utah (45 percent conservative, 37 percent moderate, 13 percent liberal), followed by Indiana (42 percent conservative, 39 percent moderate, 13 percent liberal). The most liberal states were Massachusetts (26 percent conservative, 42 percent moderate, 26 percent liberal), New York (29 percent conservative, 39 percent moderate, 26 percent liberal), and New Jersey (28 percent conservative, 40 percent moderate, 26 percent liberal).*

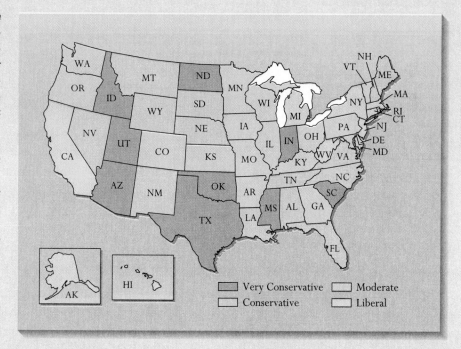

*Source:* Gerald C. Wright, Robert S. Erikson, and John P. McIver, "Public Opinion and Policy Liberalism in the American States," *American Journal of Political Science* 31 (November 1987): 980–1001.

and morality in social affairs. Conservatives wish to retain our historical commitments to individual freedom from governmental controls, reliance on individual initiative and effort for self-development, a free-enterprise economy with a minimum of governmental intervention, and rewards for initiative, skill, risk, and hard work—views consistent with the early classical liberalism of Locke, Jefferson, and the nation's Founders, discussed at the beginning of this chapter. The result is a confusion of ideological labels: modern conservatives claim to be the true inheritors of the (classical) liberal tradition.

## PEOPLE IN POLITICS

## P.J. O'Rourke, Conservative with a Sense of Humor

"Giving money and power to government is like giving whiskey and car keys to teenage boys," according to political humorist P.J. O'Rourke. Two of his books—*Parliament of Whores* (1991), dealing with the American political system, and *Give War a Chance* (1994), describing international politics, have topped the best-seller lists. Describing himself as a "cigar-smoking conservative," O'Rourke actually bashes Republicans as well as Democrats:

When you look at the Republicans you see the scum off the top of business. When you look at the Democrats you see the scum off the top of politics. Personally, I prefer business. A businessman will steal from you directly instead of getting the IRS to do it for him. And when Republicans ruin the environment, destroy the supply of affordable housing, and wreck the industrial infrastructure, at least they make a buck off it. The Democrats just do these things for fun.

O'Rourke describes his life as a youth growing up in Toledo, Ohio:

My own family was poor when I was a kid, though I didn't know it; I just thought we were broke. My father died, and my mother married a drunken bum who shortly thereafter died himself. . . . But I hon-

estly didn't know we were poor until just now, when I was researching poverty levels.

He counts himself lucky, because no one coddled or sympathized with his family's distress. His mother never went on welfare. In the "bad old days," he was simply expected to shut up, behave, and work hard. O'Rourke started out as a Republican but joined the counterculture of the 1960s. Yet he says he was never a Democrat: "I went from being a Republican, to being a Maoist, then back to being a Republican again." He won a scholarship to Miami University of Ohio and later Johns Hopkins. In 1972, he went to work for *National Lampoon,* and on the strength of his irreverent articles he was elevated to editor-in-chief in 1978. Later he moved to Hollywood to write movie scripts, including Rodney Dangerfield films, then returned to New York to become an editor of *Rolling Stone.*

A frequent speaker on university campuses, O'Rourke reflects a distinctly conservative view of government: "A little government and a little luck are necessary in life but only a fool trusts either of them. . . . The whole idea of government is: if enough people get together and act in concert, they can take something and not pay for it." His latest book, *Age and Guile Beat Youth, Innocence, and a Bad Haircut* (1995), describes his ideological journey from youthful radicalism to his current mature (?) conservatism: "I was once younger than anyone ever has been. And on drugs. At least I hope I was on drugs. I'd hate to think that those were my sober and well-considered thoughts."

*Source:* P.J. O'Rourke, *Parliament of Whores* (New York: Atlantic Monthly Press, 1991); and *Age and Guile Beat Youth, Innocence, and a Bad Haircut* (New York: Atlantic Monthly Press, 1995).

Modern conservatism does indeed incorporate many classical liberal ideals, but it also has a distinct ideological tradition of its own. Conservatism is less optimistic about human nature (see *People in Politics:* "P.J. O'Rourke, Conservatism with a Sense of Humor"). Traditionally, conservatives have recognized that human nature includes elements of irrationality, ignorance, hatred, and violence. Thus they have been more likely to place their faith in *law* and *traditional values* than in popular fads, trends, or emotions. To conservatives, the absence of law does not mean freedom but, rather, exposure to the tyranny of terrorism and violence. They believe that without the guidance of traditional values, people would soon come to grief through the unruliness of their passions, destroying both themselves and others. Conservatives argue that strong institutions—family, church, and community—are needed to repress individuals' selfish and immoral impulses and to foster civilized ways of life.

*Modern Liberalism: Governmental Power to "Do Good"*   Modern **liberalism** combines a belief in a strong government to provide economic security and protection for civil rights with a belief in freedom from government intervention in social conduct. Modern liberalism retains the classical liberalism commitment to individual dignity, but it emphasizes the importance of social and economic security for the whole population as a prerequisite to individual self-development. Classical liberalism looked with suspicion on government as a potential source of "interference" with personal freedom, but modern liberalism looks on the power of government as a positive force for eliminating social and economic conditions that adversely affect people's lives and impede their self-development. The modern liberal approves of the use of governmental power to ensure the general welfare and to correct the perceived ills of society (see *People in Politics:* "Barbara Boxer, Defending Liberalism")

Today's liberals believe they can change people's lives through the exercise of governmental power: end racial and sexual discrimination, abolish poverty, eliminate slums, create jobs, uplift the poor, provide medical care for all, educate the masses, protect the environment, and instill humanitarian values in everyone. The prevailing impulse is to "do good," to perform public services, and to assist the least fortunate in society, particularly the poor and minorities. Modern liberalism is impatient with what it sees as slow progress through individual initiative and private enterprise toward the solution of socioeconomic problems, so it seeks to use the power of the national government to find immediate and comprehensive solutions to society's troubles.

Modern liberalism continues to recognize the individual's right to own private property, but it imposes on the property owner social and economic obligations that are designed to reduce capitalism's hardships. It assumes that businesses will be privately owned but subject to considerable governmental regulation. Modern liberals are committed to a significant enlargement of the public (governmental) sector of society in education, welfare, housing, recreation facilities, transportation, urban renewal, medicine, employment, child care, and other areas. Modern liberalism envisions a larger role for government in the future: setting new goals, managing the economy, meeting popular wants, and redirecting national resources away from private wants toward public needs.

Modern liberalism defines equality somewhat differently from the way classical liberalism does. Classical liberalism stresses the value of equality of opportunity. Individuals should be free to make the most of their talents and skills, but differ-

**Liberalism:** A belief in the value of strong government to provide economic security and protection for civil rights, combined with a belief in personal freedom from government intervention in social conduct.

## Barbara Boxer, Defending Liberalism

Perhaps no one has been more successful in defending liberal causes in Congress than California's outspoken U.S. senator, Barbara Boxer. Her political resumé boasts of awards and honors from such organizations as Planned Parenthood (abortion rights), the Sierra Club (environmental causes), Mobilization against AIDS, Anti-Defamation League (civil rights), and Public Citizen (consumer affairs).

A graduate of Brooklyn College with a B.A. in economics, Boxer worked briefly as a stockbroker before moving to San Francisco, where she became a journalist and later a campaign aide to a local congressional representative. Her political career is based in Marin County, a wealthy, trendy, upper-class, liberal community north of San Francisco, where she first won elected office as member of the County Board of Supervisors. She was elected to the U.S. House of Representatives from her Marin County district in 1982 and quickly won a reputation as one of the most liberal members of the

House. Appointed to the House Armed Services Committee, she became a leading critic of defense spending and virtually every weapon requested by the military.

When her state's liberal Democratic senator, Alan Cranston, announced he would not seek reelection to the Senate in the wake of his censure in the Keating Five affair, Boxer sought the open seat. Her opponent, conservative Republican radio and TV commentator Bruce Herschensohn, hammered at Boxer's 143 overdrafts at the House bank, her frequent absenteeism, and her extensive use of congressional perks. But with the help of Clinton's 1992 landslide (47 to 32 percent) victory over George Bush in California, Boxer eked out a 48 to 45 percent victory over Herschensohn. Her victory, together with that of Dianne Feinstein, gave California a historical first—two women U.S. senators.

Boxer quickly emerged as a powerful force in the U.S. Senate on behalf of abortion rights. She led the Senate fight for a federal law protecting abortion clinics from obstruction by demonstrators. On the Environmental and Public Works Committee she helped block efforts to relax federal environmental regulations. And she led the movement to oust Republican Senator Bob Packwood from the Senate on charges of sexually harassing staff members.

ences in wealth or power that are a product of differences in talent, initiative, risk taking, and skill are accepted as natural. In contrast, modern liberalism contends that individual dignity and equality of opportunity depend in some measure on *reduction of absolute inequality* in society. Modern liberals believe that true equality of opportunity cannot be achieved where there are significant numbers of people suffering from hunger, remediable illness, or extreme hardships in the conditions of life. Thus modern liberalism supports government efforts to reduce inequalities in society.

*Neo-Conservatism and Neo-Liberalism* Ideologies continually evolve. Both liberalism and conservatism in the United States have thus changed to meet new challenges and altered conditions. For example, in the 1960s and 1970s many liberals became disillusioned with large-scale, costly bureaucratic government programs. They were still concerned with poverty, discrimination, crime, ignorance, and pollution, but they came to believe that many government programs were ineffective or were making things worse. As they saw it, government was overloaded with tasks that should be left to the individual, the family, the church, or the free-market system. These liberals won the label **neo-conservatives** (new conservatives) in recognition of their changing views toward less government intervention in society. Most neo-conservatives ended up in the Republican Party.

Other traditional liberals retained their faith in the power of government to solve social problems, but they sought new programs to restore the nation's economic health. Unlike old liberals, who placed social issues first on their agenda, these new liberals were convinced that little progress on social problems could be expected unless the economy is healthy. Thus they argued that government must take an active role in promoting and directing the nation's industrial growth. These **neo-liberals** were generally critical of the traditional interest-group liberals. They worried that traditional liberals would sacrifice American growth, productivity, and competitive edge in world markets to satisfy the demands of union leaders, protection-seeking industries, and other special interests. During the 1980s neo-liberals helped form the Democratic Leadership Council (with Arkansas Governor Bill Clinton as chair) to push their "new" Democratic agenda within the Democratic Party (see *People in Politics:* "Bill Clinton's Lifelong Campaign for the Presidency" in Chapter 11).

## IDEOLOGICAL BATTLEGROUNDS: FOUR PERSPECTIVES

If Americans aligned themselves along a single liberal-conservative dimension, politics in the United States would be easier to describe but far less interesting (see *What Do You Think?* "Are You a Liberal or a Conservative?"). We might define the liberal-conservative dimension as generally referring to the role of government in society, with liberals favoring an active, powerful government and conservatives favoring a limited, noninterventionist government. But many Americans make a distinction between *social conduct* and *economic affairs* in their views of the proper role of government. So it is possible to map ideology in the United States in a two-dimensional framework based (1) on whether people prefer more or less government (2) in either social or economic affairs. The result is the identification of four possible ideological types: liberals, conservatives, populists, and libertarians (see Figure 2-8). Interestingly, in the battle over ideas, think tanks have arisen that mirror these ideological types in their approach to policy (see *Up Close:* "Think Tanks: The Battle of Ideas").

*Liberals*   Liberals generally prefer an active, powerful government in economic affairs—a government that provides a broad range of public services; regulates business; protects civil rights; protects consumers and the environment; provides generous unemployment, welfare, and Social Security benefits; and reduces economic inequality. But many of these same liberals would limit the government's power to regulate social conduct. They oppose restrictions on abortion; oppose school prayer; favor "decriminalizing" marijuana, public intoxication, and vagrancy; oppose government restrictions on speech, press, and protest; oppose the death penalty; and strive to protect the rights of criminal defendants. Liberalism is the prevailing ideology among college professors, while most college students think of themselves as "middle-of-the-road" (see *Up Close* "Ideology on the Campus: Students versus Professors").

**Neo-Conservative:** Traditional liberal concerns about the nation's social problems, but disillusionment with large-scale, costly bureaucratic government programs as solutions.

**Neo-Liberal:** Continued faith in the power of government to solve social problems, but with priority given to stimulating economic growth over traditional liberal welfare programs.

*Liberals' concern about efforts to curtail social welfare programs reflects their support of strong government, whereas conservatives' demands for tax cuts reflect their preference for government that encourages self-reliance and individual initiative.*

FIGURE 2-8 **Mapping Ideologies: The Role of Government**

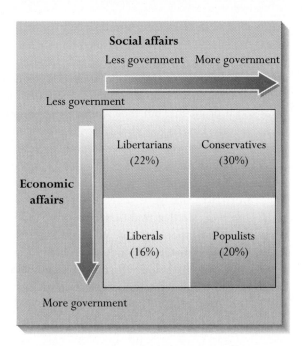

\*Percentages are based on combined responses to national survey questions asking whether government should do more "to solve our country's problems" or "to promote traditional values," as reported in *American Enterprise,* 5 (May/June 1994): 91. Figures do not total 100 percent because of "Don't Know" and "Other" responses.

*Conservatives*    In contrast, conservatives generally prefer limited noninterventionist government in economic affairs—a government that relies on free markets to provide and distribute goods and services; minimizes its regulatory activity; limits social welfare programs to the "truly needy"; keeps taxes low; and rejects schemes to equalize income or wealth. On the other hand, conservatives would strengthen government's power to regulate social conduct. They support restrictions on abortion; endorse school prayer; favor a war on drugs and pornography; support the death penalty; and advocate tougher criminal penalties.

Thus, neither liberals nor conservatives in the United States take a consistent view toward the role of government. Most liberals today would expand government power in economic affairs and civil rights yet limit its power to regulate many areas of social conduct. Most conservatives would restrict government power in economic affairs and civil rights yet expand its power to regulate social conduct.

*Populists*    The term **populism** is frequently used to describe the philosophy of people who are liberal on economic affairs but conservative on social matters. These people are really very consistent in their view toward the role of government. They favor a strong government to regulate business and provide economic security, and they also favor a strong government to control social conduct. They believe strongly in tradition, law, and morality in social affairs. While few people use the term *populist* to describe themselves, populists may actually make up a large portion of the electorate. Liberal politicians can appeal for their votes by stressing economic issues, while conservative politicians can appeal to them by stressing social issues.

**Populism:** A belief in the value of strong government to control business, provide economic security, and regulate social conduct, combined with a belief in tradition, law, and morality in social affairs.

# Are You a Liberal or a Conservative?

Not everyone consistently takes a liberal or a conservative position on every issue. But if you agree with more positions under one of the following "liberal" or "conservative" lists, you are probably ready to label yourself ideologically.

| | YOU ARE **LIBERAL** IF YOU AGREE THAT | YOU ARE **CONSERVATIVE** IF YOU AGREE THAT |
|---|---|---|
| Economic policy | Government should regulate business to protect the public interest<br>The rich should pay higher taxes to support public services for all<br>Government spending for social welfare is a good investment in people | Free-market competition is better at protecting the public than government regulation<br>Taxes should be kept as low as possible<br>Government welfare programs destroy incentives to work |
| Crime | Government should place primary emphasis on alleviating the social conditions (poverty, joblessness, etc.) that cause crime | Government should place primary emphasis on providing more police and prisons and stop courts from coddling criminals |
| Social policy | Government should protect the right of women to choose abortion and fund abortions for poor women<br>Government should pursue affirmative action programs on behalf of minorities and women in employment, education, etc.<br>Government should keep religious prayers and ceremonies out of schools and public places | Government should restrict abortion and not use taxpayer money for abortions<br>Government should not grant preferences to anyone based on race or gender<br>Government should allow prayers and religious observances in schools and public places |
| National security policy | Government should support "human rights" throughout the world<br>Military spending should be reduced now that the Cold War is over | Government should pursue the "national interest" of the United States<br>Military spending must reflect a variety of new dangers in this post–Cold War period |
| YOU GENERALLY DESCRIBE YOURSELF AS: | "caring"<br>"compassionate"<br>"progressive" | "responsible"<br>"moderate"<br>"sensible" |
| AND YOU DESCRIBE YOUR POLITICAL OPPONENTS AS: | "extremists"<br>"right-wing radicals"<br>"reactionaries" | "knee jerks"<br>"bleeding hearts"<br>"left-wing radicals" |

# Think Tanks:
# The Battle of Ideas

Ideas have power, and the nation's think tanks battle to control the flow of ideas. Think tanks are private organizations, independent of government, that seek to influence policy making through books, articles, editorials, media interviews, and direct communication with government officials. Think tanks recruit scholars, writers, and former government officials to study policy questions and develop policy recommendations, which are then circulated among the press and television, interest groups, congressional committees and staff, and executive agencies.

Think tanks are financed by private foundations, corporations, and wealthy individuals, as well as by the sale of the books and magazines they produce. They are usually governed by a board of trustees chosen in large measure for their ability to raise funds. Individual think tanks, even those that claim to provide unbiased, expert policy advice, tend to develop ideological identifications.

Among the most influential national think tanks are the Brookings Institution, the American Enterprise Institute, the Heritage Foundation, the Cato Foundation, and the Progressive Policy Institute. These five think tanks are active in a broad range of policy questions. Other think tanks may be equally influential in a specialized policy arena—for example the Council on Foreign Relations, the Urban Institute, and Resources for the Future.

*Brookings Institution*   The Brookings Institution is the oldest and perhaps the most influential think tank in Washington, despite the growing influence of competing think tanks over the years. Brookings staffers dislike the institution's reputation as a "liberal think tank" and deny that Brookings can set national priorities. Yet the Harvard historian writing team of Leonard and Mark Silk describe Brookings as the central locus of the Washington "policy network." The Brookings Institution was started early in the twentieth century with grants from Robert Brookings, a wealthy St. Louis merchant; Andrew Carnegie, founder of U.S. Steel (now USX); John D. Rockefeller, founder of the Standard Oil Company (now Exxon); and Robert Eastman, founder of Kodak Corporation. Its recommendations for economy and efficiency in government led to the Budget and Accounting Act of 1921, which established the annual unified federal budget. (Before 1921, each department submitted separate budget requests to Congress.) In the 1960s, the Brookings Institution, with grants from the Ford Foundation, helped design the War on Poverty. Today Brookings continues to influence federal tax and spending policies and social programs. Its journal, the *Brookings Review,* is read by a small but influential circle in Washington.

*American Enterprise Institute*   For many years, Republicans dreamed of a "Brookings Institution for Republicans" that would help offset the liberal bias of Brookings. Beginning in the late 1970s,

*Libertarians*   People who are adherents of **libertarianism** are sometimes described as economic conservatives and social liberals, yet they are really very consistent in their preference for minimal government intervention in both economic and social affairs. They oppose government interference both in the marketplace and in the private lives of citizens. They are against most environmental regulations, consumer protection laws, antidrug laws, and government restrictions on abortion. They favor a small government with limited functions, privatization of many government services, minimal welfare benefits, and low taxes. They also oppose defense spending, foreign aid, and U.S. involvement in world affairs.

**Libertarianism:** A preference for minimal government intervention in both economic and social affairs.

CHAPTER 2 • POLITICAL CULTURE: IDEAS IN CONFLICT

that role was assumed by the American Enterprise Institute (AEI). AEI attracted many distinguished neo-conservative scholars who were beginning to have doubts about big government. AEI publishes a journal, the *American Enterprise,* which regularly reports on American public opinion and comments on policy questions.

*Heritage Foundation* Conservative business-people, who once shunned Washington circles, gradually came to understand that without an institutional base in the capital they could never establish a strong and continuing influence in the policy network. The result of their efforts to build "a solid institutional base" and establish "a reputation for reliable scholarship and creative problem-solving" is the Heritage Foundation. The initial funding came from Colorado business executive–brewer Joseph Coors, who was later joined by two drugstore magnates, Jack Eckerd of Florida and Lewis I. Lehrman of New York. Heritage boasts that it accepts no government grants or contracts and that it has a larger number of individual contributors than any other think tank. It prides itself on being "on the top of the news" with quick "backgrounders"—reports and memoranda ready at the drop of a press release. Despite the emphasis on current, topical, and brief analyses, its flagship publication, *Policy Review,* has gained respect in academic circles. Heritage has also encouraged the formation of a loose network of state and regional think tanks.

*Cato Institute* The Cato Institute is a small think tank committed to libertarian ideas. It came to Washington in 1981 as an offspring of the Libertarian Party but gradually entered mainstream policy debates with free-market, limited-government, and antiregulatory recommendations. Conservatives generally applaud Cato's efforts to free the economy from government intervention and reduce the size of government but cringe at its call to legalize drugs. Cato also opposes spending for defense and foreign aid, and it urges a general withdrawal of the United States from world politics. It publishes *Cato Policy Review* as well as the more scholarly *Cato Journal.*

*Progressive Policy Institute* The Progressive Policy Institute was founded in 1989 to serve as an institutional base for efforts to move the Democratic Party and the nation toward growth-oriented economic policies. The institute is an outgrowth of the Democratic Leadership Council, formerly chaired by then-governor Bill Clinton of Arkansas. It advocates policies "designed to reverse America's slide, stimulate broad upward mobility and foster a more inclusive, more democratic capitalism." It seeks to renew the public sector by redesigning government along more entrepreneurial and less bureaucratic lines. Ideas generated by people affiliated with the Progressive Policy Institute often find their way into *Washington Monthly,* a lively magazine that generally reflects neo-liberal politics.

# DISSENT IN THE UNITED STATES

Dissent from the principal elements of American political culture—individualism, free enterprise, democracy, and equality of opportunity—has arisen over the years from both the *left* and the *right*. Despite their professed hostility toward each other, **radicals** on the left and right share many characteristics. Both are usually **extremist.** They reject democratic politics, compromise, and coalition building as immoral, and they assert the supremacy of the "people" over laws, institutions, and individual rights. Extremists view politics with hostility, although they may make cynical use of democratic politics as a short-term tactical means to their goals.

**Radicalism:** The advocacy of immediate and drastic changes in society, including the complete restructuring of institutions, values, and beliefs. Radicals may exist on either the extreme left or extreme right.

**Extremism:** The rejection of democratic politics and the assertion of the supremacy of the "people" over laws, institutions, and individual rights.

# Ideology on the Campus: Students versus Professors

Today most college students think of themselves as "middle-of-the-road." Among those who choose an ideological label, liberals slightly outnumber conservatives. A generation ago, students were much more likely to be liberal. In the early 1970s, the war in Vietnam still raged, the military draft loomed large in young people's lives, political activism in the form of protests and demonstrations was common on campus, and drugs and nonconforming lifestyles were more in evidence. In this environment, liberals outnumbered conservatives among students by 2 to 1. Students of the 1980s confronted a different world: the Vietnam War and the military draft were history; competition for jobs was greater, and a college education no longer guaranteed a middle-class life; affirmative action programs assisted minorities in education and employment; and political activism seemed to them a distraction from the more important task of career preparation. In this environment, fewer students described themselves as liberals, and conservatives gained near parity. Recently liberals and conservatives have been almost evenly matched on campus.

In contrast, professors' politics are decidedly liberal—more liberal than the general population's and more liberal than their students.' In a national sample of college professors, 51 percent described themselves as liberal, 17 percent as middle-of-the-road, and 28 percent as conservative. But there are distinct differences among faculty groups. Faculty in the humanities and social sciences are overwhelmingly political liberals. Liberals outnumber conservatives in the physical and biological sciences by 2 or 3 to 1. In engineering, liberals and conservatives are nearly equal; in law and business, conservatives outnumber liberals.

**Political ideology of entering freshmen**

| Year | Liberal | Middle of the road | Conservative |
|------|---------|--------------------|--------------|
| 1970 | 37% | 45% | 18% |
| 1976 | 28% | 56% | 16% |
| 1982 | 21% | 60% | 19% |
| 1987 | 21% | 59% | 20% |
| 1990 | 23% | 55% | 21% |
| 1995 | 25% | 53% | 22% |

Percent (0 10 20 30 40 50 60 70 80 90 100)

**Political ideology of professors**

| | Liberal | Middle of the road | Conservative |
|------|---------|--------------------|--------------|
| All | 51% | 17% | 28% |
| Humanities | 76% | 9% | 15% |
| Social Sciences | 72% | 14% | 14% |
| Biological Sciences | 61% | 17% | 23% |
| Physical Sciences | 54% | 19% | 26% |
| Engineering | 40% | 22% | 38% |
| Law | 36% | 22% | 42% |
| Business | 31% | 17% | 52% |

Percent (0 10 20 30 40 50 60 70 80 90 100)

☐ Liberal   ☐ Middle of the road   ☐ Conservative

*Source:* American Council on Education, *The American Freshman* (Los Angeles: Higher Education Research Institute, University of California at Los Angeles, published annually); and Carnegie Foundation for the Advancement of Teaching, reported in *American Enterprise* 2 (July/August 1991): 86–87.

Conspiracy theories are popular among extremists. For example, the left sees a conspiracy among high government, corporate, and military chieftains to profit from war; the right sees a conspiracy among communists, intellectuals, the United Nations, and Wall Street bankers to subordinate the United States to a world government. The historian Richard Hofstadter referred to this tendency as "the paranoid style of politics."[15] Both the left and right are intolerant of the opinions of others and are willing to disrupt and intimidate those with whom they disagree. Whether shouting down speakers or disrupting meetings or burning crosses and parading in hoods, the impulse to violence is often present in those who subscribe to radical politics.

*Antidemocratic Ideologies* Dissent in the United States has historical roots in antidemocratic movements that originated primarily outside the borders of this country. These movements have spanned the political spectrum from far right to far left.

At the far-right end of this spectrum lies **fascism,** an ideology that asserts the supremacy of the state and/or race over individuals. The goal of fascism is unity of people, nation, and leadership—in the words of Adolf Hitler: *"Ein Volk, Ein Reich, Ein Fuehrer* (One People, One Nation, One Leader). Every individual, every interest, and every class are to be submerged for the good of the nation. Against the rights of liberty or equality, fascism asserts the duties of service, devotion, and discipline. Its goal is the development of a superior type of human being, with qualities of bravery, courage, genius, and strength. The World War II defeat of the two leading fascist regimes in history—Adolf Hitler's Nazi Germany and Benito Mussolini's Fascist Italy—did not extinguish fascist ideas. Elements of fascist thought are found today in extremist movements in both the United States and Europe.

**Marxism** arose out of the turmoil of the Industrial Revolution as a protest against social evils and economic inequalities. Karl Marx (1818–83), its founder, was not an impoverished worker but rather an upper-middle-class intellectual unable to find an academic position. Benefiting from the financial support of his wealthy colleague Frederick Engels, Marx spent years writing *Das Kapital* (1867)

**Fascism:** A political ideology in which the state and/or race is assumed to be supreme over individuals.

**Marxism:** The theories of Karl Marx, among them that capitalists oppress workers and that worldwide revolution and the emergence of a classless society are inevitable.

*Political extremists of the left and right often have more in common than they would like to admit. While decidedly different in their political philosophies, both members of right-wing American neo-Nazi groups and members of left-wing communist groups reject democratic politics and assert the supremacy of the "people" over laws, institutions, and individual rights.*

a lengthy work describing the evils of capitalism, especially the oppression of workers and the inevitability of revolution and a classless society. The two men collaborated on a popular pamphlet entitled *The Communist Manifesto* (1848), which called for a workers' revolution: "Workers of the world, unite. You have nothing to lose but your chains."

It fell to Vladimir Lenin (1870–1924) to implement Marx and Engels's revolutionary ideology in the Russian Revolution in 1917. According to **Leninism,** the key to a successful revolution is the organization of small, disciplined, hard-core groups of professional revolutionaries into a centralized totalitarian party. To explain why Marx's predictions about the ever-worsening conditions of the masses under capitalism proved untrue (workers' standards of living in Western democracies rose rapidly in the twentieth century), Lenin devised the theory of imperialism: advanced capitalist countries turned to war and colonialism, exploiting the Third World, in order to make their own workers relatively prosperous.

**Communism** is the outgrowth of Marxist-Leninist ideas about the necessity of class warfare, the inevitability of a worldwide proletarian revolution, and the concentration of all power in the "vanguard of the proletariat"—the Communist Party. Communism justifies violence as a means to attain power by arguing that the bourgeoisie (the capitalistic middle class) will never voluntarily give up its control over "the means of production" (the economy). Democracy is only "window dressing" to disguise capitalist exploitation. The Communist Party justifies authoritarian single-party rule as the "dictatorship of the proletariat." In theory, after a period of rule by the Communist Party, all property will be owned by the government, and a "classless" society of true communism will emerge.

**Socialism** shares with communism a condemnation of capitalist profit making as exploitative of the working classes. Communists and socialists agree on the "evils" of industrial capitalism: the concentration of wealth, the insensitivity of the profit motive to human needs, the insecurities and suffering brought on by the business cycle, the conflict of class interests, and the tendency of capitalist nations to involve themselves in imperialist wars. However, socialists are committed to the democratic process as a means of replacing capitalism with collective ownership of economic enterprise. Socialists generally reject the notion of violent revolution as a way to replace capitalism and instead advocate peaceful, constitutional roads to socialism. Moreover, many socialists are prepared to govern in a free society under democratic principles, including freedom of speech and press and the right to organize political parties and oppose government policy. Socialism is egalitarian, seeking to reduce or eliminate inequalities in the distribution of wealth. It would attempt to achieve equality of results, rather than mere equality of opportunity.

*The End of History?*    Much of the history of the twentieth century has been the struggle between democratic capitalism and totalitarian communism. Thus, the collapse of communism in Eastern Europe and the Soviet Union, as well as the worldwide movement toward free markets and democracy, has been labeled the **end of history.**[16] Democratic revolutions were largely inspired by the realization that free-market capitalism provided much higher standards of living than socialism. The economies of Eastern Europe were falling further and further behind the economies of the capitalist nations of the West. Similar comparative observations of the successful economies of the Asian capitalist "Four Tigers"—

**Leninism:** The theories of Vladimir Lenin, including among them that advanced capitalist countries turned toward war and colonialism to make their own workers relatively prosperous.

**Communism:** A system of government in which a single totalitarian party controls all means of production and distribution of goods and services.

**Socialism:** A system of government involving collective or government ownership of economic enterprise, with the goal being equality of results, not merely equality of opportunity.

**End of history:** The collapse of communism and the worldwide movement toward free markets and political democracy.

South Korea, Taiwan, Singapore, and Hong Kong—even inspired China's communist leadership to experiment with market reforms. Communism destroyed the individual's incentive to work, produce, innovate, save, and invest in the future. Under communism, production for government goals (principally a strong military) came first; production for individual needs came last. The result was long lines at stores, shoddy products, and frequent bribery of bureaucrats to obtain necessary consumer items. More important, perhaps, the concentration of both economic and political power in the hands of a central bureaucracy proved to be incompatible with democracy. Communism relies on central direction, force, and repression. Communist systems curtail individual freedom and prohibit the development of separate parties and interest groups outside of government.

Capitalism does not *ensure* democracy; some capitalist nations are authoritarian. But economic freedom inspires demands for political freedom. Thus market reforms, initiated by communist leaders to increase productivity, led to democracy movements, and those movements eventually dismantled the communist system in Eastern Europe and the old Soviet Union.

*Academic Radicalism*   Marxism survives on campuses today largely as an academic critique of the functioning of capitalism.[17] It provides some disaffected academics with ideas and language to attack everything that disturbs them about the United States—from poverty, racism, and environmental hazards to junk food, athletic scholarships, and obnoxious television advertising—conveniently blaming the "profit motive" for many of the ills of American society.

Contemporary radicals argue that the institutions of capitalism have conditioned people to be materialistic, competitive, and even violent. The individual has been transformed into a one-dimensional person in whom genuine humanistic values are repressed.[18] Profitability, rather than humanistic values, remains the primary criterion for decision making in the capitalist economy, and thus profitability is the reason for poverty and misery despite material abundance. Without capitalist institutions, life would be giving, cooperative, and compassionate. Only a *radical restructuring* of social and economic institutions will succeed in liberating people from these institutions to lead humanistic, cooperative lives.

To American radicals, the problem of social change is truly monumental, because capitalist values and institutions are deeply rooted in this country. Since most people are not aware that they are oppressed and victimized, the first step toward social change is consciousness raising—that is, making people aware of their misery.

The agenda of academic radicalism has been labeled **politically correct (PC)** thinking. Politically correct thinking views American society as racist, sexist, and homophobic. Overt bigotry is not the real issue, but rather Western institutions, language, and culture, which systematically oppress and victimize women, "people of color," gays, and others. Thus, PC thinking encompasses a broad assault on the institutions, language, and culture of Western civilization.

Academic radicalism "includes the assumption that Western values are inherently oppressive, that the chief purpose of education is political transformation, and that all standards are arbitrary."[19] In PC thinking, "everything is political." Therefore curriculum, courses, and lectures—even language and demeanor—are judged according to whether they are politically correct or not. Universities have

**Politically correct (PC):** Repression of attitudes, speech, and writings that are deemed racist, sexist, homophobic (antihomosexual), or otherwise "insensitive."

always been centers for the critical examination of institutions, values, and culture, but PC thinking does not really tolerate open discussion or debate. Opposition is denounced as "insensitive," racist, sexist, or worse, and intimidation is not infrequent (see "Political Correctness versus Free Speech on Campus" in Chapter 14).

## SUMMARY NOTES

Ideas are sources of power. They provide people with guides for determining right and wrong and with rationales for political action. Political institutions are shaped by the values and beliefs of the political culture, and political leaders are restrained in their exercise of power by these ideas.

- The American political culture is a set of widely shared values and beliefs about who should govern, for what ends, and by what means.
- Americans share many common ways of thinking about politics. Nevertheless, there are often contradictions between professed values and actual conditions, problems in applying abstract beliefs to concrete situations, and even occasional conflict over fundamental values.
- Individual liberty is a fundamental value in American life. The classical liberal tradition that inspired the nation's Founders included both political liberties and economic freedoms.
- Equality is another fundamental American value. The nation's Founders believed in equality before the law; yet political equality, in the form of universal voting rights, required nearly two centuries to bring about.
- Equality of opportunity is a widely shared value; most Americans are opposed to artificial barriers of race, sex, religion, or ethnicity barring individual advancement. But equality of results is not a widely shared value; most Americans support a "floor" on income and well-being for their fellow citizens but oppose placing a "ceiling" on income or wealth.
- Income inequality has increased in recent years primarily as a result of economic and demographic changes. Most Americans believe that opportunities for individual advancement are still available, and this belief diminishes the potential for class conflict.

- Liberal and conservative ideologies in American politics present somewhat different sets of values and beliefs, even though they share a common commitment to individual dignity and private property. Generally, liberals favor an active, powerful government to provide economic security and protection for civil rights but oppose government restrictions on social conduct. Generally, conservatives favor minimal government intervention in economic affairs and civil rights but support many government restrictions on social conduct.
- Many Americans who identify themselves as liberals or conservatives are not always consistent in the application of their professed views. Populists are liberal on economic issues but conservative in their views on social issues. Libertarians are conservative on economic issues but liberal in their social views.
- Liberal and conservative ideas evolve over time in response to new challenges and changing conditions. Neo-conservatives share the historical classical liberal concerns about the nation's social problems but no longer believe that solutions can be found in large-scale, costly bureaucratic government programs. Neo-liberals retain their faith in the power of government but focus their attention on efforts to promote economic growth as a prerequisite to solving social problems.
- The collapse of communism in Eastern Europe and the former Soviet Union and the worldwide movement toward free markets and democracy have undermined support for socialism throughout the world. Yet Marxism survives in academic circles as a critique of the functioning of capitalism.

# SELECTED READINGS

EBENSTEIN, WILLIAM, and EDWIN FOGELMAN. *Today's Isms: Communism, Fascism, Capitalism, Socialism,* 10th ed. Englewood Cliffs, N.J.: Prentice Hall, 1994. A concise description and history of the major isms.

HENRY, WILLIAM A., III. *In Defense of Elitism.* New York: Doubleday, 1994. A humorous as well as persuasive attack on the "myths" that everyone is alike (or should be), that a just society will produce equal success for everyone, and that "the common man" is always right.

HUNTINGTON, SAMUEL P. *American Politics: The Promise of Disharmony.* Cambridge, Mass.: Harvard University Press, 1981. An examination of the gaps between the promise of the American ideals of liberty and equality and the performance of the American political system.

MCCLOSKY, HERBERT, and ALIDA BRILL. *Dimensions of Tolerance: What Americans Believe about Civil Liberties.* New York: Russell Sage Foundation, 1983. An argument, based on public opinion surveys, that political leaders apply norms of political tolerance more consistently than the mass public does.

MCCLOSKY, HERBERT, and JOHN ZALLER. *The American Ethos: Public Attitudes toward Capitalism and Democracy.* Cambridge, Mass.: Harvard University Press, 1984. An explanation of the American political culture based on analysis of public opinion surveys of both leaders and the mass public. The cultural foundations of both democracy and capitalism are examined, as well as the potential for conflict among these ideals.

SMITH, JAMES A. *The Idea Brokers.* New York: Free Press, 1991. A description of the rise of think tanks and "the new policy elite" that inhabit them.

VERBA, SIDNEY, and GARY R. ORREN. *Equality in America: The View from the Top.* Cambridge, Mass.: Harvard University Press, 1985. An examination of the attitudes of leaders of various sectors of American society toward equality of opportunity and equality of results.

WATTENBERG, BEN J. *Values Matter Most.* New York: Free Press, 1995. An argument that sound values rather than economic concerns will drive American politics in the future.

WOLFF, EDWARD N. *Top Heavy.* New York: Twentieth Century Fund, 1995. A fact-filled report on increasing inequality of wealth in America, together with a proposal to tax wealth as well as income.

# THE CONSTITUTION LIMITING GOVERNMENTAL POWER

## CONSTITUTIONAL GOVERNMENT

Constitutions govern government. **Constitutionalism**—a government of laws, not of people—means that those who exercise governmental power are restricted in their use of it by a higher law. To place individual freedoms

---

## ASK YOURSELF ABOUT POLITICS

**1** Was the original Constitution of 1787 a truly democratic document?
Yes ⬤　No ⬤

**2** Should citizens have the opportunity to vote directly on national government policies such as tax rates or funding for abortion?
Yes ⬤　No ⬤

**3** Should a large state such as California, with 32 million people, elect more U.S. senators than a small state such as Wyoming, with only half a million people?
Yes ⬤　No ⬤

**4** Should federal laws always supersede state laws?
Yes ⬤　No ⬤

**5** Should the president be able to act independently to send U.S. troops into military action in places like Somalia and Bosnia if there is no formal declaration of war?
Yes ⬤　No ⬤

**6** Should the Constitution be amended to require Congress to pass only balanced budgets?
Yes ⬤　No ⬤

**7** Should the Constitution be amended to guarantee that equality of rights shall not be denied on account of sex?
Yes ⬤　No ⬤

In a democracy "of the people, by the people, and for the people," who really has the power to govern? Who decides about war and taxes? Are strong national government and personal liberty compatible? Can majorities limit individual rights? America's founders struggled with such questions, and in resolving them established the oldest existing constitutional government.

beyond the reach of government and beyond the reach of majorities, a constitution must truly limit and control the exercise of authority by government. It does so by setting forth individual liberties that the government—even with majority support—cannot violate.

A **constitution** legally establishes government authority. It sets up governmental bodies (such as the House of Representatives, the Senate, the presidency, and the Supreme Court in the United States). It grants them powers. It determines how their members are to be chosen. And it prescribes the rules by which they make decisions.

Constitutional decision making is deciding how to decide; that is, it is deciding on the rules for policy making. It is not policy making itself. Policies will be decided later, according to the rules set forth in the constitution.

A constitution cannot be changed by the ordinary acts of governmental bodies; change can come only through a process of general popular consent.[1] The U.S. Constitution, then, is superior to ordinary laws of Congress, orders of the president, decisions of the courts, acts of the state legislatures, and regulations of the bureaucracies. Indeed, the Constitution is "the supreme law of the land."

To be effective in protecting the individual from government, a constitution must be respected—by both the people and the government. Government officials must believe that they are in fact limited by the constitution, and private citizens must believe that they are in fact protected by it. The constitution must be taken seriously if it is to be effective in limiting government and protecting the liberties of individuals.

## THE CONSTITUTIONAL TRADITION

Americans are strongly committed to the idea of a written constitution to establish governments and limit their powers. The Constitutional Convention of 1787 in fact had many important antecedents.

**Constitutionalism:** A government of laws, not people, operating on the principle that governmental power must be limited, that government officials should be restrained in their exercise of power over individuals.

**Constitution:** The legal structure of a political system, establishing governmental bodies, granting their powers, determining how their members are selected, and prescribing the rules by which they make their decisions. Considered basic or fundamental, a constitution cannot be changed by ordinary acts of governmental bodies.

*The Magna Carta, 1215*   English lords, traditionally required to finance the kings' wars, forced King John to sign the Magna Carta, a document guaranteeing their feudal rights and setting the precedent of a limited government and monarchy.

*The Mayflower Compact, 1620*   Puritan colonists, while still aboard the *Mayflower,* signed a compact establishing a "civil body politic . . . to enact just and equal laws . . . for the general good of the colony; unto which we promise all due submission and obedience." After the Puritans landed at Plymouth, in what is today Massachusetts, they formed a colony based on the Mayflower Compact, thus setting a precedent of a government established by contract with the governed.

*The Colonial Charters, 1630–1732*   Charters authorizing colonies in America were granted by royal action, either by officially granting proprietary rights, as in Maryland (granted by the king to Lord Baltimore), Pennsylvania (to William Penn), and Delaware (also to Penn); or by granting royal commissions to companies to establish governments, as in Virginia, Massachusetts, New Hampshire,

New York, New Jersey, Georgia, and North and South Carolina. Only in Connecticut and Rhode Island were royal charters granted directly to the colonists themselves. They drew up their charters and presented them to the king, setting a precedent in America for written documents.

The "Charter Oak Affair" of 1685–88 began when James II became displeased with his Connecticut subjects and issued an order for the repeal of the Connecticut Charter. In 1687, Sir Edmund Andros went to Hartford, dissolved the colonial government, and demanded that the charter be returned. But Captain John Wadsworth hid it in an oak tree. After the so-called Glorious Revolution in England in 1688, the charter was taken out and used again as the fundamental law of the colony. Subsequent British monarchs silently acquiesced in this restoration of rights, and the affair strengthened the notion of loyalty to the constitution rather than to the king.

*The Declaration of Independence, 1776*  The First Continental Congress, a convention of delegates from twelve of the thirteen original colonies, came together in 1774 to protest British interference in American affairs. But the Revolutionary War did not begin until April 19, 1775. The evening before, British regular troops marched out from Boston to seize arms stored by citizens in Lexington and Concord, Massachusetts. At dawn the next morning, the Minutemen—armed citizens organized for the protection of their towns—engaged the British regulars in brief battles, then harassed them all the way back to Boston. In June of that year, the Second Continental Congress appointed George Washington commander-in-chief and sent him to Boston to take command of the American militia forces surrounding the city. Still, popular support for the Revolution remained limited, and even many members of the Continental Congress hoped only to force changes—not to split off from Britain.

*After numerous drafts by Thomas Jefferson, which included such changes as eliminating a condemnation of slavery to appease North Carolina and Georgia, the Declaration of Independence was accepted by the majority of the Continental Congress on July 4, 1776. The document then became "the unanimous declaration of the thirteen United States of America" on July 19, and was signed by all members of the Continental Congress on August 2. Shown in this painting are (left to right) Benjamin Franklin, Thomas Jefferson, Robert Livingston, John Adams, and Roger Sherman.*

As this hope died, however, the Continental Congress came to view a formal Declaration of Independence as necessary to give legitimacy to their cause and establish the basis for a new nation. Accordingly, on July 2, 1776, the Continental Congress "Resolved, that these United Colonies are, and, of right, ought to be free and independent States." Thomas Jefferson had been commissioned to write a justification for the action, which he presented to the Congress on July 4, 1776. In writing the Declaration of Independence, Jefferson lifted several phrases directly from the English political philosopher John Locke (see Chapter 1) asserting the rights of individuals, the contract theory of government, and the right of revolution. The declaration was signed first by the president of the Continental Congress, John Hancock.

The Revolutionary War ended when British General Charles Cornwallis surrendered at Yorktown in October 1781. But even as the war was being waged, the new nation was creating the framework of its government.

*The Articles of Confederation, 1781–89*   Although Richard Henry Lee, a Virginia delegate to the Continental Congress, first proposed that the newly independent states form a confederation on July 6, 1776, the Continental Congress did not approve the Articles of Confederation until November 15, 1777, and the last state, Maryland, did not sign them until March 1, 1781. Under the Articles, Congress was a single house in which each state had two to seven members but only one vote. Congress itself created and appointed executives, judges, and military officers. It also had the power to make war and peace, conduct foreign affairs, and borrow and print money. But Congress could *not* collect taxes or enforce laws directly; it had to rely upon the states to provide money and enforce its laws. The United States under the Articles was really a confederation of nations. Within this "firm league of friendship" (Article III of the Articles of Confederation), the national government was thought of as an alliance of independent states, not as a government "of the people."

## TROUBLES CONFRONTING A NEW NATION

Two hundred years ago the United States was struggling to achieve nationhood. The new U.S. government achieved enormous successes under the Articles of Confederation: it won independence from the world's most powerful colonial nation, defeated vastly superior forces in a prolonged war for independence, established a viable peace, won powerful allies (such as France) in the international community, created an effective army and navy, established a postal system, and laid the foundations for national unity. But despite the successes in war and diplomacy, the political arrangements under the Articles were unsatisfactory to many influential groups—notably, bankers and investors who held U.S. government bonds, plantation owners, real estate developers, and merchants and shippers.

*Financial Difficulties*   Under the Articles of Confederation, Congress had no power to tax the people directly. Instead, Congress had to ask the states for money to pay its expenses, particularly the expenses of fighting the long and costly War of Independence with Great Britain. There was no way to force the states to make their payments to the national government. In fact, about 90 percent of the funds requisitioned by Congress from the states was never paid, so

Congress had to borrow money from wealthy patriot investors to fight the war. Without the power to tax, however, Congress could not pay off these debts. Indeed, the value of U.S. governmental bonds fell to about 10 cents for every dollar's worth, because few people believed the bonds would ever be paid off. Congress even stopped making interest payments on these bonds.

*Commercial Obstacles*    Under the Articles of Confederation, states were free to tax the goods of other states. Without the power to regulate interstate commerce, the national government was unable to protect merchants from heavy tariffs imposed on shipments from state to state. Southern planters could not ship their agricultural products to northern cities without paying state-imposed tariffs, and northern merchants could not ship manufactured products from state to state without interference. Merchants, manufacturers, shippers, and planters all wanted to develop national markets and prevent the states from imposing tariffs or restrictions on interstate trade. States competed with one another by passing low tariffs on foreign goods (to encourage the shipment of goods through their own ports) and high tariffs against one another's goods (to protect their own markets). The result was a great deal of confusion and bad feeling—as well as a great deal of smuggling.

*Currency Problems*    Under the Articles, the states themselves had the power to issue their own currency, regulate its value, and require that it be accepted in payment of debts. States had their own "legal tender" laws, which required creditors to accept state money if "tendered" in payment of debt. As a result, many forms of money were circulating: Virginia dollars, Rhode Island dollars, Pennsylvania dollars, and so on. Some states (Rhode Island, for example) printed a great deal of money, creating inflation in their currency and alienating banks and investors whose loans were being paid off in this cheap currency. If creditors refused payment in a particular state's currency, the debt could be abolished in that state. So finances throughout the states were very unstable, and banks and creditors were threatened by cheap paper money.

*Civil Disorder*    In several states, debtors openly revolted against tax collectors and sheriffs attempting to repossess farms on behalf of creditors who held unpaid mortgages. The most serious rebellion broke out in the summer of 1786 in western Massachusetts, where a band of 2,000 insurgent farmers captured the courthouses in several counties and briefly held the city of Springfield. Led by Daniel Shays, a veteran of the Revolutionary War battle at Bunker Hill, the insurgent army posed a direct threat to investors, bankers, creditors, and tax collectors by burning deeds, mortgages, and tax records to wipe out proof of the farmers' debts. Shays's Rebellion, as it was called, was finally put down by a small mercenary army, paid for by well-to-do citizens of Boston.

Reports of Shays's Rebellion filled the newspapers of the large eastern cities. George Washington, Alexander Hamilton, James Madison, and many other prominent Americans wrote their friends about it. The event galvanized property owners to support the creation of a strong central government capable of dealing with "radicalism." Only a strong central government, they wrote one another, could "insure domestic Tranquility," guarantee "a republican form of government," and protect property "against domestic violence." It is no accident that all of these phrases appear in the Constitution of 1787.

*In an attempt to prevent the foreclosure of farms by creditors, Revolutionary War veteran Daniel Shays led an armed mass of citizens in a march on a western Massachusetts courthouse. This uprising, which came to be known as Shays's Rebellion, exposed the Confederation's military weakness and increased support for a strong central government.*

*The Road to the Constitutional Convention*    In the spring of 1785, some wealthy merchants from Virginia and Maryland met at Alexandria, Virginia, to try to resolve a conflict between the two states over commerce and navigation on the Potomac River and Chesapeake Bay. George Washington, the new nation's most prominent citizen, took a personal interest in the meeting. As a wealthy plantation owner and a land speculator who owned more than 30,000 acres of land upstream on the Potomac, Washington was keenly interested in commercial problems under the Articles of Confederation. He lent his great prestige to the Alexandria meeting by inviting the participants to his house at Mount Vernon. Out of this conference came the idea for a general economic conference for all of the states to be held in Annapolis, Maryland, in September 1786.

The Annapolis Convention turned out to be a key stepping-stone to the Constitutional Convention of 1787. Instead of concentrating on commerce and navigation between the states, the delegates at Annapolis, including Alexander Hamilton and James Madison, called for a general constitutional convention to suggest remedies to what they saw as defects in the Articles of Confederation.

On February 21, 1787, the Congress called for a convention to meet in Philadelphia for the "sole and express purpose" of revising the Articles of Confederation and reporting to the Congress and the state legislatures "such alterations and provisions therein as shall, when agreed to in Congress and confirmed by the states, render the federal Constitution adequate to the exigencies of government and the preservation of the union." Notice that Congress did not authorize the convention to write a new constitution or to call constitutional conventions in the states to ratify a new constitution. State legislatures sent delegates to Philadelphia expecting that their task would be limited to revising the Articles and that revisions would be sent back to Congress and state legislatures for their approval. But that is not what happened.

## THE NATION'S FOUNDERS

The fifty-five delegates to the Constitutional Convention, which met in Philadelphia in the summer of 1787, quickly discarded the congressional mandate to merely "revise" the Articles of Confederation. The Virginia delegation, led by James Madison, arrived before a quorum of seven states had assembled and used the time to draw up an entirely new constitutional document. After the first formal session opened on May 25 and George Washington was elected president of the convention, the Virginia Plan became the basis of discussion. Thus, at the very beginning of the convention, the decision was made to scrap the Articles of Confederation altogether, write a new constitution, and form a new national government.[2]

The Founders were very confident of their powers and abilities. They had been selected by their state legislatures (only Rhode Island, dominated by small farmers, refused to send a delegation). When Thomas Jefferson, then serving in the critical post of ambassador to France (the nation's military ally in the Revolutionary War), first saw the list of delegates, he exclaimed: "It is really an assembly of demigods." Indeed, among the nation's notables, only Jefferson and John Adams (then serving as ambassador to England) were absent. The eventual success of the convention, and the ratification of the new Constitution, resulted in part from the enormous prestige, experience, and achievements of the delegates themselves.

George Washington was the new nation's most popular and prestigious citizen (see *People in Politics:* "George Washington, Founder of a Nation"). Not only preeminent as a military leader and respected hero, he was also one of the richest people in the United States. In addition to his large estate on the Potomac, he possessed many thousands of acres of undeveloped land in western Virginia, Maryland, Pennsylvania, Kentucky, and the Northwest Territory. He owned major shares in the Potomac Company, the James River Company, the Bank of Columbia, and the Bank of Alexandria. And he held large amounts in U.S. bonds and securities. Thus, he was personally concerned about obstacles to interstate commerce, unstable currencies, and the inability of Congress to pay its debts.

The foremost financial leader in the nation in 1787 was a delegate from Pennsylvania, Robert Morris. This Philadelphia banker and business leader owned scores of ships that traded throughout the world, engaged in iron manufacturing, speculated in real estate, controlled the Bank of North America in Philadelphia, and underwrote a large share of the debts of the United States during and after the Revolutionary War. Later in his life, his financial empire collapsed, probably because of overspeculation, and he died in debt. But at the time of the convention, Morris stood at the center of America's financial structure.

The Founders were extraordinarily well educated. At a time when very few men on the North American continent had gone to college, the Founders were conspicuous for their educational attainment. More than half the delegates had been educated at Harvard (founded in 1636), William and Mary (1693), Yale (1701), the University of Pennsylvania (1740), Columbia (1754), Princeton (1746), or in England. The tradition of legal training for political decision makers, which has continued in the United States to the present, was already evident.

## George Washington, Founder of a Nation

From the time he took command of the American Revolutionary forces in 1775 until he gave his Farewell Address to the nation in 1796 and returned to his Mount Vernon plantation, George Washington (1732–99) was, indeed, "First in war, first in peace, first in the hearts of his countrymen." His military success, combined with his diplomacy and practical political acumen, gave him overwhelming moral authority, which he used to inspire the Constitutional Convention, to secure the ratification of the Constitution, and then to guide the new nation through its first years.

Washington was raised on a Virginia plantation and inherited substantial landholdings, including his Mount Vernon plantation on the Potomac River. He began his career as a surveyor. His work took him deep into the wilderness of America's frontier. This experience later served him well when, at age 21, he was commissioned by the governor of Virginia to explore "the Forks of the Ohio" (now Pittsburgh, Pennsylvania) and extend British claims against French interests west of the Allegheny Mountains. In 1753 Washington's application for a regular commission in the British army was rejected, but he was appointed a major and later promoted to lieutenant colonel in the Virginia militia.

In 1754 he led a small force toward the French Fort Duquesne, but after a brief battle at makeshift "Fort Necessity," he was obliged to retreat. In 1755

British Major General Edward Braddock asked the young militia officer to accompany his heavy regiments on a campaign to dislodge the French from Fort Duquesne. Braddock disregarded Washington's warnings about concealed ways of fighting in the New World; Braddock's parading redcoat forces were ambushed by the French and Indians near Pittsburgh, and the general was killed. Washington rallied what remained of the British forces and led them in a successful retreat back to Virginia.

Washington was viewed by Virginians as a hero, and at age 22 he was appointed by the Virginia Assembly "Colonel of the Virginia Regiment and Commander in Chief of all Virginia Forces." But regular British officers ridiculed the militia forces and asserted their authority over Washington. British General John Forbes occupied Fort Duquesne, renamed it Fort Pitt, and gave Washington's men the task of garrisoning it.

In 1759, having completed his service in the French and Indian Wars, Washington left his military post and returned to plantation life. He married a wealthy widow, Martha Custis, expanded his plantation holdings, and prospered in western land speculation.

The Virginia legislature elected Washington to attend the First Continental Congress in September 1774. Washington was the most celebrated veteran of the French and Indian Wars who was still young enough (42) to lead military forces in a new struggle. John Adams of Massachusetts was anxious to unite the continent in the coming contest, and he persuaded the Second Continental Congress to give Washington command of the American revolutionary forces surrounding the British army in Boston. Upon accepting command in 1775, Washington declined a salary and modestly suggested that his experience "may not be equal to the task."

About a dozen delegates were active lawyers in 1787, and about three dozen had legal training.

The Founders also had extensive experience in governing. Many had participated in all the key events of the previous years, from the First Continental Congress in 1774, to the Declaration of Independence, the Articles of Confederation, and the successful conclusion of the Revolutionary War. Eight of the fifty-five delegates had signed the Declaration of Independence. Eleven delegates had served as

Washington faced what appeared to be insurmountable odds in his campaigns against the British army. His ragtag soldiers were no match for the well-trained and better-equipped British troops. In addition, America's citizen-soldiers were only obligated to brief periods of enlistment, which, combined with a high rate of desertion, nearly resulted in the collapse of Washington's army on several occasions. Through it all Washington persevered by employing many of the tactics later defined as the principles of guerrilla warfare. By retreating deep into Pennsylvania's Valley Forge, Washington avoided defeat and saved his army. His bold Christmas night attack against Hessian troops at Trenton, New Jersey, encouraged French intervention on America's behalf. Slowly Washington was able to wear down the British resolve to fight. In the end, he succeeded in trapping a British army at Yorktown, Virginia. Assisted by a French naval blockade, he accepted the surrender of Lord Cornwallis and 8,000 of his men on October 19, 1781. As a result, peace negotiations were opened in Paris.

Perhaps Washington's greatest contribution to democratic government occurred in 1783 in Newburgh, New York, near West Point, where the veterans of his Continental Army were encamped. Despite their hardships and ultimate victory in the Revolutionary War, these soldiers remained unpaid by Congress. Indeed, Congress ignored a series of letters, known as the Newburgh Addresses, that threatened military force if Congress continued to deny benefits to the veterans. Washington was invited to Newburgh by officers who hoped he would agree to lead a military coup against the Congress. But when Washington mounted the platform he denounced the use of force and the "infamous propositions" contained in their earlier addresses to Congress. There is little doubt that he could have chosen to march on the Congress with his veteran army and install himself as military dictator. World history is filled with revolutionary army leaders who did so. But Washington chose to preserve representative government.

One of the few noncontroversial decisions of the Constitutional Convention in 1787 was the selection of George Washington to preside over the meetings. He took little part in the debates; however, his enormous prestige helped to hold the convention together and later to win support for the new Constitution.

When the first Electoral College voted on the presidential candidates, Washington received all sixty-nine votes. John Adams was elected vice-president. Washington steered a steady course for the new nation by maintaining a strict neutrality toward warring Europe, and in his Farewell Address, he warned against foreign entanglements, as well as the formation of political parties and party spirit, which, he said, "agitates the community with ill-founded jealousies."

George Washington died on December 14, 1799, in his home at Mount Vernon. During Washington's war service, the highest rank granted him by Congress was that of lieutenant-general. In 1976, Congress granted Washington the nation's highest military rank, General of the Armies, and confirmed him forever as the senior officer on United States Army rolls.

*Source:* George Washington, Farewell Address, September 17, 1796, in *Documents of American History,* eds. Henry Steele Commager and Milton Cantor, 10th ed. (Englewood Cliffs, N.J.: Prentice Hall, 1988), 1:172.

officers in Washington's army in the Revolutionary War. Forty-two Founders had already served in the Congress. More than forty held high offices in state governments, including three who were state governors.

Above all, the delegates at Philadelphia were cosmopolitan. They approached political, economic, and military issues from a "continental" point of view. Unlike most Americans in 1787, their loyalties extended beyond their states. They were truly nationalists.[3]

# CONSENSUS IN PHILADELPHIA

The Founders shared many ideas about government. We often focus our attention on *conflict* in the Convention of 1787 and the compromises reached by the participants, but the really important story of the Constitution is the *consensus* that was shared by these men of influence.

*Liberty and Property*    The Founders had read John Locke and absorbed his idea that the purpose of government is the protection of individual liberty and property. They believed in a natural law, superior to any human-made laws, that endowed each person with certain inalienable rights—the rights to life, liberty, and property. They believed that all people were equally entitled to these rights, although most of the Founders, including slave owners George Washington and Thomas Jefferson, were aware that their belief in personal liberty for all people ran contrary to the practice of slavery.

*Social Contract*    The Founders believed that government originated in an implied contract among people. People agreed to establish government, obey laws, and pay taxes in exchange for protection of their natural rights. This social contract gave government its legitimacy—a legitimacy that rested on the consent of the governed, not with gods, or kings, or force. If governments violate individual liberty, they break the social contract and lose their legitimacy.

*Representative Government*    While most of the world's governments in 1787 were hereditary monarchies, the Founders believed the people should have a voice in choosing their own representatives in government. They opposed hereditary aristocracy and titled nobility. Instead, they sought to forge a republic. **Republicanism** meant government by representatives of the people. The Founders expected the masses to consent to be governed by their leaders—men of principle and property with ability, education, and a stake in the preservation of liberty. The Founders believed that the people should have only a limited role in directly selecting their representatives—that they should vote for members of the House of Representatives but that senators, the president, and members of the Supreme Court should be selected by others more qualified to judge their ability.

*Limited Government*    The Founders believed that unlimited power was corrupting and that the concentration of power was dangerous. They believed in a written constitution that limited the scope of governmental power. They also believed in dividing power within government by creating separate bodies able to check and balance one another's powers.

*Nationalism*    Most important, the Founders shared a belief that a strong **national** government with power to govern directly, rather than through state governments, was essential "to establish Justice, insure domestic Tranquility, provide for the common defense, promote the general Welfare, and secure the Blessings of Liberty." Not everyone in America shared this enthusiasm for a strong federal government; indeed, opposition forces, calling themselves Anti-Federalists, almost succeeded in defeating the new Constitution. But the leaders meeting in Philadelphia in the summer of 1787 were convinced of the need for a strong central government that would share power with the states.

**Republicanism:** Government by representatives of the people rather than directly by the people themselves.

**Nationalism:** The belief that shared cultural, historical, linguistic, and social characteristics of a people justify the creation of a government encompassing all of them; the resulting nation-state should be independent and legally equal to all other nation-states.

# CONFLICT IN PHILADELPHIA

Consensus on basic principles of government was essential to the success of the Philadelphia convention. But conflict over the implementation of these principles not only tied up the convention for an entire summer but later threatened to prevent ratification by the states of the document it produced.

*Representation*    Representation was the most controversial issue in Philadelphia. Following the election of George Washington as president of the convention, Governor Edmund Randolph of Virginia rose to present a draft of a new constitution. The Virginia Plan proposed a two-house legislature: the lower house was to be chosen by the people of the states, with representation according to population; the upper house was to be chosen by the lower house (see Table 3-1). Congress was to have the broad power to "legislate in all cases in which the separate states are incompetent, or in which the harmony of the United States may be interrupted." Congress was to have the power to nullify state laws that it believed violated the Constitution, thus ensuring the national government's supremacy over the states. The Virginia Plan also proposed a *parliamentary* form of government, that is, one in which the legislature (Congress) chose the principal executive officers of the government as well as federal judges. Finally, the Virginia Plan included a curious "council of revision," with the power to veto acts of Congress.

Delegates from New Jersey, New York, and Delaware objected strongly to the great power given to the national government in the Virginia Plan and the plan's failure to recognize the role of the states in the composition of that government. After several weeks of debate, William Paterson of New Jersey submitted a counterproposal. The New Jersey Plan called for a Congress in which each state, regardless of its population, had one vote, just as under the Articles of Confederation. But unlike the Articles, the New Jersey Plan proposed separate executive and judicial branches of government and the expansion of the powers of Congress

| TABLE 3-1 CONSTITUTIONAL COMPROMISE | | |
|---|---|---|
| *The Virginia Plan* | *The New Jersey Plan* | *The Connecticut Compromise The Constitution of 1787* |
| A two-house legislature, with the lower house directly elected based on population and the upper house elected by the lower. | A one-house legislature, with equal state representation, regardless of population. | A two-house legislature, with numerical representation in the directly elected House and equal state representation in the indirectly elected Senate. |
| Broad legislative power, with veto power over laws passed by state legislatures. | Same legislative power as under Articles of Confederation, plus power to levy some taxes and to regulate commerce. | Broad legislative power, including power to tax and to regulate commerce. |
| President and cabinet elected by legislature. | Separate plural executive, elected by Congress, removable by petition from majority of state governors. | Single executive, chosen by an Electoral College. |
| National judiciary elected by the legislature. | Judiciary, appointed by executive. | Judiciary appointed by president and confirmed by Senate. |
| "Council of Revision," with power to veto laws of Congress. | A National Supremacy Clause similar to that found in Article VI of 1787 Constitution. | National Supremacy Clause: the Constitution is "the supreme Law of the Land." |

to include levying taxes and regulating commerce. Moreover, the New Jersey Plan included the now-famous National Supremacy Clause, declaring that the Constitution and federal laws would supersede state constitutions and laws.

Debate over representation in Congress raged into July 1787. At one point, the convention actually voted for the Virginia Plan, 7 votes to 3, but without New York, New Jersey, and Delaware, the new nation was not really viable. Eventually, Roger Sherman of Connecticut came forward with a compromise. The Connecticut Compromise established two houses of Congress: in the upper house, the Senate, each state would have two members regardless of its size; in the lower body, the House of Representatives, each state would be represented according to population. Legislation would have to pass both houses to be enacted. This compromise was approved by the convention on July 16.

*Slavery*    Another conflict absorbing the attention of the delegates was slavery. In 1787, slavery was legal everywhere except in Massachusetts. Nevertheless, the delegates were too embarrassed to use the word *slave* or *slavery* in their debates or in the Constitution itself. Instead, they referred to "other persons" and "persons held to service or labour."

Planters and slaveholders believed that persons held in slavery should be counted in representation afforded the states, especially if taxes were to be levied on a population basis (which meant counting slaves as persons). Nonslaveholders believed that "the people" counted for representation purposes should include only free persons. The Connecticut Plan included the now-infamous Three-fifths Compromise: three-fifths of the slaves of each state would be counted for purposes both of representation in the House of Representatives and of apportionment for direct taxes.

Slave owners also sought protection for their human "property" in the Constitution itself. They were particularly concerned about slaves running away to other states and claiming their freedom. So they succeeded in writing into the Constitution (Article IV, Section 2) a specific guarantee: "No persons held to Service or Labour in one State . . . escaping into another, shall . . . be discharged from such Service or Labour, but shall be delivered up on Claim of the Party to whom such Service or Labour may be due."

Yet another compromise dealt with the slave trade. The capture, transportation, and "breaking in" of African slaves was considered a nasty business, even by southern planters. Many wealthy Maryland and Virginia plantations were already

*Though hotly debated, the issue of slaveholding was not resolved by the Founders in either the Declaration of Independence or the Constitution. As a result, the practice of buying and selling slaves—and the debate over this practice—continued for years to come, until political conflict exploded in the Civil War.*

well supplied with slaves and thus could afford the luxury of conscience to call for an end to the slave trade. But other planters from the less-developed southern states, particularly South Carolina and Georgia, needed additional slave labor. The final compromise prohibited the slave trade—but not before the year 1808, thereby giving the planters twenty years to import all the slaves they needed before the slave trade ended.

*Voter Qualifications*   Another important conflict centered on qualifications for voting and holding office in the new government. Most of the delegates believed that voters as well as officeholders should be men of property. (Only Benjamin Franklin went so far as to propose universal *male* suffrage.) But delegates representing different kinds of property argued over the specific wording of property qualifications. Merchants, bankers, and manufacturers objected to property qualifications for officeholding that were expressed as land ownership. James Madison, a plantation owner himself, was forced to admit that "landed possessions were no certain evidence of real wealth. Many enjoyed them who were more in debt than they were worth."

After much debate, the convention approved a constitution without any expressed property qualifications for voting or holding office, except those that the states might impose themselves: "The Electors in each State shall have the Qualifications requisite for Electors of the most numerous Branch of the State Legislature." At the time, every state had property qualifications for voting, and women were not permitted to vote or hold office. (The New Jersey Constitution of 1776 enfranchised women as well as men who owned property, but in 1887, a new state law limited the vote to "free white male citizens.")

## RESOLVING THE ECONOMIC ISSUES

The Founders were just as concerned with "who gets what, when, and how" as today's politicians are. Important economic interests were at stake in the Constitution. Historian Charles A. Beard pointed out that the delegates to the Constitutional Convention were men of wealth: planters, slaveholders, merchants, manufacturers, shippers, bankers and investors, and land speculators. Moreover, most of the delegates owned Revolutionary War bonds that were now worthless and would remain so unless the national government could obtain the tax revenues to pay them off[4] (see *A Conflicting View:* "An Economic Interpretation of the Constitution"). But it is certainly not true that the Founders acted only out of personal interest. Wealthy delegates were found on both sides of constitutional debates, arguing principles as well as economic interests.[5]

*Levying Taxes*   A central purpose of the Constitution was to enable the national government to levy its own **taxes,** so that it could end its dependence upon state contributions and achieve financial credibility. The very first power given to Congress in Article I, Section 8 is the power to tax: "The Congress shall have Power To lay and collect Taxes, Duties, Imposts and Excises, to pay the Debts and provide for the common Defence and general Welfare."

The financial credit of the United States and the interests of Revolutionary War bondholders were guaranteed by Article VI in the Constitution, which specifically declared that the new government would be obligated to pay the debts of the old

**Taxes:** Compulsory payment to the government.

# An Economic Interpretation of the Constitution

Charles Beard, historian and political scientist, provided the most controversial historical interpretation of the origin of American national government in his landmark book *An Economic Interpretation of the Constitution* (1913). Not all historians agree with Beard's interpretation—particularly his emphasis on economic forces—but all concede that it is a milestone in understanding the U.S. Constitution. Beard closely studied unpublished financial records of the U.S. Treasury Department and the personal letters and financial accounts of the fifty-five delegates to the Philadelphia convention. He concluded that the movement for the Constitution of the United States was originated and carried through principally by five groups of economic interests. He summarized these financial interests as:

- *Public security interests* (persons holding U.S. bonds from the Revolutionary War: thirty-seven of the fifty-five delegates). The taxing power was of great benefit to the holders of public securities, particularly when it was combined with the provision in Article VI that "all Debts contracted and Engagements entered into, before the Adoption of this Constitution, shall be as valid against the United States under this Constitution, as under the Confederation." That is, the national government would be obliged to pay off all those investors who held U.S. bonds, and the taxing power would give the national government the ability to do so on its own.

- *Merchants and manufacturers* (persons engaged in shipping and trade: eleven of the fifty-five delegates). The Interstate Commerce Clause, which eliminated state control over commerce, and the provision in Article I, Section 9, which prohibited the states from taxing exports, created a free-trade area, or "common market," among the thirteen states.

- *Bankers and investors* (twenty-four of fifty-five delegates). Congress is given the power to make bankruptcy laws, to coin money and regulate its value, to fix standards of weights and measures, to punish counterfeiting, to establish post offices and post roads, to pass copyright and patent laws to protect authors and inventors, and to punish piracies and felonies committed on the high seas. Each of these powers is a specific asset to bankers, investors, merchants, authors, inventors, and shippers.

- *Western land speculators* (persons who purchased large tracts of land west of the

government. Indeed, the nation's first secretary of the treasury, Alexander Hamilton, made repayment of the national debt the first priority of the Washington Administration.

The original Constitution placed most of the tax burden on consumers in the form of **tariffs** on goods imported into the United States. For more than a century, these tariffs provided the national government with its principal source of revenue. Tariffs were generally favored by American manufacturers, who wished to raise the price paid for foreign goods to make their home-produced goods more competitive. No taxes were permitted on *exports,* a protection for southern planters, who exported most of their tobacco and, later, cotton. Direct taxes on individuals were prohibited (Article I, Section 2) except in proportion to *population.* This provision prevented the national government from levying direct taxes in proportion to *income* until the Sixteenth Amendment (income tax) was ratified in 1913.

The power to tax and spend is given to Congress, not to the president or executive agencies. Instead, the Constitution is very specific: "No Money shall be

**Tariff:** A tax imposed on imported products (also called a custom's duty).

Appalachian Mountains, fourteen of the fifty-five delegates). If western settlers were to be protected from the Indians, and if the British were to be persuaded to give up their forts in Ohio and open the way to American westward expansion, the national government could not rely upon state militias but must have an army of its own.

- **Slave owners** (fifteen of the fifty-five delegates). Protection against domestic insurrection also appealed to the southern slaveholders' deep-seated fear of a slave revolt. The Constitution permitted Congress to outlaw the *import of slaves* after the year 1808. But most southern planters were more interested in protecting their existing property and slaves than they were in extending the slave trade, and the Constitution provided an explicit advantage to slaveholders in Article IV, Section 2 (later revoked by the Thirteenth Amendment, which abolished slavery):

No Person held to Service or Labour in one State, under the Laws thereof, escaping into another, shall, in Consequence of any Law or Regulation therein, be discharged from such Service or Labour, but shall be delivered up on Claim of the Party to whom such Service or Labour may be due.

Beard argued that the members of the Philadelphia convention that drafted the Constitution were, with a few exceptions, immediately, directly, and personally interested in, and derived economic advantages from, the establishment of the new system. But many historians disagree with Beard's emphasis on the economic motives of the Founders. The Constitution, they point out, was adopted in a society that was fundamentally democratic, and it was adopted by people who were primarily middle-class property owners, especially farmers, rather than owners of businesses. The Constitution was not just an economic document, although economic factors were certainly important. Since most of the people were middle-class and owned private property, practically all Americans were interested in the protection of property.

Moreover, in the struggle over ratification of the Constitution, it is clear that some people of prestige, reputation, and property opposed it. Influential Anti-Federalists deplored the undemocratic features of the Constitution, and their criticism about the omission of a bill of rights led directly to the inclusion of the first ten amendments. Supporters of the Constitution were forced to retreat from their demand for unconditional ratification, and they agreed to add the Bill of Rights as amendments as soon as the first Congress was convened under the Constitution.

drawn from the Treasury, but in Consequence of Appropriations made by Law." This is the constitutional basis of Congress's "power of the purse."

*Regulating Commerce*   The new Constitution gave Congress the power to "regulate Commerce with foreign Nations, and among the several States" (Article I, Section 8), and it prohibited the states from imposing tariffs on goods shipped across state lines (Article I, Section 10). This power created what we call today a **common market;** it protected merchants against state-imposed tariffs and stimulated trade among the states. States were also prohibited from "impairing the Obligation of Contracts"—that is, passing any laws that would allow debtors to avoid their obligations to banks and other lenders.

*Protecting Money*   The Constitution also ensured that the new national government would control the money supply. Congress was given the power to coin money and regulate its value. More important, the states were prohibited from

**Common market:** Unified trade area in which all goods and services can be sold or exchanged free from customs or tariffs.

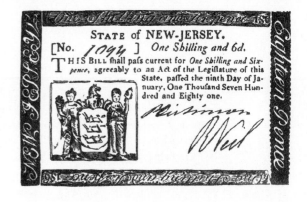

*Under the Articles of Confederation, each state issued its own currency. Differences in currency regulation from state to state led to financial uncertainty and inflation. By creating a national currency and putting the national government in charge of the money supply, the Founders hoped to restore stability and control inflation.*

issuing their own paper money, thus protecting bankers and creditors from the repayment of debts in cheap state currencies. (No one wanted to be paid for goods or labor in Rhode Island's inflated dollars.) If only the national government could issue money, the Founders hoped, inflation could be minimized.

## PROTECTING NATIONAL SECURITY

At the start of the Revolutionary War, the Continental Congress had given George Washington command of a small regular army—"Continentals"—paid for by Congress and also had authorized him to take command of state militia units. During the entire war, most of Washington's troops had been state militia. (The "militia" in those days was composed of every free adult male; each was expected to bring his own gun.) Washington himself had frequently decried the militia units as undisciplined, untrained, and unwilling to follow his orders. He wanted the new United States to have a *regular* army and navy, paid for by the Congress with its new taxing power, to back up the state militia units.

*War and the Military Forces*   Congress was authorized to "declare War," to raise and support a regular army and navy, and to make rules regulating these forces. It was also authorized to call up the militia, as it had done in the Revolution, in order to "execute the Laws of the Union, suppress Insurrections and repel Invasions." When the militia are called into national service, they come under the rule of Congress and the command of the president.

The United States relied primarily on militia—citizen-soldiers organized in state units—until World War I. The regular U.S. Army, stationed in coastal and frontier forts, directed most of its actions against Native Americans. The major actions in America's nineteenth-century wars—the War of 1812 against the British, the Mexican War of 1846–48, the Civil War in 1861–65, and the Spanish-American War in 1898—were fought largely by citizen-soldiers from these state units.

*Commander-in-Chief*   Following the precedent set in the Revolutionary War, the new president, who everyone expected to be George Washington, was made "Commander in Chief of the Army and Navy of the United States, and of the Militia of the several States, when called into the actual Service of the United States." Clearly, there is some overlap in responsibility for national defense: Congress has the power to declare war, but the president is Commander-in-Chief. During the

next two centuries, the president would order U.S. forces into 200 or more military actions, but Congress would declare war only five times. Conflict between the president and Congress over war-making powers continues to this day.

*Foreign Affairs*    The national government also assumed full power over foreign affairs and prohibited the states from entering into any "Treaty, Alliance, or Confederation." The Constitution gave the president, not Congress, the power to "make Treaties" and "appoint Ambassadors." However, the Constitution stipulated that the president could do these things only "by and with the Advice and Consent of the Senate," indicating an unwillingness to allow the president to act autonomously in these matters. The Senate's power to "advise and consent" to treaties and appointments, together with the congressional power over appropriations, gives the Congress important influence in foreign affairs. Nevertheless, the president remains the dominant figure in this arena.

## THE STRUCTURE OF THE GOVERNMENT

The Constitution that emerged from the Philadelphia convention on September 17, 1787, founded a new government with a unique structure. That structure was designed to implement the Founders' beliefs in nationalism, limited government, republicanism, the social contract, and the protection of liberty and property. The Founders were realists; they did not have any romantic notions about the wisdom and virtue of "the people." James Madison wrote: "A dependence on the people is, no doubt, the primary control on the government; but experience has taught mankind the necessity of auxiliary precautions." The key structural arrangements in the Constitution—national supremacy, federalism, republicanism, separation of powers, checks and balances, and judicial review—all reflect the Founders' desire to create a strong national government while at the same time ensuring that it would not become a threat to liberty or property.

*National Supremacy*   The heart of the Constitution is the National Supremacy Clause of Article VI:

> This Constitution, and the Laws of the United States which shall be made in Pursuance thereof; and all Treaties made, or which shall be made, under the Authority of the United States, shall be the supreme Law of the Land; and the Judges in every State shall be bound thereby, any Thing in the Constitution or Laws of any State to the Contrary notwithstanding.

This sentence ensures that the Constitution itself is the supreme law of the land and that laws passed by Congress supersede state laws. This National Supremacy Clause establishes the authority of the Constitution and the United States government.

*Federalism*   The Constitution *divides power* between the nation and the states (see Chapter 4). It recognizes that both the national government and the state governments have independent legal authority over their own citizens: both can pass their own laws, levy their own taxes, and maintain their own courts. The states have an important role in the selection of national officeholders—in the apportionment of congressional seats and in the allocation of electoral votes for president. Most important, perhaps, both the Congress and three-quarters of the states must consent to changes in the Constitution itself.

*Republicanism*   To the Founders, a *republican* government meant the delegation of powers by the people to a small number of gifted individuals "whose wisdom may best discern the true interest of their country, and whose patriotism and love of justice, will be least likely to sacrifice it to temporary or partial considerations."[6] The Founders believed that enlightened leaders of principle and property with ability, education, and a stake in the preservation of liberty could govern the people better than the people could govern themselves. So they gave the voters only a limited voice in the selection of government leaders.

The Constitution of 1787 created *four* decision-making bodies, each with separate numbers, terms of office, and selection processes (see Table 3-2). Note that

| TABLE 3-2   DECISION-MAKING BODIES IN THE CONSTITUTION OF 1787 | | | |
| --- | --- | --- | --- |
| *House of Representatives* | *Senate* | *President* | *Supreme Court* |
| Members allotted to each state "according to their respective numbers," but each state guaranteed at least one member. Two-year terms. Selected by "the People of the several States. | "Two senators from each State." Six-year terms. Selected by state legislatures (changed to direct election by the people by the Seventeenth Amendment in 1913). | A single executive. A four-year term. Selected by "Electors," appointed in each state "in such Manner as the Legislature thereof may direct" and equal to the total number of U.S. senators and House members to which the state is entitled in Congress. | No size in the Constitution, but by recent tradition, nine. Life terms. Appointed by the president, "by and with the Advice and Consent of the Senate." |

in the *original* Constitution only one of these four bodies—the House of Representatives—was to be directly elected by the people. The other three were removed from direct popular control: state legislatures selected U.S. senators; "electors" (chosen at the discretion of the state legislatures) selected the president; the president appointed Supreme Court and other federal judges.

*Democracy?*    The Founders believed that government rests ultimately on "the consent of the governed." But their notion of republicanism envisioned decision making by *representatives* of the people, not the people themselves. The U.S. Constitution does not provide for *direct* voting by the people on national questions; that is, unlike many state constitutions today, it does not provide for national **referenda.** Moreover, as noted earlier, only the House of Representatives (sometimes referred to even today as "the people's house") was to be elected directly by voters in the states.

These republican arrangements may appear "undemocratic" from our perspective today, but in 1787 this Constitution was more democratic than any other governing system in the world. Although other nations were governed by monarchs, emperors, chieftans, and hereditary aristocracies, the Founders recognized that government depended on the *consent of the governed*. Later democratic impulses in America greatly altered the original Constitution (see "Constitutional Change" later in this chapter) and reshaped it into a much more democratic document.

# SEPARATION OF POWERS AND CHECKS AND BALANCES

The Founders believed that unlimited power was corrupting and that the concentration of power was dangerous. James Madison wrote: "Ambition must be made to counteract ambition." The **separation of powers** within the national government—the creation of separate legislative, executive, and judicial branches in Articles I, II, and III of the Constitution—was designed to place internal controls on governmental power. Power is not only apportioned among three branches of government, but, perhaps more important, each branch is given important **checks and balances** over the actions of the others (see Figure 3-1). According to Madison, "The constant aim is to divide and arrange the several offices in such a manner as that each may be a check on the other."

No bill can become a law without the approval of both the House and the Senate. The president shares legislative power through the power to sign or to veto laws of Congress, although Congress may override a presidential veto with a two-thirds vote in each house. The president may also suggest legislation, "give to the Congress Information of the State of the Union, and recommend to their Consideration such Measures as he shall judge necessary and expedient." Finally, the president may also convene special sessions of Congress.

However, the president's power of appointment is shared by the Senate, which confirms Cabinet and ambassadorial appointments. The president must also secure the advice and consent of the Senate for any treaty. The president must execute the laws, but it is Congress that provides the money to do so. The president and the rest of the executive branch may not spend money that

**Referenda:** Proposed laws or constitutional amendments submitted to the voters for their direct approval or rejection; found in state constitutions but not in the U.S. Constitution.

**Separation of powers:** The constitutional allocation of powers among the three branches of the national government—legislative, executive, and judicial.

**Checks and balances:** Constitutional provisions giving each branch of the national government certain checks over the actions of other branches.

FIGURE 3-1 The Separation of Powers and Checks and Balances

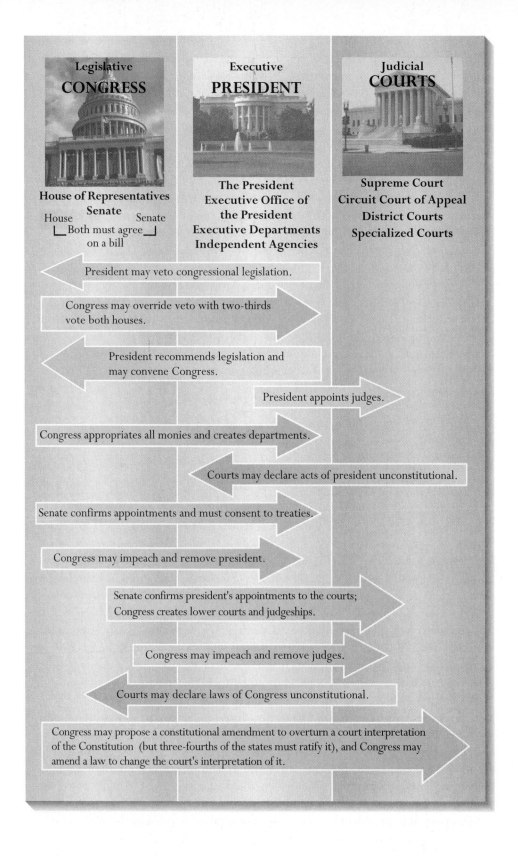

The Separation of Powers and Checks and Balances

**Legislative**
**CONGRESS**

**Executive**
**PRESIDENT**

**Judicial**
**COURTS**

House of Representatives
Senate
House     Senate
└ Both must agree ┘
on a bill

The President
Executive Office of
the President
Executive Departments
Independent Agencies

Supreme Court
Circuit Court of Appeal
District Courts
Specialized Courts

President may veto congressional legislation.

Congress may override veto with two-thirds vote both houses.

President recommends legislation and may convene Congress.

President appoints judges.

Congress appropriates all monies and creates departments.

Courts may declare acts of president unconstitutional.

Senate confirms appointments and must consent to treaties.

Congress may impeach and remove president.

Senate confirms president's appointments to the courts; Congress creates lower courts and judgeships.

Congress may impeach and remove judges.

Courts may declare laws of Congress unconstitutional.

Congress may propose a constitutional amendment to overturn a court interpretation of the Constitution (but three-fourths of the states must ratify it), and Congress may amend a law to change the court's interpretation of it.

has not been appropriated by Congress. Congress must also authorize the creation of executive departments and agencies. Finally, Congress may impeach and remove the president from office for "Treason, Bribery, or other High Crimes and Misdemeanors."

Members of the Supreme Court are appointed by the president and confirmed by the Senate. Traditionally, this court has nine members, but Congress may determine the number of justices. More important, Congress must create lower federal district courts as well as courts of appeal. Congress must also determine the number of these judgeships and determine the jurisdiction of federal courts. But the most important check of all is the Supreme Court's power of judicial review.

**Judicial review,** which is not specifically mentioned in the Constitution itself, is the power of the judiciary to overturn laws of Congress and the states and actions of the president that the courts believe violate the Constitution (see "Judicial Power," Chapter 13). Judicial review, in short, ensures conformity with the Constitution.

Many Federalists, including Alexander Hamilton, believed that the Constitution of 1787 clearly implied that the Supreme Court could invalidate any laws of Congress or presidential actions that it believed to be unconstitutional. Hamilton wrote in 1787 that "Limited government . . . can be preserved in no other way than through the medium of courts of justice, whose duty it is to declare all acts contrary to the manifest tenor of the Constitution void."[7] But it was not until *Marbury v. Madison* in 1803 that Chief Justice John Marshall asserted a Supreme Court ruling that the Supreme Court possessed the power of judicial review over laws of Congress. (See *People in Politics:* "John Marshall and Early Supreme Court Politics" in Chapter 13.)

## CONFLICT OVER RATIFICATION

Today the U.S. Constitution is a revered document, but in the winter of 1787–88, the Founders had real doubts about whether they could get it accepted as "the supreme Law of the Land." Indeed, the Constitution was ratified by only the narrowest of margins in the key states of Massachusetts, Virginia, and New York.

The Founders adopted a **ratification** procedure that was designed to enhance chances for acceptance of the Constitution. The ratification procedure written into the new Constitution was a complete departure from what was then supposed to be the law of the land, the Articles of Confederation, in two major ways. First, the Articles of Confederation required that amendments be approved by *all* of the states. But since Rhode Island was firmly in the hands of small farmers, the Founders knew that unanimous approval was unlikely. So they simply wrote into their new Constitution that approval required only nine of the states. Second, the Founders called for special ratifying conventions in the states rather than risk submitting the Constitution to the state legislatures. Since the Constitution placed many prohibitions on the powers of states, the Founders surmised that special constitutional ratifying conventions would be more likely to approve the document than would state legislatures.

The Founders enjoyed some important tactical advantages over the opposition. The Constitutional Convention was secret; potential opponents did not know

**Judicial review:** The power of the U.S. Supreme Court to declare laws of Congress and the states, and the actions of the president, unconstitutional and legally invalid.

**Ratification:** The power to approve or reject decisions made by representatives. State legislators or state conventions must ratify constitutional amendments submitted by Congress. The U.S. Senate must ratify treaties made by the president.

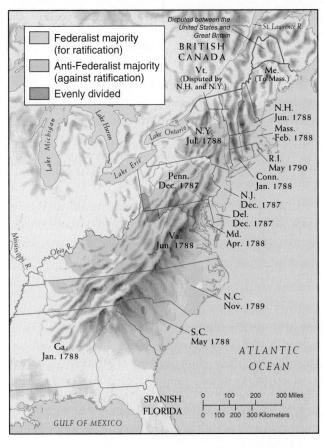

FIGURE 3-2    The Fight over Ratification

Federalist majority (for ratification)

Anti-Federalist majority (against ratification)

Evenly divided

*Source:* Richard B. Morris, ed., *Encyclopedia of American History* (New York: Harper & Row, 1965), p. 118.

what was coming out of it. The Founders called for ratifying conventions as quickly as possible so that the opposition could not get itself organized. Many state conventions met in the winter, so it was difficult for some rural opponents of the Constitution to get to their county seats to vote (see Figure 3-2).

The Founders also waged a very professional (for 1787–88) media campaign in support of the Constitution. James Madison, Alexander Hamilton, and John Jay issued a series of eighty-five press releases, signed simply "Publius," on behalf of the Constitution. Major newspapers ran these essays, which were later collected and published as *The Federalist Papers* (see *People in Politics:* "James Madison and the Control of 'Faction'"). The essays provide an excellent description and explanation of the Constitution by three of its writers and even today serve as a principal reference for political scientists and judges faced with constitutional ambiguities. Two of the most important are reprinted in the Appendix to this textbook.

Nevertheless, opponents of the Constitution—the Anti-Federalists—almost succeeded in defeating the document in New York and Virginia. They charged that the new Constitution would create an "aristocratic tyranny" and pose a threat to the "spirit of republicanism." They argued that the new Senate would be an aristocratic upper house and the new president a ruling monarch. They complained that these officers were not responsible to the people. They also argued that the new national government would trample state governments and deny the people of the states the opportunity to handle their own political and economic affairs. Virginia

## James Madison and the Control of "Faction"

The most important contributions to American democracy by James Madison (1751–1836) were his work in helping to write the Constitution and his insightful and scholarly defense of it during the ratification struggle. Indeed, Madison is more highly regarded by political scientists and historians as a *political theorist* than as the fourth president of the United States.

Madison's family owned a large plantation, Montpelier, near present-day Orange, Virginia. Private tutors and prep schools provided him with a thorough background in history, science, philosophy, and law. He graduated from the College of New Jersey (now Princeton University) at eighteen and assumed a number of elected and appointed positions in Virginia's colonial government. In 1776, Madison drafted a new Virginia Constitution. While serving in Virginia's Revolutionary assembly, he met Thomas Jefferson; the two became lifetime political allies and friends. In 1787, Madison represented Virginia at the Constitutional Convention and took a leading role in its debates over the form of a new federal government. Many of the ideas in his Virginia Plan were incorporated into the Constitution.

Madison's political insights are revealed in *The Federalist Papers,* a series of eighty-five essays published in major newspapers in 1787–88, all signed simply "Publius." Alexander Hamilton and John Jay contributed some of them, but Madison wrote the two most important essays: Number 10, which explains the nature of political conflict (faction) and how it can be "controlled"; and Number 51, which explains the system of separation of powers and checks and balances (both reprinted in the Appendix of this textbook). According to Madison, "controlling faction" was the principal task of government.

What creates faction? According to Madison, conflict is part of human nature. In all societies, we find "a zeal for different opinions concerning religion, concerning government, and many other points," as well as "an attachment to different leaders ambitiously contending for preeminence and power." Even

when there are no serious differences among people, these "frivolous and fanciful distinctions" will inspire "unfriendly passions" and "violent conflicts."

Clearly, Madison believed conflict could arise over just about any matter. Yet "the most common and durable source of factions, has been the various and unequal distribution of property." That is, economic conflicts between rich and poor and between people with different kinds of wealth and sources of income are the most serious conflicts confronting society.

Madison argued that factions could best be controlled in a republican government extending over a large society with a "variety of parties and interests." He defended republicanism (representative democracy) over "pure democracy," which he believed "incompatible with personal security, or the rights of property." And he argued that protection against "factious combinations" can be achieved by including a great variety of competing interests in the political system so that no one interest will be able to "outnumber and oppress the rest." Modern pluralist political theory (see Chapter 1) claims Madison as a forerunner.

Madison served in the House of Representatives from 1789 to 1797 and was largely responsible for writing the first ten amendments to the Constitution—the Bill of Rights. While in the House, Madison became concerned over the expanding power of the national government led by Hamilton and his Federalist Party. Once a proponent of a strong central government, Madison shifted to a more moderate position and split with the Federalists. Frustrated with politics, he retired to his estate in 1797 until Thomas Jefferson appointed him secretary of state in 1801. He negotiated the Louisiana Purchase and was Jefferson's handpicked successor to the presidency in 1809.

As president, Madison unfortunately allowed the nation to become embroiled in Europe's Napoleonic Wars. Conflict with the British over shipping rights and the impressment of American sailors led to a declaration of war against Great Britain in 1812. The war went badly for the United States; in 1814, Madison and the government were forced to flee Washington as the British burned the Capitol. After achieving an uneasy peace with Britain in 1815, Madison retired from politics, again following the footsteps of Thomas Jefferson by becoming president of the University of Virginia in 1826. Madison died at Montpelier on June 28, 1836.

patriot Patrick Henry urged the defeat of the Constitution "to preserve the poor Commonwealth of Virginia." Finally, their most effective argument was that the new Constitution lacked a bill of rights to protect individual liberty from government abuse (see *A Conflicting View:* "Objections to the Constitution by an Anti-Federalist").

## A BILL OF RIGHTS

It may be hard to imagine today, but the original Constitution had no **bill of rights.** This was a particularly glaring deficiency because many of the new state constitutions proudly displayed these written guarantees of individual liberty.

The Founders certainly believed in limited government and individual liberty, and they did write a few liberties into the body of the Constitution, including protection against ex post facto laws, a limited definition of treason, a guarantee of the writ of habeas corpus, and a guarantee of trial by jury (see Chapter 14).

The Federalists argued that there was really no need for a bill of rights because: (1) the national government was one of enumerated powers only and could not exercise any power not expressly granted in the Constitution; (2) the power to limit free speech or press, or establish a religion, or otherwise restrain individual liberty was not among the enumerated powers; (3) therefore it was not necessary to specifically deny these powers to the new government. But the Anti-Federalists were unwilling to rest fundamental freedoms on a thin thread of logical inference from the notion of enumerated powers. They wanted specific written guarantees that the new national government would not interfere with the rights of individuals or the powers of the states. So Federalists at the New York, Massachusetts, and Virginia ratifying conventions promised to support the addition of a bill of rights to the Constitution in the very first Congress.

A young representative in the new House, James Madison, rose in 1789 and presented a bill of rights that he had drawn up after reviewing more than 200 recommendations sent from the states. Interestingly, the new Congress was so busy debating new tax laws that Madison had a difficult time attracting attention to his bill. Eventually, in September 1789, Congress approved a Bill of Rights as ten **amendments** to the Constitution and sent them to the states. (Congress actually passed twelve amendments. One was never ratified; another, dealing with pay raises for Congress, was not ratified by the necessary three-quarters of the states until 1992.) The states promptly ratified the first ten amendments to the Constitution (see Table 3-3), and they took effect in 1791.

The Bill of Rights was originally designed to limit the powers of the new *national* government. The Bill of Rights begins with the command "Congress shall make no law. . . ." It was not until after the Civil War that the Constitution was amended to also prohibit *states* from violating individual liberties. The Fourteenth Amendment, ratified in 1868, includes the command "No State shall. . . ." It prohibits the states from depriving any person of "life, liberty or property, without due process of law," or abridging "the privileges or immunities of citizens of the United States," or denying any person "equal protection of the laws." Today, virtually all of the liberties guaranteed in the Constitution protect individuals not only from the national government but also from state governments. (See also *Compared to What?* "Written Constitutions in the World.")

**Bill of Rights:** Written guarantees of basic individual liberties; the first ten amendments to the U.S. Constitution.

**Amendment:** A change in a bill or a law or a constitution.

CHAPTER 3 • THE CONSTITUTION: LIMITING GOVERNMENTAL POWER

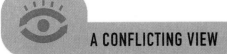

# Objections to the Constitution by an Anti-Federalist

Virginia's George Mason was a delegate to the Constitutional Convention of 1787, but he refused to sign the final document and became a leading opponent of the new Constitution. Mason was a wealthy plantation owner and a heavy speculator in western (Ohio) lands. He was a friend of George Washington, but he considered most other political figures of his day to be "babblers" and he generally avoided public office. However, in 1776 he authored Virginia's Declaration of Rights, which was widely copied in other state constitutions and later became the basis for the Bill of Rights. Although an ardent supporter of states' rights, he attended the Constitutional Convention of 1787 and, according to James Madison's notes on the proceedings, was an influential force in shaping the new national government. His refusal to sign the Constitution and his subsequent leadership of the opposition to its ratification made him the recognized early leader of the Anti-Federalists.

Mason's first objection was that there was no Bill of Rights in the original Constitution. But he also objected to the powers of the new U.S. Senate, which was not directly elected by the people in the original Constitution, and to the powers given to the federal courts and the president. He was wary of the Necessary and Proper Clause, correctly predicting that it would be used to preempt the powers of the states.

In his "objections to the Constitution" Mason wrote:

> There is no declaration of rights; and the laws of the general government being paramount to the laws and constitutions of the several States, the declaration of rights in the separate States are no security.

The Senate has the power of altering all money-bills, and of originating appropriations of money, and the salaries of the officers of their own appointment in conjunction with the President of the United States; although they are not the representatives of the people, or amenable to them.

The judiciary of the United States is so constructed and extended as to absorb and destroy the judiciaries of the several States; thereby rendering law as tedious, intricate and expensive, and justice as unattainable by a great part of the community, as in England, and enabling the rich to oppress and ruin the poor.

By declaring all treaties supreme laws of the land, the Executive and the Senate have, in many cases, an exclusive power of legislation; which might have been avoided by proper distinctions with respect to treaties, and requiring the assent of the House of Representatives, where it could be done with safety.

Under their own construction of the general clause at the end of the enumerated powers, the Congress may grant monopolies in trade and commerce, constitute new crimes, inflict unusual and severe punishments, and extend their power as far as they shall think proper; so that the State Legislatures have no security for the powers now presumed to remain to them; or the people for their rights.

Note that virtually all of Mason's objections to the original Constitution had to be remedied at a later date. The Bill of Rights was added as the first ten amendments. Eventually (1913) the Seventeenth Amendment provided for the direct election of U.S. senators. The president by custom and law came to rely upon a cabinet and later the National Security Council to provide "proper information and advice." And Mason correctly predicted that the federal judiciary would eventually render the law "tedious, intricate, and expensive" and that the Necessary and Proper Clause, which he refers to as "the general clause at the end of the enumerated powers," would be used to expand congressional powers at the expense of the states.

TABLE 3-3    THE BILL OF RIGHTS

**Guaranteeing Freedom of Expression**

First Amendment prohibits government from abridging freedom of speech, press, assembly, and petition.

**Guaranteeing Religious Freedom**

First Amendment prohibits government from establishing a religion or interfering with the free exercise of religion.

**Affirming the Right to Bear Arms
and Protecting Citizens from Quartering Troops**

Second Amendment guarantees the right to bear arms.

Third Amendment prohibits troops from occupying citizens' home in peacetime.

**Protecting the Rights of Accused Persons**

Fourth Amendment protects against unreasonable searches and seizures.

Fifth Amendment requires an indictment by a grand jury for serious crimes; prohibits the government from trying a person twice for the same crime; prohibits the government from taking life, liberty, or property without due process of law; and prohibits the government from taking private property for public use without fair compensation to the owner.

Sixth Amendment guarantees a speedy and public jury trial, the right to confront witnesses in court, and the right to legal counsel for defense.

Seventh Amendment protects the right to a jury trial in civil cases.

Eighth Amendment prohibits the government from setting excessive bail or fines or inflicting cruel and unusual punishment.

**Protecting the Rights of People and States**

Ninth Amendment protects all other unspecified rights of the people.

Tenth Amendment reserves to the states or to the people those powers neither granted to the federal government nor prohibited to the states in the Constitution.

# CONSTITUTIONAL CHANGE

The purpose of a constitution is to govern government—to place limits on governmental power. Thus government itself must not be able to alter or amend a constitution easily. Yet the U.S. Constitution has changed over time, sometimes by formal amendment and other times by judicial interpretation, presidential and congressional action, and general custom and practice.

*Amendments*    A constitutional amendment must first be proposed, and then it must be ratified. The Constitution allows two methods of *proposing* a constitutional amendment: (1) by passage in the House and the Senate with a two-thirds vote; or (2) by passage in a national convention called by Congress in response to petitions by two-thirds of the state legislatures. Congress then chooses the method of *ratification,* which can be either: (1) by vote in the legislatures of three-fourths of the states; or (2) by conventions called for that purpose in three-fourths of the states (see Figure 3-3; see also *What Do You Think?* "Should We Amend the Constitution to Require a Balanced Budget?").

Of the four possible combinations of proposal and ratification, the method involving proposal by a two-thirds vote of Congress and ratification by three-

# Written Constitutions in the World

In 1787, the idea of a written constitution establishing a national government and limiting its power was unprecedented. Today most nations boast of a written constitution defining government institutions and setting forth "rights" of the people. Nations sometimes refer to their constitutions as "Basic Laws" or "Fundamental Laws." But few constitutions actually limit government power.

Many of today's nations achieved independence after World War II, and most national constitutions have been written since 1948. Many constitutions are symbolic. Like the Preamble to the U.S. Constitution—which declares our national goals in general terms but is not enforceable in court—they set forth ideals but no specific procedures for their realization or enforcement. Many constitutions reflect the Universal Declaration of Human Rights adopted by the United Nations in 1948, and like it confuse rights as legally enforceable protections against government with desirable social and economic conditions.

The Declaration's many rights include:

- "Rights to life, liberty, and security of person."
- Freedom from "torture or cruel, inhuman, or degrading treatment or punishments."
- Freedom from "arbitrary arrest, detention, or exile."
- Freedom from "arbitrary interference with privacy, family, home, or correspondence or attacks upon honor and reputation."
- "Right to leave any country and return."
- "Right to marry and form a family."
- "Rights to own property."
- "Freedom of thought, conscience, and religion."
- "Freedom of opinion and expression."
- "Freedom of peaceful assembly and association."
- "Right to social security.
- "Right to work . . . and to protection against unemployment."
- "Right to equality for equal work."
- "Right to just and feasible remuneration."
- "Rights to form and to join trade unions."
- "Right to rest and leisure."
- "Right to an adequate standard of living."
- "Right to education . . . [which] shall be free at least in the elementary and fundamental stages."

- "Right to freely participate in the cultural life of the community to enjoy the arts and to share in scientific advancement and its benefits."

A survey of the constitutions of 142 nations calculated the percentage with provisions dealing with human rights and economic rights.

**Human rights**

| Right | Percent |
|-------|---------|
| Rights of defendants | 88% |
| Protection of private life | 80.4% |
| Personal liberty/security | 66.9% |
| Freedom of movement | 57% |
| Right to life | 45% |
| Prohibition of slavery | 47.2% |
| Prohibition of torture | 46.5% |
| Right of asylum | 31.7% |
| Right to privacy | 26.1% |

0 10 20 30 40 50 60 70 80 90 100
Percent

**Economic rights**

| Right | Percent |
|-------|---------|
| Right to property | 83.1% |
| Right to form or join unions | 59.2% |
| Right to work | 55% |
| Fair remuneration or equal payment | 32.4% |
| Right to rest and leisure | 32.4% |
| Right to free choice of work | 28% |
| Right to strike | 25.3% |

0 10 20 30 40 50 60 70 80 90 100
Percent

*Source:* United Nations General Assembly, *Universal Declaration of Human Rights,* December 6, 1948, 2d sess., Doc. A/811; Hene van Maarseveen and Ger van der Tang, *Written Constitutions: A Computerized Comparative Study* (Dobbs Ferry, N.Y.: Oceans Publications, 1978).

# Should We Amend the Constitution to Require a Balanced Budget?

Every year the U.S. government goes deeper into debt. It is now nearly $5 trillion in debt, a figure equal to $18,000 for every man, woman, and child in the nation. This debt is owed to banks, insurance companies, investment firms, and anyone else who buys U.S. government bonds. Government interest payments to holders of the debt now amount to more than 20 percent of governmental expenditures. The debt need not ever be paid off, but future generations of American taxpayers must continue to pay the annual interest costs.

Governmental expenditures have exceeded revenues for every one of the last thirty years. Democrats and Republicans, liberals and conservatives, have all contributed to government deficits; they differ only in where they place the blame. Conservatives blame "runaway" government entitlement programs, such as Social Security and Medicare, as well as large-scale spending programs for welfare, education, job training, and agriculture. Liberals claim that the nation's high deficits result largely from cutting the taxes of the wealthy during the Reagan Administration. Democrats point out that the nation's largest annual deficits occurred in the Reagan and Bush Administrations. Republicans argue that Democrats in the Congress are responsible for these deficits because they failed to cut domestic spending as Republican presidents wished.

Regardless of who is to blame, the implications of the debt are serious. The painful legacy of these annual deficits will linger for generations. Interest payments on the debt consume about $1 out of every $5 of federal expenditures. This means that taxpayers can receive at most only $4 of public goods and services for every $5 paid to the federal government.

The simplest solution to the federal deficit is to have the president and Congress prepare and pass only *balanced* budgets. But that solution has eluded policy makers for more than thirty years. Neither presidents nor Congresses, Democrats nor Republicans, have been willing to reduce expenditures or raise taxes enough to balance budgets. Indeed, deficit spending allows elected politicians to spend heavily on their constituents while shifting the full costs to younger generations, who are either too young to vote or who vote less often than older people.

In 1995, the House of Representatives by a vote of 300 to 132 passed an amendment to the Constitution requiring a balanced budget by 2002 (or the second year after ratification, whichever is later). But the amendment failed by a single vote in the U.S. Senate to get the necessary two-thirds majority that would have sent it to the states for ratification. One Republican senator, Mark Hatfield (Oregon), broke party ranks to defeat the amendment. Six Democratic senators who had previously supported a Balanced Budget Amendment switched to the opposition when the amendment appeared close to passage. One of the strongest lobbying groups opposing the amendment was the National Association of Retired Persons, which feared that a balanced budget might mean less generous Social Security payments.

**Public Opinion on a Balanced Budget Amendment**

| Year | Favor | Oppose | No Response |
|------|-------|--------|-------------|
| 1985 | 49% | 27% | 24% |
| 1987 | 53% | 23% | 24% |
| 1992 | 59% | 24% | 17% |
| 1996 | 71% | 22% | 7% |

☐ Favor  ☐ Oppose  ☐ No Response

*Source:* Gallup opinion reports.

For almost twenty years, citizens' groups, led by the National Taxpayers Union, have tried to take the alternate route to amending the Constitution—getting two-thirds of the states to call a national constitutional convention to write a Balanced Budget Amendment. This route would bypass Congress in proposing the amendment; three-quarters of the states would still be required to ratify it. Over half of the states have passed such a resolution at one time or another. But this path to amending the Constitution has never been successful, and it is not likely that such a convention will ever be convened. There is widespread agreement, however, that if Congress ever proposed a Balanced Budget Amendment, three-quarters of the states would quickly ratify it.

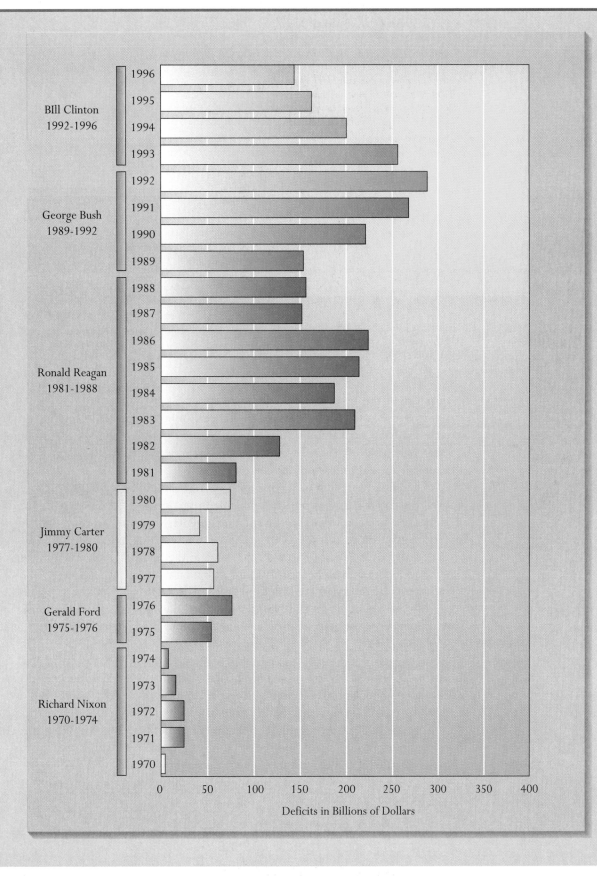

Deficits in Billions of Dollars

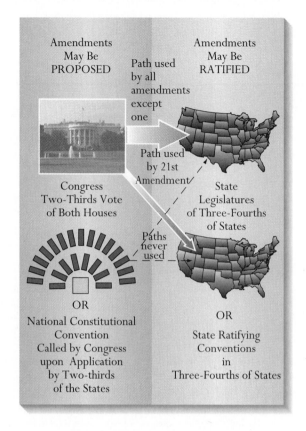

**FIGURE 3-3** **Constitutional Amendment Process**

*The Constitution set up two alternative routes for proposing amendments and two for ratifying them. One of the four possible combinations has actually been used for all except one (Twenty-first) amendment. However, in our time, there have been persistent calls for a constitutional convention to propose new amendments permitting school prayer, making abortion illegal, and requiring a balanced national budget.*

quarters of the legislatures has been used for all the amendments except one. Only for the Twenty-first Amendment's repeal of Prohibition did Congress call for state ratifying conventions (principally because Congress feared that southern Bible Belt state legislatures would vote against repeal). The method of proposal by national convention has never been used.

In addition to the Bill of Rights, most of the constitutional amendments ratified over the nation's 200 years have expanded our notion of democracy. Today, the Constitution includes twenty-seven amendments, which means that only seventeen (out of more than 10,000) proposed amendments have been ratified since the passage of the Bill of Rights. Some, such as the Equal Rights Amendment, had strong support in both houses of Congress but failed to receive sufficient votes for ratification by the states (see *Up Close:* "ERA: Three States Short"). It is possible to classify the amendments that have been ratified into the broad categories of constitutional processes, prohibition, income tax, individual liberty, and voting rights (see Table 3-4).

*Judicial Interpretations* Some of the greatest changes in the Constitution have come about not by formal amendment but by interpretations of the document by courts, Congresses, and presidents.

Through judicial review, the U.S. Supreme Court has come to play the major role in interpreting the meaning of the Constitution. This power is itself largely an interpretation of the Constitution (see "Judicial Power" in Chapter 13). Over the years, the federal courts have been much more likely to strike down laws of the states than laws of Congress.

TABLE 3-4    AMENDMENTS TO THE CONSTITUTION SINCE THE BILL OF RIGHTS

**Perfecting Constitutional Processes**

Eleventh Amendment (1798): forbids federal court suits against a state by citizens of another state or nation.

Twelfth Amendment (1804) provides separate ballots for president and vice-president in the Electoral College to prevent confusion.

Twentieth Amendment (1933) determines the dates for the beginning of the terms of Congress (January 3) and the president (January 20).

Twenty-second Amendment (1951) limits the president to two terms.

Twenty-fifth Amendment (1967) provides for presidential disability.

Twenty-seventh Amendment (1992) prevents Congress from raising its own pay in a single session.

**The Experiment with Prohibition**

Eighteenth Amendment (1919) prohibits the manufacture, sale, or transportation of intoxicating liquors.

Twenty-first Amendment (1933) repeals the Eighteenth Amendment.

**The Income Tax**

Sixteenth Amendment (1913) allows Congress to tax incomes.

**Expanding Liberty**

Thirteenth Amendment (1865) abolishes slavery.

Fourteenth Amendment (1868) protects life, liberty, and property and the privileges and immunities of citizenship, and provides equal protection of the law.

**Expanding Voting Rights**

Fifteenth Amendment (1870) guarantees that the right to vote shall not be denied because of race.

Seventeenth Amendment (1913) provides for the election of senators by the people of each state.

Nineteenth Amendment (1920) guarantees that the right to vote shall not be denied because of sex.

Twenty-third Amendment (1961) gives the District of Columbia electoral votes for presidential elections.

Twenty-fourth Amendment (1964) guarantees that the right to vote shall not be denied because of failure to pay a poll tax or other tax.

Twenty-sixth Amendment (1971) guarantees that the right to vote shall not be denied persons eighteen years of age or older.

The Supreme Court has given meaning to many of our most important constitutional phrases. Among the most important examples of constitutional change through judicial interpretation are the important meanings given to the Fourteenth Amendment:

- Deciding that "equal protection of the laws" requires an end to segregation of the races (*Brown v. Board of Education of Topeka,* 1954, and subsequent decisions).
- Deciding that "liberty" includes a woman's right to choose an abortion, and that the term *person* does not include the unborn fetus (*Roe v. Wade,* 1973, and subsequent decisions).

## ERA: Three States Short

Amending the U.S. Constitution is no easy task. It requires not only a two-thirds vote in both houses of Congress, reflecting *national* support, but also ratification by three-fourths of the states, reflecting widespread support within the *states*. The fate of the Equal Rights Amendment, popularly known as ERA, illustrates the need for nationwide consensus in order to amend the Constitution.

The Equal Rights Amendment is a simple statement to which the vast majority of Americans agree, according to public opinion polls: "Equality of rights under the law shall not be denied or abridged by the United States or any state on account of sex." Congress passed ERA in 1972 with far more than the necessary two-thirds vote; ERA won by 84 to 8 in the Senate and 354 to 24 in the House. Both Republicans and Democrats supported ERA, and it was endorsed by Presidents Richard Nixon, Gerald Ford, and Jimmy Carter and most other national political leaders and organizations. ERA won quick ratification in about half the states.

But by 1975, a new and powerful Stop ERA movement had developed in the states that slowed the amendment's progress toward ratification. By 1978, thirty-five state legislatures had ratified ERA. This was three states short of the necessary thirty-eight (three-quarters) states. (However, five states voted to rescind their earlier ratification. There is some disagreement about the validity of rescissions. Most constitutional scholars do not believe a state can rescind its earlier ratification of a constitutional amendment, and there is no language in the Constitution regarding rescission.)

Leaders of the ERA movement called upon Congress to grant an unprecedented extension beyond the traditional seven years to continue the battle for ratification. (The Constitution, Article V, does not specify how long states can consider a constitutional amendment.) Congress (by simple majority vote) granted ERA an additional three years for state ratification; the new limit was 1982, a full ten years after Congress proposed the amendment. Even so, last-ditch attempts failed to pass ERA in Florida, Illinois, and North Carolina, where the battle was close. Unlike his predecessors in the Oval Office, President Ronald Reagan opposed ERA, although he did not take an active role in defeating it.

State legislators had become uncomfortable with ERA when the Stop ERA movement successfully demonstrated that many of the supposed beneficiaries opposed the amendment. "Ladies in pink" came to state capitals to lobby against the amendment wearing pink, bringing apple pies, and generally adopting traditional symbols of femininity. Stop ERA activist Phyllis Schlafly became a media celebrity. While less well organized than the leading feminist groups that supported ERA (the National Organization for Women [NOW], the League of Women Voters, the Women's Political Caucus, and others), the "ladies in pink" were very much in evidence when state legislatures took up the question of ratification.

ERA came to symbolize a larger cultural conflict in the United States. Opponents of the amendment believed that the feminist movement was weakening the institution of the family and demoralizing women who wished to devote their lives to their husbands and children. They argued that ERA would eliminate many legal protections for women—for example,

- Deciding that "equal protection of the laws" requires that every person's vote should be weighed equally in apportionment and districting plans for the House of Representatives, state legislatures, city councils, and so on (*Baker v. Carr,* 1964, and subsequent decisions).

*Presidential and Congressional Action*    Congress and the president have also undertaken to interpret the Constitution. Nearly every president, for example, has argued that the phrase "executive Power" in Article II includes more than the specific powers mentioned afterward. Thomas Jefferson purchased the

financial support in marriage and exemptions from the draft. Proponents of ERA believed that the guarantee of full sexual equality should be part of the U.S. Constitution—"the supreme law of the land"—and not rest upon state and federal law. While acknowledging that federal and state civil rights laws already prohibited sexual discrimination in employment, credit, education, and many other areas of public life, the pro-ERA forces argued that these guarantees of equality would be much more secure if they were permanently enshrined in the U.S. Constitution and therefore directly enforceable in federal courts.

Promising that "ERA won't go away," proponents of the amendment have continued to press their case. But to date Congress has not acted to resubmit ERA to the states.

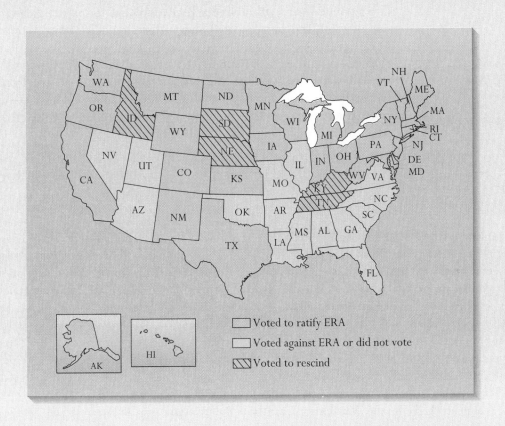

Louisiana Territory from France in 1803 even though there is no constitutional authorization for the president, or even the national government, to acquire new territory. Presidents from George Washington to Richard Nixon have argued that Congress cannot force the executive branch to turn over documents it does not wish to disclose (see Chapter 11).

Congress by law has tried to restrict the president's power as commander-in-chief by requiring that the president notify Congress when U.S. troops are sent to "situations where imminent involvement in hostilities is clearly indicated" and limiting their stay to sixty days unless Congress authorizes an extension. This War Powers Act (1973) may not ever be tested for its constitutionality, but it indicates that Congress has its own ideas about interpreting the Constitution (see Chapter 11).

*Custom and Practice*    Finally, the Constitution changes over time as a result of generally accepted customs and practice. It is interesting to note, for example, that the Constitution never mentions political parties. (Many of the Founders disapproved of parties because they caused "faction" among the people.) But soon after Thomas Jefferson resigned as President Washington's first secretary of state (in part because he resented the influence of Secretary of the Treasury Alexander Hamilton), the Virginian attracted the support of Anti-Federalists, who believed that the national government was too strong. When Washington retired from office, most Federalists supported John Adams as his successor. But many Anti-Federalists ran for posts as presidential electors as "Jefferson's men." When Adams won the presidential election of 1796, the Anti-Federalists organized themselves into a political party, the Democratic-Republicans, to oppose Adams in the election of 1800. The party secured pledges from candidates for presidential elector to cast their electoral vote for Jefferson if they won their post; then the party helped win support for its slate of electors. In this way the Electoral College was transformed from a deliberative body (where leading citizens from each state came together to decide for themselves who should be president) to a ceremonial body (where pledged electors simply cast their presidential vote for the candidate who carried their state in the presidential election).

## SUMMARY NOTES

- The true meaning of constitutionalism is the limitation of governmental power. Constitutions govern governments; they are designed to restrict those who exercise governmental power. Constitutions not only establish governmental bodies and prescribe the rules by which they make their decisions, but, more important, they also limit the powers of government.

- The American tradition of written constitutions extends back through the Articles of Confederation, the colonial charters, the Mayflower Compact, to the Magna Carta, all of which strengthened the idea of a written contract defining governmental power. The Second Continental Congress in 1776 adopted a written Declaration of Independence to justify the separation from Great Britain.

- The movement for a Constitutional Convention in 1787 was inspired by the new government's inability to levy taxes under the Articles of Confederation, its inability to fund the Revolutionary War debt, obstacles to interstate commerce, monetary problems, and civil disorders, including Shays's Rebellion.

- The nation's Founders—fifty-five delegates to the Constitutional Convention in Philadelphia in 1787—shared a broad consensus on liberty and property, the social contract, republicanism, limited government, and the need for a national government.

- The Founders compromised their differences over representation by creating two co-equal houses in the Congress: the House of Representatives, with members apportioned to the states on the basis of population and directly elected by the people for two-year terms; and the Senate, with two members allotted to each state regardless of its population and originally selected by state legislatures for six-year terms.

- The infamous slavery provisions in the Constitution—counting each slave as three-fifths of a person for purposes of taxation and representation, guaranteeing the return of escaped slaves, and postponing the end of the slave trade for twenty years—were also compromises. Voter qualifications in national elections were left to the states to determine.

- The structure of the national government reflects the Founders' beliefs in national supremacy, federalism, republicanism, separation of powers, checks and balances, and judicial review.
- The original Constitution gave the people very little influence on their government: only members of the House of Representatives were directly elected; senators were elected by state legislatures; the president was elected indirectly by "electors" chosen in each state; and members of the Supreme Court and federal judiciary were appointed for life by the president and confirmed by the Senate. Over time, the national government became more democratic through the expansion of voting rights, the enactment of civil rights laws, the direct election of senators, the emergence of political parties, and the practice of voting for presidential electors pledged to cast their vote for the candidates of one party.
- The separation of powers and checks and balances written into the Constitution was designed, in Madison's words, "to divide and arrange the several offices in such a manner as that each may be a check on the other." Judicial review was not specifically described in the original Constitution, but the Supreme Court soon asserted its power to overturn laws of Congress and the states that the Court determined to be in conflict with the Constitution.
- Opposition to the new Constitution was strong. Anti-Federalists argued that it created a national government that was aristocratic, undemocratic, and a threat to the rights of the states and the people. Their concerns resulted in the Bill of Rights: ten amendments added to the original Constitution, all designed to limit the power of the national government and protect the rights of individuals and states.
- Over time, constitutional changes have come about as a result of formal amendments, judicial interpretations, presidential and congressional actions, and changes in custom and practice. The most common method of constitutional amendment has been proposal by two-thirds vote of both houses of Congress followed by ratification by three-fourths of the states.

# SELECTED READINGS

BEARD, CHARLES. *An Economic Interpretation of the Constitution.* New York: Macmillan, 1913. A classic work setting forth the argument that economic self-interest inspired the Founders in writing the Constitution.

MADISON, JAMES, ALEXANDER HAMILTON, and JOHN JAY. *The Federalist Papers.* New York: Modern Library, 1937. These eighty-five collected essays written in 1787–88 in support of ratification of the Constitution remain the most important commentary on that document. Numbers 10 and 51 (reprinted in the Appendix) ought to be required reading for all students of American government.

MANSBRIDGE, JANE J. *Why We Lost the ERA.* Chicago: University of Chicago Press, 1986. An account of the politics of the lost ratification battle for the Equal Rights Amendment. Public opinion polls demonstrated strong national support for ERA, but the constitutional requirement for ratification by three-fourths of the states allowed a minority to exercise a veto.

MCDONALD, FORREST B. *Novus Ordo Seculorum.* Lawrence: University Press of Kansas, 1986. A description of the intellectual origins of the Constitution and the "new secular order" that it represented.

PELTASON, J. W. *Understanding the Constitution,* 13th ed. New York: Harcourt Brace, 1994. Of the many books that explain the Constitution, this is one of the best. It contains explanations of the Declaration of Independence, the Articles of Confederation, and the Constitution. The book is written clearly and is well suited for undergraduates.

ROSSITER, CLINTON L. *1787, The Grand Convention.* New York: Macmillan, 1960. A very readable account of the people and events surrounding the Constitutional Convention in 1787, with many insights into the conflicts and compromises that took place there.

STORING, HERBERT J. *What the Anti-Federalists Were For.* Chicago: University of Chicago Press, 1981. An examination of the arguments of the Anti-Federalists in opposition to the ratification of the Constitution.

TRIBE, LAURENCE H., and MICHAEL C. DORF. *On Reading the Constitution.* Cambridge, Mass.: Harvard University Press, 1991. An argument that the Constitution was a compromise charter that incorporated contending visions of government. Therefore, no single interpretation can explain the document; its meaning must emerge from continuous debate among citizens and leaders.

WOOD, GORDON S. *The Creation of the American Republic, 1776–1787.* New York: Norton, 1993. A study of the political conflicts in the new nation that led to the Constitutional Convention.

# The Constitution of the United States

## The Preamble

We the People of the United States, in Order to form a more perfect Union, establish Justice, insure domestic Tranquility, provide for the common defense, promote the general Welfare, and secure the Blessings of Liberty to ourselves and our Posterity, do ordain and establish this Constitution for the United States of America.

## Article I—The Legislative Article

### Legislative Power

*Section 1* All legislative Powers herein granted shall be vested in a Congress of the United States, which shall consist of a Senate and House of Representatives.

### House of Representatives: Composition; Qualifications; Apportionment; Impeachment Power

*Section 2* The House of Representatives shall be composed of Members chosen every second Year by the People of the several States, and the Electors in each State shall have the Qualifications requisite for Electors of the most numerous Branch of the State Legislature.

No Person shall be a Representative who shall not have attained to the Age of twenty five Years, and been seven Years a Citizen of the United States, and who shall not, when elected, be an Inhabitant of that State in which he shall be chosen.

Representatives and direct Taxes[1] shall be apportioned among the several States which may be included within this Union, according to their respective Numbers, *which shall be determined by adding to the whole Number of free Persons, including those bound to Service for a Term of Years, and excluding Indians not taxed, three fifths of all other Persons.*[2] The actual Enumeration shall be made within three Years after the first Meeting of the Congress of the United States, and within every subsequent Term of ten Years, in such Manner as they shall by Law direct. The Number of Representatives shall not exceed one for every thirty Thousand, but each State shall have at least one Representative; and until such enumeration shall be made, the State of New Hampshire shall be entitled to chuse three, Massachusetts eight, Rhode-Island and Providence Plantations one, Connecticut five, New-York six, New Jersey four, Pennsylvania eight, Delaware one, Maryland six, Virginia ten, North Carolina five, South Carolina five, and Georgia three.

When vacancies happen in the Representation from any State, the Executive Authority thereof shall issue Writs of Election to fill such Vacancies.

The House of Representatives shall chuse their Speaker and other Officers; and shall have the sole Power of Impeachment.

### Senate Composition: Qualifications, Impeachment Trials

*Section 3* The Senate of the United States shall be composed of two Senators from each State, *chosen by the Legislature thereof,*[3] for six Years; and each Senator shall have one Vote.

Immediately after they shall be assembled in Consequence of the first Election, they shall be divided as equally as may be into three Classes. The Seats of the Senators of the first Class shall be vacated at the Expiration of the second Year, of the second Class at the Expiration of the fourth Year, and of the third Class at the Expiration of the sixth Year, so that one third may be chosen every second Year; *and if Vacancies happen by Resignation, or otherwise, during the Recess of the Legislature of any State, the Executive thereof may make temporary Appointments until the next Meeting of the Legislature, which shall then fill such Vacancies.*[4]

No person shall be a Senator who shall not have attained to the Age of thirty Years, and been nine Years a Citizen of the United States, and who shall not, when elected, be an inhabitant of that State for which he shall be chosen.

The Vice President of the United States shall be President of the Senate, but shall have no Vote, unless they be equally divided.

The Senate shall chuse their other Officers, and also a President pro tempore, in the Absence of the Vice President, or when he shall exercise the Office of President of the United States.

The Senate shall have the sole Power to try all Impeachments. When sitting for that Purpose, they shall be on Oath or Affirmation. When the President of the United States is tried, the Chief Justice shall preside: And no Person shall be convicted without the Concurrence of two thirds of the Members present.

Judgment in Cases of Impeachment shall not extend further than to removal from Office, and disqualification to hold and enjoy any Office of honor, Trust or Profit under the United States; but the Party convicted shall nevertheless be liable and subject to Indictment, Trial, Judgment and Punishment, according to law.

### Congressional Elections: Times, Places, Manner

*Section 4* The Times, Places and Manner of holding Elections for Senators and Representatives, shall be prescribed in each State by the Legislature thereof; but the Congress may at any time by Law make or alter such Regulations, except as to the Places of chusing Senators.

---

[1] Modified by the 16th Amendment
[2] Replaced by Section 2, 14th Amendment

[3] Repealed by the 17th Amendment
[4] Modified by the 17th Amendment

The Congress shall assemble at least once in every Year, *and such Meeting shall be on the first Monday in December, unless they shall by Law appoint a different Day.*[5]

## Powers and Duties of the Houses

*Section 5* Each House shall be the Judge of the Elections, Returns and Qualifications of its own Members, and a Majority of each shall constitute a Quorum to do Business; but a smaller Number may adjourn from day to day, and may be authorized to compel the Attendance of absent Members, in such Manner, and under the Penalties as each House may provide.

Each House may determine the Rules of its Proceedings, punish its Members for disorderly Behaviour, and, with the Concurrence of two thirds, expel a Member.

Each House shall keep a Journal of its Proceedings, and from time to time publish the same, excepting such Parts as may in their Judgment require Secrecy; and the Yeas and Nays of the Members of either House on any question shall, at the Desire of one fifth of those Present, be entered on the Journal.

Neither House, during the Session of Congress, shall, without the Consent of the other, adjourn for more than three days, nor to any other place than that in which the two Houses shall be sitting.

## Rights of Members

*Section 6* The Senators and Representatives shall receive a Compensation for their Services, to be ascertained by Law, and paid out of the Treasury of the United States. They shall in all Cases, except Treason, Felony and Breach of the Peace, be privileged from Arrest during their Attendance at the Session of their respective Houses, and in going to and returning from the same; and for any Speech or Debate in either House, they shall not be questioned in any other Place.

No Senator or Representative, shall, during the time for which he was elected, be appointed to any civil Office under the authority of the United States, which shall have been created, or the Emoluments whereof shall have been encreased during such time; and no Person holding any Office under the United States, shall be a Member of either House during his Continuance in Office.

## Legislative Powers: Bills and Resolutions

*Section 7* All Bills for raising Revenue shall originate in the House of Representatives; but the Senate may propose or concur with Amendments as on other Bills.

Every Bill which shall have passed the House of Representatives and the Senate, shall, before it becomes a Law, be presented to the President of the United States; if he approve he shall sign it, but if not he shall return it, with his Objections to that House in which it shall have originated, who shall enter the Objections at large on their Journal, and proceed to reconsider it. If after such Reconsideration two thirds of that House shall agree to pass the Bill, it shall be sent, together with the Objections, to the other House, by which it shall likewise be reconsidered, and if approved by two thirds of that House, it shall become a Law. But in all such Cases the Votes of both Houses shall be determined by Yeas and Nays, and the Names of the Persons voting for and against the Bill shall be entered on the Journal of each House respectively. If any Bill shall not be returned by the President within ten Days (Sundays excepted) after it shall have been presented to him, the Same shall be a Law, in like Manner as if he had signed it, unless the Congress by their Adjournment prevent its Return, in which Case it shall not be a Law.

Every Order, Resolution, or Vote to which the Concurrence of the Senate and House of Representatives may be necessary (except on a question of Adjournment) shall be presented to the President of the United States; and before the Same shall take Effect, shall be approved by him, or being disapproved by him, shall be repassed by two thirds of the Senate and House of Representatives, according to the Rules and Limitations prescribed in the Case of a Bill.

## Powers of Congress

*Section 8* The Congress shall have Power To lay and collect Taxes, Duties, Imposts and Excises, to pay the Debts and provide for the common Defence and general Welfare of the United States; but all Duties, Imposts and Excises shall be uniform throughout the United States.

To borrow Money on the Credit of the United States;

To regulate Commerce with foreign Nations, and among the several States, and with the Indian Tribes;

To establish an uniform Rule of Naturalization, and uniform Laws on the subject of Bankruptcies throughout the United States;

To coin Money, regulate the Value thereof, and of foreign Coin, and fix the Standard of Weights and Measures;

To provide for the Punishment of counterfeiting the Securities and current Coin of the United States;

To establish Post Offices and post Roads;

To promote the Progress of Science and useful Arts, by securing for limited Times to Authors and Inventors the exclusive Right to their respective Writings and Discoveries,

To constitute Tribunals inferior to the supreme Court,

To define and punish Piracies and Felonies committed on the high Seas, and Offences against the Law of Nations;

To declare War, grant Letters of Marque and Reprisal, and make Rules concerning Captures on Land and Water;

To raise and support Armies, but no Appropriation of Money to that Use shall be for a longer Term than two Years;

To provide and maintain a Navy;

To make Rules for the Government and Regulation of the land and naval Forces;

To provide for calling for the Militia to execute the Laws of the Union, suppress Insurrections and repel Invasions;

To provide for organizing, arming, and disciplining, the Militia, and for governing such Part of them as may be employed in the Service of the United States, reserving to the States respectively, the Appointment of the Officers, and the Authority of training the Militia according to the discipline prescribed by Congress;

To exercise exclusive Legislation in all Cases whatsoever, over such District (not exceeding ten Miles square) as may, by Cession of particular States, and the Acceptance of Congress, become the Seat of the Government of the United States, and to exercise like Authority over all Places purchased by the Consent of the Legislature of the State in which the Same shall be, for the Erection of Forts, Magazines, Arsenals, dock-Yards, and other needful Buildings;—And

To make all Laws which shall be necessary and proper for carrying into Execution the foregoing Powers, and all other Powers vested by this Constitution in the Government of the United States, or in any Department or Officer thereof.

## Powers Denied to Congress

*Section 9* The Migration of Importation of such Persons as any of the States now existing shall think proper to admit, shall not be prohibited by the Congress prior to the Year one thousand eight hundred and eight, but a Tax or Duty may be imposed on such Importation, not exceeding ten dollars for each Person.

---

[5]Changed by the 20th Amendment

The privilege of the Writ of Habeas Corpus shall not be suspended, unless when in Cases of Rebellion or Invasion the public Safety may require it.

No Bill of Attainder or ex post facto Laws shall be passed.

No Capitation, or other direct, Tax shall be laid, unless in Proportion to the Census or Enumeration herein before directed to be taken.[6]

No Tax or Duty shall be laid on Articles exported from any State.

No Preference shall be given by any Regulation of Commerce or Revenue to the Ports of one State over those of another; nor shall Vessels bound to, or from, one State, be obliged to enter, clear, or pay Duties in another.

No Money shall be drawn from the Treasury, but in Consequence of Appropriations made by Law; and a regular Statement and Account of the Receipts and Expenditures of all public Money shall be published from time to time.

No Title of Nobility shall be granted by the United States; And no Person holding any Office of Profit or Trust under them, shall, without the Consent of Congress, accept of any present, Emolument, Office, or Title, of any kind whatever, from any King, Prince, or foreign State.

## Powers Denied to the States

*Section 10*   No State shall enter into any Treaty, Alliance, or Confederation; grant Letters of Marque and Reprisal; coin Money; emit Bills of Credit; make any Thing but gold and silver Coin a Tender in Payment of Debts; pass any Bill of Attainder, ex post facto Law, or Law impairing the Obligation of Contracts, or grant any Title of Nobility.

No State shall, without the Consent of the Congress, lay any Imposts or Duties on Imports or Exports, except what may be absolutely necessary for executing its inspection Laws: and the net Produce of all Duties and Imposts, laid by any State on Imports or Exports, shall be for the Use of the Treasury of the United States; and all such Laws shall be subject to the Revision and Controul of the Congress.

No State shall, without the Consent of Congress, lay any Duty of Tonnage, keep Troops, or Ships of War in time of Peace, enter into any Agreement or Compact with another State, or with a foreign Power, or engage in War, unless actually invaded, or in such imminent Danger as will not admit of Delay.

## Article II—THE EXECUTIVE ARTICLE

## Nature and Scope of Presidential Power

*Section 1*   The executive Power shall be vested in a President of the United States of America. He shall hold his Office during the Term of four Years and, together with the Vice President, chosen for the same Term, be elected as follows:

Each State shall appoint, in such Manner as the Legislature thereof may direct, a Number of Electors, equal to the whole Number of Senators and Representatives to which the State may be entitled in the Congress: but no Senator or Representative, or Person holding an Office of Trust or Profit under the United States, shall be appointed an Elector.

The Electors shall meet in their respective States, and vote by Ballot for two Persons, of whom one at least shall not be an Inhabitant of the same State with themselves. And they shall make a List of all the Persons voted for, and of the Number of Votes for each; which List they shall sign and certify, and transmit sealed to the Seat of the Government of the United States, directed to the President of the Senate. The President of the Senate shall, in the Presence of the Senate and House of Representatives, open all the Certificates, and the Votes shall then be counted. The Person having the greatest Number of Votes shall be the President, if such Number be a Majority of the whole Number of Electors appointed; and if there be more than one

who have such Majority and have an equal Number of Votes, then the House of Representatives shall immediately chuse by Ballot one of them for President; and if no person have a Majority, then from the five highest on the List the said House shall in like Manner chuse the President. But in chusing the President, the Votes shall be taken by States, the Representation from each State having one Vote; A quorum for this Purpose shall consist of a Member or Members from two thirds of the States, and a Majority of all the States shall be necessary to a Choice. In every Case, after the Choice of the President, the person having the greatest Number of Votes of the Electors shall be the Vice President. But if there should remain two or more who have equal Vote, the Senate shall chuse from them by Ballot the Vice President.[7]

The Congress may determine the Time of chusing the Electors, and the Day on which they shall give their Votes; which Day shall be the same throughout the United States.

No Person except a natural born Citizen, or a Citizen of the United States, at the time of the Adoption of this Constitution, shall be eligible to the Office of President; neither shall any Person be eligible to that Office who shall not have attained to the Age of thirty five Years, and been fourteen Years a Resident within the United States.

In Case of the Removal of the President from Office, or of his Death, Resignation, or Inability to discharge the Powers and Duties of the said Office, the same shall devolve on the Vice President, and the Congress may by Law provide for the Case of Removal, Death, Resignation, or Inability, both of the President and Vice President, declaring what Officer shall then act as President, and such Officer shall act accordingly, until the Disability be removed, or a President shall be elected.[8]

The President shall, at stated Times, receive for his Services, a Compensation, which shall neither be encreased nor diminished during the Period of which he shall have been elected, and he shall not receive within that Period any other Emolument from the United States, or any of them.

Before he enter on the Execution of his Office, he shall take the following Oath or Affirmation:—"I do solemnly swear (or affirm) that I will faithfully execute the Office of President of the United States, and will to the best of my Ability, preserve, protect and defend the Constitution of the United States."

## Powers and Duties of the President

*Section 2*   The President shall be the Commander in Chief of the Army and Navy of the United States, and of the Militia of the several States, when called into the actual Service of the United States, he may require the Opinion, in writing, of the principal Officer in each of the executive Departments, upon any Subject relating to the Duties of their respective Offices, and he shall have the Power to grant Reprieves and Pardons for Offences against the United States, except in Cases of Impeachment.

He shall have Power, by and with the Advice and Consent of the Senate to make Treaties, provided two thirds of the Senators present concur; and he shall nominate, and by and with the Advice and Consent of the Senate, shall appoint Ambassadors, other public Ministers and Consuls, Judges of the supreme Court, and all other Officers of the United States, whose Appointments are not herein otherwise provided for, and which shall be established by Law: but the Congress may by Law vest the Appointment of such inferior Officers, as they think proper, in the President alone, in the Courts of Law, or in the Heads of Departments.

The President shall have Power to fill up all Vacancies that may happen during the Recess of the Senate, by granting Commissions which shall expire at the End of their next Session.

*Section 3*   He shall from time to time give to the Congress Information of the State of the Union, and recommend to their Consideration such Mea-

---

[6]Modified by the 16th Amendment

[7]Changed by the 12th and 20th Amendments
[8]Modified by the 25th Amendment

sures as he shall judge necessary and expedient; he may, on extraordinary Occasions, convene both Houses, or either of them, and in Case of Disagreement between them, with Respect to the Time of Adjournment, he may adjourn them to such Time as he shall think proper; he shall receive Ambassadors and other public Ministers; he shall take Care that the Laws be faithfully executed, and shall Commission all the Officers of the United States.

*Section 4*  The President, Vice President and all civil Officers of the United States, shall be removed from Office on Impeachment for, and Conviction of, Treason, Bribery, or other High Crimes and Misdemeanors.

## ARTICLE III—THE JUDICIAL ARTICLE

### Judicial Power, Courts, Judges

*Section 1*  The judicial Power of the United States, shall be vested in one supreme Court, and in such inferior Courts as the Congress may from time to time ordain and establish. The Judges, both the supreme and inferior Courts, shall hold their Offices during good Behaviour, and shall, at stated Times, receive for their Services, a Compensation, which shall not be diminished during their Continuance in Office.

### Jurisdiction

*Section 2*  The judicial Power shall extend to all Cases, in Law and Equity, arising under this Constitution, the Laws of the United States, and Treaties made, or which shall be made, under their Authority;—to all Cases affecting Ambassadors, other public Ministers and Consuls;—to all Cases of admiralty and maritime Jurisdiction;—to Controversies to which the United States shall be a Party;—to Controversies between two or more States; *between a State and Citizens of another State;*[9]—between Citizens of different States;—between Citizens of the same State claiming Lands under Grants of different States, and between a State, or the Citizens thereof, and foreign States, Citizens, or Subjects.

In all Cases affecting Ambassadors, other public Ministers and Consuls, and those in which a State shall be Party, the supreme Court shall have original Jurisdiction. In all the other Cases before mentioned, the supreme Court shall have appellate Jurisdiction, both as to Law and Fact, with such Exceptions, and under such Regulations as Congress shall make.

The Trial of all Crimes, except in Cases of Impeachment, shall be by Jury; and such Trial shall be held in the State where the said Crimes shall have been committed; but when not committed within any State, the Trial shall be at such Place or Places as the Congress may by Law have directed.

### Treason

*Section 3*  Treason against the United States, shall consist only in levying War against them, or in adhering to their Enemies, giving them Aid and Comfort. No Persons shall be convicted of Treason unless on the Testimony of two Witnesses to the same overt Act, or on Confession in open Court.

The Congress shall have Power to declare the Punishment of Treason, but no Attainder of Treason shall work Corruption of Blood, or Forfeiture except during the Life of the Person attainted.

## ARTICLE IV—INTERSTATE RELATIONS

### Full Faith and Credit Clause

*Section 1*  Full Faith and Credit shall be given in each State to the public Acts, Records, and judicial Proceedings of every other State. And the Congress may by general Laws prescribe the Manner in which such Acts, Records and Proceedings shall be proved, and the Effect thereof.

### Privileges and Immunities; Interstate Extradition

*Section 2*  The Citizens of each State shall be entitled to all Privileges and Immunities of Citizens in the several States.

A person charged in any State with Treason, Felony or other Crime, who shall flee from Justice, and be found in another State, shall on Demand of the executive Authority of the State from which he fled, be delivered up to be removed to the State having jurisdiction of the Crime.

*No person held to Service or Labour in one State, under the Laws thereof, escaping into another, shall, in Consequence of any Law or Regulation therein, be discharged from such Service or Labour, but shall be delivered up on Claim of the Party to whom such Service or Labour may be due.*[10]

### Admission of States

*Section 3*  New States may be admitted by the Congress into this Union; but no new State shall be formed or erected within the Jurisdiction of any other State; nor any State to be formed by the Junction of two or more States, or Parts of States, without the Consent of the Legislatures of the States concerned as well as of the Congress.

The Congress shall have Power to dispose of and make all needful Rules and Regulations respecting the Territory or other Property belonging to the United States; and nothing in this Constitution shall be so construed as to Prejudice any Claims of the United States, or of any particular State.

### Republican Form of Government

*Section 4*  The United States shall guarantee to every State in this Union a Republican Form of Government, and shall protect each of them against Invasion; and on Application of the Legislature, or of the Executive (when the Legislature cannot be convened) against domestic Violence.

## ARTICLE V—THE AMENDING POWER

The Congress, whenever two thirds of both Houses shall deem it necessary, shall propose Amendments to this Constitution, or, on the Application of the Legislatures of two thirds of several States, shall call a Convention for proposing Amendments, which, in either Case, shall be valid to all Intents and Purposes, as Part of this Constitution, when ratified by the Legislatures of three fourths of the several States, or by Conventions in three fourths thereof, as the one or the other Mode of Ratification may be proposed by the Congress; Provided that no Amendment which may be made prior to the Year One thousand eight hundred and eight shall in any Manner affect the first and fourth Clauses in the Ninth Section of the first Article; and that no State, without its Consent, shall be deprived of its equal Suffrage in the Senate.

## ARTICLE VI—THE SUPREMACY ACT

All Debts contracted and Engagements entered into, before the Adoption of this Constitution, shall be as valid against the United States under the Constitution, as under the Confederation.

This Constitution, and the Laws of the United States which shall be made in Pursuance thereof; and all Treaties made, or which shall be made, under the Authority of the United States, shall be the supreme Law of the Land; and the Judges in every State shall be bound thereby, any Thing in the Constitution or Laws of any State to the Contrary notwithstanding.

The Senators and Representative before mentioned, and the Members of the several State Legislatures, and all executive and judicial Officers, both of the United States and of the several States, shall be bound by Oath or

---

[9]Modified by the 11th Amendment

[10]Repealed by the 13th Amendment

Affirmation, to support this Constitution; but no religious Test shall ever be required as a Qualification to any Office or public Trust under the United States.

## ARTICLE VII—RATIFICATION

The Ratification of the Conventions of nine States, shall be sufficient for the Establishment of this Constitution between the States so ratifying the Same.

*Done* in Convention by the Unanimous Consent of the States present the Seventeenth Day of September in the Year of our Lord one thousand seven hundred and Eighty seven and of the Independence of the United States of America the Twelfth. *In Witness whereof We have hereunto subscribed our Names.*

## AMENDMENTS

[The first ten amendments were ratified on December 15, 1791, and form what is known as the "Bill of Rights."]

## AMENDMENT 1—RELIGION, SPEECH, ASSEMBLY, AND POLITICS

Congress shall make no law respecting an establishment of religion, or prohibiting the free exercise thereof; or abridging the freedom of speech, or of the press; or the right of the people peaceably to assemble, and to petition the government for a redress of grievances.

## AMENDMENT 2—MILITIA AND THE RIGHT TO BEAR ARMS

A well regulated Milita, being necessary to the security of a free State, the right of the people to keep and bear Arms, shall not be infringed.

## AMENDMENT 3—QUARTERING OF SOLDIERS

No Soldier shall, in time of peace be quartered in any house, without the consent of the Owner, nor in time of war, but in manner to be prescribed by law.

## AMENDMENT 4—SEARCHES AND SEIZURES

The right of the people to be secure in their persons, houses, papers, and effects, against unreasonable searches and seizures, shall not be violated, and no Warrants shall issue, but upon probable cause, supported by Oath or affirmation, and particularly describing the place to be searched, and the persons or things to be seized.

## AMENDMENT 5—GRAND JURIES, SELF-INCRIMINATION, DOUBLE JEOPARDY, DUE PROCESS, AND EMINENT DOMAIN

No person shall be held to answer for a capital, or otherwise infamous crime, unless on a presentment or indictment of a Grand jury, except in cases arising in the land or naval forces, or in the Milita, when in actual service in time of War or public danger; nor shall any person be subject for the same offence to be twice put in jeopardy of life or limb; nor shall be compelled in any criminal case to be a witness against himself, nor be deprived of life, liberty, or property, without due process of law; nor shall private property be taken for public use, without just compensation.

## AMENDMENT 6—CRIMINAL COURT PROCEDURES

In all criminal prosecutions, the accused shall enjoy the right to a speedy and public trial, by an impartial jury of the State and district wherein the crime shall have been committed, which district shall have been previously ascertained by law, and to be informed of the nature and cause of the accusation; to be confronted with the witnesses against him; to have compulsory process for obtaining Witnesses in his favor, and to have the Assistance of Counsel for his defense.

## AMENDMENT 7—TRIAL BY JURY IN COMMON LAW CASES

In Suits at common law, where the value in controversy shall exceed twenty dollars, the right of trial by jury shall be preserved, and no fact tried by a jury shall be otherwise re-examined in any Court of the United States, than according to the rules of the common law.

## AMENDMENT 8—BAIL, CRUEL AND UNUSUAL PUNISHMENT

Excessive bail shall not be required, nor excessive fines imposed, nor cruel and unusual punishments inflicted.

## AMENDMENT 9—RIGHTS RETAINED BY THE PEOPLE

The enumeration in the Constitution, of certain rights, shall not be construed to deny or disparage others retained by the people.

## AMENDMENT 10—RESERVED POWERS OF THE STATES

The powers not delegated to the United States by the Constitution, nor prohibited by it to the States, are reserved to the States respectively, or to the people.

## AMENDMENT 11—SUITS AGAINST THE STATES

## [Ratified February 7, 1795]

The Judicial power of the United States shall not be construed to extend to any suit in law or equity, commenced or prosecuted against one of the United States by Citizens of another State, or by Citizens or Subjects of any Foreign State.

## AMENDMENT 12—ELECTION OF THE PRESIDENT

## [Ratified July 27, 1804]

The Electors shall meet in their respective states, and vote by ballot for President and Vice-President, one of whom, at least, shall not be an inhabitant of the same state with themselves; they shall name in their ballots the person voted for as President, and in distinct ballots the person voted for as Vice-President, and they shall make distinct lists of all persons voted for as President, and of all persons voted for as Vice-President, and of the number of votes for each, which lists they shall sign and certify, and transmit sealed to the seat of the government of the United States, directed to the President of the Senate;—The President of the Senate shall, in presence of the Senate and House of Representatives, open all the certificates and the votes shall then be counted;—The person having the greatest number of votes for President, shall be the President, if such number be a majority of the whole number of Electors appointed; and if no person have such majority, then from the persons having the highest numbers not exceeding three on the list of those voted for as President, the House of Representatives shall choose immediately, by ballot, the President. But in choosing the President, the votes shall be taken by states, the representation from each state having one vote; a quorum for this purpose shall consist of a member or members from two-thirds of the states, and a majority of all states shall be necessary to a choice. And if the House of Representatives shall not choose a President whenever the right of choice shall devolve upon them, *before the fourth day of March next following*, then the Vice-President shall act as President, as in the case of the death or other constitutional disability of the President.[11] The person having the greatest number of votes as Vice-President, shall be the Vice-President, if such a number be a majority of the whole numbers of Electors appointed, and if no person have a majority, then from the two highest numbers on the list, the Senate shall choose the Vice-President; a quorum for the purpose shall consist of two-thirds of the whole number of Senators, and a majority of the whole number shall be necessary to a choice. But no person constitutionally ineligible to the office of President shall be eligible to that of Vice-President of the United States.

## AMENDMENT 13—PROHIBITION OF SLAVERY

### [Ratified December 6, 1865]

*Section 1*  Neither slavery nor involuntary servitude, except as a punishment for crime whereof the party shall have been duly convicted, shall exist within the United States, or any place subject to their jurisdiction.

*Section 2*  Congress shall have power to enforce this article by appropriate legislation.

## AMENDMENT 14—CITIZENSHIP, DUE PROCESS, AND EQUAL PROTECTION OF THE LAWS

### [Ratified July 9, 1868]

*Section 1*  All persons born or naturalized in the United States, and subject to the jurisdiction thereof, are citizens of the United States and of the State wherein they reside. No State shall make or enforce any law which shall abridge the privileges or immunities of citizens of the United States; nor shall any State deprive any person of life, liberty, or property, without due process of law; nor deny to any person within its jurisdiction the equal protection of the laws.

*Section 2*  Representatives shall be apportioned among the several States according to their respective numbers, counting the whole number of persons in each State, excluding Indians not taxed. But when the right to vote at any election for the choice of electors for President and Vice President of the United States, Representatives in Congress, the Executive and Judicial officers of a State, or the members of the Legislature thereof, is denied to any of the male inhabitants of such State, being twenty-one[12] years of age, and citizens of the United States, or in any way abridged, except for participation in rebellion, or other crime, the basis of representation therein shall be reduced in the proportion which the number of such male citizens shall bear to the whole number of male citizens twenty-one years of age in such State.

*Section 3*  No person shall be a Senator or Representative in Congress, or elector of President and Vice President, or hold any office, civil or military, under the United States, or under any State, who, having previously taken an oath, as a member of Congress, or as an officer of the United States, or as a member of any State legislature, or as an executive or judicial officer of any State, to support the Constitution of the United States, shall have engaged in insurrection or rebellion against the same, or given aid or comfort to the enemies thereof. But Congress may by a vote of two-thirds of each House, remove such disability.

*Section 4*  The validity of the public debt of the United States, authorized by law, including debts incurred for payment of pensions and bounties for services in suppressing insurrection or rebellion, shall not be questioned. But neither the United States nor any State shall assume or pay any debt or obligation incurred in aid of insurrection or rebellion against the United States, or any claim for the loss or emancipation of any slave; but all such debts, obligations and claims shall be held illegal and void.

*Section 5*  The Congress shall have power to enforce, by appropriate legislation, the provisions of this article.

## AMENDMENT 15—THE RIGHT TO VOTE

### [Ratified February 3, 1870]

*Section 1*  The right of citizens of the United States to vote shall not be denied or abridged by the United States or by any State on account of race, color, or previous condition of servitude.

*Section 2*  The Congress shall have power to enforce this article by appropriate legislation.

## AMENDMENT 16—INCOME TAXES

### [Ratified February 3, 1913]

The Congress shall have power to lay and collect taxes on incomes, from whatever source derived, without apportionment among the several States, and without regard to any census or enumeration.

## AMENDMENT 17—DIRECT ELECTION OF SENATORS

### [Ratified April 8, 1913]

The Senate of the United States shall be composed of two Senators from each State, elected by the people thereof, for six years; and each Senator shall have one vote. The electors in each State shall have the qualifications requisite for electors of the most numerous branch of the State legislatures.

When vacancies happen in the representation of any State in the Senate, the executive authority of such State shall issue writs of election to fill such vacancies: *Provided*, That the Legislature of any State may empower the executive thereof to make temporary appointment until the people fill the vacancies by election as the legislature may direct.

This amendment shall not be so construed as to affect the election or term of any Senator chosen before it becomes valid as part of the Constitution.

## AMENDMENT 18—PROHIBITION

### [Ratified January 16, 1919 Repealed December 5, 1933 by Amendment 21]

*Section 1*  After one year from the ratification of this article the manufacture, sale, or transportation of intoxicating liquors within, the importation thereof into, or the exportation thereof from the United States and all territory subject to the jurisdiction thereof for beverage purposes is hereby prohibited.

*Section 2*  The Congress and the several states shall have concurrent power to enforce this article by appropriate legislation.

*Section 3*  This article shall be inoperative unless it shall have been ratified as an amendment to the Constitution by the legislatures of the several states, as provided in the Constitution, within seven years from the date of the submission hereof to the States by the Congress.[13]

---

[11]Changed by the 20th Amendment
[12]Changed by the 26th Amendment

[13]Repealed by the 21st Amendment

## AMENDMENT 19—FOR WOMEN'S SUFFRAGE

### [Ratified August 18, 1920]

The right of the citizens of the United States to vote shall not be denied or abridged by the United States or by any State on account of sex.

Congress shall have power, by appropriate legislation, to enforce the provision of this article.

## AMENDMENT 20—THE LAME DUCK AMENDMENT

### [Ratified January 23, 1933]

*Section 1*  The terms of the President and Vice President shall end at noon on the 20th day of January, and the terms of the Senators and Representatives at noon on the 3rd day of January, of the years in which such terms would have ended if this article had not been ratified; and the terms of their successors shall then begin.

*Section 2*  The Congress shall assemble at least once in every year, and such meeting shall begin at noon on the 3rd day of January, unless they shall by law appoint a different day.

*Section 3*  If, at the time fixed for the beginning of the term of the President, the President elect shall have died, the Vice President elect shall become President. If a President shall not have been chosen before the time fixed for the beginning of his term, or if the President elect shall have failed to qualify, then the Vice President elect shall act as President until a President shall have qualified; and the Congress may by law provide for the case wherein neither a President elect nor a Vice President elect shall have qualified, declaring who shall then act as President, or the manner in which one who is to act shall be selected, and such person shall act accordingly until a President or Vice President shall have qualified.

*Section 4*  The Congress may by law provide for the case of the death of any of the persons from whom the House of Representatives may choose a President whenever the right of choice shall have developed upon them, and for the case of the death of any of the persons from whom the Senate may choose a Vice President whenever the right of choice shall have devolved upon them.

*Section 5*  Sections 1 and 2 shall take effect on the 15th day of October following the ratification of this article.

*Section 6*  This article shall be inoperative unless it shall have been ratified as an amendment to the Constitution by the legislatures of three-fourths of the several States within seven years from the date of its submission.

## AMENDMENT 21—REPEAL OF PROHIBITION

### [Ratified December 5, 1933]

*Section 1*  The eighteenth article of amendment to the Constitution of the United States is hereby repealed.

*Section 2*  The transportation or importation into any State, Territory, or Possession of the United States for delivery or use therein of intoxicating liquors, in violation of the laws thereof, is hereby prohibited.

*Section 3*  This article shall be inoperative unless it shall have been ratified as an amendment to the Constitution by conventions in the several States, as provided in the Constitution, within seven years from the date of the submission hereof to the States by the Congress.

## AMENDMENT 22—NUMBER OF PRESIDENTIAL TERMS

### [Ratified February 27, 1951]

*Section 1*  No person shall be elected to the office of the President more than twice, and no person who has held the office of President, or acted as President, for more than two years of a term to which some other person was elected President shall be elected to the Office of the President more than once. But this Article shall not apply to any person holding the office of President when this article was proposed by the Congress, and shall not prevent any person who may be holding the office of President, or acting as President, during the term within which this Article becomes operative from holding the office of President or acting as President during the remainder of such term.

*Section 2*  This Article shall be inoperative unless it shall have been ratified as an amendment to the Constitution by the legislatures of three-fourths of the several states within seven years from the date of its submission to the States by the Congress.

## AMENDMENT 23—PRESIDENTIAL ELECTORS FOR THE DISTRICT OF COLUMBIA

### [Ratified March 29, 1961]

*Section 1*  The District constituting the seat of Government of the United States shall appoint in such manner as the Congress may direct:

A number of electors of President and Vice President equal to the whole number of Senators and Representatives in Congress to which the District would be entitled if it were a State, but in no event more than the least populous State; they shall be in addition to those appointed by the States, but they shall be considered, for the purposes of the election of President and Vice President, to be electors appointed by a State; and they shall meet in the District and perform such duties as provided by the twelfth article of amendment.

*Section 2*  The Congress shall have power to enforce this article by appropriate legislation.

## AMENDMENT 24—THE ANTI-POLL TAX AMENDMENT

### [Ratified January 23, 1964]

*Section 1*  The right of citizens of the United States to vote in any primary or other election for President or Vice President, for electors for President or Vice President, or for Senator or Representative in Congress, shall not be denied or abridged by the United States or any State by reason of failure to pay any poll tax or other tax.

*Section 2*  The Congress shall have power to enforce this article by appropriate legislation.

## AMENDMENT 25—PRESIDENTIAL DISABILITY, VICE PRESIDENTIAL VACANCIES

### [Ratified February 10, 1967]

*Section 1*  In case of the removal of the President from office or his death or resignation, the Vice President shall become President.

*Section 2*  Whenever there is a vacancy in the office of the Vice President, the President shall nominate a Vice President who shall take the office upon confirmation by a majority vote of both houses of Congress.

*Section 3*  Whenever the President transmits to the President pro tempore of the Senate and the Speaker of the House of Representatives his written declaration that he is unable to discharge the powers and duties of his office, and until he transmits to them a written declaration to the contrary, such powers and duties shall be discharged by the Vice President as Acting President.

*Section 4*  Whenever the Vice-President and a majority of either the principal officers of the executive departments, or of such other body as Congress may by law provide, transmit to the President pro tempore of the Senate and the Speaker of the House of Representatives their written declaration that the President is unable to discharge the powers and duties of his office, the Vice President shall immediately assume the powers and duties of the office as Acting President.

Thereafter, when the President transmits to the President pro tempore of the Senate and the Speaker of the House of Representatives his written declaration that no inability exists, he shall resume the powers and duties of his office unless the Vice President and a majority of either the principal officers of the executive departments, or of such other body as Congress may by law provide, transmit within four days to the President pro tempore of the Senate and the Speaker of the House of Representatives their written declaration that the President is unable to discharge the powers and duties of his office. Thereupon Congress shall decide the issue, assembling within 48 hours for that purpose if not in session. If the Congress, within 21 days after receipt of the latter written declaration, or, if Congress is not in session, within 21 days after Congress is required to assemble, determines by two-thirds vote of both houses that the President is unable to discharge the powers and duties of his office, the Vice President shall continue to discharge the same as Acting President; otherwise, the President shall resume the powers and duties of his office.

## AMENDMENT 26—EIGHTEEN-YEAR-OLD VOTE

### [Ratified July 1, 1971]

*Section 1* The right of citizens of the United States, who are eighteen years of age, or older, to vote shall not be denied or abridged by the United States or by any State on account of age.

*Section 2* The Congress shall have power to enforce this article by appropriate legislation.

## AMENDMENT 27—CONGRESSIONAL SALARIES

### [Ratified May 7, 1992]

No law, varying the compensation for the services of the Senators and Representatives, shall take effect, until an election of Representative shall be intervened.

# FEDERALISM
## DIVIDING GOVERNMENTAL POWER

## CHAPTER OUTLINE

## FEATURES

## INDESTRUCTIBLE UNION, INDESTRUCTIBLE STATES

In December 1860 South Carolina seceded from the Union and in April 1861 authorized state militia to expel U.S. troops from Fort Sumter in Charleston harbor. Although there is no provision in the Constitution for states leaving the Union, eleven southern states—South Carolina, Mississippi, Florida, Alabama, Georgia, Louisiana, Texas, Virginia, Arkansas, Tennessee, and North Carolina, in that order—argued that the Union was a voluntary association and that they were entitled to withdraw.[1] President

## ASK YOURSELF ABOUT POLITICS

**1** Should a state be able to place itself between its citizens and the national government to prevent enforcement of a law the state believes to be unconstitutional?
Yes ☐  No ☐

**2** Should the national government always have the final say in disputes with individual states?
Yes ☐  No ☐

**3** Should the national government be able to prosecute a high school student for bringing a gun to school?
Yes ☐  No ☐

**4** Should welfare benefits be the same in all states?
Yes ☐  No ☐

**5** Should each state determine its minimum age for drinking alcoholic beverages?
Yes ☐  No ☐

**6** Should each state determine its own maximum highway speed limit?
Yes ☐  No ☐

**7** Which level of government do you feel wastes the most tax money?
Federal ☐  State ☐
Local ☐

**8** In which level of government do you have the most confidence?
Federal ☐  State ☐
Local ☐

Just what should be the relationship between the national government and the states? Questions like these lie at the heart of the issue of who gets what, when, and how. They affect employment, transportation, health, education, the very air we breathe. And when there has been disagreement on them, the nation has been plunged into conflict at best, and the bloodiest war in its history at worst.

Abraham Lincoln declared these states to be in armed rebellion and sent federal troops to crush the "rebels." The result was the nation's bloodiest war: more than 250,000 battle deaths and another 250,000 deaths from disease and privation, out of a total population of less than 30 million.

Following the war, Chief Justice Salmon P. Chase confirmed what had been decided on the battlefield: "The Constitution, in all of its provisions, looks to an indestructible union, composed of indestructible states."[2]

**Federalism** divides power between two separate authorities—the nation and the states—each of which enforces its own laws directly on its citizens. Both the nation and the states pass laws, impose taxes, spend money, and maintain their own courts. Neither the nation nor the states can dissolve the Union or amend the Constitution without the consent of the other. The Constitution itself is the only legal source of authority for both the states and the nation; the states do not get their power from the national government, and the national government does not get its power from the states.

American federalism differs from a **unitary system** of government, in which formal authority rests with the national government, and whatever powers are exercised by states, provinces, or subdivisions are given to those governments by the national government. Most of the world's governments—including those of France and Britain—are unitary (see Figure 4-1).

Federalism also differs from a **confederation** of states, in which the national government relies upon the states for its authority. Under the Articles of Confederation of 1781, the United States was a confederation; the national government could not even levy taxes but instead had to ask the states for revenue. Like the United States, a number of other countries were confederations before establishing federal systems, and today new types of confederations with limited functions are being formed (see *Compared to What?* "Governmental Unions in the World").

People in the United States often think of the *federal government* when the word *government* comes up. In fact, today there are more than 86,000 American governments. These state and local governments are as important in American life as the federal government, for they are the providers of such essential day-to-day services as schools, water, and police and fire departments (see Table 4-1). However, the U.S. Constitution, the supreme law of the land, recognizes the existence of only the national government and the states. Local governments have no guarantees of power—or even existence—under the U.S. Constitution. Whatever

**Federalism:** A constitutional arrangement whereby power is divided between national and subnational governments, each of which enforces its own laws directly on its citizens and neither of which can alter the arrangement without the consent of the other.

**Unitary system:** A constitutional arrangement whereby authority rests with the national government; subnational governments have only those powers given them by the national government.

**Confederation:** A constitutional arrangement whereby the national government is created by and relies on the states for its authority.

| TABLE 4-1 HOW MANY AMERICAN GOVERNMENTS? | |
|---|---|
| U.S. government | 1 |
| States | 50 |
| Counties | 3,043 |
| Municipalities | 19,296 |
| Townships | 16,666 |
| Special districts | 33,131 |
| School districts | 14,556 |
| **All governments** | **86,743** |

*Source:* U.S. Department of Commerce, *Census of Government, 1992.*

CHAPTER 4 • FEDERALISM: DIVIDING GOVERNMENTAL POWER

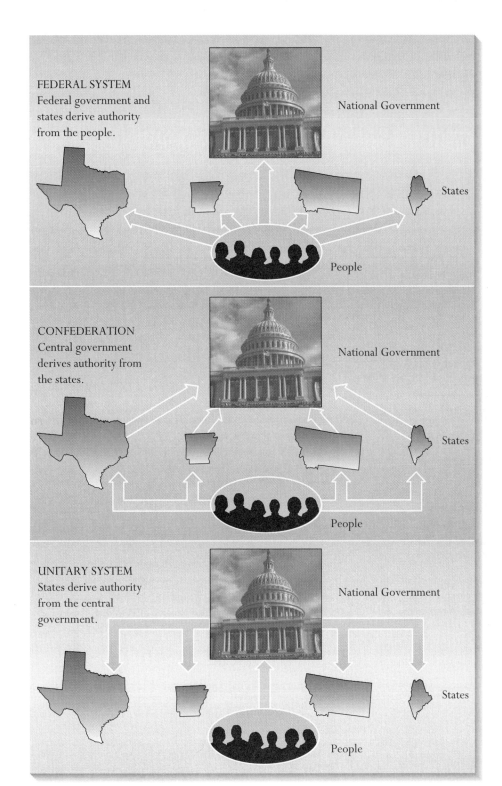

**FEDERAL SYSTEM**
Federal government and states derive authority from the people.

National Government

States

People

**CONFEDERATION**
Central government derives authority from the states.

National Government

States

People

**UNITARY SYSTEM**
States derive authority from the central government.

National Government

States

People

# Governmental Unions in the World

Confederations have played important historical roles as societies moved toward national states. The case of the United States, in which the Articles of Confederation preceded the creation of a truly national government, is not unique. For example, the eighteenth-century German confederation predated the creation of the modern German state, and the Helvetic confederation was transformed into the modern federal system of Switzerland.

## *The European Union*

Today the most important political confederation is the European Union. The EU includes fifteen member states—Austria, Belgium, Denmark, Finland, France, Germany, Greece, Ireland, Italy, Luxembourg, Netherlands, Portugal, Spain, Sweden, United Kingdom—and embraces well over 300 million people. The EU has a European Parliament, a Council of Ministers of member states, a European Commission with a president rotating among the states that serves as a bureaucracy to administer policy decisions, and a European Court of Justice to adjudicate disputes among members. The EU is a union with very specific functions granted by member states.

## *The Commonwealth of Independent States*

Currently, republics of the former Union of Soviet Socialist Republics—Armenia, Azerbaijan, Byelo-russia, Estonia, Georgia, Kazakhstan, Kyrgyzstan, Latvia, Lithuania, Moldavia, Russia, Tajikistan, Turkmenistan, Ukraine, Uzbekistan—are struggling to find an acceptable form of union. The central government of the USSR ceased to exist after December 31, 1991. The president of the new Russian Federated Republic, Boris Yeltsin, opened negotiations with other republics to create a "Commonwealth of Independent States" along lines that would resemble a confederacy. The Russian Federated Republic is itself a formal federation, and some of its states have demanded independence from Moscow. Rebellion in Chechnya was countered by a bloody military campaign in which Russian troops inflicted heavy damages on the capital city of Grozny.

## *Federal Systems*

The formal constitutions of many governments describe a federal form of government. These include Argentina, Australia, Brazil, Canada, Federal Republic of Germany, India, Malaysia, Mexico, Nigeria, Pakistan, Switzerland, United Arab Emirates, United States, and Venezuela. Yugoslavia was a federal system prior to its civil war and disintegration. Czechoslovakia was also a federal system with two republics prior to its peaceful division into two nations: Slovakia and the Czech Republic. However, despite a federal constitution, many of these governments are highly centralized, with the national government exercising a dominant role in the economic, social, and political life of the nation.

powers they have are given to them by the state government. States can create or abolish local governments, grant or withhold their powers, or change their boundaries without their consent. Some local governments have powers guaranteed in *state* constitutions, and some are even given **home rule**—the power to pass laws affecting local affairs, so long as those laws do not conflict with state or federal laws. About 60,000 of these 86,000 governments have the power to levy taxes to support activities authorized by state law.

In short, the American federal system is large and complex, with three levels of government—national, state, and local—sharing in power. Indeed, the numbers and complexity of governments in the United States make **intergovernmental relations**—all of the interactions between these governments and their officials—a major concern of political scientists and policy makers.

## WHY FEDERALISM? THE ARGUMENT FOR A "COMPOUND REPUBLIC"

The nation's Founders believed that "republican principles" would help make government responsible to the people, but they also argued that "auxiliary precautions" were necessary to protect the liberties of minorities and individuals. They believed that majority rule in a democratic government made it particularly important to devise ways to protect minorities and individuals from "unjust" and "interested" *majorities.* They believed that a federation would better protect liberty, disperse power, and manage conflict.

*Protecting Liberty*    Constitutional guarantees of individual liberty do not enforce themselves. The Founders argued that to guarantee liberty, government should be structured to encourage "opposite and rival" centers of power *within* and *among* governments. So they settled on both *federalism*—dividing powers between the national and state governments—and *separation of powers*—the dispersal of power among branches within the national government.

> In the compound republic of America, the power surrendered by the people is first divided between two distinct governments, and then the portion allotted to each subdivided among distinct and separate departments. Hence a double security arises to the rights of the people. The different governments will control each other, at the same time that each will be controlled by itself.[3]

Thus, the Founders deliberately tried to create *competition* within and among governmental units as a means of protecting liberty. Rather than rely on the "better motives" of leaders, the Founders sought to construct a system in which governments and government officials would be constrained by competition with other governments and other government officials:

> Ambition must be made to counteract ambition. The interest of the man must be connected with the constitutional rights of the place. It may be a reflection on human nature that such devices should be necessary to control the abuses of government. But what is government itself but the greatest of all reflections on human natures?[4]

**Home rule:** The power of local government to pass laws affecting local affairs, so long as those laws do not conflict with state or federal laws.

**Intergovernmental relations:** The network of political, financial, and administrative relationships among units of the federal government and those of state and local governments.

*Dispersing Power*   Federalism distributes power widely among different sets of leaders, national as well as state and local officeholders. The Founders believed that multiple leadership groups are generally more democratic than a single set of all-powerful leaders. State and local government offices also provide a political base for the opposition party when it has lost a national election. In this way, state and local governments contribute to party competition in the United States by helping to "tide over" the losing party after electoral defeat at the national level so that it can remain strong enough to challenge incumbents at the next election. And finally, state and local governments often provide a training ground for national political leaders. National leaders can be drawn from a pool of leaders experienced in state and local politics.

*Increasing Participation*   Federalism allows more people to participate in the political system. With more than 86,000 governments in the United States—state, county, municipality, township, special district, and school district—nearly a million people hold some kind of public office. The opportunity to participate doubtless contributes to popular support of the political system.

*Improving Efficiency*   Federalism also makes government more manageable and efficient. Imagine the bureaucracy, red tape, and confusion if every government activity in every local community in the nation—police, schools, roads, fire fighting, garbage collection, sewage disposal, and so forth—were controlled by a centralized administration in Washington. Government can become arbitrary when a bureaucracy far from the scene directs local officials. Thus decentralization often softens the rigidity of law.

*Ensuring Policy Responsiveness*   Federalism encourages policy responsiveness. Multiple competing governments are more sensitive to citizens' views than a single "monopoly" government. The existence of multiple governments offering different packages of benefits and costs allows a better match between citizen preferences and public policy. People and businesses can "vote with their feet" by relocating to those states and communities that most closely conform to their own policy preferences. Americans are very mobile. Mobility not only facilitates a better match between citizen preferences and public policy but also encourages competition between states and communities to offer improved services at lower costs.[5]

*Encouraging Policy Innovation*   The Founders hoped that federalism would encourage policy experimentation and innovation. Today, federalism may seem like a "conservative" idea, but it was once the instrument of liberal reformers. Federal programs as diverse as the income tax, unemployment compensation, Social Security, wage and hour legislation, bank deposit insurance, and food stamps were all state programs before becoming national undertakings. Today, much of the current "liberal" policy agenda—mandatory health insurance for workers, child-care programs, notification of plant closings, government support of industrial research and development—has been embraced by various states. The phrase *laboratories of democracies* is generally attributed to the great progressive jurist Supreme Court Justice Louis D. Brandeis, who used it in defense of state experimentation with new solutions to social and economic problems.[6]

*Managing Conflict*   Federalism allows different peoples to come together in a nation without engendering irresolvable conflict. Conflicts between geographi-

**A CONFLICTING VIEW**

# The Dark Side of Federalism

In 1963 Governor George Wallace stood in the doorway at the University of Alabama to obstruct a federal court order to admit two African-American students and integrate the university. Segregationists regularly used the argument of "states' rights" to deny equal protection of the law to African-Americans. U.S. Assistant Attorney General Nicholas Katzenbach and federal marshals were only temporarily delayed by Governor Wallace, who retreated to his office shortly after his dramatic stand in front of the television cameras. Later in his career, Wallace sought African-American votes, declaring: "I was wrong. Those days are over."

Federalism in America remains tainted by its historical association with slavery, segregation, and discrimination. An early doctrine of "nullification" was put forth by Thomas Jefferson and James Madison in the Virginia and Kentucky Resolutions of 1798, which asserted that states could nullify unconstitutional laws of Congress. Although the original use of this doctrine was to counter congressional attacks on a free press under the Alien and Sedition Acts, the doctrine was later revived to defend slavery. John C. Calhoun of South Carolina argued forcefully in the years before the Civil War that slavery was an issue for the states to decide and that the Constitution gave Congress no power to interfere with slavery in the southern states or in the new western territories.

In the years immediately following the Civil War, the issues of slavery, racial inequality, and African-American voting rights were *nationalized*. Nationalizing these issues meant removing them from the jurisdiction of the states and placing them in the hands of the national government. The Thirteenth, Fourteenth, and Fifteenth Amendments to the Constitution were enforced by federal troops in the southern states during Reconstruction. But after the Compromise of 1876 led to the withdrawal of federal troops from the southern states, legal and social segregation of African-Americans became a "way of life" in the region. Segregation was *denationalized*, which reduced national conflict over race but exacted a high price from the nation's African-American population. Segregationists asserted the states' rights argument so often in defense of racial discrimination that it became a code phrase for racism. Not until the 1950s and 1960s were questions of segregation and equality again made into *national* issues. The civil rights movement asserted the supremacy of national law and in 1954 won a landmark decision in the case of *Brown v. Board of Education of Topeka,* when the U.S. Supreme Court ruled that segregation enforced by state (or local) officials violated the Fourteenth Amendment's guarantee that no state could deny any person the equal protection of the law. Later the *national* Civil Rights Act of 1964 outlawed discrimination in private employment and businesses serving the public.

Only now that national constitutional and legal guarantees of equal protection of the law are in place is it possible to reassess the true worth of federalism. Having established that federalism will not mean racial inequality, we are now free to explore the values of decentralized government.

*In an attempt to block the admission of two African-American students from the University of Alabama in 1963, Governor George Wallace barred the door with his body in the face of U.S. federal marshals. The tactic did not succeed, and the two students were admitted.*

FEDERALISM: DIVIDING GOVERNMENTAL POWER • CHAPTER 4

103

cally separate groups in America are resolved by allowing each to pursue its own policies within its separate state or community instead of battling over a single national policy to be applied uniformly throughout the land.

*Some Important Reservations*    Despite the strengths of federalism, it is important to recognize that there are also problems with it. First of all, federalism can obstruct action on national issues. Although decentralization may reduce conflict at the national level, it may do so at the price of "sweeping under the rug" very serious national injustices (see *A Conflicting View:* "The Dark Side of Federalism"). Federalism also permits local leaders and citizens to frustrate national policy, to sacrifice national interest to local interests. Decentralized government provides an opportunity for local "NIMBYs" (people who subscribe to the motto "*Not In My Back Yard*") to obstruct airports, highways, waste disposal plants, public housing, and many other projects that would be in the national interest.

Finally, federalism permits the benefits and costs of government to be spread unevenly across the nation. For example, some states spend over twice as much on the education of each child in the public schools as other states. Welfare benefits in some states are more than twice as high as they are in other states. Taxes in some states are more than twice as high per capita as in other states. Competition among states may keep welfare benefits low in order not to encourage the immigration of poor people. Federalism obstructs uniformity in policy.

# THE ORIGINAL DESIGN OF FEDERALISM

The U.S. Constitution *originally* defined American federalism in terms of: (1) the powers expressly delegated to the national government and the Implied Powers Clause; (2) the concurrent powers exercised by both states and the national government; (3) the powers reserved to the states; (4) the powers denied by the Constitution to both the national government and the states; and (5) the constitutional provisions giving the states a role in the composition of the national government (see Figure 4-2).

**Delegated or enumerated powers:** Powers specifically mentioned in the Constitution as belonging to the national government.

**Necessary and Proper Clause:** The clause in Article I, Section 8, of the U.S. Constitution granting Congress the power to enact laws "necessary and proper" for carrying out responsibilities delegated to it. Also referred to as the Implied Powers Clause.

**Implied powers:** Powers not mentioned specifically in the Constitution as belonging to the national government but inferred as necessary and proper for carrying out enumerated powers.

*Delegated Powers*    The U.S. Constitution lists seventeen specific grants of power to Congress, in Article I, Section 8. These are usually referred to as **delegated or enumerated powers.** They include authority over war and foreign affairs; authority over the economy ("interstate commerce"); control over the money supply; and power to tax and spend "to pay the debts and provide for the common defence and general welfare." After these specific grants of power comes the power "to make all laws which shall be necessary and proper for carrying into execution the foregoing powers, and all other powers vested by this Constitution in the government of the United States or in any department or officer thereof." This statement is generally known as the **Necessary and Proper Clause,** and it is the principal source of the national government's **implied powers**—powers not specifically listed in the Constitution but inferred from those that are.

*National Supremacy*    The delegated and implied powers, when coupled with the assertion of "national supremacy" (in Article VI), ensure a powerful national government. The National Supremacy Clause is very specific in asserting the supremacy of federal laws over state and local laws:

FIGURE 4-2 **Original Constitutional Distribution of Powers**

*Under the Constitution of 1787, certain powers were delegated to the national government, other powers were shared by the national and state governments, and still other powers were reserved for state governments alone. Similarly, certain powers were denied by the Constitution to the national government, other powers were denied to both the national and state governments, and still other powers were denied only to state governments. Later amendments especially protected individual liberties.*

# POWERS GRANTED BY THE CONSTITUTION

| NATIONAL GOVERNMENT Delegated Powers | NATIONAL AND STATE GOVERNMENTS Concurrent Powers | STATE GOVERNMENTS Reserved to the States |
|---|---|---|
| **Military Affairs and Defense** <br> • Provide for the common defense (I-8) <br> • Declare war (I-8) <br> • Raise and support armies(I-8) <br> • Provide and maintain a navy (I-8) <br> • Define and punish piracies (I-8) <br> • Define and punish offenses against the law of nations (I-8) <br> • Provide for calling forth the militia to execute laws, suppress insurrections, and repel invasions (I-8) <br> • Provide for organizing, arming, and disciplining militia (I-8) <br> • Declare the punishment of treason (III-3) <br><br> **Economic Affairs** <br> • Regulate commerce with foreign nations, among the several states, and with Indian tribes (I-8) <br> • Establish uniform laws on bankruptcy (I-8) <br> • Coin money and regulate its value (I-8) <br> • Fix standards of weighs and measures (I-8) <br> • Provide for patents and copyrights (I-8) <br> • Establish post offices and post roads (I-8) <br><br> **Governmental Organization** <br> • Constitute tribunals inferior to the Supreme Court (I-8, III-1) <br> • Exercise exclusive legislative power over the seat of government and over certain military installations (I-8) <br> • Admit new states (IV-3) <br> • Dispose of and regulate territory or property of the United States (IV-3) | • Levy taxes (I-8) <br> • Borrow money (I-8) <br> • Contract and pay debts (I-8) <br> • Charter banks and corporations (I-8) <br> • Make and enforce laws (I-8) <br> • Establish courts (I-8) <br> • Provide for the general welfare (I-8) | • Regulate intrastate commerce <br> • Conduct elections <br> • Provide for public health, safety, and morals <br> • Establish local government <br> • Maintain militia (National Guard) <br> • Ratify amendments to the federal Constitution (V) <br> • Determine voter qualifications (I-2) |
| **"Implied" Powers** <br><br> • Make necessary and proper laws for carrying expressed powers into execution (I-8) | | **"Reserved" Powers** <br><br> • Powers not delegated to national government nor denied to the States by the Constitution (X) |

# POWERS DENIED BY THE CONSTITUTION

| NATIONAL GOVERNMENT | NATIONAL AND STATE GOVERNMENTS | STATE GOVERNMENTS |
|---|---|---|
| • Give preference to ports of any state (I-9) <br> • Impose tax or duty on articles exported from any state (I-9) <br> • Directly tax except by apportionment among states on population basis (I-9), now superseded as to income tax (Amendment XVI) <br> • Draw money from Treasury except by appropriation (I-9) | • Grant titles of nobility (I-9) <br> • Limit suspension of habeas corpus (I-9) <br> • Issue bills of attainder (I-10) <br> • Make ex post facto laws (I-10) <br> • Establish a religion or prohibit free exercise of religion (Amendment I) <br> • Abridge freedom of speech, press, assembly, or right of petition (Amendment I) <br> • Deny right to bear arms protected (Amendment II) <br> • Restrict quartering of soldiers in private homes (Amendment III) <br> • Conduct unreasonable searches or seizures (Amendment IV) <br> • Deny guarantees of fair trials (Amendment V, Amendment VI, and Amendment VII) <br> • Impose excessive bail or unusual punishments (Amendment VII) <br> • Take life, liberty, or property without due process (Amendment V) <br> • Permit slavery (Amendment XIII) <br> • Deny life, liberty, or property without due process of law (Amendment XIV) <br> • Deny voting because of race, color, previous servitude (Amendment XV), or sex (Amendment XIX), or age if 18 or over (Amendment XXVI) <br> • Deny voting because of nonpayment of any tax | **Economic Affairs** <br> • Use legal tender other than gold or silver coin (I-10) <br> • Issue separate state coinage (I-10) <br> • Impair the obligation of contracts (I-10) <br> • Emit bills of credit (I-10) <br> • Levy import or export duties, except reasonable inspection fees, without consent of Congress (I-10) <br> • Abridge privileges and immunities of national citizenship (Amendment XIV) <br> • Make any law that violates federal law (VI) <br> • Pay for rebellion against United States or for emancipated slaves (Amendment XIV) <br><br> **Foreign Affairs** <br> • Enter into treaties, alliances, or confederations (I-10) <br> • Make compact with a foreign state, except by congressional consent (I-10) <br><br> **Military Affairs** <br> • Issue letters of marque and reprisal (I-10) <br> • Maintain standing military forces in peace without congressional consent (I-10) <br> • Engage in war, without congressional consent, except in imminent danger or when invaded (I-10) |

"Look, the American people don't want to be bossed around by federal bureaucrats. They want to be bossed around by state bureaucrats."

This Constitution, and the laws of the United States which shall be made in pursuance thereof; and all treaties made, or which shall be made, under the authority of the United States, shall be the supreme law of the land; and the Judges in every state shall be bound thereby, any thing in the constitution or laws of any state to the contrary notwithstanding.

*Concurrent and Reserved Powers*   Despite broad grants of power to the national government, from the beginning of the Republic the states have retained considerable governing power. **Concurrent powers** are those recognized in the Constitution as belonging to *both* the national and state governments, including the power to tax and spend, make and enforce laws, and establish courts of justice. The Tenth Amendment reassured the states that "the powers not delegated to the United States . . . are reserved to the States respectively, or to the people." The states generally retain control over property and contract law; criminal law; marriage and divorce; and the provision of education, highways, and social welfare activities. The states control the organization and powers of their own local governments. Finally, the states, like the federal government, retain the power to tax and spend for the general welfare.

*Powers Denied to the States*   The Constitution denies the states some powers in order to safeguard national unity. States are specifically denied the power to coin money, enter into treaties with foreign nations, interfere with the "obligation of contracts," levy taxes on imports or exports, or engage in war.

*Powers Denied to the Nation and the States*   The Constitution denies some powers to both national and state government—namely, the powers to abridge individual rights. The Bill of Rights originally applied only to the national government; but the Fourteenth Amendment, passed by Congress in 1866 and ratified by 1868, provided that the states must also adhere to fundamental guarantees of individual liberty.

*State Role in National Government*   The states are basic units in the organizational scheme of the national government. The House of Representatives apportions members to the states by population, and state legislatures draw up the districts that elect representatives. Every state has at least one member in the House of Representatives, regardless of its population. Each state elects two U.S. senators, regardless of its population. The president is chosen by the electoral votes of the states, with each state having as many electoral votes as it has senators and representatives combined. Finally, three-fourths of the states must ratify amendments to the U.S. Constitution.

## THE EVOLUTION OF AMERICAN FEDERALISM

American federalism has evolved over 200 years from a state-centered division of power to a national-centered system of government. While the original constitutional wordings have remained in place, power has flowed toward the national government since the earliest days of the Republic. American federalism has been

**Concurrent powers:** Powers exercised by both the national government and state governments in the American federal system.

**Reserved powers:** The principle of American federalism, embodied in the Tenth Amendment, that powers not granted to the national government or specifically denied to the states in the Constitution belong to the state governments.

forged in the fires of political conflicts between states and nation, conflicts that have usually been resolved in favor of the national government.

Generalizing about the evolution of American federalism is no easy task. But let us try to describe broadly some major periods in the evolution of federalism, then look at five specific historical developments that had far-reaching impact on that evolution.

*State-Centered Federalism, 1787–1868*  From the adoption of the Constitution of 1787 to the end of the Civil War, the states were the most important units in the American federal system. It is true that during this period the legal foundation for the expansion of national power was being laid, but people looked to the states for the resolution of most policy questions and the provision of most public services. Even the issue of slavery was decided by state governments. The supremacy of the national government was frequently questioned, first by the Anti-Federalists (including Thomas Jefferson), and later by John C. Calhoun and other defenders of slavery.

*Dual Federalism, 1868–1913*  The supremacy of the national government was decided on the battlefields of the Civil War. Yet for nearly a half-century after that conflict, the national government narrowly interpreted its delegated powers, and the states continued to decide most domestic policy issues. The resulting pattern has been described as **dual federalism.** Under this pattern, the states and the nation divided most governmental functions. The national government concentrated its attention on the "delegated" powers—national defense, foreign affairs, tariffs, interstate commerce, the coinage of money, standard weights and measures, post office and post roads, and the admission of new states. State governments decided the important domestic policy issues—education, welfare, health, and criminal justice. The separation of policy responsibilities was once compared to a layer cake, with local governments at the base, state governments in the middle, and the national government at the top.[7]

*Cooperative Federalism, 1913–1964*  The distinction between national and state responsibilities gradually eroded in the first half of the twentieth century. American federalism was transformed by the Industrial Revolution and the development of a national economy; by the federal income tax in 1913, which shifted financial resources to the national government; and by the challenges of two world wars and the Great Depression. In response to the Great Depression of the 1930s, state governors welcomed massive federal public works projects under President Franklin D. Roosevelt's New Deal program. In addition, the federal government intervened directly in economic affairs, labor relations, business practices, and agriculture. Through its grants of money, the national government cooperated with the states in public assistance, employment services, child welfare, public housing, urban renewal, highway building, and vocational education.

This new pattern of federal-state relations was labeled **cooperative federalism.** Both the nation and the states exercised responsibilities for welfare, health, highways, education, and criminal justice. This merging of policy responsibilities was compared to a marble cake: "As the colors are mixed in a marble cake, so functions are mixed in the American federal system."[8] Yet even in this period of shared national-state responsibility, the national government emphasized cooperation in achieving common national and state goals. Congress generally acknowl-

**Dual federalism:** An early concept of federalism in which national and state powers were clearly distinguished and functionally separate.

**Cooperative federalism:** A model of federalism in which national, state, and local governments work together exercising common policy responsibilities.

*The massive public works projects sponsored by the federal government under President Franklin Roosevelt's New Deal during the Great Depression of the 1930s reflected the emergence of cooperative federalism. Programs of the Work Progress Administration, like the one shown here, were responsible for the construction of buildings, bridges, highways, and airports throughout the country.*

edged that it had no direct constitutional authority to regulate public health, safety, or welfare. Instead, it relied primarily on its powers to tax and spend for the general welfare, providing financial assistance to state and local governments to achieve shared goals. Congress did not usually legislate directly on local matters.

*Centralized Federalism, 1964–1980* Over the years, it became increasingly difficult to maintain the fiction that the national government was merely assisting the states to perform their domestic responsibilities. By the time President Lyndon B. Johnson launched the Great Society program in 1964, the federal government clearly had its own *national* goals. Virtually all problems confronting American society—from solid-waste disposal and water and air pollution, to consumer safety, home insulation, noise abatement, and even "highway beautification"—were declared to be national problems. Congress legislated directly on any matter it chose, without regard to its *enumerated powers* and without pretending to render merely financial assistance. The Supreme Court no longer concerned itself with the *reserved powers* of the states, and the Tenth Amendment lost most of its meaning. The pattern of national-state relations became **centralized federalism.** As for the cake analogies, one commentator observed: "The frosting had moved to the top, something like a pineapple upside-down cake."[9]

**Centralized federalism:** A model of federalism in which the national government assumes primary responsibility for determining national goals in all major policy areas and directs state and local government activity through conditions attached to money grants.

**New Federalism:** Attempts to return power and responsibility to the states and reduce the role of the national government in domestic affairs.

*New Federalism, 1980–1985* **New Federalism** was a phrase frequently applied to efforts to reverse the flow of power to Washington and to return responsibilities to states and communities. (The phrase originated in the administration of Richard M. Nixon, 1969–1974, who used it to describe general revenue sharing—making federal grants to state and local governments with few strings attached.) New Federalism was popular early in the administration of

*The Head Start Program, part of Lyndon Johnson's Great Society program, was intended initially to help prepare poor preschool children for school. The Great Society legislation marked the beginning of the era of centralized federalism.*

President Ronald Reagan, who tried to reduce federal involvement in domestic programs and encourage states and cities to undertake greater policy responsibilities themselves. The result was that state and local governments were forced to rely more on their own sources of revenue and less upon federal money. Still, centralizing tendencies in the American federal system continued. While the general public usually gave better marks to state and local governments than to the federal government, paradoxically that same public also favored greater federal involvement in policy areas traditionally thought to be state or local responsibilities (see *What Do You Think?* "Which Government Does the Best Job?")

*Representational Federalism, 1985–* Despite centralizing tendencies, it was still widely assumed prior to 1985 that the Congress could not directly legislate how state and local governments should go about performing their traditional functions. However, in its 1985 *Garcia* decision, the U.S. Supreme Court appeared to remove all barriers to direct congressional legislation in matters traditionally reserved to the states. The case arose after Congress directly ordered state and local governments to pay minimum wages to their employees. The Court dismissed arguments that the nature of American federalism and the Reserved Powers Clause of the Tenth Amendment prevented Congress from directly legislating in state affairs. It said that the only protection for state powers was to be found in the states' role in electing U.S. senators, members of the U.S. House of Representatives, and the president—a concept known as **representational federalism.**

The idea behind representational federalism is that there is no constitutional division of powers between states and nation. Federalism is defined by the role of the states in electing members of Congress and the president. The United States is said to retain a federal system because its national officials are selected from subunits of government—the president through the allocation of Electoral College votes to the states, and the Congress through the allocation of two Senate seats per state and the apportionment of representatives based on state popula-

**Representational federalism:** The assertion that there is no constitutional division of powers between the nation and the states but that the states retain a constitutional role in selecting the president and members of Congress.

# Which Government Does the Best Job?

Americans generally favor governments closer to home. Most surveys show that Americans have greater trust and confidence in their state and local governments than in the federal government. But paradoxically, Americans want the federal government to assume even more power in many *specific* policy areas, including areas traditionally thought to be state or local government responsibilities: regulation of voting, setting penalties for murder, establishing safety standards, and setting minimum wages.

**CONFIDENCE**
**How much confidence do you have in these institutions?**

YOUR LOCAL GOVERNMENT

| | |
|---|---|
| A great deal | 11 |
| Quite a lot | 20 |
| Some | 46 |
| Very little | 21 |

YOUR STATE GOVERNMENT

| | |
|---|---|
| A great deal | 6 |
| Quite a lot | 17 |
| Some | 53 |
| Very little | 23 |

THE FEDERAL GOVERNMENT

| | |
|---|---|
| A great deal | 4 |
| Quite a lot | 11 |
| Some | 47 |
| Very little | 37 |

0 10 20 30 40 50 60 70

**POWER**
**Where should power be concentrated?**

| | |
|---|---|
| State government | 64 |
| Federal government | 26 |

**WASTE**
**From which level of government do you get the LEAST for your money?**

| | | |
|---|---|---|
| Local government | 1990 | 21 |
| Local government | 1994 | 19 |
| State government | 1990 | 26 |
| State government | 1994 | 21 |
| Federal government | 1990 | 41 |
| Federal government | 1994 | 46 |

**FAIRNESS**
**Which do you think is the worst tax – that is, the LEAST fair?**

| | | |
|---|---|---|
| Federal income tax | 1980 | 36 |
| | 1987 | 30 |
| | 1994 | 27 |
| State income tax | 1980 | 10 |
| | 1987 | 12 |
| | 1994 | 7 |
| State sales tax | 1980 | 19 |
| | 1987 | 21 |
| | 1994 | 14 |
| Local property tax | 1980 | 25 |
| | 1987 | 24 |
| | 1994 | 28 |

0 10 20 30 40 50 60 70
Percent

**NATIONAL REGULATION**
**Which level of government should run the following programs?**

Welfare

| | |
|---|---|
| Federal | 38 |
| State | 40 |
| Local | 17 |

**Opportunity for minorities**

| | |
|---|---|
| Federal | 35 |
| State | 30 |
| Local | 28 |

**Air/Water Quality**

| | |
|---|---|
| Federal | 35 |
| State | 40 |
| Local | 22 |

**Public education**

| | |
|---|---|
| Federal | 21 |
| State | 47 |
| Local | 30 |

**Employment and job training**

| | |
|---|---|
| Federal | 15 |
| State | 59 |
| Local | 24 |

**Law enforcement**

| | |
|---|---|
| Federal | 15 |
| State | 36 |
| Local | 45 |

**INVOLVEMENT IN PROBLEMS**
**Which level of government should run the following programs?**

**Service to immigrants**

| | |
|---|---|
| Federal | 60 |
| State | 15 |
| Local | 6 |

**Health care for the disabled, poor, and elderly**

| | |
|---|---|
| Federal | 36 |
| State | 28 |
| Local | 18 |

**Child care**

| | |
|---|---|
| Federal | 16 |
| State | 34 |
| Local | 29 |

**Job training**

| | |
|---|---|
| Federal | 24 |
| State | 37 |
| Local | 23 |

Percent

*Note:* All figures are percentages of U.S. public in national opinion surveys. "No opinions" and "Don't knows" not shown.
*Source:* General responses on trust, power, and regulation of specific programs from Hart and Teeter for the Council for Excellence in Government, *State Legislatures* (July/August 1995); responses on fairness, waste, and involvement in specific problems from Advisory Commission on Intergovernmental Relations, *Changing Public Attitudes on Governments and Taxes* (Washington, D.C.: ACIR, 1991, 1994).

tion. Whatever protection exists for state power and independence must be found in the national political process—in the influence of state and district voters on their senators and Congress members.

The Supreme Court's ruling in the *Garcia* case raised new questions for American federalism. How is the nation to be governed if there are *no* "a priori definitions of state sovereignty," *no* "discrete limitations on the objects of federal authority," and *no* protection of state powers in the U.S. Constitution? According to the Court: "State sovereign interests . . . are more properly protected by procedural safeguards inherent in the structure of the federal system than by judicially created limitations on federal power." The Court rhetorically endorsed a federal system but left it up to the U.S. Congress, rather than the Constitution or the courts, to decide what powers should be exercised by the states and the national government. In a strongly worded dissenting opinion in the *Garcia* case, Justice Lewis Powell argued that if federalism is to be retained, the Constitution—not Congress—must divide powers. "The states' role in our system of government is a matter of constitutional law, not legislative grace. . . . [This decision] today rejects almost 200 years of the understanding of the constitutional status of federalism."[10]

# KEY DEVELOPMENTS IN AMERICAN FEDERALISM

During our nation's history, perhaps the most important developments in the evolution of federalism have been: (1) the broad interpretation of the Necessary and Proper Clause by the Supreme Court; (2) the victory of the national government in the Civil War; (3) the establishment of a national system of civil rights based upon the Fourteenth Amendment; (4) the growth of national power under the Interstate Commerce Clause; and (5) the growth of national power as federal revenues expanded as a result of the Sixteenth Amendment's income tax.

*McCulloch v. Maryland and the Necessary and Proper Clause*    Political conflict over the scope of national power is as old as the nation itself. In 1790, Secretary of the Treasury Alexander Hamilton proposed the establishment of a national bank. Congress acted on Hamilton's suggestion in 1791, establishing a national bank to serve as a depository for federal money and to aid the federal government in borrowing funds. Jeffersonians believed that the national bank was a dangerous centralization of government. They objected that the power to establish the bank was nowhere to be found in the enumerated powers of Congress. Jefferson argued that Congress had no constitutional authority to establish a bank because a bank was not "indispensably necessary" in carrying out Congress's delegated functions.

Hamilton replied that Congress could derive the power to establish a bank from grants of authority in the Constitution relating to money, in combination with the clause authorizing Congress "to make all laws which shall be necessary and proper for carrying into execution the foregoing powers." Jefferson interpreted the word *necessary* to mean "indispensable," but Hamilton argued that the national government had the right to choose the manner and means of performing its delegated functions and was not restricted to employing only those means considered indispensable in the performance of its functions.

*Since the Constitution included nothing about the establishment of a national bank, controversy raged over Hamilton's proposal to establish one in 1790. Although this suggestion was acted upon by Congress in 1791 and the first Bank of the United States was founded in Philadelphia, it took the Supreme Court's ruling in McCulloch v. Maryland in 1819 to establish that Congress has certain implied powers and that national policies take precedence over state policies.*

The question finally reached the Supreme Court in 1819, when the State of Maryland levied a tax on the national bank and the bank refused to pay it. In the case of **McCulloch v. Maryland,** Chief Justice Marshall accepted the broader Hamiltonian version of the Necessary and Proper Clause: "Let the end be legitimate, let it be within the scope of the Constitution, and all means which are appropriate, which are plainly adopted to that end, which are not prohibited but consistent with the letter and the spirit of the Constitution, are constitutional."[11]

The *McCulloch* case firmly established the principle that the Necessary and Proper Clause gives Congress the right to choose its means in carrying out the enumerated powers of the national government. Today Congress can devise programs, create agencies, and establish national laws on the basis of long chains of reasoning from the most meager phrases of the constitutional text because of this broad interpretation of the Necessary and Proper Clause. Hence, many pundits have dubbed this the "Elastic Clause," since it seems to stretch to cover just about anything.

The *McCulloch* case also made a major contribution to the interpretation of the National Supremacy Clause. Chief Justice Marshall held that Maryland's tax on the national bank was unconstitutional because it interfered with a national activity being carried out under the Constitution and laws "made in pursuance thereof." In this case, Maryland's law conflicted with the federal law establishing the national bank. From Marshall's time to the present, the National Supremacy Clause has meant that states cannot refuse to obey federal laws.

*Secession and Civil War*    The Civil War was the greatest crisis of the American federal system. Did a state have the right to oppose national law to the point of **secession**? In the years preceding the war, South Carolina's John C. Calhoun argued that the Constitution was a compact made by the *states* in their sovereign capacity rather than by the *people* in their national capacity. He contended that the federal government was an agent of the state, that the states retained their sovereignty in this compact, and that the federal government must not violate the compact, under the penalty of state nullification or even secession. Calhoun's doctrine was embodied in the constitution of the Confederacy (see *Up Close:* "Confederation Anyone?").

The question of secession was decided on the battlefield between 1861 and 1865. As Chief Justice Chase reiterated afterward, the Constitution established "an indestructible union, composed of indestructible states." Yet the states' rights doctrine and political disputes over the character of American federalism did not disappear with General Robert E. Lee's surrender at Appomattox. In addition to establishing that states cannot secede from the federal union, the Civil War led to three constitutional amendments clearly aimed at limiting state power in the interests of individual freedom. The Thirteenth Amendment eliminated slavery in the states; the Fifteenth Amendment prevented states from denying the vote on the basis of race, color, or previous enslavement; and the Fourteenth Amendment declared:

> No State shall make or enforce any law which shall abridge the privileges or immunities of citizens of the United States; nor shall any state deprive any person of life, liberty, or property, without due process of law; nor deny to any person within its jurisdiction the equal protection of the laws.

These amendments delegate to Congress the power to secure their enforcement. During the post-Civil War "Reconstruction" era (1866–1876), Congress

*McCulloch v. Maryland:* Supreme Court decision (1819) broadly interpreting national power under the Necessary and Proper Clause of the Constitution and recognizing the supremacy of federal laws over state laws under the National Supremacy Clause.

**Secession:** The withdrawal of states or provinces from a larger political union; specifically, the unsuccessful attempt by eleven southern states to break away from the federal Union that resulted in the Civil War.

CHAPTER 4 • FEDERALISM: DIVIDING GOVERNMENTAL POWER

# Confederation Anyone?

While the historical trend in the United States over 200 years has been the increasing power of the national government within a constitutional *federal* system, the history of the country includes two important *confederations:* the United States under the Articles of Confederation (1781–1788) and the Confederate States of America, formed by the seceding southern states in 1861.

## Articles of Confederation

*Article I.* The Stile of this Confederacy shall be "The United States of America."

*Article II.* Each state retains its sovereignty, freedom and independence, and every Power, Jurisdiction and right, which is not by this confederation expressly delegated to the United States, in Congress assembled.

*Article III.* The said states hereby severally enter into a firm league of friendship with each other, for their common defence, the security of their Liberties, and their mutual and general welfare, binding themselves to assist each other, against all force offered to, or attacks made upon them, or any of them, on account of religion, sovereignty, trade, or any other pretence whatever.

Note that these articles asserted that the states retained their "sovereignty, freedom and independence" and described the United States as "a firm league of friendship" among states.

Compare the Preamble to the Constitution of the Confederate States of America with the Preamble to the U.S. Constitution:

## Confederate Constitution

We the people of the Confederate States, each State acting in its sovereign and independent character, in order to form a permanent federal government, establish justice, insure domestic tranquility, and secure the blessings of liberty to ourselves and our posterity—invoking the favor and guidance of Almighty God—do ordain and establish this Constitution for the Confederate States of America.

## U.S. Constitution

We the people of the United States, in order to form a more perfect Union, establish justice, insure domestic tranquility, provide for the common defence, promote the general welfare, and secure the blessings of liberty to ourselves and our posterity, do ordain and establish this Constitution for the United States of America.

The second phrase in the Confederate Constitution—"each state acting in its sovereign and independent character"—indicates that the Confederate government was formed by a compact between *states*, not directly by the people.

passed several laws designed to enforce these amendments—laws guaranteeing the right to vote, providing remedies for the denial of rights by any person acting under "the color of law," and prohibiting discrimination in public accommodation.[12] But after 1877, Congress gave up its efforts to reconstruct southern society, and the Supreme Court held important provisions of these laws unconstitutional.[13]

*National Guarantees of Civil Rights* After World War I, the Supreme Court began to build a national system of civil rights based on the Fourteenth Amendment. The Court held that the Fourteenth Amendment prevented *states* from interfering with free speech, free press, or religious practices. Not until 1954, however, in the desegregation decision in *Brown v. Board of Education of Topeka,* did the Court begin to call for the full assertion of national authority on behalf of civil rights. When it decided that the Fourteenth Amendment prohibited

*In a long bloody war to establish national supremacy, the North's ultimate victory served to prove once and for all that the federal union cannot be dissolved.*

the states from segregating the races in public schools, the Court was asserting national authority over long-standing practices in many of the states.

Despite the clear mandate of the Supreme Court, the southern states succeeded in avoiding all but token integration for more than ten years. Yet only occasionally did resistance take the form of **interposition.** Governor Orval Faubus called out the Arkansas National Guard to prevent a federal court from desegregating Little Rock Central High School in 1957. But this interposition ended quickly when President Dwight D. Eisenhower ordered the National Guard removed and sent units of the U.S. Army to enforce national authority. In 1962, President John F. Kennedy took a similar action when Governor Ross Barnett of Mississippi personally barred the entry of an African-American student to the University of Mississippi despite a federal court order requiring his admission. These actions failed to alter the principle of national supremacy in the American political system.

*The Expansion of Interstate Commerce*   The growth of national power under the Interstate Commerce Clause of the Constitution is another important development in the evolution of American federalism. For many years, the U.S. Supreme Court narrowly defined *interstate commerce* to mean only the movement of goods and services across state lines. Until the late 1930s, it insisted that agriculture, mining, manufacturing, and labor relations were outside the reach of the delegated powers of the national government. However, when confronted with the Great Depression of the 1930s and Franklin Roosevelt's threat to add enough members to the Supreme Court to win favorable rulings, the Court yielded. It redefined *interstate commerce* to include any activity that "substantially affects" the national economy.[14] Indeed, the Court frequently approved of congressional restrictions on economic activities that had only very indirect effects on interstate commerce[15] (see *Up Close:* "Can the Federal Government Outlaw Guns in Schools?").

**Interposition:** An argument, long rejected by the Supreme Court, that a state may place itself between its citizens and the national government to prevent the enforcement of a national law believed by the state to be unconstitutional.

CHAPTER 4 • FEDERALISM: DIVIDING GOVERNMENTAL POWER

# Can the Federal Government Outlaw Guns in Schools?

Are there any limits at all to Congress's enumerated powers? Are there any areas of power truly *reserved* for the states only?

When a student, Alfonso Lopez, was apprehended at his high school carrying a .38 handgun, federal agents charged him with violating the federal Gun-Free School Zones Act of 1990. He was convicted and sentenced to six months in prison. His attorney appealed on the ground that it was beyond the constitutionally delegated powers of Congress to police local school zones; the Fifth Circuit Court agreed and the case was appealed by the U.S. government to the Supreme Court in 1995.

On April 26, 1995, the U.S. Supreme Court issued its first opinion in more than sixty years that recognized a limit to Congress's power over interstate commerce and reaffirmed the Founders' notion that the federal government has only the powers enumerated in the U.S. Constitution. Chief Justice William H. Rehnquist, writing for the majority in the 5 to 4 decision, *U.S. v. Lopez*, even cited James Madison with approval: "The powers delegated by the proposed Constitution to the federal government are few and defined. Those which are to remain in the State governments are numerous and indefinite" (*Federalist Papers*, No. 45).

After reviewing virtually all of the key Commerce Clause cases in its history, the Court determined that an activity must *substantially affect* interstate commerce in order to be regulated by Congress. "The Court has never declared that Congress may use a relatively trivial impact on commerce as an excuse for broad general resolution of state and private activities." The U.S. government argued that the Gun-Free School Zones Act was a constitutional exercise of its interstate commerce power because "possession of a firearm in a school zone may result in violent crime and that violent crime can be expected to affect the functioning of the national economy in two ways. First, the costs of violent crime are substantial and, through the mechanism of insurance, those costs are spread throughout the population. Second, violent crime reduces the willingness of individuals to travel to areas within the country that are perceived to be unsafe."

The Court rejected these arguments, holding that such tenuous reasoning would remove virtually all limits to federal power. "If we were to accept the Government's arguments, we are hard-pressed to posit any activity by an individual that Congress is without power to regulate." Moreover, "To uphold the Government's contentions here, we would have to pile inference upon inference in a manner that would bid fair to convert congressional activity under the Commerce Clause to a general police power of the sort retained by the states."

Voting with the majority were Justices Rehnquist (appointed to the Court by President Richard Nixon in 1971 and made Chief Justice by Reagan in 1986), Anthony M. Kennedy (Reagan, 1988), Sandra Day O'Connor (Reagan, 1981), Antonin Scalia (Reagan, 1986), and Clarence Thomas (Bush, 1991). Justice Stephen G. Breyer (Clinton, 1994) wrote a dissenting opinion and was joined by Justices John Paul Stevens (Ford, 1975), David Souter (Bush, 1990), and Ruth Bader Ginsburg (Clinton, 1993). Justice Breyer's dissent argued that the Court need only find that Congress has "a rational basis for finding a substantial connection between gun-related school violence and interstate commerce." He reasoned that "guns in schools significantly undermine the quality of education in our nation's classrooms" and that "education, although far more than a matter of economics, has long been inextricably intertwined with the nation's economy."

It is too early to judge the impact of this decision—whether it represents a return to traditional notions of enumerated powers of Congress and reserved powers of the state. The closeness of the vote, together with the decision's stark contrast to more than a half-century of case law on the Commerce Clause, provide no more than a hope that in the future the Supreme Court may move in the direction of strengthening federalism.

*Source: U.S. v. Lopez, 63 L.W. 4343 (1995).*

*The Federal Income Tax and Grants-in-Aid*    Even in the earliest days of the Republic, the national government was involved in public activities not specifically delegated to it by the Constitution. In the famous Northwest Ordinance of 1787, which provided for the governing of the territories west of the Appalachian Mountains, Congress made grants of land for the establishment of public schools. Then in the Morrill Land Grant Act of 1862, Congress provided grants of land to the states to promote higher education, especially agricultural and mechanical studies. Federal support for "A and M" or "land grant" universities continues today.

With the money provided Washington by the passage of the Sixteenth (income tax) Amendment in 1913, Congress embarked on cash grants to the states. Among the earliest cash grant programs were the Federal Highway Act of 1916 (highways) and the Smith-Hughes Act of 1917 (vocational education). With federal money came federal direction. For example, states that wanted federal money for highways after 1916 had to create state highway departments and submit their highway plans for approval to the U.S. Bureau of Roads (now the Federal Highway Administration in the U.S. Department of Transportation). The federal government established uniform standards of construction and even a uniform road-numbering system (U.S. 1, U.S. 30, etc.).

Shortly after these programs were begun, the U.S. Supreme Court considered the claim that these federal grants were unconstitutional intrusions into areas "reserved" for the states. But the Court upheld grants as a legitimate exercise of Congress's power to tax and spend for the general welfare.[16]

## MONEY AND POWER FLOW TO WASHINGTON

Over the years, power in the federal system has flowed to Washington because tax money has flowed to Washington. With its financial resources, the federal government has been able to offer assistance to state and local governments and thereby involve itself in just about every governmental function performed by these governments. Today, the federal government is no longer one of *enumerated* or *delegated* powers. There are really no activities *reserved* to the states. Through its power to tax and spend for the *general welfare,* the national government is now deeply involved in welfare, education, transportation, police protection, housing, hospitals, urban development, and other activities that were once the exclusive domain of state and local government (see *Up Close:* "How Congress Set a National Drinking Age").

Today, grant-in-aid programs are the single most important source of federal influence over state and local activity. A **grant-in-aid** is defined as "payment of funds by one level of government (national or state) to be expended by another level (state or local) for a specified purpose, usually on a matching-funds basis (the federal government puts up only as much as the state or locality) and in accordance with prescribed standards of requirements."[17] No state or local government is *required* to accept grants-in-aid. Participation in grant-in-aid programs is voluntary. So in theory, if conditions attached to the grant money are too oppressive, state and local governments can simply decline to participate and pass up these funds.

**Grants-in-aid:** Payments of funds from the national government to state or local governments, or from a state government to local governments, for specific purposes.

CHAPTER 4 • FEDERALISM: DIVIDING GOVERNMENTAL POWER

# How Congress Set a National Drinking Age

Traditionally the *reserved* powers of the states included protection of the health, safety, and well-being of their citizens. The *enumerated* powers of Congress in the Constitution did *not* include regulation of the sale and consumption of alcoholic beverages. Every state determined its own minimum age for drinking.

When the Twenty-sixth Amendment to the Constitution was passed in 1971, guaranteeing eighteen-year-olds the right to vote, most states lowered their minimum drinking age to eighteen. But by the early 1980s, some states had raised their minimums back to twenty-one in response to reports of teenage drinking and driving. Indeed, the National Transportation Safety Board reported that teenagers were statistically more likely to be involved in alcohol-related deaths than nonteenagers. The National Student Association, restaurant owners, and the beverage industry claimed that the selection of *all* teenagers for restriction was age discrimination. Whatever the merits of the argument, the issue was widely considered to be a *state* concern.

But the minimum drinking age became a national issue as a result of emotional appeals by groups such as Mothers Against Drunk Driving (MADD). Tragic stories told at televised committee hearings by grieving relatives of dead teenagers swept away federalism arguments. A few Congress members tried to argue that a national drinking age infringed on the powers of the state in a matter traditionally under state control. However, the new law did not directly mandate a national drinking age. Instead, it ordered the withholding of 10 percent of all federal highway funds from any state that failed to raise its minimum drinking age to twenty-one. States retained the rights to ignore the national minimum and give up a portion of their highway funds. (Congress used this same approach in 1974 in establishing a national 55-mile-per-hour speed limit.) Opponents of this device labeled it federal blackmail and a federal intrusion into state responsibilities. For some state officials,

then, the issue was not teen drinking but rather the preemption of state authority.

Proponents of the legislation cited the *national* interest in setting a uniform minimum drinking age. They argued that protecting the lives of young people outweighed the states' interest in preserving their authority. Moreover, teens were crossing state lines to drink in states with lower drinking ages. New York, for example, with a minimum drinking age of nineteen, was attracting teenagers from Pennsylvania and New Jersey, where the drinking age was twenty-one. Reports of "bloody borders" were used to justify national action to establish a uniform drinking age. While the Reagan White House had pledged to return responsibility to the states, it did not wish to offend the nation's mothers on such an emotional issue. Despite initial reservations, President Ronald Reagan supported the bill and signed it into law in 1984.

From a purely constitutional perspective, Congress simply exercised its power to spend money for the general welfare; it did not *directly* legislate in an area *reserved* to the states. Technically, states remain free to set their own minimum drinking age. Despite heated arguments in many state legislatures, virtually all of the states adopted the twenty-one-year-old minimum national drinking age by 1990.

*Appeals by groups such as Mothers Against Drunk Driving (MADD) helped overcome concerns that legislation effectively setting a national drinking age would infringe on state authority.*

FIGURE 4-3 **Purposes of Federal Grants to State and Local Governments**

*Approximately one-fifth of all state and local government revenues are derived from federal grants. Federal grants-in-aid to state and local governments are especially vital in the areas of health and welfare.*

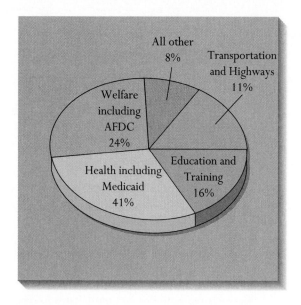

More than one-fifth of all state and local government revenues currently come from federal grants. Federal grants are available in nearly every major category of state and local government activity. So numerous and diverse are they that there is often a lack of information about their availability, purpose, and requirements. In fact, federal grants can be obtained for the preservation of historic buildings, the development of minority-owned businesses, aid to foreign refugees, the drainage of abandoned mines, riot control, and school milk. However, welfare (including Aid to Families with Dependent Children and food stamps), health (including Medicaid for the poor), and highways account for more than three-fourths of federal aid money (see Figure 4-3).

Thus, many of the special projects and ongoing programs carried out today by state and local governments are funded by grants from the federal government. These funds have generally been dispersed as categorical grants, block grants, and general revenue-sharing (GRS) grants:

- *Categorical Grant:* A grant for a specific, narrow project. The project must be approved by a federal administrative agency. Most federal aid money is distributed in the form of categorical grants. Categorical grants can be distributed on a project basis or a formula basis. Grants made on a project basis are distributed by federal administrative agencies to state or local governments that compete for project funds in their applications. Federal agencies have a great deal of discretion in selecting specific projects for support, and they can exercise direct control over the projects. Most categorical grants are distributed to state or local governments according to a fixed formula set by Congress. Federal administrative agencies may require reports and adherence to rules and guidelines, but they do not choose which specific projects to fund.

- *Block Grant:* A grant for a general governmental function, such as health, social services, law enforcement, education, or community development. State and local governments have fairly wide discretion in deciding how to spend federal block grant money within a functional area. For example, cities receiving "community development" block grants can decide for themselves about specific neighborhood development projects, housing projects, community facilities, etc. All block grants are distributed on a formula basis set by Congress.

- *General Revenue Sharing (GRS):* Formerly a money grant for state or local governments to use as they saw fit, GRS gave state and local officials wide discretion in spending federal revenues. The program was begun under President Richard M. Nixon's notion of New Federalism in the State and Local Government Fiscal Assistance Act of 1972. GRS funds were allocated to state and local governments (state governments were dropped from GRS in 1981) by a complex formula based on population, tax effort, and the income level of the population. General revenue sharing was ended in 1986 as the Reagan Administration sought to reduce the role of the federal government in domestic policy and reduce state and local government reliance on federal money.

Two modest steps toward decentralization took place under Reagan's New Federalism. First of all, general revenue sharing was ended. While the original idea behind GRS was to expand local powers by replacing many project grants with general revenues—and thus to give local officials more policy discretion—the Reagan Administration argued that most GRS funds went to traditional local government functions that local taxpayers should fund themselves. "Free" money from Washington was not spent by local officials with the same care that they exercised when spending money extracted from their own voter-taxpayers. State and local officials lobbied long and hard in Congress to retain GRS, but the pressure of the federal deficit finally ended the program in 1986.

Second, block grants replaced many categorical grant programs, notably in health services, social services, community development, alcohol and drug abuse and mental health programs, and education. Actually, the struggle in Congress between those who favored categorical grants (mostly liberals and Democrats) and those who wanted consolidation (Reagan and the Republicans) ended in a draw, with many categorical grant programs remaining independent. Finally, the Reagan Administration was successful in slowing the overall growth of federal aid programs and thus reducing the dependence of state and local governments on federal money. Total federal grant dollars *increased* during the 1980s, although not as fast as inflation or as much as in previous years (see Figure 4-4).

## COERCIVE FEDERALISM: PREEMPTIONS AND MANDATES

Traditionally, Congress avoided issuing direct orders to state and local governments. Instead, it sought to influence them by offering grants of money with federal rules, regulations, or "guidelines" attached. In theory at least, states and communities were free to forgo the money and ignore the "strings" attached to it. But increasingly Congress has undertaken direct regulation of areas traditionally reserved to the states and restricted state authority to regulate these areas. And it has issued direct orders to state and local governments to perform various services and comply with federal law in the performance of these services.

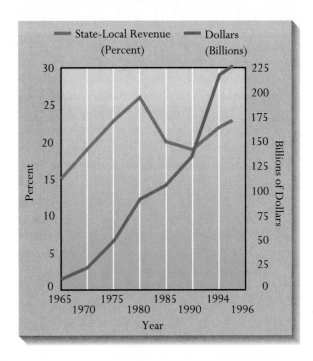

**FIGURE 4-4** **Federal Grants to State and Local Governments**

*Under the New Federalism of the 1980s, total grants-in-aid dollars to state and local governments increased, though federal money as a percentage of state and local revenue fell significantly. State and local governments had to rely more heavily on their own sources of revenue than on federal funds. But in recent years state and local reliance on federal money has begun to creep upward again.*

**Preemption:** Total or partial federal assumption of power in a particular field, restricting the authority of the states.

**Total preemption:** The federal government's assumption of all regulatory powers in a particular field.

**Partial preemption:** The stipulation that a state law on the same subject as a federal law is valid if it does not conflict with the federal law in the same area.

**Standard partial preemption:** Permission for states to regulate activities already regulated by the federal government if the state regulatory standards are at least as stringent as the federal government's.

**Mandates:** Direct federal orders to state and local governments requiring them to perform a service or to obey federal laws in the performance of their functions.

*Federal Preemptions* The supremacy of federal laws over those of the states, spelled out in the National Supremacy Clause of the Constitution, permits Congress to decide whether or not there is **preemption** of state laws in a particular field by federal law. In **total preemption,** the federal government assumes all regulatory powers in a particular field—for example, copyrights, bankruptcy, railroads, and airlines. No state regulations in a totally preempted field are permitted. **Partial preemption** stipulates that a state law on the same subject is valid as long as it does not conflict with the federal law in the same area. For example, the Occupational Safety and Health Act of 1970 specifically permits state regulation of any occupational safety or health issue on which the federal Occupational Safety and Health Administration (OSHA) has *not* developed a standard; but once OSHA enacts a standard, all state standards are nullified. Yet another form of the partial preemption, the **standard partial preemption,** permits states to regulate activities in a field already regulated by the federal government, as long as state regulatory standards are at least as stringent as those of the federal government. Usually states must submit their regulations to the responsible federal agency for approval; the federal agency may revoke a state's regulating power if it fails to enforce the approved standards. For example, the federal Environmental Protection Agency (EPA) permits state environmental regulations that meet or exceed EPA standards.

*Federal Mandates* Federal **mandates** are direct orders to state and local governments to perform a particular activity or service, or to comply with federal laws in the performance of their functions. Federal mandates occur in a wide variety of areas, from civil rights to minimum wage regulations. Their range is reflected in some recent examples of federal mandates to state and local governments:

•   *Age Discrimination Act, 1986:* Outlaws mandatory retirement ages for public as well as private employees, including police, fire fighters, and the state college and university faculty.

- *Asbestos Hazard Emergency Act, 1986:* Orders school districts to inspect for asbestos hazards and remove asbestos from school buildings when necessary.
- *Safe Drinking Water Act, 1986:* Establishes national requirements for municipal water supplies; regulates municipal waste treatment plants.
- *Clean Air Act, 1990:* Bans municipal incinerators and requires auto emission inspections in certain urban areas.
- *Americans with Disabilities Act, 1990:* Requires all state and local government buildings to promote handicapped access.
- *National Voter Registration Act, 1993:* Requires states to register voters at driver's license, welfare, and unemployment compensation offices.

State and local governments frequently complain that compliance with federal government mandates such as these imposes costs on them that are seldom reimbursed.

*"Unfunded" Mandates*   Federal mandates often impose heavy costs on states and communities. When no federal monies are provided to cover these costs, the mandates are said to be **unfunded mandates.** Governors, mayors, and other state and local officials (including Bill Clinton, when he served as governor of Arkansas) have often urged Congress to halt the imposition of unfunded mandates on states and communities. Private industries have long voiced the same complaint. Regulations and mandates allow Congress to address problems while pushing the costs of doing so onto others. In 1995, Congress finally responded to these complaints by requiring that any bill imposing unfunded costs of $50 million or more on state and local governments (as determined by the Congressional Budget Office) would be subject to an additional procedural vote; a majority must vote to waive a prohibition against unfunded mandates before such a bill can come to the House or Senate floor. But this modest restraint is not likely to be very effective.

## A DEVOLUTION REVOLUTION?

Controversy over federalism—what level of government should do what and who should pay for it—is as old as the nation itself (see *A Conflicting View:* "Liberals, Conservatives, and Federalism"). Beginning in 1995, with a new Republican majority in both houses of Congress and Republicans holding a majority of state governorships, debates over federalism were renewed. The new phrase was **devolution**—the passing down of responsibilities from the national government to the states (see *People in Politics:* "Christine Todd Whitman, On the Cutting Edge of Change in the States").

*Reliance on Block Grants*   Devolution may take the form of consolidating and transforming categorical grant-in-aid programs into block grants and giving the states greater flexibility in deciding how to spend these funds. This block grant approach is an extension of the Reagan-era New Federalism, but Reagan never succeeded in getting more than 10 percent of total federal aid money transformed into block grants. In recent years Congress has debated the issue of transforming the two largest federal aid programs—welfare and Medicaid (health care for the poor)—into block grants.

**Unfunded mandates:** Federal orders imposing costs on state and local governments (and private industry) without reimbursement.

**Devolution:** The passing down of responsibilities from the national government to the states.

# Liberals, Conservatives, and Federalism

From the earliest days of the Republic, American leaders and scholars have argued over federalism. Political interests that constitute a majority at the national level and control the national government generally praise the virtue of national supremacy. Political interests that do not control the national government but exercise controlling influence in one or more states generally see great merit in preserving the powers of the states.

In recent years, political conflict over federalism—over the division between national versus state and local responsibilities and finances—has tended to follow traditional "liberal" and "conservative" political cleavages. Generally, liberals seek to enhance the power of the *national* government because they believe that people's lives can be changed—and bettered—by the exercise of national governmental power. The government in Washington has more power and resources than do state and local governments, which many liberals regard as too slow, cumbersome, weak, and unresponsive. Thus, liberalism and centralization are closely related in American politics. The liberal argument for national authority can be summarized as follows:

• There is insufficient concern about social problems by state and local governments. The federal government must take the lead in civil rights, equal employment opportunities, care for the poor and aged, the provision of adequate medical care for all Americans, and the elimination of urban poverty and blight.
• It is difficult to achieve change when reform-minded citizens must deal with fifty state governments and more than 86,000 local governments. Change is more likely to be accomplished by a strong central government.
• State and local governments contribute to inequality in society by setting different levels of services in education, welfare, health, and other public functions. A strong national government can ensure uniformity of standards throughout the nation.
• A strong national government can unify the nation behind principles and ideals of social justice and economic progress. Extreme decentralization may favor local or regional "special" interests at the expense of the general "public" interest.

In contrast, conservatives generally seek to return power to *state and local* governments. Conservatives are skeptical about the "good" that government can do and believe that adding to the power of the national government is not an effective way of resolving society's problems. On the contrary, they argue that "government is the problem, not the solution." Excessive government regulation, burdensome taxation, and inflationary government spending combine to restrict individual freedom, penalize work and savings, and destroy incentives for economic growth. Government should be kept small, controllable, and close to the people. The conservative argument for state and local autonomy can be summarized as follows:

• Grass-roots government promotes a sense of self-responsibility and self-reliance.
• State and local governments can better adapt public programs to local needs and conditions.
• State and local governments promote participation in politics and civic responsibility by allowing more people to become involved in public questions.
• Competition between states and cities can result in improved public programs and services.
• The existence of multiple state and local governments encourages experimentation and innovation in public policy, from which the whole nation may gain.

There is no way to settle the argument over federalism once and for all. Debates about federalism are part of the fabric of American politics.

## Christine Todd Whitman, On the Cutting Edge of Change in the States

According to New Jersey's energetic governor, Christine Todd Whitman, "Time after time, Republicans and Democrats have found that things work better when states and communities set their *own* priorities, rather than being bossed around by bureaucrats in Washington." In her view, Washington should follow the lead of active Republican governors like herself—"toward less government, lower taxes, and less spending."

Christine Todd was raised in a political family; her father was Republican state chair in New Jersey. After earning a B.A. in political science from private Wheaton College in Massachusetts in 1968, she worked on the staff of the Republican National Committee in Washington, where her job was to improve GOP contacts with students and minorities. Later she returned to New Jersey, married, and devoted much of her time to raising two daughters—"my greatest accomplishment."

In 1982, Christine Todd Whitman ran for and won her first elected office, to the Somerset County, New Jersey, Board of Chosen Freeholders (county commission). In 1988, the state's Republican governor appointed her president of the New Jersey Board of Public Utilities, where she developed a statewide reputation as a consumer advocate. In 1990, the state GOP needed a sacrificial lamb to fill the ballot space opposite the popular Democratic senator, Bill Bradley. But Whitman surprised both supporters and opponents by becoming a lion on the campaign trail and nearly upsetting the long-term incumbent. Indeed, Bill Bradley's close call in 1990 (Whitman won 49 percent of the vote) helped convince him to stay out of the presidential race in 1992 and allow Bill Clinton to win the Democratic nomination.

New Jersey's voters were upset by heavy tax increases imposed on them by Governor James Florio. Whitman pounded the tax-raising Democrat in newspaper columns and a radio talk show she hosted. When Florio came up for reelection in 1992, Whitman was well positioned to oust him with a hard-hitting campaign that featured an unlikely promise to reduce state income taxes by 30 percent.

Whitman's tax pledge was widely regarded as a political gimmick. But to the surprise of many observers, she delivered on her ambitious pledge, taking advantage of the state's economic recovery, privatizing several state functions, fighting the state's public employee unions, and making state government "smaller and smarter." Critics responded that many of her spending cuts were one-shot accounting ploys, that many state costs were shifted to local governments, that spending cuts hurt the poor, and that a state fiscal crisis would eventually develop. In the meantime, Whitman's success made her a national political star and a contender for the GOP national ticket.

*Welfare Reform and Federalism*   Welfare reform turned out to be the key to devolution. Bill Clinton once promised "to end welfare as we know it," but it was a Republican Congress in 1996 that did so. After two vetoes of welfare reform by President Clinton, it was finally agreed to merge welfare reform with devolution by:

- Establishing block grants with lump-sum allocations to the states for cash welfare payments.
- Granting the states broad flexibility in determining eligibility and benefit levels for persons receiving such aid.

- Allowing states to add to welfare spending if they choose to do so but penalizing states that reduce their spending for cash aid below 75 percent of their 1996 levels.
- Allowing states to deny additional cash payments for children born to women already receiving welfare assistance, and allowing states to deny cash payments to parents under 18 who do not live with an adult and attend school.
- Denying federal benefits to illegal aliens and allowing states to deny cash assistance, Medicaid, and social services to legal immigrants.

By transferring these programs into block grants, Congress acquired greater ability to control future costs. Indeed, the driving force behind the proposals may have been less to reform welfare than the desire to save billions in future years and assist in reducing federal budget deficits.

*The Beginning of the End to Federal Entitlements?* Since Franklin Delano Roosevelt's New Deal, with its federal guarantee of cash Aid to Families with Dependent Children (AFDC), low-income mothers and children had enjoyed a legal "entitlement" to welfare payments. But welfare reform, with its devolution of responsibility for determining eligibility to the states, ends this sixty-year federal entitlement. This is a major change in federal social welfare policy (see Chapter 17) and may become a model for future shedding of federal entitlement programs.

## SUMMARY NOTES

- The struggle for power between the national government and the states over two centuries has shaped American federalism today.
- Federalism is the division of power between two separate authorities, the nation and the state, each of which enforces its own laws directly on its citizens and neither of which can change the division of power without the consent of the other.
- American federalism was designed by the Founders as an additional protection for individual liberty by providing for the division and dispersal of power among multiple units of government.
- Federalism is also defended as a means of increasing opportunities to hold public office, improving governmental efficiency, ensuring policy responsiveness, encouraging policy innovation, and managing conflict.

- However, federalism can also obstruct and frustrate national action. Narrow state interests can sometimes prevail over national interests or the interests of minorities within states. Segregation was long protected by theories of states' rights. Federalism also results in uneven levels of public services through the nation.
- Power has flowed to the national government over time, as the original state-centered division of power has evolved into a national-centered system of government. Among the most important historical influences on this shift in power toward Washington have been the broad interpretation of national power by the Supreme Court; the victory of the national government over the secessionist states in the Civil War; the establishment of a national system of civil rights based on the Four-

teenth Amendment; the growth of a national economy governed by Congress under its interstate commerce power; and the accumulation of power by the national government through its greater financial resources.

- Federal grants to state and local governments have greatly expanded the national government's powers in areas previously regarded as *reserved* to the states. State and local governments became increasingly dependent on federal money. President Ronald Reagan's New Federalism temporarily slowed the growth of federal aid.

- Federal grants are available for most state and local government activities, but welfare, health, and highways account for about three-fourths of these grants.

- Federal power in local affairs grew as a result of federal rules, regulations, and guidelines established as conditions for the receipt of federal funds. Congress generally refrained from directly legislating in areas traditionally *reserved* to the states.

- The Supreme Court in its *Garcia* decision in 1985 removed all constitutional barriers to direct congressional legislation in matters traditionally reserved to the states. The Court said that states could defend their own interests through their representation in the national government.

- Representational federalism focuses on the role of the states in electing national officials—the president through the allocation of Electoral College votes to the states, the Senate through the allocation of two seats for each state, and the House through the appointment of representatives based on the state's population.

- Current efforts at the devolution of federal responsibilities for welfare center on transforming federally determined individual entitlements to aid into block grants to the states.

# SELECTED READINGS

BEER, SAMUEL H. *To Make a Nation: The Rediscovery of American Federalism.* Cambridge, Mass.: Harvard University Press, 1993. A historical account of the development of both federalism and nationalism in American political philosophy.

DYE, THOMAS R. *American Federalism: Competition among Governments.* Lexington, Mass.: Lexington Books, 1990. A theory of "competitive federalism" is developed to argue that rivalries among governments encourage improved public services and lower taxes, restrain the growth of government, promote innovation and experimentation in public policies, inspire greater responsiveness to the preferences of citizen-taxpayers, and encourage economic growth.

ELAZAR, DANIEL J. *The American Partnership.* Chicago: University of Chicago Press, 1962. A study of the historical evolution of federalism, stressing the nation-state sharing of policy concerns and financing, from the early days of the Republic, and the politics behind the gradual growth of national power.

OSTRUM, VINCENT. *The Meaning of American Federalism.* San Francisco: ICS Press, 1991. A theoretical examination of federalism, setting forth the conditions for a self-governing rather than a state-governed society and arguing that multiple, overlapping units of government, with various checks on one another's power, provide a viable democratic system of conflict resolution.

PETERSON, PAUL E. *The Price of Federalism.* Washington, D.C.: Brookings Institution, 1995. Historical, theoretical, and empirical perspectives merged into a new, timely model of federalism that would allocate social welfare functions to the national government and education and economic development to states and communities.

PETERSON, PAUL E., BARRY C. RABE, and KENNETH K. WONG. *When Federalism Works.* Washington, D.C.: Brookings Institution, 1986. A well-developed argument that the national government is more effective in managing and financing "redistributional" policies and programs, whereas state and local governments are more effective in providing "developmental" policies and programs.

RIVLIN, ALICE M. *Reviving the American Dream.* Washington, D.C.: Brookings Institution, 1992. A comprehensive plan to restructure responsibilities between the national government and the states. The federal government would turn over to the states most of its programs in education, highways, economic development, and job training, along with common shared taxes to finance state and local efforts to revitalize the economy. The federal government would focus on welfare, Social Security, and health care, as well as international relations.

# OPINION AND PARTICIPATION
# THINKING AND ACTING IN POLITICS

## CHAPTER OUTLINE

## FEATURES

## POLITICS AND PUBLIC OPINION

For most Americans, politics is *not* as interesting as football or basketball, or the sex lives of celebrities, or prime-time television entertainment. Although politicians, pollsters, and commentators frequently assume that Americans have formed opinions on major public issues, in fact, most have not given them very much thought. Nevertheless, **public opinion** commands the attention of politicians, the news media, and political scientists.

## ASK YOURSELF ABOUT POLITICS

1. Should political leaders pay attention to public opinion polls when making decisions for the country?
Yes ☐  No ☐

2. Do you believe that your representative in Congress cares about your personal opinion on important issues?
Yes ☐  No ☐

3. Can you name the two U.S. senators from your state?
Yes ☐  No ☐

4. Is our government really legitimate when only about half the people vote in presidential elections?
Yes ☐  No ☐

5. Did you vote in the 1996 presidential election?
Yes ☐  No ☐

6. Do you identify yourself with the same political party as your family?
Yes ☐  No ☐

7. Is it appropriate for religious leaders to try to influence how people vote?
Yes ☐  No ☐

8. Has your college experience changed your political views in any way?
Yes ☐  No ☐

9. Have you ever personally called or written to your representative in Congress?
Yes ☐  No ☐

By thinking about politics and acting on your political opinions—voting, talking to friends, writing letters, joining organizations, attending meetings and rallys, contributing money, marching in demonstrations, or running for office yourself—you are participating in politics.

127

Public opinion is given a lot of attention in democracies because democratic government rests upon the consent of the governed. The question of whether public opinion *should* direct government policy has confounded political philosophers for centuries. Edmund Burke, writing in 1790, argued that democratic representatives should serve the *interests* of the people, but not necessarily conform to their *will,* in deciding questions of public policy. In contrast, other political philosophers have evaluated the success of democratic institutions by whether or not they produce policies that conform to popular opinion.

Major shifts in public opinion in America generally translate into policy change. Both the president and Congress appear to respond over time to *general* public preferences for "more" or "less" government regulation, "more" or "less" government spending, "getting tough on crime," "reforming welfare," and so on.[1] But as we shall see, public opinion is often weak, unstable, ill-informed, or nonexistent on *specific* policy issues. This gives elected officials greater flexibility in dealing with these issues, and at the same time, increases the influence of lobbyists, interest groups, reporters, commentators, and others who have direct access to policy makers. Moreover, the absence of well-formed public opinion on an issue provides interest groups and the media with the opportunity to influence policy indirectly by shaping popular opinion.

Politicians read the opinion polls. And even though many elected representatives claim that they exercise independent judgment about what is best for the nation in their decision making, we can be reasonably sure that their "independent judgment" is influenced at least in part by what they think their constituents want. Public opinion commands the attention of politicians because even if only a small number of voters cast their ballots on the basis of the candidates' policy positions, those votes are still important. The cynical stereotype of the politician who reads the opinion polls before taking stands on the issues is often embarrassingly accurate.

All this attention to public opinion has created a thriving industry in public opinion polling and **survey research.** Polls have become a fixture of American political life (see *Up Close:* "Can We Believe the Polls?"). But how much do Americans really think about politics? How informed, stable, and consistent is public opinion?

*Knowledge Levels*   Most Americans do not follow politics closely enough to develop well-informed opinions on many public issues (see Figure 5-1). Low levels of knowledge about government and public affairs make it difficult for people to form opinions on specific issues or policy proposals. Many opinion surveys ask questions about topics that people had not considered before being interviewed. Few respondents are willing to admit that they know nothing about the topic and that they have "no opinion." Respondents believe they should provide some sort of answer—even if their opinion was nonexistent before the question was asked. The result is that the polls themselves "create" opinions.[2] For example, it is unlikely that many Americans have seriously thought about, or gathered much information on, such specific issues as Aid to Families with Dependent Children (AFDC) eligibility, Medicaid cost containment, or the capital gains tax.[3]

*The "Halo Effect"*   Many respondents give "good citizen" or socially respectable answers, whether they are truthful or not, even to an anonymous interviewer. This **halo effect** leads to an *underestimation* of the true extent of prej-

**Public opinion:** The aggregate of attitudes and opinions of individuals on a significant issue.

**Survey research:** The gathering of information about public opinion by questioning a representative sample of the population.

**Halo effect:** The tendency of survey respondents to provide socially acceptable answers to questions.

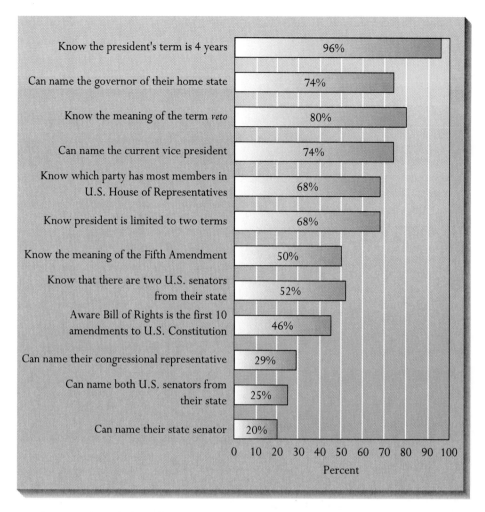

FIGURE 5-1 **What Do Americans Know about Politics?**
*Politics is not the major interest of most Americans, and as a result, knowledge about the political system is limited. Less than one-third of the general public know the names of their representatives in Congress or their U.S. senators, and knowledge of specific foreign and domestic matters is even more limited.*

Chart data:
- Know the president's term is 4 years — 96%
- Can name the governor of their home state — 74%
- Know the meaning of the term *veto* — 80%
- Can name the current vice president — 74%
- Know which party has most members in U.S. House of Representatives — 68%
- Know president is limited to two terms — 68%
- Know the meaning of the Fifth Amendment — 50%
- Know that there are two U.S. senators from their state — 52%
- Aware Bill of Rights is the first 10 amendments to U.S. Constitution — 46%
- Can name their congressional representative — 29%
- Can name both U.S. senators from their state — 25%
- Can name their state senator — 20%

Percent (0 10 20 30 40 50 60 70 80 90 100)

*Source:* Data reported in Michael X. DelliCarpini and Scott Keeter, "The U.S. Public's Knowledge of Politics," *Public Opinion Quarterly* 55 (May 1991): 583–612.

udice, hatred, and bigotry. A very common example of the halo effect is the fact that people do not like to admit that they do not vote. Surveys regularly report higher percentages of people *saying* they voted in an election than the *actual* number of ballots cast would indicate, and more people also claim to have voted for the winner of an election than actually did so (see Figure 5-2). Postelection surveys almost always produce higher percentages of people who say they voted for the winner than the actual vote tally for the winner. Apparently respondents want to be associated with the winner.

*Inconsistencies*    Since so many people hold no real opinion on political issues, the *wording* of a question frequently determines their response. People respond positively to positive phrases (for example, "helping poor people," "improving education," "cleaning up the environment") and negatively to negative phrases (for example, "raising taxes," "expanding governmental power," "restricting choice").

The wording of questions, combined with weak or nonexistent opinion, often produces inconsistent responses. For example, when asked whether they agreed or disagreed with the statement that "people should have the right to purchase a

# Can We Believe the Polls?

Survey research is a flourishing commercial enterprise. It is common in product marketing as well as in politics. There are national surveys, statewide surveys, and local market-area surveys. The national news media—notably CBS, NBC, ABC, and CNN television networks, the *New York Times* and the *Washington Post,* and *Time* and *Newsweek* magazines—regularly sponsor independent national surveys, especially during election campaigns. Major survey organizations—the American Institute of Public Opinion (Gallup), Louis Harris and Associates, National Opinion Research Center (NORC), the Roper Organization, National Election Studies (University of Michigan)—have been in business for a long time and have files of survey results going back many years. Political candidates also contract with private marketing and opinion research firms to conduct surveys in conjunction with their campaigns.

Public opinion surveys depend upon the selection of a *random sample* of persons chosen in a way that ensures that every person in the *universe* of people about whom information is desired has an equal chance of being selected for interviewing. National samples, representative of all adults or all voters, usually include only about 1,000 persons. First, geographical areas (for example, counties or telephone area codes) that are representative of all such areas in the nation are chosen. Then residential telephone numbers are randomly selected within these areas. Once the numbers have been selected at random, the poll taker does not make substitutions but calls back several times if necessary to make contact so as not to bias the sample toward people who stay at home.

Even when random selection procedures are closely followed, there is always a chance that the sample will not be truly representative of the universe. But survey researchers can estimate the *sampling error* through the mathematics of probability. The sampling error is usually expressed as a percentage range—for example, plus or minus 3 percent—above and below the sample response within which there is a 95 percent likelihood that the universe response would be found if the entire universe were questioned. For example, if 65 percent of the survey respondents favor the death penalty and the sampling error is calculated at plus or minus 3 percent, then

we can say that there is a 95 percent probability that a survey of the whole population (the universe) would produce a response of between 62 and 68 percent in favor of the death penalty.

The wording and sequence of the questions asked in any format are more an art than a science and can often determine the outcome of the poll. Indeed, "loaded" or "leading" questions are often used by *un*professional pollsters simply to produce results favorable to their side of an argument. They hope that by publicizing their results, they will create a "bandwagon effect," convincing people that most of the nation favors or opposes a particular candidate or viewpoint and therefore others should do so as well. Consider, for example, Reverend Jerry Falwell's poll asking: "Do you believe that smut peddlers should be protected by the courts and Congress, so they can openly sell pornographic materials to your children?" The overwhelming no response results were sent to Congress to influence legislation. Liberal Democratic pollster Lou Harris once asked:

> As you know, residents near the Love Canal, in the Niagara Falls, New York area, were reported to have stillbirths, cancer, deformed children, and chromosome damage as a result of the dumping of hazardous chemical wastes. How serious a problem do you think the dumping of toxic chemicals is in the country today—very serious, only somewhat serious, or hardly serious at all?

The only real surprise was that, after so obviously biased an introduction, there were still some people (7 percent of the total) who answered "hardly serious at all."

Professional pollsters strive for questions that are clear and precise, easily understood by the respondents, and as neutral and unbiased as possible. Nevertheless, because all questions have a potential bias, it is often better to examine *changes over time* in response to identically worded questions. Perhaps the best-known continuing question in public opinion polling is the presidential approval rating: "Do you approve or disapprove of the way _____ is handling his job as President?" Changes over time in public response to this question alert scholars, commentators, and presidents themselves to their public standing (see Chapter 11).

Weakly held opinions are more likely to change than strongly held opinions. Political commentators sometimes say that a particular candidate's support is "soft," meaning that his or her supporters are not very intense in their commitment, and, therefore, the polls could swing quickly away from the candidate.

Finally, widely reported news events may change public opinion very rapidly. A survey can only measure opinions at the time it is taken. A few days later public opinion may change, especially if major events are receiving heavy television coverage. Some political pollsters conduct continuous surveys until election night in order to catch last-minute opinion changes.

A common test of the accuracy of survey research is the comparison of the actual vote in presidential elections to the predictions made by the major polls (see figure). Discrepancies between the actual and predicted vote percentages are sometimes used as rough measures of the validity of surveys. Most forecasts have been fairly accurate, but the 1980 Carter-Reagan presidential contest was an exception. Opinion was extraordinarily volatile during the campaign; the lead changed several times. Last-day media coverage of the one-year anniversary of the Iranian seizure of the U.S. embassy and the continued detention of American personnel reminded people of Carter's weaknesses. Polling conducted on Sunday failed to catch persons who switched to Reagan by Tuesday (election day). It was not a problem of sample size or accuracy, but rather of rapidly changing voter opinion.

**Forecasting Errors by Major Polls in Presidential Elections**

| | Predicted Winner | Actual Winner | Error |
|---|---|---|---|
| **1996** | CLINTON | CLINTON | **1996** |
| USA Today/CNN | 52% | 49% | 3% |
| CBS/NY Times | 53% | | 4% |
| **1992** | CLINTON | CLINTON | **1992** |
| USA Today/CNN | 44% | 43% | 1% |
| Gallup | 44% | | 1% |
| **1988** | BUSH | BUSH | **1988** |
| USA Today/CNN | 55% | 54% | 1% |
| CBS/NY Times | 53% | | 1% |
| **1984** | REAGAN | REAGAN | **1984** |
| Gallup | 59.3% | | 0.3% |
| CBS/NY Times | 60.9% | 59% | 1.9% |
| ABC/Washington Post | 59.3% | | 0.3% |
| **1980** | REAGAN | REAGAN | **1980** |
| Gallup | 47% | | 4.7% |
| CBS/NY Times | 48.9% | 51.7% | 2.8% |
| NBC/AP | 48% | | 3.7% |
| **1976** | CARTER | CARTER | **1976** |
| Gallup | 48% | | 2% |
| Roper | 51% | 50% | 1% |
| NBC | 49% | | 1% |

60 50 40 30 20 10 0          0 10 20 30 40 50 60

Percent

FIGURE 5-2  Halo Effects in Reported Presidential Voting

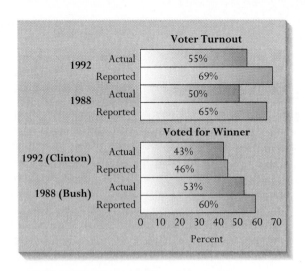

*The halo effect in survey research—the tendency of respondents to give socially acceptable answers—is easily observable in voter surveys. Many more people claim to have voted and also to have voted for the winner than actually did so.*

*Source: General Social Survey, 1994* (Chicago: National Opinion Research Center, 1995).

sexually explicit book, magazine, or movie, if that's what they want to do," an overwhelming 80 percent endorsed the statement. However, when the same respondents were also asked whether they agreed with the opposite statement that "community authorities should be able to prohibit the selling of magazines or movies they consider to be pornographic," 65 percent approved of this view as well.[4]

*Instability*    Many people answer survey questions "off the top of their head," without very serious consideration. They may hold fairly fixed attitudes—liberal or conservative, for example—but they do not bother to mentally consult their attitude when responding to a question. This often results in an apparent instability of opinions—people giving contradictory responses to the same question when asked it at different times.[5]

*Salience*    People are likely to think about issues that receive a great deal of attention in the mass media—television, newspapers, magazines. **Salient issues** are those that people think about most—issues on which they hold stronger and more stable opinions. These are issues that people feel relate directly to their own

**Salient issues:** Issues about which most people have an opinion.

PEANUTS reprinted by permission of UFS, Inc.

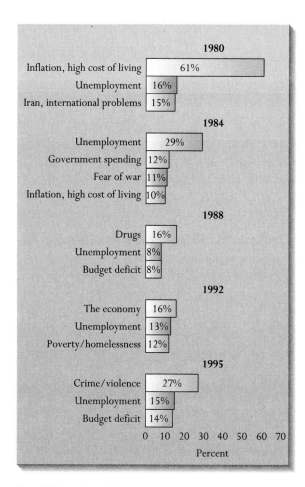

**FIGURE 5-3**  **What's to Worry About?**

*Public concerns shift over time, as indicated by changing responses to the question "What is the most important problem facing America?" In recent years, Americans have been alternately concerned about inflation, unemployment, drugs and crime, and, most recently, the economy and budget deficit.*

**1980**

| | |
|---|---|
| Inflation, high cost of living | 61% |
| Unemployment | 16% |
| Iran, international problems | 15% |

**1984**

| | |
|---|---|
| Unemployment | 29% |
| Government spending | 12% |
| Fear of war | 11% |
| Inflation, high cost of living | 10% |

**1988**

| | |
|---|---|
| Drugs | 16% |
| Unemployment | 8% |
| Budget deficit | 8% |

**1992**

| | |
|---|---|
| The economy | 16% |
| Unemployment | 13% |
| Poverty/homelessness | 12% |

**1995**

| | |
|---|---|
| Crime/violence | 27% |
| Unemployment | 15% |
| Budget deficit | 14% |

0  10  20  30  40  50  60  70
Percent

*Source:* Gallup opinion polls.

lives, such as abortion (see *Up Close:* "Abortion: The 'Hot-Button' Issue"). Salient issues are, therefore, more important in politics.

Salient issues change over time. In general, during recessions the most salient issue is "Jobs, Jobs, Jobs!"—that is, unemployment and the economy. During inflationary periods, the issue is "the high cost of living." During wartime, the war itself becomes the public's principal concern. A gasoline shortage can turn public concern toward energy issues. The Gallup Opinion Organization regularly asks Americans what they think is "the most important problem facing America." The results are shown in Figure 5-3. Over time, public interest has shifted from war, to inflation, to unemployment, to drugs, to crime. These salient issues drive the political debate of the times.

# SOCIALIZATION: THE ORIGINS OF POLITICAL OPINIONS

Where do people acquire their political opinions? Political **socialization** is the learning of political values, beliefs, and opinions (see *Compared to What?* "How 'Exceptional' Is Opinion in America?" for a look at the results of different social-

**Socialization:** The learning of values, beliefs, and opinions.

# Abortion:
# The "Hot-Button" Issue

While public opinion may be weak or nonexistent on many policy questions, there are a few "hot-button" issues in politics—issues on which virtually everyone has an opinion and many feel very intensely about.

Abortion is one such highly sensitive issue. Both *"pro-choice"* proponents of legalized abortion and *"pro-life"* opponents claim to have public opinion on their side. *Interpretation* of the poll results becomes a political activity itself. Consider, for example, responses to the *general* question posed in the graph below.

*Pro-choice* forces interpret these results as overwhelming support for legalized abortion, while *pro-life* commentators interpret these results as majority support for restricting abortion. Indeed, when the question sets forth *specific restrictions on* abortion, public opinion appears divided (see graphs on facing page.

In short, most Americans appear to want to keep some abortions legal but to place government restrictions on the practice.

*Sources:* Data derived from reports in *New York Times,* April 26, 1989; *Newsweek,* July 17, 1989; *American Enterprise* 3 (May/June, 1992): 100; National Opinion Research Center, *General Social Survey, 1994.*

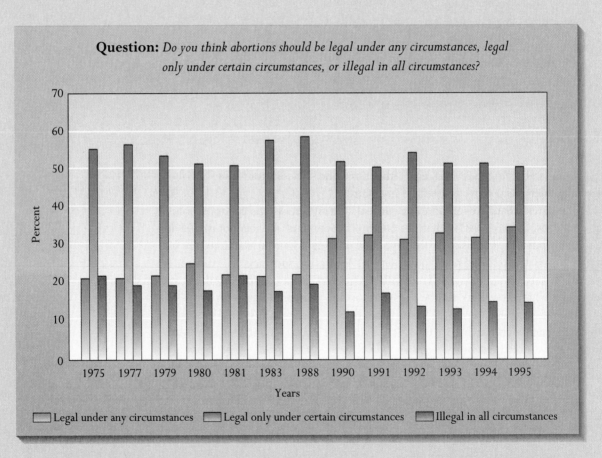

**Question:** *Do you think abortions should be legal under any circumstances, legal only under certain circumstances, or illegal in all circumstances?*

☐ Legal under any circumstances ☐ Legal only under certain circumstances ☐ Illegal in all circumstances

*Source:* Gallup Organization and National Opinion Research Center, as reported in *American Enterprise* 6 (July/August 1995): 107.

**Question:** *Please tell me whether or not you think it should be possible for a pregnant woman to obtain a legal abortion:*

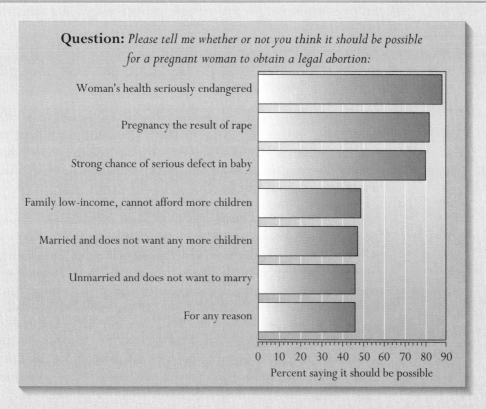

Woman's health seriously endangered

Pregnancy the result of rape

Strong chance of serious defect in baby

Family low-income, cannot afford more children

Married and does not want any more children

Unmarried and does not want to marry

For any reason

0 10 20 30 40 50 60 70 80 90

Percent saying it should be possible

---

**Question:** *Would you support or oppose the following restrictions on abortion that may come before state legislatures?*

| Support | | Oppose | Percent Difference |
|---|---|---|---|
| 54% | Medical tests must show fetus unable to survive outside womb | 33% | 21% |
| 75% | Teenagers must have parent's permission | 22% | 53% |
| 88% | Women seeking abortions must be counseled on dangers, alternatives | 9% | 79% |
| 73% | Women seeking abortions must wait 24 hours before having procedure | 27% | 46% |
| 61% | No public funds for abortion except to save a woman's life | 34% | 27% |

100 90 80 70 60 50 40 30 20 10 0          0 10 20 30 40 50 60 70 80 90 100

ization patterns in other lands). It begins early in life when a child acquires images and attitudes toward public authority. Preschool children see "police officer" and "president" as powerful yet benevolent "helpers." These figures—police officer and president—are usually the first recognized sources of authority above the parents that must be obeyed. They are usually positive images of authority at these early ages:

> Q: What does the policeman do?. . .
> A: He catches bad people.[6]

Even the American flag is recognized by most U.S. preschoolers, who pick it out when asked, "Which flag is your favorite?" These early positive perceptions about political figures and symbols may later provide *diffuse support* for the political system—a reservoir of goodwill toward governmental authority that lends legitimacy to the political order.

*Family*    The family is the first agent of socialization, and some family influences appear to stay with people over a lifetime. Children in the early school grades (3 to 5) begin to identify themselves as Republicans or Democrats. These childhood party identifications are almost always the same as those of the parents. Indeed, parent-child correspondence in party identification may last a lifetime; in one study, 66 percent of adult children who identified themselves as Democrats had parents who were Democrats, and 51 percent of the Republicans had parents with the same political identification.[7] Even the children who abandoned the party of their parents tended to become independents rather than identify with the opposition party. When parents disagree on party (one a Democrat, the other a Republican), the child is more likely to adopt the mother's party identification, though many cross-pressured children become independents. However, party identification appears to be more easily passed on from parent to child than specific opinions on policy questions. Perhaps the reason is that parental party identifications are known to children, but few families conduct specific discussions of policy questions.

*School*    Political revolutionaries once believed that the school was the key to molding political values and beliefs. After the communist revolutions in Russia in 1917 and China in 1949, the schools became the focus of political indoctrination of the population. Indeed, after World War II, U.S. military occupation forces "de-Nazified" schools in Germany and also introduced democratic principles into Japanese schools. Today political battles rage over textbooks, teaching methods, prayer in schools, and other manifestations of politics in the classroom. But there is no strong evidence of a causal relationship between what is taught in the schools and the political attitudes of students.

Certainly the schools provide the factual basis for understanding government—how the president is chosen, the three branches of government, how a law is passed. But even this elemental knowledge is likely to fade if not reinforced by additional education or exposure to the news media or discussion with family or peers.

The schools *try* to inculcate "good citizenship" values, including support for democratic rules, tolerance toward others, the importance of voting, and the legitimacy (rightfulness) of government authority. Patriotic symbols and rituals

# How "Exceptional" Is Opinion in America?

Do Americans differ much from Europeans in their social and political values? The American political culture places great value on individual liberty, limited government intervention in people's personal lives, equality of opportunity, and individual responsibility for one's own fate in life (see Chapter 2). The strong American commitment to these values has been labeled American "exceptionalism," suggesting that people in other nations, including the Western European democracies, are not as strongly committed to these values as are people in the United States.

The values of the political culture influence opinion on many specific issues. If the American political culture is truly "exceptional," Americans should differ significantly from Europeans on questions dealing with individual liberty, social mobility, and the role of government in society. And, indeed, cross-

national survey research results do show significant differences between Americans and Europeans on these issues (see table).

Americans believe strongly in an "opportunity" society where people get ahead by their own efforts. Other peoples are more committed to a "security" society where the government assumes principal responsibility for their well-being. For example, Americans are much less likely to agree that the role of government is to reduce income differences between people or to "provide everyone with a guaranteed basic income." Americans are less likely than others (with the possible exception of the independent-minded Australians) to believe that government "should provide a job for everyone who wants one." Americans are not even sure they want the government to protect them by requiring seat belts or prohibiting smoking, another indication of our preference for letting individuals determine their own fate in life. Finally, Americans, more than other free peoples, believe in the possibility of upward social mobility—"improving our standard of living."

| | Government should reduce differences between high and low incomes | Government should provide everyone with a guaranteed basic income | Government should provide a job for everyone who wants one | Wearing seat belts should be required by law | In my country, people like me have a good chance of improving our standard of living |
|---|---|---|---|---|---|
| **United States** | **29%** | **21%** | **45%** | **49%** | **72%** |
| Australia | 44 | 38 | 40 | 92 | 61 |
| Switzerland | 43 | 43 | 50 | NA | 59 |
| Great Britain | 64 | 61 | 59 | 80 | 37 |
| Netherlands | 65 | 50 | 75 | NA | 26 |
| Germany | 61 | 56 | 77 | 82 | 40 |
| Austria | 81 | 57 | 80 | 81 | 47 |
| Italy | 82 | 67 | 82 | 81 | 45 |
| Hungary | 80 | 79 | 92 | NA | 33 |

*Source:* Surveys for the International Social Survey Program by National Opinion Research Center (United States); by Social and Community Planning Research, London (Great Britain); by Zentrum fur Umfragen, Methoden, und Analysen, Mannheim (West Germany); by Ricerca Sociale e di Marketing, Milan (Italy); by Institute fur Soziologie, Graz University (Austria); by Australian National Research School of Social Sciences. Reported in *American Enterprise* I (March/April 1990): 115–117.
NA = not asked

abound in the classroom—the flag, the Pledge of Allegiance—and students are taught to respect the institutions of government. Generally the younger the student, the more positive the attitudes expressed toward political authority, as illustrated by one third-grader:

Q: What does the president do?

A: He runs the government, he decides the decisions . . . and he goes to meetings and tries to make peace and things like that.

Q: And what kind of person do you think he is?

A: Well, usually he's an honest one.

Q: Anything else?

A: Well, loyal and usually pretty smart.

Q: Why would he take the job?

A: Well, he loves his country and he wants his country to live in peace.[8]

Despite the efforts of the schools to inspire support for the political system, distrust and cynicism creep in during the high school years. While American youth retain a generally positive view of the political system, they share with adults increasing skepticism toward specific institutions and practices. During high school students acquire some ability to think along liberal-conservative dimensions. The college experience appears to produce a "liberalizing" effect: college seniors tend to be more liberal than entering freshmen (see *What Do You Think?* "College Students' Opinions"). But over the years following graduation, liberal views tend to moderate.

Why aren't the schools more effective in socializing students to democratic values? One explanation focuses on "the hidden curriculum"—the decidedly author-

## TABLE 5-1    EDUCATION AND TOLERANCE

| Tolerance | Percentage Allowing Speech, Book, Teaching (by highest degree completed) | | | | |
| --- | --- | --- | --- | --- | --- |
| | No High School | High School | Junior College | College Degree | Total |
| *If such a person wanted to make a speech in your community, should he be allowed to speak?* | | | | | |
| Atheist | 52% | 73% | 78% | 86% | 73% |
| Racist | 47 | 61 | 60 | 73 | 61 |
| Homosexual | 59 | 79 | 84 | 91 | 79 |
| *Should such a book be allowed to remain in public library?* | | | | | |
| That was against churches and religion | 47% | 69% | 75% | 81% | 69 |
| That said blacks are inferior | 49 | 65 | 67 | 75 | 66 |
| That favored homosexuality | 45 | 69 | 72 | 83 | 68 |
| *Should such a person be allowed to teach in a college or university?* | | | | | |
| Atheist | 31% | 50% | 54% | 68% | 52% |
| Racist | 33 | 41 | 45 | 52 | 42 |
| Homosexual | 47 | 71 | 79 | 83 | 71 |

*Source: General Social Survey, 1994 (Chicago: National Opinion Research Center, 1995).*

itarian structure of the classroom and the school itself. The school may teach individual participation in decision making, majority rule, respect for the rights of others, and political equality, yet the school itself is hierarchically organized, students do not elect their teachers or decide the curriculum, and they are not equal in power to the teacher or principal. Hence it is argued that this hidden curriculum undermines democratic values. Students are aware of the difference between what is taught and what is practiced.

Although there is no direct evidence that the schools can inculcate democratic values, people with more education tend to be more tolerant than those with less education and to be generally more supportive of the political system (see Table 5-1). This pattern suggests that the effects of schooling are gradual and subtle.

*Church* Religious beliefs and values may also shape political opinion. *Which* religion an individual identifies with (for example, Protestant, Catholic, Jewish) affects public opinion. So does *how important* religion is in the individual's life. It is difficult to explain exactly how religion affects political values, but we can observe differences in the opinions expressed by Protestants, Catholics, and Jews; by people who say their religious beliefs are strong versus those who say they are not; and between fundamentalists (those who believe in literal interpretation of the Bible) and nonfundamentalists. Religion shapes political attitudes on a variety of issues, including abortion, drugs, the death penalty, homosexuality, and prayer in public schools[9] (see Table 5-2). Religion also plays a measurable role in political ideology (see *What Do You Think?* "Should We Mix Politics and Religion?").

*Generational and Life-Cycle Effects* Age group differences in opinion occur on some important issues. This "generation gap" may be a product of **generational effects**—historical events that affect the views of those who lived through them. For example, the "Depression generation"—those persons who grew up during the Great Depression of the 1930s—may give greater support to government income-security programs because of this experience. The "baby boomers"—those persons who were born in the high-birth-rate years following

**Generational effects:**
Historical events that affect the views of those who lived through them.

TABLE 5-2    RELIGION AND PUBLIC OPINION

| Opinion | Affiliation | | | Faith | | Belief That the Bible Is | | |
|---|---|---|---|---|---|---|---|---|
| | Protestant | Catholic | Jew | Strong | Not Very | Literal Word of God | Inspired by God | A Book of Fables |
| Abortion for any reason should be legal | 40% | 33% | 94% | 28% | 55% | 29% | 44% | 74% |
| Legalize marijuana | 19 | 21 | 41 | 13 | 29 | 12 | 22 | 43 |
| Support death penalty | 75 | 76 | 70 | 68 | 80 | 69 | 79 | 72 |
| Remove book that favored homosexuality from library | 34 | 22 | 6 | 36 | 23 | 43 | 20 | 17 |
| Support prayer in public school | 67 | 55 | 14 | 70 | 53 | 77 | 55 | 33 |

*Source: General Social Survey, 1994* (Chicago: National Opinion Research Center, 1995).

# College Students' Opinions

College students' opinions today appear to be somewhat more conservative than they were a generation ago, although student opinion varies with the nature of the issue. Students today take a tougher line toward crime and drugs: they support the death penalty, believe the courts are too lenient with criminals, and oppose legalization of marijuana. The students of the 1970s confronted an unpopular war in Vietnam, faced a military draft, and were more likely to experiment with drugs and alternative lifestyles. Students of the 1990s confront greater economic competition and increased educational requirements for employment. Today students are more concerned with their financial future and raising a family than students were a generation ago, and less interested in "developing a meaningful philosophy of life" and keeping up with political affairs (see graph).

However, college students remain somewhat more liberal than the general population. Moreover, college seniors and graduate students are more liberal than freshmen; students at prestigious Ivy League universities are more liberal than students at state universities and community colleges; and students in humanities and social sciences are more liberal than students in engineering, physical sciences, and business. Over the years following graduation, many of these liberal predispositions tend to moderate.

The "liberalizing" effect of college may come about because of exposure to liberal professors (see Chapter 2, "Ideology on the Campus: Students versus Professors"). It may also be the result of greater exposure to the political culture. College students read more newspapers and magazines than nonstudents, watch more television news, and see and hear more political activity on the campus. They become aware of various reform movements—for example, civil rights, the women's movement, environmentalism—that noncollege people of the same age have little knowledge of. This "enlightenment" may directly promote liberal views: And even students who do not identify themselves with these movements learn what is socially acceptable and currently fashionable in educated circles.

*Source:* The American Freshman: National Norms for Fall 1972, 1980, 1994 (American Council on Education & UCLA), as reported in the *Chronicle of Higher Education,* January 13, 1995.

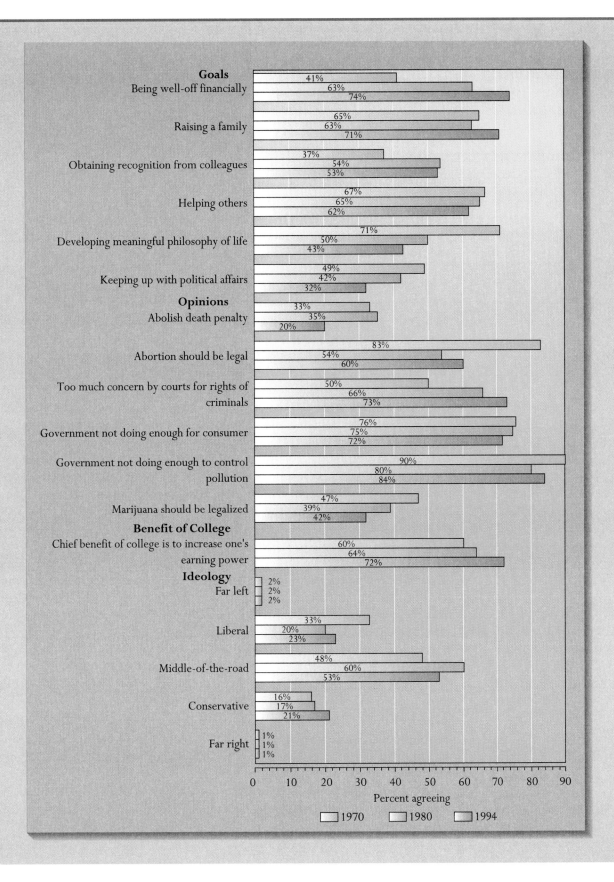

**Goals**
Being well-off financially — 41% / 63% / 74%

Raising a family — 65% / 63% / 71%

Obtaining recognition from colleagues — 37% / 54% / 53%

Helping others — 67% / 65% / 62%

Developing meaningful philosophy of life — 71% / 50% / 43%

Keeping up with political affairs — 49% / 42% / 32%

**Opinions**
Abolish death penalty — 33% / 35% / 20%

Abortion should be legal — 83% / 54% / 60%

Too much concern by courts for rights of criminals — 50% / 66% / 73%

Government not doing enough for consumer — 76% / 75% / 72%

Government not doing enough to control pollution — 90% / 80% / 84%

Marijuana should be legalized — 47% / 39% / 42%

**Benefit of College**
Chief benefit of college is to increase one's earning power — 60% / 64% / 72%

**Ideology**
Far left — 2% / 2% / 2%

Liberal — 33% / 20% / 23%

Middle-of-the-road — 48% / 60% / 53%

Conservative — 16% / 17% / 21%

Far right — 1% / 1% / 1%

0   10   20   30   40   50   60   70   80   90

Percent agreeing

☐ 1970    ☐ 1980    ☐ 1994

World War II (1946–64)—experienced the civil rights movement, the war in Vietnam, and changes in sexual morality, all of which may affect their views on many social issues.

The large size of the baby-boom generation makes their views especially important in politics. On some issues it is possible to identify a distinctive baby-boom generational viewpoint. For example, with regard to abortion, baby boomers are generally more supportive of legal abortion under various circumstances than either younger or older persons. However, over time much of the distinctiveness of the baby-boom generation has faded. As baby boomers have matured, their views have fitted more into common patterns of opinion.

A generation gap in opinion may also be a product of **life-cycle effects**—changes in life circumstances associated with age that affect one's views. Young people are expected to be idealistic. As they age and take on the responsibilities of raising children, holding a job, and paying a mortgage, they become more practical in outlook. The elderly are less amenable to social change, especially changes in morals. There is some limited evidence of life-cycle effects, but they are difficult to sort out from generational effects.[10]

*Media Influence*   Television is the major source of political information for the vast majority of Americans. More than two-thirds of Americans report that they receive "all or most" of their news from television (see Chapter 6). Moreover, Americans rate television the "most believable" channel of communication. For most Americans, newspapers, magazines, books, and radio are secondary to television as a source of political information.

But the effect of television on public opinion is not really in persuading people to take one side of an issue or another. Instead, the principal effect is in *setting the agenda* for thinking and talking about politics. Television does not tell people *what* to think, but it does tell them what to think *about* (see Chapter 6, "Mass Media: Setting the Political Agenda"). Television coverage determines matters of general public concern. Without coverage, the general public would not know about, think about, or discuss most events, personalities, and issues. Media attention creates issues, and the amount of attention given an issue determines its importance.

The media can create new opinions more easily than they can change existing ones. The media can often suggest how we feel about new events or issues—those about which we have no prior feelings or experiences. And the media can reinforce values and attitudes that we already hold. But there is very little evidence that the media can change existing values. (We shall return to the discussion of media power in Chapter 6.)

# IDEOLOGY AND OPINION

Ideology helps to shape opinion. Many people, especially politically interested and active people, approach policy questions with a fairly consistent and integrated set of principles—that is, an *ideology* (see Chapter 2). Liberal and conservative ideas about the proper role of government in the economy, about the regulation of social conduct, about equality and the distribution of income, and about civil rights influence people's views on specific policy questions.

**Life-cycle effects:** Changes in life circumstances associated with age that affect one's views.

# Should We Mix Politics and Religion?

The United States is one of the most religious societies in the world, in terms of the proportion of the people who say they believe in God (96 percent), who say God has guided them in making decisions in their life (77 percent), who say they belong to an organized religion (70 percent), who say that religion is "very important" in their own life (60 percent), and who say they attend church at least once a month (58 percent). Most Americans believe that religion should play an important role in addressing "all or most of today's problems" (64 percent), and they lament that religion is "losing its influence" in American life (69 percent).

At the same time, however, most Americans are concerned about religious leaders exercising influence in political life. Most respondents say that it is "*not* appropriate for religious leaders to talk about their political beliefs as part of their religious activities (61 percent), that "religious leaders should *not* try to influence how people vote in elections" (64 percent), and that "religious groups should *not* advance their beliefs by being involved in politics and working to affect policy" (54 percent).

Approximately 40 percent of Americans describe themselves as "born-again or evangelical Christians." They are much more likely than those who do not describe themselves in these terms (54 percent) to be Republican and conservative in their politics. Indeed, fundamentalist Christians, sometimes labeled as the "Christian right," "Christian conservatives," or "religious right" have become an important core constituency of the Republican Party. Their political strength centers on their grass-roots activism—their willingness to work hard as campaign workers, organizers, and fund raisers. Perhaps their most effective tactic in recent elections has been to produce and distribute nonpartisan "voter guides" that compare candidates on issues of interest to them, such as abortion, prayer in schools, and homosexuality. These guides do not endorse any candidates by name, but readers can easily determine who best represents the views of religious conservatives. Often these guides are distributed in churches on Sunday before election day.

But the political influence of Christian conservatives is limited by the American public's widespread view that religion and politics should not be mixed. Many church-goers as well as non-church-goers resent religious messages in the political arena. Religious broadcaster Pat Robertson fared badly as a candidate in the Republican presidential primaries in 1988. Moreover, it is difficult for "true believers" to reach out and form political alliances with groups that do not fully share their views. Fundamentalist Protestant groups have largely failed to unite with black fundamentalists or with Orthodox Catholics or Orthodox Jews. Social conservatives often find themselves at odds with economic conservatives, who often do not share their social issue agenda. Nevertheless, fundamentalist Christian groups have exercised some influence in state elections.

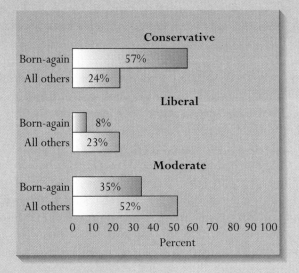

*Source:* Percentages from various Gallup opinion polls, reported in *American Enterprise* 5 (September/October, 1994): 90–93, and in *Gallup Poll Monthly,* February 1995; voter research surveys, 1992, reported in *American Enterprise* 5 (September/October 1994): 95; case studies in South Carolina, Oklahoma, Virginia, Iowa, and Minnesota, reported in John C. Green, "The Christian Right in the 1994 Elections: A View from the States," *P.S.: Political Science and Politics* 28 (March 1995): 5–23.

| TABLE 5-3    IDEOLOGY AND OPINION | | | | |
|---|---|---|---|---|
| | *Percentage Agreeing* | | | |
| | *Liberals* | *Moderates* | *Conservatives* | *Total* |
| **Equality** | | | | |
| Government should reduce income differences. | 51% | 41% | 29% | 39% |
| Government should not concern itself with income differences. | 31 | 32 | 51 | 38 |
| **Courts' treatment of criminals** | | | | |
| Too harsh | 5 | 4 | 2 | 3 |
| Not harsh enough | 76 | 83 | 89 | 82 |
| About right | 13 | 8 | 6 | 9 |
| **Social Issues** | | | | |
| Favor legalizing marijuana | 34 | 22 | 15 | 23 |
| Favor school prayer | 43 | 60 | 67 | 58 |
| Oppose busing for racial balance in public schools | 52 | 63 | 71 | 63 |

*Source: General Social Survey, 1994* (Chicago: National Opinion Research Center, 1995).

To what extent do self-described liberals and conservatives differ over specific issues? Can we predict people's stances on particular issues by knowing whether they call themselves liberal or conservative? Generally speaking, self-described liberals and conservatives do differ in their responses to specific policy questions, although some take policy positions inconsistent with their proclaimed ideology (see Table 5-3). People who describe themselves as liberal generally favor governmental efforts to reduce income inequalities and to improve the positions of African Americans, other minorities, and women. Overall, it appears that ideology and opinion are fairly well linked—that the liberal-conservative dimension is related to opinions on specific policy questions.[11]

Yet it is also true that substantial percentages of self-described conservatives take liberal policy positions, and self-described liberals take conservative positions. These inconsistencies may show that significant portions of the population do *not* consistently apply ideological principles when determining their position on specific issues. The consistent application of ideology to policy issues may be more characteristic of the interested and active few than of the mass of citizens. Or these apparent inconsistencies may arise because people are focusing on different dimensions of liberalism and conservatism when they label themselves. That is, some people who label themselves conservatives may hold traditional social views about abortion, homosexuality, prayer in the schools, crime, and pornography, but they want government to guarantee economic security. The term *populist* is sometimes applied to these social conservatives–economic liberals (see Chapter 2). Or these same people may label themselves liberal based on their view of the role of government in the economy, even though they hold traditional views about social conduct. In short, a single liberal-conservative dimension may be inadequate for describing the ideology of Americans, and this inadequacy explains the apparent inconsistencies.

CHAPTER 5 • OPINION AND PARTICIPATION

# GENDER AND OPINION

**Gender gap:** Aggregate differences in political opinions of men and women.

A **gender gap** in public opinion—a difference of opinion between men and women—occurs on only a few issues. Interestingly, a gender gap does *not* appear on women's issues—abortion, the role of women in business and politics, whether a woman's place is in the home, whether one would vote for a qualified woman for president, or whether men are better suited for political office. On these issues, men and women do not differ significantly (see Figure 5-4).

**FIGURE 5-4**  **Searching for the Gender Gap**

*Men and women do not differ significantly on gender-related issues such as abortion, but they do tend to hold different opinions on other issues and in party affiliation, suggesting the influence of gender (or at least of gender socialization) on political opinion.*

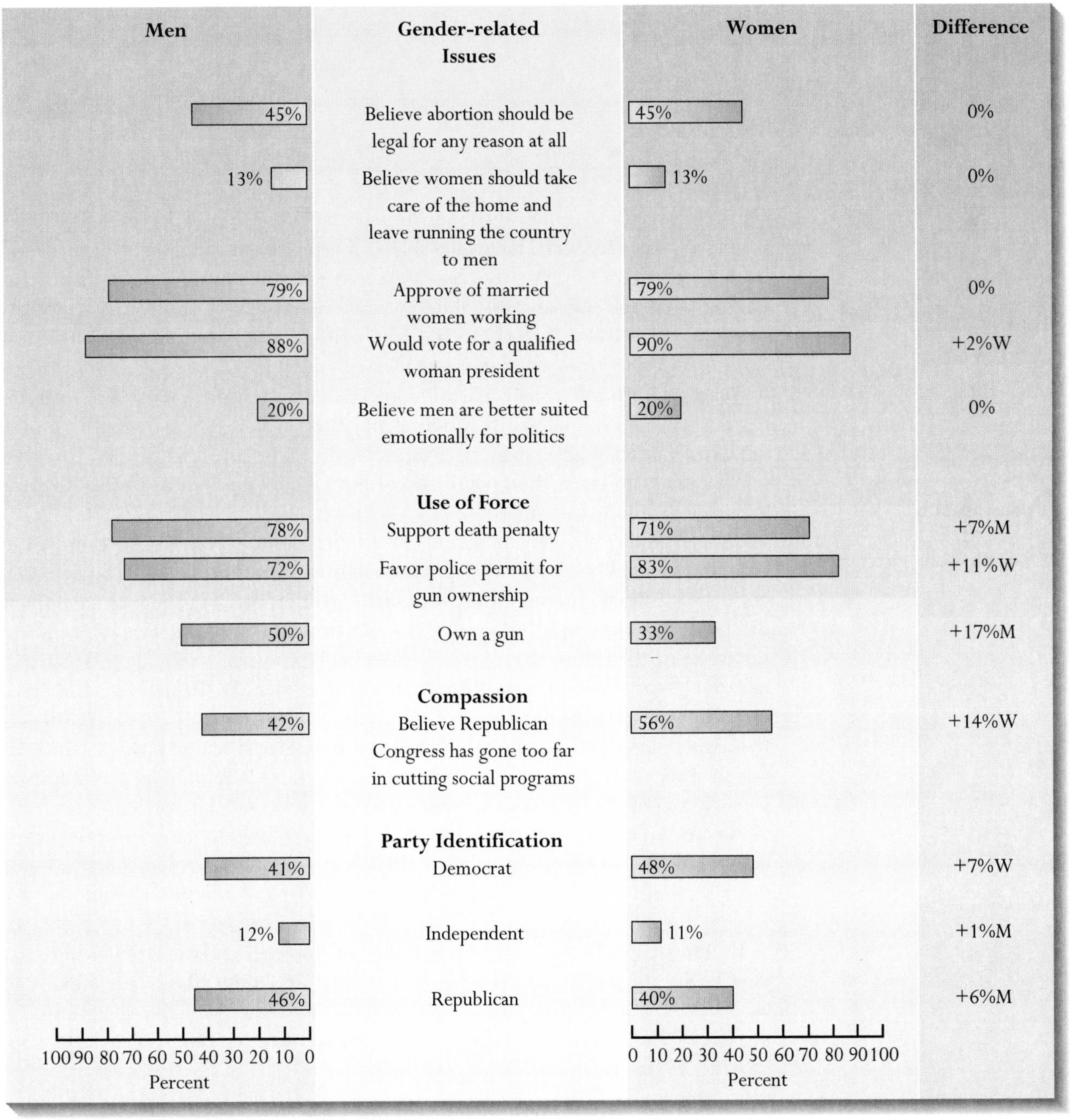

| Men | Gender-related Issues | Women | Difference |
|---|---|---|---|
| 45% | Believe abortion should be legal for any reason at all | 45% | 0% |
| 13% | Believe women should take care of the home and leave running the country to men | 13% | 0% |
| 79% | Approve of married women working | 79% | 0% |
| 88% | Would vote for a qualified woman president | 90% | +2%W |
| 20% | Believe men are better suited emotionally for politics | 20% | 0% |
| | **Use of Force** | | |
| 78% | Support death penalty | 71% | +7%M |
| 72% | Favor police permit for gun ownership | 83% | +11%W |
| 50% | Own a gun | 33% | +17%M |
| | **Compassion** | | |
| 42% | Believe Republican Congress has gone too far in cutting social programs | 56% | +14%W |
| | **Party Identification** | | |
| 41% | Democrat | 48% | +7%W |
| 12% | Independent | 11% | +1%M |
| 46% | Republican | 40% | +6%M |

100 90 80 70 60 50 40 30 20 10 0
Percent

0 10 20 30 40 50 60 70 80 90 100
Percent

*Source: General Social Survey, 1994.* (Chicago: National Opinion Research Center, 1995).

Instead, gender differences are more likely to appear on issues related to the use of force—for example, on gun control or the death penalty. While majorities of both men and women support both gun control and the death penalty, men appear to give less support to gun control and more support to the death penalty than women do. The greater propensity of men to endorse the use of force has also been observed in international affairs. Small differences between men and women have also been reported on "compassion issues," with women more likely to favor protection for the vulnerable members of society, including children, the aged, the ill, and the disabled.

Politically, the most important gender gap is in party identification. Women are more likely to identify themselves as Democrats, and men more likely to identify themselves as Republicans. This difference emerged in the 1980s, when men were more likely than women to support Republican President Ronald Reagan. (Group differences in party identification are discussed at length in Chapter 7.)

## RACE AND OPINION

Opinion over the extent of discrimination in the United States and over the causes of and remedies for racial inequality differs sharply across racial lines. Most whites believe that there is very little discrimination toward African Americans in jobs, housing, or education and that differences between whites and blacks in society occur as a result of a lack of motivation among blacks. Most blacks strongly disagree with these views and believe that discrimination continues in employment, housing, and education and that differences between whites and blacks in standards of living are "mainly due to discrimination" (see Figure 5-5). But there are important areas of agreement as well: few whites believe that blacks "have less inborn ability to learn," and majorities of both whites and blacks believe that the key to black success is education.

African Americans generally support a more positive role for government in reducing inequality in society. Approximately two out every three believe that government should do more to reduce income differences between rich and poor. Blacks favor busing to achieve racial balance in public schools, a view that is not shared by many whites. Given these preferences for a strong role for government, it is not surprising that more blacks than whites identify themselves as liberals. Note, however, that about one-quarter of blacks identify themselves as conservative. And indeed, on certain social issues—crime, drugs, school prayers—majorities of blacks take conservative positions. However, black support for the death penalty is significantly less than white support.

African Americans are much more likely than whites to support governmental actions and programs to improve the position of blacks and other minorities. Levels of support for affirmative action depend on the wording of the question, but regardless of wording, blacks are more likely to support racial and minority preferences than whites. For example, both blacks and whites say they "favor affirmative action programs in business," with blacks more likely to do so than whites. However, if the question specifies "preferential treatment" for blacks and minorities, whites oppose affirmative action, while blacks support it.

FIGURE 5-5  **Black and White Opinions**

*Blacks and whites differ over the extent of discrimination in America as well as over its causes and remedies. Blacks and whites also differ on economic issues, but are in fairly close agreement on a number of social issues.*

| Whites | Discrimination | Blacks | Difference |
|---|---|---|---|
| | Do you feel that compared to whites, blacks... | | |
| 72% | get equal pay for equal work? | 31% | +41%W |
| 51% | are treated equally by the justice system? | 17% | +34%W |
| | On the average, blacks have worse jobs, income, and housing than white people. Do you think these differences are because most blacks... | | |
| 21% | have less inborn ability to learn? | 16% | +5%W |
| 62% | do not have the motivation or will power to pull themselves out of poverty? | 36% | +26%W |
| 52% | don't have the education it takes to rise out of poverty? | 68% | +16%B |
| | Most people agree that, on the average, blacks have worse jobs, income, and housing than whites. Do you think the differences are... | | |
| 7% | mainly due to discrimination? | 70% | +63%B |
| | **Satisfaction with Financial Condition** | | |
| 31% | Pretty well satisfied | 18% | +13%W |
| 44% | More or less satisfied | 42% | +2%W |
| 25% | Not satisfied | 40% | +15%B |
| | **Government should reduce income differences between rich and poor** | | |
| 47% | Agree | 67% | +20%B |
| | **Favor busing for racial balance in public schools** | | |
| 29% | Agree | 60% | +31%B |
| | **Social Issues** | | |
| 84% | Courts are not harsh enough with criminals | 77% | +7%W |
| 80% | Oppose legalizing marijuana | 81% | +1%B |
| 54% | Favor school prayer | 69% | +15%B |
| 77% | Favor death penalty | 51% | +26%W |
| | **Affirmative Action** | | |
| 55% | Favor affirmative action programs in business for blacks and other minorities. | 82% | +27%B |
| 16% | We should make every effort to improve the position of blacks and other minorities even if it means giving them preferential treatment. | 67% | +51%B |
| 12% | Blacks and minorities should receive hiring preference to make up for past discrimination. | 51% | +39%B |
| 16% | Blacks and minorities should receive preference in college admissions to make up for past inequality. | 58% | +42%B |
| 74% | Chances are likely these days that a white person won't get admitted to a college while a less qualified black person gets admitted instead. | 24% | +50%W |

100  80  60  40  20  0
Percent

0  20  40  60  80  100
Percent

*Source:* Views on discrimination derived from data reported in *American Enterprise* 1 (January/February 1990): 96, 103; opinions on affirmative action derived from *American Enterprise* 2 (September/October 1991): 82–83; other questions from the *General Social Survey, 1994* (Chicago: National Opinion Research Center, 1995).

## POLICY AND OPINION

Does public opinion determine government policy? It is widely assumed that in a democracy government policy will be heavily influenced by public opinion. Yet, as noted earlier, public opinion is weak or nonexistent on many policy questions; it is frequently inconsistent and unstable; and it is poorly informed about many policy issues. Under these circumstances, political leaders—presidents and members of Congress, bureaucrats, judges, and other public officials—are relatively unconstrained by mass opinion in policy decisions. Moreover, in the absence of well-formed public opinion on an issue, other political actors—lobbyists and lawyers, interest group spokespersons, journalists and commentators, television reporters and executives—can influence public policy by communicating directly with government officials, claiming to represent the public. They can also influence public policy indirectly by molding and shaping public opinion.

The weakness of public opinion on many policy issues increases the influence of elites—that small group of people who are interested and active in public affairs; who call or write their elected representatives; who join organizations and contribute money to causes and candidates; who attend meetings, rallies, and demonstrations; and who hold strong opinions on a wide variety of public issues. According to political scientist V. O. Key, Jr., the linkage between ordinary citizens and democratic government depends heavily on "that thin stratum of persons referred to variously as the political elite, the political activists, the leadership echelons, or the influentials."[12] Thus political *participation* appears to be the essential link between opinion and policy.

## INDIVIDUAL PARTICIPATION IN POLITICS

Democracies provide a variety of ways for individuals to participate in politics. People may run for, and win, public office; take part in marches, demonstrations, and protests; make financial contributions to political candidates or causes; attend political meetings, speeches, and rallies; write letters to public officials or to newspapers; wear a political button or place a bumper sticker on their car; belong to organizations that support or oppose particular candidates or take stands on public issues; attempt to influence friends while discussing candidates or issues; and vote in elections. Individuals may also participate in politics passively, by simply following political issues and campaigns in the media, acquiring knowledge, forming opinions about public affairs, and expressing their views to others. These forms of political participation can be ranked according to their order of frequency (see Figure 5-6). Only a little more than half of the voting-age population votes in presidential elections, and far fewer vote in state and local elections.

## SECURING THE RIGHT TO VOTE

Popular participation in government is part of the very definition of democracy. The long history of struggle to secure the right to vote—**suffrage**—reflects the democratizing of the American political system.

**Suffrage:** The legal right to vote.

CHAPTER 5 • OPINION AND PARTICIPATION

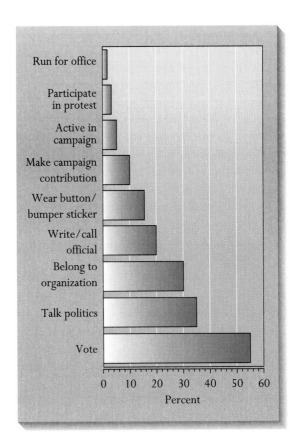

FIGURE 5-6 **Political Participation**

*Only a small percentage of the American people are actively engaged in the political process, yet they receive most of the media attention. Less than 1 percent of the population runs for office at any level of government, and only about half of all voting-age Americans bother to go to the polls.*

*The Elimination of Property Qualifications, 1800–1840*    The Constitution of 1787 left it to the states to determine voter qualifications. The Founders generally believed that only men of property had a sufficient "stake in society" to exercise their vote in a "responsible" fashion. However, the Founders could not agree on the wording of property qualifications for insertion into the Constitution, so they left the issue to the states, feeling safe in the knowledge that at the time every state had property qualifications for voting. Yet over time, Jeffersonian and Jacksonian principles of democracy, including confidence in the judgment of ordinary citizens, spread rapidly in the new Republic. The states themselves eliminated most property qualifications by 1840. Thus before the Civil War (1861–65), the vote had been extended to virtually all *white males* over twenty-one years of age.

*The Fifteenth Amendment, 1870*    The first important limitation on state powers over voting came with the ratification of the Fifteenth Amendment: "The right of citizens of the United States to vote shall not be denied or abridged by the United States or by any state on account of race, color, or previous condition of servitude." The object of this amendment, passed by the Reconstruction Congress after the Civil War and ratified in 1870, was to extend the vote to former black slaves and prohibit voter discrimination on the basis of race. The Fifteenth Amendment also gave Congress the power to enforce black voting rights "by appropriate legislation." The states retain their right to determine voter qualifications, *as long as they do not practice racial discrimination,* and Congress has the power to pass legislation ensuring black voting rights.

**White primary:** Democratic Party primary elections in many southern counties in the early part of the twentieth century that excluded blacks from voting.

**Literacy test:** An examination of a person's ability to read and write as a prerequisite to voter registration; outlawed by Voting Rights Act (1965) as discriminatory.

*Continued Denial of Voting Rights, 1870–1964*   For almost 100 years after the adoption of the Fifteenth Amendment, white politicians in the southern states were able to defeat its purposes. Social and economic pressures and threats of violence were used to intimidate many thousands of would-be black voters.

There were also many "legal" methods of disenfranchisement, including a technique known as the **white primary.** So strong was the Democratic Party throughout the South that the Democratic nomination for public office was tantamount to election. Thus *primary elections* to choose the Democratic nominee were the only elections in which real choices were made. If blacks were prevented from voting in Democratic primaries, they could be effectively disenfranchised. Therefore, southern state legislatures resorted to the simple device of declaring the Democratic Party in southern states a private club and ruling that only white people could participate in its elections—that is, in primary elections. Blacks were free to vote in "official" general elections, but all whites tacitly agreed to support the Democratic, or "white man's," Party in general elections, regardless of their differences in the primary. Not until 1944, in *Smith v. Allwright,* did the Supreme Court declare the white primary unconstitutional and bring primary elections under the purview of the Fifteenth Amendment.

From an estimated 5 percent of voting-age blacks registered in southern states in the 1940s, black registration rose to an estimated 20 percent in 1952, 25 percent in 1956, 28 percent in 1960, and 39 percent in 1964. But this last figure was still only about half of the comparable figure for white registration in the South. Despite the Fifteenth Amendment, many local registrars in the South succeeded in barring black registration by an endless variety of obstacles, delays, and frustrations. Application forms for registration were lengthy and complicated; even a minor error, like underlining rather than circling in the "Mr.—Mrs.—Miss" set of choices, as instructed, would lead to rejection. **Literacy tests** were the most common form of disenfranchisement. Many a black college graduate failed to interpret "properly" the complex legal documents that were part of the test.

*Passage of the Voting Rights Act of 1965 opened the voting booth to millions of black voters formerly kept from the polls by a variety of discriminatory regulations in the South. Here African Americans in rural Alabama in 1966 line up at a local store to cast their votes in a primary that focused on an issue central to their existence—segregation.*

White applicants for voter registration were seldom asked to go through these lengthy procedures.

**Poll taxes:** Taxes imposed as a prerequisite to voting; prohibited by the Twenty-fourth Amendment.

*The Civil Rights Act, the Twenty-fourth Amendment, and the Voting Rights Act, 1964–65*   The Civil Rights Act of 1964 made it unlawful for registrars to apply unequal standards in registration procedures or to reject applications because of immaterial errors. It required that literacy tests be in writing and made a sixth-grade education a presumption of literacy. In 1970, Congress outlawed literacy tests altogether.

The Twenty-fourth Amendment to the Constitution, ratified in 1964, made **poll taxes**—taxes required of all voters—unconstitutional as a requirement for voting in national elections. In 1966, the Supreme Court declared poll taxes unconstitutional in state and local elections as well.[13]

In early 1965, civil rights organizations led by Martin Luther King, Jr., effectively demonstrated against local registrars in Selma, Alabama, who were still keeping large numbers of blacks off the voting rolls. Registrars there closed their offices for all but a few hours every month, placed limits on the number of applications processed, went out to lunch when black applicants appeared, delayed months before processing black applications, and used a variety of other methods to keep blacks disenfranchised. In response to the Selma march, Congress enacted the strong Voting Rights Act in 1965. The U.S. attorney general, upon evidence of voter discrimination, was empowered to replace local registrars with federal registrars, abolish literacy tests, and register voters under simplified federal procedures. Southern counties that had previously discriminated in voting registration hurried to sign up black voters just to avoid the imposition of federal registrars. The Voting Rights Act of 1965 proved to be very effective, and Congress has voted to extend it over the years.

*The Nineteenth Amendment, 1920*   Following the Civil War, many of the women who had been active in the abolitionist movement to end slavery turned their attention to the condition of women in the United States. As abolitionists, they had learned to organize, conduct petition campaigns, and parade and demon-

*The turn of the century saw the acceleration of the women's suffrage movement. While Woodrow Wilson expressed support for granting the vote to women even before he took office in 1912, it took the activities of women "manning the homefront" during World War I to persuade the male electorate to pass the Nineteenth Amendment and give women access to the ballot box throughout the nation.*

strate. Now they sought to improve the legal and political rights of women. In 1869, the Wyoming territory adopted women's suffrage; later several other western states followed suit. But it was not until the Nineteenth Amendment was added to the U.S. Constitution in 1920 that women's right to vote in all elections was constitutionally guaranteed.

*The Twenty-Sixth Amendment, 1971*    The movement for eighteen-year-old voting received its original impetus during World War II. It was argued successfully in Georgia in 1944 that, as eighteen-year-olds were being called upon to fight and die for their country, therefore they deserved to have a voice in the conduct of government. However, this argument failed to convince adult voters in other states; qualifications for military service were not regarded as the same as qualifications for rational decision making in elections. In state after state, voters rejected state constitutional amendments designed to extend the vote to eighteen-year-olds.

Congress intervened on behalf of eighteen-year-old voting with the passage of the Twenty-sixth Amendment to the Constitution.[14] The states quickly ratified this amendment in 1971 during a period of national turbulence over the Vietnam War. Many supporters of the amendment believed that protests on the campuses and streets would be reduced if youthful protesters were given the vote.

*The National Voter Registration Act, 1993*    The National Voter Registration Act of 1993 mandates that the states offer people the opportunity to register to vote when they apply for driver's licenses or apply for welfare services. States must also offer registration by mail, and they must accept a simplified registration form prepared by the Federal Elections Commission. Finally, it bars states from removing the names of people from registration lists for failure to vote. Turnout gains from the act are likely to be modest.[15]

## WHY VOTE?

Deciding whether to cast a vote in an election is just as important as deciding which candidate to vote for. *Almost half of the voting-age population in the United States typically fails to vote even in presidential elections.* Voter **turnout**—the number of actual voters in relation to the number of people eligible to register and vote—is even lower in off-year congressional and state elections, when presidential elections are not held. Voter turnout in presidential elections steadily declined for several decades (see Figure 5-7). Then the three-way presidential race in 1992 reversed the downward trend, but the 55 percent turnout in that election was no higher than the 1972 level. Turnout in local elections (for example, city, county, school board) is even lower when these elections are held separately from national elections.

Why vote? Usually, this question is asked in the negative: Why do so many people fail to register and vote? But greater insight into the question of voter participation can be obtained if we try to understand what motivates the people who *do* go to the polls.

*The Rational Voter*    From a purely "rational" perspective, an individual should vote only if the costs of voting (time spent in registering, informing oneself about the candidates, and going to the polls) are *less* than the expected value of having

**Turnout:** The number of voters who actually cast ballots in an election, as a percentage of people eligible to register and vote.

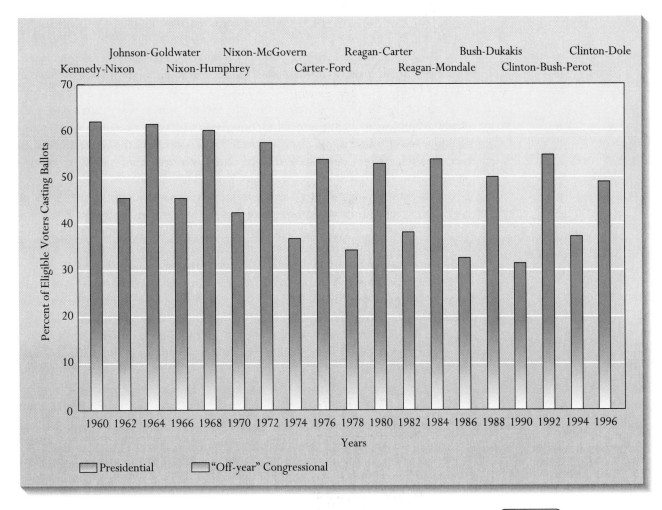

Johnson-Goldwater     Nixon-McGovern     Reagan-Carter     Bush-Dukakis     Clinton-Dole

Kennedy-Nixon     Nixon-Humphrey     Carter-Ford     Reagan-Mondale     Clinton-Bush-Perot

☐ Presidential      ☐ "Off-year" Congressional

**FIGURE 5-7**    **Voter Turnout in Presidential and Congressional Elections**

*Voter turnout is always lower in years without a presidential election. In addition, voter turnout has generally declined since 1960, even in presidential election years. The exception came in 1992, when intense interest in the contest between George Bush and Bill Clinton—spiced by the entry of independent Ross Perot—led to a higher-than-normal turnout. In 1996 fewer than half of voting-age Americans bothered to cast ballots.*

the preferred candidate win (the personal benefits gained from having one's candidate win), multiplied by the probability that one's own vote will be the deciding vote. Why vote when registering, following the political news, and getting to the polls take away time from work, family, or leisure activity? Why vote when the winner will not really change one's life for the better, or even do things much differently from what the loser would have done? Most important, why vote when the chance that one individual vote will determine who wins is very small? Thought of in this fashion, the wonder is that millions of Americans continue to vote.

The "rational" model can explain voter turnout only by adding "the intrinsic rewards of voting" to the equation. These rewards include the ethic of voting, patriotism, a sense of duty, and allegiance to democracy. People exercise their right to vote out of respect for that right rather than for any personal tangible benefit they expect to receive. They can look at the voting returns on television later in the evening, knowing that they were part of an important national event. These psychological rewards do not depend on whether a single vote determines the outcome. Millions of people vote out of a sense of duty and commitment to democracy.

*The Burden of Registration*    Voter **registration** is a major obstacle to voting. Not only must citizens care enough to go to the polls on election day; they must also expend time and energy, weeks before the election, to register. Registration occurs at a time when interest in the campaign is far from at its peak. It may involve a trip to the county courthouse and a procedure more complicated than voting itself. The registration requirement reduces voter turnout significantly. Approximately 85 percent of *registered voters* turn out for a presidential election, but this figure represents only 50 to 55 percent of the *voting-age population*. This discrepancy suggests that registration is a significant barrier to participation.

Registration is supposed to prevent fraud. Voters must identify themselves on election day and show that they have previously registered in their districts as voters; once they have voted, their names are checked off and they cannot vote again. Registration was adopted by most states in the early twentieth century as a reform designed to reduce the fraudulent voting that was often encouraged and organized by political machines. "Vote early and vote often" was the rallying cry of many party bosses, who sent their legions to the polls for repeated voting. (Registration did not end *all* voting fraud; some enterprising old party bosses continued to cast votes for registered persons who had died—"the tombstone vote"—or moved away.) But the trade-off for reducing fraud was to create an additional burden on the voter—registration.

## THE POLITICS OF VOTER TURNOUT

Politics drives the debate over easing voter registration requirements. Democrats generally favor minimal requirements—for example, same-day registration, registration by mail, and registration at welfare and motor vehicle licensing offices. They know that nonvoters are heavily drawn from groups that typically support the Democratic Party, including lower-education, lower-income, and minority groups. Republicans are often less enthusiastic about easing voting requirements, but it is politically embarrassing to appear to oppose increased participation. It is not surprising that the National Voter Registration Act of 1993, popularly known as the "Motor-Voter Act," was a product of a Democratic Congress and a Democratic president.

*The Stimulus of Competition*    The more lively the competition between parties or between candidates, the greater the interest of citizens and the larger the voter turnout. When parties and candidates compete vigorously, they make news and are given large play by the mass media. Consequently, a setting of competitive politics generates more political stimuli than does a setting with weak competition. People are also more likely to perceive that their votes count in a close contest, and thus they are more likely to cast them. Moreover, when parties or candidates are fighting in a close contest, their supporters tend to spend more time and energy campaigning and getting out the vote.

*Political Alienation*    People who feel that politics is irrelevant to their life, or who feel that they cannot personally affect public affairs, are less likely to vote than people who feel that they themselves can affect political outcomes and that these outcomes affect their life. Given the level of **political alienation** (two-

**Registration:** The requirement that prospective voters establish their identity and place of residence prior to an election in order to be eligible to vote.

**Political alienation:** The belief that politics is irrelevant to one's life and that one cannot personally affect public affairs.

thirds of respondents agree with the statement "Most public officials are not really interested in the problems of people like me"),[16] it is surprising that so many people vote. While alienation is high among voters, it is even higher among nonvoters.

*Intensity* Finally, as we might expect, people who feel strongly about politics and who hold strong opinions about political issues are more likely to vote than people who do not. For example, people who describe themselves as *extreme* liberals or *extreme* conservatives are more likely to vote than people who describe themselves as moderates.

*Explaining Turnouts* The general decline in U.S. voter turnout over the last several decades has generated a variety of explanations. This decline has occurred despite an easing of registration requirements and procedures over time. It may be a product of increasing distrust of government (see *What Do You Think?* "Can You Trust the Government?" in Chapter 1), which is related to political alienation. People who distrust the government are likely to feel that they have little influence in politics. They are therefore less likely to go to the trouble of registering and voting. The focus of the media, particularly television, on corruption in government, sex scandals involving politicians, conflicts of interest, waste and inefficiency, and negative campaign advertising may add to popular feelings of alienation.

Another explanation focuses on the expansion of the electorate to include young people eighteen to twenty-one years of age. Young people do not vote in the same proportions as older people (see Figure 5-8). After the electorate was expanded by the Twenty-sixth Amendment to include persons eighteen years of age and over, voter turnout actually dropped, from 60.9 percent in the 1968 presidential election to 55.2 percent in the 1972 presidential election, the largest turnout decline in successive presidential elections.

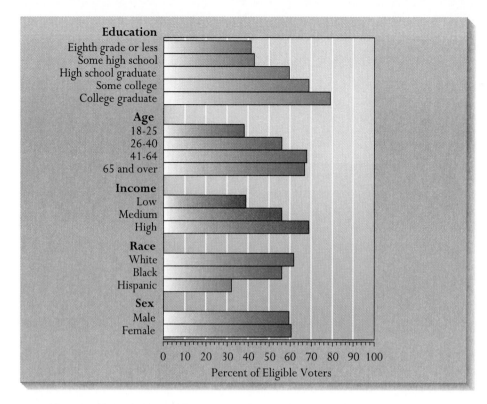

**FIGURE 5-8** **Voter Turnout by Social Groups**
*Although there is virtually no gender gap in who goes to the polls, voter turnout increases with education, age, and income. Major efforts to "get out the vote" in the African American community have raised voter turnout among blacks to nearly that of whites, but turnout among Hispanics continues to lag.*

*Source:* U.S. Bureau of the Census, *Census Population Reports,* Series P-20.

Still another explanation focuses on the declining role of party organizations in the political system. Strong party organizations, or *machines,* that canvassed neighborhoods, took citizens to the courthouse to register them, contacted them personally during campaigns, and saw to it that they got to the polls on election day have largely disappeared (see Chapter 7 and *Compared to What?* "Voter Turnout in Western Democracies.")

The rise in voter turnout in the 1992 presidential election is generally attributed to the presence in the race of a well-financed independent candidate, Ross Perot, and to popular concerns about the state of the economy. The Perot candidacy added interest and competition, as well as some uncertainty over the outcome. Perot also appealed to many people who tended to be distrustful of government and of the Democratic and Republican parties and to those who had not voted in recent elections. Moreover, slow recovery from recession worried many people during the election year, further motivating many to go to the polls and vote for change.

## VOTERS AND NONVOTERS

Who votes and who doesn't? The perceived benefits and costs of voting apparently do not fall evenly across all social groups. Nonvoting would generate less concern if voters were a representative cross section of nonvoters. But voters differ from nonvoters in politically important ways.

# Voter Turnout in Western Democracies

Other Western democracies regularly report higher voter turnout rates than the United States (see figure). Yet in an apparent paradox, Americans seem to be more supportive of their political institutions, less alienated from their political system, and even more patriotic than citizens of Western European nations. Why, then, are voter turnouts in the United States so much lower than in these other democracies?

The answer to this question lies primarily in the legal and institutional differences between the United States and the other democracies. First of all, in Austria, Australia, Belgium, and Italy, voting is *mandatory.* Penalties and the level of enforcement vary within and across these countries. Moreover, registration laws in the United States make voting more difficult than in any other country. In Western Europe, all citizens are required to register with the government and obtain identification cards. These cards are then used for admission to the polls. In contrast, voter registration is entirely voluntary in the United States, and voters must reregister if they change residences. Nearly 50 percent of the U.S. population changes residence at least once in a five-year period, thus necessitating reregistration.

Parties in the United States are more loosely organized, less disciplined, and less able to mobilize voters than are European parties. Moreover, many elections in the United States, notably elections for Congress, are not very competitive. The United States organizes congressional elections by district with winner-take-all rules, whereas many European parliaments are selected by proportional representation, with seats allocated to parties based on national vote totals. Proportional representation means every vote counts toward seats in the legislative body. Thus greater competition and proportional representation may encourage higher voter turnout in European democracies.

But there may also be cultural differences that contribute to differences in turnout. The American political culture, with its tradition of individualism and self-reliance and its reluctance to empower government (see Chapter 2), encourages Americans to resolve their problems through their own efforts rather than looking to government for solutions. Government is not as central to Americans as it is to Europeans, and therefore getting to the polls on election day is not seen as so important.

Voter turnout is substantially higher in most of the industrialized world than in the United States. In particular, nations such as Australia, where voting is mandatory, have very high turnouts. Ease of voter registration in most other nations also contributes to higher turnouts there.

*Source:* Congressional Research Service, reported in *Congressional Quarterly Weekly Report,* April 2, 1988, p. 863.

Voters are better educated than nonvoters. Education appears to be the most important determinant of voter turnout[17] (see Figure 5-8 on p. 156). It may be that schooling promotes an interest in politics, instills the ethic of citizen participation, or gives people a better awareness of public affairs and an understanding of the role of elections in a democracy. Education is associated with a sense of confidence and political *efficacy*—the feeling that one can indeed have a personal impact on public affairs.

Age is another factor affecting voter participation. Perhaps because young people have more distractions, more demands on their time in school, work, or new family responsibilities, nonvoting is greatest among eighteen- to twenty-one-year-olds. In contrast, older Americans are politically influential in part because candidates know they turn out at the polls.

High-income people are more likely to vote than are low-income people. Most of this difference stems from the fact that high-income people are more likely to be well educated and older. But poor people may also feel alienated from the political system. The poor may lack a sense of political efficacy; they may feel they have little control over their own lives, let alone over public affairs. Or the poor may simply be so absorbed in the problems of life that they have little time or energy to spend on registering and voting.[18]

Income and education differences between participants and nonparticipants are even greater when other forms of political participation are considered. Higher-income, better-educated people are much more likely to be among those who make campaign contributions, who write or call their elected representatives, and who join and work in active political organizations.[19]

Historically, race was a major determinant of nonvoting. Black voter turnout, especially in the South, was markedly lower than white voter turnout. Blacks continue today to have a slightly lower overall voter turnout than whites, but most of the remaining difference is attributable to differences between blacks and whites in educational and income levels. Blacks and whites at the same educational and income levels register and vote with the same frequency. Indeed, in cities where blacks are well organized politically, black voter turnout may exceed white voter turnout.[20]

The greatest racial disparity in voter turnout is between Hispanics and others. Low voter participation by Hispanics may be a product of language differences, lack of cultural assimilation, or noncitizenship status.

## NONVOTING: WHAT DIFFERENCE DOES IT MAKE?

How concerned should we be about low levels of participation in American politics? Certainly the democratic ideal envisions an active, participating citizenry. Democratic government, asserts the Declaration of Independence, derives its "just powers from the consent of the governed." The legitimacy of democratic government can be more easily questioned where almost half of the people fail to vote. That is, it is easier to question whether the government truly represents "the people" when only half of the people vote even in a presidential election. Voting is an expression of good citizenship, and it reinforces attachment to the nation and to democratic government. Nonvoting suggests alienation from the political system.

However, the *right* to vote is more important to democratic government than voter turnout. The nineteenth-century English political philosopher John Stuart Mill wrote, "Men, as well as women, do not need political rights in order that they might govern, but in order that they not be misgoverned."[21] As long as all adult Americans possess the right to vote, politicians must consider their interests. "Rulers in ruling classes are under a necessity of considering the interests of those who have the suffrage."[22] Democratic governments cannot really ignore the interests of anyone who can vote. People who have the right to vote, but who have voluntarily chosen not to exercise it in the past, can always change their minds, go to the polls, and "throw the rascals out."

Indeed, a huge army of nonvoters "hangs over the democratic process like a bomb ready to explode and change the course of history."[23] While some commentators view this latent "bomb" with alarm, others view it as a potential resource in hard times. The last major big surge in voting turnout occurred in 1932 in the midst of the Depression, when voters went to the polls in droves to oust incumbent Herbert Hoover and elect Franklin D. Roosevelt, who changed the role of government in the economy.

Voluntary nonvoting is not the same as being denied the suffrage. Politicians can indeed ignore the interests of people denied the vote by restrictive laws or practices or by intimidation or force. But when people *choose* not to exercise their right to vote, they may be saying that they do not believe their interests are really affected by government. The late Senator Sam Ervin is widely quoted on the topic of nonvoters:

> I'm not going to shed any crocodile tears if people don't care enough to vote. I don't believe in making it easy for apathetic lazy people. I'd be extremely happy if nobody in the United States voted except for the people who thought about the issues and made up their own minds and wanted to vote.[24]

But the "class bias" in voting presents another concern. It is frequently argued that greater overall turnout by better-educated, higher-income, older whites tilts the political system toward the interests of upper socioeconomic classes at the expense of poorer, less-educated, younger, black, and Hispanic people.[25] Thus, the people we would expect to be most in need of government help are least represented among voters. This underrepresentation not only harms their policy interests but contributes even further to their feelings of political alienation.

However, it is difficult to predict that major changes would occur in specific public policies if all socioeconomic groups voted with the same frequency. As we have already observed, rich and poor, black and white, often share the same opinions on policy issues or differ only in degree. The likely policy consequences of increased voter participation may be overestimated by scholars and commentators.[26]

## WHO ARE THE CITIZEN ACTIVISTS?

Political participation extends beyond voting to writing or calling public officials, making campaign contributions, working in campaigns, belonging to political organizations, regularly talking politics to friends, taking part in protests and demonstrations, and running for political office. Earlier we observed that only a

FIGURE 5-9    Mean
**Political Activity Scores**
*Citizen activists—people who vote, write or call public officials, make campaign contributions and work on campaigns, and join and become active in organizations—differ from nonactivists in educational level, income, ethnicity, ideological (liberal and conservative) commitment, and whether or not they receive middle-class government entitlements (Social Security, Medicare, and Veterans' benefits).*

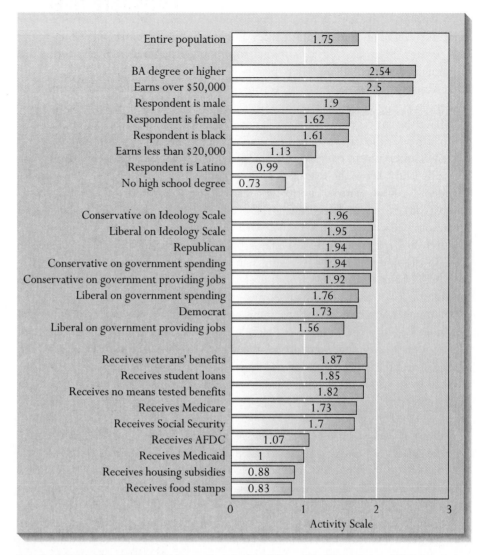

*Source:* Adapted from Sidney Verba, Kay Schlozman, Henry Brady, and Norman Nie, "Citizen Activity: Who Participates? What Do They Say?" *American Political Science Review* 87 (June 1993): 306.

small minority of Americans engage in these forms of political participation (see Figure 5-6 on p. 149)

Who are these **citizen activists?** Education and income differences between citizen activists and those who seldom or never engage in these activities are even greater than those that divide voters from nonvoters. Better-educated, higher-income people are much more likely to be among those who make campaign contributions, who write or call their elected representatives, and who join and work in active political organizations.[27] Moreover, people who receive middle-class government entitlements (Social Security, Medicare, and veterans benefits) are more politically active than those who do not, while those who receive welfare benefits (Aid to Families with Dependent Children, Medicaid, and food stamps) seldom engage in any political activity. Republicans are only slightly more active than Democrats. Finally, it is interesting to note that ideologically motivated people, both conservatives and liberals, are more active than middle-of-the-roaders (see Figure 5-9).

**Citizen activists:** People whose political participation extends beyond voting to other political activities.

# PROTEST AS POLITICAL PARTICIPATION

Protests, marches, and demonstrations are important forms of political participation. Indeed, the First Amendment guarantees the right "peaceably to assemble, and to petition the government for redress of grievances." A march to the steps of Congress, a demonstration in Lafayette Park across the street from the White House, a mass assembly of people on the Washington Mall with speakers, sign waving, and songs, and the presentation of petitions to government officials are all forms of participation protected by the First Amendment. (See *What Do You Think?* "What Forms of Protest Are Acceptable?")

**WHAT DO YOU THINK?**

## What Forms of Protest Are Acceptable?

America has a long history of protest activity. Beginning with the Boston Tea Party in 1773, when colonists illegally dumped a cargo of British tea into Boston harbor to protest an English tea tax, violent and nonviolent protest activities have accompanied nearly every major political movement in the nation's history. Nevertheless, many people disapprove of protest activity.

When Americans are asked whether or not they approve of various forms of protest, only the mildest activities win majority approval. A survey of opinion on ten forms of protest revealed that only "signing petitions," "attending lawful demonstrations," and "boycotting products" were approved by majorities of Americans. These activities, of course, are lawful. *Un*lawful protest activities—for example, "refusing to pay rent or taxes," "occupying buildings," "blocking traffic," "painting slogans on walls"—were widely disapproved of. And, as expected, violence was almost universally condemned (see graph).

Protesters must be cautious in their choice of activities. Otherwise they risk disapproval of their methods and perhaps tarnishing of their cause. Only a strong moral stand justifies illegal activities (civil disobedience), and violence is almost always counterproductive.

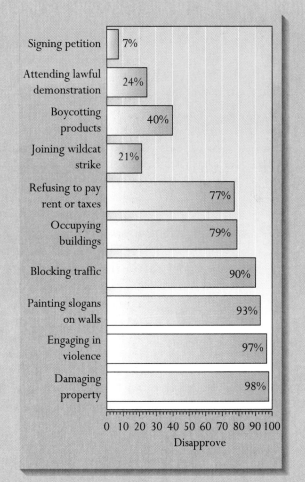

*Source:* Samuel H. Barnes and Max Kasse, eds., *Political Action* (Beverly Hills, Calif.: Sage Publications, 1979), p. 545.

*Protests*    **Protests** are generally designed to call attention to an issue and to motivate others to apply pressure on public officials. In fact, protests are usually directed at the news media rather than at public officials themselves. If protesters could persuade public officials directly in the fashion of lobbyists and interest groups, they would not need to protest. Protests are intended to generate attention and support among previously uncommitted people, enough so that the ultimate targets of the protest, public officials, will be pressured to act to redress grievances.

Coverage by the news media, especially television, is vital to the success of protest activity. The media not only carry the protesters' message to the mass public but also inform public officials about what is taking place. Protests provide the media with "good visuals"—pictorial dramatizations of political issues. The media welcome opportunities to present political issues in a confrontational fashion because confrontation helps capture larger audiences. Thus protesters and the media "use" each other to advance their separate goals.

Protests are most commonly employed by groups that have little influence in electoral politics. They were a key device of the civil rights movement at a time when many African Americans were barred from voting. In the absence of protest, the majority white population—and the public officials they elected—were at best unconcerned with the plight of blacks in a segregated society. Protests, including a dramatic march on Washington in 1963 at which Martin Luther King, Jr., delivered his inspirational "I Have a Dream" speech, called attention to the injustices of segregation and placed civil rights on the agenda of decision makers.

Protests can be effectively employed by groups that are relatively small in number but whose members feel very intensely about the issue. Often the protest is a means by which these groups can obtain bargaining power with decision makers. Protests may threaten to tarnish the reputations of government officials or private corporations, or may threaten to disrupt their daily activities or reduce their business through boycotts or pressure on customers. If the protest is successful, protest leaders can then offer to end the protest in exchange for concessions from their targets.

*Civil Disobedience*    **Civil disobedience** is a form of protest that involves breaking "unjust" laws. The purpose is to call attention to the existence of injustice. In the words of Martin Luther King, Jr., civil disobedience "seeks to dramatize the issue so that it can no longer be ignored"[28] (see *A Conflicting View:* "Sometimes It's Right to Disobey the Law," in Chapter 1). Those truly engaging in civil disobedience do not attempt to evade punishment for breaking the law but instead willingly accept the penalty. By doing so, they demonstrate not only their sincerity and commitment but the injustice of the law. Cruelty or violence directed at the protesters by police or others contributes further to the drama of injustice. Like other protest activity, the success of civil disobedience depends on the willingness of the mass media to carry the message to both the general public and the political leadership.

*Violence*    Violence can also be a form of political participation. Indeed, political violence—for example, assassinations, rioting, burning, looting—has been uncomfortably frequent in American politics over the years (see *A Conflicting View:* "American Politics as Violence," in Chapter 1). It is important to distinguish violence from protest. Peaceful protest is constitutionally protected. Often, orga-

**Protests:** Public marches or demonstrations designed to call attention to an issue and motivate others to apply pressure on public officials.

**Civil disobedience:** A form of public protest involving the breaking of laws believed to be unjust.

If a law violates the civil rights of a group of individuals, do they have not only a right but also a duty to disobey it? That was the argument advanced by the group of African American college students who sat down and asked to be served at a lunch counter in a Greensboro, North Carolina, Woolworth's store in 1960. Although jailed for their action, which violated segregation laws at the time, the young men's actions fueled the civil rights movement and helped bring about the end of segregation in America.

nized protest activity harnesses frustrations and hostilities, directs them into constitutionally acceptable activities, and thus avoids violence. Likewise, civil disobedience should be distinguished from violence. Civil disobedience breaks only "unjust" laws, without violence, and willingly accepts punishment without trying to escape.

*Effectiveness*    How effective are protests? Protests can be effective in achieving some goals under some conditions. But protests are useless or even counterproductive in pursuit of other goals under other conditions. Some generalizations about the effectiveness of protests:

- Protests are more likely to be effective when directed at specific problems or laws rather than at general conditions that cannot readily be remedied by governmental action.
- Protests are more likely to be effective when targeted toward public officials who are capable of granting the desired concession or resolving the specific problem. Protests with no specific targets, or protests directed at officials who have no power to change things, are generally unproductive.
- Protests are more likely to succeed when the goal is limited to gaining access or representation in decision making or to placing an issue on the agenda of decision makers.
- Protests are not always effective in actually getting laws changed and are even less effective in ensuring that the impact of the changes will really improve the conditions that led to the protest.

Public officials can defuse protest activity in a variety of ways. They may greet protesters with smiles and reassurances that they agree with their goals. They may disperse symbolic satisfaction without any tangible results. They may grant token concessions with great publicity, perhaps remedying a specific case of injustice while doing little to affect general conditions. Or public officials may claim to be constrained either legally or financially from doing anything—the "I-would-like-to-help-you-but-I-can't" strategy. Or public officials can directly confront the protesters by charging that they are unrepresentative of the groups they are trying to help.

## SUMMARY NOTES

- Public opinion commands the attention of elected public officials in a democracy, yet many Americans are poorly informed and unconcerned about politics; their opinions on public issues are often changeable and inconsistent. Only a few highly salient issues generate strong and stable opinions.

- Political socialization—the learning of political values, beliefs, and opinions—starts at an early age. It is influenced by family, school, church, age group, and the media.

- Ideology also shapes opinion, especially among politically interested and active people who employ fairly consistent liberal or conservative ideas in forming their opinions on specific issues.

- Race and gender also influence public opinion. Blacks and whites differ over the extent of discrimination in America, as well as over its causes and remedies. Men and women tend to differ over issues involving the use of force. In recent years, women have tended to give greater support to the Democratic Party than men have.

- Individuals can exercise power in a democratic political system in a variety of ways. They can run for public office, take part in demonstrations and protests, make financial contributions to candidates, attend political events, write letters to newspapers or public officials, belong to political organizations, vote in elections, or simply hold and express opinions on public issues.

- Securing the right to vote for all Americans required nearly 200 years of political struggle. Key victories included the elimination of property qualifications by 1840, the Fifteenth Amendment in 1870 (eliminating restrictions based on race), the Nineteenth Amendment in 1920 (eliminating

restrictions based on gender), the Civil Rights Act of 1964 and Voting Rights Act of 1965 (eliminating racial obstacles), the Twenty-fourth Amendment in 1964 (eliminating poll taxes), and the Twenty-sixth Amendment in 1971 (extending the right to vote to eighteen-year-olds).

- Nearly half of the voting-age population fails to vote even in presidential elections. Voter turnout has steadily declined in recent decades. Voter registration is a major obstacle to voting. Turnout is affected by competition as well as by feelings of political alienation and distrust of government. Young people have the poorest record of voter turnout of any age group.

- Voluntary nonvoting is not as serious a threat to democracy as denial of the right to vote. Nevertheless, the class bias in voting may tilt the political system toward the interests of higher-income, better-educated, older whites at the expense of lower-income, less-educated, younger minorities.

- Citizen activists—people who frequently contact public officials, work in political campaigns, and make political contributions—are much more likely to be well educated and ideologically motivated than politically inactive people. Activists are also more likely to be receiving middle-class government benefits.

- Protest is an important form of participation in politics. Protests are more commonly employed by groups with little direct influence over public officials. The object is to generate attention and support from previously uncommitted people in order to bring new pressure on public officials to redress grievances. Media coverage is vital to the success of protests.

# SELECTED READINGS

ASHER, HERBERT. *Polling and the Public: What Every Citizen Should Know,* 3d ed. Washington, D.C.: Congressional Quarterly Press, 1995. Explains methods of polling and how results can be influenced by wording, sampling, and interviewing techniques; also covers how polls are used by the media and in campaigns.

BARKER, LUCIUS J., and MACK H. JONES. *African Americans and the American Political System.* Englewood Cliffs, N.J.: Prentice Hall, 1994. An overview of African-American political participation and the responsiveness of the presidency, Congress, courts, parties, and interest groups.

BRACE, PAUL, and BARBARA HINCKLEY. *Follow the Leader: Opinion Polls and the Modern Presidency.* New York: Basic Books, 1992. An assessment of how presidential actions affect public opinion polls, and how presidents in turn are influenced by the polls.

CONWAY, M. MARGARET. *Political Participation in the United States,* 2d ed. Washington, D.C.: Congressional Quarterly Press, 1991. A comprehensive summary of who participates in politics and why.

ERIKSON, ROBERT S., NORMAN R. LUTTBEG, and KENT L. TEDIN. *American Public Opinion,* 3d ed. New York: Macmillan, 1988. A comprehensive review of the forces influencing public opinion and an assessment of the influence of public opinion in American politics.

GREENSTEIN, FRED I. *Children and Politics.* New Haven, Conn.: Yale University Press, 1985. Early research on what children know about politics and how they learned it.

PAGE, BENJAMIN I., and ROBERT Y. SHAPIRO. *The Rational Public: Fifty Years of Trends in Americans' Policy Preferences.* Chicago: University of Chicago Press, 1992. An argument that government policies generally reflect public opinion.

REICHLY, A. JAMES. *Religion in American Public Life.* Washington, D.C.: Brookings Institution, 1985. The impact of religion on American politics is reviewed from 1790 through 1985, with specific discussions of religious differences in public opinion.

STIMSON, JAMES A. *Public Opinion in America: Moods, Cycles, and Swings.* Boulder, Colo.: Westview Press, 1992. A systematic analysis of swings and cycles in "policy moods" that roughly correspond to liberal and conservative views toward the effectiveness of government in dealing with perceived problems.

WALD, KENNETH D. *Religion and Politics in the United States,* 3d ed. Washington D.C.: Congressional Quarterly Press, 1996. An explanation of the impact of religion on American political culture, the policy process, and voting behavior.

ZALLER, JOHN R. *The Nature and Origins of Mass Opinion.* New York: Cambridge University Press, 1992. An effort to develop and test a conceptual model of how people form political preferences, how political views and arguments diffuse through the population, and how people evaluate this information and convert their reactions into public opinion.

# MASS MEDIA
# SETTING THE
# POLITICAL AGENDA

## ASK YOURSELF ABOUT POLITICS

1 Are media professionals—news reporters, editors, anchors—the true voice of the people in public affairs?
Yes ☐  No ☐

2 Do the media mirror what is really news, rather than deciding what's important and making it news?
Yes ☐  No ☐

3 Is television a more believable source of news than newspapers?
Yes ☐  No ☐

4 Should the media report on all aspects of the private lives of public officials?
Yes ☐  No ☐

5 Do the media report equally fairly on Democratic and Republican candidates for office?
Yes ☐  No ☐

6 Should the media be legally required to be fair and accurate in reporting political news?
Yes ☐  No ☐

7 Are you more alienated than attracted by the media's coverage of politics?
Yes ☐  No ☐

8 Is your choice of candidates in elections affected by their advertising?
Yes ☐  No ☐

## THE POWER OF THE MEDIA

Politics—the struggle over who gets what, when, and how—is largely carried out in the **mass media.** The arenas of political conflict are the various media of mass communication—television, newspapers, magazines, radio, books, recordings, motion pictures, the Internet (see *Up Close:* "Media Is a Plural Noun"). What we know about politics comes to us largely through these media. Unless we ourselves are admitted to the White House Oval Office or the committee rooms of Congress or dinner parties at foreign embassies, or unless we ourselves attend political rallies and demonstrations or travel to distant battlefields, we must rely on the mass media to tell us about politics. Furthermore, few of us ever have the opportunity to personally evaluate the character of presidential candidates or cabinet members or

Ask yourself how much of your knowledge about politics in America comes from television and newspapers and the radio. What you know about politics and how you participate are, in fact, largely determined by the power of the media to decide what they want you to know.

FIGURE 6-1 **The National
News Media**

*A handful of media outlets in the
United States serve as the major
sources of news information for the
American public. Television is by far
the most influential source today,
with most Americans getting their
news primarily from TV. The growth
of cable television in recent years
has accelerated this trend, with
CNN becoming the "crisis network"—the place to turn to see a
war, an earthquake, or any other
major event.*

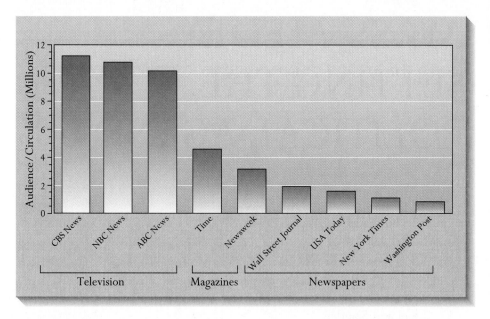

*Source:* Television viewers reported by A. C. Nielsen and Company for 1994; newspaper circulation for 1994 as reported in
*Editor and Publisher,* May 14, 1994.

members of Congress, or to learn their views on public issues by talking with
them face-to-face. Instead, we must learn about people as well as events from the
mass media.

Great power derives from the control of information. *Who knows what* helps to
determine *who gets what.* The media not only provide an arena for politics; they are
themselves players in that arena. The media not only report on the struggles for
power in society; they are themselves participants in those struggles. The media
have long been referred to as America's "fourth branch" of government, and for
good reason.

Media power is concentrated in the leading television networks (ABC, CBS,
NBC, and CNN), the nation's leading newspapers *(New York Times, Washington Post,
Wall Street Journal),* and broad-circulation news magazines *(Newsweek, Time,* and *U.S.
News and World Report)* (see Figure 6-1). The reporters, anchors, editors, and producers of these *prestige* news organizations constitute a relatively small group of
people in whose hands rests the power to decide what we will know about people, events, and issues.

Television is the most powerful medium of communication. It is the first true
*mass* communication medium. Virtually every home in America has a television
set, and the average home has the set turned on for about *seven* hours a day. More
important, television is "the most believable" source of news (see Figure 6-2). But
the power of television derives from both its large audiences and its ability to
communicate emotions as well as information. Television's power is found in its
visuals—angry faces in a rioting mob, police beating an African American
motorist, wounded soldiers being unloaded from a helicopter—scenes that convey an emotional message. Moreover, television focuses on the faces of individuals as well as on their words, portraying honesty or deception, humility or arro-
gance, compassion or indifference, humor or meanness, and a host of other
personal characteristics. Skillful politicians understand that *what* one says may not
be as important as *how* one says it. Image triumphs over substance on television.

**Mass media:** All means of
communication with the general
public, including television,
newspapers, magazines, radio,
books, recordings, motion
pictures, and the Internet.

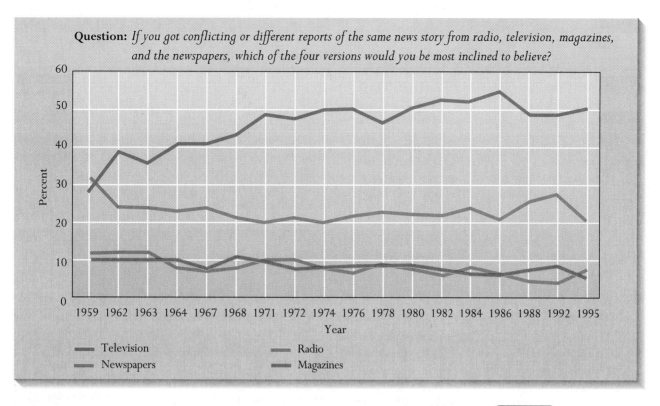

**Question:** *If you got conflicting or different reports of the same news story from radio, television, magazines, and the newspapers, which of the four versions would you be most inclined to believe?*

Television
Newspapers
Radio
Magazines

FIGURE 6-2  The Believability of News Sources

Media people themselves often deny that they exercise great power. They sometimes claim that they only "mirror" reality. They like to think of themselves as unbiased reporters who simply narrate happenings and transmit videotaped portrayals of people and events as they really are. Occasionally, editors or reporters or anchors will acknowledge that they make important decisions about

*Members of the media enjoy far greater access than most Americans to politicians, particularly national figures such as the president. Thus the media's presentation of these figures significantly shapes the political knowledge and opinions of average citizens.*

# Media Is a Plural Noun

For most of us, politics is a *mediated* experience. What we know about our political world comes to us not from personal experience but through the mass media. We can broaden our political knowledge by regularly monitoring all types of media.

*Television*   For many years, national television was dominated by three networks—American Broadcasting Company (ABC), Columbia Broadcasting System (CBS), and National Broadcasting Company (NBC). As late as 1970, they captured over 90 percent of the television audience. Today most of the nation's 1,000 local commercial TV stations remain affiliated with one or another of the networks. Local stations usually restrict themselves to local news coverage and then broadcast the network "feeds" of the "evening news" for national coverage. But technological developments, notably cable television and satellite broadcasting, destroyed the comfortable oligopoly of ABC, CBS, and NBC.

Today, two-thirds of the nation's homes have cable TV. Cable News Network (CNN), begun by independent entrepreneur Ted Turner, is a major competitor in news broadcasting; with its around-the-clock coverage, it dominates crisis reporting, as it did during the Gulf War. C-SPAN regularly broadcasts congressional proceedings and other Washington events. Other cable channels offer viewers a wide choice of sports broadcasting (ESPN), music (MTV), satellite "superstations" (Ted Turner's TNT), and pay television (HBO and Showtime).

*Radio*   The nation's 10,000 radio stations are about evenly divided between AM and FM band broadcasting. Most programming features music, but *talk radio* is growing in both listeners and political importance. Talk show hosts take telephone calls that often signal popular concerns and emotions. Often the hosts themselves are highly opinionated (for example, conservative Rush Limbaugh) and enjoy a national following.

*Newspapers*   Over 70 percent of the adult population read one or another of the nation's 1,600 daily newspapers. The nation's *prestige* newspapers—the *New York Times, Washington Post,* and *Wall Street Journal*—are regularly read by government officials, corporate chieftains, interest group leaders, and other media people.

*Magazines*   The leading weekly news magazines—*Time* (4.6 million), *Newsweek* (3.2 million), and *U.S. News and World Report* (2.3 million)—reach a smaller but more politically attentive audience. Magazines of political commentary—for example, the *Nation* (liberal), *New Republic* (liberal), *National Review* (conservative), *American Spectator* (conservative), *Public Interest* (neo-conservative), and *Washington Monthly* (neo-liberal, anti-establishment)—reach very small but politically active audiences. The newer *George,* edited by John F. Kennedy, Jr., offers light, breezy, people-oriented coverage of current politics.

*Motion Pictures*   Most of the 250 or so feature films produced and distributed in the United States each year are commercial ventures designed to attract theater-going (younger) audiences. Controversy over the effects of the sex and violence shown on the screen are almost as old as the movie industry itself. A system of industry self-regulation, with its *G, GP, R,* and *NC-17* (formerly *X*) ratings, was designed to deflect criticism and avoid government intervention.

A generation ago the movie industry generally avoided movies with a social or political "message." As one wit at a major studio quipped: "If I want to send a message, I use Western Union." But independent producers broke the major studio monopoly, and today Hollywood regularly produces movies with liberal social and political themes.

*Books and Recordings*   About half of all Americans claim to have read a book in the past year. About half of the 50,000 books published each year are textbooks for elementary or secondary schools or colleges and universities. Most of the "trade" books marketed in shopping mall bookstores across the country have little political content. However, a few books each year capture the attention of politically minded readers and help shape debate among opinion leaders. Most of the 700 million records sold each year, mainly to young people, feature romantic themes. But some popular recordings incorporate a political message. Folk music has a tradition of social protest; rap music often voices racial concerns; country music often reflects populist and patriotic themes.

*The Internet*    The newest of the media now in play in politics is the Internet. Its use is recent enough that formal studies of its effectiveness are just being begun. But people in public life—from the president, to members of Congress, to interest groups, to local party organizers—have taken advantage of its presence to establish Web "home pages" and bulletin boards, and all the major online services have "chat groups" for political exchange. Several large media companies have ventured onto the Internet with politically oriented Web sites. Time Inc. and Cable News Network have a site called All Politics (http://allpolitics.com), and ABC News, *The Washington Post, Newsweek,* and *The National Journal* have joined forces to produce Politics Now (http://www.politics.now.com).

*Source:* U.S. Bureau of the Census, *Statistical Abstract of the United States, 1995,* p. 572. Data for 1995-98 are projections.

The White House Home Page on the World Wide Web.

what stories, people, events, or issues will be covered in the news, how much time or space they will be given, what visuals will be used, and what sources will be quoted. They may also occasionally acknowledge that they provide interpretations of the news and that their personal politics affect these interpretations. A few media people may even recognize that they can set the agenda for political decision making by focusing special attention on particular issues. For example, *ABC World News Tonight with Peter Jennings* regularly incorporates a report entitled "The American Agenda" into its broadcasts. But whether or not the editors, reporters, producers, or anchors acknowledge their own power, it is clear that they do more than passively "mirror" reality.

## SOURCES OF MEDIA POWER

Government and the media are natural adversaries. (Thomas Jefferson once wrote that he would prefer newspapers without government to a government without newspapers. But after serving as president, he wrote that people who never read newspapers are better informed than those who do, because ignorance is closer to the truth than the falsehoods spread by newspapers.) Public officials have long been frustrated by the media. But the U.S. Constitution's First Amendment guarantee of a free press anticipates this conflict between government and the media. It prohibits government from resolving this conflict by silencing its critics.

Media professionals—television and newspaper reporters, editors, anchors, and producers—are not neutral observers of American politics but rather are active participants. They not only report events but discover events to report, assign them political meaning, and predict their consequences (see *People in Politics:* "Stars of the Network News: Rather, Jennings, and Brokaw"). They seek to challenge government officials, debate political candidates, and define the problems of society. They see their profession as a "sacred trust" and themselves as the true voice of the people in public affairs. As the celebrated Watergate reporter Carl Bernstein put it: "The job of the press is not to follow Ronald Reagan's or George Bush's agenda, but to make its *own* decisions about what's important for the country."[1]

*Newsmaking*　Deciding what is "news" and who is "newsworthy"—**newsmaking**—is the most important source of media power. It is only through the media that the general public comes to know about events, personalities, and issues. Media attention makes topics public, creates issues, and elevates personalities from obscurity to celebrity. Each day editors, producers, and reporters must select from millions of events, topics, and people those that will be videotaped, written about, and talked about. The media can never be a "picture of the world" because the whole world cannot be squeezed into the picture. The media must decide what is and is not "news."

Decisions about what will be news not only influence popular discussion but also cue public officials about topics they must turn their attention to. Politicians cannot respond to reporters' questions by saying, "I don't know," or "That's not important," or "No comment." Media attention to a topic requires public officials to respond to it. Moreover, the media decide how important an issue or person or event is by their allocation of time and space. Topics that are given early place-

**Newsmaking:** Deciding what events, topics, presentations, and issues will be given coverage in the news.

## Stars of the Network News: Rather, Jennings, and Brokaw

Television news strives for credibility. Anchors are chosen not only for their personal appearance but also for the credibility they can lend to the news. The recognized all-time champion of credibility was CBS's Walter Cronkite, who for many years was "the most trusted man in America," according to all of the national polls.*

Each night nearly 40 million Americans watch one of three men: Dan Rather, Peter Jennings, or Tom Brokaw. No other individuals—not presidents, movie stars, or popes—have had such extensive contact with so many people. These network celebrities are recognized and heard by more people than anyone else on the planet. The networks demand that an anchor be the network's premier journalist, principal showman, top editor, star, symbol of news excellence, and single most important living logo.

Anchors, then, are both celebrities and newspeople. They are chosen for their mass appeal, but they must also bring journalistic expertise to their jobs. The anchors help select from thousands of hours of videotapes and hundreds of separate stories that will be squeezed into the twenty-two minutes of nightly network news (eight minutes being reserved for commercials). Each minute represents approximately 160 spoken words; the total number of words on the entire newscast is less than found on a single newspaper page. These inherent restrictions of the medium give great power to the anchors and their executive producers through their selection of

what Americans will see and hear about the world each night.

All three network anchors are middle-aged, Anglo-Saxon, male Protestants. All share liberal and reformist social values and political beliefs.

Dan Rather, who deliberately projects an image of emotional intensity, has created both strong attachments and heated animosities among his audiences. He is most despised by conservatives because of his undisguised and passionate liberal views. Rather worked his way up through the ranks of CBS news following graduation from Sam Houston State College. He was a reporter and news director for the CBS affiliate station in Houston, then chief of the CBS London Bureau, and later Vietnam correspondent. He came to national prominence in 1966 as a CBS White House correspondent and took over the anchor position from Walter Cronkite in 1981.

The Canadian-born Peter Jennings projects an image of thoughtful, urbane sophistication. He is widely traveled (his father was a journalist), but his formal education ended in the tenth grade. ABC's *World News Tonight with Peter Jennings* devotes slightly more time to international news than do its rival news shows.

Tom Brokaw offers a calm, unemotional delivery with occasional touches of wry humor. Brokaw graduated from the University of South Dakota and started his career at an Omaha television station. He anchored local news in Atlanta and Los Angeles before moving up to the post of NBC White House correspondent in 1973. He hosted the NBC *Today* show from 1976 to 1982, and his show biz and talk show host experience has served him well as anchor of the NBC nightly news since then. He is less ideological than Rather or Jennings and can appear relaxed and friendly with Republicans as well as Democrats.

The ratings race among the anchors is very close. Indeed, the closeness of those ratings may be driving the shows toward even more sensational themes, violent confrontations, and dramatic hype. Although all current shows have commentators, they are used less often; and it is now almost mandatory to end the show with a crowd-pleasing human interest story.

*Alex S. Jones, "The Anchors," *New York Times Magazine*, July 27, 1986, p. 14.

ment on the newscast and several minutes of airtime or that receive front-page newspaper coverage with headlines and pictures are believed to be important by viewers and readers.

Politicians have a love-hate relationship with the media. They need media attention to promote themselves, their message, and their programs. They crave the exposure, the name recognition, and the celebrity that the media can confer. At the same time, they fear attack by the media. They know that the media are active players in the political game, not just passive spectators. The media seek sensational stories of sin, sexuality, corruption, and scandal in government to attract viewers and readers, and thus the media pose a constant danger to politicians. Politicians understand the power of the media to make or break their careers.

"Making the news"—attracting media attention—has become a well-practiced art form in politics. The media jealously guard their power to grant or withhold public attention, but politicians, aspiring "celebrities," publicists, public relations firms, and interest groups all regularly try to influence the news. The result is an overflow of "media events"—activities arranged primarily to attract media coverage. Generally, the more bizarre, dramatic, and sensational the event, the more likely it is to make the news. It may be a march, a demonstration, a dramatic confrontation, or an emotional illustration of some injustice. Or it may be a press conference to which television and newspaper reporters are invited—whether or not there is any real news to announce. Or it may be a politician's visit to a factory or coal mine, or a walk through an inner-city neighborhood, or an inspection of a fire or other disaster site. During political campaigns, each day is a scramble to get just a few seconds on the network news—a *sound bite* of the candidate pronouncing a particularly striking phrase.

*Agenda Setting*    **Agenda setting** is the power to decide what will be decided. It is the power to define society's "problems," to create political issues, and to set forth alternative solutions. Deciding which issues will be addressed by government may be even more important than deciding how the issues will be resolved. The distinguished political scientist E. E. Schattschneider once wrote: "He who determines what politics is about runs the country."[2]

The real power of the media lies in their ability to set the political agenda for the nation. This power grows out of their power to decide what is news. Media coverage determines what both citizens and public officials regard as "crises" or "problems" or "issues" to be resolved. Conditions that are ignored by the media seldom get on the agenda of political leaders. Media attention forces public officials to speak on the topic, take positions, and respond to questions. Media *inat-tention* allows problems to be ignored by government. "TV is the Great Legitimator. TV confers reality. Nothing happens in America, practically everyone seems to agree, until it happens on television."[3]

Political issues do not just "happen." The media are crucial to their development. Organized interest groups, professional public relations firms, government bureaucracies, political candidates, and elected officials all try to solicit the assistance of the media in shaping the political agenda. Creating an issue, publicizing it, dramatizing it, turning it into a "crisis," getting people to talk about it, and ultimately forcing government to do something about it are the tactics of agenda setting. The participation of the mass media is vital to their success.[4]

**Agenda setting:** Deciding what will be decided; defining the problems and issues to be addressed by decision makers.

*Interpreting*    The media not only decide what will be news, they also interpret the news for us. Editors, reporters, and anchors provide each story with an *angle*—an interpretation that places the story in a context and speculates about its meaning and consequences. The interpretation tells us what to think about the news.

Interpretation of television news begins with the *lead-in*—usually a statement about the importance of the news item or its relationship to other events. The selection of *visuals* is crucial to the interpretation, because people remember a picture better than words. The *voice-over* tells us what the visuals mean. A *recap* statement may summarize the meaning of the story.

News is presented in "stories." Reporters do not report facts; they tell stories. The story structure gives meaning to various pieces of information. Some common angles or themes of news stories are:

- *Good guys versus bad guys:* for example, corrupt officials, foreign dictators, corporate polluters, and other assorted villains versus honest citizens, exploited workers, endangered children, or other innocents
- *Little guys versus big guys:* for example, big corporations, the military, or insensitive bureaucracies versus consumers, taxpayers, poor people, or the elderly
- *Appearance versus reality:* for example, the public statements of government officials or corporate executives versus whatever contradicting facts hardworking investigative reporters can find

News is also "pictures." A story without visuals is not likely to be selected as television news in the first place. The use of visuals reinforces the *angle*. A close-up shot can reveal hostility, insincerity, or anxiety on the face of villains or can show fear, concern, sincerity, or compassion on the face of innocents. To emphasize elements of a story, an editor can stop the action, use slow motion, zoom the lens, add graphics, cut back and forth between antagonists, cut away for audience reaction, and so on. Videotaped interviews can be spliced to make the interviewees appear knowledgeable, informed, and sincere or, alternatively, ignorant, insensitive, and mean-spirited. The media jealously guard the right to edit interviews themselves, rejecting virtually all attempts by interviewees to review and edit their own interviews.

Interpretation also occurs in the selection of *sources*—people who are presented as experienced and knowledgeable. The media select sources who express the media's views about an issue. Even when the media present both sides of a controversy, the choice of spokespersons can tilt the debate. If the media support a cause, they can select spokespersons who are personally appealing, articulate, and attractive. If they oppose a cause, they can select people who are unattractive, bumbling, confused, or obnoxious.

*Socializing*    The media have power to socialize audiences to the political culture. News, entertainment, and advertising all contribute to **socialization**—to the learning of political values. Socialization through television begins in early childhood and continues throughout life. Most of the political information people learn comes to them through television—specific facts as well as general values. Election coverage, for example, shows "how democracy works," encourages

*Groups hoping for free media coverage of their cause can improve their chances by framing their protests in dramatic form. Here several environmental groups protesting offshore drilling in Florida express their concerns in the kinds of graphics that will broadcast well. They have also pitted their struggle in terms of "average Americans versus insensitive industry"—another aspect designed to appeal to broadcasters.*

**Socialization:** The learning of a culture and its values.

political participation, and legitimizes the winner's control of government. Advertising shows Americans desirable middle-class standards of living even while it encourages people to buy automobiles, detergent, and beer, and entertainment programming socializes them to "acceptable" ways of life. Political values such as racial tolerance, sexual equality, and support for law enforcement are reinforced in countless situation comedies, police shows, and made-for-TV movies. Realistic "docudramas" seize on specific political themes, from abortion, to homosexuality, to drug use, to child abuse, to AIDS. Entertainment news programming such as the highly popular *60 Minutes* is now regular prime-time fare. Thirty years ago, television avoided political controversy in its entertainment programs. Today it thrives on political controversy.

*Persuading*    The media, in both paid advertising and news and entertainment programming, engage in direct efforts to change our attitudes, opinions, and behavior. Newspaper editorials have traditionally been employed for direct persuasion. A great deal of the political commentary on television news and interview programs is aimed at persuading people to adopt the views of the commentators. Even many entertainment programs and movies are intended to promote specific political viewpoints. But most direct persuasion efforts come to us through paid advertising.

Corporations may use their advertising dollars not only to promote sales of their product but also to convey the message that they are good citizens—sensitive to the environment, concerned with worker and consumer safety, devoted to providing more and better jobs, goods, and services to America.

Political campaigning is now largely a media battle, with paid political advertisements as the weapons. Candidates rely on professional campaign management firms, with their pollsters, public relations specialists, advertising production people, and media consultants, to carry on the fight.

Governments and political leaders must rely on persuasion through the mass media to carry out their programs. Presidents can take their message directly to people in televised speeches, news conferences, and the yearly State of the Union message. Presidents by custom are accorded television time whenever they request it. In this way, they can go over the heads of Congress and even the media executives and reporters themselves to communicate directly with the people.

In short, persuasion is central to politics, and the media are the key to persuasion.

## THE POLITICS OF THE MEDIA

The politics of the media are shaped by (1) their *economic interest,* (2) their *professional environment,* and (3) their *ideological leanings.* The economic interests of the media are primarily to attract and hold readers and viewers. Television networks and commercial stations charge advertisers on the basis of audience estimates made by the rating services. One rating service, A. C. Nielsen and Company, places electronic boxes in a national sample of television homes and calculates the proportion of these homes that watch a program (the rating), as well as the proportion of homes with their sets turned on that watch a particular program (the share). Newspapers' advertising revenue is based primarily on circulation figures.

In short, the business of the media is to gather mass audiences to sell to advertisers.

*Sensationalism*  The economic interest of the media—the need to capture and hold audience attention—creates a bias toward "hype" in the selection of news, its presentation, and its interpretation. To attract viewers and readers, the media bias the news toward violence, conflict, scandal, corruption, sex, scares of various sorts, and the personal lives of politicians and celebrities. News is selected primarily for its emotional impact on audiences; its social, economic, or political significance is secondary to the need to capture attention.

News must "touch" audiences personally, arouse emotions, and hold the interest of people with short attention spans. Scare stories—street crime, drug use, AIDS, nuclear power plant accidents, global warming, and a host of health alarms—make "good" news, for they cause viewers to fear for their personal safety. The sex lives of politicians, once by custom off-limits to the press, are now public "affairs." Scandal and corruption among politicians, as well as selfishness and greed among business executives, are regular media themes.

*Negativism*  The media are biased toward bad news. Bad news attracts larger audiences than good news. Television news displays a pervasive bias toward the negative in American life—in government, business, the military, politics, education, and everywhere else. Bad-news stories on television outnumber good-news stories by at least 3 to 1.[5]

Good news gets little attention. For example, television news watchers are not likely to know that illegal drug use is declining in the United States; that both the air and water are measurably cleaner today than in past decades; that the nuclear power industry has the best safety record of any major industry in the United States; and that the aged in America are wealthier and enjoy higher incomes than the nonaged. Television has generally failed to report these stories

*"Bad news" is far more likely to make the news than is "good news." Viewers sit up and take notice of disasters like the bombing of the Federal Building in Oklahoma City.*

or, even worse, has implied that the opposite is true.[6] Good news—stories about improved health statistics, longer life spans, better safety records, higher educational levels, for example—seldom provides the dramatic element needed to capture audience attention. The result is an overwhelming bad-news bias, especially on television.

*Muckraking*   The professional environment of reporters and editors predisposes them toward an activist style of journalism once dubbed **muckraking.** Reporters today view themselves as "watchdogs" of the public trust. They see themselves in noble terms—enemies of corruption, crusaders for justice, defenders of the disadvantaged. "The watchdog function, once considered remedial and subsidiary . . . [is now] paramount: the primary duty of the journalists is to focus attention on problems and deficits, failures and threats."[7] Their professional models are the crusading "investigative reporters" who expose wrongdoing in government, business, the military, and every other institution in society—except the media.

Many reporters go beyond the watchdog role and view themselves as adversaries of government. They feel that their first obligation is to attack wrongdoing—to expose greed, lawlessness, and evil in high places—so that citizens will force their government to reform. The working hypothesis almost universally shared among correspondents is that politicians are suspect: their public images are probably false, their public statements disingenuous, their moral pronouncements hypocritical, and their motives self-serving. Correspondents see it as their job to expose politicians by unmasking their disguises, debunking their claims, and piercing their rhetoric. In short, until proven otherwise, political figures of any party or persuasion are presumed to be opponents. Even on entertainment shows, politicians are usually depicted as corrupt, hypocritical, and self-seeking, and business executives as crooked, greedy, and insensitive. Reporters are particularly proud of their work when it results in official investigations.

The activist role that the media have taken upon themselves means that the personal values of reporters, editors, producers, and anchors are a very important element of American politics. If the media limited themselves to a neutral observer role, then the political views of these people might have less of an impact on politics. Most newspeople argue that they do not allow their personal values to affect the news. But newspeople—like all of us—rely on their personal values in making decisions, including decisions about what is "newsworthy."

*Liberalism*   The political values of the media are decidedly liberal and reformist. Political scientist Doris A. Graber writes about the politics of the media: "Economic and social liberalism prevails, as does a preference for an internationalist foreign policy, caution about military intervention, and some suspicion about the ethics of established large institutions, particularly government."[8]

The media elite—the executives, producers, reporters, editors, and anchors—are clearly liberal or left-leaning in their political news. One study of news executives reported that 63 percent described themselves as "left-leaning," only 27 percent as "middle-of-the-road," and 10 percent as "right-leaning." Newsmakers describe themselves as either "independent" (45 percent) or Democratic (44 percent); very few (9 percent) admit to being Republican.[9] (see *Up Close:* "The Hollywood Liberals").

**Muckraking:** Journalistic exposés of corruption, wrongdoing, or mismanagement in government, business, and other institutions of society.

CHAPTER 6 • MASS MEDIA: SETTING THE POLITICAL AGENDA

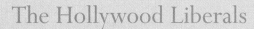

# The Hollywood Liberals

The motion picture and television industry centered in Hollywood has a profound effect on the nation's political culture. Much of the commercial product of Hollywood—both television entertainment programming and motion pictures—is directed toward young people. They are the heaviest watchers of television and the largest buyers of movie tickets. Thus Hollywood plays an important role in socializing young Americans to their political world.

With a few exceptions, Hollywood producers, directors, writers, studio executives, and actors are decidedly liberal in their political views, especially when compared with the general public. Of the Hollywood elite, over 60 percent describe themselves as liberal and only 14 percent as conservative, whereas in the general public, self-described conservatives outnumber liberals by a significant margin. Hollywood leaders are five times more likely to be Democrats than Republicans, although many claim to be independents. And on both economic and social issues, the Hollywood elite is significantly more liberal than the nation's general public or college-educated public (see figure).

The question remains, however, how much political influence Hollywood exercises over its audiences. Many television shows and motion pictures have little political content; they are designed almost exclusively to entertain, to gather the largest audiences for advertisers, and to sell theater tickets. Even shows or movies with political themes or pronounced political biases may not influence audiences as much as Hollywood would wish.

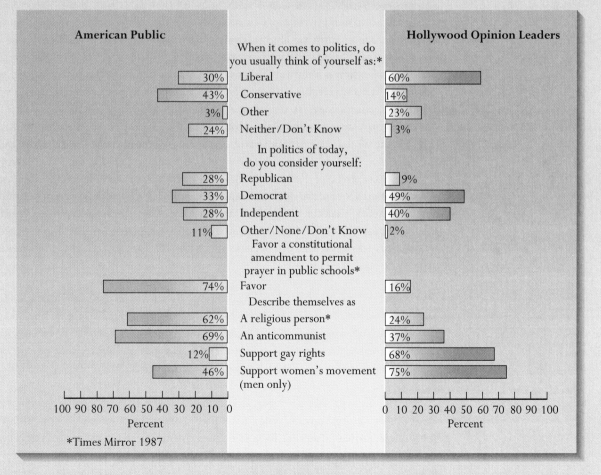

| American Public | When it comes to politics, do you usually think of yourself as:* | Hollywood Opinion Leaders |
|---|---|---|
| 30% | Liberal | 60% |
| 43% | Conservative | 14% |
| 3% | Other | 23% |
| 24% | Neither/Don't Know | 3% |
| | In politics of today, do you consider yourself: | |
| 28% | Republican | 9% |
| 33% | Democrat | 49% |
| 28% | Independent | 40% |
| 11% | Other/None/Don't Know | 2% |
| | Favor a constitutional amendment to permit prayer in public schools* | |
| 74% | Favor | 16% |
| | Describe themselves as | |
| 62% | A religious person* | 24% |
| 69% | An anticommunist | 37% |
| 12% | Support gay rights | 68% |
| 46% | Support women's movement (men only) | 75% |

American Public: 100 90 80 70 60 50 40 30 20 10 0 — Percent

*Times Mirror 1987

Hollywood Opinion Leaders: 0 10 20 30 40 50 60 70 80 90 100 — Percent

*Source:* David Prindle, "Hollywood Liberalism," *Social Science Quarterly* 74 (March 1993): 121.

A few conservative commentators are added to the liberal stew in order to add spice. Since controversy holds viewer attention, conservatives such as George Will, William F. Buckley, and Patrick Buchanan regularly play a confrontational role on news and talk shows. Talk *radio* is the one medium where conservatism prevails, among both hosts and call-ins (see *People in Politics:* "Rush Limbaugh, Bashing Liberals").

## MEDIATED ELECTIONS

Political campaigning is largely a media activity, and the media, especially television, shape the nation's electoral politics.

*The Media and Candidate-Voter Linkage*   The media are the principal link between candidates and the voters. At one time, political party organizations performed this function, with city, ward, and precinct workers knocking on doors, distributing campaign literature, organizing rallies and candidate appearances, and getting out the vote on election day. But television has largely replaced party organizations and personal contact as the means by which candidates communicate with voters. Candidates come directly into the living room via television—on the nightly news, in broadcast debates and interviews, and in paid advertising.

Media campaigning requires candidates to possess great skill in communications. Candidates must be able to project a favorable media *image*. The image is a composite of the candidate's words, mannerisms, appearance, personality, warmth, friendliness, humor, and ease in front of a camera. Policy positions have less to do with image than the candidate's ability to project personal qualities—leadership, compassion, strength, and character.

Television places an especially important emphasis on personal communication skills. Print media—newspapers and magazines—communicate only what is said. But *television communicates not only what is said but also how it is said.* For example, newspaper reports of Ronald Reagan's commonplace speeches and time-worn slogans failed to capture his true audience appeal—the folksy, warm, comfortable, reassuring manner, the humor and humility, and the likable personality that made Reagan "the Great Communicator." Reagan prevailed over hostile reporters, editors, and commentators because he was able to effectively communicate directly to mass audiences.

*The Media and Candidate Selection*   The media strongly influence the early selection of candidates. Media coverage creates *name recognition,* an essential quality for any candidate. Early media "mentions" of senators, governors, and other political figures as possible presidential contenders help to sort out the field even before the election year begins. Conversely, media inattention can condemn aspiring politicians to obscurity.

The media sort out the serious candidates early in a race. They even assign front-runner status—which may be either a blessing or a curse, depending on subsequent media coverage. In presidential primaries, the media play the *expectations game*—setting vote margins that the front-runner must meet in order to maintain *momentum*. If the front-runner does not win by a large enough margin, the media may declare the runner-up the "real" winner.

# Rush Limbaugh, Bashing Liberals

Welcome to the *Rush Limbaugh Show,* featuring "the number-one talk show host in America," according to Rush himself. Limbaugh believes politics should be fun, but what is fun for him enrages liberal groups, variously labeled by Limbaugh as "environmental wackos," "croissant people," and "femi-Nazis." Whether his popularity is due to his politics or his showmanship, he has the most popular radio talk show in the country, and his television show is thriving.

Limbaugh hails from Cape Girardeau, Missouri. His father was a successful attorney, but Rush never had much interest in education. He dropped out of Southeast Missouri State University after two semesters, and his father helped him get a job at his hometown radio station. For years Limbaugh roamed the country as a struggling radio DJ, news reader, and commentator. He thought he had left radio forever when he landed a job with the Kansas City Royals baseball club as a marketing manager, but in 1983, he went back to radio, working as a commentator on KMBZ in Kansas City.

After a few months of work, KMBZ fired Limbaugh for being too controversial. His next stop was Sacramento, where he filled in for his liberal-bashing predecessor, Morton Downey, Jr. In 1988, he was offered his own show in New York, where through word-of-mouth and his own self-promotion, Rush hit it big.

The *Rush Limbaugh Show* combines entertainment with current events that involve liberal issues. NOW conventions, Ted Kennedy, environmental activists, and Jane Fonda are typical targets. Limbaugh asserts that *he* is the response to the liberal media, and therefore he is not required to give equal time to the other side because "I am equal time."

All callers are carefully screened, and only occasionally does Limbaugh accept a liberal caller. He has a policy of not having guests on the show, but "well . . . I'll make an exception for the president." Listeners can never be quite sure when Rush is serious or "Hey, we're just having fun here, lighten up."

Limbaugh and other radio and television talk show hosts represent the new "call-in democracy." They are the first to sense the public mood, often receiving calls within an hour of a political event. Callers are not necessarily representative of the general public. Rather, they are usually the most intense and outraged of citizens. But they are an early warning sign for wary politicians.

---

This sorting out of candidates by the media influences not only voters, but—more important—financial contributors. The media-designated favorite is more likely to receive campaign contributions; financial backers do not like to waste money on losers. And as contributions roll in, the favorite can buy more television advertising, adding momentum to the campaign.

In presidential elections, the media sorting process places great emphasis on the early primary states, particularly New Hampshire, whose primary in early February is customarily the first contest in a presidential election year. Less than 1 percent of convention delegates are chosen by this small state, but media coverage is intense, and the winner quickly becomes the media-designated front-runner.[10]

Perhaps the most striking example of media influence in presidential politics occurred in 1968 when anti–Vietnam War candidate Senator Eugene McCarthy challenged President Lyndon Johnson in the Democratic primary in New Hampshire. Johnson won with 60 percent of the vote, but the media reported

McCarthy's 40 percent as a "stunning surprise," even a "moral victory." This deeply embarrassed President Johnson, who announced his decision not to seek reelection on March 31.

*The Media and the Horse Race*   The media give election campaigns **horse-race coverage**—reporting on who is ahead or behind, what the candidates' strategies are, how much money they are spending, and, above all, what their current standing in the polls is. Such stories account for more than half of all television news coverage of an election. Additional stories are centered on *campaign* issues—controversies that arise on the campaign trail itself, including verbal blunders by the candidate—and *character* issues, such as the sex life of the candidate. In contrast, *policy* issues typically account for fewer than one-quarter of the television news stories on a presidential election campaign.

*The Media as Campaign Watchdogs*   The media's bad-news bias is evident in election campaigns as well as in general news reporting. Negative stories about all presidential candidates outnumber positive stories by margins of 2 to 1 or more.[11] The media generally see their function in political campaigns as reporting on the weaknesses, blunders, and vulnerabilities of the candidates (see *What Do You Think?* "Should Media Report on the Private Lives of Public Officials?"). It might be argued that exposing the flaws of the candidates is an important function in a democracy. But the media's negative reporting about candidates and generally skeptical attitude toward their campaign speeches, promises, and advertisements may contribute to political alienation and cynicism among voters.

The media focus intense scrutiny on the personal lives of candidates—their marriages, sex lives, drug or alcohol use, personal finances, past friendships, military service, club memberships, and any other potential sources of embarrassment. Virtually any past error in judgment or behavior by a candidate is given heavy coverage. But the media defend their attention to personal scandal on the ground that they are reporting on the "character issue." Voters must have information on candidates' character as well as on their policy positions.

*The Media and Political Bias*   The media are very sensitive to charges of bias toward candidates or parties. Media people are overwhelmingly liberal and Democratic but generally try to deflect charges of political bias during an election campaign by giving almost equal coverage to both Democratic and Republican candidates. Moreover, the media report negatively on both Republicans and Democrats, although some scholars count more negative stories about Republican candidates.

The media are generally more critical of front-runners than of underdogs during a campaign. A horse race loses audience interest if one horse gets too far ahead, so the media tend to favor the underdog. "Frontrunners and incumbents consistently experienced the least balanced, least favorable news coverage."[12] During the long presidential primary season, media attacks on an early favorite may result in gains for the underdog, who then becomes the new object of attack.

## FREEDOM VERSUS FAIRNESS

Complaints about the fairness of media are as old as the printing press. Most early newspapers in America were allied with political parties; they were not expected

**Horse-race coverage:** Media coverage of electoral campaigns that concentrates on who is ahead and who is behind, and neglects the issues at stake.

# Should the Media Report on the Private Lives of Public Officials?

Historically, reputable newspapers and magazines declined to carry stories about the sex lives of political figures. This unwritten ethic of journalism protected Presidents Franklin D. Roosevelt, Dwight D. Eisenhower, and John F. Kennedy during their political careers. But today, journalistic ethics (if there are any at all) do not limit reporting of sexual charges, rumors, or innuendos or public questioning of candidates and appointees about whether they ever "cheated on their spouse," "smoked marijuana," or "watched pornographic movies."

The media's rationale is that these stories reflect on the *character* of a candidate and hence deserve reporting to the general public as information relevant to their choice for national leadership. Yet it seems clear that scandalous stories are pursued by the media primarily for their commercial value. Sex sells; it attracts viewers and readers. But the media's focus on sexual scandal and other misconduct obscures other issues. Politicians defending themselves from personal attack cannot get their political themes and messages across to voters. Moreover, otherwise qualified people may stay out of politics to avoid the embarrassment to themselves and their families that results from invasion of personal privacy.

But Bill Clinton demonstrated that a presidential candidate could survive scandalous sex charges. Gennifer Flowers held a national press conference to publicize her charges of a long-term sexual affair with the governor of Arkansas. Clinton responded with a dramatic appearance before millions of viewers on the popular *60 Minutes,* immediately after the 1992 Super Bowl broadcast. With his wife, Hillary, at his side, he candidly acknowledged marital difficulties in the past but reassured viewers that he and his wife had chosen to make their marriage work. While he declined to describe details of their private lives, he went further than any other presidential candidate in talking publicly about personal matters.

The graph below illustrates Americans' divisions over the issue of publicizing officials' private lives.

**Question:** *For each of the following stories about public officials, please tell me whether you feel it should almost always be reported, whether it should sometimes be reported depending on the circumstances, or whether it should almost never be reported.*

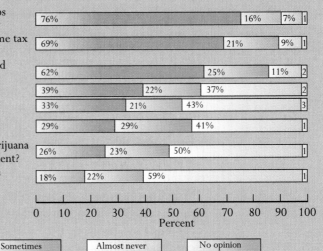

*When a public official:*

| | Almost always | Sometimes | Almost never | No opinion |
|---|---|---|---|---|
| Used military aircraft for personal trips without reimbursing the government? | 76% | 16% | 7% | 1 |
| Is found to have not paid federal income tax one time in the past? | 69% | 21% | 9% | 1 |
| Is found to have exaggerated his record of military service? | 62% | 25% | 11% | 2 |
| Is having an extramarital affair? | 39% | 22% | 37% | 2 |
| Is a homosexual? | 33% | 21% | 43% | 3 |
| Attended a party at which cocaine was used? | 29% | 29% | 41% | 1 |
| Is found to have been arrested for marijuana possession when he was a college student? | 26% | 23% | 50% | 1 |
| Had an extramarital affair six or seven years ago? | 18% | 22% | 59% | 1 |

*Source:* Gallup poll, May 8, 1991.

## Muzzle the Media to Win the War

Media images of war influence public opinion. George Washington understood clearly the importance of maintaining public support in order to conduct a prolonged war; many of his military operations during the Revolution were designed primarily to maintain support and confidence in the war effort. Many in the U.S. military believe that the loss of popular support for the war in Vietnam was the cause of America's defeat: the U.S. military was not defeated on the battlefield, it was defeated at home, with the media playing a major role through hostile reporting and televising pictures of battlefield carnage. In recent years, the Defense Department has been extremely sensitive to media coverage of military operations.

Operation Desert Storm began on the night of January 16, 1991, with live coverage of U.S. air attacks on Baghdad provided by CNN and narrated by Bernard Shaw and Peter Arnett. Earlier, the Iraqi government had ousted CBS, ABC, and NBC from the city; CNN held a monopoly on news reporting from the enemy capital. But its privileged position soon embroiled CNN in controversy. Critics charged correspondent Peter Arnett with serving as an instrument of Iraqi propaganda, especially after he reported that U.S. bombs had hit a "baby milk" factory, when it was actually a disguised chemical weapons facility.

The American public was about evenly divided over allowing broadcasts from the enemy capital or permitting Iraqi leader Saddam Hussein to make his case over American airwaves. After the war, Arnett conceded that Iraq's government permitted his heavily censored broadcasts to serve its own interest in drawing world attention to civilian casualties. But he argued that this story deserved to be told. He added: "I was in Baghdad not for the American government, nor even for the United States . . . [but] for the people who look at CNN . . . in 105 countries." But it was precisely Arnett's attitude—that reporters should not take sides—that angered the American public. They believed American journalists should play on the American "team" in the fashion of World War II combat reporters.

Meanwhile, the American media complained bitterly about military restrictions on their travel and reporting. Most Gulf War news came from official military briefings. The military itself supplied the dramatic videotapes of "smart bombs" destroying military targets with virtually unerring accuracy. Reporters claimed that their independent stories were unduly altered or delayed and blamed their military escorts for inhibiting soldiers from speaking freely to them. News accounts began to denounce the Pentagon restrictions as dictatorial, and some reporters tried to bypass the system by striking out on their own. Among them were CBS correspondent Bob Simon and his crew, who were captured by Iraqi soldiers and spent the war as POWs.

The military succeeded in maintaining strong public support for the war and in enhancing the public's trust and confidence in the military, despite the antiwar bias in news reporting itself. Three out of five "sources" quoted during the war were critical of U.S. policy. The networks aired as many pictures of

to be fair in their coverage. It was only in the early 1900s that many large newspapers broke their ties with parties and proclaimed themselves independent. And it was not until the 1920s and 1930s that the norms of journalistic professionalism and accuracy gained widespread acceptance.

The Constitution protects the *freedom* of the press; it was not intended to guarantee *fairness*. The First Amendment's guarantee of freedom of the press was originally designed to protect the press from government attempts to silence criticism. Over the years, the U.S. Supreme Court has greatly expanded the meaning of the free press guarantee.

*Critics charged that Peter Arnett's broadcasts for CNN during the Gulf War, which were censored by the Iraqi government, amounted to propaganda for that government. But the network defended its decision to air the film from inside Baghdad, arguing that any coverage was more informative than none at all and that other networks had been banned from broadcasting.*

civilian damage as they did of all combat operations, implying that the military was waging war against innocent civilians. The only positive reporting by the media was on the troops themselves.

The rapid and successful conclusion of the Gulf War leaves many issues unresolved. In a longer war, would the media's bad-news bias, or its outright opposition to a war effort, undermine public sup-port and contribute to defeat? Are military restrictions on the flow of information from the battlefield justified? Do American media organizations have any obligation to suppress stories that might, if broadcast, cost American lives?

*Source:* Interview on *Larry King Live,* Cable News Network, March 8, 1991; *Media Monitor,* (March 1991): 5–6.

*No Prior Restraint*    The Supreme Court has interpreted freedom of the press to mean that government may place no **prior restraint** on speech or publication (that is, before it is said or published). Originally, this doctrine was designed to prevent the government from closing down or seizing newspapers. Today the doctrine prevents the government from censoring any news items. In the famous case of the Pentagon Papers, the *New York Times* and *Washington Post* undertook to publish secret information stolen from the files of the State Department and Defense Department regarding U.S. policy in Vietnam while the war was still in progress.[13] No one disputed the fact that stealing the secret material was illegal.

**Prior restraint:** The power of government to prevent publication or to require approval before publication; generally prohibited by the First Amendment.

What was at issue was the ability of the government to prevent the publication of stolen documents in order to protect national security. The Supreme Court rejected the national security argument and reaffirmed that the government may place no prior restraint on publication. If the government wishes to keep military secrets, it must not let them fall into the hands of the American press (see *A Conflicting View:* "Muzzle the Media to Win the War").

*Press versus Electronic Media*    In the early days of radio, broadcast channels were limited, and anyone with a radio transmitter could broadcast on any frequency. As a result, interference was a common frustration of early broadcasters. The industry petitioned the federal government to regulate and license the assignment and use of broadcast frequencies.

The Federal Communications Commission (FCC) was established in 1934 to allocate broadcast frequencies and license stations for "the public interest, convenience and necessity." The act clearly instructed the FCC: "Nothing in this Act shall be understood or construed to give the Commission the power of censorship." However, the FCC views a broadcast license and exclusive right to use a particular frequency as a *public trust*. Thus broadcasters, unlike newspapers and magazines, are licensed by a government agency and must operate in the *public interest*.

*The Equal-Time Requirement*    The Federal Communications Commission requires radio and television stations that provide airtime to a political candidate to offer competing candidates the same amount of airtime at the same price. Stations are not required to give free time to candidates, but if stations choose to give free time to one candidate, they must do so for the candidate's opponents. But this **equal-time rule** does not apply to newscasts, news specials, or even long documentaries; nor does it apply to talk shows like *Larry King Live* (see *People in Politics:* "Larry King Live"). Nor does it apply to presidential press conferences or presidential addresses to the nation, although the networks now generally offer free time for a "Republican response" to a Democratic president, and vice versa. A biased news presentation does not require the network or station to grant equal time to opponents of its views. And it is important to note that newspapers, unlike radio and television, have *never* been required to provide equal time to opposing views (see *Compared to What?* "America's TV Culture in Perspective").

## LIBEL AND SLANDER

Communications that wrongly damage an individual are known in law as **libel** (when written) and **slander** (when spoken). The injured party must prove in court that the communication caused actual damage and that it was either false or defamatory. A damaging falsehood or words or phrases that are defamatory (such as, "Joe Jones is a rotten son of a bitch") are libelous and are not protected by the First Amendment from lawsuits seeking compensation.

*Public Officials*    Over the years, the media have sought to narrow the protection afforded public officials against libel and slander. In 1964, the U.S. Supreme Court ruled in the case of *New York Times v. Sullivan* that public officials did not have

**Equal-time rule:** A Federal Communications Commission requirement that broadcasters who sell time to any political candidate must make equal time available to opposing candidates at the same price.

**Libel:** Writings that are false and malicious and intended to damage an individual.

**Slander:** Oral statements that are false and malicious and intended to damage an individual.

CHAPTER 6 • MASS MEDIA: SETTING THE POLITICAL AGENDA

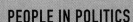

## Larry King Live

Who turned presidential politics into talk show entertainment? A strong argument can be made that Larry King was personally responsible for changing the nature of presidential campaigning. It was Larry King who nudged frequent talk show guest Ross Perot into the presidential arena. And it was Larry King who demonstrated to the candidates that the talk show format was a better way to reach out to the American people than the news shows.

Larry King's supremacy in talk show politics came late in life, after a half-century of hustling and hard knocks, no college education, bouts of gambling followed by bankruptcy, and multiple marriages. King has written five books about himself, describing his rise from Brooklyn neighborhoods, his friendships with Jackie Gleason, Frank Sinatra, and other celebrities, and his hard-scrabble life. As he tells it, he hung around a New York radio station for five years before taking a bus to Miami to try his luck first as a disk jockey and later as a sports announcer. After a decade in Miami, he had his own TV interview show, a talk show on radio, and a newspaper column, and he was color commentator for the Miami Dolphins. He lived the fast life, running up huge debts and dealing in shady financial transactions. He was arrested in 1971 on grand larceny charges; they were dropped only because the statute of limitations had expired. He lost his TV and radio shows and his newspaper column. He ended up in Shreveport, Louisiana, doing play-by-play for the World Football League's Shreveport Steamers. In 1975, he was bankrupt, but back in Miami doing radio. In 1978, he moved to Washington to launch his mutual network radio talk show. As radio talk shows gained popularity, so did King. When CNN started twenty-four—hour broadcasting in 1982, the new TV network turned to King to do an evening interview show, *Larry King Live*. At first, the show merely filled the space between the evening and the late news. A decade later, the show was making news itself.

King's success is directly attributable to his accommodating style. He actually listens to his guests; he lets them speak for themselves; he unashamedly plugs their books, records, and movies. He does *not* attack his guests; he does not assume the adversarial, abrasive style preferred by reporters like Sam Donaldson, Dan Rather, and Mike Wallace. An old-fashioned liberal himself, King appears comfortable interviewing politicians of every stripe. He holds his own ego in check and lets guests talk about themselves. He tosses "softball" questions: "If I were to interview the president about an alleged sexual affair, I wouldn't ask if he'd had one, I'd ask him, 'How does it feel to read these things about yourself?'"

With his emphasis on feelings, emotions, and motives rather than on facts, it is little wonder that King's style attracts politicians . . . or that *Larry King Live* is the highest-rated show on CNN.

*Source: Time,* October 5, 1992, p. 76.

---

a right to recover damages for false statements unless they are made with "malicious intent."[14] The **Sullivan rule** requires public officials not only to show that the media published or broadcast false and damaging statements but also to prove that they did so knowing at the time that their statements were false and damaging or that they did so with "reckless disregard" for the truth or falsehood of their statements. The effect of the Sullivan rule is to free the media to say virtually anything about public officials. Indeed, the media have sought to expand the definition of "public officials" to "public figures"—that is, to include virtually anyone they choose as the subject of a story.

**Sullivan rule:** A court guideline that false and malicious statements regarding public officials are protected by the First Amendment unless it can be proven that they were known to be false at the time they were made or were made with "reckless disregard" for their truth or falsehood.

# America's TV Culture in Perspective

America is a TV culture. Americans rely more on television for news and entertainment than people in other advanced industrial nations do. Perhaps more important, Americans have greater confidence in the media than other peoples do. Consider, for example, the question, "Would you say you have a great deal of confidence, only some confidence, hardly any confidence, or no confidence at all in the media—press, radio, and television?" When this question was asked of a national sample of Americans, 69 percent responded that they had a great deal or at least some confidence in the media. But majorities in four other countries—France, Great Britain, Germany, and Spain—said they had little or no confidence in the media (see "confidence in the media" figure).

How much do the media influence key decisions in society? A majority of people in both the United States and these same European nations believe that the media exert a large influence on public opinion. Americans appear to be closer to unanimity on this point (88 percent) than are Europeans. When people are asked how much influence the media exerts on particular governing institutions—the executive, the legislature, and the judiciary—Americans are much more likely to perceive strong media influence than are Europeans (see "media influence" figure).

*Source:* Adapted from Lawrence Parisot, "Attitudes about the Media: A Five Country Study," *Public Opinion* 43 (January/February 1988): 18, 60.

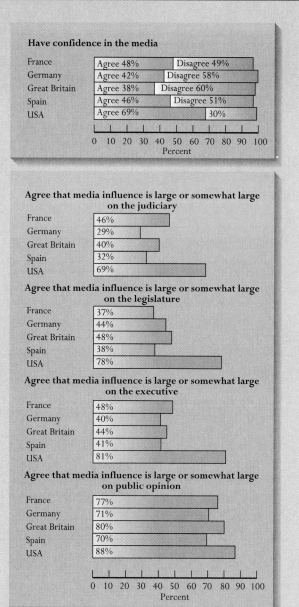

*"Absence of Malice"* The First Amendment protects the right of the media to be biased, unfair, negative, sensational, and even offensive. Indeed, even *damaging falsehoods* may be printed or broadcast as long as the media can show that the story was not deliberately fabricated by them with malicious intent. In a CBS documentary, *The Uncounted Enemy: A Vietnam Deception,* broadcast in 1982, Mike Wallace charged General William C. Westmoreland, former commander of U.S.

forces in Vietnam, with a "conspiracy" to deceive Congress, the president, and the American people about enemy troop strength. The documentary made no attempt to present different sides of the story or even to acknowledge that different intelligence analysts could arrive at different conclusions about enemy strength. CBS deleted all information and testimony it received supporting General Westmoreland's position from the broadcast and spliced and doctored tapes and distorted quotes to make interviewees appear to attack the general when the full interview showed them to be defending him. By any journalistic standard the broadcast was unfair and biased.[15]

But the Constitution protects the right of a free press to be unfair. CBS did not have to prove that the general deceived his superiors; all CBS needed to show was that it had a reasonable basis for believing that he did. At the libel trial, CBS produced a surprise witness, Westmoreland's own intelligence chief in Vietnam, who said that the general "withheld" intelligence estimates from Washington. The general withdrew his suit in exchange for a statement from CBS affirming the general's patriotism and "long and faithful service to his country." But CBS paid no monetary damages and declared it would "stand by the broadcast" despite "minor procedural violations of CBS news standards."

*Shielding Sources*   The media argue that the First Amendment allows them to refuse to reveal the names of their sources, even when this information is required in criminal investigations and trails. Thus far, the U.S. Supreme Court has not given blanket protection to reporters to withhold information from court proceedings. However, a number of states have passed *shield laws* protecting reporters from being forced to reveal their sources.

# MEDIA EFFECTS: SHAPING POLITICAL LIFE

What effects do the media have on public opinion and political behavior? Let us consider media effects on (1) information and agenda setting, (2) values and opinions, and (3) behavior. These categories of effects are ranked by the degree of influence the media are likely to have over us. The strongest effects of the media are on our information levels and societal concerns. The media also influence values and opinions, but the strength of media effects in these areas is diluted by many other influences. Finally, it is most difficult to establish the independent effect of the media on behavior.

*Information and Agenda-Setting Effects*   The media strongly influence what we know about our world and how we think and talk about it. Years ago, foreign policy expert Bernard Cohen, in the first book to assess the effects of the media on foreign policy, put it this way: "The mass media may not be successful in telling people what to think, but the media are stunningly successful in telling their audience what to think about"[16] (see *Up Close:* "The Media Age").

However, **information overload** diminishes the influence of the media in determining what we think about. There are so many communications directed at us that we cannot possibly process them all in our minds. A person's ability to recall a media report depends on repeated exposure to it and reinforcement through personal experience. For example, an individual who has a brother in a

**Information overload:** A situation in which individuals are subjected to so many communications that they cannot make sense of them.

## The Media Age

The print media—newspapers, magazines, books—have played a major role in American politics since colonial times. But the electronic media—radio, television, and cable television—are relatively new forces.

Radio was widely introduced into American homes in the 1920s and 1930s, allowing President Franklin D. Roosevelt to become the first "media president"—directly communicating with the American people through radio "fireside chats." After World War II, the popularity of television spread quickly; between 1950 and 1960, the percentage of homes with TV sets grew from 9 to 87.

Some notable political media innovations over the years:

- *1952:* The first paid commercial TV ad in a presidential campaign appeared, on behalf of Dwight D. Eisenhower. The black-and-white ad began with a voice-over—"Eisenhower answers the nation!"—followed by citizens asking favorable questions and Eisenhower responding, and ending with a musical jingle: "I like Ike." Though crude by current standards, it nevertheless set a precedent in media campaigning.
- *1952:* The "Checkers Speech" by Eisenhower's running mate, Richard M. Nixon, represented the first direct television appeal to the people over the heads of party leaders. Nixon was about to be dumped from the Republican ticket for hiding secret slush-fund money from campaign contributors. He went on national television with

an emotional appeal, claiming that the only personal item he ever took from a campaign contributor was his daughters' little dog, Checkers. Thousands of viewers called and wired in sympathy. Ike kept Nixon on the ticket.

- *1960:* The first televised debate between presidential candidates featured a youthful, handsome John F. Kennedy against a shifty-eyed Richard M. Nixon with a pronounced "five o'clock shadow." Nixon doggedly scored debater points, but JFK presented a cool and confident image and spoke directly to the viewers. The debate swung the popular tide toward Kennedy, who won in a very tight contest. Nixon attributed his defeat to his failure to shave before the broadcast.
- *1964:* The first "negative" TV ad was the "Daisy Girl" commercial sponsored by the Lyndon Johnson campaign against Republican conservative Barry Goldwater. It implied that Goldwater would start a nuclear war. It showed a little girl picking petals off a daisy while an ominous voice counted down "10-9-8-7 . . ." to a nuclear explosion, followed by a statement that Lyndon Johnson could be trusted to keep the peace.
- *1976:* President Gerald Ford was the first incumbent president to agree to a televised debate. (No televised presidential debates were held in the Nixon-Humphrey race in 1968 or in the Nixon-McGovern race in 1972. Apparently Nixon had learned his lesson.) Ford stumbled badly, and Jimmy Carter went on to victory. President Carter was unable to dodge debating Reagan in 1980, and televised debates became a political institution.

trouble spot in the Middle East is more likely to be aware of reports from that area of the world. But too many voices with too many messages cause most viewers to block out a great deal of information.

Information overload may be especially heavy in political news. Television tells most viewers more about politics than they really want to know. Political scientist Austin Ranney writes: "The fact is that for most Americans politics is still far from being the most interesting and important thing in life. To them, politics is usually

*The first televised presidential election debates were in 1960 between Senator John F. Kennedy and then Vice-President Richard Nixon. Nixon came armed with statistics, but his dour demeanor, "five o'clock shadow," and stiff presentation fared poorly in contrast to Kennedy's open, relaxed, confident air.*

- *1982:* CNN (Cable News Network), introduced by the maverick media mogul Ted Turner, began twenty-four-hour broadcasting.
- *1991:* The Persian Gulf War was the first war to be fought live on television. (While film and videotape reports of the Vietnam War had been important molders of public opinion in America, the technology of that era did not allow live reporting. In the Gulf War, the Iraqi government permitted CNN to continue live broadcasts from Baghdad, including spectacular coverage of the first night's air raids on the city.
- *1992:* In the presidential election, television talk shows became a major focus of the campaign. Wealthy independent candidate Ross Perot actu-

ally conducted an all-media campaign, rejecting in-person appearances in favor of such media techniques as half-hour "infomercials."

- *1994-95:* The arrest and trial of celebrity O.J. Simpson on murder charges so dominated the national news that more television time was devoted to the O.J. story than to the actions of the president and Congress.
- *1996:* The presidential election was given less television time and newspaper space than previous elections. Clinton's large lead throughout the campaign, public boredom with Whitewater and other scandals, and Dole's lackluster performance frustrated reporters in search of drama. Network TV news gave Clintion twice as much postive coverage as Dole.

confusing, boring, repetitious, and above all irrelevant to the things that really matter in their lives."[17]

*Effects on Values and Opinions*   The media often tell us how we *should* feel about news events or issues—especially those about which we have no prior feelings or experiences. The media can reinforce values and attitudes that we already hold. However, the media seldom change our preexisting values or opinions.

**Selective perception:**
Mentally screening out information or opinions with which one disagrees.

**Television malaise:**
Generalized feelings of distrust, cynicism, and powerlessness stemming from television's emphasis on the negative aspects of American life.

Media influence over values and opinions is reduced by **selective perception**—mentally screening out information or opinions with which one disagrees. People tend to see and hear only what they want to see and hear. For example, television news concentration on scandal, abuse, and corruption in government has not always produced the liberal, reformist values among viewers that media people expected. On the contrary, the focus of network executives on governmental scandals—Watergate, the Iran-Contra scandal, the sexual antics of politicians, congressional check kiting, and so on—has produced feelings of general political distrust and cynicism toward government and the political system. These feelings have been labeled **television malaise**—a combination of social distrust, political cynicism, feelings of powerlessness, and disaffection from parties and politics that seems to stem from television's emphasis on the negative aspects of American life.

The media do not *intend* to create television malaise; they are performing their self-declared watchdog role. They expect their stories to encourage liberal reform of our political institutions. But the result is often alienation rather than reform.

*Direct Effects on Public Opinion* Can the media change public opinion, and if so, how? For many years, political scientists claimed that the media had only "minimal effects" on public opinions and behavior. This early view was based largely on the fact that newspaper editorial endorsements seldom affected people's votes. But serious research on the effects of television tells a different story. The Center for Media and Public Affairs, a private nonpartisan organization that regularly analyzes the content of news stories on television, has demonstrated a close relationship between the public's ratings of presidential performance in office as revealed in national polls and the positive or negative television news coverage of the president (see Figure 6-3). The rise and fall of Bill Clinton's public approval ratings follow closely on the heels of good/bad television news stories.

**FIGURE 6-3** **Clinton's Evaluation over Time**
*Television coverage of the president—the percentage of good-news versus bad-news stories on the evening news—appears to affect the general public's approval ratings of presidential performance.*

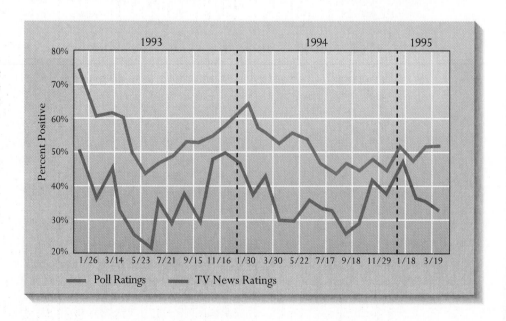

CHAPTER 6 • MASS MEDIA: SETTING THE POLITICAL AGENDA

In an extensive study of eighty policy issues over fifteen years, political scientists examined public opinion polls on various policy issues at a first point in time, then media content over a following interval of time, and finally public opinion on these same issues at the end of the interval. The purpose was to learn if media content—messages scored by their relevance to the issue, their salience in the broadcast, their pro/con direction, the credibility of the news source, and quality of the reporting—changed public opinion. Although most people's opinions remained constant over time (opinion at the first time period is the best predictor of opinion at the second time period), opinion *changes* were heavily influenced by media messages. The authors concluded that "news variables alone account for nearly half the variance in opinion change." They also reported that:

- Anchors, reporters, and commentators have the greatest impact on opinion change. Television newscasters have high credibility and trust with the general public. Their opinions are crucial in shaping mass opinion.
- Independent experts interviewed by the media have a substantial impact on opinion, but not as great as newscasters themselves.
- A popular president can also shift public opinion somewhat. On the other hand, unpopular presidents do not have much success as opinion movers.
- Interest groups on the whole have a slightly negative effect on public opinion. "In many instances they seem to actually have antagonized the public and created a genuine adverse effect"; such cases include Vietnam War protesters, nuclear freeze advocates, and other demonstrators and protesters, even peaceful ones.[18]

*Effects on Behavior*   There have been many studies of the effects of the media on behavior—studies of the effects of TV violence, studies of the effects of television on children, and studies of the effects of obscenity and pornography.[19] It is difficult to generalize from these studies. However, it appears that television is more likely to reinforce behavioral tendencies than to change them. For example, televised violence may trigger violent behavior in children who are already predisposed to such behavior, but televised violence has little behavioral effect on average children.[20] Nevertheless, we know that television advertising sells products. And we know that political candidates spend millions to persuade audiences to go out and vote for them on election day. Both manufacturers and politicians create name recognition, employ product differentiation, try to associate with audiences, and use repetition to communicate their messages. These tactics are designed to affect our behavior both in the marketplace and in the election booth.

Political ads are more successful in motivating a candidate's supporters to go to the polls than they are in changing opponents into supporters. It is unlikely that voters who dislike a candidate or are committed to another candidate will be persuaded by political advertising to change their votes. But many potential voters are undecided, and the support of many others is "soft." Going to the polls on election day requires effort: people have errands to do, it may be raining, they may be tired. Television advertising is more effective with the marginal voters.

# SUMMARY NOTES

- The mass media in America not only report on the struggle for power; they are participants themselves in that struggle.

- It is only through the media that the general public comes to know about political events, personalities, and issues. Newsmaking—deciding what is or is not "news"—is a major source of media power. Media coverage not only influences popular discussion but also forces public officials to respond.

- Media power also derives from the media's ability to set the agenda for public decision making—to determine what citizens and public officials will regard as "crises," "problems," or "issues" to be resolved by government.

- The media also exercise power in their interpretation of the news. News is presented in story form; pictures, words, sources, and story selection all contribute to interpretation.

- The media play a major role in socializing people to the political culture. Socialization occurs in news, entertainment, and advertising.

- The politics of the media are shaped by their economic interest in attracting readers and viewers. This interest largely accounts for the sensational and negative aspects of news reporting.

- The professional environment of newspeople encourages an activist, watchdog role in politics and government. The politics of most newspeople are liberal and Democratic.

- Political campaigning is largely a media activity. The media have replaced the parties as the principal linkage between candidates and voters. But the media tend to report the campaign as a horse race, at the expense of issue coverage, and to focus more on candidates' character than on their voting records or issue positions.

- The First Amendment guarantee of freedom of press protects the media from government efforts to silence or censor them and allows the media to be "unfair" when they choose to be. The Federal Communication Commission exercises some modest controls over the electronic media, since the rights to exclusive use of broadcast frequencies is a *public trust.*

- Public officials are afforded very little protection by libel and slander laws. The Supreme Court's Sullivan rule allows even damaging falsehoods to be written and broadcast as long as newspeople themselves do not deliberately fabricate lies with "malicious intent" or "reckless disregard."

- Media effects on political life can be observed in (1) information and agenda setting, (2) values and opinions, and (3) behavior—in that order of influence. The media strongly influence what we know about politics and what we talk about. The media are less effective in changing existing opinions, values, and beliefs than they are in creating new ones. Nevertheless, the media can change many people's opinions, based upon the credibility of news anchors and reporters. Direct media effects on behavior are limited. Political ads are more important in motivating supporters to go to the polls, and in swinging undecided or "soft" voters, than in changing the minds of committed voters.

# SELECTED READINGS

ANSOLABEHERE, STEPHEN, ROY BEHR, and SHANTO IYENGAR. *The Media Game: American Politics in the Television Age.* New York: Macmillan, 1993. A comprehensive text assessing the changes in the political system brought about by the rise of television since the 1950s.

FALLOWS, JAMES. *Breaking the News: How the Media Undermine American Democracy.* New York: Pantheon Books, 1996. An argument that today's arrogant, cynical, and scandal-minded news reporting is turning readers and viewers away and undermining support for democracy.

GRABER, DORIS A. *Mass Media and American Politics,* 4th ed. Washington, D.C.: Congressional Quarterly Press, 1992. A wide-ranging description of media effects on campaigns, parties, and elections, as well as on social values and public policies.

LICHTER, ROBERT S., STANLEY ROTHMAN, and LINDA S. LICHTER. *The Media Elite.* Bethesda, Md.: Adler and Adler, 1986. A thorough study of the social and political values of top leaders in the mass media, based on extensive interviews of key people in the most influential media outlets.

LIMBAUGH, RUSH. *The Way Things Ought to Be*. New York: Simon & Schuster, 1992. Humor and bombast by the popular conservative radio and television personality.

MEDVED, MICHAEL. *Hollywood versus America*. New York: HarperCollins, 1992. An assault on the entertainment establishment, charging it with corrupting American culture with "sleaze and self-indulgence," a "preference for the perverse," and "a bias for the bizarre" that bashes religion, the family, business, the military, and American institutions generally.

PATTERSON, THOMAS E. *Out of Order*. New York: Random House, 1994. The antipolitical bias of the media poisons national election campaigns; policy questions are ignored in favor of the personal characteristics of candidates, their campaign strategies, and their standing in the horse race.

PRINDLE, DAVID F. *Risky Business*. Boulder, Colo: Westview Press, 1993. An examination of the politics of Hollywood, its liberalism, activism, self-indulgence, and celebrity egotism.

SABATO, LARRY J. *Feeding Frenzy: How Attack Journalism Has Transformed American Politics*. New York: Free Press, 1992. A strong argument that the media prefer "to employ titillation rather than scrutiny" and as a result produce "trivialization rather than enlightenment."

WATTENBERG, BEN J. *The Good News Is the Bad News Is Wrong*. New York: Simon & Schuster, 1984. An incisive description of the media bad-news bias and the long-term effects of negative news reporting on society.

WEST, DARRELL M. *Air Wars*. Washington, D.C.: Congressional Quarterly Press, 1993. An assessment of the effects of television advertisements in election campaigns from 1952 through 1992.

# POLITICAL PARTIES
## ORGANIZING POLITICS

## THE POWER OF ORGANIZATION

In the struggle for power, organization grants advantage. Italian political scientist Gaetano Mosca once put it very succinctly: "A hundred men acting uniformly in concert, with a common understanding, will triumph over a thousand men who are not in accord and can be dealt with one by one."[1] Thus, politics centers on organization—on organizing people to win office and to influence public policy.

## ASK YOURSELF ABOUT POLITICS

**1** Generally speaking, how would you identify yourself: as a Republican, Democrat, Independent, or something else?
Republican ⬭　　Democrat ⬭
Independent ⬭　　Other ⬭

**2** Which major political party better represents the interests of people like yourself?
Republican ⬭　　Democrat ⬭

**3** Does the Republican Party favor the rich more than the middle class or poor?
Yes ⬭　　No ⬭

**4** Does the Democratic Party favor the poor more than the middle class or rich?
Yes ⬭　　No ⬭

**5** Which major party does a better job of protecting the Social Security system?
Republican ⬭　　Democrat ⬭

**6** Which major party does a better job of handling foreign affairs?
Republican ⬭　　Democrat ⬭

**7** Should elected officials be bound by their party's platform?
Yes ⬭　　No ⬭

**8** Should the two-party system be eliminated in favor of more parties representing greater diversity of principles and policies?
Yes ⬭　　No ⬭

How much power do political parties really have to determine who gets what in America? We hear the terms Republican and Democratic linked to people and to policies, but do these parties have real power beyond that of organizing for elections?

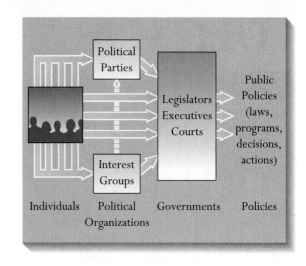

**FIGURE 7-1** **Political Organizations as Intermediaries**

*All political organizations function as intermediaries between individuals and government. Parties are concerned primarily with winning elected office, while interest groups are concerned with influencing policy.*

**Political organizations**—parties and interest groups—function as intermediaries between individuals and government. They organize individuals to give them power in selecting government officials—who governs—and in determining public policy—for what ends. Generally, **political parties** are more concerned with winning public office in elections than with influencing policy, while **interest groups** are more directly concerned with public policy and involve themselves with elections only to advance their policy interests (see Figure 7-1). In other words, parties and interest groups have an informal division of functions, with parties focusing on personnel and interest groups focusing on policy. Yet both organize individuals for more effective political action.

# AMERICAN PARTIES: A HISTORICAL PERSPECTIVE

Parties are *not* mentioned in the Constitution. Indeed the nation's Founders regarded both parties and interest groups as "factions"—citizens united by "some common impulse of passion, or of interest, adverse to the rights of other citizens, or to the permanent and aggregate interests of the community." The Founders viewed factions as "mischievous" and "dangerous."[2] Yet the emergence of parties was inevitable as people sought to organize themselves to exercise power over who governs (see Figure 7-2).

*The Emergence of Parties: Federalists and Democratic-Republicans*
In his Farewell Address, George Washington warned the nation about political parties: "Let me . . . warn you in the most solemn manner against the baneful effects of the spirit of party generally."[3] As president, Washington stood above the factions that were coalescing around his secretary of treasury, Alexander Hamilton, and around his former secretary of state, Thomas Jefferson. Jefferson had resigned from Washington's cabinet in 1793 to protest the fiscal policies of Hamilton, notably his creation of a national bank and repayment of the state's Revolutionary War debts with federal funds. Washington had endorsed Hamilton's policies, but so great was the first president's prestige that Jefferson and his followers

**Political organizations:**
Parties and interest groups that function as intermediaries between individuals and government.

**Political parties:**
Organizations that seek to achieve power by winning public office.

**Interest group:** A political organization concerned with public policy and involved in the electoral process only to further those policy aims.

CHAPTER 7 • POLITICAL PARTIES: ORGANIZING POLITICS

FIGURE 7-2  **Change and Continuity in the American Party System**

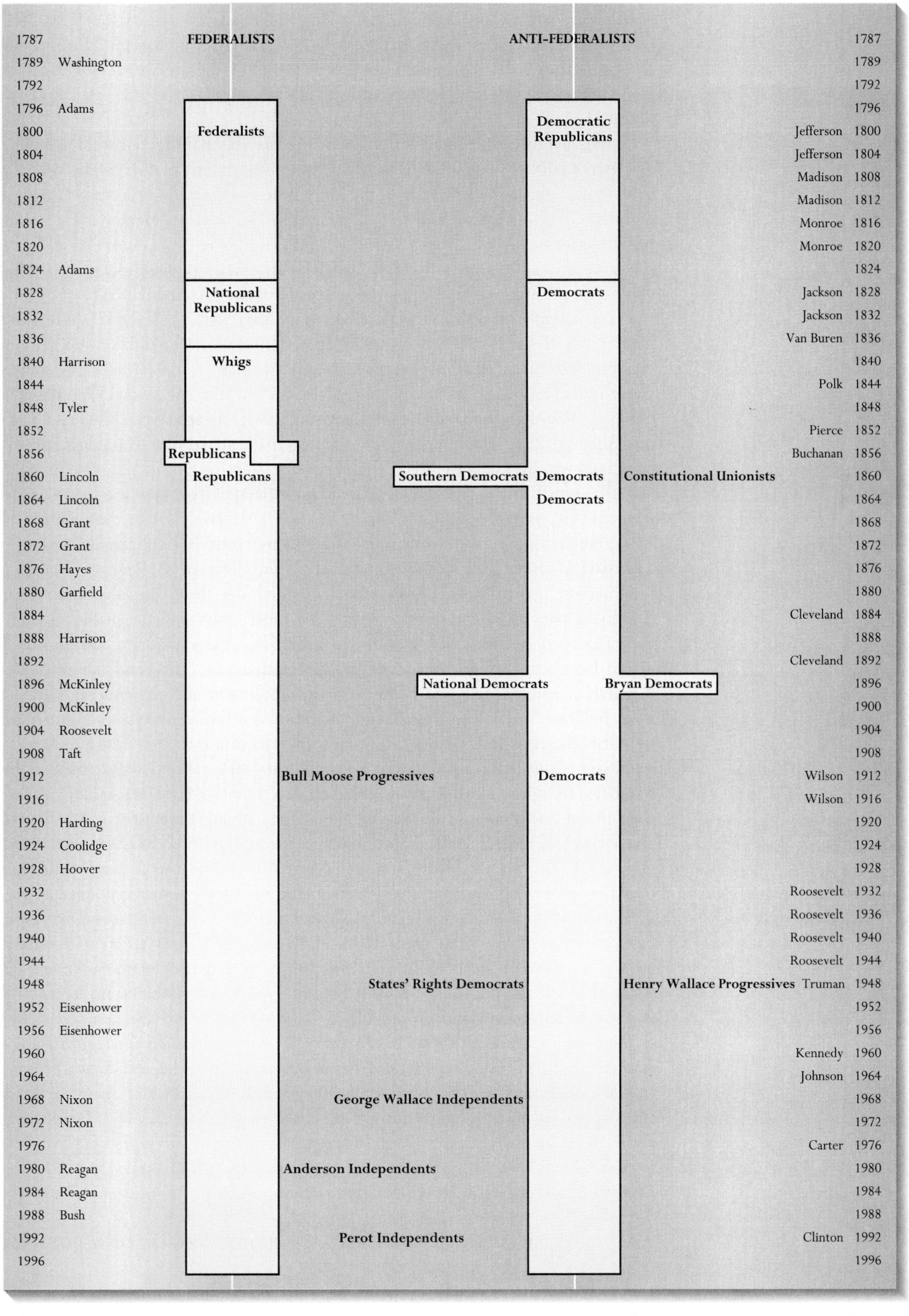

| Year | (Federalist line) | FEDERALISTS | | | ANTI-FEDERALISTS | | (Anti-Federalist line) | Year |
|------|------|------|------|------|------|------|------|------|

1787 — FEDERALISTS — ANTI-FEDERALISTS — 1787
1789 — Washington — 1789
1792 — 1792
1796 — Adams — 1796
1800 — **Federalists** — **Democratic Republicans** — Jefferson 1800
1804 — Jefferson 1804
1808 — Madison 1808
1812 — Madison 1812
1816 — Monroe 1816
1820 — Monroe 1820
1824 — Adams — 1824
1828 — **National Republicans** — **Democrats** — Jackson 1828
1832 — Jackson 1832
1836 — Van Buren 1836
1840 — Harrison — **Whigs** — 1840
1844 — Polk 1844
1848 — Tyler — 1848
1852 — Pierce 1852
1856 — **Republicans** — Buchanan 1856
1860 — Lincoln — **Republicans** — **Southern Democrats** **Democrats** **Constitutional Unionists** — 1860
1864 — Lincoln — **Democrats** — 1864
1868 — Grant — 1868
1872 — Grant — 1872
1876 — Hayes — 1876
1880 — Garfield — 1880
1884 — Cleveland 1884
1888 — Harrison — 1888
1892 — Cleveland 1892
1896 — McKinley — **National Democrats** **Bryan Democrats** — 1896
1900 — McKinley — 1900
1904 — Roosevelt — 1904
1908 — Taft — 1908
1912 — **Bull Moose Progressives** **Democrats** — Wilson 1912
1916 — Wilson 1916
1920 — Harding — 1920
1924 — Coolidge — 1924
1928 — Hoover — 1928
1932 — Roosevelt 1932
1936 — Roosevelt 1936
1940 — Roosevelt 1940
1944 — Roosevelt 1944
1948 — **States' Rights Democrats** **Henry Wallace Progressives** Truman 1948
1952 — Eisenhower — 1952
1956 — Eisenhower — 1956
1960 — Kennedy 1960
1964 — Johnson 1964
1968 — Nixon — **George Wallace Independents** — 1968
1972 — Nixon — 1972
1976 — Carter 1976
1980 — Reagan — **Anderson Independents** — 1980
1984 — Reagan — 1984
1988 — Bush — 1988
1992 — **Perot Independents** — Clinton 1992
1996 — 1996

directed their fire not against Washington but against Hamilton, John Adams, and their supporters, who called themselves **Federalists** after their leaders' outspoken defense of the Constitution during the ratification process. By the 1790s, Jefferson and Madison, as well as many **Anti-Federalists** who had initially opposed the ratification of the Constitution, began calling themselves Republicans or Democratic-Republicans, terms that had become popular after the French Revolution in 1789.

Adams narrowly defeated Jefferson in the presidential election of 1796. This election was an important milestone in the development of the parties and the presidential election system. For the first time, two candidates campaigned as members of opposing parties, and candidates for presidential elector in each state pledged themselves as "Adams's men" or "Jefferson's men." By committing themselves in advance of the actual presidential vote, these pledged electors enabled voters in each state to determine the outcome of the presidential election.

Party activity intensified in anticipation of the election of 1800. Jefferson's Democratic-Republican Party first saw the importance of organizing voters, circulating literature, and rallying the masses to their causes. Many Federalists viewed this early party activity with disdain. Indeed, the Federalists even tried to outlaw public criticism of the federal government by means of the Alien and Sedition Acts of 1798, which among other things made it a crime to publish false or malicious writings against the (Federalist) Congress or president or to "stir up hatred" against them. These acts directly challenged the newly adopted First Amendment guarantees of freedom of speech and press. But in the election of 1800, the Federalists went down to defeat. Democratic-Republican electors won a **majority** (more than half the votes cast) in the Electoral College.

However, the original Constitution provided that each presidential elector could cast two votes; the person getting the most votes won the presidency and the runner-up won the vice-presidency. If no one won a majority, the president would be elected by the House of Representatives. In 1800, each Democratic-Republican elector cast one of his votes for Jefferson and the other for Aaron Burr, Jefferson's vice-presidential running mate. But the result was an unintended tie between Jefferson and Burr, throwing the election into the House of Representatives. (The Twelfth Amendment, ratified in 1804, remedied the problem by requiring electors to cast separate votes for president and vice-president). A few disgruntled Federalists in the House considered giving Burr their votes just to embarrass Jefferson, and the ambitious Burr encouraged this chicanery. But in the end, the House selected Jefferson. President Adams and the Federalists turned over the reigns of government to Jefferson and the Democratic-Republicans.

The election of 1800 was a landmark in American democracy—the first time that control of government passed peacefully from one party to another on the basis of an election outcome. As commonplace as that may seem to Americans today, the peaceful transfer of power from one group to another remains a rarity in political systems around the world.

Jefferson's Democratic-Republican Party—later to be called the Democrats—was so successful that the Federalist Party never regained the presidency or control of Congress. The Federalists tended to represent merchants, manufacturers, and shippers, who were concentrated in New York and New England. The Democratic-Republicans tended to represent agrarian interests, from large plantation owners to small farmers. In the mostly agrarian America of the early 1800s, the Democratic-Republican Party prevailed. Jefferson easily won reelection in 1804,

**Federalists:** Those who supported the U.S. Constitution during the ratification process and who later formed a political party in support of John Adams's presidential candidacy.

**Anti-Federalists:** Those who opposed the ratification of the U.S. Constitution and the creation of a strong national government.

**Majority:** Election by more than 50 percent of all votes cast in the contest.

CHAPTER 7 • POLITICAL PARTIES: ORGANIZING POLITICS

and his allies James Madison and James Monroe overwhelmed their Federalist opponents in subsequent presidential elections. By 1820, the Federalist Party had ceased to exist. Indeed, for a few years, it seemed as if the new nation had ended party politics.

*Jacksonian Democrats and Whigs*    Partisan politics soon reappeared, however. The Democratic-Republicans had already begun to fight among themselves by the 1824 presidential election. After winning a **plurality** (at least one more vote than anyone else in the race), but not a majority, of the popular and Electoral College vote and then losing in a close decision by the factionalized House of Representatives, Jackson led his supporters to found a new party, the **Democratic Party,** to organize popular support for his 1828 presidential bid against then-President John Quincy Adams.

Jacksonian ideas both *democratized* and *nationalized* the party system. Under Jackson, the Democratic Party began to mobilize voters on behalf of the party and its candidates. It pressed the states to lower property qualifications for voting in order to recruit new Democratic Party voters. The electorate expanded from 365,000 voters in 1824 to well over a million in 1828 and over 2 million in 1840. The Democratic Party also pressed the states to choose presidential electors by popular vote rather than by state legislatures. Thus Jackson and his Democratic successor, Martin Van Buren, ran truly national campaigns directed at the voters in every state.

At the same time, Jackson's opponents formed the Whig Party, named after the British party of that name. Like the British Whigs, who opposed the power of the king, the American Whigs charged "King Andrew" with usurping the powers of Congress and the people. The Whigs quickly adopted the Democrats' tactics of national campaigning and popular organizing. By 1840, the Whigs were able to gain the White House, running William Henry Harrison—nicknamed "Old Tippecanoe" from his victory at Tippecanoe over Native Americans in 1811—and John Tyler and featuring the slogan "Tippecanoe and Tyler too."

*Post–Civil War Republican Dominance*    Whigs and Democrats continued to share national power until the slavery conflict that ignited the Civil War destroyed the old party system. The Republican Party had formed in 1854 to oppose the spread of slavery to the western territories. By the election of 1860, the slavery issue so divided the nation that four parties offered presidential candidates: Lincoln the Republican, Stephen A. Douglas the Northern Democrat, John C. Breckinridge the Southern Democrat, and John Bell the Constitutional Union Party candidate. No party came close to winning a majority of the popular vote, but Lincoln won in the Electoral College.

The new party system that emerged from the Civil War featured a victorious **Republican Party** that generally represented the northern industrial economy and a struggling Democratic Party that generally represented a southern agricultural economy. The Republican Party won every presidential election from 1860 to 1912 except for two victories by Democratic reformer and New York governor Grover Cleveland.

Yet the Democratic Party offered a serious challenge in the election of 1896 and realigned the party affiliations of the nation's voters. The Democratic Party nominated William Jennings Bryan, a talented orator and a religious fundamentalist. Bryan sought to rally the nation's white "have-nots" to the Democratic Party

**Plurality:** Election by at least one vote more than any other candidate in the race.

**Democratic Party:** One of the main parties in American politics; it traces its origins to Thomas Jefferson's Democratic-Republican Party, acquiring its current name under Andrew Jackson in 1828.

**Republican Party:** One of the two main parties in American politics; it traces its origins to the antislavery and nationalist forces that united in the 1850s and nominated Abraham Lincoln for president in 1860.

*The 1837 cartoon on the left, showing outgoing democratic President Andrew Jackson riding a donkey, is the first use of the donkey as a symbol for the Democratic party. The cartoon on the right, by Thomas Nast (1840–1902), is an early example of the use of the elephant as a symbol for the Republican party. It was Nast who popularized both symbols.*

banner, particularly the debt-ridden farmers of the South and West. His plan was to stimulate inflation (and thus enable debtors to pay their debts with "cheaper," less valuable dollars) by making plentiful western-mined "free silver" the monetary standard rather than gold. He defeated Cleveland's faction and the "Gold Democrats" in the 1896 Democratic Party convention with his famous Cross of Gold speech: "You shall not crucify mankind upon a cross of gold."

But the Republican Party rallied its forces in perhaps the most bitter presidential battle in history. It sought to convince the nation that high tariffs, protection for manufacturers, and a solid monetary standard would lead to prosperity for industrial workers as well as the new tycoons. The campaign, directed by Marcus Alonzo Hanna, attorney for John D. Rockefeller's Standard Oil Company, spent an unprecedented $16 million (an amount in inflation-adjusted dollars that has never been equaled) to elect Republican William McKinley, advertised as the candidate who would bring a "full dinner pail" to all. The battle also produced one of the largest voter turnouts in history. McKinley won in a landslide. Bryan ran twice again but lost by even larger margins. The Republican Party solidified the loyalty of industrial workers, small business owners, bankers, and large manufacturers, as well as voting blacks who respected "the party of Lincoln" and despised the segregationist practices of the southern Democratic Party.

So great was the Republican Party's dominance in national elections that only a split among Republicans enabled the Democrat Woodrow Wilson to capture the presidency in 1912. Republican Theodore Roosevelt (who became president following McKinley's assassination and had won reelection in 1904) sought to recapture the presidency from his former protégé, Republican William Howard Taft. In the **GOP** convention ("Grand Old Party," as the Republicans began labeling themselves), party regulars rejected the unpredictable Roosevelt in favor of Taft, even though Roosevelt had won the few primary elections that had recently been initiated. An irate Teddy Roosevelt launched a third, progressive party, the "Bull Moose," which actually outpolled the Republican Party in the 1912 election, the only time a third party has surpassed one of the two major parties in U.S. history. But the result was a victory for the former Princeton political science professor

**GOP:** "Grand Old Party"—a popular label for the Republican Party.

CHAPTER 7 • POLITICAL PARTIES: ORGANIZING POLITICS

Woodrow Wilson. Following Wilson's two terms, Republicans again reasserted their political dominance with victories by Warren G. Harding, Calvin Coolidge, and Herbert Hoover.

*The New Deal Democratic Party*   The promise of prosperity that empowered the Republican Party and held its membership together faded in the light of the Great Depression. The U.S. stock market crashed in 1929, and by the early 1930s, one-quarter of the labor force was unemployed. Having lost confidence in the nation's business and political leadership, in 1932 American voters turned out incumbent Republican President Herbert Hoover in favor of Democrat Franklin D. Roosevelt, who promised the country a **New Deal**.

More than just bringing the Democrats to the White House, the Great Depression marked another party realignment. This time traditionally Republican voting groups changed their affiliation and enabled the Democratic Party to dominate national politics for a generation. This realignment actually began in 1928 when Democratic presidential candidate Al Smith, a Catholic, won many northern, urban, ethnic voters away from the Republican Party. By 1932, a majority New Deal Democratic coalition had been formed in American politics. It consisted of:

* Working classes and union members, especially in large cities
* White ethnic groups who had previously aligned themselves with Republican machines
* Catholics and Jews
* African Americans, who ended their historic affiliation with the party of Lincoln to pursue new economic and social goals
* Poor people, who associated the New Deal with expanded welfare and Social Security programs
* Southern whites, who had provided the most loyal block of Democratic voters since the Civil War.

To be sure, this majority coalition had many internal factions: southern "Dixiecrats" walked out of the Democratic Party convention in 1948 to protest a party platform that called for an end to racial discrimination in employment. But the promise of a New Deal, with its vast array of government supports for workers,

**New Deal:** The policies of President Franklin D. Roosevelt during the depression of the 1930s that helped form a Democratic Party coalition of urban working class, ethnic, Catholic, Jewish, poor, and Southern voters.

*Franklin Roosevelt campaigning among coal miners in West Virginia during the presidential election campaign of 1932. Roosevelt's optimism and "can-do" attitude in the face of the Great Depression helped cement the New Deal Democratic coalition that won him the presidency.*

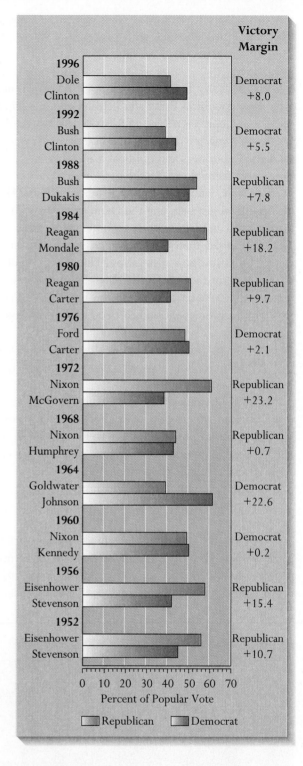

**FIGURE 7-3** The Parties in Presidential Voting

*Despite the dominance of the Democratic Party in terms of numbers of registered voters, Republicans have won seven of the eleven presidential elections since 1952, indicating that, at the presidential level, voters are not always loyal to their party.*

**Fair Deal:** The policies of President Harry Truman extending Roosevelt's New Deal and maintaining the Democratic Party's voter coalition.

aged, disabled, widows and children, and farmers, held this coalition together reasonably well. President Harry Truman's **Fair Deal** proved that the coalition could survive its founder, Franklin Roosevelt. Republican Dwight D. Eisenhower made inroads into this coalition by virtue of his personal popularity and the Republican Party's acceptance of most New Deal programs. But John F. Kennedy's "New Frontier" demonstrated the continuing appeal of the Democratic Party tradition.

Lyndon Johnson's **Great Society** went further than the programs of any of his predecessors in government intervention in the economic and social life of the nation. Indeed, it might be argued that the excesses of the Great Society laid the foundation for a political reaction that eventually destroyed the old Democratic coalition and led to yet another new party alignment (see Figure 7-3).

*A New Republican Majority*    The American political system underwent massive convulsions in the late 1960s as a result of both the civil rights revolution at home and an unpopular war in Vietnam. Strains were felt in all of the nation's political institutions, from the courts to the Congress to the presidency. And when Lyndon Johnson announced his decision not to run for reelection in 1968, the Democratic Party erupted in a battle that ultimately destroyed its majority support among presidential voters.

At the 1968 Democratic Party convention in Chicago, Vice-President Hubert Humphrey controlled a majority of the delegates inside the convention hall, but antiwar protesters dominated media coverage outside the hall. When Chicago police attacked unruly demonstrators with batons, the media broadcast to the world an image of the nation's turmoil. In the presidential campaign that followed, both candidates—Democrat Hubert Humphrey and Republican Richard Nixon—presented nearly identical positions supporting the U.S. military commitment in Vietnam while endorsing a negotiated, "honorable" settlement of the war. But the image of the Democratic Party became associated with the street protesters. Inside the convention hall, pressure from women and minorities led party leaders to adopt changes in the party's delegate selection process for future conventions to assure better representation of these groups—at the expense of Democratic officeholders (see "Making Party Rules" later in this chapter for more details).

*Battles between "hippie" demonstrators and police in Chicago during the Democratic National Convention in 1968 bolstered Republicans' arguments that government by the Democrats had led to a breakdown in fundamental values and that the nation must shift gears in order to restore "law and order."*

In 1972, the Democratic Party convention strongly reflected the views of anti-war protesters, civil rights advocates, feminist organizations, and liberal activists generally. The visibility of these activists, who appeared to be well to the left of both Democratic Party voters and the electorate in general, allowed the Republican Party to portray the Democratic presidential nominee, George McGovern, as an unpatriotic liberal, willing to "crawl to Hanoi" and to sacrifice the nation's honor for peace. It also allowed the Republicans to characterize the new Democratic Party as soft on crime, tolerant of disorder, and committed to racial and sexual quotas in American life. Richard Nixon, never very popular personally, was able to win in a landslide in 1972. The Watergate scandal and Nixon's forced resignation only temporarily stemmed the tide of "the new Republican majority." Democrat Jimmy Carter's narrow victory over Republican Gerald R. Ford in 1976 owed much to the latter's pardon of Nixon.

*The Reagan Coalition*    Under the leadership of Ronald Reagan, the Republican Party was able to assemble a majority coalition that dominated presidential elections in the 1980s, giving Reagan landslide victories in 1980 and 1984 and George Bush a convincing win in 1988. The **Reagan Coalition** consisted of:

- Economic conservatives concerned about high taxes and excessive government regulation, including business and professional voters who had traditionally supported the Republican Party
- Social conservatives concerned about crime, drugs, and racial conflict, including many white ethnic voters and union members who had traditionally voted Democratic
- Religious fundamentalists concerned about such issues as abortion and prayer in schools
- Southern whites concerned about racial issues, including affirmative action programs
- Internationalists and anticommunists who wanted the United States to maintain a strong military force and to confront Soviet-backed Marxist regimes around the world.

Reagan held this coalition together in large part through his personal popularity and his infectious optimism about the United States and its future. Although sometimes at odds with one another, economic conservatives, religious fundamentalists, and internationalists could unite behind the "Great Communicator." Reagan's presidential victory in 1980 helped to elect a Republican majority to the U.S. Senate and encouraged Democratic conservatives in the Democrat-controlled House of Representatives to frequently vote with Republicans. As a result, Reagan got most of what he asked of Congress in his first term: cuts in personal income taxes, increased spending for national defense, and slower growth of federal regulatory activity. With the assistance of the Federal Reserve Board, inflation was brought under control. But Reagan largely failed to cut government spending as he had promised, and the result was a series of huge federal deficits. Reagan appointed conservatives to the Supreme Court and the federal judiciary (see Chapter 13), but no major decisions were reversed (including the *Roe v. Wade* decision protecting abortion); social conservatives had to be content with the president's symbolic support.

**Reagan Coalition:** A combination of economic and social conservatives, religious fundamentalists, and defense-minded anticommunists who rallied behind Republican President Ronald Reagan.

CHAPTER 7 • POLITICAL PARTIES: ORGANIZING POLITICS

During these years, the national Democratic Party was saddled with an unpopular image as the party of special-interest groups. As more middle-class and working-class voters deserted to the GOP, the key remaining loyal Democratic constituencies were African Americans and other minorities, government employees, union leaders, liberal intellectuals in the media and universities, feminist organizations, and environmentalists. Democratic presidential candidates Walter Mondale in 1984 and Michael Dukakis in 1988 were obliged to take liberal positions to win the support of these groups in the primary elections. Later both candidates sought to move toward the center of the ideological battleground in the general election. But Republican Party strategists were able to "define" Mondale and Dukakis through negative campaign advertising (see Chapter 8) as liberal defenders of special-interest groups. The general conservative tilt of public opinion in the 1980s added to the effectiveness of the GOP strategy of branding Democratic presidential candidates with the "*L* word" *(liberal)*.

*Clinton and the "New" Democrats*    Yet even while Democratic candidates fared poorly in presidential elections, Democrats continued to maintain control of the House of Representatives, to win back control of the U.S. Senate in 1986, and to hold more state governorships and state legislative seats than the Republicans. Thus the Democratic Party retained a strong leadership base on which to rebuild itself.

During the 1980s, Democratic leaders among governors and senators came together in a **Democratic Leadership Council** to create a "new" Democratic Party closer to the center of the political spectrum. The chair of the Democratic Leadership Council was the young, energetic, and successful governor of Arkansas, Bill Clinton. The concern of the council was that the Democratic Party's traditional support for social justice and social welfare programs was overshadowing its commitment to economic prosperity. Many council members argued that a healthy economy was a prerequisite to progress in social welfare. The council became closely identified with *neo-liberal* arguments (see Chapter 2) about the need for government to stimulate economic growth, productivity, and competitiveness in world markets. Not all Democrats agreed with the council agenda. African-American leaders (including the Reverend Jesse Jackson), as well as liberal and environmental groups, feared that the priorities of the council would result in the sacrifice of traditional Democratic Party commitments to minorities, the poor, and the environment.

In the 1992 presidential election, Bill Clinton was in a strong position to take advantage of the faltering economy under George Bush, to stress the "new" Democratic Party's commitment to the middle class, and to avoid being labeled as a liberal defender of special interests. At the same time, he managed to rally the party's core activist groups—liberals, intellectuals, African Americans, feminists, and environmentalists. Many liberals in the party deliberately soft-pedaled their views during the 1992 election in order not to offend voters, hoping to win with Clinton and then fight for liberal programs later. Clinton won with 43 percent of the vote, to George Bush's 38 percent. Independent Ross Perot captured a surprising 19 percent of the popular vote, including many voters who were alienated from both the Democratic and Republican Parties. Once in office, Clinton appeared to revert to liberal policy directions rather than pursue the more moderate line he had espoused as a "new" Democrat. Yet polls continued to suggest that voters favored *moderate* and *conservative* political labels, as well as many specific

**Democratic Leadership Council:** An organization of party leaders who sought to create a "new" Democratic Party to appeal to middle-class, moderate voters.

policy proposals that Clinton opposed, including a Balanced Budget Amendment, congressional term limits, and cutbacks in social welfare spending. As Clinton's ratings sagged, the opportunity arose for a Republican resurgence.

*Republican Resurgence*    A political earthquake shook Washington in the 1994 congressional elections, when the Republicans for the first time in forty years captured the House of Representatives, regained control of the Senate, and captured a majority of the nation's governorships. Not a single Republican incumbent lost, while Democratic incumbents lost two Senate, thirty-five House, and five governor races. Republicans won a large majority of open-seat races and for the first time in history won more seats in the South than the Democrats. This southern swing to the Republicans in congressional elections seemed to confirm the realignment of southern voters that had begun earlier in presidential elections. Just two years after a Democratic president had been elected, the GOP won its biggest nationwide victory since the Great Depression.

*Clinton Holds On*    Following the Republican victory, the Democratic Party was in disarray. The new Republican House Speaker, Newt Gingrich, appeared to seize national policy leadership; Clinton was widely viewed as a failed president. But the Republicans quickly squandered their political opportunity. They had promised much—a balanced federal budget, congressional term limits, a middle-class tax cut, welfare reform, and more—but they delivered little. Majority Leader Bob Dole failed by one vote to pass the Balanced Budget Amendment in the Senate. President Clinton took an unexpectedly hard line toward GOP spending cuts, vetoing several budget bills. When the federal government officially "closed down" for lack of appropriated funds, the public appeared to blame Republicans. Polls showed a dramatic recovery in the president's approval ratings. Clinton skillfully portrayed GOP leaders, especially Newt Gingrich, as "extremists" and himself as a responsible moderate prepared to trim the budget, reduce the deficit, and reform welfare, "while still protecting Medicare, Medicaid, education, and the environment." By early 1996 Clinton had set the stage for his reelection campaign.

Bill Clinton is the first Democratic president to be *re*-elected since Franklin D. Roosevelt. Clinton rode to victory on a growing economy. In 1996 most Americans thought the nation's economy was excellent or good (57 percent), compared to very few (19 percent) who thought so when Bush had sought reelection in 1992. They were willing to put aside doubts about Clinton's character, and ignored Republican Bob Dole's call for tax reductions. Clinton won with 49 percent of the popular vote to Dole's 41 percent and Perot's 8 percent. But Clinton's victory failed to rejuvenate the Democratic Party's fortunes across the country. The GOP retained its majorities in both houses of Congress.

# POLITICAL PARTIES AND DEMOCRATIC GOVERNMENT

"Political parties created modern democracy and modern democracy is unthinkable save in terms of parties."[4] Traditionally, political scientists have praised parties as indispensable to democratic government. They have argued that parties are essential for organizing popular majorities to exercise control over government. The development of political parties in all the democracies of the world testifies to the underlying importance of parties to democratic government. But political parties in the United States have lost their preeminent position as instruments of democracy. Other structures and organizations in society—interest groups, the mass media, independent campaign organizations, primary elections, social welfare agencies—now perform many of the functions traditionally regarded as prerogatives of political parties. Nevertheless, the Democratic and Republican parties remain important organizing structures for politics in the United States.

*"Responsible" Parties in Theory*    In theory, political parties function in a democracy to organize majorities around broad principles of government in order to win public office and enact these principles into law. A "responsible" party should:

- Adopt a platform setting forth its principles and policy positions.
- Recruit candidates for public office who agree with the party's platform.
- Inform and educate the public about the platform.
- Organize and direct campaigns based on platform principles.
- Organize the legislature to ensure party control in policy making.
- Hold its elected officials responsible for enacting the party's platform.

*If* responsible, disciplined, policy-oriented parties competed for majority support, *if* they offered clear policy alternatives to the voters, and *if* the voters cast their ballots on the basis of these policy options, *then* the winning party would have a "policy mandate" from the people to guide the course of government. In that way, the democratic ideal of government by majority rule would be implemented (see *Up Close:* "The Republican 'Contract with America'").

*Winning Wins over Principle*    The **responsible party model** never accurately described the American party system. The major American parties have been loose coalitions of individuals and groups seeking to attract sufficient votes to gain control of government. *Winning has generally been more important than any principles or policies.* America's major parties must appeal to tens of millions of voters in every section of the nation and from all walks of life. If a major party is to acquire a majority capable of controlling the U.S. government, it cannot limit its appeal by relying on a single unifying principle. Instead, it must form coalitions of voters from as many sectors of the population as it can. Major American parties therefore usually do not emphasize particular principles or ideologies so much as try to find a common ground of agreement among many different people. This emphasis does not mean that there are no policy differences between the American parties. On the contrary, each party tends to appeal to a distinctive coalition of interests, and therefore each party expresses somewhat distinctive policy views (see *What Do You Think?* "Popular Images of the Democratic and Republican Parties").

In their efforts to win, major American political parties strive to attract the support of the large numbers of people near the center of public opinion. It is generally true that there are more votes at the center of the ideological spectrum—the middle-of-the-road—than on the extreme liberal or conservative ends. Thus *there is no real incentive for vote-maximizing parties to take strong policy positions in opposition to each other.* As the Democratic and Republican policy positions

**Responsible Party Model:** A system in which competitive parties adopt a platform of principles, recruiting candidates and directing campaigns based on the platform, and holding their elected officials responsible for enacting it.

# The Republican "Contract with America"

In the 1994 congressional election campaign, the Republican House leader Newt Gingrich of Georgia sought to revive the *responsible* party model, setting forth ten policy proposals in a "Contract with America" signed by more than 300 of his party's House candidates. The contract urged voters to send Republican congressional candidates to Washington to implement this national policy agenda, and it promised to bring these proposals to a floor vote if the Republicans won a majority of seats in the House of Representatives.

The policy stands in the Contract with America were reasonably specific as campaign promises, and they enjoyed overwhelming popularity with the public. They included a Balanced Budget Amendment to the Constitution (supported by 85 percent of the public), line-item veto power to the president (supported by 77 percent), placing a two-year limit on welfare payments and denying these payments to teenage mothers (supported by 79 percent), a $500 per child tax credit for middle-income families (supported by 83 percent), a cut in the capital gains tax (supported by 58 percent), and congressional term limits (supported by 73 percent). The only hedge was that the contract promised only to bring these items up for a vote, not necessarily to pass them. And only Republican House members signed the Contract with America, not Republican senators. Nevertheless, the contract was much more specific than the vague party platforms ritualistically adopted at the Democratic and Republican conventions every four years.

The Republican victory in the 1994 congressional elections was one of historic proportions. The GOP captured control of the Senate 53 to 47 and, more important, for the first time in forty years, control of the House of Representatives 230 to 204 (with 1 independent). It was the most sweeping party victory in recent congressional history.

Yet it is doubtful that the Contract with America reestablished the responsible party model in American politics. First of all, it is by no means certain that the Republican victories in the 1994 midterm election are attributable to voter support for the policy

*Newt Gingrich addresses the rally on Capitol Hill in September 1994 in which Republican congressional candidates pledged their support for the Contract with America.*

proposals in the contract. Opinion polls indicated that the vast majority of voters (80 percent) had never heard of the Contract with America. Voters were generally dissatisfied with Congress and identified the ruling Democratic Party with "politics as usual." It might be argued that the voters wanted "change," but it is not clear what kind of change they wanted. Indeed, President Bill Clinton interpreted the outcome as the voters' endorsement of a continuation of his own policies, admitting only that "they were not satisfied with the progress we had made."

Second, to reestablish the responsible party model, the Republicans in Congress were obliged to deliver on their promises, that is, to *enact* the major provisions of the Contract with America, not merely promise to vote on them.

But key items in the Contract never became law. Perhaps the most important promise—the Balanced Budget Amendment to the Constitution—lost by a single vote in the Senate. Congressional term limits failed in the House and were never even voted on in the Senate. Stalemate ensued when the president and Congress could not agree on how to balance the budget. Only welfare reform and the presidential item veto became law. By promising more in the Contract than it could deliver, the Republican-controlled Congress lost public support over time. By 1996 opinion polls showed that majorities of Americans disapproved of House Speaker Newt Gingrich and the GOP Congress.

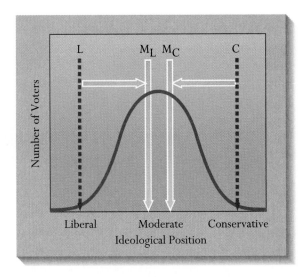

(FIGURE 7-4)    **Winning versus Principle**

*Why don't we have a party system based on principles, with a liberal party and a conservative party, each offering the voters a real ideological choice? Let's assume that voters generally choose the party that is* closest *to their own ideological position. If the liberal party (L) took a strong ideological position to the left of most voters, the conservative party (C) would move toward the center, winning more moderate votes, even while retaining its conservative supporters, who would still prefer it to the more liberal opposition party. Likewise, if the conservative party took a strong ideological position to the right of most voters, the liberal party would move to the center and win. So both parties must abandon strong ideological positions and move to the center, becoming moderate in the fight for support of moderate voters.*

approach the center, the parties seem to echo each other, and critics attack them as Tweedledee and Tweedledum (see Figure 7-4).

*The Erosion of Traditional Party Functions*    Parties play only a limited role in campaign organization and finance. Campaigns are generally directed by professional campaign management firms or by the candidates' personal organizations, not by parties. Campaigns are financed largely by contributions solicited directly by the candidates or by their personal representatives, with the parties making only modest financial contributions. Party organizations have largely been displaced in campaign activity by professional firms, media consultants, pollsters, and others hired by the candidates themselves (see Chapter 8).

American political parties also play only a limited role in recruiting candidates for elected office. Most political candidates today are self-recruited. People initiate their own candidacies, first contacting friends and financial supporters. Especially in state and local races, candidates contact party officials only as a courtesy, if at all. However, candidates running for federal offices generally seek the support of their party's leaders to strengthen their own credibility as candidates.

The major American political parties cannot really control who their **nominee**—the party's entry in a general election race—will be. Rather, party **nominations** for most elected offices are won in *primary elections*. In a **primary election,** registered voters select from among a party's members who meet minimum legal standards and choose to run. The primary winner then becomes

**Nominee:** A political party's entry in a general election race.

**Nomination:** A political party's selection of its candidate for a public office.

**Primary elections:** Elections to choose party nominees for public office; may be open or closed.

# Popular Images of the Democratic and Republican Parties

What do Americans think of the Democratic and Republican Parties? Generally speaking, the Democratic Party has been able to maintain an image of "the party of the common people," while the Republican Party has long been saddled with an image of "favoring the rich."

But when it comes to popular perceptions of each party's ability to deal with problems confronting the nation, the Democratic and Republican Parties appear evenly matched. The Republican Party is trusted to "do a better job" in handling foreign affairs and maintaining a strong national defense. It is also seen as better able to fight crime and illegal drugs. Finally, the Republican Party enjoys a reputation of being better at "holding down taxes."

The Democratic Party enjoys its greatest advantage on "compassion issues" like helping the poor, the elderly, and the homeless. And the Democrats have long enjoyed the support of the high-voter-turnout over-sixty-five age group because it is trusted to do a better job "protecting the Social Security system."

*Source:* Surveys by the Gallup and CBS News/*New York Times*, reported in *American Enterprises* (March/April 1994); 78–80.

**Question**: *In general, do you think the (Republican/Democrat) party favors the rich?*

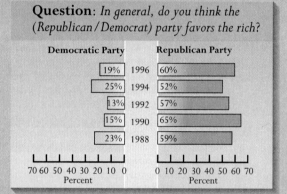

| Democratic Party | | Republican Party |
|---|---|---|
| 19% | 1996 | 60% |
| 25% | 1994 | 52% |
| 13% | 1992 | 57% |
| 15% | 1990 | 65% |
| 23% | 1988 | 59% |

Percent / Percent

**Question**: *Regardless of how you usually vote, do you think the Democratic Party or the Republican Party is:*

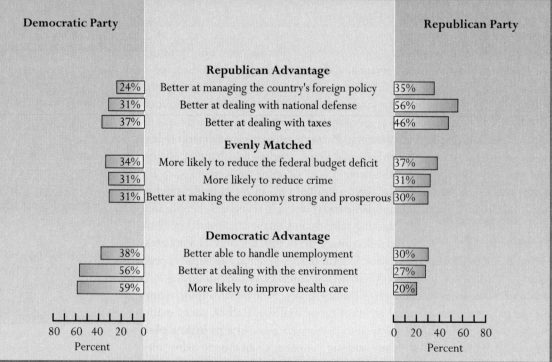

| Democratic Party | | Republican Party |
|---|---|---|
| **Republican Advantage** | | |
| 24% | Better at managing the country's foreign policy | 35% |
| 31% | Better at dealing with national defense | 56% |
| 37% | Better at dealing with taxes | 46% |
| **Evenly Matched** | | |
| 34% | More likely to reduce the federal budget deficit | 37% |
| 31% | More likely to reduce crime | 31% |
| 31% | Better at making the economy strong and prosperous | 30% |
| **Democratic Advantage** | | |
| 38% | Better able to handle unemployment | 30% |
| 56% | Better at dealing with the environment | 27% |
| 59% | More likely to improve health care | 20% |

Percent / Percent

the party's nominee. Party leaders may endorse a candidate in a primary election and may even work to try to ensure the victory of their favorite, but the voters in that party's primary select the nominee.

Once nominated, candidates have little need of their parties, since they usually communicate directly with voters through the mass media. Television has replaced the party organization as the principal medium of communication between candidates and voters. Candidates no longer rely much on party workers to carry their message from door to door. Instead, candidates can come directly into the voters' living room via television.

Even if the American parties wanted to take stronger policy positions and to enact them into law, they would not have the means to do so. *American political parties have no way to bind their elected officials to the party platform or even to their campaign promises.* Parties have no strong disciplinary sanctions to use against members of Congress who vote against the party's policy position. The parties cannot deny them renomination. At most, the party's leadership in Congress can threaten the status, privileges, and pet bills of disloyal members (see Chapter 10). Party cohesion, where it exists, is more a product of like-mindedness than of party discipline.

Finally, American political parties no longer perform social welfare functions—trading off social services, patronage jobs, or petty favors in exchange for votes. Traditional party organizations, or **machines,** especially in large cities, once helped immigrants get settled in, found **patronage** jobs in government for party workers, and occasionally provided aid to impoverished but loyal party voters. But *government bureaucracies have replaced the political parties as providers of social services.* Government employment agencies, welfare agencies, civil service systems, and other bureaucracies now provide the social services once undertaken by political machines in search of votes.

## PARTIES AS ORGANIZERS OF ELECTIONS

Despite the erosion of many of their functions, America's political parties survive as the principal institutions for organizing elections. Party nominations organize electoral choice by narrowing the field of aspiring office seekers to the Democratic and Republican candidates in most cases. Very few independents are elected to high political office in the United States. Democratic or Republican Party nominations are sought by most serious aspirants for state and national office—though as Ross Perot proved in 1992, there are exceptions (see *Up Close:* "Independent Politics: The Perot Factor"). Nonpartisan elections—elections in which there are no party nominations and all candidates run without an official party label—are common only in local elections, for city council, county commission, school board, and so on. Party conventions are still held in many states and every presidential year, but these conventions seldom have the power to determine the parties' nominees for public office.

*Party Conventions*   Historically, party nominations were made by caucus or convention. The **caucus** was the earliest nominating process; party leaders (party chairs, elected officials, and "bosses") would simply meet several months before the election and decide upon the party's nominee themselves. The early presidents—Thomas Jefferson, James Madison, James Monroe, and John Quincy Adams—were nominated by caucuses of Congress members. Complaints about the exclusion of people from this process led to nominations by convention—

**Machine:** Tightly disciplined party organization, headed by a boss, that relies on material rewards—including patronage jobs—to control politics.

**Patronage:** Appointment to public office based on party loyalty.

**Caucus:** A nominating process in which party leaders select the party's nominee.

# Independent Politics: The Perot Factor

Although no independent candidate has ever made it to the White House, independent presidential candidates have affected the outcome of the race between the major party candidates. For example, Teddy Roosevelt's 1912 "Bull Moose" effort split off enough votes from Republican William Howard Taft to allow Democrat Woodrow Wilson to win. But the American two-party system historically has discounted the electoral chances of independent candidates.

Texas billionaire Ross Perot, however, initially seemed to defy the conventional wisdom about independent candidates. In 1992 he motivated tens of thousands of supporters in a grass-roots effort, "United We Stand, America," that succeeded in placing his name on the ballot in all fifty states. And Perot himself promised to resolve the financial obstacle by spending "whatever it takes" from his own huge fortune to mount a "world-class campaign." He ended up spending about $70 million (almost all of it his own money), an amount roughly equivalent to that spent by each of the major party candidates.

Perot's popular support mushroomed to 35 percent in the polls by late spring, higher than any independent candidate's support in the history of modern polling. His twangy Texas quotes captivated audiences,

yet he carefully avoided taking clear policy positions. Perot promised only to "fix things," appealing to voters as a successful "can do" business executive challenging the political "establishment." Perot's political support came mostly from the center of the political spectrum—people who identified themselves as independents rather than as Democrats or Republicans and people who considered themselves middle of the road rather than liberal or conservative.

But "Perot mania" began to fade once the media started tearing down the candidate they had helped to create. Perot himself blamed Republican "dirty tricksters" for the negative publicity, and no doubt many of the media leads were supplied by the Bush camp. In July, at the start of the Democratic convention, Perot announced his withdrawal from the race, though he never removed his name from the ballot in any state and actually continued to fund his petition drives. Many Perot supporters were deeply disappointed or angry with the temperamental tycoon. In September, he staged a "poll" of his "volunteers" and cited the results as a call to reenter the campaign.

Perot launched the first real electronic campaign—shunning the usual daily flying circus of cross-country airport speeches, rallies, photo ops, and press conferences in favor of TV talk show appearances, spot commercials, and paid half-hour "infomercials." With pointer in hand, Perot flipped through charts depicting the nation's economic problems.

Perot's blunt Texas talk clearly "won" the first presidential debate. "If it's time for action, I have the experience that counts. If it's time for gridlock and talk and finger-pointing, I'm the wrong man." In all three debates, Clinton and Bush treated Perot with kid gloves, not wanting to alienate his middle-class supporters. The debates rehabilitated Perot's candidacy.

In the end, Perot garnered 19 percent of the popular vote, the highest percentage won by a third party candidate since Teddy Roosevelt in 1912. Moreover, the Perot campaign played a major part in increasing overall voter turnout for the first time in more than thirty years. Perot's candidacy prevented Bill Clinton from claiming majority support, holding the winner to 43 percent of the total votes cast. But Perot's voters were spread across the nation. He failed to win in a single state, and thus came up with no electoral votes.

Perot's 1996 presidential campaign "sequel" never really got off the ground. First he teased his followers about whether he would run again, and even recruited former Colorado Governor Richard Lamm to enter the race to be the nominee of his new Reform Party, only to humiliate him later in an awkward "electronic" nominating convention. With only 5 to 6 percent support in the early polls and no real chance of winning any electoral votes, Perot was excluded from the presidential debates. Rather than spend his own money this time, he accepted taxpayer-funded presidential campaign money.

But in his second national campaign Perot was no longer a media novelty. Indeed, in many appearances on *Larry King Live,* he often appeared brusque, prickly, irritating, and autocratic. His key issues—deficit reduction and opposition to international trade agreements—seemed less compelling to voters in a thriving economy. On election day he won fewer than half of the votes he had garnered four years earlier, and again failed to win any state's electoral votes.

**Ward:** A division of a city for electoral or administrative purposes or as a unit for organizing political parties.

**Precinct:** A subdivision of a city, county, or ward for election purposes.

large meetings of delegates sent by local party organizations—starting in 1832. Andrew Jackson was the first president to be nominated by convention. The convention was considered more democratic than the caucus.

For nearly a century, party conventions were held at all levels of government—local, state, and national. City or county conventions included delegates from local **wards** and **precincts,** who nominated candidates for city or county office, for the state legislature, or even for the House of Representatives when a congressional district fell within the city or country. Only Nebraska has nonpartisan elections for its unicameral (one-house) state legislature. State conventions included delegates from counties and nominated governors, U.S. senators, and other statewide officers. State parties chose delegates to the Republican and Democratic national conventions every four years to nominate a president.

*Party Primaries*    Today, primary elections have largely replaced conventions as the means of selecting the Democratic and Republican nominees for public

*Political parties as organizers of elections. (a) The Executive Committee of the Republican National Convention in Chicago in 1880. Conventions emerged as the main way for parties to select candidates in the nineteenth century. (b) Bob Dole celebrates after winning a crucial set of primaries on Super Tuesday. Today party candidates are determined by primary elections rather than by convention. (c) Parties also seek to attract voters through registration drives. (d) President Clinton campaigning on his way to the Democratic National Convention in Chicago. Parties provide the organizational structure for political campaigns.*

*(a)*

*(b)*

*(c)*

*(d)*

CHAPTER 7 • POLITICAL PARTIES: ORGANIZING POLITICS

office.[5] Primary elections, introduced as part of the progressive reform movement of the early twentieth century, allow the party's voters to choose the party's nominee directly. The primary election was designed to bypass the power of party organizations and party leaders and to further democratize the nomination process. It generally succeeded in doing so, but it also had the effect of seriously weakening political parties, since candidates seeking a party nomination need only appeal to party *voters*—not *leaders*—for support in the primary election.[6]

Primary elections to choose each party's nominee may be open or closed. **Closed primaries** allow only voters who are registered as Democrats or Republicans to vote in their party's primaries. Voters who wish to cast ballots in a particular party's primary must declare their party affiliation sometime before the primary. Persons registered as independents cannot vote in either party's primary. Thus closed primaries tend to discourage people from officially registering as independents, even if they think of themselves as independent. About half the states hold closed primaries.[7] **Open primaries** allow voters to choose on election day in which party primary they wish to participate. Anyone, regardless of prior party affiliation, may choose to vote in either party's primary. Voters simply request the ballot of *one* party or the other. (Only in Alaska and Washington can primary voters cast ballots in *both* party primaries.) About half the states hold open primaries. Open primaries provide opportunities for voters to *cross over* party lines and vote in the primary of the party they usually do not support. One concern about open primaries is their potential for **raiding**—an organized effort by one party to get its members to cross over in a primary and defeat an attractive candidate in the opposition party's primary, thus strengthening the raiding party's chances in the general election. However, there is little evidence that large numbers of voters connive in such a fashion.

Some states hold a **runoff primary** when no candidate receives a majority or a designated percentage of the vote in the party's first primary election. A runoff primary is limited to the two highest vote-getters in the first primary. Runoff elections are more common in the southern United States.[8] In most states, only a plurality of votes is needed to win a primary election.

*General Elections* Several months after the primaries and conventions, the **general election** (usually held in November, on the first Tuesday after the first Monday for presidential and most state elections) determines who will occupy elective office. Winners of the Democratic and Republican primary elections must face each other—and any independent or minor-party candidates—in the general election. Voters in the general election may chose any candidate, regardless of how they voted earlier in their party's primary or whether they voted in the primary at all.

Independent and minor-party candidates can get on the general election ballot, although the process is usually very difficult. Most states require that independent candidates file a petition with the signatures of several thousand registered voters. The number of signatures varies from state to state and office to office, but it may range up to 5 or 10 percent of *all* registered voters—a very large number that, in a big state especially, presents a difficult obstacle. The same petition requirements usually apply to minor parties, though some states automatically carry a minor party's nominee on the general election ballot if that party's candidate or candidates received a certain percentage (for example, 10 percent) of the vote in the previous general election.

**Closed primaries:** Primary elections in which voters must declare (or have previously declared) their party affiliation and can cast a ballot only in their own party's primary election.

**Open primaries:** Primary elections in which a voter may cast a ballot in either party's primary election.

**Raiding:** An organized effort by one party to get its members to cross over in a primary and defeat an attractive candidate in the opposition party's primary.

**Runoff primary:** An additional primary held between the top two vote-getters in a primary where no candidate has received a majority of the vote.

**General election:** Election to choose among candidates nominated by parties and/or independent candidates who gained access to the ballot by petition.

# WHERE'S THE PARTY?

The Democratic and Republican parties are found in different political arenas (see Figure 7-5). There is, first of all, the **party-in-the-electorate**—the voters who identify themselves as Democrats or Republicans and who tend to vote for the candidates of their party. The party-in-the-electorate appears to be in decline today. Party loyalties among voters are weakening. More people identify themselves as independents, and more **ticket splitters** divide their votes between candidates of different parties for different offices in the same general election, and more voters cast their ballots without regard to the party affiliation of the candidates than ever before.

The second locus of party activity is the **party-in-the-government**—officials who received their party's nomination and won the general election. The party-in-the-government includes members of Congress, state legislators and local government officials, and elected members of the executive branch, including the president and governors.

Party identification and loyalty among elected officeholders (the party-in-the-government) are generally stronger than party identification and loyalty among the party-in-the-electorate. Nevertheless, party loyalties among elected officials have also weakened over time. (We will examine the role of parties in Congress in Chapter 9 and the president's party role in Chapter 10.)

Finally, there is the **party organization**—national and state party officials and workers, committee members, convention delegates, and others active in the party. The Democratic and Republican party organizations formally resemble the

**FIGURE 7-5** **Where's the Party?**
*Even among Americans who strongly identify with a major party, there are differences among those who are strictly members of the party-in-the-electorate (voters), those who are members of the party-in-the-government (elected officials), and those who are members of the party organization (national and state party committee members).*

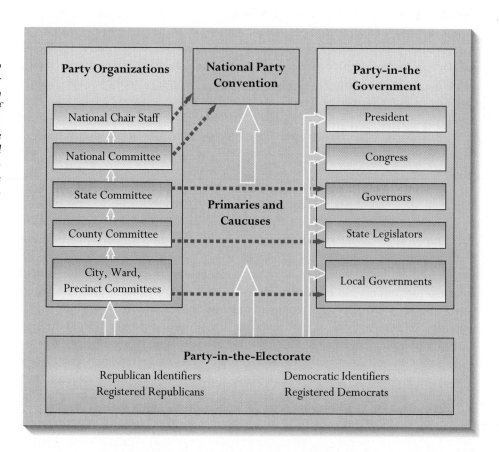

CHAPTER 7 • POLITICAL PARTIES: ORGANIZING POLITICS

American federal system, with national committees, officers and staffs, and national conventions, 50 state committees, and more than 3,000 county committees with city, ward, and precinct levels under their supervision. State committees are not very responsive to the direction of the national committee, and in most states, city and county party organizations operate quite independently of the state committees. In other words, there is no real hierarchy of authority in American parties.

*National Party Structure*    The Democratic and Republican national party conventions possess *formal* authority over the parties. They meet every four years not only to nominate candidates for president and vice-president but also to adopt a party platform, choose party officers, and adopt rules for the party's operation. Because the convention is a large body that meets only three or four days, however, its real function is to ratify decisions made by national party leaders— including the presidential nominee, who has already been chosen in primary elections throughout the country.

The Democratic and Republican National Committees, made up of delegates from each state and territory, are supposed to govern party affairs *between* conventions. But the *real* work of the national party organizations is undertaken by the national party chairs and staff. The national chair is officially chosen by the national committee but is actually chosen by the party's presidential candidate. If the party wins the presidency, the national chair usually serves as a liaison with the president for party affairs. If the party loses, the chair may be replaced before the next national convention. The national chair is supposed to be neutral in the party's primary battles, but when an incumbent president is seeking reelection, the national chair and staff lean very heavily in the president's favor (see *People in Politics:* "Ron Brown, Serving Party and Country").

The power of the national chair and staff lies in their ability to raise campaign funds and assist the party's candidates in presidential and congressional elections. The Republican National Committee's (RNC) staff took the lead in fund raising in the 1980s, devising sophisticated computerized mailing lists and a huge file of potential contributors. The RNC used these funds to assist Republican candidates in House and Senate races, commission polls, develop campaign themes, analyze voter trends, and promote the party as a whole in national advertising. The success of the RNC inspired the Democratic National Committee (DNC) to emulate these activities. By 1992, the DNC was able to match the RNC in fund raising.

*State Party Organizations*    State party organizations consist of a state committee, a state chair who heads the committee, and a staff working at the state capital. Democratic and Republican state committees vary from state to state in composition, organization, and function. The state party chair is generally selected by the state committee, but this selection is often dictated by the party's candidate for governor. Membership on the state committee may range from about a dozen up to several hundred. The members may be chosen through party primaries or by state party conventions. Generally, representation on state committees is allocated by counties, but occasionally other units of government are recognized in state party organizations.

Most state party organizations maintain full-time staffs, including an executive director and public relations, fund-raising, and research people. These organizations help to raise campaign funds for their candidates, conduct registration

## Ron Brown, Serving Party and Country

The first African American to become chair of a major political party, Ron Brown preferred to be known as the person who regained the White House for the Democrats in 1992. A long time Washington lobbyist and insider, Brown's goal was to unite the Democratic Party: "We'll all work together, brown, black, yellow, and white." Democratic leaders described Brown as a team player who avoided racial and ethnic politics and concerned himself with the process of electing Democrats to national office.

Brown grew up in Harlem. Both of his parents were college graduates, and his father managed the Theresa Hotel, next to the Apollo Theater. As a youth, Brown was exposed to the upper strata of black society in New York, including many of the famous entertainers who played the Apollo. He attended an exclusive New York preparatory school and went on to graduate from Middlebury College in Vermont. At Middlebury, Brown was the only African-American student in his freshman class. He was popular among his classmates and was invited to join a then all-white fraternity. When the national organization prohibited Brown's membership, his Middlebury fraternity brothers renounced their national affiliation. The college also stood by Ron Brown and barred all exclusionary fraternities from campus. Brown later became a trustee of Middlebury College.

After a stint in the Army, Brown earned a law degree at St. John's University and became a Washington lobbyist for the National Urban League. He worked as a deputy campaign manager for Senator Edward Kennedy in 1979–80, becoming Kennedy's general counsel and staff director. From 1981 to 1985, he was a deputy director of the Democratic National Committee; in 1988, he managed Jesse Jackson's presidential campaign. Brown then joined the powerful Washington lawyer-lobbying firm of Patton, Boggs, and Blow.

It was Brown's role in bringing Jackson and his supporters into the Dukakis camp in 1988 that propelled him to the party's chair. Brown's negotiating skills resolved the platform differences between the candidates. Both candidates were able to save face, and a serious racial split within the Democratic Party was averted. As national chair, Brown proved to be an impressive fund raiser; under his leadership the Democrats gained four congressional seats in the 1989 off-year elections, including Dan Quayle's former seat in Indiana. And in 1992 he led the Democratic Party back into the White House.

As comfortable on the tennis courts as in national politics, Brown proved to be an extremely likable and popular national chair. As Michael Dukakis said: "If Ron were a pop singer, he would have cross-over appeal." Brown vowed: "I promise you my chairmanship will not be about race, it will be about the races we win"—and win he did. In return, President Bill Clinton named Brown to his cabinet as secretary of commerce, the first African American ever to hold that post. An active commerce secretary, Brown traveled the world in search of economic opportunities. He died in a tragic airplane crash in Bosnia while seeking American investments in that embattled region.

drives, provide advice and services to their nominees, and even recruit candidates to run in election districts and for offices where the party would otherwise have no names on the ballot. Services to candidates may include advertising and media consulting, advice on election law compliance, polling, research (including research on opponents), registration and voter identification, mailing lists, and even seminars on campaign techniques.

State committees are also supposed to direct the campaigns for important statewide elections—governors and U.S. senators. They are supposed to serve as central coordinating agencies for these election campaigns and as the party's principal fund-raising organization in the state. However, today the role of the state committee is very often limited, since most candidates have their own campaign organizations.

*Legislative Party Structures*  The parties organize the U.S. Senate and House of Representatives, and they organize most state legislatures as well. The majority party in the House meets in caucus to select the Speaker of the House as well as the House majority leader and whip (see "Organizing Congress: Party and Leadership" in Chapter 10). The minority party elects its own minority leader and whip. The majority party in the Senate elects the president pro tempore, who presides during the (frequent) absences of the vice-president, as well as the Senate majority leader and whip. The minority party in the Senate elects its own minority leader and whip. Committee assignments in both the House and Senate are allocated on a party basis; committee chairs are always majority-party members.

*County Committees*  The nation's 3,000 Republican and 3,000 Democratic county chairs probably constitute the most important building blocks in party organization in the nation. City and county party officers and committees are chosen in local primary elections; they cannot be removed by state or national party authorities.

## NATIONAL PARTY CONVENTIONS

The Democratic and Republican parties are showcased every four years at the national party **convention**. The official purpose of these four-day, fun-filled events is the nomination of the presidential candidates and their vice-presidential running mates. Yet the presidential choices have already been made in the parties' **presidential primaries** and caucuses earlier in the year. By midsummer convention time, delegates pledged to cast their convention vote for the presidential candidates have already been selected. Not since 1952, when the Democrats took three convention ballots to select Adlai Stevenson as their presidential candidate, has convention voting gone beyond the first ballot. The possibility exists that in some future presidential race no candidate will win a majority of delegates in the primaries and caucuses, and the result will be a *brokered* convention in which delegates will exercise independent power to select the party nominee. But this event is unlikely.

The Democratic and Republican national conventions are really televised party rallies, designed to showcase the presidential nominee, confirm the nominee's choice for a running mate, and inspire television viewers to support the party and its candidates in the forthcoming general election. Indeed, the national party conventions are largely media events, carefully staged to present an attractive image of the party and its nominees. Party luminaries jockey for key time slots at the podium, and the party prepares slick videotaped commercials touting its nominee for prime-time presentation.

*Convention Delegates*  Over time, the spread of presidential primary elections has taken the suspense out of the national party conventions. As late as 1968, fewer than half of the delegates were selected in primary elections. But today the selection of more than 80 percent of pledged delegates by the party's

**Convention:** A nominating process in which delegates from local party organizations select the party's nominees.

**Presidential primaries**: Primary elections in the states in which voters in each party can choose presidential candidates for their parties' nomination. Outcomes help determine the distribution of pledged delegates to the parties' national nominating conventions.

**Delegate:** An accredited voting member of a party's national presidential nominating convention.

primary voters has greatly diminished the role of party officials in presidential selection.

Both parties award **delegates** to each state in rough proportion to the number of party voters in the state. Democratic Party rules currently require that all popularly elected delegates from each state be awarded to the presidential candidates according to their proportion of that state's primary or caucus vote, after the candidates reach a 15 percent vote threshold. Republican Party rules allow states either to apportion their delegates according to the primary or caucus vote or to adopt a winner-take-all system of awarding all state delegates to the state's primary election victor.

Convention delegates are generally party activists, ideologically motivated and strongly committed to their presidential candidates.[9] Democratic delegates are much more *liberal* than Democratic voters, and Republican delegates are more *conservative* than Republican voters (see Figure 7-6). There is a slight tendency for Democratic and Republican delegates to differ in social backgrounds; there are usually more African Americans, women, and union members among Democratic delegates than among Republican delegates.

*Making Party Rules*    National party conventions make rules for the party, including rules governing the selection of delegates at the next party convention. Democrats are especially likely to focus on delegate selection rules. In 1972, the Democratic Party responded to charges that African Americans, women, and other minorities were underrepresented among the delegates by appointing a special commission chaired by Senator George McGovern to "reform" the party. The McGovern Commission took "affirmative steps" to ensure that the next convention would include "goals" for the representation of African Americans, women, and other minorities among the delegates in proportion to their presence in the Democratic electorate. The effect of these reforms was to reduce the influence of

**FIGURE 7-6**    **Ideologies of Convention Delegates**
*Democratic and Republican Party activists, including convention delegates, are far more likely to hold divergent liberal and conservative views than voters generally or even their party's voters.*

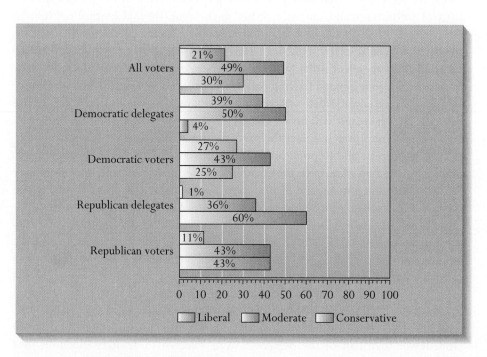

*Source:* Data reported by *Washington Post*, August 16, 1992.

Democratic officeholders (members of Congress, governors, state legislators, and mayors) at the convention and to increase the influence of ideologically motivated activists. Later rule changes eliminated the *unit vote,* in which all delegates from a state were required to vote with the majority of the state's delegation, and required that all delegates pledged to a candidate vote for that candidate unless *released* by the candidate.

Then, in the 1980s, the Democratic Leadership Council pressed the party to reserve some convention delegate seats for **superdelegates**—elected officials and party leaders not bound to one candidate—with the expectation that these delegates would be more moderate than the liberal party activists. The notion was that the superdelegates would inject more balanced, less ideological political judgments into convention deliberations, thus improving the party's chances of victory in the general elections. As a result, many Democratic senators, governors, and members of Congress now attend the convention as superdelegates. If presidential candidates ever fail to win a majority of delegates in the primaries, these superdelegates may someday control a nomination.

*Party Platforms*   National conventions also write party **platforms,** setting out the party's goals and policy positions. Because a party's platform is not binding on its nominees, platform *planks* are largely symbolic, though they often provide heated arguments and provide distinct differences between the parties to present to voters (see *Up Close:* "Democratic and Republican Platforms: Can You Tell the Difference?").

*Selecting a Running Mate*   Perhaps the only suspense remaining in national party conventions centers on the presidential nominee's choice of a vice-presidential running mate. In 1956, Democratic presidential nominee Adlai Stevenson threw open the choice of a vice-presidential nominee to the convention, which chose Tennessee Senator Estes Kefauver over young Massachusetts Senator John F. Kennedy. Normally, however, the choice is made by the presidential nominee. Even a presidential candidate who has decided on a running mate well in advance of the convention may choose to wait until the convention to announce the choice; otherwise there would be little real "news value" to the convention, and the television networks would give less coverage to it. By encouraging speculation about who the running mate will be, the candidate and the convention manager can sustain media interest. (For a discussion of various strategies in selecting a running mate, see "The Vice-Presidential Waiting Game" in Chapter 11.)

The convention *always* accepts the presidential candidate's recommendation for a running mate. No formal rules require the convention to do so, but it would be politically unacceptable for the convention to override the first important decision of the party's presidential nominee. Convention delegates set aside any personal reservations they may have and unanimously endorse the presidential nominee's choice.

*Campaign Kickoff*   The final evening of the national conventions is really the kickoff for the general election campaign. The presidential nominee's acceptance speech tries to set the tone for the fall campaign. Party celebrities, including defeated presidential candidates, join hands at the podium as a symbol of party unity. Presidential and vice-presidential candidates, spouses, and families assemble under balloons and streamers, amid the happy noise and hoopla, to signal the start of the general election campaign.[10]

**Superdelegates:** Delegates to the Democratic Party national convention selected because of their position in the government or the party and not pledged to any candidate.

**Platform:** A statement of principles adopted by a political party at its national convention (specific portions of the platform are known as *planks*); a platform is *not* binding on the party's candidates.

## Democratic and Republican Platforms: Can You Tell the Difference?

These statements have been selected from the Democratic and Republican platforms in 1996. They differ in both tone and substance on various issue areas. Can you correctly guess which statements are taken from the Democratic platform and which from the Republican?

### Civil Rights

**A.** We continue to lead the fight to end discrimination on the basis of race, gender, religion, age, ethnicity disability, and sexual orientation. [Our] Party has always supported the Equal Rights Amendment, and we are committed to ensuring full equality for women and to vigorously enforce the Americans with Disabilities Act. We support continued efforts, like the Employment Non-Discrimination Act, to end discrimination against gay men and lesbians and further their full inclusion in the life of the nation.

**B.** The sole source of equal opportunity for all is equality before the law. Therefore, we oppose discrimination based on sex, race, age, creed, or national origin and will vigorously enforce anti-discrimination statutes. We reject the distortion of those laws to cover sexual preference, and we endorse the Defense of Marriage Act to prevent states from being forced to recognize same-sex unions. Because we believe rights inhere in individuals, not in groups, we will attain our nation's goal of equal rights without quotas or other forms of preferential treatment.

### Abortion

**A.** [We] stand behind the right of every woman to choose, consistent with *Roe v. Wade,* regardless of ability to pay. . . It is a fundamental constitutional liberty that individual Americans—not government—can best take responsibility for making the most difficult and intensely personal decisions regarding reproduction.

**B.** The unborn child has a fundamental individual right to life which cannot be infringed. We support a human life amendment to the Constitution. We oppose using public revenues for abortion and will not fund organizations which advocate it. We support the appointment of judges who respect traditional family values and the sanctity of innocent human life.

## THE PARTY VOTERS

**Party identification:** Self-described identification with a political party, usually in response to the question: "Generally speaking, how would you identify yourself: as a Republican, Democrat, independent, or something else?"

Traditionally, the Democratic Party has been able to claim to be the majority party in the United States (see Figure 7-7). In opinion polls, those who "identified" with the Democratic Party generally outnumbered those who "identified" with the Republican Party. (**Party identification** is determined by response to the question: "Generally speaking, how would you identify yourself: as a Republican, Democrat, independent, or something else?") But the Democratic Party advantage among the voters has eroded over time, partly as a result of a gradual increase in the number of people who call themselves independents and partly as a result of recent Republican gains.[11]

## Taxes

**A.** We want to strengthen middle-class families by providing a $500 tax cut for children. We want to cut taxes to help families pay for education after high school and to guarantee the first two years of college. We want people to be able to use their IRA's to buy a first home, deal with a medical emergency, or provide for education. We want to cut taxes for small businesses that invest in the future and set up pensions for their workers. And we want to cut taxes for people who are self-employed and self-insured so their health care is more affordable.

**B.** American families deserve better. They should be allowed to keep more of their hard-earned money so they can spend on their priorities, as opposed to sending ever-increasing amounts to Washington to be spent on the priorities of federal bureaucrats.

In response to this unprecedented burden confronting America, we support an across-the-board, 15-percent tax cut to marginal tax rates. We believe such a cut should be the first step towards reducing overall tax burdens while promoting the economic growth that will raise family incomes and our overall standard of living.

## Welfare

**A.** Now, because of [us], national welfare reform is going to make work and responsibility the law of the land. Thanks to [us], the new welfare bill includes the health care and child care people need so they can go to work confident their children will be cared for. Thanks to [us] the new welfare bill imposes time limits and real work requirements—so anyone who can work, does work, and so that no one who can work can stay on welfare forever. Thanks to [us] the new welfare bill cracks down on deadbeat parents and requires minor mothers to live at home with their parent or with another responsible adult.

**B.** The key to welfare reform is restoring personal responsibility and encouraging two-parent households. The path to that goal lies outside of official Washington. All able-bodied adults must be required to work, either in private sector jobs or in community work projects. Illegal aliens must be ineligible for all but emergency benefits. And a firm time limit for receipt of welfare must be enforced.

Because illegitimacy is the most serious cause of child poverty, we will encourage States to stop cash payments to unmarried teens and set a family cap on payments for additional children. When benefits of any kind are extended to teen mothers, they must be conditioned upon their attendance at school and their living at home with a parent, adult relative or guardian.

All **A** entries are Democrat. All **B** entries are Republican.

---

*Growing Numbers of Independents*   Over time, Americans have grown disenchanted with both parties. Both the Democratic and Republican parties have lost *identifiers,* while numbers of *independent identifiers* have increased substantially. Indeed, in recent years more people have identified themselves as independents than as either Democrats or Republicans.

*Dealignment*   **Dealignment** describes the decline in attractiveness of the political parties to the voters, the growing reluctance of people to identify themselves with either party, and a decrease in reliance on a candidate's party affiliation in voter choice. Dealignment is evident not only in the growing numbers of self-described independents but also in the declining numbers of those who iden-

**Dealignment:** Declining attractiveness of the parties to the voters, a reluctance to identify strongly with a party, and a decrease in reliance on party affiliation in voter choice.

FIGURE 7-7 **Party Identification in the Electorate**

*For many years, the Democratic Party enjoyed a substantial lead in party identification among voters. This Democratic lead eroded somewhat following the election of Republican President Ronald Reagan in 1980. Independent identification over the years has risen, suggesting that many voters have become disillusioned with both parties. Relatively few people consider themselves "strong" Democrats or Republicans.*

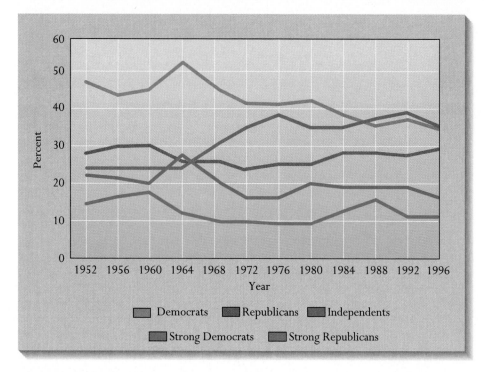

*Source:* Data from National Election Studies, University of Michigan.

tify themselves as "strong" Democrats or Republicans. In short, the electorate is less partisan than it once was.

*Party Loyalty in Voting* Despite the decline in partisan identification in the electorate, it is important to note that *party identification is a strong influence in voter choice in elections.* Most voters cast their ballot for the candidate of their party. This is true in presidential elections (see Figure 7-8) and even more true in congressional and state elections. Those who identify themselves as Democrats are somewhat more likely to vote for a Republican presidential candidate than those who identify themselves as Republicans are to vote for a Democratic presidential candidate. Republican Ronald Reagan was able to win more than one-quarter of self-identified Democrats in 1980 and 1984, earning these crossover voters the label "Reagan Democrats."[12]

*Realignment?* While Democratic Party loyalty has eroded over the last twenty years, it is not clear whether or not this erosion is a classic party **realignment.**[13] Most scholars agree that party realignments occurred in the presidential elections of 1824 (Jackson, Democrats), 1860 (Lincoln, Republicans), 1896 (Bryan, Democrats), 1932 (Roosevelt, Democrats). This historical sequence gave rise to a theory that realigning elections occur every thirty-six years. According to this theory, the election of 1968 should have been a realigning one. It is true that Richard Nixon's 1968 victory marked the beginning of a Republican era in presidential election victories that was broken only by Jimmy Carter in 1976. But there was relatively little shifting of the party loyalties of major social groups, and the Democratic Party remained the dominant party in the electorate and in Congress.

**Realignment:** A long-term shift in social group support for various political parties that creates new coalitions in each party.

226        CHAPTER 7 • POLITICAL PARTIES: ORGANIZING POLITICS

The Democratic Party still receives *disproportionate* support from Catholics, Jews, African Americans, less-educated and lower-income groups, blue-collar workers, union members, and big-city residents. The Republican Party still receives *disproportionate* support from Protestants, whites, more-educated and higher-income groups, white-collar workers, nonunion workers, and suburban and small-town dwellers. Disproportionate support does not mean that these groups *always* give a majority of their votes to the indicated party, but only that they give that party a larger percentage of their votes than the party receives from the general electorate. This pattern of social group voting and party identification has remained relatively stable, even though the GOP has made some gains among many of the traditionally Democratic groups (see Figure 7-9). The only major *shift* in social group support has occurred among southern whites. This group has

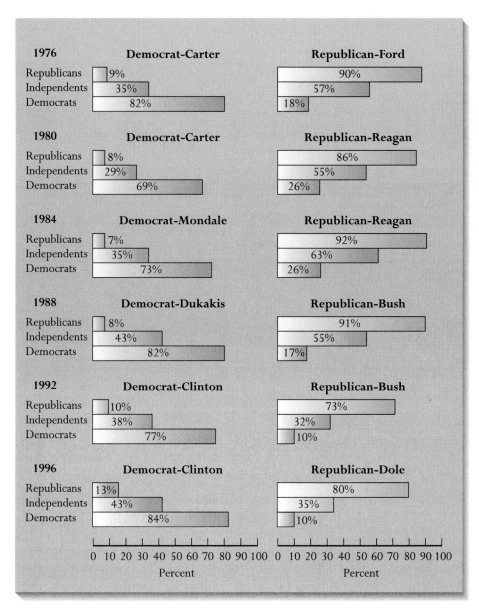

**FIGURE 7-8**    Republican, Democratic, and Independent Voters in Presidential Elections

*As the percentages here indicate, in recent years registered Democrats have been more likely to "cross over" and vote for a Republican candidate for president than registered Republicans have been to vote for the Democratic presidential candidate.*

Source: *New York Times.*

FIGURE 7-9

**Social Group Support for the Democratic and Republican Parties**

*The Democratic Party draws disproportionate support from low income, less educated, Catholic, Jewish, and African American voters. The Republican Party relies more heavily on support from high income, college-educated, white Protestant voters.*

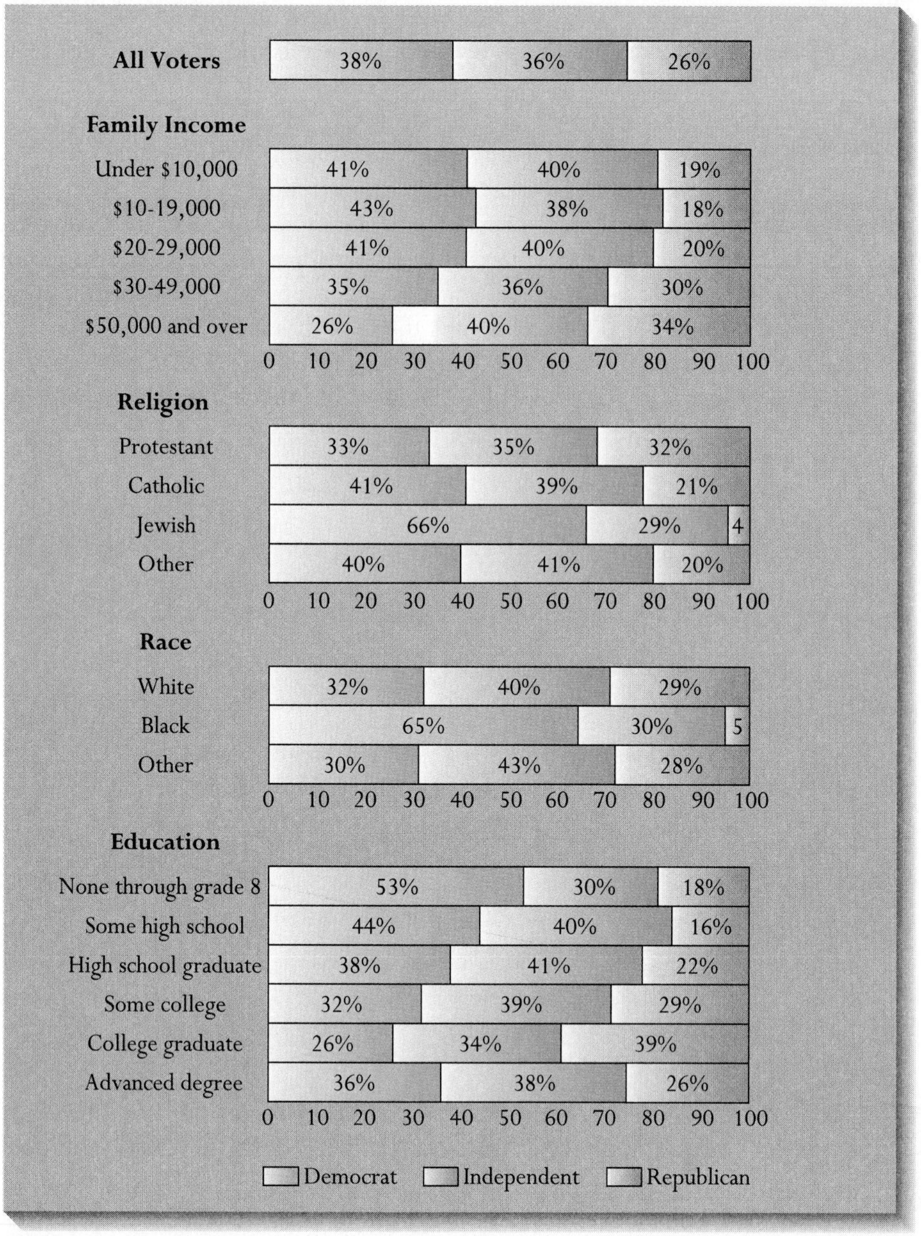

**All Voters** 38% | 36% | 26%

**Family Income**
| | Democrat | Independent | Republican |
|---|---|---|---|
| Under $10,000 | 41% | 40% | 19% |
| $10-19,000 | 43% | 38% | 18% |
| $20-29,000 | 41% | 40% | 20% |
| $30-49,000 | 35% | 36% | 30% |
| $50,000 and over | 26% | 40% | 34% |

**Religion**
| | Democrat | Independent | Republican |
|---|---|---|---|
| Protestant | 33% | 35% | 32% |
| Catholic | 41% | 39% | 21% |
| Jewish | 66% | 29% | 4 |
| Other | 40% | 41% | 20% |

**Race**
| | Democrat | Independent | Republican |
|---|---|---|---|
| White | 32% | 40% | 29% |
| Black | 65% | 30% | 5 |
| Other | 30% | 43% | 28% |

**Education**
| | Democrat | Independent | Republican |
|---|---|---|---|
| None through grade 8 | 53% | 30% | 18% |
| Some high school | 44% | 40% | 16% |
| High school graduate | 38% | 41% | 22% |
| Some college | 32% | 39% | 29% |
| College graduate | 26% | 34% | 39% |
| Advanced degree | 36% | 38% | 26% |

□ Democrat □ Independent □ Republican

*Source:* Data from National Election Studies, University of Michigan.

shifted from heavily Democratic in party identification to a substantial Republican preference. Thus it is questionable whether a true party realignment has occurred.[14] (See *Across the USA:* "Democratic and Republican Party Strength in the States.")

## THIRD-PARTY PROSPECTS

There is widespread disillusionment in the United States with "politics as usual." This is reflected in the distrust expressed by Americans in their government (see *What Do You Think?* "Can You Trust the Government?" in Chapter 1), in their belief

## Democratic and Republican Party Strength in the States

*The Democratic and Republican parties compete in every state. Indeed, party competition within states has increased as the once heavily Democratic states of the "Solid South" have developed stronger Republican Party ties. But some voters have favored candidates of one party in gubernatorial and congressional elections and the other in presidential elections in recent years.*

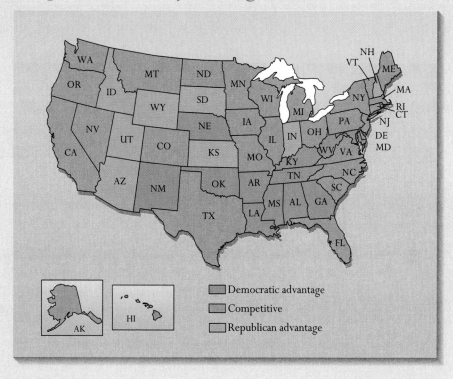

that the government is "run by a few big interests looking out for themselves" (see *What Do You Think? "Is Government Run by a Few Big Interests Looking Out for Themselves?"* in Chapter 1), and in their increasing dealignment from the Republican and Democratic Parties. The public mood provides fertile ground for the emergence of **third parties** and independent candidates.

*Third-Party Popularity*    In recent years, polls have reported that a majority of Americans favor the idea of a third party. The support for the *general idea* of a third party is usually favored by 55 to 65 percent of the American public.[15] But this support for the general idea has never been matched by voter support for *specific* third-party or independent presidential candidates (see Table 7-1). And even the most popular of these candidates have failed to win the electoral votes of very many states (see *Up* Close: "Understanding the Electoral College" in Chapter 8). Third-party and independent movements in the twentieth century have been short-lived; by the next election, their supporters have been reabsorbed into the two-party system.

**Third party:** A political party that challenges the two major parties in an election.

| TABLE 7-1  TWENTIETH-CENTURY THIRD-PARTY PROSPECTS | | |
|---|---|---|
| Third-Party Presidential Candidates | Popular Vote (percentage) | Electoral Votes (number) |
| Theodore Roosevelt, 1912 Progressive (Bull Moose) Party | 27.4% | 88 |
| Ross Perot, 1992 Independent | 18.9 | 0 |
| Robert M. La Follette, 1924 Progressive Party | 16.6 | 13 |
| George C. Wallace, 1968 American Independent Party | 13.5 | 46 |
| Ross Perot, 1996 Reform Party | 8.5 | 0 |
| John Anderson, 1980 Independent | 6.6 | 0 |

*The Detached Center*   Dissatisfaction with the Democratic and Republican Parties and their presidential candidates rose to new highs in 1996. Legions of self-identified political independents as well as ideologically self-identified moderates provided support for an assault on the two-party system. Popular U.S. Senator Bill Bradley, in announcing his early retirement from the Senate, seemed to summarize the central problem confronting moderates: "The political debate has settled into two familiar ruts," he said. "The Republicans are infatuated with the 'magic' of the market and reflexively criticize government as the enemy of freedom, and the Democrats distrust the market, preach government as the answer to our problems and prefer the bureaucrats they know to the consumer they can't control."[16]

*Ideological Separation of the Parties*   As ideologically driven political activists have gained influence in the Democratic and Republican parties, many moderate voters have been turned away. Often the fierce rhetoric of core Democratic activists (public employee unionists, feminists, environmentalists, and outspoken African-American leaders) has alienated centrists and independents, just as the uncompromising stands of core Republican activists (religious fundamentalists, immigration opponents, anti-abortion activists) have done. Earlier we observed that vote-maximizing parties would avoid extreme liberal or conservative positions and converge at the broad center of American opinion (see Figure 7-4). But often party activists in both parties—people who contribute money, work in campaigns, staff the party offices, vote regularly in party primaries, and frequently win seats as convention delegates—are more ideologically motivated than the general electorate. Many liberals among Democratic activists and many conservatives among Republican activists are concerned primarily with their party's ideological stance, and they resist compromises designed to make their party more appealing to centrist voters. Moderates become disillusioned with both parties, and opportunities emerge for centrist, independent candidates.

*Reform Party Prospects.*   In 1996 Ross Perot was successful in getting his Reform Party on the ballot in all fifty states. The party's convention spanned two weekends, between which members were asked to participate in a complicated electronic voting scheme. Perot himself emerged the predictable winner, and former Colorado governor Richard Lamm an embittered loser. But despite convincing evidence of continued popular disillusionment with "politics as usual"—only 49 percent of the voting-age population cast ballots in 1996, the lowest turnout in seventy years—the Reform Party failed to challenge the major parties. Perhaps independents were disenchanted with the autocratic style of Ross Perot and the Reform Party's too-close identification with the outspoken billionaire.

## WHY THE TWO-PARTY SYSTEM PERSISTS

The two-party system is deeply ingrained in American politics. While third parties have often made appearances in presidential elections, no third-party candidate has ever won the Oval Office. (Lincoln's new Republican Party in 1860 might be counted as an exception, but it quickly became a major party.) Very few third-party candidates have won seats in Congress. Since many other democracies have multiple-party systems, the question arises as to why has the United States had a two-party system throughout its history (see also *A Conflicting View*: "Trash the Two-Party System").

*Cultural Consensus*     One explanation of the nation's two-party system focuses on the broad consensus supporting the American political culture (see Chapter 2). The values of democracy, capitalism, free enterprise, individual liberty, religious freedom, and equality of opportunity are so widely shared that no party challenging these values has ever won much of a following. There is little support in the American political culture for avowedly fascist, authoritarian, or other antidemocratic parties. Moreover, the American political culture includes a strong belief in the separation of church and state. Political parties with religious affiliations, common in European democracies, are absent from American politics. Socialist parties have frequently appeared on the scene under various labels—the Socialist Party, the Socialist Labor Party, the Socialist Workers Party, and the Communist Party. But the largest popular vote ever garnered by a socialist candidate in a presidential election was the 6 percent won by Eugene V. Debs in 1912. In contrast, socialist parties have frequently won control of European governments.

On broad policy issues, most Americans cluster near the center. This general consensus tends to discourage multiple parties. There does not appear to be sufficient room for them to stake out a position on the ideological spectrum that would detach voters from the two major parties.

This cultural explanation blends with the influence of historical precedents. The American two-party system has gained acceptance through custom. The nation's first party system developed from two coalitions, Federalists and Anti-Federalists, and this dual pattern has been reinforced over two centuries.

*Winner-Take-All Electoral System*     Yet another explanation of the American two-party system focuses on the electoral system itself. Winners in presidential and congressional elections, as well as in state gubernatorial and legislative elections, are usually determined by a plurality, winner-take-all vote. Even

# Trash the Two-Party System

The American party system is being abandoned by the voters for good reason: it no longer offers voters principled policy choices to resolve the nation's pressing problems. This is the thrust of the argument by political scientist Theodore J. Lowi. The Democratic and Republican parties no longer perform any of the crucial tasks of parties in a democratic system—setting forth principled policy positions, recruiting candidates who support those positions, informing and educating the public, organizing majorities to support the party's policy positions, and then enforcing party discipline on officeholders. According to Lowi:

> One of the best-kept secrets in American politics is that the two-party system has long been brain dead—kept alive by support systems like state electoral laws that protect the established parties from rivals and by Federal subsidies and so-called campaign reform. The two-party system would collapse in an instant if the tubes were pulled and the IV's were out.

Both parties have dodged the really difficult issues of American politics—crime, welfare, taxes, and deficits. Instead, they have resorted to personal attacks on the opposition and have focused on scandal and corruption rather than fundamental policy choices.

Lowi argues that a strong third-party movement in America would reinvigorate politics and inspire national leaders to confront real policy issues:

> With three parties, no party needs to seek a majority or pretend that it is a majority. What a liberating effect this would have on party leaders and candidates to go after constituencies composed of 35 percent rather

than 51 percent of the voters. A three-party system would be driven more by issues, precisely because parties fighting for pluralities can be clearer in their positions.

Not only would a new third party be a source of new ideas, but the Democratic and Republican Parties would also have stronger incentives to be more policy oriented, because they would no longer seek to win over a majority of voters. With real issues at stake in a three-party election, voter turnout would increase, as would all forms of political participation. Ross Perot's 1992 candidacy motivated thousands of people to circulate petitions, knock on doors, and make telephone calls for their hero; millions of others signed his petitions. Reinvigorated parties would not need to rely so much on "dehumanizing" television campaigning but instead could go back to personal political activity.

Finally, Lowi argues that a three-party system in Congress would allow that body to function more like a parliamentary system. (If three parties caused the president to be chosen by the House of Representatives, so much the better, says Lowi.) With three parties in Congress, the president would have more bargaining leeway to enact major legislative programs. "A third party would play the role of honest broker and policy manager, because it would hold a balance of power in many important and decisive issues."

What do you think? Would a strong third party help resolve policy gridlock, inspire political participation, and give the president bargaining power in Congress? Or would it further divide the American people, complicate even further the problem of finding consensus, and lead to even more party squabbling in Congress?

*Source:* Theodore J. Lowi, "The Party Crasher," *New York Times Magazine,* August 30, 1992.

in elections that require a majority of more than 50 percent to win—which may involve a runoff election—only one party's candidate wins in the end. Because of the winner-take-all nature of U.S. elections, parties and candidates have an overriding incentive to broaden their appeal to a plurality or majority of voters. Losers come away empty-handed. There is not much incentive in such a system for a party to form to represent the views of 5 or 10 percent of the electorate.

Americans are so accustomed to winner-take-all elections that they seldom consider alternatives. In some countries, legislative bodies are elected by **proportional representation,** whereby all voters cast a single ballot for the party of their choice and legislative seats are then apportioned to the parties in proportion to their total vote in the electorate (see *Compared to What?* "Political Parties of the World"). Minority parties are assured of legislative seats, perhaps with as little as 10 or 15 percent of the vote. If no party wins 50 percent of the votes and seats, the parties try to form a coalition of parties to establish control of the government. In these nations, party coalition building to form a governing majority occurs *after* the election rather than *before* the election, as it does in winner-take-all elections systems.

*Legal Access to the Ballot*   Another factor in the American two-party system may be electoral system barriers to third parties. While the Democratic and Republican nominees are automatically included on all general election ballots, third-party and independent candidates face difficult obstacles in getting their names listed. In presidential elections, a third-party candidate must meet the varied requirements of fifty separate states to appear on their ballots along with the Democratic and Republican nominees. These requirements often include filing petitions signed by up to 5 or 10 percent of registered voters. In addition, states require third parties to win 5 or 10 percent of the vote in the last election in order to retain their position on the ballot in subsequent elections. In 1980, independent John Anderson gained access to the ballot in all fifty states, as did independent Ross Perot in 1992. But just doing so required a considerable expenditure of effort and money that the major parties were able to avoid.

## THIRD PARTIES IN THE U.S. SYSTEM

Despite the cultural and electoral barriers to victory, third parties, more accurately called minor parties, are a common feature of American politics. These parties can be roughly classified by the role they play in the political system.

*Ideological Parties*   **Ideological parties** exist to promote an ideology rather than to win elections. They use the electoral process to express their views and to rally activists to their cause, and they measure success not by victory at the polls but by their ability to bring their name and their views to the attention of the American public. The socialist parties, which have run candidates in virtually every presidential election in this century, are prime examples of ideological parties in the United States (see also *Up Close:* "The Libertarian Party: A Dissenting Voice").

*Protest Parties*   **Protest parties** arise around popular issues or concerns that the major parties have failed to address. An important historical example of a protest party is the Populist Party of the late 1800s. It arose as a protest by midwestern farmers against eastern railroads, "trusts" and monopolies, and the gold

**Proportional representation:** An electoral system that allocates seats in a legislature based on the proportion of votes the parties receive in a national election.

**Ideological party:** A third party that exists to promote an ideology rather than to win elections.

**Protest party:** A third party that arises in response to issues of popular concern that have not been addressed by the major parties.

# Political Parties of the World

Party politics vary throughout the world, but some general patterns are apparent. Multiparty systems occur in nations with proportional representation, while two-party systems occur in nations with winner-take-all elections. France has a unique two-step electoral system: all parties run candidates in a first election, and the top two candidates in each district face off in a second election. In Germany, half of the Bundestag (national legislature) is chosen by proportional representation and half by winner-take-all district elections. Both the German and French electoral systems support a multiparty system, although two-party coalitions dominate government. Small communist parties are found in multiparty Western democracies, but wherever the Communist Party has taken power, it has established a one-party system. Most two-party systems have one party oriented more toward free markets and another party more toward a welfare state or democratic socialism.

| Nation | System | Major Parties | Party Orientation |
|---|---|---|---|
| Australia | Two-party, winner-take-all elections | Liberal Party<br>Labor Party | Free enterprise<br>Democratic socialism |
| Austria | Multiparty, proportional representation | Austrian Socialist Party<br>Austrian Peoples Party<br>Austrian Freedom Party | Democratic socialism<br>Christian democratic and conservative<br>Free enterprise, anti-immigration |
| Canada | Multiparty, winner-take-all elections | Liberal Party<br>Progressive Conservative Party<br>Le Parti Quebecois<br>New Democratic Party | Free enterprise, social reform<br>Conservative, preservation of Canada<br>Political sovereignty for Quebec<br>Democratic socialism |
| China, People's Republic | One-party system | Communist Party of China | Revolutionary class struggle, "market socialism" |
| Cuba | One-party system | Communist Party of Cuba | Revolutionary class struggle, socialism |

standard. The Populists threatened to capture the wave of popular support for railroad regulation, cheap money, and antimonopoly legislation, and thus they endangered the established Democratic and Republican Parties. But when the Democratic Party nominated William Jennings Bryan in 1896, the Populist Party officially endorsed Bryan and subsequently disappeared as a significant independent political organization. Later, Republican President Theodore Roosevelt would voice Populist "trust-busting" themes, stealing the rhetoric of the early Populist Party. Populist ideas were set forth again in a new Progressive Party, which nominated Robert M. La Follette for president in 1924; both the Democ-

| Nation | System | Major Parties | Party Orientation |
|--------|--------|---------------|-------------------|
| France | Multiparty, two elections, winner-take-all elections | Rally for the Republic<br>Union for French Democracy<br>Socialist Party<br>Unified Socialist Party<br>Radical Socialist Party<br>Communist Party<br>National Front<br>Greens | Nationalism, "Gaulist"<br>Centrist, European outlook<br>Democratic socialism<br>Socialism, no compromise<br>Socialism, compromise with center<br>Communist society<br>Anti-immigration<br>Environmentalism |
| Germany | Multiparty, half proportional representation, half winner-take-all elections | Christian Democratic Union<br>Social Democratic Party<br>Free Democratic Party<br>Greens | Christian conservative<br>Democratic socialism<br>Free Enterprise<br>Environmentalism, disarmament |
| Japan | Multiparty with a single dominant party, mixture of proportional representation and winner-take-all elections | Liberal Democratic<br>Japan Socialist Party<br>Komeito Party<br>Japan Communist Party | Free enterprise<br>Democratic socialism<br>"Clean government"<br>"Scientific socialism" |
| Israel | Multiparty with two major alignments proportional representation | Likud Alignment<br>Labour Alignment<br>Liberal Party<br>National Religious Party<br>Communist Party | Nationalism<br>Democratic socialism<br>Free enterprise<br>Religious orthodoxy<br>Marxism-Leninism |
| United Kingdom | Modified two-party, winner-take-all elections | Conservative Party<br>Labour Party<br>Liberal Party | Free enterprise<br>Social welfare state<br>Free enterprise, centrist |

ratic and Republican Parties nominated conservative candidates that year, helping La Follette to win almost 17 percent of the popular vote.

Not all major protest movements have been accompanied by the formation of third parties. Indeed, protest leaders have often argued that a third-party effort distracts the movement from a more effective strategy of capturing control of one or both of the major parties. The labor-union-organizing movement of the 1930s and the civil rights and antiwar movements of the 1960s did *not* spark a separate third party but instead worked largely *within* the dominant Democratic Party to advance their goals.

## The Libertarian Party: A Dissenting Voice

Would you like to see the federal income tax repealed, the Internal Revenue Service abolished, foreign aid ended, all U.S. troops brought home from overseas, and individual choice "in all matters" from abortion, to gun control, to drug use? Would you like to eliminate government farm subsidies, end federal support for public broadcasting, science, and the arts, and "privatize" education and "chari-tize" welfare? These are the campaign promises of the Libertarian Party, whose presidential candidates names appeared on the ballot in all fifty states in 1992 and 1996.

The Libertarian Party is unique in its uncompro-mising commitment to the classical liberal, eigh-teenth-century ideals of John Locke and Adam Smith. Libertarians oppose all interference by government in the private lives of citizens. They support unregu-lated free markets and the protection of private prop-erty rights. Thus they oppose environmental regula-tions, consumer protection laws, and civil rights laws that infringe on private property or "take" property for government use without just compensation to owners. They also oppose government efforts to reg-ulate private morals—including laws outlawing drug use, prostitution, gambling, and pornography—believing that these activities should be the exclusive choice of consenting individuals. Libertarians are strict noninterventionists in international affairs; they are opposed to the North Atlantic Treaty Organiza-tion (NATO) alliance, to foreign aid, to military involvements outside of U.S. territory, and to virtu-ally all spending for national defense.

While the Libertarian Party candidate for presi-dent regularly receives less than 1 percent of the pop-ular vote, Libertarian ideas have entered the nation's policy debates and influenced both major parties. Republican candidates have frequently adopted Liber-tarian arguments on behalf of deregulation of market activities; Democratic candidates frequently use Lib-ertarian arguments about individual "choice" in the areas of abortion, school prayer, and homosexual activity. And both the Democratic and Republican parties have vocal "isolationist" wings that borrow Libertarian, noninterventionist arguments against foreign aid, international alliances, and military expenditures. Thus the Libertarian Party, like other ideological parties, functions to promote ideas rather than win elections.

*Single-Issue Parties*   **Single-issue parties** have frequently formed around a particular cause. Single-issue parties are much like protest parties, although some-what narrower in their policy focus. The Greenback Party of the late 1800s shared with the Populists a desire for cheap inflated currency in order to ease the burden of debt and mortgage payments by farmers. But the Greenback Party focused on a single remedy: an end to the gold standard and the issuance of cheap currency—"greenbacks."

Perhaps the most persistent of minor parties over the years has been the Pro-hibition Party. It achieved temporary success with the passage of the Eighteenth Amendment to the U.S. Constitution in 1919, which prohibited the manufacture, sale, or transportation of "intoxicating liquors," only to see its "noble experiment" fail and be repealed by the Twenty-first Amendment. Actually, the prohibitionists' successes were more directly attributable to their interest-group activity—lobby-ing in Congress and in state legislatures—than to the electoral threat of the Pro-hibition Party.

**Single-issue party:** A third party formed around one particular cause.

*After declining to run for another term in 1908 and encouraging the Republican Party to nominate William Howard Taft to fill his position, Teddy Roosevelt felt ready to return to the White House in 1912. When the Republican Party nominated President Taft again, Roosevelt formed his own independent party—the Progressive (Bull Moose) Party—and won more votes than any other third-party candidate in U.S. history, but still failed to win the presidency.*

*Splinter Parties*   Finally, many third parties in American politics are really **splinter parties**—parties formed by a dissatisfied faction of a major party. Splinter parties may form around a particular individual, as did the Progressive (Bull Moose) Party of Theodore Roosevelt in 1912. As a popular ex-president, Teddy Roosevelt won more than 27 percent of the popular vote, outpolling Republican candidate William Howard Taft but allowing Democrat Woodrow Wilson to win the presidency.

Splinter parties also may emerge from an intense intraparty policy dispute. For example, in 1948, the States' Rights (Dixiecrat) Party formed in protest to the civil rights (fair employment practices) plan in the Democratic Party platform of that year and nominated Strom Thurmond for president. In 1968, George Wallace's American Independent Party won nearly 14 percent of the popular vote. Wallace attacked school desegregation and busing to achieve racial balance in schools, as well as crime in the streets, welfare "cheats," and meddling federal judges and bureaucrats. He abandoned his third-party organization in 1972 to run in the Democratic presidential primary elections. Following some Democratic primary victories, he was shot and disabled for life.

**Splinter party:** A third party formed by a dissatisfied faction of a major party.

## SUMMARY NOTES

- Organization grants advantage in the struggle for power. Political parties organize individuals and groups to exercise power in democracies by winning elected office.
- Political parties are not mentioned in the U.S. Constitution, yet they have played a central role in American political history. Major party realignments have occurred at critical points in American history, as major social groups shifted their political loyalties.

- In theory, political parties are "responsible" organizations that adopt a principled platform, recruit candidates who support the platform, educate the public about it, direct an issue-oriented campaign, and then organize the legislature and ensure that their candidates enact the party's platform.
- But in the American two-party system, winning office by appealing to the large numbers of people at the center of the political spectrum becomes more important than promoting strong policy posi-

tions. American parties cannot bind elected officials to campaign promises anyway.

- American parties have lost many of their traditional functions over time. Party nominations are won by individual candidates in primary elections rather than through selection by party leaders. Most political candidates are self-selected; they organize their own campaigns. Television has replaced the party as the principal means of educating the public. And government bureaucracies, not party machines, provide social services.

- Nevertheless, the parties continue to organize electoral choice. Democratic or Republican party nominations provide access to the general election ballot. Few independents are elected to high political office.

- Party nominations are won in primary elections as earlier caucus and convention methods of nomination have largely disappeared. Party primary elections in the various states may be open or closed and may or may not require runoff primaries. The nominees selected in each party's primary election then battle each other in the general election.

- The parties battle in three major arenas. The *party-in-the electorate* refers to party identification among voters. The *party-in-the-government* refers to party identification and organization among elected officials. The *party organization* refers to party offices at the local, state, and national levels.

- The Democratic and Republican Parties are structured to include national party conventions, national committees with chairs and staff, congressional party organizations, state committees, and county and local committees.

- Since presidential nominations are now generally decided in primary elections, with pledged delegates selected before the opening of the national conventions, and party platforms are largely symbolic and wholly unenforceable on the candidates, the conventions have become largely media events designed to kick off the general election campaign. Only in the unlikely event that no presidential candidate wins a majority of delegates in the primaries could there again be a *brokered* convention. Making party rules does occupy a great deal of the delegates' time, however.

- *Dealignment* refers to a decline in the attractiveness of the parties to the voters, a growing reluctance of people to identify strongly with either party, and greater voter willingness to cross party lines. Despite dealignment, party identification remains a strong influence in voter choice.

- Opinion polls indicate that most Americans support the general idea of a third party, but throughout the twentieth century no third-party presidential candidate won very many votes.

- In the United States, many aspects of the political system—including cultural consensus, the winner-take-all electoral system, and legal restrictions to ballot access—place major obstacles in the way of success for third parties and independent candidates. While never successful at gaining federal office in significant numbers, ideological, protest, single-issue, and splinter third parties have often been effective at getting popular issues on the federal agenda.

# SELECTED READINGS

DOWNS, ANTHONY. *An Economic Theory of Democracy.* New York: Harper & Row, 1957. The classic work describing rational-choice winning strategies for political parties and explaining why there is no incentive for vote-maximizing parties in a two-party system to adopt widely separate policy positions.

ROSENSTONE, STEVEN J., ROY L. BEHR, and EDWARD H. LAZARUS. *Third Parties in America.* Princeton, N.J.: Princeton University Press, 1984. A review of the history of third parties in American politics with an analysis of the various causes of third-party movements.

SCHATTSCHNEIDER, E. E. *Party Government.* New York: Holt, Rinehart and Winston, 1942. A classic argument on behalf of more disciplined, centralized, principled, "responsible" parties.

SORAUF, FRANK J., and PAUL ALLEN BECK. *Party Politics in America,* 7th ed. New York: HarperCollins, 1992. The authoritative text on the American party system—party organizations, the parties in government, and the parties in the electorate.

SUNQUIST, JAMES L. *Dynamics of the Party System*. Washington, D.C.: Brookings Institution, 1983. A historical perspective on the American party system, describing the key periods of realignment.

WATTENBERG, MARTIN P. *The Decline of American Political Parties, 1952–1988*. Cambridge, Mass.: Harvard University Press, 1990. An authoritative discussion of increasing negative attitudes toward the parties and the growing dealignment in the electorate.

ZEIGLER, HARMON. *Political Parties in Industrial Democracies*. Itasca, Ill.: Peacock Publishers, 1992. An insightful comparative analysis of parties and interest groups in Western European nations, Japan, and the United States.

chapter

8

# CAMPAIGNS AND ELECTIONS
## DECIDING WHO GOVERNS

## CHAPTER OUTLINE

## FEATURES

## ELECTIONS IN A DEMOCRACY

Democratic government is government by "the consent of the governed." Elections give practical meaning to this notion of "consent." Elections allow people to choose among competing candidates and parties and to decide who will occupy public office. Elections give people the opportunity to pass judgment on current officeholders, either by reelecting them (granting continued consent) or by throwing them out of office (withdrawing consent).

## ASK YOURSELF ABOUT POLITICS

1. Should elections be mandates for a party's or candidate's policy priorities?
   Yes ⬭  No ⬭

2. Should elected officials be bound by their campaign promises?
   Yes ⬭  No ⬭

3. Do you think that personal ambition, rather than civic duty, motivates most politicians?
   Yes ⬭  No ⬭

4. Do career politicians serve their constituents better than those who go into politics for just a short time?
   Yes ⬭  No ⬭

5. Should people vote on the basis of a candidate's personal character rather than his or her policy positions?
   Yes ⬭  No ⬭

6. Would you vote for a candidate who used "dirty tricks" to discredit an opponent?
   Yes ⬭  No ⬭

7. Should heavy campaign contributors have greater access to "their" elected officials than ordinary citizens?
   Yes ⬭  No ⬭

8. Should presidents be elected by a direct popular vote rather than by the Electoral College?
   Yes ⬭  No ⬭

What real power do you have in a democracy? By casting ballots, citizens in a democracy have the power to determine who will represent them, who will make up the government under which they live. You, then, are an integral part of the democratic process every time you vote in an election.

**Mandate:** The perception of popular support for a program or policy based on the margin of electoral victory won by a candidate who proposed it during a campaign.

In a representative democracy, elections function primarily to choose personnel to occupy public office—to decide "who governs." But elections also have an indirect influence on public policy, allowing voters to influence policy directions by choosing between candidates or parties with different policy priorities. Thus, elections indirectly influence "who gets what"—that is, the outcomes of the political process.

*Elections as Mandates?*   It is difficult to argue that elections serve as "policy mandates"—that is, that elections allow voters to direct the course of public policy. Frequently, election winners claim a **mandate**—overwhelming support from the people—for their policies and programs. But for elections to serve as policy mandates, four conditions have to be met:

1.   Competing candidates have to offer clear policy alternatives.
2.   The voters have to cast their ballots on the basis of these policy alternatives alone.
3.   The election results have to clearly indicate the voters' policy preferences.
4.   Elected officials have to be bound by their campaign promises.[1]

As we shall see, none of these conditions is fully met in American elections. Often candidates do not differ much on policy questions, or they deliberately obscure their policy positions to avoid offending groups of voters. Voters themselves frequently pay little attention to policy issues in elections but rather vote along traditional party lines or group affiliations, or on the basis of the candidate's character, personality, or media image.

Moreover, even in elections in which issues seem to dominate the campaign, the outcome may not clearly reflect policy preferences. Candidates take stands on a variety of issues. It is never certain on which issues the voters agreed with the winner and on which issues they disagreed yet voted for the candidate anyway.

Finally, candidates often fail to abide by their campaign promises once they are elected. Some simply ignore their promises, assuming voters have forgotten about

*President Clinton celebrates his reelection with his wife, Hillary Rodham Clinton, and their daughter, Chelsea. Clinton is the first Democrat to win a second term since Franklin Roosevelt. He fell just shy of 50 percent of the vote, however, and faces a Republican Congress.*

the campaign. Others point to changes in circumstances or conditions as a justification for abandoning a campaign pledge.

*Retrospective Judgment* Voters can influence future policy directions through retrospective judgments about the performance of incumbents, by either reelecting them or throwing them out of office.[2] Voters may not know what politicians will do in the future, but they can evaluate how well politicians performed in the past. When incumbent officeholders are defeated, it is reasonable to assume that voters did not like their performance and that newly elected officials should change policy course if they do not want to meet a similar fate in the next election. It is not always clear what the defeated incumbents did in office that led to their ouster by the voters. Nor, indeed, can incumbents who won reelection assume that all of their policies are approved of by a majority of voters. But retrospective voting provides an overall judgment of how voters evaluate performance in office.

Retrospective voting is probably more important in presidential elections than in congressional elections. And most speculation about retrospective voting centers on the economy. Incumbent presidents seeking reelection in hard economic times have been regularly defeated by voters, and other candidates of the party in power during an economic downturn may suffer as well.

*Protection of Rights* Elections provide protection against official abuse. The English political philosopher John Stuart Mill wrote:

> Men, as well as women, do not need political rights in order that they might govern, but in order that they not be misgoverned. . . . Rulers in ruling classes are under a necessity of considering the interests of those who have the suffrage; but of those who are excluded, it is in their option whether they will do so or not, and however honestly disposed, they are in general too fully occupied with things they must attend to, to have much room in their thoughts for anything which they can with impunity disregard.[3]

The long struggle for African-American voting rights in the United States was premised on the belief that once blacks acquired the right to vote, government would become more responsive to their concerns. In signing the Voting Rights Act of 1965, President Lyndon Johnson expressed this view: "The vote is the most powerful instrument ever devised by man for breaking down injustice and destroying the terrible walls which imprison men because they are different from other men."[4] The subsequent history of racial politics in America (see Chapter 15) suggests that the vote is more effective in eliminating discriminatory laws than it is in resolving social or economic inequities. Nevertheless, *without* the vote, we can be certain that government would have very little incentive to respond to popular needs.

## POWER AND AMBITION

Personal ambition is a driving force in politics. Politics attracts people for whom *power*—the drive to shape the world according to one's own beliefs and values— and *celebrity*—the public attention, deference, name recognition, and social status

*In 1996 most voters said that "compared to four years ago" they were "better off" or "about the same," rather than "worse off." This generally favorable retrospective judgment on Clinton's first term undermined Dole's chances of unseating the Democratic president.*

that accompany public office—are more rewarding than money, leisure, or privacy. "Political office today flows to those who want it enough to spend the time and energy mastering its pursuit. It flows in the direction of ambition—and talent."[5]

Political ambition is the most distinguishing characteristic of elected office-holders. The people who run for and win public office are not necessarily the most intelligent, best informed, wealthiest, or most successful business or professional people. At all levels of the political system, from presidential candidates and members of Congress, to governors and state legislators, to city council and school board members, it is the most politically ambitious people who are willing to sacrifice time, family and private life, and energy and effort for the power and celebrity that come with public office.

Most politicians publicly deny that personal ambition is their real motivation for seeking public office. Rather, they describe their motives in highly idealistic terms: "civic duty," "service to community," "reforming the government," "protecting the environment," "bringing about change." These responses reflect the norms of our political culture. People are not supposed to enter politics to satisfy *personal* ambitions but rather to achieve *public* purposes. Many politicians do not really recognize their own drive for power or how much they crave celebrity. But if there were no personal rewards in politics, no one would run for office.

To achieve their ambitions, politicians must meet certain basic requirements and possess several key talents and skills.

*Constitutional Requirements for Office*    The constitutional requirements for presidential and congressional candidates are very few:

- *President:* A natural-born citizen of the United States, a resident for at least fourteen years, and at least thirty-five years of age (Article II, Section 1). The Twenty-second Amendment to the U.S. Constitution, passed in 1951 after Franklin D. Roosevelt's unprecedented four elections to the presidency, imposes one more restriction: A person cannot be elected president more than twice, or more than once if having served more than two years of another president's term.
- *U.S. Senate:* A resident of the state from which elected, a citizen of the United States for at least nine years, and at least thirty years of age (Article I, Section 3).
- *U.S. House of Representatives:* A resident of the state from which elected, a citizen of the United States for at least seven years, and at least twenty-five years of age (Article I, Section 2).

*Political Entrepreneurship*    One talent required of politicians is of **political entrepreneurship**—the ability to sell themselves to others as candidates, to raise money from contributors, to organize people to work on their behalf, and to communicate and publicize themselves through the media. Political parties no longer recruit candidates; candidates recruit themselves. Nor do interest groups recruit candidates; candidates seek out interest groups to win their support.

**Political entrepreneurship:** The ability to sell oneself as a candidate for public office, including skills of organizing, fund raising, communicating, and publicizing.

*Political Temperament*    Perhaps the most important personal qualification is the willingness to work long and hard, to live, eat, and breathe politics every day. Occasionally people win high office who really do not like political campaigning; they view it as a torture they must endure in order to gain office and exercise power. But most successful politicians are people who really like politics—the meetings, appearances, speeches, interviews, hand shaking—and really enjoy interacting with other people (see *People in Politics:* "Colin Powell: Saying No to Presidential Politics").

*Communication Skills*    Another important personal qualification is the ability to communicate with others. Politicians must know how to talk, and talk, and talk—to large audiences, in press conferences and interviews, on television, to reporters, to small groups of financial contributors, on the phone, at airports and commencements, to their staffs, on the floor of Congress or the state legislature. It matters less what politicians say than how they look and sound saying it. They must communicate sincerity, compassion, confidence, and good humor, as well as ideas.

*Professionalism*    Politics is becoming increasingly professionalized. "Citizen officeholders"—people with business or professional careers who get into politics part-time or for short periods of time—are being driven out of political life by career politicians—people who enter politics early in life as a full-time occupation and expect to make it their career. Politics increasingly demands all of a politician's time and energy. At all levels of government, from city council to state legislatures to the U.S. Congress, political work is becoming full-time and year-round. It is not only more demanding to *hold* office than it was a generation ago but also far more demanding to *run* for office. Campaigning has become more time consuming, more technically sophisticated, and much more costly over time.

*Careerism*    Professional political careers begin at a relatively early age. Politically ambitious young people seek out internships and staff positions with members of Congress, with congressional committees, in state legislators' or governors' offices, in mayors' offices, or in council chambers. Others volunteer to work in political campaigns. Many find political mentors from whom they learn how to

*President Clinton prepares for an interview with reporters from the television news show 60 Minutes. Successful politicians are skilled communicators; most truly enjoy the hard work and constant interaction with other people their careers entail.*

# Colin Powell, Saying No To Presidential Politics

Colin Powell embodies the American Dream: "a black kid of no early promise from an immigrant family of limited means who was raised in the South Bronx and somehow rose to become the National Security Adviser to the President of the United States and then Chairman of the Joint Chiefs of Staff." He also rose to be the American public's preferred choice for president of the United States, yet decided that he did not have the "passion and commitment" for political life that he "felt every day of my thirty-five years as a soldier." Powell became the first person in modern political history to opt out of a presidential race while leading all other candidates, including the incumbent president, in the opinion polls.

Born in Harlem to Jamaican immigrant parents, Powell recounts his youth as proof that "it is possible to rise above conditions." After graduation from Morris High School in the South Bronx, Powell, encouraged by his parents, enrolled at The City College of New York on a ROTC scholarship. In 1958 he graduated with a degree in geology at the top of his ROTC class and was commissioned a second lieutenant in the United States Army. Powell went to South Vietnam as a military adviser in 1962 and returned for a second tour in 1968. In Vietnam, he was awarded two Purple Hearts, a Bronze Star for Valor, and the Legion of Merit.

In 1972, Powell returned to the classroom to pursue a master's degree in business administration from George Washington University and accept an appointment to the prestigious White House Fellows Program. As a White House Fellow, Powell was assigned to the Office of Management and Budget, where he worked under Caspar Weinberger, later secretary of defense in the Reagan Administration. Powell's career was on a fast track after his White House duty.

Powell was recalled to Washington in 1983 by Defense Secretary Weinberger to become senior military adviser to the secretary. During the invasion of Grenada in October of that year, Powell was assigned the task of running interference for the military against meddling White House and National Security Council staff. Later Powell was active on behalf of Secretary Weinberger in opposing arms sales to Iran; he was overruled by President Ronald Reagan, but his memo urging that Congress be notified of the arms transfers would later give him good standing with the Congress after the Iran-Contra scandal became public.

President George Bush chose General Powell in 1989 to head the Joint Chiefs of Staff—the nation's highest military position. It was Powell who helped convince the president that if military force were to be used to oust Saddam Hussein from Kuwait, it must be overwhelming and decisive force, not gradual, limited escalation as in Vietnam. Powell's televised briefings during the course of the war assured the American people of the competence and effectiveness of the U.S. military. The Gulf War victory restored the morale of U.S. military forces and the confidence of the American people in its military leadership. Powell retired from the army in 1993 when his term as chair of the Joint Chiefs of Staff ended and proceeded to write his inspiring autobiography, *My American Journey*.

To a great many Americans, Powell seemed to offer the nation what it most needed: a decisive leader with integrity and character, a political outsider untarnished by "politics as usual," and an African American whose "American Journey" could serve as a model for all and ease the nation's racial divisions. He was frequently compared to Dwight D. Eisenhower, whose military leadership in World War II ushered him into the White House. Like Ike, Powell waited until after army retirement to declare himself a Republican and announce his support for a balanced federal budget, tax cuts, and a reduction in the size of government. He expressed moderate views on abortion rights and some forms of affirmative action and offered to help "the party of Lincoln move once again close to the spirit of Lincoln." Yet after "prayerful consideration," he announced to a disappointed nation that he would not be a candidate for president of the United States "or any elective office" in 1996.

*Source:* Colin Powell, *My American Journey* (New York: Random House, 1995).

organize campaigns, contact financial contributors, and deal with the media. Soon they are ready to run for local office or the state legislature. Rather than challenge a strong incumbent, they may wait for an open seat to be created by retirement, by reapportionment, or by its holder seeking another office. Or they may make an initial attempt against a strong incumbent of the opposition party in order to gain experience and win the appreciation of their own party's supporters for a good effort. Over time, running for and holding elective office becomes their career. They work harder at it than anyone else, in part because they have no real private-sector career to return to in case of defeat.

*Lawyers in Politics*    The prevalence of lawyers in politics is an American tradition. Among the fifty-five delegates to the Constitutional Convention in 1787, some twenty-five were lawyers. The political dominance of lawyers is even greater today, with lawyers filling more than half of U.S. Senate seats and nearly half of the seats in the U.S. House of Representatives.

It is sometimes argued that lawyers dominate in politics because of the parallel skills required in law and politics. Lawyers represent clients, so they can apply their professional experience to represent constituents in Congress. Lawyers are trained to deal with statutory law, so they are assumed to be reasonably familiar with the United States Code (the codified laws of the United States government) when they arrive in Congress to make or amend these statutes.

But it is more likely that people attracted to politics decide to go to law school, fully aware of the tradition of lawyers in American politics. Moreover, political officeholding at the state and local level as well as in the national government can help a struggling lawyer's private practice through free public advertising and opportunities to make contacts with potential clients. Finally, there are many special opportunities for lawyers to acquire public office in "lawyers only" posts as judges and prosecuting attorneys in federal, state, and local governments. Law school graduates who accept modest salaries as U.S. attorneys in the Justice Department or in state or county prosecuting offices can gain invaluable experience for later use in either private law practice or politics.

Most of the lawyers in the Congress, however, have become professional politicians over time. They have left their legal practices behind; they are not partners in the nation's most prestigious law firms. If they left Congress, they would have to rebuild their legal careers.

# THE ADVANTAGES OF INCUMBENCY

In theory, elections offer voters the opportunity to "throw the rascals out." But in practice, voters seldom do so. **Incumbents,** people already holding public office, have a strong advantage when they seek reelection. The reelection rates of incumbents for *all* elective offices—city council, mayor, state legislature, governor, and especially Congress—are very high. Since 1950, more than 90 percent of all members of the House of Representatives who have sought reelection have been successful. (Even in 1994, when Republicans wrested control of the House from the Democrats, the incumbent reelection rate was 92 percent. Only 35 of 382 incumbents seeking reelection lost, but all 35 were Democrats.) The success rate of U.S. Senate incumbents is not as great, but it is still impres-

**Incumbent:** A candidate currently in office seeking reelection.

sive; since 1950, more than 70 percent of senators seeking reelection have been successful.

Why do incumbents win so often? This is a particularly vexing question, inasmuch as so many people are distrustful of government and hold politicians in low esteem. Congress itself is the focal point of public disapproval and even ridicule. Yet people seem to distinguish between Congress as an institution—which they distrust—and their own members of Congress—whom they reelect. The result is something of a contradiction—popular members of Congress serving in an unpopular Congress (see *What Do You Think:* Why Do Voters Reelect Members of an Unpopular Congress?" in Chapter 10).

*Name Recognition*    One reason for incumbents' success is that they begin the campaign with greater *name recognition* than their challengers, simply because they are the incumbent and their name has become familiar to their constituents over the previous years. Much of the daily work of all elected officials, especially members of Congress, is really public relations. Name recognition is a strategic advantage at the ballot box, especially if voters have little knowledge of policy positions or voting records. Voters tend to cast ballots for recognizable names over unknowns. Cynics have concluded that there is no such thing as bad publicity, only publicity. Even in cases of well-publicized scandals, incumbent members of Congress have won reelection; presumably voters preferred "the devil they knew" to the one they did not.

The somewhat lower rate of reelection of Senate versus House members may be a result of the fact that Senate challengers are more likely to have held high-visibility offices—for example, governor or member of Congress—before running for the Senate. Thus Senate challengers often enjoy some name recognition even before the campaign begins. Greater media attention to a statewide Senate race also helps to move the challenger closer to the incumbent in public recognition. In contrast, House challengers are likely to have held less visible local or state legislative offices or to be political novices, and House races attract considerably less media attention than do Senate races.

*Campaign Finances*    Incumbents have a strong advantage in raising campaign funds, simply because individuals and groups seeking access to those already in office are inspired to make contributions (see Figure 8-1). Challengers have no immediate favors to offer; they must convince a potential contributor that they will win office and also that they are devoted to the interests of their financial backers.[6]

Contributing individuals and organizations—especially **political action committees (PACs)**—show a strong preference for incumbents over challengers. They do not wish to offend incumbent officeholders by contributing to their challengers; doing so risks both immediate retribution and future "freezing out" in the likely event of the challengers' defeat. Thus only when an incumbent has been especially hostile to an organization's interest or in rare cases where an incumbent seems especially vulnerable will a PAC support a challenger. Yet challengers need even larger campaign war chests than incumbents to be successful. Challengers must overcome the greater name recognition of incumbents, their many resources, and their records of constituency service. Thus even if incumbents and challengers had equal campaign treasuries, incumbents would enjoy the advantage.

**Political action committee (PAC):** A corporation, union, or other interest group that pools contributions to support political candidates.

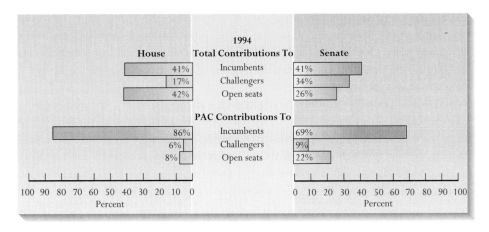

Source: U.S. Federal Election Commission, *FEC Report on Financial Activity* (biennial).

FIGURE 8-1

**Congressional Campaign Contributions to Incumbents versus Challengers, 1994**

*Incumbents enjoy a strong advantage over challengers in raising campaign contributions. The incumbent advantage in the Senate is not as great as in the House, perhaps because Senate challengers are likely to be well-known former officeholders themselves. Political action committees (PACs) representing organized interest groups are even more likely than individuals to support incumbents.*

*Office Resources* Successful politicians use their offices to keep their names and faces before the public in various ways—public appearances, interviews, speeches, and press releases. Incumbents make full use of the **franking privilege** (free use of the U.S. mails) to send self-promotional newsletters to tens of thousands of households in their district at taxpayers' expense. They travel on weekends to their district virtually year-round, using tax-funded travel allowances, to make local appearances, speeches, and contacts.

Members of Congress have large staffs working every day over many years with the principal objective of ensuring the reelection of their members. Indeed, Congress is structured as an "incumbent-protection society" organized and staffed to help guarantee the reelection of its members (see "Home Style" in Chapter 10.) Service to constituents occupies the energies of congressional office staffs both in Washington and in local district offices established for this purpose. Casework wins voters one at a time: tracing lost Social Security checks, ferreting out which federal loans voters qualify for and helping them with their applications, and performing countless other personal favors. These individual "retail-level" favors are supplemented by larger-scale projects that experienced members of Congress can bring to their district or state (roads, dams, post offices, buildings, schools, grants, contracts) or even undesirable projects (landfills, waste disposal sites, halfway houses) that they can keep out of their district. The longer incumbents have occupied the office, the more favors they have performed and the larger their networks of grateful voters.

## CAMPAIGN STRATEGIES

Campaigning is largely a media activity, especially in presidential and congressional campaigns. Media campaigns are highly professionalized, relying on public relations and advertising specialists, professional fund raisers, media consultants, and pollsters. Campaign management involves techniques that strongly resemble those employed in marketing commercial products. Professional media campaign management includes developing a **campaign strategy;** compiling computerized mailing lists and invitations for fund-raising events; selecting a campaign theme and coming up with a desirable candidate image; monitoring the progress

**Franking privilege:** Free use of the U.S. mails granted to members of Congress to promote communication with constituents.

**Campaign strategy:** A plan for a political campaign, usually including a theme, an attempt to define the opponent or the issues, and an effort to coordinate images and messages in news broadcasts and paid advertising.

of the campaign with continual polling of the voters; producing television tapes for commercials, newspaper advertisements, signs, bumper stickers, and radio spots; selecting clothing and hairstyles for the candidate; writing speeches and scheduling appearances; and even planning the victory party.

*Selecting a Theme*   Finding the right theme or slogan for a campaign is essential; this effort is not greatly different from that of launching an advertising campaign for a new detergent. A successful theme is one that characterizes the candidate or the electoral choice confronting the voters. A campaign theme need not be controversial; indeed, it need not even focus on a specific issue. It might be as simple as "a leader you can trust"—an attempt to "package" the candidate as competent and trustworthy.

Most media campaigns focus on candidates' personal qualities rather than on their stands on policy issues. Professional campaigns are based on the assumption that a candidate's "image" is the most important factor affecting voter choice. This image is largely devoid of issues, except in very general terms; for example, "tough on crime," "stands up to the special interests," "fights for the taxpayer," or "cares about you."

*"Defining" the Opponent*   A media campaign also seeks to "define" the opponent in negative terms. The original negative TV ad is generally identified as the 1964 "Daisy Girl" commercial, aired by the Lyndon B. Johnson presidential campaign (see *Up Close:* "Dirty Politics"). Over time, the techniques of negative ads have been refined; weaknesses in opponents are identified and dramatized in emotionally forceful thirty-second spots. The 1988 George Bush presidential campaign is considered the most successful negative campaign at the national level. With Bush far behind in the polls at the beginning of the campaign, the Bush team aired a series of "attack videos" portraying Democrat Michael Dukakis as an unpatriotic liberal who furloughed murderers, befouled harbors, and spurned the American flag. Negative ads can serve a purpose in exposing the record of an opponent. The Bush campaign defended them as necessary because Dukakis's unpopular liberal positions on taxing, spending, and the death penalty were not known by most voters at the beginning of the campaign. But negative campaigns risk an opponent's counterattack charges of "mudslinging," "dirty tricks," and "gutter politics." In 1992, Bill Clinton's "negatives" were "high"—that is, polls revealed that many voters were aware of his alleged faults and worried about them. Bush declined to make an issue of Clinton's marital infidelities, fearing backlash for "mudslinging"; but Bush hit hard at Clinton's avoidance of the draft and participation in anti-Vietnam War demonstrations. In 1996 Dole again sought to make Clinton's "character" an issue. But in both races Clinton skillfully kept the focus of the campaign on the economy. Polls indicated that voters were willing to overlook Clinton's character flaws in assessing his presidential qualifications.

Research into the opponent's public and personal background provides the data for negative campaigning. Previous speeches and writings can be mined for embarrassing or mean-spirited statements. The voting record of the opponent can be scrutinized for unpopular policy positions. Any evils that occurred during an opponent's term of office can be attributed to him or her, either directly ("She knew and conspired in it") or indirectly ("He should have known and done something about it"). Personal scandals or embarrassments can be developed as evi-

*Pat Buchanan donned a coonskin hat and hefted a flintlock rifle during his failed bid for the Republican presidential nomination. Campaign strategists schedule appearances that draw media attention and are consistent with a candidate's theme and image.*

CHAPTER 8 • CAMPAIGNS AND ELECTIONS: DECIDING WHO GOVERNS

# Dirty Politics

Political campaigning frequently turns ugly with negative advertising that is vicious and personal. It is widely believed that television's focus on personal character and private lives—rather than on policy positions and governmental experience—encourages negative campaigning. But vicious personal attacks in political campaigns began long before television. They are nearly as old as the nation itself.

"If Jefferson is elected," proclaimed Yale's president in 1800, "the Bible will be burned and we will see our wives and daughters the victims of legal prostitution." In 1864, *Harper's Weekly* decried the "mud-slinging" of the day, lamenting that President Abraham Lincoln was regularly referred to by his opponent as a "filthy storyteller, despot, liar, thief, braggart, buffoon, monster, Ignoramus Abe, robber, swindler, tyrant, fiend, butcher, and pirate."

Television's first memorable attack advertisement was the "Daisy Girl" commercial broadcast by Lyndon Johnson's presidential campaign in 1964 against his Republican opponent, Barry Goldwater. While never mentioning Goldwater by name, the purpose of the ad was to "define" him as a warmonger who would plunge the world into a nuclear holocaust. The ad opens with a small, innocent girl standing in an open field plucking petals from a daisy and counting, "1, 2, 3 . . .". When she reaches 9, an ominous adult male voice begins a countdown: "10, 9, 8 . . ." as the camera closes in on the child's face. At "zero," a mushroom cloud appears, reflected in her eyes, and

envelopes the screen. Lyndon Johnson's voice is heard: "These are the stakes."

The infamous Willie Horton ad, broadcast by an independent organization supporting Republican George Bush in 1988, portrayed Democrat Michael Dukakis as weak on crime prevention. It featured a close-up mug shot of a very threatening convicted murderer, Willie Horton, with a voice proclaiming that "Dukakis not only opposes the death penalty, he allowed first-degree murderers to have weekend passes from prison. One was Willie Horton who murdered a boy in a robbery, stabbing him nineteen times. Despite a life sentence, Horton received ten weekend passes from prison." A final photo shows Dukakis, with a voice-over announcing: "Weekend prison passes, Dukakis weak on crime."

Clinton's 1996 negative TV ads described Dole as "wrong in the past, wrong for the future" and featured unflattering black-and-white photos of an aging Dole standing with Newt Gingrich. Dole's campaign found an old MTV show tape of Clinton joking about past drug use.

What are the effects of negative advertising? First of all, it works more often than not. Controlled experiments indicate that targets of attack ads are rated less positively by people who have watched these ads. Rarely do viewers penalize candidates for airing negative messages. Professional campaign managers are aware of the effectiveness of negative ads, and there is little likelihood that such ads will disappear over time. But another important effect of negative advertising is to make voters more cynical about politics and government in general. Indeed, there is some evidence that negative campaigning by opposing candidates reduces voter turnout.

What, if anything, can be done? Government regulation of political speech directly contravenes the First Amendment. American democracy has survived negative campaigning for a long time. Some reform proposals have called for candidates to appear in person on camera when delivering an attack statement, or for media monitoring and criticism of attack messages as well as correction of erroneous positive claims. But it is unlikely that these reforms would have much of an impact on negative campaigning.

*Source:* Kathleen Hall Jamieson, *Dirty Politics: Deception, Distraction, and Democracy* (New York: Oxford University Press, 1992); also Stephen Ansolabehere et al, "Does Attack Advertising Demobilize the Electorate?" *American Political Science Review* 88 (December 1994):829-38.

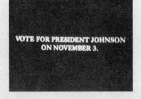

*Four frames from Lyndon Johnson's 1964 "Daisy Girl" commercial.*

dence of "character." If campaign managers fear that highly personal attacks on an opponent will backfire, they may choose to "leak" the information to reporters and try to avoid attribution of the story to themselves or their candidate.

*Using Focus Groups and Polling*   Focus-group techniques can help in selecting campaign themes and identifying negative characteristics in opponents. A **focus group** is a small group of people who are brought together to view videotapes, listen to specific campaign appeals, and respond to particular topics and issues. Media professionals then develop a campaign strategy around "hot-button" issues—issues that generate strong responses by focus groups—and avoid themes or issues that fail to elicit much interest.

The results of focus-group work can then be tested in wider polling. Polling is a central feature of professional campaigning. Serious candidates for national and statewide offices almost always employ their own private polling firms, distinct from the national survey organizations that supply the media with survey data. Initial polling is generally designed to determine candidates' "name recognition"—the extent to which the voters recognize the candidates—and whatever positive and negative images are already associated with their names.

Special polling techniques that ask respondents to choose between mock candidates who are said to espouse various positions can further determine what a "winning candidate profile" looks like. And survey results on what issues are uppermost in the minds of the voters and where they stand on these issues are essential in developing a campaign strategy. "High negatives" of potential opponents may suggest an "attack" strategy, exploiting the weaknesses of the opponents. High negatives for the candidate suggest the need for a strategy to overcome these images.

For example, if the candidate is seen as too rich or too upper class or too "out of touch" with common people, then the campaign will show the candidate in blue jeans hanging out with factory workers in beer and pizza places. If the candidate's private life is under suspicion, then the campaign will feature appearances with a loving spouse and family attending church services. If the candidate is perceived as "too liberal," then centrist themes will be stressed; if seen as "too conservative," then moderation, warmth, and compassion will be emphasized. Astute campaign managers try not to completely reverse a candidate's previous political stances in order to deflect charges of "flip-flopping" and to avoid unintended images of insincerity or untrustworthiness.

Campaign polling is highly professionalized, with telephone banks with multiple lines, trained interviewers, and computer-assisted-telephone-interviewing (CATI) software that records and tabulates responses instantly and sends the results to campaign managers. In well-financed campaigns, polling is continual throughout the campaign, so that managers can assess progress on a daily basis.

During the campaign, polls chart the candidate's progress and, perhaps more important, help assess the effectiveness of specific campaign themes. If the candidate appears to be gaining support, the campaign stays on course. But if the candidate appears to be falling in the polls, the campaign manager comes under intense pressure to change themes and strategies. As election day nears, the pressure increases on the trailing candidate to "go negative"—to launch even more scathing attacks on the opponent.

**Focus group:** In a political context, a small number of people brought together in a comfortable setting to discuss and respond to themes and issues, allowing campaign managers to develop and analyze strategies.

CHAPTER 8 • CAMPAIGNS AND ELECTIONS: DECIDING WHO GOVERNS

*Incumbent versus Challenger Strategies*   Campaign strategies vary by the offices being sought, the nature of the times, and the imagination and inventiveness of the candidates' managers. But incumbency is perhaps the most important factor affecting the choice of a strategy. The challenger must attack the record of the incumbent, deplore current conditions in the city, state, or nation, and stress the need for change. Challengers are usually freer to take the offensive; incumbents must defend their record in office and either boast of accomplishments during their term or blame the opposition for blocking them. Challengers frequently opt for the "outsider" strategy, capitalizing on distrust and cynicism toward government.

The incumbent's electoral fortunes are often tied to current conditions, notably the state of the economy. Incumbents who feel fairly secure may opt for a strategy placing them "above the political fray" as dedicated and patriotic public servants largely ignoring (and thus trivializing) the attacks of challengers. For example, incumbent presidents may opt for the "Rose Garden strategy," remaining near the White House and performing presidential functions on the nightly news or traveling abroad and appearing "presidential" in photo sessions in world capitals. As George Bush found in 1992, however, this strategy can backfire if voters see the president as ignoring problems back home.

*News Management*   Television is the real battleground of the media campaign in national elections. The campaign is planned to get the maximum favorable "free" exposure on the evening news as well as to saturate the media with paid commercial advertising. Media events are planned each day, with visual images too good for television news to ignore. A well-managed media campaign will coordinate themes and images for both free news exposure and paid commercials. Images may shift during the campaign as issues arise and as each side tries to "define" the other. Candidates battle each other in a war of television ads and sound bites.

News management is the key to the media campaign. News coverage of the candidates is more credible in the eyes of viewers than paid advertisements. Each day a candidate must do something interesting and "newsworthy," that is, likely to be reported as news. Thus, each day of the campaign is organized to win favorable coverage on the nightly television news and in the next day's newspapers. Pictures are as important as words. Candidates must provide good **photo ops** to the media—pictures of themselves appearing in settings or backgrounds that emphasize their themes. Thus, for example, if the theme is patriotism, then the candidate appears with war veterans, at a military base, or at a flag factory. If the theme is education, the candidate appears at a school; if crime control, then with police officers; if environmentalism, then in a wilderness area; if the economy, then at a closed factory or unemployment line or soup kitchen for the homeless.

*Words* must also be carefully chosen for television reports. Themes must be stated in concise and catchy **sound bites** that will register in the viewers' minds. Candidates now understand that the news media will select only a few seconds of an entire day of speech making for broadcast. The average length of a network news sound bite has shrunk from forty-five to seven seconds over the last twenty years. Thus extended or serious discussion of issues during a campaign is sacrificed to the need for one-liners on the nightly news. Indeed, if a campaign theme cannot fit on a bumper sticker, it is too complex.

**Photo ops:** Staged opportunities for the media to photograph the candidate in a favorable setting.

**Sound bites:** Concise and catchy phrases that attract media coverage.

# Change, with Moderation: Clinton's Winning Strategy in 1996

At the start of the 1992 presidential race, Democratic strategists were painfully aware that Republicans had won five of the previous six presidential elections. Northern liberal Democrats—Humphrey, McGovern, Mondale, Dukakis—had lost in campaigns in which Republicans had captured moderate as well as conservative voters. The strategic problem was diagnosed as follows: The party's liberal candidates enjoyed an advantage in primary elections, where low turnouts magnified the influence of the party's liberal constituencies; but in the general election, liberal candidates who won the party's nomination fared poorly among moderate swing voters.

*Becoming a "New Democrat"*   Bill Clinton had spent nearly twenty years shaping his image as a youthful "New Democrat" and positioning himself to run for president as a "moderate." He avoided the "liberal" tag with tough talk about workfare, the death penalty, and personal responsibility. He emphasized economic growth over income redistribution. He referred to government spending as "investment." His "putting people first" theme emphasized help for the middle class and avoided direct references to traditional Democratic groups: African Americans, feminists, environmentalists, labor unions, government employees.

*Handling the Character Issue*   Bill Clinton almost lost the prize he had sought for a lifetime early in the 1992 Democratic primaries, when Gennifer Flowers held a nationally televised press conference to announce that she had had a long-term affair with him. Rumors of marital infidelity had shadowed Clinton for many years. The same problem had driven Gary Hart out of the presidential race in 1988. But a tenacious Bill Clinton decided to confront the "bimbo issue" head-on. When Don Hewitt, producer of *60 Minutes*, offered Clinton a Sunday night prime-time interview just after the Super Bowl, the candidate accepted. With wife Hillary at his side, Bill Clinton told a huge nationwide audience that his marriage had survived shaky moments but it was rock-solid now. He correctly calculated that the public was increasingly disgusted with the media's focus on sexual scandal.

*1992: Focusing on Change*   Clinton's 1992 campaign strategy was to hammer home, over and over again, a single theme: the economy is in bad shape, and the nation demands change. Yet in late spring, the most powerful voice for economic change in the nation was that of Ross Perot. Clinton was running *third* in the polls, trailing both President Bush and the independent billionaire. But Perot's focus on the economy and the need for change was detaching millions of middle-class voters from Bush and sending the president's popularity rating into a nosedive.

With the prospect of a three-man race looming, some Clinton strategists urged their candidate to jettison his moderate image in favor of cultivating the core liberal constituencies of the Democratic Party and thus eke out a plurality victory. But Clinton rejected this advice and insisted on sticking with the original game plan—moderation and change.

The Democratic convention was a celebration of Clinton's good fortune and sound political judgment. When the temperamental Perot unexpectedly withdrew from the race, millions of his disillusioned supporters were set adrift at precisely the moment that Clinton was broadcasting his message of change to national audiences. Perot's middle-class, independent supporters flocked to Clinton's banner. By the end of the Democratic convention, Clinton had soared to a 20-point lead in the polls.

*Taking Advantage of Opponent's Mistakes*   Clinton's single-minded focus on the economy and the need for change contrasted with the unfocused rambling of the Bush campaign. The Bush team at first implausibly tried to claim the "change" theme for itself, only to have voters ask why the president hadn't sought change in the previous four years. A subsequent attempt to focus on "family values" met with only limited success. Bush's attempts to remind voters of America's victories in the Cold War and the Gulf War seemed to backfire: They only proved that the president had focused his energies on foreign affairs rather than on problems at home. Bush's claim that the economy was not all that bad only seemed to show that he was "out of touch" with the people.

*Setting a Favorable Agenda*   Clinton went into the presidential debates in 1992 with one simple goal—to keep the focus of the campaign on the economy. Bush had a much more challenging task—to refocus the campaign on Clinton's character and somehow overcome the Democrat's lead in the polls. Bush tried to tag Clinton as a Vietnam War protestor and draft-dodger who lacked the personal stature to be commander-in-chief. But in the first debate Clinton nimbly deflected Bush's attack: "Your father was right to stand up to Joe McCarthy. You were wrong to attack my patriotism." Bush was awkward and uncomfortable in the attack mode.

In the final days of the campaign, Bush finally hit his stride with a fierce attack on Clinton's character. Could "Slick Willie"—a taxer, a spender, a liberal, a draft dodger, an antiwar demonstrator, and a liar—be trusted to run the country? But Bush's theme was negative and failed to give voters a reason to vote *for* the president. The Clinton team wanted the election to be a referendum on the economy, not on their candidate's character. In the end, that is what they got.

While Clinton emerged only 5 percentage points ahead of Bush in the popular vote, the nation's desire for change was clearly evident in the combined votes for Clinton and Perot. Fully 62 percent of the voters chose to vote against incumbent president George Bush. Clinton prevailed in one of the toughest political campaigns in American history because he skillfully presented himself to the voters as an agent of change.

### 1996: Becoming Presidential

In his reelection campaign Bill Clinton reshaped his image into that of a responsible, centrist president—a president whose tireless efforts had improved the economy, reduced annual federal deficits, lowered the crime rate, and saved Medicare and Medicaid from mean-spirited Republicans in Congress. He shifted the public's attention away from his controversial early initiatives in office—his large tax increase, his confrontation with the military over homosexuals, and his unsuccessful national health care proposal. Instead, he focused on a series of modest but popular positions—for example, the family leave act, portable health insurance, minimum two-day hospital stays following childbirth, the V-chip, school uniforms, a ban on assault weapons—positions that appealed especially to women voters. As incumbent president, he sailed through the presidential primaries in 1996 with no opposition.

### "Defining" Bob Dole

General Colin Powell was the only potential opponent who led Clinton in presidential choice polls. When Powell removed himself from contention, a loud sigh of relief was heard in the White House. Bob Dole—an aging, dour, occasion-

ally grumpy, long-time congressional leader—was a welcome opponent. Indeed, as polls consistently reported Clinton's 20-plus percentage point lead over Dole, the only concern in the Clinton camp was overconfidence.

With the economy growing, the president had only to ask, "Are you better off now than when I took office?" But the Clinton campaign also sought to "define" Bob Dole as "wrong in the past, wrong for the future." Indeed, from the beginning Bob Dole seemed ill-suited as a presidential candidate: a Washington insider when the voters distrusted Washington; a congressional leader when Congress was the least-trusted branch of government; an aging World War II veteran out of touch with the baby boomer electorate. Clinton television ads showed Dole acknowledging that "I voted against Medicare," raising fears among Dole's own senior generation voters. A modest Dole "bounce" in the polls after the GOP convention was quickly washed away.

### Building the Bridge

The Clinton theme was an upbeat "bridge to the 21st century," suggesting his own forward-looking posture and subtly reminding voter's of Dole's age. In the debates, Clinton remained cool, confident, unrattled, and "presidential" in the face of Dole's barbs. "No insult," he said at one point, "ever cleaned up a toxic waste dump." Dole's promise of a 15 percent tax cut went unheeded by voters more concerned with federal deficits. Polls reported that although Americans thought Dole was more "honest and trustworthy" than Clinton, they still preferred Clinton as president. Clinton was judged the clear winner of the debates, but viewership was down. The campaign was the dullest in recent times, as reflected in a half-century-record low voter turnout (48 percent). An embarrassing last-minute flap over Democratic campaign contributions from foreign sources seemed to raise Perot's vote just enough to prevent the president from winning 50 percent of the electorate. The final vote was Clinton 49 percent, Dole 41 percent, Perot 8 percent, with 2 percent going to minor party candidates.

Clinton won a second term—the first Democratic president since Franklin Roosevelt to do so— but he failed to win a policy mandate. Republicans maintained control of both houses of Congress, and scandals and investigations promised to follow the Clintons throughout their White House years. But Bill Clinton had again successfully shaped a winning image.

Consequently, each day's campaigning is a series of photo ops and sound bites, all prepared with the evening news in mind. Between events, candidates must scramble to various funding-raising events—dinners, parties, personal meetings with large contributors. Thus candidates balance their time between "getting out the message" and finding ways to pay for the message and its transmittal.

*Paid Advertising*   Television "spot" ads must be prepared prior to and during the campaign. They involve employing expensive television advertising and production firms well in advance of the campaign and keeping them busy revising and producing new ads throughout the campaign to respond to changing issues or opponents' attacks. Commercial advertising is the most expensive aspect of the campaign. Heavy costs are incurred in the production of the ads and in the purchase of broadcast time. The Federal Communications Commission (FCC) does not permit television networks or stations to charge *more* than standard commercial rates for political ads, but these rates are high enough. Networks and stations are required to offer the same rates and times to all candidates, but if one candidate's campaign treasury is weak or exhausted, an opponent can saturate broadcast airtime.

*Free Airtime*   All candidates seek free airtime on news and talk shows, but the need to gain free exposure is much greater for underfunded candidates. They must go to extremes in devising media events, and they must encourage and participate in free televised debates. The debate format is particularly well suited for candidates who cannot match their opponents in paid commercial advertising. Thus, well-funded and poorly funded candidates may jockey over the number and times of public debates.

## MONEY IN ELECTIONS

The professionalization of campaigning and the heavy costs of a media campaign (especially television) drive up the costs of running for office. Generally, campaign costs for presidential and congressional races can be broken down in terms of television production (20 to 25 percent), television time (40 to 50 percent), polling (5 to 10 percent), paid staff (5 to 10 percent), office overhead and candidate travel (5 to 10 percent), and the costs of fund-raising events and solicitations (20 to 25 percent). Altogether, in a presidential election year, campaign spending by all presidential and congressional candidates, the Democratic and Republican parties, and independent political organizations tops *$1 billion*. Fund raising to meet these costs is the most important hurdle for any candidate for public office (see *A Conflicting View:* "Reforming Campaign Finance").

**Federal Election Commission (FEC):** Agency charged with enforcing federal election laws and disbursing public presidential campaign funds.

*The Federal Election Commission*   The **Federal Election Commission (FEC)** is responsible for enforcing limits on individual and organizational contributions to all federal elections, administering the public funding of presidential campaigns, and requiring full disclosure of all campaign financial activity in presidential and congressional elections. Enforcement of these federal election and campaign finance laws lies in the hands of the six-member FEC. Appointed by the president to serve staggered six-year terms, commission members are traditionally split 3 to 3 between Republicans and Democrats.

*Presidential Campaign Costs*    What does it cost to run for president? It is no easy task to add up all of the various costs of a presidential campaign. Costs are incurred in both the primaries and the general election. Contributions and disbursements are made by: (1) the presidential campaign organizations of each candidate, (2) the Democratic and Republican parties, and (3) independent organizations unconnected with a candidate or party. All three types of financing are regulated by the FEC. A serious presidential candidate must be prepared to raise and spend $20 million or more in the primary elections and $70 million or more in the general election.

*Congressional Campaign Costs*    Campaign costs for House and Senate races vary a great deal across the country, depending on the size of the state, the costs of television time in various "market areas," and a host of other local factors. However, the average U.S. Senate candidate spends about $4 million (incumbents, $5 million; challengers, $3 million), with some races costing as much as $10 million or more. (The current record is held by Republican Michael Huffington, whose *losing* 1994 campaign in California cost more than $28 million, most of it his own; his Democratic opponent, Dianne Feinstein, spent "only" about $12 million.) The average candidate for the U.S. House of Representatives spends about $450,000 (incumbents, $550,000; challengers, $225,000). Incumbents spend more than challengers because incumbents get more in campaign contributions. Winners generally spend more than losers.

*Sources of Money*    Where does the money come from? The FEC limits individual contributions to a candidate to $1,000 per election and organizational contributions to $5,000 per election (see Table 8-1). But there are many ways in which individuals and organizations can legally surmount these limits. Contribu-

| TABLE 8-1    FEDERAL CAMPAIGN SPENDING LIMITS | | | |
|---|---|---|---|
| | *Contribution to Any Candidate or Candidate Committee* | *Contribution to Any National Party Committee* | *Contribution to Any PAC or Other Political Committee* |
| *Time Period* | *Per Election** | *Per Calendar Year* | *Per Calendar Year* | *Per Calendar Year Total* |
| Individual | $1,000 | $20,000 | $5,000 | $25,000 |
| Multicandidate committee** | $5,000 | $15,000 | $5,000 | no limit |
| Other political committee | $1,000 | $20,000 | $5,000 | no limit |

*Primary and general elections count as two separate elections, so this contribution can effectively be doubled during a normal election year in states with primaries.

**Multicandidate committees, commonly known as political action committees, or PACs, are those with more than fifty contributors that have been registered for at least six months and that have made contributions to five or more federal candidates.

# Reforming Campaign Finance

Battles over campaign finance reform reflect conflict between the parties. Historically, Republicans enjoyed a greater ability to raise money from their more affluent loyalists. Democrats were usually more dependent upon organizations and political action committee (PAC) money. Moreover, Democrats tended to protect the interests of incumbents, since they had control of both the House and Senate for most of the last forty years. As the minority party in Congress, Republicans were somewhat more sympathetic to the interests of challengers. But that sympathy for challengers largely evaporated with the Republican congressional victory in 1994. Rather, each member of Congress, Democrat or Republican, tends to view reform proposals from his or her own political perspective.

Political scientist Frank Sorauf writes: "Nothing colors the politics of regulating campaign finance as much as the central fact that the Congress is regulating its own electoral activity. . . . The members of Congress know campaign finance at first hand, and they know that even the slightest change in the structure of regulations may have considerable consequences for their own political careers."*

*Reform Goals* Ideally, reform of campaign financing should minimize the opportunity for cor-

ruption, inspire voter confidence in the integrity of the political system, equalize influence between rich and poor, encourage competitive elections by giving challengers a fair chance against incumbents, and at the same time preserve free speech and the right of people to promote their views at election time. But it is not clear that any reform proposals could achieve all of these goals at once.

*Eliminate PACs?* Proposals to outlaw PACs and ban all contributions by corporations, unions, and interest groups raise constitutional questions about the right of groups to express their preferences and participate in the electoral process. The Supreme Court might strike down a congressional attempt to ban PACs as a violation of the First Amendment. Republicans might gain more from such a ban than Democrats; if PAC or organization money were to be eliminated, individual contributions would become the only game in town, a situation that might favor Republicans. Eliminating PACs might also hide the special-interest sources of campaign contributions. The reporting requirements of the Federal Election Commission (FEC) now make it clear where PAC money goes. But if individual donors became the sole source of campaign funds, their interests would be hidden, even if their names were recorded, because few people would know what interests the donors represented. Eliminating PACs would increase the influence of lawyers and political brokers who contact people

tors may give a candidate $1,000 for each member of their family in a primary election and then another $1,000 per member in the general election. Organizations may generate much more than the $5,000 limit by "bundling" (combining) $1,000 contributions from individual members. Both individuals and organizations can give money to the parties for "party building" or "voter registration" activity, as long as this **soft money** is not spent directly on the presidential campaign. Independent organizations can spend money beyond the limits set by the FEC for a presidential candidate or party in order to promote their political views so long as these organizations do so "without cooperation or consultation with the candidate of his or her campaign." Finally, individuals may spend as much of their own money on their own campaigns as they wish.[7]

By law, every candidate for federal office must file periodic reports with the FEC detailing both the income and the expenditures of their campaign. Individual contributors who give an aggregate of $200 or more must be identified by name, address,

**Soft money:** Political contributions to a party for activities such as party building or voter registration, but not directly for campaigns.

and "bundle" their contributions. It would also increase the relative importance of candidates' personal wealth and ability to finance their own campaigns.

*Public Funding and Limits on Spending?* It is frequently argued that congressional elections should be publicly funded and limits placed on congressional campaign spending, just as they are in presidential elections. Most members of Congress dislike the constant chore of asking people for money. Presumably, freeing them from obligations to contributors would reduce the influence of well-heeled special interests in congressional decision making. Members of Congress would no longer be obliged to give special consideration to the requests of wealthy individual contributors and big-spending PACs. Perhaps the general public would be less cynical about Congress and more confident of the fairness of the system.

But public funding would entail limits on campaign spending for the candidates. Equal limits for congressional incumbents and challengers would grant a strong advantage to incumbents, who already have name recognition and years of constituent contacts and services working on their behalf. Indeed, skeptics charge that public funding with campaign limits is really an "incumbent protection" plan.

Finally, many taxpayers are offended by the very idea of politicians using tax dollars to run for public office. Indeed, four out of five taxpayers refuse even to check off one dollar of their taxes for presidential campaigns.

*Banning "Soft" Money?* Money has a way of flowing around regulatory obstacles. Currently, the FEC allows individuals to contribute up to $20,000 in "soft money" to political parties. Soft money allows big contributors ("fat cats") to exercise disproportionate influence in party politics. But this soft money also gives the parties what little direct influence they have over members of Congress. Cutting off party funding would further weaken the party system.

In addition, it might prove extremely difficult to regulate brokering and bundling of individual contributions. Under current laws, a broker or "intermediary" collecting campaign contributions must report the names of the original donor and the recipient candidate. But how could the government ban individuals from hosting a cocktail party, inviting wealthy guests, persuading them to give to a candidate, suggesting how the checks should be made out, collecting the checks, and handing them to the candidate? Banning individuals or organizations from expressing their views during an election, independently of a party or candidate, would clearly violate the freedoms of speech and press guaranteed by the First Amendment.

*Frank Sorauf, *Inside Campaign Finance* (New Haven, Conn.: Yale University Press, 1992), p. 191.

occupation, and employer. All PAC and party contributions, no matter how large or small, must also be itemized. In addition, PACs themselves must file reports with the FEC at least four times a year, detailing both the contributions received by the PAC and the names of candidates and other groups that received the PAC's donations.

*Fund Raising* Most campaign funds for presidential primaries, as well as for senatorial and congressional elections, come from individual contributions. About 7 to 10 percent of the population claims in national surveys to have contributed to candidates running for public office. Contributors are disproportionately high-income, well-educated, older people with strong partisan views (see Figure 8-2). There are networks of contributors in every state, and campaign staffs use sophisticated computerized mailing lists and telephone directories of regular Democratic and Republican and liberal and conservative contributors to solicit funds (see *Up Close:* "How to Raise $20 Million for a Political Campaign").

Fund raising occupies more of a candidate's time than any other campaign activity. Candidates must personally contact as many individual contributors as possible. They work late into the evening on the telephone with potential contributors. Fund-raising dinners, cocktail parties, barbecues, fish frys, and so on are scheduled nearly every day of a campaign. The candidate is expected to appear personally to "press the flesh" of big contributors. Movie and rock stars and other assorted celebrities may also be asked to appear at fund-raising affairs to generate attendance. Dinners may run $250 to $1,000 per plate in presidential affairs, though often less in Senate or House campaigns. Tickets may be "bundled" to well-heeled individual contributors or sold in blocks to organizations. Fund-raising techniques are limited only by the imagination of the campaign manager.

*Organizational Contributions*   Organizations channel their campaign contributions through political action committees. Corporations and unions are not allowed to contribute directly from corporate or union funds, but they may form PACs to seek contributions from managers and stockholders and their families, or

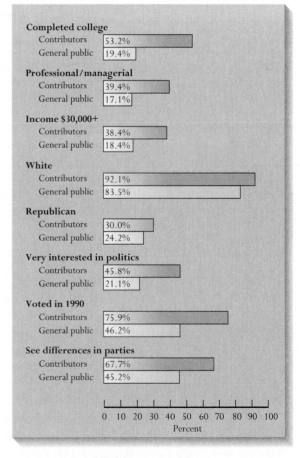

( FIGURE 8-2 )

**Characteristics of Political Contributors**

*Contributors to political campaigns generally have better educations, higher incomes, and more professional positions than most Americans. They also are far more likely than average Americans to vote regularly and to hold strongly partisan views.*

**Completed college**
Contributors 53.2%
General public 19.4%

**Professional/managerial**
Contributors 39.4%
General public 17.1%

**Income $30,000+**
Contributors 38.4%
General public 18.4%

**White**
Contributors 92.1%
General public 83.5%

**Republican**
Contributors 30.0%
General public 24.2%

**Very interested in politics**
Contributors 45.8%
General public 21.1%

**Voted in 1990**
Contributors 75.9%
General public 46.2%

**See differences in parties**
Contributors 67.7%
General public 45.2%

0  10  20  30  40  50  60  70  80  90  100
Percent

*Source:* Center for Political Studies, University of Michigan, *1990 National Election Study.* Data provided by the Interuniversity Consortium for Political and Social Research.

CHAPTER 8 • CAMPAIGNS AND ELECTIONS: DECIDING WHO GOVERNS

# How to Raise $20 Million for a Political Campaign

The 1996 presidential primary schedule—thirty-five state primary elections scheduled in just twenty-nine days in February and March—placed a premium on the ability of contending Republican candidates to raise "early money." The serious candidates all sought to raise at least $20 million in campaign contributions *before* the first primary election. (Only mega-millionaire publisher Steve Forbes could afford to pay his campaign expenses out of his own pocket.) This meant that presidential campaign activity actually stretched out over two years; candidates spent most of 1995 in fund-raising activity, preparing for the primary and general election battles of 1996.

Asking people for money is something candidates endure rather than enjoy. Preparing for the campaign means mostly "schmoozing" with affluent donors rather than meeting voters, discussing issues, or formulating policy positions. Perhaps the most common fund-raising activity is the large $1,000-per-plate dinner session, at a big hotel or convention center, with celebrity introductions followed by a rousing speech by the candidate and as much schmoozing at the tables as possible. A 1,000-person event at that

price produces almost a $1 million, minus modest expenses. The first $250 of each person's contribution is matched by federal funds, so the potential income from such an event is $1.25 million. Each ticket represents the Federal Election Commission limit on individual contributions, but tickets can be sold in blocks or tables to families or groups.

However, it is not easy to sell $1,000 tickets. Less-affluent donors can be solicited for cocktail parties and luncheons where the goal may be to obtain twenty-five or fifty contributions of at least $250. Candidates may schedule two or three of these more modest events each day. Success depends on old-fashioned "pyramiding" of friends—donors asked to identify ten or twenty people who might come to such an event, and these donors in turn pressed to identify ten or twenty more friends to do the same.

Finally, direct-mail solicitation from carefully screened lists of potential donors can also produce campaign money. Direct mail can reach people who may be inclined to donate $25 to $100. The problem is that this method is very costly, with 50 to 75 percent of the money received from direct mailing going to the cost of producing and mailing the solicitation. "Hot" mailing lists are those that produce the most money; they are cherished by candidates and their finance managers.

---

union workers and their families. PACs are organized not only by corporations and unions but also by trade and professional associations, environmental groups, and liberal and conservative ideological groups. The wealthiest PACs are based in Washington, D.C. Most PAC money goes to congressional campaigns, which receive no federal funding (see "Getting to Capitol Hill" in Chapter 10). PAC contributions go overwhelmingly to incumbent officeholders (see Figure 8-3). PACs may not give more than $5,000 to any candidate for a federal office, but since there are no limits to the number of candidates that a PAC may support, there are no overall limits on total PAC contributions.

*Federal Funding of Presidential Elections*   Federal funding is available to presidential candidates in both primary and general elections. Candidates seeking the nomination in presidential primary elections can qualify for federal funds by raising $5,000 from private contributions no greater than $250 each in each of

FIGURE 8-3    **Sources of Congressional Campaign Funds, 1994**

*Most congressional campaign money comes from individual contributors. Political action committee contributions are heavily weighted in favor of incumbents. Challengers often must rely on their own money.*

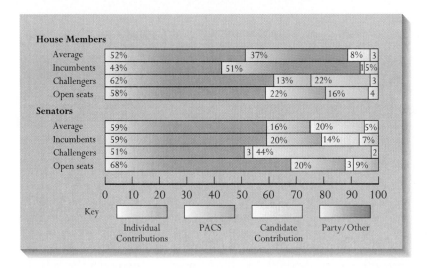

**House Members**

| | Individual Contributions | PACS | Candidate Contribution | Party/Other |
|---|---|---|---|---|
| Average | 52% | 37% | 8% | 3 |
| Incumbents | 43% | 51% | 1 | 5% |
| Challengers | 62% | 13% | 22% | 3 |
| Open seats | 58% | 22% | 16% | 4 |

**Senators**

| | Individual Contributions | PACS | Candidate Contribution | Party/Other |
|---|---|---|---|---|
| Average | 59% | 16% | 20% | 5% |
| Incumbents | 59% | 20% | 14% | 7% |
| Challengers | 51% | 3 | 44% | 2 |
| Open seats | 68% | 20% | 3 | 9% |

*Source:* Federal Election Commission.

twenty states. In the general election, Democratic and Republican nominees are funded equally at levels determined by the FEC. In order to receive federal funding, presidential candidates must agree to FEC limits on their campaign spending in both primary and general elections. (Until 1992, all presidential candidates agreed to the FEC limits and accepted federal funding; but independent Texas billionaire H. Ross Perot funded his own campaign that year, rejecting federal funds, and publishing mogul Steve Forbes rejected federal funds in 1996 and paid for his own unsuccessful Republican presidential primary race.) Federal funding pays about one-third of the primary campaign costs of presidential candidates and all the official presidential campaign organization costs in the general election. The parties also receive federal funds for their nominating conventions and general

*Senator Bob Kerry of Nebraska, head of the Democratic Senatorial Campaign Committee, greets contributors at a Democratic fundraising event.*

election activities. Third-party candidates can receive federal reimbursement after the election if they get 5 percent of the vote; otherwise they must bear the full cost of the campaign themselves.

Federal funding is financed by a one-dollar "checkoff" box on individual income tax returns. All taxpayers are asked whether they wish one dollar of their tax payments to go into the federal presidential election campaign fund. But taxpayers have grown increasingly reluctant to have their tax dollars spent for political campaigning, even though the one-dollar contribution does not increase their taxes. Today only about 15 percent of taxpayers check off a dollar for presidential campaign funding.

House Speaker Newt Gingrich with movie star Arnold Schwarzenegger. Politicians often seek the support of celebrities to boost their campaigns and help raise funds.

*Why People Contribute*    Those who contribute to presidential and/or congressional campaign funds do so for a variety of reasons. Some contributors are ideologically motivated. They make their contributions based on their perception of the ideological position of the candidate (or perhaps their perception of the candidate's opponent). They may make contributions to congressional candidates across the country who share their policy views. Liberal and conservative networks of contributors can be contacted through specialized mailing lists—for example, liberals through television producer Norman Lear's People for the American Way and conservatives through North Carolina Senator Jesse Helms's National Congressional Club. Feminists have been effective in soliciting individual contributions across the country and funneling them very early in a campaign to women candidates through EMILY's list (see *Up Close:* "EMILY's List"). Ideological contributors may only get the satisfaction of knowing that they are financially backing their cause in the political process. Some contributors simply enjoy the opportunity to be near and to be seen with high-ranking politicians. Presidents pose for photos with big contributors, who later frame the photos and hang them in their office to impress their friends, associates, and customers.

## WHAT DO CONTRIBUTORS "BUY"?

What does money buy in politics? A cynic might say that money can buy anything—for example, special appropriations for public works directly benefiting the contributor, special tax breaks, special federal regulations. Scandals involving the direct (quid pro quo) purchase of special favors, privileges, exemptions, and treatments have been common enough in the past, and they are likely to continue in the future. But campaign contributions are rarely made in the form of a direct trade-off for a favorable vote. Such an arrangement risks exposure as bribery and may be prosecuted under the law. Campaign contributions are more likely to be made without any *explicit* quid pro quo but rather with a general understanding that the contributor has confidence in the candidate's good judgment on issues directly affecting the contributor. The contributor expects the candidate to be smart enough to figure out how to vote in order to keep the contributions coming in the future.

*Access to Policy Makers*    Large contributors expect to be able to call or visit and present their views directly to "their" officeholders. At the presidential level, major contributors who cannot get a meeting with the president expect to meet

## EMILY's List

Fund raising is the greatest obstacle to mounting a successful campaign against an incumbent. And the most difficult problem facing challengers is raising money *early* in the campaign, when they have little name recognition and little or no standing in the polls.

EMILY's list is a politically adroit and effective effort to support liberal women candidates by infusing *early money* into their campaigns. EMILY stands for Early Money Is Like Yeast, because "it makes the dough rise." Early contributions provide the initial credibility that a candidate, especially a challenger, needs in order to solicit additional funds from individuals and organizations. EMILY is a fund-raising network of thousands of contributors, each of whom pays $100 to join and pledges to give at least $100 to two women from a list of candidates prepared by EMILY's leaders. Most of the contributors are professional women who appreciate EMILY's screening of pro-choice, liberal women candidates around the country. In 1992, EMILY helped distribute more than $3 million among some three dozen liberal Democratic women candidates for Congress.

EMILY's list was begun by a wealthy heir to a founder of IBM, Ellen Malcolm. Malcolm graduated from Hollins College in Virginia in 1969 and joined the liberal public interest group Common Cause as a volunteer. She later joined the staff of the National Women's Political Caucus. In 1980, she established her own private foundation, Windom Fund, to channel money to women and minority groups. (She reportedly invented the Windom name to preserve her own anonymity as the benefactor.) She created EMILY's list in 1985.

Women challengers for congressional races traditionally faced frustration in fund raising. Incumbent male officeholders enjoyed a huge fund-raising advantage because contributors expected them to win and therefore opened their wallets to gain access and good will. Contributing to women challengers, even by people who supported their views, was often considered a waste of money. EMILY's list has helped to overcome defeatism among both women candidates and contributors.

U.S. Senator Barbara Mikulski of Maryland testified that a $100,000 early contribution from EMILY's list in her 1986 campaign was crucial to her election, as did Ann Richards, who received $100,000 through EMILY's list in her 1990 Texas gubernatorial campaign.

*Senator Barbara Milkulski, Democrat of Maryland and a beneficiary of EMILY's list, at a news conference.*

at least with high-level White House staff or cabinet officials. At the congressional level, major contributors usually expect to meet or speak directly with their representative or senator. Members of Congress boast of responding to letters, calls, or visits by any constituent, but contributors can expect more immediate and direct response than noncontributors can. Lobbyists for contributing organizations routinely expect and receive a hearing from members of Congress.

*Assistance*    Many individual large contributors do business with government agencies. They expect any representative or senator they have supported to intervene on their behalf with these agencies, sometimes acting to cut red tape, ensure fairness, and expedite their cases, and other times pressuring the agencies for a favorable decision. Officials in the White House or the cabinet may also be expected to intervene on behalf of major contributors. There is little question raised when the intervention merely expedites consideration of a contributor's case, but pressure to bend rules or regulations to get favorable decisions raises ethical problems for officeholders (see "Congressional Ethics" in Chapter 10).

# THE PRESIDENTIAL CAMPAIGN: THE PRIMARY RACE

The phrase *presidential fever* refers to the burning political ambition required to seek the presidency. The grueling presidential campaign is a test of strength, character, endurance, and determination. It is physically exhausting and mentally and emotionally draining. Every aspect of the candidates' lives—and the lives of their families—is subject to investigation and microscopic inspection by the news media. Most of this coverage is critical, and much of it is unfair. Yet candidates are expected to handle it all with grace and humor, from the earliest testing of the waters through a full-fledged campaign.

*Media Mentions*    Politicians with presidential ambitions may begin by promoting presidential *mentions* by media columnists and commentators. The media help to identify "presidential timber" years in advance of a presidential race simply by drawing up lists of potential candidates, commenting on their qualifications, and speculating about their intentions. Mentions are likely to come to prominent governors or senators who start making speeches outside of their state, who grab the media spotlight on a national issue, or who simply let it be known to the media "off the record" that they are considering a presidential race. Visiting New Hampshire and giving speeches there is viewed as "testing the waters" and a signal of presidential ambitions.

*Presidential Credentials*    Political experience as vice-president, governor, U.S. senator, or member of Congress not only inspires presidential ambition but also provides vital experience in political campaigning. However, virtually all presidential candidates testify that the presidential arena is far more challenging than politics at any other level. The experience of running for and holding high public office appears to be a political requirement for the presidency. Some recent presidential aspirants (Independent Ross Perot, Republican Steve Forbes, and Republican Patrick Buchanan) have tried to make a virtue of their lack of previous political office holding, no doubt hoping to attract support from the many Americans who disdain "politics as usual." But in the Twentiety Century no major party nominee for president has not previously held office as vice-president, governor, U.S. senator, or member of Congress except World War II hero General Dwight D. Eisenhower (see Table 8-2).

| | **TABLE 8-2** POLITICAL EXPERIENCE OF PRESIDENTIAL CANDIDATES, 1948–1996, AND MAJOR ELECTIVE OFFICE HELD PRIOR TO NOMINATION | |
|---|---|---|
| | *Republican Nominees* | *Democratic Nominees* |
| 1996 | Bob Dole<br>U.S. Senator, Kansas | Bill Clinton<br>President<br>Governor of Arkansas |
| 1992 | George Bush<br>President<br>Vice-president | Bill Clinton<br>Governor of Arkansas |
| 1988 | George Bush<br>Vice-president | Michael Dukakis<br>Governor of Massachusetts |
| 1984 | Ronald Reagan<br>President<br>Governor of California | Walter Mondale<br>Vice-president<br>U.S. senator, Minnesota |
| 1980 | Ronald Reagan<br>Governor of California | Jimmy Carter<br>President<br>Governor of Georgia |
| 1976 | Gerald Ford<br>President by succession<br>Vice-president<br>U.S. representative, Michigan | Jimmy Carter<br>Governor of Georgia |
| 1972 | Richard M. Nixon<br>President<br>Vice-president<br>U.S. senator, California | George McGovern<br>U.S. senator, South Dakota |
| 1968 | Richard M. Nixon<br>Vice-president<br>U.S. senator, California | Hubert H. Humphrey<br>Vice-president<br>U.S. senator, Minnesota |
| 1964 | Barry Goldwater<br>U.S. senator, Arizona | Lyndon B. Johnson<br>President by succession<br>Vice-president<br>U.S. senator, Texas |
| 1960 | Richard M. Nixon<br>Vice-president<br>U.S. senator, California | John F. Kennedy<br>U.S. senator, Massachusetts |
| 1956 | Dwight D. Eisenhower<br>President | Adlai E. Stevenson<br>Governor of Illinois |
| 1952 | Dwight D. Eisenhower<br>General of the Army<br>(no previous elected office) | Adlai E. Stevenson<br>Governor of Illinois |
| 1948 | Thomas E. Dewey<br>Governor of New York | Harry S. Truman<br>U.S. senator, Missouri |

*The Decision to Run*   The decision to run for president involves complex personal and political calculations. Ambition to occupy the world's most powerful office must be weighed against the staggering costs—emotional as well as financial—of a presidential campaign.

Serious planning, organizing, and fund raising must begin at least two years before the general election. A staff must be assembled—campaign managers and strategists, fund raisers, media experts, pollsters, issue advisers and speech writ-

CHAPTER 8 • CAMPAIGNS AND ELECTIONS: DECIDING WHO GOVERNS

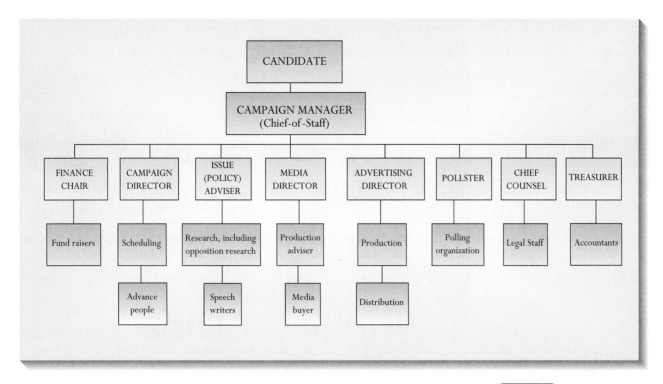

```
                    ┌──────────────────┐
                    │    CANDIDATE     │
                    └──────────────────┘
                             │
                ┌──────────────────────────┐
                │    CAMPAIGN MANAGER       │
                │    (Chief-of-Staff)       │
                └──────────────────────────┘
```

FINANCE CHAIR — Fund raisers

CAMPAIGN DIRECTOR — Scheduling — Advance people

ISSUE (POLICY) ADVISER — Research, including opposition research — Speech writers

MEDIA DIRECTOR — Production adviser — Media buyer

ADVERTISING DIRECTOR — Production — Distribution

POLLSTER — Polling organization

CHIEF COUNSEL — Legal Staff

TREASURER — Accountants

**FIGURE 8-4** **Typical Campaign Organization**

*Campaign organizations vary, but most assign someone to perform these tasks: funding, scheduling and appearances, speech writing, media production and buying, polling, advertising, legal compliance, and check writing, even if, in local campaigns, all these tasks must be performed by the candidate or his or her family members.*

ers, lawyers and accountants—and supporters must be identified in key states throughout the nation. Paid as well as volunteer workers must be assembled (see Figure 8-4). Leaders among important interest groups must be contacted. A general campaign strategy must be developed, an organization put in place, and several millions of dollars in campaign contributions pledged in advance of the race.

Often the decision to run hinges on whether initial pledges of campaign contributions appear adequate. At a minimum, a serious candidate must be able to raise $100,000 to receive matching funds from the FEC. More realistically, a serious candidate must be able to fund creditable campaigns in the early primary and caucus states, especially New Hampshire. Down the road, the serious candidate must be able to anticipate contributions of $20 million or more for primary elections.

*A Strategy for the Primaries*   The road to the White House consists of two separate races—the primary elections and caucuses leading to the Democratic and Republican party nominations, and the general election. Each of these races requires a separate strategy. The primary race requires an appeal to party activists and the more ideologically motivated primary voters in key states. The general election requires an appeal to the less partisan, less attentive, more ideologically moderate general election voters. Thus the campaign strategy developed to win the nomination must give way after the national conventions to a strategy to win the November general election.

*The New Hampshire Primary*   The primary season begins in the winter snows of New Hampshire, traditionally the first state to hold a presidential primary election. New Hampshire is far more important *strategically* to a presidential campaign than it is in delegate strength. As a small state, New Hampshire supplies

Republican presidential hopefuls join hands after a televised debate in New Hampshire in October, 1995. The strategic importance of the New Hampshire primary, the first of the primary season, far outweighs the state's electoral importance. From the left are Pennsylvania Senator Arlen Specter, Texas Senator Phil Gramm, Alan Keyes, former Tennessee Governor Lamar Alexander, Stephen Forbes, Kansas Senator Bob Dole, Pat Buchanan, California Representative Robert Dornan, Morrey Taylor, and Indiana Senator Richard Lugar.

fewer than 1 percent of the delegates at the Democratic and Republican conventions. But the New Hampshire primary looms very large in media coverage and hence in overall campaign strategy. While the popular Iowa party caucuses are held even earlier, New Hampshire is the nation's first primary, and the media begin speculating about its outcome and reporting early state poll results months in advance (see Table 8-3).

The "expectations" game is played with a vengeance. Media polls and commentators set the candidates' expected vote percentages, while the candidates and their spokespersons try to deflate these expectations. On election night, the candidates' **spin doctors** sally forth among the crowds of television and newspaper reporters to give a favorable interpretation to the outcome. The candidates themselves appear at campaign headquarters (and, they hope, on national television) to give the same favorable "spin" to the election results. But the media itself—par-

**Spin doctor:** A practitioner of the art of "spin control," or manipulation of media reporting to favor one's own candidate.

### TABLE 8-3 REPUBLICANS AT THE STARTING GATE

**Question:** *If asked to vote for a Republican nominee for president today [March 1995], for whom would you vote?*

| | | |
|---|---|---|
| Robert Dole | Senate majority leader | 43% |
| Phil Gramm | Senator from Texas | 16 |
| Pete Wilson | Governor of California | 4 |
| Lamar Alexander | Former governor of Tennessee | 4 |
| Pat Buchanan | Political commentator | 6 |
| Richard Lugar | Senator from Indiana | 3 |
| Arlen Specter | Senator from Pennsylvania | 2 |
| Robert Dornan | Member of Congress from California | 1 |
| Alan Keyes | Former State Department official | 1 |

*Source:Time/*CNN poll reported in *Time,* March 13, 1995, p. 69. © 1995 Time Inc. Reprinted by permission.

ticularly the television network anchors and reporters and commentators—interpret the results for the American people, determining the early favorites in the presidential "horse race."

New Hampshire provides the initial *momentum* for the presidential candidates. "Momentum" is more than just a media catchword. The Democratic and Republican winners in New Hampshire have demonstrated their voter appeal—their "electability." Favorable New Hampshire results inspire more financial contributions and thus the resources needed to carry the fight into the next group of primary elections. Unfavorable New Hampshire results tend to dry up contributions; weak candidates may be forced into an early withdrawal.

*The Front-End Strategy*   A **front-end strategy** places heavy emphasis on the results from New Hampshire and other early primary states. This strategy involves spending all or most of the candidate's available resources—time, energy, and money—on the early primary states, in the hopes that early victories will provide the momentum, in media attention and financial contributions, to continue the race. The front-end strategy became especially important in 1996, owing to the decisions of New York and California, with their lush harvests of convention delegates, to move up their primary elections to March dates. Traditionally the front-end strategy had been the choice of lesser-known candidates who lacked initial support from major interest groups and party financial "fat cats." As a small, rural state, New Hampshire encouraged "retail" politics—face-to-face, door-to-door, handshaking campaigning that is less expensive than media campaigning in large urban states like New York and California. But the "front-end loading" of the 1996 primary election schedule made it especially important for candidates to raise "early money." This obstacle appeared to discourage many potential GOP candidates by early 1995, including former Housing Secretary Jack Kemp, former Defense Secretary Richard Cheney, former Vice-President Dan Quayle, and former Education Secretary William Bennett, all "mentioned" for the GOP nomination.

*Super Tuesday Southern Strategy*   The primary road leads from New Hampshire to **Super Tuesday**—a cluster of primaries held in early March including Texas and Florida, the biggest prizes among the southern states. The decision of these states to hold early primaries on the same day was inspired by moderate Democrats in the 1980s who believed that their party's presidential losses in general elections were occurring because the nominees were too liberal. By holding presidential primaries in more moderate or conservative states early in the race, they hoped to give momentum to moderate candidates. (This strategy appeared to backfire in 1984 and 1988, when liberal Jesse Jackson won several southern state presidential primaries. But in 1992, the strategy worked well for Arkansas governor Bill Clinton by overcoming the effects of Paul Tsongas's win in New Hampshire.) However, in 1996 several states moved their primary elections ahead of the Super Tuesday states, including delegate-rich New York.

*Big-State Strategy*   Presidential aspirants who begin the race with widespread support among party activists, heavy financial backing, and strong endorsements from the major interest groups can focus their attention on the big-state primaries. A **big-state strategy** generally requires more money, more

**Front-end strategy:** A presidential political campaign strategy in which a candidate focuses on winning early primaries to build momentum.

**Super Tuesday:** A cluster of presidential primaries held in early March that includes important southern states.

**Big-state strategy:** A presidential political campaign strategy in which a candidate focuses on winning primaries in large states because of their high delegate counts.

# Understanding the Electoral College

The president of the United States is not elected by nationwide *popular* vote but rather by a majority of *electoral votes* of the states. The Constitution grants each state a number of electors equal to the number of its congressional representatives and senators combined (see map). Since representatives are apportioned to the states on the basis of population, the electoral vote of the states is subject to change after each ten-year census. No state has fewer than three electoral votes, since the Constitution guarantees every state two U.S. senators and at least one representative. The Twenty-third Amendment granted three electoral votes to the District of Columbia even though it has no voting members of Congress.

Voters in presidential elections are actually choosing a slate of presidential electors pledged to vote for their party's presidential and vice-presidential candidates. The names of electors seldom appear on the ballot, only the names of the candidates and their parties. The slate that wins a *plurality* of the popular vote in a state (more than any other slate, not necessarily a majority) casts *all* of the state's vote in the Electoral College. This "winner-take-all" system in the states is not mandated by the Constitution; a state legislature could allocate a state's electoral votes in proportion to the split in the popular vote. The winner-take-all system in the states helps ensure that the Electoral College produces a majority for one candidate. Indeed, winning candidates usually garner a heavy majority in the Electoral College, even when they win the nationwide popular vote by only a modest margin.

The Electoral College never meets at a single location; rather, electors meet at their respective state capitals to cast their ballots around December 15, following the general election on the first Tuesday after the first Monday of November. The results are sent to the presiding officer of the Senate, the vice-president, who in January presides over their count in the presence of both houses of Congress and formally announces the results. These procedures are usually considered a formality, but the U.S. Constitution does not *require* that electors cast their vote for the winning presidential candidate in their state, and occasionally "faithless electors" disrupt the process.

If no candidate wins a majority of electoral votes, the House of Representatives chooses the president from among the three candidates with the largest number of electoral votes, with each state casting *one* vote. The Constitution does not specify how House delegations should determine their vote, but by House rules, the state's vote goes to the candidate receiving a majority vote in the delegation.

Only two presidential elections have ever been decided formally by the House of Representatives. In 1800, Thomas Jefferson and Aaron Burr tied in the Electoral College because the Twelfth Amendment had not yet been adopted to separate presidential from vice-presidential voting; all the Democratic-Republican electors voted for both Jefferson and Burr, creating a tie. In 1824, Andrew Jackson won the popular vote and more electoral votes than anyone else but failed to get a majority. The House chose John Quincy Adams over Jackson, causing a popular uproar and ensuring Jackson's election in 1828.

In addition, in 1876, the Congress was called upon to decide which electoral results from the southern states to validate; a Republican Congress chose to validate enough electoral votes to allow Republican Rutherford B. Hayes to win, even though Democrat Samuel Tilden had won more popular votes. Hayes promised the Democratic southern states that in return for their acknowledgement of his presidential claim, he would end the military occupation of the South.

Finally, in 1888, the Electoral College vote failed to reflect the popular vote. Benjamin Harrison received 233 electoral votes to incumbent president Grover Cleveland's 168, even though Cleveland won about 90,000 more popular votes than Harrison. Harrison served a single lackluster term; Cleveland was elected for a second time in 1892, the only president to serve two nonconsecutive terms.

Constitutional proposals to reform the Electoral College have circulated for nearly 200 years, but none has won widespread support. These reform proposals have included: (1) election of the president by direct national popular vote; (2) allocation of each state's electoral vote in proportion to the popular vote each candidate received in the state; (3) allocation of electoral votes to winners of each congressional district and two to the statewide winners; (4) requirement that all electoral votes be cast for the state's winner, eliminating the possibility of faithless electors.

But most reform proposals create as many problems as they resolve. If the president is to be elected by direct nationwide popular vote, should a plurality vote be sufficient to win? Or should a national runoff be held in the event that no one receives a majority in the first election? Would proportional allocation of electoral votes encourage third-party candidates to enter the race in order to deny the leading candidate a majority?

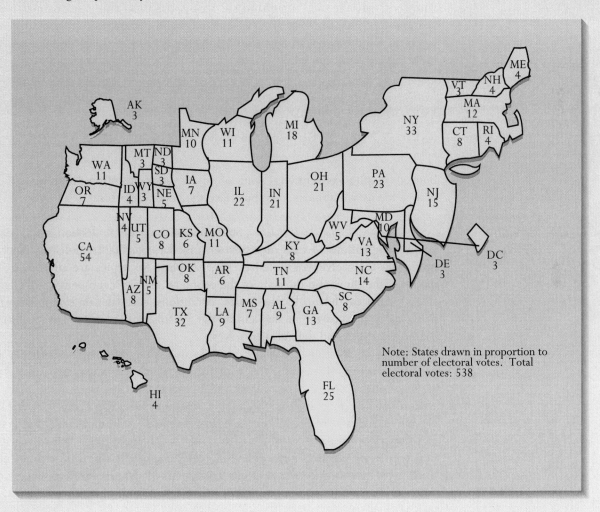

Note: States drawn in proportion to number of electoral votes. Total electoral votes: 538

*In this map, each state is drawn in a size relative to the number of Electoral College votes it represented after the 1990 census.*

*Source:* Holly Idelson, "Count Adds Seats in Eight States," *Congressional Quarterly* Weekly Report 48 (December 29, 1990), p. 4220.

The "uncrowned" presidential nominee usually submits his choice for vice-president in the runup to the party's national convention. Here Jack Kemp, Bob Dole's 1996 running mate, accepts the nomination of the Republican Party at their national convention in San Diego.

**Electoral College:** The 538 presidential electors apportioned among the states according to their congressional representation (plus 3 for the District of Columbia) whose votes officially elect the president and vice-president of the United States.

workers, and better organization than a front-end strategy. But the big states—California, New York, Pennsylvania, Ohio, and Michigan—have the most delegates. The results of these primaries may determine the Democratic and Republican nominees, assuming that most or all of them are won by the same candidates. During the late March and April primaries, weaker candidates usually announce their withdrawals. It is rare that more than two candidates in each party survive as credible candidates into May and June. By this stage of the race, many uncommitted delegates begin to commit themselves and their convention vote to the leader.

*Convention Showplace*   Once a presidential candidate has enough votes to assure nomination, this "uncrowned" winner must prepare for the party's convention. Organizing and orchestrating convention forces, dominating the platform and rules writing, enjoying the nominating speeches and the traditional roll call of the state delegations, mugging for the television camera when the nominating vote goes "over the top," submitting the vice-presidential nominee's name for convention approval, and preparing and delivering a rousing acceptance speech to begin the fall campaign are just a few of the many tasks awaiting the winner—and the winner's campaign team.

# THE PRESIDENTIAL CAMPAIGN: THE GENERAL ELECTION BATTLE

Buoyed by the conventions—and often by postconvention "bounces" in the polls—the new nominees must now face the general electorate.

*General-Election Strategies*   Strategies in the general election are as varied as the imaginations of campaign advisers, media consultants, pollsters, and the candidates themselves. As noted earlier, campaign strategies are affected by the nature of the times and the state of the economy; by the incumbent or challenger status of the candidate; by the issues, conditions, scandals, or events currently being spotlighted by the media; and by the dynamics of the campaign itself as the candidates attack and defend themselves.

Presidential election campaigns must focus on the **Electoral College.** The president is not elected by the national popular vote total but rather by a majority of the *electoral* votes of the states. Electoral votes are won by plurality, winner-take-all popular voting in each of the states (see *Up Close:* "Understanding the Electoral College"). Thus a narrow plurality win in a state delivers *all* of that state's electoral votes. Big-state victories, even by very narrow margins, can deliver big electoral prizes. The biggest prizes are California with 54 electoral votes, New York with 33, and Texas with 32. With a total 538 electoral votes at stake, *the winner must garner victories in states with a minimum of 270 electoral votes.*

*Targeting the Swing States*   In focusing on the most populous states, with their large electoral votes, candidates must decide which of these states are "winnable," then direct their time and energy and money to these *swing states*. Candidates cannot afford to spend too much effort in states that already seem to be solidly in their column, although they must avoid the perception that they are ignoring these strong bases of support. Neither can candidates waste much effort on states that already appear to be solidly in their opponent's column. So the swing states receive most of the candidates' time, attention, and television advertising money.

*Regional Alignments*    A glance at the Electoral College vote results in recent elections (see *Across the USA:* "How the States Voted") suggests that Republican candidates depend heavily on electoral votes from the South and the Mountain States. Florida and Texas are the keys to Republican presidential election strength. The Democratic presidential electoral base is found in the Northeast and upper Midwest. Even when Democratic candidates have lost in New York, Massachusetts, Pennsylvania, Illinois, Michigan, and Wisconsin, the vote margin in these states has been fairly close. California, with its prize of 54 electoral votes, is the most important swing state. California voters supported the Republican ticket in every election from 1968 to 1988; their swing to the Democratic ticket in 1992 and 1996 was a key component of Clinton's victories. Among the Republican "must win" states, Dole held on to Texas but lost Florida.

*The Presidential Debates*    The nationally televised presidential debates are the central feature of the general election campaign. These debates attract more viewers than any other campaign event. Moreover, they enable a candidate to reach undecided voters and the opponent's supporters, as well as the candidate's own partisans. Even people who usually pay little attention to politics may be drawn in by the drama of the confrontation (see *Up Close:* "The Presidential Debates").

The debates allow viewers an opportunity to see and hear candidates together and to compare their responses to questions as they stand side by side. The debates give audiences a better view of the candidates than they can get from thirty-second commercial ads or seven-second news sound bites. Viewers can at least judge how the candidates react under pressure.

However, the debates emphasize candidate "image" over substantive policy issues. Candidates must appear "presidential." They must appear confident, compassionate, concerned, and good humored. They must not appear uncertain or unsure of themselves, or aloof or out-of-touch with viewers, or easily upset by hostile questions. They must avoid verbal slips or gaffes or even unpolished or awkward gestures. They must remember that the debates are not really debates so much as joint press conferences in which the candidates respond to questions with rehearsed "mini-speeches" and practiced sound bites.[8]

Indeed, a great deal of predebate time is spent "prepping" the candidate. Mock debate sessions are held with "sparring partners" representing the opponent and the questioners. Winning sound bites and "zingers" are rehearsed for use at key moments in the debate. Spin doctors are prepared to collar the press after the debate to argue that their candidate won. Media interpretation of who won influences popular perceptions of who won. To date, no candidate who has been perceived as losing the debates has ever won the presidential election.

# How the States Voted

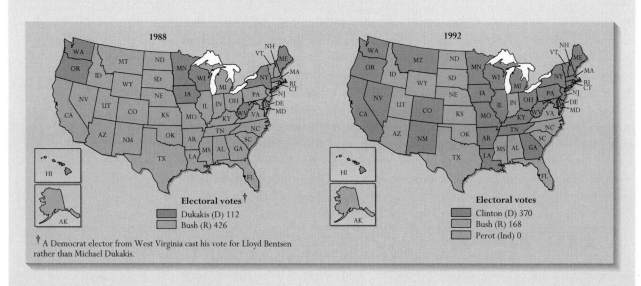

**1988**

**Electoral votes** †
- Dukakis (D) 112
- Bush (R) 426

† A Democrat elector from West Virginia cast his vote for Lloyd Bentsen rather than Michael Dukakis.

**1992**

**Electoral votes**
- Clinton (D) 370
- Bush (R) 168
- Perot (Ind) 0

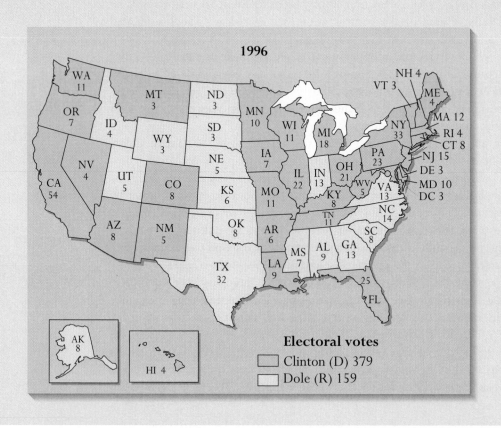

**1996**

**Electoral votes**
- Clinton (D) 379
- Dole (R) 159

# THE VOTER DECIDES

Understanding the reasons behind the voters' choice at the ballot box is a central concern of candidates, campaign strategists, commentators, and political scientists. Perhaps no other area of politics has been investigated so thoroughly as voting behavior. Survey data on voter choice have been collected for presidential elections for the past half century.[9] We know that voters cast ballots for and against candidates for a variety of reasons—party affiliation, group interests, characteristics and images of the candidates themselves, the economy, and policy issues. But forecasting election outcomes remains a risky business.

*Party Affiliation*   Although many people *claim* to vote for "the person, not the party," party identification remains a powerful influence in voter choice. Party ties among voters have weakened over time, with increasing proportions of voters labeling themselves as independents or only weak Democrats or Republicans, and more voters opting to split their tickets or cross party lines than did so a generation ago (see Chapter 7). Nevertheless, party identification remains one of the most important influences on voter choice. Party affiliation is more important in congressional than in presidential elections, but even in presidential elections the tendency to see the candidate of one's own party as "the best person" is very strong.

Consider the last four presidential elections (see Figure 8-5). Self-identified Republicans voted overwhelmingly for Reagan in 1984, for Bush in 1988, for Bush in 1992, and for Dole in 1996. Self-identified Democrats voted overwhelmingly for Mondale in 1984, Dukakis in 1988, and Clinton in 1992 and 1996.

Because Republican identifiers are outnumbered in the electorate by Democratic identifiers, Republican presidential candidates, and many Republican congressional candidates as well, *must* appeal to independent and Democratic crossover voters. The success of Republican presidential candidates for many years—Richard Nixon, Ronald Reagan, and George Bush in 1988—can be attributed largely to their success in winning the independent vote as well as a small yet significant vote from Democrats. But Perot won many independent voters in 1992, and Clinton won more independents than Bush did.
Update to come

*Group Voting*   We already know that various social and economic groups give disproportionate support to the Democratic and Republican parties (see Chapter 7). So it comes as no surprise that recent Democratic presidential candidates have received disproportionate support from African Americans, Catholics, Jews, less-educated and lower-income voters, and union workers; while Republican presidential candidates have fared better among whites, Protestants, and better-educated and higher-income voters (see Figure 8-6). That is, these groups have given a larger percentage of their vote to the Democratic or Republican candidates than the candidate received from the total electorate.

Among the more interesting group voting patterns is the serious *gender gap* affecting recent Republican candidates. While Reagan won the women's vote in both 1980 and 1984, his vote percentages among men were considerably higher than among women. Bush lost the women's vote in both 1988 and 1992. In 1996 the gender gap widened, with a stunning 54 percent of women voting for Clinton as opposed to 38 percent for Dole.[10] African Americans have long constituted the

# The Presidential Debates

Presidential debates attract more viewers than any other campaign activity. They produce vastly greater audiences than the candidates could garner by any other means. Most campaign activities—speeches, rallies, motorcades—reach only supporters. Such activities may inspire supporters to go to the polls, contribute money, and even work to get others to vote their way. But televised debates reach undecided voters as well as supporters, and they allow candidates to be seen by supporters of their opponent. Debates allow people to directly compare the responses of each candidate. Even if issues are not really discussed in depth, people see how presidential candidates react as human beings under pressure.

*Kennedy-Nixon* Televised presidential debates began in 1960 when John F. Kennedy and Richard M. Nixon confronted each other on a bare stage before an America watching on black-and-white TV sets. Nixon was the vice-president in the popular presidential administration of Dwight Eisenhower; he was also an accomplished college debate team member. He prepared for the debates as if they were college debates, memorizing facts and arguments. But he failed to realize that image triumphs over substance on television. Nixon was shifty-eyed and clearly in need of a shave or more makeup to hide his pronounced "five o'clock shadow." By contrast, Kennedy was handsome, cool, confident; whatever doubts the American people may have had regarding his youth and inexperience were dispelled by his polished manner. Radio listeners tended to think that Nixon won, and debate coaches scored him the winner. But television viewers preferred the glamorous young Kennedy. The polls shifted in Kennedy's direction after the debate, and he won in a very close general election. Nixon blamed his makeup man.

*Carter-Ford* President Lyndon Johnson avoided debating in 1964, and Nixon, having learned his lesson, declined to debate in 1968 and 1972. Thus televised presidential debates did not resume until 1976, when incumbent president Gerald Ford, perceiving that he was behind in the polls, agreed to debate challenger Jimmy Carter. Ford made a series of verbal slips—saying, for example, that the nations of Eastern Europe were free from Soviet domination. In that same year, the first vice-presidential debate was held. In it, Republican Robert Dole's biting comments appeared mean-spirited in contrast to Democrat Walter Mondale's "Boy Scout" image. Both Carter and Mondale were widely perceived as having "won" their debates, and they went on to victory in the general election.

*Reagan-Carter and Reagan-Mondale* It was Ronald Reagan who demonstrated the true power of television. Reagan had lived his life in front of a camera. It was the principal tool of both of his trades—actor and politician. In 1980, incumbent president Jimmy Carter attempted to portray Reagan as a mean-spirited conservative ideologue who was a threat to peace. Carter talked rapidly and seriously about programs, figures, and budgets. But Reagan was master of the stage; he was relaxed, confident, joking. He appeared to treat the president of the United States as an overly aggressive, impulsive younger man, regrettably given to exaggeration ("There you go again."). When it was all over, it was clear to most viewers that Carter had been bested by a true professional in media skills.

However, in the first of two televised debates with Walter Mondale in 1984, Reagan's skills of a lifetime seemed to desert him. He stumbled over statistics and groped for words. Mondale was respectful of the presidency, somewhat stiff and ill-at-ease before the cameras but nevertheless clearheaded in his responses. Reagan's poor performance raised the only issue that might conceivably defeat him—his age. The president had looked and sounded *old*.

In preparation for the second debate, Reagan decided, without telling his aides, to lay the perfect trap for his questioners. When asked about his age and capacity to lead the nation, he responded with a serious deadpan expression to a hushed audience and waiting America: "I want you to know that I will not make age an issue in this campaign. I am not going to exploit for political purposes [pause] my opponent's youth and inexperience." The studio audience broke into uncontrolled laughter. Even Mondale had to laugh. With a classic one-liner, the president buried the age issue and won not only the debate but the election.

**Bush-Dukakis**   In 1988, Michael Dukakis ensured his defeat with a cold, detached performance in the presidential debates, beginning with the very first question. When CNN anchor Bernard Shaw asked: "Governor, if Kitty Dukakis were raped and murdered, would you favor an irrevocable death penalty for the killer?" The question demanded an emotional reply. Instead, Dukakis responded with an impersonal recitation of his stock positions on crime, drugs, and law enforcement. Bush seized the opportunity to establish an intimate, warm, and personal relationship with the viewers: "I do believe some crimes are so heinous, so brutal, so outrageous . . . I do believe in the death penalty." Voters responded to Bush, electing him.

**Clinton-Bush-Perot**   The three-way presidential debates of 1992 drew the largest television audiences in the history of presidential debates. In the first debate, Ross Perot's Texas twang and down-home folksy style stole the show. Chided by his opponents for having no governmental experience, he shot back: "Well they have a point. I don't have any experience in running up a $4 trillion dollar debt. I don't have any experience in gridlock government. I don't have any experience in creating the worst public school system in the industrialized world, the most violent crime-ridden society in the industrialized world. But I do have a lot of experience in getting things done." Perot's popularity in the polls, hardly visible at all fol-

lowing his earlier abrupt withdrawal from the race, suddenly sprang to life again.

But it was Bill Clinton's smooth performance in the second debate, with its talk-show format, that seemed to wrap up the election. Ahead in the polls, Clinton appeared at ease walking about the stage and responding to audience questions with sympathy and sincerity. By contrast, George Bush appeared stiff and formal, and somewhat ill-at-ease with the "unpresidential" format. Bush made a modest comeback in the third and final debate with hard-hitting attacks on Clinton as a "waffler," but his modest recovery was too little and too late.

**Clinton-Dole**   A desperate Bob Dole, running 20 points behind, faced a newly "presidential" Bill Clinton in their two 1996 debates. (Perot's poor standing in the polls led to his exclusion.) Dole tried to counter his image as a grumpy old man in the first encounter; his humor actually won more laughs from the audience than the president's more stately comments. Dole injected more barbs in the second debate, complaining of "ethical problems in the White House" and repeating the mantra "I keep my word," suggesting that Clinton did not. But Clinton remained cool and comfortable, ignoring the challenger and focusing on the nation's economic health. Viewers, most of whom were already in Clinton's court, judged him the winner of both debates.

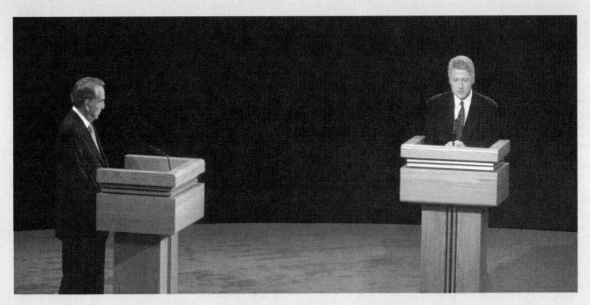

**FIGURE 8-5** Party, Ideology, and Nature of the Times in Presidential Voting

*Those who identify themselves as members of a major political party are highly likely to vote for the presidential candidates of their party. Likewise, those who identify themselves as liberals are more likely than average to vote for Democrats, while those who identify themselves as conservatives are more likely to vote for Republicans in presidential elections. In addition, voters who see the economic picture as better are more likely to vote for the incumbent, while those who are concerned about the nation's economy are more likely to vote against the incumbent.*

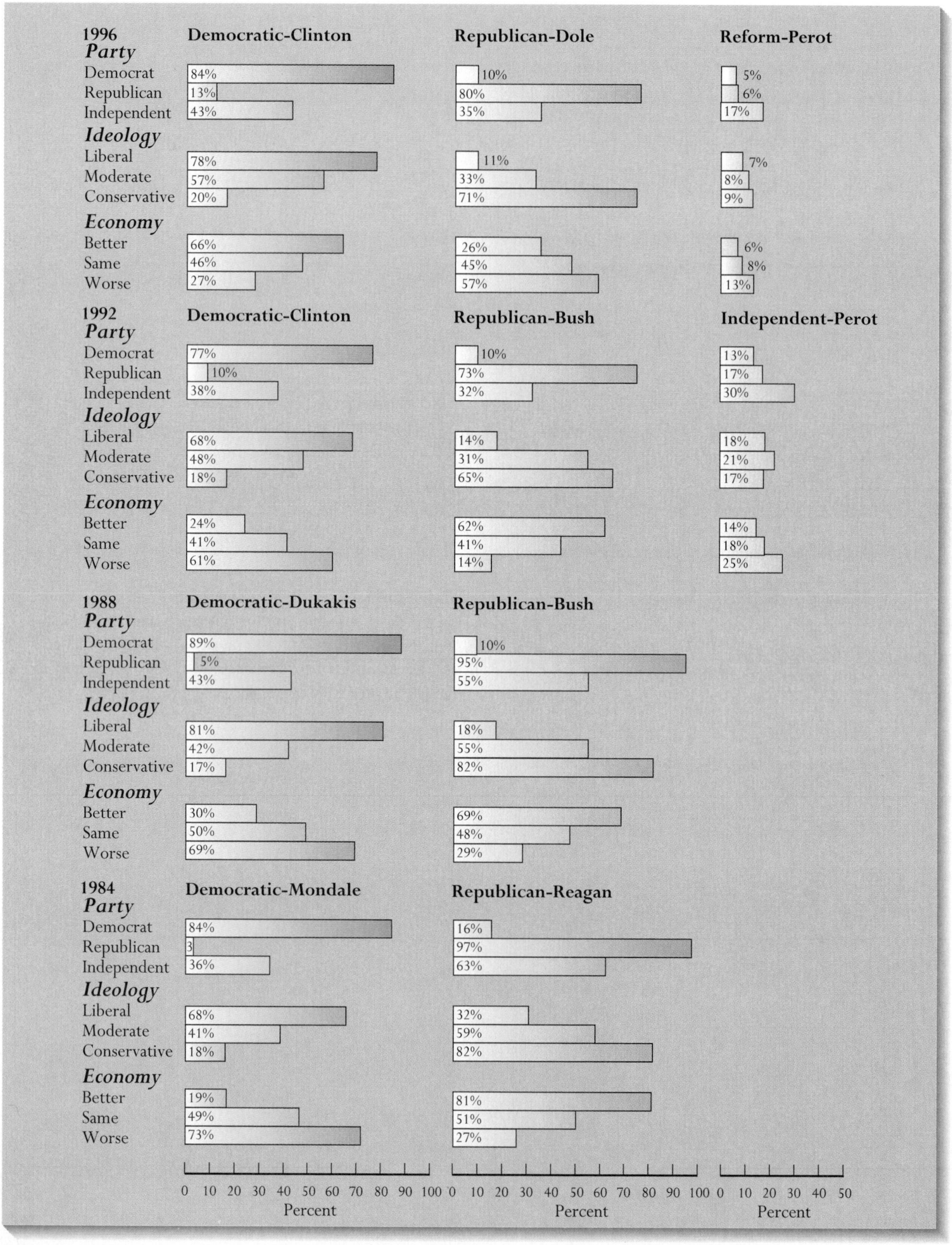

**1996**

| | Democratic-Clinton | Republican-Dole | Reform-Perot |
|---|---|---|---|
| **Party** | | | |
| Democrat | 84% | 10% | 5% |
| Republican | 13% | 80% | 6% |
| Independent | 43% | 35% | 17% |
| **Ideology** | | | |
| Liberal | 78% | 11% | 7% |
| Moderate | 57% | 33% | 8% |
| Conservative | 20% | 71% | 9% |
| **Economy** | | | |
| Better | 66% | 26% | 6% |
| Same | 46% | 45% | 8% |
| Worse | 27% | 57% | 13% |

**1992**

| | Democratic-Clinton | Republican-Bush | Independent-Perot |
|---|---|---|---|
| **Party** | | | |
| Democrat | 77% | 10% | 13% |
| Republican | 10% | 73% | 17% |
| Independent | 38% | 32% | 30% |
| **Ideology** | | | |
| Liberal | 68% | 14% | 18% |
| Moderate | 48% | 31% | 21% |
| Conservative | 18% | 65% | 17% |
| **Economy** | | | |
| Better | 24% | 62% | 14% |
| Same | 41% | 41% | 18% |
| Worse | 61% | 14% | 25% |

**1988**

| | Democratic-Dukakis | Republican-Bush |
|---|---|---|
| **Party** | | |
| Democrat | 89% | 10% |
| Republican | 5% | 95% |
| Independent | 43% | 55% |
| **Ideology** | | |
| Liberal | 81% | 18% |
| Moderate | 42% | 55% |
| Conservative | 17% | 82% |
| **Economy** | | |
| Better | 30% | 69% |
| Same | 50% | 48% |
| Worse | 69% | 29% |

**1984**

| | Democratic-Mondale | Republican-Reagan |
|---|---|---|
| **Party** | | |
| Democrat | 84% | 16% |
| Republican | 3 | 97% |
| Independent | 36% | 63% |
| **Ideology** | | |
| Liberal | 68% | 32% |
| Moderate | 41% | 59% |
| Conservative | 18% | 82% |
| **Economy** | | |
| Better | 19% | 81% |
| Same | 49% | 51% |
| Worse | 73% | 27% |

Percent scales: 0 10 20 30 40 50 60 70 80 90 100 (Democratic and Republican columns); 0 10 20 30 40 50 (Reform/Independent column)

*Source:* Based on Gallup poll surveys; data for 1996 from *New York Times*, November 6, 1996.

FIGURE 8-6 **Group Voting in Presidential Elections**

*Despite a great deal of attention in the popular press to a supposed gender gap in recent presidential elections, majorities of both women and men have given their support to the winning candidates. Likewise, voters in all age groups have basically followed the "majority-for-winner" formula. However, race, income, and education level do appear to influence voting patterns, with minorities, the poor, and those with little education voting heavily for Democratic candidates.*

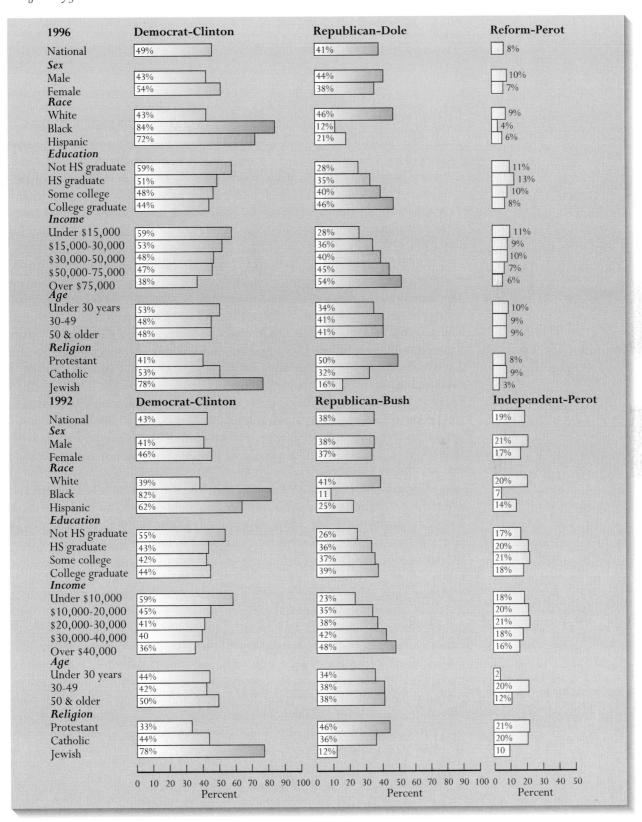

| 1996 | Democrat-Clinton | Republican-Dole | Reform-Perot |
|---|---|---|---|
| National | 49% | 41% | 8% |
| **Sex** | | | |
| Male | 43% | 44% | 10% |
| Female | 54% | 38% | 7% |
| **Race** | | | |
| White | 43% | 46% | 9% |
| Black | 84% | 12% | 4% |
| Hispanic | 72% | 21% | 6% |
| **Education** | | | |
| Not HS graduate | 59% | 28% | 11% |
| HS graduate | 51% | 35% | 13% |
| Some college | 48% | 40% | 10% |
| College graduate | 44% | 46% | 8% |
| **Income** | | | |
| Under $15,000 | 59% | 28% | 11% |
| $15,000-30,000 | 53% | 36% | 9% |
| $30,000-50,000 | 48% | 40% | 10% |
| $50,000-75,000 | 47% | 45% | 7% |
| Over $75,000 | 38% | 54% | 6% |
| **Age** | | | |
| Under 30 years | 53% | 34% | 10% |
| 30-49 | 48% | 41% | 9% |
| 50 & older | 48% | 41% | 9% |
| **Religion** | | | |
| Protestant | 41% | 50% | 8% |
| Catholic | 53% | 32% | 9% |
| Jewish | 78% | 16% | 3% |

| 1992 | Democrat-Clinton | Republican-Bush | Independent-Perot |
|---|---|---|---|
| National | 43% | 38% | 19% |
| **Sex** | | | |
| Male | 41% | 38% | 21% |
| Female | 46% | 37% | 17% |
| **Race** | | | |
| White | 39% | 41% | 20% |
| Black | 82% | 11 | 7 |
| Hispanic | 62% | 25% | 14% |
| **Education** | | | |
| Not HS graduate | 55% | 26% | 17% |
| HS graduate | 43% | 36% | 20% |
| Some college | 42% | 37% | 21% |
| College graduate | 44% | 39% | 18% |
| **Income** | | | |
| Under $10,000 | 59% | 23% | 18% |
| $10,000-20,000 | 45% | 35% | 20% |
| $20,000-30,000 | 41% | 38% | 21% |
| $30,000-40,000 | 40 | 42% | 18% |
| Over $40,000 | 36% | 48% | 16% |
| **Age** | | | |
| Under 30 years | 44% | 34% | 2 |
| 30-49 | 42% | 38% | 20% |
| 50 & older | 50% | 38% | 12% |
| **Religion** | | | |
| Protestant | 33% | 46% | 21% |
| Catholic | 44% | 36% | 20% |
| Jewish | 78% | 12% | 10 |

0 10 20 30 40 50 60 70 80 90 100  Percent
0 10 20 30 40 50 60 70 80 90 100  Percent
0 10 20 30 40 50  Percent

*Source:* Based on data from the Gallup poll surveys.

most loyal group of Democratic voters, regularly giving the Democratic presidential nominee 85 to 90 percent or more of their vote. The Hispanic vote is heavily Democratic, although a significant portion of Hispanics, notably Cuban Americans in Florida, are solidly Republican. Catholics are still more Democratic than Protestants, but Catholics favored Republican Ronald Reagan in 1980 and 1984. Catholics drifted back to the Democratic column in 1996.

*Candidate Image*  In an age of direct communication between candidates and voters via television, the image of candidates and their ability to relate to audiences have emerged as important determinants of voter choice. As party and group identifications have moderated and independent and middle-of-the-road identifications among voters have grown, the personal characteristics of candidates have become central to many voters. Indeed, the personal qualities of candidates are most important in the decision of less partisan, less ideological voters. Candidate image is most important in presidential contests, inasmuch as presidential candidates are personally more visible to the voter than candidates for lesser offices.[11]

It is difficult to identify exactly what personal qualities appeal most to voters. Warmth, compassion, strength, confidence, honesty, sincerity, good humor, appearance, and "character" all seem important. "Character" has become a central feature of media coverage of candidates (see Chapter 6). Reports of extramarital affairs, experimentation with drugs, draft dodging, cheating in college, shady financial dealings, conflicts of interest, or lying or misrepresenting facts receive heavy media coverage because they attract large audiences. But it is difficult to estimate how many voters are swayed by "character" issues.

Attractive personal qualities can win support from opposition party identifiers and people who disagree on the issues. John F. Kennedy's handsome and youthful appearance, charm, self-confidence, and disarming good humor defeated the heavy-jowled, shifty-eyed, defensive, and ill-humored Richard Nixon. Ronald Reagan's folksy mannerisms, warm humor, and comfortable rapport with television audiences justly earned him the title "the Great Communicator." Reagan disarmed his critics by laughing at his own personal flubs—falling asleep at meetings, forgetting names—and by telling his own age jokes. His personal appeal won more Democratic voters than any other Republican candidate has won in modern history, and he won the votes of many people who disagreed with him on the issues.

An important reservation regarding image voting: While many voters cite favorable or unfavorable personal characteristics of the candidates as the reason for their vote, it turns out that Democratic voters usually perceive favorable attributes in Democratic candidates and unfavorable attributes in Republican candidates, while Republican voters see just the opposite. In other words, the voters' perceptions of the candidates' personal qualities are influenced by the voters' party identifications and perhaps by their group affiliations as well. Thus evaluations of the candidates' personal characteristics may not be a significant independent determinant of voter choice, especially for people who identify themselves as strong Democrats or Republicans.

## TABLE 8-4 Economic Conditions and the Vote for Incumbent Party Presidential Candidates, 1932–1996

| | Change in Disposable Personal Income (percentage) | Incumbent Party's Nominee | Vote for Incumbent Party Presidential Candidate (percentage of popular vote) | Outcome |
|---|---|---|---|---|
| 1996 | +2.5 | Clinton | 49.0 | Win |
| 1992 | +1.9 | Bush | 37.7 | Loss |
| 1988 | +3.8 | Bush | 53.4 | Win |
| 1984 | +4.9 | Reagan | 58.8 | Win |
| 1980 | −1.1 | Carter | 41.0 | Loss |
| 1976 | +2.6 | Ford* | 48.0 | Loss |
| 1972 | +2.9 | Nixon | 60.7 | Win |
| 1968 | +2.9 | Humphrey* | 42.7 | Loss |
| 1964 | +5.5 | Johnson | 61.1 | Win |
| 1960 | +1.5 | Nixon | 49.7 | Loss |
| 1956 | +2.9 | Eisenhower | 57.4 | Win |
| 1952 | +1.3 | Stevenson | 44.4 | Loss |
| 1948 | +3.7 | Truman | 49.6 | Win |
| 1944 | +2.6 | Roosevelt | 53.4 | Win |
| 1940 | +5.4 | Roosevelt | 54.7 | Win |
| 1936 | +11.3 | Roosevelt | 60.1 | Win |
| 1932 | −13.9 | Hoover | 39.6 | Loss |

*Losses despite growth in excess of 2%.

*The Economy* Fairly accurate predictions of voting outcomes in presidential elections can be made from models of the American economy. Economic conditions at election time—recent growth or decline in personal income, the unemployment rate, consumer confidence, and so on—are related to the vote given the incumbent versus the challenger. Ever since the once-popular Republican incumbent Herbert Hoover was trounced by Franklin Roosevelt as the Great Depression of the 1930s deepened, politicians have understood that voters hold the incumbent party responsible for hard economic times.

Perhaps no other lesson has been as well learned by politicians; hard economic times hurt incumbents and favor challengers. Considering change in disposable personal income (income less taxes) shows an interesting pattern in presidential elections. A brief look at presidential election results since 1932 (see Table 8-4) suggests the following axioms:

- The better the economy during an election year, the greater the popular vote percentage for the incumbent party's presidential candidate.
- If personal income growth is less than 2 percent during an election year, the incumbent party's presidential candidate loses.
- However, a growth rate in excess of 2 percent does not ensure an incumbent party victory, as Republican Gerald Ford and Democrat Hubert Humphrey learned.

Thus, the economy may not be the only important factor in presidential voting, but it is certainly a factor of great importance.

There is some evidence that it is *not* voters' *own* personal economic well-being that affects their vote but rather voter perception of *general* economic conditions. People who perceive the economy as getting worse are likely to vote against the incumbent party, while people who think the economy is getting better support the incumbent.[12] Thus, voters who thought the economy was getting *worse* in 1992 supported challenger Bill Clinton over incumbent president George Bush. And more than twice as many people thought the economy was getting worse in that year than getting better. But the reverse was true in 1996; more people thought the economy was *better,* and the people who thought so voted heavily for incumbent Bill Clinton.

*Issue Voting*   Casting one's vote exclusively on the basis of the policy positions of the candidates is rare. Most voters are unaware of the specific positions taken by the candidates on the issues. Indeed, voters often believe that their preferred candidate agrees with them on the issues, even when this is not the case. In other words, voters project their own policy views onto their favorite candidate more often than they decide to vote for a candidate because of his or her position on the issues.

However, when asked specifically about issues, voters are willing to name those they care most about. Voters do not always make their choices based on a candidate's stated policy positions, but voters *do* strongly favor candidates whose policy views they assume match their own. Only when a key issue takes center stage do voters really become aware of what the candidates actually propose to do. In both the 1992 and 1996 elections, the economy was the issue that voters cared about most. In both elections, Clinton won the votes of the people most concerned about the economy (see Table 8-5). Clinton also won the strong support of people (especially senior citizens) concerned with Medicare and Social Security, as well as people concerned about education. Taxes, the deficit, and foreign policy were Bob Dole's best issues.

**TABLE 8-5   ISSUES THE VOTERS CARED ABOUT IN 1996**

*Vote of Those Who Listed Issue as Most Important*

| Rank | Issue | Clinton | Dole | Perot |
|------|-------|---------|------|-------|
| 1 | Economy/jobs | 60% | 28% | 10% |
| 2 | Medicare/Social Security | 69 | 24 | 6 |
| 3 | Taxes | 18 | 75 | 6 |
| 4 | Deficit | 29 | 53 | 17 |
| 5 | Education | 79 | 16 | 3 |
| 6 | Foreign policy | 30 | 60 | 9 |

CHAPTER 8 • CAMPAIGNS AND ELECTIONS: DECIDING WHO GOVERNS

# Tracking the Campaign

Voter swings in loyalty during presidential campaigns suggest that the outcome of elections is by no means certain at the outset (see graphs). Tracking polls during the 1992 campaign showed large swings in opinion in midsummer—the time of the Democratic and Republican nominating conventions. In contrast, tracking polls in 1996 showed uncommon stability in Clinton's large lead over Dole throughout the campaign.

At the start of his 1992 reelection bid, George Bush enjoyed a comfortable lead in the polls. But in late spring, the independent candidacy of Ross Perot eroded Bush's support. Bill Clinton was mired in third place. The Bush campaign launched a strong attack on Perot, calling him temperamentally unfit to be president and encouraging the press to delve into his financial dealings and penchant for investigating

his opponents. Perot's support began to drop in the polls, and he abruptly announced his withdrawal from the race on July 16—the start of the Democratic convention. Perot supporters were set adrift at precisely the moment that Bill Clinton was benefiting from favorable television coverage of the Democratic convention. Clinton soared ahead in the polls. The race narrowed somewhat in the fall, but Clinton never lost his lead.

In contrast to the volatile 1992 campaign, the presidential campaign of 1996 was so stable that voters appeared to lose interest. Clinton maintained a comfortable lead all year, dipping only slightly during the GOP convention in August and peaking during the September bombing of Iraq. Perot never mounted a serious threat. Clinton's margin of victory, however, was somewhat narrower than the tracking polls had forecast.

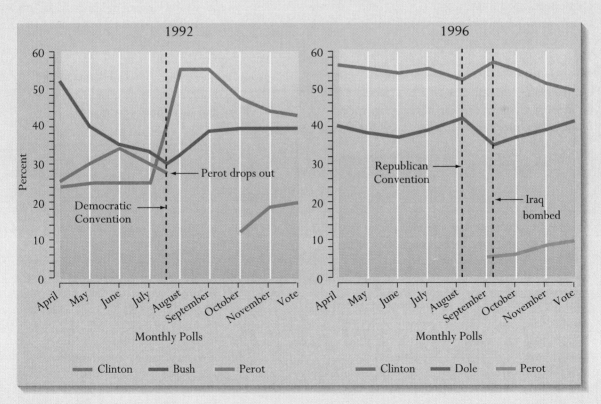

**The "Horse Race": Tracking the Presidential Campaigns in the Polls**

# SUMMARY NOTES

In a democracy, elections decide "who governs." But they also indirectly affect public policy, influencing "who gets what."

- Although winning candidates often claim a mandate for their policy proposals, in reality few campaigns present clear policy alternatives to the voters, few voters cast their ballots on the basis of policy considerations, and the policy preferences of the electorate can seldom be determined from election outcomes.
- Nevertheless, voters can influence future policy directions through retrospective judgments about the performance of incumbents, returning them to office or turning them out. Most retrospective voting appears to center on the economy.
- Personal ambition for power and celebrity drives the decision to seek public office. Political entrepreneurship, professionalism, and careerism have come to dominate political recruitment; lawyers have traditionally dominated American politics.
- Incumbents begin campaigns with many advantages: name recognition, financial support, good will from services they perform for constituents, large-scale public projects they bring to their districts, and the other resources of office.
- Campaigning for office is largely a media activity, dominated by professional advertising specialists, fund raisers, media consultants, and pollsters.

- The professionalization of campaigning and the heavy costs of a media campaign drive up the costs of running for office. These huge costs make candidates heavily dependent on financial support from individuals and organizations. Fund raising occupies more of a candidate's time than any other campaign activity.
- Campaign contributions are made by politically active individuals and organizations, including political action committees. Many contributions are made in order to gain access to policy makers and assistance with government business. Some contributors are ideologically motivated; others merely seek to rub shoulders with powerful people.
- Presidential primary election strategies emphasize appeals to party activists and core supporters, including the more ideologically motivated primary voters.
- In the general election campaign, presidential candidates usually seek to broaden their appeal to moderate, centrist voters while holding onto their core supporters. Campaigns must focus on states where the candidate has the best chance of gaining the 270 electoral votes needed to win.
- Voter choice is influenced by party identification, group membership, perceived image of the candidates, economic conditions, and, to a lesser extent, ideology and issue preferences.

# SELECTED READINGS

CONWAY, M. MARGARET. *Political Participation in the United States,* 2d ed. Washington, D.C.: Congressional Quarterly Press, 1991. Standard text on political participation in American politics, incorporating the research literature on who participates, how, and with what effect.

FIORINA, MORRIS P. *Retrospective Voting in American National Elections.* Princeton, N.J.: Princeton University Press, 1988. Argues that retrospective judgments guide voter choice in presidential elections.

FLANAGAN, WILLIAM H., and NANCY H. ZINGALE. *Political Behavior of the American Electorate,* 8th ed. Washington, D.C.: Congressional Quarterly Press, 1994. A brief but comprehensive summary of the extensive research literature on the effects of party identification, opinion, ideology,

the media, and candidate image on voter choice and election outcomes.

IYENGAR, SHANTO, and STEPHEN ANSOLABEHERE. *Going Negative: How Political Advertisements Shrink and Polarize the Electorate.* New York: Free Press, 1996. The real problem with negative political ads is not that they sway voters to support one candidate over another, but that they reinforce the belief that all are dishonest and cynical.

MATALIN, MARY, and JAMES CARVILLE. *All's Fair: Love, War and Running for President.* New York: Random House and Simon & Schuster, 1994. Inside the presidential campaign of George Bush and Bill Clinton in 1992 by their respective campaign directors, who were romantically involved and married after the campaign.

POMPER, GERALD M. *The Election of 1992.* Chatham, N.J.: Chatham Publishing Co., 1993. Thorough analysis of the primary and general election campaigns in both parties, the general election campaign, and popular and electoral vote outcomes. Previous editions cover the elections of 1976, 1980, 1984, and 1988.

ROSENSTONE, STEVEN. *Forecasting Presidential Elections.* New Haven, Conn.: Yale University Press, 1985. A discussion of the models employed to forecast presidential election outcomes based on unemployment, inflation, and personal income statistics.

SORAUF, FRANK J. *Inside Campaign Finance.* New Haven, Conn.: Yale University Press, 1992. A comprehensive description of campaign financing in America, individual contributions, PACs, party funds, independent organizations, soft money, middlemen and brokers, and so on,

# INTEREST GROUPS
## GETTING THEIR SHARE AND MORE

## CHAPTER OUTLINE

Interest-Group Power
Origins of Interest Groups
The Organized Interests in Washington
Leaders and Followers
Washington Representatives: Lobbyists for Hire
The Fine Art of Lobbying
PAC Power
Lobbying the Bureaucracy
Lobbying the Courts
Politics as Interest-Group Conflict

## FEATURES

*Up Close:* Superlobby: The Business Roundtable
*People in Politics:* Marion Wright Edelman, Lobbying for the Poor
*Up Close:* How Harry and Louise Killed Hillary's Health Plan
*Up Close:* The Christian Coalition: Organizing the Faithful
*People in Politics:* Ralph Nader, People's Lobbyist
*Up Close:* NRA: Top Gun in Washington
*Up Close:* AARP: The Nation's Most Powerful Interest Group
*What Do You Think?* Is It What You Know or Who You Know?

## INTEREST-GROUP POWER

Organization is a means to power—to determining who gets what in society. Interest groups are organizations that seek to influence government policy. Organization concentrates power, and concentrated power prevails over unorganized interests.

The First Amendment to the Constitution recognizes "the right of the people peaceably to assemble, and to petition the government for a redress of grievances." Americans thus enjoy a fundamental right to organize themselves to influence government.

## ASK YOURSELF ABOUT POLITICS

❶ Do special interest groups in America obstruct the majority of citizens' wishes on public policy?
Yes ⬭ No ⬭

❷ Should people join an interest group such as the American Association of Retired Persons for its discounts, magazines, and travel guides even if they disagree with its policy goals?
Yes ⬭ No ⬭

❸ Should state and local governments use taxpayers' money to lobby Congress to get federal funds?
Yes ⬭ No ⬭

❹ Should former government officials be allowed to lobby their former colleagues?
Yes ⬭ No ⬭

❺ Should religious groups organize themselves to influence public policy?
Yes ⬭ No ⬭

❻ Should interest groups be prohibited from making large campaign contributions in their effort to influence public policy?
Yes ⬭ No ⬭

❼ If a lobbyist makes a campaign contribution to a Congress member, hoping to gain support for a bill, is this a form of bribery?
Yes ⬭ No ⬭

❽ Is organized interest-group activity a significant cause of government gridlock?
Yes ⬭ No ⬭

What role do interest groups play in politics? Their organization, their money, and their influence in Washington raise the possibility that interest groups, rather than individuals, may in fact hold the real power in politics. They may be the "who" that determines the "what" that the rest of us get.

*Electoral versus Interest-Group Systems*    The *electoral system* is organized to represent geographically defined constituencies—states and congressional districts in Congress. The *interest-group system* is organized to represent economic, professional, ideological, religious, racial, gender, and issue constituencies.[1] In other words, the interest group system supplements the electoral system by providing people with another avenue of participation. Individuals may participate in politics by supporting candidates and parties in elections, and also by joining **interest groups**—organizations that pressure government to advance their interests.

Interest-group activity provides more direct representation of policy preferences than electoral politics. At best, individual voters can influence government policy only indirectly through elections (see Chapter 8). Elected politicians try to represent many different—and even occasionally conflicting—interests. But interest groups provide concentrated and direct representation of policy views in government.

*Checking Majoritarianism*    The interest-group system gives voice to special interests, while parties and the electoral system cater to the majority interest. Indeed, interest groups are often defended as a check on **majoritarianism**—the tendency of democratic governments to allow the faint preferences of a majority to prevail over the intense feelings of minorities. However, the interest group system is frequently attacked because it obstructs the majority from implementing its preferences in public policy. Interest group power was once described and defended by a California state senator:

> About 90 percent of all legislation is conceived by special interests. It is merchandised by special interests. And probably less than 5 percent is inspired by governors, by individual legislators, by government itself. You say "Oh, isn't that evil!" The answer is, hell no, it isn't evil. That's what democracy is all about.[2]

*Concentrating Benefits While Dispersing Costs*    Interest groups seek special benefits, subsidies, privileges, and protections from the government. The costs of these *concentrated* benefits are usually *dispersed* to all taxpayers, none of whom individually bears enough added cost to merit spending time, energy, or money to organize a group to oppose the benefit. Thus the interest-group system concentrates benefits to the few and disperses costs to the many. The system favors small, well-organized, homogeneous interests that seek the expansion of government activity at the expense of larger but less well organized citizen-taxpayers. Over long periods of time, the cumulative activities of many special interest groups, each seeking concentrated benefits to themselves and dispersed costs to others, result in what has been termed **organizational sclerosis**—a society so encrusted with subsidies, benefits, regulations, protections, and special treatments for organized groups that work, productivity, and investment are discouraged and everyone's standard of living is lowered.

# ORIGINS OF INTEREST GROUPS

James Madison viewed interest groups—which he called "factions"—as a necessary evil in politics. He defined a faction as "a number of citizens, whether amounting to a majority or a minority of the whole, who are united and actuated

**Interest groups:** Organizations that seek to influence government policy.

**Majoritarianism:** The tendency of democratic governments to allow the faint preferences of the majority to prevail over the intense feelings of minorities.

**Organizational sclerosis:** Society encrusted with so many special benefits to interest groups that everyone's standard of living is lowered.

by some common impulse of passion, or of interest, adverse to the rights of other citizens, or to the permanent and aggregate interests of the community." He believed that interest groups not only conflict with each other but, more important, also conflict with the common good. Nevertheless, Madison believed that the origin of interest groups was to be found in human nature—"a zeal for different opinions concerning religion, concerning government, and many other points"—and therefore impossible to eliminate from politics.[3]

*Protecting Economic Interests*    Madison believed that "the most common and durable source of factions, has been the various and unequal distribution of property." With genuine insight, he identified *economic interests* as the most prevalent in politics: "a landed interest, a manufacturing interest, a mercantile interest, a moneyed interest, with many lesser interests."[4] From Madison's era to the present, businesspeople and professionals, bankers and insurers, farmers and factory workers, merchants and shippers have organized themselves to press their demands upon government (see *Up Close:* "Superlobby: The Business Roundtable").

*Advancing Social Movements*    Major social movements in American history have spawned many interest groups. Abolitionist groups were formed before the Civil War to fight slavery. The National Association for the Advancement of Colored People (NAACP) emerged in 1910 to fight segregation laws and to rally public support against lynching and other violence against African Americans. Farm organizations emerged from the populist movement of the late nineteenth century to press demands for railroad rate regulation and easier credit terms. The small trade unions that workers formed in the nineteenth century to improve their pay and working conditions gave way to large national unions in the 1930s as workers sought protection for the rights to organize, bargain collectively, and strike. The success of the women's suffrage movement led to the formation of the League of Women Voters in the early twentieth century, and a generation later the feminist movement inspired the National Organization for Women (NOW).

*Seeking Government Benefits*    As government expands its activities, it creates more interest groups. Wars create veterans' organizations. The first large veterans' group—the Grand Army of the Republic—formed after the Civil War and successfully lobbied for bonus payments to veterans over the years. Today the American Legion, the Veterans of Foreign Wars, and the Vietnam Veterans of America engage in lobbying the Congress and monitor the activities of the Department of Veterans Affairs. As the welfare state grew, so did organizations seeking to obtain benefits for their members, including the nation's largest interest group, the American Association of Retired Persons (AARP). Over time, organizations seeking to protect and expand welfare benefits for the poor also emerged (see *People in Politics:* "Marian Wright Edelman, Lobbying for the Poor"). Federal grant-in-aid programs to state and local governments inspired the development of governmental interest groups—the Council of State Governments, the National League of Cities, the National Governors Association, the U.S. Conference of Mayors, and so on—so that it is not uncommon today to see governments lobby other governments. Expanded government support for education led to political activity by the National Education Association, the American Federation

# Superlobby: The Business Roundtable

The Business Roundtable was established in 1972 "in the belief that business executives should take an increased role in the continuing debates about public policy." The organization is composed of the chief executives of the 200 largest corporations in America and is financed through corporate membership fees. For many years, the U.S. Chamber of Commerce, the National Association of Manufacturers, the Business Council, and hundreds of industry associations such as the powerful American Petroleum Institute had represented business in traditional interest-group fashion. Why did business create this superorganization? The Business Roundtable itself says:

> The answer is that business leaders believed there was a need that was not being filled, and they invented the Roundtable to fill it. They wanted an organization in which the chief executive officers of leading enterprises take positions and advocate those positions. . . . The Roundtable therefore was formed with two major goals:
>
> 1. to enable chief executives from different corporations to work together to analyze specific issues affecting the economy and business; and
>
> 2. to present government and the public with knowledgeable, timely information, and with practical, positive suggestions for action.*

In brief, traditional interest-group representation was inadequate for the nation's top corporate leadership. It wished to come together *itself* to decide upon public policy and press its views in Washington.

The power of the Business Roundtable stems in part from its "firm rule" that a corporate chief executive officer (CEO) cannot send a substitute to its meetings. Moreover, corporate CEOs lobby the Congress in person rather than sending paid lobbyists. Members of Congress are impressed when the chair of IBM appears at a congressional hearing on business regulation or when the chair of GTE speaks to a congressional committee about taxation, or when the chair of Prudential talks to Congress about Social Security, or when the head of B. F. Goodrich testifies before the Senate Judiciary Committee about antitrust policy. One congressional staff member explained: "If a corporation sends its Washington representative to our office, he's probably going to be shunted over to a legislative assistant. But the chairman of the board is going to get in to see the senator." Another aide echoed those sentiments: "Very few members of Congress would not meet with the president of a Business Roundtable corporation."**

The work of the Business Roundtable is organized by means of fifteen task forces on various issues of priority to its members. For example, there are task forces on antitrust policy, energy, the environment, inflation, government regulation, health, Social Security, taxation, and welfare. Roundtable task forces send their recommendations to a forty-five-member policy committee for formal approval before the initiation of a lobbying campaign. Thus Roundtable executives are speaking for an apparently unified business community, as opposed to what might appear to be the narrower interests of a single industry.

The Business Roundtable has experienced both victories and defeats in Congress. During the Ford and Carter administrations, the Roundtable successfully opposed the creation of a new federal consumer protection agency comparable to the Environmental Protection Agency. During the Reagan years, the Roundtable was at the forefront of "deregulation" and tax cutting. But the Roundtable lost a lengthy battle over mandated family leaves in 1993 when the Congress sent the Family Leave Act to President Bill Clinton to sign as his first major legislative victory. The Roundtable also was defeated in its opposition to the expansion of the Clean Air Act of 1990, which it believes imposes excessive compliance costs on industry and handicaps American corporations in global competition. So even with all of its prestige and resources, the Business Roundtable does not win all of its battles.

*Quotations about the reasons for the establishment of the Business Roundtable from Business Roundtable public statement, "What the Roundtable Is," January 1988.
**\*Time* April 13, 1981, pp. 76–77.

*(a)*

*(b)*

*(c)*

*(d)*

*(e)*

*(f)*

From (a) the Whiskey Rebellion of 1794 to (b) violent early union protests like the Haymarket Riot of 1886 to (c) Carrie Nation's battle to ban liquor and (d) the women's suffrage movement of the late nineteenth and early twentieth centuries to (e) the civil rights marches of the 1960s and (f) the gay rights marches of the 1990s, protest has had a long and strong history for interest groups in the United States. While some protests have been violent and others peaceful, by addressing key issues of the time, all have prompted public debate and many have resulted in changes in public policy.

## Marian Wright Edelman, Lobbying for the Poor

As founder and president of the Children's Defense Fund, Marian Wright Edelman has become legendary in Washington as a persuasive and persistent lobbyist on behalf of civil rights and social welfare legislation. A close friend of the Kennedy family, Edelman regularly testifies at Senate committee hearings, providing rapid-fire statistics on the effects of poverty on African-American children. Each year the Children's Defense Fund, with a staff of more than 100 in its Washington headquarters and an $8 million annual budget, produces numerous reports on infant mortality, homelessness, prenatal care, child nutrition, drug use, child abuse, teenage pregnancy, and single-parent households.

Marian Wright grew up in segregated rural South Carolina, the academically gifted daughter of a Baptist minister with a strong commitment to social justice. At an early age, she worked at the Wright House for the Aged, which her father had established. She entered all-black Spelman College in Atlanta and studied abroad at the Sorbonne in Paris and the University of Geneva, intending to take up a career in the foreign service. But Wright changed her career plans when she became involved in the early civil rights struggles in Atlanta. After graduating from Spelman, she entered Yale Law School to prepare herself in civil rights law. Upon her graduation in 1963, she immediately went to work for the National Association for the Advancement of Colored People Legal Defense Fund and traveled to Mississippi, where for four years she undertook the

dangerous work of defending civil rights workers. In 1967 she met Peter Edelman, a Harvard Law School graduate and legislative aide to Senator Robert Kennedy; together they persuaded Kennedy to personally tour the most poverty-stricken areas of the Mississippi Delta, where the senator directly confronted hungry children living in miserable conditions.

The following year Wright and Edelman were married and settled in Washington, where she established the Washington Research Project, a public interest research and lobbying organization on behalf of President Lyndon Johnson's War on Poverty. She maintained her Washington base even while directing the Harvard University Center for Law and Education during the several years that her husband served as vice-president of the University of Massachusetts. In 1973, she organized the Children's Defense Fund in Washington with the support of private foundation grants and government grants and contracts. Part think tank and part lobbying organization, the Children's Defense Fund describes itself as an advocate for millions of "voiceless and voteless," neglected and abused, poor children. It was the principal lobbying group behind the Head Start program as well as federal child care and family leave legislation.

Marian Wright Edelman is especially effective as an advocate of social welfare programs with her lively style, sense of urgency, and wealth of information about children in poverty. "The real joy comes from achieving results, when you really see you've got a law that will protect children from being abused, that will provide them with proper health care and dental care. My greatest reward will be seeing thirteen million poor children lifted out of poverty."*

*New York Times, February 27, 1986, p. A10.

of Teachers, the American Association of Land Grant Colleges and Universities, and other educational groups.

*Responding to Government Regulation*   As more businesses and professions came under government regulation in the twentieth century, more organizations formed to protect their interests, including such large and powerful groups as the American Medical Association (doctors), the American Bar Association (lawyers), and the National Association of Broadcasters (broadcasters). Indeed, the issue of regulation—whether of public utilities, interstate transportation, mine safety, medicines, or children's pajamas—always causes the formation of interest groups. Some form to demand regulation, while others form to protect their members from regulatory burdens.

# THE ORGANIZED INTERESTS
# IN WASHINGTON

The Washington telephone directory lists hundreds of organizations with their own offices in the capital and hundreds of additional firms of paid lawyers and lobbyists. Trade and professional associations and corporations have the most lobbies in Washington, D.C., but unions, public interest groups, farm groups, and organized interests representing such groups as minorities, women, and the elderly also recognize that they need to be "where the action is." There are more than 22,000 national nonprofit organizations in the United States, several thousand of which are officially registered in Washington as lobbyists.[5] Among this huge assortment of organizations, many of which are very influential in their highly specialized fields, are a number of very well known interest groups. Even a partial list of organized interest groups provides some idea of both the depth and the breadth of such associations in U.S. political life and of the complexities facing modern legislators in trying to please such vastly different groups (see Table 9-1).

*Business and Trade Organizations*   Traditionally, economic organizations have dominated interest-group politics in Washington. There is ample evidence that economic interests continue to play a major role in national policy making, despite the rapid growth over the last several decades of consumer and environmental organizations. Certainly in terms of the sheer number of organizations with offices and representatives in Washington, business and professional groups and occupational and trade associations predominate. More than half of the organizations with offices in Washington are business or trade associations, and another 15 percent are professional associations.

Business interests are represented, first of all, by large inclusive organizations, such as the U.S. Chamber of Commerce, representing thousands of local chambers of commerce across the nation; the National Association of Manufacturers; the Business Roundtable, representing the nation's largest corporations; and the National Federation of Independent Businesses, representing small business.

Specific business interests are also represented by thousands of **trade associations.** These associations can closely monitor the interests of their specialized memberships. Among the most powerful of these associations are the American Bankers Association, the American Gas Association, the American Iron and Steel Institute, the National Association of Real Estate Boards, the American Petroleum Institute, and the National Association of Broadcasters.

In addition, many individual corporations and firms achieve representation in Washington by opening their own lobbying offices or by hiring experienced professional lobbying and law firms.

**Trade associations:** Interest groups composed of businesses in specific industries.

TABLE 9-1   MAJOR ORGANIZED INTEREST GROUPS BY TYPE

**Business**
Business Roundtable
National Association of Manufacturers
National Federation of Independent Businesses
National Small Business Association
U.S. Chamber of Commerce

**Trade**
American Bankers Association
American Gas Association
American Iron and Steel Institute
American Petroleum Institute
American Truckers Association
Automobile Dealers Association
Home Builders Association
National Association of Broadcasters
National Association of Real Estate Boards

**Professional**
American Bar Association
American Medical Association
Association of Trial Lawyers
National Education Association

**Union**
AFL-CIO
American Federation of State, County, and Municipal Employees
American Federation of Teachers
International Brotherhood of Teamsters
International Ladies' Garment Workers Union
National Association of Letter Carriers
United Auto Workers
United Steel Workers
United Postal Workers

**Agricultural**
American Farm Bureau Federation
National Cattlemen's Association

National Farmers Union
National Grange
National Milk Producers Federation
Tobacco Institute

**Women**
League of Women Voters
National Organization for Women

**Public Interest**
Common Cause
Consumer Federation of America
Public Citizen
Public Interest Research Groups

**Ideological**
American Conservative Union
Americans for Constitutional Action (conservative)
Americans for Democratic Action (liberal)
People for the American Way (liberal)
National Conservative Political Action Committee (conservative)

**Single-Issue**
Mothers against Drunk Driving
National Abortion Rights Action League
National Rifle Association
National Right-to-Life Committee
Planned Parenthood Federation of America
National Taxpayers Union

**Environmental**
Environmental Defense Fund
Greenpeace
National Wildlife Federation
Natural Resources Defense Council
Nature Conservancy
Sierra Club
Wilderness Society

**Religious**
American Jewish Committee
Anti-Defamation League of B'nai B'rith
Christian Coalition
National Council of Churches
U.S. Catholic Conference

**Civil Rights**
American Civil Liberties Union
American Indian Movement
Mexican-American Legal Defense and Education Fund
National Association for the Advancement of Colored People
National Urban League
Rainbow Coalition
Southern Christian Leadership Conference

**Age-Related**
American Association of Retired Persons
Children's Defense Fund

**Veterans**
American Legion
Veterans of Foreign Wars
Vietnam Veterans of America

**Defense**
Air Force Association
American Security Council
Army Association
Navy Association

**Government**
National Association of Counties
National Conference of State Legislators
National Governors Association
National League of Cities
U.S. Conference of Mayors

*Professional Associations*   Professional associations rival business and trade organizations in lobbying influence. The American Bar Association (ABA), the American Medical Association (AMA), and the National Education Association (NEA) are three of the most influential groups in Washington. For example, the American Bar Association, which includes virtually all of the nation's practicing attorneys, and its more specialized offspring, the American Association of Trial

Lawyers, have successfully resisted efforts to reform the nation's tort laws (see "America Drowning in a Sea of Lawsuits," Chapter 13).

The AMA is regularly listed among the highest-spending lobbying organizations each year. For many years, the AMA successfully fought off national health insurance plans, arguing that socialized medicine would erode quality medical care. But when Medicare for the aged and Medicaid for the poor were pushed forward by President Lyndon Johnson in 1965, the AMA switched tactics, supporting the legislation as a means of bringing vast sums of tax money into the nation's health-care system. The strategy proved immensely profitable: Medicare and Medicaid are the fastest-growing programs in the federal budget, contributing heavily to medical cost inflation. Government payments also now account for nearly one-third of the average doctor's income.

In recent years, the AMA and other powerful lobbies such as the Health Insurance Association of America have fought government efforts to regulate costs and practices (see *Up Close:* "How Harry and Louise Killed Hillary's Health Plan"). The AMA has been forced to accept government payment schedules for various procedures, but the cost of physicians' care continues to rise as more procedures are prescribed. The AMA remains vigorously opposed to any limits on physicians' decisions about care for their patients.

Only about 45 percent of the nation's physicians are members of the AMA, down from nearly 75 percent thirty years ago. Many physicians believe that they are better represented by more specialized medical groups (for example, the American College of Surgeons, the American Academy of Family Physicians, the American Society of Internal Medicine), especially in negotiations over government fee schedules for particular procedures.

*Organized Labor*  Labor organizations have declined in membership over the last several decades. The percentage of the nonagricultural work force belonging to unions has declined from about 35 percent in the 1950s to 16 percent in the 1990s. This decline has occurred primarily as a result of changes in the economy: rapid growth of professional, managerial, finance, technical, sales, and service employment, where unions are weakest; and slower growth or stagnation of manufacture, mining, and construction employment, where unions are strongest. Yet even in manufacturing, union membership today is only about 25 percent of the work force.

Nevertheless, labor unions remain a major political influence in Congress and the Democratic Party. The AFL-CIO is a federation of more than 100 separate unions with more than 14 million members. The AFL-CIO has long maintained a large and capable lobbying staff in Washington, and it provides both financial contributions and campaign services (registration, get-out-the-vote, information, endorsements) for members of Congress it favors. Many of the larger individual unions also maintain offices in Washington and offer campaign contributions and services.

*Farm Organizations*  Even though the farm population of the United States has declined from about 25 percent of the total population in the 1930s to less than 3 percent today, farmers—especially large agricultural producers—remain a very potent political force in Washington. Agricultural interests are organized both into large inclusive groups, such as the American Farm Bureau Federation and the National Grange, and into very effective specialized groups, such as the

## How Harry and Louise Killed Hillary's Health Plan

The importance of health care reform to the Clinton presidency was reflected in Hillary Clinton's personal assumption of the leadership of the President's Task Force on Health Care Reform, the committee formed to devise a comprehensive health care plan for the nation. She chose Ira Magaziner, a close friend of Bill's since their days together as Rhodes Scholars at Oxford University, to be her top aide in health care policy. From the very beginning of their work, Hillary Clinton and Ira Magaziner sought to exclude interest groups from the deliberations of the task force; its membership was secret and its meetings were private. While this tactic may have facilitated the writing of the 1,342-page health care plan that eventually emerged from the task force, it also contributed to its rejection by the American people and its defeat in Congress.

The Clinton plan involved a comprehensive restructuring of the nation's health care system. Among its many provisions:

- creation of government health care purchasing alliances around the country to purchase health care for all citizens from HMOs, hospitals, physician groups, nursing homes, and so on
- extension of health insurance to all citizens and legal residents, through "mandates" on employers

to provide 80 percent of the cost of insurance for their employees and their dependents, with government subsidies available for low-paid workers and unemployed persons

- provision of comprehensive benefits including prescription drugs, mental health and drug abuse treatment, preventive check ups, and all pregnancy-related services, including abortion.

The American Medical Association, representing the nation's physicians, realized that government purchasing organizations would favor HMOs, eventually forcing virtually all the nation's doctors into these organizations and eliminating most independent medical practices. The AMA initially offered to work with Hillary Clinton and Ira Magaziner to come up with a plan that would protect "patient choice" of physicians and medical care. But the AMA was rebuffed in its efforts and excluded from deliberations of the task force. Eventually, the AMA went into opposition.

Initially business groups seemed divided over the plan, with big business, as represented by the Business Roundtable, unopposed to mandated coverage, since most big business already provided medical insurance to their employees. But the National Federation of Independent Businesses, representing small business, was strongly opposed, claiming that mandated insurance would raise costs and prices and eliminate jobs. The U.S. Chamber of Commerce joined in opposition, promoting instead its own business-friendly health care program.

National Milk Producers and the National Cattlemen's Association. Small and low-income farmers are represented by the National Farmers Union.

*Women's Organizations*    Women's organizations date back to the antislavery societies in pre–Civil War America. The first generation of feminists—Lucretia Mott, Elizabeth Cady Stanton, Lucy Stone, and Susan B. Anthony—learned to organize, hold public meetings, and conduct petition campaigns as abolitionists. After the Civil War, women were successful in changing many state laws that abridged the property rights of married women and otherwise treated them as "chattel" (property) of their husbands. Women were also prominent in the Anti-Saloon League, which succeeded in outlawing prostitution and gambling in every

The Catholic Church and the Protestant fundamentalist Christian Coalition led the opposition to government-funded abortions under the plan. The Catholic Church offered to change sides if Hillary would drop abortion services, but feminist organizations and pro-choice groups convinced her to keep abortion in the plan.

The powerful senior citizens lobby, led by the American Association of Retired Persons, was only lukewarm in its support of the plan. To satisfy this group, the Clinton plan left Medicare for the aged untouched and indeed even offered to add prescription drugs to its long list of benefits. But the AARP never really rallied its troops behind the Clinton plan.

The key to the defeat of the Clinton plan was the skillful media blitz unleashed by the insurance industry, led by the Health Insurance Association of America. Their multimillion-dollar television advertising campaign featured "Harry and Louise," a yuppie couple who worried convincingly about bureaucratic interference in health care, soaring costs, and eventual rationing of health care.

The Harry and Louise ads appeared to shift public opinion over time. Full support for the Clinton program dropped between September 1993 and September 1994 from 23 to 16 percent; outright rejection rose from 15 percent to 30 percent, with more than 50 percent demanding "major changes." Among the objections fostered in the ads, together with percentages of popular agreement:

| | *Percentage Agreeing It Is a "Big Concern about the Clinton Health Plan"* |
|---|---|
| You might not have good choices of doctors or hospitals | 72% |
| The cost of your medical care will go up | 70 |
| Some expensive medical services will not be available to all who need them | 69 |
| Taxes will have to be increased to pay for the plan | 68 |
| The quality of your medical care will decline | 64 |
| The plan would create another large and inefficient government bureaucracy | 59 |

The insurance industry combined an *outside strategy*—using television ads to convince Americans of the dangers of the Clinton plan and generating thousands of calls and letters to Congress members—with an *inside strategy*—direct lobbying of Congress members, especially those who were recipients of medical and insurance industry political action committee contributions. By late summer 1994 it was clear that the Clinton plan was dead. Hillary Clinton cast the blame on the "special interests" who she believed had misled the American people. Other commentators faulted the Clinton administration for failing to include key interest groups in the preparation of the plan and winning their cooperation.

state except Nevada and provided a major source of support for the Eighteenth Amendment (Prohibition). In the early twentieth century, the feminist movement concentrated on obtaining the vote (suffrage) for women. Today the League of Women Voters, a broad-based organization that provides information to voters, backs registration and get-out-the-vote drives, and generally supports measures seeking to ensure honesty and integrity in government.

Interest in feminist politics revived in the wake of the civil rights movement of the 1960s. New organizations sprang up to compete with the conventional activities of the League of Women Voters by taking a more activist stance toward women's issues. The largest of these organizations is the National Organization for Women (NOW), founded in 1966.

*Religious Groups* Churches and religious groups have a long history of involvement in American politics—from the pre-Civil War antislavery crusades, to the prohibition effort in the early twentieth century, to the civil rights movement of the 1960s. The leadership for the historic Civil Rights Act of 1964 came from the Reverend Martin Luther King, Jr., and his Southern Christian Leadership Conference. Today religious groups span the political spectrum, from liberal organizations such as the National Council of Churches and Anti-Defamation League of B'nai B'rith, to conservative and fundamentalist organizations, such as the Christian Coalition, often referred to as the "religious right" (see *Up Close:* "The Christian Coalition: Organizing the Faithful").

*Public Interest Groups* **Public interest groups** claim to represent broad classes of people—consumers, voters, reformers, or the public as a whole. Groups with lofty-sounding names—such as Common Cause, Public Citizen, and the Consumer Federation of America—perceive themselves as balancing the narrow, "selfish" interests of business organizations, trade associations, unions, and other "special" interests. Public interest groups generally lobby for greater government regulation of consumer products, public safety, campaign finance, and so on. Their reform agenda, as well as their call for a larger regulatory role for government, makes them frequent allies of liberal ideological groups, civil rights organizations, and environmental groups. Many public interest groups were initially formed in the 1970s by group "entrepreneurs" who saw an untapped "market" for the representation of these interests.

Among the most influential public interest groups are Common Cause, a self-styled "citizens' lobby," and the sprawling network of organizations created by consumer advocate Ralph Nader (see *People in Politics:* "Ralph Nader, People's Lobbyist"). Common Cause tends to focus on election law reform, public financing of elections, and limitations on political contributions. The Nader organization began as a consumer protection group focusing on auto safety but soon spread to encompass a wide variety of causes.

*Single-Issue Groups* Like public interest groups, **single-issue groups** appeal to principle and belief. But as their name implies, single-issue groups concentrate their attention on a single cause. They attract the support of individuals with a strong commitment to that cause. Single-issue groups have little incentive to compromise their position. They exist for a single cause; no other issues really matter to them. They are by nature passionate and often shrill. Their attraction to members is the intensity of their beliefs.

Among the most vocal single-issue groups in recent years have been the organizations on both sides of the abortion issue. The National Abortion Rights Action League (NARAL) describes itself as "pro-choice" and opposes any restrictions on a woman's right to obtain an abortion. The National Right-to-Life Committee describes itself as "pro-life" and opposes abortion for any reason other than to preserve the life of the mother. Other prominent single-issue groups include the National Rifle Association (see *Up Close:* "NRA: Top Gun in Washington") and Mothers against Drunk Driving (MADD).

*Ideological Groups* **Ideological organizations** pursue liberal or conservative agendas, often with great passion and considerable financial resources derived from true-believing contributors. The ideological groups rely heavily on

**Public interest groups:**
Interest groups that claim to represent broad classes of people or the public as a whole.

**Single-issue groups:**
Organizations formed to support or oppose government action on a specific issue.

**Ideological organizations:**
Interest groups that pursue ideologically based (liberal or conservative) agendas.

CHAPTER 9 • INTEREST GROUPS: GETTING THEIR SHARE AND MORE

# The Christian Coalition: Organizing the Faithful

Christian fundamentalists, whose religious beliefs are based on a literal reading of the Bible, have become a more significant political force in the United States through effective organization. Perhaps the most influential Christian fundamentalist organization today is the Christian Coalition with nearly 2 million active members throughout the country. Its director, Ralph Reed, expresses the importance of organization: "You have to organize, organize, organize, and build and build, and train and train, so that there is a permanent vibrant structure of which people can be a part."*

Fundamentalist Christians are opposed to abortion, pornography, and homosexuality; they favor the recognition of religion in public life, including prayer in schools; and they despair at the decline of traditional family values in American culture, including motion pictures and television broadcasting. Historically fundamentalist Protestant churches avoided politics as profane and concentrated evangelical efforts at saving individual souls. Their few ventures into worldly politics—notably the prohibition movement in the early twentieth century—ended in defeat. Their strength tended to be in the southern, rural, and poorer regions of the country. They were widely ridiculed on the national media.

In the 1960s, television evangelism emerged as a religious force in the United States. The Reverend Pat Robertson founded the Christian Broadcasting Network (CBN) to air his popular *700 Club* and later purchased the Family Channel. But efforts by social conservatives to build a "moral majority" for political action largely failed, as did Robertson's presidential candidacy in 1988. "Televangelists," including Jerry Falwell and Tammy Fay Baker, suffered popular disdain following some well-publicized scandals. As president, Ronald Reagan gave symbolic support to the political agenda of social and religious conservatives, but concentrated instead on the concerns of economic conservatives (for deregulation and tax reduction) and anticommunist conservatives (for a military buildup and challenge to the Soviet Union).

Robertson eventually turned over his embattled political organization, the Christian Coalition, to a young, energetic, professional political organizer, Ralph Reed.

Under Reed's direction, the Christian Coalition has risen in political influence across the country—in local politics, school board elections, state legislative and governors' races, and congressional politics. Building from the grass roots, in local communities and churches, Reed has made the Christian Coalition perhaps the most powerful religious-based lobby in the nation. While officially nonpartisan, the coalition represents an important force in Republican politics; religious fundamentalists may constitute as much as one-third of the party's voter support. The Christian Coalition does not officially endorse candidates, but its voter guides clearly indicate which candidates reflect the coalition's position on major issues. The distribution of more than 33 million of these guides, mostly in churches on the weekend before the Tuesday election, was credited with helping Republicans capture control of Congress in 1994.

The political influence of the Christian Coalition in Republican politics, and the "religious right" generally, ensures that most GOP candidates for public office publicly express support for a "profamily" agenda. Indeed, the Christian Coalition issued its own "Contract with the American Family," following the lead of the Newt Gingrich–inspired "Contract with America," that summarizes the policy views of the coalition and many religious fundamentalists. These views included a constitutional amendment allowing prayer in public schools; vouchers for parents to send their children to private, religious schools; tax credits to families with children; banning late-term abortions as well as banning the use of taxpayer funds to pay for abortions; restrictions on pornography on cable television; and a requirement that criminals make restitution to their victims after release. According to Reed, fundamentalist Christians "have finally gained a place at the table, a sense of legitimacy, and a voice in the conversation we call democracy."**

*Time,* May 15, 1995, p. 35.
**Congressional Quarterly Weekly Report,* May 20, 1995, p. 1449.

# Ralph Nader, People's Lobbyist

Much of the credit for the growth of public-interest groups in recent decades goes to Ralph Nader, the self-appointed "people's lobbyist" who achieved national celebrity as an advocate of consumer protection laws. From seat belts and nonsmoking sections to nuclear power regulation, insurance rates, food and drug legislation, and worker safety, Nader's influence has been widely felt in American society.

The child of Lebanese immigrants who operated a small bakery in Winsted, Connecticut, Nader graduated from the Woodrow Wilson School of Public and International Affairs at Princeton University magna cum laude, then went on to Harvard Law, where he earned an LL.B. with distinction in 1958. After a short stint in the army, Nader opened a private law practice in Hartford, Connecticut, but soon left to travel throughout the world, working as a free-lance journalist for the *Christian Science Monitor.*

An article that Nader wrote for the *Harvard Law Review* on auto design and safety brought him to the attention of then-Acting Secretary of Labor (now U.S. senator from New York) Daniel Patrick Moynihan. Moynihan hired the young attorney as a staff consultant on highway safety. While employed at the Department of Labor, Nader wrote and published a book, *Unsafe at Any Speed* (1965), which charged that General Motors Corporation preferred styling to safety. Nader was thrust further into the national spotlight when he sued General Motors for invading his privacy by hiring private detectives to investigate him. With his $16 million in settlement money (plus substantial royalty and speaking income), Nader began to construct an organizational colossus (see figure). In 1969, Nader founded his Washington-based Center for Study of Responsive Law and staffed it with aggressive young lawyers. These "Nader's Raiders" launched attacks against a number of federal regulatory agencies for lax enforcement.

In 1971, Nader started Public Citizen, Inc., to enlist members of the general public in a broad array of causes. Nader has also formed a number of organizations that address more specific topics, such as the Citizens for Tax Justice, Aviation Consumer's Action, Center for Auto Safety, and Congress Watch. Nader was instrumental in the creation of the Occupational Safety and Health Administration and the Consumer Product Safety Commission, but Congress rejected his idea for a federal consumer protection agency.

Nader's independence and altruism, his contempt for bureaucratic lethargy and incompetence, and his posture as David fighting the corporate Goliaths of the world have appealed to idealistic young people at colleges and universities across the nation. Capitalizing on his campus popularity, Nader has formed hundreds of Public Interest Research Groups (PIRGs) and has overcome the "free-rider" problem by pressuring university administrators on many campuses to add PIRG dues to student activities fees.

Nader has resigned from direct participation in most of the organizations he founded, leaving them to be managed by a new generation of consumer advocates. He continues to live in a low-rent boardinghouse in Washington, D.C., reportedly wearing one of the twelve pairs of shoes that he bought at an army PX in 1958. "I'm not an idealist. I think of myself as being very practical because I want to be effective. . . . Traditional reformers . . . didn't follow through by politically mobilizing a concerned constituency."

Nader ran for president in 1996 as a Green Party (environmental protection) candidate. He succeeded in getting his name on the ballot in California and several other states. But he campaigned very little and refused to solicit contributions. In public appearances he often seemed argumentative and self-righteous. He ended up with less than one percent of the popular vote nationwide.

*Source:* Adapted from "The Ralph Nader Trust," *Forbes,* September 17, 1990, pp. 120–21, by permission of Forbes Magazine; quotation from *Newsmakers* (Detroit: Gale Research, 1989), p. 360.

# The Nader Network

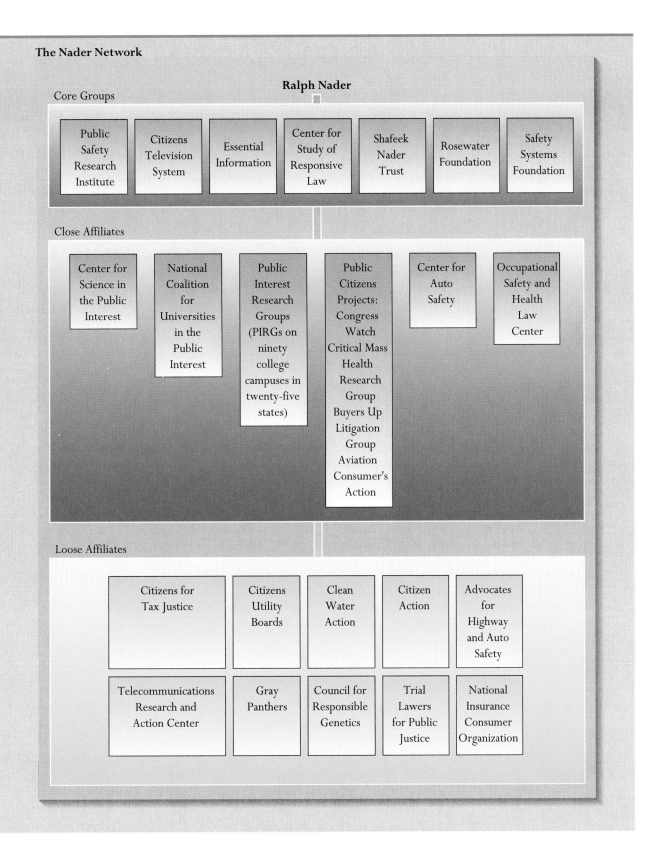

**Ralph Nader**

**Core Groups**

| | | | | | | |
|---|---|---|---|---|---|---|
| Public Safety Research Institute | Citizens Television System | Essential Information | Center for Study of Responsive Law | Shafeek Nader Trust | Rosewater Foundation | Safety Systems Foundation |

**Close Affiliates**

| | | | | | |
|---|---|---|---|---|---|
| Center for Science in the Public Interest | National Coalition for Universities in the Public Interest | Public Interest Research Groups (PIRGs on ninety college campuses in twenty-five states) | Public Citizens Projects: Congress Watch Critical Mass Health Research Group Buyers Up Litigation Group Aviation Consumer's Action | Center for Auto Safety | Occupational Safety and Health Law Center |

**Loose Affiliates**

| | | | | |
|---|---|---|---|---|
| Citizens for Tax Justice | Citizens Utility Boards | Clean Water Action | Citizen Action | Advocates for Highway and Auto Safety |
| Telecommunications Research and Action Center | Gray Panthers | Council for Responsible Genetics | Trial Lawers for Public Justice | National Insurance Consumer Organization |

# NRA: Top Gun in Washington

The National Rifle Association exemplifies the powerful single-interest lobby: it is large, well organized, passionate, and focused on a single issue—gun control. The NRA is against it. More than 3 million dues-paying members, together with advertising revenue, provide NRA with a full treasury to carry its message to Congress, the bureaucracy, the courts, and the general public through the media.

The NRA began after the Civil War to improve marksmanship among "Yankees" (whose skills had proved decidedly inferior to those of the "Rebels"). Ulysses S. Grant was an early NRA president. For many years, the U.S. Army sold its surplus arms through the NRA.

NRA members share interests in hunting, marksmanship, and gun collecting. The organization publishes the *American Hunter* and the *American Rifleman* for its members and offers them free insurance against loss or theft of their firearms or injury from hunting and shooting accidents. NRA members view hunting, shooting, and gun collecting as recreational activities, and they view themselves as responsible, law-abiding citizens, which most of them are. They believe that efforts to reduce crime by taking guns away from law-abiding citizens are misguided. NRA members pride themselves on education, training, and responsibility in gun safety. More important, they see gun ownership as a symbol of independence, self-reliance, and freedom in America.

NRA lobbying activities began in earnest during the congressional debate over the Gun Control Act of 1968, introduced after the assassinations of Senator Robert F. Kennedy and Martin Luther King, Jr. The act banishes mail-order sales of firearms and ammunition; prohibits sale of firearms to convicted felons; establishes licensing of all firearm dealers by the federal Bureau of Alcohol, Tobacco, and Firearms; requires dealers to keep records on all firearm sales; and calls for registration for ownership of automatic weapons. The NRA succeeded in defeating a proposed federal ban on all handguns and federal registration of all gun owners.

Gun ownership is widespread in the United States. More than 150 million firearms are in the hands of the nation's 265 million people. Half of all American families questioned in public opinion surveys admit to owning guns. In opinion polls, a majority of Americans oppose any outright ban on the possession or sale of handguns, yet a majority also favor "stricter" laws governing handguns (see graph).

The NRA argues that any restriction on owning a gun is a step toward the prohibition and confiscation of all guns. Following every highly publicized gun incident—attempted assassinations of presidents Gerald Ford and Ronald Reagan, the shooting of John Lennon, and so on—gun control advocates have urged a ban on handguns. But so far, the NRA has successfully fought off national legislation to ban handguns, to register them, or to license owners.

The NRA's success in Congress is generally attributed to its organizational skills and the intensity of its feelings on the single issue of gun control. Its legislative strategy is to direct antigun sentiments toward increasing the penalties for using a gun to commit a crime. Thus the NRA supports federal and state laws imposing such penalties.

The NRA also supplies technical information and research findings to Congress. For example, the group distributed studies showing that violent crime rates in states with very restrictive gun laws (New York, Massachusetts, New Jersey, and Illinois) are just as high as violent crime rates in states without restrictive gun laws. The organization focuses on studies showing that gun laws have no effect on violent crime rates, on crimes committed with guns, or even on gun ownership. The NRA acknowledges Fed-

computerized mailings to solicit funds from persons identified as holding liberal or conservative views. The oldest of the established ideological groups is the liberal Americans for Democratic Action (ADA), well known for its annual liberalism ratings of members of the Congress according to their support for or rejection of programs of concern. The American Conservative Union (ACU) also

eral Bureau of Investigation figures showing that 62 percent of all murders are committed with guns (supplying accurate information to Congress, even when the data may appear to undermine the group's position, is important for maintaining its reputation as a reliable information source) but contends that "guns do not kill people, people kill people," and that banning guns only deprives law-abiding citizens of their constitutional rights while doing nothing to prevent criminals from using guns. Moreover, the NRA's political action committee funnels millions of dollars into congressional campaign coffers. It credits itself with playing a key roll in the defeat of many House supporters of gun control in 1994.

But the NRA has suffered some serious defeats in recent years. Congress passed the Brady Law in 1993 over strong NRA opposition; the law requires a waiting period for the purchase of a handgun to allow for a police criminal records check on buyers. (The law is named for former Reagan Press Secretary James Brady, who was permanently disabled in the attempted assassination of President Reagan in 1991. His wife, Sarah Brady, was a very effective advocate of handgun control.) The NRA also failed to stop Congress from adding a ban on the sale of "assault weapons," usually defined as semiautomatic rifles and machine pistols, from the Crime Control Act of 1994.

In addition, the NRA has run into severe public relations problems in recent years. It has had a long history of conflict with the Bureau of Alcohol, Tobacco, and Firearms (ATF), the federal agency responsible for the enforcement of federal gun laws. The NRA has frequently protested the ATF's heavy-handed enforcement tactics, including its attack on the Branch Davidian compound in Waco, Texas, resulting in the deaths of more than seventy people. (A reference in NRA literature to ATF agents as "jack booted government thugs" prompted the well-publicized resignation of George Bush from the organization.) When the bombing of the Oklahoma City

Federal Building in 1995, and resulting deaths of over 160 people, was linked to antigovernment extremists, the NRA was castigated by President Bill Clinton for contributing to antigoverment sentiments in the nation.

**Public Opinion on Gun Control**

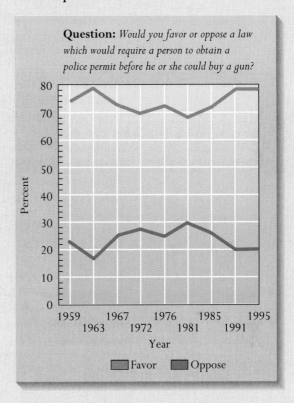

*While responses have varied somewhat over time, most Americans do believe some gun control laws are needed, with most favoring licensing of handguns similar to licensing of cars. Nevertheless, over the years, the National Rifle Association has been extremely effective in halting many proposed restrictions on gun ownership.*

*Source:* General Social Survey.

rates members of Congress each year. Overall, Democrats do better on the liberal list and Republicans on the conservative list, though both parties include some members whose policies frequently put them on the opposite side of the fence from the majority of their fellow party members (see Table 9-2). Other interest groups, such as the AFL-CIO, the National Taxpayers Union, and the

TABLE 9-2  IDEOLOGICAL INTEREST GROUP SCORES FOR VOTING IN CONGRESS

|  | Americans for Democratic Action (liberal) | American Conservative Union (conservative) |
|---|---|---|
| House |  |  |
| Average Republicans | 14 | 82 |
| Average Democrats | 67 | 18 |
| Senate |  |  |
| Average Republicans | 18 | 76 |
| Average Democrats | 25 | 22 |
| Most Liberal Senators |  |  |
| Paul Simon (D-Ill.) | 100 | 0 |
| Tom Harkin (D-Iowa) | 100 | 0 |
| Paul Sarbanes (D-Md.) | 100 | 0 |
| Edward Kennedy (D-Mass.) | 95 | 0 |
| John Kerry (D-Mass.) | 95 | 5 |
| Paul Wellstone (D-Minn.) | 95 | 5 |
| Frank Lautenberg (D-N.J.) | 95 | 5 |
| Daniel Patrick Moynihan (D-N.Y.) | 95 | 0 |
| Most Liberal Republican Senators |  |  |
| William Cohen (R-Maine) | 65 | 43 |
| James Jeffords (R-Vt.) | 65 | 10 |
| Most Conservative Senators |  |  |
| Jesse Helms (R-N.C.) | 5 | 100 |
| Daniel Coats (R-Ind.) | 5 | 100 |
| Don Nickles (R-Okla.) | 0 | 95 |
| Phil Gramm (R-Tex.) | 0 | 95 |
| Connie Mack (R-Fla.) | 15 | 90 |
| Mitch McConnell (R-Ky.) | 0 | 90 |
| Robert Smith (R-N.H.) | 10 | 90 |
| Strom Thurmond (R-S.C.) | 10 | 90 |
| Most Conservative Democratic Senators |  |  |
| Ernest Hollings (D-S.C.) | 55 | 62 |

Source: Reported in *Congressional Quarterly Weekly Report*, May 2, 1992. Updates by author.

National Abortion Rights Action League, also rate members of Congress, but these groups have a narrower focus than the ADA and ACU. Yet another prominent ideological group, People for the American Way, was formed by television producer Norman Lear *(All in the Family, Maude)* to coordinate the efforts of liberals in the entertainment industry as well as the general public, but issues no ratings.

*Government Lobbies*   The federal government's grant-in-aid programs to state and local governments (see Chapter 4) have spawned a host of lobbying efforts by these governments in Washington, D.C. Thus state and local government taxpayers foot the bill to lobby Washington to transfer federal taxpayers' revenues to states and communities. The National Governors Association occupies a beautiful marble building, the Hall of the States, in Washington, along with representatives of the separate states and many major cities. The National League of Cities and the National Association of Counties also maintain large Washington offices, as does the U.S. Conference of Mayors. The National Conference of State Legislators sends its lobbyists to Washington from its Denver headquarters. These groups pursue a wide policy agenda and often confront internal disputes. But they are united in their support for increased federal transfers of tax revenues to states and cities.

# LEADERS AND FOLLOWERS

Organizations require leadership. And over time leaders develop a perspective somewhat different from that of their organizations' membership. A key question in interest-group politics is how well organization leaders represent the views of their members.

*Interest-Group Entrepreneurs*   People who create organizations and build membership in those organizations—**interest-group entrepreneurs**—have played a major role in strengthening the interest-group system in recent decades. These entrepreneurs help overcome a major obstacle to the formation of strong interest groups—the *free-rider* problem.

**Free-riders** are people who benefit from the efforts of others but do not contribute to the costs of those efforts. Not everyone feels an obligation to support organizations that represent their interests or views. Some people feel that their own small contribution will not make a difference in the success or failure of the organization's goals and, moreover, that they will benefit from any successes even if they are not members. Indeed, most organizations enroll only a tiny fraction of the people they claim to represent.

The task of the interest group entrepreneur is to convince people to join the organization, either by appealing to their sense of obligation or by attracting them through tangible benefits.

*Marketing Membership*   Interest-group entrepreneurs make different appeals for membership depending on the nature of the organization. Some appeal to passion or purpose, as, for example, those who seek to create ideological (liberal or conservative) organizations, public interest organizations committed to environmental or consumer protection or governmental reform, and single-issue organizations devoted to the support or opposition of a single policy issue (gun control, abortion, and so on). Entrepreneurs of these organizations appeal to people's sense of duty and commitment to the cause rather than to material rewards of membership. By using sophisticated computerized mailing lists, they can solicit support from sympathetic people.[6]

Business, trade, and professional organizations usually offer their members many tangible benefits in addition to lobbying on behalf of their economic interests. These benefits may include magazines, journals, and newsletters that provide access to business, trade, and professional information as well as national conventions and meetings that serve as social settings for the development of contacts,

**Interest-group entrepreneurs:** Leaders who create organizations and market memberships.

**Free-riders:** People who do not belong to an organization or pay dues, yet nevertheless benefit from its activities.

friendships, and business and professional relationships. Some organizations also offer discount travel and insurance, credit cards, and the like that go only to dues-paying members.

It is generally easier to organize smaller, specialized economic interests than larger, general, noneconomic interests. People more easily recognize that their own membership is important to the success of a small organization, and economic interests are more readily calculated in dollar terms.

Large organizations with broad goals—such as advancing the interests of all veterans or all retired people or all automobile drivers—must rely even more heavily on tangible benefits to solicit members. Indeed, some organizations have succeeded in recruiting millions of members (for example, the AARP with 30 million members, the American Automobile Association with 28 million members), most of whom have very little knowledge about the policy positions or lobbying activities of the organization. These members joined to receive specific benefits—magazines, insurance, travel tips, discounts. Leaders of these organizations may claim to speak for millions of members, but it is unlikely that these millions all share the policy views expressed by the leaders.

*Organizational Democracy and Leader/Member Agreement*  Most organized interest groups are run by a small group of leaders and activists. Few interest groups are governed democratically; members may drop out if they do not like the direction their organization is taking but rarely do they have the opportunity to directly challenge or replace the organization's leadership. Relatively few members attend national meetings, vote in organizational elections, or try to exercise influence within their organization. Thus the leadership may not always reflect the views of the membership, especially in large organizations that rely heavily on tangible benefits to recruit members. Leaders of these organizations enjoy considerable freedom in adopting policy positions and negotiating, bargaining, and compromising in the political arena.

The exception to this rule is the single-issue group. Because the strength of these groups is in the intensity of their members' beliefs, the leaders of such groups are closely tied to their members' views. They cannot bargain or compromise these views or adopt policy positions at variance with those of their members.

*Class Bias in Membership*  Americans are joiners. A majority of the population belong to at least one organization, most often a church. Yet membership in organized interest groups is clearly linked to socioeconomic status. Membership is greatest among professional and managerial, college-educated, and high-income persons.[7]

The class bias of organized groups varies according to the organization. Unions (which frequently are not voluntary) recruit from the working class. Public interest groups draw disproportionately from the university educated. The average member of Common Cause has a family income twice the national average; 43 percent have completed graduate school or a professional school. Studies of comparable groups document the upper-class bias in environmental groups. Likewise, there is a middle- to upper-class bias in business, trade, and professional organizations. Moreover, the leaders and activists in interest groups are even *higher* in social status than the membership.

# WASHINGTON REPRESENTATIVES: LOBBYISTS FOR HIRE

Washington is a labyrinth of interest representatives—lawyers and law firms; independent consultants; public and governmental relations firms; business, professional, and trade associations; and advocates of special causes. It is estimated that more than 14,000 people in Washington fit the definition of **lobbyist**—a person working to influence government policies and actions. These figures suggest that there are at least twenty-five lobbyists for every member of Congress.

*Who Are the Lobbyists?*    Lobbyists in Washington, D.C., represent a broad array of concerns (see Table 9-3). They share a common goal—to influence the making and enforcing of laws—and common tactics to achieve this goal. Many lobbyists are the employees of interest group organizations who devote all of their efforts to their sponsors. Other lobbyists are located in independent law, consulting, or public relations firms that take on clients for fees. Independent lobbyists, especially law firms, are often secretive about whom they represent, especially when they represent foreign governments. Lobbyists frequently prefer to label their activities as "government relations," "public affairs," "regulatory liaison," "legislative counseling," or merely "representation."

In reality, many independent lawyers and lobbyists in Washington are "fixers" who offer to influence government policies for a price. Many are former government officials—former Congress members, cabinet secretaries, White House aides, and the like—who "know their way around." Their personal connections help to "open doors" to allow their paying clients to "just get a chance to talk" with top officials.

*Regulation of Lobbies*    The Constitution's First Amendment guarantee of the right "to petition the government for a redress of grievances" protects lobbying. But the government can and does regulate lobbying activities, primarily through disclosure laws. The Regulation of Lobbying Act requires lobbyists to register and to report how much they spend, but definitions of *lobbying* are unclear and enforcement is weak. Many large lobbying groups—for example, the National Association of Manufacturers, the National Bankers Association, and Americans for Constitutional Action—have never registered as lobbyists. These organizations

## TABLE 9-3   TYPES OF LOBBYISTS

| | |
|---|---|
| Business, trade, and professional organization officers (approximately 2,200 organizations) | 5,000 |
| Representatives of individual corporations | 1,500 |
| Representatives of special causes | 2,500 |
| Lawyers registered as lobbyists | 3,000 |
| Public and governmental relations | 2,500 |
| Political action committee officers | 200 |
| Think tank officers | 150 |

*Source: Washington Representatives, 1995* (Washington, D.C.: Columbia Books, 1995).

**Lobbyist:** A person working to influence government policies and actions.

claim that because lobbying is not their "principal" activity, they need not register under the law. In addition, financial reports of lobbyists grossly underestimate the extent of lobbying in Congress because the law requires report of only money spent for direct lobbying before Congress, not money spent for public relations. Another weakness in the law is that it applies only to attempts to influence Congress; it does not regulate lobbying activities in administrative agencies or the executive branch.

Tax laws require nonprofit organizations to refrain from direct lobbying in order to retain their tax-free status. Under current tax law, individual contributions to nonprofit charitable and educational organizations are tax deductible, and the income of these organizations is tax-free. But these organizations risk losing these tax preferences if a "substantial part" of their activities is "attempting to influence legislation." Thus, for example, Washington think tanks such as the Brookings Institution, the American Enterprise Institute, and the Heritage Foundation (see *Up Close*: "Think Tanks: The Battle of Ideas" in Chapter 2) refrain from direct lobbying even though they make policy recommendations. But the line between public affairs "education" and "lobbying" is very fuzzy.

## THE FINE ART OF LOBBYING

Any activity directed at a government decision maker with the hope of influencing decisions is a form of **lobbying.** (The term arose from the practice of waiting in the lobbies of legislative chambers to meet and persuade legislators.) For organized interests, lobbying is continuous—in congressional committees, in congressional staff offices, at the White House, at executive agencies, at Washington cocktail parties. If a group loses a round in Congress, it continues the fight in the agency in charge of executing the policy, or it challenges the policy in the courts. The following year it resumes the struggle in Congress: it fights to repeal the offending legislation, to weaken amendments, or to reduce the agency's budget enough to cripple enforcement efforts.

Lobbying techniques are as varied as the imagination of interest group leaders, but such activities generally fall into seven categories: (1) public relations; (2) access; (3) information; (4) grass-roots mobilization; (5) protests and demonstrations; (6) coalition building; and (7) campaign support. In the real world of Washington power struggles, all these techniques may be applied simultaneously, or innovative techniques may be discovered and applied at any time (see Figure 9-1).

*Public Relations*    Many interest groups actually spend more of their time, energy, and resources on **public relations**—developing and maintaining a favorable climate of opinion in the nation—than on direct lobbying of Congress. The mass media—television, magazines, newspapers—are saturated with expensive ads by oil companies, auto companies, chemical manufacturers, trade associations, teachers' unions, and many other groups, all seeking to create a favorable image for themselves with the general public. These ads are designed to go well beyond promoting the sale of particular products; they portray these organizations as patriotic citizens, protectors of the environment, providers of jobs, defenders of family values, and supporters of the American way of life. Generally,

**Lobbying:** Activities directed at government officials with the hope of influencing their decisions.

**Public relations:** Building and maintaining goodwill with the general public.

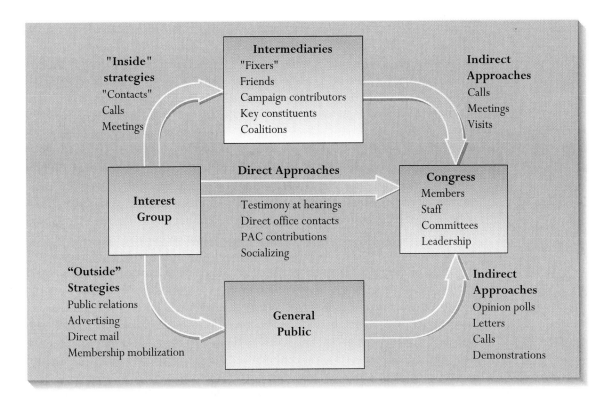

**FIGURE 9-1** **A Guide to the Fine Art of Lobbying**
*Interest groups seek to influence public policy both directly through lobbying and campaign contributions (inside strategy) and indirectly through public relations efforts to mold public opinion (outside strategy).*

business interests have an advantage in the area of public relations since public relations and sales and market activities are synonymous. But paid advertising is less credible than news stories and media commentary. Hence interest groups generate a daily flood of press releases, media events, interviews, reports, and studies for the media.

*Access* "Opening doors" is a major business in Washington. To influence decision makers, organized interests must first acquire **access** to them. Individuals who have personal contacts in Congress, the White House, or the bureaucracy (or who say they do) sell their services at high prices. Washington law firms, public relations agencies, and consultants—often former insiders—all offer their connections, along with their advice, to their clients. The personal prestige of the lobbyist, together with the group's perceived political influence, helps open doors in Washington.

Washington socializing is often an exercise in access—rubbing elbows with powerful people. Well-heeled lobbyists regularly pay hundreds, even thousands, of dollars per plate at fund-raising dinners for members of Congress. Lobbyists regularly provide dinners, drinks, travel, vacations, and other amenities to members of Congress, their families, and congressional staff, as well as to White House and other executive officials. (Until recently, *honoraria*—direct payments to members of Congress for speaking to an organization—were common, but congressional ethics legislation now prohibits honoraria for House members and limits annual honoraria income for senators to 27 percent of their salaries.) These favors are rarely provided on a direct quid pro quo basis in exchange for votes. Rather, they are designed to gain access—"just a chance to talk."

**Access:** Meeting and talking with decision makers, a prerequisite to direct persuasion.

*Information*   Once lobbyists gain access, their knowledge and information become valuable resources to those they lobby. Members of Congress and their staffs look to lobbyists for *technical expertise* on the issue under debate as well as *political information* about the group's position on the issue. Members of Congress must vote on hundreds of questions each year, and it is impossible for them to be fully informed about the wide variety of bills and issues they face. Consequently many of them (and administrators in the executive branch as well) come to depend on trusted lobbyists.

Lobbyists also spend considerable time and effort keeping informed about bills affecting their interests. They must be thoroughly familiar with the "ins and outs" of the legislative process—the relevant committees and subcommittees, their schedules of meetings and hearings, their key staff members, the best moments to act, the precise language for proposed bills and amendments, the witnesses for hearings, and the political strengths and weaknesses of the legislators themselves. In their campaign to win congressional and bureaucratic support for their programs, lobbyists engage in many different types of activities. Nearly all testify at congressional hearings and make direct contact with government officials on issues that affect them. In addition, lobbyists provide the technical reports and analyses used by congressional staffs in their legislative research. Engaging in protest demonstrations is a less common activity, in part because it involves a high risk of alienating some members of Congress (see Table 9-4).

Experienced lobbyists develop a reputation for accurate information. Most successful lobbyists do not supply faulty information; their success depends on maintaining the trust and confidence of decision makers. A reputation for honesty is as important as a reputation for influence.

*Grass-Roots Mobilization*   Many organized interests lobby Congress from both the *outside* and the *inside*. From the outside, organizations seek to mobilize **grass-roots lobbying** of members of Congress by their constituents. Lobbyists frequently encourage letters and calls from "the folks back home." Larger

**Grass-roots lobbying:**
Attempts to influence government decision making by inspiring constituents to contact their representatives.

| TABLE 9-4   ACTIVITIES OF PROFESSIONAL LOBBYISTS | |
| --- | --- |
| *Activity* | *Lobbyists Participating in Activity* |
| Testifying at hearings | 99% |
| Contacting government officials directly | 98 |
| Making informal contacts over meals, and so on | 95 |
| Presenting research results | 92 |
| Helping write legislation | 85 |
| Mounting grass-roots lobbying campaigns | 80 |
| Telling legislators the impact of legislation in their districts | 75 |
| Pursuing litigation | 72 |
| Publicizing candidates' voting records | 44 |
| Making in-kind (work, skill) contributions to campaigns | 24 |
| Endorsing candidates publicly | 22 |
| Engaging in protests or demonstrations | 20 |

*Source:* Kay Lehman Schlozman and John T. Tierney, *Organized Interests and American Democracy* (New York: Harper and Row, 1986), p. 150.

organized interests often have local chapters throughout the nation and can mobilize these local affiliates to apply pressure when necessary. Lobbyists encourage influential local people to visit the office of a member of Congress personally or to make a personal phone call on behalf of the group's position. And, naturally, members are urged to vote for or against certain candidates, based on their policy stances (see *Up Close:* "AARP: The Nation's Most Powerful Interest Group").

Experienced lawmakers recognize attempts by lobby groups to orchestrate "spontaneous" grass-roots outpourings of cards and letters. Pressure mail is often identical in wording and content. Nevertheless, members of Congress dare not ignore a flood of letters and telegrams from home, for the mail shows that constituents are aware of the issue and care enough to sign their names.

Another grass-roots tactic is to mobilize the press in the home district of a member of Congress. Lobbyists may provide news, analyses, and editorials to local newspapers and then clip favorable articles to send to lawmakers. Lobby groups may also buy advertisements in hometown newspapers.

*Protests and Demonstrations*   Interest groups occasionally employ protests and demonstrations to attract media attention to their concerns and thereby apply pressure on officials to take action. For these actions to succeed in getting issues on the agenda of decision makers in Congress, in the White House, and in executive agencies, participation by the media, especially television, is essential. The media carry the message of the protest or demonstration both to the general public and directly to government officials (see "Protest as Political Participation" in Chapter 5).

Organized interest groups most often resort to protests and demonstrations when (1) they are frustrated in more traditional "inside" lobbying efforts; and/or (2) they wish to intensify pressure on officials at a specific point in time. Demonstrations typically attract media attention for a short time only. But media coverage of specific events can carry a clear message—for example, farmers driving tractors through Washington to protest farm conditions; motorcyclists conducting a giant "bike-in" to protest laws requiring helmets; cattle raisers driving steers down the Washington Mall to protest beef prices. The potential drawbacks to such activities are that the attention is short-lived and that the group's reputation may be tarnished if the protest turns nasty or violent.

*Coalition Building*   Interest groups frequently seek to build **coalitions** with other groups in order to increase their power. Coalitions tend to form among groups with parallel interests: for example, the National Organization for Women, the League of Women Voters, and the National Abortion Rights Action League on women's issues. Coalitions usually form temporarily around a single piece of legislation in a major effort to secure or prevent its passage.

*Campaign Support*   Perhaps the real key to success in lobbying is the campaign contribution. Interest-group contributions not only help lobbyists gain access and a favorable hearing but also help elect people friendly to the group's goals. As the costs of campaigning increase, legislators must depend more heavily on the contributions of organized interests.

Most experienced lobbyists avoid making electoral threats. Amateur lobbyists sometimes threaten legislators by vowing to defeat them at the next election, but

**Coalition:** A joining together of interest groups (or individuals) to achieve a common goal.

# AARP: The Nation's Most Powerful Interest Group

The American Association of Retired Persons (AARP) is the nation's largest and most powerful interest group, with nearly 33 million members. The AARP's principal interests are the Social Security and Medicare system programs, the nation's largest and most expensive entitlements. It led the fight in Congress against the Balanced Budget Amendment to the Constitution.

Like many other interest groups, the AARP has grown in membership not only by appealing to the political interests of retired people but also by offering a wide array of material benefits. For an $8 annual fee, members are offered a variety of services, including discounted rates on home, auto, and life insurance; discounted mail-order drugs; tax advisory services; discounted rates on hotels, rental cars, and so on; a newsletter; and a semimonthly magazine, *Modern Maturity*.

Senior citizens are the most politically powerful age group in the population. They constitute 28 percent of the voting-age population, but because of their high voter turnout rates, they constitute more than one-third of the voters on election day. Persons over sixty-five average a 68 percent turnout rate in presidential elections and a 61 percent rate in congressional elections. In contrast, the turnout rate for those aged eighteen to twenty-one is 36 percent in presidential elections and 19 percent in congressional elections. In short, the voting power of senior citizens is twice that of young people. No elected official can afford to offend the seniors, and seniors strongly support generous Social Security and Medicare benefits.

The power of the "gray lobby" is clearly evident in the federal budget (see graph). The federal government invests very little in education, training, and social services for young people. Yet the federal government's most costly function is the support of the nation's senior citizens. Social Security, Medicare, and federal retirement programs now account for almost 40 percent of all federal spending.

At present there are no "means" (low-income) tests for Social Security and Medicare. These benefits go to the wealthy among the aged as well as the poor. And overall, the aged have higher average incomes and much more wealth than the rest of the population. Poverty among persons over sixty-five is 2 full percentage points below the national average. Seniors also are much more likely than other Americans to own their own homes with paid mortgages, to have larger bank accounts, and to own stocks and bonds.

But the political power of senior citizens is so great that prospects for limiting current or even future increases in government benefits for the elderly are slim. Social Security is said to be the "third rail of American politics—touch it and you're dead."

Critics of the AARP argue that its lobbyists in Washington do not fairly represent the views of the nation's senior citizens, that few of its members know what its lobbying arm does at the nation's capital. AARP keeps its dues low, and consequently its membership high, through its business ties with insurance companies, its magazine advertising revenue, and commercial royalties revenues for endorsing products and services. Only about one-third of its revenues come from members' dues. Its critics argue that its many business ties should bar it from claiming tax-free status as a nonprofit charitable and education organization.

**Young and Old in the Federal Budget**

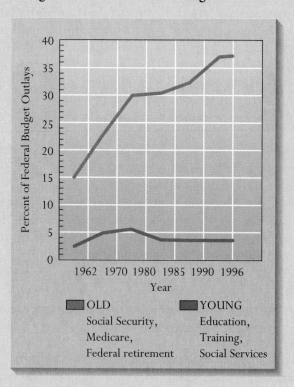

Source: *Budget of the United States Government, 1996.*

Interest groups use campaign contributions to gain access to legislators and help elect people favorable to their goals. The National Rifle Association, for example, has contributed substantially over the years to Senator Phil Gramm of Texas, an opponent of gun control, shown here addressing workers at a gun factory.

this tactic usually produces a hostile reaction among members of Congress. Legislators are likely to respond to crude pressures by demonstrating their independence and voting against the threatening lobbyist. Moreover, experienced members of Congress know that such threats are empty; lobbyists can seldom deliver enough votes to influence the outcome of an election.

Experienced lobbyists also avoid offering a campaign contribution in exchange for a specific vote.[8] Crude "vote buying" (bribery) is illegal and risks repulsing politicians who refuse bribes. **Bribery,** when it occurs, is probably limited to very narrow and specific actions—payments to intervene in a particular case before an administrative agency; payments to insert a very specific break in a tax bill or a specific exemption in a trade bill; payments to obtain a specific contract with the government. Bribery on major issues is very unlikely; there is too much publicity and there are too many participants for bribery to be effective (but see *Up Close:* "The Keating Five: Service to Constituents, for a Price?" in Chapter 10).

Instead of bribery, organized interests contribute to an incumbent member of Congress over a long period of time and leave it to the lawmaker to figure out how to retain their support. Only when a legislator consistently works against an organized interest will it consider contributing to that lawmaker's opponent in an election.

## PAC POWER

Organized interest groups channel their campaign contributions through **political action committees (PACs).** PACs are organized by corporations, labor unions, trade associations, ideological and issue-oriented groups, and cooperatives and nonprofit corporations to solicit campaign contributions and distribute them to political candidates.

**Bribery:** Giving or offering anything of value in an effort to influence government officials in the performance of their duties.

**Political action committees (PACs):** Organizations that solicit and receive campaign contributions from corporations, unions, trade associations, and ideological and issue-oriented groups, and their members, then distribute these funds to political candidates.

TABLE 9-5   THE GROWTH OF PACS

|  | 1974 | 1980 | 1988 | 1995 |
|---|---|---|---|---|
| Corporate | 89 | 1,206 | 1,816 | 1,670 |
| Labor | 201 | 297 | 354 | 334 |
| Trade and professional | 318 | 576 | 786 | 804 |
| Ideological issue | — | 374 | 1,115 | 1,002 |
| All other | — | 98 | 197 | 172 |
| Total | 608 | 2,551 | 4,268 | 3,982 |

*Source:* Federal Election Commission, July 1995.

*Origins*   The first PACs were created by organized labor to circumvent prohibitions against using union dues to finance elections. Corporations, like labor unions, had long been prohibited from making direct campaign contributions. Prior to passage of the Federal Election Campaign Act of 1974, which encouraged corporations to create their own PACs, PACs were relatively rare. But once begun, the PAC tide could not be stemmed (see Table 9-5). Today corporate PACs far outnumber labor PACs. Trade and professional associations quickly organized their own PACs. Soon entrepreneurs for ideological, environmental, and single-issue groups created PACs. Increasingly political candidates turned to PACs as a major source of campaign financing.

## TABLE 9-6   THE BIG MONEY PACS

**Corporate PACs**

American Telephone and Telegraph Company Inc. Political Action Committee (AT&T PAC)

Federal Express Corporation Political Action Committee (FEPAC)

Philip Morris Political Action Committee (PHIL-PAC)

United Parcel Service Political Action Committee (UPS PAC)

Waste Management Inc. Employees' Better Government Fund (WMI PAC)

**Labor PACs**

AFL-CIO Committee on Political Education (COPE)

American Federation of State, County, and Municipal Employees (PEOPLE)

Communications Workers of America Committee on Political Education (CWA-COPE)

Teamsters Union Democratic/Republican/ Independent Voter Education Committee

National Education Association Political Action Committee

United Auto Workers (UAW V CAP)

**Ideological and Issue PACs**

Conservative Campaign Fund

Council for a Livable World (environmental)

EMILY'S List (women candidates)

GOPAC (conservative)

National Abortion Rights Action League Political Action Committee

National Committee to Preserve Social Security and Medicare Political Action Committee

National Right-to-Life Political Action Committee

National Rifle Association Victory Fund

**Trade Associations**

American Bankers Association Political Action Committee

American Medical Association Political Action Committee

Association of Trial Lawyers of America Political Action Committee

National Association of Home Builders Political Action Committee (BUILD-PAC)

National Automobile Dealers Association Election Action Committee

National Association of Broadcasters Television and Radio Political Action Committee

Realtors' Political Action Committee

*Source:* Congressional Quarterly, *Washington Information Directory, 1994–1995.*

*Regulation*    PACs are regulated by the Federal Election Commission (FEC), which requires them to register and report their finances and political contributions periodically. A registered PAC that has received contributions from more than fifty people and has contributed to at least five campaigns is eligible to contribute $5,000 to any candidate (per election), $15,000 to a party's national committee, and $5,000 to any other PAC. These limits mean that PACs can give five times as much to candidates in each election as can individuals, who are limited to $1,000. Individuals may, however, give $5,000 to any PAC. Thus the 1974 reform act, while intended to reform campaign financing, actually encouraged the growth of PACs and PAC power.

*Distributing PAC Money*    PACs are vastly more important than political parties in financing campaigns. Also, because PAC contributions are in larger lumps than individual contributions, PAC contributions often attract more attention from members of Congress. PACs are also easier for politicians to deal with since there are far fewer PACs (about 4,000) than voters. The PACs listed in Table 9-6 give millions of dollars each year to finance the campaigns of their potential allies.

Most PACs use their campaign contributions to acquire access and influence with decision makers. Corporate, trade, and professional PAC contributions go overwhelmingly to incumbents, regardless of party. Leaders of these PACs know that incumbents are rarely defeated, and they do not wish to antagonize even unsympathetic members of Congress by backing challengers. However, ideological and issue-oriented PACs are more likely to allocate funds according to the candidates' policy positions and voting records.

Overall, Democratic candidates for Congress rely more heavily on PAC funds than do Republican candidates. Labor PACs give almost all of their contributions to Democrats. Corporate, trade, and business PACs favor incumbents of both parties, who are far more likely than their challengers to receive large contributions from PACs. Ideological and issue-oriented PACs give money to challengers as well as incumbents; in recent years, these groups collectively favored Democrats, as environmental, abortion rights, and elderly groups proliferated (see Table 9-7).

| TABLE 9-7  CAMPAIGN CONTRIBUTIONS FROM PACs TO CONGRESSIONAL ELECTIONS | | |
| --- | --- | --- |
| | *1994* | *1990* |
| **House** | | |
| Democratic incumbents | 51% | 58% |
| Democratic challengers | 25 | 29 |
| Democratic open-seat candidates | 31 | 34 |
| Republican incumbents | 36 | 41 |
| Republican challengers | 11 | 10 |
| Republican open-seat candidates | 22 | 28 |
| **Senate** | | |
| Democratic incumbents | 20 | 26 |
| Democratic challengers | 15 | 14 |
| Democratic open-seat candidates | 20 | 19 |
| Republican incumbents | 27 | 23 |
| Republican challengers | 3 | 18 |
| Republican open-seat candidates | 24 | 38 |

*Source:* Federal Election Commission.

The pattern of contributing to incumbents is particularly significant in the House of Representatives, where Democratic incumbents usually get more than half of their campaign funds from PACs. PAC money is less important in the Senate than in the House. While PAC contributions account for almost 40 percent of House campaign contributions, they only account for about 20 percent of Senate campaign contributions. Actually PACs contribute more *dollars* to the average senator than to the average House member. But since Senate campaigns cost so much more than House campaigns, PAC contributions are *proportionally* less. Senators must rely more on individual contributions than House members do.

## LOBBYING THE BUREAUCRACY

Lobbying does not cease after a law is passed. Rather, interest groups try to influence the implementation of the law. Interest groups know that bureaucrats exercise considerable discretion in policy implementation (see the discussion of "Bureaucratic Power" in Chapter 12). Thus many interests spend as much or more time and energy trying to influence executive agencies than Congress.

Lobbying the bureaucracy involves various types of activities, including monitoring regulatory agencies for notices of new rules and regulatory changes; providing reports, testimony, and evidence in administrative hearings; submitting contract and grant applications and lobbying for their acceptance; and monitoring the performance of executive agencies on behalf of group members. Groups may try to influence the creation of a new agency to carry out the law or influence the assignment of implementation to an existing "friendly" agency. They may try to influence the selection of personnel to head the implementing agency. They may lobby the agency to devote more money and personnel to enforcement of the law (or less, depending on a group's preference). They may argue for strict rules and regulations—or loose interpretations of the law—by the implementing agencies. Lobbyists frequently appear at administrative hearings to offer information. They often undertake to sponsor test cases of administrative regulations on behalf of affected members. In short, lobbying extends throughout the government.[9]

*Iron Triangles*   In general, interest groups strive to maintain close working relationships with the departments and agencies that serve their members or regulate their industries. Conversely, bureaucracies seek to nourish relationships with powerful "client" groups that are capable of pressuring Congress to expand their authority and increase their budgets. Both bureaucracies and interest groups seek close working relationships with the congressional committees that exercise jurisdictions over their policy function. Finally, members of Congress seek the political and financial support of powerful interest groups, and members also seek to influence bureaucrats to favor supportive interest groups.

The mutual interests of congressional committee members, organized groups, and bureaucratic agencies come together to form what has been labeled the "iron triangles" of American government. **Iron triangles** refer to stable relationships among interest groups, congressional committees, and administrative agencies functioning in the same policy area. Each of the three sides of these triangles depends upon the support of the other two; their cooperation serves their own interests (see Figure 9-2).

**Iron triangles:** Mutually supportive relationships among interest groups, government agencies, and legislative committees with jurisdiction over a specific policy area.

CHAPTER 9 • INTEREST GROUPS: GETTING THEIR SHARE AND MORE

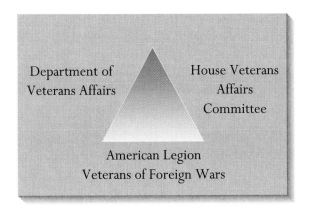

FIGURE 9-2 **Iron Triangles**
*The "iron triangle" approach provides a convenient way to look at the interrelationship among interest groups, executive agencies, and congressional committees. As this example shows, veterans' interest groups work closely with both the Department of Veterans Affairs (executive agency) and the House Veterans Affairs Committee.*

In an iron triangle, bureaucracies, interest groups, and congressional committees "scratch each other's back." Bureaucrats get political support from interest groups in their requests for expanded power and authority and increased budgetary allocations. Interest groups get favorable treatment of their members by the bureaucracy. Congressional committee members get political and financial support from interest groups, as well as favorable treatment for their constituents and contributors who are served or regulated by the bureaucracy.

Iron triangles are more likely to develop in specialized policy areas over which there is relatively little internal conflict. For example, the Maritime Administration in the Department of Transportation has developed close relationships with shipbuilders and maritime unions as well as with the House Merchant Marine Committee.[10]

However, conflict, rather than cooperation, is more likely to characterize bureaucratic-congressional-interest group relationships when powerful, diverse interests are at stake. For example, the Occupational Safety and Health Administration is caught between the demands of labor unions and industry groups. The U.S. Forest Service is caught between the demands of environmental groups and the lumber industry. The Environmental Protection Agency is pressured by environmental groups as well as by industry and agriculture. These kinds of conflicts break open the iron triangles or prevent them from forming in the first place.

*Policy Networks*    Generally, we think of American government in terms of the separate branches—Congress, the president and the bureaucracy, and the courts—with interest groups portrayed as external to government itself. But it is also possible to envision government as a series of **policy networks**—interactions in a common policy area among interest group leaders and lobbyists, members of Congress and their staff personnel, executive agency officials, lawyers and consultants, foundation and think tank people, and even reporters and journalists assigned to the field. Policy networks develop among people who share some knowledge and interest in a policy field—for example, weapons procurement, housing, environment, transportation, or energy—and who regularly interact with each other in the policy arena. Policy networks may include people who differ strongly with each other as well as people who share similar views. What they have in common is their policy expertise and regular interaction. They can participate in negotiations and reach compromises as well as try to outwit and outmaneuver each other.

**Policy networks:** Interaction in a common policy area, among lobbyists, elected officials, staff personnel, bureaucrats, journalists, and private-sector experts.

*Revolving Doors*    It is not uncommon in Washington for people in a policy network to switch jobs—moving from a post in the government to a job in the private sector, or vice versa, or moving to different posts within the government. In one example, an individual might move from a job in a corporation (Pillsbury or General Mills) to the staff of an interest group (American Farm Bureau Federation), and then to the executive agency charged with implementing policy in the field (U.S. Department of Agriculture) or to the staff of a House or Senate committee with jurisdiction over the field (House Agricultural Committee or Senate Agriculture, Nutrition, and Forestry Committee). The common currency of moves within a network is both policy expertise and contacts within the field.

The term **revolving doors** is often used to criticize people who move from a government post (where they acquired experience, knowledge, and personal contacts) to a job in the private sector as a consultant, lobbyist, or salesperson. Defense contractors may recruit high-ranking military officers or Defense Department officials to help sell weapons to their former employers. Trade associations may recruit congressional staffers, White House staffers, or high-ranking agency heads as lobbyists, or these people may leave government service to start their own lobbying firms. Attorneys from the Justice Department, the Internal Revenue Service, and federal regulatory agencies may be recruited by Washington law firms to represent clients in dealings with their former employers. Following retirement, many members of Congress turn to lobbying their former colleagues.

Concern about revolving doors centers not only on individuals cashing in on their knowledge, experience, and contacts obtained through government employment but also on the possibility that some government officials will be tempted to tilt their decisions in favor of corporations, law firms, or interest groups that promise these officials well-paid jobs after they leave government employment (see *What Do You Think?* "Is It What You Know or Who You Know?").

The Ethics in Government Act limits postgovernment employment in an effort to reduce the potential for corruption. Former members of Congress are not permitted to lobby Congress for one year after leaving that body. Former employees of executive agencies are not permitted to lobby their agency for one year after leaving government service, and they are not permitted to lobby their agency for two years on any matter over which they had any responsibility while employed by the government. President Bill Clinton requires top officials in his administration to sign a pledge that they will not lobby their former agencies for five years and that they will never represent a foreign government.

## LOBBYING THE COURTS

Interest groups play an important role in influencing federal courts. Many of the key cases brought to the federal courts are initiated by interest groups. Indeed, **litigation** is becoming a favored instrument of interest group politics. Groups that oppose a new law or an agency's action often challenge it in court as unconstitutional or as violating the law. Interest groups bring issues to the courts by (1) supplying the attorneys for individuals who are parties to a case; (2) bringing suits to the courts on behalf of classes of citizens; or (3) filing companion **amicus curiae** (literally "friend of the court") arguments in cases in which they are

**Revolving doors:** The movement of individuals from government positions to jobs in the private sector, using the experience, knowledge, and contacts they acquired in government employment.

**Litigation:** A legal dispute brought before a court.

**Amicus curiae:** Person or group other than the defendant or the plaintiff or the prosecution that submits an argument in a case for the court's consideration.

# Is It What You Know or Who You Know?

A majority of paid lobbyists in Washington come to their jobs from government. The "revolving door" complaint is that these people exploit their government experience for private gain. A survey of Washington lobbyists revealed that 55 percent had held some government position before becoming a lobbyist. More had worked in the executive branch than in Congress, and a few had worked in both branches of government. Full-time staff lobbyists for interest groups had somewhat less government experience than independent lawyer lobbyists (78 percent of whom had government experience) and professional lobbying consultants (62 percent of whom had government experience).

How helpful is this experience, and, more important, is it "what you know" or "who you know" that counts most in lobbying? The "good old boy" theory of lobbying suggests that success depends mostly on contacts with officials, knowing them personally and maintaining warm relations with them, so that when they are asked to do something, they are most likely to respond favorably. But the knowledge theory of lobbying suggests that success is more a product of (1) knowledge about legislative and bureaucratic processes; and (2) substantive policy expertise.

When lobbyists themselves are asked questions on this topic, they acknowledge that government experience is important in lobbying (see table). Some 87 percent of lobbyists reported that their time in government was helpful in their present work; 80 percent said that it helped them to gain familiarity with the policy-making process; and 70 percent reported that it gave them familiarity with the issues. Government experience is also helpful in making contacts with decision makers. Contacts made through congressional experience appear to be more important than contacts made through executive branch experience. But, according to the lobbyists themselves, "what you know" is more important than "who you know."

**Helpfulness of Government Experience**

|  | *Responses by Lobbyists with Congressional Experience* | *Responses by Lobbyists with Executive Experience* |
|---|---|---|
| Government experience provides: |  |  |
| Issue familiarity | 72% | 72% |
| Knowledge of decision-making process | 92 | 81 |
| Contacts in administration | 48 | 53 |
| Contacts in Congress | 87 | 49 |

*Source:* Derived from Robert H. Salisbury et al., "Who You Know versus What You Know: The Uses of Government Experience for Washington Lobbyists," *American Journal of Political Science* 33 (February 1989): 175–195.

interested. The number of interest groups that choose to involve themselves in a pending court case can be staggering. Abortion, for example, a very "hot topic" in the U.S. judicial system over the last twenty years, prompted a total of seventy-seven interest groups to file amicus curiae briefs in an attempt to sway members of the Supreme Court in 1989 (see Table 9-8).[11]

TABLE 9-8 AMICUS CURIAE: PETITIONING THE SUPREME COURT ON ABORTION

*Amicus Curiae Briefs Filed in Webster v. Reproductive Health Services (1989)*

| *Pro-abortion Rights* | *Anti-abortion Rights* |
|---|---|
| 1. American Civil Liberties Union | 1. Agudeth Israel of America |
| 2. 281 American historians | 2. Alabama Lawyers for Unborn Children |
| 3. American Jewish Congress et al. | 3. Edward Allen |
| 4. American Library Association and Freedom to Read Foundation | 4. American Academy of Medical Ethics |
| 5. American Medical Association et al. | 5. American Association of Pro-Life Ob-Gyns et al. |
| 6. American Nurses Association et al. | 6. American Collegians for Life et al. |
| 7. American Public Health Association et al. | 7. American Family Association |
| 8. American Psychological Association | 8. American Life League |
| 9. Americans for Democratic Action et al. | 9. Association for Public Justice et al. |
| 10. Americans United for Separation of Church and State | 10. Attorneys general of Louisiana, Arizona, Idaho, Pennsylvania, Wisconsin |
| 11. Association of Reproductive Health Professionals et al. | 11. Birthright, Inc. |
| 12. Attorneys general of California, Colorado, Massachusetts, New York, Texas, Vermont | 12. Catholic Health Association of the United States |
| 13. Bioethicists for Privacy | 13. Catholics United for Life et al. |
| 14. California National Organization for Women et al. | 14. Center for Judicial Studies and 56 members of Congress |
| 15. Canadian Women's Organizations et al. | 15. 250 state legislators |
| 16. Catholics for a Free Choice et al. | 16. 69 members of Pennsylvania General Assembly |
| 17. Center for Population Options et al. | 17. Christian Advocates Serving Evangelism |
| 18. 140 members of Congress | 18. Covenant House and Good Counsel |
| 19. 3 committees of the Bar of New York City | 19. Doctors for Life et al. |
| 20. 167 scientists and physicians | 20. Feminists for Life et al. |
| 21. Group of American law professors | 21. Focus on Family et al. |
| 22. International Women's Health Organization et al. | 22. Free Speech Advocates |
| 23. National Association of Public Hospitals | 23. Holy Orthodox Church |
| 24. National Association of Women Lawyers et al. | 24. Human Life International |
| 25. National Coalition against Domestic Violence | 25. International Right to Life Federations |
| 26. National Council of Negro Women et al. | 26. Larry Joyce |
| 27. National Family Planning et al. | 27. Knights of Columbus |
| 28. National Organization for Women | 28. Lutheran Church—Missouri Synod |
| 29. 77 organizations committed to equality | 29. James Joseph Lynch, Jr. |
| 30. Population-Environmental Balance et al. | 30. Paul Marx |
| 31. 608 state legislators | 31. 127 members of Missouri General Assembly |
| 32. 2,887 women who had abortions et al. | 32. Missouri Catholic Conference |
| | 33. Bernard Nathanson, M.D. |
| | 34. National Legal Foundation |
| | 35. National Right-to-Life Committee |
| | 36. New England Christian Action Council |
| | 37. Right-to-Life Advocates |
| | 38. Right-to-Life League of Southern California |
| | 39. Rutherford Institute et al. |
| | 40. 53 members of Congress |
| | 41. Southern Center for Law and Ethics |
| | 42. Southwest Life and Law Center |
| | 43. United States (Office of Solicitor General) |
| | 44. U.S. Catholic Conference |
| | 45. Austin Vaughn and Crusade for Life |

*Source: Webster v. Reproductive Health Services,* 492 U.S. 490 (1989).
Numbers before each entry signify the number of signatures on a brief from individuals.

The nation's most powerful interest groups all have legal divisions specializing in these techniques. The American Civil Liberties Union is one of the most active federal court litigants on behalf of criminal defendants (see *Up Close:* "Politics and the ACLU" in Chapter 14). The early civil rights strategy of the National Association for the Advancement of Colored People (NAACP) was directed by its Legal Defense Fund under the leadership of Thurgood Marshall (see *People in Politics:* "Thurgood Marshall" in Chapter 15). The NAACP chose to sponsor a suit by Linda Brown against the Board of Education in her hometown—Topeka, Kansas—in order to win a historic desegregation decision.[12] The National Abortion Rights Action League (NARAL) is active in sponsoring legal challenges to abortion restrictions. The Environmental Defense Fund and the Natural Resources Defense Council specialize in environmental litigation.

The special rules of judicial decision making preclude direct lobbying of judges by interest groups (see "The Special Rules of Judicial Decision Making" in Chapter 13). Directly contacting federal judges about a case, letter writing, telephoning, and demonstrating outside of federal courtrooms are all considered inappropriate conduct. They inspire more resentment than support among federal judges. However, interest groups have been very active in direct lobbying of Congress over judicial appointments. Key interest groups supporting abortion rights—the National Abortion Rights Action League, People for the American Way, the National Organization for Women, and so on—have played a central role in recent confirmation battles (see *Up Close:* "The Confirmation of Clarence Thomas" in Chapter 13).

## POLITICS AS INTEREST-GROUP CONFLICT

Politics can be viewed as a struggle among interest groups over government policy. Interest groups, rather than individual citizens, can be viewed as the principal participants in American politics.

*Pluralism as Democratic Politics*    Pluralism (see Chapter 2) is the idea that democracy can be preserved in a large, complex society through individual membership in interest groups that compete, bargain, and compromise over government policy. Individuals are influential in politics only when they act as part of, or on behalf of, groups. (Only leaders of organizations participate directly in policy making.) The group becomes the essential bridge between the individual and the government. Pluralists argue that interest-group politics is a natural extension of the democratic ideals of popular participation in government, freedom of association, and competition over public policy.

Pluralism portrays public policy at any given time as the equilibrium reached in the struggle among interest groups to influence policy (see Figure 9-3). This equilibrium is determined by the relative influence of interest groups. Changes in the relative influence of any interest group can be expected to result in changes in public policy; policy will move in the direction desired by the groups gaining in influence and away from the desires of groups losing influence.

According to this view of political life, government plays a passive role, merely "refereeing" group struggles. Public policy at any given moment represents the "equilibrium" point of the group pressures—the balance of competing interests. The job of politicians is to function as "brokers" of group interests, arranging compromises and balancing interests.

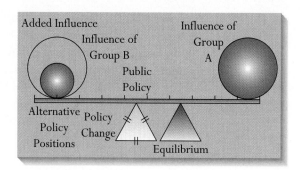

FIGURE 9.3 **The Interest-Group Model**

*According to pluralist theorists, policy in a democracy is the result of various special interest groups "reaching equilibrium"—arriving at a compromise position that requires all parties to give up something but gives all parties something they wanted.*

*Balancing Group Power*    Pluralism assumes that compromises *can* be arranged and that interests *can* be balanced in relatively stable fashion. It assumes that no single interest will ever become so dominant that it can reject compromise and proceed to impose its will on the nation without regard for the interests of other people. This assumption is based upon several beliefs. The first is that interest groups act as a check upon each other and that a system of *countervailing power* will protect the interests of all. For example, the power of big business will be checked by the countervailing power of big labor and big government.

A second belief is that *overlapping group membership* will tend to moderate the demands of particular groups and lead to compromise. Since no group can command the undivided loyalty of all its members, its demands will be less drastic and its leaders more amenable to compromise. If the leaders of any group go too far with their demands, those of its members who also belong to other groups endangered by these immoderate demands will balk.

A third belief is that radical programs and doctrinaire demands will be checked by the large, unorganized, but potentially significant *latent interest group* that is composed of all Americans who believe in toleration, compromise, and democratic processes.

*Interest-Group Politics: How Democratic?*    There are several problems with accepting pluralism as the legitimate heir to classic democratic theory. Democratic theory envisions public policy as the rational choice of individuals with equal influence who evaluate their needs and reach a majority decision with due regard for the rights of others. This traditional theory does not view public policy as a product of interest-group pressures. In fact, classical democratic theorists viewed interest groups and even political parties as intruders into an individualistic brand of citizenship and politics. Today critics of pluralism charge that interest groups dominate the political arena, monopolize access to governmental power, and thereby restrict individual participation rather than enhance it.

Pluralism contends that different groups of leaders make decisions about different issues, but critics charge that these leaders do not necessarily compete with each other. Rather, groups of leaders often allow other groups of leaders to govern their own spheres of influence without interference. Accommodation, rather than competition, may be the prevailing style of leadership interaction: "You scratch my back, and I'll scratch yours."

Another assumption of pluralism is that group membership enhances the individual's influence on policy. But only rarely are interest groups democratically governed. Individuals may provide the numerical strength for organizations, but interest groups are usually run by a small elite of officers and activists. Leaders of corporations, banks, labor unions, medical associations, and bar associations—whose views and agendas often differ from those of their membership—remain in control year after year. Very few people attend meetings, vote in organizational elections, or make their influence felt within their organization.

Finally, pluralists hope that the power of diverse institutions and organizations in society will roughly balance out and prevent the emergence of a power monopoly. Yet inequality of power among organizations is commonplace. Examples abound of narrow, organized interests achieving their goals at the expense of the broader, unorganized public. Furthermore, producer interests, bound together by economic ties, usually dominate less well organized consumer groups and groups based on noneconomic interests. Special interests seeking governmental subsidies, payments, and "entitlements" regularly prevail over the broader yet unorganized interests of taxpayers.

*Interest-Group Politics: Gridlock and Paralysis*    Even if the pluralists are correct that the public interest is only the equilibrium of special interest claims, some consensus among major interest groups is required if government is to function at all. Democracies require a sense of community and common purpose among the people. If the demands of special interests displace the public interest, government cannot function effectively. Uncompromising claims by conflicting special interests create policy *gridlock*. Yet if politicians try to placate every special interest, the result is confusing, contradictory, and muddled policy—or worse, no policy at all.

Interest group paralysis and the resulting inability of government to act decisively to resolve national problems weaken popular confidence in government. "The function of government is to govern. A weak government, a government which lacks authority, fails to perform its function, is immoral in the same sense in which a corrupt judge, a cowardly soldier, or an ignorant teacher, is immoral."[13]

Over time, the continued buildup of special protections, privileges, and treatments in society results in "institutional sclerosis." Economist Mancur Olson argues that the accumulation of special interest subsidies, quotas, and protections leads to economic stagnation. Interest groups focus on gaining distributive advantages—a larger share of the pie for themselves—rather than on growth of the whole economy—a larger pie.[14] Major interest groups are more interested in winning income transfers to themselves through government action than in promoting the growth of national income. The more entrenched the interest group system becomes, the slower the growth of the national economy.

# SUMMARY NOTES

- Organizations concentrate power, and concentrated power prevails over diffused power. Interest groups are organizations that seek to influence government policy.
- The interest-group system supplements the electoral system as a form of representation. The electoral system is designed to respond to broad,

majority preferences in geographically defined constituencies. The interest-group system represents narrower, minority interests in economic, professional, ideological, religious, racial, gender, and issue constituencies.

- Interest groups originated to protect economic interests, to advance social movements, to seek government benefits, and to respond to government activity. As government has expanded into more sectors of American life, more interest groups have formed to influence government policy.

- Washington lobbying groups represent a wide array of organized interests. But business, trade, and professional associations outnumber labor union, women's, public interest, single-issue, and ideological groups.

- Interest-group formation has been aided in recent decades by entrepreneurs who create and build group memberships. They urge people to join organizations either by appealing to their sense of obligation or by providing an array of direct tangible benefits.

- Most organized groups are dominated by small groups of leaders and activists. Few groups are governed democratically; members who oppose the direction of the organization usually drop out rather than challenge the leadership. Group membership and especially group leadership overrepresent educated, upper-middle-class segments of the population.

- Lobbying activities include advertising and public relations, obtaining access to government officials, providing them with technical and political information, mobilizing constituents, building coalitions, organizing demonstrations, and providing campaign support. Bribery is illegal, and most lobbyists avoid exacting specific vote promises in exchange for campaign contributions.

- Organized political action committees (PACs) proliferated following the 1974 "reform" of campaign finance laws. Most PAC money goes to incumbents; interest-group leaders know that incumbents are rarely defeated.

- The mutual interests of organized groups, congressional committees, and bureaucratic agencies sometimes come together to form "iron triangles" of mutual support and cooperation in specific policy areas. In many policy areas, loose "policy networks" emerge among people who share an interest and expertise—though not necessarily opinions—about a policy and are in regular contact with each other.

- The "revolving door" problem emerges when individuals use the knowledge, experience, and contacts obtained through government employment to secure high-paying jobs with corporations, law firms, lobbying and consulting firms, and interest groups doing business with their old agencies.

- Interest groups influence the nation's courts not only by providing financial and legal support for issues of concern to them but also by lobbying Congress over judicial appointments.

- Pluralism views interest-group activities as a form of democratic representation. According to the pluralists, public policy reflects the equilibrium of group influence and a reasonable approximation of society's preferences. Competition among groups, overlapping group memberships, and latent interest groups all combine to ensure that no single group dominates the system.

- Critics of pluralism warn that interest groups may monopolize power and restrict individual participation in politics rather than enhance it. They note that interest groups are not usually democratically governed, nor are their leaders or members representative of the general population. They warn that accommodation rather than competition may characterize group interaction and that narrow producer interests tend to achieve their goals at the expense of broader consumer (taxpayer) interests.

- The growing power of special interests, when combined with the declining power of parties and the fragmentation of government, may lead to gridlock and paralysis in policy making. The general public interest may be lost in the conflicting claims of special interests.

## SELECTED READINGS

BIRNBAUM, JEFFREY H., and ALAN S. MURRAY. *Showdown at Gucci Gulch: Lobbyists, Lawmakers and the Unlikely Triumph of Tax Reform.* New York: Vintage, 1987. An entertaining case study of how tax reform in 1986 passed over the strenuous objections of the well-paid Gucci-dressed lobbyists.

CIGLER, ALLAN J., and BURDETT A. LOOMIS, EDS. *Interest Group Politics,* 4th ed. Washington, D.C.: Congressional Quarterly Press, 1994. A collection of essays examining interest group politics.

HREBENAR, RONALD J. *Interest Group Politics in America,* 3rd ed. New York: M.E. Sharpe, 1996. A concise, readable, and timely introduction to the study of group power.

LOWI, THEODORE J. *The End of Liberalism.* New York: Norton, 1969. The classic critique of "interest group liberalism," describing how special interests contribute to the growth of government and the development of "clientism."

MUCCIARONI, GARY. *Public Policy and Private Interests.* Washington: Brookings, 1995. Identifying the factors that contribute to the victory or defeat of producer groups—firms, industries, professional and trade associations—in the policy process.

OLSON, MANCUR. *The Logic of Collective Action.* Cambridge, Mass.: Harvard University Press, 1965. A highly theoretical inquiry into the benefits and costs to individuals of joining groups and the obstacles (including the free-rider problem) to forming organized interest groups.

OLSON, MANCUR. *The Rise and Decline of Nations.* New Haven, Conn.: Yale University Press, 1982. Argues that, over time, the development of powerful special interest lobbies has led to institutional sclerosis, inefficiency, and slowed economic growth.

SCHLOZMAN, KAY LEHMANN, and JOHN T. TIERNEY. *Organized Interests and American Democracy.* New York: Harper and Row, 1986. Comprehensive examination of interest groups in American politics, with original survey data from Washington lobbyists.

STERN, PHILIP M. *Still the Best Congress Money Can Buy.* Washington: Regnery Press, 1992. A muckraking account of interest group activities and PAC contributions and how they threaten democratic government.

TRUMAN, DAVID B. *The Governmental Process.* New York: Knopf, 1951. The classic description and defense of interest-group pluralism.

WALKER, JACK L. *Mobilizing Interest Groups in America: Patrons, Professions, and Social Movements.* Ann Arbor: University of Michigan Press, 1991. A study of mobilization and maintenance of interest groups, based on large-scale mail surveys of Washington-based membership associations. It includes chapters on how and why organizations are formed, what inducements members are offered, and what influences leaders' choices of strategy.

# CONGRESS
# POLITICS ON CAPITOL HILL

## CHAPTER OUTLINE

## FEATURES

## THE POWERS OF CONGRESS

James Madison argued that the control of "faction" was "the principal task of modern legislation."[1] He meant that in enacting laws, legislators were really balancing interests, finding compromises, and resolving conflicts. Public policies—laws, regulations, and budgets—represent temporary balances of power among conflicting interests. As the relative power of these interests changes over time, new laws, amendments, and increases or decreases in funding will be enacted, reflecting new balances of power.

## ASK YOURSELF ABOUT POLITICS

**1** Should members of Congress be limited in the number of terms they can serve?
Yes ◯  No ◯

**2** Should congressional districts be drawn to ensure that minorities win seats in Congress in rough proportion to their populations in the states?
Yes ◯  No ◯

**3** Should a party's candidates for Congress across the country join together and pledge to support specific policy positions?
Yes ◯  No ◯

**4** Would the nation be better served if the president and the majority in Congress were from the same party?
Yes ◯  No ◯

**5** Is it ethical for Congress members to pay special attention to requests for assistance by people who make large campaign contributions?
Yes ◯  No ◯

**6** Are there too many lawyers in Congress?
Yes ◯  No ◯

**7** Are members of Congress obliged to vote the way their constituents wish, even if they personally disagree?
Yes ◯  No ◯

**8** Are members of Congress obligated to support bills submitted to them by a president of their own party?
Yes ◯  No ◯

Who are the members of Congress? How did they get there, and how do they manage to stay there? How did Congress—the official institution for deciding who gets what in America—get its powers, and how does it use them?

327

*Constitutional Powers*   The Constitution gives very broad powers to Congress. "All legislative Powers herein granted shall be vested in a Congress of the United States, which shall consist of a Senate and House of Representatives." The nation's Founders envisioned Congress as the first and most powerful branch of government. They equated national powers with the powers of Congress and gave Congress the most clearly specified role in national government.

Article I empowers Congress to levy taxes, borrow and spend money, regulate interstate commerce, establish a national money supply, establish a post office, declare war, raise and support an army and navy, establish a court system, and pass all laws "necessary and proper" to implement these powers. Congress may also propose amendments to the Constitution or call a convention to do so. Congress admits new states. In the event that no presidential candidate receives a majority of votes in the Electoral College, the House of Representatives selects the president. The Senate is called on for "advice and consent" to treaties and approves presidential nominations to executive and judicial posts. The House has the power to impeach, and the Senate to try, any officer of the U.S. government, including the president. Congress may also conduct investigations on any topic it chooses, discipline its own members, and regulate its internal affairs (see Table 10-1).

*Institutional Conflict*   Over two centuries, the separate branches of the national government—the Congress, the presidency and the executive branch, and the Supreme Court and federal judiciary—have struggled for power and pre-

---

**TABLE 10-1   CONSTITUTIONAL POWERS OF CONGRESS**

| Powers of Both House and Senate | Powers of House Only | Powers of Senate Only |
|---|---|---|
| • Appropriate money ⎫ the "power • Authorize borrowing ⎬ of the purse" • Levy taxes ⎭ <br> • Regulate currency and punish counterfeiting <br> • Establish post office and post roads <br> • Make bankruptcy laws <br> • Regulate interstate and foreign commerce <br> • Establish rules of naturalization <br> • Fix weights and measures <br> • Make patent and copyright law <br> • Provide for government of District of Columbia <br> • Admit new states <br> • Establish lower federal courts <br> • Propose amendments to the Constitution <br> • Declare war ⎫ <br> • Raise and support military forces ⎬ War-making Powers <br> • Provide for militia ⎭ <br> • "Make all laws which shall be necessary and proper for carrying into Execution the foregoing Powers, and all other powers vested by this Constitution in the Government of the United States" ⎬ Implied Powers | • Originate tax bills <br> • Bring impeachment charges | • Advise and consent to (ratify) treaties <br> • Confirm appointments to Supreme Court and federal judiciary, ambassador, cabinet, and other high executive posts <br> • Try impeachments |

---

CHAPTER 10 • CONGRESS: POLITICS ON CAPITOL HILL

eminence in governing. This struggle for power among the separate institutions is precisely what the Founders envisioned. In writing the Constitution, they sought to create "opposite and rival interests" among the separate branches of the national government. "The constant aim," explained Madison, "is to divide and arrange the several offices in such a manner as that each may be a check on the other."[2] From time to time, first the Congress, then the presidency, and occasionally the Supreme Court have appeared to become the most powerful branch of government.

Throughout much of the twentieth century, Congress ceded leadership in national policy making to the president and the executive branch. Congress largely responded to the policy initiatives and spending requests originating from the president, executive agencies, and interest groups. Congress did *not* merely ratify or "rubber stamp" these initiatives and requests; it played an independent role in the policy-making process. But this role was essentially a deliberative one, in which Congress accepted, modified, amended, or rejected the policies and budget requests initiated by others.

It is easier for the Congress to obstruct the policy initiatives of the president than it is to assume policy leadership itself. Congress can defeat presidential policy proposals, deny presidential budget requests, delay or reject presidential appointments, investigate executive agencies, hold committee hearings to spotlight improprieties, and generally immobilize the executive branch. It can investigate and question nominees for the Supreme Court and the federal judiciary; it can legislate changes in the jurisdiction of the federal courts; and it can try to reverse court decisions by amending laws or the Constitution itself. The Congress can even threaten to impeach the president or federal judges. But these are largely reactive, obstructionist actions, usually accompanied by a great deal of oratory.

In recent years, however, Congress has attempted to reassert national leadership. This effort was especially obvious in the 104th Congress, elected in 1994 and controlled by Republicans for the first time in forty years. The House of Representatives, under Speaker Newt Gingrich, undertook to set the nation's policy agenda in its "Contract with America" (see Chapter 7, *Up Close:* "The Republican 'Contract with America'"). Although most of the promises in this contract failed to pass and some were vetoed by the president, the important institutional lesson was that the House of Representatives *can* seize the policy initiative from time to time. Nevertheless, over the long term, national leadership and policy initiative have tended to shift from Congress to the president.

*Dividing Congressional Power: House and Senate*   Congress must not only share national power with the executive and judicial branches of government; it must share power within itself. The framers of the Constitution took the advice of the nation's eldest diplomat, Benjamin Franklin: "It is not enough that your legislature should be numerous; it should also be divided. . . . One division should watch over and control the other, supply its wants, correct its blunders, and cross its designs, should they be criminal or erroneous."[3] Accordingly, the U.S. Congress is **bicameral**—composed of two houses (see Figure 10-1).

No law can be passed and no money can be spent unless both the House of Representatives and the Senate pass identical laws. Yet the House and the Senate have very different constituencies and terms. The House consists of 435 voting members, elected from districts within each state apportioned on the basis of

**Bicameral:** Any representative legislative body that consists of two separate chambers or houses; in the United States, the Senate represents 50 statewide voter constituencies, while the House of Representatives represents voters in 435 separate districts.

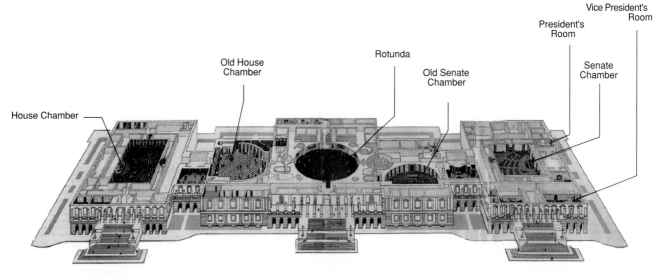

Vice President's
Room

President's
Room

Rotunda

Old House
Chamber

Old Senate
Chamber

Senate
Chamber

House Chamber

**FIGURE 10-1**  **Corridors of Power in Congress**

*The architecture and floor plan of the Capitol Building in Washington reflect the bicameral division of Congress, with one wing for the House of Representatives and one for the Senate.*

equal population. (The average congressional district since the 1990 census has a population of 571,700; the House also includes nonvoting delegates from Puerto Rico, the District of Columbia, Guam, the Virgin Islands, and American Samoa.) All House members face election every two years. The Senate consists of 100 members serving six-year terms, elected by statewide constituencies. Senate terms are staggered so that one-third of senators are elected every two years.

Congress was designed to represent local and state interests in policy making. The House of Representatives, with its two-year terms, was designed to be more responsive to the popular mood. Representatives are fond of referring to their chamber as "the people's House." The Constitution requires that all revenue-raising bills originate in the House. The Senate was designed to be a more deliberative body, with its members serving six-year terms and, until passage of the Seventeenth Amendment in 1913, chosen by state legislatures, not directly by voters. Indeed, the Senate is the more prestigious body. House members frequently give up their seats to run for the Senate, while the reverse has seldom occurred. Moreover, the Senate exercises certain powers not given to the House: the power to ratify treaties and the power to confirm federal judges, ambassadors, cabinet members, and other high executive officials.

*Domestic versus Foreign and Defense Policy*   Congress is more powerful in domestic than in foreign and military affairs. It is freer to reject presidential initiatives in domestic policy areas—for example, welfare, health, education, the environment, or taxation. But Congress usually follows presidential leadership in foreign and defense policy. Constitutionally, the president and Congress share power in these arenas. The president is "Commander-in-Chief" of the armed forces, but only Congress can "declare war." The president appoints and receives ambassadors and "makes Treaties," but the Senate must confirm appointments and provide "advice and consent" to treaties. Historically presidents have led the nation in matters of war and peace. Presidents have sent U.S. troops beyond the borders of the United States in military actions on more than 200 occasions. In contrast, Congress has formally declared war only five times: the War of 1812, the Mexican War in 1846, the Spanish-American War in 1898, World War I in 1917, and World War II in 1941. Congress did not declare war in the Korean War (1950–53), the Vietnam War (1965–73), or the Persian Gulf War (1991).

The Vietnam experience inspired Congress to try to reassert its powers over war and peace. Military embarrassment, prolonged and indecisive fighting, and accumulating casualties—all vividly displayed on national television—encouraged Congress to challenge presidential war-making power. The War Powers Act of 1973, passed over the veto of President Richard Nixon, who was weakened by the Watergate scandal, sought to curtail the president's power to commit U.S. military forces to combat (see "Commander-in-Chief" in Chapter 11). But this act has not proven effective, and both Republican and Democratic presidents have continued to exercise war-making powers.

*The Power of the Purse* Congress's real power in both domestic and foreign (defense) policy centers on its **power of the purse**—its power over federal taxing and spending. Only Congress can "lay and collect Taxes, Duties, Imposts and Excises" (Article I, Section 8), and only Congress can authorize spending: "No Money shall be drawn from the Treasury, but in Consequence of Appropriations made by Law" (Article I, Section 9).

Congress jealously guards these powers. Presidents initiate taxing and spending policies by sending their budgets to the Congress each year (see "The Bureaucracy and the Budgetary Process" in Chapter 12 for details). But Congress has the last word on taxing and spending. The most important bills that Congress considers each year are usually the budget resolutions setting ceilings on various categories of expenditures and the later appropriations bills authorizing specific expenditures. It is often in these appropriations bills that Congress exercises its greatest influence over national policy. Thus, for example, the Congress's involvement in foreign affairs centers on its annual consideration of appropriations for foreign aid, its involvement in military affairs centers on its annual deliberations over the defense appropriations bill, and so on.

*Oversight of the Bureaucracy* Congressional **oversight** of the federal bureaucracy is a continuing process by which Congress reviews the activities of the executive branch. The *formal* rationale of oversight is to determine whether the purposes of laws passed by Congress are being achieved by executive agencies and whether appropriations established by Congress are being spent as intended. Often the *real* purpose is to influence executive branch decisions, secure favorable treatment for friends and constituents, embarrass presidential appointees, undercut political support for particular programs or agencies, lay the political groundwork for budgetary increases or decreases for an agency, or simply enhance the power of congressional committees and subcommittees and those who chair them.

Oversight is carried out primarily through congressional committees and subcommittees. Individual senators and representatives can engage in a form of oversight simply by writing or calling executive agencies, but committees and their staffs carry on the bulk of oversight activity. Because committees and subcommit-

**Power of the purse:** Congress's exclusive, constitutional power to authorize expenditures by all agencies of the federal government.

**Oversight:** Congressional monitoring of the activities of executive branch agencies to determine if the laws are being faithfully executed.

tees specialize in particular areas of policy making, each tends to focus its oversight activities on particular executive departments and agencies. Oversight is particularly intense during budget hearings. Subcommittees of both the House and the Senate Appropriations Committees are especially interested in how money is being spent by the agencies they oversee.

Oversight often begins when special interest groups or constituents complain about bureaucratic performance. While minor complaints can be resolved by members of Congress or their staffs contacting the executive agency involved, executive officials may also be called to a congressional committee or subcommittee hearing to explain and defend their actions. Sitting before a hostile congressional committee in the glare of television cameras and responding to unfriendly questions can be embarrassing and unpleasant. Thus executive officials have a powerful motivation to comply with the wishes of a member of Congress and escape such treatment.

*Agenda Setting and Media Attention* **Congressional hearings** and investigations often involve agenda setting—bringing issues to the public's attention and placing them on the national agenda. For agenda-setting purposes, congressional committees or subcommittees need the assistance of the media. Televised hearings and investigations are perhaps the most effective means by which Congress can attract attention to issues as well as to itself and its members.

Hearings and investigations are similar in some ways, but hearings are usually held on a specific bill in order to build a record of both technical information (what is the problem and how legislation might be crafted to resolve it) and political information (who favors and who opposes various legislative options). In contrast, investigations are held on alleged misdeeds or scandals. While the U.S. Supreme Court has held that there must be some "legislative purpose" behind a **congressional investigation,** that phrase has been interpreted very broadly indeed.[4]

The *formal* rationale for congressional investigations is that Congress is seeking information to assist in its lawmaking function. But from the earliest Congress to the present, the investigating powers of Congress have often been used for political purposes: to rally popular support for policies or programs favored by Congress; to attack the president, high officials in the administration, or presidential policies or programs; to focus media attention and public debate on particular issues; or simply to win media coverage and popular recognition for members of Congress. Congressional investigators have the legal power to subpoena witnesses (force them to appear), administer oaths, cross-examine, compel testimony, and bring criminal charges for contempt (refusing to cooperate) and perjury (lying). These powers can be exercised by Congress's regular committees and subcommittees and by committees appointed especially to conduct a particular investigation.

Congress cannot impose criminal punishments as a result of its investigations. (This would be a *bill of attainder* forbidden by Article I, Section 9 of the Constitution.) But the information uncovered in a congressional investigation can be turned over to the U.S. Department of Justice, which may proceed with its own criminal investigation and perhaps indictment and trial of alleged wrongdoers in federal courts.

Congressional investigations have long been used as an opportunity for Congress to expose wrongdoing on the part of executive branch officials. The first

**Congressional hearings:**
Congressional committee sessions in which members listen to witnesses who provide information and opinions on matters of interest to the committee, including pending legislation.

**Congressional investigation:**
Congressional committee hearings on alleged misdeeds or scandals.

CHAPTER 10 • CONGRESS: POLITICS ON CAPITOL HILL

congressional investigation (1792) examined why General Arthur St. Clair had been defeated by the Indians in Ohio; the Crédit Mobilier investigations (1872–73) revealed scandals in the Grant Administration; the Select Committee on Campaign Practices, known universally as the "Watergate Committee," exposed the activities of President Richard Nixon's inner circle that led to impeachment charges and Nixon's forced resignation; a House and Senate Joint Select Committee conducted the "Iran-Contra" investigation in the Reagan Administration; and the Senate Special Whitewater Committee investigated matters related to Bill and Hillary Clinton's real estate investments in Arkansas.

*Conflict Management*   Congress plays a central role in managing the nation's conflicts. Congressional hearings and investigations and the media attention they generate allow conflicts to be aired, give groups and individuals an opportunity to plead their policy preferences, and familiarize the general public with the operations of government. Public hearings and even floor debate help to legitimize law and government. These activities help persuade citizens that laws have a purpose and rationale, that Congress studies and deliberates over the laws it passes, and that Congress is trying to cope with the problems of society.

# CONGRESSIONAL APPORTIONMENT AND REDISTRICTING

The Constitution states that "Representatives . . . shall be apportioned among the several states . . . according to their respective Numbers." It orders an "actual enumeration" (census) every ten years. And it provides that every state shall have at least one representative, in addition to two senators, regardless of population. But the Constitution is silent on the size of the House of Representatives. Congress itself determines its own size; for more than a century, it allowed itself to grow to accommodate new states and population growth. In 1910, it fixed the membership of the House at 435.

*Apportionment*   **Apportionment** refers to the allocation of House seats to the states after each ten-year census. The Constitution does not specify a mathematical method of apportionment; Congress adopted a complex "method of equal proportion" in 1929, which so far has withstood court challenges (see *Across the USA:* "Apportionment of House Seats, 1990s," which shows the current apportionment, together with the states that gained and lost seats after the 1990 census).

*Malapportionment*   The Constitution does not determine how the states should apportion seats among their own citizens. State legislatures were long notorious for their **malapportionment**—congressional (and state legislative) districts with grossly unequal numbers of people. Most congressional districts were within 15 percent of the national average, but some had twice the average number of people per district, while others had only half as many. In 1962, for example, Georgia's congressional districts varied in size from a rural district of 272,154 to an Atlanta district of 823,860. In a district twice the size of the average district, the value of an individual's vote was heavily

**Apportionment:** The allocation of legislative seats to jurisdictions based upon population. Seats in the U.S. House of Representatives are apportioned to the states on the basis of their population after every ten-year census.

**Malapportionment:** Unequal numbers of people in legislative districts resulting in inequality of voter representation.

# Apportionment of House Seats, 1990s

*When the number of seats in the House of Representatives stays constant, as it has at 435 seats since 1910, each census requires a reapportionment of seats among the states. States such as Arizona, which gained population between 1980 and 1990, gained seats. States such as Illinois, which lost population in that same period, lost seats. Changing population statistics do not affect Senate seats, however, since the Constitution stipulates that every state shall have two senators, elected by all voters in the state, regardless of the state's population.*

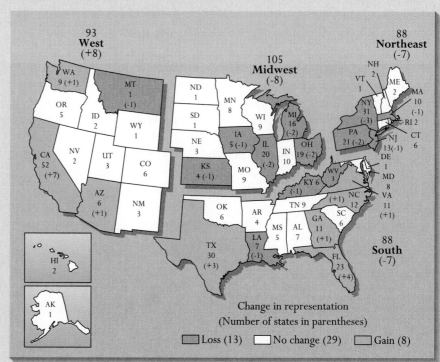

diluted. In a district half the size of the average, the value of an individual's vote was greatly magnified.

*Enter the Supreme Court* Prior to 1962, the Supreme Court refused to intervene in apportionment, holding that this question belonged to the state legislatures and that the federal courts should avoid this "political thicket." So the Supreme Court's decision in the landmark case *Baker v. Carr* (1962) came as a surprise. The Court ruled that inequalities in voters' influence resulting from different-size districts violated the Equal Protection Clause of the Fourteenth Amendment. The case dealt with a complaint about Tennessee's state legislative districts, but the Court soon extended its holding to congressional districts as well.[5] "The conception of political equality from the Declaration of Independence to Lincoln's Gettysburg Address, to the Fourteenth, Fifteenth, Seventeenth, and Nineteenth Amendments, can mean only one thing—one person, one vote."[6]

The shift in the Supreme Court's policy raised a new question: How equal must districts be in order to guarantee voters "equal protection of the law"? The courts

have ruled that only official U.S. Census figures may be used: estimated changes since the last census may *not* be used. In recent years, the courts have insisted on nearly exact mathematical equality in congressional districts.

*Redistricting*   **Redistricting** refers to the drawing of boundary lines of congressional districts following the census. After each census, some states gain and others lose seats, depending on whether their populations have grown faster or slower than the nation's population. In addition, population shifts within a state may force districting changes. Congressional district boundaries are drawn by state legislatures in each state; a state's redistricting act must pass both houses of the state legislature and win the governor's signature (or be passed over a gubernatorial veto). The U.S. Justice Department and the federal judiciary are also deeply involved in redistricting issues, particularly questions of whether or not redistricting disadvantages African Americans or other minorities.

*Gerrymandering*   **Gerrymandering** is the drawing of district lines for political advantage (see Figure 10-2). The population of districts may be equal, yet the district boundaries are drawn in such a fashion as to grant advantage or disadvantage to specific groups of voters. Gerrymandering has long been used by parties in control of the state legislatures to maximize their seats in Congress and state legislatures.

Gerrymandering, with the aid of sophisticated computer-mapping programs and data on past voting records of precincts, is a highly technical task. But consider a simple example where a city is entitled to three representatives and the eastern third of the city is Republican while the western two-thirds is Demo-

**Redistricting:** Drawing of
legislative district boundary lines
following each ten-year census.

**Gerrymandering:** Drawing
district boundary lines for
political advantage.

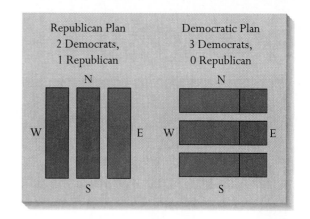

**FIGURE 10-3** **Gerry-mandering in Action**

*Depending on how an area is divided into districts, the result may benefit one party or the other. In this example, dividing the area so that one district has virtually all the Republicans gives that party a victory in that district, while ceding the other two districts to the Democrats. In contrast, Democrats benefit when Republican voters are divided among the three districts so that their votes are splintered.*

cratic (see Figure 10-3). If the Republicans could draw the district lines, they might draw them along a north-south direction to allow their party to win in one of the three districts. In contrast, if Democrats could draw the district lines, they might draw them along an east-west direction to allow their party to win all three districts by diluting the Republican vote. Such dividing up and diluting of a strong minority to deny it the power to elect a representative is called **splintering.** Often gerrymandering is not as neat as our example; district lines may twist and turn, creating grotesque patterns in order to achieve the desired effects. Another gerrymandering strategy—**packing**—is the heavy concentration of one party's voters in a single district in order to "waste" their votes and allow modest majorities of the party doing the redistricting to win in other districts.

*Partisan Gerrymandering*    Generally, partisan gerrymandering does *not* violate federal court standards for "equal protection" under the Fourteenth Amendment. There is no constitutional obligation to allocate seats "to the contending parties in proportion to what their anticipated statewide vote will be."[7] However, the federal courts may intervene in political gerrymandering if it "consistently degrades a voter's or a group of voters' influence on the political process as a whole."[8] These vague standards set forth by the U.S. Supreme Court open the door to judicial intervention in particularly grievous cases of partisan gerrymandering.

*Seats-Votes Relationship*    One way to determine whether partisan gerrymandering has occurred is to compare the total statewide vote compiled by all of one party's candidates with the proportion of congressional seats it won. Extreme and persistent differences in the seats-votes relationship may signal the existence of partisan gerrymandering. For example, if a party's candidates win 60 percent of the total votes cast in all legislative elections but only 40 percent of the seats, we might conclude that partisan gerrymandering is to blame. But it is normal for a party that wins a slight majority of votes to win a few more seats than its majority vote position would predict. Unlike many European democracies, the United States does not employ *proportional representation;* hence there is no expectation of proportionality in the seats-votes relationship. However, for Congress as a whole, the seats-votes relationship has been reasonable, with the majority party winning only a few percentage of seats in the House more than congressional votes nationwide (see Figure 10-4).

**Splintering:** Redistricting in which a strong minority is divided up and diluted to prevent it from electing a representative.

**Packing:** Redistricting in which partisan voters are concentrated in a single district, "wasting" their majority vote and allowing the opposition to win by modest majorities in other districts.

CHAPTER 10 • CONGRESS: POLITICS ON CAPITOL HILL

| Democratic Party Percentage of Total Votes Cast | | Percentage of Seats Won | Democratic Party Percentage Difference |
|---|---|---|---|
| 45.5 | 1994 | 46.8 | +1.3 |
| 50.8 | 1992 | 59.3 | +8.5 |
| 52.9 | 1990 | 61.4 | +8.5 |
| 53.4 | 1988 | 59.8 | +6.4 |
| 54.5 | 1986 | 59.3 | +4.8 |
| 52.1 | 1984 | 58.2 | +6.1 |
| 55.2 | 1982 | 61.8 | +6.6 |
| 50.4 | 1980 | 55.9 | +5.5 |
| 53.6 | 1978 | 63.7 | +10.1 |

60 40 20 0 Percent          0 20 40 60 Percent

**FIGURE 10-4** The Seats-Votes Relationship in Congressional House Elections

*As the statistics here show, efforts by Democratic political leaders to gerrymander congressional districts to their party's favor have met with only some success. The percentage of House seats won by Democrats have been slightly higher than the percentage of votes cast for congressional Democratic candidates nationwide. In 1994, for the first time in forty years, Democratic candidates collectively failed to win a majority of congressional votes cast, and they lost control of the House.*

Source: *Statistical Abstract of the United States, 1992*, p. 257; updated by author.

*The Politics of Redistricting*  Congressional district boundaries are drawn by state legislatures and governors, unless federal courts rule that these bodies have acted illegally and step in to undertake the task themselves. Thus party control of state legislatures and governorships across the nation influences partisan gerrymandering and the protection of incumbents. During the reapportionment following the 1990 census, seventy-one state legislative chambers were controlled by Democrats, twenty-three were controlled by Republicans, five were tied, and one (Nebraska) was officially nonpartisan. Moreover, twenty-eight states had Democratic governors, versus twenty with Republican governors and two (Alaska and Connecticut) with independent governors. As a result, the Democrats were well positioned to protect Democratic seats in the House of Representatives through careful, partisan redistricting plans. Republicans in many states were obliged to appeal to the courts and the Justice Department for relief. (In some cases, Republicans championed efforts to create African-American and Hispanic districts, hoping to "pack" traditional Democratic-voting minorities into a few districts and thereby improve Republican chances in the remaining districts.) But political gerrymandering could not save the Democratic Congress in 1994. Republican House candidates nationwide won more than 54 percent of the total congressional votes cast and captured 230 seats (53 percent) in the House of Representatives.

*Racial Gerrymandering*  Racial gerrymandering to disadvantage African Americans and other minorities violates both the Equal Protection Clause of the Fourteenth Amendment and the Voting Rights Act of 1965. The Voting Rights Act specifies that redistricting in states with a history of voter discrimination or low voter participation must be "cleared" in advance with the U.S. Justice Department. The act extends special protection not only to African American voters but also to Hispanic, Native American, Alaska Native, and Asian voters.

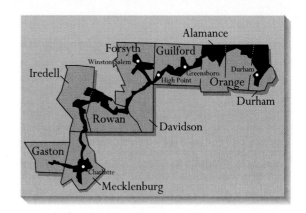

**FIGURE 10-5** **Affirmative Racial Gerrymandering**

*North Carolina's Twelfth Congressional District was drawn up to be a "majority-minority" district by combining African-American communities over a wide region of the state. The U.S. Supreme Court in* Shaw v. Reno *(1993) ordered a court review of this district to determine whether it incorporated any common interest other than race.*

In 1982, Congress strengthened the Voting Rights Act by outlawing any electoral arrangement that has the *effect* of weakening minority voting power. This *effects test* replaced the earlier *intent test,* under which redistricting was outlawed only if boundaries were intentionally drawn to dilute minority political influence. In *Thornburg v. Gingles* (1986), the Supreme Court interpreted the effects test to require state legislatures to redistrict their states in a way that maximizes minority representation in Congress and the state legislatures.[9] The effect of this ruling was to require **affirmative racial gerrymandering**—the creation of predominately African-American and minority districts (labeled "majority-minority" districts) whenever possible. Following the 1990 census, redistricting in legislatures in states with large minority populations was closely scrutinized by the U.S. Justice Department and the federal courts. The result was a dramatic increase in African-American and Hispanic representation in Congress.

Yet the Supreme Court has expressed constitutional doubts about bizarre-shaped districts based *solely* on racial composition. In a controversial 5 to 4 decision, Justice Sandra Day O'Connor wrote: "Racial gerrymandering, even for remedial purposes, may balkanize us into competing racial factions. . . . A reapportionment plan that includes in one district individuals who have little in common with one another but the color of their skin bears an uncomfortable resemblance to political apartheid"[10] (see Figure 10-5). And the Court has held that the use of race as the "predominant factor" in dividing district lines is unconstitutional: "When the state assigns voters on the basis of race, it engages in the offensive and demeaning assumption that voters of a particular race, because of their race, think alike, share the same political interests and will prefer the same candidates at the polls."[11]

## GETTING TO CAPITOL HILL

Members of Congress are independent political entrepreneurs—selling themselves, their services, and their personal policy views to the voters in 435 districts and 50 states across the country. They initiate their own candidacies, raise most of their campaign funds from individual contributors, put together personal campaign organizations, and get themselves elected with relatively little help from their party. Their reelection campaigns depend on their ability to raise funds from individuals and interest groups and on the services and other benefits they provide to their constituents.

**Affirmative racial gerrymandering:** Drawing district boundary lines to maximize minority representation.

CHAPTER 10 • CONGRESS: POLITICS ON CAPITOL HILL

*Who Runs for Congress?*    Members of Congress come from a wide variety of backgrounds, ranging from acting and professional sports to medicine and the ministry (see *People in Politics:* "Sonny Bono, Celebrity Congressman"). However, exceptionally high percentages of senators and representatives have prior experience in at least one of three fields—law, business, or public service (see Table 10-2). Members of Congress are increasingly career politicians—people who decided early in life to devote themselves to running for and occupying public office.[12] The many lawyers, by and large, are *not* practicing attorneys. Rather, the typical lawyer-legislator is a political activist with a law degree. These are people who graduated from law school and immediately sought public jobs—as federal or state prosecuting attorneys, or as attorneys for federal or state agencies, or as staff assistants in congressional, state, or city offices. They used their early job experiences to make political contacts and learn how to organize a political campaign, find financial contributors, and deal with the media. Another group of Congress members are former businesspeople—not employees of large corporations, but people whose personal or family businesses brought them into close contact with government and their local community, in real estate, insurance, franchise dealerships, community banks, and so forth. Another likely background for a political career is the media; reporting and broadcasting develop both the skills and the contacts needed for political entrepreneurship.

*Competition for Seats*    Careerism in Congress is aided by the electoral advantages enjoyed by incumbents over challengers. Greater name recognition, advantages in raising campaign funds, and the resources of congressional offices

**TABLE 10-2    OCCUPATIONAL BACKGROUNDS OF MEMBERS OF CONGRESS, 1995–1997**

|  | House | | | Senate | | | Congress |
|---|---|---|---|---|---|---|---|
|  | D | R | Total | D | R | Total | Total |
| Acting/entertainment | 0 | 1 | 1 | 0 | 0 | 0 | 1 |
| Aeronautics | 0 | 2 | 2 | 1 | 0 | 1 | 3 |
| Agriculture | 7 | 12 | 19 | 3 | 5 | 8 | 27 |
| Business/banking | 56 | 75 | 131 | 12 | 12 | 24 | 155 |
| Clergy | 1 | 1 | 2 | 0 | 1 | 1 | 3 |
| Education | 45 | 20 | 66 | 6 | 5 | 11 | 77 |
| Engineering | 2 | 3 | 5 | 0 | 0 | 0 | 5 |
| Homemaking | 0 | 1 | 1 | 0 | 0 | 0 | 1 |
| Journalism | 11 | 12 | 24 | 7 | 2 | 9 | 33 |
| Labor officials | 2 | 0 | 2 | 0 | 0 | 0 | 2 |
| Law | 122 | 59 | 181 | 33 | 25 | 58 | 239 |
| Law enforcement | 8 | 2 | 10 | 0 | 0 | 0 | 10 |
| Medicine | 4 | 2 | 6 | 0 | 0 | 0 | 6 |
| Military | 0 | 0 | 0 | 0 | 1 | 1 | 1 |
| Professional sports | 0 | 1 | 1 | 1 | 0 | 1 | 2 |
| Public service | 51 | 36 | 87 | 8 | 2 | 10 | 97 |
| Real estate | 9 | 17 | 26 | 2 | 3 | 5 | 31 |

*Source: Congressional Quarterly,* November 12, 1994.

*Note:* Because some members have more than one occupation, totals are higher than membership of Congress.

## PEOPLE IN POLITICS

## Sonny Bono, Celebrity Congressman

Few freshmen in Congress attract media attention as much as the former pop singer and songwriter Sonny Bono. Bono made a show-biz career in the 1970s as the butt of his former wife, Cher's, jokes, playing a good-natured, self-deprecating, straight man on the top-rated CBS television show *The Sonny and Cher Comedy Hour.* Today, he projects a political persona not too distant from his familiar celebrity image. Yet despite little formal education (Bono dropped out of high school at age sixteen), he is convinced he has molded himself into a capable lawmaker. "People said to me, 'You can't write songs.' 'You can't play an instrument.' But I've got ten gold records. I can do this job too."

Bono is the son of Sicilian immigrants who divorced when he was very young, leaving him to pursue his own interests, which focused on music. He spent many difficult years as a delivery boy, butcher's assistant, waiter, and truck driver, while trying to write songs. He finally caught on as a record promoter, arranging, engineering, and producing records as well as continuing to write songs and singing backup for groups. Following the breakup of his first marriage, he met an extraordinarily talented sixteen-year-old runaway, later to become the superstar Cher. They married, and Bono devoted his time to writing songs for her and promoting her career. Their big break came in 1965 with the hit song "I Got You Babe." More hits followed and "Sonny and Cher" rose to the top of the pop world.

Cher divorced Bono in 1974 , and his show business career faded while she went on to superstardom. Eventually Bono opened a restaurant in Palm Springs, California, that became a profitable business. A run-in with the local planning board bureaucracy, with its stringent regulations, led Bono into his first political race. He ran for mayor of Palm Springs as a pro-growth candidate in 1988, and despite the many barbs he suffered, he defeated six opponents in a landslide victory. By most accounts, he was a very successful mayor, revitalizing the city with a new amphitheater, golf course, racetrack, and a host of concerts and film festivals. Bono stumbled badly in 1992 in the California primary race for Republican U.S. Senate nomination, receiving only 17 percent of the vote. But having caught political fever, he persevered in building up support in the state GOP. When the local Republican Congress member decided to retire in 1994, Bono was well positioned to compete for the open seat. He had studied conservative Republican positions, and he deflected attacks on his background with good humor, turning his political inexperience to his advantage. He defeated a more-experienced candidate in the GOP primary and another in the general election to win a solid 56 percent of the vote in his conservative, Republican-leaning district.

all combine to limit competition for seats in Congress and to reelect the vast majority of incumbents (see "The Advantages of Incumbency" in Chapter 8). A congressional district in which the incumbent regularly wins by a large margin (55 to 60 percent or more of the vote) is regarded as a **safe seat.** More than two-thirds of the members of the House of Representatives sit comfortably in safe seats. Even incumbents elected by close margins enjoy many advantages over challengers. The result is a reelection percentage for House members that usually exceeds 90 percent (see *What Do You Think?* "Term Limits for Members of Congress?"). The average reelection rate for U.S. Senators is more than 75 percent (see Figure 10-6).

**Safe seat:** A legislative district in which the incumbent regularly wins by a large margin of the vote.

CHAPTER 10 • CONGRESS: POLITICS ON CAPITOL HILL

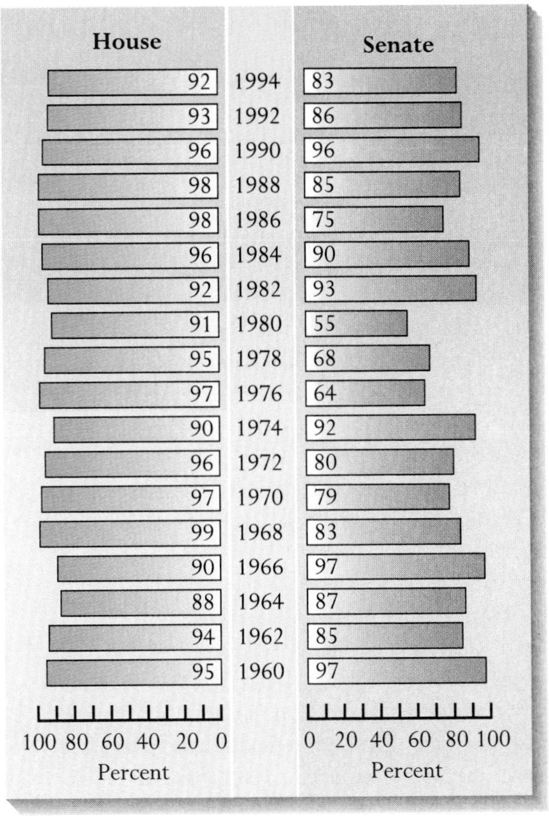

| House | Year | Senate |
|---|---|---|
| 92 | 1994 | 83 |
| 93 | 1992 | 86 |
| 96 | 1990 | 96 |
| 98 | 1988 | 85 |
| 98 | 1986 | 75 |
| 96 | 1984 | 90 |
| 92 | 1982 | 93 |
| 91 | 1980 | 55 |
| 95 | 1978 | 68 |
| 97 | 1976 | 64 |
| 90 | 1974 | 92 |
| 96 | 1972 | 80 |
| 97 | 1970 | 79 |
| 99 | 1968 | 83 |
| 90 | 1966 | 97 |
| 88 | 1964 | 87 |
| 94 | 1962 | 85 |
| 95 | 1960 | 97 |

House: Percent 100 80 60 40 20 0
Senate: Percent 0 20 40 60 80 100

**FIGURE 10-6  Incumbent Advantage**

*Despite periodic movements to "throw the bums out," voters in most districts and states routinely reelect their members of Congress. While incumbents do not always retain their seats, the odds are strongly in their favor. In recent decades, more than 90 percent of representatives and 75 percent of senators who have sought reelection have been returned to Congress by voters in their districts or states.*

Aspirants for congressional careers are well advised to wait for open seats. **Open seats** in the House of Representatives are created when incumbents retire or vacate the seat to run for higher office. These opportunities occur on average in about 10 percent of House seats in each election. But every ten years reapportionment creates many new opportunities to win election to Congress. Reapportionment creates new seats in states gaining population, just as it forces out some incumbents in states losing population. Redistricting also threatens incumbents with new constituencies, where they have less name recognition, no history of casework, and perhaps no common racial or ethnic identification. Thus forced retirements and electoral defeats are more common in the first election following each ten-year reapportionment and redistricting of Congress.

Senate races are somewhat more competitive. Senate challengers are usually people who have political experience and name recognition as members of the House or governors or other high state officials. Even so, most Senate incumbents seeking reelection are victorious over their challengers (see *What Do You Think?* "Why Do Voters Reelect Members of an Unpopular Congress?").

*Turnover*  Despite a high rate of reelection of incumbents in Congress, **turnover** of membership in recent years has been fairly high. Turnover occurs more frequently as a result of retirement, resignation (sometimes to run for higher office), or reapportionment (and the loss of an incumbent's seat) than it does a result of an incumbent's being defeated in a bid for reelection.

**Open seat:** A seat in a legislature for which no incumbent is running for reelection.

**Turnover:** Replacement of members of Congress by retirement or resignation, by reapportionment, or (more rarely) by electoral defeat, usually expressed as a percentage of members newly elected.

CONGRESS: POLITICS ON CAPITOL HILL • CHAPTER 10

## WHAT DO YOU THINK?

# Term Limits for Members of Congress?

Declining confidence in government and increasing distrust of politicians have fueled a national grassroots movement to limit the terms of public officials—notably members of Congress and state legislators. Term limits are very popular with voters. National polls regularly report that 70 percent or more of Americans favor congressional term limits. However, the enthusiasm of the general public for term limits is more than matched by the intense opposition the proposal meets on Capitol Hill. It is not likely that members of Congress will ever vote to limit their own terms of office, especially since a constitutional amendment to do so requires two-thirds of the members of both houses to vote to limit their own legislative careers.

At the Constitutional Convention of 1787, Roger Sherman commented that Congress should be composed of "citizen-legislators" who would be expected to "return home and mix with the people." He feared that "by remaining at the seat of government, they would acquire the habits of the place, which might differ from those of their constituents." But after brief consideration, the convention dropped the idea of limiting congressional terms. The president's term was not constitutionally limited until the adoption of the Twenty-second Amendment in 1951. (This amendment was passed largely in reaction to Franklin D. Roosevelt's election to four terms in office, breaking the tradition of a two-term presidency set by George Washington.) In addition, some twenty-five states restrict governors to two terms, and four additional states restrict them to one term.

Proponents of term limits argue that citizen-legislators have largely been replaced by career politicians. Over time, professional officeholders become isolated from the lives and concerns of average citizens; they acquire an "inside the Beltway" (a reference to the circle of interstate highways that surrounds Washington, D.C.) mentality. They respond to the media, to polls, and to interest groups but have no direct feeling for how their constituents live. Terms limits, proponents argue, would force politicians to return home and live under the laws that they make.

Proponents also argue that term limits would increase competition in the electoral system. Creating "open-seat" races on a regular basis would encourage more people to seek public office. Incumbents continually win reelection not because they are the most qualified people in their districts but rather because of the many electoral advantages granted by incumbency itself. The large margins by which incumbents win discourage good people from challenging them.

Opponents of term limits argue that they infringe on the voters' freedom of choice. If voters are upset with the performance of Congress or their state legislature, they can always "throw the rascals out." If they want to limit the terms of their own members of Congress, they can do so by not reelecting them. But if voters wish to keep popular, able, experienced, and hard-working legislators in office, they should be permitted to do so. Experience is a valuable asset in Washington. Voters may reasonably want to be represented by members of Congress with knowledge and experience in public affairs.

Opponents argue that inexperienced legislators would be forced to rely more on the policy information supplied them by bureaucrats, lobbyists, and

*The Congressional Electorate* Congressional elections generally fail to arouse much interest among voters. Indeed, only about 60 percent of the general public can name one U.S. senator from their state, and only about 40 percent can name both of their U.S. senators. Members of the House of Representatives fare no better: less than half of the general public can name their representative.[13] But even constituents who know the names of their congressional delegation seldom

staff people. Term limits would weaken the institution of Congress, leaving it less capable of checking the power of the special interests. But proponents counter this argument by observing that the closest relationships have developed between lobbyists and senior members of Congress who have interacted professionally and socially over the years. And they note that the most powerful lobbying groups in Washington strongly oppose term limits.

If the question were left to voters in the states, Congress would certainly confront term limits. Term limits have won by landslide margins almost everywhere they have appeared on referenda ballots (although voters in these states have continued to reelect incumbents).

However, the U.S. Supreme Court ruled in 1995 that the states cannot themselves limit the terms of their members of Congress:

> Such a state-imposed restriction is contrary to the "fundamental principle of our representative democracy," embodied in the Constitution that "the people should choose whom they please to govern them" *Powell v. McCormack* (1969). Allowing individual states to adopt their own qualifications for Congressional service would be inconsistent with the framers' vision of a uniform national legislature representing the people of the United States. If the qualifications set forth in the text of the Constitution are to be changed, that text must be amended.

Justice John Paul Stevens, writing for the majority in the controversial 5-4 decision, set forth two key arguments in opposition to state-imposed congressional term limits: first, that the power to do so is *not* among the powers reserved to the states by the Tenth Amendment, and second, that the Founders intended age, citizenship, and residency be the *only* qualifications for members of Congress.

> [Arkansas argues] that the Constitution contains no express prohibition against state added qualifications, and that Amendment 73 is therefore an appropriate exercise of a state's reserved power to place additional restrictions on the choices that its own voters may make. We disagree for two independent reasons. First, we conclude that the power to add qualifications is not within the "original powers" of the states, and thus is not reserved to the states by the 10th Amendment. Second, even if states possessed some original power in this area, we conclude that the framers intended the Constitution to be the exclusive source of qualifications for members of Congress, and that the framers thereby "divested" states of any power to add qualifications.

But Justice Clarence Thomas, in his dissenting opinion, set forth a compelling argument on behalf of the powers reserved to the people of the states by the Tenth Amendment:

> It is ironic that the Court bases today's decision on the right of the people to "choose whom they please to govern them." The majority therefore defends the right of the people of Arkansas to "choose whom they please to govern them" by invalidating a provision that won nearly 60 percent of the votes cast in a direct election and that carried every Congressional district in the state.
>
> I dissent. Nothing in the Constitution deprives the people of each state of the power to prescribe eligibility requirements for the candidates who seek to represent them in Congress. The Constitution is simply silent on this question. And where the Constitution is silent, it raises no bar to action by the states or the people.

know anything about the policy positions of these elected officials or about their votes on specific issues. Turnout in congressional *general elections* averages only about 35 percent in off-year (nonpresidential) elections. Turnout in congressional *primary elections* seldom exceeds 15–20 percent of persons eligible to vote. This lack of public attentiveness to congressional elections gives a great advantage to candidates with high name recognition—generally the incumbents.

# Why Do Voters Reelect Members of an Unpopular Congress?

Congress is the least popular branch of government. Today confidence in Congress appears to have reached an all-time low (see graph on page 345).

What accounts for this lack of popularity? The inability of Congress to deal effectively with national problems, particularly deficit spending, may be to blame. The growing belief that members of Congress "spend more time thinking about their own political futures than they do in passing legislation" may contribute. Well-publicized congressional scandals, pay raises, and lavish "perks" offend taxpayers. Congress also shares in the general decline in popular trust in government.

But in an apparent paradox, most voters *approve of their own* representative (see figure). Individual members of Congress are generally popular, even while Congress itself is the object of popular distrust and ridicule. A majority of voters believe that their own representatives "deserve reelection."

The apparent contradiction of popular members of Congress serving in an unpopular Congress can be explained in part by the differing expectations Americans have of Congress and their own representatives. Americans expect Congress to deal with national issues, but they expect their own representatives to deal with local concerns and even personal problems. Members of Congress understand this concern and consequently devote a great deal of their time and energy to constituent service. Indeed,

many members of Congress try to dissociate themselves from Congress, attacking Congress in their own campaigns and contributing to negative images of the institution. Finally, the national news media are highly critical in their treatment of Congress, but local news media frequently portray local members of Congress in a more favorable light.

## Percentage of Those Expressing Approval of Their Representatives and Congress

| My Representative | | Congress | Percentage Difference |
|---|---|---|---|
| 62 | 1978 | 31 | −31% |
| 60 | 1990 | 38 | −22% |
| 60 | 1996 | 31 | −29% |

80 60 40 20 0
Percent

0 20 40 60 80
Percent

While the *most* popular institutions in the United States change from year to year, Congress has never been highly popular. In recent years, it has ranked at the *bottom* of the list among institutions surveyed.

*Source:* 1973 and 1990 surveys by the Gallup Organization, reported in *American Enterprise,* January–February 1991, p. 83; 1992 survey by Louis Harris reported in *American Enterprise,* May–June 1992, p. 103; 1995 by Gallup Organization.
*Note:* Gallup's questions center on confidence in the "institutions" themselves, while Harris's surveys ask about "the people running them." In addition, Gallup offered respondents four options—"a great deal," "quite a lot," "some," or "very little"—while Harris offered only three options, dropping "quite a lot."

*Independence of Congressional Voting* Congressional voting is largely independent of presidential voting. The same voters who elected Republican presidents in 1968, 1972, 1980, 1984, and 1988 simultaneously elected Democratic majorities to the House of Representatives. It is unlikely that voters who supported Republican presidential candidates deliberately sought to impose *divided party government* on the nation. Rather, they cast their presidential and congressional votes on the basis of differing expectations of presidents versus members of Congress.[14]

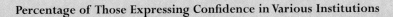

**Percentage of Those Expressing Confidence in Various Institutions**

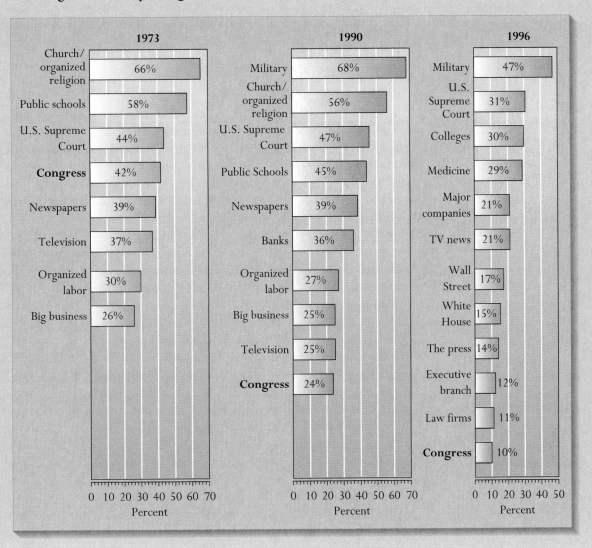

| 1973 | | 1990 | | 1996 | |
|---|---|---|---|---|---|
| Church/organized religion | 66% | Military | 68% | Military | 47% |
| Public schools | 58% | Church/organized religion | 56% | U.S. Supreme Court | 31% |
| U.S. Supreme Court | 44% | U.S. Supreme Court | 47% | Colleges | 30% |
| **Congress** | 42% | Public Schools | 45% | Medicine | 29% |
| Newspapers | 39% | Newspapers | 39% | Major companies | 21% |
| Television | 37% | Banks | 36% | TV news | 21% |
| Organized labor | 30% | Organized labor | 27% | Wall Street | 17% |
| Big business | 26% | Big business | 25% | White House | 15% |
| | | Television | 25% | The press | 14% |
| | | **Congress** | 24% | Executive branch | 12% |
| | | | | Law firms | 11% |
| | | | | **Congress** | 10% |

*Percent*

*Congressional Campaign Spending and Fund Raising*   Congressional campaigns can be classified as either incumbent-versus-challenger or open-seat campaigns. In most incumbent-versus-challenger races, incumbents heavily outspend their challengers (see Table 10-3). In open-seat races, Democratic and Republican candidates spend about the same amounts. Raising the $550,000 it can take to hold onto or win a House seat or the $4 million for a successful Senate campaign is a major job in and of itself. Even incumbents who face little or no competition still work hard at fund raising, "banking" contributions against some

TABLE 10-3  CONGRESSIONAL CAMPAIGN SPENDING

|                             | House     | Senate      |
|-----------------------------|-----------|-------------|
| Average incumbent           | $559,929  | $4,685,444  |
| Average challenger          | $239,352  | $3,999,492  |
| Average open-seat candidate | $588,722  | $3,001,013  |

*Source:* Based on data from Norman J. Ornstein, Thomas E. Mann, and Michael J. Malbin. *Vital Statistics in Congress 1995–96* (Washington, D.C.: American Enterprise Institute, 1996).

future challenger. Large campaign chests, assembled well in advance of an election, can also be used to frighten off would-be challengers. Campaign funds can be used to build a strong personal organization back home, finance picnics and other festivities for constituents, expand the margin of victory, and develop a reputation for invincibility that may someday protect against an unknown challenger.[15]

Incumbents generally receive more money from political action committees (PACs) than challengers do (see "Money in Elections" in Chapter 8). PACs usually avoid funding challengers, and they are very cautious about funding candidates in open-seat races. The strategies behind PAC campaign contributions differ according to the nature of the PAC—whether it is a business or corporate PAC, a union PAC, an ideological PAC, or a single-issue PAC (see "PAC Power" in Chapter 9). Most business and corporate PACs are very pragmatic: they fund incumbents, regardless of party, in order to gain and maintain access to decision makers. Union PACs generally fund Democrats, based on the Democratic Party's perceived support for the goals of organized labor. Ideological PACs usually base their contributions on the perceived "correctness" of the voting records of members of Congress.

Challengers must rely far more heavily on their own resources than do incumbents, though all candidates are free to spend as much of their own money as they wish. Parties account for only a small fraction of congressional campaign financing.

*The Historic Democratic Party Dominance of Congress*   For forty years (1954–94) Democrats enjoyed an advantage in congressional races, so much so that the Democratic Party was said to have a "permanent majority" in the House of Representatives (see Figure 10-7). Thus, the Republican victory in the congressional election of 1994 was widely described as a political "earthquake." It gave the GOP control of the House of Representatives for the first time in four decades, as well as control of the Senate.

The historic Democratic dominance of Congress was attributed to several factors. First, over those four decades more voters identified themselves with the Democratic Party than with the Republican Party (see Chapter 7). Party identification plays a significant role in congressional voting; it is estimated that 75 percent of those who identify themselves with a party cast their vote for the congressional candidate of their party.[16] Second, the Democratic advantage was buttressed by the fact that many voters considered local rather than national conditions when casting congressional votes. House campaigns were usually 435 separate local contests emphasizing personal qualities of the candidates and their abil-

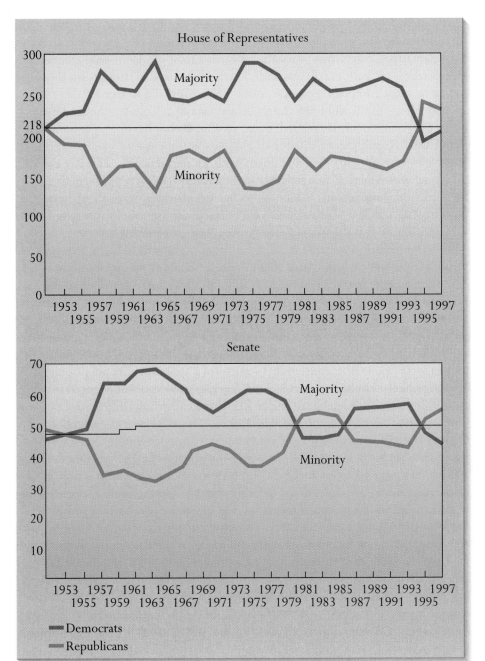

FIGURE 10-7 **Party Control of the House and Senate**

*Except for two very brief periods, Democrats continuously controlled both the House of Representatives and the Senate for more than forty years. The Democratic Party's "permanent" control of Congress was ended in 1994 when Republicans won majorities in both houses. Republicans retained control of Congress despite President Clinton's victory in 1996.*

ity to serve their district's constituents. Voters may have wanted to curtail *overall* federal spending in Washington (a traditional Republican promise), but they wanted a member of Congress who would "bring home the bacon." Although both Republican and Democratic congressional candidates usually promised to bring money and jobs to their districts, Democratic candidates appeared more creditable on such promises as their party generally supported large domestic spending programs. Finally, Democratic congressional candidates over those years enjoyed the many advantages of incumbency. It was thought that only death or retirement would dislodge many of them from their seats.

*The Republican congressional victory in 1994 brought many younger conservative members to the House, including J. C. Watts of Oklahoma.*

*The Republican "Revolution"?*   The sweeping Republican victory in 1994 surprised many analysts, especially the party's capture of control of the House of Representatives.[17] Just two years after a Democratic president won election and Democrats won substantial majorities in both houses of Congress, the GOP gained its most complete victory in many years. How did it happen?

First of all, the Republican congressional candidates, under the leadership of Newt Gingrich, largely succeeded in *nationalizing* the midterm congressional election. That is, Republican candidates sought to exploit the voters' general skepticism about government and disenchantment with its performance. The Republicans' "Contract with America" was an effort to rally voters to a party platform that called for limits on government. While voters were unfamiliar with all of its specific promises (see *Up Close:* "The Republican 'Contract with America'" in Chapter 8), they correctly sensed that the Republicans favored "less government."

The Democratic advantage in bringing "pork"—lucrative federal projects—to their districts was turned against them. Indeed, the most powerful House Democratic incumbent, Speaker Thomas S. Foley of Washington, was unable to convince his constituents in 1994 that his twenty years of service to them and his impressive record of bringing pork to the district justified his reelection. Foley became the first Speaker of the House in more than 100 years to suffer defeat in a bid for reelection.

The GOP's capture of control of both houses of Congress in 1994 for the first time in forty years raised conservatives' hopes of a "revolution" in public policy. The new Republican House Speaker, Newt Gingrich, was the acknowledged leader of the revolution, with Republican Senate Majority Leader Bob Dole in tow. But soon the revolution began to fizzle out. The House failed to muster the necessary two-thirds majority for a constitutional amendment to impose congressional term limits, and the Senate failed to do so on behalf of a balanced budget amendment.

But worse was yet to come for the Republicans. Congress passed several budget resolutions aimed at balancing the federal budget in seven years, only to see them vetoed. Clinton positioned himself as the defender of popular programs—Medicare, Medicaid, education, and the environment—consistently referring to congressional efforts to reduce the rate of growth in these programs as "cuts." The failure of Congress and the president to agree on appropriations temporarily shut down the federal government. To the surprise of the Republican leadership, opinion polls reported that Americans blamed the GOP Congress for the gridlock. Clinton's approval ratings rose, while Newt Gingrich was portrayed as a mean-spirited "extremist." Eventually Congress and the president agreed on a compromise budget, a welfare reform bill, and health insurance portability (see Chapter 17).

Republicans succeeded in maintaining their control of Congress despite Clinton's reelection in 1996. Collectively, the voters seemed to say that they preferred divided government, that they wanted a Republican Congress that would press for a balanced budget, but that they also wanted a Democratic president who would defend popular middle-class entitlement programs. In short, voters seemed reluctant to allow either party to govern unchaperoned by the other.

## LIFE IN CONGRESS

"All politics is local," declared former House Speaker Thomas P. "Tip" O'Neill, himself the master of both Boston ward politics and the U.S. House of Representatives. Attention to the local constituency is the key to survival and success in congressional politics. If Congress often fails to deal responsibly with national problems, the explanation lies in part with the design of the institution. House members must devote primary attention to their districts and Senate members to their states. Only *after* their constituencies are served can they turn their attention to national policy making.

*The "Representativeness" of Congress*    The Constitution requires only that members of the House of Representatives be (1) residents of the state they represent (they need not live in their congressional district, though virtually all do so); (2) U.S. citizens for at least seven years; and (3) at least twenty-five years old. Senators must also be residents of the state they represent, but they must be at least thirty years old and U.S. citizens for at least nine years.

African-American membership in Congress is higher today than at any time in the history of the institution (see Figure 10-8). African Americans were first elected to Congress following the Civil War—seven black representatives and one senator served in 1875. But with the end of Reconstruction, black membership in Congress fell to a single seat in the House from 1891 to 1955. Following the Civil Rights Act of 1964 and the Voting Rights Act of 1965, black membership in Congress rose steadily. Redistricting following the 1990 census resulted in many new "majority-minority" congressional districts. Following the 1992 elections, black membership in the House rose from 26 to 39, with most elected from predominately African-American districts. As a result, while African Americans today make up a little more than 12 percent of the U.S. population, they make up a little less than 9 percent of the House membership. Hispanic membership in the House is now 19; Hispanics now account for 9 percent of the U.S. population but only about 4 percent of House membership (see *People in Politics:* "Carol Moseley Braun and Ben Nighthorse Campbell, Minority Faces in Congress").

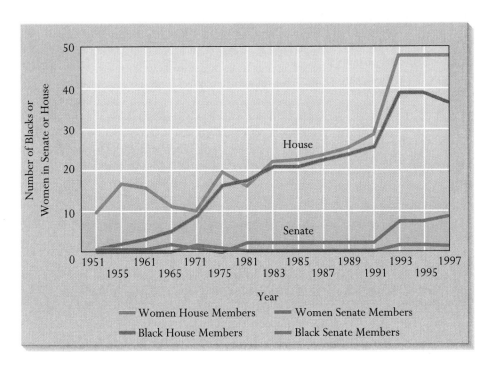

**FIGURE 10-8    Women and African Americans in Congress, 1951–1997**
*Although the House of Representatives is still far short of "looking like America," in recent years the number of African American and female members has risen noticeably. Both groups made particularly impressive advances in the 1992 elections; as did Hispanics. While there are now nine women serving in the Senate (six Democrats and three Republicans), there is still only one African-American member of that body (a woman, Democrat Carol Moseley Braun of Illinois).*

## Carol Moseley Braun and Ben Nighthorse Campbell, Minority Faces in Congress

Among the more noteworthy people serving in the U.S. Senate today are two prominent members of minority groups—Democrat Carol Moseley Braun, the first African-American woman ever to serve in the Senate, and Republican Ben Nighthorse Campbell, the first Native American to do so.

*Carol Moseley Braun* Carol Moseley Braun, the daughter of a police officer and a medical technician, grew up in Chicago. After obtaining a law degree from the University of Chicago, she went to work for Harold Washington, Chicago's first black mayor. In 1978, she won a seat in the state legislature, where she served for more than a decade. As Chicago's Cook County recorder of deeds, she was given little chance to unseat the incumbent Democratic senator Alan Dixon when she announced her candidacy for the Senate in 1992. But in a three-way primary battle, Moseley Braun capitalized on anti-incumbent sentiments in her own party as well as on discomfort over the Senate's handling of sexual harassment allegations by Anita Hill. Her surprise win over Dixon brought her national attention and heavy campaign contributions from women's groups across the nation. Her Republican opponent, a wealthy conservative lawyer who had served in minor posts in the Reagan and Bush administrations, offered little challenge. (Stronger Republican personalities had avoided the race, believing that Dixon was unbeatable.) Moseley Braun campaigned on a strong liberal platform— abortion rights, universal health care, defense cuts, and higher spending for education and job training. Illinois voters opted for change, giving Bill Clinton a 48–35 percent victory over George Bush, and giving Moseley Braun a comfortable 55–45 percent victory. As expected, Moseley Braun quickly emerged in the U.S. Senate as a spokesperson for minority and women's concerns, including backing legislation requiring tougher enforcement of child support and sexual harassment prohibitions in the military.

*Ben Nighthorse Campbell* In an age of slick Ivy League career politicians, the colorful style of Ben Nighthorse Campbell is a welcome relief. Campbell is part Native American and an official chief of the Northern Cheyenne nation. Growing up with an alcoholic father and a mother suffering from tuberculosis, he dropped out of high school and joined the Air Force, then later worked his way through the California State University at San Jose by driving a truck. Along the way, Campbell took up judo and won a spot on the U.S. Olympic team. His business skills in marketing Indian jewelry allowed him to go into cattle ranching and horse training in southwest Colorado and to win election to the House of Representatives in an upset in 1986. In 1988 and 1990, Colorado voters reelected him with more than 70 percent of the vote.

As a member of the House Agriculture Committee, Campbell was strongly supportive of ranching and mining interests, portraying himself as a social liberal and a fiscal conservative. When he announced his intention to run for the seat of retiring Democratic Senator Tim Wirth, environmental groups rushed to support his opponents, including former three-term governor Richard Lamm. But the witty and outspoken Campbell easily captured the Democratic nomination in a three-way race and entered the general election race with a wide lead over Republican state senator Terry Considine. The gap narrowed somewhat as Considine launched attack ads claiming Campbell was a pawn of the oil and mining companies, but Campbell, with his ponytail and trademark string tie, kept the confidence of Colorado voters and won a convincing 55–45 victory.

Campbell shocked his Democratic colleagues in the Senate in early 1995 when he announced his switch to the Republican Party. During his first two years in the Senate as a Democrat, he had given only lukewarm support to this party and President Bill Clinton, complaining that his moderate views were often out of sync with the Democratic leadership. Yet even while announcing his switch, he warned his new Republican colleagues that he would continue to support liberal positions on many social issues, including abortion.

Women made impressive gains in the Senate as well. Four new women senators—all Democrats—were elected in 1992: Dianne Feinstein and Barbara Boxer from California, Patty Murray from Washington, and Carol Moseley Braun from Illinois. They joined Democrat Barbara Mikulski from Maryland. Democrat Mary Landrieu was elected from Louisiana in 1996. Republican Kay Hutchison was elected in 1993 to fill the Texas Senate seat vacated by Treasury Secretary Lloyd Bentsen, and Republican Olympia Snowe won Maine's Senate seat vacated by the retirement of the Democratic Senate Leader George Mitchell. Susan Collins, also from Maine, became the third Republican woman in the Senate in 1996. While this is the largest delegation of women ever to serve together in the U.S. senate, it is still only 9 percent of that body.

*Congressional Staff*   Congress is composed of a great deal more than 535 elected senators and representatives. Congressional staff and other support personnel now total more than 25,000 people—a huge increase from the 1950s, when only about 3,000 people worked in Congress. Each representative has a staff of twenty or more people, usually headed by an administrative assistant and including legislative assistants, constituent service personnel, office managers, secretaries, and aides of various sorts. Senators frequently have staffs of thirty to fifty or more people. All representatives and senators are provided with offices both in Washington and in their home districts and states. In addition, representatives receive more than $500,000 apiece for office expenses, travel, and staff, and senators receive $2 million or more, depending on the size of their state's population. Overall, Congress spends more than *$2 billion* on itself each year.

Congressional staff people exercise great influence over legislation.[18] Many experienced "Hill rats" have worked for the same member of Congress for many years. They become very familiar with "their" member's political strengths and vulnerabilities and handle much of the member's contacts with interest groups and constituents. Staff people, more than members themselves, move the legislative process—scheduling committee hearings, writing bills and amendments, and tracking the progress of such proposals through committees and floor proceed-

*A member of Congress meets with his staff in his offices in Washington, D.C. Congressional staff play a key role in the legislative process.*

ings. By working with the staff of other members of Congress or the staff of committees and negotiating with interest-group representatives, congressional staff are often able to work out policy compromises, determine the wording of legislation, or even outline "deals" for their member's vote (all subject to later approval by their member). With multiple demands on their time, members of Congress come to depend on their staff not only for information about the content of legislation but also for political recommendations about what position to take regarding it. Indeed, staff have become so important in the internal operations of Congress that members have less direct contact with each other than in the past, a situation that often makes modern congressional relations impersonal.

Staff people also handle the bulk of constituent services. Staff *caseworkers* labor in both Washington, D.C., and the member's home district to satisfy constituent requests. About 40 percent of congressional staff workers are assigned to the home district or state offices. These staff activities contribute heavily to the advantage current members of Congress have when seeking reelection.

In addition to the personal staffs of members of Congress, congressional committees have their own staffs, ranging in size from 25 to more than 200 persons. Committee staffs are generally beholden to the committee chair and are often replaced when a new chair is named. Minority committee members do control some committee staff positions, however.

*Support Agencies*   In addition to the thousands of personal and committee staff who are supposed to assist members of Congress in research and analysis, four congressional support agencies provide Congress with information: the Library of Congress, the General Accounting Office, the Congressional Budget Office, and the Office of Technology Assessment.

- The Library of Congress and its Congressional Research Service (CRS) are the oldest congressional support agencies. Members of Congress can turn to the Library of Congress for references and information. The Congressional Research Service responds to direct requests of members for factual information on virtually any topic. It tracks major bills in Congress and produces summaries of each bill introduced. This information is available on computer terminals in members' offices.
- The General Accounting Office (GAO) has broad authority to oversee the operations and finances of executive agencies, to evaluate their programs, and to report its findings to Congress. Established as an arm of Congress in 1921, the GAO largely confined itself to financial auditing and management studies in its early years but expanded to more than 5,000 employees in the 1970s and undertook a broad agenda of policy research and evaluation. Most GAO studies and reports are requested by members of Congress and congressional committees, but the GAO also undertakes some studies on its own initiative.
- The Congressional Budget Office (CBO) was created by the Congressional Budget and Impoundment Act of 1974 to strengthen Congress's role in the budgeting process. It was designed as a congressional counterweight to the president's Office of Management and Budget (see Chapter 14). The CBO supplies the House and Senate budget committees with its own budgetary analyses and economic forecasts, sometimes challenging those found in the president's annual budget.

- The Office of Technology Assessment (OTA) was created in 1972 to provide Congress with its own source of expertise on scientific and technical matters. The OTA responds to requests for information and analyses from congressional committees rather than from individual members.

Note that both the CBO and the OTA were created at a time when Congress was growing in power relative to a presidency weakened by Vietnam and Watergate. In these same years, Congress encouraged the GAO to undertake a more active and critical role relative to executive agencies. Thus the growth of congressional staff and supporting agencies is tied to the struggle for power between the legislative and executive branches.

*Workload*  Members of Congress claim to work twelve- to fifteen-hour days: two to three hours in committee and subcommittee meetings; two to three hours on the floor of the chamber; three to four hours meeting with constituents, interest groups, other members, and staff in their offices; and two to three hours attending conferences, events, and meetings in Washington.[19] Members of Congress may introduce anywhere from ten to fifty bills in a session of Congress. (A "session" convenes in January following a congressional election and extends for two years, until after the next election.) Most bills are introduced merely to exhibit the member's commitment to a particular group or issue. Cosigning a popular bill is a common practice; particularly popular bills may have 100 or 200 cosigners in the House of Representatives. While thousands of bills are introduced, only 600 to 800 are passed in a session. Many bills are *private bills* designed to correct a perceived injustice affecting a particular person. Still others make only minor changes or corrections in federal statutes or regulations. Probably fewer than a third of the bills enacted have any significant effect on policy. Congress may also make its opinion known by passing a **resolution,** a declaration that lacks the force of law and does not require the president's signature.

Members of Congress resent the notion that they are overpaid, underworked, pampered, self-seeking, corrupt, and ineffective. They respond to the bell calling them to the floor for a recorded vote 900 to 1,000 times a session. Each representative is a member of two standing committees and four subcommittees, and each senator may be a member of nine to twelve committees and subcommittees. Thousands of committee and subcommittee meetings are scheduled each session.

*Pay and Perks*  Taxpayers can relate directly to what members of Congress spend on themselves, even while millions—and even billions—of dollars spent on government programs remain relatively incomprehensible. Taxpayers thus were enraged when Congress, in a late-night session in 1991, raised its own pay from $89,500 to $129,000. Congress claimed the pay raise was a "reform" since it was coupled with a stipulation that members of Congress would no longer be allowed to accept "honoraria" from interest groups for their speeches and appearances, thus supposedly reducing members' dependence on outside income. Many angry taxpayers saw only a 44 percent pay raise, in the midst of a national recession, for a Congress that was doing little to remedy the nation's problems. By 1995, automatic cost-of-living increases, also enacted by Congress, had raised members' pay to $133,600.

As the pay-raise debate raged in Washington, several states resurrected a constitutional amendment originally proposed by James Madison. Though passed by

**Resolution:** A congressional declaration that does not have the force of law and therefore does not require the president's signature.

the Congress in 1789, it had never been ratified by the necessary three-quarters of the states. The 203-year-old amendment, requiring a House election to intervene before a congressional pay raise can take effect, was added as the Twenty-seventh Amendment when ratified by four states (for a total of thirty-nine) in 1992.

Even more damaging to public confidence in Congress have been revelations about the "perks" (privileges) accorded its members. For example, Congress had long maintained its own "bank"—actually more like an employee credit union—where members deposited their pay and wrote checks. Overdrafts were common, as members regularly wrote checks in anticipation of pay deposits. Some members clearly abused the privilege, writing hundreds of overdrafts totaling tens of thousands of dollars. Technically, no government (taxpayer) funds were involved. But when the "check-kiting" scandal was reported by the media in 1992, most people believed that members of Congress were abusing their power. Other perks also came under fire—travel and office expenses, the free congressional health club, free medical clinic, free parking, free video studios for making self-promotional tapes, free mailing privileges, and a subsidized dining room, gift shop, and barber shop.

## HOME STYLE

Members of Congress spend as much time politically cultivating their districts and states as they do legislating. *Home style* refers to the activities of senators and representatives in promoting their images among constituents and personally attending to constituents' problems and interests.[20] These activities include members' allocations of their personnel and staff resources to constituent services; members' personal appearances in the home district or state to demonstrate personal attention; and members' efforts to explain their Washington activities to the voters back home.

*Casework*    **Casework** is really a form of "retail" politics. Members of Congress can win votes one at a time by helping constituents on a personal level. Casework can involve everything from tracing lost Social Security checks and Medicare claims to providing information about federal programs, solving problems with the Internal Revenue Service, and assisting with federal job applications. Over time, grateful voters accumulate and give incumbents a heavy advantage in low-turnout elections. Congressional staff do much of the actual casework, but letters go out over the signature of the member of Congress. One estimate of staff work suggests that House members' offices process more than 100 cases a week on average, and senators' offices process more than 300.[21] Senators and representatives blame the growth of government for increasing casework, but it is also clear that members solicit casework, constantly reminding constituents to bring their problems to their member of Congress.

*Pork Barrel*    **Pork-barreling** describes the efforts of senators and representatives to "bring home the bacon"—to bring federally funded projects, grants, and contracts that primarily benefit a single district or state to their home constituencies. Opportunities for pork-barreling have never been greater: roads, dams,

**Casework:** Services performed by legislators or their staff on behalf of individual constituents.

**Pork-barreling:** Legislation designed to make government benefits, including jobs and projects used as political patronage, flow to a particular district or state.

*Pork is in the eye of the beholder. These workers in Dallas are protesting the closing of the federally funded Superconducting Supercollider, a multibillion dollar project intended to advance research in particle physics. Some saw it as pork, others as essential to keeping the United States in the forefront of science research.*

parks, and post offices are now overshadowed by redevelopment grants to city governments, research grants to universities, weapons contracts to local plants, "demonstration" projects of all kinds, and myriad other "goodies" tucked inside each year's annual appropriations bills. Members of Congress understand the importance of supporting each other's pork-barrel projects, cooperating in the "incumbent protection society." Even though pork-barreling adds to the public's negative image of Congress as an institution, individual members gain local popularity for the benefits they bring to home districts and states.

*Pressing the Flesh*    Senators and representatives spend a great deal of time in their home states and districts. While congressional sessions last virtually all year, members of Congress find ways to spend more than a hundred days per year at home.[22] It is important to be seen at home—giving speeches and attending dinners, fund-raising events, civic occasions, and so on. To accommodate this aspect of home style, Congress usually follows a Tuesday-to-Thursday schedule of legislative business, allowing members to spend longer weekends in their home districts. Congress also enjoys long recesses during the late summer and over holidays.

*Puffing Images*    To promote their images back home, members make generous use of their *franking privilege* (free mailing) to send their constituents newsletters, questionnaires, biographical material, and information about federal programs. Newsletters "puff" the accomplishments of the member; questionnaires are designed more to flatter voters than to assess opinions; and informational brochures tout federal services members claim credit for providing and defending. Congress's penchant for self-promotion has also kept pace with the media and electronic ages. Congress now provides its members with television studios and support for making videotapes to send to local stations in home districts, and all members have addresses on the Internet.

# ORGANIZING CONGRESS: PARTY AND LEADERSHIP

Congress is composed of people who think of themselves as leaders, not followers. They got elected without much help from their party. Yet they realize that their chances of attaining their personal goals—getting reelected and influencing policy—are enhanced if they cooperate with each other.[23]

*Party Organizations in Congress*  The Democratic and Republican party organizations within the House of Representatives and the Senate are the principal bases for organizing Congress (see Figure 10-9). The leadership of each house of Congress, although nominally elected by the entire chamber, is actually chosen by secret ballot of the members of each party at a "conference" or caucus (see Table 10-4).

The parties and their leaders do not choose congressional candidates, nor can they deny them renomination; all members of Congress are responsible for their own primary and general election success. But party leadership in each chamber *can* help incumbents achieve their reelection goals. Each party in the House and Senate sponsors a campaign committee that channels some campaign funding to party members seeking reelection, though these Republican and Democratic congressional and senatorial campaign committees contribute less money than either PACs or individuals to the candidates.[24] Rather, good relations between members and their party's leadership are more important in the quest for power and influence in Washington.

Occasionally, the congressional party leaders are urged to exercise more discipline over their members, to ensure that they support the party's position on key votes. Theoretically, party leaders in the House and Senate could do so by denying disloyal members appointment to preferred committees, by regularly burying their favorite bills, by cutting their pork-barrel projects from the budget, or by denying them party campaign funds. But except in very extreme cases, party leaders have been reluctant to employ these punishments. Members of Congress cherish their independence. They respect each other's need to get reelected. A mem-

| TABLE 10-4 | LEADERSHIP IN CONGRESS, 1997–1999 | |
|---|---|---|
| | *Senate* | |
| President Pro Tempore | Strom Thurmond (R-S.C.) | |
| Majority Leader | Trent Lott (R-Miss.) | |
| Majority Whip | Don Nickles (R-Okla.) | |
| Minority Leader | Tom Daschle (D-S.D.) | |
| Minority Whip | Wendell Ford (D-Ky.) | |
| | *House* | |
| Speaker | Newt Gingrich (R-Ga.) | |
| Majority Leader | Dick Armey (R-Tex.) | |
| Majority Whip | Tom DeLay (R-Tex.) | |
| Minority Leader | Richard Gephardt (D-Mo.) | |
| Minority Whip | David Bonior (D-Mich.) | |

ber's vote lost today may be won next week if the member is not alienated by disciplinary action.

*In the House: "Mr. Speaker"* In the House of Representatives, the key leadership figure is the **Speaker of the House,** who serves as both presiding officer of the chamber and leader of the majority party. The Twenty-fifth Amendment to the Constitution stipulates that if the president and vice-president simultaneously become unable to serve for any reason, the Speaker is to become president. In the House, the Speaker has many powers. The Speaker decides who shall be recognized to speak on the floor and rules on points of order (with advice from the parliamentarian), including whether a motion or amendment is germane (relevant) to the business at hand. The Speaker decides to which committees new bills will be assigned and can schedule or delay votes on a bill. The Speaker appoints members of select, special, and conference committees and names majority party members to the Rules Committee. And the Speaker controls both patronage jobs and office space in the Capitol. While the norm of fairness requires the Speaker to apply the rules of the House consistently, the Speaker is elected by the majority party and is expected to favor that party. However, the effectiveness and success of the Speaker really rest "less on formal rules than on personal prestige, sensitivity to member needs, ability to persuade and skill at mediating disputes"[25] (for a look at the style of the current Speaker, see *People in Politics:* "Speaker Newt").

*House Leaders and Whips* The Speaker's principal assistant is the **majority leader (majority floor leader).** The majority leader formulates the party's legislative program in consultation with other party leaders and steers the program through the House. The majority leader also must persuade committee leaders to support the aims of party leaders in acting on legislation before their committees. Finally, the majority leader arranges the legislative schedule with the cooperation of key party members.

The minority party in the House selects a **minority leader (minority floor leader),** whose duties correspond to those of the majority leader, except that the minority leader has no authority over the scheduling of legislation. The minority leader's principal duty has been to organize the forces of the minority party to counter the legislative program of the majority and to pass the minority party's bills. It is also the minority leader's duty to consult ranking minority members of House committees and to encourage them to adopt party positions and to follow the lead of the president if the minority party controls the White House.

In both parties, **whips** assist floor leaders in keeping track of the whereabouts of party members and in pressuring them to vote the party line. Whips are also responsible for ensuring the attendance of party members at important roll calls and for canvassing their colleagues as to their likely support for or opposition to party-formulated legislation. Finally, whips are involved regularly in the formation of party policy and the scheduling of legislation.

*In the Senate: "Mr. President"* The Constitution declares the vice-president of the United States to be the presiding officer of the Senate. But vice-presidents seldom exercise this senatorial responsibility, largely because the presiding officer of the Senate has very little power. Having only 100 members, the Senate usually does not restrict debate and has fewer scheduling constraints than the House. The only significant power of the vice-president is the right to cast a deciding vote in

**Speaker of the House:** The presiding officer of the House of Representatives.

**Majority (floor) leader:** In the House, the majority party leader and second in command to the Speaker; in the Senate, the leader of the majority party.

**Minority (floor) leader:** In both the House and Senate, the leader of the opposition party.

**Whip:** In both the House and Senate, a party leader who assists floor leaders and is next in command to those leaders.

FIGURE 10-9 **The Organization of Congress**

*Aside from naming the Speaker of the House as head of that body's operations and the vice-president as overseer of Senate deliberations, t stitution is silent on the organization of Congress. Political parties have filled this gap: both majority and minority parties have their ov ership, which governs the appointment of members to the various committees, where the work of Congress actually takes place.*

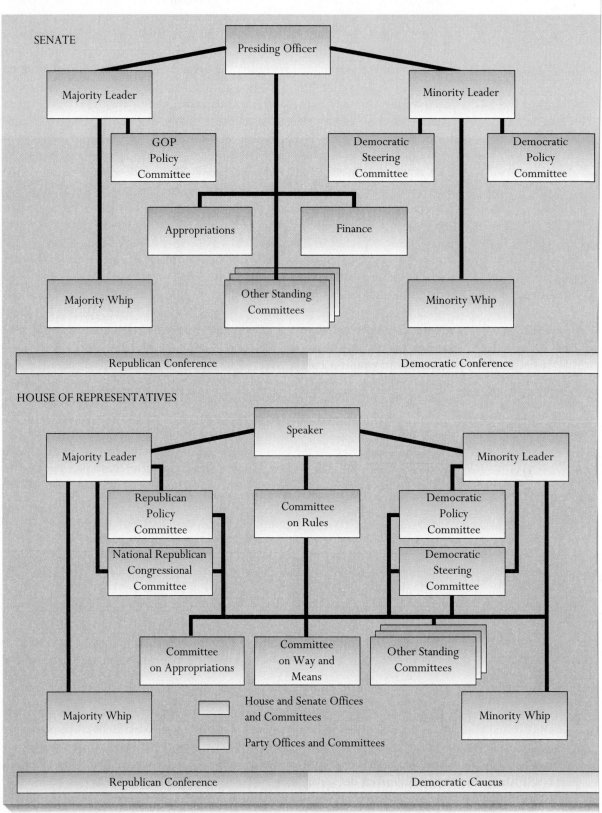

the event of a tie on a Senate roll call. In the usual absence of the vice-president, the Senate is presided over by a *president pro tempore*. This honorific position is traditionally granted by the majority party to one of its senior stalwarts. The job of presiding over the Senate is so boring that neither the vice-president nor the president pro tempore is found very often in the chamber. Junior senators are often asked to assume the chore. Nevertheless, speeches on the Senate floor begin with the salutation "Mr. President."

*Senate Majority and Minority Leaders* Senate leadership is actually in the hands of the Senate majority leader, but the Senate majority leader is not as powerful in that body as the Speaker is in the House. With fewer members, all of whom perceive themselves as powerful leaders, the Senate is less hierarchically organized than the House. The Senate majority leader's principal power is scheduling the business of the Senate and recognizing the first speaker in floor debate. To be effective in policy making, the majority leader must be skilled in interpersonal persuasion and communication. Moreover, in the media age, the Senate majority leader must also be a national spokesperson for the party, along with the Speaker of the House. With a Democrat in the White House, Republican Senate Leader Bob Dole and Republican Speaker of the House Newt Gingrich emerged as their party's leaders (see *People in Politics:* "Bob Dole, Running for President and Running the Senate"). The minority party leader in the Senate represents the opposition in negotiations with the majority leader over Senate business. With the majority leader, the minority party leader tends to dominate floor debate in the Senate.

*Career Paths within Congress* Movement up the party hierarchy in each house is the most common way of achieving a leadership position. The traditional succession pattern in the House is from whip to majority leader to Speaker. In the Senate, Republicans and Democrats frequently resort to election contests in choosing their party leaders, yet both parties have increasingly adopted a two-step succession route from whip to leader. Once in office, leaders in both parties are rarely removed.[26]

# IN COMMITTEE

Much of the real work of Congress is done in committee. The floor of Congress is often deserted; C-SPAN focuses on the podium, not the empty chamber. Members dash to the floor when the bell rings throughout the Capitol signaling a roll-call vote. Otherwise they are found in their offices or in the committee rooms, where the real work of Congress is done.

*Standing Committees* The committee system provides for a division of labor in the Congress, assigning responsibility for work and allowing members to develop some expertise. The committee system is as old as the Congress itself: the very first Congress regularly assigned the task of wording bills to selected members who were believed to have a particular expertise. Soon a system of **standing committees**—permanent committees that specialize in a particular area of legislation—emerged. House committees have thirty to forty members and Sen-

**Standing committee:** A permanent committee of the House or Senate that deals with matters within a specified subject area.

## Speaker Newt

Newt Gingrich is the most powerful Speaker of the House in modern times. In the midterm congressional elections of 1994, the Republican Party not only captured control of the U.S. Senate but also for the first time in forty years won control of the House of Representatives. The GOP victory enabled the brash, brilliant, and pugnacious southern conservative, Newt Gingrich, to assume the office of Speaker. Indeed, Gingrich sees himself as the architect of his party's stunning victory. It was Gingrich who composed the Republican "Contract with America" (see *Up Close:* "The Republican 'Contract with America,'" in Chapter 7). He sought to nationalize the House election, which had historically been decided on local issues and personalities in 435 separate districts, by setting forth clear party positions on key issues and pledging to bring them to a vote if Republicans won control of the House. With the contract, Gingrich seized the policy initiative away from the president.

Newt Gingrich was born in a military hospital in 1943 while his father was fighting in World War II. Highly opinionated even as a youngster, Newt was more comfortable with books than classmates. He was voted "most intellectual" in his senior year in high school. He attended college on a federal war orphans scholarship, and he took educational exemptions during the Vietnam War. He majored in history and earned a Ph.D. from Tulane University in 1971.

Gingrich was a young professor of history at West Georgia College when he first ran for Congress, in 1974. Twice he ran and lost in a traditionally Democratic district, but on his third try, in 1978, he won election to the House by projecting a strong conservative image. Upon his arrival in Washington, he rejected the traditional apprentice role for freshman members and chose instead to organize his fellow Republican conservatives. Gingrich sought not only to challenge the liberal Democratic majority leadership of the House but also to push moderate Republican minority leaders toward a more aggressive conservative stance. Gingrich quickly acquired a reputation as a "bomb thrower"—a pugnacious, guerrilla fighter—even within his own party. In 1986, he took control of a political action committee, GOPAC, dedicated to helping Republicans get elected. In this role he won the loyalty of many House Republicans to whom he directed money.

Gingrich mounted vicious attacks on Democrats in the Congress, even forcing the resignation of former House Speaker Jim Wright (Tex.) on ethics charges. In 1989, Gingrich challenged a more senior and more moderate Republican for the post of minority whip, the second highest post in the minority party in the House. He won a narrow victory with the support of many of the more conservative

ate committees fifteen to twenty members each. The proportions of Democrats and Republicans on each committee reflect the proportions of Democrats and Republicans in the House and Senate as a whole. Thus the majority party has a majority of members on every committee; and every committee is chaired by a member of the majority party. The minority membership on each committee is led by the *ranking minority member,* the minority party committee member with the most seniority.

The principal function of standing committees is the screening and drafting of legislation. With 6,000 to 8,000 or more bills introduced each session, the screening function is essential. The standing committees are the gatekeepers of Congress; less than 10 percent of the legislation introduced will pass the Congress. With rare exceptions, bills are not submitted to a vote by the full member-

Republican members. He opposed Republican President George Bush's agreement with congressional leaders to raise taxes in 1990, correctly perceiving the voters' wrath over Bush's broken "No new taxes!" promise. Although the media despised Gingrich's politics, his aggressive style made news, and soon Gingrich became the spokesperson for House Republicans. The soft-spoken moderate minority leader, Bob Michel (Ill.), decided to retire, and Gingrich assumed the GOP leadership post.

As a player of "hardball politics," Gingrich often finds himself on the receiving end of personal attacks. Democrats have filed several ethics complaints against the Speaker over his political action committee GOPAC and its contributions, over his televised college course, "Renewing American Civilization" and the sources of its funding, and over his contract with publisher HarperCollins to write two books. After charges that a $4.5 million advance on royalties represented an unethical "cashing in on his office," he declined the huge advance payment in favor of a standard author's contract. National polls suggest that he is not personally very popular with the American people; Gingrich believes this is a price that a revolutionary leader must pay.

Gingrich's popular image suffered during his budget battles with President Clinton. The president was successful in portraying Gingrich's proposed spending cuts as "radical" and in blaming the Speaker for the deadlock that temporarily shut down the government.

Gingrich sees himself as a modern "Third Wave" (Information Age) conservative who seeks to "revolutionize" government in America:

Government does some things very well. It defends the nation. It keeps the peace. It freed the slaves. It builds useful things, like the Panama Canal, and enables valuable research, like discovering the cure for polio. It can shape market forces creating the right incentives for saving or investing. Those are things government can do. . . .

Where Lyndon Johnson went wrong was that he thought government could do it all. In the 1960s, government crowded out private sector voluntarism. Secular bureaucracy crowded out spiritual commitment.

What was the result? The welfare state, a vast structure which leads to 12-year-olds getting pregnant, 14-year-olds getting killed, 17-year-olds dying of AIDS and 18-year-olds getting diplomas they can't read. . . . Our generation must replace, not repair, the welfare state. The welfare state has failed.

If Thomas Edison invented the electric light today, Dan Rather would report it on CBS News as "the candlemaking industry is threatened." You would get a downer. You would get a story explaining that electricity kills. At least three politicians would pass a bill banning electricity.*

*Newsweek, April 10, 1995, pp. 20–25; Time, December 25, 1995. See also Newt Gingrich, To Renew America (New York: HarperCollins, 1995).

ship of the House or Senate without prior approval by the majority of a standing committee. Moreover, committees do not merely sort through bills assigned to them to find what they like. Rather, committees—or more often their subcommittees—draft (write) legislation themselves. Committees may amend, rewrite, or write their own bills. Committees are "little legislatures" within their own policy jurisdictions. Each committee guards its own policy jurisdiction jealously; jurisdictional squabbles are common.

*Decentralization and Subcommittees* Congressional subcommittees within each standing committee further decentralize the legislative process. At present, the House has about 90 subcommittees and the Senate about 70 subcommittees, each of which functions independently of its full committee (see

TABLE 10-5    STANDING COMMITTEES IN CONGRESS

### Senate

| | |
|---|---|
| Agriculture, Nutrition, and Forestry | Foreign Relations |
| Appropriations | Governmental Affairs |
| Armed Services | Indian Affairs |
| Banking, Housing, and Urban Affairs | Judiciary |
| Budget | Labor and Human Resources |
| Commerce, Science, and Transportation | Rules and Administration |
| Energy and Natural Resources | Small Business |
| Environment and Public Works | Special Aging |
| Finance | Veterans Affairs |

### House

| | |
|---|---|
| Agriculture | National Security |
| Appropriations | Resources |
| Banking and Financial Services | Rules |
| Budget | Science |
| Commerce | Small Business |
| Economic and Educational Opportunities | Standards of Official Conduct |
| Government Reform and Oversight | Transportation and Infrastructure |
| House Oversight | Veterans Affairs |
| International Relations | Ways and Means |
| Judiciary | |

*Note:* Select Committees in Senate: Aging, Ethics, Intelligence; Select Committee in House: Intelligence.

Table 10-5). Subcommittees have fixed jurisdictions (for example, the House International Relations Committee has subcommittees on Africa, Asia and the Pacific, International Economic Policy, International Operations and Human Rights, and the Western Hemisphere); they meet and schedule their own hearings; and they have their own staffs and budgets. However, bills recommended by subcommittee still require full standing committee endorsement before being reported to the floor of the House or Senate. Full committees usually, but not always, ratify the decisions of their subcommittees.

Subcommittees decentralize power in Congress. Interest groups no longer concentrate their attention on a few senior standing committee chairs and party leaders. Rather, they concentrate on those subcommittees dealing most directly with their concerns. Likewise, executive agencies must respond to subcommittees with policy oversight. Both lobbyists and bureaucrats must seek out "their" subcommittee and try to win the support of the chair and perhaps the ranking minority member. (For example, agents of the postal workers' union, the U.S. Postal Service, and private competitors such as Federal Express and United Parcel Service all converge on the Post Office and Civil Service subcommittee of the Senate Governmental Affairs Committee.) The result has been hundreds of policy networks, each featuring subcommittee members and staff, lobbyists with an interest in the subcommittee's field, and bureaucrats in the executive branch charged with implementing congressional policy in that field.

Chairing a committee or subcommittee gives members of Congress the opportunity to exercise power, attract media attention, and thus improve their chances of reelection. Often committees have become "fiefdoms" over which their chairs

# Bob Dole: Running the Senate, and then Running for President

Bob Dole's withered right arm is a permanent reminder of the personal sacrifice he made fighting for his country more than fifty years ago. The last national leader from the World War II generation, Dole spent thirty-five years in Congress, eleven of them as Senate Republican leader. In 1996, at the age of 73, he became the oldest person ever nominated for president by a major party.

Dole was a high school athlete in tiny Russell, Kansas, who went on to the University of Kansas, waiting tables at a fraternity house and hoping to win an athletic scholarship. But the army called him to war in 1943, and by 1945, Lieutenant Dole was leading a platoon of the Tenth Mountain Division against German forces in northern Italy. He was nearly blown apart by mortar and machine gun fire and lay bloodsoaked on the battlefield for nine hours. Two medics were killed trying to reach him before he was finally dragged to a field hospital. His right arm was shattered, his collarbone and vertebrae were broken, and he was paralyzed from the neck down. He would spend the next three years in hospitals, surviving several close brushes with death from secondary infections. In 1947 the people of Russell contributed to a fund to pay for his travel to Chicago, where a specialist performed seven grueling operations on him for no charge. His long, torturous rehabilitation included learning to walk, eat, and dress himself again. He married his physical therapist, finished college, and enrolled at tiny Washburn Municipal University law school in Topeka in 1952.

But even before he finished law school, Dole won a seat in the Kansas legislature at the age of twenty-six. He would not be out of public office for the next forty-seven years. He was district attorney for Russell County, Kansas, for four terms, then a Kansas state congressman for four terms. In 1968 he was elected to the U.S. Senate and was reelected by large margins in subsequent elections. He divorced his first wife in 1972 and married Elizabeth Hanford Dole, a member of the Federal Trade Commission,

in 1975. She later became secretary of transportation in the Reagan administration and now heads the American Red Cross.

In 1976 Dole was Gerald Ford's vice-presidential running mate on the unsuccessful Republican ticket. In that campaign Dole gained a reputation as a "hatchet man," especially in comparison to the boy scout image of Walter Mondale, the Democratic candidate for vice-president. Dole is perhaps one of the wittiest elected officials in Washington, but on television his quips often seem bitter and caustic.

In his eight years in the House and twenty-seven in the Senate, Dole developed a reputation as an honest bargainer, negotiator, and compromiser. He supported big spending programs for his farm constituents, including food stamps and school lunches, as well as programs for veterans and handicapped people, yet he also fought against government deficits. In 1983 his Republican colleagues in the Senate elected him their leader. Rather than pursuing an ideological agenda, Dole led by conciliation and compromise. He supported Bush's tax increase in 1990, the landmark Americans with Disabilities Act, and the Brady Gun Control Act. These votes raised doubts among his party's conservatives, yet his lifetime rating on over 12,000 roll call votes by the American Conservative Union was 82 out of 100.

Following the Republican congressional victories in 1994, Dole appeared to be overshadowed by House Speaker Newt Gingrich. But as Newt's public image soured, Dole again emerged as the Republican party's leading spokesman. In his quest for the presidency in 1996, Dole's long service made him the favorite of the GOP establishment. Although Pat Buchanan rallied the party's die-hard conservatives to win the New Hampshire primary, Dole convinced Republican voters that it was his turn to lead the party. Although Dole would tout his rural roots in Russell, Kansas, most Americans viewed him as a lifetime Washington insider. But running the Senate and running for president proved incompatible. In May 1996, his voice choked with emotion, Dole resigned from the Senate he loved to invigorate his campaign:

> My time to leave this office has come, and I will seek the presidency with nothing to fall back on but the judgment of the people, and nowhere to go but the White House or home.

exercise complete control and jealously guard their power. This situation allows a very small number of House and Senate members to block legislation. Many decisions are not really made by the whole Congress. Rather they are made by subcommittee members with a special interest in the policy under consideration. In addition, the subcommittee system is fragmented and more easily dominated by special interests who need only to "capture" a few members to influence policy making in their area of interest.

While the committee system may satisfy the desire of members to gain power, prestige, and reelection opportunities, it weakens responsible government in the Congress as a whole. Party leaders in the Congress—notably the House Speaker and Senate majority leader—have less authority to push the party's legislative agenda through the Congress. Speaker Newt Gingrich was especially effective in pressuring House Republican chairs into producing the legislation called for by the "Contract with America" within the first 100 days of the new Congress. But Senate Majority Leader Bob Dole was unable to push his senior committee chairs in the same fashion. Frequently new members of Congress complain about the power of committees and subcommittees and the senior members who chair them. In 1995, the new Republican majority in the House streamlined that body's committee structure, eliminating several standing committees, reducing the number of subcommittees, and setting six-year term limits for chairs. (See *Up Close:* "The House Tries to Reform Itself.") The Senate, however, retained its traditional committee structure and rules.

*Committee Membership*  Given the power of the committee system, it comes as little surprise to learn that members of Congress have a very keen interest in their committee assignments. Members strive for assignments that will give them

## The House Tries to Reform Itself

For years reformers had urged the Congress, especially the House of Representatives, to review its rules to expedite lawmaking, focus more attention on national issues, respond to popular concerns, and become a more open, accountable body. On the first day of the 104th Congress in January 1995, the newly elected Republican majority, with considerable Democratic support, enacted a series of rules changes that went a long way toward reforming House operations. Among the rules changes enacted:

- Total numbers of committee and subcommittee staff were cut by one-third.
- Three standing committees were abolished, reducing the total from twenty-two to nineteen, and a new rule limited each standing committee to no more than five subcommittees (except for Appropriations, thirteen; Government Reform and Oversight, seven; and Transportation and Infrastructure, six).
- Funding for the House's twenty-eight "caucuses" was eliminated, from the powerful Congressional Black Caucus to the less influential Hunger Caucus, Space Caucus, Textile Caucus, and Sunbelt Caucus.
- Members were limited to serving on no more than two standing committees and four subcommittees.
- Chairs were prohibited from casting proxy votes, and committees were instructed to publish all members' votes on all bills.
- Committees and subcommittees were barred from closing meetings except to protect national security, law enforcement, or ethics investigations.
- The Speaker may no longer send a bill to more than one committee simultaneously for consideration.
- The Speaker may serve no more than four consecutive two-year terms, and committee chairs are limited to three consecutive terms in these posts.
- Commemorative legislation—for example, bills designating "National Drinking Water Week," "Be Kind to Animals Day," or "Boy Scout of the Year"— may no longer be introduced or considered.
- A three-fifths majority of members voting will be required to pass a bill raising income taxes.

Most of these reforms were welcomed by congressional conservatives and scholars. The supermajority requirement to pass tax increases was challenged as unconstitutional, inasmuch as the Constitution specifies supermajority votes only for constitutional amendments, overriding presidential vetoes, Senate trial on impeachment, and Senate ratification of treaties. But the courts may decide not to intervene in House rules. However, future Congresses can vote to change these rules again. And historically, changes trumpeted as "reforms" have often created new problems. Whether these new rules, or indeed the future performance of Congress, can rehabilitate its reputation with the American people remains to be seen.

influence in Congress, allow them to exercise power in Washington, and ultimately improve their chances for reelection. For example, a member from a big city may seek a seat on Banking, Finance, and Urban Affairs, while a member from a farm district may seek a seat on Agriculture and a member from a district with a large military base may seek a seat on National Security or Veterans Affairs. Everyone seeks a seat on Appropriations, since both the House and Senate Appropriations Committees have subcommittees on each area of federal spending.

Party leadership in both the House and Senate largely determines committee assignments. These assignments are given to new Democratic House members by the Democratic Steering and Policy Committee; new Democratic senators receive their assignments from the Senate Democratic Steering Committee. New Republican members receive their committee assignments from the Republican

Committee on Committees in both houses. The leadership generally tries to honor new members' requests and improve their chances for reelection, but since incumbent members of committees are seldom removed, openings on powerful committees are infrequent.

*Seniority*  Committee chairs are elected in the majority party caucus. But the **seniority system** governs most movement into committee leadership positions. The seniority system ranks all committee members in each party according to the length of time they have served on the committee. If the majority party chair exits the Congress or leaves the committee, that position is filled by the next *ranking majority party member.* New members of a committee are initially added to the bottom of the ranking of their party; they climb the seniority ranking by remaining on the committee and accruing years of seniority. Members who stay in Congress but "hop" committees are usually placed at the bottom of their new committee's list.

The seniority system has a long tradition in the Congress. The advantage is that it tends to reduce conflict among members, who otherwise would be constantly engaged in running for committee posts. It also increases the stability of policy direction in committees over time. Critics of the system note, though, that the seniority system grants greater power to members from "safe" districts—districts that offer little electoral challenge to the incumbent. (Historically in the Democratic Party, these districts were in the conservative South, and opposition to the seniority system developed among liberal northern Democrats. But in recent years, many liberal big-city Democrats gained seniority and the seniority system again became entrenched.) The seniority rule for selecting committee chairs has been violated on only a few notable occasions.

*Committee Hearings*  The decision of a congressional committee to hold public hearings on a bill or topic is an important one. It signals congressional interest in a particular policy matter and sets the agenda for congressional policy making. Ignoring an issue by refusing to hold hearings on it usually condemns it to oblivion. Public hearings allow interest groups and government bureaucrats to present formal arguments to Congress. Testimony comes mostly from government officials, lobbyists, and occasional experts recommended by interest groups or committee staff members. Hearings are usually organized by the staff under the direction of the chair. Staff members contact favored lobbyists and bureaucrats and schedule their appearances. Committee hearings are regularly listed in the *Washington Post* and are open to the public. Indeed, the purpose of many hearings is not really to inform members of Congress but instead to rally public support behind an issue or a bill. The media are the real target audience of many public hearings, with committee members jockeying in front of the cameras for a "sound bite" on the evening news.

*Markup*  Once hearings are completed, the committee's staff is usually assigned the task of writing a report and **drafting a bill.** The staff's bill generally reflects the chair's policy views. But the staff draft is subject to committee **markup**—a line-by-line consideration of the wording of the bill. Markup sessions are frequently closed to the public in order to expedite work. Lobbyists are forced to stand in the hallways, buttonholing members as they go into and out of committee rooms.

It is in markup that the detailed work of lawmaking takes place. Markup sessions require patience and skill in negotiation. Committee or subcommittee chairs

**Seniority system:** The custom whereby the member of Congress who has served the longest on the majority side of a committee becomes its chair and the member who has served the longest on the minority side becomes its ranking member.

**Drafting a bill:** The actual writing of a bill in legal language.

**Markup:** The line-by-line revision of a bill in committee by editing each phrase and word.

may try to develop consensus on various parts of the bill, either within the whole committee or within the committee's majority. In marking up a bill, members of a subcommittee must always remember that the bill must pass in both the full committee and on the floor of the chamber. While they have considerable freedom in writing their own policy preferences into law, especially on the details of the legislation, they must give some consideration to the views of these larger bodies. Consultations with party leadership are not infrequent.

Most bills "die" in committee. Some are voted down, but most are simply ignored. Bills introduced simply to reassure constituents or interest groups that a representative is committed to "doing something" for them generally die quietly. But House members who really want action on a bill can be frustrated by committee inaction. The only way to force a floor vote on a bill opposed by a committee is to get a majority (218) of House members to sign a **discharge petition.** Out of hundreds of discharge petition efforts, only a few dozen have succeeded. The Senate also can forcibly "discharge" a bill from committee by simple majority vote; but since senators can attach any amendment to any bill they wish, there is generally no need to go this route.

## ON THE FLOOR

A favorable *report* by a standing committee of the House or Senate places a bill on the *calendar*. The word "calendar" is misleading, since bills on the calendar are not considered in chronological order, and many die on the calendar without ever reaching the floor.

*House Rules Committee*   Even after a bill has been approved by a standing committee, getting it to the floor of the House of Representatives for a vote by the full membership requires favorable action by the Rules Committee. The Rules Committee acts as a powerful "traffic cop" for the House. In order to reach the floor, a bill must receive a rule from the Rules Committee. The Rules Committee can kill a bill simply by refusing to give it a rule. A **rule** determines when the bill will be considered by the House and how long the debate on the bill will last. More important, a rule determines whether amendments from the floor will be permitted and, if so, how many. A **closed rule** forbids House members from offering any amendments and speeds up consideration of the bill in the form submitted by the standing committee. A **restricted rule** allows certain specified amendments to be considered. An **open rule** permits unlimited amendments.

When a bill comes to the floor, the full House must decide whether to adopt the Rules Committee rule, but it almost always does so. Most key bills are brought to the floor of the House with fairly restrictive rules. In recent sessions, about three-quarters of all bills reaching the floor were restricted, while an additional 10 to 15 percent were fully closed. Only a few bills were open.

*Senate Floor Traditions*   The Senate has no rules committee but relies instead upon a *unanimous consent agreement* negotiated between the majority and minority leader to govern consideration of a bill. The unanimous consent agreement generally specifies when the bill will be debated, what amendments will be considered, and when the final vote will be taken. But as the name implies, a

**Discharge petition:** A petition signed by at least 218 House members to force a vote on a bill within a committee that opposes it.

**Rule:** Stipulation attached to a bill in the House of Representatives that governs its consideration on the floor, including when and for how long it can be debated and how many (if any) amendments may be appended to it.

**Closed rule:** A rule that forbids adding any amendments to a bill under consideration by the House.

**Restricted rule:** A rule that allows specified amendments to be added to a bill under consideration by the House.

**Open rule:** A rule that permits unlimited amendments to a bill under consideration by the House.

single senator can object to a unanimous consent agreement and thus hold up Senate consideration of a bill. Senators do not usually do so, because they know that a reputation for obstructionism will imperil their own favorite bills at a later date. Once accepted, a unanimous consent agreement is binding on the Senate and cannot be changed without another unanimous consent agreement. To get unanimous consent, Senate leaders must consult with all interested senators. Unanimous consent agreements have become more common in recent years as they have become more specific in their provisions.

The Senate cherishes its tradition of unrestricted floor debate. Senators may speak as long as they wish or even try to **filibuster** a bill to death by talking nonstop and tying up the Senate for so long that the leadership is forced to drop the bill in order to go on to other work. Senate rules also allow senators to place a "hold" on a bill, indicating their unwillingness to grant unanimous consent to its consideration. Debate may be ended only if sixty or more senators vote for **cloture,** a process of petition and voting that limits the debate. A cloture vote requires a petition signed by sixteen senators; two days must elapse between the petition's introduction and the cloture vote. If cloture passes, then each senator is limited to one hour of debate on the bill. Despite the obstacles to cloture, in recent years it has been used with increasing frequency.

Senate floor procedures also permit unlimited amendments to be offered, even those that are not *germane* to the bill. A **rider** is an amendment to a bill that is not germane to the bill's purposes.

These Senate traditions of unlimited debate and unrestricted floor amendments give individual senators considerably more power over legislation than individual representatives enjoy.

*Floor Voting*   The key floor votes are usually on *amendments* to bills rather than on their final passage. Indeed, "killer amendments" are deliberately designed to defeat the original purpose of the bill. Other amendments may water down the bill so much that it will have little policy impact. Thus the true policy preferences of senators or representatives may be reflected more in their votes on amendments than their vote on final passage. Members may later claim to have supported legislation on the basis of their vote on final passage, even though they earlier voted for amendments designed to defeat the bill's purposes.

Members may also obscure their voting records by calling for a voice vote—simply shouting "aye" or "nay"—and avoiding recording of their individual votes. In contrast, a **roll-call vote** involves the casting of individual votes, which are reported in the *Congressional Record* and are available to the media and the general public. Electronic voting machines in the House allow members to insert their cards and record their votes automatically. The Senate, truer to tradition, uses no electronic counters.

*Conference Committees*   The Constitution requires that both houses of Congress pass a bill with identical wording. However, many major bills pass each house in different forms, not only with different wording but sometimes with wholly different provisions. Occasionally the House or the Senate will resolve these differences by reconsidering the matter and passing the other chamber's version of the bill. But about 15 percent of the time, serious differences arise and bills are assigned to **conference committees** to reach agreement on a single version for resubmission to both houses.

**Filibuster:** A delaying tactic by a senator or group of senators, using the Senate's unlimited debate rule to prevent a vote on a bill.

**Cloture:** A vote to end debate—that is, to end a filibuster—that requires a three-fifths vote of the entire membership of the Senate.

**Rider:** An amendment to a bill that is not germane to the bill's purposes.

**Roll-call vote:** A vote of the full House or Senate on which all members' individual votes are recorded and made public.

**Conference committee:** A meeting between representatives of the House and Senate to reconcile differences over provisions of a bill passed by both houses.

CHAPTER 10 • CONGRESS: POLITICS ON CAPITOL HILL

**FIGURE 10-10** **How a Bill Becomes a Law**

*This diagram depicts the major hurdles a successful bill must overcome in order to be enacted into law. Few bills introduced travel this full path; less than 10 percent of bills introduced are passed by Congress and sent to the president for approval or veto. Bills fail at every step along the path, but most die in committees and subcommittees, usually from inaction rather than from being voted down.*

**Bill Introduction**

**Subcommittee Hearings**

**Committee Action**

**Floor Action**

**Conference Action**

**Presidential Decision**

### HOUSE

Bill is introduced and assigned to a committee, which refers it to the appropriate subcommittee.

**Subcommittee**
Subcommittee holds hearings and "marks up" the bill. If the bill is approved in some form, it goes to the full committee.

**Committee**
Full committee considers the bill. If the bill is approved in some form, it is "reported" to the full House and placed on the House calendar.

**Rules Committee**
Rules Committee issues a rule to govern debate on the floor. Sends it to the full House.

**Full House**
Full House debates the bill and may amend it. If the bill passes and it is in a form different from the Senate version, it must go to a conference committee.

### SENATE

Bill is introduced and assigned to a committee, which refers it to the appropriate subcommittee.

**Subcommittee**
Subcommittee holds hearings, debates provisions and "marks up" the bill. If a bill is approved, it goes to the full committee.

**Committee**
Full committee considers the bill. If the bill is approved in some form, it is "reported" to the full Senate and placed on the Senate calendar.

**Leadership**
Majority and minority leaders "unanimous consent" agreements schedule full Senate debate and vote on the bill.

**Full Senate**
Full Senate debates the bill. Senate may amend it. If the bill passes and is in a form different from the House version, it must go to a conference committee.

**Conference Committee**
Conference committee of senators and representatives meets to reconcile differences between bills. When agreement is reached, a compromise bill is sent back to both the House and the Senate.

**President**
President signs or vetoes the bill. Congress can override a veto by a two-thirds majority vote in both the House and Senate.

**LAW**

Conference committees are temporary, with members appointed by the leadership in each house, usually from among the senior members of the committees that approved the bills. Since conference committee members are also members of the relevant standing committees in the House and Senate, the conference battle is often between these separate committees—for example, between the House and Senate Appropriations Committees. Traditionally, conference committee "reports" parallel Senate versions of the bill more closely than House versions. Conference committees write a single compromise version of the bill that must be passed by both houses *without amendments* in order to become law. Conferees often try to persuade their counterparts from the other chamber that "if we surrender on this point, our house will defeat the bill." Once agreement is reached in conference, conference committee members are expected to support the bill in their respective houses. Figure 10-10 summarizes the lawmaking process.

Conference committees can be very powerful. Their final bill is usually (though not always) passed in both houses and sent to the president for approval. In resolving differences between the House and the Senate versions, the conference committee makes many final policy decisions. While conference committees have considerable leeway in striking compromises, they focus on points of disagreement and usually do not change provisions already approved by both houses.

## DECISION MAKING IN CONGRESS

How do senators and representatives decide about how they will vote on legislation? From an almost limitless number of considerations that go into congressional decision making, a few factors recur across a range of voting decisions: party loyalty, presidential support or opposition, constituency concerns, interest-group pressures, and the personal values and ideologies of members themselves.[27]

*Party Voting*    Party remains a significant influence on congressional voting. **Party votes** are roll-call votes on which a majority of voting Democrats oppose a majority of voting Republicans. Over the years, party votes have occurred in roughly *half* of all roll-call votes in Congress. Party votes decline slightly in election years (when representatives and senators are most concerned with how they look to voters). Partisanship in Congress, as reflected in the percentage of party votes, has risen steadily in recent years. New highs in partisan votes were recorded in 1995. Party votes appear more frequently in the House than in the Senate (see Figure 10-11).

**Party unity** is measured by the percentage of Democrats and Republicans who stick by their party on party votes. Republican party unity has remained at fairly constant levels (75-85 percent) in both the House and the Senate over the past twenty years. Until recently, Democratic Party cohesion was weakened by the frequent defection of southern Democrats. But in the last several sessions, Democratic Party unity in the House has matched that of the Republican Party, with both parties holding the votes of over 80 percent of their members.

Why does party continue to be an important influence in congressional voting when party leaders cannot deny renomination to members or influence party primary elections in districts or states? First of all, Democratic and Republican members of Congress tend to be ideologically distinct. Democratic members of both the House and Senate are more liberal on social and economic issues than are

**Party vote:** A majority of Democrats voting in opposition to a majority of Republicans.

**Party unity:** The percentage of Democrats and Republicans who stick with their party on party votes.

CHAPTER 10 • CONGRESS: POLITICS ON CAPITOL HILL

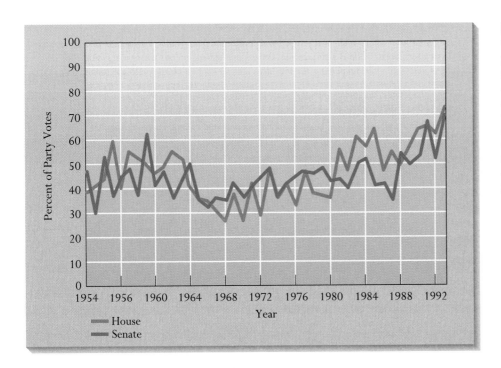

FIGURE 10-11    **Party Voting in Congress**
*Partisanship varies over time in Congress. For many years, between 30 and 60 percent of votes in the House and Senate were party votes—votes on which a majority of Democrats were in opposition to a majority of Republicans—but in recent years the percentage has risen, indicating an increasingly partisan environment in Congress.*

Republican members. Thus ideological like-mindedness accounts for much of the party cohesion observed in congressional roll-call votes.

Conflict between the parties occurs frequently on domestic social and economic issues—welfare, housing and urban affairs, health, business regulation, taxing, and spending. On civil rights issues, voting often follows party lines on amendments and other preliminary matters but then swings to **bipartisan** voting on a final bill. This pattern suggests that the parties tend to agree on the general goals of civil rights legislation but not on the means. Traditionally, bipartisanship was the goal of both presidents and congressional leaders on foreign and defense policy issues. Since the Vietnam War, however, Democrats in the House have been more critical of U.S. military involvements (and defense spending in general) than have Republicans, though many Democrats in the Senate have continued to support presidential initiatives.

Party may also influence congressional voting even when ideology is not a concern. Members of Congress run under party labels. (Only one Independent, Vermont's Bernard Sanders, serves in the House.) So there is some incentive for Democrats and Republicans in Congress to improve the image of their parties generally. The party leadership tries to appeal to party loyalty whenever it can. Members do have an interest in seeing their party win majority status in their chamber. Majority status means committee and subcommittee chairs, control over committee and subcommittee budgets and staff, and a better opportunity to get pork-barrel legislation passed. Finally, party leaders in the House and Senate do have modest favors to disperse. In short, party loyalty is not an insignificant factor in congressional voting.

*Presidential Support or Opposition*    Presidential influence in congressional voting is closely tied to party. Presidents almost always receive their greatest support from members of their own party (see Figure 10-12). Indeed,

**Bipartisan:** Agreement by members of both the Democratic and the Republican parties.

FIGURE 10-12 **Congressional Voting in Support of the President, 1977–1995**

*Presidents always receive more support in Congress from members of their own party. Democratic presidents Jimmy Carter and Bill Clinton could count on winning large majorities of Democratic members' votes, while Republican presidents Ronald Reagan and George Bush won large majorities of GOP members' votes. Percentages indicate congressional votes supporting the president on votes on which the president took a position.*

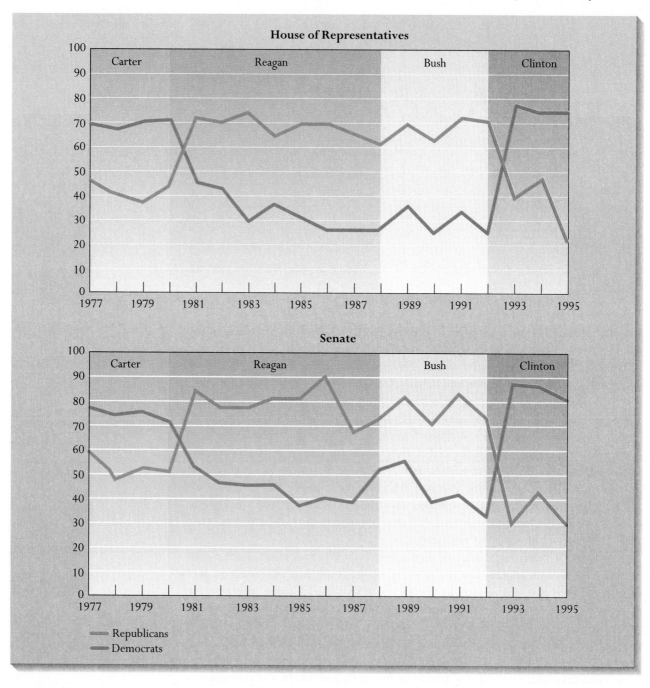

*Source:* Norman J. Ornstein, *Vital Statistics on Congress* (Washington, D.C.: Congressional Quarterly Press, 1996); updated by author.

the policy *gridlock* associated with *divided government*—in past decades, a Republican president and a Democratic-controlled Congress, but in 1995 and 1996 a Democratic president and a Republican-controlled Congress—arises directly from the tendency of the opposition party to obstruct the president's policy proposals.

Presidential influence is diluted not only by party opposition but also by the electoral independence of members of Congress. Winning presidential candidates have been unable to pull many of their party's congressional candidates into office with them. Only Dwight Eisenhower in 1952, Lyndon Johnson in 1964, and Ronald Reagan in 1980 succeeded in helping elect many of their party's candidates to Congress. It is interesting to note that in these cases the new president was highly successful in winning Congress members' votes, even many from the opposition party (see Reagan in 1981 in Figure 10-12).

The decentralization of power in the congressional committee system also limits the president's ability to influence voting. The president cannot simply negotiate with the leadership of the House and Senate but instead must deal with scores of committee and subcommittee chairs and ranking members. To win the support of so many members of Congress, presidents often must agree to insert pork into presidential bills, promise patronage jobs, or offer presidential assistance in campaign fund raising.

If negotiations break down, presidents can "go over the heads" of Congress, using the media to appeal directly to the people to support presidential programs and force Congress to act. The president has better access to the media than Congress has. But such threats and appeals can only be effective when (1) the president himself is popular with the public (no president used media powers more effectively than Ronald Reagan); and (2) the issue is one about which constituents can be made to feel intensely.

Finally, presidents can threaten to veto legislation. This threat, expressed or implied, confronts congressional leaders, committee chairs, and sponsors of a bill with several options. They must decide whether to (1) modify the bill to overcome the president's objections; (2) try to get two-thirds of both houses to commit to overriding the threatened veto; or (3) pass the bill and dare the president to veto it, then make a political issue out of the president's opposition. Historically, less than 5 percent of vetoes have been overridden by the Congress. Unless the president is politically very weak (as Richard Nixon was during the Watergate scandal), Congress cannot count on overriding a veto. If members of Congress truly want to address an important problem and not just define a political issue, they must negotiate with the White House to write a bill the president will sign.

*Constituency Influence*   Constituency influence in congressional voting is most apparent on issues that attract media attention and discussion and generate intense feelings among the general public. If many voters in the home state or district know about an issue and have intense feelings about it, members of Congress almost always defer to their constituents' feelings, regardless of the position of their party's leadership or even their own personal feelings.[28] Members of Congress from *safe seats* seem to be just as attuned to the interests of their constituents as members from competitive seats.

Constituency influence is particularly important on economic issues. Members from districts heavily dependent on a particular industry are routinely found protecting and advancing the interests of that industry. This kind of constituency representation is not unlike pork-barrel politics.

Constituencies may also exercise a subtle influence by conditioning the personal views of members. Many members were born, were raised, and continue to live in the towns they represent; over a lifetime they have absorbed and internalized the views of their communities. Moreover, some members of Congress feel an obligation to represent their constituents' opinions even when they personally disagree.

Members of Congress have considerable latitude in voting against their constituents' opinions if they choose to do so. Constituents, as noted earlier, lack information about most policy issues and the voting records of their senators and representatives. Even when constituents know about an issue and feel strongly about it, members can afford to cast a "wrong" vote from time to time. A long record of home-style politics—casework, pork-barreling, visits, public appearances, and so on—can isolate members of Congress from the wrath generated by their voting records. Only a long string of "wrong" votes on issues important to constituents is likely to jeopardize an incumbent.

*Interest-Group Influence*   Inside the Washington Beltway, the influence of interest groups, lobbyists, and fund raisers on members of Congress is well understood. This influence is seldom talked about back home or on the campaign trail, except perhaps by challengers. Lobbyists have their greatest effects on the *details* of public policy. Congressional decisions made in committee rooms, at markup sessions, and around conference tables can mean billions of dollars to industries and tens of millions to individual companies. Pressures from competing interest groups can be intense, as lobbyists buttonhole lawmakers and try to win legislative amendments that can make or break business fortunes. One of the most potent tools in the lobbyist's arsenal is money. The prohibitive cost of modern campaigning has dictated that dollars are crucial to electoral victory, and virtually all members of Congress spend more time than they would like courting it, raising it, and stockpiling it for the next election.

Voters may be wrong when they think that all members of Congress are crooks, but they are not far off the mark when they worry that their own representatives may be listening to two competing sets of constituents—the real constituents back home in the district and the cash constituents who come calling in Washington, D.C.[29]

*Personal Values*   It was the eighteenth-century English political philosopher Edmund Burke, himself a member of Parliament, who told his constituents: "You choose a member indeed; but when you have chosen him, he is not a member of Bristol, but he is a member of *Parliament*." Burke defended the classic notion of representatives as *trustees* who are obligated to use their own best judgment about what is good for the nation as a whole. In this theory, representatives are not obligated to vote the views of their constituents. This notion contrasts with the idea of representatives as *delegates* who are obligated to vote according to the views of their constituents regardless of their own personal viewpoint.

While democratic political philosophers have pondered the merits of trustee versus delegate representation over the centuries, the question only rarely arises in actual congressional deliberations. In many cases, members' own personal views and those of their constituents are virtually identical. (However, there is some evidence that members themselves may exaggerate the knowledge and issue-oriented tendencies of voters, since those most likely to communicate directly with their members of Congress are among the most knowledgeable and issue-oriented people in the district.)[30] Even when legislators perceive conflicts between their own views and those of their constituents, most attempt to find a compromise between these competing demands rather than choose one role or another exclusively. The political independence of members of Congress—their independence from party, combined with the ignorance of their constituents about most policy issues—allows members to give great weight to their own personal ideologies in voting.

## CUSTOMS AND NORMS

Over time, institutions develop customs and norms of behavior to assist in their functioning. These are not merely quaint and curious folkways; they promote the purposes of the institution. Congressional customs and norms are designed to help members work together, to reduce interpersonal conflict, to facilitate bargaining and promote compromise, and in general to make life in Congress a little more pleasant.

Consider, for example, the celebrated custom of members of Congress referring to each other in elaborately courteous terms: "my distinguished colleague from Ohio," "the honorable representative from Pennsylvania," and the like. By custom, even bitter partisan enemies in Congress are expected to avoid harsh personal attacks on each other. The purpose of this custom is to try to maintain an atmosphere in which people who hold very different opinions can nevertheless function with some degree of decorum. Unfortunately, many of these customs and norms of behavior are breaking down. Individual ambition and the drive for power and celebrity have led to a decline in courtesy, cooperation, and respect for traditional norms. One result is that it has become increasingly difficult for Congress to reach agreement on policy issues. Another result is that life in Congress is increasingly tedious, conflict-filled, and unpleasant.

Democrats in the House of Representatives display a blow-up of a newspaper headline mocking House speaker Newt Gingrich, to the objection of House Republicans. These kinds of displays are becoming increasingly common as traditional congressional norms of decorum and courtesy break down.

*The Demise of the Apprenticeship Norm*   Not too many years ago, "the first rule"[31] of congressional behavior was that new members were expected to be seen but not heard on the floor, to be studious in their committee work, and to be cooperative with party leaders. But the institutional norm of apprenticeship was swept aside in the 1970s as increasingly ambitious and independent senators and representatives arrived on Capitol Hill. Today new members of Congress feel free to grab the spotlight on the floor, in committee, and in front of television cameras. "The evidence is clear, unequivocal, and overwhelming: the [apprenticeship] norm is simply gone."[32] Nevertheless, experienced members are more active and influential in shaping legislation than are new members.[33]

*Specialization and Deference*   The committee system encourages members of Congress to specialize in particular policy areas. Even the most independent and ambitious members can perceive the advantage of developing power and expertise in an area especially relevant to their constituents. Traditionally, members who developed a special expertise and accumulated years of service on a standing committee were deferred to in floor proceedings. These specialists were "cue givers" for party members when bills or amendments were being voted upon. Members are still likely to defer to specialized committee members when the issues are technical or complicated, or when the issue is outside of their own area of policy specialization, but deference is increasingly rare on major public issues.

*Bargaining*   Bargaining is central to the legislative process. Little could be achieved if individual members were unwilling to bargain with each other for votes both in committees and on the floor. A willingness to bargain is a long-standing functional norm of Congress.

Members of Congress are not expected to violate their consciences in the bargaining process. On the contrary, members respect one another's issues of conscience and receive respect in return. On most issues, however, members can and do bargain their support. "Horse trading" is very common in committee work. "Congressional committees are natural settings for bargaining. In many cases the decisions made in congressional committees are ratified on the floor of the House or, to a lesser extent, the floor of the Senate; hence, to wait until a bill reaches the floor before striking bargains is to wait too long."[34] Members may bargain in their own personal interest, in the interests of constituents or groups, or even in the interests of their committee with members of other committees. Since most bargaining occurs in a committee setting, it is seldom a matter of public record. The success and reputation of committee chairs are largely dependent on their ability to work out bargains and compromises.

Bargaining can assume different forms. Explicit trade-offs such as "If you vote for my bill, I'll vote for yours" are the simplest form of bargaining, but implicit understandings may be more common. Members may help other members in anticipation of receiving reciprocal help at some future unspecified time. Moreover, representatives who refuse to cooperate on a regular basis may find little support for their own bills. Mutual "back scratching" allows members to develop a reservoir of IOUs for the future. Building credit is good business for most members; one can never tell when one will need help in the future.

Bargaining requires a certain kind of integrity. Members of Congress must stick to their agreements. They must not consistently ask too high a price for their cooperation. They must recognize and return favors. They must not renege on promises. They must be trustworthy.

Conference committee bargaining is essential if legislation acceptable to both houses is to be written. Indeed, it is expected that conferees from each house will bargain and compromise their differences. "Every House-Senate conference is expected to proceed via the methods of 'give and take,' 'trading back and forth,' 'pulling and hauling,' 'horse-trading and compromise,' 'splitting the difference,' etc."[35]

*Reciprocity*   The norm of *reciprocity*—favors rendered should be repaid in kind—supports the bargaining process. Reciprocity may mean simply supporting a bill that is important to a colleague. But it may also extend to committees and subcommittees. In order to minimize intercommittee disputes over legislation, jurisdiction, or appropriations, "committees negotiate treaties of reciprocity ranging from 'I will stay out of your specialty if you will stay out of mine,' to 'I'll support your bill if you will support mine.'"[36]

The norm of reciprocity facilitates compromise and agreement and getting the work of Congress accomplished. Members who were willing to accept "half a loaf" traditionally accomplished more than those who insisted on a "whole loaf." But the norm of reciprocity may have weakened in recent years.

*Logrolling*   Perhaps the most celebrated and reviled form of reciprocity, **logrolling** is mutual agreement to support projects that primarily benefit individual members of Congress and their constituencies. Logrolling is closely associated with pork-barrel legislation. Yet it can occur in virtually any kind of legislation. Even interest-group lobbyists may logroll with each other, promising to support each other's legislative agendas.

*Leader-Follower Relations*   Since leaders have few means of disciplining members, they must rely heavily on their bargaining skills to solicit cooperation and get the work of Congress accomplished. Party leaders can appeal to members' concerns for their party image among the voters. Individual majority members want to keep their party in the majority—if for no other reason than to retain their committee and subcommittee chairs. Individual minority members would like their party to win control of their house in order to assume the power and privileges of committee and subcommittee chairs. Party leaders must appeal to more than partisanship to win cooperation, however.

To secure cooperation, leaders can grant—or withhold—some tangible benefits. A member of the House needs the Speaker's support to get recognition, to have a bill called up, to get a bill scheduled, to see to it that a bill gets assigned to a preferred committee, to get a good committee assignment, to help a bill get out of the Rules Committee, for example.

Party leaders may also seek to gain support from their followers by doing favors that ease their lives in Washington, advance their legislative careers, and help them with their reelection. Favors from party leaders place members under obligation to respond to leaders' requests at a later time. Members themselves like to build up a reservoir of good feeling and friendship with the leadership, knowing that eventually they will need some favors from the leadership.

**Logrolling:** Bargaining for agreement among legislators to support each other's favorite bills, especially projects that primarily benefit individual members and their constituents.

# CONGRESSIONAL ETHICS

While critics might consider the phrase *congressional ethics* to be an oxymoron, the moral climate of Congress today is probably better than in earlier eras of American history. Nevertheless, Congress as an institution has suffered from well-publicized recent scandals that have prompted calls for reform (see *Up Close:* "The Keating Five: Service to Constituents for a Price?").

*Ethics Rules*  Congress has an interest in maintaining the integrity of the institution itself and the trust of the people. Thus Congress has established its own rules of ethics. These rules include:

- *Financial disclosure:* All members must file personal financial statements each year.
- *Honoraria:* Members cannot accept fees for speeches or personal appearances.
- *Campaign funds:* Surplus campaign funds cannot be put to personal use. (A loophole allowed members elected before 1980 to keep such funds if they left office before January 1, 1993. A record number of House members resigned in 1992; many of them kept substantial amounts of campaign money.)
- *Gifts:* Members may not accept gifts worth more than $200 for representatives and $300 for senators (with annual increases in these amounts for inflation).
- *Free travel:* Members may not accept free travel from private corporations or individuals for more than four days of domestic travel and seven days of international travel per year. (Taxpayer-paid "junkets" to investigate problems at home or abroad or attend international meetings are not prohibited.)
- *Lobbying:* Former members may not lobby Congress for at least one year after retirement.

These limited rules have not gone very far in restoring popular trust in Congress. Indeed, the "check-kiting" scandals in 1992 and media reporting of the various perks available to members of Congress were very damaging to the reputation of Congress. Yet these practices were not prohibited by ethics rules.

*Expulsion*  The Constitution gives Congress the power to discipline its own members. "Each House may . . . punish its Members for disorderly Behaviour, and, with the Concurrence of two thirds, expel a Member." But the Constitution fails to define *disorderly behavior.*

It seems reasonable to believe that criminal conduct falls within the constitutional definition of *disorderly behavior.* Bribery is a criminal act: it is illegal to solicit or receive anything of value in return for the performance of a government duty. During its notorious Abscam investigation in 1980, the Federal Bureau of Investigation set up a "sting" operation in which agents posing as wealthy Arabs offered bribe money to members of Congress while secretly videotaping the transactions. Six representatives and one senator were convicted. But criminal conviction does not automatically result in expulsion from Congress. In the Abscam case, only one

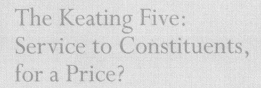

# The Keating Five:
# Service to Constituents,
# for a Price?

The case of the Keating Five dates back to 1985, when Charles H. Keating, owner of California-based Lincoln Savings and Loan, ran into difficulties with the Federal Home Loan Bank Board, which regulates the savings and loan industry. Keating invested Lincoln's government-insured funds in a wide variety of risky stocks, bonds, and commercial real estate ventures. When the Bank Board regulators charged that he had violated savings and loan regulations, Keating began to line up prominent politicians to pressure the board to drop its "vendetta" against him, among them U.S. Senators Alan Cranston (D-Calif.), John Glenn (D-Ohio), Donald W. Riegle (D-Mich.), Dennis DeConcini (D-Ariz.), and John McCain (R-Ariz.).

Most of the senators' work on behalf of Keating consisted of contacting regulators and urging speedy and favorable consideration of his case. Regulators appeared ready to close down the shaky Lincoln S&L in early 1987 in order to save its remaining assets and limit the taxpayers' responsibility for additional losses. But Keating arranged to have his senators meet with top regulators and pressure them to postpone for two years the government's decision to close down the bankrupt S&L, a decision that eventually cost U.S. taxpayers $2 *billion.*

How did Keating win the active support of five U.S. senators in his fight against the Bank Board? Keating contributed a total of $1.5 million to their campaign chests and political causes. Nearly $1 million of these contributions went to Senator Alan Cranston; specific contributions of $250,000, $250,000, and $500,000 were made within days of Cranston's calls and meetings with Bank Board officials. Senator John Glenn received a total of $242,000 from Keating, and John McCain received

$110,000. Dennis DeConcini and Donald Riegle, who received $85,000 and $78,250, respectively, later returned those monies.

The key question in the subsequent Senate Ethics Committee investigation in 1991 was whether there was any direct connection between Keating's payments and the actions of the five senators on behalf of their benefactor. Bribery is an illegal exchange of official actions for payment. When Keating himself was asked whether his large campaign contributions brought him political influence, he replied: "I certainly hope so." Keating was later tried and convicted on fraud charges stemming from his S&L operations.

But Senator Cranston contended that he was just performing a service for a constituent. His "everyone does it" defense cited his own and other senators' efforts on behalf of defense contractors, automobile manufacturers, and others seeking specific government benefits and subsidies. "Nothing I did violated any law or specific Senate rule. . . . There is no evidence that I ever agreed to help Charles Keating in return for a contribution."*

But the Senate Ethics Committee found that Cranston's "impermissible pattern of conduct violated established norms of behavior in the Senate . . . [and] was improper and repugnant." The committee "strongly and severely reprimanded" Cranston but took no further action due to "extenuating circumstances. . . . Senator Cranston is in poor health . . . [and] has announced his intention not to seek reelection to the Senate." The Senate Ethics Committee also determined that the other four senators—DeConcini, Glenn, McCain, and Riegle— were guilty of "poor judgment" in conduct that gave "the appearance of impropriety." But the Ethics Committee offered little in the way of future guidance in handling constituent services and campaign contributions.

*U.S. Senator Alan Cranston, statement in the U.S. Senate, reported in *Congressional Quarterly Weekly Report,* November 23, 1991, p. 3437.

*Senator Harrison Williams, Jr. (D-N.J.), is shown here with FBI Agent Richard Farhardt, who is posing as an Arab sheik named Yassire Habib as part of the FBI's Abscam "sting" operation revealed in 1981. Williams, along with four members of the House of Representatives, was convicted of criminal conspiracy and accepting bribes to introduce legislation that would have benefited Abdul Enterprises (the name "Abdul scam" being shortened to "Abscam"), a business front established by the FBI as part of the "sting."*

defendant, Representative Michael Ozzie Myers (D-Pa.) was expelled, becoming the first member to be expelled since the Civil War. (Two other House members and the senator resigned rather than face expulsion, and the other three representatives were defeated for reelection. Perhaps the most interesting result of the Abscam investigation: only *one* member of Congress approached by the FBI, Democratic Senator Larry Presler of South Dakota, turned down the bribe.) The powerful chair of the House Appropriations Committee, Democrat Dan Rostenkowski (Ill.) was indicted by a federal grand jury in 1994 for misuse of congressional office funds. He refused to resign from Congress, but his Chicago constituents voted him out of office. Democratic Representative Mel Reynolds (Ill.) resigned in 1995, following his criminal conviction on charges of sexual misconduct. (A special election to fill his vacated seat was won by Jesse Jackson, Jr., son of the popular preacher, commentator, and former Democratic presidential contender.) Republican Senator Robert Packwood (Oreg.) resigned in 1995 in order to avoid official expulsion following a Senate Ethics Committee report charging him with numerous counts of sexual harassment of female staff.

*Censure*    A lesser punishment in the Congress than expulsion is official **censure.** Censured members are obliged to "stand in the well" and listen to the charges read against them. It is supposed to be a humiliating experience and fatal to one's political career. In 1983, two members of Congress were censured for sexual misconduct with teenage congressional pages. Both were obliged to "stand in the well." Representative Daniel B. Crane (R-Ill.), who acknowledged a sexual relationship with a female page, was subsequently defeated for reelection. But

**Censure:** A public reprimand for wrongdoing, given to a member standing in the chamber before Congress.

Representative Gerry E. Studds (D-Mass.), who admitted to a homosexual relationship with a male teenage page, won reelection.

The threat of censure can be a potent one, though. In 1989, Speaker of the House Jim Wright (D-Tex.) was found to have circumvented ethics rules regarding outside financial payments to a member. He received heavy royalties on sales to interest groups of a book he authored. He also accepted large gifts from supporters, including the free use of an expensive condominium. He resigned the Speaker's post as well as his seat in Congress. Democratic Whip Tony Coelho (D-Calif.) also resigned in the face of ethics charges that year.

## SUMMARY NOTES

- The Constitution places all of the delegated powers of the national government in the Congress. The Founders expected Congress to be the principal institution for resolving national conflicts, balancing interests, and deciding who gets what. Today, Congress is a central battleground in the struggle over national policy. Congress generally does not initiate but responds to policy initiatives and budget requests originating from the president, the bureaucracy, and interest groups. Over time, the president and the executive branch, together with the Supreme Court and federal judiciary, have come to dominate national policy making.

- The Congress represents local and state interests in policy making. The Senate's constituencies are the 50 states, and the House's constituencies are 435 separate districts. Both houses of Congress, but especially the House of Representatives, wield power in domestic and foreign affairs primarily through the "power of the purse."

- Congressional powers include oversight and investigation. These powers are exercised primarily through committees. While Congress claims these powers are a necessary part of lawmaking, their real purpose is usually to influence agency decision making, to build political support for increases or decreases in agency funding, to lay the political foundation for new programs and policies, and to capture media attention and enhance the power of members of Congress.

- Congress is gradually becoming more "representative" of the general population in terms of race and gender. Redistricting, under federal court interpre-

tations of the Voting Rights Act, has increased African-American and Hispanic representation in Congress. And women have significantly increased their presence in Congress in recent years. Nevertheless, women and minorities do not occupy seats in Congress proportional to their share of the general population.

- Members of Congress are independent political entrepreneurs. They initiate their own candidacies, raise their own campaign funds, and get themselves elected with very little help from their party. Members of Congress are largely career politicians who skillfully use the advantages of incumbency to stay in office. Incumbents outspend challengers by large margins. Interest group political action committees and individual contributors strongly favor incumbents. Congressional elections are seldom focused on great national issues but rather on local issues and personalities and the ability of candidates to "bring home the bacon" from Washington and serve their constituents.

- Congress as an institution is not very popular with the American people. Scandals, pay raises, "perks," and privileges reported in the media have hurt the image of the institution. Nevertheless, individual members of Congress remain popular with their districts' voters.

- Members of Congress spend as much time on "home-style" activities—promoting their images back home and attending to constituents' problems—as they do legislating. Casework wins votes one at a time, gradually accumulating political support back home, and members often support each other's "pork-barrel" projects.

- Despite the independence of members, the Democratic and Republican party structures in the House and Senate remain the principal bases for organizing Congress. Party leaders in the House and Senate generally control the flow of business in each house, assigning bills to committees, scheduling or delaying votes, and appointing members to committees. But leaders must bargain for votes; they have few formal disciplinary powers. They cannot deny renomination to recalcitrant members.

- The real legislative work of Congress is done in committees. Standing committees screen and draft legislation; with rare exceptions, bills do not reach the floor without approval by a majority of a standing committee. The committee and subcommittee system decentralizes power in Congress. The system satisfies the desires of members to gain power, prestige, and electoral advantage, but it weakens responsible government in the Congress as a whole. All congressional committees are chaired by members of the majority party. Seniority is still the major determinant of power in Congress.

- In order to become law, a bill must win committee approval and withstand debate in both houses of Congress. The rules attached to a bill's passage in the House can significantly help or hurt its chances. Bills passed with differences in the two houses must be reworked and passed in identical form in both.

- In deciding how to vote on legislation, Congress members are influenced by party loyalty, presidential support or opposition, constituency concerns, interest group pressures, and their own personal values and ideology. Party majorities oppose each other on roughly half of all roll-call votes in Congress. Presidents receive the greatest support in Congress from members of their own party.

- The customs and norms of Congress help to reduce interpersonal conflict, facilitate bargaining and compromise, and make life more pleasant on Capitol Hill. They include the recognition of special competencies of members, a willingness to bargain and compromise, mutual "back scratching" and logrolling, reciprocity, and deference toward the leadership. But traditional customs and norms have weakened over time as more members have pursued independent political agendas.

- Congress establishes its own rules of ethics. The Constitution empowers each House to expel its own members for "disorderly conduct" by a two-thirds vote, but expulsion has seldom occurred. Some members have resigned to avoid expulsion, while others have been officially censured yet remained in Congress.

## SELECTED READINGS

FENNO, RICHARD F. *Home Style.* Boston: Little Brown, 1978. The classic description of how attention to constituency by members of Congress enhances their reelection prospects. Home-style activities, including casework, pork-barreling, travel and appearances back home, newsletters, and surveys, are described in detail.

FIORINA, MORRIS P. *Congress: Keystone to the Washington Establishment,* 2d ed. New Haven, Conn.: Yale University Press, 1989. A lively description of members of Congress as independent political entrepreneurs serving themselves by serving local constituencies and ensuring their own reelection, often at the expense of the national interest.

GINGRICH, NEWT. *To Renew America.* New York: HarperCollins, 1995. The Republican Speaker of the House describes the "third wave information age" that will "empower and enhance" the lives of Americans and the "liberals, lawyers, and bureaucrats" who will try to block it to maintain their own power.

KAPTOR, MARCY. *Women of Congress.* Washington: Congressional Quarterly Press, 1996. An account of the progress of women toward longer tenure, greater seniority, and more influential committee appointments and how women in Congress still differ from men on these factors.

OLESZEK, WALTER J. *Congressional Procedures and the Policy Process,* 4th ed. Washington, D.C.: Congressional Quarterly Press, 1995. An explanation of the interaction between congressional rules and policy making that includes a description of committee and floor procedures and an explanation of the role of the leadership.

ORNSTEIN, NORMAN J., THOMAS E. MANN, and MICHAEL J. MALBIN. *Vital Statistics on Congress.* Washington, D.C.:

Congressional Quarterly Press, 1996. Published biennially. Excellent source of data on members of Congress, congressional elections, campaign finance, committees and staff, workload, and voting alignments.

PARKER, GLENN R. *Characteristics of Congress.* Englewood Cliffs, N.J.: Prentice Hall, 1989. A well-documented account of the independence of members of Congress and their attention to their home districts, the decentralization of Congress and the weakness of party leadership, the development of "cozy triangles" among interest groups, committees, and bureaucratic agencies, and other behaviors in Congress that make it an "incumbent protection society."

SINCLAIR, BARBARA. *Legislators, Leaders, and Lawmaking: The U.S. House of Representatives in the Postreform Era.* Baltimore: Johns Hopkins University Press, 1995. A systematic examination of the role of majority party leadership in meshing the goals of individual members with the collective goals of the House.

# THE PRESIDENT
# WHITE HOUSE
# POLITICS

## CHAPTER OUTLINE

Presidential Power
Constitutional Powers of the President
Political Resources of the President
Chief Executive
Chief Legislator and Lobbyist
Global Leader
Commander-in-Chief
The Vice-Presidential Waiting Game

## FEATURES

*What Do You Think?* How Would You Rate the Presidents?
*What Do You Think?* Is Presidential Character the Key to
    Performance?
*Up Close:* Watergate and the Limits of Presidential Power
*A Conflicting View:* Liberals, Conservatives, and Presidential Power
*People in Politics:* Bill Clinton: The Ambivalent Presidency
*Up Close:* Iran-Contra and the White House Staff

## PRESIDENTIAL POWER

Americans look to their president for "Greatness." The presidency embodies the popular "great man" view of history and public affairs—attributing progress in the world to the actions of particular individuals. Great presidents are those associated with great events—George Washington with the founding of the nation, Abraham Lincoln with the preservation of the Union, Franklin D. Roosevelt with the nation's emergence from economic depression and victory in World War II (see *What Do You Think?* "How Would You Rate the Presidents?"). People tend to believe that the president is responsible for "peace and prosperity" as well as for "change." They expect their president to present a "vision" of America's future and to symbolize the nation.

*The Symbolic President*    The president personifies American government for most people. People expect the president to act decisively and effectively to deal with national problems. They expect the president to be

## ASK YOURSELF ABOUT POLITICS

**1** Do you approve of the way the president is handling his job?
Yes ⬭   No ⬭

**2** Should presidents have the power to take actions not specifically authorized by law or the Constitution that they believe necessary for the nation's well-being?
Yes ⬭   No ⬭

**3** Should the Senate reject a president's cabinet appointments if it disagrees with their policy pronouncements?
Yes ⬭   No ⬭

**4** Should Congress rally to support a president's decision to send U.S. troops into action even if it disagrees with the decision?
Yes ⬭   No ⬭

**5** In addition to formal treaties, should all agreements with other countries require the approval of the Senate?
Yes ⬭   No ⬭

**6** Should Congress have the authority to call home U.S. troops sent by the president to engage in military actions overseas?
Yes ⬭   No ⬭

**7** Should Congress undertake to impeach and remove a president whose policy decisions damage the nation?
Yes ⬭   No ⬭

**8** Is presidential performance more related to character and personality than to policy positions?
Yes ⬭   No ⬭

How much power does the president of the United States really have—over policies, over legislation, over the budget, over how this country is viewed by other nations, even over how it views itself?

"compassionate"—to show concern for problems confronting individual citizens.[1] The president, while playing these roles, is the focus of public attention and is the nation's leading celebrity. Presidents receive more media coverage than any other person in the nation, for everything from their policy statements to their heart flutters to their favorite foods.

*Managing Crises*   In times of crisis, the American people look to their president to take action, to provide reassurance, and to protect the nation and its people. It is the president, not the Congress or the courts, who is expected to speak on behalf of the American people in times of national triumph and tragedy.[2]

The president gives expression to the nation's pride in victory. The nation's heroes are welcomed and its championship sports teams are feted in the White House Rose Garden. The president also gives expression to the nation's sadness in tragedy and strives to help the nation go forward. When the *Challenger* spacecraft disintegrated before the eyes of millions of television viewers in 1986, President Ronald Reagan canceled his State of the Union Address and went on national television to give voice to the nation's feelings about the disaster and to explain it to children: "I want to say something to the schoolchildren of America who were watching the live coverage of the shuttle's takeoff. I know it is hard to understand, but sometimes painful things like this happen. It's part of the process of exploration and discovery. It's all part of taking a chance and expanding man's horizons. The future doesn't belong to the faint-hearted. It belongs to the brave."

*Providing Policy Leadership*   The president is expected to set policy priorities for the nation. Most policy initiatives originate in the White House and various departments and agencies of the executive branch, then are forwarded to Congress with the president's approval. Presidential programs are submitted to Congress in the form of messages, including the president's annual State of the Union Address, and in the Budget of the United States Government, which the president presents each year to Congress.

As a political leader, the president is expected to mobilize political support for policy proposals. It is not enough for the president to send policy proposals to Congress. The president must rally public opinion, lobby members of Congress, and win legislative battles. To avoid being perceived as weak or ineffective, presidents must get as much of their legislative programs through Congress as possible. Presidents use the threat of a veto to prevent Congress from passing bills they oppose; when forced to veto a bill, they fight to prevent an override of the veto. The president thus is responsible for "getting things done" in the policy arena (see *What Do You Think?* "Is Presidential Character the Key to Performance?").

*Managing the Economy*   The American people hold the president responsible for maintaining a healthy economy. Presidents are blamed for economic downturns, whether or not governmental policies had anything to do with market conditions. The president is expected to "Do Something!" in the face of high unemployment, declining personal income, high mortgage rates, rising inflation, or even a stock market crash. Herbert Hoover in 1932, Gerald Ford in 1976, Jimmy Carter in 1980, and George Bush in 1992—all incumbent presidents defeated for reelection during recessions—learned the hard way that the general public holds the president responsible for hard economic times. Presidents must have an economic "game plan" to stimulate the economy—tax incentives to spur

# How Would You Rate the Presidents?

From time to time, historians have been asked to rate U.S. presidents (see table). Historian Arthur Schlesinger surveyed fifty-five leading historians first in 1948, then again in 1962. Although later surveys included much larger numbers of historians, the ratings given the presidents have been remarkably consistent. Abraham Lincoln, George Washington, Franklin Roosevelt, Woodrow Wilson, and Thomas Jefferson are universally recognized as the greatest American presidents.

It is more difficult for historians to rate recent presidents; the views of historians are influenced by current political controversies. Often the passage of time allows scholars to make more objective evaluations. Both Jimmy Carter and Richard Nixon may be evaluated higher by future historians than they are today. How would you rate Ronald Reagan, George Bush, and Bill Clinton?

| Schlesinger (1948) | Schlesinger (1962) | Dodder (1970) | DiClerico (1977) | Tribune (1982) | Murray (1982) |
|---|---|---|---|---|---|
| **Great** | **Great** | **Accomplishments of Administration** | **Ten Greatest Presidents** | **Ten Best Presidents** | **Presidential Rank** |
| 1. Lincoln | 1. Lincoln | 1. Lincoln | 1. Lincoln | 1. Lincoln (best) | 1. Lincoln |
| 2. Washington | 2. Washington | 2. F. Roosevelt | 2. Washington | 2. Washington | 2. F. Roosevelt |
| 3. F. Roosevelt | 3. F. Roosevelt | 3. Washington | 3. F. Roosevelt | 3. F. Roosevelt | 3. Washington |
| 4. Wilson | 4. Wilson | 4. Jefferson | 4. Jefferson | 4. T. Roosevelt | 4. Jefferson |
| 5. Jefferson | 5. Jefferson | 5. T. Roosevelt | 5. T. Roosevelt | 5. Jefferson | 5. T. Roosevelt |
| 6. Jackson | **Near Great** | 6. Truman | 6. Wilson | 6. Wilson | 6. Wilson |
| **Near Great** | 6. Jackson | 7. Wilson | 7. Jackson | 7. Jackson | 7. Jackson |
| 7. T. Roosevelt | 7. T. Roosevelt | 8. Jackson | 8. Truman | 8. Truman | 8. Truman |
| 8. Cleveland | 8. Polk | 9. L. Johnson | 9. Polk | 9. Eisenhower | 9. J. Adams |
| 9. J. Adams | Truman (tie) | 10. Polk | 10. J. Adams | 10. Polk (10th best) | 10. L. Johnson |
| 10. Polk | 9. J. Adams | 11. J. Adams | | **Ten Worst Presidents** | 11. Eisenhower |
| **Average** | 10. Cleveland | 12. Kennedy | | 1. Harding (worst) | 12. Polk |
| 11. J. Q. Adams | **Average** | 13. Monroe | | 2. Nixon | 13. Kennedy |
| 12. Monroe | 11. Madison | 14. Cleveland | | 3. Buchanan | 14. Madison |
| 13. Hayes | 12. J. Q. Adams | 15. Madison | | 4. Pierce | 15. Monroe |
| 14. Madison | 13. Hayes | 16. Taft | | 5. Grant | 16. J. Q. Adams |
| 15. Van Buren | 14. McKinley | 17. McKinley | | 6. Fillmore | 17. Cleveland |
| 16. Taft | 15. Taft | 18. J.Q. Adams | | 7. A. Johnson | 18. McKinley |
| 17. Arthur | 16. Van Buren | 19. Hoover | | 8. Coolidge | 19. Taft |
| 18. McKinley | 17. Monroe | 20. Eisenhower | | 9. Tyler | 20. Van Buren |
| 19. A. Johnson | 18. Hoover | 21. A. Johnson | | 10. Carter (10th worst) | 21. Hoover |
| 20. Hoover | 19. B. Harrison | 22. Van Buren | | | 22. Hayes |
| 21. B. Harrison | 20. Arthur | 23. Arthur | | | 23. Arthur |
| **Below Average** | Eisenhower (tie) | 24. Hayes | | | 24. Ford |
| 22. Tyler | 21. A. Johnson | 25. Tyler | | | 25. Carter |
| 23. Coolidge | **Below Average** | 26. B. Harrison | | | 26. B. Harrison |
| 24. Fillmore | 22. Taylor | 27. Taylor | | | 27. Taylor |
| 25. Taylor | 23. Tyler | 28. Buchanan | | | 28. Tyler |
| 26. Buchanan | 24. Fillmore | 29. Fillmore | | | 29. Fillmore |
| 27. Pierce | 25. Coolidge | 30. Coolidge | | | 30. Coolidge |
| **Failure** | 26. Pierce | 31. Pierce | | | 31. Pierce |
| 28. Grant | 27. Buchanan | 32. Grant | | | 32. A. Johnson |
| 29. Harding | **Failure** | 33. Harding | | | 33. Buchanan |
| | 28. Grant | | | | 34. Nixon |
| | 29. Harding | | | | 35. Grant |
| | | | | | 36. Harding |

These ratings result from surveys of scholars ranging in number from 55 to 950.

*Source:* Arthur Murphy, "Evaluating the Presidents of the United States," *Presidential Studies Quarterly* 14 (1984): 117–26.

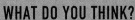

## Is Presidential Character the Key to Performance?

Are political ideology and policy issues the keys to presidential performance? Or is presidential performance more a product of an individual's character and personality?

Was Watergate a product of "character flaws" in Richard Nixon? He was suspicious of others, almost paranoid, keeping an "enemies list" in the Oval Office. His suspicious nature led him to approve of "dirty tricks" against his opponents, sure that they were doing the same to him. Increasingly, he isolated himself from all except his closest aides. He came to view Watergate as a conspiracy among his liberal opponents in Congress and the news media to reverse the outcome of his landslide election in 1972. He became rigid in his stance on releasing information. Can we conclude that Nixon's "negative" personality led to his forced resignation?

In contrast, did Ronald Reagan survive the Iran-Contra crisis because of his more open, congenial, and optimistic personality? Reagan's "soft-hearted" nature and his tendency to view policy questions in very personal terms may have led him to respond to the emotional appeals of the hostage families to negotiate for the hostages' release, despite a firm announced policy against dealing with terrorists. Later, he openly cooperated with investigators, personally testifying to what he knew about the affair.

His relaxed, easygoing style of administration allowed him to make a creditable claim that he did not know anything about the scheme to direct profits from arms deals to the Contras. Many Americans faulted him for trading arms for the hostages, but they forgave his many oversights, in part because they trusted his motives. Can we conclude that Reagan's "positive" personality helped him survive the crisis and leave office with high approval ratings?

Political scientist James David Barber claims that we can classify presidents according to: (1) their activism—that is, how energetic and assertive they are in leadership; and (2) their enjoyment of politics and public service. With these two dimensions Barber believes we can understand presidential performance fairly well. The table shows Barber's classification scheme and how he assesses most twentieth-century presidents.

Barber believes that the people best suited for the presidency are "active-positive" politicians who creatively shape their environment and enjoy the give-and-take exchanges of political life. Those most ill suited are the "active-negative" types—driven personalities who are compelled to feverish activity yet doomed by rigidity and personal frustration in their approach to the job. However, critics doubt that Barber's generalizations are based on sufficient evidence. Barber rated Gerald Ford an active-positive type, but others think of Ford more as a passive-positive type. Some observers think Carter belongs as much in the negative category as in the positive. Many people judge

investments, spending proposals to create jobs, plans to lower interest rates. In today's global economy, they must also develop programs to improve America's international "competitiveness."

Presidents themselves are partly responsible for these public expectations. Incumbent presidents have been quick to take credit for economic growth, low inflation, low interest rates, and low unemployment. And presidential candidates in recessionary times invariably promise "to get the economy moving again."

However, public expectations far exceed presidential power to ensure prosperity for all. The U.S. economy is not easily manipulated by *anything* the government does (see Chapter 16), be it changes in taxing, spending, or interest rates. The American economy also is increasingly influenced by global forces—oil prices, recessions in other nations, trade restrictions—beyond the direct control of the U.S. government. Finally, the president must share control with Congress on

Reagan to be an "active," not a "passive" type. Disagreements over where to place individual presidents may mean that this scheme is more confusing than helpful, that it is more likely to tell us about the politics of the classifiers than about the character of the classified.

Where should we place George Bush in this classification scheme? His presidency was widely perceived as schizophrenic—active in foreign affairs but passive in domestic policy. He displayed strength, perseverance, and decisiveness in the Gulf War but passivity, weakness, and vacillation on economic policy at home. He was positive, friendly, courteous, and likable in face-to-face encounters with world leaders but was often stiff and uncomfortable on the political campaign trail.

According to Barber's definition of character, Bill Clinton is clearly active and positive. He obviously enjoys political campaigning, and his energy level may be higher than any president in recent time. But questions about his "character" (defined in terms of personal ethical behavior) have followed him throughout his political career.

Even if Barber's analysis is accurate, is it useful in deciding whom to vote for? For whom should we vote, for example, if all the candidates are "active-positive"? Further, using strict character criteria to screen candidates probably would have prevented the moody and often-depressed Abraham Lincoln from winning office. In addition to a presidential candidate's character, voters want and deserve to know the candidate's policy positions.

Perhaps too much emphasis is placed on presidential personality and character. Psychologists tend to emphasize the personal more than the institutional. But the personality of the president is at best only one factor. Presidential success or failure is probably due more to social, economic, and political forces at work in the nation during a president's term than to that president's personality. This is not to say that the president's character, integrity, and leadership styles are unimportant. But these considerations are only one set of concerns, and they may be less important than our institutional structures and processes.

**Barber's Classification of Presidential Character**

*Energy Level in Politics*

| | | Active | Passive |
|---|---|---|---|
| *Emotional Attitude Toward Politics* | *Positive* | Franklin Roosevelt<br>Harry Truman<br>John F. Kennedy<br>Gerald Ford<br>Jimmy Carter | William H. Taft<br>Warren G. Harding<br>Ronald Reagan |
| | *Negative* | Richard Nixon<br>Lyndon Johnson<br>Herbert Hoover<br>Woodrow Wilson | Dwight Eisenhower<br>Calvin Coolidge |

James David Barber, *The Presidential Character*, 4th ed. (Englewood Cliffs, N.J.: Prentice Hall, 1992).

issues of taxing and spending and with an independent Federal Reserve Board on issues of interest rates.

*Managing the Government*  As the chief executive of a mammoth federal bureaucracy with 2.8 million civilian employees, the president is responsible for implementing policy—that is, for achieving policy goals. Policy making does not end when a law is passed. Policy implementation involves issuing orders, creating organizations, recruiting and assigning personnel, disbursing funds, overseeing work, and evaluating results. It is true that the president cannot perform all of these tasks personally. But the ultimate responsibility for implementation—in the words of the Constitution, "to take Care that the Laws be faithfully executed"— rests with the president. Or as the sign on Harry Truman's desk put it: "THE BUCK STOPS HERE."

*While far less glamorous than the job of commander-in-chief of the U.S. armed forces, commanding the nation's bureaucracy and over-seeing the running of the civilian government usually occupies far more of a president's time. Here President Clinton discusses the budget at a meeting of his Cabinet.*

*The Global President*　　Nations strive to speak with a single voice in international affairs; for the United States, the global voice is that of the president. As commander-in-chief of the armed forces of the United States, the president is a powerful voice in foreign affairs. Efforts by Congress to speak on behalf of the nation in foreign affairs and to limit the war-making power of the president have been generally unsuccessful. It is the president who orders American troops into combat. It is the president's finger that rests on the nuclear trigger.

## CONSTITUTIONAL POWERS OF THE PRESIDENT

Popular expectations of presidential leadership far exceed the formal constitutional powers granted to the president. Compared with the Congress, the president has only modest constitutionally expressed powers (see Table 11-1). Nevertheless, presidents throughout the years have pointed to a variety of clauses in Article II to support their rights to do everything from doubling the land area of the nation through purchase (Thomas Jefferson) to sending U.S. troops to keep the peace in Bosnia (Bill Clinton).

*Who May Be President?*　　To become president, the Constitution specifies that a person must be a natural-born citizen at least thirty-five years of age and a resident of the United States for fourteen years. (For more on modern career paths to the presidency, see Figure 11-1.)

Initially, the Constitution put no limit on how many terms a president could serve. George Washington set a precedent for a two-term maximum that endured until Franklin Roosevelt's decision to run for a third term in 1940 (and a fourth term in 1944). In reaction to Roosevelt's lengthy tenure, in 1947 Congress proposed the Twenty-second Amendment (ratified in 1951), which officially

TABLE 11-1   THE CONSTITUTIONAL POWERS OF THE PRESIDENT

**Chief Administrator**
Implement policy: "take Care that the Laws be faithfully executed" (Article II, Section 3)
Supervise executive branch of government
Appoint and remove executive officials (Article II, Section 2)
Prepare executive budget for submission to Congress (by law of Congress)

**Chief Legislator**
Initiate policy: "give to the Congress Information of the State of the Union, and
    recommend to their Consideration such Measures as he shall judge necessary and
    expedient" (Article II, Section 3)
Veto legislation passed by Congress, subject to override by a two-thirds vote in both
    houses
Convene special session of Congress "on extraordinary Occasions" (Article II, Section 3)

**Chief Diplomat**
Make treaties "with the Advice and Consent of the Senate" (Article II, Section 2)
Exercise the power of diplomatic recognition: "receive Ambassadors" (Article II, Section 3)
Make executive agreements (by custom and international law)

**Commander-in-Chief**
Command U.S. armed forces: "The president shall be Commander in Chief of the Army
    and Navy" (Article II, Section 2)
Appoint military officers

**Chief of State**
"The executive Power shall be vested in a President" (Article II, Section 1)
Grant reprieves and pardons (Article II, Section 2)
Represent the nation as chief of state
Appoint federal court and Supreme Court judges (Article II, Section 2)

restricts the president to two terms (or one full term if a vice-president must complete more than two years of the previous president's term).

*Presidential Succession*   Until the adoption of the Twenty-fifth Amendment in 1967, the Constitution had said little about presidential succession, other than designating the vice-president as successor to the president "in Case of the Removal, . . . Death, Resignation, or Inability" and giving Congress the power to decide "what Officer shall then act as President" if both the president and vice-president are removed. The Constitution was silent on how to cope with serious presidential illnesses. It contained no provision for replacing a vice-president. The incapacitation issue was more than theoretical: James A. Garfield lingered months after being shot in 1881; Woodrow Wilson was an invalid during his last years in office (1919–20); Dwight Eisenhower suffered serious heart attacks in office; and Ronald Reagan was in serious condition following an assassination attempt in 1981.

The Twenty-fifth Amendment stipulates that when the vice-president and a majority of the cabinet notify the speaker of the House and the president pro tempore of the Senate in writing that the president "is unable to discharge the powers and duties of his office," then the vice-president becomes *acting* president. To resume the powers of office, the president must then notify Congress in writing that "no inability exists." If the vice-president and a majority of cabinet officers do

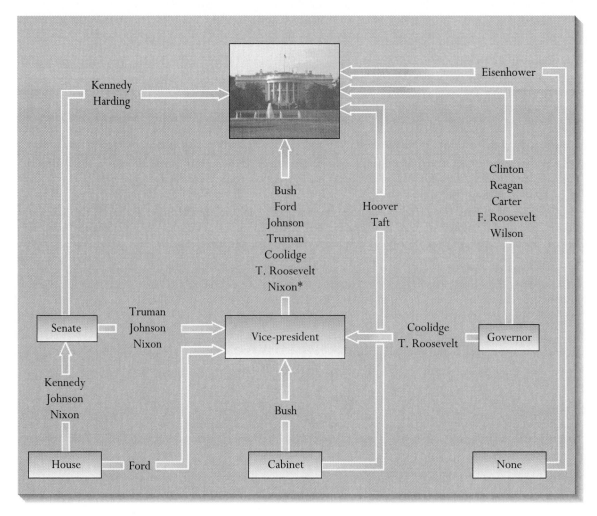

**FIGURE 11.1** Twentieth-Century Career Paths to the White House

*Throughout the twentieth century, Americans have selected their presidents almost exclusively from the ranks of experienced politicians. Except for Dwight Eisenhower, every modern president has held high federal or state office before entering the White House.*

*Richard Nixon served as vice-president under Dwight Eisenhower, 1953–61 but failed to win election to the presidency directly from that office in 1960. He was also defeated for the governorship of California in 1962 but was nominated and elected president in 1968.

not agree that the president is capable of resuming office, then the Congress "shall decide the issue" within twenty-one days. A two-thirds vote of both houses is required to replace the president with the vice-president.

The disability provisions of the amendment have never been used, but the succession provisions have been. The Twenty-fifth Amendment provides for the selection of a new vice-president by presidential nomination and confirmation by a majority vote of both houses of Congress. When Vice-President Spiro Agnew resigned in the face of bribery charges in 1973, President Richard Nixon nominated the Republican leader of the House, Gerald Ford, as vice-president; and when Nixon resigned in 1974, Ford assumed the presidency and made Nelson Rockefeller, governor of New York, his vice-president. Thus, Gerald Ford's two-year tenure in the White House marked the only time in history when the man serving as president had not been elected to either the presidency or the vice-presidency. (If the offices of president and vice-president are both vacated, then Congress by law has specified the next in line for the presidency as the Speaker of the House of Representatives, followed by the president pro tempore of the Senate, then the cabinet officers, beginning with the secretary of state.)

*Impeachment*　The Constitution grants Congress the power of **impeachment** over the president, vice-president, and "all civil Officers of the United States" (Article II, Section 4). Technically, impeachment is a charge similar to a criminal indictment brought against an official. The power to bring charges of impeachment is given to the House of Representatives. The power to try all impeachments is given to the Senate, and "no Person shall be convicted without the Concurrence of two thirds of the Members present" (Article I, Section 3). Impeachment by the House and conviction by the Senate only remove an official from office; a subsequent criminal trial is required to inflict any other punishment.

The Constitution specifies that impeachment and conviction can only be for "Treason, Bribery, or other High Crimes and Misdemeanors." These words clearly indicate that Congress is not to impeach presidents, federal judges, or any other officials simply because Congress disagrees with their decisions or policies. Indeed, the phrase implies that only serious criminal offenses can result in impeachment, not political disagreements, disputes, or conflicts. Nevertheless, politics *was* at the root of the nation's only presidential impeachment—that of President Andrew Johnson in 1867. Johnson was a southern Democrat who had remained loyal to the Union. Lincoln had chosen him as vice-president in 1864 as a gesture of national unity. A Republican House impeached him on a party-line vote, but following a month-long trial in the Senate, the "guilty" vote fell one short of the two-thirds needed for removal.[3] In our times, Richard Nixon resigned after the House Judiciary Committee recommended impeachment but before a vote by the full House (see *Up Close:* "Watergate and the Limits of Presidential Power").

*Presidential Pardons*　The Constitution grants the president the power to "grant Reprieves and Pardons." This power derives from the ancient right to appeal to the king to reverse errors of law or justice that may have occurred in the court system. The presidential pardon power is absolute: the president may grant pardons to anyone for any reason. The most celebrated use of the presidential pardon was President Ford's blanket pardon of former President Nixon "for all offenses against the United States which he, Richard Nixon, has committed or may have committed or taken part in." Ford defended the pardon as necessary to end "the bitter controversy and divisive national debate" and reunite the nation, but criticism from those who wished to see Nixon prosecuted for his actions in office may have helped cause Ford's defeat in the 1976 election.

*Executive Power*　The Constitution declares that the "executive Power" shall be vested in the president, but it is unclear whether this statement grants the president any powers that are not specified later in the Constitution or given to the president by acts of Congress. In other words, does the grant of "executive Power" give presidents constitutional authority to act as they deem necessary *beyond* the actions specified elsewhere in the Constitution or specified in laws passed by Congress?

Contrasting views on this question have been offered over two centuries (see *A Conflicting View:* "Liberals, Conservatives, and Presidential Power"). President William Howard Taft provided the classic *narrow* interpretation of executive power:

> The true view of the executive function is, as I conceive it, that the president can exercise no power which cannot be fairly and reasonably traced to some

**Impeachment:** The equivalent of a criminal charge against an elected official; removal of the impeached official from office depends on the outcome of a trial.

# Watergate and the Limits of Presidential Power

Richard Nixon was the only president ever to resign the office. He did so to escape certain impeachment by the House of Representatives and a certain guilty verdict in trial by the Senate. Yet Nixon's first term as president included a number of historic successes. He negotiated the first-ever strategic nuclear arms limitation treaty, SALT I, with the Soviet Union. He changed the global balance of power in favor of the Western democracies by opening relations with the People's Republic of China and dividing the communist world. In his second term, he withdrew U.S. troops from Vietnam, negotiated a peace agreement, and ended one of America's longest and bloodiest wars. But his remarkable record is forever tarnished by his failure to understand the limits of presidential power.

In early 1972, Nixon's attorney general, John Mitchell, became head of the Committee to Re-Elect the President (CREEP). Mitchell hired ex-CIA agent and author of spy novels E. Howard Hunt, Jr., and former FBI agent G. Gordon Liddy to gather intelligence about the Democratic opposition. On the night of June 17, 1972, five men with burglary tools and wiretapping devices were arrested in the offices of the Democratic National Committee in the Watergate Building in Washington, together with Hunt and Liddy, who had directed the break-in and bugging, and James W. McCord, Jr., security coordinator for CREEP. All pleaded guilty and were convicted, but U.S. District Court Judge John J. Sirica believed that the defendants were shielding whoever had ordered and paid for the operation.

While there is no evidence that Nixon himself ordered or had any prior knowledge of the break-in,

When the U.S. Supreme Court ruled that there is no "executive privilege" of a president to withhold possible evidence of illegal activities, Richard Nixon was forced to surrender tape recordings of conversations between himself and his closest aides. Arguing that the quality of the tape recordings made it difficult to distinguish what was being said, Nixon released "official" transcripts along with the tapes. Rather than placating his enemies, however, the transcripts provided evidence of Nixon's participation in the Watergate cover-up.

he discussed the advisability of payoffs to buy the silence of the defendants with his chief of staff, H.R. Halderman, and White House advisers John Ehrlichman and John Dean. Hunt and the burglars subsequently received money and were told that later executive clemency was possible if they remained silent about Mitchell's involvement. Nixon hoped his landslide electoral victory in November 1972 would put the matter to rest.

But a series of sensational revelations in the *Washington Post* kept the story alive. Using an inside source known only as Deep Throat, Bob Woodward and Carl Bernstein, investigative reporters for the *Post*, alleged

specific grant of power or justly implied and included within such express grant as proper and necessary to its exercise. Such specific grants must be either in the federal constitution or in the pursuance thereof. There is no undefined residuum of power which can be exercised which seems to him to be in the public interest.[4]

Theodore Roosevelt, Taft's bitter opponent in a three-way race for the presidency in 1912, expressed the opposite view:

that key members of Nixon's reelection committee and White House staff were actively involved in the break-in and, more important, in the subsequent attempts at a cover-up. Judge Sirica threatened Liddy and McCord with long prison sentences unless they told him who had ordered the break-in and made the cover-up payments. Liddy refused and subsequently served fifty-two months in Lewisburg federal penitentiary; McCord confessed and received a light sentence. Seven Nixon associates, including Mitchell, Ehrlichman, and Halderman, were indicted on charges of conspiracy to obstruct justice.

In February 1973, the U.S. Senate formed a Special Select Committee on Campaign Activities—the "Watergate Committee"—to delve into Watergate and related activities. The committee's nationally televised hearings enthralled millions of viewers with lurid stories of "the White House horrors." John Dean broke with the White House and testified before the committee that he had earlier warned Nixon that the cover-up was "a cancer growing on the presidency." Then, in a dramatic revelation, the committee—and the nation—learned that President Nixon maintained a secret tape-recording system in the Oval Office. Hoping that the tapes would prove or disprove charges of Nixon's involvement in the cover-up, the committee issued a subpoena to the White House. Nixon refused to comply, arguing that the constitutional separation of powers gave the president an "executive privilege" to withhold his private conversations from Congress.

However, Special Prosecutor Archibald Cox convinced Judge Sirica to subpoena Nixon's tapes for the government's continuing criminal investigation. Nixon ordered Attorney General Elliot Richardson to fire Cox. Richardson, and later his deputy, William Ruckelshaus, refused and were themselves fired before Nixon finally persuaded the next-in-command, Solicitor General Robert Bork, to fire Cox. The so-called Saturday Night Massacre proved futile, however. Public outcry forced Nixon to appoint a new special prosecutor, Leon Jaworski, and to grant him even greater independence than Cox. Jaworski continued to press for the tapes, and the U.S. Supreme Court, voting 8 to 0 on *United States v. Richard M. Nixon,* ordered Nixon to turn over the tapes to the court.

On May 9, 1974, the Judiciary Committee of the House of Representatives, chaired by Peter Rodino (D-N.J.) convened to consider a series of articles of impeachment against President Nixon. Despite the rambling nature of the tapes, committee members interpreted them as confirming Nixon's involvement in the payoffs and cover-up. The committee passed two articles of impeachment: one accused Nixon of obstructing justice in the Watergate investigation; the other accused him of misusing his executive power and disregarding his constitutional duty to ensure that the laws be faithfully executed. Informed by congressional leaders of his own party that impeachment by a majority of the House and removal from office by two-thirds of the Senate were assured, on August 9, 1974, Richard Nixon resigned his office.

On September 8, 1974, new President Gerald R. Ford pardoned former President Nixon "for all offenses against the United States which he, Richard Nixon, has committed or may have committed or taken part in" during his presidency. In accepting the pardon, Nixon expressed remorse over Watergate and acknowledged grave errors of judgment, but he did not admit personal guilt. Upon his death in 1994, Nixon was eulogized for his foreign policy successes.

I decline to adopt the view that what was imperatively necessary for the nation could not be done by the president unless he could find some specific authorization to do it. My belief was that it was not only his right but his duty to do anything that the needs of the nation demanded, unless such action was forbidden by the Constitution or by the laws.[5]

While the constitutional question has never been fully resolved, history has generally sided with those presidents who have taken an expansive view of their

# Liberals, Conservatives, and Presidential Power

Liberals traditionally endorsed strong presidential leadership, viewing the president as a powerful initiator of social change. Franklin D. Roosevelt succeeded in ushering in the New Deal welfare state by presidential leadership, and Harry Truman was a feisty proponent of a liberal Fair Deal. Moderate Dwight Eisenhower was criticized by liberals for failing to use his great popularity to advance civil rights or social welfare programs. Liberals urged John F. Kennedy to be an activist president and strongly endorsed Lyndon Johnson's Great Society programs in education, welfare, and health. In his influential book *Presidential Power,* Harvard professor Richard E. Neustadt urged presidents to constantly strive to acquire as much power as possible because their constitutional authority is limited, noting that only by using their powers of persuasion can presidents achieve great change. Roosevelt was portrayed as the model for the modern president because he "had a love affair with power" as well as self-confidence, ambition, political experience, and knowledge of how to deal with people. Congress was generally viewed as a slow, cumbersome obstruction to social progress. Liberal reform required forceful national leadership, and only the president could fulfill this role.

But liberals had a change of heart when presidents Lyndon Johnson and Richard Nixon pursued the Vietnam War. Liberals complained that both presidents were *too* powerful: "Each man was driven, tending to excess, compulsive in seeking control, taking frustration hard."* What liberals had earlier praised as the *use* of presidential power was now described as the *abuse* of power. Liberal historian Arthur M. Schlesinger, Jr., attacked "the Imperial Presidency" and called for greater congressional power to restrain presidential actions, especially in war.** Liberals argued that Lincoln, Roosevelt, and Truman acted in wartime emergencies but that Johnson and Nixon had usurped Congress's war-making powers and thereby threatened our constitutional system. The Watergate scandals revealed further misuses of power and lawless actions.

Following the resignation of President Richard Nixon in 1974, Congress tried to reestablish its position as the first branch of government. It reasserted its authority in war making, in intelligence operations, and in the budgetary process. The War Powers Act of 1973 requires congressional approval within sixty days of the president's deployment of military forces; the Budget and Impoundment Control Act of 1974 establishes Congress's own budget office and prevents the president from impounding funds without congressional approval; and the Case Act requires the president to submit executive agreements to the Senate. Two weakened presidents—Republican Ger-

powers. John F. Kennedy expressed the modern view of the constitutional presidency:

> The Constitution is a very wise document. It permits the president to assume just about as much power as he is capable of handling. . . . I believe that the president should use whatever power is necessary to do the job unless it is expressly forbidden by the Constitution.[6]

*Some Historical Examples*    U.S. history is filled with examples of presidents acting independently, beyond specific constitutional powers or laws of Congress. Among the most notable:

ald Ford and Democrat Jimmy Carter—suffered from the "post-Watergate" paralysis. President Ford lamented: "As a member of Congress for twenty-five years, I clearly understand the powers and obligations of the Senate and the House under our Constitution. But as president for eighteen months, I also understand that Congress is trying to go too far!"

Conservatives were traditionally concerned about the concentration of power in the presidency. But by 1980, conservatives were calling for policy *changes:* lowering tax rates, slowing the growth of government, reducing the burdens of regulation, and restoring America's military power. Only strong presidential leadership could bring about these changes, and conservatives found that leadership in Ronald Reagan. Ronald Reagan liked to compare himself with Franklin D. Roosevelt: both presidents used the power, prestige, and media access of their office to redirect the nation. Like Roosevelt, Reagan had a clear vision and sense of the direction in which he wanted to move the nation; and, especially in his first term, he was extraordinarily successful in achieving his goals. Conservatives soon found themselves bashing the liberal Democratic Congress for failing to follow the president's lead in spending cuts and regulatory reform. Liberals, now well entrenched in Congress, were forced to defend that institution, seizing on the Iran-Contra affair in Reagan's second term to rekindle memories of Watergate and "the Imperial Presidency."

The sweeping Republican congressional victory in 1994, ending forty years of Democratic control of the House of Representatives and giving the GOP control of the Senate as well, again shifted the stances of liberals and conservatives regarding presidential power. Conservatives in the House under the speakership of Newt Gingrich reasserted the power of Congress, while liberals praised the checking powers of the president, Democrat Bill Clinton. The initiative in policy leadership seemed to shift to the House of Representatives as it proceeded to act on the Republican "Contract with America." But it soon became clear that a majority party in Congress cannot enact its own agenda over the opposition of the president.

Today, both liberals and conservatives have come to understand that the nation is poorly served by a weak presidency. The American people want strength in the presidency and in their presidents. Weakening the president does *not* mean turning back power to Congress or to the people. Weakening the president only means strengthening the special interests, deadlocking the legislative process, and crippling the ability of the government to deal with threats abroad and problems at home.

*Richard E. Neustadt, *Presidential Power* (New York: Wiley, 1960).
**Arthur M. Schlesinger, Jr., *The Imperial Presidency* (Boston: Houghton Mifflin, 1973).

- George Washington issued a Proclamation of Neutrality during the war between France and Britain following the French Revolution, thereby establishing the president's power to make foreign policy.
- Thomas Jefferson, who prior to becoming president argued for a narrow interpretation of presidential powers, purchased the Louisiana Territory despite the fact that the Constitution contains no provision for the acquisition of territory, let alone authorizing presidential action to do so.
- Andrew Jackson ordered the removal of federal funds from the national bank and removed his secretary of the treasury from office, establishing the president's power to *remove* executive officials, a power not specifically mentioned in the Constitution.

- Abraham Lincoln, asking "Was it possible to lose the nation yet preserve the Constitution?" established the precedent of vigorous presidential action in national emergencies: he blockaded southern ports, declared martial law in parts of the country, and issued the Emancipation Proclamation, all without constitutional or congressional authority.
- Franklin D. Roosevelt, battling the Great Depression during the 1930s, ordered the nation's banks to close temporarily. Following the Japanese attack on Pearl Harbor in 1941, he ordered the incarceration without trial of many thousands of Americans of Japanese ancestry living on the West Coast.

*Checking Presidential Power*   President Harry Truman believed that "the president has the right to keep the country from going to hell," and he was willing to use means beyond those specified in the Constitution or authorized by Congress. In 1952, while U.S. troops were fighting in Korea, steelworkers at home were threatening to strike. Rather than cross organized labor by forbidding the strike under the terms of the Taft-Hartley Act of 1947 (which he had opposed), Truman chose to seize the steel mills by executive order and continue their operations under U.S. government control. The U.S. Supreme Court ordered the steel mills returned to their owners, however, acknowledging that the president may have inherent powers to act in a national emergency but arguing that Congress had provided a legal remedy—however distasteful to the president. Thus the president can indeed act to keep the country from "going to hell," but if Congress has already acted to do so, the president must abide by the law.

*Executive Privilege*   Over the years, presidents and scholars have argued that the Constitution's establishment of a separate executive branch of government entitles the president to **executive privilege**—the right to keep confidential communications from other branches of government. Public exposure of internal executive communications would inhibit the president's ability to obtain candid advice from subordinates and would obstruct the president's ability to conduct negotiations with foreign governments or to command military operations.

But Congress has never recognized executive privilege. It has frequently tried to compel the testimony of executive officials at congressional hearings. Presidents have regularly refused to appear themselves at congressional hearings and have frequently refused to allow other executive officials to appear or divulge specific information, citing executive privilege. The federal courts have generally refrained from intervening in this dispute between the executive and legislative branches. However, the Supreme Court has ruled that the president is not immune from court orders when illegal acts are under investigation. In *United States v. Nixon* (1974), the U.S. Supreme Court acknowledged that while the president might legitimately claim executive privilege where military or diplomatic matters are involved, such a privilege cannot be invoked in a criminal investigation. The Court ordered President Nixon to surrender tape recordings of White House conversations between the president and his advisers during the Watergate scandal.

*Presidential Impoundment*   The Constitution states that "no Money shall be drawn from the Treasury, but in Consequence of appropriations made by Law" (Article I, Section 9). Clearly the president cannot spend money *not* appropriated

**Executive privilege:** The right of a president to withhold from other branches of government confidential communications within the executive branch; while posited by presidents, it has been upheld by the Supreme Court only in limited situations.

by Congress. But the Constitution is silent on whether the president *must* spend all of the money appropriated by Congress for various purposes. Presidents from Thomas Jefferson onward frequently refused to spend money appropriated by Congress, an action referred to as **impoundment.** But taking advantage of a presidency weakened by the Watergate scandal, the Congress in 1974 passed the Budget and Impoundment Control Act, which requires the president to spend all appropriated funds. The act does provide, however, that presidents may send Congress a list of specific **deferrals**—items on which they wish to postpone spending—and **rescissions**—items they wish to cancel altogether. Congress by *resolution* (which cannot be vetoed by the president) may restore the deferrals and force the president to spend the money. Both houses of Congress must approve a rescission; otherwise the government must spend the money.

*The Constitution's Congressional Tilt*   The Constitution, reflecting the Founders' view of the preeminence of the legislative branch, gives the last word to the Congress in disputes with the president:

- The Congress can override the president's veto of legislation if it can muster a two-thirds vote in both houses.
- The Congress can impeach and remove the president from office.
- Only the Congress can appropriate money.
- Major presidential appointments require Senate confirmation.
- The president is obliged by the Constitution to "take Care that the Laws be faithfully executed"—that is, the *laws of Congress*—regardless of any personal feelings about these laws.

Thus, Congress is *constitutionally* positioned to dominate American government. But it is the president who *politically* dominates the nation's public affairs.

# POLITICAL RESOURCES OF THE PRESIDENT

The real sources of presidential power are not found in the Constitution. The president's power is the *power to persuade.* As Harry Truman put it: "I sit here all day trying to persuade people to do things they ought to have sense enough to do without my persuading them. . . . That's all the powers of the president amount to."[7]

The president's political resources are potentially very great. The nation looks to the president for leadership, for direction, for reassurance. The president is the focus of public and media attention. The president has the capacity to mobilize public opinion, to communicate directly with the American people, and to employ the symbols of office to advance policy initiatives in both foreign and domestic affairs.

*The Reputation for Power*   A reputation for power is itself a source of power. Presidents must strive to maintain the image of power in order to be effective. A president perceived as powerful can exercise great influence abroad with foreign governments and at home with the Congress, interest groups, and the executive bureaucracy. A president perceived as weak, unsteady, bumbling, or error-prone will soon become unpopular and ineffective.

**Impoundment:** Refusal by a president to spend monies appropriated by Congress; outlawed except with congressional consent by the Budget and Impoundment Control Act of 1974.

**Deferrals:** Items on which a president wishes to postpone spending.

**Rescissions:** Items on which a president wishes to cancel spending.

*Presidential Popularity*    Presidential popularity with the American people is a political resource. Popular presidents cannot always transfer their popularity into foreign policy successes or legislative victories, but popular presidents usually have more success than unpopular presidents.

Presidential popularity is regularly tracked in national opinion polls. For more than forty years, national surveys have asked the American public: "Do you approve or disapprove of the way———is handling his job as president?" (see Figures 11-2, 11-3). Analyses of variations over time in these poll results suggest some generalizations about presidential popularity.[8]

Presidential popularity is usually high at the beginning of a president's term of office, but this period can be very brief. The American public's high expectations for a new president can turn sour within a few months. A president's popularity will vary a great deal during a term in office, with sharp peaks and steep valleys in the ratings. But the general trend is downward.[9] Presidents usually recover some popularity at the end of their first term as they campaign for reelection.

Presidential popularity rises during crises. People "rally 'round the president" when the nation is confronted with an international threat or the president initiates a military action.[10] President George Bush, for example, registered the all-time high in presidential ratings during the Persian Gulf War. Likewise, the invasion of Grenada in 1983 and Panama in 1989 rallied support to the president. But prolonged warfare and stalemate erode popular support. In both the Korean and the Vietnam Wars, initial public approval of the president and support for the war eroded over time as military operations stalemated and casualties mounted.[11]

Major scandals also hurt presidential popularity and effectiveness. The Watergate scandal produced a low of 22 percent approval for Nixon just prior to his resignation. Reagan's generally high approval ratings were blemished by the Iran-Contra scandal hearings in 1987, but he ultimately left office with the highest approval rating of any outgoing president.

**FIGURE 11-2**    **Presidential Popularity over Time**

*Americans expect a great deal from their presidents and are quick to give these leaders the credit—and the blame—for major events in the nation's life. In general, public approval (as measured by response to the question "Do you approve or disapprove of the way———is handling the job of president?") is highest at the beginning of a new president's term in office and declines from that point. Major military confrontations generally raise presidential ratings initially but can (as in the case of Lyndon Johnson) cause dramatic decline if the conflict drags on. In addition, public approval of the president is closely linked to the nation's economic health. When the economy is in recession, Americans tend to take a negative view of the president.*

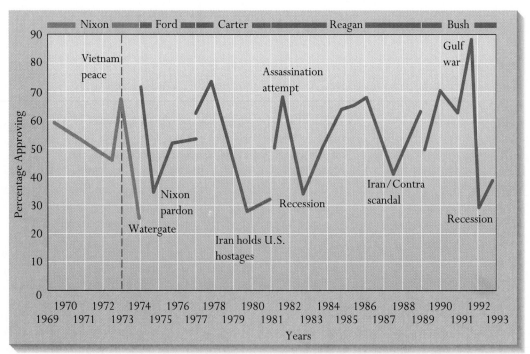

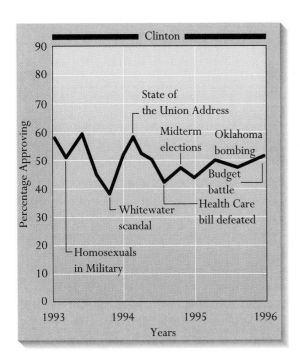

FIGURE 11-3 **Bill Clinton's Popularity Ratings** *Despite a healthy economy, Bill Clinton's job approval ratings generally remained mediocre. Dips in popularity occurred with his opening of military service to homosexuals, press coverage of the Whitewater scandal, and the defeat of his health care bill. But following the terrorist bombing of the Federal Building in Oklahoma City and his later battles with Congress over the budget, Clinton moved above the critical 50 percent approval level and maintained a positive rating throughout the 1996 presidential campaign.*

Finally, economic recessions erode presidential popularity. Every president in office during a recession has suffered loss of popular approval, including President Reagan during the 1982 recession. But no president suffered a more precipitous decline in approval ratings than George Bush, whose popularity plummeted from its Gulf War high of 89 percent to a low of 37 percent in only a year, largely as a result of recession.

*Access to the Media*　　The president dominates the news more than any other single person. All major television networks, newspapers, and news magazines have reporters (usually their most experienced and skilled people) covering the "White House beat."[12] The presidential press secretary briefs these reporters daily. The president also may appear in person in the White House press room at any time. Presidents regularly use this media access to advance their programs and priorities.

Presidential press conferences can help mobilize popular support for presidential programs. Presidents often try to focus attention on particular legislative issues, and they generally open press conferences with a lengthy policy statement on these issues. But reporters' questions and subsequent reporting often refocus the press conference in other directions. The president cannot control the questions or limit the subject matter of press conferences. Indeed, the president cannot even ensure that the television networks—ABC, CBS, and NBC—will carry a presidential press conference live, although CNN, with its all-news format, always does so.

Presidents may also use direct television addresses from the White House. President Reagan, who held relatively few press conferences, made heavy use of national prime-time television appeals to mobilize support for his programs. Reagan's appeals frequently resulted in a deluge of telephone calls, wires, and letters to Congress in support of the president. George Bush and Bill Clinton were far less successful in this approach. Presidents must also weigh the drawbacks of television addresses. The networks now routinely give opposition leaders television time to respond following the president's address.

Finally, presidents can try to mobilize popular support for a program by public appearances, addresses, and speeches. The national meetings or conventions of influential groups such as the American Newspaper Association, the American Legion, the National Association of Manufacturers, the U.S. Chamber of Commerce, and the National Association for the Advancement of Colored People can provide a forum. So can college and university commencements.

*Party Leadership*     Presidents are leaders of their party, but this role is hardly a source of great strength. It is true that presidents select the national party chair, control the national committee and its Washington staff, and largely direct the national party convention. Incumbent presidents can use this power to defeat challengers *within* their own parties. President Ford used this power to help defeat challenger Ronald Reagan in 1976; President Carter used it to help defeat challenger Ted Kennedy in 1980; and President Bush used it against challenger Pat Buchanan in 1992. But the role of party leader is of limited value to a president, since the parties have few controls over their members (see Chapter 7).

In some instances, however, presidents have found it preferable *not* to provide support for some of their party's congressional candidates. Even Ronald Reagan, who frequently made speeches and appearances at fund-raising events on behalf of Republican candidates, declined to campaign for some Republican candidates running against conservative Democrats who had supported his tax-cutting measures in Congress. Presidents of both parties have also decided on occasion not to risk future retaliation in legislative politics by actively opposing the reelection of incumbents in safe districts.

Nevertheless, presidents enjoy much stronger support in Congress from members of their own party than from members of the opposition party. Some of the

*President Clinton answers questions during a press conference. These meetings with the press can be a double-edged sword. They give the president an opportunity to present his point of view to the public, but they also allow the press to raise issues a president might rather avoid.*

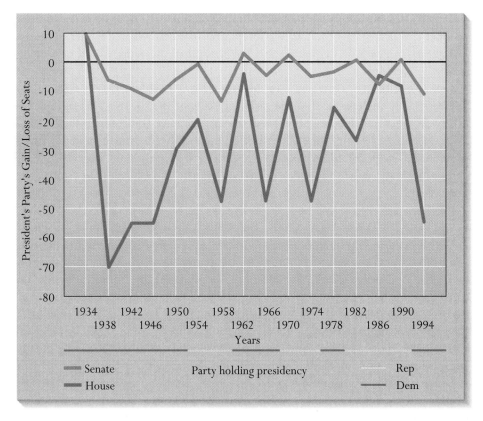

FIGURE 11-4 Losses by President's Party in Midterm Elections, 1934–1994

*The president's party tends to lose seats in the House of Representatives in midterm elections (congressional elections in a nonpresidential election year). More often than not, the president's party has also lost some Senate seats. Note that the graph shows the net gains or losses in the House and Senate seats by the president's party. When the president was a Democrat, there were lost Democratic seats; when the president was a Republican, there were lost Republican seats.*

*Source:* Norman J. Ornstein, Thomas E. Mann, and Michael J. Malbin, *Vital Statistics on Congress* (Washington, D.C.: Congressional Quarterly Press, 1996), p. 55.

president's party support in Congress is a product of shared ideological values and policy positions. But Republican Congress members do have some stake in the success of a Republican president, as do Democratic members in the success of a Democratic president. Unsuccessful presidents may cost their seats at the next election. Popular presidents may produce those few extra votes that make the difference for party candidates in close congressional districts.

Presidential popularity tends to wane after the first-year "honeymoon," and opposition to presidential programs rises among voters. As a result, the president's party tends to lose House seats in midterm congressional elections. The Democrats' loss of fifty-four House seats and nine Senate seats in 1994 was one of the worst congressional party defeats in modern times (see Figure 11-4). The president's party's record in the Senate in midterm elections also shows a negative trend, even though only one-third of Senate seats are up for election.

## CHIEF EXECUTIVE

The president is the chief executive of the nation's largest bureaucracy—2.8 million civilian employees, sixty independent agencies, fourteen departments, and the large Executive Office of the President. The formal organizational chart of the federal government places the president at the head of this giant structure (see Figure 12-1, "The Federal Bureaucracy," in Chapter 12). Yet the president cannot command this bureaucracy in the fashion of a military officer or a corporation president. When Harry Truman was preparing to turn over the White House to Dwight Eisenhower, he predicted that the general of the army would not understand the presidency: "He'll sit here and say 'Do this! Do that!' and nothing will happen. Poor Ike—it won't be a bit like the army. He'll find it very frustrating." Truman vastly underestimated the political skills of the former general, but the crusty Missourian clearly understood the frustrations confronting the nation's chief executive. The president does not command the executive branch of government but rather stands at its center—persuading, bargaining, negotiating, and compromising to achieve goals (see *People in Politics:* "Bill Clinton: The Ambivalent Presidency").

*The Constitutional Executive*   The Constitution is vague about the president's authority over the executive branch. It vests executive power in the presidency and grants the president authority to appoint principal officers of the government "by and with the Advice and Consent of the Senate." Under the Constitution, the president may also "require the Opinion, in writing, of the principal Officer of each of the executive Departments, upon any Subject relating to the Duties of their respective Offices." This awkward phrase presumably gives the president the power to oversee operations of the executive departments. Finally, and perhaps most important, the president is instructed to "take Care that the Laws be faithfully executed."

At the same time, Congress has substantial authority over the executive branch. Through its lawmaking abilities, Congress can establish or abolish executive departments and regulate their operations. Congress's "power of the purse" allows it to determine the budget of each department each year and thus to limit or broaden or even "micromanage" the activities of these departments. Moreover, Congress can pressure executive agencies by conducting investigations, calling administrators to task in public hearings, and directly contacting agencies with members' own complaints or those of their constituents.

*Executive Orders*   Presidents frequently use **executive orders** to implement their policies. Executive orders may direct specific federal agencies to carry out the president's wishes, or they may direct all federal agencies to pursue the president's preferred course of action. In any case, they must be based on either a president's constitutional powers or on powers delegated to the president by laws of Congress. Presidents regularly issue 50 to 100 executive orders each year,[13] but some stand out. In 1948, President Harry Truman issued Executive Order 9981 to desegregate the U.S. armed forces. In 1967, President Lyndon Johnson issued Executive Order 11246 to require that private firms with federal contracts institute affirmative action programs.

*Appointments*   Presidential power over the executive branch derives in part from the president's authority to appoint and remove top officials. Presidents can shape policy by careful attention to top appointments—cabinet secretaries, assistant secretaries, agency heads, and White House staff. The key is to select people who share the president's policy views and who have the personal qualifications to do an effective job. However, in cabinet appointments political considerations weigh heavily: unifying various elements of the party; appealing for interest group

**Executive order:** A formal regulation governing executive branch operations issued by the president.

support; rewarding political loyalty; providing a temporary haven for unsuccessful party candidates; achieving a balance of racial, ethnic, and gender representation.[14] The appointment power gives the president only limited control over the executive branch of government. Of the executive branch's 2.8 million civilian employees, the president actually appoints only about 3,000. The vast majority of federal executive branch employees are civil servants—recruited, paid, and protected under civil service laws—and are not easily removed or punished by the president (see "Bureaucratic Politics" in Chapter 12). Cabinet secretaries and heads of independent regulatory agencies require congressional confirmation, but presidents can choose their own White House staff without the approval of Congress.

Presidents have only limited power to remove the heads of independent regulatory agencies. By law, Congress sets the terms of these officials. Federal Communications Commission members are appointed for seven years; Securities and Exchange Commission members for five years; and Federal Reserve Board members, responsible for the nation's money supply, enjoy the longest term of any executive officials—fourteen years. Congress's responsibility for term length for regulatory agencies is supposed to insulate them, in particular their quasi-judicial responsibilities, from "political" influence. The effect is simply to substitute bureaucratic politics for presidential politics (see "Bureaucratic Politics" in Chapter 12).

Even having a presidential appointee at the helm of a department does not always guarantee the president control over that department. Many political appointees are stymied by the career bureaucrats in departments and agencies who have the knowledge, skills, and experience to function with little or no supervision from their nominal political chiefs. Rather than carrying out the president's policies, some appointees "go native": they yield to the career bureaucrats, adopt the prevailing customs and values of their agencies, and seek the support of the bureaucrats, interest groups, and congressional committees that determine the agencies' future.

Republican presidents have an especially difficult task controlling the bureaucracy because a majority of career bureaucrats are Democratic voters.[15] When President Nixon tried to deal with this problem by shifting power from executive departments to his White House staff, the unhappy result was that the White House staff itself became a large and powerful bureaucracy, frequently locked in conflict with executive departments. President Reagan instead tried appointing committed conservatives to head key agencies, only to see them isolated and undermined by angry bureaucrats. Some lower-level bureaucrats supplied the media and Congress with damaging reports about Reagan appointees' activities (see "Bureaucratic Politics" in Chapter 12).

Career bureaucrats know that they can outlast political heads of agencies and departments. Indeed, the median tenure of top executive officials is only two years. Department and agency heads normally require a year or more to learn the programs, issues, problems, and personalities of their domains. With frequent turnover, it is difficult for the president to provide stable direction to the bureaucracy.

*Budget*   Presidential authority also derives from the president's role in the budgetary process. The Constitution makes no mention of the president with regard to expenditures; rather, it grants the power of the purse to Congress.

# Bill Clinton:
# The Ambivalent Presidency

No one doubts that William Jefferson Clinton is one of the most intelligent men ever to occupy the Oval Office, and that his knowledge of the details of government and public policy exceeds that of any other recent president. But with no fixed ideological compass, the Clinton presidency has suffered "deep, near terminal ambivalence." Throughout his first term he weighed conflicting advice from moderates and liberals with reference to a single, overriding goal—reelection. Now in his second term, he is free to pursue a consistent course for his presidency. But he is more likely to continue to pursue multiple directions simultaneously.

*Getting Started*  Born Billy Blythe in rural Hope, Arkansas, three months after his father's death in an automobile accident (he assumed his stepfather's name of Clinton at age 15), young Bill learned that persistence and tenacity were the keys to success and acclaim. As a teenage delegate to Boys Nation, he won a handshake from President John F. Kennedy in 1963. He chose to attend Georgetown University in Washington to be near the nation's centers of power. As soon as he arrived in the capital he called on his state's senator, William J. Fulbright, Chairman of the Senate Foreign Relations Committee, and won a part-time job as a legislative aide. Clinton won a Rhodes Scholarship to Oxford University with the help of Senator Fulbright, himself a former Rhodes scholar. He never completed a degree at Oxford, but he cultivated friendships that would later enhance his public career. In London he helped organize anti-Vietnam War demonstrations, even while he worried that his antiwar activities might someday come back to haunt his political ambitions. When he received a draft notice, he promptly enrolled in the ROTC program at the University of Arkansas, making himself temporarily ineligible for the draft, even while acknowledging that his real plans were to go to Yale Law School.

*The Nation's Youngest Governor*  Upon graduation from Yale, Clinton turned down offers to return to Washington as a congressional staff aide. He was anxious to launch his own political career, and he knew that the road to elective office ran through his home state. Trying to capitalize on the Watergate scandal, he challenged a veteran Republican congressman in 1974. As a young antiwar activist with long sixties-style hair, a Yale and Oxford background, and liberal friends such as Hillary Rodham coming from Washington to help in the campaign, he could have lost by a wide margin in conservative Arkansas. Instead, he came within a few votes of defeating a strong incumbent. When the state's elected attorney general vacated the post to run for Congress, Clinton mounted a successful campaign to replace him. In 1978 Clinton jumped into the open gubernatorial contest and became the nation's youngest governor at age 32.

*Remolding His Image*  As governor, Clinton first pushed a broad program of liberal reform for Arkansas, increasing taxes and expenditures. But he appeared to be an arrogant, crusading, liberal politician, out of touch with his conservative Arkansas constituency. He was defeated for reelection in 1980. His defeat "forever influenced the way he approached government and politics." He proceeded to remold himself into a political moderate, calling for workfare to replace welfare, supporting the death penalty, and working to create a favorable business climate in Arkansas. He cut his hair, and his wife began using her married name so as not to offend social conservatives. The moderate strategy proved successful; he was elected governor once again in 1982. By most accounts, Bill Clinton was a successful governor. He focused on economic development and education. He declared himself an environmentalist but granted concessions to his state's giant chicken industry. His many compromises and accommodations led the *Arkansas Democrat Gazette* to label him "Slick Willie."

Bill Clinton's view that only a moderate Democrat could succeed in winning the presidency was reinforced by Michael Dukakis's disastrous defeat in 1988. Just as he had shaped his image to fit his Arkansas constituents, Clinton molded his national image as a "New Democrat"—concerned with economic growth, favoring workfare over welfare, acting tough on crime, and willing to stand up to traditional core Democratic interest groups such as labor unions, minorities, and government employees. He used his tenure as chairman of the centrist Democratic Leadership Conference (DLC) to promote himself as a moderate, pro-business, pro-investment Democrat, capable of winning back the support of the white middle class. He promised everything to everybody: "We can be pro-growth and pro-environment, we can be pro-business and pro-labor, we can make government work again by making it more aggressive and leaner and more effective at the same time, and we can be pro-family and pro-choice."

*First Term Flip-Flops*  Bill Clinton won the White House in 1992 with only 43 percent of the popular vote, hardly a mandate for comprehensive policy change. His first major battle—to protect military service for homosexuals—proved a disaster. Military chiefs, led by the popular General Colin Powell, resisted, and Clinton was forced to beat a retreat. He succeeded in getting the Democratic-controlled Congress to pass a large tax increase, raising the top marginal income tax rate from 31 to nearly 40 percent. But in his second year, he stumbled badly in his massive national health care program, and his approval ratings sagged.

The sweeping Republican congressional victory in 1994 posed very important political choices for Clinton. Should he respond by moving back to the center, moderating his big spending plans, cooperating with Republicans in Congress on budget cutting and welfare reform, and moving away from the policies advocated by traditional core Democratic constituencies—feminists, environmentalists, union officials, government employees, and African American and civil rights organizations? Or should he continue to fight for liberal policies and large-scale government programs, challenging the Republican Congress to reject his initiatives, and then campaign for reelection by castigating Congress?

Typically, Clinton followed *both* paths simultaneously. He pressured Senate Democrats to defeat the Balanced Budget Amendment and proceeded to veto several Republican balanced budget plans. When the government temporarily "shut down," Clinton uncharacteristically stood firm and shifted blame to the Republican Congress. He cast himself as the defender of "Medicare, Medicaid, education, and the environment" against mean-spirited Republican budget cutters. The Oklahoma City bombing seemed to warn the nation about the dangers of "extremism." Clinton's approval ratings began a long rise.

*Shifting Toward Mini-Policies*  Election year brought still more policy shifts. Earlier he had announced "The era of big government is over." He signed the Republican welfare bill that he had vetoed twice. Then he reassured enraged liberals by vetoing a congressional ban on late-term "partial birth" abortions. But winning back the family vote—especially moderate, middle-class women—became the focus of his attention.

Rather than champion large-scale change in the fashion of Roosevelt's New Deal, Clinton shifted to what might be labeled the "Small Deal"—an assembly of small changes easily understood by the American people and not costing very much. This shift toward mini-policies—V-chips, school uniforms, gun control, time off for family emergencies, longer stays in maternity wards, etc.—paid off handsomely at the polls. Although men appeared to divide their votes evenly between Clinton and Dole, the president won women voters by a stunning 54 to 38 margin.

*Building "A Bridge to the 21st Century"*  At the start of his second term Clinton seemed to acknowledge that he had no mandate for new, large-scale government programs. He modestly observed in his election night victory speech: "Tonight we proclaim that the vital American center is alive and well." But even if he sought to return to a liberal agenda—to massive government interventions to solve social and economic problems—it is not likely that a Republican Congress would allow him to get very far. Indeed, Republicans and conservatives claim that he won reelection as a deficit-cutting, welfare-reforming, more-cops-on-the-beat president—that is, by "stealing" traditional Republican issues. And both Clintons face continued scrutiny in a variety of investigations, detracting from the administration's ability to focus on policy issues. Yet the important issues will not disappear: how to achieve a balanced budget; how to slow the growth of entitlement spending, especially Medicare; how to implement welfare reform; how to maintain a growing economy. So the "bridge to the 21st century" will likely remain a political battleground.

Indeed, for nearly 150 years, executive departments submitted their budget requests directly to the Congress without first submitting them to the president. But with the passage of the Budget and Accounting Act in 1921, Congress established the Office of Management and Budget (originally named the Bureau of the Budget) to assist the president in preparing an annual Budget of the United States Government for presentation to the Congress. The president's budget is simply a set of recommendations to the Congress. Congress must pass appropriations acts before the president or any executive department or agency may spend money. Congress can and frequently does alter the president's budget recommendations.

The Office of Management and Budget is the largest agency in the Executive Office of the President. All requests for congressional appropriations must clear OMB first, a requirement that gives OMB great power over the executive branch. Since almost all agencies request more money than they can receive, OMB has primary responsibility for reviewing and reducing departmental and agency requests (subject to their appeal to the president). OMB also continuously scrutinizes the organization and operations of executive agencies in order to recommend changes and improve efficiency and economy. Like other members of the White House staff, the top officials of OMB are appointed by and responsible solely to the president, who relies on them to reflect presidential goals and priorities.

With the Senate's consent, the president also appoints three professional economists of high standing to the Council of Economic Advisers (CEA). Created by the Employment Act of 1946, CEA analyzes trends in the economy and recommends to the president the fiscal and monetary policies necessary to avoid depression and inflation (see "Economic Decision Making" in Chapter 16).

*The Cabinet*    The **cabinet** is not mentioned in the U.S. Constitution; it has no formal powers. It consists of the secretaries of the executive departments and others the president may designate, including the vice-president, the Ambassador to the United Nations, the Director of the Central Intelligence Agency and the Special Trade Representative. According to custom, cabinet officials are ranked by the date their departments were created (see Table 11-2). Thus, the secretary of state is the senior cabinet officer, followed by the secretary of the treasury. They sit next to the president at cabinet meetings; heads of the newest departments sit at the far ends of the table. The Defense Department was created by law in 1947, but the secretary of defense inherits the traditional posts—and rank—of the secretary of war and the secretary of the navy, which were created by the first Congress of the United States.

The cabinet rarely functions as a decision-making body. Cabinet officers in the United States are powerful because they head giant administrative organizations. The secretary of state, the secretary of defense, the secretary of the treasury, the attorney general, and, to a lesser extent, the other departmental secretaries are all people of power and prestige. But seldom does a strong president hold a cabinet meeting to decide important policy questions. More frequently, presidents know what they want and hold cabinet meetings only to help promote their views. Presidents who have tried to use the cabinet as a policy-making body have been disappointed. George Washington was frustrated by constant feuding between his secretary of the treasury, Alexander Hamilton, and his secretary of state, Thomas Jefferson. President Jimmy Carter promised

**Cabinet:** The heads (secretaries) of the executive departments together with other top officials accorded cabinet rank by the president; only occasionally does it meet as a body to advise and support the president.

TABLE 11-2   THE CABINET DEPARTMENTS

| Department | Created |
|---|---|
| State | 1789 |
| Treasury | 1789 |
| Defense* | 1947 |
| Justice | 1789 |
| Interior | 1849 |
| Agriculture** | 1889 |
| Commerce | 1913 |
| Labor | 1913 |
| Health and Human Services*** | 1953 |
| Housing and Urban Development | 1965 |
| Transportation | 1966 |
| Energy | 1977 |
| Education | 1979 |
| Veterans Affairs | 1989 |

*Formerly the War and Navy Departments, created in 1789 and 1798, respectively.

**Agriculture Department created in 1862; made part of cabinet in 1889.

***Originally Health, Education, and Welfare; reorganized in 1979, with the creation of a separate Department of Education.

"cabinet government" but soon found that meetings were little more than "adult show and tell." The cabinet is too large for serious discussion; its members are not necessarily familiar with issues beyond their own department's sphere of activity; they are preoccupied with managing large bureaucracies. Finally, cabinet members are frequently appointed not for policy guidance but to cement the president's relationships with interest groups—agriculture, veterans, labor, and so forth—or to provide the administration with racial, ethnic, or gender balance.

The Constitution requires that "Officers of the United States" be confirmed by the Senate. In the past, the Senate rarely rejected a presidential cabinet nomination; the traditional view was that presidents were entitled to pick their own people and even make their own mistakes. In recent years, however, the confirmation process has become more partisan and divisive, with the Senate conducting lengthy investigations and holding public hearings on presidential cabinet nominees. In 1989, the Senate rejected President Bush's nomination of John Tower as secretary of defense in a partisan battle featuring charges that the former Texas senator was a heavy drinker. In 1993, President Clinton was obliged to withdraw the nomination of Zoe Baird as attorney general following Senate hearings featuring the charge that she had employed an illegal alien as a babysitter and had failed to pay the woman's Social Security taxes. The intense public scrutiny and potential for partisan attacks, together with financial disclosure and conflict-of-interest laws, may be discouraging some well-qualified people from accepting cabinet posts.

*The National Security Council*   The National Security Council (NSC) is really an "inner cabinet" created by law in 1947 to advise the president and coordinate foreign, defense, and intelligence activities. The president is chair, and the vice-president, secretary of state, secretary of defense, and director of the Office of Emergency Planning (a minor unit in the Executive Office) are participating members. The chair of the Joint Chiefs of Staff and the director of the Central Intelligence Agency serve as advisers to the NSC, which is headed by the Special Assistant to the President for National Security Affairs. The purposes of the council are to advise and coordinate policy, but in the Iran-Contra scandal, a staff member of the NSC, Lt. Col. Oliver North, undertook to implement security policy. Various investigative committees strongly recommended that the NSC staff confine itself to an advisory role.

*White House Staff* Today, presidents exercise their powers chiefly through the White House staff.[16] This staff includes the president's closest aides and advisers. Over the years, the White House staff has grown from Roosevelt's small "brain trust" of a dozen advisers to several hundred people, many with impressive titles, such as assistant to the president, deputy assistant to the president, special assistant to the President, and counsel to the president.

Senior White House staff members are trusted political advisers, often personal friends and long-time associates of the president. Some enjoy office space in the White House itself and daily contact with the president (see Figure 11-5). Appointed without Senate confirmation, their loyalty is to the president alone, not to departments, agencies, or interest groups. Their many tasks include:

- Providing the president with sound advice on everything from national security to congressional affairs, policy development, and electoral politics.
- Monitoring the operations of executive departments and agencies and evaluating the performance of key executive officials.
- Setting the president's schedule, determining whom the president will see and call, where and when the president will travel, and where and to whom the president will make personal appearances and speeches.

Above all, the staff must protect their boss, steering the president away from scandal, political blunders, and errors of judgment.

The senior White House staff normally includes a chief of staff, the national security adviser, a press secretary, the counsel to the president (an attorney), a director of personnel (patronage appointments), and assistants for political affairs, legislative liaison, management, and domestic policy. Staff organization depends on each president's personal taste. Some presidents have organized their staffs hierarchically, concentrating power in the chief of staff. Others have maintained direct contact with several staff members.

## CHIEF LEGISLATOR AND LOBBYIST

The president has the principal responsibility for the initiation of national policy. Indeed, about 80 percent of the bills considered by Congress originate in the executive branch. Presidents have a strong incentive to fulfill this responsibility: The American people hold them responsible for anything that happens in the

FIGURE 11-5 **The Clinton Administration's Corridors of Power**

*Presidents allocate office space in the White House according to their own desires. An office located close to the president's is considered an indication of the power of the occupant.*

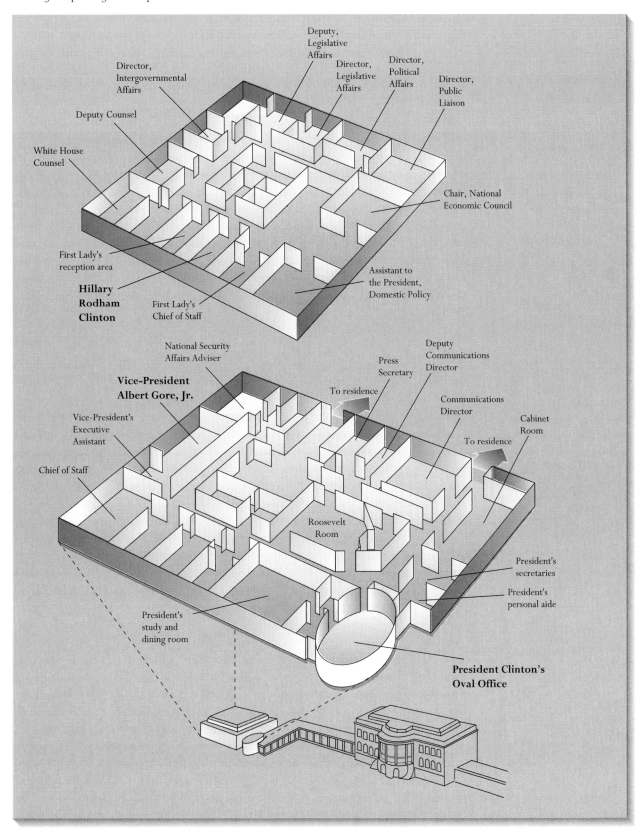

nation during their term of office, whether or not they have the authority or capacity to do anything about it.

*Policy Initiation*    The Founders understood that the president would be responsible for policy initiation. The Constitution requires the president to "give to the Congress Information of the State of the Union," to "recommend to their Consideration such Measures as he shall judge necessary and expedient" (Article II, Section 3). "On extraordinary Occasions" the president may call a recessed Congress into special session. Each year the principal policy statement of the president comes in the State of the Union message to Congress. It is followed by the president's Budget of the United States Government, which sets forth the president's programs with price tags attached. Many other policy proposals are developed by executive departments and agencies, transmitted to the White House for the president's approval or "clearance," and then sent to Congress.

Congress may not accept all or even most of the president's proposals. Indeed, from time to time it may even try to develop its own legislative agenda in competition with the president's, as in the Republican "Contract with America" in 1995. But the president's legislative initiatives usually set the agenda of congressional decision making. No other actor in the political system has the capability of the president to set agendas in given policy areas. As one experienced Washington lobbyist put it: "Obviously when the president sends up a bill, it takes first place in the queue. All other bills take second place."[17]

*White House Lobbying*    Presidents do not simply send their bills to Congress and then await the outcome. The president is also expected to be the chief lobbyist on behalf of the administration's bills as they make their way through the legislative labyrinth. The White House staff includes "legislative liaison" people—lobbyists for the president's programs. They organize the president's legislative proposals, track them through committee and floor proceedings, arrange committee appearances by executive department and agency representatives, count votes, and advise the president on when and how to "cut deals" and "twist arms."

To be successful, presidents must persuade members of Congress that it is in their interest to support presidential programs. Presidential influence, as indicated by role-call votes in Congress, is significantly weaker on domestic issues than on foreign policy issues.[18] The president's domestic policy is constantly challenged by powerful interest groups, by entrenched bureaucrats reluctant to follow their president's leadership, and by members of Congress with their own policy agendas. The president cannot appeal to national unity in the face of external threats when lobbying Congress on domestic issues.

Presidents are not without resources in lobbying Congress. They may exchange many favors, large and small, for the support of individual members. They can help direct "pork" to a member's district, promise White House support for a member's pet project, and assist in resolving a member's problems with the bureaucracy. Presidents also may issue or withhold invitations to the White House for prestigious ceremonies, dinners with visiting heads of state, and other glittering social occasions—an effective resource because most members of Congress value the prestige associated with close White House "connections."

The president may choose to "twist arms" individually—by telephoning and meeting with wavering members of Congress. Arm twisting is generally reserved for the president's most important legislative battles. There is seldom time for a president to contact individual members of Congress personally about many bills in various stages of the legislative process—in subcommittee, full committee, floor consideration, conference committee, and final passage—in both the House and the Senate. Instead, the president must rely on White House staff for most legislative contacts and use personal appeals sparingly.

*The Honeymoon*    The **honeymoon period** at the very start of a president's term offers the best opportunity to get the new administration's legislative proposals enacted into law. Presidential influence in Congress is generally highest at this time both because the president's personal popularity is typically at its height and because the president can claim the recent election results as a popular mandate for key programs. Sophisticated members of Congress know that votes cast for a presidential candidate are not necessarily votes cast for that candidate's policy position (see "The Voter Decides" in Chapter 8). But election results signal members of Congress, in a language they understand well, that the president is politically popular and that they must give the administration's programs careful consideration. President Lyndon Johnson succeeded in getting the bulk of his Great Society program enacted in the year following his landslide victory in 1964. Ronald Reagan pushed through the largest tax cut in American history in the year following his convincing electoral victory over incumbent president Jimmy Carter in 1980. Bill Clinton was most successful with the Congress during his first year in office, in 1993, even winning approval for a major tax increase as part of a deficit-reduction package.

*Presidential "Box Scores"*    How successful are presidents in getting their legislation through Congress? *Congressional Quarterly* regularly compiles "box scores" of presidential success in Congress—percentages of presidential victories on congressional votes on which the president took a clear-cut position. The measure does not distinguish between bills that were important to the president and bills that may have been less significant. But viewed over time (see Figure 11-6), the presidential box scores provide interesting insights into the factors affecting the president's legislative success.

The most important determinant of presidential success in Congress is party control. Presidents are far more successful when they face a Congress controlled by their own party. Democratic presidents John F. Kennedy and Lyndon Johnson enjoyed the support of Democratic-controlled Congresses and posted average success scores over 80 percent. Jimmy Carter was hardly a popular president, yet he enjoyed the support of a Democratic Congress and an average of 76.8 percent presidential support. Republican presidents Richard Nixon and Gerald Ford fared poorly with Democrat-controlled Congresses. Republican president Ronald Reagan was very successful in his first term when he faced a Democratic House and a Republican Senate, but after Democrats took over both houses of Congress, Reagan's success rate plummeted. During the Reagan and Bush presidencies, divided party control of government (Republicans in the White House and Democrats controlling one or both houses of Congress) was said to produce **gridlock**—the political inability of the government to act decisively on the nation's problems. President Bill Clinton's notable achievements when Democrats controlled the Congress (1993–94), contrasted with his dismal record in dealing with a Republican-controlled Congress (1995–96), provide a vivid illustration of the importance of party in determining a president's legislative success. Clinton's

**Honeymoon period:** Early months of a president's term in which his popularity with the public and influence with the Congress are generally high.

**Gridlock:** Political stalemate between the executive and legislative branches arising when one branch is controlled by one major political party and the other by the other party.

FIGURE 11-6 **Presidential Success Scores in Congress**

*Presidential "box scores"—the percentage of times that a bill endorsed by the president is enacted by Congress—are closely linked to the strength of the president's party in Congress. For example, both Dwight D. Eisenhower and Ronald Reagan benefited from having a Republican majority in the Senate in their first terms and suffered when Democrats gained control of the Senate in their second terms. Democratic control of both houses of Congress resulted in significantly higher box scores for Democratic presidents John Kennedy, Lyndon Johnson, and Jimmy Carter than for Republicans Richard Nixon, Gerald Ford, and George Bush. Clinton was very successful in his first two years when the Democrats controlled Congress, but when the Republicans won control following the 1994 midterm election, Clinton's box score plummeted.*

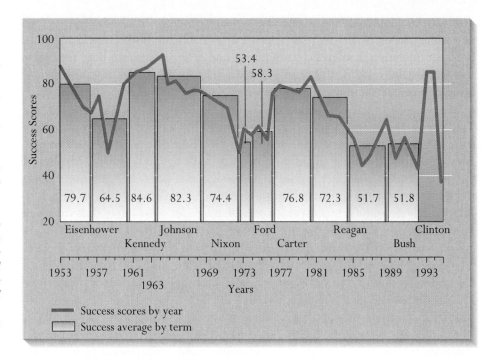

*Source: Congressional Quarterly, January 27, 1996.*

**Veto:** Rejection of a legislative act by the executive branch; in the U.S. federal government, overriding of a veto requires a two-thirds majority in both houses of Congress.

**Pocket veto:** The effective veto of a bill when Congress adjourns within ten days of passing it and the president fails to sign it.

**Override:** Voting in Congress to enact legislation vetoed by the president; requires a two-thirds vote in both the House and Senate.

"box score" plummeted from 86 percent to a record low of 36 percent following the election of a Republican Congress.

*The Veto Power*    The **veto** is the president's most powerful weapon in dealing with Congress. The veto is especially important to a president facing a Congress controlled by the opposition party. Even the *threat* of a veto enhances the president's bargaining power with Congress.[19] Confronted with such a threat, congressional leaders must calculate whether they can muster a two-thirds vote of both houses to override the veto.

To veto a bill passed by the Congress, the president sends to Congress a veto message specifying reasons for not signing it. If the president takes no action for ten days (excluding Sundays) after a bill has been passed by Congress, the bill becomes law without the president's signature. However, if Congress has adjourned within ten days of passing a bill and the president has not signed it, then the bill does not become law; this outcome is called a **pocket veto.**

A bill returned to Congress with a presidential veto message can be passed into law over the president's opposition by a two-thirds vote of both houses. (A bill that has received a pocket veto cannot be overridden because the Congress is no longer in session.) In other words, the president needs only to hold the loyalty of more than one-third of *either* the House or the Senate to sustain a veto. If congressional leaders cannot count on the votes to **override,** they are forced to bargain with the president. "What will the president accept?" becomes a key legislative question.

The president's bargaining power with Congress has been enhanced over the years by a history of success in sustaining presidential vetoes.[20] Only two presidents—Franklin Pierce and Andrew Johnson—had more than 15 percent of their vetoes overturned. One-third of U.S. presidents *never* had a veto overridden by the Congress (see Table 11-3). From George Washington to Bill Clinton, more

## TABLE 11-3  PRESIDENTIAL VETOES

| President | Total Vetoes* | Vetoes Overridden | Percent of Vetoes Sustained |
|---|---|---|---|
| Washington | 2 | 0 | 100% |
| Adams | 0 | 0 | — |
| Jefferson | 0 | 0 | — |
| Madison | 7 | 0 | 100 |
| Monroe | 1 | 0 | 100 |
| Adams | 0 | 0 | — |
| Jackson | 12 | 0 | 100 |
| Van Buren | 0 | 0 | — |
| Harrison | 0 | 0 | — |
| Tyler | 9 | 1 | 90 |
| Polk | 3 | 0 | 100 |
| Taylor | 0 | 0 | — |
| Fillmore | 0 | 0 | — |
| Pierce | 9 | 5 | 64 |
| Buchanan | 7 | 0 | 100 |
| Lincoln | 6 | 0 | 100 |
| A. Johnson | 29 | 15 | 66 |
| Grant | 94 | 4 | 96 |
| Hayes | 13 | 1 | 93 |
| Garfield | 0 | 0 | — |
| Arthur | 12 | 1 | 92 |
| Cleveland | 413 | 2 | 99 |
| B. Harrison | 44 | 1 | 98 |
| Cleveland | 170 | 5 | 97 |
| McKinley | 42 | 0 | 100 |
| T. Roosevelt | 82 | 1 | 99 |
| Taft | 39 | 1 | 98 |
| Wilson | 44 | 6 | 88 |
| Harding | 6 | 0 | 100 |
| Coolidge | 50 | 4 | 93 |
| Hoover | 37 | 3 | 93 |
| F. Roosevelt | 633 | 9 | 99 |
| Truman | 250 | 12 | 95 |
| Eisenhower | 181 | 2 | 99 |
| Kennedy | 21 | 0 | 100 |
| L. Johnson | 30 | 0 | 100 |
| Nixon | 43 | 5 | 90 |
| Ford | 66 | 12 | 85 |
| Carter | 31 | 2 | 94 |
| Reagan | 78 | 8 | 91 |
| Bush | 46 | 1 | 98 |
| Clinton (through 1995) | 11 | 1 | 91 |
| Total | 2,522 | 102 | 96 |

*Regular vetoes plus pocket vetoes.

*Source: Vital Statistics on American Politics* (Washington, D.C.: Congressional Quarterly Press, 1995), p. 258. Updated by author.

than 96 percent of all presidential vetoes have been sustained. For example, while Bush was unable to achieve much success in getting his own legislative proposals enacted by a Democratic Congress, he was extraordinarily successful in saying no. Of Bush's many vetoes, only one (regulation of cable TV) was overridden by Congress.[21] Clinton did not veto any bills when Democrats controlled Congress, but he began a series of vetoes in his struggle with the Republican Congress elected in 1994. He was able to sustain almost all of his vetoes because Republicans did not have two-thirds of the seats in both houses and most Democratic Congress members stuck with their president.

*The Line-Item Veto*  For many years, presidents, both Democratic and Republican, petitioned Congress to give them the **line-item veto**—the ability to veto some provisions of a bill while accepting other provisions. The lack of presidential line-item veto power was especially frustrating when dealing with appropriations bills because the president could not veto specific pork-barrel provisions from major spending bills for defense, education, housing, welfare, and so on. Finally, in 1996 Congress granted the president authority to "cancel" spending items in any appropriation act, any new entitlement, or any limited tax benefit. Such cancellation would take effect immediately unless blocked by a special "disapproval bill" passed by Congress. The president could veto the disapproval bill, and a two-thirds vote of both houses would be required to override the veto.

Potentially, this veto shifts enormous power to the president. A president could use it to threaten individual lawmakers with cancellation of their pet spending projects if they fail to support the president on certain legislation. Opponents of the line-item veto challenge its constitutionality, arguing that it transfers legislative power—granted by the Constitution only to Congress—to the president. The line-item veto would go into effect starting in 1997 for a trial period of seven years.

## GLOBAL LEADER

The president of the United States is the leader of the world's largest and most powerful democracy. During the Cold War, the president of the United States was seen as the leader of the "free world." The threat of Soviet expansionism, the huge military forces of the Warsaw Pact, and Soviet-backed guerrilla wars around the world all added to the global role of the American president as the defender of democratic values. In today's post–Cold War world, Western Europe and Japan are formidable economic competitors and no longer routinely defer to American political leadership. Yet if a new, stable world order based on democracy and self-determination is to emerge, the president of the United States must provide the necessary leadership.

Global leadership is based upon a president's powers of persuasion. Presidents are more persuasive when the American economy is strong, when American military forces are perceived as ready and capable, and when the president is seen as having the support of the American people and Congress. America's allies as well as its enemies perceive the president as the controlling force over U.S. foreign and military policy. Only occasionally do they seek to bypass the president and appeal to the Congress or to American public opinion.

Presidents sometimes prefer their global role to the much more contentious infighting of domestic politics. Abroad, presidents are treated with great dignity as

**Line-item veto:** The power of the chief executive to reject some portions of a bill without rejecting all of it.

head of the world's most powerful state. In contrast, at home presidents must confront hostile and insulting reporters, backbiting bureaucrats, demanding interest groups, and contentious members of Congress.

*Foreign Policy*   As the nation's chief diplomat, the president has the principal responsibility for formulating U.S. foreign policy. The president's constitutional powers in foreign affairs are relatively modest. Presidents have the power to make treaties with foreign nations "with the Advice and Consent of the Senate." Presidents may negotiate with nations separately or through international organizations such as the North Atlantic Treaty Organization (NATO) or the United Nations, where the president determines the U.S. position in that body's deliberations. The Constitution also empowers the president to "appoint Ambassadors, other public Ministers, and Consuls" and to "receive Ambassadors." This power of **diplomatic recognition** permits a president to grant legitimacy to or withhold it from ruling groups around the world (to declare or refuse to declare them "rightful"). Despite controversy, President Franklin Roosevelt officially recognized the communist regime in Russia in 1933, Richard Nixon recognized the communist government of the People's Republic of China in 1972, and Carter recognized the communist Sandinistas' regime in Nicaragua in 1979. To date, all presidents have withheld diplomatic recognition of Fidel Castro's government in Cuba.

Presidents have expanded on these modest constitutional powers to dominate American foreign policy making. In part, they have done so as a product of their role as commander-in-chief. Military force is the ultimate diplomatic language. During wartime, or when war is threatened, military and foreign policy become inseparable. The president must decide upon the use of force and, equally important, when and under what conditions to order a cease-fire or an end to hostilities.

Presidents have also come to dominate foreign policy as a product of the customary international recognition of the head of state as the legitimate voice of a government. While nations may also watch the words and actions of the American Congress, the president's statements are generally taken to represent the official position of the United States government.

*Treaties*   Treaties the president makes "by and with the Advice and Consent of the Senate" are legally binding upon the United States. The Constitution specifies that "all Treaties made . . . under the Authority of the United States, shall be the supreme Law of the Land; and the Judges in every State shall be bound thereby" (Article VI). Thus treaty provisions are directly enforceable in federal courts.

Although presidents may or may not listen to "advice" from the Senate on foreign policy, no formal treaty is valid unless "two-thirds of the Senators present concur" to its ratification. While the Senate has ratified the vast majority of treaties, presidents must be sensitive to Senate concerns. The Senate defeat of the Versailles Treaty in 1920, which formally ended World War I and established the League of Nations, prompted Presidents Roosevelt and Truman to include prominent Democratic and Republican members of the Senate Foreign Relations Committee in the delegation that drafted the United Nations Treaty in 1945 and later the NATO Treaty in 1949.

*Executive Agreements*   Over the years, presidents have come to rely heavily on **executive agreements** with other governments rather than formal treaties. An executive agreement signed by the president of the United States has much the

*President Clinton addresses guests at a White House dinner honoring Jacques Chirac during a state visit by the French president in January, 1996. Our president has the principal responsibility for formulating U.S. foreign policy, making him the nation's chief diplomat.*

**Diplomatic recognition:** The power of the president to grant "legitimacy" to or withhold it from a government of another nation (to declare or refuse to declare it "rightful").

**Executive agreement:** An agreement with another nation signed by the president of the United States but less formal (and hence potentially less binding) than a treaty because it does not require Senate confirmation.

same effect in international relations as a treaty. However, an executive agreement does not require Senate ratification. Presidents have asserted that their constitutional power to execute the laws, command the armed services, and determine foreign policy gives them the authority to make agreements with other nations and heads of state without obtaining approval of the U.S. Senate. Unlike treaties, executive agreements do not supersede laws of the United States or of the states with which they conflict, but they are otherwise binding upon the United States.

The use of executive agreements in important foreign policy matters was developed by President Franklin Roosevelt. Prior to his administration, executive agreements had been limited to minor matters. But in 1940, Roosevelt agreed to trade fifty American destroyers to England in exchange for naval bases in Newfoundland and the Caribbean. Roosevelt was intent upon helping the British in their struggle against Nazi Germany, but before the Japanese attack on Pearl Harbor in 1941, isolationist sentiment in the Senate was too strong to win a two-thirds ratifying vote for such an agreement. Toward the end of World War II, Roosevelt at the Yalta Conference and Truman at the Potsdam Conference negotiated secret executive agreements dividing the occupation of Germany between the Western Allies and the Soviet Union and granting the Soviet Union territory in the Japanese Kurile Islands in exchange for its entry into the war against Japan.

Congress has sometimes objected to executive agreements as usurping its own powers. In the Case Act of 1972, Congress required the president to inform Congress of all executive agreements within sixty days, but the act does not limit the president's power to make agreements. It is easier for Congress to renege on executive agreements than on treaties that the Senate has ratified. In 1973, President Nixon signed an executive agreement with South Vietnamese President Nguyen Van Thieu pledging that the United States would "respond with full force" if North Vietnam violated the Paris Peace Agreement that ended American participation in the Vietnam War. But when North Vietnam reinvaded the south in 1975,

*Though still part of the "Big Three" along with Prime Minister Winston Churchill of Great Britain (left) and Marshal Josef Stalin of the Soviet Union (right), it was a gravely ill President Franklin Roosevelt (middle) who traveled to Yalta, a port on Russia's Crimean peninsula, and negotiated secret executive agreements dividing Germany among the Allies in 1945. Germany remained divided until 1989 when protesters tore down the Berlin Wall and the Soviet Union under Mikhail Gorbachev acquiesced in the unification of Germany under a democratic government.*

CHAPTER 11 • THE PRESIDENT: WHITE HOUSE POLITICS

Congress rejected President Gerald Ford's pleas for renewed military aid to the South Vietnamese government, and Ford knew that it had become politically impossible for the United States to respond with force.

*Intelligence*   The president is responsible for the intelligence activities of the United States. Presidents have undertaken intelligence activities since the founding of the nation. During the Revolutionary War, General George Washington nurtured small groups of patriots living behind British lines who supplied him with information on Redcoat troop movements.[22] Today, the director of central intelligence (DCI) is appointed by the president (subject to Senate confirmation) and reports directly to the president. The DCI coordinates the activities of the Central Intelligence Agency, the National Security Agency (which maintains electronic broadcasts around the world), and the secret National Reconnaissance Office (which obtains information from satellites), as well as the intelligence activities of the Department of Defense.

The Central Intelligence Agency (CIA) is directly supervised by the DCI. It is responsible for the analysis, preparation, and distribution of intelligence to the president and the National Security Council. It is also responsible for the collection of human intelligence—reports obtained from foreign sources by CIA caseworkers around the world. And the CIA is responsible for all **covert action**—activities in support of the national interest of the United States that would be ineffective or counterproductive if their sponsorship were to be made public. For example, one of the largest covert actions undertaken by the United States was the support, for nearly ten years, of the Afghan rebels fighting Soviet occupation of their country during the Afghanistan War (1978–92). Public acknowledgment of such aid would have assisted the Soviet-backed regime in Afghanistan to claim that the rebels were not true patriots but rather "puppets" of the United States. The rebels themselves did not wish to acknowledge U.S. aid publicly, even though they knew it was essential to the success of their cause. Hence Presidents Carter and Reagan aided the Afghan rebels through covert action.

Covert action is, by definition, secret. And secrecy spawns elaborate conspiracy theories and flamboyant tales of intrigue and deception. In fact, most covert actions consist of routine transfers of economic aid and military equipment to pro-U.S. forces that do not wish to acknowledge such aid publicly. While most covert actions would have widespread support among the American public if they were done openly, secrecy opens the possibility that a president will undertake to do by covert action what would be opposed by Congress and the American people if they knew about it.

In the atmosphere of suspicion and distrust engendered by the Watergate scandal, Congress passed intelligence oversight legislation in 1974 requiring a written "presidential finding" for any covert action and requiring that members of the House and Senate Intelligence Committees be informed of all covert actions. The president does not have to obtain congressional approval for covert actions; but Congress can halt such actions if it chooses to do so. For example, in 1982, Congress passed the controversial Boland Amendment, which ordered the president and executive branch not to spend federal funds to assist the Contra rebel forces in Nicaragua in their efforts to overthrow the Sandinistas' regime. The Reagan Administration's efforts to get around the Boland Amendment led directly to the Iran-Contra scandal (see *Up Close:* "Iran-Contra and the White House Staff").

**Covert action:** A secret intelligence activity outside U.S. borders undertaken with specific authorization by the president; acknowledgment of U.S. sponsorship would defeat or compromise its purpose.

**UP CLOSE**

# Iran-Contra and the White House Staff

Ronald Reagan entered the White House with a strong sense of mission: to restore American military strength and respect in world councils, to reduce the size of government and the burdens of regulation, and to strengthen the economy by lowering taxes. Reagan knew in what direction he wanted to take the country, but he seldom involved himself in the details of policy or its implementation. Instead he relied heavily on the White House staff and key Cabinet officers to guide his presidency.

President Reagan was strongly committed to the support of pro-Western resistance movements in communist-dominated nations. He believed that the Soviet "evil empire" should be rolled back, not merely contained, and that the United States should assist "freedom fighters" in Afghanistan, Angola, and Nicaragua. While Congress supported these actions in Afghanistan and Angola, it decided in 1982 to cut off U.S. aid to the Contra rebel forces fighting the Soviet-backed Sandinista regime in Nicaragua. The Boland Amendment specifically prohibited all executive branch agencies, including the Central Intelligence Agency and Defense Department, from sending any more aid to the Contras. But Reagan clearly communicated to his White House staff (especially his national security advisers Robert McFarlane and later John Poindexter) his desire to find ways to keep the Contra movement supplied. A National Security Council staff officer, Marine Lieutenant Colonel Oliver North, was especially active in soliciting assistance for the Contras from private sources and from friendly foreign governments in a deliberate effort to circumvent the congressional ban. While these efforts no doubt antagonized key members of Congress, the president's problems deepened when the Contra aid issue became enmeshed in a more serious affair.

In 1985, Reagan issued a strong policy statement against international terrorism: "The United States gives terrorists no rewards and no guarantees. We make no concessions, we make no deals." Yet in November 1986, a Lebanese newspaper disclosed that the United States had been secretly shipping arms to Iran in an effort to secure the release of Americans held hostage in Lebanon by Iranian-backed terrorists. It was later revealed that National Security Adviser Robert McFarlane and Lieutenant Colonel Oliver North had been directly involved in these arms-for-hostages dealings. President Reagan initially denied that the arms shipments were a ransom-for-hostages deal, but upon thorough investigation, the Tower Commission, an independent commission assigned to investigate the incident, reported: "Whatever the intent, almost from the beginning the initiative became a series of arms-for-hostages deals."

But the worst news was yet to be revealed. At a nationally televised press conference, Attorney General Ed Meese revealed that money paid by the Iranians for the weapons shipments had been diverted to the Contras. The scheme to divert the "profits" from the arms deals to the Contras had been concocted by North, with the knowledge of McFarlane and Poindexter, and perhaps CIA director William Casey (who became seriously ill and died before the investigation was complete). There is no direct evidence or testimony that Reagan himself knew of the scheme to direct profits from Iranian dealings to the Contras, but the president's strong support of the Contra cause led North to believe that the president approved of the diversion of arms-sales money.

Trading arms for hostages with the hated regime in Iran was enough to send President Reagan's approval ratings into a steep decline. His presidency was badly shaken; there were murmurs on Capitol Hill about beginning impeachment proceedings. It

## COMMANDER-IN-CHIEF

Global power derives primarily from the president's role as commander-in-chief of the armed forces of the United States. Presidential command over the armed forces is not merely symbolic; presidents may issue direct military orders to

---

was the worst moment of the previously popular president's eight years in office. The president fired Poindexter and North and appointed a blue-ribbon commission headed by former U.S. Senator John Tower to investigate the affair and a special prosecutor to undertake criminal investigations (which, despite years of effort and expenditures, produced very little in the way of results).

Congress held its own nationally televised hearings. His Marine Corps uniform covered with a chestful of medals, Lieutenant Colonel Oliver North created a media sensation at the hearings. During his six days in the spotlight of national television, North captured the imagination and sympathy of many Americans and put the Congress on the defensive in its own hearings. Thousands of telegrams poured into Congress attacking the investigators and praising the patriotism of the colonel. Visitors—many sporting "Ollie North for President" T-shirts—crowded the Capitol, cheering North. Weeks after his testimony, opinion polls gave North a more favorable rating than either the president or the Congress. North was eventually convicted of having lied earlier to Congress about aid to the Contras, but his conviction was overturned on appeal.

What factors explain the Iran-Contra affair? The Tower Commission attributes the problem primarily to President Reagan's "management style":

> The president's management style is to put the principal responsibility for policy review and implementation on the shoulders of his advisors. . . . At no time did he insist upon accountability and performance review.*

Others have attributed the affair to Reagan's strong ideological views and his deliberate recruitment of White House staff members who shared his passions. The Reagan Administration encouraged ideological zealotry. The arms deal and the diversion of funds to the Contras in Nicaragua "were motivated by ideol-

ogy and carried out by zealots who had contempt for foreign policy professionals."**

Still others have cited the constitutional separation of powers in foreign policy making, and the resulting conflict that arose when Congress undertook to deny funds for a foreign policy (support for the Contras) strongly endorsed by the president. General Brent Scowcroft, later to become President Bush's national security adviser, said that the

> Contra controversy is really a constitutional confrontation between an executive who has a foreign policy which he believes deeply is important to the United States and a Congress which is ambivalent or negative about it and wants to do something else. What the hearings did not do was to examine how to make the system work when there is this kind of impasse.***

Presidents have always dominated foreign policy and have traditionally withheld information from Congress. Reagan was no different from most of his predecessors; he saw the separation of powers as crippling and sought to avoid it. Hence North's view of Congress as the enemy is not without precedent. But the Reagan Administration was chastened by the joint congressional committee's minority (Republican) report:

> The Constitution gives important foreign policy powers to both Congress and the President. Neither can accomplish very much over the long term by trying to go it alone.****

*The Tower Commission Report (New York: Times Books, 1987), p. 80.
**William Schneider, "Iran-Contra Affair's Basic Flaw Was Ideology," National Journal, March 7, 1987, p. 571.
***Frances FitzGerald, "Reagan's Band of True Believers," New York Times Magazine, April 24, 1987, p. 38.
****Joel Brinkley, ed., Report of the Congressional Committees Investigating the Iran-Contra Affair (New York: Times Books, 1988).

troops in the field. As president, Washington personally led troops to end the Whiskey Rebellion in 1794; Abraham Lincoln issued direct orders to his generals in the Civil War; Lyndon Johnson personally chose bombing targets in Vietnam; and George Bush personally ordered the Gulf War cease-fire after 100 hours of ground fighting. All presidents, whether they are experienced in world affairs or not, soon learn after taking office that their influence throughout the world is heavily dependent upon the command of capable military forces.

Constitutionally, war-making power is divided between the Congress and the president. Article I, Section 8, says: "The Congress shall have Power . . . to . . . provide for the common Defence . . . to declare War . . . to raise and support Armies . . . to provide and maintain a Navy . . . to make Rules for the Government and Regulation of the land and naval forces." Article II, Section 2, says: "The President shall be Commander in Chief of the Army and Navy of the United States." In defending the newly written Constitution, the *Federalist Papers* construed the president's war powers narrowly, implying that the war-making power of the president was little more than the power to defend against imminent invasion when Congress was not in session.

In reality, however, presidents have exercised their powers as commander-in-chief to order U.S. forces into military action overseas on many occasions—from John Adams's ordering of U.S. naval forces to attack French ships in 1789–99 to George Bush's Operation Desert Storm in 1991. The Supreme Court has consistently refused to hear cases involving the war powers of the president and Congress. Supreme Court Chief Justice William H. Rehnquist wrote before he was elevated to the Court:

> It has been recognized from the earliest days of the Republic, by the President, by Congress, and by the Supreme Court, that the United States may lawfully engage in armed hostilities with a foreign power without Congressional declaration of war. Our history is replete with instances of "undeclared wars" from the war with France in 1789–1800 to the Vietnamese War.[23]

Thus, although Congress retains the formal power to "declare war," in modern times wars are seldom "declared." Instead, they begin with direct military actions, and the president, as commander-in-chief of the armed forces, determines what those actions will be. Historically, Congress accepted the fact that only the president has the information-gathering facilities and the ability to act with the speed and secrecy required for military decisions during the periods of crisis. Not until the Vietnam War, and later during the Persian Gulf War, was there serious congressional debate over whether the president has the power to commit the nation to war.

*War Powers Act*    In the early days of the Vietnam War, the liberal leadership of the nation strongly supported the effort, and no one questioned the president's power to commit the nation to war. By 1969, however, many congressional leaders had withdrawn their support of the war. With a new Republican president and a Democratic Congress, congressional attacks on presidential policy became much more partisan.

Antiwar members of Congress made several attempts to end the war by cutting off money for U.S. military activity in Southeast Asia. Such legislation only passed after President Nixon announced a peace agreement in 1973, however. It is important to note that Congress has *never* voted to cut off funds to support American armies while they were in the field.

Congress also passed the **War Powers Act,** designed to restrict presidential war-making powers, in 1973. (President Nixon vetoed the bill, but the Watergate affair undermined his support in Congress, which overrode his veto.) The act has four major provisions:

**War Powers Act:** A bill passed in 1973 to limit presidential war-making powers; it restricts when, why, and for how long a president can commit U.S. forces and requires notification of and, in many cases, approval by Congress.

1. In the absence of a congressional declaration of war, the president can commit armed forces to hostilities or to "situations where imminent involvement in hostilities is clearly indicated by the circumstances" *only:*

   To repel an armed attack on the United States or to forestall the "direct and imminent threat of such an attack."

   To repel an armed attack against U.S. armed forces outside the United States or to forestall the threat of such attack.

   To protect and evacuate U.S. citizens and nationals in another country if their lives are threatened.

2. The president must report promptly to Congress the commitment of forces for such purposes.

3. Involvement of U.S. forces must be no longer than sixty days unless Congress authorizes their continued use by specific legislation.

4. Congress can end a presidential commitment by resolution, an action that does not require the president's signature.

*Presidential Noncompliance*   The War Powers Act raises constitutional questions. A commander-in-chief clearly can order U.S. forces to go anywhere. Presumably, Congress cannot constitutionally command troops, yet that is what the act attempts to do by specifying that troops must come home if Congress orders them to do so or if Congress simply fails to endorse the president's decision to commit them. No president—Democrat or Republican—can allow Congress to usurp this presidential authority. Thus, since the passage of the War Powers Act, presidents have continued to undertake military actions, including:

*President Bush visits troops in Saudi Arabia in November 1990, during the buildup to the Persian Gulf War. As commander-in-chief, the president has the authority to send U.S. forces abroad into combat or into peacekeeping missions.*

- President Gerald Ford ordered U.S. forces to attack a Cambodian island in 1975 to free the U.S. merchant ship *Mayaguez;* forty-one marines died in the attack. Ford notified the Congress of his action only after the attack.
- President Jimmy Carter did not notify Congress before ordering U.S. military forces to attempt a rescue of American embassy personnel held hostage by Iran in 1980.
- After President Reagan had committed troops to "peacekeeping" in Lebanon in 1982, Congress invoked the War Powers Act and attempted to limit U.S. marines to an eighteen-month stay. The president maintained that the act was unconstitutional and made it clear that the administration would keep the troops there as long as it desired. Only the deaths of 241 marines in a suicidal attack by an Islamic faction persuaded President Reagan to withdraw U.S. troops from Lebanon in 1983.
- In 1983, U.S. troops invaded the tiny Caribbean island of Grenada in the wake of a procommunist coup there. Informed after the fact, Congress chose not to invoke the War Powers Act in view of the invasion's rapid success.
- President Bush ignored the provisions of the War Powers Act in ordering the invasion of Panama in 1989 and in sending U.S. forces to Saudi Arabia in August 1990, following Saddam Hussein's invasion of Kuwait.
- Bush also claimed he had the constitutional power to order U.S. military forces to liberate Kuwait from Iraqi occupation, whether or not Congress authorized the action. Bush ordered military preparations to begin, and despite misgivings Congress voted to authorize the use of force a few days

before U.S. air attacks began. Rapid military victory in the ensuing Gulf War silenced congressional critics.

• President Clinton ordered U.S. troops into Bosnia as part of a NATO "peacekeeping" operation in 1995.

The War Powers Act is not only constitutionally questionable but also politically weak. The president almost always enjoys great popular support in the initial stages of an international conflict. At this point, members of Congress are likely to be swept along and to endorse the president's action rather than invoking the War Powers Act and appearing unsupportive of U.S. troops. Only if the fighting goes badly, becomes protracted, or fails to produce decisive results is the War Powers Act likely to be invoked by Congress. Thus the War Powers Act remains largely a symbolic reminder to presidents that if things go badly, the Congress will desert them.

*Presidential Use of Military Force in Domestic Affairs* Democracies are generally reluctant to use military force in domestic affairs. Yet the president has the constitutional authority to "take Care that the Laws be faithfully executed" and, as commander-in-chief of the armed forces, can send them across the nation as well as across the globe. The Constitution appears to limit presidential use of military forces in domestic affairs to protecting states "against domestic Violence" and only on Application of the [state] Legislature or the [state] Executive (when the Legislature cannot be convened)" (Article IV, Section 4). Although this provision would seem to require states themselves to request federal troops before they can be sent to quell domestic violence, historically presidents have not waited for state requests to send troops when federal laws, federal court orders, or federal constitutional guarantees are being violated.

Relying on their constitutional duty to "faithfully execute" federal laws and their command over the nation's armed forces, presidents have used military force in domestic disputes since the earliest days of the Republic. In 1894, for example, members of the American Railway Union rioted rather than obey a court order to cease their strike against the Pullman Palace Car Company, prompting President Grover Cleveland to order federal troops and 5,000 newly deputized federal marshals to Chicago to quell the strike and arrest Eugene V. Debs, the union's founder and leader. The Supreme Court rejected arguments that President Cleveland acted unconstitutionally in the absence of the state's request for federal troops and held that federal troops could be used to enforce a federal court order designed to remove "obstructions to the freedom of interstate commerce."[24]

Yet another significant example of a president's use of military force in domestic affairs was Dwight Eisenhower's 1957 dispatch of U.S. troops to Little Rock, Arkansas, to enforce a federal court's desegregation order. In this case, the president acted directly *against* the expressed wishes of the state's governor, Orval Faubus, who had posted state units of the National Guard at the entrance of Central High School to prevent the admission of black students that had been ordered by the federal court. Eisenhower officially called Arkansas's National Guard units into federal service, took personal command of them, and then ordered them to leave the high school. Ike then replaced the Guard units with U.S. federal troops under orders to enforce desegregation. Eisenhower's action marked a turning point in the struggle over school desegregation. The Supreme Court's historic desegregation decision in *Brown v. Board of Education of Topeka* might have been rendered meaningless had not the president chosen to use military force to secure compliance.

Despite a Supreme Court ruling that segregation in education was illegal, many southern states continued to try to keep their schoolhouse doors closed to blacks. Here Elizabeth Eckford, a fifteen-year-old resident of Little Rock, Arkansas, is denied entry to Central High School by a member of the National Guard under the orders of Governor Orval Faubus. Not until President Dwight Eisenhower sent the 101st Airborne Division to Little Rock were the High Court's desegregation orders enforced.

# THE VICE-PRESIDENTIAL WAITING GAME

The principal responsibility of the vice-president is to be prepared to assume the responsibilities of the president. The phrase describing the job as "a heartbeat away from the presidency" is historically relevant: eight vice-presidents have become president following the death of their predecessor. But vice-presidents have not always been well prepared; Harry Truman, who succeeded Franklin Roosevelt while World War II still raged, had never even been informed about the secret atomic bomb project.

*Political Selection Process*   The political process surrounding the initial choice of vice-presidential candidates does not necessarily produce the persons best qualified to occupy the White House. It is, indeed, a "crap shoot",[25] if it produces a person well qualified to be president, it is only by luck. Candidates may *claim* that they select running mates who are highly qualified to take over as president, but this claim is seldom true.

Vice-presidential candidates are chosen to give political "balance" to the ticket, to attract voters who might otherwise desert the party or stay home. Traditionally, Democratic presidential candidates sought to give ideological and geographical balance to the ticket. Northern liberal presidential candidates (Adlai Stevenson, John Kennedy) selected southern conservatives (John Sparkman, Estes Kefauver, Lyndon Johnson) as their running mates. Hubert Humphrey ignored the tradition in choosing Maine Senator Edmund Muskie in 1968; and Walter Mondale selected New York Congresswoman Geraldine Ferraro in a bold move to exploit the gender gap. Liberal Massachusetts Governor Michael Dukakis returned to the earlier Democratic tradition, choosing to run with conservative Texas Senator Lloyd Bentsen. Bill Clinton sought a different kind of balance: Al Gore's military service in Vietnam and his unimpeachable family life helped offset reservations about Clinton's avoidance of the draft and his past marital troubles.

Traditionally, Republican presidential candidates sought to accommodate either the conservative or moderate "wing" of their party in their vice-presidential selections. Moderate Eisenhower chose conservative Nixon. Conservative Barry Goldwater's selection of William Miller, an unknown conservative congressman, ensured his loss of moderate support in 1964. In 1980, conservative Reagan first asked his moderate predecessor, Gerald Ford, to join him on the ticket before turning to his moderate primary opponent George Bush, who in 1988 tapped conservative Senator Dan Quayle.

Seldom do presidential candidates give great weight to the presidential qualifications of their running mates. Bush reportedly never personally interviewed Quayle to assess his understanding of the issues or competence to serve as president. Instead, Bush relied on his campaign manager's judgment that Quayle's youthful appearance would attract baby-boom voters and that Quayle's conservative voting record would satisfy the Republican right wing. Bush was said to be wary of selecting a strong political figure such as Robert Dole or Jack Kemp, preferring someone who would be as loyal to him as he had been to Reagan. Almost immediately, the press exposed Quayle's lack of experience and qualifications to be president. But it was Quayle's pitiful performance against the more experienced Bentsen in the nationally televised vice-presidential debate that spotlighted the younger man's lack of presidential stature. When Quayle noted that his age and political experience were the same as those of John F. Kennedy in 1960, Bentsen responded: "Senator, you're no Jack Kennedy." The brief sound bite captured Quayle's vulnerability.

In 1996 Bob Dole gambled big in choosing the popular and charismatic, but opinionated and unpredictable Jack Kemp as his running mate. Far behind in the polls, Dole could not afford a "safe" choice. He needed the former star quarterback of the Buffalo Bills to add excitement to the ticket, even at the risk of seeing Kemp call plays not approved by the coach.

*Vice-Presidential Roles*   Presidents determine what role their vice-presidents will play in their administration. Constitutionally, the only role given the vice-president is to preside over the Senate and to vote in case of a tie in that body. Presiding over the Senate is so tiresome that vice-presidents perform it only on rare ceremonial occasions, but they have occasionally cast important tie-breaking votes. If the president chooses not to give the vice-president much responsibility, the vice-presidency becomes what its first occupant, John Adams, described as "the most insignificant office that ever the invention of man contrived or his imagination conceived." One of Franklin Roosevelt's three vice-presidents, the salty Texan John Nance Garner, put it more pithily, saying that the job "ain't worth a bucket of warm spit" (reporters of that era may have substituted "spit" for Garner's actual wording.)

The political functions of vice-presidents are more significant than their governmental functions. Vice-presidents are obliged to support their president and the administration's policies. But sometimes a president will use the vice-president to launch strongly partisan political attacks on opponents while the president remains "above" the political squabbles and hence more "presidential." Richard Nixon served as a partisan "attack dog" for Eisenhower, then gave Spiro Agnew

this task in his own administration. George Bush was a much more reserved vice-president, but Dan Quayle renewed the tradition of the vice-president as political "hit man." The attack role allows the vice-president also to help cement political support for the president among highly partisan ideologues. Vice-presidents are also useful in campaign fund raising. Large contributors expect a personal touch; the president cannot be everywhere at once, so the vice-president is frequently a guest at political fund-raising events. Presidents also have traditionally sent their vice-presidents to attend funerals of world leaders and placed them at the head of governmental commissions.

Vice-presidents themselves strive to play a more significant policy-making role, often as senior presidential adviser and confidant. Recent presidents have encouraged the development of the vice-presidency along these lines. Walter Mondale, the first modern vice-president to perform this function, had an office in the White House next to the president's, had access to all important meetings and policy decisions, and was invited to lunch privately each week with President Carter. As vice-president, George Bush claimed to have participated in every major decision of the Reagan Administration. Vice-President Al Gore was routinely stationed behind President Clinton during major policy pronouncements. Thus, the senior advisory role is becoming institutionalized over time.

*The Waiting Game* Politically, vice-presidents are obliged to play a tortuous waiting game. They can use their time in office to build a network of contacts that can later be tapped for campaign contributions, workers, and support in their own race for the presidency, should they decide to run. But winning the presidency following retirement of their former boss requires a delicate balance. On the one hand, they must show loyalty to the president in order to win the president's endorsement and also to help ensure that the administration in which they participated is judged by voters to be a success. At the same time, vice-presidents must demonstrate that they have independent leadership qualities and a policy agenda of their own to offer voters. This dilemma becomes more acute as their boss's term nears its end.

Historically, only a few sitting vice-presidents have won election to the White House: John Adams (1797), Thomas Jefferson (1801), Martin Van Buren (1837), and George Bush (1988). In addition, four vice-presidents won election in their own right after entering the Oval Office as a result of their predecessors' death: Theodore Roosevelt (1901), Calvin Coolidge (1923), Harry Truman (1945), and Lyndon Johnson (1963). Only one nonsitting former vice-president has been elected president: Richard Nixon (1968, after losing to Kennedy in 1960). Thus, out of the forty-six men who served the nation as vice-president through 1992, only nine were ever elected to higher office.

## SUMMARY NOTES

- The American presidency is potentially the most powerful office in the world. As head of state, the president symbolizes national unity and speaks on behalf of the American people to the world. And as commander-in-chief of the armed forces, the president has a powerful voice in national and international affairs. The president also symbolizes government for the American people, reassuring them in times of hardship and crises.

- As head of the government, the president is expected to set forth policy priorities for the nation, to manage the economy, to mobilize political support for the administration's programs in Congress, to manage the giant federal bureaucracy, and to recruit people for policy-making positions in both the executive and judicial branches of government.

- Popular expectations of presidential leadership far exceed the formal constitutional powers of the president: chief administrator, chief legislator, chief diplomat, commander-in-chief, and chief of state. The vague reference in the Constitution to "executive Power" has been used by presidents to justify actions beyond those specified elsewhere in the Constitution or in laws of Congress.

- It is the president's vast political resources that provide the true power base of the presidency. These include the president's reputation for power, personal popularity with the public, access to the media, and party leadership position.

- Presidential popularity and power are usually highest at the beginning of the term of office. Presidents

are more likely to be successful in Congress during this honeymoon period. Presidents' popularity also rises during crises, especially during international threats and military actions. But prolonged indecision and stalemate erode popular support, as do scandals and economic recessions.

- As chief executive, the president oversees the huge federal bureaucracy. Presidential control of the executive branch is exercised through executive orders, appointments and removals, and budgetary recommendations to Congress. But the president's control of the executive branch is heavily circumscribed by Congress, which establishes executive departments and agencies, regulates their activities by law, and determines their budgets each year.

- Presidents are expected not only to initiate programs and policies but also to shepherd them through Congress. Presidential success scores in Congress indicate that presidents are more successful early in their term of office. Presidents who face a Congress controlled by the opposition party are far less successful in winning approval for their programs than presidents whose party holds a majority.

- The veto is the president's most powerful weapon in dealing with Congress. The president needs to hold the loyalty of only one more than one-third of either the House or the Senate to sustain a veto. Few vetoes are overridden. The threat of a veto enables the president to bargain in Congress for more acceptable legislation.

- During the long years of the Cold War, the president of the United States was the leader of the "free world." In the post–Cold War world, the president is still the leader of the world's most powerful democracy and is expected to exercise global leadership on behalf of a stable world order.

- Presidents have come to dominate foreign policy through treaty making, executive agreements, control of intelligence activities, and international recognition of their role as head of state. Above all, presidents have used their power as commander-in-chief of the armed forces to decide when to make war and when to seek peace.

- The global power of presidents derives primarily from this presidential role as commander-in-chief. Constitutionally, war-making power is divided between Congress and the president, but histori-

cally, it has been the president who has ordered U.S. military forces into action. In the War Powers Act, Congress tried to reassert its war-making power after the Vietnam War, but the act has failed to restrain presidents. Presidents have also used the armed forces in domestic affairs to "take Care that the Laws be faithfully executed."

- The principal responsibility of the vice-president is to be prepared to assume the responsibilities of the president. However, the selection of the vice-president is dominated more by political concerns than by consideration of presidential qualifications. Aside from officially presiding over the U.S. Senate, vice-presidents perform whatever roles are assigned them by the president.

# SELECTED READINGS

BARBER, JAMES DAVID. *The Presidential Character: Predicting Performance in the White House,* 4th ed. Englewood Cliffs, N.J.: Prentice Hall, 1992. An updated version of Barber's original thesis that a president's performance in office is largely a function of active/passive and positive/negative character; includes classifications of twentieth-century presidents through Reagan.

BRACE, PAUL, and BARBARA HINKLEY. *Follow the Leader.* New York: Basic Books, 1992. The most marked increases in public approval of the president came on the heels of international crises, especially when the president responds with bold and decisive action.

BRODY, RICHARD A. *Assessing Presidents: The Media, Elite Opinion, and Public Support.* Stanford, Calif.: Stanford University Press, 1991. Develops the thesis that media and elite interpretations of presidential actions shape public evaluations of the president; includes analysis of the president's "honeymoon," "rally round the president" events, and the rise and fall of public approval ratings.

DICLERICO, ROBERT E. *The American President,* 4th ed. Englewood Cliffs: Prentice Hall, 1995. Comprehensive text on the presidency, focusing on selection, power, accountability, decision-making, personality, and leadership.

DREW, ELIZABETH. *On the Edge: The Clinton Presidency.* New York: Simon & Schuster, 1994. A reporter's inside account of the Clinton presidency—"ambitious and uncertain, looking to the future and bounded by the past."

EDWARDS, GEORGE C., III. *At the Margins: Presidential Leadership of Congress.* New Haven, Conn.: Yale University Press, 1989. A systematic examination of the factors affecting

presidential success in Congress, including presidential popularity, party support, and lobbying efforts.

KESSLER, RONALD. *Inside the White House.* New York: Pocket Books, 1995. Muckraking accounts of the "hidden lives" of presidents, from Lyndon Johnson to Bill Clinton.

LOWI, THEODORE. *The Personal President.* Ithaca, N.Y.: Cornell University Press, 1987. An examination of the presidency from the perspective of the public and its reliance on the president for reassurance in crises.

MARANISS, DAVID. *First in His Class.* New York: Simon & Schuster, 1995. A biography of Bill Clinton, describing his overriding ambition, talent for politics, perseverance in the face of adversity, eagerness to please everyone, and tendency to shade the truth.

MILKUS, STANLEY, and MICHAEL NELSON. *The American Presidency: Origins and Development, 1776–1990.* Washington D.C.: Congressional Quarterly Press, 1990. A comprehensive history of the presidency that argues that the institution is best understood by examining its development over time; describes the significant presidential actions in the early days of the Republic that shaped the office, as well as the modern era in which the president has replaced Congress and the political parties as the leading instrument of popular rule.

NEUSTADT, RICHARD E. *Presidential Power.* New York: Wiley, 1960. The classic argument that the president's power is the power to persuade, that the formal constitutional powers of the presidency provide only a framework for the president's use of persuasion, public prestige, reputation for power, and other personal attributes to exercise real power.

# THE BUREAUCRACY
## BUREAUCRATIC POLITICS

## ASK YOURSELF ABOUT POLITICS

**1** Do bureaucrats in Washington have too much power?
Yes ⬭ No ⬭

**2** Do you believe that the bureaucrats in Washington really believe in the value of the programs they administer?
Yes ⬭ No ⬭

**3** Should the U.S. Postal Service and Amtrak be required to break even rather than receiving government subsidies to cover their deficits?
Yes ⬭ No ⬭

**4** Should the federal bureaucracy be managed by nonpartisan professionals rather than people politically loyal to the president?
Yes ⬭ No ⬭

**5** Should the federal bureaucracy at all levels reflect the gender and minority ratios of the total civilian workforce?
Yes ⬭ No ⬭

**6** Do you believe that the bureaucrats in Washington waste a lot of the money we pay in taxes?
Yes ⬭ No ⬭

**7** Do you believe that the federal government is spending more money but delivering less service?
Yes ⬭ No ⬭

**8** Do you believe that bureaucratic regulations of all kinds are suffocating America?
Yes ⬭ No ⬭

Power in Washington is not only exercised by the president, Congress, and courts, but also by 2.8 million federal bureaucrats—neither elected nor accountable to ordinary citizens—who determine in large measure who gets what in America.

## BUREAUCRATIC POWER

Political conflict does not end after a law has been passed by Congress and signed by the president. The arena for conflict merely shifts from Capitol Hill and the White House to the **bureaucracy**—to the myriad departments, agencies, and bureaus of the federal executive branch that implement the law. Despite the popular impression that policy is decided by the president and Congress and merely implemented by the federal bureaucracy, in

431

fact policy is also made by the bureaucracy. Indeed, it is often remarked that "implementation is the continuation of policy-making by other means." The Washington bureaucracy is a major base of power in the American system of government—independent of Congress, the president, the courts, and the people. Indeed, controlling the bureaucracy has become a major challenge of democratic government (see *What Do You Think?* "Do Bureaucrats in Washington Have Too Much Power?").

*The Nature of Bureaucracy* "Bureaucracy" has become a negative term equated with red tape,[1] paper shuffling, duplication of effort, waste and inefficiency, impersonality, senseless regulations, and unresponsiveness to the needs of "real" people. But bureaucracy is really a form of social organization found not only in governments but also in corporations, armies, schools, and many other societal institutions. The German sociologist Max Weber described bureaucracy as a "rational" way for society to organize itself that is characterized by:

- **Chain of command:** A hierarchical structure of authority in which command flows downward.
- **Division of labor:** Work is divided among many specialized workers in an effort to improve productivity.
- **Specification of authority:** Clear lines of responsibility with positions and units reporting to superiors.
- **Goal orientation:** Organizational goals determining structure, authority, and rules.
- **Impersonality:** All persons within the bureaucracy treated on "merit" principles, and all "clients" served by the bureaucracy treated equally according to rules; all activities undertaken according to rules; records maintained to assure rules are followed.[2]

Thus, according to Weber's definition, General Motors and IBM, the U.S. Marine Corps, the U.S. Department of Education, and all other institutions that are organized according to these principles are "bureaucracies."

*The Growth of Bureaucratic Power* Bureaucratic power has grown with advances in technology and increases in the size and complexity of society. The standard explanation for the growth of bureaucratic power in Washington is that Congress and the president do not have the time, energy, or expertise to handle the details of policy making. A related explanation is that the increasing complexity and sophistication of technology require that technical experts ("technocrats") actually carry out the intent of Congress and the president. Neither the president nor the 535 members of Congress can look after the myriad details involved in environmental protection, occupational safety, air traffic control, or thousands of other responsibilities of government. So the president and Congress create bureaucracies, appropriate money for them, and authorize them to draw up detailed rules, regulations, and "guidelines" that actually govern the nation. Bureaucratic agencies receive only vague and general directions from the president and Congress. Actual governance is in the hands of the Environmental Protection Agency, the Occupational Safety and Health Administration, the Federal Aviation Administration, and hundreds of similar agencies (see Figure 12-1).

**Bureaucracy:** Departments, agencies, bureaus, and offices that perform the functions of government.

**Chain of command:** The hierarchical structure of authority in which command flows downward; typical of a bureaucracy.

**Division of labor:** The division of work among many specialized workers in a bureaucracy.

**Specification of authority:** The clear lines of responsibility with positions and units reporting to superiors in a bureaucracy.

**Goal orientation:** Organizational goals that determine structure, authority, and rules in a bureaucracy.

**Impersonality:** The treatment of all persons within a bureaucracy on the basis of "merit" and of all "clients" served by the bureaucracy equally according to rule.

FIGURE 12-1    The Federal Bureaucracy

*Although the president has constitutional authority over the operation of the executive branch, Congress creates departments and agencies and appropriates their funds, and Senate approval is needed for presidential appointees to head departments.*

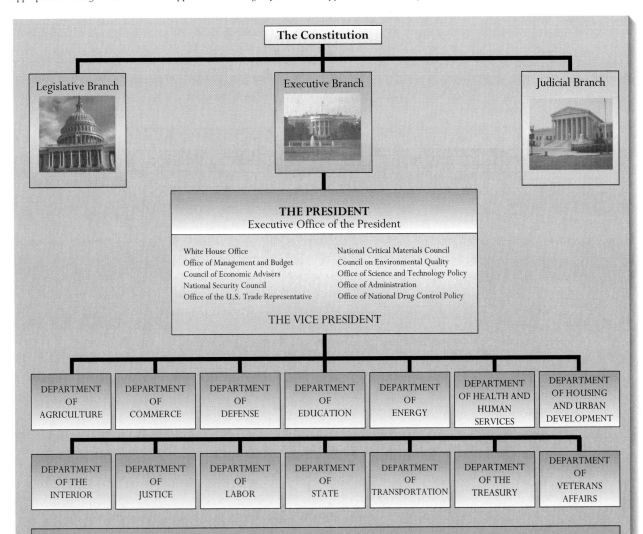

**The Constitution**

**Legislative Branch**

**Executive Branch**

**Judicial Branch**

**THE PRESIDENT**
Executive Office of the President

White House Office
Office of Management and Budget
Council of Economic Advisers
National Security Council
Office of the U.S. Trade Representative

National Critical Materials Council
Council on Environmental Quality
Office of Science and Technology Policy
Office of Administration
Office of National Drug Control Policy

THE VICE PRESIDENT

| DEPARTMENT OF AGRICULTURE | DEPARTMENT OF COMMERCE | DEPARTMENT OF DEFENSE | DEPARTMENT OF EDUCATION | DEPARTMENT OF ENERGY | DEPARTMENT OF HEALTH AND HUMAN SERVICES | DEPARTMENT OF HOUSING AND URBAN DEVELOPMENT |
|---|---|---|---|---|---|---|
| DEPARTMENT OF THE INTERIOR | DEPARTMENT OF JUSTICE | DEPARTMENT OF LABOR | DEPARTMENT OF STATE | DEPARTMENT OF TRANSPORTATION | DEPARTMENT OF THE TREASURY | DEPARTMENT OF VETERANS AFFAIRS |

### INDEPENDENT ESTABLISHMENTS AND GOVERNMENT CORPORATIONS

ACTION
Administrative Conference of the U.S.
African Development Foundation
Central Intelligence Agency
Commission on Civil Rights
Commission on National and Community Service
Commodity Futures Trading Commission
Consumer Product Safety Commission
Defense Nuclear Facilities Safety Board
Environmental Protection Agency
Equal Employment Opportunity Commission
Export–Import Bank of the U.S.
Farm Credit Administration
Federal Communications Commission
Federal Deposit Insurance Corporation
Federal Election Commission

Federal Emergency Management Agency
Federal Housing Finance Board
Federal Labor Relations Authority
Federal Maritime Commission
Federal Mediation and Conciliation Service
Federal Mine Safety and Health Review Commission
Federal Reserve System
Federal Retirement Thrift Investment Board
Federal Trade Commission
General Services Administration
Inter–American Foundation
Interstate Commerce Commission
Merit Systems Protection Board
National Aeronautics and Space Administration
National Archives and Records Administration
National Capital Planning Commission

National Credit Union Administration
National Labor Relations Board
National Mediation Board
National Railroad Passenger Corporation (Amtrak)
National Science Foundation
National Transportation Safety Board
Nuclear Regulatory Commission
Occupational Safety and Health Review Commission
Office of Government Ethics
Office of Personnel Management
Office of Special Counsel
Panama Canal Commission
Peace Corps
Pennsylvania Avenue Development Corporation
Pension Benefit Guaranty Corporation

Postal Rate Commission
Railroad Retirement Board
Resolution Trust Corporation
Securities and Exchange Commission
Selective Service System
Small Business Administration
Tennessee Valley Authority
Thrift Depositor Protection Oversight Board
Trade and Development Agency
U.S. Arms Control and Disarmament Agency
U.S. Information Agency
U.S. International Development Cooperation Agency
U.S. International Trade Commission
U.S. Postal Service

Source: Chart prepared by U.S. Bureau of the Census.

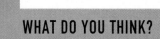

# Do Bureaucrats in Washington Have Too Much Power?

Americans have always been suspicious of government power. Opinion polls regularly report that Americans believe "the federal government in Washington" has "too much power." A majority also believe that "major corporations" and "television news" have too much power.

But among federal government agencies, the tax collecting Internal Revenue Service (IRS) is clearly the most feared. The power of the Central Intelligence Agency (CIA) and the Bureau of Alcohol, Tobacco and Firearms (ATF) also appear to raise concerns among Americans, no doubt in part because of adverse publicity in recent years. (The CIA was deeply embarrassed by the revelation that a high officer, Aldrich Ames, had been paid millions of dollars by Russian agents to work secretly on their behalf; the ATF was strongly criticized for attacking the Branch Davidian compound in Waco, Texas in 1993.)

In contrast, the U.S. military enjoys a favorable reputation among most Americans, 80 percent of whom believe it has "about the right amount of power" or "not enough." Local government in America and local police are also perceived as having about the right amount or not enough power.

**Question:** *As I read off the following, please tell me whether you think it has too much power in the United States today, about the right amount of power, or not enough power.*

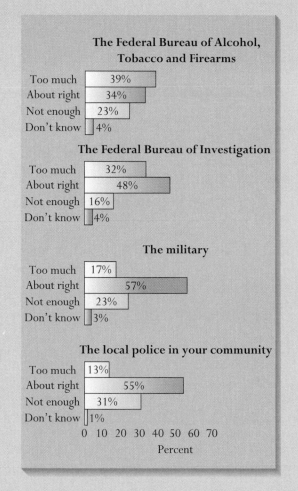

### The Internal Revenue Service
- Too much: 63%
- About right: 32%
- Not enough: 3%
- Don't know: 2%

### The federal government in Washington
- Too much: 60%
- About right: 29%
- Not enough: 8%
- Don't know: 3%

### Television news
- Too much: 56%
- About right: 36%
- Not enough: 7%
- Don't know: 1%

### The Central Intelligence Agency
- Too much: 42%
- About right: 37%
- Not enough: 9%
- Don't know: 12%

### The Federal Bureau of Alcohol, Tobacco and Firearms
- Too much: 39%
- About right: 34%
- Not enough: 23%
- Don't know: 4%

### The Federal Bureau of Investigation
- Too much: 32%
- About right: 48%
- Not enough: 16%
- Don't know: 4%

### The military
- Too much: 17%
- About right: 57%
- Not enough: 23%
- Don't know: 3%

### The local police in your community
- Too much: 13%
- About right: 55%
- Not enough: 31%
- Don't know: 1%

Percent

*Source:* Gallup Poll, 1995.

But there are also political explanations for the growth of bureaucratic power. Congress and the president often deliberately pass vague and ambiguous laws. These laws allow elected officials to show symbolically their concerns for environmental protection, occupational safety, and so on, yet avoid the controversies surrounding actual application of those lofty principles. Bureaucracies must then give practical meaning to these symbolic measures by developing specific rules and regulations. If the rules and regulations prove unpopular, Congress and the president can blame the bureaucrats and pretend that these unpopular decisions are a product of an "ungovernable" Washington bureaucracy.

Finally, as the bureaucracy itself has grown in size and influence, it has become its own source of power. Bureaucrats have a personal stake in expanding the size of their own agencies and budgets and adding to their own regulatory authority. They can mobilize their "client" groups (interest groups that directly benefit from the agency's programs, such as environmental groups on behalf of the Environmental Protection Agency, farm groups for the Department of Agriculture, the National Education Association for the Department of Education) in support of larger budgets and expanded authority.

*Bureaucratic Power: Implementation*    Bureaucracies are not *constitutionally* empowered to decide policy questions. But they do so, nevertheless, as they perform their tasks of implementation, regulation, and adjudication.

**Implementation** is the development of procedures and activities to carry out policies legislated by Congress. It may involve creating new agencies or bureaus or assigning new responsibilities to old agencies. It often requires bureaucracies to translate laws into operational rules and regulations and usually to allocate resources—money, personnel, offices, supplies—to the new function. All of these tasks involve decisions by bureaucrats—decisions that drive how the law will actually affect society. In some cases, bureaucrats delay the development of regulations based on a new law, assign enforcement responsibility to existing offices with other higher-priority tasks, and allocate few people with limited resources to the task. In other cases, bureaucrats act forcefully in making new regulations, insist on strict enforcement, assign responsibilities to newly created aggressive offices with no other assignments, and allocate a great deal of staff time and agency resources to the task. Interested groups have a strong stake in these decisions, and they actively seek to influence the bureaucracy.

*Bureaucratic Power: Regulation*    **Regulation** involves the development of formal rules for implementing legislation. The federal bureaucracy publishes about 60,000 pages of rules in the *Federal Register* each year. The Environmental Protection Agency (EPA) is especially active in developing regulations governing the handling of virtually every substance in the air, water, or ground. The rule-making process for federal agencies is prescribed by an Administrative Procedures Act, first passed in 1946 and amended many times. Generally, agencies must:

1. Announce in the *Federal Register* that a new regulation is being considered.
2. Hold hearings to allow interested groups to present evidence and arguments regarding the proposed regulation.
3. Conduct research on the proposed regulation's economic and environmental impacts.

**Implementation:** The development by the federal bureaucracy of procedures and activities to carry out policies legislated by Congress; it includes regulation as well as adjudication.

**Regulation:** The development by the federal bureaucracy of formal rules for implementing legislation.

4. Solicit "public comments" (usually the arguments of interest groups).

5. Consult with higher officials, including the Office of Management and Budget.

6. Publish the new regulation in the *Federal Register*.

Regulatory battles are important because formal regulations that appear in the *Federal Register* have the effect of law. Congress can amend or repeal a regulation only by passing new legislation and obtaining the president's signature. Controversial bureaucratic regulations often remain in place because Congress is slow to act, because key committee members block corrective legislation, or because the president refuses to sign bills overturning the regulation.

*Bureaucratic Power: Adjudication*   **Adjudication** involves bureaucratic decisions about individual cases. While rule making resembles the legislative process, adjudication resembles the judicial process. In adjudication, bureaucrats decide whether a person or firm is failing to comply with laws or regulations and, if so, what penalties or corrective actions are to be applied. Regulatory agencies and commissions—for example, the National Labor Relations Board, the Federal Communications Commission, the Equal Employment Opportunity Commission, the Federal Trade Commission, the Securities and Exchange Commission—are heavily engaged in adjudication. Their elaborate procedures and body of previous decisions closely resemble the court system. Some agencies authorize specific hearing officers, administrative judges, or appellate divisions to accept evidence, hear arguments, and decide cases. Individuals and firms involved in these proceedings usually hire lawyers specializing in the field of regulation. Administrative hearings are somewhat less formal than a court trial, and the "judges" are employees of the agency itself. Losers may appeal to the federal courts, but the record of agency success in the federal courts discourages many appeals.

*Bureaucratic Power: Administrative Discretion*   Much of the work of bureaucrats is administrative routine—issuing Social Security checks, printing forms, delivering the mail. Routines are repetitive tasks performed according to established rules and procedures. Yet bureaucrats almost always have some discretion in performing even the most routine tasks. Discretion is greatest when cases do not exactly fit established rules, or when more than one rule might be applied to the same case, resulting in different outcomes. The Internal Revenue Service administers the hundreds of thousands of rules developed to implement the U.S. Tax Code, but each IRS auditing agent has wide discretion in deciding which rules to apply to a taxpayer's income, deductions, business expenses, and so on. Indeed, identical tax information submitted to different IRS offices almost always results in different estimates of tax liability. But even in more routine tasks, from processing Medicare applications to forwarding mail, individual bureaucrats can be friendly and helpful or hostile and obstructive.[3]

*Bureaucratic Power: To What End?*   Bureaucrats generally believe strongly in the value of their programs and the importance of their tasks. Senior military officers and civilian officials of the Department of Defense believe in the importance of a strong national defense, and top officials in the Social Security Administration are committed to maintaining the integrity of the retirement system and

**Adjudication:** Decision making by the federal bureaucracy as to whether or not an individual or organization has complied with or violated government laws and/or regulations.

# Why Government Grows, and Grows, and Grows

What accounts for the growth of government activity? Many theories offer explanations. These theories are not mutually exclusive; indeed, probably all of the forces they identify contribute to government growth.

*Societal Demands: Wagner's Law* In the nineteenth century, economist Adolf Wagner proposed a "law of increasing state activity"—the notion that government activity increased faster than economic output in all developing societies.* He attributed this growth to a variety of factors including increasing demands in a developed society for social services such as education, welfare, and public health.

*Wars and Crises* Another theory is based on the fact that during periods of social upheaval, especially war or economic turmoil, people willingly accept higher-than-normal levels of taxation. During these periods, then, government grows. But after the stressful period is over, government size does *not* return to its previous levels. Instead, governments substitute new expenditures for those accepted during the crisis. Thus, expenditures increase during crisis periods but never return to the precrisis levels after the crisis passes.

*Fiscal "Illusion"* This explanation assumes that government officials can increase revenues, and then expenditures, by altering tax-collecting devices so that voters do not realize how much money government is actually taking from them. The federal income tax grew very rapidly *after* the introduction of federal tax "withholding" in 1943. Since that time, wage earners have not received all of the money they earn and have come to perceive the missing portion as "belonging" to the federal government. This illusion is also aided by government-mandated withholding of Social Security taxes.

*Bureaucratic Expansionism* Bureaucrats and legislators have a personal interest in expanding government budgets. Bureaucrats want to increase the amount of money they can spend and the number of employees under their supervision. Legislators want to increase the resources over which they have jurisdiction and to enhance the government benefits bestowed on their constituents.

*Interest-Group Pressures* This explanation assumes that interest groups want to increase the size of government programs that benefit their own members. Benefits are visible and concentrated. Costs are invisible in many cases or are of less significance to those who will clearly benefit. As each interest group is motivated to act on behalf of its own members, largely ignoring the associated costs, government grows.

*Politicians Seeking Votes* Politicians in competitive elections frequently promise their constituents visible and exaggerated benefits while hiding or minimizing the costs to other voters. When these promises become policies, government grows.

*Cumulative Unintended Consequences* The current size of the government is the result of previous efforts to solve earlier problems. Once established, bureaucracies and programs live on, even when their original tasks no longer need doing. Over the years, the effects of all these decisions accumulate beyond what anyone originally intended.

*Incrementalism* Governments expand because decision making is incremental. Presidents and members of Congress focus on a narrow range of new policy proposals and *increases* or *decreases* in the budget. Old programs are never reviewed as a whole every year. The value of existing programs is seldom reconsidered.

*Adolf Wagner's major work is *Grundlegung der Politischen Ökonomie* (Leipzig, 1883). This work is discussed at length in Alan T. Peacock and Jack Wiseman, *The Growth of Public Expenditures in the United Kingdom* (Princeton, N.J.: Princeton University Press, 1961).

serving the nation's senior citizens. Beyond these public-spirited motives, bureaucrats, like everyone else, seek higher pay, greater job security, and added power and prestige for themselves.

These public and private motives converge to inspire bureaucrats to seek to expand the powers, functions, and budgets of their departments and agencies. Rarely do bureaucrats request a reduction in authority, the elimination of a program, or a decrease in their agency's budget. Rather, over time, "budget maximization"—expanding the agency's budget as much as possible—becomes a driving force in government bureaucracies. This is especially true of discretionary funds. **Discretionary funds** are those that bureaucrats have flexibility in deciding how to spend, rather than money committed by law to specific purposes.[4] Thus bureaucracies continually strive to add new functions, acquire more authority and responsibility, and increase their budgets and personnel. Bureaucratic expansion is just one of the reasons that government grows over time (see *Up Close:* "Why Government Grows, and Grows, and Grows").

# THE FEDERAL BUREAUCRACY

The federal bureaucracy—officially the executive branch of the United States government—consists of about 2.8 million civilian employees (plus 1.4 million persons in the armed forces) organized into fourteen cabinet departments, sixty independent agencies, and a large Executive Office of the President (see Figures 12-1 and 12-2). The expenditures of *all* governments in the United States—the federal government, the 50 state governments, and some 86,000 local governments—now amount to more than $2.5 *trillion* (roughly 35 percent of the U.S. gross domestic product). About two-thirds of this—more than $1.6 *trillion* a year (more than 23 percent of GDP)—is spent by the federal government. In contrast, at the start of the century, the federal government was very small relative to state and local governments, and federal spending was only about 2 percent of GDP. Nevertheless, government spending in the United States remains relatively modest compared to that of many nations (see *Compared to What?* "The Size of Government in Other Nations").

*Cabinet Departments*    Cabinet departments employ about 60 percent of all federal workers. Each of the fourteen departments is headed by a secretary (with the exception of the Justice Department, which is headed by the attorney general) who is appointed by the president and must be confirmed by the Senate. Each department is hierarchically organized; each has its own organization chart. Although organizational patterns differ among departments, the chart for the Department of Health and Human Services shown in Figure 12-3 is typical.

Government departments vary widely in the budgetary funds they control and in the number of personnel (see Table 12-1). The largest budget belongs to the Department of Health and Human Services (HHS), primarily spent through its Social Security and Medicare and Medicaid outlays, which account for about 40 percent of all federal spending. The largest organization in the federal bureaucracy in terms of personnel is the Department of Defense (DOD), with nearly 1 million civilian employees in addition to 1.4 million military personnel. The Department of Defense is unique in that the civilian heads of the "Departments" of the Army, Navy, and Air Force are given the title "secretary" even though they really

**Discretionary funds:**
Budgeted funds not earmarked for specific purposes but available to be spent in accordance with the best judgment of a bureaucrat.

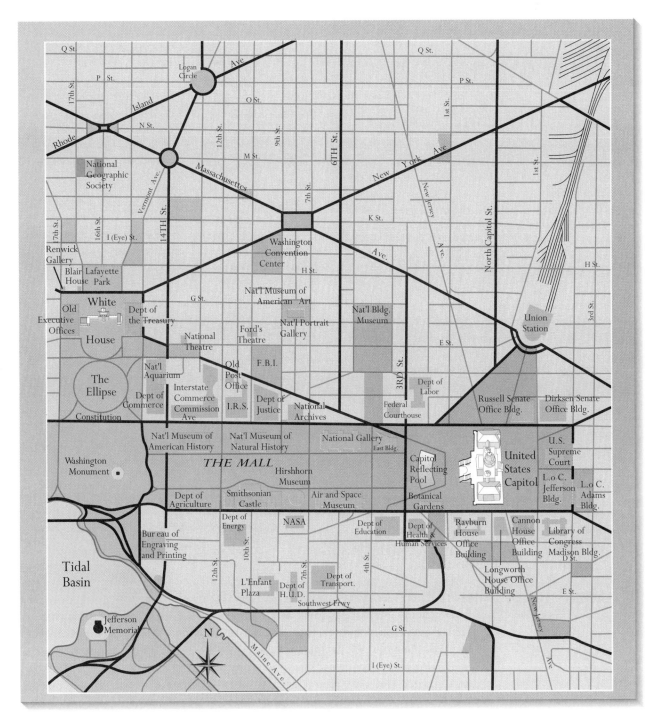

The following labels appear on the map:

Q St. · Logan Circle · Ave. · Q St. · 17th St. · P St. · P St. · Island · 1st St. · O St. · N St. · Rhode · 12th St. · 9th St. · 6TH St. · New York · Ave. · National Geographic Society · Vermont Ave. · Massachusettes · New Jersey · North Capitol St. · M St. · 14TH St. · K St. · 1st St. · H St. · 7th St. · Ave. · 7th St. · 16th St. · I (Eye) St. · Renwick Gallery · Washington Convention Center · H St. · 3rd St. · Blair House · Lafayette Park · G St. · H St. · Nat'l Museum of American Art · Nat'l Bldg. Museum · Union Station · Old Executive Offices · White · Dept of the Treasury · Nat'l Portrait Gallery · E St. · House · National Theatre · Ford's Theatre · The Ellipse · Nat'l Aquarium · F.B.I. · 3RD St. · Dept of Commerce · Interstate Commerce Commission Ave · Old Post Office · Dept of Justice · National Archives · Dept of Labor · Russell Senate Office Bldg. · Dirksen Senate Office Bldg. · Constitution · I.R.S. · Federal Courthouse · Nat'l Museum of American History · Nat'l Museum of Natural History · National Gallery · East Bldg. · U.S. Supreme Court · Washington Monument · THE MALL · Hirshhorn Museum · Capitol Reflecting Pool · United States Capitol · L.o C. Jefferson Bldg. · L.o C. Adams Bldg. · Dept of Agriculture · Smithsonian Castle · Air and Space Museum · Botanical Gardens · Dept of Energy · NASA · Dept of Education · Dept of Health & Human Services · Rayburn House Office Building · Cannon House Office Building · Library of Congress Madison Bldg. · Bureau of Engraving and Printing · 10th St. · 12th St. · 7th St. · 4th St. · D St. · Tidal Basin · L'Enfant Plaza · Dept of H.U.D. · Dept of Transport. · Longworth House Office Building · E St. · Southwest Frwy · New Jersey · Jefferson Memorial · N · Maine Ave. · G St. · Ave. · I (Eye) St.

FIGURE 12-2 Corridors of Power in the Bureaucracy

*This map shows the location of the major departments of the federal bureaucracy in Washington, D.C.*

function as undersecretaries to the Secretary of Defense. This anomaly is a product of historical tradition: a secretary of war headed a separate War Department (created 1789) and the secretary of the navy headed a separate Department of the Navy (created 1798) until the creation of a unified Department of Defense in 1947.

Cabinet status confers great legitimacy on a governmental function and prestige on the secretary, thus strengthening that individual's voice in the government. Therefore the elevation of an executive department to cabinet level often reflects

# The Size of Government in Other Nations

How does the size of the public sector in the United States compare with the size of the public sector in other countries? There is a great deal of variation in the size of government across countries. Government spending accounts for nearly three-fifths of the total output in Denmark, Sweden, and the Netherlands. Approximately one-half of the total income of Italy, Austria, Greece, France, Belgium, and Germany is channeled through the public sector. The high level of government spending in these countries primarily reflects greater public-sector involvement in the provision of housing, health care, retirement insurance, and aid to the poor and unemployed. The size of the public sectors in Australia, Japan, and Switzerland are approximately the same as in the United States, while the size of government in South Korea and Hong Kong, two Asian nations where income has grown very rapidly in recent decades, is substantially smaller than that of the United States.

**Governmental Percentage of Gross Domestic Product**

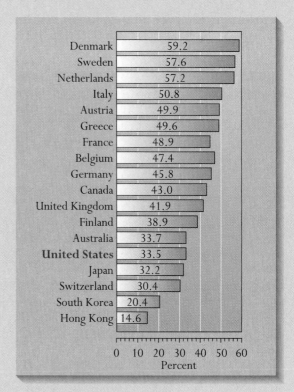

| Country | Percent |
|---|---|
| Denmark | 59.2 |
| Sweden | 57.6 |
| Netherlands | 57.2 |
| Italy | 50.8 |
| Austria | 49.9 |
| Greece | 49.6 |
| France | 48.9 |
| Belgium | 47.4 |
| Germany | 45.8 |
| Canada | 43.0 |
| United Kingdom | 41.9 |
| Finland | 38.9 |
| Australia | 33.7 |
| **United States** | 33.5 |
| Japan | 32.2 |
| Switzerland | 30.4 |
| South Korea | 20.4 |
| Hong Kong | 14.6 |

*Source: OECD Economic Outlook, June 1990.*

political considerations as much as or more than national needs. Strong pressures from "client" interest groups (groups principally served by the department), as well as presidential and congressional desires to pose as defenders and promoters of particular interests, account for the establishment of all of the newer departments. President Woodrow Wilson appealed to the labor movement in 1913 when he separated out a Department of Labor from the earlier business-dominated Department of Commerce and Labor. President Lyndon Johnson demonstrated his concern for urban problems by creating the Department of Housing and Urban Development in 1965.

Presidents have differed greatly in their opinions of what is "important enough" for a cabinet inclusion. In 1979, President Jimmy Carter sought support from teachers and educational administrators when he created a separate Department of Education and changed the name of the former Department of Health, Education, and Welfare to the Department of Health and Human Services (perhaps finding the phrase "human services" more politically acceptable than "welfare"). President Ronald Reagan, never a favorite of educational groups, tried and failed to "streamline" government by abolishing the Department of Education. But Reagan himself added a cabinet post, elevating the Veterans Administration to the Department of Veterans Affairs in an attempt to ingratiate himself with veterans. President Clinton promised to elevate the Environmental Protection Agency (EPA) to a cabinet department.

*Cabinet Department Functions*   The relative power and prestige of each cabinet-level department is a product not only of its size and budget but also of the importance of its function. By custom, the "pecking order" of departments—and therefore the prestige ranking of their secretaries—is determined by their years of origin. Thus, the Departments of State, Treasury, Defense (War), and Justice, created by the First Congress in 1789, head the protocol list of departments. Overall, the duties of the fourteen cabinet-level departments of the executive branch cover an enormous range—everything from providing mortgage insurance to protecting the nation from nuclear attack.

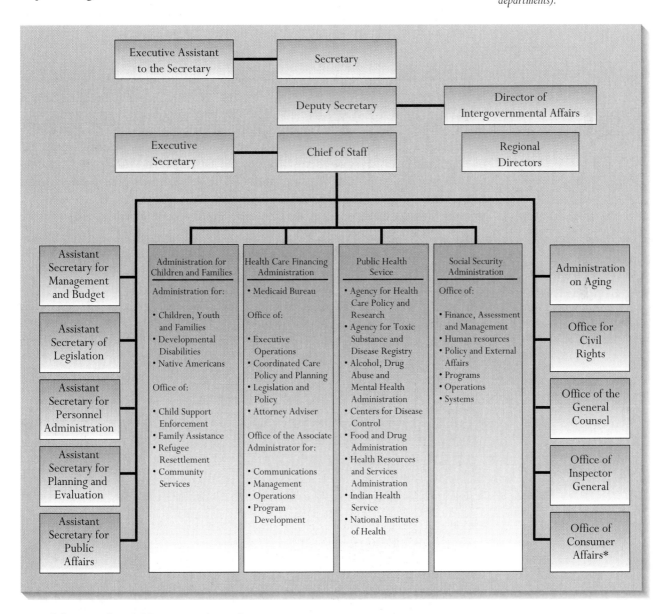

*Located administratively in HHS, but reports to the president.

TABLE 12-1 EXECUTIVE DEPARTMENTS' SIZE AND BUDGETS

|  | Personnel (thousands) | Budgets ($ billions) |
|---|---|---|
| Agriculture | 128.3 | 62.3 |
| Commerce | 38.1 | 4.1 |
| Defense | 982.8 | 281.9 |
| Education | 5.1 | 30.7 |
| Energy | 20.9 | 15.7 |
| Health and Human Services | 131.2 | 713.1 |
| Housing and Urban Development | 13.7 | 26.3 |
| Interior | 85.3 | 7.3 |
| Justice | 96.9 | 13.5 |
| Labor | 17.9 | 35.8 |
| State | 25.7 | 5.5 |
| Transportation | 70.6 | 37.3 |
| Treasury | 161.9 | 386.1 |
| Veterans Affairs | 260.2 | 37.9 |
| All Independent Agencies | 978.3 | 78.4 |

*Source: Statistical Abstract of the United States, 1995,* and *Budget of the United States Government, 1996.* Personnel figures are for 1992; budget figures, for 1996.

- *State* (1789): Advises the president on the formation and execution of foreign policy; negotiates treaties and agreements with foreign nations; represents the United States in the United Nations and in the more than fifty major international organizations and maintains U.S. embassies abroad; issues U.S. passports and, in foreign countries, visas to the United States.
- *Treasury* (1789): Serves as financial agent for the U.S. government; issues all payments of the U.S. government according to law; manages the debt of

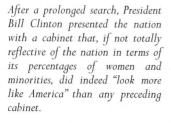

*After a prolonged search, President Bill Clinton presented the nation with a cabinet that, if not totally reflective of the nation in terms of its percentages of women and minorities, did indeed "look more like America" than any preceding cabinet.*

the U.S. government by issuing and recovering bonds and paying their interest; collects taxes owed to the U.S. government; collects taxes and enforces laws on alcohol, tobacco, and firearms and on customs duties; manufactures coins and currency.

- *Defense* (1947, formerly the War Department, created in 1789, and the Navy Department, created 1798): Provides the military forces needed to deter war and protect the national security interest; includes the Departments of the Army, Navy, and Air Force.
- *Justice* (1789): Enforces all federal laws, including consumer protection, antitrust, civil rights, drug, and immigration and naturalization; maintains federal prisons.
- *Interior* (1849): Has responsibility for public lands and natural resources, for American Indian reservations, and for people who live in island territories under U.S. administration; preserves national parks and historical sites.
- *Agriculture* (1889): Works to improve and maintain farm income and to develop and expand markets abroad for agricultural products; safeguards standards of quality in the food supply through inspection and grading services; administers rural development, credit, and conservation programs; administers food stamp program.
- *Commerce* (1913): Encourages the nation's international trade, economic growth, and technological advancement; conducts the census; provides social and economic statistics and analyses for business and government; maintains the merchant marine; grants patents and registers trademarks.
- *Labor* (1913): Oversees working conditions; administers federal labor laws; protects workers' pension rights; sponsors job training programs; keeps track of changes in employment, price, and other national economic indicators.
- *Health and Human Services* (1953 as Health, Education, and Welfare; reorganized with Education as a separate department in 1979): Administers social welfare programs for the elderly, children, and youths; protects the health of the nation against impure and unsafe foods, drugs, and cosmetics; operates the Centers for Disease Control; funds the Medicare and Medicaid programs; and operates the Social Security system.
- *Housing and Urban Development* (1965): Is responsible for programs concerned with housing needs, fair housing opportunities, and the improvement and development of the nation's communities; administers mortgage insurance programs, rental subsidy programs, and neighborhood rehabilitation and preservation programs.
- *Transportation* (1966): Is responsible for the nation's highway planning, development, and construction; also urban mass transit, railroads, aviation, and the safety of waterways, ports, highways, and oil and gas pipelines.
- *Energy* (1977): Is responsible for the research, development, and demonstration of energy technology; marketing of federal electric power; energy conservation; the nuclear weapons program; regulation of energy production and use; and collection and analysis of energy data.
- *Education* (1979): Administers and coordinates most federal assistance to education.
- *Veterans Affairs* (1989): Operates programs to benefit veterans and members of their families.[5]

*Independent Regulatory Commissions* Independent regulatory commissions differ from cabinet departments in their function, organization, and accountability to the president. Their function is to *regulate* a sector of society—transportation, communications, banking, labor relations, and so on (see Table 12-2). These commissions are empowered by Congress both to make and to enforce rules, and they thus function in a quasi-judicial fashion. To symbolize their impartiality, many of these organizations are headed by *commissions,* usually with five to ten members, rather than by a single director or secretary. Major policy decisions are made by majority vote of the commission. Finally, these agencies are more independent of the president than are cabinet departments. Their governing commissions are appointed by the president and confirmed by the Senate in the same fashion as cabinet secretaries, but their terms are fixed; they cannot be removed by the president.[6] These provisions are designed to insulate regulators from direct partisan or presidential pressures in their decision making.

A few powerful regulatory agencies remain inside cabinet departments. The most notable are the Food and Drug Administration (FDA), which remains in the Department of Health and Human Services and has broad authority to prevent the sale of drugs not deemed by the agency to be both "safe" and "effective"; the Occupational Health and Safety Administration (OSHA) in the Department of Labor, with authority to make rules governing any workplace in America; and the most powerful government agency of all, the Internal Revenue Service in the Treasury Department, with its broad authority to interpret the tax code, maintain records on every American, and investigate and punish alleged violations of the tax code.

*Independent Agencies* Congress has created a number of independent agencies outside of any cabinet department. Like cabinet departments, these agencies are hierarchically organized with a single head—usually called an "administrator"—who is appointed by the president and confirmed by the Senate. Administrators have no fixed terms of office and can be dismissed by the president; thus they are independent only insofar as they report directly to the president rather than through a cabinet secretary. Politically, this independence ensures that their interests and budgets will not be compromised by other concerns, as may occur in agencies located within departments. (For more on their operations, see "Regulatory Battles" later in this chapter.)

Perhaps the most powerful independent agency is the Environmental Protection Agency (EPA), which is responsible for implementing federal legislation dealing with clean air, safe drinking water, solid waste disposal, pesticides, radiation, and toxic substances. EPA establishes and enforces comprehensive and complex standards for thousands of substances in the environment. It enjoys the political support of influential environmental interest groups, including the Environmental Defense Fund, Friends of the Earth, National Audubon Society, National Wildlife Federation, Natural Resources Defense Council, Sierra Club, and the Wilderness Society.

*Government Corporations* Government corporations are created by Congress to undertake independent commercial enterprises. They resemble private corporations in that they typically charge for their services. Like private corporations, too, they are usually governed by a chief executive officer and a board of directors, and they can buy and sell property and incur debts.

CHAPTER 12 • THE BUREAUCRACY: BUREAUCRATIC POLITICS

## TABLE 12-2 MAJOR REGULATORY BUREAUCRACIES

| Commission | Date Created | Primary Functions |
| --- | --- | --- |
| Federal Communications Commission (FCC) | 1934 | Regulates interstate and foreign communications by radio, television, wire, and cable. |
| Food and Drug Administration (FDA) | 1930 | Sets standards of safety and efficacy for foods, drugs, and medical devices. |
| Federal Home Loan Bank | 1932 | Regulates savings and loan associations that specialize in making home mortgage loans. |
| Federal Maritime Commission | 1961 | Regulates the waterborne foreign and domestic offshore commerce of the United States. |
| Federal Reserve Board (FRB) | 1913 | Regulates the nation's money supply by making monetary policy, which influences the lending and investing activities of commercial banks and the cost and availability of money and credit. |
| Federal Trade Commission (FTC) | 1914 | Regulates business to prohibit unfair methods of competition and unfair or deceptive acts or practices. |
| National Labor Relations Board (NLRB) | 1935 | Protects employees' rights to organize; prevents unfair labor practices. |
| Securities and Exchange Commission (SEC) | 1934 | Regulates the securities and financial markets (such as the stock market). |
| Occupational Safety and Health Administration (OSHA) | 1970 | Issues workplace regulations; investigates, cites, and penalizes for noncompliance |
| Consumer Product Safety Commission (CPSC) | 1972 | Protects the public against product-related deaths, illnesses, and injuries. |
| Commodity Futures Trading Commission | 1974 | Regulates trading on the futures exchanges as well as activities of commodity exchange members, public brokerage houses, commodity salespersons, trading advisers, and pool operators. |
| Nuclear Regulatory Commission (NRC) | 1974 | Regulates and licenses the users of nuclear energy. |
| Federal Energy Regulatory Commission (formerly Federal Power Commission) | 1977 | Regulates the transportation and sale of natural gas, the transmission and sale of electricity, the licensing of hydroelectric power projects, and the transportation of oil by pipeline. |
| Equal Employment Opportunity Commission (EEOC) | 1964 | Investigates and rules on charges of racial, gender, and age discrimination by employers and unions, in all aspects of employment. |
| Environmental Protection Agency (EPA) | 1970 | Issues and enforces pollution control standards regarding air, water, solid waste, pesticides, radiation, and toxic substances. |

*Source:* The United States Government Manual 1994/95 (Washington, D.C.: Government Printing Office, 1994).

*Cleaning up an oil spill on a California beach. The Environmental Protection Agency is perhaps the most powerful independent agency in the bureaucracy.*

Presumably, government corporations perform a service that the private enterprise system has been unable to carry out adequately. The first government corporation was the Tennessee Valley Authority, created by President Franklin Roosevelt during the Depression to build dams and sell electricity at inexpensive rates to impoverished citizens in the mid-South. In 1970, Congress created Amtrak to restore railroad passenger service to the United States. Originally, the U.S. Post Office was a cabinet-level department, but in 1971, it became the U.S. Postal Service, a government corporation with a mandate from Congress to break even. But when the Postal Service and other government corporations run recurring deficits in their operations, Congress has provided subsidies to make up the difference.

*Contractors and Consultants*    How has the federal government grown enormously in power and size, yet kept its number of employees at roughly the same level in recent years? The answer is found in the spectacular growth of private firms that live off federal contracting and consulting fees.

Nearly one-fifth of all federal government spending flows through private contractors: for supplies, equipment, services, leases, and research and development. An army of scientists, economists, education specialists, management consultants, transportation experts, social scientists, and others are scattered across the country in universities, think tanks, consulting firms, and laboratories. Many are concentrated in the "beltway bandit" firms surrounding Washington, D.C.

The federal grant and contracting system is enormously complex; an estimated 150,000 federal contracting offices in nearly 500 agencies oversee thousands of outside contractors and consultants.[7] Although advertised bidding is required by law, most contracts and grants are awarded without competition through negotiation with favored firms or "sole source contracts" with organizations believed by bureaucrats to be uniquely qualified. Even when federal agencies issue public requests for proposals, often a favored contractor has been alerted and advised by bureaucrats within the agency about how to win the award.

## BUREAUCRACY AND DEMOCRACY

Traditionally, conflict over government employment centered on the question of partisanship versus competence. Should the federal bureaucracy be staffed by people politically loyal to the president, the president's party, or key members of Congress? Or should it be staffed by nonpartisan people selected on the basis of merit and protected from "political" influence?[8]

*The Spoils System*   Historically, government employment was allocated by the **spoils system**—selecting employees on the basis of party loyalty, electoral support, and political influence. Or as Senator William Marcy said in 1832, "They see nothing wrong in the rule that to the victors belong the spoils of the enemy."[9] The spoils system is most closely associated with President Andrew Jackson, who viewed it as a popular reform of the earlier tendency to appoint officials on the basis of kinship and class standing. Jackson sought to bring into government many of the common people who had supported him. Later in the nineteenth century, the bartering and sale of government jobs became so scandalous and time-consuming that presidents complained bitterly about the task. And when President James Garfield was shot and killed in 1881 by a disgruntled job seeker, the stage was set for reform.

*The Merit System*   The **merit system**—government employment based on competence, neutrality, and protection from partisanship—was introduced in the Pendleton Act of 1883. The act created the Civil Service Commission to establish a system for selecting government personnel based on merit, as determined by competitive examinations. In the beginning, "civil service" coverage included only about 10 percent of total federal employees. Over the years, however, more and more positions were placed under civil service, primarily at the behest of presidents who sought to "freeze in" their political appointees. By 1978, more than 90 percent of federal employees were covered by civil service or other merit systems.[10]

The civil service system established a uniform General Schedule (GS) of job grades from GS 1 (lowest) to GS 15 (highest), with an Executive Schedule added later for top managers and pay ranges based on an individual's time in the grade. Each grade has specific educational requirements and examinations. College graduates generally begin at GS 5 or above; GS 9 through GS 12 are technical and supervisory positions; and GS 13, 14, and 15 are midlevel management and highly specialized positions. The Executive Schedule (the "supergrades") are reserved for positions of greatest responsibility. (In 1995, annual pay ranged from roughly $20,000 to $35,000 for Grades 5–8, up to $50,000 to $90,000 for Grades 13–15, and over $100,000 for some Executive Schedule positions.) When a position in a federal agency opens up, the agency is supposed to receive the names of the three

*During the administration of Andrew Jackson, the spoils system was perhaps more overt than at any other time in the history of the U.S. federal government. Jackson claimed he was trying to involve more of the "common folk" in the government, but his selection of advisers on the basis of personal friendship rather than qualifications sometimes caused him difficulties.*

**Spoils system:** Selection of employees for government agencies on the basis of party loyalty, electoral support, and political influence.

**Merit system:** Selection of employees for government agencies on the basis of competence, with no consideration of an individual's political stance and/or power.

people earning the highest examination scores for that position grade. The agency is supposed to hire one of the three, with the other two remaining at the top of the register for the next opening. But agencies often set highly specialized job qualifications that relatively few applicants possess, and special preferences abound in federal employment regulations.

Once hired and retained through a brief probationary period, a federal civil servant cannot be dismissed except for "cause." Firing a federal employee requires giving the employee:

- Written notice at least thirty days in advance of a hearing to determine incompetence or misconduct.
- A statement of cause, indicating specific dates, places, and actions cited as incompetent or improper.
- The right to a hearing and decision by an impartial official, with the burden of proof falling on the agency that wishes to fire the employee.
- The right to have an attorney and to present witnesses in the employee's favor at the hearing.
- The right to appeal any adverse action to the Merit Systems Protection Board.
- The right to appeal any adverse action by the board to the U.S. Court of Appeals.
- The right to remain on the job and be paid until all appeals are exhausted.

About two-thirds of all federal civilian jobs come under the General Schedule system, with its written examinations and/or training, experience, and educational requirements. Most of the other one-third of federal civilian employees are part of the "excepted services"; they are employed by various agencies that have their own separate merit systems, such as the Federal Bureau of Investigation, the Central Intelligence Agency, the U.S. Postal Service, and the State Department Foreign Service. The military also has its own system of recruitment, promotion, and pay.

*The Problem of Responsiveness*   The civil service system, like most "reforms," eventually created problems at least as troubling as those in the system it replaced. First of all, there is the problem of a *lack of responsiveness* to presidential direction. Civil servants, secure in their protected jobs, can be less than cooperative toward their presidentially appointed department or agency heads. They can slow or obstruct policy changes with which they personally disagree. Each bureau and agency develops its own "culture," usually in strong support of the governmental function or client group served by the organization. Changing the culture of an agency is extremely difficult, especially when a presidential administration is committed to reducing its resources, functions, or services. Bureaucrats' powers of policy obstruction are formidable: they can help mobilize interest group support against the president's policy; they can "leak" damaging information to sympathizers in Congress or the media to undermine the president's policy; they can delay and/or "sabotage" policies with which they disagree.

*The Problem of Productivity*   Perhaps the most troublesome problem in the federal bureaucracy has involved *productivity*—notably the inability to improve job performance because of the difficulties in rewarding or punishing civil servants.

"Merit" salary rewards have generally proven ineffective in rewarding the performance of federal employees. More than 99 percent of federal workers regularly receive annual "merit" pay increases. Moreover, over time, federal employees have secured higher grade classifications and hence higher pay for most of the job positions in the General Schedule. This "inflation" in GS grades, combined with regular increases in salary and benefits, has resulted in many federal employees' enjoying higher pay and benefits than employees in the private sector performing similar jobs.

At the same time, very poor performance often goes largely unpunished. Severe obstacles to firing a civil servant result in a rate of dismissal of about one-tenth of 1 percent of all federal employees. It is doubtful that only such a tiny fraction are performing unsatisfactorily. A federal executive confronting a poorly performing or nonperforming employee must be prepared to spend more than a year in extended proceedings to secure a dismissal. Often costly substitute strategies are devised to work around or inspire the resignation of unsatisfactory federal employees—assigning them meaningless or boring tasks, denying them promotions, transferring them to distant or undesirable locations, removing secretaries or other supporting resources, and the like.

*Civil Service Reform*   Presidents routinely try to remedy some of the problems in the system (see *Up Close:* "Al Gore, 'Reinventing' Government"). When President Jimmy Carter sponsored the Civil Service Reform Act of 1978, he noted: "There is not enough merit in the merit system. There is inadequate motivation because we have too few rewards for excellence and too few penalties for unsatisfactory work."[11] The act replaced the Civil Service Commission with the Office of Personnel Management (OPM) and made OPM responsible for recruiting, examining, training, and promoting federal employees. Unlike the Civil Service Commission, OPM is headed by a single director responsible to the president. The act also sought to (1) streamline procedures through which individuals could be disciplined for poor performance; (2) establish merit pay for middle-level managers; and (3) create a Senior Executive Service (SES) composed of about 8,000 top people designated for higher Executive Schedule grades and salaries who also might be given salary bonuses, transferred among agencies, or demoted, based upon performance.

But like many reforms, this act failed to resolve the major problems—the responsiveness and productivity of the bureaucracy. No senior executives were fired, demoted, or involuntarily transferred. The bonus program proved difficult to implement: there are few recognized standards for judging meritorious work in the public service, and bonuses often reflect favoritism as much as merit.[12] Because the act creates a separate Merit Systems Protection Board to hear appeals by federal employees from dismissals, suspensions, and demotions, rates of dismissal for all grades have not changed substantially from earlier days.

*Bureaucracy and Representation*   In addition to the questions of responsiveness and productivity, there is also the question of the representativeness of the federal bureaucracy. Today, the federal bureaucracy *as a whole* reflects fairly well the gender and minority ratios of the U.S. population. Nearly 49 percent of the total civilian work force is female, 16.5 percent is black, and 5.2 is Hispanic. However, a close look at *top* bureaucratic positions reveals a somewhat different picture. As Table 12-3 shows, only 9.1 percent of federal "executive"

# Al Gore, "Reinventing" Government

How can we overcome "the bankruptcy of bureaucracy"—the waste, inefficiency, impersonality, and unresponsiveness of large government organizations? Solving the problem of bureaucracy is perceived as overcoming "the routine tendency to protect turf, to resist change, to build empires, to enlarge one's sphere of control, to protect projects and programs regardless of whether or not they are any longer needed."* The answer, according to current reformers, is to "reinvent government"—to focus on the needs of citizens, not bureaucrats, to inject competition into public service provision, to use market incentives whenever possible, to decentralize, and to encourage agencies to be mission-driven rather than rule-driven.

The notion of "reinventing government" gained popularity among centrist Democrats even before the Clinton administration arrived in Washington. Some Democratic Party constituencies—notably government employees and their unions, teachers and their unions, and environmental groups—are concerned about the antibureaucratic thrust of many of the new reforms and fear the loss of government jobs to private contractors. But Clinton campaigned on the pledge to make government more efficient and responsive. Upon taking office, he assigned this task to Al Gore.

Vice-presidents traditionally undertake symbolic roles in presidential administrations, but Al Gore responded to his assignment with considerable energy and enthusiasm, promptly producing a 168-page report of the National Performance Review, *Creating a Government That Works Better and Costs Less.*** The report includes 384 specific recommendations designed to put the "customer" (U.S. citizen) first, to "empower" government employees to get results, to cut red tape, to introduce competition and a market orientation wherever possible, and to decentralize government decision making. Many previous bureaucratic reform efforts had floundered, from Hoover Commission studies in the Truman and Eisenhower years to the Grace Commission in the Reagan Administration. But Bill Clinton boasted that the new effort

*Making a point about red tape and bureaucratic inefficiency, President Clinton and Vice President Al Gore walk past two fork lifts loaded with reams of federal rules and regulations before announcing their plans for "reinventing" government.*

would succeed because Vice-President Gore was given the responsibility not just to devise recommendations but to oversee their implementation as well.

How successful has Al Gore been at "reinventing" federal government? Periodically Gore has published "status reports" on the implementation of his National Performance Review recommendations. As expected, these reports present glowing accounts of "reinvention," bureaucratic "cultural change," "cutting red tape," and "putting customers first." But even after discounting for puffery, it seems clear that some progress has been achieved. The most impressive evidence is the overall decline in federal employment.

*David Osborne and Ted Gaebler, *Reinventing Government: How the Entrepreneurial Spirit Is Transforming the Public Sector* (New York: Addison-Wesley, 1992), pp. 23–24.
**Al Gore, *Creating a Government That Works Better and Costs Less* (Washington, D.C.: Government Printing Office, 1993).

## TABLE 12-3  WOMEN AND MINORITIES IN THE FEDERAL BUREAUCRACY

|  | Percentage Female | Percentage Minority* | Percentage Black | Percentage Hispanic |
|---|---|---|---|---|
| Overall | 48.7% | 27.8% | 16.5% | 5.2% |
| By pay grade |  |  |  |  |
| Lowest GS 1–4 | 74.8 | 43.2 | 29.4 | 7.0 |
| GS 5–8 | 53.5 | 34.6 | 23.1 | 6.1 |
| GS 9–12 | 32.9 | 22.1 | 11.8 | 5.0 |
| GS 13–15 | 17.0 | 13.7 | 6.8 | 2.9 |
| Executive | 9.1 | 8.1 | 5.0 | 2.3 |
| U.S. population | 51.1 | 28.7 | 12.1 | 9.0 |

Source: Statistical Abstract of the United States, 1994, p. 346. Figures are for 1992.

*Blacks and Hispanics, plus American Indians, Alaska Natives, Asians, and Pacific Islanders.

positions (levels GS 16–18) are filled by women, only 5.0 percent by blacks, and only 2.3 percent by Hispanics (see *People in Politics:* "Henry Cisneros, HUD Secretary"). Thus, the federal bureaucracy, like other institutions in American society, is *un*representative of the general population in its top executive positions.

## BUREAUCRATIC POLITICS

To whom is the federal bureaucracy really accountable? The president, Congress, or itself? Article II, Section 2, of the Constitution places the president at the head of the executive branch of government, with the power to "appoint Ambassadors, other public Ministers and Consuls, Judges of the Supreme Court, and all other Officers of the United States . . . which shall be established by Law." Appointment of these officials requires "the Advice and Consent of the Senate"—that is, a majority vote in the Senate. The Constitution also states that "the Congress may by Law vest the Appointment of such inferior Officers, as they think proper, in the President alone." If the bureaucracy is to be made accountable to the president, we would expect the president to directly appoint *policy-making* executive officers. But it is difficult to determine exactly how many positions are truly "policy making."

*Presidential "Plums"*    The president retains direct control over about 3,000 federal jobs. Some 700 of these jobs are considered policy-making positions. They include presidential appointments authorized by law—cabinet and subcabinet officers, judges, U.S. marshals, U.S. attorneys, ambassadors, and members of various boards and commissions. The president also appoints a large number of "Schedule C" jobs throughout the bureaucracy, which are described as "confidential or policy-determining" in character. Each new presidential administration goes through many months of internal squabbling, high-powered lobbying, and scrambling to fill these posts. Applicants with congressional sponsors, friends in the White House, or a record of loyal campaign work for the president compete for these "plums." Political loyalty must be weighed against administrative competence.

# Henry Cisneros, HUD Secretary

Fulfilling his campaign promise to make government "look like America," in 1993 newly elected president Bill Clinton turned to the nation's mayors in selecting two Hispanic members for his cabinet: former Denver mayor Federico Peña as secretary of transportation and former San Antonio mayor Henry Cisneros as secretary of housing and urban development.

Henry Cisneros brings an impressive background of education and experience to the Department of Housing and Urban Development (HUD). His grandfather, a Mexican revolutionary and newspaper editor who fled to the United States in 1926 to escape the heavy hand of the Mexican government, established a printshop in the "Colonia Mexicana" in San Antonio and became a leader of the Hispanic community in the city. Cisneros's father was a civilian administrator in the Department of Defense and a colonel in the Army Reserve.

Young Henry did not grow up in a *barrio* but rather in a distinctively middle-class Mexican-American neighborhood in San Antonio. He graduated with honors from Texas A&M and went on to earn a master's degree at the John F. Kennedy School of Government at Harvard University and a Ph.D. in public administration at George Washington University. He spent a year as a White House Fellow and a year as a research fellow at the Massachusetts Insti-

tute of Technology before returning home to teach at the University of Texas at San Antonio and at Trinity University.

Cisneros entered city politics at a time when Hispanics were beginning to mobilize against the traditional "Anglo" power structure. In the early 1970s, local Hispanic leaders had organized protests in San Antonio to force the city government to improve public services in the poor *barrios*. Cisneros, first elected to the city council in 1975, was instrumental in resolving some of the conflicts between his Mexican-American constituents and Anglo businesspeople. In 1981, proclaiming "Now is the time, compadres!" Cisneros defeated a wealthy Anglo insurance executive in a close election for mayor. Cisneros's promising political career was set back by a well-publicized extramarital affair; a chastised Cisneros left the mayor's office in 1989 to devote more time to his family.

As Secretary of Housing and Urban Development, Henry Cisneros has the challenging task of making the federal bureaucracy more responsive to the problems of the nation's cities while recognizing that "we can't go back to the big bureaucracy answers of the 1960s." HUD programs focus on public housing, but Cisneros argues that various federal departments must coordinate their activities in order to cope with the multifaceted problems of cities. HUD was created in 1965, partly in response to deadly rioting in the Watts section of Los Angeles that year. In 1992, rioting in south-central Los Angeles, following the first well-publicized Rodney King trial, indicated that conditions in the nation's inner cities had not changed much in more than twenty-five years, or perhaps had grown even worse. Secretary Cisneros and HUD face a truly monumental task.

**Whistleblower:** An employee of the federal government or of a firm supplying the government who reports waste, mismanagement, and/or fraud by a government agency or contractor.

*Whistleblowers* The question of bureaucratic responsiveness is complicated by the struggle between the president and Congress to control the bureaucracy. Congress expects federal agencies and employees to respond fully and promptly to its inquiries and to report candidly on policies, procedures, and expenditures. **Whistleblowers** are federal employees (or employees of a firm supplying the government) who report government waste, mismanagement, or fraud to the media or to congressional committees or who "go public" with their policy disputes with their superiors. Congress generally encourages whistleblowing as a means of getting information and controlling the bureaucracy, but the president and agency heads whose policies are under attack are often less kindly disposed toward whistleblowers. In 1989, Congress passed the Whistleblower Protection Act, which established an independent agency to guarantee whistleblowers protection against unjust dismissal, transfer, or demotion.

*Agency Cultures*  Over time, every bureaucracy tends to develop its own "culture"—beliefs about the values of the organization's programs and goals and close associations with the agency's client groups and political supporters. Many government agencies are dominated by people who have been in government service most of their lives, and most of these people have worked in the same functional field most of their lives. They believe that their work is important, and they resist efforts by either the president or Congress to reduce the activities, size, or budget of their agency. Career bureaucrats tend to support enlargement of the public sector—to enhance education, welfare, housing, environmental and consumer protection, and so on.[13] Bureaucrats not only share a belief in the need for government expansion but also stand to benefit directly from increased authority, staffing, and funding as government takes on new and enlarged responsibilities.

*Friends and Neighbors*  Bureaucracies maintain their own cultures in part by staffing themselves. Informal practices in recruitment often circumvent civil service procedures. Very few people ever get hired by taking a federal civil service examination administered by OPM and then sitting and waiting to be called for an interview by an agency. Most bureaucratic hiring actually comes about through "networks" of personal friends and professional associates. People inside an agency contact their friends and associates when a position first becomes vacant; they then send their friends to OPM to formally qualify for the job. Thus inside candidates learn about an opening well before it appears on any list of vacant positions and can tailor their applications to the job description. Agencies may even send a "name request" to OPM, ensuring that the preselected person will appear on the list of qualified people. In this way, individuals sometimes move through many jobs within a specific policy network—for example, within environmental protection, within transportation, or within social welfare—shifting between the federal bureaucracy, state or local government, and private firms or interest groups in the same field. Network recruiting generally ensures that the people entering a bureaucracy will share the same values and attitudes of the people already there.

# THE BUREAUCRACY AND THE BUDGETARY PROCESS

The federal government's annual budget battles are the heart of political process. Budget battles decide who gets what and who pays the cost of government. The budget is the single most important policy statement of any government.

The president is responsible for submitting the annual Budget of the United States Government—with estimates of revenues and recommendations for expenditures—for consideration, amendment, and approval by the Congress. But the president's budget reflects the outcome of earlier bureaucratic battles over who gets what. Despite highly publicized wrangling between the president and Congress each year—and occasional declarations that the president's budget is "DOA" (dead on arrival)—final congressional appropriations rarely deviate by more than 2 or 3 percent from the original presidential budget. Thus the president and the Office of Management and Budget in the Executive Office of the President have real budgetary power.

*The Office of Management and Budget*   The Office of Management and Budget (OMB) has the key responsibility for budget preparation. In addition to this major task, OMB has related responsibilities for improving the organization and management of the executive agencies, for coordinating the extensive statistical services of the federal government, and for analyzing and reviewing proposed legislation.

Preparation of the budget starts a full sixteen to eighteen months *before* the beginning of the **fiscal year** for which it is intended. In other words, work began in January 1996 on the budget for the fiscal year beginning October 1, 1997, and ending September 30, 1998. Budgets are named for the fiscal year in which they *end*, so this example describes the work on the Budget of the United States Government, Fiscal Year 1998, or more simply, FY98.

The process begins when OMB, after preliminary consultations with the executive agencies and in accord with presidential policy, develops targets or ceilings within which the agencies are encouraged to build their requests (see Figure 12-4). Budget materials and instructions then go to the agencies, with the request that the forms be completed and returned to OMB. This request is followed by about three months of arduous work by agency budget officers, department heads, and the "grass-roots" bureaucracy in Washington, D.C., and out in the field. Budget officials at the bureau level check requests from the smaller units, compare them with previous years' estimates, hold conferences, and make adjustments. The process of checking, reviewing, modifying, and discussing is repeated on a larger scale at the department level. The heads of agencies are expected to submit their completed requests to OMB by July or August. Although these requests usually remain within target levels, occasionally they include some "over-ceiling" items (requests above the suggested ceilings). With the requests of the spending agencies at hand, OMB begins its own budget review, including hearings at which top agency officials support their requests as convincingly as possible. Frequently OMB must say "NO," that is, reduce agency requests. On rare occasions, dissatisfied agencies may ask the budget director to take their cases to the president.

*The President's Budget*   In December, the president and the OMB director devote much time to the document, which by now is approaching its final stages of assembly. They and their staffs "blue-pencil," revise, and make last-minute changes, as well as prepare the president's message that accompanies the budget to Congress. Although the completed document includes a revenue plan with general estimates for taxes and other income, it is primarily an expenditure budget. (Revenue and tax policy staff work center in the Treasury Department, not in the Office of Management and Budget.) In late January, the president presents Congress with the Budget of the United States Government for the fiscal year beginning October 1. After the budget is in legislative hands, the president may recommend further alterations as needs dictate.

**Fiscal year:** Yearly government accounting period, not necessarily the same as the calendar year. The federal government's fiscal year begins October 1 and ends September 30.

FIGURE 12-4   The Budget Process

*Development, presentation, and approval of the federal budget for any fiscal year takes almost two full years. The executive branch spends more than a year on the process before Congress even begins its review and revision of the president's proposals. The problems of implementing the budgeted programs then fall to the federal bureaucracy.*

| | WHO | WHAT | WHEN |
|---|---|---|---|
|  **Presidential budget making** | President and OMB | OMB presents long-range forecasts for revenues and expenditures to the president. President and OMB develop general guidelines for all federal agencies. Agencies are sent guidelines and forms for their budget requests. | January February March |
| | Executive agencies | Agencies prepare and submit budget requests to OMB. | April May June July |
| | OMB and agencies | OMB reviews agency requests and holds hearings with agency officials. | August September October |
| | OMB and president | OMB presents revised budget to president. President and OMB write budget message for Congress. | November December |
| | President | President presents budget for the next fiscal year to Congress. | January |
|  **Congressional budget process** | CBO and congressional committees | CBO reviews taxing and spending proposals and reports to House and Senate budget committees. | February– May |
| | Congress; House and Senate budget committees | Committees present first concurrent resolution, which sets overall total for budget outlays in major categories. Full House and Senate vote on resolution. Committees are instructed to stay within Budget Committee's resolution. | May June |
| | Congress; House and Senate appropriations committees and budget committees | Appropriations committees and subcommittees draw up detailed appropriations bills and submit them to budget committees for second concurrent resolution. The full House and Senate vote on "reconciliations" and second (firm) concurrent resolution. | July August September |
| | Congress and president | House and Senate pass various appropriations bills (nine to sixteen bills, by major functional category, such as "defense"). Each is sent to president for signature. (If sucessfully vetoed, a bill is revised and resubmitted to the president.) | September October |
|  **Executive budget implementation** | Congress and president | Fiscal year for all federal agencies begins October 1. If no appropriations bill for an agency has been passed by Congress and signed by the president, Congress must pass and the president sign a continuing resolution to allow the agency to spend at last years's level until a new appropriations bill is passed. If no continuing resolution is passed, the agency must officially cease spending government funds and must officially shut down. | After October 1 |

*House and Senate Budget Committees*   The Constitution gives Congress the authority to decide how the government should spend its money: "No money shall be drawn from the Treasury, but in Consequence of Appropriations made by Law" (Article I, Section 9). The president's budget is sent initially to the House and Senate Budget Committees, which rely on their own bureaucracy, the Congressional Budget Office (CBO), to review the president's budget. Based on the CBO's assessment, these committees draft a first **budget resolution** (due May 15) setting forth target goals to guide congressional committees regarding specific appropriations and revenue measures. If proposed spending exceeds the targets in the budget resolution, the resolution comes back to the floor in a reconciliation measure. A second budget resolution (due September 15) sets binding budget figures for committees and subcommittees considering appropriations. In practice, however, these two budget resolutions are often folded into a single measure because Congress does not want to argue the same issues twice.

*Congressional Appropriations Committees*   Congressional approval of each year's spending is usually divided into thirteen separate appropriations bills (acts), each covering separate broad categories of spending (for example, defense, labor, human services and education, commerce, justice). These appropriations bills are drawn up by the House and Senate Appropriations Committees and their specialized subcommittees, which function as overseers of agencies included in their appropriations bills. Committee work in the House of Representatives is usually more thorough than it is in the Senate; the committee in the Senate tends to be a "court of appeal" for agencies opposed to House action. Each committee, moreover, has about ten largely independent subcommittees, each reviewing the requests of a particular agency or a group of related functions. Specific appropriations bills are taken up by the subcommittees in hearings. Departmental officers answer questions on the conduct of their programs and defend their requests for the next fiscal year; lobbyists and other witnesses testify. While committees and subcommittees have broad discretion in allocating funds to the agencies they monitor, they must stay within overall totals set forth in the second budget resolution adopted by Congress.

*Appropriations Acts*   In examining the interactions between Congress and the federal bureaucracy over spending, it is important to distinguish between appropriations and authorization. An **authorization** is an act of Congress that establishes a government program and defines the amount of money it may spend. Authorizations may be for one or several years. However, an authorization does not actually provide the money that has been authorized; only an **appropriations act** can do that. In fact, appropriations acts, which are usually for a single fiscal year, are almost always *less* than authorizations; deciding how much less is the real function of the Appropriations Committees and subcommittees. (By its own rules, Congress cannot appropriate money for programs it has not already authorized.) Appropriations acts include both obligational authority and outlays.

**Obligational authority** permits a government agency to enter into contracts that will require the government to make payments beyond the fiscal years in question. **Outlays** must be spent in the fiscal year for which they are appropriated.

**Budget resolution:** A congressional bill setting forth target budget figures for appropriations to various government departments and agencies.

**Authorization:** An act of Congress that establishes a government program and defines the amount of money it may spend.

**Appropriations act:** A congressional bill that provides money for programs authorized by Congress.

**Obligational authority:** A feature of some appropriations acts by which an agency is empowered to enter into contracts that will require the government to make payments beyond the fiscal year in question.

**Outlays:** Actual dollar amounts to be spent by the federal government in a fiscal year.

*Continuing Resolutions and "Shutdowns"*   All appropriations acts *should* be passed by both houses and signed by the president into law before October 1, the date of the start of the fiscal year. However, it is rare for Congress to meet this deadline, so the government usually finds itself beginning a new fiscal year without a budget. Constitutionally, any U.S. government agency for which Congress does not pass an appropriations act may not draw money from the Treasury and thus is obliged to shut down. To get around this problem, Congress usually adopts a **continuing resolution** that authorizes government agencies to keep spending money for a specified period at the same level as in the previous fiscal year.

A continuing resolution is supposed to grant additional time for Congress to pass, and the president to sign, appropriations acts. But occasionally this process has broken down in the heat of political combat over the budget: the time period specified in a continuing resolution has expired without agreement on appropriations acts or even on a new continuing resolution. Shutdowns occurred during the bitter battle between President Bill Clinton and the Republican-controlled Congress over the Fiscal Year 1996 budget. In theory, the absence of either appropriations acts or a continuing resolution should cause the entire federal government to "shut down," that is, to cease all operations and expenditures for lack of funds. But in practice, such shutdowns have been only partial, affecting only "nonessential" government employees and causing relatively little disruption.

## THE POLITICS OF BUDGETING

Budgeting is very political. Being a good "bureaucratic politician" involves (1) cultivating a good base of support for requests among the public at large and among people served by the agency; (2) developing interest, enthusiasm, and support for one's program among top political figures and congressional leaders; (3) winning favorable coverage of agency activities in the media; and (4) following strategies that exploit opportunities[14] (see *Up Close:* "Bureaucratic Budget Strategies").

*Budgeting Is "Incremental"*   The most important factor determining the size and content of the budget each year is last year's budget. Decision makers generally use last year's expenditures as a *base*; active consideration of budget proposals generally focuses on new items and requested increases over last year's base. The budget of an agency is almost never reviewed as a whole. Agencies are seldom required to defend or explain budget requests that do *not* exceed current appropriations; but requested increases *do* require explanation and are most subject to reduction by OMB or Congress.

The result of **incremental budgeting** is that many programs, services, and expenditures continue long after there is any real justification for them. When new needs, services, and functions arise, they do not displace older ones but rather are *added* to the budget. Budget decisions are made incrementally because policy makers do not have the time, energy, or information to review every dollar of every budget request every year. Nor do policy makers wish to refight every political battle over existing programs every year. So they generally accept last year's base spending level as legitimate and focus attention on proposed increases for each program.

Reformers have proposed "sunset" laws requiring bureaucrats to justify their programs every five to seven years or else the programs go out of existence, as

**Continuing resolution:** A congressional bill that authorizes government agencies to keep spending money for a specified period at the same level as in the previous fiscal year; passed when Congress is unable to enact final appropriations measures by October 1.

**Incremental budgeting:** A method of budgeting that focuses on requested increases in funding for existing programs, accepting as legitimate their previous year's expenditures.

## Bureaucratic Budget Strategies

How do bureaucrats go about "maximizing" their resources? Some of the most common budgetary strategies of bureaucrats are listed below. It is important to remember that most bureaucrats believe strongly in the importance of their tasks; they pursue these strategies not only to increase their own power and prestige but also to better serve their client groups and the entire nation.

- *Spend it all:* Spend all of your current appropriation. Failure to use up an appropriation indicates that the full amount was unnecessary in the first place, which in turn implies that your budget should be cut next year.
- *Ask for more:* Never request a sum less than your current appropriation. It is easier to find ways to spend up to current appropriation levels than it is to explain why you want a reduction. Besides, a reduction indicates your program is not growing, and this is an embarrassing admission to most government administrators. Requesting an increase, at least enough to cover "inflation," demonstrates the continued importance of your program.
- *Put vital programs in the "base":* Put top-priority programs into the basic budget—that is, that part

of the budget that is within current appropriation levels. The Office of Management and Budget (OMB) and legislative committees will seldom challenge programs that appear to be part of existing operations.

- *Make new programs appear "incremental":* Requested increases should appear to be small and should appear to grow out of existing operations. Any appearance of a fundamental change in a budget should be avoided.
- *Give them something to cut:* Give the OMB and legislative committees something to cut. Normally it is desirable to submit requests for substantial increases in existing programs and many requests for new programs, in order to give higher political authorities something to cut. This approach enables authorities to "save" the public untold millions of dollars and justify their claim of promoting "economy" in government. Giving them something to cut also diverts attention from the basic budget with its vital programs.
- *Make cuts hurt:* If your agency is faced with a real budget cut—that is, a reduction from last year's appropriation—announce pending cuts in vital and popular programs in order to stir up opposition to the cut. For example, the National Park Service might announce the impending closing of the Washington Monument. Never acknowledge that cuts might be accommodated by your agency without reducing basic services.

well as **zero-based budgeting** that would force agencies to justify every penny requested—not just requested increases. In theory, sunset laws and zero-based budgeting would regularly prune unnecessary government programs, agencies, and expenditures and thus limit the growth of government and waste in government (see *What Do You Think?* "How Much Money Does the Government Waste?"). But in reality, sunset laws and zero-based budgeting require so much effort in justifying already accepted programs that executive agencies and legislative committees grow tired of the effort and return to incrementalism.

The "incremental" nature of budgetary politics helps reduce political conflicts and maintain stability in governmental programs. As bruising as budgetary battles are today, they would be much worse if the president or Congress undertook to review the value of *all* existing expenditures and programs each year. Comprehensive budgetary review would "overload the system" with political conflict by refighting every policy battle every year.[15]

**Zero-based budgeting:** A method of budgeting that demands justification for the entire budget request of an agency, not just its requested increase in funding.

# How Much Money Does the Government Waste?

Bureaucracy is often associated in the public's mind with waste and inefficiency. But it is very difficult to determine objectively how much money government really wastes. People disagree on the value of various government programs. What is "waste" to one person may be a vital governmental function to another. One very conservative south Georgia farmer once explained politics to his son: "There's only three things that government should ever do—defend our country in war, keep the highways paved, and provide the peanut allotment." But even those who believe a government program is necessary may still believe that some of the money going to that program is wasted by the bureaucracy.

Indeed, over the last twenty years, nearly two-thirds of Americans have described the government as wasting "a lot" of money rather than "some" or "not very much" (see graphs). Belief in the wastefulness of government rose during the Vietnam War and Watergate years, just as confidence and trust in government declined.

Is public opinion correct in estimating that "a lot" of money is wasted? The General Accounting Office is an arm of Congress with broad authority to audit the operations and finances of federal agencies. GAO audits have frequently found fraud and mismanagement amounting to 10 percent or more of the spending of many agencies it has reviewed, which suggests that $160 *billion* of the overall federal budget of $1.6 trillion may be wasted.* Citizens' commissions studying the federal bureaucracy place an even higher figure on waste. The Grace Commission estimated waste at more than 20 percent of federal spending, more than enough to eliminate annual deficits.**

*General Accounting Office, *Federal Evaluation Issues* (Washington, D.C.: General Accounting Office, 1989).
**President's Private Sector Survey on Cost Control* (Grace Commission Report) (Washington, D.C.: Government Printing Office, 1984).

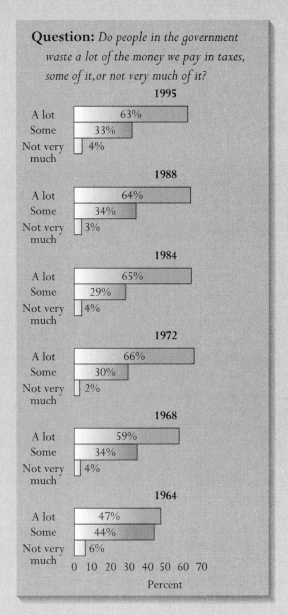

**Question:** *Do people in the government waste a lot of the money we pay in taxes, some of it, or not very much of it?*

*Source:* National Election Studies.

*Budgeting Is Nonprogrammatic*   Budgeting is *nonprogrammatic* in that an agency budget typically lists expenditures under ambiguous phrases: "personnel services," "contractual services," "travel," "supplies," "equipment." It is difficult to tell from such a listing exactly what programs the agency is spending its money on. Such a budget obscures policy decisions by hiding programs behind meaningless phrases. Even if these categories are broken down into line items (for example, under "personnel services," the line item budget might say, "John Doaks, Assistant Administrator, $65,000"), it is still next to impossible to identify the costs of various programs.

For many years, reformers have called for budgeting by programs. **Program budgeting** would require agencies to present budgetary requests in terms of the end products they will produce or at least to allocate each expense to a specific program. However, bureaucrats are often unenthusiastic about program budgeting; it certainly adds to the time and energy devoted to budgeting, and many agencies are reluctant to describe precisely what it is they do and how much it really costs to do it. Moreover, some political functions are best served by *nonprogram* budgeting. Agreement comes more easily when the items in dispute can be treated in dollars instead of programmatic differences. Congressional Appropriations Committees can focus on increases or decreases in overall dollar amounts for agencies rather than battle over even more contentious questions of what individual programs are worthy of support.

## REGULATORY BATTLES

Bureaucracies regulate virtually every aspect of American life. Interest rates on loans are heavily influenced by the Federal Reserve Board. The National Labor Relations Board protects unions and prohibits "unfair labor practices." Safety in automobiles and buses is the responsibility of the National Transportation Safety Board. The Federal Deposit Insurance Corporation insures bank accounts. The Federal Trade Commission orders cigarette manufacturers to place a health warning on each pack. The Equal Employment Opportunity Commission investigates complaints about racial and sexual discrimination in jobs. The Consumer Product Safety Commission requires that toys be large enough that they cannot be swallowed by children. The Federal Communications Commission bans tobacco advertisements on television. The Environmental Protection Agency requires automobile companies to limit exhaust emissions. The Occupational Safety and Health Administration requires construction firms to place portable toilets at work sites. The Food and Drug Administration decides what drugs your doctor can prescribe. The list goes on and on. Indeed, it is difficult to find an activity in public or private life that is not regulated by the federal government (see *A Conflicting View:* "Bureaucratic Rules Are Suffocating America").

Federal regulatory bureaucracies are legislators, investigators, prosecutors, judges, and juries—all wrapped into one. They issue thousands of pages of rules and regulations each year; they investigate thousands of complaints and conduct thousands of inspections; they require businesses to submit hundreds of thousands of forms each year; they hold hearings, determine "compliance" and "noncompliance," issue corrective orders, and levy fines and penalties. Most economists agree that regulation adds to the cost of living, is an obstacle to innovation and productivity, and hinders economic competition. Most regulatory commissions

**Program budgeting:** Identifying items in a budget according to the functions and programs they are to be spent on.

**Capture theory of regulation:** A theory describing how some regulated industries come to benefit from government regulation and how some regulatory commissions come to represent the industries they are supposed to regulate rather than representing "the people."

# Bureaucratic Rules Are Suffocating America

Today, bureaucratic regulations of all kinds—environmental controls, workplace safety rules, municipal building codes, government contracting guidelines—have become so numerous, detailed, and complex that they are stifling initiative, curtailing economic growth, wasting billions of dollars, and breeding popular contempt for law and government.

Consider, for example, the Environmental Protection Agency's rules and regulations, now *seventeen volumes* of fine print. Under one set of rules, before any land on which "toxic" waste was once used can be reused by anyone for any purpose, it must be cleaned to near perfect purity. The dirt must be made cleaner than soil that has never been used for anything. The result is that most new businesses choose to locate on virgin land rather than incur the enormous expense of cleaning dirt, and a great deal of land previously used by industry sits vacant while new land is developed.

Consider the plight of Mother Teresa and the Sisters of Charity who tried to renovate a vacant building in New York City to serve the homeless. Their renovation plan incorporated their own vow of poverty; they excluded dishwashers, automatic laundering machines, and elevators. The nuns were pledged to do those tasks by hand and to climb stairs to their own rooms on the third and fourth floors. But the New York City bureaucracy ruled that all new or renovated multifloor buildings must have elevators, adding $100,000 or more to the cost. After two years of bureaucratic hearings and appeals, Mother Teresa gave up the project: "The Sisters felt they could use the money much more usefully for soup and sandwiches."

These and similar examples of "the death of common sense" in bureaucratic regulations are set forth by critic Philip K. Howard, who argues that:

> Our regulatory system has become an instructional manual. It tells us and the bureaucrats exactly what to do and how to do it. Detailed rule after detailed rule addresses every eventuality or at least every situation that lawmakers and bureaucrats can think of. Is it a coincidence that almost every encounter with government is an exercise in frustration? . . . We have constructed a system of regulatory law that basically outlaws common sense.*

The result is that we direct our energy and wealth into defensive measures, designed not to improve our lives but to avoid tripping over senseless rules. People come to see government as their adversary and government regulations as obstacles in their lives.

Bureaucrats become more concerned with following rules than with promoting sensible outcomes. They seek to protect themselves by following detailed rules and by focusing on time-consuming and costly procedures (paperwork, forms, hearings, appeals, and delays) rather than the actual effect of their decisions. Following procedures substitutes for personal responsibility.

The remedy is to force both citizen and bureaucrat to take responsibility for achieving the goals set forth by law—that is, to use their judgment. This approach means granting greater discretion to bureaucrats in implementing the purposes of law and holding them accountable for outcomes. It means requiring them to use common sense, to be flexible and fair.

*Philip K. Howard, *The Death of Common Sense: How Law Is Suffocating America* (New York: Random House, 1995), pp. 10–11.

are independent; they are not under an executive department, and their members are appointed for long terms by a president who has little control over their activities.

*Traditional Agencies: Capture Theory*   The **capture theory of regulation** describes how some regulated industries come to benefit from government regulation and how some regulatory commissions come to represent the industries they are supposed to regulate rather than representing "the people." Historically, regulatory commissions have acted against only the most wayward members of an industry. By attacking those businesses that gave the industry bad publicity, the commissions actually helped improve the public's opinion of the industry as a whole. Regulatory commissions provided symbolic reassurance to the public that the behavior of the industry was proper. Among the traditional regulatory agencies that have been accused of becoming too close to their regulated industry are the Federal Communications Commission (FCC, the communications industry, including the television networks), the Securities and Exchange Commission (SEC, the securities industry and stock exchanges), the Federal Reserve Board (FRB, the banking industry), and National Labor Relations Board (NLRB, unions).

Close relationships between the regulatory bureaucracies and their client industries often arise from the government's need to obtain technical information and recruit experts. Commission members often come from the industry they are supposed to regulate, and after a few years in government, the "regulators" return to high-paying jobs in the industry, creating the *revolving door problem* described in Chapter 9. In addition, many regulatory commissions attract young attorneys fresh from law school to their staffs. Industry siphons off the "best and the brightest" of these, offering them much higher-paying jobs as defenders against government regulation.[16] In essence, taxpayers foot the bill to train people in the intricacies of government regulation, and these people then fight the agencies designed to protect those same taxpayers.

Over the years, then, some industries have come to support their regulatory bureaucracies. Industries have often strongly opposed proposals to reduce government controls. Proposals to deregulate railroads, interstate trucking, and airlines have met with substantial opposition from both the regulatory bureaucracies and the regulated industries, working together. Indeed, when President Ronald Reagan moved to abolish the Civil Aeronautics Board in 1984, it was the airline industry that objected most strongly.

*The Newer Regulators: The Activists*   In recent decades, Congress created several new "activist" regulatory agencies in response to the civil rights movement, the environmental movement, and the consumer protection movement. Unlike traditional regulatory agencies, the activist agencies do not regulate only a single industry; rather, they extend their jurisdiction to all industries. The Equal Employment Opportunity Commission (EEOC), the Environmental Protection Agency (EPA), and the Occupational Safety and Health Administration (OSHA) pose serious challenges to the business community. Many businesspeople argue that EEOC rules designed to prevent racial and sexual discrimination in employment and promotion (affirmative action guidelines) ignore the problems of their industry or their labor market and overlook the costs of training or the availability of qualified minorities and women. Likewise, many of OSHA's thousands of safety regulations appear costly and ridiculous to people in industry. The complaint about EPA is that it seldom considers the cost of its rulings to business or the consumer. Industry representatives contend that EPA should weigh the costs of its regulations against the benefits to the environment.

**Deregulation:** The lifting of government rules and bureaucratic supervision from business and professional activity.

*Deregulation*   The demand to deregulate American life was politically very popular in the 1980s, even though **deregulation** made only limited progress in curtailing the power of the regulatory bureaucracies. Arguments for deregulation centered on the heavy costs of compliance with regulations, the burdens these costs imposed on innovation and productivity, and the adverse impact of regulatory activity on the global competitiveness of American industry.

The costs of maintaining the regulatory bureaucracies is small compared with the costs incurred by businesses and consumers in complying with their regulations. The most common estimates of the costs of compliance run between $300 billion and $500 billion a year, or one-quarter of the federal budget. But these costs never appear on the federal budget. They are borne by private business and individual consumers (see *Up Close:* "The Invisible Costs of Regulation").

But deregulation has made very little progress in Washington. In 1978, Jimmy Carter succeeded in getting Congress to deregulate the airline industry. Against objections by the industry itself, which *wanted* continued regulation, the Civil Aeronautics Board was stripped of its powers to allocate airline routes to various carriers and to set rates. At the end of 1984, the board went out of existence, the first major regulatory agency ever to be abolished. With the airlines free to choose where to fly and what to charge, competition on heavily traveled routes (such as from New York to Los Angeles) reduced fares dramatically, while prices rose on less-traveled routes served by a single airline. Competition caused airline profits to decline and financially weak airlines to declare bankruptcy. Also, during the 1980s the Interstate Commerce Commission (ICC), the first regulatory commission ever established by the federal government, dating from 1887, was stripped of most of its power to set railroad and trucking rates. The ICC itself was finally abolished in 1995.

*Reregulation*    Deregulation threatens to diminish politicians' power and to eliminate bureaucrats' jobs. It forces industries to become competitive and diminishes the role of interest group lobbyists. So in the absence of strong popular support for deregulation, pressures to continue and expand regulatory activity will always be strong in Washington.

Airline deregulation brought about a huge increase in airline travel, from roughly 15 million passengers in 1980 to 42 million in 1990.[17] The airlines doubled their seating capacity and made more efficient use of their aircraft through the development of "hub-and-spoke" networks. Air safety continued to improve; fatalities per millions of miles flown declined; and by taking travelers away from far more dangerous highway travel, overall transportation safety was enhanced. But these favorable outcomes were overshadowed by complaints about congestion at major airports and increased flight delays, especially at peak hours. The major airports are publicly owned, and governments have been very slow in responding to increased air traffic. Congestion and delays are widely publicized, and politicians respond to complaints by calling for reregulation of airline travel.

Reregulation also gained impetus from the financial disaster in the savings and loan industry. During the 1970s, deregulation of the financial industry allowed savings and loan companies to expand well beyond their traditional function of providing home mortgage loans. Removing limits on the interest rates savings and loan firms could pay on deposits forced them to compete for depositors, which encouraged them to make riskier loans to recover their higher costs. But because the federal government guaranteed deposits (up to $100,000) through the Federal Deposit Insurance Corporation, the savings and loan companies were really risking money guaranteed by American taxpayers. Fraud and mismanagement played

*While deregulation of the airline industry has caused fares to decrease on heavily competitive routes, critics charge that it has contributed to higher rates on non-competitive routes as airlines struggle to make up for income lost on popular commutes. In addition, increased competition and fare wars have driven many airlines, small and large, into bankruptcy, decreasing competition in the industry and forcing thousands of workers into the unemployment lines.*

# The Invisible Costs of Regulation

The explosive growth in federal regulations in the last two decades has added heavy costs to the American economy. The costs of regulations do not appear in the federal budget: rather, they are paid for by businesses, employees, and consumers. Indeed, politicians prefer a regulatory approach to the environment, health, and safety precisely because it forces costs on the private sector—costs that are largely invisible to voters and taxpayers. Yet as the costs of regulation multiply for American businesses, the prices of their products rise in world markets. Unless other nations place similar restrictions on their businesses, American firms face a competitive disadvantage.

How large is the regulatory bill? Proponents of a regulatory activity usually object to estimating its cost. Politicians who wish to develop an image as protectors of the environment, of consumers, of the disabled, and so on do not want to call attention to the costs of their legislation. Only recently has the Office of Management and Budget even attempted to estimate the costs of federal regulatory activity. Overall, regulatory activity costs Americans between $300 billion and $500 billion a year, an amount equal to about one-quarter of the total federal budget. This means that each of America's 100 million households pays about $4,000 per year in the hidden costs of regulation. Paperwork requirements consume more than 5 billion hours of people's time, mostly to comply with the administration by the Internal Revenue Service of the tax laws. However, the costs of environmental controls, including the Environmental Protection Agency's enforcement of clean air and water and hazardous waste disposal regulations, are the fastest-growing regulatory costs.

The real question is whether the *benefits* of this regulatory activity—for example, cleaner air and water, safer disposal of toxic wastes, safer consumer products, fewer workplace injuries, fewer highway deaths, protections against discrimination, improved access for disabled, and so on—are greater or less than the costs. But assessing the value of benefits is extraordinarily difficult. Many people object on ethical grounds to economic estimates of the value of a human life saved.

Regulation places a heavy burden on innovations and productivity. The costs and delays in winning permission for a new product tend to discourage invention and to drive up prices. For example, new drugs are difficult to introduce in the United States because the Food and Drug Administration (FDA) typically requires up to ten years of testing. Western European nations are many years ahead in their number of life-saving drugs available; they speak of the "drug lag" in the United States. Critics charge that if aspirin were proposed for marketing today, it would not be approved by the FDA. Recently activists have succeeded in speeding up FDA approval of drugs to treat AIDS, but the agency has continued to delay the introduction of drugs to treat other diseases.

Competition declines when regulatory bureaucracies license and limit entry into a field. The cost of complying with federal reporting requirements is an obstacle to the survival of small businesses. And larger businesses must cope with reams of reports on employee relations, taxes, Social Security, affirmative action, occupational safety and health, environmental impact, and so on. Only the largest corporations have high-priced legal staffs prepared to do battle with the regulators, and only the largest corporations can afford the expensive delays involved in obtaining governmental approval. But all of these costs and delays hurt American business in global competition with foreign firms that do not confront these obstacles.

a role in the disaster, but the real problem was the "moral hazard" created by allowing these companies free rein with government-guaranteed funds. (If the U.S. government is going to guarantee deposits, then it must regulate their use. Or alternatively, if the financial industry is to be deregulated, then the government must also end its deposit insurance.) The federal government was obliged to spend about $200 billion to "bail out" the savings and loan industry and to reimburse insured depositors for their losses. The savings and loan disaster has resulted in tightened federal regulation of banking and savings institutions.

# CONGRESSIONAL CONSTRAINTS ON THE BUREAUCRACY

Bureaucracies are unelected hierarchical organizations, yet they must function within democratic government. To wed bureaucracy to democracy, ways must be found to ensure that bureaucracy is responsible to the people. Controlling the bureaucracy is a central concern of democratic government.

The federal bureaucracy is responsible to all three branches of government—the president, the Congress, and the courts. While the president is the nominal head of the executive agencies, Congress—through its power to create or eliminate and fund or fail to fund these agencies—exerts its full share of control.

Most of the structure of the executive branch of government (see Figure 12-1) is determined by laws of Congress. Congress has the constitutional power to create or abolish executive departments and independent agencies, or to transfer their functions, as it wishes. Congress can by law expand or contract the discretionary authority of bureaucrats. It can grant broad authority to agencies in vaguely written language—thereby adding to the power of bureaucracies, which can then determine themselves how to define and implement their own authority. In contrast, narrow and detailed laws place constraints on the bureaucracy.

In addition to specific constraints on particular agencies, Congress has placed a number of general constraints on the entire federal bureaucracy. Among the more important laws governing bureaucratic behavior are:

- *Administrative Procedures Act* (1946): Requires that agencies considering a new rule or policy give public notice in the *Federal Register,* solicit comments, and hold public hearings before adopting the new measures.
- *Freedom of Information Act* (1966): Requires agencies to allow citizens (and the media) to inspect all public records, with some exceptions for intelligence, current criminal investigations, and personnel actions.
- *Privacy Act* (1974): Requires agencies to keep confidential the personal records of individuals, notably their Social Security files and income tax records.

*Senate Confirmation of Appointments*   The U.S. Senate's power to confirm presidential appointments gives it some added influence over the bureaucracy.[18] It is true that once nominated and confirmed, cabinet secretaries and regulatory commission members can defy the Congress; only the president can remove them from office. Senators usually try to impress their own views upon presidential appointees seeking confirmation, however. Senate committees holding confirmation hearings often subject appointees to lengthy lectures on how the members believe their departments or agencies should be run. In extreme cases, when presidential appointees do not sufficiently reflect the views of Senate leaders, their confirmation can be held up indefinitely or, in very rare cases, defeated in a floor vote on confirmation.

*Congressional Oversight*   Congressional oversight of the federal bureaucracy is a continuing activity.[19] Congress justifies its oversight activities on the ground that its lawmaking powers require it to determine whether the purposes of the laws it passed are being carried out. Congress has a legitimate interest in communicating legislative *intent* to bureaucrats charged with the responsibility of implementing laws of Congress. But often oversight activities are undertaken to influence bureaucratic decision making. Members of Congress may seek to secure favorable treatment for friends and constituents, try to lay the political groundwork for increases or decreases in agency appropriations, or simply strive to enhance their own power or the power of their committees or subcommittees over the bureaucracy.

Oversight is lodged primarily in congressional committees and subcommittees (see "In Committee" in Chapter 10) whose jurisdictions generally parallel those of executive departments and agencies. However, all too frequently, agencies are required to respond to multiple committee inquiries in both the House and the Senate. For example, the secretary of defense may be called to testify before both the House National Security and Senate Armed Forces committees, as well as the Defense Appropriations subcommittees of both the House and Senate Appropriations Committees, the Government Operations Committee of the House and the Senate Governmental Affairs Committee overseeing defense contracts, and the Senate Foreign Relations and House Foreign Affairs Committees. But the committee system in Congress often results in the development of close relationships between specific committees and subcommittees and their staffs and particular departments and agencies (see "Iron Triangles and Policy Networks" in Chapter 9).

Congressional committee hearings are a major form of oversight activity. Agency officials may be called to testify before congressional committees or subcommittees to explain their actions, decisions, and policies. Bureaucrats are reluctant to argue with members of Congress, even when their bureaucratic actions or policies are well within the authority previously granted them by laws of Congress. Bureaucrats know that angry members of Congress, especially committee and subcommittee chairs, can undertake to rewrite the laws governing the authority of the agency or, worse, that an angry Congress can cut the agency's requested budget appropriations.

*Congressional Appropriations*   The congressional power to grant or to withhold the budget requests of bureaucracies and the president is perhaps Congress's most potent weapon in controlling the bureaucracy. Spending authorizations for executive agencies are determined by standing committees with jurisdiction in various policy areas, such as armed services, judiciary, education, and labor (see Table 10-4), while appropriations are determined by the House and Senate Appropriations Committees, and more specifically their subcommittees with particular jurisdictions. These committees and subcommittees exercise great power over executive agencies. The Defense Department, for example, must seek *authorizations* for new weapons systems from the House and Senate Armed Services Committees and *appropriations* to actually purchase these weapons from the House and Senate Appropriations Committees, especially their Defense Appropriations subcommittees.

Congress frequently undertakes to control the specific policies and actions of executive agencies through strings it attaches to appropriations measures. Con-

*Attorney General Janet Reno holds a gas mask as she answers questions from a House committee investigating the Justice Department's handling of the 1993 raid on the Branch Davidian compound in Waco, Texas.*

gressional committees and subcommittees may write detailed instructions into appropriations acts about how money is to be spent, thus denying either the president or the bureaucracy any real discretion in implementing programs. For example, in some cases, the Defense Department has been forced to buy weapons it does not need or want simply because an influential member of Congress wrote a pork-barrel provision into the defense appropriations act.

*Congressional Investigation*   Congressional investigations offer yet another tool for congressional oversight of the bureaucracy. Historically, congressional investigations have focused on scandal and wrongdoing in the executive branch (see "Oversight of the Bureaucracy" in Chapter 10). Occasionally, investigations even produce corrective legislation, although they more frequently produce changes in agency personnel, procedures, or policies. Investigations are more likely to follow media reports of waste, fraud, or scandal than to uncover previously unknown problems. In other words, investigations perform a political function for Congress—assuring voters that the Congress is taking action against bureaucratic abuses. Studies of routine bureaucratic performance are likely to be undertaken by the General Accounting Office (GAO), an arm of Congress and frequent critic of executive agencies. GAO may undertake studies of the operations of executive agencies on its own initiative but more often responds to requests for studies by specific members of Congress.

*Casework*   Perhaps the most frequent congressional oversight activities are calls, letters, and visits to the agencies by individual members of Congress seeking to influence particular actions on behalf of themselves or their constituents. A great deal of congressional **casework** involves intervening with executive agencies on behalf of constituents[20] (see Chapter 10). Executive departments and agencies generally try to deal with congressional requests and inquiries as favorably and rapidly as the law allows. Pressure from a congressional office will lead bureaucrats to speed up an application, correct an error, send information, review a case, or reinterpret a regulation to favor a client with congressional contacts. But bureaucrats become very uncomfortable when asked to violate established regulations on behalf of a favored person or firm (see *Up Close:* "The Keating Five: Service to Constituents, for a Price?" in Chapter 10). The line between serving constituents and unethical or illegal attempts to influence government agencies is sometimes very difficult to discern.

*The Legislative Veto*   Congress has employed the legislative veto from time to time in an effort to control bureaucratic and presidential actions. A **legislative veto** is a provision in a law that requires executive agencies to submit regulations or actions to the Congress before they take effect and allows Congress to veto them by passing a resolution in *either* one or both houses. The purpose of the legislative veto is to allow Congress to review and reverse executive decisions. Congress has most often used the legislative veto to involve itself in specific arms sales to foreign countries.

In 1983, the case of the *Immigration and Naturalization Service v. Chadha*,[21] however, the Supreme Court held that no congressional resolution has the force of law unless signed by the president (or passed over a presidential veto by a two-thirds vote of both houses). The constitutional separation of powers and checks and balances does not allow the Congress to bypass the president's veto power over legislation. If Congress wants an executive agency to refrain from taking a particular

**Casework:** Services performed by legislators and their staffs on behalf of individual constituents.

**Legislative veto:** A provision in a law that requires executive agencies to submit regulations or actions to the Congress before they take effect and allows Congress to veto them by passing a resolution in either one or both houses; struck down by the Supreme Court.

*Lobbying Washington can take many forms. While most professional lobbyists operate quietly within the halls of the nation's capital, groups of private citizens often take to the streets to get their message across. But while demonstrations may capture the attention of the media, and thus may force bureaucrats and politicians at least to consider a group's cause, the attention span of both media and Washington power-brokers can be extremely short. Here people with disabilities demonstrate in front of the White House for continued support of attendant care.*

action or making a particular rule, it must pass a bill to do so and send that bill to the president for signing. Note, however, that the *Chadha* decision does not prevent Congress from requiring the president or an executive agency to submit plans and proposals to Congress and allow Congress time to pass a *law* preventing their implementation. Nor does it prevent Congress from simply pressing executive agencies to rescind proposed rules or actions by threatening to reduce appropriations or curtail authority in the future.

## INTEREST GROUPS AND BUREAUCRATIC DECISION MAKING

Interest groups understand that great power is lodged in the bureaucracy. Indeed, interest groups exercise an even closer oversight of bureaucracy than do the president, Congress, and courts—largely because their interests are directly affected by day-to-day bureaucratic decisions. Interest groups focus their attention on the particular departments and agencies that serve or regulate their own members or that function in their chosen policy field. For example, the American Farm Bureau Federation monitors the actions of the Department of Agriculture; environmental lobbies—such as the National Wildlife Federation, the Sierra Club, and the Environmental Defense Fund—watch over the Environmental Protection Agency as well as the National Park Service; the American Legion, Veterans of Foreign Wars, and Vietnam Veterans "oversee" the Department of Veterans Affairs. Thus specific groups come to have a proprietary interest in "their" specific departments and agencies. Departments and agencies understand that their "client" groups have a continuing interest in their activities.

Many bureaucracies owe their very existence to strong interest groups that successfully lobbied Congress to create them. The Environmental Protection Agency owes its existence to the environmental groups, just as the Equal Employment Opportunity Commission owes its existence to civil rights groups. Thus, many bureaucracies nourish interest groups' support to aid in expanding their authority and increasing their budgets (see "Iron Triangles and Policy Networks" in Chapter 9).

Interest groups can lobby bureaucracies directly by responding to notices of proposed regulations, testifying at public hearings, and providing information and commentary. Or interest groups can lobby Congress either in support of bureaucratic activity or to reverse a bureaucratic decision. Interest groups may also seek to "build fires" under bureaucrats by holding press conferences, undertaking advertising campaigns, and soliciting media support for agency actions. Or interest groups may even seek to influence bureaucracies through appeals to the federal courts.

## JUDICIAL CONSTRAINTS ON THE BUREAUCRACY

Judicial oversight is another source of restraint on the bureaucracy. Bureaucratic decisions are subject to review by the federal courts. Federal courts can even issue *injunctions* (orders) to an executive agency *before* it issues or enforces a regulation or undertakes a particular action. Thus the judiciary poses a check upon bureaucratic power.

*Judicial Standards of Bureaucratic Behavior*   Historically, the courts have stepped in when agency actions have violated laws passed by Congress, when agencies have exceeded the authority granted them under the laws, when the agency actions have been adjudged "arbitrary and unreasonable," and when agencies have failed in their legal duties under the law. The courts have also restrained the bureaucracy on procedural grounds—ensuring proper notice, fair hearings, rights of appeal, and so on. In short, appeal to the courts must cite failures of agencies to abide by substantive or procedural laws.

Judicial oversight tends to focus on (1) whether or not agencies are acting beyond the authority granted them by Congress; and (2) whether or not they are abiding by rules of procedural fairness. It is important to realize that the courts do not usually involve themselves in the *policy* decisions of bureaucracies. If policy decisions are made in accordance with the legal authority granted agencies by Congress, and if they are made with procedural fairness, the courts generally do not intervene.

*Bureaucrats' Success in Court*   Bureaucracies have been very successful in defending their actions in federal courts. Individual citizens and interest groups seeking to restrain or reverse the actions or decisions of executive agencies have been largely *un*successful. One study reported that the Federal Trade Commission won 91 percent of the cases they argued before the Supreme Court; the National Labor Relations Board won 75 percent; and the Internal Revenue Service won 73 percent. Only the Immigration and Naturalization Service had a mediocre record of 56 percent.[22] Independent agencies enjoy greater support from the courts than cabinet departments.[23]

What accounts for this success? Bureaucracies have established elaborate administrative processes to protect their decisions from challenge on procedural grounds. Regulatory agencies have armies of attorneys, paid for out of tax monies, who specialize in these narrow fields of law. It is very expensive for individual citizens to challenge agency actions. Corporations and interest groups must weigh the costs of litigation against the costs of compliance before undertaking a legal challenge of the bureaucracy. Excessive delays in court proceedings, sometimes extending to several years, add to the time and expense of challenging bureaucratic decisions.

# SUMMARY NOTES

- The Washington bureaucracy—the departments, agencies, and bureaus of the executive branch of the federal government—is a major base of power in American government. Political conflict does not end when a law is passed by Congress and signed by the president. The arena merely shifts to the bureaucracy.

- Bureaucratic power has grown with increases in the size of government, advances in technology, and the greater complexity of modern society. Congress and the president do not have the time, resources, or expertise to decide the details of policy across the wide range of social and economic activity in the nation. Bureaucracies must draw up the detailed rules and regulations that actually govern the nation. Often laws are passed for their symbolic value; bureaucrats must give practical meaning to these laws. And the bureaucracy itself is not sufficiently powerful to get laws passed adding to its authority, size, and budget.

- Policy implementation is the development of procedures and activities and the allocation of money, personnel, and other resources to carry out the tasks mandated by law. Implementation includes regulation—the making of detailed rules based upon the law—as well as adjudication—the application of laws and regulations to specific cases. Bureaucratic power increases with increases in administrative discretion.

- Bureaucracies usually seek to expand their own powers, functions, and budgets. Most bureaucrats believe strongly in the value of their own programs and the importance of their tasks. And bureaucrats, like everyone else, seek added power, pay, and prestige. Bureaucratic expansion contributes to the growth of government.

- The federal bureaucracy consists of 2.8 million civilian employees in fourteen cabinet departments and more than sixty independent agencies, as well as a large Executive Office of the President. Federal employment is not growing, but federal spending, especially for entitlement programs, is growing rapidly. Today federal spending amounts to more than 23 percent of GDP, and federal, state, and local government spending combined amounts to about 35 percent of GDP.

- Historically, political conflict over government employment centered on the question of partisanship versus competence. Over time, the "merit system" replaced the "spoils system" in federal employment, but the civil service system raised problems of responsiveness and productivity in the bureaucracy. Civil service reform efforts have not really resolved these problems.

- The president's control of the bureaucracy rests principally on the powers to appoint and remove policy-making officials, to recommend increases and decreases in agency budgets, and to recommend changes in agency structure and function.

- But the bureaucracy has developed various means to insulate itself from presidential influence. Bureaucrats have many ways to delay and obstruct policy decisions with which they disagree. Whistleblowers may inform Congress or the media of waste, mis-

management, or fraud. A network of friends and professional associates among bureaucrats, congressional staffs, and client groups helps create a "culture" within each agency and department. The bureaucratic culture is highly resistant to change.

- Women and minorities are represented in overall federal employment in proportion to their percentages of the U.S. population. However, women and minorities are not proportionately represented in the higher levels of the bureaucracy.

- Budget battles over who gets what begin in the bureaucracy as departments and agencies send their budget requests forward to the president's Office of Management and Budget. OMB usually reduces agency requests in line with the president's priorities. The president submits spending recommendations to Congress early each year in the Budget of the United States Government. Congress is supposed to pass its appropriations acts prior to the beginning of the fiscal year, October 1, but frequently falls behind schedule.

- Budgeting is incremental, in that last year's agency expenditures are usually accepted as a base and attention is focused on proposed increases. Incrementalism saves time and effort and reduces political conflict by not requiring agencies to justify every dollar spent, only proposed increases each year. Nonprogrammatic budgeting also helps reduce conflict over the value of particular programs. The result, however, is that many established programs continue long after the need for them has disappeared.

- Bureaucracies regulate virtually every aspect of our lives. The costs of regulation are borne primarily by business and consumers; they do not appear in the federal budget. In part for this reason, a regulatory approach to national problems appeals to elected officials who seek to obscure the costs of government activity. It is difficult to calculate the true costs and benefits of much regulatory activity. After a brief period of deregulation in the 1980s, regulation has regained popular favor.

- Congress can exercise control over the bureaucracy in a variety of ways: by creating, abolishing, or reorganizing departments and agencies; by altering their authority and functions; by requiring bureaucrats to testify before congressional committees; by undertaking investigations and studies through the General Accounting Office; by intervening directly on behalf of constituents; by instructing presidential nominees in Senate confirmation hearings and occasionally delaying or defeating nominations; and especially by withholding or threatening to withhold agency appropriations or by writing very specific provisions into appropriations acts.

• Interest groups also influence bureaucratic decision making directly by testifying at public hearings and providing information and commentary, and indi-rectly by contacting the media, lobbying Congress, and initiating lawsuits.

• Judicial control of the bureaucracy is usually limited to determining whether agencies have exceeded the authority granted them by law or have abided by the rules of procedural fairness. Federal bureaucracies have a strong record of success in defending themselves in court.

## SELECTED READINGS

BENNETT, LINDA M., and STEPHEN E. BENNETT. *Living with Leviathan.* Lawrence, Kans.: University of Kansas Press, 1990. An analysis of public opinion regarding the size and power of government in America; it argues that partisan identification and liberal-conservative ideological orientations are not as important in determining attitudes toward governmental power as trust and confidence in government and ideas about what government should do.

DERTHICK, MARTHA. *Agency under Stress: The Social Security Administration in American Government.* Washington, D.C.: Brookings Institution, 1990. An examination of how political conflicts between interest groups and their constituencies lead to vague and contradictory laws that make agency implementation prone to failure. The author focuses on the political conflicts surrounding Social Security disability review during the 1980s.

GORE, AL. *Creating a Government That Works Better and Costs Less.* Washington, D.C.: Government Printing Office, 1993. Specific recommendations for "reinventing" government by making citizens "customers," introducing competition, cutting red tape, and privatizing government services.

GORMLY, WILLIAM T. *Taming the Bureaucracy.* Princeton, N.J.: Princeton University Press, 1989. An examination of the formal and informal controls over the bureaucracy by the president, Congress, interest groups, and the courts, with a discussion of the problems of making the bureaucracy accountable and proposals for reform.

HOWARD, PHILIP K. *The Death of Common Sense: How Law Is Suffocating America.* New York: Random House, 1995. Outrageous stories of bureaucratic senselessness coupled with a plea to allow bureaucrats flexibility in achieving the purposes of laws and holding them accountable for outcomes.

JOHNSON, RONALD N., and GARY D. LIBECAP. *The Federal Civil Service System and the Problem of Bureaucracy.* Chicago: University of Chicago Press, 1994. A convincing argument that civil service was not a product of a moral crusade by reformers against politicians but rather a result of presidents and Congresses competing to maximize their power.

ROURKE, FRANCIS E. *Bureaucracy, Politics and Public Policy.* 4th ed. Boston: Little, Brown, 1988. A classic examination of the power of the bureaucracy in policy making: its sources of power in expertise, advice, and discretion; and its ability to mobilize clientele groups and the public to influence the president and Congress. Updated with discussions of "antibureaucratic ferment" and the resiliency of bureaucracies.

SCHICK, ALLEN. *The Federal Budget: Politics, Policy, Process.* Washington, D.C.: Brookings Institution, 1995. A comprehensive explanation of the federal budgetary process.

WILDAVSKY, AARON. *The New Politics of the Budgetary Process.* Glenview, Ill.: Scott Foresman, 1988. The revised version of the classic work on politics and incrementalism in budgeting, including strategies by bureaucrats, the Office of Management and Budget, the president, and Congress, with emphasis on the collapse of political consensus, the entitlements problem, and the failure of budget-balancing efforts.

WILSON, JAMES Q. *Bureaucracy: What Government Agencies Do and Why They Do It.* New York: Basic Books, 1989. In the author's words, "an effort to depict the essential features of bureaucratic life in the government agencies of the United States." Examining what really motivates middle-level public servants, Wilson argues that congressional attempts to "micromanage" government activities hamper the ability of bureaucrats to do their jobs.

# COURTS
# JUDICIAL POLITICS

## CHAPTER OUTLINE

## FEATURES

## JUDICIAL POWER

"There is hardly a political question in the United States which does not sooner or later turn into a judicial one."[1] This observation by French diplomat and traveler Alexis de Tocqueville, though made in 1835, is even more accurate today. It is the Supreme Court and the federal judiciary, rather than the president or Congress, that has taken the lead in deciding many of the most heated issues of American politics. It has undertaken to:

- Eliminate racial segregation and decide about affirmative action
- Ensure separation of church and state and decide about prayer in public schools
- Determine the personal liberties of women and decide about abortion
- Define the limits of free speech and free press and decide about obscenity, censorship, and pornography
- Ensure equality of representation and require legislative districts to be equal in population

## ASK YOURSELF ABOUT POLITICS

**1** Have the federal courts grown too powerful?
Yes ☐  No ☐

**2** Is it really democratic to allow federal court judges, who are appointed, not elected, and serve for life, to overturn laws of an elected Congress and president?
Yes ☐  No ☐

**3** Should the Constitution be interpreted in terms of the original intentions of the Founders rather than the morality of society today?
Yes ☐  No ☐

**4** Should Congress limit monetary awards in lawsuits to actual losses and prohibit multimillion-dollar awards for "pain and suffering"?
Yes ☐  No ☐

**5** Should a president appoint only judges who agree with his judicial philosophy?
Yes ☐  No ☐

**6** Should the Senate confirm Supreme Court appointees who oppose abortion?
Yes ☐  No ☐

**7** Should the Supreme Court be able to decide whether or not there can be organized prayer in schools?
Yes ☐  No ☐

Do the Supreme Court and the federal judiciary in fact have the real power to shape public policies in the United States?

- Define the rights of criminal defendants, prevent unlawful searches, limit the questioning of suspects, and prevent physical or mental intimidation of suspects
- Decide the life-or-death issue of capital punishment

Courts are "political" institutions. Like Congress, the president, and the bureaucracy, courts decide who gets what in American society. Judges do not merely "apply" the law to specific cases. Years ago, former Supreme Court Justice Felix Frankfurter explained why this mechanistic theory of judicial objectivity fails to describe court decision making:

> The meaning of "due process" and the content of terms like "liberty" are not revealed by the Constitution. It is the Justices who make the meaning. They read into the neutral language of the Constitution their own economic and social views. . . . Let us face the fact that five Justices of the Supreme Court are the molders of policy rather than the impersonal vehicles of revealed truth.[2]

*Constitutional Power*   The Constitution grants "the judicial Power of the United States" to the Supreme Court and other "inferior Courts" that Congress may establish. The Constitution guarantees that the Supreme Court and federal judiciary will be politically independent: judges are appointed, not elected, and hold their appointments for life (barring commission of any impeachable offenses). It also guarantees that their salaries will not be reduced during their time in office. The Constitution goes on to list the kinds of cases and controversies that the federal courts may decide. The list is very broad; almost any issue can become a federal case. Federal judicial power extends to any case arising under the Constitution and federal laws and treaties, to cases in which officials of the federal government or of foreign governments are a party, and to cases between states or between citizens of different states.

*Interpreting the Constitution: Judicial Review*   The Constitution is the "supreme Law of the Land" (Article VI). Judicial power is the power to decide cases and controversies and, in doing so, to decide what the Constitution and laws of Congress really mean. This authority—together with the guaranteed independence of judges—places great power in the Supreme Court and the federal judiciary. Indeed, because the Constitution takes precedence over laws of Congress as well as state constitutions and laws, it is the Supreme Court that ultimately decides whether Congress, the president, the states, and their local governments have acted constitutionally.

The power of **judicial review** is the power to invalidate laws of Congress or of the states that conflict with the U.S. Constitution. Judicial review is not specifically mentioned in the Constitution but has long been inferred from it. Even before the states had approved the Constitution, Alexander Hamilton wrote in his 1787 support of that document that "limited government . . . can be preserved in practice no other way than through the medium of courts of justice, whose duty it is to declare all acts contrary to the manifest tenor of the Constitution void."[3] But it was the historic decision of *Marbury v. Madison* (1803)[4] that officially established judicial review as the most important judicial check on congressional power (see *People in Politics:* "John Marshall and Early Supreme Court Politics"). Writing for the majority, Chief Justice Marshall constructed a classic statement in

**Judicial review:** The power of the courts, especially the Supreme Court, to declare laws of Congress, laws of the states, and actions of the president unconstitutional and invalid.

# John Marshall and Early Supreme Court Politics

John Marshall was a dedicated Federalist. A prominent Virginia lawyer, he was elected a delegate to Virginia's Constitution-ratifying convention, where he was instrumental in winning his state's approval of the document in 1788. Later Marshall served as secretary of state in the administration of John Adams, where he came into conflict with Adams's vice-president, Thomas Jefferson.

In the election of 1800, Jefferson's Democratic-Republicans crushed Adams's Federalist Party. But Adams, taking advantage of the fact that his term of office would not expire until the following March,* sought to pack the federal judiciary with Federalists. The lame-duck Federalist majority in the Senate confirmed the appointments, and John Marshall was sworn in as Chief Justice of the Supreme Court on February 4, 1801. Many of these "midnight appointments" came at the very last hours of Adams's term of office.

At that time, a specified task of the secretary of state was to deliver judicial commissions to new judges. When Marshall left his position as secretary of state to become Chief Justice, several of these commissions were still undelivered. Jefferson and the Democratic-Republicans were enraged over this last-minute Federalist chicanery, so when Jefferson assumed office in March, he ordered his new secretary of state, James Madison, not to deliver the remaining commissions. William Marbury, one of the disappointed Federalist appointees, brought a lawsuit to the Supreme Court, asking it to issue a writ of mandamus ("we command") to James Madison, ordering him to do his duty and deliver the valid commission.

The Judiciary Act of 1789, which established the federal court system, had included a provision granting original jurisdiction to the Supreme Court to issue writs of mandamus. The case, therefore, came directly to new Chief Justice John Marshall, who had failed to deliver the commission in the first place. (Today, we expect justices who are personally involved in a case to "recuse" themselves—that is, not to participate in that case, allowing the other justices to make the decision—but Marshall's actions were typical of his time.)

John Marshall realized that if he issued a direct order to Madison to deliver the commission, Madison would probably ignore it. The Court had no way to enforce such an order, and Madison had the support of President Jefferson. Issuing the writ would create a constitutional crisis in which the Supreme Court would most likely lose power. On the other hand, if the Court failed to pronounce Madison's actions unlawful, it would lose legitimacy.

Marshall resolved his political dilemma with a brilliant judicial ploy. Writing for the majority in *Marbury v. Madison,* he announced that Madison was wrong to withhold the commission but that the Supreme Court could not issue a writ of mandamus because Section 13 of the Judiciary Act of 1789, which gave the Court original jurisdiction in the case, was unconstitutional. Giving the Supreme Court *original* jurisdiction conflicted with Article III, Section 2, of the Constitution, which gives the Supreme Court original jurisdiction only in cases affecting "Ambassadors, other public Ministers and Consuls, and those in which a State shall be a Party." "In all other Cases," the Constitution states that the Court shall have appellate jurisdiction. Thus, Section 13 of the Judiciary Act was unconstitutional.

By declaring part of an act of Congress unconstitutional, Marshall accomplished multiple political objectives. He avoided a showdown with the executive branch that would undoubtedly have weakened the Court. He left Jefferson and Madison with no Court order to disobey. At the same time, Marshall forced Jefferson and the Democratic-Republicans to acknowledge the Supreme Court's power of judicial review—the power to declare an act of Congress unconstitutional. (To do otherwise would have meant acknowledging Marbury's claim.) Thus Marshall sacrificed Marbury's commission to a greater political goal—enhancing the Supreme Court's power.

*Not until the adoption of the Twentieth Amendment in 1933 was the president's inauguration moved up to January.

judicial reasoning as he proceeded step by step to infer judicial review from the Constitution's Supremacy (Article VI) and Judicial Power (Article III, Section 1) Clauses:

- The Constitution is the supreme law of the land, binding on all branches of government: legislative, executive, and judicial.
- The Constitution deliberately establishes a government with limited powers.
- Consequently, "an act of the legislature repugnant to the Constitution is void." If this were not true, the government would be unchecked and the Constitution would be an absurdity.
- Under the judicial power, "It is emphatically the province and duty of each of the judicial departments to say what the law is."
- "So if a law be in opposition to the Constitution . . . the court must determine which of these conflicting rules governs the case. This is the very essence of judicial duty."
- "If, then, the courts are to regard the Constitution, and the Constitution is superior to any ordinary act of the legislature, the Constitution, and not such ordinary act, must govern the case to which they both apply."
- Hence, if a law is repugnant to the Constitution, the judges are duty bound to declare that law void in order to uphold the supremacy of the Constitution.

The power of the federal courts to invalidate *state* laws and constitutions that conflict with federal laws or the federal Constitution is easily defended. Article VI states that the Constitution and federal laws and treaties are the supreme law of the land, "any Thing in the Constitution or Laws of any State to the Contrary notwithstanding." Indeed, the Constitution specifically obligates state judges to be "bound" by the Constitution and federal laws and to give these documents precedence over state constitutions and laws in rendering decisions. Federal court power over state decisions is probably essential to maintaining national unity: fifty different state interpretations of the meaning of the Constitution or of the laws and treaties of Congress would create unimaginable confusion. Thus, the power of federal judicial review over state constitutions, laws, and court decisions is seldom questioned.

Today, the power of federal courts to invalidate laws of Congress and actions of the president is also widely accepted. No serious challenge to the power of judicial review has emerged in American politics. But we still might ask: Why should an appointed court's interpretation of the Constitution prevail over the views of an elected Congress and an elected president? Members of Congress and presidents swear to uphold the Constitution, and we can assume that they do not pass laws they believe to be unconstitutional. Since both houses of Congress and the president must approve laws, why should federal courts be allowed to set aside these decisions? Is not judicial review, especially by unelected justices appointed for life, undemocratic?

*The Use of Judicial Review*  Judicial review is potentially the most powerful weapon in the hands of the Supreme Court. It enables the Court to assert its power over the Congress, the president, and the states and to substitute its own

| Years | Federal Laws | State Laws |
|---|---|---|
| 1790–99 | 0 | 0 |
| 1800–39 | 1 | 19 |
| 1840–59 | 1 | 16 |
| 1860–99 | 20 | 141 |
| 1900–39 | 43 | 300 |
| 1940–69 | 23 | 267 |
| 1970–89 | 36 | 352 |
| 1990–94 | 3 | 31 |

*Source:* Harold W. Stanley and Richard G. Niemi, eds., *Vital Statistics on American Politics,* 5th ed. (Washington, D.C.: Congressional Quarterly Press, 1995), p. 286.

judgment for that of other branches of the federal government and the states. However, the Supreme Court has been fairly restrained in its use of judicial review to void acts of Congress. Prior to the Civil War, the Supreme Court invalidated very few laws of any kind. Since that time, however, the general trend has been for the U.S. Supreme Court to strike down more *state* laws as unconstitutional. In contrast, the Court has been relatively restrained in its rejection of *federal* laws. Indeed, since *Marbury v. Madison,* the Court has overturned only about 127 federal laws in whole or in part (see Table 13-1), a very tiny fraction of the more than 60,000 laws passed by Congress over two centuries.

Nevertheless, some of the laws overturned by the Supreme Court have been very important. In 1857, the Court ruled in the case of *Dred Scott v. Sandford*[5] that the Missouri Compromise of 1820, which had restricted the expansion of slavery into U.S. territories, was invalid; this decision helped to bring about the Civil War. The Court overturned several important New Deal laws in the early 1930s in a direct effort to restrict the federal government's role in regulating the economy. The Court's frontal attack on President Franklin Roosevelt and the Democratic Congress created a constitutional crisis when Roosevelt responded with a proposal to "pack" the Court, to increase its traditional nine-member size to fifteen, so that his additional appointees—New Deal supporters—would dominate. (There is no constitutional provision specifying nine members; Congress could, if it chose to do so, change the number of justices on the Court.) The Court reversed its anti-New Deal stance in the late 1930s (inspiring the jibe "A switch in time saved nine") and began to interpret the federal government's powers much more broadly.[6] In *Buckley v. Valeo* (1976),[7] the Court struck down provisions of the Federal Election Campaign Act that had limited the amount individuals could spend to finance their own campaigns or express their own independent political views. And in *INS v. Chadha* (1973),[8] the Court invalidated the legislative veto (see Chapter 12) by which Congress had sought to intervene in executive branch matters. In *United States v. Lopez* (1995), the Supreme Court struck down Congress's Gun-Free School Zones Act as an unconstitutional expansion of the interstate commerce power and an invasion of powers reserved to the states. Overall, however, the Supreme Court's use of judicial review against the Congress has been restrained.

The Supreme Court has only rarely challenged presidential power. The Court has overturned presidential policies both on the grounds that they conflicted with laws of Congress and on the grounds that they conflicted with the Constitution. In *Ex parte Milligan* (1866),[9] for example, the Court held (somewhat belatedly) that President Abraham Lincoln could not suspend the writ of habeas corpus in rebellious states during the Civil War. In *Youngstown Sheet and Tube Co. v. Sawyer* in 1952,[10] it declared President Harry Truman's seizure of the nation's steel mills during the Korean War to be illegal. In 1974, it ordered President Richard Nixon to turn over taped White House conversations to the special Watergate prosecutor, leading to Nixon's forced resignation.[11]

The Supreme Court has used its power of judicial review far more frequently to invalidate state laws. Some of these decisions had impact far beyond the individual states on trial. For example, the historic 1954 decision in *Brown v. Board of Education of Topeka*, declaring segregation of the races in public schools to be unconstitutional, struck down the laws of twenty-one states[12] (see Chapter 15). The 1973 *Roe v. Wade* decision, establishing the constitutional right to abortion, struck down antiabortion laws in more than forty states.[13]

*Interpreting Federal Laws*   The power of the Supreme Court and the federal judiciary does not rest on judicial review alone. The courts also make policy in their interpretation of **statutory laws**—the laws of Congress. Frequently, Congress decides that an issue is too contentious to resolve. Members of Congress cannot themselves agree on specific language, so they write, sometimes deliberately, vague, symbolic language into the law—words and phrases like "fairness," "equitableness," "good faith," "good cause," and "reasonableness"—effectively shifting policy making to the courts by giving courts the power to read meaning into these terms.

*The Supreme Court's Policy Agenda*   The Supreme Court, and federal courts generally, deal with a very wide range of policy issues. However, the overwhelming majority of cases decided by the Court involve disputes that arise out of government activity—disputes in which a government or a government agency is one party and an individual or firm is the contending party. The Supreme Court dominates policy making in the areas of (1) civil rights and the treatment of women and minorities; (2) the procedural rights of criminal defendants; and (3) freedom of speech, press, and religion. It is estimated that more than half of all the cases decided by the Supreme Court involve these three issue areas.[14] Some of these cases involve interpretations of statutory law, especially the Civil Rights Act of 1964, the Voting Rights Act of 1965, and later amendments of these acts by Congress. But in most civil rights and civil liberties cases, the Court must determine the meaning of the Constitution itself—the meaning of the First Amendment's freedom of speech and press and religion, the meaning of the Equal Protection Clause of the Fourteenth Amendment, and the meaning of the Due Process Clause of the Fifth and Fourteenth Amendments.

The Court is active in determining the nature of American federalism (see Chapter 4), resolving disputes between states and the federal government. It has also played a key role in refereeing the struggle for power between Congress and the president. Finally, the Court devotes considerable attention to government regulatory activity—environmental protection, banking and securities regulation,

**Statutory laws:** Laws made by act of Congress or the state legislatures, as opposed to constitutional law.

labor-management relations. The Supreme Court is noticeably absent from the areas of national defense and international relations, leaving these issues to the president and Congress to resolve.

## ACTIVISM VERSUS SELF-RESTRAINT

Supreme Court Justice Felix Frankfurter once wrote: "The only check upon our own exercise of power is our own sense of self-restraint. For the removal of unwise laws from the statute books, appeal lies not to the courts but to the ballot and to the processes of democratic government."[15]

*Judicial Self-Restraint*    The idea behind **judicial self-restraint** is that judges should not read their own philosophies into the Constitution and should avoid direct confrontations with Congress, the president, and the states whenever possible. The argument for judicial self-restraint is that federal judges are not elected by the people and therefore should not substitute their own views for the views of elected representatives. Judicial activism encourages people to believe that federal courts—rather than Congress, the president, or state governments—should decide all important matters. As Justice Sandra Day O'Connor (see *People in Politics:* "Sandra Day O'Connor, Holding the Middle Ground") argued in her Senate confirmation hearings: "The courts should interpret the laws, not make them. . . . I do not believe it is a function of the Court to step in because times have changed or social mores have changed."[16]

*Wisdom versus Constitutionality*    A law may be unwise, unjust, or even stupid and yet still be constitutional. One should not equate the wisdom of a law with its constitutionality, and the Court should decide only the constitutionality and not the wisdom of a law. Justice Oliver Wendell Holmes once lectured a younger colleague, sixty-one-year-old Justice Harlan Stone, on this point:

> Young man, about 75 years ago I learned that I was not God. And so, when the people . . . want to do something I can't find anything in the Constitution expressly forbidding them to do, I say, whether I like it or not, "Goddamn it, let 'em do it."[17]

However, the actual role of the Supreme Court in the nation's power struggles suggests that the Court indeed often equates wisdom with constitutionality. People frequently cite broad phrases in the Fifth and Fourteenth Amendments establishing constitutional standards of "due process of law" and "equal protection of the laws" when attacking laws they believe are unfair or unjust. Most Americans have come to believe that unwise laws must be unconstitutional. If so, then the courts must be the final arbiters of fairness and justice.

*Original Intent*    Should the Constitution be interpreted in terms of the intentions of the Founders or according to the morality of society today? Most jurists agree that the Constitution is a living document, that it must be interpreted by each generation in the light of current conditions, and that to do otherwise would soon render the document obsolete. But in interpreting the document, whose

**Judicial self-restraint:** Self-imposed limitation on judicial power by judges deferring to the policy judgments of elected branches of government.

## PEOPLE IN POLITICS

# Sandra Day O'Connor, Holding the Middle Ground

For nearly 200 years, the U.S. Supreme Court was America's most exclusive all-male club. After 101 male justices, Sandra Day O'Connor was named to the Supreme Court by President Ronald Reagan in 1981. On the High Court, O'Connor has succeeded in molding a moderate bloc of votes that holds the balance of power on the Supreme Court between liberal and conservative blocs. More important, perhaps, O'Connor has taken the lead in shaping Court policy on women's issues, including the most controversial issue of all—abortion.

Sandra Day grew up on her family's large Arizona ranch, graduated from Stanford with honors, and went on to Stanford Law School, where she finished near the top of her class (along with Chief Justice of the Supreme Court William Rehnquist, who was first in the class). After graduation, she married John Jay O'Connor, a Phoenix attorney, and had three sons. She entered Arizona politics about the time her youngest son entered school. In 1969, she was appointed to fill a vacancy in the Arizona State Senate and was later elected twice to that body, where she rose to become majority leader in 1973. She left the Arizona legislature in 1975 to become a Phoenix trial judge and in 1979 was appointed by a Democratic governor to the Arizona Court of Appeals, an intermediate court that does not hear major constitutional issues.

O'Connor had some business experience: she was formerly a director of the First National Bank of Arizona and Blue Cross/Blue Shield of Arizona. But until her appointment to the U.S. Supreme Court, she was an obscure state court judge. Her service as a Republican leader in the Arizona State Senate qualified her as a moderately conservative party loyalist. However, it appears that her professional and political friendships had more to do with bringing her to President Ronald Reagan's attention than her record as a jurist. She had known both Justice Rehnquist and former Chief Justice Warren Burger for many years, and Barry Goldwater, Arizona's senior U.S. senator and Republican warhorse, had been her mentor in Arizona Republican politics. When Reagan's political advisers told him during the presidential campaign that he was not doing well among women voters (he opposed the Equal Rights Amendment), he responded by pledging to appoint a woman to the Supreme Court. Reagan's fulfillment of his campaign pledge was a politically popular decision. Feminist groups felt forced to support the appointment, even though O'Connor's record in Arizona was moderately conservative.

In her early Court deliberations, Justice O'Connor generally reflected the moderate conservatism of recent Republican appointees, but on gender questions she took an independent role from the beginning. Over time, her independent course has made her a swing vote on many key policy issues, from affirmative action to abortion. Indeed, her leadership of the Court on the abortion issue has preserved the constitutional right to abortion.

**Original intent:** A judicial philosophy under which judges attempt to apply the values of the Founders to current issues.

values should prevail—the values of the judges or the values of the Founders? The doctrine of **original intent** takes the values of the Founders as expressed in the text of the Constitution and attempts to apply these values to current conditions. Defenders of original intent argue that the words in the document must be given their historical meaning and that that meaning must restrain the courts as well as the legislative and executive branches of government. That is, the Supreme Court should not set aside laws made by elected representatives unless they conflict with the original intent of the Founders. Judges who set aside laws that do not accord with their personal views of today's moral standards are simply substituting their own morality for that of elected bodies. Such decisions lack democratic legitimacy because there is no reason why judges' moral views should prevail over those of elected representatives.

*Judicial Activism*    The doctrine of original intent carries little weight with proponents of judicial activism. The idea behind **judicial activism** is that the Constitution is a living document whose strength lies in its flexibility and that judges should shape constitutional meaning to fit the needs of contemporary society. The argument for judicial activism is that viewing the Constitution as a broad and flexible document saves the nation from having to pass dozens of new constitutional amendments to accommodate changes in society. Instead, the courts need to give contemporary interpretations to constitutional phrases, particularly general phrases such as "due process of law" (Fifth Amendment), "equal protection of the laws" (Fourteenth Amendment), "establishment of religion" (First Amendment), and "cruel and unusual punishment" (Eighth Amendment).

*Stare Decisis*    Conflicts between judicial activism and judicial self-restraint are underscored by questions of whether to let past decisions stand or to find constitutional support for overturning them. The principle of **stare decisis,** which means that the issue has already been decided in earlier cases, is a fundamental notion in law. Reliance on **precedent** gives stability to the law; if every decision were new law, then no one would know what the law is from day to day. Yet the Supreme Court has discarded precedent in many of its most important decisions: *Brown v. Board of Education* (1954), which struck down laws segregating the races; *Baker v. Carr* (1962), which guaranteed equal representation in legislatures; *Roe v. Wade* (1973), which made abortion a constitutional right; and many other classic cases. Former Justice William O. Douglas, a defender of judicial activism, justified disregard of precedent as follows:

> The decisions of yesterday or of the last century are only the starting points. . . . A judge looking at a constitutional decision may have compulsions to revere the past history and accept what was once written. But he remembers above all else that it is the Constitution which he swore to support and defend, not the gloss which his predecessors may have put on it. So he comes to formulate his own laws, rejecting some earlier ones as false and embracing others. He cannot do otherwise unless he lets men long dead and unaware of the problems of the age in which he lives do his thinking for him.[18]

*Rules of Restraint*    Even an activist Supreme Court adheres to some general rules of judicial self-restraint, however, including:

- The Court will pass upon the constitutionality of legislation only in an actual case; it will not advise the president or Congress on constitutional questions.
- The Court will not anticipate a question on constitutional law; it does not decide hypothetical cases.
- The Court will not formulate a rule of constitutional law broader than that required by the precise facts to which it must be applied.

**Judicial activism:** The making of new law through judicial interpretations of the Constitution.

**Stare decisis:** The judicial precept that the issue has already been decided in earlier cases and that the earlier decision need only be applied in the specific case before the bench; the rule in most cases, it comes from the Latin for "the decision stands."

**Precedent:** The legal principle that previous decisions should determine the outcome of current cases; the basis for stability in law.

- The Court will not pass upon a constitutional question if some other ground exists upon which it may dispose of the case.
- The Court will not pass upon the validity of a law if the complainants fail to show that they have been injured by the law, or if the complainants have availed themselves of the benefits of the law.
- When doubt exists about the constitutionality of a law, the Court will try to interpret the law so as to give it a constitutional meaning and avoid the necessity of declaring it unconstitutional.
- Complainants must have exhausted all remedies available in lower federal courts or state courts before the Supreme Court will accept review.
- The Court will invalidate a law only when a constitutional issue is *crucial* to the case and is substantial, not trivial.
- Occasionally the Court defers to Congress and the president, classifies an issue as a political question, and refuses to decide it. The Court has generally stayed out of foreign and military policy areas.
- If the Court holds a law unconstitutional, it will confine its decision to the particular section of the law that is unconstitutional; the rest of the statute stays intact.

# STRUCTURE AND JURISDICTION OF FEDERAL COURTS

The federal court system consists of three levels of courts—the Supreme Court, the Courts of Appeals, and the district courts—together with various special courts (see Figure 13-1). Only the Supreme Court is established by the Constitution, although the number of justices is determined by Congress. Article III authorizes Congress to establish such "inferior Courts" as it deems appropriate. Congress has designed a hierarchical system with a U.S. Court of Appeals divided into 12 regional circuit courts, a federal circuit, and 89 district courts in the fifty states and one each in Puerto Rico and the District of Columbia. Table 13-2 describes their **jurisdiction** and distinguishes between **original jurisdiction**—where cases are begun, argued, and initially decided—and **appellate jurisdiction**—where cases begun in lower courts are argued and decided on **appeal.**

The Supreme Court is the "court of last resort" in the United States, but it hears only a very small number of cases each year. In a handful of cases, the Supreme Court has original jurisdiction; these concern primarily disputes between states (or states and residents of other states), disputes between a state and the federal government, and disputes involving foreign dignitaries. However, most Supreme Court cases are appellate decisions involving cases from state supreme courts or cases tried first in a U.S. District Court.

*District Courts*   **District courts** are the original jurisdiction trial courts of the federal system. Each state has at least one district court, and larger states have more (New York, for example, has four). There are more than 600 federal district judges, each appointed for life by the president and confirmed by the Senate. The president also appoints a U.S. marshall for each district to carry out orders of the court and maintain order in the courtroom. District courts hear criminal cases prosecuted by the Department of Justice as well as civil cases. As trial courts, the

**Jurisdiction:** The power of a court to hear a case in question.

**Original jurisdiction:** Refers to a particular court's power to serve as the place where a given case is initially argued and decided.

**Appellate jurisdiction:** A particular court's power to review a decision or action of a lower court.

**Appeal:** In general, requests that a higher court review cases decided at a lower level. In the Supreme Court, certain cases are designated as appeals under federal law; formally, these must be heard by the Court.

**District courts:** The original jurisdiction trial courts of the federal system.

**Grand juries:** Juries called to hear evidence and decide whether defendants should be indicted and tried.

**Petit (regular) juries:** Juries called to determine guilt or innocence.

**Circuit courts:** The twelve appellate courts that make up the middle level of the federal court system.

**Briefs:** Documents submitted by an attorney to a court, setting out the facts of the case and the legal arguments in support of the party represented by the attorney.

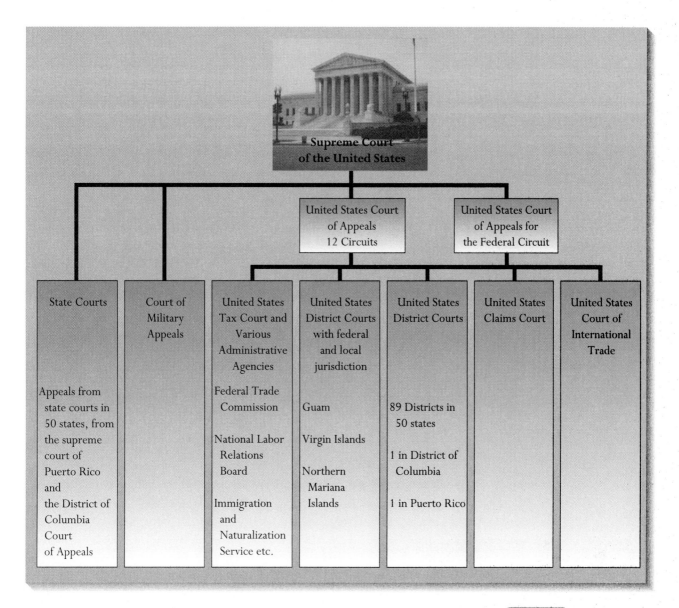

| Supreme Court of the United States | | | | | | |
|---|---|---|---|---|---|---|
| | **United States Court of Appeals 12 Circuits** | | | **United States Court of Appeals for the Federal Circuit** | | |
| State Courts | Court of Military Appeals | United States Tax Court and Various Administrative Agencies | United States District Courts with federal and local jurisdiction | United States District Courts | United States Claims Court | United States Court of International Trade |
| Appeals from state courts in 50 states, from the supreme court of Puerto Rico and the District of Columbia Court of Appeals | | Federal Trade Commission<br><br>National Labor Relations Board<br><br>Immigration and Naturalization Service etc. | Guam<br><br>Virgin Islands<br><br>Northern Mariana Islands | 89 Districts in 50 states<br><br>1 in District of Columbia<br><br>1 in Puerto Rico | | |

district courts make use of both **grand juries** (called to hear evidence and, if warranted, to indict a defendant by bringing formal criminal charges) and **petit (regular) juries** (which determine guilt or innocence). District courts may hear as many as 300,000 cases in a year, including 50,000 criminal cases.

*Courts of Appeals*   Federal **circuit courts** (see *Across the USA:* "Geographic Boundaries of Federal Courts") are appellate courts. They do not hold trials or accept new evidence but consider only the records of the trial courts and oral or written arguments **(briefs)** submitted by attorneys. Federal law guarantees everyone the right to appeal, so the Court of Appeals has little discretion in this regard. Appellate judges themselves estimate that more than 80 percent of all appeals are frivolous—that is, without any real basis. There are more than a hundred circuit judges, each appointed for life by the president subject to confirmation by the Senate. Normally, these judges serve together on a panel to hear appeals. More than 90 percent of the cases decided by the Court of Appeals end

**FIGURE 13-1**   **Structure of Federal Courts**

*As this diagram shows, the federal court system of the United States is divided into three levels: the courts of original jurisdiction (state courts, military courts, tax courts, district courts, claims courts, and international trade courts), U.S. Courts of Appeals (which hear appeals from all lower courts except state and military panels), and the U.S. Supreme Court, which can hear appeals from all sources.*

TABLE 13-2   JURISDICTION OF FEDERAL COURTS

| Supreme Court of the United States | United States Courts of Appeals | United States District Courts |
|---|---|---|
| Appellate jurisdiction (cases begin in a lower court); hears appeals, at its own discretion, from: | No original jurisdiction; hear only appeals from: | Original jurisdiction over cases involving: |
| 1. Lower federal courts | 1. Federal district courts | 1. Federal crimes |
| 2. Highest state courts | 2. U.S. regulatory commissions | 2. Civil suits under the federal law |
| Original jurisdiction (cases begin in the Supreme Court) over cases involving: | 3. Certain other federal courts | 3. Civil suits between citizens of different states where the amount exceeds $50,000 |
| 1. Two or more states | | 4. Admiralty and maritime cases |
| 2. The United States and a state | | 5. Bankruptcy cases |
| 3. Foreign ambassadors and other diplomats | | 6. Review of actions of certain federal administrative agencies |
| 4. A state and a citizen of a different state (if begun by the state) | | 7. Other matters assigned to them by Congress |

*Justices of the Supreme Court. Front row, from the left: Antonin Scalia, John Paul Stevens, Chief Justice William Rehnquist, Sandra Day O'Connor, and Anthony Kennedy. Back Row, from the left: Ruth Bader Ginsburg, David Souter, Clarence Thomas, and Stephen Breyer.*

at this level. Further appeal to the Supreme Court is not automatic; it must be approved by the Supreme Court itself. Since the Supreme Court hears very few cases, in most cases the decision of the circuit court becomes law.

*Supreme Court*   The Supreme Court of the United States is the final interpreter of all matters involving the Constitution and federal laws and treaties, whether the case began in a federal district court or in a state court. Appeals to

# Geographic Boundaries of Federal Courts

*For administrative convenience, the U. S. District Courts are organized into twelve circuits (regions), plus the Federal Circuit (Washington, D. C.). Within each region, circuit court judges form panels to hear appeals from district courts.*

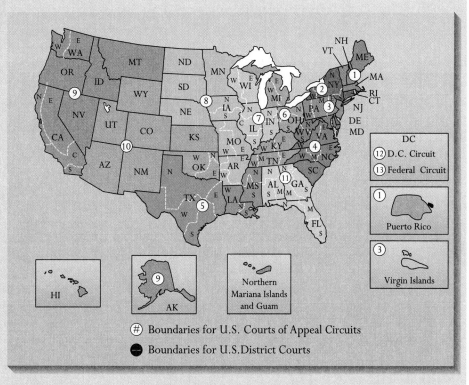

● Boundaries for U.S. Courts of Appeal Circuits
● Boundaries for U.S. District Courts

the U.S. Supreme Court may come from a state court of last resort (usually a state's supreme court) or from lower federal courts. The Supreme Court determines whether to accept an appeal and consider a case. It may do so when there is a "substantial federal question" presented in a case or when there are "special and important reasons," or it may reject a case—with or without explaining why.

In the early days of the Republic, the size of the Supreme Court fluctuated, but since 1869 the membership has remained at nine: the Chief Justice and eight associate justices. The Supreme Court is in session each year from October through June, hearing oral arguments, accepting written briefs, conferring, and rendering opinions.

*Appeals from State Courts* Each of the fifty states maintains its own courts. The federal courts are not necessarily superior to those courts; state and federal courts operate independently. State courts have original jurisdiction in

# America Drowning Itself in a Sea of Lawsuits

America is threatening to drown itself in a sea of lawsuits. Civil suits in the nation's courts exceed 10 *million* per year. There are more than 805,000 lawyers in the United States (compared to about 650,000 physicians), more than three times as many as in 1960. These lawyers are in business, and their business is litigation. Generating business means generating lawsuits. And just as businesses search for new products, lawyers search for new legal principles upon which to bring lawsuits. They seek to expand legal liability for civil actions—that is, to expand the definition of civil wrongdoings, or torts.

Unquestionably, the threat of lawsuits is an important safeguard for society, compelling individuals, corporations, and government agencies to behave responsibly toward others. Because victims require compensation for *actual* damages incurred by the wrongdoing of others, liability laws protect all of us.

But we need to consider the social costs of frivolous lawsuits, especially those brought without any merit but initiated in the hope that individuals or firms will offer a settlement just to avoid the expenses of defending themselves. Legal expenses and excessive jury awards leveled against corporations increase insurance premiums for businesses and service providers, including physicians and hospitals. The risk of lawsuits forces physicians to practice "defensive medicine," ordering expensive tests, multiple consultations with specialists, and expensive procedures not because they are adjudged medically necessary but rather to protect themselves from the possibility of a lawsuit.

*Product Liability*   The threat of lawsuits discourages new products from entering the marketplace by raising their cost through extensive testing and perhaps modification to ensure near-perfect safety.

Virtually any accident involving a commercial product can inspire a product liability suit. An individual who gets cut opening a can of peas can sue the canning company. A woman who spills hot coffee on herself while driving sues the fast food restaurant for making the coffee too hot. Real estate brokers are sued by buyers unhappy in their new homes. Bar owners are sued by persons injured by intoxicated patrons driving home. Hotels pay damages to persons raped in their rooms. Coastal cities with beaches are successfully sued by relatives of persons who drowned in the ocean.

*Third-Party Suits*   Defendants in civil cases are not necessarily the parties directly responsible for damages to the plaintiff. Instead, wealthier third parties, who may indirectly contribute to an accident, are favorite targets of lawsuits. For example, if a drunk driver injures a pedestrian but the driver has only limited insurance and small personal wealth, a shrewd attorney will sue the bar that sold the driver the drinks instead of the driver. Insurance premiums have risen sharply for physicians seeking malpractice insurance, as have premiums for recreation facilities, nurseries and day care centers, motels, and restaurants. Trial lawyers have been successful in coaxing ever-larger damage awards out of juries, especially against corporations, insurance companies, and governments. Many of these awards are reduced on appeal, but the trend in awards is unmistakably upward.

most criminal and civil cases. Since the U.S. Supreme Court has appellate jurisdiction over state supreme courts as well as over lower federal courts, the Supreme Court oversees the nation's entire judicial system, but the great bulk of cases begin and end in the state court systems. The federal courts do not interfere once a case has been started in a state court except in very rare circumstances. And Congress has stipulated that legal disputes between citizens of different states must involve $50,000 or more to be heard in federal courts.

*"Pain and Suffering" Awards*   High jury awards in liability cases, sometimes running into tens of millions of dollars, cover much more than the doctor bills, lost wages, and cost of future care for injured parties. Most large damage awards are for *pain and suffering*. Pain and suffering awards are *added* compensation for the victim, beyond actual costs for medical care and lost wages.

*"Joint and Several" Liability*   A legal rule known as *joint and several liability* allows a plaintiff to collect the entire award from any party that contributed in any way to an accident if other defendants cannot pay. If, for example, a drunk driver crosses a median strip and crashes into another car, leaving its driver crippled, the victim may sue the city for not placing a guard railing in the median strip. The rule encourages trial lawyers to sue the party "with the deepest pockets," that is, the wealthiest party rather than the party most responsible for the accident. Unsophisticated juries can be emotionally manipulated into granting huge damage awards, especially against businesses, municipalities, and insurance companies.

*Contingency Fees*   Many lawsuits are initiated by lawyers who charge fees on a contingency basis; the plaintiff pays nothing unless the attorney wins an award. Up to half of that award may go to the attorney in expenses and fees. Trial attorneys argue that many people could not afford to bring civil cases to court without a contingency fee contract.

*Reform Proposals*   Legal reform centers on discouraging the worst abuses of the system. Some of the most common reform proposals are:

- *Loser pay rule:* requiring the losing party in a civil action to pay the attorney fees and court costs of the winning party. This rule would discourage baseless suits designed to force settlements by threatening defendants with high costs. It encourages strong cases since claimants know that they would be reimbursed for costs if they win.
- *Contingency fees limits:* requiring that the parties suffering damages, rather than attorneys, receive the bulk of court awards. A related reform would require attorneys to provide written notice of all expenses, charges, and fees to their clients.
- *"Pain and suffering" damage caps:* limiting awards for noneconomic damages as well as "punitive" awards to $250,000.
- *Ending "joint and several" liability:* limiting the responsibility of any defendant to his or her actual contribution to the wrongdoing rather than holding the wealthiest defendant responsible for all damages.

*Reform Politics*   Reforming the nation's liability laws presents major challenges to the political system. The reform movement can count on support from some normally powerful interest groups—insurance companies, manufacturers, drug companies, hospitals, and physicians. Sensing its popularity with voters, Republican House candidates included legal reform in their 1994 "Contract with America." But legal reform is an anathema to the legal profession itself, notably the powerful Association of Trial Lawyers. And lawyers compose the single largest occupational background of Congress members—indeed, of politicians generally.

Moreover, parties to cases in state courts must "exhaust their remedies"—that is, appeal their case all the way through the state court system—before the federal courts will hear an appeal. Appeals from state supreme courts go directly to the U.S. Supreme Court and not to a federal district or circuit court. Such appeals are usually made on the grounds that a federal question is involved in the case—that is, a question has arisen regarding the application of the Constitution or a federal law.

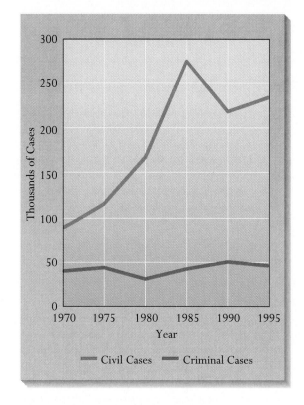

**FIGURE 13-2** **Caseloads in Federal Courts**

*Increasing caseloads in the federal courts have placed a heavy burden on prosecutors and judges. While the increase in civil suits in the federal courts is the result of more plaintiffs insisting on taking their cases to the federal level both originally and on appeal, the increase in criminal cases is the result of Congress's decision to make more crimes—especially drug-related crimes—federal offenses and to pursue such criminals more vigorously.*

*Source: Statistical Abstract of the United States, 1996, p. 213.*

*Federal Cases* Some 10 million civil and criminal cases are begun in the nation's courts each year (see *A Conflicting View:* "America Drowning Itself in a Sea of Lawsuits"). Fewer than 300,000 (3 percent) of the cases are begun in the federal courts. About 5,000 are appealed to the Supreme Court each year, but the Court hears only about 200 of them. The Constitution "reserves" general police powers to the states. That is, civil disputes and most crimes—murder, robbery, assault, and rape—are normally state offenses rather than federal crimes and thus are tried in state and local courts.

Federal court caseloads have risen in recent years (see Figure 13-2), in part because more civil disputes are being brought to federal courts. In addition, the U.S. Justice Department is prosecuting more criminal cases as federal law enforcement agencies—such as the Federal Bureau of Investigation (FBI), Drug Enforcement Administration (DEA), Internal Revenue Service (IRS), and Bureau of Alcohol, Tobacco and Firearms (ATF)—have stepped up their investigations. Most of this recent increase is attributable to enforcement of federal drug laws.

Traditionally, federal crimes were offenses directed against the U.S. government, its property, or its employees or were offenses involving the crossing of state lines. Over the years, however, Congress has greatly expanded the list of federal crimes so that federal and state criminal court jurisdictions often overlap, as they do, for example, in most drug violations.

# THE SPECIAL RULES
# OF JUDICIAL DECISION MAKING

Courts are political institutions that resolve conflict and decide about public policy. But unlike Congress, the presidency, and the bureaucracy, the courts employ highly specialized rules in going about their work.

*Cases and Controversies*   One overriding characteristic of the way courts work is that they do not initiate policy but rather wait until a case or controversy is brought to them for resolution. A case must involve two disputing parties, one of which must have incurred some real damage as a result of the action or inaction of the other. Federal courts do *not* render "advisory" opinions about pending legislation or executive actions. They do *not* issue policy declarations or decide hypothetical cases. Federal courts do *not* render opinions about whether or not proposed laws of Congress are constitutional. Rather, the courts wait until disputing parties bring a case to them that requires them to interpret the meaning of a law or determine its constitutionality in order to resolve the case. Only then do courts render opinions.

The vast majority of cases do *not* involve important policy issues. Courts determine the guilt or innocence of criminal defendants. Courts enforce contracts and award damages to victims of negligence in **civil cases.** And courts render these decisions on the basis of established law. Only occasionally do courts make significant policy decisions.

*Adversarial Proceedings*   Underlying judicial decision making is the assumption that the best way to decide an issue is to allow two disputing parties to present arguments on each side. Judges in the United States do not investigate cases, question witnesses, or develop arguments themselves (as they do in some European countries). This **adversarial system** depends upon quality of argument on each side, which means it often depends upon the capabilities of attorneys. There is no guarantee that the adversarial process will produce the best policy outcomes.

*Standing*   To bring an issue into court as a case, individuals or firms or interest groups must have **standing;** that is, they must be directly harmed by a law or action. People cannot "go to court" simply because they do not like what the government is doing. Merely being taxpayers does not entitle people to claim that they are damaged by government actions.[19] Individuals or firms automatically have standing when they are prosecuted by the government for violation of laws or regulations. Thus one way to gain standing in order to challenge the legality of a regulation or the constitutionality of a law is to violate the regulation or law and invite the government to prosecute.

In recent years, however, the federal courts have liberalized the definition of standing to permit more individuals and groups to bring issues to the courts. Indeed, political conflicts are now more likely to be resolved in the judicial arena than ever before.

To sue the government, plaintiffs must show that they have suffered financial damages, loss of property, or physical or emotional harm as a direct result of

**Civil cases:** Noncriminal court proceedings in which a plaintiff sues a defendant for damages in payment for harm inflicted.

**Adversarial system:** The method of decision making in which an impartial judge or jury or decision maker hears arguments and reviews evidence presented by opposite sides.

**Standing:** A requirement that the party who files a lawsuit have a legal stake in the outcome.

*The settlement of a class action suit on behalf of women claiming silicone gel breast implants made them sick prompted the Dow Corning company to declare bankruptcy in 1995. Here Karen Berger, author of a book about implants, holds one up at a press conference.*

**Plaintiffs:** Parties initiating suits and claiming damages. In criminal cases, the state acts as plaintiff on behalf of an injured society and requests fines and/or imprisonment as damages. In civil suits, the plaintiff is the injured party and seeks monetary damages.

**Defendants:** Parties against whom a criminal or civil suit is brought.

**Sovereign immunity:** The legal doctrine that individuals can sue the government only with the government's consent.

**Class action suits:** Cases initiated by parties acting on behalf of themselves and all others similarly situated.

**Contingency fees:** Fees paid to attorneys to represent the plaintiff in a civil suit and receive in compensation an agreed-upon percentage of damages awarded (if any).

the government's action. (The party initiating a suit and claiming damages is the **plaintiff;** the party against whom a suit is brought is the **defendant.** The ancient legal doctrine of **sovereign immunity** means that one cannot sue the government without the government's consent. But by law, the U.S. government allows itself to be sued in a wide variety of contract and negligence cases. A citizen can also personally sue to force government officials to carry out acts that they are required by law to perform or for acting contrary to law. The government does not allow suits for damages as a result of military actions.

*Class Action Suits*   **Class action suits** are cases brought into court by individuals on behalf not only of themselves but also of all other persons "similarly situated." That is, the party bringing the case is acting on behalf of a "class" of people who have suffered the same damages from the same actions of the defendant. One of the most famous and far-reaching class action suits was *Brown v. Board of Education of Topeka* (1954). In it the plaintiff, Linda Brown of Topeka, Kansas, sued her local board of education on behalf of herself and all other black pupils who were forced to attend segregated schools, charging that such schools violated the Equal Protection Clause of the Fourteenth Amendment. When she won the case, the Court's ruling affected not only Linda Brown and the segregated public schools in Topeka but also all other black pupils similarly situated across the nation (see Chapter 15).

Since the *Brown* case, class action suits have grown in popularity. These suits have enabled attorneys and interest groups to bring multi-million-dollar suits against corporations and governments for damages to large numbers of people, even when none of them has individually suffered sufficient harm to merit bringing a case to court. For example, an individual overcharged by an electric utility would not want to incur the expense of suing for the return of a few dollars. But if attorneys sue the utility on behalf of a large number of customers similarly overcharged, the result may be a multi-million-dollar settlement from which the attorneys can deduct their hefty fees. In recent years, the courts have tightened the rules governing class action suits in order to stem the huge tide of suits generated by the legal profession. Today, federal courts generally require attorneys bringing class action suits to notify each member of the class on whose behalf the case is said to be brought.

*Legal Fees*   Going to court requires financial resources. Criminal defendants are guaranteed an attorney, without charge if they are poor, by the Sixth Amendment's guarantee of "Assistance of Counsel" (see Chapter 14).[20] Persons who wish to bring a *civil* suit against governments or corporations must still arrange for the payment of legal fees, however. The most common arrangement is the **contingency fee,** in which plaintiffs agree to pay expenses and share one-third or more of the money damages with their lawyers if the case is won. If the case is lost, neither plaintiffs nor their lawyers receive anything for their labors. Lawyers do not usually participate in such arrangements unless the prospects for winning the case are good and the promised monetary reward is substantial. Civil suits against the government have increased since Congress enacted a law requiring governments to pay the attorneys' fees of citizens who successfully bring suit against public officials for violation of their constitutional rights.

*Remedies and Relief* Judicial power has vastly expanded through court determination of remedies and relief. These are the orders of a court following a decision that are designed to correct a wrong. In most cases, judges simply fine or sentence criminal defendants to jail or order losing defendants in civil suits to pay monetary damages to the winning plaintiffs. In recent years, however, federal district court judges have issued sweeping orders to governments to correct constitutional violations. For example, a federal district judge took over operation of the Boston public schools for more than ten years to remedy *de facto* (an existing, though not necessarily deliberate, pattern of) racial segregation. A federal district judge ordered the city of Yonkers, New York, to build public housing in white neighborhoods. A federal district judge took over the operation of the Alabama prison system to ensure proper prisoner treatment. A federal district judge ordered the Kansas City, Missouri, school board to increase taxes to pay for his desegregation plan. (This case reached the Supreme Court, which held that a federal court does have the power to levy taxes—a power reserved to the legislature in English-speaking countries for centuries—when necessary to implement a constitutional guarantee.)[21]

# THE POLITICS OF SELECTING JUDGES

The Constitution specifies that all federal judges, including justices of the Supreme Court, shall be appointed by the president and confirmed by a majority vote of the Senate. Judicial recruitment is a political process: presidents almost always appoint members of their own party to the federal courts. More than 80 percent of federal judges have held some political office prior to their appointment to the court. More important, political philosophy now plays a major role in the selection of judges. Thus the appointment of federal judges has increasingly become an arena for conflict between presidents and their political opponents in the Senate.

*The Politics of Presidential Selection* Presidents have a strong motivation to select judges who share their political philosophy. Judicial appointments are made for life. The Constitution stipulates that federal judges "shall hold their Offices during good Behaviour." Though a rather vague phrase, it has come to mean a virtually guaranteed life term. A president cannot remove a judge for any reason, and Congress cannot impeach judges just because it dislikes their decisions.

This independence of the judiciary has often frustrated presidents and Congresses. Presidents who have appointed people they thought were liberals or conservatives to the Supreme Court have sometimes been surprised by the decisions of their appointees. It is estimated that about one-quarter of the justices of the Supreme Court have deviated from the political expectations of the presidents who appointed them.[22] For example, Chief Justice Earl Warren, perhaps the most liberal and activist chief justice in the Court's history, was appointed by Republican President Dwight Eisenhower. Previously the governor of California, Warren lacked judicial experience and received his appointment as a reward for swinging his state's delegation to Eisenhower at the 1952 Republican national convention. Eisenhower later complained that the Warren appointment was "the biggest damn mistake I ever made."

It is important to recognize that presidents' use of political criteria in selecting judges has a democratic influence on the courts. Presidents can campaign on the pledge to make the courts more liberal or conservative through their appointive powers, and voters are free to cast their ballots on the basis of this pledge. For example, Bill Clinton's promise to appoint judges more liberal on the abortion issue influenced some voters in 1992.

*Political Litmus Test*    Traditionally, presidents and senators have tried to discern where a Supreme Court candidate fits on the continuum of liberal activism versus conservative self-restraint. Democratic presidents and senators usually prefer liberal judges who express an activist philosophy. Republican presidents usually prefer conservative judges who express a philosophy of judicial self-restraint. Appointing members of their own party has given presidents a fairly high success rate in obtaining their preferences in the federal judiciary as a whole. Table 13-3 reports a survey of federal district and appellate judges. In this poll, 75 percent of judges appointed by Democrats claimed to be politically liberal. While only 37 percent of Republicans claimed conservative ideology, 69 percent of them espoused a conservative philosophy of judicial restraint and 85 percent were generally opposed to government regulation of business.

Until very recently, both the president and the Senate denied using any political "litmus test" in judicial recruitment. A **litmus test** generally refers to recruitment based on a nominee's stand on a single issue. Since the Supreme Court ruling on *Roe v. Wade* (1973), however, the single issue of abortion has come to dominate the politics of judicial recruitment. While Presidents Ronald Reagan and George Bush denied applying a litmus test on this issue, many observers believe that their nominees were selected with the expectation that they would help reverse *Roe v. Wade*. President Clinton was forthright in his pledge to nominate only justices who specifically support the *Roe v. Wade* decision.

*Competence and Ethics*    While competence and ethics may be of lesser importance than party and political philosophy, they are serious considerations for the attorney general and Justice Department as they assist the president in screening nominees for federal judgeships. Given the close scrutiny to which the media and the Senate now subject nominees, even minor violations of laws or moral standards can lead to Senate rejection, especially when senators dislike a candidate's judicial philosophy. Questions of competence and ethics can seldom be separated from politics.

*The Politics of Senate Confirmation*    All presidential nominations for the federal judiciary, including the Supreme Court, are sent to the Senate for confirmation. The Senate refers them to its powerful Judiciary Committee, which holds hearings, votes on the nomination, and then reports to the full Senate, where floor debate may precede the final confirmation vote.

The Senate's involvement in federal district judgeships traditionally centered on the practice of **senatorial courtesy.** If senators from the president's party from the same state for which an appointment was being considered disapproved of a nominee, their Senate colleagues would defeat the nomination. But if the president and senators from that party agreed on the nomination, the full Senate, even if controlled by the opposition, customarily confirmed the nomination. Dur-

**Litmus test:** In political terms, a person's stand on a key issue that determines whether he or she will be appointed to public office or supported in electoral campaigns.

**Senatorial courtesy:** The custom of the U.S. Senate with regard to presidential nominations to the judiciary to defer to the judgment of senators from the president's party from the same state as the nominee.

TABLE 13-3    IDEOLOGY AND OPINION AMONG FEDERAL JUDGES

| | Republican Appointees | Democratic Appointees |
|---|---|---|
| **Political Ideology** | | |
| Liberal | 28 | 75 |
| Conservative | 37 | 17 |
| **Judicial Philosophy** | | |
| Courts show too much concern for criminals. | 44 | 16 |
| Judges should apply the law, leave the rest to legislators. | 69 | 51 |
| **Economics** | | |
| The poor are poor due to circumstances beyond their control. | 33 | 50 |
| Less regulation of business is good for the country. | 85 | 54 |
| Government should not guarantee jobs. | 70 | 36 |
| Government should ensure a good standard of living. | 27 | 57 |
| Government should reduce the income gap between rich and poor. | 44 | 78 |
| **Sex and Morality** | | |
| Extramarital sex is wrong. | 71 | 63 |
| Homosexuals should not teach in public schools. | 60 | 22 |
| Adult homosexual relations are wrong. | 77 | 59 |
| **Affirmative Action** | | |
| Special preference should be given to blacks in hiring. | 41 | 62 |
| Special preference should be given to women in hiring. | 22 | 47 |
| **The Environment** | | |
| Environmental problems are not as serious as thought. | 47 | 19 |

*Source:* Athea K. Nagai, Stanley Rothman, and S. Robert Lichter, "The Verdict on Federal Judges," *Public Opinion* 10 (November/December 1987): 52–58.

ing the Reagan-Bush years, however, partisan divisions between these Republican presidents and Senate Democrats eroded the tradition of senatorial courtesy.

Supreme Court nominations have always received close political scrutiny in the Senate. Over the last two centuries, the Senate has rejected or refused to confirm about 20 percent of presidential nominees to the High Court, but only five nominees in this century (see Table 13-4). In the past, most senators believed that presidents deserved to appoint their own judges; the opposition party would get its own opportunity to appoint judges when it won the presidency. Only if the Senate found some personal disqualification in a nominee's background (for

| Nominee | President | Year | Vote |
|---|---|---|---|
| Earl Warren | Eisenhower | 1954 | NRV* |
| John Marshall Harlan | Eisenhower | 1955 | 71–11 |
| William J. Brennan | Eisenhower | 1957 | NRV |
| Charles Whittaker | Eisenhower | 1957 | NRV |
| Potter Stewart | Eisenhower | 1959 | 70–17 |
| Byron White | Kennedy | 1962 | NRV |
| Arthur Goldberg | Kennedy | 1962 | NRV |
| Abe Fortas | Johnson | 1965 | NRV |
| Thurgood Marshall | Johnson | 1967 | 69–11 |
| Abe Fortas** | Johnson | 1968 | Withdrawn*** |
| Homer Thornberry | Johnson | 1968 | No action |
| Warren Burger | Nixon | 1969 | 74–3 |
| Clement Haynsworth | Nixon | 1969 | Defeated 45–55 |
| G. Harrold Carswell | Nixon | 1970 | Defeated 45–51 |
| Harry Blackmun | Nixon | 1970 | 94–0 |
| Lewis Powell | Nixon | 1971 | 89–1 |
| William Rehnquist | Nixon | 1971 | 68–26 |
| John Paul Stevens | Nixon | 1975 | 98–0 |
| Sandra Day O'Connor | Reagan | 1981 | 99–0 |
| William Rehnquist** | Reagan | 1986 | 65–33 |
| Antonin Scalia | Reagan | 1986 | 98–0 |
| Robert Bork | Reagan | 1987 | Defeated 42–58 |
| Douglas Ginsburg | Reagan | 1987 | Withdrawn |
| Anthony Kennedy | Reagan | 1988 | 97–0 |
| David Souter | Bush | 1990 | 90–9 |
| Clarence Thomas | Bush | 1991 | 52–48 |
| Ruth Bader Ginsburg | Clinton | 1993 | 96–3 |
| Stephen G. Breyer | Clinton | 1994 | 87–9 |

*Source:* Congressional Quarterly, *The Supreme Court: Justice and the Law* (Washington, D.C.: Congressional Quarterly, 1983), p. 179; updated by the author.

*No recorded vote.

**Elevation to Chief Justice.

***Nomination withdrawn after Senate vote failed to end filibuster against nomination; vote was 45–43 to end filibuster, and two-thirds majority was required.

example, financial scandal, evidence of racial or religious bias, judicial incompetence) would a nominee likely be rejected. But publicity and partisanship over confirmation of Supreme Court nominees have increased markedly in recent years (see *Up Close:* "The Bork Battle").

## WHO IS SELECTED?

What background and experiences are brought to the Supreme Court? Despite often holding very different views on the laws, the Constitution, and their interpretation, the justices of the U.S. Supreme Court tend to share a common back-

# The Bork Battle

The U.S. Senate's rejection of President Ronald Reagan's nomination of Judge Robert H. Bork in 1987 set a new precedent in Senate confirmation of Supreme Court nominees. The Senate rejected Bork because of his views, not because he lacked judicial qualifications. On the contrary, no appointee to the Supreme Court was ever more qualified in terms of scholarship, judicial experience, and knowledge of the law than Judge Bork. As a law school professor at the University of Chicago and Yale University, he had written many scholarly volumes and articles on constitutional law; he had served as solicitor general of the United States and as a judge of the prestigious U.S. Court of Appeals for the District of Columbia, where he had written hundreds of opinions. But Bork had a reputation for "conservative activism"—a desire to better reflect the "original intent" of the Constitution's framers by rolling back some of the Supreme Court's broad interpretations of privacy rights, free speech, and equal protection of the law. Perhaps most controversial were his views on *Roe v. Wade*; he had labeled the Court's striking down of state laws prohibiting abortion as "wholly unjustifiable judicial usurpation of state legislative authority."

Unlike previous nominees, Bork was subjected by the Senate Judiciary Committee to extensive case-by-case questioning in nationally televised confirmation hearings, during which the bearded, scholarly Bork presented a poor TV image. The Democrat-controlled Judiciary Committee in the U.S. Senate rejected his nomination. A second unfortunate nominee, Douglas H. Ginsberg, withdrew in the face of press reports that he had smoked marijuana. Finally, President Reagan submitted the name of a relatively unknown nominee, Anthony M. Kennedy, who testified that he had "no overriding theory of [constitutional] interpretation" and "no fixed or immutable ideas," and the Senate confirmed the appointment.

Victory in the Bork battle encouraged liberal interest groups to closely scrutinize the personal lives

*Robert Bork testifying at his confirmation hearing.*

and political views of subsequent nominees by President Bush. Groups such as People for the American Way (headed by Hollywood producer Norman Lear), the National Abortion Rights Action League, and the National Organization for Women were committed to opposing any nominee who would restrict abortion rights. When William Brennan retired in 1990, the intense political conflict surrounding Supreme Court nominations forced President Bush to search for a nominee who had never spoken out on key issues or rendered any decision on them. Judge David Souter, an obscure justice of the New Hampshire Supreme Court, fit this nomination strategy as the "stealth nominee": he had written very little about the law and had dealt with few national issues as a state court judge. When Senate committee members pressed for his views on abortion and other issues likely to come before the Court, Souter declined to answer, citing the need to retain a judicial posture of neutrality on pending cases. With no personal scandal in his background and no ideological grounds for rejection, Souter was confirmed, but the determination of the Senate to do more than "rubber-stamp" presidential appointments continued. Indeed, the Bork battle set the stage for an even more controversial political struggle—the confirmation of Justice Clarence Thomas.

TABLE 13-5   THE SUPREME COURT

| Justice | Age at Appointment | President Who Appointed | Law School | Position at Time of Appointment | Years as a Judge |
|---|---|---|---|---|---|
| William H. Rehnquist | | | | | |
|    Original appointment | 47 | Nixon (1971) | Stanford | Asst. Attorney General | 0 |
|    Chief Justice | 61 | Reagan (1986) | | | 15 |
| John Paul Stevens | 50 | Ford (1976) | Northwestern | U.S. Court of Appeals | 5 |
| Sandra Day O'Connor | 51 | Reagan (1981) | Stanford | State Court | 6 |
| Antonin Scalia | 50 | Reagan (1988) | Harvard | U.S. Court of Appeals | 4 |
| Anthony M. Kennedy | 51 | Reagan (1988) | Harvard | U.S. Court of Appeals | 12 |
| David H. Souter | 50 | Bush (1990) | Harvard | State Supreme Court | 13 |
| Clarence Thomas | 43 | Bush (1991) | Yale | U.S. Court of Appeals | 2 |
| Ruth Bader Ginsburg | 60 | Clinton (1993) | Columbia | U.S. Court of Appeals | 13 |
| Stephen G. Breyer | 56 | Clinton (1994) | Harvard | U.S. Court of Appeals | 14 |

ground of education at the nation's most prestigious law schools and prior judicial experience.

*Law Degrees*   There is no constitutional requirement that Supreme Court justices be attorneys, but every person who has ever served on the High Court has been trained in law. Moreover, a majority of the justices have attended one or another of the nation's most prestigious law schools—Harvard, Yale, and Stanford (see Table 13-5).

*Judicial Experience*   Historically, about half of all Supreme Court justices have been federal or state court judges. The emphasis on judicial experience has been even greater in recent years; in anticipation of intense scrutiny by the Democrat-controlled Senate Judiciary Committee, Republican presidents Reagan and Bush nominated only people with judicial experience. Historically, however, about one-quarter of justices have come to the Court directly from private practices. Many justices have served some time as U.S. attorneys in the Department of Justice early in their legal careers. Relatively few have held elected political office; among today's justices, only Sandra Day O'Connor ever won an election (to the Arizona state legislature), but one chief justice—William Howard Taft—previously held the nation's highest elected post, the presidency.

*Age*   Most justices have been in their fifties when appointed to the Court. Presumably this is the age at which people acquire the necessary prominence and experience to bring themselves to the attention of the White House and Justice Department as potential candidates. At the same time, presidents seek to make a lasting imprint on the Court, and candidates in their fifties can be expected to serve on the Court for many more years than older candidates with the same credentials.

*Race and Gender*   No African American had ever served on the Supreme Court until President Lyndon Johnson's appointment of Thurgood Marshall in 1967. A Howard University Law School graduate, Marshall had served as counsel for the National Association for the Advancement of Colored People Legal Defense Fund and had personally argued the historic *Brown v. Board of Education* case before the Supreme Court in 1954. He served as solicitor general of the United States under President Lyndon Johnson before his elevation to the High Court.

Upon Marshall's retirement in 1991, President George Bush sought to retain minority representation on the Supreme Court, choosing Clarence Thomas. Bush's hopes for a smooth confirmation process in the Senate were dashed, however, when allegations of sexual harassment by Thomas created a firestorm of controversy before his eventual approval (see *Up Close:* "The Confirmation of Clarence Thomas").

No woman had served on the Supreme Court prior to the appointment of Sandra Day O'Connor by President Ronald Reagan in 1981. O'Connor was Reagan's first Supreme Court appointment. Though a relatively unknown Arizona state court judge, she had the powerful support of Arizona Republican Senator Barry Goldwater and Stanford classmate Justice William Rehnquist. The second woman to serve on the high court, Ruth Bader Ginsburg, had served as an attorney for the American Civil Liberties Union while teaching at Columbia Law School and had argued and won several important gender discrimination cases. President Jimmy Carter appointed her in 1980 to the U.S. Court of Appeals, where she acquired a reputation as a judicial moderate. President Bill Clinton elevated her to the Supreme Court in 1993.

*Class*   No one ever rose from more humble beginnings to the nation's highest Court, or any other top position in government, than Clarence Thomas. But Thomas is definitely an exception (see Table 13-6). Despite the appointments of Clarence Thomas, Thurgood Marshall, Sandra Day O'Connor, and Ruth Bader Ginsburg, the backgrounds of the 108 Supreme Court justices from 1789 to the present have been weighted in favor of white Protestant males over the age of fifty. The classic description of a Supreme Court justice written more than thirty years ago still applies more often than not:

> white, generally Protestant . . . ; fifty to fifty-five years of age at the time of . . . appointment; Anglo-Saxon ethnic stock. . . . ; high social status; reared in an urban environment; member of a civic-minded, politically active, economically comfortable family; legal training; some type of public office; generally well-educated.[23]

## SUPREME COURT DECISION MAKING

The Supreme Court sets its own agenda: it decides what it wants to decide. Of the more than 5,000 requests for hearing that come to its docket each year, the Court issues opinions on only about 200 cases. Another 150 or so cases are decided *summarily* (without opinion) by a Court order either affirming or reversing the lower-court decision. The Supreme Court refuses to rule at all on the vast

## The Confirmation of Clarence Thomas

Television coverage of Senate confirmation hearings on Clarence Thomas's appointment to the Supreme Court in 1991 captivated a national audience. The battle pitted blacks against whites (as well as against other blacks), men against women, and liberals against conservatives. The conflict raised just about every "hot-button" issue in American politics, from abortion rights and affirmative action to the most explosive new issue—sexual harassment.

Born to a teenage mother who earned $10 a week as a maid, Clarence Thomas and his brother lived in a dirt-floor shack in Pin Point, Georgia, where they were raised by strict, hardworking grandparents who taught young Clarence the value of education and sacrificed to send him to a Catholic school. He excelled academically and went on to mostly white Immaculate Conception Seminary College in Missouri to study for the Catholic priesthood. But when he overheard a fellow seminarian express satisfaction at the assassination of Dr. Martin Luther King, Jr., Thomas left the seminary in anger and enrolled at Holy Cross College, where he helped found the college's Black Student Union, and went on to graduate with honors and to win admission to Yale Law School.

Upon graduating from Yale, Thomas took a job as assistant attorney general in Missouri and later became a congressional aide to Republican Missouri Senator John Danforth. Despite misgivings about accepting a "black" post in government, in 1981 Thomas accepted the post as head of the Office of Civil Rights in the Department of Education, using the position to speak out on self-reliance, self-discipline, and the value of education. In 1982, he was named chair of the Equal Employment Opportunity

Commission (EEOC), where he successfully eliminated much of that agency's financial mismanagement and aggressively pursued individual cases of discrimination. At the same time, he spoke out against racial "quotas" and imposed minority hiring goals only on employers with proven records of discrimination. In 1989, President Bush nominated him to the U.S. Court of Appeals, and he was easily confirmed by the Senate.

In tapping Thomas for the Supreme Court, the White House reasoned that the liberal groups who had blocked the earlier nomination of conservative Robert Bork would be reluctant to launch personal attacks on an African American. The White House also believed that blacks would be divided; some might oppose Thomas because of his conservative views, but others might take pride in his remarkable rise from extreme poverty. With the opposition fractured, the White House saw an opportunity to push a strong conservative nominee through the Democrat-dominated Senate Judiciary Committee and win confirmation by the full Senate.

At first the Thomas nomination progressed fairly well in the media and in the Senate. The Senate Judiciary Committee, led by chair Joseph Biden, divided along party lines, with Democrat Dennis DeConcini siding with the Republicans to create a tie vote. The confirmation was forwarded to the full Senate, where at least sixty senators were prepared to vote for the nominee.

Behind the scenes, liberal interest groups, including the National Abortion Rights Action League, People for the American Way, and the National Organization for Women, were searching for evidence to discredit Thomas. On the third day of the hearings, a University of Oklahoma law professor, Anita Hill, a former legal assistant to Thomas both at the Department of Education and later at the Equal Employment Opportunity Commission, contacted the staff

majority of cases that are submitted to it. Thus the rhetorical threat to "take this all the way to the Supreme Court" is usually an empty one. It is important, however, to realize that a refusal to rule also creates law by allowing the decision of the lower court to stand. That is why the U.S. Circuit Courts of Appeals are powerful bodies.

of the Judiciary Committee with charges that Thomas had sexually harassed her in both jobs. Initially, Hill declined to make her charges public, but when Senator Biden refused to circulate anonymous charges, she agreed to be interviewed by the Federal Bureau of Investigation and went on to give a nationally televised press conference, elaborating on her charges against Thomas. Her bombshell became a media extravaganza, and the Senate Judiciary Committee reopened hearings.

Thomas himself flatly denied the charges. Appealing to the huge national television audience watching the proceedings live, he declared, "This is not American; this is Kafkaesque. It has got to stop. It must stop for the benefit of future nominees and our country. Enough is enough. . . ." A convincing witness on her own behalf, Anita Hill began by saying that only three months after coming to the civil rights office in the Department of Education, Thomas, who was then single, asked her to go out with him. Hill stated that though she declined, Thomas continued to ask her out and initiated sexual conversations with her that included references to pubic hair, penis size, and sex with animals.

Chair Biden and other Democrats on the committee treated Hill with great deference, asking her to talk about her feelings and provide even more explicit details of Thomas's alleged misconduct. But Senator Arlen Specter, a Republican moderate with a history of strong support for abortion rights, was not convinced that Hill was telling the truth. Why, he asked, with her legal education and knowledge of civil rights, had she failed to report this harassment? Why did she accept another job at the EEOC from Thomas if she had been harassed by him earlier at the Department of Education? Why had she made many calls to Thomas over the years leaving messages with his secretary such as "Please call."

Given a final opportunity to rebut Hill's charges, Thomas did so very emphatically: "This is a circus. It's a national disgrace. And from my standpoint as a black American, as far as I'm concerned, it is a high-tech lynching for uppity blacks who in any way deign to think for themselves. . . ." And, indeed, the confirmation process had exploded into a lurid show. The only restraint was Biden's rule that no questions would be asked about either Clarence Thomas's or Anita Hill's sex life. But the damage was done anyway, not only to Clarence Thomas and Anita Hill but to the Senate confirmation process.

In the end, there was no objective way to determine who was telling the truth. Too often the truth in Washington is determined by opinion polls. An astonishing 86 percent of the general public said they had watched the televised hearings. A majority of blacks as well as whites and a majority of women as well as men sided with the nominee.* In a fitting finale to the bitter and sleazy conflict, the final Senate confirmation vote was 52 to 48, the closest vote in the history of such confirmations. The best that can be said about the affair was that it placed the issue of sexual harassment on the national agenda.

*Gallup opinion reports, October 15, 1991, p. 209.

**Writt of certiorari:** A writ issued by the Supreme Court, at its discretion, to order a lower court to prepare the record of a case and send it to the Supreme Court for review. Most cases come to the Court as petitions for writs of certiorari.

*Setting the Agenda: Granting Certiorari*  Most cases reach the Supreme Court when a party in a case appeals to the Court to issue a **writ of certiorari** (literally to "make more certain"), a decision by the Court to require a lower federal or state court to turn over its records on a case.[24] To "grant certiorari"—that is, to decide to hear arguments in a case and render a decision—the Supreme

TABLE 13-6    BACKGROUNDS OF SUPREME COURT JUSTICES

| All U.S. Supreme Court Justices, 1789 to Present | *Number of Justices*<br>(Total = 108) |
|---|---|
| **Occupation or Position before Appointment** | |
| Private legal practice | 25 |
| State judgeship | 22 |
| Federal judgeship | 26 |
| U.S. attorney general | 7 |
| Deputy or assistant U.S. attorney general | 2 |
| U.S. solicitor general | 2 |
| U.S. senator | 6 |
| U.S. representative | 2 |
| State governor | 3 |
| Federal executive posts | 10 |
| Other | 3 |
| **Religious Background** | |
| Protestant | 84 |
| Roman Catholic | 9 |
| Jewish | 7 |
| Unitarian | 7 |
| No religious affiliation | 1 |
| **Age on Appointment** | |
| Under 40 | 4 |
| 41–50 | 30 |
| 51–60 | 59 |
| 61–70 | 15 |
| **Political Party Affiliation** | |
| Federalist (to 1835) | 13 |
| Democratic-Republican (to 1828) | 7 |
| Whig (to 1861) | 2 |
| Democrat | 44 |
| Republican | 42 |
| **Sex** | |
| Male | 106 |
| Female | 2 |
| **Race** | |
| Caucasian | 106 |
| African American | 2 |

*Source:* Congressional Quarterly, *Congressional Quarterly's Guide to the U.S. Supreme Court* (Washington, D.C.: Congressional Quarterly, 1979); *Congressional Quarterly's Guide to Government, Spring 1983* (Washington, D.C., 1982); updated to 1996 by author.

Court relies on its *rule of four:* four justices must agree to do so. Deciding which cases to hear takes up a great deal of the Court's time.

What criteria does the Supreme Court use in choosing its policy agenda—that is, in choosing the cases it wishes to decide? The Court rarely explains why it accepts or rejects cases, but there are some general patterns. First, the Court accepts cases involving issues that the justices are interested in. The justices are clearly interested in the area of First Amendment freedoms—speech, press, and religion. Members of the Court are also interested in civil rights issues under the Equal Protection Clause of the Fourteenth Amendment and the civil rights laws and in overseeing the criminal justice system and defining the Due Process Clauses of the Fifth and Fourteenth Amendments.

In addition, the Court seems to feel an obligation to accept cases involving questions that have been decided differently by different circuit courts of appeals. The Supreme Court generally tries to see to it that "the law" does not differ from one circuit to another. Likewise, the Supreme Court usually acts when lower courts have made decisions clearly at odds with Supreme Court interpretations in order to maintain control of the federal judiciary. Finally, the Supreme Court is more likely to accept a case in which the United States government is a party and requests a review, especially when an issue appears to be one of overriding importance to the government. In fact, the U.S. government is a party in almost half of the cases that are decided by the Supreme Court.

*Hearing Arguments*   Once the Supreme Court places a case on its decision calendar, attorneys for both sides submit written briefs on the issues. The Supreme Court may also allow interest groups to submit **amicus curiae** (literally, "friend of the court") briefs. This process allows interest groups direct access to the Supreme Court. In the affirmative action case of *University of California Regents v. Bakke* (1978),[25] the Court accepted 59 amicus curiae briefs representing more than 100 interest groups.

The United States government frequently submits amicus curiae arguments in cases in which it is not a party. The solicitor general of the United States is responsible for presenting the government's arguments both in cases in which the government is a party and in cases in which the government is merely an amicus curiae.

Oral arguments before the Supreme Court are a time-honored ritual of American government. They take place in the marble "temple"—the Supreme Court building across the street from the U.S. Capitol in Washington, D.C. (see Figure 13-3). The justices, clad in their black robes, sit behind a high "bench" and peer down at the attorneys presenting their arguments. Arguing a case before the Supreme Court is said to be an intimidating experience. Each side is usually limited to either a half-hour or an hour of argument, but justices frequently interrupt with their own pointed questioning. Court watchers sometimes try to predict the Court's decision from the tenor of the questioning. Oral argument is the most public phase of Supreme Court decision making, but no one really knows whether these arguments ever change the justices' minds.

*In Conference*   The actual decisions are made in private conferences among the justices. These conferences usually take place on Wednesdays and Fridays and cover the cases argued orally during the same week. The Chief Justice (currently William Rehnquist; see *People in Politics:* "William Rehnquist, Leading the Conservative Bloc") presides, and only justices (no law clerks) are present. It is customary for the Chief Justice to speak first on the issues, followed by each associate justice in order of seniority. A majority must decide which party wins or loses and whether a lower court's decision is to be affirmed or reversed.

*Writing Opinions*   The *written* opinion determines the actual outcome of the case (votes in conference are not binding). When the decision is unanimous, the

**Amicus curiae:** Literally, "friend of the court"; a person, private group or institution, or government agency that is not a party to a case but that participates in the case (usually through submission of a brief) at the invitation of the court or on its own initiative.

FIGURE 13-3 **Corridors of**

**Power in the Supreme Court**
*This cutaway shows the location of the principal offices and chambers of the Supreme Court building.*

THE SUPREME COURT

1. Courtyards
2. Solicitor General's Office
3. Lawyers' Lounge
4. Marshall's Office
5. Main Hall
6. Court Room
7. Conference and Reception Rooms

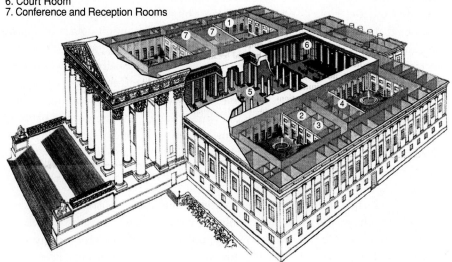

Chief Justice traditionally writes the opinion. In the case of a split decision, the Chief Justice may take on the task of writing the **majority opinion** or assign it to another justice in the majority. If the Chief Justice is in the minority, the senior justice in the majority makes the assignment. Writing the opinion of the Court is the central task in Supreme Court policy making. Broadly written opinions may effect sweeping policy changes; narrowly written opinions may decide a particular case but have very little policy impact. The reasons cited for the decision become binding law, to be applied by lower courts in future cases. Yet despite the crucial role of opinion writing in Court policy making, most opinions are actually written by law clerks who are only recent graduates of the nation's prestigious law schools. The justices themselves read, edit, correct, and sometimes rewrite drafts prepared by clerks, but clerks may have a strong influence over the position taken by justices on the issues.

In addition, the views of the legal profession itself—as reflected by the American Bar Association (ABA) as well as the numerous law reviews published by law schools—influence the Court in subtle yet important ways. Often new interpretations of laws or the Constitution first appear in prestigious law journals, then are borrowed by Supreme Court clerks preparing drafts of opinions by justices, and finally become law when incorporated into majority opinions.

A draft of the opinion is circulated among members of the majority. Any majority member who disagrees with the reasoning in the opinion, and thus disagrees with the policy that is proposed, may either negotiate changes in the opinion with others in the majority or write a concurring opinion. A **concurring opinion** agrees with the decision about which party wins the case but sets forth a different reason for the decision, proposing, in fact, a different policy position.

Justices in the minority must also agree on a **dissenting opinion.** The dissenting opinion sets forth the views of justices who disagree with both the decision and the majority reasoning. Dissenting opinions do not have the force of

**Majority opinion:** An opinion in a case that is subscribed to by a majority of the judges who participated in the decision.

**Concurring opinion:** An opinion by a member of a court that agrees with the result reached by the court in the case but disagrees with or departs from the court's rationale for the decision.

**Dissenting opinion:** An opinion by a member of a court that disagrees with the result reached by the court in the case.

# William Rehnquist, Leading the Conservative Bloc

In the more than 200 years of Supreme Court history, the Court has contained some of the finest legal minds of its time (as well as its share of less-than-brilliant legalists). Only three men, however, have been "promoted" from the post of associate justice to chief justice: Edward D. White (Chief Justice from 1910 to 1921), Harlan F. Stone (Chief Justice from 1941 to 1946), and the current Chief Justice, William H. Rehnquist.

Rehnquist grew up in the affluent Milwaukee suburb of Shorewood, where his mother was a civic activist and local Republican leader. After serving in the Army Air Corps during World War II as a weather observer in North Africa, he took advantage of the G.I. Bill to attend Stanford University, where he graduated Phi Beta Kappa with a degree in political science in 1948. He went on to graduate school at Harvard, earning a master's degree, then returned to Stanford to attend law school, finishing at the top of his class and winning the chance to serve as a clerk for the late Justice Robert H. Jackson, one of the Court's more conservative thinkers. When his internship at the Supreme Court ended, Rehnquist moved to Arizona to begin private practice. In Phoenix, he became active in the Arizona State Republican Party and worked on the presidential campaigns of Barry Goldwater in 1964 and Richard Nixon in 1968.

Following Nixon's election, Rehnquist went to Washington as assistant attorney general. On several occasions, Rehnquist publicly criticized the Supreme Court as having gone too far in protecting the rights of the accused.

When a seat on the Supreme Court became open in 1971, Nixon, who had pledged in his campaign to appoint "judicial conservatives" to the Court, nominated Rehnquist, anticipating that the relatively young conservative (age forty-seven) would serve for a long time. The nomination sparked a debate in the Senate over what Rehnquist's opponents labeled his "ultraconservative" philosophy. Numerous civil rights groups and liberals spoke against him in the Senate Judiciary Committee's hearings, but Rehnquist successfully defended his positions, responding calmly and professionally to hostile questions by Senators Edward Kennedy and Birch Bayh. The Senate voted 68 to 26 in favor of confirming the nomination.

Rehnquist arrived at the Court just as it was beginning to reconcile years of judicial activism under recently retired Chief Justice Earl Warren with the more restrained approach of Chief Justice Warren Burger. But Burger never followed a true conservative or restraintist position; the Chief Justice frequently led the Court in upholding defendants' rights, court-ordered desegregation, and affirmative action plans. As a result, Rehnquist wrote so many "lone dissenting" opinions that his law clerks presented him with a Lone Ranger doll. In *Roe v. Wade* in 1973, Rehnquist wrote in his dissenting opinion (which only Justice Byron White joined) that "Abortion involves the purposeful termination of potential life" and is therefore "beyond the rubric of personal privacy."

Over time Rehnquist began to find additional support on the Court for his positions, not because he had changed but because the Court membership changed. In 1986, after fifteen years on the Court, Rehnquist was nominated by President Reagan to the position of Chief Justice upon Burger's retirement. At the same time, Reagan nominated another strong conservative, Antonin Scalia, to take Rehnquist's seat as associate justice. Again Rehnquist came under sharp attack in the Senate Judiciary Committee, but no one really doubted his brilliance in constitutional law. The Senate tradition of confirming presidential nominees (barring evidence of incompetence or lack of ethics) still held sway, and Rehnquist was confirmed.

With the appointment of this conservative leader to the most conservative Court in fifty years, many observers looked for major changes in the High Court's decisions. Instead, Rehnquist has wound up the leader of only the most conservative members on the Court.

law. They are written both to express opposition to the majority view and to appeal to a future Court to someday modify or reverse the position of the majority.

Occasionally, the Court is unable to agree on a clear policy position on particularly vexing questions. If the majority is strongly divided over the reasoning behind their decision and as many as four justices dissent altogether from the decision, lower courts will lack clear guidance and future cases will be decided on a case-by-case basis, depending on multiple factors occurring in each case (see, for example, "Affirmative Action in the Courts" in Chapter 15). The absence of a clear opinion of the Court, supported by a unified majority of the justices, invites additional cases, keeping the issue on the Court's agenda until such time (if any) as the Court establishes a clear policy on the issue.

*Voting Blocs*   Although liberal and conservative voting blocs on the Court are visible over time, on any given case particular justices may deviate from their perceived ideological position. Many cases do not present a liberal-conservative dimension. Each case presents a separate set of facts, and even justices who share a general philosophy may perceive the central facts of a case differently. Moreover, the liberal-versus-conservative dimension sometimes clashes with the activist-versus-self-restraint dimension. While we generally think of liberals as favoring activism and conservatives self-restraint, occasionally those who favor self-restraint are obliged to approve of legislation that violates their personal conservative beliefs because opposing it would substitute their judgment for that of elected officials. So ideological blocs are not always good predictors of voting outcomes on the Court.

Over time, the composition of the Supreme Court has changed, as has the power of its various liberal and conservative voting blocs (see Table 13-7). The liberal bloc, headed by Chief Justice Earl Warren, dominated Court decision making from the mid-1950s through the end of the 1960s. The liberal bloc gradually weakened following President Richard Nixon's appointment of Warren Burger as

| TABLE 13-7   LIBERAL AND CONSERVATIVE VOTING BLOCS ON THE SUPREME COURT | | | |
|---|---|---|---|
| | *The Warren Court* 1968 | *The Burger Court* 1975 | *The Rehnquist Court* 1996 |
| Liberal | Earl Warren Hugo Black William O. Douglas Thurgood Marshall William J. Brennan Abe Fortas | William O. Douglas Thurgood Marshall William J. Brennan | John Paul Stevens Ruth Bader Ginsburg Stephen G. Breyer |
| Moderate | Potter Stewart Byron White | Potter Stewart Byron White Lewis Powell Harry Blackmun | Anthony Kennedy Sandra Day O'Connor David Souter |
| Conservative | John Marshall Harlan | Warren Burger William Rehnquist | William Rehnquist Antonin Scalia Clarence Thomas |

Chief Justice in 1969, but not all of Nixon's appointees joined the conservative bloc; Justice Harry Blackmun and Justice Lewis Powell frequently joined in voting with the liberal bloc. Among Nixon's appointees, only William Rehnquist has consistently adopted conservative positions. President Gerald Ford's only appointee to the Court, John Paul Stevens, began as a moderate and drifted to the liberal bloc. As a result, the Burger Court, while generally not as activist as the Warren Court, still did not reverse any earlier liberal holdings.

President Ronald Reagan, who had campaigned on a pledge to restrain the liberal activism of the Court, tried to appoint conservatives. His first appointee, Sandra Day O'Connor, turned out to be less conservative than expected, especially on women's issues and abortion rights. When Chief Justice Burger retired in 1986, Reagan seized on the opportunity to strengthen the conservative bloc by elevating Rehnquist to Chief Justice and appointing a strong conservative, Antonin Scalia, to the Court. Reagan added Anthony Kennedy to the Court in 1988, giving Rehnquist and the conservative bloc the opportunity to form a majority if they could win over Byron White, a moderately conservative justice and the Court's senior member, having been appointed by President John F. Kennedy in 1962. Had President Reagan succeeded in getting the powerful conservative voice of Robert Bork on the Court, it is possible that many earlier liberal decisions, including *Roe v. Wade,* would have been reversed. But the Senate rejected Bork (see *Up Close:* "The Bork Battle"); David Souter, the man ultimately confirmed, compiled a moderate record.

Liberals worried that the appointment of conservative Clarence Thomas as a replacement for the liberal Thurgood Marshall would give the conservative bloc a commanding voice in Supreme Court policy making. But no solid conservative majority emerged. Justices Rehnquist, Scalia, and Thomas are considered the core of the conservative bloc, but they must win over at least two of the more moderate justices in order to form a majority in a case. President Bill Clinton's appointees, Ruth Bader Ginsburg and Stephen G. Breyer, came to the Court with reputations as moderate judges, but they have generally supported liberal views on the Supreme Court. On key questions, the moderate bloc has the deciding vote (see *Up Close:* "Privacy, Abortion, and the Constitution").

# CHECKING COURT POWER

Many people are concerned about the extent to which we now rely on a non-elected judiciary to decide key policy issues rather than depending upon a democratically elected president or Congress. Harvard Law School professor Archibald Cox, who became famous as the first Watergate prosecutor, warned that

> excessive reliance upon courts, instead of self-government through democratic processes, may deaden the people's sense of moral and political responsibility for their own future, especially in matters of liberty, and may stunt the growth of political capacity that results from the exercise of the ultimate powers of decision.[26]

## Privacy, Abortion, and the Constitution

No other issue has generated more emotional, political, and legal controversy for the Supreme Court than abortion. Yet prior to the 1973 Court decision in *Roe v. Wade,* abortion was not a significant issue in American national politics. Since the 1800s, abortions for any purpose other than saving the life of the mother had been criminal offenses under most state laws. About a dozen states acted in the late 1960s to permit abortions in cases of rape or incest or to protect the physical (and, in some cases, mental) health of the mother. Relatively few abortions were performed under these laws, however, because of the red tape involved—review of each case by several concurring physicians, approval of a hospital board, and so forth. Then in 1970, New York, Alaska, Hawaii, and Washington enacted laws that in effect permitted abortion at the request of the woman involved and the concurrence of her physician. During this period, a growing pro-abortion coalition formed, including the American Civil Liberties Union, a new National Association for the Repeal of Abortion Laws, Planned Parenthood, and women's organizations, including the National Organization for Women.

*The Right to Privacy* Meanwhile, the Supreme Court was developing a new constitutional right—the right of privacy—partly in response to a case brought to it by Planned Parenthood in 1965. When Estelle Griswold opened a birth control clinic on behalf of the Planned Parenthood League of Connecticut, the state found her in violation of a Connecticut law prohibiting the use of contraceptives. She challenged the constitutionality of the statute, and in its ruling in *Griswold v. Connecticut* the Supreme Court struck down the law by a vote of 7 to 2. Voting for the majority were William J. Brennan, Tom Clark, William O. Douglas, Arthur Goldberg, John Marshall Harlan, Earl Warren, and Byron R. White. Dissenting were Hugo Black and Potter Stewart.

While the majority agreed that a right to privacy could be found in the Constitution, members of the majority could not agree on where it was to be found. Justice Douglas found it in "the penumbras formed by emanations from" the First, Third, Fourth, Ninth, and Fifteenth Amendments. Justices Goldberg, Warren, and Brennan found it in the Ninth Amendment: "The enumeration of the Constitution of certain rights, shall not be contrived to deny or disparage others retained by the people." Justice Harlan found the right in the word "liberty" in the Fourteenth Amendment. The fact that Griswold dealt with reproduction gave encouragement to groups advocating abortion rights.

*Roe v. Wade* In 1969, Norma McCorvey sought an abortion in Texas, but the doctor refused, citing a state law prohibiting abortion except to save a woman's life. McCorvey bore the child and gave it up for adoption but then enlisted the aid of two young attorneys, Linda Coffee and Sarah Weddington, who challenged the Texas law in federal courts on a variety of constitutional grounds, including the right to privacy. Amicus curiae briefs were filed by a wide assortment of groups on both sides of the issue. McCorvey became "Jane Roe," and the case became one of the most controversial in the Court's history.[1]

Again divided 7 to 2 (despite membership changes), the Supreme Court ruled that the constitutional right of privacy as well as the Fourteenth Amendment's guarantee of "liberty" included a woman's decision to bear or not to bear a child. The Court ruled that the word "person" in the Constitution did *not* include the unborn child; therefore, the Fifth and Fourteenth Amendments' guarantee of "life, liberty, or property" did not protect the "life" of the fetus. The Court also ruled that a state's power to protect the health and safety of the mother could not justify any restriction on abortion in the first three months of pregnancy. Between the third and sixth months of pregnancy, a state could set standards for abortion procedures in order to protect the health of women, but a state could not prohibit abortions. Only in the final three months could a state prohibit or regulate abortion to protect the unborn. Voting with the majority were Harry A. Blackmun, William J. Brennan, Warren Burger, William O. Douglas, Thurgood Marshall, Lewis Powell, and Potter Stewart. Dissenting were William Rehnquist and Byron R. White.

Rather than end the political controversy over abortion, *Roe v. Wade* set off a conflagration. A new movement was mobilized to restrict the scope of the decision and if possible to bring about its overturn. Congress defeated efforts to pass a constitutional amendment restricting abortion or declaring that life begins at conception. However, when Congress banned the use of federal funds under Medicaid (medical care for the poor) for abortions except to protect the life of a woman, the Supreme Court upheld the ban, holding that there was no constitutional obligation for governments to pay for abortions.[2]

*The Battle over Restrictions*   Initial efforts by some states to restrict abortion ran into Supreme Court opposition. In the face of repeated challenges, the Court held that states may not require that all abortions be performed in hospitals; require parental consent for all minors; require that physicians inform women of particular risks associated with abortion or provide information about fetal development; or require a twenty-four-hour waiting period between authorizing and performing an abortion.

Opponents of abortion won a victory in *Webster v. Reproductive Health Services* in 1989.[3] In this case, the Supreme Court upheld a Missouri law denying public funds for abortions that were not necessary to preserve the life of the woman and denying the use of public facilities or employees in performing or assisting in abortions. More important, the justices recognized the state's "interest in the protection of human life when viability is possible" and upheld Missouri's requirement for a test of "viability" after twenty weeks and a prohibition on abortions of a viable fetus except to save a woman's life.

The vote on *Webster* was a signal to pro-life groups that the Supreme Court's position was changing. Rehnquist and White had dissented in the original *Roe v. Wade* case; they were now joined in upholding restrictions on abortion by three new Reagan appointees, Sandra Day O'Connor, Anthony Kennedy, and Antonin Scalia. Dissenting were Harry A. Blackmun, William J. Brennan, Thurgood Marshall, and John Paul Stevens.

*Reaffirming Roe v. Wade*   Abortion has become such a polarizing issue that "pro-choice" and "pro-life" groups are generally unwilling to search out a middle ground. Yet the current Supreme Court appears to have chosen a policy of affirming a woman's right to abortion while upholding modest restrictions, as evidenced by the Court's ruling in *Planned Parenthood of Pennsylvania v. Casey* (1992).[4]

In this case, the Supreme Court considered a series of restrictions on abortion enacted by Pennsylvania: that physicians must inform women of risks and alternatives; that women must wait twenty-four hours after requesting an abortion before having one; and that minors must have the consent of parents or a judge. It struck down the requirement that spouses be notified.

Justice Sandra Day O'Connor took the lead in forming a moderate, swing bloc on the Court, consisting of herself, Anthony Kennedy, and David Souter. (Harry A. Blackmun and John Paul Stevens voted to uphold *Roe v. Wade* with *no* restrictions, making the vote 5 to 4.) Her majority opinion strongly reaffirmed the fundamental right of abortion, both on the basis of the Fourteenth Amendment and on the principle of stare decisis. But the majority also upheld states' rights to protect any fetus that reached the point of "viability." The Court went on to establish a new standard for constitutionally evaluating restrictions: they must not impose an "undue burden" on women seeking abortion or place "substantial obstacles" in her path. All of Pennsylvania's restrictions met this standard and were upheld except spousal notification.

Despite outcries from both pro-choice and pro-life forces, the Casey decision puts the Supreme Court almost exactly where opinion polls suggest most Americans are: generally supporting a woman's right to choose an abortion early in pregnancy but also supporting many restrictions on the exercise of that right.

[1]*Roe v. Wade*, 410 U.S. 113 (1973).
[2]*Harris v. McRae*, 448 U.S. 297 (1980).
[3]*Webster v. Reproductive Health Services*, 492 U.S. 490 (1989).
[4]*Planned Parenthood v. Casey*, 510 U.S. 110 (1992).

*Legitimacy as a Restraint in the Judiciary*   Court authority derives from legitimacy rather than force. By that we mean that the courts depend upon their authority being seen as rightful, on people perceiving an obligation to abide by court decisions whether they agree with them or not. The courts have no significant force at their direct command. Federal marshals, who carry out the orders of federal courts, number only a few thousand. Courts must rely primarily upon the executive branch for enforcement of their decisions.

Today most Americans believe that Supreme Court decisions are authoritative statements about the Constitution and that people have an obligation to obey these decisions whether they agree with them or not. Thus public opinion constrains other public officials—from the president, to governors, to school superintendents, to law enforcement officials—to obey Supreme Court decisions. Their constituents do not hold them personally responsible for unpopular actions that are ordered by the Supreme Court or federal judges. On the contrary, their constituents generally expect them to comply with court decisions.

The institutional legitimacy of the federal courts was tested in the civil rights battles of the 1950s and 1960s. In 1957, Governor Orval Faubus of Arkansas used state National Guard troops to halt federal marshals from escorting black students into a segregated Little Rock high school pursuant to a federal court order. President Dwight Eisenhower had his personal doubts about the wisdom of federal court-ordered desegregation, but the governor's open defiance of a federal court order could not be tolerated by a president sworn "to preserve, protect, and defend the Constitution of the United States." Eisenhower ordered U.S. Army troops to Little Rock to enforce the federal court's order, a decision that proved a historic turning point in the civil rights movement. But Eisenhower's decision also greatly strengthened federal courts, ensuring that the full force of the federal government would be used to gain compliance with their decisions.

Widespread opposition to Supreme Court policy can obstruct and delay its implementation. For example, the Supreme Court's 1963 ruling that prayer and Bible-reading exercises in public schools violated the No Establishment Clause of the First Amendment was very unpopular (see Chapter 14). Many public school systems simply ignored the decision. Enforcement required individuals or groups in school districts throughout the country to bring separate suits in federal courts. In school districts where no one strongly objected to prayer or where objectors did not have the will or resources to bring suit against school officials, the practice continued. Congress did not feel disposed to cut off federal funds to schools that allowed prayer, and the president was not disposed to send federal troops into the schools to halt Bible reading. Only gradually were prayers and other religious observances deleted from public school exercises.

*Compliance with Court Policy*   Federal and state court judges must apply Supreme Court policies when ruling on cases in their own courts.[27] Occasionally lower courts will express their disagreement with the Supreme Court in an opinion, even when they feel obliged to carry out the High Court's policy. At times, lower federal and state courts will try to give a narrow interpretation to a Supreme Court decision with which they disagree. But judges who seek to defy the Supreme Court face the ultimate sanction of reversal on appeal by the losing party. Professional pride usually inspires judges to avoid reversals of their judgments by higher courts even though a long record of reversals is not grounds for impeachment or removal of a federal judge.

Public officials who defy Supreme Court rulings risk lawsuits and court orders mandating compliance. Persons injured by noncompliance are likely to file suit against noncomplying officials, as are interest groups that monitor official compliance with the policies they support. These suits are expensive and time-consuming and are potentially embarrassing to government officials and agencies. Once a court order is issued, continued defiance can result in fines and penalties for contempt of court.

The president of the United States is subject to federal court orders. Historically, this notion has been challenged: early presidents believed that they were separate and at least co-equal to the courts and that their own determination about the legality or constitutionality of their own acts could not be overturned by the courts. President Andrew Jackson could—and did—say: "John Marshall has made his decision. Now let him enforce it," expressing the view that the president was not obliged to enforce court decisions that he disagreed with.[28] But in the course of 200 years, the courts—not the president—have gained in legitimacy as the final authority on the law and the Constitution. Today a president who openly defied the Supreme Court would lose any claims to legitimacy and would risk impeachment by Congress.

The case of Richard Nixon illustrates the weakness of a modern president who would even consider defying the Supreme Court. When Nixon sought to invoke executive privilege to withhold damaging tapes of White House conversations in the Watergate investigation (see *Up Close:* "Watergate and the Limits of Presidential Power" in Chapter 11), federal district judge John Sirica rejected his claim and ordered that the tapes be turned over to the special prosecutor in the case. In arguments before the Supreme Court, Nixon's lawyers contended that the president would not have to comply with a Supreme Court decision to turn over the tapes. Yet when the Court ruled unanimously against him, Nixon felt bound to comply and released tapes that were very damaging to his cause. But Nixon understood that refusal to abide by a Supreme Court decision would most assuredly have resulted in impeachment. Under the circumstances, compliance was the better of two unattractive choices.[29]

*Presidential Influence on Court Policy*   The president and Congress can exercise some restraint over court power through the checks and balances built into the Constitution. Using the office's powers of appointment, presidents have effectively modified the direction of Supreme Court policy and influenced lower federal courts as well. Certainly presidents must await the death or retirement of Supreme Court justices and federal judges, and presidents are constrained by the need to secure Senate confirmation of their appointees. However, over time presidential influence on the courts can be significant. During their combined twelve years in the White House, Ronald Reagan and George Bush were able to fill 70 percent of federal district and appellate court judgeships and six of nine Supreme Court positions with their own appointees. As noted earlier, however, their appointees did not always reflect these presidents' philosophy of judicial self-restraint in rendering decisions. Nevertheless, the federal courts tilted in a somewhat more conservative direction. President Bill Clinton's appointments generally strengthened liberal, activist impulses throughout the federal judiciary.

*Congressional Checks on the Judiciary* The Constitution gives Congress control over the structure and jurisdiction of federal district and appellate courts, but congressional use of this control has been restrained. Only the Supreme Court is established by the Constitution; Article III gives Congress the power to "ordain and establish" "inferior" courts. In theory, Congress could try to limit court jurisdiction to hear cases that Congress did not wish it to decide. Congress has used this power to lighten the federal courts' workload; for example, Congress has limited the jurisdiction of federal courts in cases between citizens of different states by requiring that the dispute involve more than $50,000. But Congress has never used this power to change court policy—for example, by removing federal court jurisdiction over school prayer cases or desegregation cases. Indeed federal courts would probably declare unconstitutional any congressional attempt to limit their power to interpret the Constitution by limiting jurisdiction.

Likewise while Congress could, in theory, expand membership on the Supreme Court, the custom of a nine-member Supreme Court is now so deeply ingrained in American government that "court packing" is politically unthinkable. Franklin Roosevelt's unsuccessful 1937 attempt to expand the Supreme Court was the last serious assault on its membership. However, President Jimmy Carter succeeded in getting Congress to add a large number of federal district judgeships, and he used these new posts to appoint more women and minorities to the federal judiciary.

A more common congressional constraint on the Supreme Court is amending statutory laws to reverse federal court interpretations of these laws that Congress believes are in error. Thus when the Supreme Court decided that civil rights laws did not mandate a cutoff of all federal funds to a college upon evidence of discrimination in a single program but only the funds for that program,[30] Congress amended its own laws to require the more sweeping remedy. Likewise, when the Supreme Court ruled that existing civil rights legislation put the burden of proof of discrimination on plaintiffs rather than employers, Congress passed the Civil Rights Act of 1991, which requires employers to show why tests and other recruitment practices are a "business necessity." While members of Congress frequently berate the Court for what they see as misreading of the laws, all Congress needs to do to reverse a Court interpretation of those laws is to pass amendments to them.

Constitutional amendment is the only means by which the Congress and the states can reverse a Supreme Court interpretation of the Constitution itself. After the Civil War, the Thirteenth Amendment abolishing slavery reversed the Supreme Court's *Dred Scott* decision (1857) that slavery was constitutionally protected. The Sixteenth Amendment (1913) gave Congress the power to impose an income tax, thus reversing the Supreme Court's earlier decision in *Pollock v. Farmer's Loan*[31] holding income taxes illegal (1895). But recent attempts to reverse Supreme Court interpretations of the Constitution by passing constitutional amendments on the issues of prayer in public schools, busing, and abortion have all failed to win congressional approval. The barriers to a constitutional amendment are formidable: a two-thirds vote of both houses of Congress and ratification by three-quarters of the states. Thus for all practical purposes, the Constitution is what the Supreme Court says it is.

Congress can impeach federal court judges, but only for committing crimes, not for their decisions. Although impeachment is frequently cited as a constitutional check on the judiciary, it has no real influence over judicial policy making. Only five federal court judges have ever been impeached by the House, convicted by the Senate, and removed from office, though two others were impeached and another nine resigned to avoid impeachment. In 1989, Federal District Court Judge Alcee Hastings became the first sitting judge in more than fifty years to be impeached, tried, and found guilty by the Congress. He was convicted by the Senate of perjury and conspiracy to obtain a $150,000 bribe; but a federal district court judge ruled that he should have been tried by the full Senate, not a special committee of the Senate. Hastings declared the ruling a vindication; in 1992, he won a congressional seat in Florida, becoming the first person ever to become a member of the House after being impeached by that same body. Even criminal convictions do not ensure removal from office, although judges have resigned under fire.

# SUMMARY NOTES

- Great power is lodged in the Supreme Court of the United States and the federal judiciary. These courts have undertaken to resolve many of the most divisive conflicts in American society. The judicial power is the power to decide cases and controversies, and in so doing to decide the meaning of the Constitution and laws of Congress.

- The power of judicial review is the power to invalidate laws of Congress or of the states that the federal courts believe conflict with the U.S. Constitution. This power is not specifically mentioned in the Constitution but was derived by Chief Justice John Marshall from the Supremacy Clause and the meaning of judicial power in Article III.

- The Supreme Court has been fairly restrained in its use of judicial review with regard to laws of Congress and actions of presidents; it has more frequently overturned state laws. The federal courts also exercise great power in the interpretation of the laws of Congress, especially when statutory language is vague.

- Arguments over judicial power are reflected in the conflicting philosophies of judicial activism and judicial self-restraint. Advocates of judicial restraint argue that judges must not substitute their own views for those of elected representatives and that the remedy for unwise laws lies in the legislature, not the courts. Advocates of judicial activism argue that the courts must view the Constitution as a liv-

ing document and that its meaning must fit the needs of a changing society.

- The federal judiciary consists of three levels of courts—the Supreme Court, the U.S. Courts of Appeals, and the U.S. District Courts. The district courts are trial courts that hear both civil and criminal cases. The courts of appeals are appellate courts and do not hold trials but consider only the record of trial courts and the arguments (briefs) of attorneys. More than 90 percent of federal cases end in appeals courts. The Supreme Court can hear appeals from state high courts as well as lower federal courts. The Supreme Court hears only about 200 cases a year.

- Courts function under general rules of restraint that do not bind the president or Congress. The Supreme Court does not decide hypothetical cases or render advisory opinions. The principle of stare decisis, or reliance on precedent, is not set aside lightly.

- The selection of Supreme Court justices and federal judges is based more on political considerations than legal qualifications. Presidents almost always appoint judges from their own party, and presidents increasingly have sought judges who share their ideological views. However, because of the independence of judges once they are appointed, presidents have sometimes been disappointed in the decisions of their appointees. In addition, Senate approval of nominees has become increasingly politicized, with problems most evident when different parties control the White House and the Senate.

- The Supreme Court sets its own agenda for policy making, usually by granting or withholding certiorari. Generally four justices must agree to grant certiorari for a case to be decided by the Supreme Court. The Supreme Court has been especially active in policy making in interpreting the meaning of the Fourteenth Amendment's guarantee of "equal protection of the laws," as well as of the civil rights and voting rights acts of Congress. It has also been active in defining the meaning of freedom of press, speech, and religion in the First Amendment and "due process of law" in the Fifth Amendment. The federal courts are active in overseeing government regulatory activity. But federal courts have generally left the areas of national security and international relations to the president and Congress. In addition, the Court tends to accept cases involving questions decided differently by different courts of appeal, cases in which lower courts have challenged Supreme Court interpretations, and cases in which the U.S. government is a party and it requests review.

- Liberal and conservative blocs on the Supreme Court can be discerned over time. Generally, liberals have been judicial activists while conservatives have been restraintists. Today a moderate bloc appears to hold the balance of power.

- Court power derives primarily from legitimacy rather than force. Most Americans believe that Supreme Court decisions are authoritative statements about the Constitution and that people have an obligation to obey these decisions whether they agree with them or not. While early presidents thought of themselves as constitutional co-equals with the Supreme Court and not necessarily bound by Court decisions, today it would be politically unthinkable for a president to ignore a court order.

- There are very few checks on Supreme Court power. Presidents may try to influence Court policy through judicial nominations, but once judges are confirmed by the Senate they can pursue their own impulses. Congress has never tried to use its power to limit the jurisdiction of federal courts in order to influence judicial decisions.

- Only by amending the Constitution can Congress and the states reverse a Supreme Court interpretation of its meaning. Congress can impeach federal judges only for committing crimes, not for their decisions.

# SELECTED READINGS

ABRAHAM, HENRY J. *The Judicial Process,* 8th ed. New York: Oxford University Press, 1991. A comprehensive survey of judicial politics and processes. It provides an introduction to the nature and sources of law, as well as the organization, functioning, and staffing of the courts.

————. *Justices and Presidents,* 3d ed. New York: Oxford University Press, 1992. A history of the presidential appointments to the Supreme Court and the politics surrounding their nomination and confirmation.

BAUM, LAWRENCE. *The Supreme Court,* 4th ed. Washington, D.C.: Congressional Quarterly Press, 1992. A readable introduction to the Supreme Court as a political institution, covering the selection and confirmation of judges, the nature of the issues decided by courts, the process of judicial decision making, and the impact of Supreme Court decisions.

EPSTEIN, LEE, JEFFREY A. SEGAL, HAROLD J. SPAETH, and THOMAS G. WALKER. *The Supreme Court Compendium.* Washington, D.C.: Congressional Quarterly Press, 1994. A comprehensive collection of data on the High Court, including key decisions organized by subject, backgrounds and voting of justices, and nominations and confirmations.

JOHNSON, CHARLES A., and BRADLEY C. CANNON. *Judicial Policies: Implementation and Impact.* Washington, D.C.: Congressional Quarterly Press, 1984. An examination of how court policies are implemented and how their impact is felt by citizens and governments.

NAGEL, ROBERT F. *Judicial Power and American Character.* New York: Oxford University Press, 1994. A critique of judicial reasoning as a mask for the exercise of power.

SCHWARTZ, BERNARD. *A History of the Supreme Court.* New York: Oxford University Press, 1995. A comprehensive one-volume history of the nation's highest court and the influence the Court has had on American politics and society.

Woodward, Bob, and Scott Amestry. *The Brethren*. New York: Simon & Schuster, 1979. A behind-the-scenes account of decision making in the Supreme Court, purporting to expose how the justices maneuver, argue, intrigue, and compromise over major issues.

U.S. Supreme Court decisions are available at most public and university libraries as well as at law libraries in volumes of *United States Reports*. Court opinions are cited by the names of the parties, for example, *Brown v. Board of Education of Topeka,* followed by a reference number such as 347 U.S. 483 (1954). The first number in the citation (347) is the volume number; "U.S." refers to *United States Reports;* the subsequent number is the page on which the decision begins; the year the case was decided is in parentheses.

# chapter 14

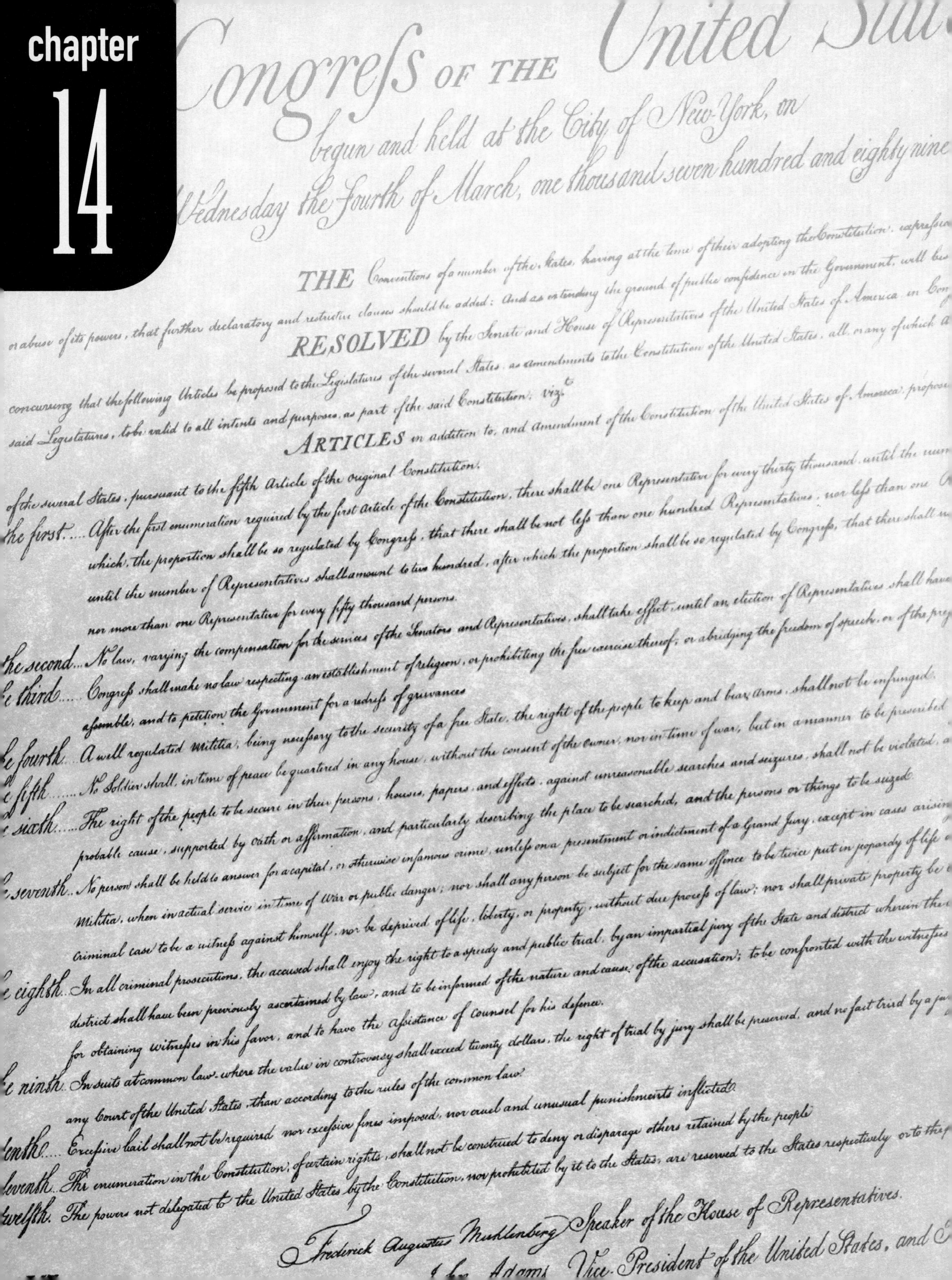
Congress of the United Stat[es]
begun and held at the City of New-York, on
[W]ednesday the Fourth of March, one thousand seven hundred and eighty nine
THE Conventions of a number of the States, having at the time of their adopting the Constitution, expressi[ng]
or abuse of its powers, that further declaratory and restrictive clauses should be added: And as extending the ground of public confidence in the Government, will bes[t]
RESOLVED by the Senate and House of Representatives of the United States of America in Con[gress]
concurring that the following Articles be proposed to the Legislatures of the several States, as amendments to the Constitution of the United States, all, or any of which a[...]
said Legislatures, to be valid to all intents and purposes, as part of the said Constitution; viz.[t]
ARTICLES in addition to, and Amendment of the Constitution of the United States of America, propos[ed]
of the several States, pursuant to the fifth Article of the original Constitution.
[T]he first..... After the first enumeration required by the first Article of the Constitution, there shall be one Representative for every thirty thousand, until the num[ber]
which, the proportion shall be so regulated by Congress, that there shall be not less than one hundred Representatives, nor less than one R[...]
until the number of Representatives shall amount to two hundred, after which the proportion shall be so regulated by Congress, that there shall n[...]
nor more than one Representative for every fifty thousand persons.
[T]he second... No law, varying the compensation for the services of the Senators and Representatives, shall take effect, until an election of Representatives shall have [...]
[Th]e third..... Congress shall make no law respecting an establishment of religion, or prohibiting the free exercise thereof; or abridging the freedom of speech, or of the pre[ss]
assemble, and to petition the Government for a redress of grievances.
[Th]e fourth... A well regulated Militia, being necessary to the security of a free State, the right of the people to keep and bear Arms, shall not be infringed.
[Th]e fifth...... No Soldier shall, in time of peace be quartered in any house, without the consent of the Owner, nor in time of war, but in a manner to be prescribed [...]
[Th]e sixth..... The right of the people to be secure in their persons, houses, papers, and effects, against unreasonable searches and seizures, shall not be violated, a[...]
probable cause, supported by Oath or affirmation, and particularly describing the place to be searched, and the persons or things to be seized.
[Th]e seventh.. No person shall be held to answer for a capital, or otherwise infamous crime, unless on a presentment or indictment of a Grand Jury, except in cases arisin[g]
Militia, when in actual service in time of War or public danger; nor shall any person be subject for the same offence to be twice put in jeopardy of life o[r]
criminal case to be a witness against himself, nor be deprived of life, liberty, or property, without due process of law; nor shall private property be t[...]
[Th]e eighth.. In all criminal prosecutions, the accused shall enjoy the right to a speedy and public trial, by an impartial jury of the State and district wherein the[...]
district shall have been previously ascertained by law, and to be informed of the nature and cause of the accusation; to be confronted with the witnesses [...]
for obtaining witnesses in his favor, and to have the Assistance of Counsel for his defence.
[Th]e ninth. In suits at common law, where the value in controversy shall exceed twenty dollars, the right of trial by jury shall be preserved, and no fact tried by a ju[ry]
any Court of the United States, than according to the rules of the common law.
[T]enth..... Excessive bail shall not be required, nor excessive fines imposed, nor cruel and unusual punishments inflicted.
[E]leventh.. The enumeration in the Constitution, of certain rights, shall not be construed to deny or disparage others retained by the people.
[T]welfth. The powers not delegated to the United States by the Constitution, nor prohibited by it to the States, are reserved to the States respectively, or to the pe[ople]
Frederick Augustus Muhlenberg Speaker of the House of Representatives.
[Jo]hn Adams Vice-President of the United States, and [...]

# POLITICS AND PERSONAL LIBERTY

## CHAPTER OUTLINE

## FEATURES

## POWER AND INDIVIDUAL LIBERTY

To the authors of the Declaration of Independence, individual liberty was inherent in the human condition. It was not derived from governments or even from constitutions. Rather, governments and constitutions existed to make individual liberty more secure:

> We hold these truths to be self-evident, that all men are created equal, that they are endowed by their Creator with certain unalienable Rights, that among these are Life, Liberty and the pursuit of Happiness. That to secure these rights, Governments are instituted among Men, deriving their just powers from the consent of the governed.

## ASK YOURSELF ABOUT POLITICS

**1** Do you think the government has become so large and powerful that it poses a threat to the rights and freedoms of ordinary citizens?
Yes ☐ No ☐

**2** Do you believe that using tax funds to pay tuition at church-affiliated schools violates the separation of church and state?
Yes ☐ No ☐

**3** Should advocating revolution to overthrow the U.S. government be outlawed?
Yes ☐ No ☐

**4** Should we have the right to burn the American flag?
Yes ☐ No ☐

**5** Should federal or local governments be able to censor what motion pictures are shown in public theaters?
Yes ☐ No ☐

**6** Should organizations like the Ku Klux Klan and the American Nazi Party be permitted to hold marches and rallies?
Yes ☐ No ☐

**7** Do law-abiding citizens have a constitutional right to carry a handgun for self-protection?
Yes ☐ No ☐

**8** Do you believe that the death penalty violates the Constitution's prohibition against "cruel and unusual punishments"?
Yes ☐ No ☐

Government power defends your most basic rights to life, liberty, and the pursuit of happiness while at the same time ensuring that all other Americans have the same rights. The Founders guaranteed individual liberty in the earliest days of our nation through the first ten amendments to the Constitution—our Bill of Rights.

*Authority and Liberty*    To avoid the brutal life of a lawless society, where the weak are at the mercy of the strong, people form governments and endow them with powers to secure peace and self-preservation (see *People and Politics:* "Thomas Hobbes and the Need for Leviathan" in Chapter 1). People voluntarily relinquish some of their individual freedom to establish a government that is capable of protecting them from their neighbors as well as from foreign aggressors. This government must be strong enough to maintain its own existence or it cannot defend the rights of its citizens.

But what happens when a government becomes too strong and infringes on the liberties of its citizens? How much liberty must individuals surrender to secure an orderly society? This is the classic dilemma of free government: people must create laws and governments to protect their freedom, but the laws and governments themselves restrict freedom.

*Democracy and Personal Liberty*    When democracy is defined only as a *decision-making process*—widespread popular participation and rule by majority—it offers little protection for individual liberty. Democracy must also be defined to include *substantive values*—a recognition of the dignity of all individuals and their equality under law. Otherwise, some people, particularly "the weaker party, or an obnoxious individual" would be vulnerable to deprivations of life, liberty, or property simply by decisions of majorities (see "The Paradox of Democracy" in Chapter 1). Indeed, the "great object" of the Constitution, according to James Madison, was to preserve popular government yet at the same time to protect individuals from "unjust" majorities.[1]

The purpose of the Constitution—and especially its Bill of Rights, the first ten amendments, passed by the First Congress in September 1789 and ratified by the states—is to limit governmental power over the individual, that is, to place personal liberty beyond the reach of government (see Table 14-1). Each individual's rights to life, liberty, and property, due process of law, and equal protection of the law are not subject to majority vote. Or, as Supreme Court Justice Robert Jackson once declared:

> The very purpose of a Bill of Rights was to withdraw certain subjects from the vicissitudes of political controversy, to place them beyond the reach of majorities and officials, and to establish them as legal principles to be applied by the courts. One's right to life, liberty, and property, to free speech, a free press, freedom of worship and assembly, and other fundamental rights may not be submitted to vote: they depend on the outcome of no elections.[2]

*Nationalizing the Bill of Rights*    The Bill of Rights begins with the words "*Congress* shall make no law . . . ," indicating that it was originally intended to limit only the powers of the federal government. The Bill of Rights was added to the Constitution because of fear that the *federal* government might become too powerful and encroach on individual liberty. But what about encroachments by state and local governments and their officials? For more than one hundred years, the U.S. Supreme Court, reflecting what it saw as the intentions of the framers, refused to make the protections of the Bill of Rights binding on state and local governments. States had their own constitutions with many of the same rights, but state constitutions were enforceable only in state courts.[3]

TABLE 14-1   CONSTITUTIONALLY PROTECTED RIGHTS

*The Bill of Rights*

The first ten amendments to the Constitution of the United States, passed by the First Congress of the United States in September 1789 and ratified by the states in December 1791.

| AMENDMENTS | PROTECTIONS |
|---|---|
| **First Amendment: Religion, Speech, Press, Assembly, Petition**<br>Congress shall make no law respecting an establishment of religion, or prohibiting the free exercise thereof; or abridging the freedom of speech, or of the press; or the right of the people peaceably to assemble, and to petition the Government for a redress of grievances. | Prohibits government establishment of religion.<br>Protects the free exercise of religion.<br>Protects freedom of speech.<br>Protects freedom of the press.<br>Protects freedom of assembly.<br>Protects the right to petition government "for a redress of grievances." |
| **Second Amendment: Right to Bear Arms**<br>A well regulated Militia, being necessary to the security of a free State, the right of the people to keep and bear Arms, shall not be infringed. | Protects the right of people to bear arms and states to maintain militia (National Guard) units. |
| **Third Amendment: Quartering of Soldiers**<br>No Soldier shall, in time of peace, be quartered in any house, without the consent of the Owner, nor in time of war, but in a manner to be prescribed by law. | Prohibits forcible quartering of soldiers in private homes in peacetime, or in war without congressional authorization. |
| **Fourth Amendment: Searches and Seizures**<br>The right of the people to be secure in their persons, houses, papers, and effects, against unreasonable searches and seizures, shall not be violated, and no Warrants shall issue, but upon probable cause, supported by Oath or affirmation, and particularly describing the place to be searched, and the persons or things to be seized. | Protects against "unreasonable searches and seizures."<br>Requires warrants for searches of homes and other places where there is a reasonable expectation of privacy.<br>Judges may issue search warrants only with "probable cause"; and such warrants must be specific regarding the place to be searched and the things to be seized. |
| **Fifth Amendment: Grand Juries, Double Jeopardy, Self-Incrimination, Due Process, Protection against Government Takings of Property**<br>No person shall be held to answer for a capital, or otherwise infamous crime, unless on a presentment or indictment of a Grand jury, except in cases arising in the land or naval forces, or in the Militia, when in actual service in time of war or public danger; nor shall any person be subject for the same offence to be twice put in jeopardy of life or limb; nor shall he be compelled in any criminal case to be a witness against himself, nor be deprived of life, liberty, or property, without due process of law; nor shall private property be taken for public use, without just compensation. | Requires that, before trial for a serious crime, a person (except military personnel) must be indicted by a grand jury.<br>Prohibits double jeopardy (trial for the same offense a second time after being found innocent).<br>Prohibits the government from forcing any person in a criminal case to be a witness against himself.<br>Prohibits the government from taking life, liberty, or property "without due process of law."<br>Prohibits government from taking private property without paying "just compensation." |
| **Sixth Amendment: Fair Trial**<br>In all criminal prosecutions, the accused shall enjoy the right to a speedy and public trial, by an impartial jury of the State and district wherein the crime shall have been committed, which district shall have been previously ascertained by law, and to be informed of the nature and cause of the accusation; to be confronted with the witnesses against him; to have compulsory process for obtaining witnesses in his favor, and to have the Assistance of Counsel for his defense. | Requires that the accused in a criminal case be given a speedy and public trial, and thus prohibits prolonged incarceration without trial or secret trials.<br>Requires that trials be by jury and take place in the district where the crime was committed.<br>Requires that the accused be informed of the charges, have the right to confront witnesses, have the right to force supporting witnesses to testify, and have the assistance of counsel. |

TABLE 14-1    CONSTITUTIONALLY PROTECTED RIGHTS, CONTINUED

| AMENDMENTS | PROTECTIONS |
|---|---|
| **Seventh Amendment: Trial by Jury in Civil Cases**<br>In Suits at common law, where the value in controversy shall exceed twenty dollars, the right of trial by jury shall be preserved, and no fact tried by a jury, shall be otherwise reexamined in any Court of the United States, than according to the rules of the common law. | Requires a jury trial in civil cases involving more than twenty dollars.<br>Limits the degree to which factual questions decided by a jury may be reviewed by another court. |
| **Eighth Amendment: Bail, Fines and Punishment**<br>Excessive bail shall not be required, nor excessive fines imposed, nor cruel and unusual punishments inflicted. | Prohibits excessive bail.<br>Prohibits excessive fines.<br>Prohibits cruel and unusual punishment. |
| **Ninth Amendment: Unspecified Rights Retained by People**<br>The enumeration in the Constitution, of certain rights, shall not be construed to deny or disparage others retained by the people. | Protection of unspecified rights (including privacy) that are not listed in the Constitution. The Constitution shall not be interpreted to be a complete list of rights retained by the people. |
| **Tenth Amendment: Rights Reserved to the States**<br>The powers not delegated to the United States by the Constitution, nor prohibited by it to the States, are reserved to the States respectively, or to the people. | States retain powers that are not granted by the Constitution to the national government or prohibited by it to the states. |

## Rights in the Text of the Constitution

Several rights were written into the text of the Constitution in 1787 and thus precede in time the adoption of the Bill of Rights.

| | |
|---|---|
| **Article I Section 9: Habeas Corpus, Bills of Attainder, and Ex Post Facto Laws**<br>The privilege of the Writ of Habeas Corpus shall not be suspended, unless when in Cases of Rebellion or Invasion the public Safety may require it.<br>No Bill of Attainder or ex post facto Law shall be passed. | Habeas corpus prevents imprisonment without a judge's determination that a person is being lawfully detained.<br>Prohibition of bills of attainder prevents Congress (and states) from deciding people guilty of a crime and imposing punishment without trial.<br>Prohibition of ex post facto laws prevents Congress (and states) from declaring acts to be criminal that were committed before the passage of a law making them so. |

## Thirteenth and Fourteenth Amendments

The Bill of Rights begins with the words "Congress shall make no law . . ." indicating that it initially applied only to the *federal* government. While states had their own constitutions that guarantee many of the same rights, for more than a century the Bill of Rights did not apply to state and local governments. Following the Civil War, the Thirteenth, Fourteenth, and Fifteenth (voting rights) Amendments were passed, restricting *state* governments and their local subdivisions. But not until many years later did the U.S. Supreme Court, in a long series of decisions, apply the Bill of Rights against the states.

| | |
|---|---|
| **Thirteenth Amendment**<br>Neither slavery nor involuntary servitude, except as a punishment for crime whereof the party shall have been duly convicted, shall exist within the United States, or any place subject to their jurisdiction. | Prohibits slavery or involuntary servitude except for punishment by law; applies to both governments and private citizens. |
| **Fourteenth Amendment**<br>All persons born or naturalized in the United States, and subject to the jurisdiction thereof, are citizens of the United States and of the State wherein they reside. No State shall make or enforce any law which shall abridge the privileges or immunities of citizens of the United States; nor shall any State deprive any person of life, liberty, or property, without due process of law; nor deny to any person within its jurisdiction the equal protection of the laws. | Protects "privileges and immunities of citizenship."<br>Prevents deprivation of life, liberty, or property "without due process of law"; this phrase incorporates virtually all of the rights specified in the Bill of Rights.<br>Prevents denial of "equal protection of the laws" for all persons. |

With the addition of the Fourteenth Amendment to the Constitution following the Civil War, the question of the applicability of the Bill of Rights to the states arose anew. The Fourteenth Amendment includes the words "No State shall . . ."; its provisions are directed specifically at states. This amendment was designed to secure equality for newly freed slaves, but its provisions guaranteed that no one could be denied "the privileges or immunities of citizens," "life, liberty, or property," "due process of law," or "equal protection of the laws." Do these general phrases incorporate the protections of the Bill of Rights—make them applicable against *state* actions?

Initially, the U.S. Supreme Court rejected the argument that the Privileges or Immunities Clause[4] and the Due Process Clause[5] incorporated the Bill of Rights. But beginning in the 1920s, the Court handed down a long series of decisions that gradually brought about the **incorporation** of almost all of the protections of the Bill of Rights into the "liberty" guaranteed against state actions by the Due Process Clause of the Fourteenth Amendment. In *Gitlow v. New York* (1925), the Court ruled that "freedom of speech and of the press—which are protected by the First Amendment from abridgment by Congress—are among the fundamental personal rights and liberties protected by the due process clause of the Fourteenth Amendment from impairment by the states."[6] Over time, the Court applied the same reasoning in incorporating almost all provisions of the Bill of Rights into the Fourteenth Amendment's Due Process Clause (see Table 14-2).

# FREEDOM OF RELIGION

Americans are a very religious people. Belief in God and church attendance are more widespread in the United States than in any other advanced industrialized nation. Although many early American colonists came to the new land to escape religious persecution, they frequently established their own government-supported churches and imposed their own religious beliefs on others. Puritanism was the official faith of colonial Massachusetts, and Virginia officially established the Church of England. Only two colonies (Maryland and Rhode Island) provided for full religious freedom. In part to lessen the potential for conflict among the states, the framers of the Bill of Rights sought to prevent the new national government from establishing an official religion or interfering with religious exercises.[7] The very first words of the First Amendment set forth two separate prohibitions on government: "Congress shall make no law respecting an *establishment of religion,* or prohibiting the *free exercise* thereof." These two restrictions on government power—the Free Exercise Clause and the No Establishment Clause—guarantee separate religious freedoms.

*Free Exercise of Religion*    The **Free Exercise Clause** prohibits government from restricting religious beliefs or practices. Although the wording of the First Amendment appears absolute ("Congress shall make no law . . ."), the U.S. Supreme Court has never interpreted the phrase to protect *any* conduct carried on in the name of religion. In the first major decision involving this clause, the Court ruled in 1879 that polygamy could be outlawed by Congress in Utah Territory even though some Mormons argued that it was part of their religious faith.

**Incorporation:** In constitutional law, the application of almost all of the Bill of Rights to the states through the Fourteenth Amendment.

**Free Exercise Clause:** A clause in the First Amendment to the Constitution that prohibits the federal government from restricting religious beliefs and practices.

TABLE 14-2   THE NATIONALIZATION OF THE BILL OF RIGHTS

| Year | Amendment | Protection | Case |
|------|-----------|------------|------|
| 1925 | First | Freedom of speech | *Gitlow v. New York* |
| 1931 | First | Freedom of press | *Near v. Minnesota* |
| 1932 | Sixth | Rights to counsel in capital cases | *Powell v. Alabama* |
| 1937 | First | Freedom of assembly | *DeJonge v. Oregon* |
| 1940 | First | Free exercise of religion | *Cantwell v. Connecticut* |
| 1947 | First | No establishment of religion | *Everson v. Board of Education* |
| 1948 | Sixth | Public trial | *In re Oliver* |
| 1949 | Fourth | No unreasonable searches and seizures | *Wolf v. Colorado* |
| 1962 | Eighth | No cruel and unusual punishments | *Robinson v. California* |
| 1963 | Sixth | Right to counsel in felony cases | *Gideon v. Wainwright* |
| 1964 | Fifth | Freedom from self-incrimination | *Malloy v. Hagan* |
| 1967 | Sixth | Speedy trial | *Klopfer v. North Carolina* |
| 1968 | Sixth | Jury trial in all criminal cases | *Duncan v. Louisiana* |
| 1969 | Fifth | No double jeopardy | *Benton v. Maryland* |

*In 1990, the Supreme Court ruled against two Native Americans who had been fired from their jobs as drug counselors for taking peyote during religious ceremonies of the Native American Church. The Court maintained that the Free Exercise Clause does not exempt individuals from complying with valid laws regulating conduct. In this picture, a Native American holy man performs a ceremony outside the court as it hears arguments on the case.*

The Court distinguished between faith and behavior, saying that "Congress was deprived of all legislative power over mere opinion [by the First Amendment], but was left free to reach actions which were in violation of social duties."[8] The Court also employed the Free Exercise Clause to strike down as unconstitutional an attempt by a state to prohibit private religious schools and force all children to attend public schools.[9] This decision protects the entire structure of private religious schools in the nation.

Later, the Supreme Court elaborated on its distinction between religious belief and religious practice. *Beliefs* are protected absolutely, but with regard to religious *practices,* the Court has generally upheld governmental restrictions when enacted for valid secular purposes.[10] Thus, the government can outlaw religious practices that threaten health, safety, or welfare. The Free Exercise Clause does *not* confer the *right* to practice human sacrifice or even the ceremonial use of illegal drugs.[11] Individuals must comply with valid and neutral laws even if these laws restrict religious practices.

But the Supreme Court has continued to face many difficulties in applying its "valid secular test" to specific infringements of religious freedom. When some Amish parents refused to allow their children to attend any school beyond the eighth grade, the State of Wisconsin argued that its universal compulsory school attendance law had a valid purpose: the education of children. The Amish parents argued that high school exposed their children to worldly influences and values contrary to their religious beliefs. The Supreme Court sided with the Amish, deciding that their religious claims outweighed the legitimate interests of the state in education.[12] But the Supreme Court approved of an Internal Revenue Service action revoking the tax-exempt status of Bob Jones University because of its rules against interracial dating or marriage among its students. The school argued that its rule was based on religious belief, but the Court held that the government had "an overriding interest in eradicating racial discrimination in education."[13] And the Supreme Court struck down an attempt by a Florida city to outlaw the Santeria (a mix of Catholicism and voodoo) practice of slaughtering animals in religious ceremonies.[14]

*No Establishment of Religion*　　Various meanings have been ascribed to the First Amendment prohibition against the "establishment" of religion. The first meaning—what the writers of the Bill of Rights had in mind—is that it merely prohibits the government from officially recognizing and supporting a national church, like the Church of England in that nation. A second meaning is somewhat broader: the government may not prefer one religion over another or demonstrate favoritism toward or discrimination against any particular religion, but it might recognize and encourage religious activities in general. The most expansive meaning is that the **No Establishment Clause** creates "a wall of separation between church and state" that prevents government from endorsing, aiding, sponsoring, or encouraging any or all religious activities. In 1947, Justice Hugo Black, writing for the Court majority, gave the following definition of this **wall of separation doctrine.**

> Neither a state nor the Federal Government can set up a church. Neither can pass laws which aid one religion, aid all religions, or prefer one religion over another. Neither can force nor influence a person to go to or to remain away from church . . . or force him to profess a belief or disbelief in any religion. . . . No tax in any amount, large or small, can be levied to support any religious activities or institutions, whatever they may be called, or whatever form they may adopt to teach or practice religion. Neither a state nor the Federal Government can, openly or secretly, participate in the affairs of any religious organizations or groups and vice versa. In the words of Jefferson, the clause against establishment of religion by law was intended to erect "a wall of separation between Church and State."[15]

Yet even while erecting this high rhetorical wall between church and state, the Court in this case upheld a state's provision of school bus service to parochial school pupils at public expense on the grounds that the buses did not directly aid religion but merely helped all children in the community proceed safely to and from school.[16] Although the Supreme Court has generally voiced its support for the wall-of-separation doctrine, on several occasions it has permitted cracks to develop in the wall. In allowing public schools to give pupils regular releases from school to attend religious instructions given outside of the school, Justice William O. Douglas wrote that the state and religion need not be "hostile, suspicious or even unfriendly."[17]

*What Constitutes "Establishment"?*　　It has proven difficult for the Supreme Court to reconcile this wall-of-separation interpretation of the First Amendment with the fact that religion plays an important role in the life of most Americans. Public meetings, including sessions of the Congress, often begin with prayers;[18] coins are inscribed with the words "In God We Trust"; and the armed forces provide chaplains for U.S. soldiers.

The Supreme Court has set forth a three-part *Lemon test* for determining whether a particular state law constitutes "establishment" of religion and thus violates the First Amendment. To be constitutional, a law affecting religious activity:

**No Establishment Clause:** A clause in the First Amendment to the Constitution that is interpreted to require the separation of church and state.

**Wall of separation doctrine:** The Supreme Court's interpretation of the No Establishment Clause that laws may not have as their purpose aid to one religion or aid to all religions.

1. Must have a secular purpose.

2. As its primary effect, must neither advance nor inhibit religion.

3. Must not foster "an excessive government entanglement with religion."[19]

Using this three-part test the Supreme Court held that it was unconstitutional for a state to pay the costs of teachers' salaries or instructional materials in parochial schools. The justices argued that this practice would require excessive government controls and surveillance to ensure that funds were used only for secular instruction and thus involved "excessive entanglement between government and religion." However, the Court has upheld the use of tax funds to provide students attending church-related schools with nonreligious textbooks, lunches, and transportation. And the Court has upheld a state's granting of tax credits to parents whose children attend private schools, including religious schools.[20] The Court has also upheld government grants of money to church-related colleges and universities for secular purposes.[21]

The High Court has upheld tax exemptions for churches on the grounds that "the role of religious organizations as charitable associations, in furthering the secular objectives of the state has become a fundamental concept in our society."[22] It held that schools must allow after-school meetings on school property by religious groups if such a privilege is extended to nonreligious groups.[23] Deductions on federal income tax returns for church contributions are also constitutional. The Supreme Court allows states to close stores on Sundays and otherwise set aside that day, as long as there is a secular purpose—such as "rest, repose, recreation and tranquility"—in doing so.[24] However, the Supreme Court has held that a Christmas nativity scene on public property is an official "endorsement" of Christian belief and therefore violates the No Establishment Clause of the First Amendment.[25]

*Prayer in the School*   The Supreme Court's most controversial interpretation of the No Establishment Clause involved the question of prayer and Bible-reading ceremonies conducted by public schools. The practice of opening the school day with prayer and Bible-reading ceremonies was once widespread in American public schools. To avoid the denominational aspects of these ceremonies, New York State's Board of Regents substituted the following nondenominational prayer, which it required to be said aloud in each class in the presence of a teacher at the beginning of each school day: "Almighty God, we acknowledge our dependence upon Thee, and we beg Thy blessings upon us, our parents, our teachers, and our country." New York argued that this brief prayer did not violate the No Establishment Clause, because the prayer was denominationally neutral and because student participation in the prayer was voluntary. However, in *Engle v. Vitale* (1962), the Supreme Court stated that "the constitutional prohibition against laws respecting an establishment of a religion must at least mean in this country it is no part of the business of government to compose official prayers for any group of the American people to recite as part of a religious program carried on by government." The Court pointed out that making prayer voluntary did not free it from the prohibitions of the No Establishment Clause, and that clause prevented the *establishment* of a religious ceremony by a government agency regardless of whether the ceremony was voluntary.[26]

One year later, in the case of *Abington School District v. Schempp,* the Court considered the constitutionality of Bible-reading ceremonies in the public schools. Here again, even though the children were not required to participate, the Court found that Bible reading as an opening exercise in the schools was a religious ceremony. The justices went to some trouble in the majority opinion to point out that they were not "throwing the Bible out of the schools." They specifically stated that the *study* of the Bible or of religion, when presented objectively and as part of a secular program of education, did not violate the First Amendment; but religious *ceremonies* involving Bible reading or prayer established by a state or school did.[27]

State efforts to encourage "voluntary prayer" in public schools have also been struck down by the Supreme Court as unconstitutional. When the state of Alabama authorized a period of silence for "meditation or voluntary prayer" in public schools, the Court ruled that this action was an "establishment of religion." The Court said the law had no secular purpose, that it conveyed "a message of state endorsement and promotion of prayer," and that its real intent was to encourage prayer in public schools. In a stinging dissenting opinion, Chief Justice Warren Burger noted that the Supreme Court itself opened its session with a prayer and that both houses of Congress opened every session with prayers led by official chaplains paid by the government. "To suggest that a moment of silence statute that includes the word *prayer* unconstitutionally endorses religion manifests not neutrality but hostility toward religion."[28]

*Religious Freedom Restoration?*   Congress sought to intervene in government-religion disputes with a Religious Freedom Restoration Act in 1993. Traditionally, the Supreme Court had employed a "compelling interest" test to decide whether government could ban a religious practice; that is, the government had to prove a compelling public interest to justify even a nondiscriminatory law or regulation that infringed on the free exercise of religion.[29] But when the Court appeared to relax that test and to hold that religious beliefs cannot excuse persons from compliance with *any* otherwise valid law, Congress saw an opportunity to align itself with religion. It acted to exempt people from government laws or regulations that burden their religious freedom unless the government can prove that the burden is "the least restrictive means of furthering a compelling interest."[30]

*Although the Supreme Court ruled in 1962 (Engle v. Vitale) that even voluntary prayer in public schools was an unconstitutional violation of the separation of church and state under the First Amendment, the question of prayer in the schools remains a heated one. Indeed, recent court rulings regarding nondenominational prayers at graduation ceremonies and sporting events have, if anything, further confused the issue.*

# FREEDOM OF SPEECH

Although the First Amendment is absolute in its wording ("Congress shall pass *no* law . . . abridging the freedom of speech"), the Supreme Court has never been willing to interpret this statement as a protection of *all* speech. What kinds of speech does the First Amendment protect from government control, and what kinds of speech may be constitutionally prohibited?

*Clear and Present Danger Doctrine*   The classic example of speech that can be prohibited was given by Justice Oliver Wendell Holmes in 1919: "The most stringent protection of free speech would not protect a man in falsely shouting 'fire' in a theater and causing a panic."[31] While Holmes recognized that the government may prevent speech that creates a serious and immediate danger to society, he objected to government attempts to stifle critics of its policies, such as the

Espionage Act of 1917 and the Sedition Act of 1918. The Sedition Act prohibited, among other things, speech that was meant to discourage the sale of war bonds; "disloyal" speech about the government, the Constitution, the military forces, or the flag of the United States; and speech that urged the curtailment of war production. In the case of *Gitlow v. New York,* the majority supported the right of the government to curtail any speech that "tended to subvert or imperil the government," but Holmes dissented, arguing that "Every idea is an incitement. It offers itself for belief and if believed it is acted on unless some other belief outweighs it."[32] Unless the expression of an idea created a *serious and immediate danger,* Holmes argued that it should be tolerated and combated or defeated only by the expression of better ideas. This standard for determining the limits of free expression became known as the **clear and present danger doctrine.** Government should not curtail speech merely because it *might tend* to cause a future danger: "The question in every case is whether the words used are used in such circumstances and are of such a nature as to create a clear and present danger that they will bring about the substantive evils that Congress has a right to prevent."[33] Holmes's dissent inspired a long struggle in the courts to strengthen constitutional protections for speech and press (see *Up Close:* "The American Civil Liberties Union").

Although Holmes was the first to use the phrase "clear and present danger," it was Justice Louis D. Brandeis who later developed the doctrine into a valuable constitutional principle that the Supreme Court gradually came to adopt. Brandeis explained that the doctrine involved two elements: (1) the clearness or seriousness of the expression; and (2) the immediacy of the danger flowing from the speech. With regard to immediacy he wrote:

> No danger flowing from speech can be deemed clear and present, unless the incidence of the evil apprehended is so imminent that it may befall before there is opportunity for full discussion. If there be time to expose through discussion the falsehood and fallacies, to avert the evil by the processes of education, the remedy to be applied is more speech, not enforced silence.

And with regard to seriousness he wrote:

> Moreover, even imminent danger cannot justify resort to prohibition [of speech] . . . unless the evil apprehended is relatively serious. Prohibition of free speech and assembly is a measure so stringent that it would be inappropriate as the means for averting a relatively trivial harm to society. . . . There must be the probability of serious injury to the State.[34]

*Preferred Position Doctrine* Over the years, the Supreme Court has given the First Amendment freedom of speech, press, and assembly a special **preferred position** in Constitutional law. These freedoms are especially important to the preservation of democracy. If speech, press, or assembly are prohibited by government, the people have no way to correct the government through democratic processes. Thus, the burden of proof rests upon the *government* to justify any restrictions on speech, writing, or assembly.[35] In other words, any speech or writing is presumed constitutional unless the government proves that a serious and immediate danger would ensue if the speech were allowed (see *What Do You Think?* "Advocating Hate and Violence").

**Clear and present danger doctrine:** A standard used by the courts to determine whether speech may be restricted; only speech that creates a serious and immediate danger to society may be restricted.

**Preferred position:** Refers to the tendency of the courts to give preference to the First Amendment rights to speech, press, and assembly when faced with conflicts.

# The American Civil Liberties Union

The American Civil Liberties Union (ACLU) is one of the largest and most active interest groups devoted to litigation in the country. Its Washington offices employ a staff of several hundred people; it counts on some 5,000 volunteer lawyers across the country; and it has affiliates in every state and most large cities. The ACLU claims that its sole purpose is defense of civil liberty, that it has no other political agenda, that it defends the Communist Party and the Ku Klux Klan alike—not because it endorses their beliefs but because "the Bill of Rights is the ACLU's only client."* And indeed on occasion it has defended the liberties of Nazis, Klansmen, and other right-wing extremists to express their unpopular views. But most ACLU work has involved litigation on behalf of liberal causes, such as abortion rights, resistance to military service, support for affirmative action, and opposition to the death penalty.

The ACLU was founded in 1920 by Roger Baldwin, a wealthy radical activist who opposed both capitalism and war. Baldwin graduated from Harvard University and briefly taught sociology at Washington University in St. Louis. He refused to be drafted during World War I and served a year's imprisonment for draft violation. In prison, Baldwin joined the Industrial Workers of the World (IWW or the "Wobblies"), a radical labor union that advocated violence to achieve its goals. In the early 1920s, the ACLU defended socialists, "Bolsheviks," labor organizers, and pacifists against government coercion, including those arrested in the "Red Scare" raids of Attorney General Alexander Mitchell Palmer.

Later the ACLU concentrated its efforts on the defense of First Amendment freedoms of speech, press, religion, and assembly. ACLU member Felix Frankfurter, later a Supreme Court Justice, set the tone: "Civil liberty means liberty for those whom we do not like or even detest." In the famous "Monkey Trial" of 1925, the ACLU helped defend schoolteacher John Scopes for having taught the theory of evolution in violation of Tennessee state law. Later, it played a supporting role in the litigation efforts of the National Association for the Advancement of Colored People in the elimination of segregation; it defended Vietnam War protesters; it brought cases

In 1978 the ACLU defended the right of American Nazis to march in the Chicago suburb of Skokie, Illinois, home to many survivors of the Nazi holocaust in Europe.

to court to ban prayer and religious exercise in public schools; it has opposed the death penalty and fought for abortion rights; and it defended the rights of people to burn the American flag as a form of symbolic speech.

The ACLU's decision to defend the right of the American Nazi Party to march through Skokie, Illinois, a Chicago suburb with a large Jewish population, including some Holocaust survivors, created a crisis in the organization. The ACLU had defended Nazis and Klansmen before, but the Skokie case engendered more publicity than any earlier cases involving right-wing extremists. Many members quit the organization and financial contributions temporarily declined.

Today, the ACLU is racked by internal arguments over politically correct speech codes and over whether "hate crimes" (crimes committed with racist, sexist, antihomosexual, and similar motives) should invoke harsher sentences than the same crimes committed for other motives. "Pure" First Amendment defenders in the organization oppose speech codes and hate crime legislation, while many liberal members rationalize these penalties on speech and thought.

Former Supreme Court Chief Justice Earl Warren once said of the ACLU, "It is difficult to appreciate how far our freedoms might have eroded had it not been for the Union's valiant representation in the courts of the constitutional rights of people of all persuasions."**

*William A. Donohue, *The Politics of the American Civil Liberties Union* (New Brunswick: Transaction Books, 1985), p. 3.
**Quoted in *ACLU Annual Report,* 1977, cited in ibid., p. 2.

# Advocating Hate and Violence

Following the 1995 bombing of the federal building in Oklahoma City that left 187 people dead, President Bill Clinton lashed out against the "loud and angry voices in America today" advocating hate and violence on the nation's radio airwaves. "They spread hate; they leave the impression, by their very words, that violence is acceptable." He attacked "right-wing extremists" who "try to keep some people as paranoid as possible and the rest of us all torn up and upset with each other." He complained that they portray "the government as bad, the government as the enemy" and by so doing they encourage terrorism. By implication, he blamed conservative talk show hosts for the Oklahoma bombing. Was the president right? Or was he exploiting the tragedy to attack his political opponents?

There is no doubt that a great deal of speech in America today preaches hate, encourages armed insurrection, and recommends violence. (Indeed, for an argument that historically much of American politics has centered on violence, see *A Conflicting View:* "American Politics as Violence" in Chapter 1). G. Gordon Liddy (the second most listened-to radio talk show host after Rush Limbaugh) advised his listeners to take "head shots" at federal Bureau of Alcohol, Tobacco and Firearms (ATF) agents if they invaded their home because the agents usually wore bullet-proof vests. (It was ATF agents who initially raided the Branch Davidian compound in Waco, Texas, because it suspected the group of owning unregistered automatic weapons; four agents were killed, and after a fifty-one-day stand-off, a Federal Bureau of Investigation raid with tanks ended with a fire that killed seventy residents.)

The men accused of the Oklahoma bombing had ties to hate organizations. Armed extremism is advo-cated by many groups, from property-rights radicals and tax protesters to survivalists, "militias," and white supremacists. Extremists in the antiabortion movement have claimed that the murder of abortionists is justifiable to save lives of the unborn. Bomb-making books are available in public libraries and on the Internet, the global computer network. Yet most Americans are able to distinguish between speech and action. They believe that extremist groups, including "militias," are "dangerous" (80 percent), and they think the federal government "should spy on them and monitor their activities (68 percent). However, they doubt that radio talk show hosts encourage violence:

**Question**: *Do you think comments by some nationally syndicated radio talk show hosts helped create an environment that encouraged the bombing in Oklahoma City?*

Yes 33%
No 53%

0 10 20 30 40 50 60 70 80 90 100
Percent

And a majority still see the federal government itself as a threat to freedom:

**Question**: *Do you think the federal government has become so powerful that it poses a threat to the rights and freedoms of citizens?*

Yes 52%
No 44%

0 10 20 30 40 50 60 70 80 90 100
Percent

Source: Time/CNN Poll reported in Time, May 8, 1995.

*The Cold War Challenge*   Despite the Supreme Court's endorsement of the clear and present danger and preferred position doctrines, in times of perceived national crisis the courts have been willing to permit some government restrictions of speech, press, and assembly. At the outbreak of World War II, just prior to United States entry into that world conflict, Congress passed the Smith Act, which stated:

It shall be unlawful for any person to knowingly or willfully advocate, abet, advise, or teach the duty, necessity, desirability, or propriety of overthrowing or destroying any government in the United States by force or violence, or by the assassination of any officer of any such government.

Congress justified its action in terms of national security, initially as a protection against fascism during World War II, then later as a protection against communist revolution in the early days of the Cold War.

In 1949, the Department of Justice prosecuted Eugene V. Dennis and ten other top leaders of the Communist Party of the United States for violation of the Smith Act. A jury found them guilty of violating the act, and the party leaders were sentenced to jail terms ranging from one to five years. In 1951, the case of *Dennis v. United States* came to the Supreme Court on appeal. In upholding the conviction of the Communist Party leaders, the Court seemed to abandon Brandeis's idea that "present" meant "before there is opportunity for full discussion."[36] It seemed to substitute clear and *probable* for clear and *present*.

Since that time, however, the Supreme Court has returned to a policy closer to the original clear and present danger doctrine. As the Cold War progressed, Americans grew to view communism as a serious threat to democracy, but not a *present* danger. The overthrow of the American government advocated by communists was not an incitement to *immediate* action. A democracy must not itself become authoritarian to protect itself from authoritarianism. In later cases, the Supreme Court held that the mere advocacy of revolution, apart from unlawful action, is protected by the First Amendment.[37] It struck down federal laws requiring communist organizations to register with the government,[38] laws requiring individuals to sign "loyalty oaths,"[39] laws prohibiting communists from working in defense plants,[40] and laws stripping passports from Communist Party leaders.[41] In short, once the perceived Cold War crisis began to fade, the Supreme Court reasserted the First Amendment rights of individuals and groups.

*Symbolic Speech* The First Amendment's guarantees of speech, press, and assembly are broadly interpreted to mean **freedom of expression.** Political expression encompasses more than just words. For example, when Mary Beth Tinker and her brothers were suspended for wearing black armbands to high school to protest the Vietnam War, they argued that the wearing of armbands constituted **symbolic speech** protected by the First Amendment. The Supreme Court agreed, noting that the school did not prohibit all wearing of symbols but instead singled out this particular expression for disciplinary action.[42] The Court also held that wearing Ku Klux Klan hoods and gathering together to burn a cross[43] and even burning the American flag (see *What Do You Think:* "Do We Have a Constitutional Right to Burn the American Flag?")[44] are protected expression. However, burning one's draft card does not constitute protected speech and exempt the burner from legal penalties for failure to carry such a card. The Court "cannot accept the view that an apparently limitless variety of conduct can be labeled 'speech.'"[45]

The Supreme Court continues to wrestle with the question of what kinds of conduct are symbolic speech protected by the First Amendment and what kinds of conduct are outside of this protection. Symbolic speech, like speech itself, cannot be banned just because it offends people. "If there is only one bedrock principle underlying the First Amendment, it is that the Government may not prohibit

**Freedom of expression:** Collectively, the First Amendment rights to free speech, press, and assembly.

**Symbolic speech:** Actions other than speech itself but protected by the First Amendment because they constitute political expression.

*The Supreme Court has ruled that Ku Klux Klan cross burnings constitute symbolic speech protected by the First Amendment.*

# Do We Have a Constitutional Right to Burn the American Flag?

Flag waving is an American political tradition. The American flag symbolizes nationhood and national unity. Most states and the federal government have laws forbidding "desecration" of the flag.

Flag desecration is a physical act, but it also has symbolic meaning—for example, hatred of the United States or opposition to government policies. At the 1984 Republican national convention in Dallas, Gregory Lee Johnson joined a protest march against Reagan Administration policies, then doused an American flag with kerosene and set fire to it. As it burned, he and others chanted: "America, the red, white, and blue, we spit on you." Police arrested Johnson and charged him with violating a Texas law against flag desecration. The American Civil Liberties Union came to Johnson's defense, arguing that flag burning is "symbolic speech" protected by the First Amendment.

In the case of *Texas v. Johnson* (1989), a majority of Supreme Court justices argued that "Johnson's burning of the flag was conduct sufficiently imbued with elements of communication to implicate the First Amendment." They declared that when speech and conduct are combined in the same expressive act, the government must show that it has "a sufficiently important interest in regulating the non-speech element to justify incident limitations on First Amendment freedoms." In this case, "preserving the flag as a symbol of nationhood and national unity" was not deemed sufficiently important to justify limiting Johnson's freedom of expression.*

The Court's decision caused a political uproar. President George Bush immediately condemned it, and public opinion polls showed massive opposition to it. Congress quickly passed the Flag Protection Act of 1989, mandating a one-year jail sentence and $1,000 fine for anyone who "knowingly mutilates, defaces, physically defiles, burns, maintains on the floor or ground, or tramples upon, any flag of the United States." But just as promptly, the Supreme Court, by the same 5–4 vote, struck down the new federal law as unconstitutional, using the same reasoning as expressed in the *Johnson* case.

Congress was not finished with the issue. Its next effort centered on the passage of a constitutional amendment: "The Congress and the states shall have the power to prohibit physical desecration of the flag of the United States." Since Congress was controlled by the Democrats, Republicans were convinced that the failure to pass the amendment would hurt Democratic Party candidates in the next election. (A June 1990 Gallup Poll revealed that 68 percent of Americans supported a constitutional amendment protecting the flag.) But Democratic leaders argued that the proposed amendment would alter the Bill of Rights and that Republicans were trying to "politicize the flag." The Democratic leadership also called for a quick vote to forestall efforts to rally strong public support for the amendment. Republicans led the fight for the amendment, but the political appeal of supporting the flag pulled a large number of Democratic members of the House to their side. Supporters paid homage to the flag:

> Too many people have paid for it with their blood. Too many people have marched behind it. Too many kids and parents and widows have accepted this triangle as the last remembrance of their loved ones. Too many to have this ever demeaned.

Opponents frequently quoted the Supreme Court's majority opinion:

> The way to preserve the flag's special role is not to punish those who feel differently about these matters. It is to persuade them that they are wrong. . . . We can imagine no more appropriate response to burning a flag than waving one's own, no better way to counter a flag-burner's message than by saluting the flag that burns. . . . We do not consecrate the flag by punishing its desecration, for in doing so we dilute the freedom that this cherished emblem represents.**

In the end, the flag amendment was defeated when it garnered a majority of House votes but fewer than required to pass a constitutional amendment by the necessary two-thirds vote. Likewise, a majority of the Senate has voted several times in favor of the amendment, but it has always fallen short of the necessary two-thirds vote.

*Texas v. Johnson, 491 U.S. 397 (1989).
**Quotations from *Congressional Quarterly,* June 23, 1990, p. 2004.

the expression of an idea simply because society finds the idea itself offensive or disagreeable."[46]

*Speech and Public Order*   The Supreme Court has wrestled with the question of whether speech can be prohibited when it stirs audiences to public disorder, not because the speaker urges lawless action but because the audience reacts to the speech with hostility. In short, can a speaker be arrested because of the *audience's* disorderly behavior? In an early case, the Supreme Court fashioned a *fighting words doctrine,* to the effect that words that "ordinary men know are likely to cause a fight" may be prohibited.[47] But later the Court seemed to realize that this doctrine, if broadly applied, could create a huge constitutional hole in the First Amendment guarantee of free speech. Authorities could curtail speech simply because it met with audience hostility. The Court recognized that "speech is often provocative and challenging. It may . . . have profound unsettling effects . . . That is why freedom of speech, while not absolute, is nevertheless protected against censorship."[48] In recent years, the Court has consistently refused to allow government authorities to ban speech *before* it has occurred simply because they believe it *may* create a disturbance.

In recent years, many colleges and universities have undertaken to ban speech that is considered racist, sexist, homophobic, or otherwise "insensitive" to the feelings of women and minorities. Varieties of "speech codes," "hate codes," and sexual harassment regulations that prohibit verbal expressions raise serious constitutional questions, especially at state-supported colleges and universities. The First Amendment does not exclude insulting or offensive racist or sexist words or comments from its protection (see *Up Close:* "Political Correctness versus Free Speech on Campus").

*Commercial Speech*   Do First Amendment freedoms of expression apply to commercial advertising? The Supreme Court has frequently asserted that **commercial speech** is protected by the First Amendment. The Court held that states cannot outlaw price advertising by pharmacists[49] or advertising for services by attorneys[50] and that cities cannot outlaw posting "For Sale" signs on property, even in the interests of halting white flight and promoting racially integrated neighborhoods. Advertising is the "dissemination of information" and is constitutionally protected.[51]

However, the Court has also been willing to weigh the First Amendment rights of commercial advertisers against the public interest served by regulation.[52] In other words, the Court seems to suspend its preferred position doctrine with regard to commercial advertising and to call for a "balancing of interests." Thus the Supreme Court has allowed the Federal Communications Commission to regulate the contents of advertising on radio and television and even to ban advertising for cigarettes. The Federal Trade Commission enforces "truth" in advertising by requiring commercial packages and advertisers to prove all claims for their products.

*Libel and Slander*   Libel and slander have never been protected by the First Amendment against subsequent punishment (see "Libel and Slander" in Chapter 6). Once a communication is determined to be libelous or slanderous, it is outside of the protection of the First Amendment. The Courts have traditionally defined "libel" as a "damaging falsehood." However, if plaintiffs are public officials they must prove that the statements made about them are not only false and

**Commercial speech:**
Advertising communications given only partial protection under the First Amendment to the Constitution.

# Political Correctness versus Free Speech on Campus

Universities have a very special responsibility to protect freedom of expression. The free and unfettered exchange of views is essential to the advancement of knowledge—the very purpose of universities. For centuries universities have fought to protect academic freedom from pressures arising from the world *outside* of the campus—governments, interest groups, financial contributors—arguing that the university must be a protected enclave for free expression of ideas. But the latest threat to academic freedom arises from *within* universities—from efforts by administrations, faculty, and campus groups to suppress ideas, opinions, and language that are not "politically correct" (PC). PC activists seek to suppress opinions and expressions they consider to be racist, sexist, "homophobic," or otherwise "insensitive" to specified groups.*

*Speech Codes* The experience at the University of Michigan with its "Policy on Discrimination and Discriminatory Harassment" illustrates the battles occurring on many campuses over First Amendment rights. In 1988, a series of racial incidents on campus prompted the university to officially ban "any behavior verbal or physical" that "stigmatized" an individual "on the basis of race, ethnicity, religion, sex, sexual orientation, ancestry, age, marital status, handicap, or Vietnam-era veteran status" or that created "an intimidating, hostile, or demeaning environment for educational pursuits." A published guide provided examples of banned activity, which included:

- A male student makes remarks in class like "women just aren't as good in this field as men."
- Jokes about gay men and lesbians.
- Commenting in a derogatory way about a particular person or group's physical appearance or sexual orientation, or their cultural origins, or religious beliefs.

*Free Speech* In 1989, "John Doe," a psychology graduate student studying gender differences in personality traits and mental differences, filed suit in federal court requesting that the University of Michigan policy be declared a violation of the First Amendment. (He was permitted by the court to remain anonymous because of fear of retribution.) He was joined in his complaint against the university by the American Civil Liberties Union.

In its decision, the court acknowledged that the University had a legal responsibility to prevent racial or sexual discrimination or harassment. However, it did *not* have a right to

> establish an anti-discrimination policy which had the effect of prohibiting certain speech because it disagreed with ideas or messages sought to be conveyed. . . . Nor could the University proscribe speech simply because it was found to be offensive, even gravely so, by large numbers of people. . . . These principles acquire a special significance in the University setting, where the free and unfettered interplay of competing views is essential to the institution's educational mission. . . . While the Court is sympathetic to the University's obligation to ensure educational opportunities for all of its students, such efforts must not be at the expense of free speech.**

It seems ironic that students and faculty now must seek the protection of the federal courts from attempts by universities to limit speech. Traditionally, universities themselves fought to protect academic freedom. Academic freedom included the freedom of faculty and students to express themselves in the classroom, on the campus, and in writing, on controversial and sensitive topics, including race and gender. It was recognized that students often express ideas that are biased or ill-informed, immature, or crudely expressed. But students were taught that the remedy for offensive language or off-color remarks or ill-chosen examples was more-enlightened speech, not suppression.

*Dinesh D'Souza, *Illiberal Education: The Politics of Race and Sex on Campus* (New York: Vintage Books, 1992).
**John Doe v. University of Michigan, 721 F. Supp. 852 (1989).

damaging but also "made with actual malice"—that is, with knowledge that they are false or with "reckless disregard" of the truth—in order to prove libel.[53]

## OBSCENITY AND THE LAW

Obscene materials of all kinds—words, publications, photos, drawings, films—are also exempt from First Amendment protection. Most states ban the publication, sale, or possession of obscene material, and Congress bans its shipment in the mails. Because obscene material is not protected by the First Amendment, it can be banned without even an attempt to prove that it results in antisocial conduct. In other words, it is not necessary to show that obscene material would result in a clear and present danger to society, the test used to decide the legitimacy of *speech*. In order to ban obscene materials, the government need only prove that they are *obscene*.

Defining "obscenity" has confounded legislatures and the courts for years, however. State and federal laws often define pornography and obscenity in such terms as "lewd," "lascivious," "filthy," "indecent," "disgusting"—all equally as vague as "obscene." "Pornography" is simply a synonym for "obscenity." *Soft-core pornography* usually denotes nakedness and sexually suggestive poses; it is less likely to confront legal barriers. *Hard-core pornography* usually denotes explicit sexual activity. After many fruitless efforts by the Supreme Court to come up with a workable definition of "pornography" or "obscenity," a frustrated Justice Potter Stewart wrote in 1974: "I shall not today attempt further to define [hard-core pornography] . . . But *I know it when I see it.*"[54]

*A Narrow Definition of Obscenity: The Roth Standards*   The Court's first comprehensive effort to define "obscenity" came in *Roth v. United States* (1957). Although the Court upheld Roth's conviction for distributing pornographic magazines through the mails, it defined "obscenity" somewhat narrowly: "Whether to the average person applying contemporary community standards, the dominant theme of the material, taken as a whole, appeals to prurient interests."[55]

Note that the material must be obscene to the *average* person, not to children or particular groups of adults who might be especially offended by pornography. The standard is "contemporary," suggesting that what was once regarded as obscene might be acceptable today. Later, the *community standard* was clarified to mean the "society at large," not a particular state or local community.[56] The material must be "considered as a whole," meaning that even if a work includes some obscene material, it is still acceptable if its "dominant theme" is something other than "prurient."[57] The Court added that a work must be "utterly without redeeming social or literary merit" in order to be judged obscene.[58] The Court never really said what a "prurient" interest was but reassured everyone that "sex and obscenity are not synonymous."[59]

*A Broader Definition of Obscenity: The Miller Standards*   The effect of the Roth decision, and the many and varied attempts by lower courts to apply its slippery standards, tended to limit law enforcement efforts to combat pornography during the 1960s and 1970s. The Supreme Court itself came under ridicule when it was learned that the justices had set up a movie room in the basement of the Supreme Court building to view films that had been brought before them in obscenity cases.[60]

So the Supreme Court tried again, in *Miller v. California* (1973), to give law enforcement officials some clearer standards in determining obscenity. While the Court retained the "average person" and "contemporary" standards, it redefined "community" to mean the *local* community rather than the society at large. It also defined "prurient" as "patently offensive" representations or descriptions of "ultimate sex acts, normal or perverted, actual or simulated," as well as "masturbation, excretory functions, and lewd exhibition of the genitals." It rejected the earlier requirement that the work had to be "utterly without redeeming social value" in order to be judged obscene, and it substituted instead "lacks serious literary, artistic, political, or scientific value."[61]

The effect of the Supreme Court's *Miller Standards* has been to increase the likelihood of conviction in obscenity-pornography cases.[62] It is easier to prove that a work lacks serious value than to prove that it is utterly without redeeming merit. Nevertheless, the *local community standard* allows sales of pornographic materials (by most people's standards) in adult bookstores and X-rated video stores in many cities throughout the nation.

*Child Pornography*   The Supreme Court has struck hard against child pornography—the "dissemination of material depicting children engaged in sexual conduct regardless of whether the material is obscene." Such conduct includes any visual depiction of children performing sexual acts or lewdly exhibiting their genitals. The Court held that safe-guarding children used in films or photographs from sexual exploitation and abuse was "a government objective of overriding importance."[63] In such cases, the existence of the material itself is evidence that a crime has been committed. Thus the test for *child* pornography is much stricter than the *Miller* standards.

# FREEDOM OF THE PRESS

Democracy depends upon the free expression of ideas. Authoritarian regimes either monopolize press, radio, and television facilities themselves or subject them to strict licensing and censorship of their content. The idea of a free and independent press is deeply rooted in the evolution of democratic government.

*No Prior Restraint Doctrine*  Long before the Bill of Rights was written, English law protected newspapers from government restrictions or licensing prior to publication—a practice called **prior restraint.** This protection, however, does not mean that publishers are exempt from *subsequent punishment* for libelous, obscene, or other illegal publications. Prior restraint is more dangerous to free expression, since it allows the government to censor the work prior to publication and forces the defendants to *prove* that their material should *not* be censored. In contrast, subsequent punishment requires a trial in which the government must prove that the defendant's published materials are unlawful.

In 1695, the great English jurist William Blackstone described the meaning of a free press as freedom from *prior* censorship:

> The liberty of the press . . . consists in laying no previous restraints upon publications, and not in freedom from censure for criminal matter when published. Every freeman has an undoubted right to lay what sentiments he pleases before the public. To forbid this is to destroy the freedom of the press; but if he published what is improper, mischievous or illegal, he must take the consequences of his own temerity.[64]

In *Near v. Minnesota* (1931), a muckraking publication accusing local officials of trafficking with gangsters had been barred from publishing under a Minnesota law that prohibited the publication of a "malicious, scandalous or defamatory newspaper." The Supreme Court, quoting Blackstone with approval, struck down the law as unconstitutional. Although *Near v. Minnesota* was a landmark decision affirming the *no-prior-restraint doctrine,* a close reading of the majority opinion reveals that the doctrine was not presented as absolute. Chief Justice Charles Evans Hughes noted that prior government censorship might be constitutional "if publication . . . threatened the country's safety in times of war."[65] Presumably, the government can prevent the publication of information on troop movements, invasion plans, or other military information when lives are at stake.

The question of whether or not the government can restrain publication of stories that present a serious threat to national security remains unanswered. For example, can the government restrain the press from reporting in advance on the time and place of an impending U.S. military action, thereby warning an enemy and perhaps adding to American casualties? In the most important case on this question, *New York Times v. United States* (1971), the Supreme Court upheld the right of the newspaper to publish secret documents that had been stolen from State Department and Defense Department files. The material covered U.S. policy decisions in Vietnam, and it was published while the war was still being waged. But five separate (concurring) opinions were written by justices in the majority as well as two dissenting opinions. Only two justices (Hugo Black and William O. Douglas) argued that government can *never* restrain any

**Prior restraint:** Government actions to restrict publication of a magazine, newspaper, or books on grounds of libel, obscenity, or other legal violations prior to actual publication of the work.

While self-ratings by the movie industry have thus far kept it from government regulation, recent ratings have caused an uproar, both within the film industry and among the movie-going public. Just what separates an "R" film from an "NC-17" (formerly "X")? When Midnight Cowboy first appeared in 1969, it was rated "X," but, with no changes, it was re-rated as "R" after winning the Oscar for the best picture. More recently, critics have charged that the violence and steamy sex scenes of Basic Instinct went far beyond "R" standards, but it avoided an "NC-17" rating only because it was the product of a major film studio that was able to pressure the ratings board.

publication regardless of the seriousness or immediacy of the harm. Others in the majority cited the government's failure to show proof in this case that publication "would surely result in direct, immediate, and irreparable damage to our nation or its people."[66] Presumably, if the government had produced such proof, the case might have been decided differently. The media interprets the decision as a blanket protection to publish anything it wishes regardless of harm to government or society.

*Film Censorship*   The no-prior-restraint doctrine was developed to protect the print media—books, magazines, newspapers. When the motion picture industry was in its infancy, the Supreme Court held that films were "business, pure and simple" and were not entitled to the protection of the First Amendment.[67] But as films grew in importance, the Court gradually extended First Amendment freedoms to cover motion pictures.[68] However, the Supreme Court has *not* given the film industry the same strong no-prior-restraint protection it has given the press. The Court has approved government requirements for prior submission of films to official censors, so long as (1) the burden of proof that the film is obscene rests with the censor; (2) a procedure exists for judicial determination of the issue; and (3) censors are required to act speedily.[69] To avoid government-imposed censorship the motion picture industry adopted its own system of rating films:

G: suitable for all audiences
PG: parental guidance suggested
PG-13: parental guidance strongly suggested for children under thirteen
R: restricted to those seventeen or older unless accompanied by a parent or guardian
NC-17: no one under seventeen admitted

Some city governments have sought to restrict showing of NC-17 films, and their restrictions have been upheld by the Courts.[70]

*Radio and Television Censorship*   The Federal Communications Commission was created in 1934 to allocate broadcast frequencies and to license stations. The exclusive right to use a particular frequency is a "public trust." Thus, broadcasters, unlike newspapers and magazines, are licensed by the government and subject to government rules. While the First Amendment protects broadcasters, the Supreme Court has recognized the special obligations that may be imposed on them in exchange for the exclusive right to use a broadcast frequency. "No one has a First Amendment right to a license or to monopolize a radio frequency; to deny a station license because 'the public interest' requires it, is not a denial of free speech."[71] Thus the Court has upheld FCC-imposed "equal time" and "fairness" rules against broadcasters, even while striking down state attempts to impose the same rules on newspapers.[72]

*Media Claims for Special Rights*   The news media make various claims to special rights arising out of the First Amendment's guarantee of a free press. Reporters argue, for example, that they should be able to protect their news sources and are not obliged to give testimony in criminal cases when they have obtained evidence in confidence. However, the only witnesses the Constitution exempts from compulsory testimony are defendants themselves, who enjoy the Fifth Amendment's protection against "self-incrimination." The Supreme Court has flatly rejected reporters' claims to a privilege against compulsory testimony. "We cannot seriously entertain the notion that the First Amendment protects a newsman's agreement to conceal the criminal conduct of his source, or evidence thereof, on the theory that it is better to write about a crime than to do something about it."[73] The Court also has rejected the argument that media notes and records are confidential; instead, it sided with law enforcement officials who had used a valid warrant to search the *Stanford Daily*'s offices for photos showing demonstrators who had attacked police.[74]

Despite these rulings, reporters regularly boast of their willingness to go to jail to protect sources, and many have done so. But the media have also pressured the nation's legislatures for protection. Congress has passed the Privacy Protection Act, which sharply limits the ability of law enforcement officials to search press offices, and many states have passed **shield laws** specifically protecting reporters from giving testimony in criminal cases.

*Conflicting "Rights"*    The conflict between reporters' "rights" to protect their sources under shield laws and the constitutional right of individuals to face their accusers when on trial is just one example of the many conflicts over "rights" in American life. In the case of shield laws, the courts have ruled that "rights" granted by law are not equal to rights granted by the constitution and have imprisoned those who try to hide behind these laws. Sometimes, however, conflict pits two constitutional rights against one another, as when a judge places a **gag order** on individuals involved in a case. In such cases, the court has essentially decreed that the First Amendment rights of free speech and freedom of the press must be postponed so that the right of an individual to receive a fair and impartial trial is not destroyed.

*The Information Highway*    New technologies continue to challenge courts in the application of First Amendment principles. Currently the Internet, the global computer communication network, allows users to gain access to information worldwide. Thousands of electronic bulletin boards give computer users with communication modems access to everything from bomb-making instructions and sex conversations to obscene photos and even child pornography. Many commercial access services ban obscene messages and exclude bulletin boards with racially or sexually offensive commentary. But can *government* try to ban such material from the Internet without violating First Amendment freedoms? A Federal Appeals Court decision in 1996 held that the Internet deserved the "broadest possible" free speech protection and struck down a federal law banning "indecent" material on the Internet.

# FREEDOM OF ASSEMBLY AND PETITION

The First Amendment guarantees "the right of the people peaceably to assemble, and to petition the government for redress of grievances." The right to organize political parties and interest groups derives from the right of assembly. And freedom of petition protects most lobbying activities.

**Shield laws:** Laws in some states that give reporters the right to refuse to name their sources or to release their notes in court cases; may be overturned by the courts when such refusals jeopardize a fair trial for a defendant.

**Gag order:** An order by a judge banning discussion or reporting of a case in order to ensure a fair and impartial trial.

*The Right of Association*   Freedom of assembly includes the right to form and join organizations and associations. In an important case during the early civil rights movement, the state of Alabama attempted to harass the National Association for the Advancement of Colored People by requiring it to turn over its membership lists to authorities. The Supreme Court held the state's action to be an unconstitutional infringement of the freedom of association.[75]

The Supreme Court has also protected the right of students to form organizations. "First Amendment rights are available to teachers and students. It can hardly be argued that either teachers or students shed their constitutional rights at the school house gate."[76] Attempts by a college or university to deny official recognition to a student organization based on its views violates the right of association.

*Protests, Parades, and Demonstrations*   Freedom of assembly includes the right to peacefully protest, parade, and demonstrate. Authorities may, within reasonable limits, enact restrictions regarding the time, place, and manner of an assembly so as to preserve public order, smooth traffic flow, freedom of movement, and even peace and quiet. But these regulations cannot be unevenly applied to groups with different views. Thus authorities may require a permit to parade, but they cannot deny a permit to a group because of the nature of their cause. For example, the Supreme Court held that city authorities in Skokie, Illinois, acted unconstitutionally in prohibiting the American Nazi Party from holding a march in that city even though it was populated with large numbers of Jewish survivors of the Holocaust.[77] (As *What Do You Think?* "Freedom of Assembly for Whom?" illustrates, however, many Americans disagree with this interpretation.)

Pro-choice and pro-life activists clash outside the Supreme Court after a ruling on abortion. Pro-life activists picketing abortion clinics have tested the limits of freedom of assembly.

*Picketing*   Assemblies of people have a high potential for creating a public disturbance. Parades block traffic and litter the streets; loudspeakers assault the ears of local residents and bystanders; picket lines may block the free passage of others. Although the right of assembly is protected by the First Amendment, its exercise involves conduct as well as expression, and therefore it is usually subject to greater government regulation than expression alone. The Court has generally upheld reasonable use of public property for assembly, but it has not forced *private* property owners to accommodate speeches or assemblies. Airport terminals, shopping malls, and other open forums, which may or may not be publicly owned, have posed problems for the courts.

Freedom of assembly is currently being tested by opponents of abortion such as Operation Rescue that picket abortion clinics, hoping to embarrass and dissuade women from entering them. Generally the Courts have placed strict limits on these demonstrations to ensure that people can move freely in and out of the clinics. Freedom of assembly does not include the right to block access to public or private buildings. And when abortion opponents demonstrated at the residence of a physician who performed abortions, the Supreme Court upheld a local ordinance barring assemblies in residential neighborhoods.[78] Physically obstructing access to buildings almost always violates state or local laws, as does the threat or use of force by picketers. In 1994 Congress passed a federal law guaranteeing access to abortion clinics, arguing that the federal government should act to guarantee a recognized constitutional right.

# Freedom of Assembly for Whom?

The general public lags far behind the Supreme Court, and well behind persons trained in the law, in adherence to the prevailing constitutional norms of freedom of assembly. While most Americans express general support for the right to hold mass protests and demonstrations, they are unwilling to extend police protection to unpopular groups or to risk any protests that "might" result in violence. When the same questions are asked of a national sample of lawyers and judges, there is much greater understanding of the constitutional principles at stake and a much greater willingness to protect demonstrators.

The First Amendment right of assembly does not depend upon the views of the group that is meeting. If a community regularly allows its civic auditorium to be used by organizations, it cannot deny use to a particular organization on the basis of its unpopular views. But the general public appears quite willing to deny the use of a community facility to advocates of unpopular causes. For example, while the right of association protects even Nazis, it is not likely that many university administrations would permit such an organization to meet on campus unless confronted with a court order to do so. And while persons trained in the law are generally more cognizant of First Amendment rights, even lawyers do not uniformly endorse the exercise of the right of assembly for all groups.

| What is your position on the following activities? | General Public | Lawyers and Judges |
|---|---|---|
| **Mass student protest demonstrations** | | |
| should be allowed by college officials as long as they are nonviolent. | 68% | 88% |
| have no place on the college campus and participating students should be punished. | 21 | 9 |
| neither/undecided | 12 | 3 |
| **When groups like the Nazis or other extreme groups require police protection at their rallies and marches, the community should** | | |
| supply and pay for whatever police protection is needed. | 18 | 67 |
| prohibit such groups from holding rallies because of the costs and damages incurred. | 57 | 14 |
| neither/undecided | 25 | 20 |
| **Should a community allow its civic auditorium to be used by** | | |
| Protestant groups who want to hold a revival meeting? | | |
| Yes | 69 | 74 |
| No | 16 | 17 |
| right to life groups to preach against abortion? | | |
| Yes | 65 | 81 |
| No | 18 | 10 |
| gay liberation movements to organize for homosexual rights? | | |
| Yes | 26 | 65 |
| No | 59 | 26 |
| atheists who want to preach against God and religion? | | |
| Yes | 18 | 66 |
| No | 71 | 24 |
| foreign radicals who want to express their hatred of America? | | |
| Yes | 6 | 32 |
| No | 87 | 52 |
| **If some students at a college want to form a "Campus Nazi Club"** | | |
| they should be allowed to do so. | 17 | 67 |
| college officials should ban such clubs from campus. | 67 | 24 |
| neither/undecided | 16 | 9 |

*Source:* Data from Herbert McClosky and Alida Brill, *Dimensions of Tolerance* (New York: Russell Sage Foundation, 1983).

# THE RIGHT TO BEAR ARMS

The Second Amendment to the U.S. Constitution states: "A well regulated Militia, being necessary to the security of a free State, the right of the people to keep and bear Arms, shall not be infringed."

*Bearing Arms*    What is meant by the right of the people "to keep and bear arms"? One view is that the Second Amendment confers on Americans an *individual* constitutional right, like the First Amendment freedom of speech or press (see *Across the USA:* "Gun Control and the Second Amendment"). The history surrounding the adoption of the Second Amendment reveals the concern of colonists with attempts by despotic governments to confiscate the arms of citizens and render them helpless to resist tyranny. James Madison wrote in the *Federalist Papers,* No. 46 that "the advantage of being armed which the Americans possess over the people of almost every other nation, forms a barrier against the enterprise of [tyrannical] ambition."[79] The Second Amendment was adopted with little controversy; most state constitutions at the time, like Pennsylvania's, declared that "the people have a right to bear arms for the defense of themselves and the state." Early American political rhetoric was filled with praise for an armed citizenry able to protect its freedoms by force if necessary.

The violent conclusion of the attempt by the Bureau of Alcohol, Tobacco and Firearms to enforce federal gun laws against the Branch Davidians in Waco, Texas. Members of citizen militia groups regard the ATF as a threat to their freedom to bear arms.

*State Militias*    Many constitutional scholars argue that the Second Amendment protects only the *collective* right of the states to form militias—that is, their right to maintain National Guard units. They focus on the qualifying phrase "a well-regulated Militia, being necessary to the security of a free State." The Second Amendment merely prevents Congress from denying the states the right to organize their own military units. If the Founders had wished to create an individual right to bear arms, they would not have inserted the phrase about a "well-regulated militia." (Opponents of this view argue that the original definition of a militia included all free males over eighteen.) Interpreted in this fashion, the Second Amendment does *not* protect private groups who form themselves into militias, nor does it guarantee citizens the right to own guns.

*Citizen "Militias"*    In recent years, self-styled citizen "militias" have cropped up across the nation. They are armed groups who more or less regularly get together dressed in camouflage to engage in military tactics and training. They generally view federal government agencies, and often the United Nations, as potential threats to their freedom. They view themselves as modern-day descendants of the American patriot militias who fought in the Revolutionary War. Indeed, the Militia Act of 1792 *required* "every free white male citizen of the respective states, resident therein, who is or shall be of the age of 18 years and under the age of 45 years" to be enrolled in the militia and equipped with "a good musket," a bayonet, and "24 rounds of ammunition." This law was not changed until 1912, when National Guard units replaced state militia.

Citizen militia groups frequently come into conflict with federal firearms regulations. Enforcement of these regulations is the responsibility of the Bureau of Alcohol, Tobacco and Firearms. It was the ATF's violent efforts to enforce federal gun laws that led to the deaths of more than seventy people at the Branch

# Gun Control and the Second Amendment

*One subject of contention in the debate over gun control is whether or not law abiding citizens should be permitted to carry concealed handguns. Laws on this issue vary from state to state.*

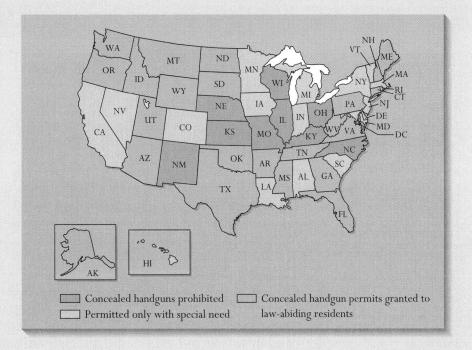

☐ Concealed handguns prohibited  ☐ Concealed handgun permits granted to
☐ Permitted only with special need     law-abiding residents

Attempts at gun control legislation frequently follow murders or assassination attempts on prominent figures. The Federal Gun Control Act of 1968 was a response to the assassinations of Senator Robert F. Kennedy and Martin Luther King, Jr., in that year. It banned mail-order sales of handguns and required that manufacturers place serial numbers on all firearms, that dealers record all sales, and that dealers be licensed by the Bureau of Alcohol, Tobacco and Firearms. In 1993, Congress passed the Brady Act, requiring a seven-day waiting period for the purchase of a handgun. The act is named for James S. Brady, former press secretary to President Ronald Reagan, who was severely wounded in the 1981 attempted assassination of the president. The Crime Control Act of 1994 banned the manufacture or sale of "assault weapons," generally defined to include both automatic and semi-automatic rifles and machine pistols. Opponents of these acts believe they are empty political gestures that erode the Second Amendment right to bear arms.

Proponents of gun control cite the U.S. Supreme Court decision in *United States v. Miller* (1939). In this case, the Court considered the constitutionality of the federal National Firearms Act of 1934, which, among other things, prohibited the transportation of sawed-off shotguns in interstate commerce. The defendant claimed that Congress could not infringe upon his right to keep and bear arms. But the Court responded that a sawed-off shotgun had no "relationship to the preservation or efficiency of a well-regulated militia."\* The clear implication of this decision is that the right to bear arms refers only to a state's right to maintain a militia. But even if an individual has a constitutional right to own a gun, the Supreme Court is likely to approve of reasonable restrictions on that right, including waiting periods for purchases, reporting, and registration. No constitutional right is viewed as absolute.

The Second Amendment does not necessarily include the right to carry a hidden gun. Currently about half of the states grant concealed weapons carrying permits to applicants who have never been convicted of a felony. (Generally a "concealed weapon" refers to a handgun carried on a person or within immediate reach in an automobile.) Nine states and the District of Columbia prohibit the carrying of concealed weapons altogether. Other states require applicants for permits to prove that they have a specific need to carry a weapon.

\**United States v. Miller*, 307 U.S. 174 (1939).

Davidian compound in Waco, Texas, in 1993. Radical militia groups have pledged to enforce their right to bear arms with violence if necessary.

## CRIME, VIOLENCE, AND THE CONSTITUTION

Crime, violence, and social disorder are common ills confronting all societies (see *Compared to What?* "Crime and Punishment"). But democratic societies must balance any remedies with respect for the dignity of individuals. For democratic societies, government repression, invasions of privacy, and police misconduct are evils at least as dangerous as crime and violence. It is not surprising that half of the amendments in the Bill of Rights are related to matters involving criminal justice.

*Crime in America*   How much crime is there in America? Official **crime rates** are based on the Federal Bureau of Investigation's *Uniform Crime Reports,* but these annual FBI reports themselves are based on crimes reported to state and local law enforcement agencies. The FBI has established a uniform classification of certain crimes: *violent crimes* (crimes against persons)—murder and nonnegligent manslaughter, forcible rape, robbery, and aggravated assault; and *property crimes* (crimes against property only)—burglary, larceny, arson, and theft, including auto theft (see Table 14-3).

*Crime Rates*   National crime rates have risen dramatically yet unevenly over the past few decades. From 1965 to 1975, crime rates more than doubled, and "law and order" became an important political issue. In the early 1980s, crime rates leveled off and even declined slightly from their record years (see Figure 14-1). Many speculated that this pattern reflected age-group changes in the population: the early rise in crime reflected the large numbers of baby boomers reaching "crime-prone" age groups (fifteen to twenty-four) at that time. Crime rates leveled off when this age group was no longer increasing as a percentage of the population and were expected to keep falling. But instead, crime rates moved upward again. The new factor in the crime rate equation

**TABLE 14-3**   OFFICIAL CRIME RATES (OFFENSES REPORTED TO POLICE PER **100,000** POPULATION)

|  | 1980 | 1985 | 1990 | 1995 |
|---|---|---|---|---|
| **Crime against Persons** | | | | |
| Murder | 10 | 8 | 9 | 8 |
| Forcible rape | 37 | 34 | 41 | 37 |
| Robbery | 251 | 217 | 257 | 221 |
| Aggravated assault | 299 | 279 | 424 | 423 |
| Total | 597 | 538 | 732 | 689 |
| **Crimes against Property** | | | | |
| Total | 5,353 | 4,637 | 5,089 | 4,611 |
| **All Reported Crimes** | | | | |
| Total | 5,950 | 5,175 | 5,821 | 5,300 |

**Crime rates:** Numbers of crimes reported to law enforcement authorities in relation to the population.

# Crime and Punishment

The United States has the dubious distinction of leading all other advanced industrial nations in both crime rates and the proportion of its population behind bars. In cross-national victimization surveys, almost 30 percent of Americans say they were a victim of a crime in the last year. Even more shocking perhaps is the murder rate in the United States, which is more than twice as high as Germany's and nearly eight times higher than Japan's (see table).

With a crime rate higher than any other advanced nation's, it is no surprise that the incarceration rate (the number of persons imprisoned per 100,000 population) in the United States is also higher. Crackdowns on drug crimes, mandatory sentencing laws in many states, and a high rate of returns to prison have doubled the U.S. prison population since 1980. Indeed, imprisonment in the United States is more common than in South Africa or Russia, two nations widely regarded as having severe penal codes.

| | Victimization (percent population saying they have been victim of a crime in previous year, 1989) | Murder Rate (murders reported to police, per 100,000 population, 1990) | Incarceration Rate (prisoners per 100,000 population, 1990) |
|---|---|---|---|
| United States | 28.8% | 9.4 | 426 |
| Canada | 28.1 | 5.5 | — |
| Australia | 27.8 | 4.5 | 72 |
| Netherlands | 26.8 | — | 40 |
| Denmark | — | 5.2 | 68 |
| France | 19.4 | 4.6 | 81 |
| Germany | 21.9 | 4.2 | 85 |
| Belgium | 17.7 | 2.8 | 65 |
| Spain | 24.6 | 2.3 | 76 |
| Switzerland | 15.6 | 2.3 | 73 |
| Italy | — | 7.2 | 60 |
| Norway | 16.5 | 2.0 | 48 |
| United Kingdom | 19.4 | 2.0 | 97 |
| Austria | — | 1.8 | 77 |
| Ireland | — | 1.0 | 55 |
| Finland | 15.9 | 0.7 | 73 |
| Japan | 9.3 | 1.2 | 45 |

Source: Jan J. M. Van Dijik et al., *Experiences of Crime across the World,* 2d ed. (Deventer, Netherlands: Kluwer, 1991, p. 174; Andrew J. Shapiro, *We're Number One* (New York: Vintage Books, 1992), p. 120.

appeared to be the widespread popularity of "crack" cocaine and other illegal drugs. Perhaps as many as one-half of all crimes today are drug-related (see *A Conflicting View:* "Legalize Drugs to Reduce Crime"). Contrary to the general public's perception, the overall crime rate in the United States has declined slightly since 1991.

*Victimization*    Many crimes are not reported to the police and therefore cannot be counted in the official crime rates shown in Table 14-3. In an effort to learn the real amount of crime in the nation, the U.S. Justice Department regularly

# Legalize Drugs to Reduce Crime

Drug offenses currently account for almost half of all prison sentences meted out by federal courts.* The average federal sentence for drug crimes—possession, trafficking, or manufacturing of illegal substances—is seven years; the federal minimum sentence for possession of illegal drugs is five years. Almost half of the federal prison population is serving time for drug offenses. Nearly 1 million persons are arrested each year for drug violations. The United States imprisons a larger proportion of its population than any other advanced nation. Is all this too high a price to pay for the "war on drugs"?

The U.S. government's National Institute on Drug Abuse regularly surveys Americans to ask whether they have ever used particular drugs and whether they have used them in the past year or month. These surveys suggest that about 15 million people, or 6 percent of the U.S. population, have used an illicit drug in the previous thirty days (see figure). Marijuana is the most commonly used illicit drug, followed by cocaine. There are an estimated 12 million regular users of marijuana, or about 5 percent of the population, although many more have smoked it at least once. According to the survey evidence, the numbers of people using illicit drugs has declined in recent years. However, the U.S. Drug Enforcement Administration (DEA) reports increased numbers of cocaine seizures and drug arrests each year. There appear to be no significant reductions in the volume of drugs entering the country or reaching the streets.

The failure of antidrug policies to produce any significant reductions in drug supply or demand, coupled with the high costs of enforcement and the loss of civil liberties, has caused some observers to propose the legalization of drugs and government control of their production and sales. "Prohibition" failed earlier in the century to end alcohol consumption, and the crime, official corruption, and enormous cost of futile efforts to stop drinking eventually forced the nation to end Prohibition. Similarly, it is argued that the legalization of drugs would end organized crime's profit monopoly over the drug trade, raise billions of dollars by legally taxing drugs, end the strain on relations with Latin American nations caused by efforts to eradicate drugs, and save additional billions in enforcement costs that could be used for education and treatment. If drugs were legally obtainable under government supervision, it is argued that many of society's current problems would be alleviated: the crime and violence associated with the drug trade, the corruption of public officials, the spread of diseases associated with drug use, and the many infringements of personal liberty associated with antidrug wars.

But even the suggestion of drug legalization offends Americans who believe that legalization would greatly expand drug use in the country. Cheap, available drugs would greatly increase the numbers of addicted persons, creating a "society of zombies" that would destroy the social fabric of the nation. Cocaine and heroin are far more habit forming than alcohol, and legalization would encourage the development of newer and even more potent and addictive synthetic drugs. Whatever the health costs of drug abuse today, it is argued that legalization would produce public health problems of enormous magnitude. Whatever the damages to society from drug-related crime and efforts to prohibit drugs, the damages to society from cheap, available drug usage would be far greater.

*Statistical Abstract of the United States, 1994, p. 212.

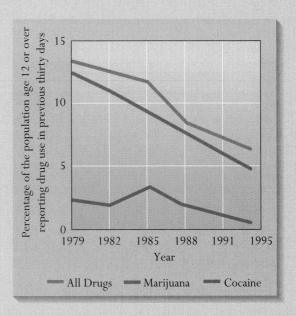

Source: U.S. Substance Abuse and Mental Health Services Administration, Natural Household Survey on Drug Abuse, 1994.

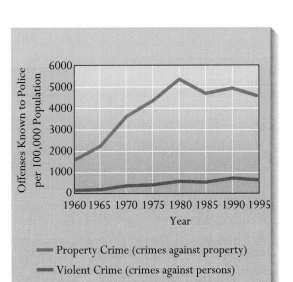

FIGURE 14-1    Crime Rates

Offenses Known to Police per 100,000 Population

6000
5000
4000
3000
2000
1000
0

1960 1965 1970 1975 1980 1985 1990 1995
Year

—— Property Crime (crimes against property)
—— Violent Crime (crimes against persons)

surveys a national sample of people, asking whether they have been a victim of a crime during the past year.[80] These surveys reveal that the **victimization rate** is many times greater than the official crime rate. Between 30 and 40 million of the nation's 265 million inhabitants say that they have been a victim of a crime in the preceding year; 6 million say they have been victims of violent crime. The number of forcible rapes is three to five times greater than the number reported to police, burglaries three times greater, and robbery more than twice the reported rate. Only auto theft and murder statistics are reasonably accurate, indicating that most people call the police when their car is stolen or someone is murdered.

Why do people fail to report crime to the police? The most common reason given by interviewees is the feeling that police cannot be effective in dealing with the crime. Other reasons included the feeling that the crime was "a private matter" or that the victim did not want to harm the offender. Fear of reprisal was mentioned less frequently, usually in cases of assaults and family crimes.[81]

## RIGHTS OF CRIMINAL DEFENDANTS

While society needs the protection of the police, it is equally important to protect society from the police. Arbitrary searches and arrests, imprisonment without trial, forced confessions, beatings and torture, secret trials, tainted witnesses, excessive punishments, and other human rights violations are all too common throughout the world. The U.S. Constitution limits the powers of the police and protects the rights of the accused (see Table 14-4).

*The Guarantee of the Writ of Habeas Corpus*    One of the oldest and most revered rights in English common law is the right to obtain a **writ of habeas corpus,** which is a court order directing public officials who are holding a person in custody to bring the prisoner into court and explain the reasons for confinement. If a judge finds that the prisoner is being unlawfully detained, or finds that there is not sufficient evidence that a crime has been committed or that the prisoner could have committed it, the judge must order the prisoner's release.

**Victimization rate:** The incidence of crime as reported in public opinion polls; exceeds the crime rate because it takes into account individuals who are victimized but decline to take the issue to the police.

**Writ of habeas corpus:** A court order directing public officials who are holding a person in custody to bring the prisoner into court and explain the reasons for confinement; the right to habeas corpus is protected by Article I of the Constitution.

TABLE 14-4   INDIVIDUAL RIGHTS IN THE CRIMINAL JUSTICE PROCESS

| Process | Rights |
|---|---|
| **Investigation by law enforcement officers**<br>Expectation that police act lawfully. | **Fourth Amendment: Protection against unreasonable searches and seizures**<br>Warranted searches for sworn "probable cause." Exceptions: consent searches, safety searches, car searches, and searches incident to a valid arrest. |
| **Arrest**<br>Arrests based on warrants issued by judges and magistrates.<br>Arrests based on crimes committed in the presence of law enforcement officials.<br>Arrests for "probable cause." | **Fifth Amendment: Protection against self-incrimination**<br>Miranda rules (see Figure 14-2)<br><br>**Habeas Corpus**<br>Police holding a person in custody must bring that person before a judge with cause to believe that a crime was committed and the prisoner committed it. |
| **Hearing and bail**<br>Preliminary hearing in which prosecutor presents testimony that a crime was committed and probable cause for charging the accused. | **Eighth Amendment: No excessive bail**<br>Defendant considered innocent until proven guilty; release on bail and amount of bail depends on seriousness of crime, trustworthiness of defendant, and safety of community. |
| **Indictment**<br>Prosecutor, or a grand jury in federal cases, issues formal document naming the accused and specifying the charges. | **Fifth Amendment: Grand Jury (federal)**<br>Federal prosecutors (but not necessarily state prosecutors) must convince a grand jury that a reasonable basis exists to believe that the defendant committed a crime and he or she should be brought to trial. |
| **Arraignment**<br>Judge reads indictment to the accused and ensures that the accused understands charges and rights and has counsel.<br>Judge asks defendant how to choose a plea: Guilty, *nolo contendere* (no contest), or not guilty. If defendant pleads guilty or no contest, a trial is not necessary and defendant proceeds to sentencing. | **Sixth Amendment: Right to Counsel**<br>Begins in investigation stage, when officials become "accusatory," extends throughout criminal justice process.<br>Free counsel for indigent defendants. |
| **Trial**<br>Impartial judge presides as prosecuting and defense attorneys present witnesses and evidence relevant to guilt or innocence of defendant and make arguments to the jury. Jury deliberates in secret and issues a verdict. | **Sixth Amendment: Right to a speedy and public trial**<br>Impartial jury.<br>Right to confront witnesses.<br>Right to compel favorable witnesses to testify.<br><br>**Fourth Amendment: Exclusionary rule**<br>Illegally obtained evidence cannot be used against defendant. |
| **Sentencing**<br>If the defendant is found not guilty, the process ends. Defendants who plead guilty or no contest and defendants found guilty by jury are sentenced by fine, imprisonment, or both by the judge. | **Eighth Amendment: Protection against cruel and unusual punishments** |
| **Appeal**<br>Defendants found guilty may appeal to higher courts for reversal of verdict or a new trial based on errors made anywhere in the process. | **Fifth Amendment: Protection against double jeopardy**<br>Government cannot try a defendant again for the same offense. |

Thus the writ of habeas corpus is a means to test the legality of any imprisonment.

The writ of habeas corpus was considered so fundamental to the framers of the Constitution that they included it in the original text of Article I: "The privilege of the Writ of Habeas Corpus shall not be suspended, unless when in Cases of Rebellion or Invasion the public Safety may require it." Despite the qualifying phrase, the Supreme Court has never sanctioned suspension of the writ of habeas corpus even during wartime. President Abraham Lincoln suspended the writ of habeas corpus in several areas during the Civil War, but in the case of *Ex parte Milligan* (1866), the Supreme Court ruled that the president had acted unconstitutionally.[82] (With the war over, however, the Court's decision had no practical effect.) Again, in 1946, the Supreme Court declared that the military had had no right to substitute military courts for ordinary courts in Hawaii during World War II, even though Hawaii was in an active theater of war.[83] State courts cannot issue writs of habeas corpus to federal officials, but federal judges may issue such writs to state officials whenever there is reason to believe that a person is being held in violation of the Constitution or laws of the United States.

*The Prohibition of Bills of Attainder and Ex Post Facto Laws*    Like the guarantee of habeas corpus, protection against bills of attainder and ex post facto laws was considered so fundamental to individual liberty that it was included in the original text of the Constitution. A **bill of attainder** is a legislative act inflicting punishment without judicial trial. An **ex post facto law** is a retroactive criminal law that works against the accused—for example, a law that makes an act criminal after the act is committed or a law that increases the punishment for a crime and applies it retroactively. Both the federal government and the states are prevented from passing such laws.

The fact that relatively few cases of bills of attainder or ex post facto laws have come to the federal courts does not diminish the importance of these protections. Rather, it testifies to the widespread appreciation of their importance in a free society.

*Unreasonable Searches and Seizures*    Individuals are protected by the Fourth Amendment from "unreasonable searches and seizures" of their private "persons, houses, papers, and effects." The Fourth Amendment lays out specific rules for searches and seizures of evidence: "No warrants shall issue, but upon probable cause, supported by Oath or affirmation, and particularly describing the place to be searched, and the persons or things to be seized." Judges cannot issue a **search warrant** just to let police see if an individual has committed a crime; there must be "probable cause" for such issuance. The indiscriminate searching of whole neighborhoods or groups of people is unconstitutional and is prevented by the Fourth Amendment's requirement that the place to be searched must be specifically described in the warrant. The requirement that the things to be seized must be described in the warrant is meant to prevent "fishing expeditions" into an individual's home and personal effects on the possibility that some evidence of unknown illegal activity might crop up. The only exception is if police, in the course of a valid search for a specified item, find other items whose very possession is a crime—for example, illicit drugs.

But the courts also permit police to undertake various other "reasonable" searches *without* a warrant: searches in connection with a valid arrest; searches to

**Bill of attainder:** A legislative act inflicting punishment without judicial trial; forbidden under Article I of the Constitution.

**Ex post facto law:** A retroactive criminal law that works against the accused; forbidden under Article I of the Constitution.

**Search warrant:** A court order permitting law enforcement officials to search a location in order to seize evidence of a crime; issued only for a specified location, in connection with a specific investigation, and on submission of proof that "probable cause" exists to warrant such a search.

*Unlike soldiers in a conventional war, U.S. police officers face restraints on how far they can go in their war on crime. While some charge that these restrictions have made it easy for criminals to escape the consequences of their actions, others argue that forcing law enforcement officials to follow the law is not only reasonable but also results in stronger cases and increased chances of conviction.*

protect the safety of police officers; searches to obtain evidence in the immediate vicinity and in the suspect's control; searches to preserve evidence in danger of being immediately destroyed; and searches with the consent of a suspect. Indeed, most police searches today take place without warrant under one or another of these conditions. The Supreme Court has also allowed automobile searches and searches of open fields without warrants in many cases. The requirement of "probable cause" has been very loosely defined; even a "partially corroborated anonymous informant's tip" qualifies as "probable cause" to make a search, seizure, or arrest.[84] And if the police, while making a warranted search or otherwise lawfully on the premises, see evidence of a crime "in plain view," they may seize such evidence without further authorization.[85]

*Arrests*    The Supreme Court has not applied the warrant requirement of the Fourth Amendment to arrests. Rather, the Court permits arrests without warrants (1) when a crime is committed in the presence of an officer; and (2) when an arrest is supported by "probable cause" to believe that a crime has been committed by the person apprehended.[86] However, the Court has held that police may not enter a home to arrest its occupant without either a warrant for the arrest or the consent of the owner.[87]

*Indictment*    The Fifth Amendment requires that an **indictment** be issued by a **grand jury** before a person may be brought to trial on a felony offense. This provision was designed as a protection against unreasonable and harassing prosecutions by the government. In principle, the grand jury is supposed to determine whether the evidence submitted to it by government prosecutors is sufficient to place a person on trial. In practice, however, grand juries spend very little time deliberating on the vast majority of cases. Neither defendants nor their attorneys are permitted to testify before grand juries without the prosecution's permission, which is rarely given. Thus the prosecutor controls the information submitted to grand juries and instructs them in their duties. In almost all cases, grand juries accept the prosecution's recommendations with little or no discussion. Thus, grand juries, whose hearings are secret, do not provide much of a check on federal prosecutors, and their refusal to indict is very rare.

*Self-Incrimination and the Right to Counsel*    Freedom from self-incrimination had its origin in English common law; it was originally designed to prevent persons from being tortured into confessions of guilt. It is also a logical

**Indictment:** Determination by a grand jury that sufficient evidence exists to warrant trial of an individual on a felony charge; necessary before an individual can be brought to trial.

**Grand jury:** A jury charged only with determining whether sufficient evidence exists to support indictment of an individual on a felony charge; the grand jury's decision to indict does not represent a conviction.

CHAPTER 14 • POLITICS AND PERSONAL LIBERTY

extension of the notion that individuals should not be forced to contribute to their own prosecution, that the burden of proof rests upon the state. The Fifth Amendment protects people from both physical and psychological coercion.[88] It protects not only accused persons at their own trial but also witnesses testifying in trials of other persons, civil suits, congressional hearings, and so on. Thus "taking the Fifth" has become a standard phrase in our culture: "I refuse to answer that question on the grounds that it might tend to incriminate me." The protection also means that judges, prosecutors, and juries cannot use the refusal of people to take the stand at their own trial as evidence of guilt. Indeed, a judge or attorney is not even permitted to imply this to a jury, and a judge is obligated to instruct a jury *not* to infer guilt from a defendant's refusal to testify.

It is important to note that individuals may be forced to testify when they are not themselves the object of a criminal prosecution. Government officials may extend a grant of **immunity from prosecution** to a witness in order to compel testimony. Under a grant of immunity, the government agrees not to use any of the testimony against the witness; in return, the witness provides information that the government uses to prosecute others who are considered more dangerous or more important than the immune witness. Because such grants ensure that nothing the witnesses say can be used against them, immunized witnesses cannot refuse to answer under the Fifth Amendment.

The Supreme Court under Chief Justice Earl Warren greatly strengthened the Fifth Amendment protection against self-incrimination and the right to counsel in a series of rulings in the 1960s:

- *Gideon v. Wainwright* (1963): Equal protection under the Fourteenth Amendment requires that free legal counsel be appointed for all indigent defendants in all criminal cases.[89]
- *Escobedo v. Illinois* (1964): Suspects are entitled to confer with counsel as soon as police investigation focuses on them or once "the process shifts from investigatory to accusatory."[90]
- *Miranda v. Arizona* (1966): Before questioning suspects, a police officer must inform them of all their constitutional rights, including the right to counsel (appointed at no cost to the suspect if necessary) and the right to remain silent. Although suspects may knowingly waive these rights, the police cannot question anyone who at any point asks for a lawyer or declines "in any manner" to be questioned. If the police commit an error in these procedures, the accused goes free, regardless of the evidence of guilt.[91] Figure 14-2 shows a typical "Miranda rights" card carried by police to ensure that they issue the proper warnings to those under arrest.

It is very difficult to determine the extent to which these decisions have really hampered efforts to halt the rise in crime in the United States. Studies of police behavior following these decisions show that at first police committed many procedural errors and guilty persons were freed, but after a year or so of adjustment to the new rules, successful prosecutions rose to the same level achieved before the decisions.[92]

*The Exclusionary Rule*   Illegally obtained evidence and confessions may *not* be used in criminal trials. If police find evidence of a crime in an illegal search or if they elicit statements from suspects without informing them of their rights to

**Immunity from prosecution:** A grant by the government to an individual of freedom from prosecution on a particular charge in return for testimony by that individual that might otherwise be self-incriminating.

| METROPOLITAN POLICE DEPARTMENT | WAIVER |
|---|---|
| Warning As To Your Rights | |

**METROPOLITAN POLICE DEPARTMENT**
Warning As To Your Rights

You are under arrest. Before we ask you any questions you must understand what your rights are.

You have the right to remain silent. You are not required to say anything to us at any time or to answer any questions. Anything you say can be used against you in court.

You have the right to talk to a lawyer for advice before we question you and to have him with you during questioning.

If you cannot afford a lawyer and want one, a lawyer will be provided for you.

If you want to answer questions now without a lawyer present, you will still have the right to stop answering at any time. You also have the right to stop answering at any time until you talk to a lawyer.

**WAIVER**

1. Have you read or had read to you the warning as to your rights?_____

2. Do you understand these rights? _____

3. Do you wish to answer any questions? _____

4. Are you willing to answer questions without having an attorney present? _____

5. Signature of defendant on line below.

_____

6. Time _____ Date _____

7. Signature of officer _____

8. Signature of witness _____

**FIGURE 14-2** **The Miranda Warning**
*Since the U.S. Supreme Court's ruling in the case of* Miranda v. Arizona *in 1966, law enforcement officials at all levels have routinely carried "Miranda Rights" cards, which they read to accused individuals immediately after their arrest. This procedure has largely eliminated defendants' abilities to obtain dismissals and/or acquittals on the basis of ignorance of their rights or lack of proper counsel.*

**Exclusionary rule:** A rule of law that evidence found in an illegal search or resulting from an illegally obtained confession may not be admitted at trial.

remain silent or to have counsel, the evidence or statements produced are not admissible in a trial. This **exclusionary rule** is one of the more controversial procedural rights that the Supreme Court has extended to criminal defendants. The rule is also unique to the United States: in Great Britain evidence obtained illegally may be used against the accused, although the accused may bring charges against the police for damages.

The rule provides *enforcement* for the Fourth Amendment guarantee against unreasonable searches and seizures, as well as the Fifth Amendment guarantee against compulsory self-incrimination and the guarantee of counsel. Initially applied only in federal cases, in *Mapp v. Ohio* (1961) the Supreme Court extended the exclusionary rule to all criminal cases in the United States.[93] A *good faith exception* is made "when law enforcement officers have acted in objective good faith or their transgressions have been minor."[94] But the exclusionary rule is frequently attacked for the high price it extracts from society—the release of guilty criminals. Why punish society because of the misconduct of police? Why not punish police directly, perhaps with disciplinary measures imposed by courts that discover errors, instead of letting guilty persons go free?

*Bail Requirements* The Eighth Amendment says only that "*excessive* bail shall not be required." This clause does not say that pretrial release on bail will be available to all. The Supreme Court has held that "in our society liberty is the norm, and detention prior to trial or without trial is the carefully limited exception." Pretrial release on bail can be denied on the basis of the seriousness of the crime (bail is often denied in murder cases), the trustworthiness of the defendant (bail is often denied when the prosecution shows that the defendant is likely to flee before trial), or, in a more controversial exception, when "no release conditions will reasonably assure the safety of any other person or the community."[95] If the court does not find any of these exceptions, it must set bail no higher than an amount reasonably calculated to ensure the defendant's later presence at trial.

Most criminal defendants cannot afford the bail money required for pretrial release. They must seek the services of a bail bondsman, who charges a heavy fee for filing the bail money with the court. The bail bondsman receives all of the bail money back when the defendant shows up for trial. But even if the defendant is found innocent, the bail bondsman retains the charge fee. Thus the system discriminates against poor defendants who cannot pay the fee.

*Fair Trial*    The original text of the Constitution guaranteed jury trials in criminal cases, and the Sixth Amendment went on to correct weaknesses the framers saw in the English justice system at that time—closed proceedings, trials in absentia (where the defendant is not present), secret witnesses, long delays between arrest and trial, biased juries, and the absence of defense counsel. Specifically, the Sixth Amendment guarantees:

- The right to a speedy and public trial.
- An impartial jury chosen from the state or district where the crime was committed.
- The right to confront (cross-examine) witnesses against the accused.
- The right of the accused to compel (subpoena) favorable witnesses to appear.
- The right of the accused to be represented by counsel.

Over the years the courts have elaborated on these elements of a fair trial so that today trial proceedings follow a rigidly structured format. First, attorneys make opening statements. The prosecution describes the crime and how it will prove beyond a reasonable doubt that the defendant committed it. The defense attorney argues either that the crime did not occur or that the defendant did not do it. Next, each side, again beginning with the prosecution, calls witnesses who first testify on "direct examination" for their side, then are cross-examined by the opposing attorney. Witnesses may be asked to verify evidence that is introduced as "exhibits." Defendants have a right to be present during their own trials (although an abusive and disruptive defendant may be considered to have waived his or her right to be present and be removed from the courtroom).[96] Prosecution witnesses must appear in the courtroom and submit to cross-examination (although special protection procedures, including videotaped testimony, may be used for children).[97] Prosecutors are obliged to disclose any information that might create a reasonable doubt about the defendant's guilt,[98] but the defendant may not be compelled to disclose incriminating information.

After all of the witnesses offered by both sides have been heard and cross-examined, prosecution and defense give their closing arguments. The burden of proof "beyond a reasonable doubt" rests with the prosecution; the defense does not need to prove that the accused is innocent, only that reasonable doubt exists regarding guilt.

Juries must be "impartial": they must not have prejudged the case or exhibit bias or prejudice or have a personal interest in the outcome. Judges can dismiss jurors for "cause." During jury selection, attorneys for the prosecution and defense are

*Judge Lance Ito presiding at the trial of O. J. Simpson. The televised trial consumed the American public for months, focusing attention on the strengths and weaknesses of the jury system.*

allowed a fixed number of "peremptory" challenges of jurors (although they cannot do so on the basis of race).[99] Jury selection is often regarded by attorneys as the key to the outcome of a case; both sides try to get presumed sympathetic people on the jury. In well-publicized cases, judges may "sequester" a jury (keep them in a hotel away from access to the mass media) in order to maintain impartiality. Judges may exclude press or television to prevent trials from becoming spectacles if they wish.[100] By tradition, English juries have had twelve members; however, the Supreme Court has allowed six-member juries in non-death-penalty cases.[101] Also by tradition, juries should arrive at a unanimous decision. If a jury cannot do so, judges declare a "hung" jury and the prosecutor may schedule a retrial. Only a "not guilty" prevents retrial of a defendant. Traditionally, it was believed that a lack of unanimity raised "reasonable doubt" about the defendant's guilt. But the Supreme Court has permitted nonunanimous verdicts in some cases.[102]

*Plea Bargaining*   Few criminal cases actually go to trial. More than 90 percent of criminal cases are plea bargained.[103] In **plea bargaining,** the defendant agrees to plead guilty and waives the right to a jury trial in exchange for concessions made by the prosecutor, perhaps the dropping of more serious charges against the defendant or a pledge to seek a reduced sentence or fine. Some critics of plea bargaining view it as another form of leniency in the criminal justice system that reduces its deterrent effects. Other critics view plea bargaining as a violation of the Constitution's protection against self-incrimination and guarantee of a fair jury trial. Prosecutors, they say, threaten defendants with serious charges and stiff penalties in order to force a guilty plea. Still other critics see plea bargaining as an "under-the-table" process that undermines respect for the criminal justice system.

Yet it is vital to the nation's court system that most defendants plead guilty. The court system would quickly break down from overload if any substantial proportion of defendants insisted on jury trials.

## THE DEATH PENALTY

Perhaps the most heated debate in criminal justice policy today concerns capital punishment. Opponents of the death penalty argue that it violates the prohibition against "cruel and unusual punishments" in the Eighth Amendment to the Constitution. They also argue that the death penalty is applied unequally. A large proportion of those executed have been poor, uneducated, and nonwhite. In contrast, many Americans feel that justice demands strong retribution for heinous crimes—a life for a life. A mere jail sentence for a multiple murderer or rapist-murderer seems unjust compared with the damage inflicted upon society and the victims. In many cases, a life sentence means less than ten years in prison under the current early-release and parole policies in many states. Convicted murderers have been set free, and some have killed again.

*Prohibition against Unfair Application*   Prior to 1971, the death penalty was officially sanctioned by about half of the states. Federal law also retained the death penalty. However, no one had actually suffered the death penalty since 1967 because of numerous legal tangles and direct challenges to the constitutionality of capital punishment.

**Plea bargaining:** The practice of allowing defendants to plead guilty to lesser crimes than those with which they were originally charged in return for reduced sentences.

In *Furman v. Georgia* (1972), the Supreme Court ruled that capital punishment, as then imposed, violated the Eighth and Fourteenth Amendment prohibitions against cruel and unusual punishment and due process of law. The justices' reasoning in the case was very complex. Only Justices William J. Brennan and Thurgood Marshall declared that capital punishment itself is cruel and unusual. The other justices in the majority felt that death sentences had been applied unfairly; some individuals received the death penalty for crimes for which many others received much lighter sentences. These justices left open the possibility that capital punishment would be constitutional if it was specified for certain kinds of crime and applied uniformly.[104]

After this decision, a majority of states rewrote their death penalty laws to try to ensure fairness and uniformity of application. Generally, these laws mandate the death penalty for murders committed during rape, robbery, hijacking, or kidnapping; murder of prison guards; murder with torture; and multiple murders. They call for two trials to be held—one to determine guilt or innocence and another to determine the penalty. At the second trial, evidence of "aggravating" and "mitigating" factors must be presented; if there are aggravating factors but no mitigating factors, the death penalty is mandatory.

*Death Penalty Reinstated*    The revised death penalty laws were upheld in a series of cases that came before the Supreme Court in 1976. The Court concluded that "the punishment of death does *not* invariably violate the Constitution." The majority decision noted that the framers of the Bill of Rights had accepted death as a common penalty for crime. While acknowledging that the Constitution and its amendments must be interpreted in a dynamic fashion, reflecting changing moral values, the Court's majority noted that most state legislatures have been willing to reenact the death penalty and hundreds of juries have been willing to impose that penalty. Thus "a large proportion of American society continues to regard it as an appropriate and necessary criminal sanction." Moreover, the Court held that the social purposes of retribution and deterrence justify the use of the death penalty; this ultimate sanction is "an expression of society's moral outrage at particularly offensive conduct."[105]

The Court reaffirmed that *Furman v. Georgia* struck down the death penalty only where it was invoked in "an arbitrary and capricious manner." A majority of the justices upheld the death penalty in states where the trial was a two-part proceeding, provided that during the second part the judge or jury was given relevant information and standards for deciding whether to impose the death penalty. The Court approved the consideration of "aggravating and mitigating circumstances." The Court also called for automatic review of all death sentences by state supreme courts to ensure that none is imposed under the influence of passion or prejudice, that aggravating factors are supported by the evidence, and that the sentence is not disproportionate to the crime. However, the court disapproved of state laws making the death penalty mandatory in all first-degree murder cases, holding that such laws were "unduly harsh and unworkably rigid."

*Racial Bias*    The death penalty has been challenged as a violation of the Equal Protection Clause of the Fourteenth Amendment because of racial bias in the application of the punishment. White murderers are just as likely to receive the death penalty as black murderers. However, some statistics show that if the *victim* is white there is a greater chance that the killer will be sentenced to death than if the victim is black. Nevertheless, the U.S. Supreme Court has ruled that statistical disparities in the race of victims by itself does not bar the use of the death penalty in all cases. There must be evidence of racial bias against a particular defendant in order for the Court to reverse a death sentence.[106]

*Delays*   Once imposed, the death penalty is, of course, irreversible. It is the ultimate punishment, and it must not be imposed if there is any doubt whatsoever about the defendant's guilt. Yet how many opportunities should death row inmates have to challenge their convictions and sentences? The writ of habeas corpus is guaranteed in the Constitution, but how many habeas corpus petitions should federal courts allow a condemned prisoner to submit? Attorneys for prisoners often generate new claims for last-minute appeals, expecting that federal courts will delay executions for future hearings and adjudications. Sometimes these claims are repetitive and frivolous. Currently, multiple appeals and writs by prisoners mean more than a decade between death sentence and execution.

In recent years, the Supreme Court has limited habeas corpus petitions of prisoners who have already exhausted their appeals and filed one claim in federal court and lost, and prisoners who failed to follow state rules of appeal. But what if genuine new evidence is uncovered after all appeals have been exhausted? Prisoners must then rely on governors' pardons (or, in federal cases, a presidential pardon).

# SUMMARY NOTES

- Laws and government are required to protect individual liberty. Yet laws and governments themselves restrict liberty. To resolve this dilemma, constitutions seek to limit governmental power over the individual. In the U.S. Constitution, the Bill of Rights is designed to place certain liberties beyond the reach of government.

- Initially the Bill of Rights applied against only the federal government, not state or local governments. But over time, the Bill of Rights was nationalized, as the Supreme Court applied the Due Process Clause of the Fourteenth Amendment to all governments in the United States.

- Freedom of religion encompasses two separate restrictions on government: government must not establish religion or prohibit its free exercise. While the wording of the First Amendment is absolute ("Congress shall make no law. . .") the Supreme Court has allowed some restrictions on religious practices that threaten health, safety, or welfare.

- The Supreme Court's efforts to maintain "a wall of separation" between church and state have proven difficult and controversial. The Court's banning of prayer and religious ceremony in public schools

more than thirty years ago remains politically unpopular today.

- The Supreme Court has never adopted the absolutist position that all speech is protected by the First Amendment. The Court's clear and present danger doctrine and its preferred position doctrine recognize the importance of free expression in a democracy, yet the Court has permitted some restrictions on expression, especially in times of perceived national crisis.

- The Supreme Court has placed obscenity outside of the protection of the First Amendment, but it has encountered considerable difficulty in defining "obscenity."

- Freedom of the press prevents government from imposing prior restraints (censorship) on the news media except periodically in wartime, when it has been argued that publication would result in serious harm or loss of life. The Supreme Court has allowed greater government authority over radio and television than over newspapers, on the grounds that radio and television are given exclusive rights to use specific broadcast frequencies.

- The First Amendment guarantee of the right of

assembly and petition protects the organization of political parties and interest groups. It also protects the right of people to peacefully protest, parade, and demonstrate. Governments may, within reasonable limits, restrict these activities for valid reasons but may not apply different restrictions to different groups based on the nature of their views.

- The Second Amendment guarantees "the right of the people to keep and bear arms." However, it is frequently argued that this is not an individual right to possess a gun, but rather a collective right of the states to maintain National Guard units.

- Crime rates in the United States are higher than in most other nations in the world. Yet a free society must balance any remedies to the crime problem against potential infringements of the rights of its citizens.

- The Constitution includes a number of important procedural guarantees in the criminal justice system: the writ of habeas corpus; prohibitions against bills of attainder and ex post facto laws; protection against unreasonable searches and seizures; protection against self-incrimination; guarantee of legal counsel; protection against excessive bail; guaran-

tee of a fair public and speedy trial by an impartial jury; the right to confront witnesses and to compel favorable witnesses to testify; and protection against cruel or unusual punishment.

- The Supreme Court's exclusionary rule helps to enforce some of these procedural rights by excluding illegally obtained evidence and self-incriminating statements from criminal trials. In the 1960s, Court interpretations of the Fourth and Fifth Amendments strengthened the rights of criminal defendants. Police procedures adjusted quickly, and today there is little evidence that procedural rights greatly hamper law enforcement.

- Few criminal cases go to trial. Most are plea bargained, with the defendant pleading guilty in exchange for reduced charges and/or a lighter sentence. While this practice is frequently criticized, without plea bargaining the nation's criminal court system would break down from case overload.

- The Supreme Court has ruled that the death penalty is not a "cruel and unusual punishment," but the Court has insisted on fairness and uniformity of application.

# SELECTED READINGS

ELSHTAIN, JEAN BETHKE. *Democracy on Trial.* New York: Basic Books, 1995. A "communitarian" argument that America's emphasis on personal rights erodes the common good and subverts democracy.

GARROW, DAVID. *Liberty and Sexuality: The Right to Privacy and the Making of Roe v. Wade.* New York: Macmillan, 1994. A historical account of the background and development of the right to sexual privacy.

HENTOFF, NAT. *Free Speech for Me—But Not for Thee.* New York: HarperCollins, 1992. An account of how both the right and the left in America try to suppress the opinions of those who disagree with them.

———. *The First Freedom,* 2d edition. New York: Delacorte, 1988. A history of the development and interpretation of the freedom of speech guarantee of the First Amendment.

HICKOK, EUGENE W., ed. *The Bill of Rights: Original Meaning and Current Understanding.* Charlottesville, Va.: University Press of Virginia, 1991. Essays on civil liberty and current controversies surrounding individual liberties guaranteed in the Bill of Rights.

KOBYLKA, JOSEPH F. *The Politics of Obscenity.* Westport, Conn.: Greenwood Press, 1991. A comprehensive review

of Supreme Court obscenity decisions, arguing that the *Miller* case in 1973 was a turning point away from a more permissive to a more restrictive approach toward sexually oriented material. It examines the litigation strategies of the American Civil Liberties Union and other groups in obscenity cases.

LEWIS, ANTHONY. *Gideon's Trumpet.* New York: Random House, 1964. The extraordinary story of Clarence Gideon and how his handwritten habeas corpus plea made its way to the U.S. Supreme Court, resulting in the guarantee of free legal counsel for poor defendants in felony cases.

MCCLOSKY, HERBERT, and ALIDA BRILL. *Dimensions of Tolerance.* New York: Russell Sage Foundation, 1983. Using public opinion surveys, the authors assess popular and elite support for constitutional liberties; they conclude that intolerance is widespread in the mass public but that community and legal elites give greater support to constitutional principles.

REICHLEY, A. JAMES. *Religion in American Public Life.* Washington, D.C.: Brookings Institution, 1986. A survey of the impact of religion and religious groups in American politics since the nation's founding.

# POLITICS AND CIVIL RIGHTS

## CHAPTER OUTLINE

## FEATURES

## ASK YOURSELF ABOUT POLITICS

**1** Does the U.S. Constitution require the government to be colorblind with respect to different races in all its laws and actions?
Yes ⬭  No ⬭

**2** If a city's schools are mostly black and the surrounding suburban schools are mostly white, should busing be used to achieve a better racial balance?
Yes ⬭  No ⬭

**3** Are differences between blacks and whites in average income mainly a product of discrimination?
Yes ⬭  No ⬭

**4** Do you generally favor affirmative action programs for women and minorities?
Yes ⬭  No ⬭

**5** Do you believe that racial and sexual preferences in employment and education discriminate against white males?
Yes ⬭  No ⬭

**6** Should gender equality receive the same level of legal protection as racial equality?
Yes ⬭  No ⬭

**7** Do dirty jokes and foul language at work constitute sexual harassment?
Yes ⬭  No ⬭

## THE POLITICS OF EQUALITY

*Equality* has been the central issue of American politics throughout the history of the nation. It is the issue that sparked the nation's only civil war, and it continues today to be the nation's most vexing political concern.

Conflict begins over the very definition of "equality" (see "Dilemmas of Equality" in Chapter 2). While Americans agree in the abstract that everyone is equal, they disagree over what they mean by "equality." Traditionally, "equality" meant "equality of *opportunity*": an equal opportunity to develop individual talents and abilities and to be rewarded for work, initiative, merit, and achievement. Over time, the issue of equality has shifted to "equality of *results*": an equal sharing of income and material rewards. With this shift in definition has come political conflict over the question of what, if anything,

Equality has long been the central issue of American politics. What do we mean by equality? And what, if anything, should government do to achieve it?

government should do to narrow the gaps between rich and poor, men and women, blacks and whites, and all other groups in society. Achieving greater equality of results requires government policies that modify the effects of equality of opportunity—that is, policies leading to **redistribution** of income, wealth, jobs, promotions, admissions, and other benefits.

A related issue arises over whether "equality" is to be defined in individual or group terms. Traditionally, Americans thought of equality as the fair treatment of all *individuals,* rather than the treatment afforded particular *groups* such as racial and ethnic minorities, women, or handicapped people. Inequality among groups takes on even greater political significance than inequality among individuals. Disparities between men and women, blacks and whites, and various ethnic groups spur political activity, as people in disadvantaged groups come to see their common plight and organize themselves for remedial political action.[1]

The nation's long struggle over equality has produced a number of constitutional and legal milestones in civil rights. These are summarized in Table 15-1. Much of the politics of civil rights centers on the development and interpretation of these guarantees of equality.

# SLAVERY, SEGREGATION, AND THE CONSTITUTION

In penning the Declaration of Independence in 1776, Thomas Jefferson argued eloquently that "All men are created equal." Yet from 1619, when the first slaves were brought to Jamestown, Virginia, until 1865, when the Thirteenth Amendment to the Constitution outlawed the practice, slavery was a way of life in the United States. Africans were captured, enslaved, transported to America, bought and sold, and used as personal property.

*Slavery and the Constitution*  The Constitution of 1787 recognized and protected slavery in the United States. Article I stipulated that slaves were to be counted as three-fifths of a person for purposes of representation and taxation; it also prohibited any federal restriction on the importation of slaves until 1808. Article IV even guaranteed the return of escaped slaves to their owners. The Founders were aware that the practice of slavery contradicted their professed belief in "equality," and this contradiction caused them some embarrassment. Thus they avoided the word "slave" in favor of the euphemism "person held to Service or Labour" in writing the Constitution.

Supreme Court Chief Justice Roger Taney, ruling in the notorious case of *Dred Scott v. Sandford* in 1857, reflected the racism that prevailed in early America:

> They had for more than a century before been regarded as beings of an inferior order, and altogether unfit to associate with the white race, either in social or political relations; and so far inferior, that they had no rights which the white man was bound to respect; and that the negro might justly and lawfully be reduced to slavery for his benefit. He was bought and sold, and treated as an ordinary article of merchandise and traffic, whenever a profit could be made by it. This opinion was at that time fixed and universal in the civilized portion of the white race.[2]

**Redistribution:** Government policies meant to shift assets from one group to another.

CHAPTER 15 • POLITICS AND CIVIL RIGHTS

TABLE 15-1    GUARANTEES OF CIVIL RIGHTS

### Thirteenth Amendment (1865)

Neither slavery nor involuntary servitude, except as a punishment for crime whereof the party shall have been duly convicted, shall exist within the United States, or any place subject to their jurisdiction.

### Fourteenth Amendment (1868)

No State shall make or enforce any law which shall abridge the privileges or immunities of citizens of the United States; nor shall any State deprive any person of life, liberty, or property, without due process of law; nor deny to any person within its jurisdiction the equal protection of the laws.

### Fifteenth Amendment (1870)

The rights of the citizens of the United States to vote shall not be denied or abridged by the United States or by any State on account of race, color, or previous condition of servitude.

### Nineteenth Amendment (1920)

The right of the citizens of the United States to vote shall not be denied or abridged by the United States or by any State on account of sex.

### Civil Rights Acts of 1866, 1871, and 1875

Acts passed by the Reconstruction Congress following the Civil War. The Civil Rights Act of 1866 guaranteed newly freed persons the right to purchase, lease, and use real property. The Civil Rights Act of 1875 outlawed segregation in privately owned businesses and facilities, but in the Civil Rights Cases (1883), the Supreme Court declared the Act an unconstitutional expansion of federal power, ruling that the Fourteenth Amendment limits only "State" actions. Other provisions of these acts were generally ignored for many decades. But the Civil Rights Act of 1871 has been revived in recent decades; the act makes it a federal crime for any person acting under the authority of state law to deprive another of rights protected by the Constitution.

### Civil Rights Act of 1957

The first civil rights law passed by Congress since Reconstruction. It empowers the U.S. Justice Department to enforce voting rights, established the Civil Rights Division in the Justice Department, and created the Civil Rights Commission to study and report on civil rights in the United States.

### Civil Rights Act of 1964

A comprehensive enactment designed to erase racial discrimination in both public and private sectors of American life. Major titles of the act: I. outlaws arbitrary discrimination in voter registration and expedites voting rights suits; II. bars discrimination in public accommodations, such as hotels and restaurants, that have a substantial relation to interstate commerce; III. and IV. authorize the national government to bring suits to desegregate public facilities and schools; V. extends the life and expands the power of the Civil Rights Commission; VI. provides for withholding federal funds from programs administered in a discriminatory manner; VII. establishes the right to equality in employment opportunities.

### Civil Rights Act of 1968

Prohibits discrimination in the advertising, financing, sale, or rental of housing, based on race, religion, or national origin and, as of 1974, sex. A major amendment to the act in 1988 extended coverage to the handicapped and to families with children.

### Voting Rights Act

Enacted by Congress in 1965 and renewed and expanded in 1970, 1975, and 1982, this law has sought to eliminate restrictions on voting that have been used to discriminate against blacks and other minority groups. Amendments in 1975 (1) required bilingual ballots in all states; (2) required approval by the Justice Department or a federal court of any election law changes in states covered by the act; (3) extended legal protection of voting rights to Hispanic Americans, Asian Americans, and Native Americans. The 1982 act provides that intent to discriminate need not be proven if the results demonstrate otherwise. Although the 1982 extension does not require racial quotas for city councils, school boards, or state legislatures, a judge may under the law redraw voting districts to give minorities maximum representation.

---

Taney's decision in this case interpreted the Constitution in terms of the *original intent* of the Founders. The ruling upheld slavery and the constitutional guarantee given slave owners for the return of slaves escaping to nonslave states.

*Emancipation and Reconstruction*    A growing number of Americans, especially members of the **abolition movement,** disagreed with Taney. In 1860, internal party divisions over the slavery issue led to a four-way race for the pres-

**Abolition movement:** A social movement before the Civil War whose goal was to abolish slavery throughout the United States.

idency and the election of Abraham Lincoln. Although personally opposed to slavery, Lincoln had promised during the campaign not to push for abolition of slavery where it existed. Many southerners were unconvinced, however, and on December 20, 1860 (three months before Lincoln's inauguration), South Carolina became the first state to secede from the Union, touching off the Civil War.

The Civil War was the nation's bloodiest war. (Combined deaths of Union and Confederate forces matched the nation's losses in World War II, even though the nation's population in 1860 was only 31 million compared to 140 million during World War II.) Very few families during the Civil War did not experience a direct loss from that conflict. As casualties mounted, northern Republicans joined abolitionists in calling for emancipating, or freeing, the slaves simply to punish the Rebels. They knew that much of the South's power depended on slave labor. Lincoln also knew that if he proclaimed that the war was being fought to free the slaves, military intervention by the British on behalf of the South was less likely. Accordingly, on September 22, 1862, Lincoln issued his Emancipation Proclamation. Claiming his right as commander-in-chief of the army and navy, he declared that, as of January 1, 1863, "all persons held as slaves within any State, or designated part of a State, the people whereof shall then be in rebellion against the United States, shall be then, thenceforward, and forever free." The Emancipation Proclamation did not come about as a result of demands by the people. It was a political and military action by the president intended to help preserve the Union.

The Emancipation Proclamation freed slaves in the seceding states, and the Thirteenth Amendment in 1865 abolished slavery everywhere in the nation. But freedom did not mean civil rights. The Fourteenth Amendment, passed in 1867 by a Republican Congress that intended to reconstruct southern society after the Civil War and ratified the next year, made "equal protection of the laws" a command for every state to obey. The Fifteenth Amendment, passed in 1869 and ratified in 1870, prohibited federal and state governments from abridging the right to vote "on account of race, color, or previous condition of servitude." In addition, Congress passed a series of civil rights laws in the 1860s and 1870s guaranteeing the newly freed slaves protection in the exercise of their constitutional rights. Between 1865 and the early 1880s, the success of Reconstruction was evident in widespread black voting throughout the South, the presence of many blacks in federal and state offices, and the admission of blacks to theaters, restaurants, hotels, and public transportation.[3]

*The Imposition of Segregation*   Political support for Reconstruction policies soon began to erode. In the Compromise of 1877, the national government agreed to end military occupation of the South, give up its efforts to rearrange southern society, and lend tacit approval to white supremacy in that region. In return, the southern states pledged their support to the Union, accepted national supremacy, and agreed to permit the Republican presidential candidate, Rutherford B. Hayes, to assume the presidency, although the Democratic candidate, Samuel Tilden, had received more popular votes in the disputed election of 1876.

As white southerners regained political power and blacks lost the protection of federal forces, the Supreme Court moved to strike down Reconstruction laws. In the Civil Rights Cases of 1883, the Supreme Court declared federal civil rights laws preventing discrimination by private individuals to be unconstitutional.[4] By denying Congress the power to protect blacks from discrimination by businesses and individuals, the Court paved the way for the imposition of segregation as the prevailing social system of the South. In the 1880s and 1890s, white southerners imposed segregation in public accommodations, housing, education, employment, and almost every other sector of private and public life. By 1895, most southern states had passed laws *requiring* racial segregation in education and in public accommodations. At the time, more than 90 percent of the African-American population of the United States lived in these states.

Segregation became the social instrument by which African Americans were "kept in their place"—that is, denied social, economic, educational, and political equality. In many states, **Jim Crowism** followed them throughout life: birth in a segregated hospital ward, education in a segregated school, residence in segregated housing, employment in a segregated job, eating in segregated restaurants, and burial in a segregated graveyard. Segregation was enforced by a variety of public and private sanctions, from lynch mobs to country-club admission committees. But government was the principal instrument of segregation in both the southern and the border states of the nation. (For a look at the political reactions of African Americans to segregation, see *Up Close:* "African-American Politics in Historical Perspective.")

*Early Court Approval of Segregation*   Segregation was imposed despite the Fourteenth Amendment's guarantee of "equal protection of the laws." In the 1896 case of *Plessy v. Ferguson,* the Supreme Court upheld state laws requiring segregation. Although segregation laws involved state action, the Court held that segregation of the races did not violate the Equal Protection Clause of the Fourteenth Amendment so long as people in each race received equal treatment. Schools and other public facilities that were **separate but equal** were constitutional, the Court ruled.

> The object of the amendment was undoubtedly to enforce the absolute equality of the two races before the law, but in the nature of things it could not have been intended to abolish distinctions based upon color, or to enforce social, as distinguished from political, equality, or a commingling of the two races upon terms unsatisfactory to either. Laws permitting, and even requiring, their separation in places where they are liable to be brought into contact do not necessarily imply the inferiority of either race to the other, and have been generally, if not universally, recognized as within the competency of the state legislatures in the exercise of their police power.[5]

*Early Dissent: "Our Constitution Is Colorblind"*   A lone dissenting voice in *Plessy v. Ferguson* spoke out against this separate-but-equal doctrine. Justice John Marshall Harlan set forth a great principle of individual liberty when he wrote:

> In view of the Constitution, in the eye of the law, there is in this country no superior, dominant, ruling class of citizens. There is no caste here. Our Constitution is colorblind, and neither knows nor tolerates classes among citizens. In respect to civil rights all citizens are equal before the law.

But this **colorblind standard** remained a dissenting view, and it continues to be a dissenting view even today.

**Jim Crowism:** The second-class-citizen status conferred on blacks by southern segregation laws; derived from a nineteenth-century song-and-dance act (usually performed by a white man in blackface) that stereotyped blacks.

**Separate but equal:** The ruling of the Supreme Court in the case of *Plessy v. Ferguson* (1896) to the effect that segregated facilities were legal as long as the facilities were equal.

**Colorblind standard:** The view that laws should take *no* account of race at all, that they should neither discriminate against nor grant preference to any individual based on race.

# African-American Politics in Historical Perspective

Many early histories of Reconstruction paid little attention to the political responses of African Americans to the imposition of segregation. But there were at least three distinct types of response: accommodation to segregation; the formation of a black protest movement and resort to legal action; and migration out of the South (to avoid some of the worst consequences of white supremacy) coupled with political mobilization of black voters in large northern cities.

*Accommodation*    The foremost African-American advocate of accommodation to segregation was well-known educator Booker T. Washington (1856–1915). Washington enjoyed wide popularity among both white and black Americans. He was an adviser to two presidents (Theodore Roosevelt and William Howard Taft) and was highly respected by white philanthropists and government officials. In his famous Cotton States' Exposition speech in Atlanta in 1895, Washington assured whites that blacks were prepared to accept a separate position in society: "In all things that are purely social we can be as separate as the fingers, yet one as the hand in all things essential to mutual progress."*

Washington's hopes for black America lay in a program of self-help through education. He himself had attended Hampton Institute in Virginia, where the curriculum centered around practical trades for African Americans. Washington obtained some white philanthropic support in establishing his own Tuskegee Institute in Tuskegee, Alabama, in 1881. His first students helped build the school. Early curricula at Tuskegee emphasized immediately useful vocations, such as farming, teaching, and blacksmithing. One of Tuskegee's outstanding faculty members, George Washington Carver, researched and developed uses for southern crops. Washington urged his

*Booker T. Washington*

students to stay in the South, to acquire land, and to build homes, thereby helping to eliminate ignorance and poverty.

*Protest*    While Booker T. Washington was urging African Americans to make the best of segregation, a small group was organizing in support of a declaration of black resistance and protest that would later rewrite American public policy. The leader of this group was W.E.B. Du Bois (1868–1963), a historian and sociologist at Atlanta University. In 1905, Du Bois and a few other black intellectuals met in Niagara Falls, Canada, to draw up a platform intended to "assail the ears" and sear the consciences of white Americans. The Niagara Statement listed the major injustices perpetrated against African Americans since Reconstruction: the loss of voting rights, the imposition of Jim Crow laws and segregated public schools, the denial of equal job opportunities, the existence of inhumane conditions in southern prisons, the exclu-

*W.E.B. Dubois*

sion of blacks from West Point and Annapolis, and the federal government's failure to enforce the Fourteenth and Fifteenth Amendments. Out of the Niagara meeting came the idea of a nationwide organization dedicated to fighting for African Americans, and on February 12, 1909, the one-hundredth anniversary of Abraham Lincoln's birth, the National Association for the Advancement of Colored People (NAACP) was founded.

Du Bois himself was on the original board of directors of the NAACP, though a majority of the early board members and financial contributors were white. Du Bois was also the NAACP's first director of research and the editor of its magazine, *Crisis*. The NAACP began a long and eventually successful campaign to establish black rights through legal action. Over the years, this organization brought hundreds of court cases at the local, state, and federal court levels on behalf of African Americans denied their constitutional rights.

*Migration and Political Mobilization*    World War I provided an opportunity for restive blacks in the South to escape the worst abuses of white supremacy by migrating en masse to northern cities. Between 1916 and 1918, an estimated half-million African Americans moved north to fill the labor shortage caused by the war effort. Most arrived in big northern cities only to find more poverty and segregation, but at least they could vote, and they did not encounter laws requiring segregation in public places.

The progressive "ghettoization" of African Americans—their migration from the rural South to the urban North and their increasing concentration in central cities—had profound political, as well as social, implications. The ghetto provided an environment conducive to political mobilization. As early as 1928, African Americans in Chicago were able to elect one of their own to the U.S. House of Representatives. The election of Oscar de Priest, the first black member of Congress from the North, signaled a new turn in American urban politics by announcing to white politicians that they would have to reckon with the black vote in northern cities. The black ghettos would soon provide an important element in a new political coalition that was about to take form: the Democratic Party of Franklin Delano Roosevelt.

The increasing concentration of African Americans in large, politically competitive, "swing" states provided black voters with new political power—not only to support the Democratic Party coalition in national politics but also to elect African Americans to local public office. Today African-American mayors serve, or have served, in cities as diverse as New York, Chicago, Los Angeles, Detroit, Philadelphia, Atlanta, and New Orleans.

*Quoted in Henry Steele Commager, ed., *The Struggle for Racial Equality* (New York: Harper & Row, 1967), p. 19.

# EQUAL PROTECTION OF THE LAWS

The initial goal of the civil rights movement was to eliminate segregation laws, especially segregation in public education. Only after this battle was well under way could the civil rights movement turn to the fight against segregation and discrimination in all sectors of American life, *private* as well as *public*.

*The NAACP and the Legal Battle* The National Association for the Advancement of Colored People (NAACP) and its Legal Defense and Education Fund led the fight to abolish lawful segregation. As chief legal counsel to the fund, Thurgood Marshall (see *People in Politics:* "Thurgood Marshal, Advocate of Equal Protection") began a long legal campaign to ensure equal protection of the law for African Americans. Initially, the NAACP's strategy focused on achieving the "equal" portion of the separate-but-equal doctrine. Segregated facilities, including public schools, were seldom "equal," even with respect to physical conditions, teachers' salaries and qualifications, curricula, and other tangible factors. In other words, southern states failed to live up even to the segregationist doctrine of separate but equal. In a series of cases, Marshall and other NAACP lawyers convinced the Supreme Court to act when segregated facilities were clearly unequal. For example, the Court ordered the admission of individual blacks to white public universities where evidence indicated that separate black institutions were inferior or nonexistent.[6]

But Marshall's goal was to prove that segregation itself was inherently unequal whether or not facilities were equal in all tangible respects. In other words, Marshall sought a reversal of *Plessy v. Ferguson* and a ruling that separation of the races was unconstitutional. In 1952, Marshall led a team of NAACP lawyers in a suit to admit Linda Brown to the white public schools of Topeka, Kansas, one of the few segregated school systems where white and black schools were equal with respect to buildings, curricula, teachers' salaries, and other tangible factors. In choosing the *Brown* suit, the NAACP sought to prevent the Court from simply ordering the admission of black pupils because tangible facilities were not equal and to force the Court to review the doctrine of segregation itself.

*Brown v. Board of Education of Topeka* On May 17, 1954, the Court rendered its historic decision in the case of *Brown v. Board of Education of Topeka*:

> Segregation of white and colored children in public schools has a detrimental effect upon the colored children. The impact is greater when it has the sanction of law, for the policy of separating the races is usually interpreted as denoting the inferiority of the Negro group. A sense of inferiority affects the motivation of a child to learn. Segregation with the sanction of law, therefore, has a tendency to retard the educational and mental development of Negro children and to deprive them of some of the benefits they would receive in a racially integrated school system. Whatever may have been the extent of psychological knowledge of the time of *Plessy v. Ferguson,* this finding is amply supported by modern authority. Any language in *Plessy v. Ferguson* contrary to this source is rejected. . . . We conclude that in the field of public education the doctrine of "separate but equal" has no place. Separate educational facilities are inherently unequal.[7]

CHAPTER 15 • POLITICS AND CIVIL RIGHTS

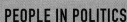
## Thurgood Marshall, Advocate of Equal Protection

The modern civil rights movement in the United States began with the historic Supreme Court decision in *Brown v. Board of Education of Topeka* in 1954. And the individual most responsible for bringing about that decision was Thurgood Marshall (1908–93), then chief counsel for the NAACP Legal Defense Fund. Marshall directed the NAACP's legal strategy against segregation, and he personally argued the *Brown* case before the Supreme Court. His later appointment to the Supreme Court as the first African American to serve on that body was a fitting recognition of his immense contribution to civil rights law in the United States.

Marshall grew up in Baltimore, the son of a railroad car steward. He attended all-black Lincoln University in Chester, Pennsylvania, and following his cum laude graduation in 1930 he entered Howard University Law School in Washington, D.C. Shortly after graduation in 1933, Marshall became counsel for the Baltimore chapter of the NAACP. In 1940, he became the director and chief counsel of the NAACP's newly formed and semi-autonomous Legal Defense and Education Fund, a position he held for more than twenty years.

Marshall coordinated the NAACP's broad legal attack against discrimination in voting, housing, public accommodations, and education. He personally argued thirty-two cases for the NAACP before the Supreme Court, winning twenty-nine of them, including the landmark decision in the *Brown* case. President John F. Kennedy appointed Marshall as a judge on the U.S. Circuit Court of Appeals in 1961. Four years later, President Lyndon Johnson appointed him solicitor general of the United States in 1965, making Marshall the first African American to serve as the nation's chief counsel. In that capacity, Marshall personally argued nineteen more cases before the Supreme Court, including the important case of *South Carolina v. Katzenbach,* upholding the constitutionality of the Voting Rights Act.* Announcing Marshall's appointment to the Supreme Court, President Johnson noted that few other attorneys in the history of the nation had ever argued as many cases before the Supreme Court as Thurgood Marshall. Marshall was confirmed by a vote of 69 to 11 in the Senate in 1967.

In his more than two decades on the Supreme Court, Marshall was the most consistent member of the liberal voting bloc. He regularly voted against restrictions on abortions, against capital punishment, and for affirmative action and racial set-aside programs. Upon his retirement in 1991, his seat on the Court was taken by Clarence Thomas.

*South Carolina v. Katzenbach*, 383 U.S. 301 (1966).

---

The Supreme Court decision in *Brown* was symbolically very important. Although it would be many years before any significant number of black children would attend previously all-white schools in the South, the decision by the nation's highest court stimulated black hopes and expectations. Indeed, *Brown* started the modern civil rights movement. As the African-American psychologist Kenneth Clark wrote:

> This [civil rights] movement would probably not have existed at all were it not for the 1954 Supreme Court school desegregation decision, which provided a tremendous boost to the morale of blacks by its clear affirmation that color is irrelevant to the rights of American citizens.[8]

*Enforcing Desegregation*   The *Brown* ruling struck down the laws of twenty-one states as well as congressional laws segregating the schools of the District of Columbia.[9] Such a far-reaching exercise of judicial power was bound to meet with difficulties in enforcement, and the Supreme Court was careful not to risk its own authority. It did not order immediate national desegregation but rather required state and local authorities, under the supervision of federal district courts, to proceed with "all deliberate speed" in desegregation.[10] For more than fifteen years, state and school districts in the South waged a campaign of resistance to desegregation. Delays in implementing school desegregation continued until 1969, when the Supreme Court rejected a request by Mississippi officials for further delay, declaring that all school districts were obligated to end their dual school systems "at once" and "now and hereafter" to operate only integrated schools.[11]

*Busing and Racial Balancing*   Federal district judges enjoy wide freedom in fashioning remedies for past or present discriminatory practices by governments. If a federal district court anywhere in the United States finds that any actions by governments or school officials have contributed to racial imbalances (for example, drawing school district attendance lines that separate black and white pupils), the judge may order the adoption of a desegregation plan to overcome racial imbalances produced by official action. A large number of cities have come under federal district court orders to improve racial balances in their schools through busing.

In the important case of *Swann v. Charlotte-Mecklenburg County Board of Education* (1971), the Supreme Court upheld:

1. The use of racial balance requirements in schools and the assignment of pupils to schools based on race.
2. "Close scrutiny" by judges of schools that are predominantly of one race.
3. Gerrymandering of school attendance zones as well as "clustering" or "grouping" of schools to achieve racial balance.
4. Court-ordered busing of pupils to achieve racial balance.[12]

The Court was careful to note, however, that racial imbalance in schools is not itself grounds for ordering these remedies unless it is also shown that some present or past governmental action contributed to the imbalance.

In the absence of any governmental actions contributing to racial imbalance, states and school districts are *not* required by the Fourteenth Amendment to integrate their schools. For example, where central-city schools are predominantly black and suburban schools are predominantly white owing to residential patterns, cross-district busing is not required unless some official action brought about these racial imbalances. Thus, in 1974 the Supreme Court threw out a lower federal court order for massive busing of students between Detroit and fifty-two suburban school districts.[13] Although Detroit city schools are 70 percent black and the suburban schools almost all white, none of the area school districts segregated students within their own boundaries. This important decision means that largely black central cities that are surrounded by largely white suburbs will remain segregated in practice because there are not enough white students living within the city boundaries to achieve integration.

While the first conflicts over integration in the public schools erupted in the segregated southern states, northern cities have been the focus of most unrest over school integration in recent years. When federal judges ordered the busing of schoolchildren outside their neighborhoods in order to achieve racial balances citywide, parents and politicians in some northern cities responded with a ferocity equal to any earlier southern protest. In Boston, many parents initially boycotted the busing order, refusing to send their children to school at all or establishing private schools and even attacking busloads of minority children arriving at formerly white schools. Even today, changes in busing plans have the potential to arouse violent reactions in Boston.

Many school districts in the South and elsewhere have operated under federal court supervision for many years. How long should court supervision continue, and what standards are to be used in determining when desegregation has been achieved once and for all? The Rehnquist-led Supreme Court in recent years has undertaken to free some school districts from direct federal court supervision. Where the last vestiges of state-sanctioned discrimination have been removed "as far as practicable," the Supreme Court has allowed lower federal courts to dissolve racial balancing plans even though imbalances due to residential patterns may continue to exist.[14]

## THE CIVIL RIGHTS ACTS

The early goal of the civil rights movement was to eliminate discrimination and segregation practiced by *governments,* particularly states and school districts. When the civil rights movement turned to *private* discrimination—discrimination practiced by private owners of restaurants, hotels, motels, and stores; private employers, landlords, and real estate agents; and others who were not government officials—it had to take its fight to the Congress. The Constitution does not govern the activities of private individuals. Only Congress at the national level could outlaw discrimination in the private sector. Yet prior to 1964, Congress had been content to let the courts struggle with the question of civil rights. New political tactics and organizations were required to put the issue of equality on the agenda of Congress.

*Martin Luther King, Jr., and Nonviolent Direct Action*   Leadership in the struggle to eliminate discrimination and segregation from private life was provided a young African-American minister, Martin Luther King, Jr. (see *People in Politics:* "Martin Luther King, Jr., 'I Have a Dream'"). Under King, the civil rights

# Martin Luther King, Jr., "I Have a Dream"

"If a man hasn't discovered something he will die for, he isn't fit to live."*

For Martin Luther King, Jr., (1929–1968), civil rights was something to die for, and before he died for the cause, he would shatter a century of southern segregation and set a new domestic agenda for the nation's leaders. King's contributions to the development of nonviolent direct action won him international acclaim and the Nobel Peace Prize.

King's father was the pastor of one of the South's largest and most influential African-American congregations, the Ebenezer Baptist Church in Atlanta, Georgia. Young Martin was educated at Morehouse College in Atlanta and received a Ph.D. in religious studies at Boston University. Shortly after beginning his career as a Baptist minister in Montgomery, Alabama, in 1955, a black woman, Rosa Parks, refused to give up her seat to whites on a Montgomery bus, setting in motion a year-long bus boycott in that city. Only twenty-six years old, King was thrust into national prominence as the leader of that boycott, which ended in the elimination of segregation on the city's buses. In 1957, King founded the Southern Christian Leadership Conference (SCLC) to provide encouragement and leadership to the growing nonviolent protest movement against segregation.

Perhaps the most dramatic application of nonviolent direct action occurred in Birmingham, Alabama, in the spring of 1963. Under King's direction, the SCLC had chosen that city as a major site for demonstrations during the centennial year of the Emancipation Proclamation. By its own description the "Heart of Dixie," Birmingham was the most rigidly segregated large city in the United States at the time. King believed that if segregation could be successfully challenged in Birmingham, it might begin to crumble throughout the South. Thousands of African Americans, ranging from schoolchildren to senior citizens, staged protest marches in Birmingham from May 2 to May 7. Although the demonstrators conducted themselves in a nonviolent fashion, police and firefighters under the direction of Police Chief Eugene "Bull" Connor attacked the demonstrators with fire hoses, cattle prods, and police dogs, all in clear view of national television cameras. Thousands of demonstrators were dragged off to jail, including King. (It was at this time that King wrote his "Letter from Birmingham Jail," explaining and defending nonviolent direct action.) But Connor's "victory" was short-lived. Pictures of police brutality flashed throughout the nation and the world, touching the consciences of many white Americans.

King was also the driving force behind the most massive application of nonviolent direct action in U.S. history: the great "March on Washington" in August 1963, during which more than 200,000 black and white marchers converged on the nation's capital. The march ended at the Lincoln Memorial, where King delivered his most eloquent appeal, entitled "I Have a Dream."

I still have a dream. It is a dream deeply rooted in the American dream. I have a dream that one day this nation will rise up and live out the true meaning of its creed: "We hold these truths to be self-evident, that all men are created equal."

**Nonviolent direct action:** A strategy used by civil rights leaders such as Martin Luther King, Jr., in which protesters break "unjust" laws openly but in a "loving" fashion in order to bring the injustices of such laws to public attention.

movement developed and refined political techniques for use by American minorities, including **nonviolent direct action.** Nonviolent direct action is a form of protest that involves breaking "unjust" laws in an open, "loving," nonviolent fashion. The purpose of nonviolent direct action is to call attention—to "bear witness"—to the existence of injustice. In the words of Martin Luther King, Jr., such civil disobedience "seeks to dramatize the issue so that it can no longer be ignored[15] (see *A Conflicting View:* "Sometimes It's Right to Disobey the Law" in Chapter 1).

I have a dream that one day on the red hills of Georgia, sons of former slaves and sons of former slave-owners will be able to sit down together at the table of brotherhood.

I have a dream that one day, even in the state of Mississippi, a state sweltering with the heat of injustice, sweltering with the heat of oppression, will be transformed into an oasis of freedom and justice.

I have a dream my four little children will one day live in a nation where they will not be judged by the color of their skin but by content of their character. . . .

And when this happens, and when we allow freedom to ring, when we let it ring from every village and hamlet, from every state and city, we will be able to speed up that day when all of God's children—black men and white men, Jews and Gentiles, Catholics and Prostestants—will be able to join hands and to sing in the words of the old Negro spirtual, "Free at last, free at last; thank God Almighty, we are free at last."**

It was in the wake of the March on Washington that President John F. Kennedy sent to the Congress a strong civil rights bill that would be passed after his death—the Civil Rights Act of 1964. That same year, King received the Nobel Peace Prize.

Yet even after passage of this act, voting registrars in many southern counties continued to keep African Americans off of the voting rolls through a variety of discriminatory tactics. In 1965, King again took action. Selma, the county seat of Dallas County, Alabama, was chosen as the site to dramatize the voting rights problem. King organized a fifty-mile march from Selma to the state capitol in Montgomery. He didn't get very far. Acting on orders of Governor George Wallace to disband the marchers, state troopers did so with a vengeance—

using tear gas, nightsticks, and whips. This time, however, the national government intervened: in his capacity as commander-in-chief of the armed forces, President Lyndon Johnson ordered the National Guard to protect the demonstrators, and the march continued. During the march, Johnson went on television to address a special joint session of Congress, urging passage of new legislation to assure African Americans the right to vote, and Congress responded with the Voting Rights Act of 1965.

White racial violence in the early 1960s, including murders and bombings of black and white civil rights workers, shocked and disgusted many whites in both the North and the South. In 1963, Medgar Evers, the NAACP's state chair for Mississippi, was shot to death by a sniper as he entered his Jackson home. That same year, a bomb killed four young black girls attending Sunday school in Birmingham. On the evening of April 3, 1968, King spoke to a crowd in Memphis, Tennessee, in eerily prophetic terms. "I just want to do God's will. And He's allowed me to go to the mountain. And I've looked over, and I've seen the promised land. I may not get there with you. But I want you to know tonight, that we, as a people will get to the promised land. So I'm happy tonight. I'm not worried about anything. I'm not fearing any man."*** On the night of April 4, 1968, the world's leading exponent of nonviolence was killed by an assassin's bullet.

*Martin Luther King, Jr., speech, June 23, 1963, Detroit, Michigan.
**Martin Luther King, Jr., "I Have a Dream" speech, August 28, 1963, at the Lincoln Memorial, Washington, D.C., printed in David J. Garrow, *Bearing the Cross: Martin Luther King, Jr., and the Southern Christian Leadership Conference* (New York: Vintage Books, 1988), pp. 283–84.
***Martin Luther King, Jr., speech, April 3, 1968, Memphis, Tennessee, in ibid., p 621.

King formed the Southern Christian Leadership Conference (SCLC) in 1957 to develop and direct the growing nonviolent direct action movement. During the next few years, the SCLC overshadowed the older NAACP in leading the fight against segregation. Where the NAACP had developed its strategy of court litigation to combat discrimination by *governments,* now the SCLC developed nonviolent direct action tactics to build widespread popular support and to pressure Congress to outlaw discrimination by *private businesses.*

In the Civil Rights March of 1963 more than 200,000 people marched peacefully on Washington, D.C. to end segregation. It was here that Martin Luther King, Jr., delivered his famous "I Have a Dream" speech.

The year 1963 was perhaps the most important for nonviolent direct action. The SCLC focused its efforts in Birmingham, Alabama, where King led thousands of marchers in a series of orderly and peaceful demonstrations. When police attacked the marchers with fire hoses, dogs, and cattle prods—in full view of national television cameras—millions of viewers around the country came to understand the injustices of segregation. The Birmingham action set off demonstrations in many parts of the country. The theme remained one of nonviolence, and it was usually whites rather than blacks who resorted to violence in these demonstrations. Responsible black leaders remained in control of the movement and won widespread support from the white community.

The culmination of King's nonviolent philosophy was a huge yet orderly march on Washington, D.C., held on August 28, 1963. More than 200,000 blacks and whites participated in the march, which was endorsed by many civic leaders, religious groups, and political figures. The march ended at the Lincoln Memorial, where Martin Luther King, Jr., delivered his most eloquent appeal, entitled "I Have a Dream." Congress passed the Civil Rights Act of 1964 by better than a two-thirds favorable vote in both houses; it won the overwhelming support of both Republican and Democratic members of Congress.

*The Civil Rights Act of 1964*   Signed into law on July 4, 1964, the Civil Rights Act of 1964 ranks with the Emancipation Proclamation, the Fourteenth Amendment, and the *Brown* case as one of the most important steps toward full equality for African Americans. Among its most important provisions:

*Title II:* It is unlawful to discriminate or segregate persons on the grounds of race, color, religion, or national origin in any public accommodation, including hotels, motels, restaurants, movies, theaters, sports arenas, entertainment houses, and other places that offer to serve the public. This prohibition extends to all business establishments whose operations affect interstate commerce or whose discriminatory practices are supported by state action.

*Title VI:* Each federal department and agency is to take action to end discrimination in all programs or activities receiving federal financial assistance in any form. This action may include termination of financial assistance to persistently discriminatory agencies.

*Title VII:* It is unlawful for any employer or labor union to discriminate against any individual in any fashion in employment, because of the individual's race, color, religion, sex, or national origin. The Equal Employment Opportunity Commission is established to enforce this provision by investigation, conference, conciliation, persuasion, and, if need be, civil action in federal court.

*The Civil Rights Act of 1968*   For many years "fair housing" had been considered the most sensitive area of civil rights legislation. Discrimination in the sale and rental of housing was the last major civil rights problem on which Congress took action. Discrimination in housing had not been mentioned in the comprehensive Civil Rights Act of 1964. Prohibiting discrimination in the sale or rental of housing affected the constituencies of northern members of Congress; earlier public accommodations provisions had their greatest effect in the South.

Prospects for a fair housing law were poor at the beginning of 1968. However, when Martin Luther King, Jr., was assassinated on April 4, the mood of Congress and the nation changed dramatically. Congress passed a fair housing law as tribute to the slain civil rights leader. The Civil Rights Act of 1968 prohibited the following forms of discrimination:

- Refusal to sell or rent a dwelling to any person on the basis of race, color, religion, or national origin.
- Discrimination against a person in the terms, conditions, or privileges of the sale or rental of a dwelling.
- Indicating a preference or discrimination based on race, color, religion, or national origin in advertising the sale or rental of a dwelling.
- Inducing persons to sell a dwelling by referring to the entry into the neighborhood of persons of a particular race, religion, or national origin.

## EQUALITY: OPPORTUNITY VERSUS RESULTS

Although the gains of the civil rights movement were immensely important, these gains were primarily in *opportunity* rather than in *results*. The civil rights movement of the 1960s did not bring about major changes in the conditions under which most African Americans lived in the United States. Racial politics today center around the *actual* inequalities between blacks and whites in incomes, jobs, housing, health, education, and other conditions of life.

*Continuing Inequalities*   The issue of inequality today is often posed as differences in the "life chances" of blacks and whites. Figures can reveal only the bare outline of an African American's "life chances" in this society (see Table 15-2). The average income of a black family is 60 percent of the average white family's income. About one-third of all black families live below the recognized poverty line, while only about 12 percent of white families do so. The black unemployment rate is more than twice as high as the white unemployment rate. Blacks are less likely to hold prestigious executive jobs in professional, managerial, clerical, or sales work. They do not hold many skilled craft jobs in industry but are concentrated in operative, service, and laboring positions. The civil rights movement opened up new opportunities for African Americans. But equality of *opportunity* is not the same as equality of *results*.

*Policy Choices*   What public policies should be pursued to achieve equality in America? Is it sufficient that government eliminate discrimination, guarantee equality of opportunity, and apply colorblind standards to both blacks and whites? Or should government take **affirmative action** to overcome the results of past unequal treatment of blacks—preferential or compensatory treatment to assist black applications for university admissions and scholarships, job hiring and promotion, and other opportunities for advancement in life?

*Shifting Goals in Civil Rights Policy*   For decades, the emphasis of government policy was on equal *opportunity*. This early nondiscrimination approach began with President Harry Truman's decision to desegregate the armed forces in 1948 and carried through to Title VI and Title VII of the Civil Rights Act of 1964, which eliminated discrimination in federally aided projects and private employment.

**Affirmative action:** Any program, whether enacted by a government or by a private organization, whose goal is to overcome the results of past unequal treatment of minorities and/or women by giving members of these groups preferential treatment in admissions, hiring, promotions, or other aspects of life.

## TABLE 15-2  MINORITY LIFE CHANCES

|  | *Median Income of Families* | | | | |
|---|---|---|---|---|---|
|  | 1970 | 1975 | 1980 | 1985 | 1993 |
| White | $10,236 | $14,268 | $21,904 | $29,152 | $39,300 |
| Black | 6,279 | 8,779 | 12,674 | 16,786 | 21,542 |
| Hispanic | — | 9,551 | 14,716 | 19,027 | 23,654 |

|  | *Percentage of Persons below Poverty Level* | | | |
|---|---|---|---|---|
|  | 1975 | 1980 | 1985 | 1993 |
| White | 9.7% | 10.2% | 11.4% | 12.2% |
| Black | 31.3 | 32.5 | 31.3 | 33.1 |
| Hispanic | 26.9 | 25.7 | 29.0 | 30.6 |

|  | *Unemployment Rate* | | |
|---|---|---|---|
|  | 1980 | 1985 | 1994 |
| White | 6.3% | 6.2% | 5.3% |
| Black | 14.3 | 15.1 | 11.5 |
| Hispanic | 10.1 | 10.5 | 9.9 |

|  | *Education: Percentage of Persons over Twenty-Five Completing:* | |
|---|---|---|
|  | High School | College |
| White | 82% | 23% |
| Black | 73 | 13 |
| Hispanic | 53 | 9 |

*Source: Statistical Abstract of the United States, 1995,* pp. 420, 476, 480.

Gradually, however, the goal of the civil rights movement shifted from the traditional aim of equality of opportunity through nondiscrimination alone to affirmative action involving the establishment of "goals and timetables" to achieve greater equality of results between blacks and whites. While avoiding the term **quota,** the notion of affirmative action tests the success of equal opportunity by observing whether blacks achieve admissions, jobs, and promotions in proportion to their numbers in the population.

*Affirmative Action*  Affirmative action programs were initially developed in the federal bureaucracy. Federal executive agencies were authorized by the Civil Rights Act of 1964 to develop "rules and regulations" for desegregating any organization or business receiving federal funds. In 1965, President Lyndon B. Johnson signed Executive Order 11246, requiring all federal agencies and businesses contracting with the federal government to practice affirmative action. In 1972, the U.S. Office of Education issued guidelines that mandated "goals" for university admissions and faculty hiring of minorities and women. The Equal Employment Opportunity Commission (EEOC), established by the Civil Rights Act of 1964, is responsible for monitoring affirmative action programs in private employment.

Federal officials generally measure "progress" in affirmative action in terms of the number of disadvantaged group members admitted, employed, or promoted. The pressure to show "progress" can result in relaxation of traditional measures of qualifications, such as test scores and educational achievement. Advocates of affirmative action argue that these measures are not good predictors of performance

**Quota:** A provision of some affirmative action programs in which specific numbers or percentages of positions are open only to minorities and/or women.

CHAPTER 15 • POLITICS AND CIVIL RIGHTS

on the job or in school and are biased in favor of white culture. State and local governments, schools, colleges and universities, and private employers are under pressure to drop these standards.

## AFFIRMATIVE ACTION IN THE COURTS

The constitutional question posed by affirmative action programs is whether or not they discriminate against whites in violation of the Equal Protection Clause of the Fourteenth Amendment. A related question is whether or not affirmative action programs discriminate against whites in violation of the Civil Rights Act of 1964, which prohibits discrimination "on account of race," not just discrimination against blacks. Clearly, these are questions for the Supreme Court to resolve, but unfortunately the Court has failed to develop clear-cut answers.

*Reporters talking to Allan Bakke in 1978 after the Supreme Court ruled that the University of California Davis Medical School had discriminated against him because of his race when it denied him admission.*

*The Bakke Case* In the absence of a history of racial discrimination, the Supreme Court has been willing to scrutinize affirmative action programs to ensure that they do not directly discriminate against whites. In *University of California Regents v. Bakke* (1978), the Supreme Court struck down a special admissions program for minorities at a state medical school on the grounds that it excluded a white applicant because of his race and violated his rights under the Equal Protection Clause.[16] Allan Bakke applied to the University of California Davis Medical School two consecutive years and was rejected; in both years, black applicants with significantly lower grade point averages and medical aptitude test scores were accepted through a special admissions program that reserved sixteen minority places in a class of one hundred.[17] The University of California did not deny that its admissions decisions were based on race. Instead, it argued that its racial classification was "benign," that is, designed to assist minorities. The special admissions program was designed to (1) "reduce the historical deficit of traditionally disfavored minorities in medical schools and the medical profession"; (2) "counter the effects of societal discrimination"; (3) "increase the number of physicians who will practice in communities currently underserved"; and (4) "obtain the educational benefits that flow from an ethnically diverse student body."

The Supreme Court held that these objectives were legitimate and that race and ethnic origin *may* be considered in reviewing applications to a state school without violating the Fourteenth Amendment's Equal Protection Clause. However, the Court also held that a separate admissions program for minorities with a specific quota of openings that were unavailable to white applicants *did* violate the Equal Protection Clause. The Court ordered the university to admit Bakke to its medical school and to eliminate the special admissions program. It recommended that California consider an admissions program developed at Harvard, which considers disadvantaged racial or ethnic background as a "plus" in an overall evaluation of an application but does not set numerical quotas or exclude any person from competing for all positions.

Reaction to the decision was predictable: supporters of affirmative action, particularly government officials from affirmative action programs, emphasized the Supreme Court's willingness to allow minority status to be considered a positive factor; opponents emphasized the Supreme Court's unwillingness to allow quotas that exclude whites from competing for some positions. Since Bakke had "won" the case, many observers felt that the Supreme Court was not going to permit racial quota systems.

*Affirmative Action as a Remedy for Past Discrimination*    The Supreme Court has continued to approve of affirmative action programs where there is evidence of past discriminatory practices. In *United Steelworkers of America v. Weber* (1979), the Supreme Court approved a plan developed by a private employer and a union to reserve 50 percent of higher paying, skilled jobs for minorities. Kaiser Aluminum Corporation and the United Steelworkers Union, under federal government pressure, had established a program to get more blacks into skilled technical jobs; only 2 percent of the skilled jobs were held by blacks in the plant in question, while 39 percent of the local work force was black. When Weber, a white male, was excluded from the training program while blacks with less seniority and fewer qualifications were accepted, he filed suit in federal court claiming that the plan violated Title VII of the Civil Rights Act of 1964 by discriminating against him because of his race. But the Supreme Court held that "employers and unions in the private sector [are] free to take such race-conscious steps to eliminate manifest racial imbalances in traditionally segregated job categories. We hold that Title VII does not prohibit such . . . affirmative action plans." Weber's reliance on the clear language of Title VII was "misplaced." According to the Court, it would be "ironic indeed" if the Civil Rights Act were used to prohibit voluntary private race-conscious efforts to overcome the past effects of discrimination.[18] In *United States v. Paradise* (1987), the Court upheld a rigid 50 percent black quota system for promotions in the Alabama Department of Safety, which had excluded blacks from the ranks of state troopers prior to 1972 and had not promoted any blacks higher than corporal prior to 1984. In a 5 to 4 decision, the majority stressed the long history of discrimination in the agency as a reason for upholding the quota system. Whatever burdens imposed on innocent parties were outweighed by the need to correct the effects of past discrimination.[19]

*Case Questioning Affirmative Action*    The Supreme Court has continued to express concern about whites who are directly and adversely affected by government action solely because of their race. In *Firefighters Local Union 1784 v. Stotts* (1984), the Court ruled that a city could not lay off white firefighters in favor of black firefighters with less seniority.[20] In *City of Richmond v. Crosen Co.* (1989), the Supreme Court held that a minority **set-aside program** in Richmond, Virginia, which mandated that 30 percent of all city construction contracts must go to "blacks, Spanish-speaking, Orientals, Indians, Eskimos, or Aleuts," violated the Equal Protection Clause of the Fourteenth Amendment.[21]

It is important to note that the Supreme Court has never adopted the color-blind doctrine, first espoused by Justice Harlan in his dissent from *Plessy v. Ferguson,* that "Our Constitution is colorblind, and neither knows nor tolerates classes among citizens." If the Equal Protection Clause required that the laws of the United States and the states be truly colorblind, then no racial guidelines, goals, or quotas would be tolerated. Occasionally this view has been expressed in recent minority dissents.[22]

However, the Court has held that racial classifications in law must be subject to "strict scrutiny." This means that race-based actions by government—any disparate treatment of the races by federal, state, or local public agencies—must be found necessary to remedy past proven discrimination, or to further clearly identified,

**Set-aside program:** A program in which a specified number or percentage of contracts must go to designated minorities.

compelling, and legitimate government objectives. Moreover, race-based actions must be "narrowly tailored" so as not to adversely affect the rights of individuals. In striking down a federal construction contract "set-aside" program for small businesses owed by racial minorities, the Court expressed skepticism about governmental racial classifications: "There is simply no way of determining what classifications are 'benign' and 'remedial' and what classifications are in fact motivated by illegitimate notions of racial inferiority or simple racial politics."[23]

*Absence of a Clear Constitutional Principle*   The Supreme Court's decisions on affirmative action have not provided the nation with a clear and coherent interpretation of the Constitution. There is no clear rule of law, or legal test, or constitutional principle that tells us what is permissible and what is prohibited in the way of racially conscious laws and practices. Each affirmative action program must be judged separately.

Nevertheless, over time some general tendencies in Supreme Court policy can be identified. Affirmative action programs are *more likely to be found constitutional* when:

- They are adopted in response to a past proven history of discrimination.
- They are "narrowly tailored" so as not to adversely affect the rights of individuals.
- They do not absolutely bar whites or men from competing or participating.
- They serve clearly-identified, compelling, and legitimate government objectives.

## AFFIRMATIVE ACTION IN CONGRESS

The battle over affirmative action has been waged in the Congress as well as in the courts. Members of Congress are very much aware of survey results showing that most Americans favor affirmative action when it is expressed in the abstract. But they are equally aware that the poll results are much different when "preferences" or "quotas" are mentioned. So Congress, ever mindful of the polls, has tried to find a way to advance affirmative action while avoiding direct reference to preferences or quotas.

*Getting into Specifics*   The Civil Rights Act of 1964, Title VII, bars racial or sexual discrimination in employment. But how can persons who feel that they have been passed over for jobs or promotions go about the task of proving that discrimination was involved? Evidence of direct discrimination is often difficult to obtain. Can underrepresentation of minorities or women in a work force be used as evidence of discrimination in the absence of any evidence of direct discriminatory practices? If an employer uses a requirement or test that has a disparate effect on minorities or women, who has the burden of proof of showing that the requirement or test is relevant to effective job performance?

The Supreme Court responded to both of these questions in its interpretation of the Civil Rights Act in *Wards Cove Packing Co., Inc. v. Antonio* in 1989.[24] In a controversial 5 to 4 decision, the Court held that statistical imbalances in race or gender in the workplace were not sufficient evidence by themselves to prove discrimination. And the Court ruled that it was up to plaintiffs to prove that an employer had no business reason for requirements or tests that had an adverse impact on minorities or women. This decision clearly made it more difficult to prove job discrimination.

*Civil Rights and Women's Equity Act of 1991*    Civil rights groups were highly critical of what they regarded as the Supreme Court's "narrowing" of the Civil Rights Act protections in employment. They turned to Congress to rewrite portions of the Civil Rights Act to "restore" these protections. Business lobbies, however, believed that accepting statistical imbalances as evidence of discrimination or that shifting the burden of proof to employers would result in hiring by "quotas" simply to avoid lawsuits. After nearly two years of negotiations on Capitol Hill and a reversal of President George Bush's initial opposition, Congress produced the Civil Rights and Women's Equity Act of 1991.

Congress sought to deflect criticism of this act as a "quota bill" by specifically including an antiquota provision: nothing in the bill is to be "construed to require, encourage, or permit an employer to adopt hiring or promotion quotas on the basis of race, color, religion, sex or national origin, and the use of such quotas shall be deemed to be an unlawful employment practice."[25] Among the more important provisions of the act:

- *Statistical imbalances:* The mere existence of statistical imbalance in an employer's work force is not, by itself, sufficient evidence to prove discrimination. However, statistical imbalances may be evidence of employment practices (rules, requirements, academic qualifications, tests) that have a "disparate impact" on minorities or women.
- *Disparate employment practices:* Employers bear the burden of proof that any practice that has a "disparate impact" is necessary and has "a significant and manifest relationship to the requirements for effective job performance."
- *Penalties:* The act gives victims of discrimination both compensating money awards (usually back pay and attorney's fees) as well as punitive money awards, unlimited for racial discrimination but limited to $150,000 for sex discrimination (a disparity in the law that women's groups have vowed to remedy).

## NEW DEBATES OVER AFFIRMATIVE ACTION

Martin Luther King, Jr., had a dream, that "our children will one day live in a nation where they will not be judged by the color of their skin but by the content of their character." What united "all of God's children—black men and white men, Jews and Gentiles, Catholics and Protestants . . . to join hands and to sing . . . 'free at last'" during the civil rights movements of the 1960s was the inspiring principle that everyone—regardless of race, sex, color, or ethnicity—is entitled to equal protection of the laws.[26] What has happened to the dream?

*Individual Rights versus Group Benefits*    Over time, the civil rights movement shifted its focus from *individual rights* to *group benefits*. Affirmative action programs classify people by group membership, thereby challenging a deeply rooted American value—that people be judged on individual attributes like character and achievement rather than race, color, or gender. Racial and gender preferences are currently encountered in hiring and promotion practices in private and public employment and in college and university admissions, scholarships, and faculty recruitment. A personal commitment to "diversity" in the work force and in the student body and the faculty has become a requirement for promotion to high administrative position. "New" groups—homosexuals, for example—seek to include themselves among the preferred groups. The predictable result has been increased intergroup tension and conflict nearly everywhere—on the job, in schools, on college campuses.

*Rising Opposition to Preferences*    Blacks and whites have come to hold very different opinions about the extent of discrimination in American society today and about what, if anything, should be done about it (see *Up Close:* "Black and White Opinion on Affirmative Action"). Few Americans object to actions taken to remedy proven discrimination by private employers, public officials, or university administrations. But increasing resentment among whites toward preferential treatment of minorities has weakened political support for civil rights laws. Yet another stereotype has emerged—the "angry white male," who is likely to blame affirmative action for personal setbacks in life. Some early supporters of affirmative action have come to view race-conscious programs as no longer necessary; they argue that disadvantages in society today are more class-based than race-based. If preferences are to be granted at all, they should be based on economic disadvantage, not race. Some misgivings have been also expressed by a few African American scholars about unfair stigmatizing of the supposed beneficiaries of affirmative action—a resulting negative stereotyping of blacks as unable to get ahead on merit alone. Race-conscious government policies, they argue, have been more hurtful than helpful.[27]

*Arguments for Continuing Affirmative Action*    Most Americans agree that discrimination still exists in American society, even if they do not agree on what should be done about it. Many supporters of affirmative action would ideally prefer a colorblind society—Martin Luther King, Jr.'s, dream remains the ultimate goal for the nation—but they see race-conscious policies as a continuing necessity to remedy current discrimination and bad effects of past discrimination. "If we abandon affirmative action we return to the old white boy network."[28]

*The California Civil Rights Initiative*    The rethinking of affirmative action was inspired by a citizen's initiative placed on the ballot in California by popular petition. The California Civil Rights Initiative would add the following key phrase to that state's constitution:

> Neither the state of California nor any of its political subdivisions or agents shall use race, sex, color, ethnicity or national origin as a criterion for either discriminating against, or granting preferential treatment to, any individual or group in the operation of the State's system of public employment, public education or public contracting.

Supporters argue that this initiative leaves all existing federal and state civil rights protections intact. It simply extends the rights of all previously protected groups to all of the state's citizens. The only preferences prohibited are those based on

# Black and White Opinion on Affirmative Action

Blacks and whites differ over the extent of discrimination in American society today and what, if anything, should be done about it. Blacks are far more likely than whites to believe that racial discrimination is the principal reason why blacks, on the average, have lower incomes and poorer housing than whites. While 70 percent of blacks believe that these differences are "mainly due to discrimination," only 47 percent of whites think so.

*Affirmative Action*  Given these different views on the extent of discrimination, it is not surprising that blacks and whites also differ on "affirmative action." There is widespread debate over the meaning of the term affirmative action. Insofar as it is interpreted to mean greater effort to make sure that *opportunities* are equally open to all—that is, making sure that schools and jobs are equally available to all

races and both sexes—there is little controversy over its desirability. But affirmative action becomes controversial when it is interpreted to mean equality of *results* in admissions, jobs, and promotions. And the proposed use of "preferences" and "quotas" to ensure equality of results among races and sexes produces polarization of opinion among Americans.

Levels of support for affirmative action often depend on the wording of the question. If the question is posed simply in terms of support for or opposition to "affirmative action," without specifying preferences or quotas, then whites as well as blacks favor it.

Moreover, if affirmative action is defined in terms of "encouraging" minorities or providing job training or special education "to make them better qualified," most Americans, both black and white, are supportive. However, black and white opinion diverges sharply over preferences and quotas for minorities and women.

*Source: American Enterprise,* January/February, 1990, pp. 96–97; Gallup poll, reported in *USA Today,* March 24, 1995.

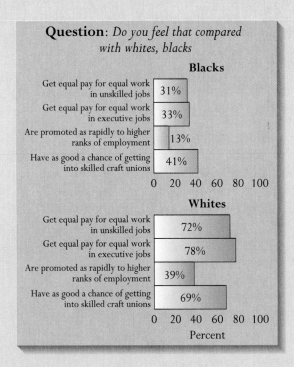

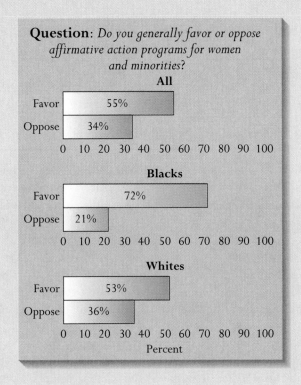

**Question**: *Do you favor or oppose providing job training for minorities and women to make them qualified for better jobs?*

**All**

Favor 82%
Oppose 17%

0 10 20 30 40 50 60 70 80 90 100

**Blacks**

Favor 94%
Oppose 6%

0 10 20 30 40 50 60 70 80 90 100

**Whites**

Favor 80%
Oppose 18%

0 10 20 30 40 50 60 70 80 90 100

Percent

**Question**: *Do you favor or oppose providing special educational classes for minorities and women to make them better qualified for college?*

**All**

Favor 75%
Oppose 22%

0 10 20 30 40 50 60 70 80 90 100

**Blacks**

Favor 90%
Oppose 9%

0 10 20 30 40 50 60 70 80 90 100

**Whites**

Favor 73%
Oppose 24%

0 10 20 30 40 50 60 70 80 90 100

Percent

**Question**: *Do you favor or oppose making a certain number of scholarships at public colleges and universities available only to minorities and women?*

**All**

Favor 31%
Oppose 67%

0 10 20 30 40 50 60 70 80 90 100

**Blacks**

Favor 51%
Oppose 45%

0 10 20 30 40 50 60 70 80 90 100

**Whites**

Favor 27%
Oppose 71%

0 10 20 30 40 50 60 70 80 90 100

Percent

**Question**: *Do you favor or oppose establishing quotas that require schools to admit a certain number of minorities and women as students?*

**All**

Favor 39%
Oppose 57%

0 10 20 30 40 50 60 70 80 90 100

**Blacks**

Favor 70%
Oppose 27%

0 10 20 30 40 50 60 70 80 90 100

**Whites**

Favor 35%
Oppose 61%

0 10 20 30 40 50 60 70 80 90 100

Percent

race, sex, color, ethnicity, and national origin. It does *not* restrict the state from granting preferential treatment to individuals based upon socioeconomic disadvantage, physical disability, or veteran's status. The initiative was approved by 54 percent of California voters in 1996, but its implementation faces challenges in federal courts.

# GENDER EQUALITY AND THE FOURTEENTH AMENDMENT

The historical context of the Fourteenth Amendment implies its intent to guarantee equality for newly freed slaves, but the wording of its Equal Protection Clause applies to "any person." Thus, the text of the Fourteenth Amendment could be interpreted to bar any gender differences in the law, in the fashion of the proposed Equal Rights Amendment. But the Supreme Court has never interpreted the Equal Protection Clause to give the same level of protection to gender equality as to racial equality. Indeed, in 1873 the Supreme Court specifically rejected arguments that this clause applied to women. The Court once upheld a state law banning women from practicing law, arguing that: "The natural and proper timidity and delicacy which belongs to the female sex evidently unfits it for many of the occupations of civil life. . . . The paramount destiny and mission of women are to fulfill the noble and benign offices of wife and mother. This is the law of the Creator."[29]

*Early Feminist Politics*    The earliest active feminist organizations grew out of the pre-Civil War antislavery movement (see *Up Close:* "A Declaration of Women's Rights, 1848"). There the first generation of feminists—including Lucretia Mott, Elizabeth Cady Stanton, Lucy Stone, and Susan B. Anthony—learned to organize, hold public meetings, and conduct petition campaigns. After the Civil War, women were successful in changing many state laws that abridged the property rights of married women and otherwise treated them as "chattel" (property) of their husbands. By the early 1900s activists were also successful in winning some protections for women in the workplace, including state laws limiting women's hours of work, working conditions, and physical demands. At the time, these laws were regarded as "progressive."

The most successful feminist efforts of the 1800s centered on protection of women in families. The perceived threats to women's well-being were their husbands' drinking, gambling, and consorting with prostitutes. Women led the Anti-Saloon League, succeeded in outlawing gambling and prostitution in every state except Nevada, and provided the major source of moral support for the Eighteenth Amendment (Prohibition).

In the early twentieth century, the feminist movement concentrated on women's suffrage—the drive to guarantee women the right to vote. The early suffragists employed mass demonstrations, parades, picketing, and occasional disruption and civil disobedience—tactics similar to those of the civil rights movement of the 1960s. The culmination of their efforts was the 1920 passage of the Nineteenth Amendment to the Constitution: "The right of citizens of the United States to vote shall not be denied or abridged by the United States or by any State on account of sex." The suffrage movement spawned the League of Women Voters; in

# A Declaration of Women's Rights, 1848

The movement for women's rights in the United States is nearly as old as the nation itself. In 1776, Abigail Adams wrote to her husband, John Adams, at the Second Continental Congress while it was debating whether to declare American independence:

> I long to hear that you have declared an independency. And in the new code of laws which I suppose it will be necessary for you to make, I desire you would remember the ladies, and be more generous and favorable to them than your ancestors. . . . If particular care and attention is not paid to the ladies, we are determined to foment a rebellion and will not hold ourselves bound by any laws in which we have no voice or representation.

The political movement forecast by Abigail Adams did not really emerge until a generation later, however. The origins of the women's rights movement lie in the antislavery crusade, in which women played the major role. When a delegation of American women was excluded from the World Anti-Slavery Convention in London in 1840, they realized that the cause of emancipation affected them as well as slaves. On July 19, 1848, Elizabeth Cady Stanton, Lucretia Mott, and several hundred other women reformers met in Seneca Falls, New York, where they drew up "The Seneca Falls Declaration of Sentiments and Resolutions." The resolution parallels the Declaration of Independence and reads in part:

> We hold these truths to be self-evident: that all men and women are created equal; that they are endowed by their Creator with certain inalienable rights; that among these are life, liberty, and the pursuit of happiness. . . .
>
> The history of mankind is a history of repeated injuries and usurpations, on the part of man toward woman, having in direct object the establishment of an absolute tyranny over her. To prove this, let facts be submitted to a candid world.
>
> He has never permitted her to exercise her inalienable right to the elective franchise.
>
> He has compelled her to submit to laws, in the formation of which she had no voice. . . .
>
> He has made her, if married, in the eye of the law, civilly dead.

> He has taken from her all rights in property, even to the wages she earns. . . .
>
> He has monopolized nearly all the profitable employments, and from those she is permitted to follow, she receives but a scanty remuneration. . . .
>
> He has denied her the facilities for obtaining a thorough education, all colleges being closed against her.
>
> He allows her in Church, as well as State, but a subordinate position, claiming Apostolic authority for her exclusion from the ministry, and, with some exceptions, from any public participation in the affairs of the Church.
>
> He has created a false public sentiment by giving to a world a different code of morals for men and women, by which moral delinquencies which exclude women from society, are not only tolerated, but deemed of little account in man. . . .
>
> Now, in view of this entire disfranchisement of one-half the people of this country, their social and religious degradation—in view of the unjust laws above mentioned, and because women do feel themselves aggrieved, oppressed, and fraudulently deprived of their most sacred rights, we insist that they have immediate admission to all the rights and privileges which belong to them as citizens of the United States.

*Elizabeth Cady Stanton, one of the authors of the Seneca Falls Declaration, addressing a meeting.*

addition to women's right to vote, the League has sought protection of women in industry, child welfare laws, and honest election practices.

*Judicial Scrutiny of Gender Classifications*   In the 1970s, the Supreme Court became responsive to arguments that sex discrimination might violate the Equal Protection Clause of the Fourteenth Amendment. In *Reed v. Reed* (1971), it ruled that sexual classifications in the law "must be reasonable and not arbitrary, and must rest on some ground of difference having fair and substantial relation to . . . important governmental objectives."[30] This is a much more relaxed level of scrutiny than the Supreme Court gives to racial classification in the law. Since then, the Court has also ruled:

- A state can no longer set different ages for men and women to become legal adults[31] or purchase alcoholic beverages.[32]
- Women cannot be barred from police or firefighting jobs by arbitrary height and weight requirements.[33]
- Insurance and retirement plans for women must pay the same monthly benefits (even though women on the average live longer).[34]
- Schools must pay coaches in girls' sports the same as coaches in boys' sports.[35]

*Continuing Gender Differences*   The Supreme Court continues to wrestle with the question of whether some gender differences can be recognized in law. The question is most evident in laws dealing with sexual activity and reproduction. The Court has upheld statutory rape laws that make it a crime for an adult male to have sexual intercourse with a female under the age of eighteen, regardless of her consent. "We need not to be medical doctors to discern that young men and young women are not similarly situated with respect to the problems and the risks of sexual intercourse. Only women may become pregnant, and they suffer disproportionately the profound physical, emotional and psychological consequences of sexual activity."[36]

Women's participation in military service, particularly combat, raises even more controversial questions regarding permissible gender classifications. The Supreme Court appears to have bowed out of this particular controversy. In upholding Congress's draft registration law for men only, the Court ruled that "the constitutional power of Congress to raise and support armies and to make all laws necessary and proper to that end is broad and sweeping."[37] Congress and the Defense Department are responsible for determining assignments for women in the military. Women have recently won assignments to air and naval combat units but remain excluded from combat infantry, armor, artillery, and special forces.

*Aims of the Equal Rights Amendment*   The proposed Equal Rights Amendment to the U.S. Constitution (see *Up Close:* "ERA: Three States Short" in Chapter 3) was worded very broadly: "Equality of rights under the law shall not be denied or abridged by the United States or any State on account of sex." Had it been ratified by the necessary thirty-eight states, it would have eliminated most, if not all, gender differences in the law. Without ERA, many important guarantees of equality for women rest upon laws of Congress rather than upon the Constitution.

# GENDER EQUALITY IN THE ECONOMY

As cultural views of women's roles in society have changed and economic pressures on family budgets have increased, women's participation in the labor force has risen. The gap between women's and men's participation in the nation's work force is closing over time.[38] With the movement of women into the work force, feminist political activity has shifted toward economic concerns—gender equality in education, employment, pay, promotion, and credit.

*Employees of the Mitsubishi automobile plant in Normal, Illinois, demonstrated outside the offices of the Equal Employment Opportunity Commission in Chicago in April, 1996, in support of the company after it became the target of a sexual harassment investigation. The company provided transportation to the demonstration and paid the workers for the day.*

*Gender Equality in Civil Rights Laws*   Title VII of the Civil Rights Act of 1964 prevents sexual (as well as racial) discrimination in hiring, pay, and promotions. The Equal Employment Opportunity Commission, the federal agency charged with eliminating discrimination in employment, has established guidelines barring stereotyped classifications of "men's jobs" and "women's jobs." The courts have repeatedly struck down state laws and employer practices that differentiate between men and women in hours, pay, retirement age, and so forth.

The Federal Equal Credit Opportunity Act of 1974 prohibits sex discrimination in credit transactions. Federal law prevents banks, credit unions, savings and loan associations, retail stores, and credit card companies from denying credit because of sex or marital status. However, these businesses may still deny credit for a poor or nonexistent credit rating, and some women who have always maintained accounts in their husband's name may still face credit problems if they apply in their own name.

Title IX of the Education Act Amendment of 1972 deals with sex discrimination in education. This federal law bars discrimination in admissions, housing, rules, financial aid, faculty and staff recruitment and pay, and—most troublesome of all—athletics. The latter problem has proven very difficult because men's football and basketball programs have traditionally brought in the money to finance all other sports, and men's football and basketball have received the largest share of school athletic budgets.

*The Earnings Gap*   Despite protections under federal laws, women continue to earn substantially less than men do. Today women, on average, earn only about 71 percent of what men do (see Figure 15-1). This earnings gap is not primarily a product of **direct discrimination;** women in the same job with the same skills, qualifications, experience, and work record are not generally paid less than men. Such direct discrimination has been illegal since the Civil Rights Act of 1964. Rather, the earnings gap is primarily a product of a division in the labor market between traditionally male and female jobs, with lower salaries paid in traditionally female occupations[39] (see *Compared to What?* "The Earnings Gap in Democratic Nations").

*The Dual Labor Market and "Comparable Worth"*   The existence of a "dual" labor market, with male-dominated "blue collar" jobs distinguishable from female-dominated "pink-collar" jobs, continues to be a major obstacle to economic equality between men and women. These occupational differences result from cultural stereotyping, social conditioning, and training and education—all of which narrow the choices available to women. Although significant progress has been made in reducing occupational sex segregation (see Figure 15-2), many

**Direct discrimination:** The now-illegal practice of differential pay for men versus women even when those individuals have equal qualifications and perform the same job.

FIGURE 15-1 **Median Earnings by Gender**

*The continuing "earnings gap" between men and women reflects a division in the labor market between traditionally male higher-paying occupations and traditionally female lower-paying positions.*

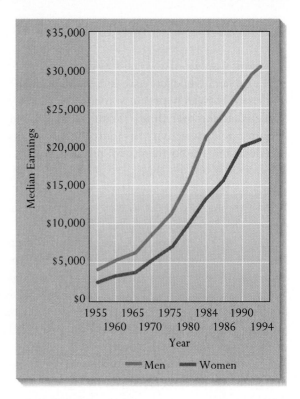

*Source: Statistical Abstract of the United States, 1995.*

observers nevertheless doubt that sexually differentiated occupations will be eliminated in the foreseeable future.

As a result of a growing recognition that the wage gap is more a result of occupational differentiation than direct discrimination, some feminist organizations have turned to a new approach—the demand that pay levels in various occupations be determined by **comparable worth** rather than by the labor market. Comparable worth goes beyond paying men and women equally for the same work and calls for paying the same wages for jobs of comparable value to the employer. Advocates of comparable worth argue that governmental agencies or the courts should evaluate traditionally male and female jobs to determine their "worth" to the employer, perhaps by considering responsibilities, effort, knowledge, and skill requirements. Jobs adjudged to be "comparable" would be paid equal wages. Government agencies or the courts would replace the labor market in the determination of wage rates.

But comparable worth raises problems of implementation: Who would decide what wages should be for various jobs? What standards would be used to decide? EEOC has rejected the notion of comparable worth and declined to recommend wages for traditionally male and female jobs. And so far, the federal courts have refused to declare that differing wages in traditionally male and female occupations constitute evidence of sexual discrimination in violation of federal law. However, some state governments and private employers have undertaken to review their own pay scales to determine if traditionally female occupations are underpaid.

*The "Glass Ceiling"* Few women have climbed the ladder to become president or chief executive officer or director of the nation's largest industrial corporations, banks, utilities, newspapers, or television networks.[40] Large numbers of

**Comparable worth:** The argument that pay levels for traditionally male and traditionally female jobs should be equalized by paying equally all jobs that are "worth about the same" to an employer.

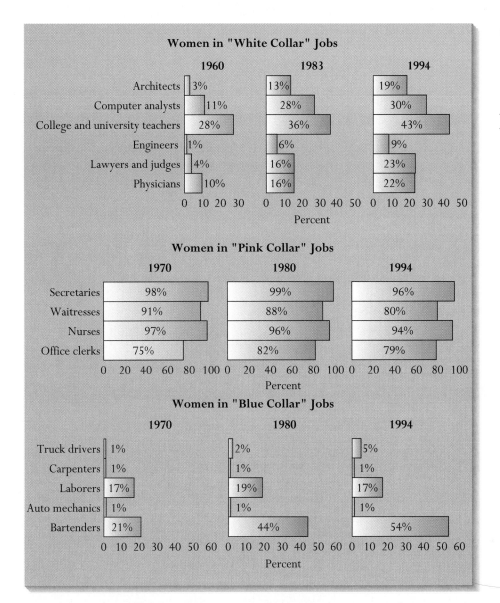

**Women in "White Collar" Jobs**

| | 1960 | 1983 | 1994 |
|---|---|---|---|
| Architects | 3% | 13% | 19% |
| Computer analysts | 11% | 28% | 30% |
| College and university teachers | 28% | 36% | 43% |
| Engineers | 1% | 6% | 9% |
| Lawyers and judges | 4% | 16% | 23% |
| Physicians | 10% | 16% | 22% |

Percent

**Women in "Pink Collar" Jobs**

| | 1970 | 1980 | 1994 |
|---|---|---|---|
| Secretaries | 98% | 99% | 96% |
| Waitresses | 91% | 88% | 80% |
| Nurses | 97% | 96% | 94% |
| Office clerks | 75% | 82% | 79% |

Percent

**Women in "Blue Collar" Jobs**

| | 1970 | 1980 | 1994 |
|---|---|---|---|
| Truck drivers | 1% | 2% | 5% |
| Carpenters | 1% | 1% | 1% |
| Laborers | 17% | 19% | 17% |
| Auto mechanics | 1% | 1% | 1% |
| Bartenders | 21% | 44% | 54% |

Percent

**FIGURE 15-2   Gender Differentiation in the Labor Market**

*Most of the earnings gap between men and women in the U.S. labor force today is the result of the different job positions held by the two sexes. Although women are increasingly entering "white-collar" occupations long dominated by men, they continue to be disproportionately concentrated in "pink-collar" service positions. "Blue-collar" jobs have been the most resistant to change, remaining a male bastion, although women bartenders now outnumber men.*

*Sources:* U.S. Department of Labor, *Employment in Perspective: Working Women* (Washington, D.C., Government Printing Office, 1983); National Research Council, National Academy of Sciences, *Women's Work, Men's Work* (Washington, D.C.: National Academy Press, 1985); U.S. Bureau of Labor Statistics, *Current Population Survey, 1994.*

women are entering the legal profession, but few are senior partners in the nation's largest and most prestigious law firms. Women are more likely to be found in the presidential cabinet than in the corporate boardroom.

The barriers to women's advancement to top positions are often very subtle, giving rise to the phrase **glass ceiling**. In explaining "why women aren't getting to the top," one observer argues that: "At senior management levels competence is assumed. What you're looking for is someone who fits, someone who gets along, someone you trust. Now that's subtle stuff. How does a group of men feel that a woman is going to fit? I think it's very hard." Or, as a woman bank executive says, "The men just don't feel comfortable."[41]

There are many other explanations, and all of them are controversial: Women choose staff assignments rather than fast-track, operating-head assignments.

**Glass ceiling:** The "invisible" barriers to women rising to the highest positions in corporations and the professions.

# The Earnings Gap in Democratic Nations

The earnings gap between men and women in the United States persists. For every dollar an American man earns in a week, an American woman earns an average of 74 cents.

In many advanced democracies, the earnings gap is significantly smaller (see graph). In France, for example, women's wages are estimated to be 82 percent of men's wages. However, in Japan, women's earnings relative to men's are much worse than in the United States: The average weekly wage of women in Japan is only half that of men.

*Source:* International Labor Organization, *We're Number One* (New York: Vintage Books, 1992), p. iii.

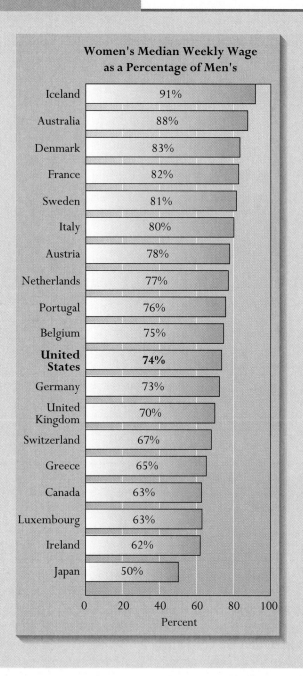

**Women's Median Weekly Wage as a Percentage of Men's**

| Country | Percent |
|---|---|
| Iceland | 91% |
| Australia | 88% |
| Denmark | 83% |
| France | 82% |
| Sweden | 81% |
| Italy | 80% |
| Austria | 78% |
| Netherlands | 77% |
| Portugal | 76% |
| Belgium | 75% |
| **United States** | **74%** |
| Germany | 73% |
| United Kingdom | 70% |
| Switzerland | 67% |
| Greece | 65% |
| Canada | 63% |
| Luxembourg | 63% |
| Ireland | 62% |
| Japan | 50% |

Women are cautious and unaggressive in corporate politics. Women have lower expectations about peak earnings and positions, and these expectations become self-fulfilling. Women bear children, and even during relatively short maternity absences they fall behind their male counterparts. Women are less likely to want to change locations than men, and immobile executives are worth less to a corporation than mobile ones. Women executives in sensitive positions come under even more pressure than men in similar posts. Women executives believe that they get much more scrutiny than men and must work harder to succeed. And at all levels, increasing attention has been paid to sexual harassment (see *What Do You Think?* "What Constitutes Sexual Harassment?"). Finally, it is important to note that affirmative action efforts by governments—notably the EEOC—are directed primarily at entry-level positions rather than senior management posts.

# HISPANIC POLITICS

Hispanics—a term the U.S. Census Bureau uses to refer to Mexican Americans, Puerto Ricans, Cubans, and others of Spanish-speaking ancestry and culture—now comprise over 10 percent of the U.S. population (see Table 15-3). The largest Hispanic subgroup is Mexican Americans. Some are descendants of citizens who lived in the Mexican territory annexed to the United States in 1848, but most have come to the United States in accelerating numbers in recent years. The largest Mexican American populations are found in Texas, Arizona, New Mexico, and California. Puerto Ricans constitute the second-largest Hispanic subgroup. Many still retain ties to the Commonwealth and move back and forth from Puerto Rico to New York. Cubans make up the third-largest subgroup; most have fled from Fidel Castro's Cuba and live mainly in the Miami metropolitan area. Each of these Hispanic groups has encountered a different experience in American life. Indeed, there is some evidence that these groups identify themselves separately, rather than as Hispanics.[42]

If all Hispanics are grouped together for statistical comparisons, their median family income level is well below whites, although somewhat higher than blacks (see Table 15-2). Hispanic poverty and unemployment rates are higher than whites and slightly lower than blacks. The percentage of Hispanics completing high school and college educations is below that of both whites and blacks, suggesting language or other cultural obstacles in education. Yet within these overall racial comparisons, there are wide disparities among subgroups as well as among individuals.

*Mexican Americans*    The Mexican American population in the southwestern United States is growing very rapidly; it doubled in size between 1980 and 1990. For many years, agricultural business encouraged immigration of Mexican farm laborers willing to endure harsh conditions for low pay. Many others came to the United State as *indocumentados*—undocumented, or illegal, aliens. In the Immigration Reform Act of 1986 Congress offered amnesty to all undocumented

| TABLE 15-3    MINORITIES IN AMERICA | | |
|---|---|---|
| | Number | Percentage of Population |
| African Americans | 33,117,000 | 12.6% |
| Hispanic Americans | 27,150,000 | 10.2 |
| Asian or Pacific Islander Americans | 9,756,000 | 3.7 |
| Native Americans | 2,226,000 | 0.8 |

*Source: Statistical Abstract of the United States, 1995.*

# What Constitutes Sexual Harassment?

The hearings on Clarence Thomas's nomination to the Supreme Court brought unprecedented levels of media scrutiny to the issue of sexual harassment. It inspired a wave of complaints to the U.S. Equal Employment Opportunity Commission, state and federal courts, corporate personnel offices, and colleges and universities. (Hollywood responded with a popular motion picture based on a best-selling book; unlike most sexual harassment complaints, however, this version cast the woman as the harasser.) Various surveys report that up to one-third of female workers say they have experienced sexual harassment on the job.\* But it is not always clear exactly what kind of behavior constitutes "sexual harassment."

The U.S. Supreme Court has provided some guidance in the development of sexual harassment definitions and prohibitions. Title VII of the Civil Rights Act of 1964 makes it "an unlawful employment practice to discriminate against any individual with respect to his [sic] compensation, terms, conditions or privileges of employment because of such individual's race, color, religion, sex, or national origin." In the employment context, the U.S. Supreme Court has approved the following definition of sexual harassment:

Unwelcome sexual advances, requests for sexual favors, and other verbal or physical conduct of a sexual nature constitute sexual harassment when (1) submission to such conduct is made either explicitly or implicitly a term or condition of an individual's employment; (2) submission to or rejection of such conduct by an individual, is used as the basis for employment decisions affecting such individual; or (3)

such conduct has the purpose or effect of unreasonably interfering with an individual's work performance or creating an intimidating, hostile, or offensive working environment.\*\*

There are no great difficulties in defining sexual harassment when jobs or promotions are conditioned on the granting of sexual favors. But several problems arise in defining a "hostile working environment." This phrase may include offensive utterances, sexual innuendos, dirty jokes, the display of pornographic material, and unwanted proposals for dates. First, it would appear to include speech and hence raise First Amendment questions regarding how far speech may be curtailed by law in the workplace. Second, the definition depends more on the subjective feelings of the individual employee about what is "offensive" and "unwanted" than on an objective standard of behavior that is easily understood by all. Justice Sandra Day O'Connor wrestled with the definition of a "hostile work environment" in *Harris v. Forklift* in 1993. She held that a plaintiff need not show that the utterances caused psychological injury but that a "reasonable person," not just the plaintiff, must perceive the work environment to be hostile or abusive. Presumably a single incident would not constitute harassment; rather, courts should consider "the frequency of the discriminatory conduct," "its severity," and whether it "unreasonably interferes with an employee's work performance."\*\*\*

What behaviors does a "reasonable person" believe to be sexual harassment? Women are somewhat more likely to perceive sexual harassment in various behaviors than men (see figure). But neither women nor men are likely to perceive it to include repeated requests for a date, the telling of dirty jokes, or comments on attractiveness—even though these behaviors often inspire formal complaints.

workers who had entered the United States prior to 1982. But the act also required employers, under threat of penalties, to hire only people who can provide documentation of their legal status in the country. The result has been an increase in discrimination against Hispanics in hiring, as well as a booming business in counterfeit green (employment) and Social Security cards.

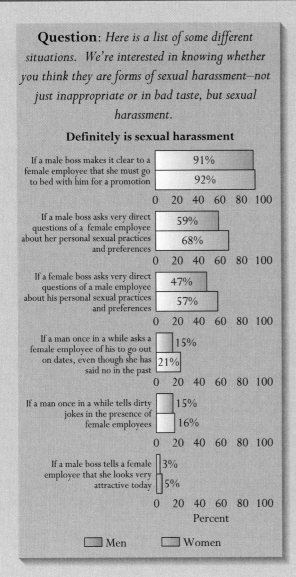

**Question**: *Here is a list of some different situations. We're interested in knowing whether you think they are forms of sexual harassment—not just inappropriate or in bad taste, but sexual harassment.*

**Definitely is sexual harassment**

If a male boss makes it clear to a female employee that she must go to bed with him for a promotion
91%
92%
0  20  40  60  80  100

If a male boss asks very direct questions of a female employee about her personal sexual practices and preferences
59%
68%
0  20  40  60  80  100

If a female boss asks very direct questions of a male employee about his personal sexual practices and preferences
47%
57%
0  20  40  60  80  100

If a man once in a while asks a female employee of his to go out on dates, even though she has said no in the past
15%
21%
0  20  40  60  80  100

If a man once in a while tells dirty jokes in the presence of female employees
15%
16%
0  20  40  60  80  100

If a male boss tells a female employee that she looks very attractive today
3%
5%
0  20  40  60  80  100
Percent

☐ Men      ☐ Women

Roper Organization as reported in *American Enterprise*, September/October 1993, p. 93.

It is important to note that many *university* policies go well beyond either Supreme Court opinion or popular opinion in defining what constitutes sexual harassment, including:

* "remarks about a person's clothing"
* "suggestive or insulting sounds"
* "leering at or ogling of a person's body"
* "nonsexual slurs about one's gender"
* "remarks that degrade another person or group on the basis of gender."

The National Association of Scholars worries that overly broad and vague definitions of sexual harassment can undermine academic freedom and inhibit classroom discussions of important yet sensitive topics including human sexuality, gender differences, sexual roles, and gender politics. Teaching and research on such topics must not be constrained by the threat that the views expressed will be labeled "insensitive," "uncomfortable," or "incorrect." Faculty must feel free to provide their best academic and professional advice to students, collectively and individually, without fear that their comments will be officially labeled as "offensive" or "unwelcome." Students must feel free to express themselves on matters of gender, whether or not their ideas are biased or immature or crudely expressed.

*Washington Post National Weekly Edition, March 7, 1993.
**Meritor Savings Bank v.Vinson, 477 U.S. 57 (1986).
***Harris v. Forklift Systems, 126 L. Ed. 2d 295 (1993).

Economic conditions in Mexico and elsewhere in Central America continue to fuel immigration, legal and illegal, to the United States. But with lower educational levels, average incomes of Mexican American families in the United States are lower and the poverty rate is higher than the general population. Although Mexican Americans have served as governors of Arizona and New Mexico and

*Many Hispanic Americans feel threatened by growing anti-immigration sentiment in states like California with large immigrant populations. In 1994 California voters passed Proposition 187, which attempted to restrict access to education, health care, and other public services for illegal immigrants.*

have won election to the U.S. Congress, their political power does not yet match their population percentages. Mexican American voter turnout is lower than other ethnic groups, perhaps because many are resident aliens or illegal immigrants not eligible to vote, or perhaps because of cultural factors that discourage political participation.[43]

*Puerto Ricans*    Residents of Puerto Rico are American citizens because Puerto Rico is a commonwealth of the United States. Puerto Rico has a government that resembles that of a state, with a constitution and elected governor and legislature, but has no voting members of the U.S. Congress and no electoral votes for president. As citizens, Puerto Ricans can move anywhere in the United States; many have immigrated to New York City.

Median family income in Puerto Rico is higher than anywhere else in the Caribbean but only half that of the poorest state in the United States. Puerto Ricans have not fared as well economically as other Hispanic groups within the United States: Puerto Ricans have lower median family incomes and higher poverty percentages, in part perhaps because of lower work force participation. One explanation centers on the history of access to federal welfare programs on the island and the resulting social dependency it fostered among some Puerto Rican families.[44]

*Cuban Americans*    Many Cuban Americans, especially those in the early waves of refugees from Castro's revolution in 1959, were skilled professionals and businesspeople, and they rapidly set about building Miami into a thriving economy. Although Cuban Americans are the smallest of the Hispanic subgroups, today they are better educated and enjoy higher incomes than the others. They are well-organized politically, and they have succeeded in electing Cuban Americans to local office in Florida and to the U.S. Congress.

*Hispanics in Congress*    Hispanic representation in the U.S. House of Representatives had risen to 18 by 1995. This figure—about 4 percent of the House membership—suggests continuing underrepresentation of the 10 percent of the U.S. population that is Hispanic. Cuban Americans tend to identify with the Republican Party, and the two Republican Hispanic House members are both Cuban Americans from the Miami area; all other Hispanic House members are Democrats.

## NATIVE AMERICANS: TRAILS OF TEARS

Christopher Columbus, having erred in his estimate of the circumference of the globe, believed he had arrived in the Indian Ocean when he first came to the Caribbean. He mistook the Arawaks there for people of the East Indies, calling them *Indios,* and this Spanish word passed into English as "Indians"—a word that came to refer to all Native American peoples. But at the time of the first European contacts, these peoples had no common ethnic identity; there were hundreds of separate cultures and languages thriving in the Americas. Although estimates vary, most historians believe that 7 to 12 million people lived in the land that is now the United States and Canada; 25 million more lived in Mexico; and as many as 60 to 70 million in all lived in the Western Hemisphere, a number comparable to Europe's population at the time.

In the centuries that followed, the Native American population of the Western Hemisphere was devastated by warfare, by famine, and, most of all, by epidemic diseases brought from Europe. Overall, the Native population fell by 90 percent, the greatest human disaster in world history. In the Europeans' conquest of the Americas, small pox was their most effective "weapon," followed by measles, bubonic plague, influenza, typhus, diphtheria, and scarlet fever. Superior military technology, together with skill in exploiting hostilities between Native nations, gradually overcame the remaining resistance. By 1910, there were only 210,000 Native Americans in the United States. Their population has slowly recovered to the current 2.2 million (less than 1 percent of the U.S. population). Many live on reservations and trust lands, the largest of which is the Navajo and Hopi enclave in the southwestern United States (see *Across the USA:* "Native American Peoples").

*The Trail of Broken Treaties*    In the Northwest Ordinance of 1787, Congress, in organizing the western territories of the new nation, declared: "The utmost good faith shall always be observed toward the Indians. Their lands and property shall never be taken from them without their consent." And later, in the

## ACROSS THE USA

# Native American Peoples

*This map shows the locations of the principal Native American reservations in the United States. Tribal governments officially govern these reservations. (Alaska Natives, including Aleuts and Eskimos, live mostly in 200 villages widely scattered across rural Alaska; twelve regional Native American corporations administer property and mineral rights on behalf of Native peoples in that state.)*

Intercourse Act of 1790, Congress declared that public treaties between the United States government and the independent Native nations would be the only legal means of obtaining "Indian" land.

As president, George Washington forged a treaty with the Creeks: in exchange for land concessions, the U.S. pledged to protect the boundaries of the Creek nation and to allow the Creeks themselves to punish all violators of their laws within these boundaries. This semblance of legality was reflected in hundreds of treaties that followed. (And indeed, in recent years some Native American nations have successfully sued in federal court for reparations and return of lands obtained in violation of the Intercourse Act of 1790 and subsequent treaties.) Yet Native lands were constantly invaded by whites. The resulting Native resistance typically led to wars that ultimately resulted in great loss of life among warriors and their families and the further loss of Native land. The cycle of invasion, resistance, military defeat, and further land concessions continued for a hundred years.

*"Indian Territories"*    Following the purchase of the vast Louisiana Territory in 1803, President Thomas Jefferson sought to "civilize" the Natives by promoting farming in "reservations" that were located west of the Mississippi River. But soon, peoples who had been forced to move from Ohio to Missouri were forced to move again to survive the relentless white expansion. President James Monroe designated as "Indian territory" most of the Great Plains west of the Missouri River. Native peoples increasingly faced three unattractive choices: assimilation, removal, or extinction.

In 1814, the Creeks, encouraged by the British during the War of 1812 to attack American settlements, faced an army of Tennessee volunteer militia led by Andrew Jackson. At the Battle of Horseshoe Bend, Jackson's cannon fire decimated the Creek warriors. In the uneven Treaty of Fort Jackson, the Creeks, Choctaws, and Cherokees were forced to concede millions of acres of land.

By 1830, the "Five Civilized Tribes" of the southeastern United States (Cherokees, Chickasaws, Choctaws, Creeks, and Seminoles) had ceded most but not all of their lands. When gold was discovered on Cherokee land in northern Georgia in 1829, whites invaded their territory. Congress, at the heeding of the old "Indian fighter" President Andrew Jackson, passed the Removal Act, ordering the forcible relocation of the Natives to Oklahoma Indian Territory. The Cherokees tried to use the whites' law to defend their land, bringing their case to the U.S. Supreme Court. When Chief Justice John Marshall held that the Cherokees were a "domestic dependent nation" that could not be forced to give up its land, President Jackson replied scornfully, "John Marshall has made his decision. Now let him enforce it." He sent a 7,000-strong army to pursue Seminoles into the huge Florida Everglades swamp and forced 16,000 Cherokees and other peoples on the infamous "Trail of Tears" march to Oklahoma in 1838.

Encroachment upon the Indian Territory of the Great Plains was not long in coming. First, the territory was crossed by the Santa Fe and Oregon Trails, and a series of military forts were built to protect travelers. In 1854, under pressure from railroad interests, the U.S. government abolished much of the Indian Territory to create the Kansas and Nebraska territories, which were immediately opened to white settlers. The Native peoples in these lands—including Potawatomis, Kickapoos, Delawares, Shawnees, Miamis, Omahas, and Missouris—were forced to sign treaties accepting vastly reduced land reservations. But large, warlike buffalo-hunting nations remained in the northern Dakotas and western Great Plains: the Sioux, Cheyennes, Arapahoes, Comanches, and Kiowas. (Other smaller peoples inhabited the Rockies to California and the Pacific Northwest; the sedentary Pueblos, Hopis, and Pimas and the migrating Apaches and Navajos occupied the Southwest.) The Plains peoples took pride in their warrior status, often fighting among themselves.

*"Indian Wars"*   The "Indian Wars" were fought between the Plains nations and the U.S. Army between 1864 and 1890. Following the Civil War, the federal government began to assign boundaries to each nation and created the Bureau of Indian Affairs (BIA) to "assist and protect" Native peoples on their "reservations." But the reservations were repeatedly reduced in size until subsistence by hunting became impossible. Malnutrition and demoralization of the Native peoples were accelerated by the mass slaughter of the buffalo; vast herds, numbering perhaps as many as 70 million, were exterminated over the years. The most storied engagement of the long war occurred at the Little Bighorn River in Montana on June 25, 1876, where Civil War hero General George Armstrong Custer led elements of the U.S. Seventh Calvary to destruction at the hands of Sioux and Cheyenne warriors led by Chief Crazy Horse, Sitting Bull, and Gall. But "Custer's last stand" inspired renewed army campaigns against the Plains peoples; the following year, Crazy Horse was forced to surrender. In 1881, destitute Sioux under Chief Sitting Bull returned from exile in Canada to surrender themselves to reservation life. Among the last peoples to hold out were the Apaches, whose famous warrior Geronimo finally surrendered in 1886. Sporadic fighting continued until 1890, when a small malnourished band of Lakota Sioux were wiped out at Wounded Knee Creek.

*The Attempted Destruction of Traditional Life*   The Dawes Act of 1887 governed federal Native American policy for decades. The thrust of the policy was to break up Native lands, allotting acreage for individual homesteads in order to assimilate Natives into the white agricultural society. Farming was to replace hunting, and traditional Native customs were to be shed for English language and schooling. But this effort to destroy culture never really succeeded. While Native peoples lost more than half of their 1877 reservation land, few lost their communal ties or accumulated much private property.

Life on the reservations was often desperate. Natives suffered the worst poverty of any group in the United States, with high rates of infant mortality, alcoholism, and other diseases. The BIA, notoriously corrupt and mismanaged, encouraged dependency and regularly interfered with religious affairs and customs.

*The New Deal*   The New Deal under President Franklin D. Roosevelt came to Native Americans in the form of the Indian Reorganization Act of 1934. This act sought to restore Native tribal structures by recognizing these nations as instruments of the federal government. Land ownership was restored, and elected Native tribal councils were recognized as legal governments. Efforts to force assimilation were largely abandoned. The BIA became more sensitive to Native culture and began employing Native Americans in larger numbers.

Yet the BIA remained "paternalistic," frequently interfering in tribal "sovereignty." Moreover, in the 1950s Congress initiated a policy of "termination" of sovereignty rights for specific nations that consented to relinquish their lands in exchange for cash payments. While only a few nations chose this course, the results were often calamitous: after the one-time cash payments were spent, Native peoples became dependent upon state social welfare services and often slipped further into poverty and alcoholism.

*The American Indian Movement*   The civil rights movement of the 1960s inspired a new activism among Native American groups. The American Indian Movement (AIM) was founded in 1968 and attracted national headlines by occupying Alcatraz Island in San Francisco Bay. Violence flared in 1972 when AIM activists took over the site of the Wounded Knee battle and fought with Federal Bureau of Investigation agents. Several Native nations succeeded in federal courts and Congress to win back lands and/or compensation for lands taken from them in treaty violations. Native culture was revitalized, and Vine Deloria's *Custer Died for Your Sins* (1969) and Dee Brown's *Bury My Heart at Wounded Knee* (1971) became national best-selling books.

*Native Americans Today*   The U.S. Constitution (Article I, Section 8) grants Congress the full power "to regulate Commerce . . . with the Indian Tribes." States are prevented from regulating or taxing Native peoples or extending their courts' jurisdiction over them unless authorized by Congress. The Supreme Court recognizes Native Americans "as members of quasi-sovereign tribal entities"[45] with powers to regulate their own internal affairs, establish their own courts, and enforce their own laws, all subject to congressional supervision. Thus, for example, many Native peoples choose to legalize gambling, including casino gambling, on reservations in states that otherwise prohibited the activity. As citizens, Native Americans have the right to vote in state as well as national elections. Those living off of reservations have the same rights and responsibilities as other citizens. Ben Nighthorse Campbell, U.S. Senator from Colorado, is the only tribal member (Northern Cheyenne) currently serving in Congress (see *People in Politics:* "Minority Faces in Congress," in Chapter 10).

The Bureau of Indian Affairs in the Department of the Interior continues to supervise reservation life, and Native Americans enrolled as members of nations and living on reservations are entitled to certain benefits established by law and treaty. Nevertheless, these peoples remain the poorest and least healthy in the United States, with high incidences of infant mortality, suicide, and alcoholism. Approximately half of all Native Americans live below the poverty line.

# THE RIGHTS OF DISABLED AMERICANS

Disabled Americans were not among the classes of people protected by the landmark Civil Rights Act of 1964. Yet they have long suffered both direct and indirect obstacles to participation in education, employment, and access to public accommodations. Throughout most of the nation's history, little thought was given to making public or private buildings or facilities accessible to blind, deaf, or mobility-impaired people.[46] Not until the Education of Handicapped Children Act of 1975 did the federal government mandate that the nation's public schools provide free education to handicapped children.

The Americans with Disabilities Act (ADA) of 1990 is a sweeping law that prohibits discrimination against disabled people in private employment, government

programs, public accommodations, and telecommunications. The act is vaguely worded in many of its provisions, requiring "reasonable accommodations" for disabled people that do not involve "undue hardship." This means disabled Americans do not have exactly the same standard of protection as minorities or women, who are protected from discrimination *regardless* of hardship or costs. (It also means that attorneys, consultants, and bureaucrats will make handsome incomes over the years interpreting the meaning of these phrases.) Specifically the ADA includes the following protections:

- *Employment:* Disabled people cannot be denied employment or promotion if, with "reasonable accommodation," they can perform the duties of the job. (Excluded from this protection are people currently using illegal drugs, gambling compulsively, or exhibiting certain other abnormal behavior.) Reasonable accommodation need not be made if doing so would cause "undue hardship" on the employer.
- *Government programs:* Disabled people cannot be denied access to government programs or benefits. New buses, taxis, and trains must be accessible to disabled persons, including those in wheelchairs.
- *Public accommodations:* Disabled people must enjoy "full and equal" access to hotels, restaurants, stores, schools, parks, museums, auditoriums, and the like. To achieve equal access, owners of existing facilities must alter them "to the maximum extent feasible"; builders of new facilities must ensure that they are readily accessible to disabled persons unless doing so is structurally impossible.
- *Communications:* The Federal Communications Commission is directed to issue regulations that will ensure that telecommunications devices for hearing- and speech-impaired people are available "to the extent possible and in the most efficient manner."

# INEQUALITY AND THE CONSTITUTION

Americans frequently claim "rights" that have no basis in the U.S. Constitution—for example, the "right" to an education, to medical care, to decent housing, to retirement benefits, to a job. Constitutions *limit* governments; they protect individuals *from* government oppression. Constitutions do not mandate that governments act wisely or compassionately, only that they behave in accordance with consistent standards in administering programs.

*Constitutional versus Legal Rights*   There is no requirement in the Constitution that governments establish education, welfare, or social security programs or that they provide housing, job training, or unemployment compensation. Whatever benefits individuals derive from these government programs, they do so as a matter of law, not as a constitutional right.

> The importance of a service performed by the State does not determine whether it must be regarded as fundamental for purposes of examination under the equal protection clause. . . . Education, of course, is not among the rights afforded explicit protection under our federal Constitution. Nor do we find any basis for saying it is implicitly so protected.[47]

*"Reasonable" Classifications*   Governments by law may classify people according to income, age, illness, disability, or any other "reasonable" standard in administering its programs. However, the Supreme Court has interpreted the Equal Protection Clause to mean only that governments may not practice "invidious" discrimination—that is, establish discriminatory classifications in the law that are "arbitrary and unreasonable" and have "no rational basis."[48] *Reasonable* classifications of individuals by law—those that serve a legitimate government purpose—are *not* unconstitutional. Yet the Equal Protection Clause obligates governments to treat equally all persons who are "similarly situated"—to treat every person who falls into a particular class in the same fashion as every other person in that class. Thus all persons who meet the eligibility requirements stated in the law must receive the same benefits. For example, if Congress establishes a public health care program for people sixty-five years of age and over (Medicare), then everyone in that age classification is entitled to the benefits of the program. Because the benefits of these programs are *legal* entitlements, not *constitutional* rights, however, Congress may choose to change the benefits or eligibility requirements at any time.

*Protections for Poor Americans*   The Constitution ensures that poor people are protected in their legal and political rights. Included among the specific protections given indigent persons:

- *Free legal counsel in criminal cases:* "From the very beginning, our state and national constitutions have laid great emphasis on procedures and substantial safeguards designed to assure fair trials before impartial tribunals in which every defendant stands equal before the law. This noble ideal cannot be realized if the poor man charged with crime has to face his accusers without the lawyer to assist him."[49]

- *No tax or financial requirement for voting:* "A state violates the equal protection clause of the Fourteenth Amendment whenever it makes the affluence of the voter or payment of any fee an electoral standard."[50] This decision extended the Twenty-fourth Amendment's ban on poll taxes for national elections to state elections as well.

But the poor cannot demand government funding as a matter of constitutional right in order to exercise other recognized rights. For example, freedom of the press does not mean that the government must buy a printing press for anyone unable to afford one. Congress, in the controversial Hyde Amendment in 1977, denied the use of Medicaid funds for poor women seeking abortions, and the Supreme Court rejected arguments that federal funding of abortions was required by the Constitution. Even though the Court reaffirmed that abortion was a constitutional right, "it simply does not follow that a woman's freedom of choice carries with it a constitutional entitlement to the financial means to avail herself of the protected choices. . . . Although the government may not place obstacles in the path of a woman's exercise of her freedom of choice, it need not remove those not of its own creation."[51]

*Income Inequality*   Governments in the United States are not under any constitutional requirement to eliminate inequality of income or wealth. (The Founders believed that "dangerous leveling" was a violation of the right to property and to use and dispose of the fruits of one's own labors.) For example, representatives of poor, black, and Hispanic groups have charged that differences in public school spending per pupil among school districts in a state discriminate unconstitutionally against poor children. While the state governments do not discriminate against the poor in their funding (on the contrary, most states have equalization programs written into state law giving more aid to schools serving poor students), it is argued that spending differences among local school districts violates the Equal Protection Clause of the Fourteenth Amendment. But the Supreme Court has ruled that disparities in school funding created by dependence on local property tax revenue and inequalities among districts in the value of property and amount of revenue raised does *not* violate the Equal Protection Clause. "We cannot say that such disparities are the product of a system that is so irrational as to be invidiously discriminatory."[52] Some *state* courts, however, have ruled that these same disparities violate *state* constitutional guarantees of equal protection.[53]

# SUMMARY NOTES

- Equality has long been the central issue of American politics. Today, most Americans agree that all individuals should have an equal opportunity to make of their lives whatever they can without artificial barriers of race, class, gender, or ethnicity. Political conflict arises over what, if anything, government should do to achieve greater equality of results—the reduction of gaps between rich and poor, men

and women, blacks and whites, and other groups in society.

- The original Constitution of 1787 recognized and protected slavery. Not until after the Civil War did the Thirteenth Amendment (1865) abolish slavery. But the Fourteenth Amendment's guarantee of "equal protection of the laws" and the Fifteenth Amendment's guarantee of voting rights were largely ignored in southern states after the federal government's Reconstruction efforts ended. Segregation was held constitutional by the U.S. Supreme Court in its "separate but equal" decision in *Plessy v. Ferguson* in 1896.

- The NAACP led the long legal battle in the federal courts to have segregation declared unconstitutional as a violation of the Equal Protection Clause of the Fourteenth Amendment. Under the leadership of Thurgood Marshall, a major victory was achieved in the case of *Brown v. Board of Education of Topeka* in 1954.

- The struggle over school desegregation continues even today. Federal courts are more likely to issue desegregation orders (including orders to bus pupils to achieve racial balance in schools) in school districts where present or past actions by government officials contributed to racial imbalances. Courts are less likely to order desegregation where racial imbalances are a product of residential patterns.

- The Courts could eliminate *governmental* discrimination by enforcing the Fourteenth Amendment of the Constitution; but only Congress could end private discrimination through legislation. Martin Luther King, Jr.'s campaign of nonviolent direct action helped to bring remaining racial injustices to the attention of Congress. Key legislation includes the Civil Rights Act of 1964, which bans discrimination in public accommodations, government-funded programs, and private employment; the Voting Rights Act of 1965, which authorizes strong federal action to protect voting rights; and the Civil Rights Act of 1968, which outlaws discrimination in housing.

- Today, racial politics center around continuing inequalities between blacks and whites in the areas of income, jobs, housing, health, education, and other conditions of life. Should the government concentrate on "equality of opportunity" and apply "colorblind" standards to both blacks and whites? Or should government take "affirmative action" to assist blacks and other minorities to overcome the results of past unequal treatment?

- Generally the Supreme Court is likely to approve of affirmative action programs when these programs have been adopted in response to a past proven history of discrimination, when they are narrowly tailored so as not to adversely affect the rights of individuals, when they do not absolutely bar whites

from participating and when they serve clearly-identified, compelling, and legitimate government objectives.

- Congress is aware that public opinion generally supports affirmative action in the abstract but that white opinion rejects the specific notions of racial preferences and quotas. Recent battles in Congress have focused on whether statistical imbalances are evidence of discrimination and whether employers should bear the burden of proof that test requirements or practices with a disparate impact on minorities are related to job performance.

- The Equal Protection Clause of the Fourteenth Amendment applies to "any person," but traditionally the Supreme Court has recognized gender differences in laws. Nevertheless, in recent years the Court has struck down gender differences where they are unreasonable or arbitrary and unrelated to legitimate government objectives.

- Gender discrimination in employment has been illegal since the passage of the Civil Rights Act of 1964. Nevertheless, differences in average earnings of men and women persist, although these differences have narrowed somewhat over time. The earnings gap appears to be mainly a product of lower pay in occupations traditionally dominated by women and higher pay in traditionally male occupations. While neither Congress nor the courts have mandated wages based on comparable worth of traditional men's and women's jobs in private employment, many governmental agencies and some private employers have undertaken to review wage rates to eliminate gender differences.

- Economic conditions in Mexico and other Spanish-speaking nations of the Western Hemisphere continue to fuel large-scale immigration, both legal and illegal, into the United States. But the political power of Mexican Americans, the nation's largest Hispanic group, does not yet match their population percentage. Their voter turnout remains lower than that of other ethnic groups in the United States.

- Since the arrival of the first Europeans on this continent, Native American peoples have experienced cycles of invasion, resistance, military defeat, and land concessions. Today Native American peoples collectively remain the poorest and least healthy of the nation's ethnic groups.

- The most recent major civil rights legislation is the Americans with Disabilities Act of 1990, which prohibits discrimination against disabled persons in private employment, government programs, public accommodations, and communications.

- The Equal Protection Clause does not bar government from treating persons in various income classes differently. However, governments must treat every individual in a class equally, and the classifications must not be "arbitrary" or "unreasonable." The poor cannot demand benefits or services as a matter of constitutional rights; but once government establishes a social welfare program by law, it must provide equal access to all persons "similarly situated."

# SELECTED READINGS

BARKER, LUCIUS J., and MACK H. JONES. *African Americans and the American Political System*, 3d ed. Upper Saddle River, N.J.: Prentice Hall, 1994. A comprehensive analysis of African-American politics, examining access to the judicial arena, the interest-group process, political parties, Congress, and the White House.

CONWAY, M. MARGARET. *Women and Public Policy: A Revolution in Progress*. Washington, D.C.: Congressional Quarterly Press, 1994. Coverage of a broad range of policy areas that affect women, including education, employment, health, marriage and family law, and child care.

FOX-GENOVESE, ELIZABETH. *Feminism Is Not the Story of My Life*. New York: Doubleday, 1995. A critique of radical feminism for failing to understand the central importance of marriage and motherhood in women's lives, and a discussion of how public policy could ease the clashing demands of work and family on women.

GLAZER, NATHAN. *Affirmative Discrimination*. Cambridge, Mass.: Harvard University Press, 1987. An argument that the focus of current civil rights policy on group rights, rather than individual rights, is not only ineffective but also destructive of race relations in America.

HACKER, ANDREW. *Two Nations*. New York: Charles Scribner's Sons, 1992. An argument that race is the principal political division in American society and that racial separation, hostilities, and inequalities are at dangerous levels today.

HERO, RODNEY E. *Latinos and the U.S. Political System*. Philadelphia: Temple University Press, 1992. A general history of political participation of major Latino groups, arguing that different cultural behaviors limit their ability to participate in the interest group system and policymaking process as currently structured.

KLUEGEL, JAMES R., and ELIOT R. SMITH. *Beliefs about Inequality*. New York: Aldine de Gruyter, 1986. A comprehensive description of Americans' beliefs and attitudes about inequality, based on extensive survey data, including evidence of changes in beliefs over time as well as inconsistencies and contradictions.

McGLEN, NANCY E., and KAREN O'CONNER. *Women, Politics, and American Society*. Upper Saddle River, N.J.: Prentice Hall, 1996. A comprehensive text contrasting women's rights and realities in politics, employment, education, reproduction, and family.

SIGELMAN, LEE, and SUSAN WELCH. *Black Americans' Views of Racial Inequality*. Cambridge, Mass.: Cambridge University Press, 1991. An analysis of survey research showing that black perceptions of racial inequality in America are considerably different from white perceptions. Though remaining optimistic about the future, blacks see discrimination as commonplace and are much more likely than whites to attribute black-white differences in education, occupation, and income to racism.

# POLITICS AND THE ECONOMY

## CHAPTER OUTLINE

## FEATURES

## POLITICS AND ECONOMICS

Earlier, we observed that one of America's foremost political scientists, Harold Lasswell, defined "politics" as "who gets what, when, and how." One of America's foremost economists, Paul Samuelson, defined "economics" as "deciding what shall be produced, how, and for whom."[1] The similarity between these definitions is based on the fact that both the political system and the economic system provide society with means for deciding about the production and distribution of goods and services. The political system involves *collective* decisions—choices made by communities, states, or nations—and relies on government *coercion* through laws, regulations, taxes, and so on to implement them. A **free-market economic system** involves *individual* decisions—choices made by millions of consumers and thousands of firms—and relies on *voluntary exchange* through buying, selling, borrowing, contracting, and so on to implement them. Both politics and markets function to transform popular demands into goods and services, to allocate costs, and to distribute goods and services.

One of the key questions in any society is how much to rely on government versus the marketplace to provide goods and services. This question of the proper relationship between governments and markets—that is, between politics and economics—is the subject of **political economy.**

## ASK YOURSELF ABOUT POLITICS

**1** Do you believe that government efforts to manage the economy usually make things better or worse?
Better ⬤    Worse ⬤

**2** Do you believe that the government should spend more during recessions to ease economic hardship even if it means larger government deficits?
Yes ⬤    No ⬤

**3** If Congress could reduce government spending, do you think the money saved should be used to balance the budget rather than to cut taxes?
Yes ⬤    No ⬤

**4** Should the government spend more money for education even if doing so increases the budget deficit?
Yes ⬤    No ⬤

**5** Do you believe that all wage earners should pay the same percentage of their income as taxes (a flat tax)?
Yes ⬤    No ⬤

**6** Would you favor ending all deductions, including those for charitable contributions, if income taxes could be lowered to no more than 17 percent?
Yes ⬤    No ⬤

**7** Is it fair for the current generation of voters to increase government debt and pass it on to future generations?
Yes ⬤    No ⬤

What is the proper relationship between government and the economy? How much influence should the government exercise over the production and distribution of goods and services in this country?

*The founder of classical economics, Scottish economist Adam Smith (1723–90), was a strong proponent of laissez-faire and free markets. He argued that government should keep out of economic matters as much as possible, relying instead on the "invisible hand" of the marketplace to rectify temporary economic problems such as recessions and inflation.*

**Free-market economic system:** An economic system in which individual choices by consumers and firms determine what shall be produced, how much, and for whom; this economic system relies on voluntary exchanges of buying and selling.

**Political economy:** The study of relationships among politics and economics and governments and markets.

**Inflation:** A rise in the *general level* of prices, not just the prices of some products.

**Recession:** A decline in the general level of economic activity, usually coupled with an

The United States is primarily a free-market economy, but the federal government strongly influences economic activity.

## COMPETING ECONOMIC THEORIES

Various economic theories compete for preeminence as guides to government involvement in a free-market economy. These theories attempt to explain the forces that influence *demand*—the willingness and ability of individuals and firms to purchase goods and services (everything from cars and houses to dry cleaning and restaurant meals)—and *supply*—the willingness and ability of other individuals and firms to produce these products. Economic theories also attempt to explain the forces that influence the economy as a whole and can result in inflation, recession, or growth. **Inflation** is a rise in the *general level* of prices, not just the prices of some products. **Recession** is a decline in the general level of economic activity, usually coupled with an increase in unemployment. *Growth* is an increase in the nation's total economic output, usually measured by the real (inflation-adjusted) gross domestic product.

*Classical Theory*   **Classical economic theory** views a market economy as a self-adjusting mechanism that will achieve full employment, maximum productivity, and stable prices if left alone by the government. The rise or fall of prices will influence the decisions of millions of people and will bring into balance the demand for and supply of goods and labor. In recessions, when workers are temporarily unemployed because the supply of workers exceeds the demand, wages (the price of labor) will fall until it again becomes profitable for businesses to have more workers at lower wages and thus to end unemployment. Similarly, when the demand for goods and services falls, business inventories will rise and firms will reduce prices (often through rebates, sales, and so forth) until demand picks up again. In inflationary periods, general increases in prices reduce demand and automatically bring it back into line with supply, unless government interferes. In the classical economic view, inflation is caused by government expansion of the money supply; when too much money is available in bank loans and currency, both prices and wages rise. But if government keeps the money supply stable, increases in the demand for money will push up interest rates, thus raising the "price" of money. An increase in interest rates will reduce the demand for money and cool inflation. In short, classical economic theory relies on the movement of prices, rather than government intervention, to counter both recession and inflation.

*Keynesian Theory*   The Great Depression of the 1930s shattered popular confidence in classical economics. During the 1930s, the unemployment rate in the United States averaged 18 percent, reaching 25 percent in the worst year, 1933. Even in 1936, seven years after the great stock market crash of 1929, unemployment remained at 18 percent of the work force, raising questions about the ability of the market to stabilize itself and ensure high employment and output.

In analyzing this worldwide economic depression, the British economist John Maynard Keynes concluded that economic instability was a product of fluctuations in *demand*. Both unemployment and lower wages reduced the demand for goods. Businesses cut production and laid off workers to adjust for lower demand for

their goods, but cuts and layoffs further reduced demand and accelerated the downward spiral. Reducing interest rates would not necessarily encourage businesses to borrow money to build new plants and create new jobs if there was no demand for their products. The economy would not expand unless demand increased. **Keynesian economic theory** suggested that the economy could fall into a recession and stay there unless government added to demand by spending more money itself and lowering taxes. This combination of spending more and taxing less means that, during a recession, government would not be able to balance its budget. Rather, during recessions government would have to incur deficits to add to demand, spending more than it receives in revenue. To counter inflationary trends, governments should take just the opposite steps. During inflations, when strong consumer demand pushes up prices, government should cut its own spending, raise taxes, and run a surplus in the budget, thus reducing overall demand.

*Employment Act of 1946*   Keynesian ideas dominated U.S. economic policy making for nearly a half century. These ideas were written into the Employment Act of 1946, specifically pledging the federal government "to promote maximum employment production and purchasing power" through its taxing and spending policies. This act created the Council of Economic Advisers to "develop and recommend to the president national economic policies" and required the president to submit to Congress an annual economic report assessing the state of the economy.

While most economists endorsed government deficits to counter recessions, it became increasingly clear over time that politicians were unable to end deficit spending after recessions were over. Politicians were more fearful of unemployment than of inflation, and since Keynesian theory portrayed these events as opposite ends of a seesaw, many politicians saw every reason to continue deficit spending. Even during inflation, politicians failed to enact the spending cuts and tax increases recommended by Keynes.

**Classical economic theory:** A school of economic thought that focuses on economic efficiency and presumes that the forces of demand and supply will automatically adjust to restore stable prices after a brief period of inflation.

**Keynesian economic theory:** A school of economic thought that calls for government intervention to control recessions and inflation; government is to increase spending and incur deficits to prop up demand during a recession and curtail spending and take in a tax surplus to reduce demand during inflationary periods.

Other problems with Keynesian economic analysis surfaced in the 1970s, when unemployment and inflation occurred simultaneously, in defiance of Keynesian theory. Forty years of Keynesian efforts to manipulate aggregate demand had produced **stagflation:** inflation and high interest rates combined with unemployment and a stagnant economy. The nation experienced runaway "double-digit" (over 10 percent) annual inflation rates and a low rate of economic growth. President Ronald Reagan dubbed Keynesian economics "the failed policies of the past."

*Supply-Side Economics*  **Supply-side economic theory** rejects Keynesianism's short-term manipulation of demand. Instead, supply-siders argue that the key is economic growth, which increases the overall supply of goods and services and thereby holds down prices, thus reducing or ending inflation altogether. More important, everyone's standard of living is improved by the availability of more goods and services at stable prices. Economic growth even increases government revenues over the long run, through additional income tax contributions.

Most supply-side economists believe that the free market is better equipped than government to bring about lower prices and more supplies of what people need and want. Government, they argue, is the problem, not the solution. Government taxing, spending, and monetary policies have promoted immediate consumption instead of investment in the future. High taxes penalize hard work, creativity, investment, and savings. Government should provide tax incentives to encourage investment and savings; tax rates should be lowered to encourage work and enterprise. Overall government spending should be held in check. Government regulations should be minimized in order to increase productivity and growth. Overall, government should act to stimulate production and supply rather than demand and consumption.

President Ronald Reagan frequently expressed his support of supply-side ideas, and he actually succeeded in getting Congress to lower federal tax rates during the 1980s. The economy grew, unemployment declined, and inflation was brought under control. But the Reagan Administration failed to cut government spending; in fact, government spending continued to increase during the Reagan years, especially defense spending. Tax cuts did not result in greatly increased revenues as predicted by some supply-side economists. Reagan had promised a balanced budget, but it was impossible to cut taxes, increase defense spending, and maintain Social Security and other popular domestic spending programs without increasing the federal deficit. Indeed, during the Reagan-Bush years the federal government ran the largest peacetime deficits in history.[2]

*Monetarist Economics*  Keynesian theory recommended not only changes in government spending and taxation to speed up or slow down demand but also changes in the money supply. During a recession, Keynes recommended expanding the supply of money available to individuals and businesses by easing bank reserve requirements (the amount banks are legally required to keep on hand and so cannot lend out) and lowering bank interest rates. Similarly, during inflationary periods, government was supposed to tighten the supply of money by increasing bank reserve requirements and increasing interest rates. Thus by increasing or decreasing the overall supply of money, government could "fine-tune" the economy.

However, **monetarist economic theory** contends that economic stability can only be achieved by holding the rate of monetary growth to the same rate as

**Stagflation:** The simultaneous occurrence of high rates of inflation and unemployment.

**Supply-side economic theory:** A school of economic thought that focuses on economic growth and argues that government taxing and spending are detrimental to such growth.

**Monetarist economic theory:** A school of economic thought that argues that economic stability can be achieved only by holding the rate of monetary growth to the rate of the economy's own growth.

CHAPTER 16 • POLITICS AND THE ECONOMY

the economy's own growth. Led by Nobel-Prize-winning economist Milton Friedman (see *People in Politics:* "Milton Friedman, In Defense of Free Markets"), monetarists challenge the view that manipulating the money supply can effectively influence economic activity. They argue that, over the long run, real income depends on actual economic output. Increasing the supply of money faster than output only creates inflation. The value of each dollar declines because there is more money to buy the same amount of goods. In short, monetarists believe that government tinkering with the money supply is the problem, not the solution.

*Clinton's Economic Policies*   The recession of the early 1990s, coupled with continuing budget deficits, fueled Bill Clinton's campaign for the presidency. Clinton initially espoused "neo-liberal" ideals (see Chapter 2) about the government's responsibility to stimulate economic growth through "investment in" (spending on) human capital—education and skill training for workers, technology advance-

## PEOPLE IN POLITICS

## Milton Friedman, In Defense of Free Markets

Economist Milton Friedman is perhaps the world's most influential spokesperson on behalf of free-market economics. He has spent a lifetime arguing that free markets are indispensable for human freedom and dignity. In 1976, Friedman was awarded a Nobel Prize in economics for his work in monetary policy.

Friedman was born in Brooklyn, New York, the son of working-class immigrants who stressed the importance of education. Young Friedman was an excellent high school student who went on to major in economics at Rutgers University, where he worked his way through college with a number of odd jobs. Upon graduation in 1932, Friedman was awarded a scholarship to attend graduate school at the University of Chicago. After earning his M.A. in economics, he worked in Washington, D.C., at various posts before returning to Columbia University for his Ph.D. in 1943. In 1946, he joined the faculty at the University of Chicago.

In his book *Studies in the Quantity Theory of Money* (1956) and in testimony before the Joint

Congressional Economic Committee, Friedman argued against the prevailing economic philosophy of John Maynard Keynes and its prescription of increased government borrowing and spending to stimulate the economy. Friedman contended that a gradual, steady, continuous rate of increase in the money supply would be the best policy for achieving stable economic growth. Friedman and other economists who support this theory are known as *monetarists*.

In Friedman's view, the chief cause of recession and inflation is fluctuation in the nation's money supply. In an influential book, *A Monetary History of the United States* (1963), Friedman presented extensive historical evidence of the effect of money supply on the economic health of the nation. But Friedman's most widely read works are his cogent defenses of individual freedom and dignity. In *Capitalism and Freedom* (1962), he argued convincingly that free markets are essential to individual freedom and that government intervention in the marketplace inevitably curtails individual liberty and substitutes the judgment of a privileged few for the decisions of the people. In his television series *Free to Choose*, he brought his free-market ideas to a wide audience. According to Friedman, "The preservation of freedom requires limiting narrowly the role of government and placing primary reliance on private property, free markets and voluntary arrangements."

ment, especially the "information highway" (computer network communications), and infrastructure development (roads, bridges, ports, airports, etc.). But these ideas all required more government spending, even while annual federal deficits remained very high. In his first year in office, Clinton pushed a major federal tax increase through a Democratic-controlled Congress (see "Tax Politics" later in this chapter), but huge federal deficits remained. These deficits prevented Clinton from pursuing a policy of more active government intervention in the economy. And the election of a Republican-controlled Congress in 1994 forced Clinton to think of how to cut rather than expand government spending. He vetoed a Republican plan to balance the federal budget by 2002, but presented his own proposal to do so "while continuing to invest in the American people."

## ECONOMIC DECISION MAKING

National **fiscal policy** focuses on the taxing, spending, and borrowing activities of the national government. Economic policy making takes place within the same system of separated powers and checks and balances that governs all federal policy making (see "Separation of Powers and Checks and Balances" in Chapter 3), with both the Congress and the president sharing responsibility for economic policy. Within the executive branch, responsibility for economic policy is divided among the White House, the Office of Management and Budget, the Treasury Department, the Council of Economic Advisers, and the powerful and independent Federal Reserve Board.

*Congress and the President*    The Constitution of the United States places all taxing, borrowing, and spending powers in the hands of Congress. Article I grants Congress the "Power To lay and collect Taxes, Duties, Imposts and Excises, to pay the Debts and provide for the common Defence and general Welfare of the United States," and "to borrow Money on the Credit of the United States." It also declares that "No Money shall be drawn from the Treasury, but in Consequence of Appropriations made by Law." For nearly 150 years the power to spend was interpreted in a limited fashion: Congress could only spend money to perform powers specifically enumerated in Article I, Section 8, of the Constitution. But the Supreme Court has since ruled that the phrase "to pay the Debts and provide for the common Defence and general Welfare" may be broadly interpreted to authorize congressional spending for any purpose that serves the general welfare. Thus today there are no constitutional limits on Congress's spending power. Congress's borrowing power has always been unlimited constitutionally; and as yet there is no constitutional requirement for a balanced budget.

The Constitution gives the president no formal powers over taxing and spending or borrowing, stating only that the president "shall . . . recommend to [Congress's] Consideration such Measures as he shall judge necessary and expedient" (Article II, Section 3). From this meager constitutional grant of power, however, presidents have gradually acquired leadership over national economic policy. The principal instrument of executive economic policy making is the Budget of the United States Government, which the president submits annually to Congress. The budget sets forth the president's recommendations for spending for the forthcoming fiscal year; revenue estimates, based on existing taxes or recommendations for new or increased tax levels; and estimates of projected deficits and the

**Fiscal policy:** Economic policies involving taxing, spending, and deficit levels.

need for borrowing when, as is almost always the case of late, spending recommendations exceed revenue estimates (see Figure 12-3, "The Budgetary Process," in Chapter 12 for more detail).

*The President's Economic Team*    The president's recommendations to Congress regarding taxing, spending, and borrowing, are influenced by advice received from three sources:

1.  The Office of Management and Budget (OMB), which is responsible for preparing the Budget of the United States Government, exerts a powerful influence on the expenditure side of the budget. OMB supervises the year-long process of checking, reviewing, and modifying the budget requests of every federal department and agency.

2.  The Department of the Treasury and the secretary of the treasury have the principal responsibility for estimating revenues and, if requested by the president, for drawing up new tax proposals and forecasting how much revenue they might produce. The Treasury Department is also responsible for managing the nation's huge national debt—the result of its cumulative annual deficits. The Treasury must continually sell **government bonds** to banks and other investors, both foreign and domestic, in order to cover payments on previous deficits as well to fund current deficits. In doing so, the Treasury Department determines interest rates on federal bonds, and it pays out interest charges on the national debt—charges that now amount to over 15 percent of all federal spending.

3.  The Council of Economic Advisers (CEA), which forecasts economic conditions and recommends economic policies, is composed of three professional economists and a small staff. In theory, the CEA gives the president unbiased forecasts of economic trends and impartial analyses of economic issues. It does so principally in the annual Economic Report of the President, which the CEA prepares. But since the president chooses the members of the CEA, it often produces economic reports that reflect the president's thinking.

*The Federal Reserve Board (the Fed)*    Most economically advanced democracies have central banks whose principal responsibility is to regulate the supply of money, both currency in circulation and bank deposits. And most of these democracies have found it best to remove this responsibility from the direct control of elected politicians. Politicians everywhere are sorely tempted to inflate the supply of money in order to fund projects and programs with newly created money instead of new taxes. Nations pay for this approach with a general rise in prices and a reduction in goods and services available to private firms and individuals—inflation. Indeed, nations whose control of the money supply has fallen victim to irresponsible governments have experienced inflation rates of 500 to 1,000 percent per year, which is to say that their money became worthless.

The Federal Reserve System of the United States is largely independent of either the president or Congress. Its independent status is a result not only of law but also of its structure. It is run by a seven-member board of governors who are appointed by the president, with the consent of the Senate, for fourteen-year terms. Members may not be removed from the board except for "cause"; no

**Government bonds:**
Certificates of indebtedness that pay interest and promise repayment on a future date.

**Federal Reserve Board (the Fed):** An independent agency of the executive branch of the federal government charged with overseeing the nation's monetary policy.

member has ever been removed since the creation of the board in 1913. The board's chair serves only a four-year term, but the chair's term overlaps that of the president, so that new presidents cannot immediately name their own chair (see *People in Politics:* "Alan Greenspan, Inflation Fighter at the Fed").

The task of the Fed is to regulate the money supply and by so doing to help avoid both inflation and recession. The Fed oversees the operation of the nation's twelve Federal Reserve Banks, which actually issue the nation's currency, called "Federal Reserve Notes." The Federal Reserve Banks are banker's banks; they do not directly serve private citizens or firms. They hold the deposits, or "reserves,"

## PEOPLE IN POLITICS

# Alan Greenspan, Inflation Fighter at the Fed

Economist Alan Greenspan was first appointed chair of the Federal Reserve Board in 1987 by President Ronald Reagan. Today, Greenspan must accommodate monetary policy to the Clinton Administration's taxing and spending policies to ensure a healthy economy.

Born in New York City, Alan Greenspan studied music at the prestigious Julliard School and enjoyed a brief but successful career as a professional saxophone player in a big swing band before returning to the classroom at New York University. He received an M.A. in economics in 1950 under the tutelage of Arthur F. Burns, who served as chair of the Federal Reserve from 1970 to 1978. After graduation, Greenspan formed his own economic consulting company, Townsend-Greenspan, which provided economic forecasts for some of America's largest corporations. In his spare time, Greenspan completed his Ph.D. at New York University and became a fan of the social philosopher and writer Ayn Rand. Greenspan embraced Rand's vision of a society in which every person could realize his or her own potential in any chosen field without government interference or regulation.

Greenspan began his public service in the Nixon Administration, serving on commissions and task forces, including the Commission on an All-Volunteer Armed Force. In 1974, President Nixon appointed Greenspan to chair the Council of Economic Advisers, a position Greenspan continued to hold under President Gerald Ford. When the Carter Administration came to Washington in 1977, Greenspan returned to running his private company.

In the early 1980s, Fed chair Paul Volker instituted a tight money policy that ultimately brought down the high rates of inflation that had plagued the nation for most of the 1970s. After initially claiming credit for what was really Volker's success in reducing inflation, the Reagan Administration, especially Secretary of the Treasury James Baker (later George Bush's secretary of state), eventually complained that Volker's anti-inflationary policies were too stringent. In August 1987, the Democrat Volker handed in his resignation and Reagan nominated Greenspan to follow him.

Like Reagan, Greenspan opposed higher taxes, but what the president had hoped would be a loyal Republican soldier often acted independently and disagreed with the administration over expanding the money supply. Greenspan's management of the Fed has been generally well received, and he has earned credibility with his fellow economists by avoiding the Washington political game. He is credited for his quick reaction to the stock market crash on October 19, 1987, when he ensured that Federal Reserve Banks would have enough cash on hand to prevent panic following the record drop in stock prices. During the 1991 recession, Greenspan pushed interest rates down to a twenty-year low and cut required Federal Reserve funds in half in order to ease credit. As independent as the Fed itself, he has frequently criticized presidents and the Congress regarding the huge federal deficits. In 1996 President Clinton nominated Greenspan for a third term as Fed chairman.

of banks; lend money to banks at "discount rates" that the Fed determines; buy and sell U.S. Government Treasury bonds; and assure regulatory compliance by private banks and protection of depositors against fraud. The Fed determines the reserve requirements of banks and otherwise monitors the health of the banking industry. The Fed also plays an important role in clearing checks throughout the banking system.

The Fed's influence over the economy is mainly through **monetary policy**— increasing or decreasing the supply of money and hence largely determining interest rates. When inflation threatens, the Fed typically acts to limit ("tighten") the supply of money and raise interest rates by (1) raising the reserve requirement of banks and thereby reducing the amount of money they have to loan out; or (2) raising the discount rate and thereby the cost of borrowing by banks; or (3) selling off government bonds to banks and others in "open market operations," thereby reducing the funds banks can lend to individuals and businesses. When economic slowdowns threaten, the Fed typically acts to expand ("ease") the money supply and lower interest rates by taking the opposite of each action described above.

Economic forecasting is risky business. Not even the best economists can always forecast whether the economy will expand, stagnate, or contract over the next six to eighteen months. Indeed, because there is always some lag between economic activity and the reporting of it in government statistics, economists are not even certain how the economy is performing at any given moment. Uncertainties open the way for political considerations to bias forecasts and hence influence recommendations for monetary policy.

As the economy grows, the money supply is generally expanded. But if the money supply expands more rapidly than the supply of goods and services, the result is inflation. In contrast, if the money supply expands too slowly, interest rates rise; and new businesses, home buyers, and consumers are restricted in their borrowing and spending, creating a drag on the economy. The drag may even precipitate a recession if "tight money" persists over time. In short, in Fed policy making, timing is everything.

While the Fed makes monetary policy, voters typically hold the president responsible for recessions. Hence the chief executive frequently tries to persuade ("jawbone") the independent Fed into lowering interest rates, especially in an election year, believing that a temporary stimulus to help win the election is worth whatever inflationary effects it might create after the election.[3] Congress, too, is usually aligned on the side of "easy" money. But Fed members are mainly bankers and economists who understand the threats posed by inflation; so are the members of the Federal Advisory Council, presidents of the twelve Federal Reserve Banks who advise the Fed. Thus tension frequently arises between the Fed, with its concern about inflation, and the president and Congress, with their concern about recession.

When the Fed deviates from the desires of the president and Congress for increases in the money supply and lower interest rates, the Fed's independence often comes under attack. Congress frequently threatens to curtail the independence of the Fed by shortening the terms of members or otherwise bringing them under the direction of the president or Congress. Despite these attempts to intimidate the Fed into abandoning its own judgment and following the lead of the president and Congress, over the years the Fed has established itself as a strong independent guardian of the nation's money supply.

**Monetary policy:** Economic policies involving the money supply and interest rates.

# THE PERFORMANCE
# OF THE AMERICAN ECONOMY

Underlying the power of nations and the well-being of their citizens is the strength of their economy—their total productive capacity. The United States produces more than $7 trillion worth of goods and services in a single year for its 265 million people—more than $25,000 worth of output for every person.

*Economic Growth*  **Gross domestic product (GDP)** is a widely used measure of the performance of the economy.[4] GDP is a nation's total production of goods and services for a single year valued in terms of market prices. It is the sum of all the goods and services that people have been willing to pay for, from wheat production to bake sales, from machine tools to maid service, from aircraft manufacturing to bus rides, from automobiles to chewing gum. GDP counts only final purchases of goods and services (that is, it ignores the purchase of steel by car makers until it is sold as a car) to avoid double counting in the production process. GDP also excludes financial transactions (such as the sale of bonds and stocks) and income transfers (such as Social Security, welfare, and pension payments) that do not add to the production of goods and services. Although GDP is expressed in current dollar prices, it is often recalculated in constant dollar terms to reflect real values over time, adjusting for the effect of inflation. GDP estimates are prepared each quarter by the U.S. Department of Commerce; these figures are widely reported and closely watched by the business and financial community.

Growth in real (constant dollar) GDP measures the performance of the overall economy. Economic recessions and recoveries are measured as fluctuations or swings in the growth of GDP. For example, a recession is usually defined as negative GDP growth in two or more consecutive quarters. Historical data reveal that periods of economic growth have traditionally been followed by periods of contraction, giving rise to the notion of *economic cycles*. Prior to 1950, economic cycles in the United States produced extreme ups and downs, with double-digit swings in real GDP. In recent decades, however, economic fluctuations have been more moderate. The United States still experiences economic cycles, but many economists believe that countercyclical government fiscal and monetary policy has succeeded in achieving greater stability (see Figure 16-1).

Voters today appear to hold the incumbent president more responsible than ever for *any* economic contraction, as George Bush learned to his sorrow in 1992. The nation experienced a modest recession in 1991 and a weak recovery in 1992. Bush correctly claimed that the 1991 recession was not very deep by historical standards and that the nation was already on the road to recovery before the election. But media reporting of continual plant closings and voters' concerns that their own jobs were not secure outweighed GDP growth figures on election day. President Clinton has enjoyed modest but continuing economic growth.

*Unemployment*  From a political standpoint, the **unemployment rate** may be the most important measure of the economy's performance. The unemployment rate is the percentage of the civilian labor force who are looking for work or waiting to return to or begin a job. Unemployment is different from not working; people who have retired or who attend school and people who do not work because of sickness, disability, or unwillingness are not considered part of the

**Gross domestic product (GDP):** A measure of economic performance in terms of the nation's total production of goods and services for a single year, valued in terms of market prices.

**Unemployment rate:** The percentage of the civilian labor force who are not working but who are looking for work or waiting to return to or to begin a job.

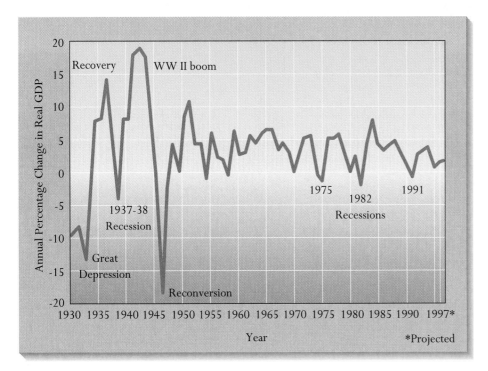

FIGURE 16-1    **Economic Growth**
*The tendency for periods of economic growth to alternate with periods of contraction has led to the concept of the business cycle—the idea that at least some fluctuation is normal, even healthy, helping to keep the economy growing in the long run by keeping prices from getting too high. In recent decades, government intervention in the economy appears to have succeeded in reducing, although not in altogether eliminating, the depths of recessions to which the nation was formerly prone.*

*Source:* U.S. Department of Commerce, *Survey of Current Busines* (Washington, D.C.: Government Printing Office, published quarterly).

labor force and so are not counted as unemployed. People who are so discouraged about finding a job that they have quit looking for work are also not counted in the official unemployment rate. The unemployed do include people who have been terminated from their last job (34 percent) or temporarily laid off from work (15 percent), as well as people who voluntarily quit (15 percent), and those who have recently entered (10 percent) or reentered (27 percent) the labor force and are now seeking employment.

The unemployment rate is measured each month by the U.S. Department of Labor. It does so by contacting a random sample of more than 50,000 households in many locations throughout the country. Trained interviewers ask a variety of questions to determine how many (if any) members of the household are either working or have a job but did not work at it because of sickness, vacation, strike, or personal reasons (employed); or whether they have no job but are available for work and actively seeking a job (unemployed). The unemployment rate fluctuates with the business cycle, reflecting recessions and recoveries (see Figure 16-2). Generally, unemployment lags behind GDP growth, going down only after the recovery has begun.

*Inflation*    The term *inflation* refers to a rise in the *general level* of prices for all goods and services. (Even when the general level of prices is stable, some prices will rise or fall.) Inflation erodes the value of the dollar because higher prices mean that the same dollars can now purchase fewer goods and services. Thus inflation erodes the value of savings, reduces the incentive to save, and hurts people who are living on fixed-dollar amounts of income. When banks and investors anticipate inflation, they raise interest rates on loans in order to cover the anticipated lower value of repayment dollars. Higher interest rates, in turn, make it

**FIGURE 16-2**

**Unemployment and Inflation**

*Economic growth during the 1980s lowered both the inflation and unemployment rates, freeing the nation from the stagflation (combined inflation and high unemployment) that had characterized much of the 1970s. Unemployment rose during the recession of 1991, while inflation remained in check. Recent years have brought good economic news—low unemployment and low inflation.*

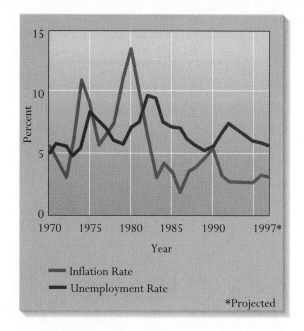

*Source: Budget of the United States Government, 1997.*

more difficult for new or expanding businesses to borrow money, for home buyers to acquire mortgages, and for consumers to make purchases on credit. Thus, inflation and high interest rates slow economic growth; in addition, government spending has an enormous effect on the economy.

# "UNCONTROLLABLE" GOVERNMENT SPENDING AND FEDERAL BUDGET PRIORITIES

The expenditures of all governments in the United States—federal, state, and local governments combined—amount to more than 35 percent of GDP (see *Up Close:* "How Big Is Government and What Does It Do?" in Chapter 1). The federal government itself spends more than $1.6 trillion each year—more than 23 percent of GDP.

*Just how bad can inflation get? Between the two world wars, inflation in Germany reached such levels that the nation's currency was often weighed, rather than counted, in order to speed transactions.*

Much of the growth of federal government spending over the years is attributed to *uncontrollables* in the federal budget. Uncontrollables are budget items committed to by past policies of Congress that are not easily changed in annual budget making. Sources of uncontrollable spending include:

- *Entitlement programs:* Federal programs that provide classes of people with a legally enforceable right to benefits are called **entitlement programs.** Entitlement programs account for more than half of all federal spending, including Social Security, welfare, Medicare and Medicaid, food stamps, federal employees' retirement pensions, and veterans' benefits (see *Up Close:* "Transfers and Entitlements Drive Government Spending"). These entitlements are benefits that past Congresses have pledged the federal government to pay. Entitlements are not really uncontrollable. Congress can always amend the basic laws that established them, but doing so is politically difficult and might be regarded as abandonment of a public trust. As more people become "entitled" to government benefits—for example, as more people reach retirement ages and claim Social Security benefits—federal spending increases.

- *Indexing of benefits:* Another reason that spending increases each year is that Congress has authorized automatic increases in benefits to match inflation. Benefits under such programs as Social Security, Supplemental Security Income, food stamps, and veteran's pensions are tied to the Consumer Price Index. This **indexing** pushes up the cost of entitlement programs each year, even when the number of recipients stays the same, thus running counter to federal efforts to restrain inflation. Moreover, because the Consumer Price Index includes interest payments for new housing and the cost of new cars and appliances, it generally overestimates the needs of older recipients for cost-of-living increases.

- *Increasing costs of in-kind benefits:* Rises in the cost of major **in-kind (noncash) benefits,** particularly the medical costs of Medicaid and Medicare, also guarantee growth in federal spending. These in-kind benefit programs have risen faster in cost than cash benefit programs.

- *Interest on the national debt:* Interest payments have grown rapidly as a percentage of all federal spending. The federal government has a long history of deficits. Not since 1969 has the federal government had a **balanced budget.** The result is a **national debt** of over $5 trillion. Each year the deficit increases, interest payments go up. Interest payments also rise with increases in interest rates. Interest payments now make up more than 15 percent of total federal spending.

- *Backdoor spending and loan guarantees:* Some federal spending does not appear on the budget. For example, spending by the Postal Service is not included in the federal budget. No clear rule explains why some agencies are in the budget and others are not, but "off-budget" agencies have the same economic effects as other government agencies. Another form of **backdoor spending** is found in government-guaranteed loans. Initially government guarantees for loans—Federal Housing Administration (FHA) housing loans, Guaranteed Student Loans, veterans' loans, and so forth—do not require federal money. The government merely promises to repay the loan if the borrower fails to do so. Yet these loans create an obligation against the government.

**Entitlement programs:** Social welfare programs that provide classes of people with legally enforceable rights to benefits.

**Indexing:** The tying of benefit levels in social welfare programs to the general price level.

**In-kind (noncash) benefits:** Benefits of a social welfare program that are not cash payments, including free medical care, subsidized housing, and food stamps.

**Balanced budget:** A government budget in which expenditures and revenues are equal, so that no deficit or surplus exists.

**National debt:** The total current debt owed by the national government, produced by deficit spending over many years.

**Backdoor spending:** Spending by agencies of the federal government whose operations are not included in the federal budget.

# Transfers and Entitlements Drive Government Spending

Traditionally, governments in the United States have provided for national defense, police and fire protection, roads, education, and other public goods and services. These "public goods" cannot readily be provided by private markets because if one individual or firm purchased them, everyone else would get a "free ride"—that is, would use them without paying. Government involvement in these areas is not surprising. But these traditional public functions are *not* responsible for the growth of government in recent years.

*Income Transfers*   Recent expansions in the relative size of government are almost exclusively the result of increased governmental involvement in "income transfer" activities. The government has become a redistributor of income from one group to another—from the working population to retirees, from the employed to the unemployed, from the taxpayers to the disadvantaged (such as low-income households with dependent children). In 1955, income transfers were about 5 percent of the GDP.

Since the mid-1970s, however, the government has been redistributing about 15 percent of total output away from producers to recipients. Most of the growth in transfers has taken place at the federal level.

*Entitlements*   Entitlement programs account for more than half of all federal spending. Virtually everyone who has examined the federal government's budget—economists, politicians, and private citizens—understands that "capping entitlements" is the only way to slow the growth of federal spending. And virtually everyone agrees that reducing federal deficits requires tax increases, spending reductions, or some combination of both. The problem is the political gridlock that has arisen over whether to rely principally on tax increases or spending reductions, and if spending reductions are to be made, over what programs will be reduced or "capped."

Note that most entitlement payments do not go to the poor. The largest share of entitlements—Social Security, Medicare, veterans' and federal retirement—goes to retirees. These three programs alone account for two-thirds of all entitlement payments. Payments to the poor and unemployed—welfare, Medicaid, and unemployment insurance—account for less than one-third of federal entitlement spending.

**Entitlements in the Federal Budget**

|  | *Billions of Dollars* | *Percentage* |
|---|---|---|
| Entitlement, Total | $982 | 60.1% |
| Social Security | 368 | 22.5 |
| Medicare | 190 | 11.6 |
| Medicaid | 120 | 7.3 |
| Federal retirement | 71 | 4.3 |
| Welfare entitlement | 166 | 10.1 |
| Veterans' benefits | 40 | 2.4 |
| Unemployment insurance | 27 | 1.6 |
| Defense | 259 | 15.8 |
| Domestic | 141 | 8.6 |
| Interest | 238 | 14.6 |
| International | 15 | 0.9 |
| Total Federal Spending | 1,635 | 100.0 |

*Source: Budget of the United States Government, 1997.*

CHAPTER 16 • POLITICS AND THE ECONOMY

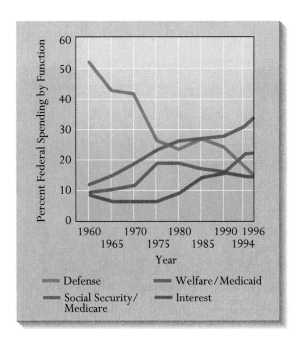

FIGURE 16-3 **Changing Federal Budget Priorities**

*Federal spending for entitlement programs (Social Security and Medicare for the aged, welfare and Medicaid for the poor) has grown rapidly over the years. In the 1960s, defense spending consumed more federal dollars and a larger share of the federal budget than any other program, but today, spending for entitlement programs far exceeds defense spending, in both dollar amounts and percentage of the federal budget.*

*Federal Budget Priorities*    Federal budget priorities have changed markedly over the last several decades. Figure 16-3 shows federal budget outlays over time for major programs as percentages of the total federal budget. Note how spending for national defense has declined very rapidly as a percentage of total federal spending. In contrast, spending for Social Security, welfare, and Medicare has grown very rapidly. Expenditures for these entitlement programs account for more than half of all federal spending today and may well keep growing, not only in dollars but also in shares of the federal budget. Medical costs are the fastest growing sector of the federal budget. Moreover, interest costs will continue to grow unless the president and Congress succeed in eliminating annual federal deficits.

## THE DEBT BURDEN

The U.S. federal government has incurred a **deficit** in every year since 1969—that is, its expenditures have exceeded its revenues (see Figure 16-4 ). The accumulated national debt is over $5 trillion, or $18,000 for every man, woman, and child in the nation. (If the federal government continues to incur annual deficits of $200 billion each year, it will add $1 trillion to the nation's total debt in five years.) This government debt is owed mostly to U.S. banks and financial institutions and private citizens who buy Treasury bonds. Only about 13 percent of the debt is owed to foreign banks and individuals. As old debt comes due, the U.S. Treasury Department sells new bonds to pay off the old; that is, it continues to "roll over" or "float" the debt. Despite its size in dollars, the debt today is smaller as a percentage of GDP than at some periods in U.S. history. For example, to pay the costs of fighting World War II, the U.S. government ran up a debt equivalent to over 100 percent of GDP. The current $5 trillion debt, though the highest in history in dollar terms, is equal to only about 68 percent of GDP (see Figure 16-5).

**Deficit:** An imbalance in the annual federal budget in which spending exceeds revenues.

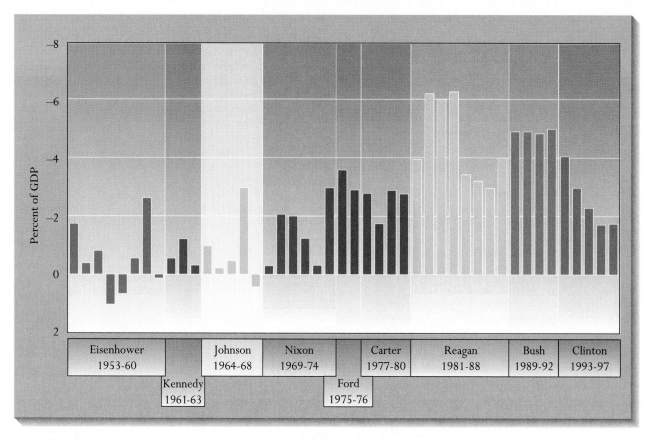

**FIGURE 16-4** **Deficits through the Years**

*This figure shows annual federal deficits as percentages of the GDP. Note that the federal government has incurred deficits every year since 1969, under both Republican and Democratic presidential administrations. President Bill Clinton's deficit reduction efforts reduced the size of annual federal deficits somewhat from the Reagan-Bush years. But without additional budget cutting by the president and Congress, deficits of $100 to $200 billion or more per year (2–3 percent of GDP) will continue indefinitely. Both the president and Congress have pledged to end annual federal deficits by the year 2002.*

**Default:** Refusal or inability to pay a debt.

The ability to float such a huge debt depends on public confidence in the United States government—confidence that it will continue to pay interest on its debt, that it will pay off the principal of bonds when they come due, and that the value of the bonds will not decline over time because of inflation.

*Default and Hyperinflation*   No one expects the United States ever to **default** on its debt—that is, to refuse to pay interest or principal when it comes due—although other debt-ridden nations have done so in the past and many threaten to do so today. But there is always the possibility that a future administration in Washington might **monetarize the debt**—that is, simply print currency and use it to pay off bondholders. Such currency would flood the nation and soon become worthless. **Hyperinflation**—annual inflation rates of 100 to 1,000 percent or more—would leave U.S. bondholders with worthless money. Both default and hyperinflation are unlikely, but the existence of a high federal deficit means that such disasters are not unthinkable.

*Interest Burden for Future Generations*   Interest payments on the national debt come from current taxes and so divert money away from *all* other government programs. Even if the federal government manages to balance its current budgets, these payments will remain obligations of the children and grandchildren of the current generation of policy makers and taxpayers. In short, today's high spending and low taxing is shifting the burden of debt from the current generation to future generations.

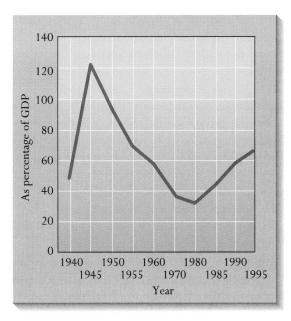

Source: Budget of the United States Government, 1997.

**FIGURE 16-5** **Federal Debt as a Percentage of GNP**
*While the absolute size of the national debt (in noninflation-adjusted dollars) has skyrocketed, it is important to note that as a percentage of GNP, the current debt is much lower than in the period immediately following World War II. At the end of the war in 1945, the total national debt was 122 percent of GNP; in contrast, today's debt is only about 68 percent of GNP.*

**Monetarize a debt:** A system of debt reduction in which a government simply prints more money and uses that money to pay its debts; because such money is more plentiful and thus worth less, inflation (and sometimes hyperinflation) results.

**Hyperinflation:** Annual inflation rates of 100 to 1,000 percent or more.

*Slowing Economic Growth* The huge federal debt and the need to sell even more government bonds each year to cover annual increases in the debt (owing to new deficits) require the U.S. Treasury Department to borrow large amounts of money each year. This money is diverted from the private sector, where it would otherwise be available as loans for starting and expanding businesses, for modernizing industrial plants and equipment, and for financing the purchase of homes, cars, appliances, and other credit items for consumers. In other words, the federal government's borrowing "crowds out" capital markets. The less capital available in the private sector, the more slowly the economy grows.

*Youthful protesters besiege the Washington headquarters of the American Association of Retired Persons, complaining about the huge deficits run up by the older generation—deficits that will burden younger generations with heavy interest payments.*

*Limiting Government Programs*   Continuing government deficits and the increasing costs of interest payments limit the president's and Congress's ability to deal with other problems confronting the nation. Any new spending for health, schools, research, or infrastructure adds to federal deficits and by so doing slows economic growth. Thus if the federal government tries to stimulate the economy by increasing its spending, it simultaneously increases already burdensome deficits, takes more money away from the private sector, and thereby threatens to undo whatever stimulative effect was intended.

*The Politics of Deficits*   Despite all the pious rhetoric about the need to "balance the budget," for decades neither presidents nor Congresses, Democrats nor Republicans, have been willing to reduce expenditures or to raise taxes to balance the budget. Deficit financing appeals to politicians. It allows them to provide high levels of government benefits while avoiding the unpopular step of raising taxes. To be sure, the burden of future interest payments is shifted to young people and future generations. But today's elected politicians know they will be long gone before these burdens are fully realized; their time frame is the next election. Many politicians are reluctant to cross swords with politically active older voters, who are more concerned with generous Social Security and Medicare benefits than with interest payments that will be paid by later generations.

*Washington's Budget Battles*   Occasionally, budget battles have temporarily "shut down" the federal government. The Constitution states that "no money shall be drawn from the Treasury, but in Consequence of Appropriations made by Law" (Art. I, Sec. 9), suggesting that if Congress fails to pass, and the president to sign, appropriations acts, the government must close for lack of funds. But when this has actually occurred, only "nonessential" offices actually have closed. After bitter and prolonged negotiations in 1995 between Democratic President Bill Clinton and Republican congressional leaders Bob Dole and Newt Gingrich, agreement was reached on a pledge to balance the budget by 2002. But battles will continue over how this goal is to be accomplished; and such a pledge does not bind the president or Congress in future years.

## THE TAX BURDEN

The tax burden in the United States is very modest compared to burdens in other advanced democracies (see *Compared to What?* "Tax Burdens in Advanced Democracies"). Federal revenues are derived mainly from (1) individual income taxes, (2) corporate income taxes, (3) Social Security payroll taxes, (4) estate and gift taxes, and (5) excise taxes and custom duties.

*Individual Income Taxes*   The **individual income tax** is the federal government's largest source of revenue (see Figure 16-6). Individual income is now taxed at five rates: 15, 28, 31, 36, and 39.6 percent, with these rising rates geared to increasing income "brackets." These are *marginal rates,* a term that economists use to mean additional. That is, income up to the top of the lowest bracket is taxed at 15 percent, additional income in the next bracket is taxed at 28 percent; up to a top marginal rate of 39.6 percent on income over $250,000. A personal exemption for each taxpayer and dependent together with a standard deduction

**Individual income tax:** Taxes on individuals' wages and other earned income, the primary source of revenue for the U.S. federal government.

# Tax Burdens in Advanced Democracies

Americans complain a lot about taxes. But from a global perspective, overall tax burdens in the United States are relatively low (see figure). Federal, state, and local taxes in the U.S. amount to about 30 percent of the gross domestic product (GDP), slightly below the burden carried by the nation's leading competitors, Japan and Germany. U.S. taxes are well below the burdens imposed in Sweden, Denmark, and other nations with highly developed welfare systems.

Top marginal tax rates in many nations were reduced during the 1980s. For example, the top rate in Great Britain was lowered from 60 to 40 percent, in Japan from 70 to 50 percent, and in Sweden from 80 to 65 percent. Both in the United States and abroad, the notion that excessively high tax rates discourage work, savings, and investment, as well as slow economic growth, won acceptance (though how high is "excessive" is obviously open to different interpretations). Moreover, in a global economy, with increased mobility of individuals and firms, pressures push nations to keep their top tax rates within reasonable limits. Corporations can shift their assets to low-tax jurisdictions, and high personal income tax rates can even threaten a "brain drain" of talented individuals.

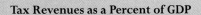

**Tax Revenues as a Percent of GDP**

for married couples and a refundable earned income tax credit ensure that the poorest families pay no income tax. (However, they still must pay Social Security taxes on wages.) Tax brackets, as well as the personal exemption and standard deduction, are indexed annually to protect against inflation.

The income tax is automatically deducted from the paychecks of employees. This "withholding" system is the backbone of the individual income tax. There is no withholding of nonwage income such as dividends on investments, but taxpayers with such income must file a "Declaration of Estimated Taxes" and pay this estimate in quarterly installments. Before April 15 of each year, all income-earning Americans must report their taxable income for the previous year to the Internal Revenue Service on its 1040 Form.

FIGURE 16-6 **Sources of Federal Income**

*Individual income taxes make up the largest portion of the federal government's revenues (43 percent). The government also relies heavily on the second largest source of its revenues, Social Security taxes.*

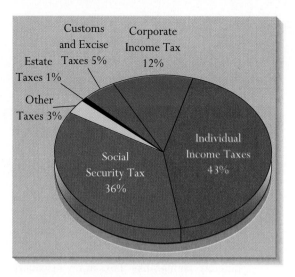

Source: Budget of the United States Government, 1997.

Americans are usually surprised to learn that half of all personal income is *not* taxed. To understand why, we must know how the tax laws distinguish between *adjusted gross income* (an individual's total money income minus expenses incurred in earning that income) and *taxable income* (that part of adjusted gross income subject to taxation). Federal tax rates apply only to *taxable* income.

**Tax expenditures** are tax revenues lost to the federal government because of exemptions, exclusions, deductions, and special treatments in tax laws. Federal government revenues from individual and business income taxes would be substantially higher were it not for special provisions in tax laws that enable taxpayers to avoid paying taxes on often-substantial sums of income. Although each of these "loopholes" supposedly has a larger social goal behind it (for example, the deductibility of mortgage interest is supposed to stimulate the purchases—and construction—of homes, keeping up the value of those assets for current homeowners and keeping the construction industry employed), critics charge that many cost far more than they are worth to society. The major tax expenditures in federal tax law are:

- Personal exemptions
- Deductibility of mortgage interest on homes
- Deductibility of property taxes on first and second homes
- Deferral of capital gains on home sales
- Deductibility of charitable contributions
- Credit for child care expenses
- Exclusion of employer contributions to pension plans and medical insurance
- Exclusion of Social Security benefits
- Exclusion of interest on public-purpose state and local bonds
- Deductibility of state and local income taxes
- Exclusion of income earned abroad
- Accelerated depreciation of machinery, equipment, and structure
- Medical expenses over 7.5 percent of income

**Tax expenditures:** Revenues lost to the federal government because of exemptions, exclusions, deductions, and special-treatment provisions in tax laws.

There is a continual struggle between proponents of special tax exemptions to achieve social goals, and those who believe the tax laws should be simplified and social goals met by direct government expenditures. Much of the political infighting in Washington involves the efforts of interest groups to obtain exemptions, exclusions, deductions, and special treatments in tax laws.[5] Former Congressman Dan Rostenkowski of Chicago, once the chair of the House Ways and Means Committee, which writes the nation's tax laws, admitted:

> We gave oil companies breaks to fuel our oil industry. We gave real estate incentives to build more housing. We sharpened our technology with research and development credits. We gave tax breaks to encourage people to save. We pile one tax benefit on top of another—each one backed with good intention.
>
> Unfortunately it didn't take too long before those with the best accountants and lawyers figured out how to beat the system . . . and the cost of government was shifted to families like those in my neighborhood who don't have the guile to play the game of hide-and-seek with the IRS. . . .
>
> In the end tax reform comes down to a struggle between the narrow interests of the few—and the broad interests of working American families.[6]

*Corporate Income Taxes*    The corporate income tax provides only about 12 percent of the federal government's total revenue. The Tax Reform Act of 1986 reduced the top corporate income tax from 46 to 34 percent (raised to 35 percent in 1993). However, prior to this act, corporations found many ways of reducing their taxable income, often to zero. The result was that many very large and profitable corporations paid little or nothing in taxes. Some of the most notorious of these corporate tax breaks were modified or eliminated in the Tax Reform Act of 1986. Religious, charitable, and educational organizations, as well as labor unions, are exempt from corporate income taxes except for income they may derive from "unrelated business activity."

Who really bears the burden of the corporate income tax? Economists differ over whether the corporate income tax is "shifted" to consumers or whether corporations and their stockholders bear its burden. The evidence on the **incidence**—that is, who actually bears the burden—of this tax is inconclusive.[7]

*Social Security Taxes*    The second largest and the fastest-growing source of federal revenue is the Social Security tax. It is withheld from paychecks as the "FICA" deduction, an acronym that helps to hide the true costs of Social Security from wage earners. To keep up with the rising number of beneficiaries and the higher levels of benefits voted for by Congress, including generous automatic cost-of-living increases each year, the Social Security tax rose to 15.3 percent. Wage income above a certain level is not subject to the Social Security tax.

Taxes collected under FICA are earmarked (by Social Security number) for the account of each taxpayer. Workers thus feel they are receiving benefits as a right rather than as a gift of the government. However, less than 15 percent of the benefits being paid to current recipients of Social Security can be attributed to their prior contributions. Current taxpayers are paying more than 85 percent of the benefits received by current retirees.

Today a majority of taxpayers pay more in Social Security taxes than income taxes. Indeed, combined employer and employee Social Security taxes now amount to nearly $8,500 for each worker at the top of the wage base. If we

**Incidence:** The actual bearer of a tax burden.

**Progressive taxation:** A system of taxation in which higher-income groups pay a larger percentage of their incomes in taxes than do lower-income groups.

**Regressive taxation:** A system of taxation in which lower-income groups pay a larger percentage of their incomes in taxes than do higher-income groups.

**Proportional (flat) taxation:** A system of taxation in which all income groups pay the same percentage of their income in taxes.

assume that the employer's share of the tax actually comes out of wages that would otherwise be paid to the employee, then more than 75 percent of all taxpayers pay more in Social Security taxes than in income taxes.

*Estate and Gift Taxes*    Taxation of property left to heirs is one of the oldest forms of taxation in the world. Federal estate taxes begin on estates of $600,000 and levy a tax of 37 percent on accounts above this level. Because taxes at death otherwise could be avoided by simply giving estates to heirs while the giver is still alive, a federal gift tax is also levied on anyone who gives gifts in excess of $10,000 annually.

*Excise Taxes and Custom Duties*    Federal excise taxes on the consumption of liquor, tobacco, gasoline, telephones, air travel, and other so-called luxury items, together with custom taxes on imports, provide about 5 percent of total federal revenues.

## TAX POLITICS

The politics of taxation centers around the question of who actually bears the heaviest burden of a tax—especially which income groups must devote the largest proportion of their income to taxes. **Progressive taxation** requires high-income groups to pay a larger percentage of their incomes in taxes than low-income groups. **Regressive taxation** takes a larger share of the income of low-income groups. **Proportional (flat) taxation** requires all income groups to pay the same percentage of their income in taxes. Note that the *percentage of income* paid in taxes is the determining factor. Most taxes take more money from the rich than the poor, but a progressive or regressive tax is distinguished by the percentages of income taken from various income groups.

*Protesters demonstrating outside the White House against tax increases. Tax policy has been a volatile issue for both Democrats and Republicans recently, as voters send conflicting messages about their preferences for tax cutting versus budget balancing.*

CHAPTER 16 • POLITICS AND THE ECONOMY

*The Argument for Progressivity*    Progressive taxation is generally defended on the principle of ability to pay; the assumption is that high-income groups can afford to pay a larger percentage of their incomes into taxes at no more of a sacrifice than that required of lower-income groups to devote a smaller proportion of their income to taxation. This assumption is based on what economists call *marginal utility theory* as it applies to money; each additional dollar of income is slightly less valuable to an individual than preceding dollars. For example, a $5,000 increase in the income of an individual already earning $100,000 is much less valuable than a $5,000 increase to an individual earning only $10,000 or to an individual with no income at all. Hence, it is argued that added dollars of income can be taxed at higher rates without violating equitable principles.

*The Argument for Proportionality*    Opponents of progressive taxation generally assert that equity can only be achieved by taxing everyone at the same percentage of their income, regardless of the size of their income (see *What Do You Think?* "Should We Enact a Flat Tax?"). Progressivity penalizes initiative, enterprise, and the risk-taking necessary to create new products and businesses. It also reduces incentives to expand and develop the nation's economy. Moreover, by taking more income from high-income groups, governments take the money that is most likely to otherwise go into business investments and stimulate economic growth. Highly progressive taxes curtail growth and make everyone poorer.

*Reagan's Reductions in Progressivity*    Certainly the most dramatic change in federal tax laws during the Reagan years was the reduction in the progressivity of individual income tax rates. The top marginal tax rate fell from 70 percent when President Reagan took office to 28 percent following enactment of tax reform in 1986. The Tax Reform Act of 1986 reduced fourteen rate brackets to only two rate brackets, 15 and 28 percent.

*"Read My Lips"*    At the Republican National Convention in 1988, presidential nominee George Bush made a firm pledge to American voters that he would veto any tax increases passed by the Democratic-controlled Congress. "Read my lips! No new taxes." Yet in a 1990 budget summit with Democratic congressional leaders, President Bush agreed to add a top marginal rate of 31 percent to the personal income tax. Breaking his solemn pledge on taxes contributed heavily to Bush's defeat in the 1992 presidential election.

*"Soak the Rich"*    Proposals to "soak the rich" are always politically very popular. President Clinton pushed Congress to raise the top marginal tax rates to 36 percent for families earning $140,000, and to 39.6 percent for families earning $250,000. But these new top rates do not raise much revenue, partly because very few people have annual incomes in these categories. High rates encourage people to seek tax-sheltered investments—to use their capital less efficiently to create tax breaks for themselves rather than to promote new business and new jobs. High taxes also encourage high-bracket taxpayers to engage in *tax avoidance* (legal methods of reducing taxes) as well as *tax evasion* (illegal methods of reducing or eliminating taxes).

*Capital Gains Taxation*    All income is *not* taxed equally under federal income tax laws. (Indeed, interest income from municipal bonds is totally tax free, encouraging many wealthy investors to put their money into these "munies.")

*George Bush's pledge "Read my lips, no new taxes" helped him to victory in 1988. But breaking the pledge in 1990 contributed heavily to his defeat in 1992.*

## Should We Enact a Flat Tax?

More than 100 years ago, Supreme Court Justice Stephen J. Field, in striking down as unconstitutional a progressive income tax enacted by Congress, predicted that such a tax would lead to class wars: "Our political contests will become a war of the poor against the rich, a war constantly growing in intensity and bitterness."* But populist sentiment in the early twentieth century—the anger of midwestern farmers toward eastern rail tycoons and the beliefs of impoverished southerners that they would never have incomes high enough to pay an income tax—helped secure the passage of the Sixteenth Amendment to the U.S. Constitution. The federal income tax passed by Congress in 1914 had a top rate of 7 percent; less than 1 percent of the population had incomes high enough to be taxed. Today the top rate is 39.6 percent (actually over 42 percent when mandated phase-outs of deductions are calculated); about half of the population pays income taxes.

The current income tax progressively penalizes all the behaviors that produce higher incomes—work, savings, investment, and initiative. And whenever incomes are taxed at different rates, people will figure out ways to take advantage of the differential. They will hire lawyers, accountants, and lobbyists to find or create exemptions, exclusions, deductions, and preferential treatments for their own sources of income. The tax laws will become increasingly lengthy and complex. Today about half of all personal income is excluded from federal income taxation. The U.S. Tax Code, originally 14 pages long, is now 9,400 pages, and Internal Revenue Service regulations interpreting the Tax Code run more than 100,000 pages.

The Internal Revenue Service (IRS) is the most intrusive of all government agencies, overseeing the finances of every tax-paying citizen and corporation in America. It maintains personal records on more than 100 million Americans and requires them to submit more than a billion forms each year. It may levy fines and penalties and collect taxes on its own initiative; in disputes with the IRS, the burden of proof falls on the taxpayer, not the agency. Its 110,000 employees spend $8 billion per year reviewing tax returns, investigating taxpayers, and collecting revenue. Americans pay an additional $30 billion for the services of tax accountants and preparers, and they waste some $200 billion in hours of record keeping and computing their taxes.

Should we replace the current federal income tax system with a simple flat tax that could be calculated on a postcard? Reformers believe that the elimination of all exemptions, exclusions, deductions, and special treatment, and the replacement of current progressive tax rates with a flat 19 percent tax on all forms of income, even excluding family incomes under $25,000, would produce just as much revenue as the current complicated system. It would sweep away the nation's army of tax accountants and lawyers and lobbyists, and increase national productivity by relieving taxpayers of millions of hours of record keeping and tax preparation. A flat tax could be filed on a post card form (see facing page). Removing progressive rates would create incentives to work, save, and invest in America. It would lead to more rapid economic growth and improve efficiency by directing investments to their most productive uses rather than to tax avoidance. It would eliminate current incentives to underreport income, overstate exemptions, and avoid and evade taxation. Finally, by exempting a generous personal and family allowance, the flat tax would be made fair.

---

The tax code distinguishes between earned income and **capital gains**—profits from the buying and selling of property, including stocks, bonds, and real estate. Currently capital gains are taxed at a top marginal rate of 28 percent, compared to the top marginal rate of 39.6 percent for earned income.

**Capital gains:** Profits from buying and selling property including stocks, bonds, and real estate.

Why should income earned from *working* be taxed at a higher rate than income earned from *investing?* The real estate industry, together with investment firms and stockbrokers, argue that high tax rates on capital gains discourage investment

Opinion polls indicated that a flat tax rate is preferred over the current progressive rate system by a large majority of Americans. However, many Americans also support deductions for home mortgages and charitable contributions. This suggests a major political weakness in the flat tax idea: even if enacted, politicians will gradually erode the uniformity, fairness, and simplicity of a flat tax by introducing popular deductions. Lobbyists for special tax treatments will continue to pressure the Congress, and, over time, deductions, exemptions, and exclusions will creep back into the tax laws.

*Pollock v. Farmer's Loan, 158 U.S. 601 (1895).

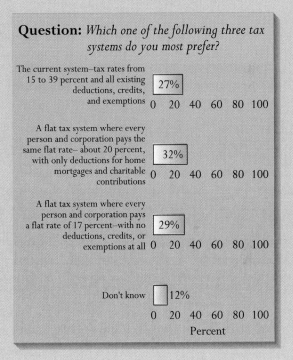

| Form 1 | Individual Wage Tax | 1995 |
|---|---|---|
| Your first name and initial (if joint return, also give spouse's name and initial) | Last name | Your social security number |
| Home address (number and street including apartment number or rural route) | | Spouse's social security number |
| City, town, or post office, state, and ZIP code | | Your occupation |
| | | Spouse's occupation |
| 1 Wages and salary | 1 | |
| 2 Pension and retirement benefits | 2 | |
| 3 Total compensation (*line 1 plus line 2*) | 3 | |
| 4 Personal allowance | | |
|    (a) 0 $16,500 for married filing jointly | 4a | |
|    (b) 0 $9,500 for single | 4b | |
|    (c) 0 $14,000 for single head of household | 4c | |
| 5 Number of dependents, not including spouse | 5 | |
| 6 Personal allowances for dependents (*line 5 multiplied by $4,500*) | 6 | |
| 7 Total personal allowances (*line 4 plus line 6*) | 7 | |
| 8 Taxable compensation (*line 3 less line 7, if positive; otherwise zero*) | 8 | |
| 9 Tax (*19% of line 8*) | 9 | |
| 10 Tax witheld by employer | 10 | |
| 11 Tax due (*line 9 less line 10, if positive*) | 11 | |
| 12 Refund due (*line 10 less line 9, if positive*) | 12 | |

**Question:** *Which one of the following three tax systems do you most prefer?*

The current system–tax rates from 15 to 39 percent and all existing deductions, credits, and exemptions — 27%

A flat tax system where every person and corporation pays the same flat rate– about 20 percent, with only deductions for home mortgages and charitable contributions — 32%

A flat tax system where every person and corporation pays a flat rate of 17 percent–with no deductions, credits, or exemptions at all — 29%

Don't know — 12%

Percent

Source: Survey by Princeton Survey Research Associates for *Newsweek*, April 6–7, 1995, reported in *American Enterprise*, July/August 1995, p. 69.

and economic growth. (But if it is true that high taxes discourage investment, high taxes must also discourage work, and both capital and labor are required for economic growth.) But the political power of investors, especially in the Republican party, places heavy downward pressure on capital gains tax rates.

A major goal of tax reform has been to treat all income equally. The Tax Reform Act of 1986 eliminated preferential treatment for capital gains, but this preference was restored by President Bush and Congress in 1991: the top rate on earned income was pushed to 31 percent while the capital gains rate stayed at 28 percent. And again in 1993, when President Clinton raised the top rate on earned income to 39.6 percent, he quietly allowed the lower capital gains rate to remain the same. But the Republican Congress has pressed to lower capital gains taxation even further, calling for additional preferential treatments for capital gains that would bring the effective tax rate on such income as low as 10 or 15 percent.

*Middle-Class Tax Cuts?* Both President Clinton and the Republican Congress promised "middle-class" tax cuts. (While politicians of both parties presume that these cuts are popular with voters, opinion polls suggest that most Americans prefer balancing the budget over tax cutting.)[8] However, Clinton and Congress argued over the dollar definition of "middle income," and partisan squabbling over the budget prevented agreement on tax cutting.

## SUMMARY NOTES

- A central policy issue is deciding how much to rely on government versus the marketplace to produce and distribute goods and services. The United States is primarily a free-market economy, but federal fiscal and monetary policies exercise a strong influence over economic activity.

- Classical economic theory views the marketplace as the most efficient means of producing and distributing goods and services. Market prices, determined by millions of individuals and thousands of firms, will adjust for recession, if government does not interfere.

- During the Great Depression of the 1930s, however, Keynesian economics came to dominate national policy making; Keynes argued that during a recession, government must apply countercyclical policies to increase demand, incurring deficits in order to add to total demand. During strong growth cycles, governments should amass surpluses to counter the threat of inflation.

- Supply-side economics focuses on stimulating growth rather than manipulating demand. Governments should lower taxes, reduce spending, and curtail regulations in order to stimulate production. The Reagan Administration lowered taxes but failed to curtail spending and thereby ran up the largest peacetime deficits in the nation's history.

- Monetarist economic theory contends that economic stability can only be achieved by holding the rate of monetary growth to the same rate as the economy's growth. It argues that government attempts to tinker with the money supply cause inflation.

- Both the president and the Congress have responsibilities for economic policy making. The independent Federal Reserve Board regulates the money supply and influences interest rates. When inflation threatens, the Fed is expected to "tighten" the money supply; when recession threatens, it is expected to "ease" the money supply.

- The performance of the economy can be measured by GDP growth and the unemployment and inflation rates. Politically the unemployment rate may be the most important of these measures of economic performance.

- Annual federal budget deficits of $200 billion or more have led to a national debt of $5 trillion dollars that grows each year. Neither Democrats nor Republicans, presidents nor Congresses, have been willing to reduce spending or raise taxes sufficiently to erase these annual deficits. The interest payments on this debt are now more than 15 percent of total federal expenditures, diverting money from all other government functions. Deficits slow economic growth by taking capital away from the private sector and keeping interest rates high.

- Tax politics centers on the question of who actually bears the burden of a tax. The individual income tax, the largest source of federal government revenue, is progressive, with higher rates levied at higher income levels. Progressive taxation is defended on the ability-to-pay principle. But half of all personal income, and a great deal of corporate income, is untaxed, owing to a wide variety of exemptions, exclusions, deductions, and special treatments on tax laws. These provisions are defended in Washington by a powerful array of interest groups.

- The Reagan Administration reduced top income tax rates from 70 to 28 percent, believing that high rates discouraged work, savings, and investment, and thereby curtailed economic growth. But George Bush agreed to an increase in the top rate to 31 percent. Bill Clinton pushed Congress to raise the top rates to 36 and 39.6 percent, arguing that rich people had benefited from Reagan's "trickle down" policies and must now be forced to bear their "fair share."

## SELECTED READINGS

AARON, HENRY J., and CHARLES L. SCHULTZE, EDS. *Setting Domestic Priorities.* Washington, D.C.: Brookings Institution, 1992. A series of policy recommendations from the liberal Brookings Institution intended to guide the Clinton Administration in dealing with health care, welfare reform, education, crime, infrastructure development, and taxation.

CLINTON, BILL, and AL GORE. *Putting People First.* New York: Times Books, 1992. Comprehensive listing of the Democratic nominees' campaign promises to reduce deficits, stimulate the economy, lower taxes, and provide for children, the elderly, families, the environment, and so on. It is interesting to compare these promises with actual presidential programs.

LIEBERMAN, CARL. *Making Economic Policy.* Englewood Cliffs, N.J.: Prentice Hall, 1991. A brief introduction to taxing, spending, monetary, and regulatory policy.

MARSHALL, WILL, and MARTIN SCHRAM, EDS. *Mandate for Change.* New York: Berkeley Books, 1993. A series of studies and recommendations for policy changes from the neo-liberal Progressive Policy Institute, focusing on enterprise economics.

PECHMAN, JOSEPH A. *Federal Tax Policy,* 5th ed. Washington, D.C.: Brookings Institution, 1987. The standard text description and analysis of federal tax policy, with recommendations from a liberal perspective.

PHILLIPS, KEVIN. *The Politics of Rich and Poor.* New York: Random House, 1990. A controversial argument that Reagan Administration economic policies made the rich richer and the poor poorer. The book is often cited to justify new and heavier taxes on affluent Americans.

SAMUELSON, ROBERT. *The Good Life and Its Discontents: The American Dream in an Age of Entitlement.* New York: Times Books, 1996. While the U.S. economy remains the world's richest and most productive, an "entitlement culture" is limiting the nation's potential and creating insecurity and dissatisfaction among Americans.

WOLFF, EDWARD N. *Top Heavy.* New York: Twentieth Century Fund Press, 1995. A study of the increasing inequality of wealth in the United States and an argument for taxing financial wealth (bank accounts, stocks, bonds, property, houses, cars, and so forth) as well as income.

# POLITICS AND SOCIAL WELFARE

## CHAPTER OUTLINE

## FEATURES

## POWER AND SOCIAL WELFARE

Social welfare policy largely determines who gets what from government—who benefits from government spending on its citizens and how much they get. This vast power has made the federal government a major *redistributor* of income from one group to another—from the working population to retirees, from the employed to the unemployed, from taxpayers to poor people. The social welfare activity of the federal government constitutes the largest and most rapidly growing portion of the federal budget (see Figure 17-1). Direct payments to individuals—Social Security, welfare, pension, and other **transfer payments**—now account for more than half of all federal government outlays.

When most Americans think of social welfare programs, they think of poor people. An estimated 35–40 million people in the United States (13–15 percent of the population) have incomes below the official **poverty line**—that is, their annual cash income falls below what is required to maintain a decent standard of living (see *Up Close:* "Who Are the Poor?"). If the approximately $1 trillion spent per year for social welfare were directly dis-

## ASK YOURSELF ABOUT POLITICS

**1** Do you believe that the government should aid people who are unable to take care of themselves, such as the very young and the very old?
Yes ⬭   No ⬭

**2** Do you think that government welfare programs perpetuate poverty?
Yes ⬭   No ⬭

**3** Should all retirees receive Social Security benefits regardless of their personal wealth or income?
Yes ⬭   No ⬭

**4** Should Medicaid pay for nursing-home care without forcing beneficiaries to use up all their savings and income?
Yes ⬭   No ⬭

**5** Should Social Security pay you back only what you have put in during your working years?
Yes ⬭   No ⬭

**6** Should the states rather than the federal government decide about welfare policy?
Yes ⬭   No ⬭

**7** Should there be a time limit on how long a person can receive welfare payments?
Yes ⬭   No ⬭

**8** Should government provide health care insurance for all Americans?
Yes ⬭   No ⬭

Through its social welfare policies, the federal government has the power to redistribute income among people. But most government payments to individuals do not go to poor people but rather to senior citizens whose voting power heavily influences elected officials.

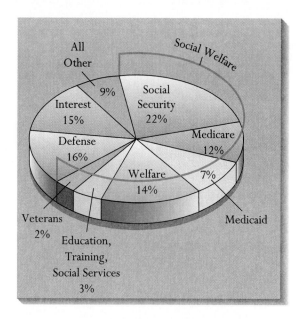

**FIGURE 17-1**  **Federal Budget Outlays**

*The social welfare activities of the United States federal government currently make up 61 percent of all government spending.*

All Other 9%

Social Welfare

Social Security 22%

Interest 15%

Medicare 12%

Defense 16%

7%

Welfare 14%

Medicaid

Veterans 2%

Education, Training, Social Services 3%

Source: Budget of the United States Government, 1996.

tributed to the nation's poor people, each poor person—man, woman, and child—would receive $25,000 per year.

Why does poverty persist in a nation where total social welfare spending is more than four times the amount needed to eliminate poverty? Because poor people are *not* the principal beneficiaries of social welfare spending. Most social welfare spending, including the largest programs—Social Security and Medicare—goes to the *nonpoor*. Only about one-fifth of federal social welfare spending is **means-tested**—that is, distributed on the basis of the recipient's income. The middle classes, not the poor, are the major beneficiaries of the nation's social welfare system.

## POVERTY IN THE UNITED STATES

How much poverty really exists in the United States? It depends on how you define the term "poverty." The official definition used by the federal government focuses on the cash income needed to maintain a "decent standard of living." The official poverty line is only a little more than one-third of the median income of all American families.[1] It takes into account the effects of inflation, rising each year with the rate of inflation. For example, in 1990, the official poverty line for an urban family of four was $13,359 per year; by 1995 the poverty line had risen to about $16,000.

*Liberal Criticism*    The official definition of poverty has many critics. Some liberal critics believe poverty is underestimated for several reasons:

1. The official definition includes cash income from welfare and Social Security, and without this government assistance, the number of poor would be much higher, perhaps 25 percent of the total population.

**Transfer payments:** Direct payments (either in cash or in goods and/or services) by governments to individuals as part of a social welfare program, not as a result of any service or contribution rendered by the individual.

**Poverty line:** The official standard regarding what level of annual cash income is sufficient to maintain a "decent standard of living"; those with incomes below this level are eligible for most public assistance programs.

**Means-tested spending:** Spending for benefits that is distributed on the basis of the recipient's income.

# Who Are the Poor?

Poverty occurs in many kinds of families and in all races and ethnic groups. However, some groups experience poverty (low income) in greater proportions than the national average (see figure).

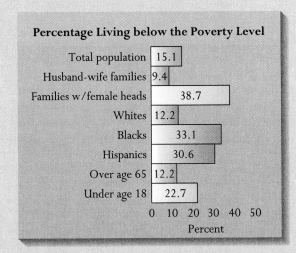

**Percentage Living below the Poverty Level**

| | |
|---|---|
| Total population | 15.1 |
| Husband-wife families | 9.4 |
| Families w/female heads | 38.7 |
| Whites | 12.2 |
| Blacks | 33.1 |
| Hispanics | 30.6 |
| Over age 65 | 12.2 |
| Under age 18 | 22.7 |

0  10  20  30  40  50
Percent

*Source: Statistical Abstract of the United States, 1995.*

Poverty is most common among families headed by women. The incidence of poverty among these families is four times greater than that for married couples. These women and their children constitute over two-thirds of all of the persons living in poverty in the United States. About one of every five children in the United States lives in poverty. These figures describe what has been labeled the "feminization of poverty" in the United States. Clearly, poverty is closely related to family structure. Today, the disintegration of the traditional husband-wife family is the single most influential factor contributing to poverty.

Blacks also experience poverty in much greater proportions than whites. Over the years, the poverty rate among blacks in the United States has been almost three times higher than the poverty rate among whites. Poverty among Hispanics is also significantly greater than among whites.

In contrast, elderly people in America experience *less* poverty than the nonaged. The aged are not poor, despite the popularity of the phrase "the poor and the aged." The percentage of persons over sixty-five years of age with low incomes is *below* the national average. Moreover, elderly people are much wealthier in terms of assets and have fewer expenses than the nonaged. They are more likely than younger people to own homes with paid-up mortgages. Medicare pays a large portion of their medical expenses. With fewer expenses, elderly people, even with relatively smaller cash incomes, experience poverty differently from the way a young mother with children experiences it. The declining poverty rate among elderly people is a relatively recent occurrence, however. Continuing increases in Social Security benefits over the years are largely responsible for this singular "victory" in the war against poverty.

2.  The official definition does not count the many "near poor," the 45–50 million Americans, or 19 percent of the population, living below 125 percent of the poverty level.

3.  The official definition does not take into account regional differences in the cost of living, climate, or accepted styles of living.

4.  The official definition does not consider what people *think* they need to live. (The poverty line is well below what most Americans think they need to survive.)

*Conservative Criticism*   Some conservative critics also challenge the official definition of poverty, arguing that:

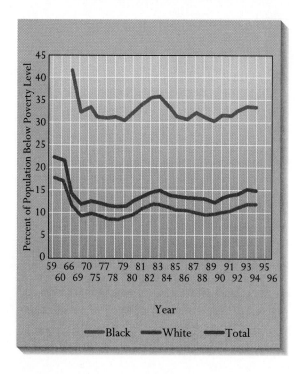

**FIGURE 17-2** **Poverty in the United States**

*Prior to 1970, poverty in the United States had been declining over time. But for the past thirty years, the poverty rate has held relatively steady at 13–15 percent of the total population. Black Americans have experienced poverty at roughly three times the rate of white Americans.*

1. It does not consider the value of family assets. Elderly people who own their own mortgage-free homes, furniture, and automobiles may have incomes below the poverty line yet not suffer hardship.

2. Many families and individuals who are officially counted as poor do not *think* of themselves as "poor people"—for example, students who deliberately postpone income to secure an education.

3. Many persons (poor and nonpoor) underreport their real income, a practice that leads to overestimates of the number of poor.

4. Most important, the official definition of poverty excludes "in-kind" (noncash) benefits given to poor people by governments. If these benefits—including food stamps, free medical care, public housing, and school lunches—were "costed out" (calculated as cash income), there may be only half as many poor people as shown in official statistics.

*Temporary Poverty*    Often, poor people are envisioned as a permanent "underclass" living most of their lives in poverty. But most poverty is not long-term. Tracing poor families over time presents a different picture of the nature of poverty from the "snapshot" view taken in any one year. For example, over the last decade 13–15 percent of the nation's population has been officially classified as poor in any one year (see Figure 17-2). However, only *some* poverty is persistent: about 6–8 percent of the population remains in poverty for more than five years. Thus about half of the people who are counted as poor are experiencing poverty for only a short period of time. For these temporary poor, welfare is a "safety net" that helps them through hard times.

*Persistent Poverty*    About half of the people on welfare rolls at any one time are *persistently poor,* that is, likely to remain on welfare for five or more years. For these people, welfare is a more permanent part of their lives.

Because they place a disproportionate burden on welfare resources, persistently poor people pose serious questions for social scientists and policy makers. Prolonged poverty and welfare dependency create an **underclass** that suffers from many social ills—teen pregnancy, family instability, drugs, crime, alienation, apathy, and irresponsibility.[2] Government educational, training, and jobs programs, as well as many other social service efforts, fail to benefit many of these people.

*Family Structure*    Poverty and welfare dependency are much more frequent among female-headed households with no husband present than among husband-wife households (see *Up Close:* "Who Are the Poor?"). Unwed parenthood may be fashionable on television, but it is ill-advised for young women hoping to avoid economic hardship for themselves and their children (see Figure 17-3).[3] Rising proportions of children living in poverty (from 15 percent in 1970 to more than 20 percent in 1995) are associated with rising proportions of births to unmarried women (see Figure 17-4). Traditionally, "illegitimacy" was held in check by powerful religious and social structures. But these structures have weakened over time, and the availability of welfare cash benefits, food stamps, medical care, and government housing has removed much of the economic hardship once associated with unwed motherhood. Indeed, it is sometimes argued that government welfare programs, however well meaning, end up perpetuating poverty and social dependency (see *A Conflicting View:* "Government as the Cause of Poverty").

*The "Truly Disadvantaged"*    The nation's largest cities have become the principal location of virtually all of the social problems confronting our society—poverty, homelessness (see *Up Close:* "Homelessness in America"), racial tension, drug abuse, delinquency, and crime. These problems are all made worse by their concentration in large cities. Yet the concentration of social ills in cities is a relatively recent occurrence; as late as 1970, there were higher rates of poverty in rural America than in the cities.

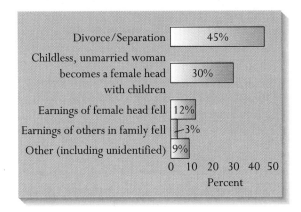

Source: Greg J. Duncan and Saul D. Hoffman, "Welfare Dynamics and the Nature of Need," paper presented at Policy Sciences Program Conference, Florida State University, Tallahassee, Florida, March 5–6, 1986, using data from University of Michigan Panel Study of Income Dynamics.

**FIGURE 17-3**    **How to Become Poor: Personal Events Associated with Welfare Reliance**
*Many individuals fall below the poverty line because of their life situations. Women and children are especially likely to suffer poverty, since divorced mothers (and their children) have the highest incidence of poverty nationwide. This has prompted some critics of modern society to argue that the cycle of poverty can only be addressed by a return to "traditional values," including the nuclear, two-parent family.*

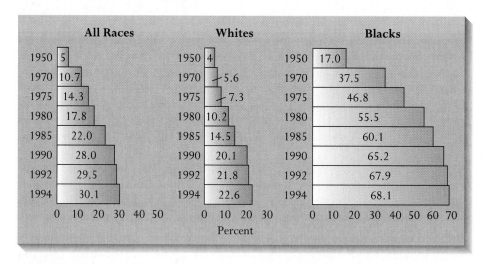

**FIGURE 17-4** **Births to Unmarried Women**

*The rate of children born to unmarried women has risen steadily since the 1950s. Although higher among African Americans than whites, it has been rising at a greater rate among whites.*

| | All Races | | Whites | | Blacks |
|---|---|---|---|---|---|
| 1950 | 5 | 1950 | 4 | 1950 | 17.0 |
| 1970 | 10.7 | 1970 | 5.6 | 1970 | 37.5 |
| 1975 | 14.3 | 1975 | 7.3 | 1975 | 46.8 |
| 1980 | 17.8 | 1980 | 10.2 | 1980 | 55.5 |
| 1985 | 22.0 | 1985 | 14.5 | 1985 | 60.1 |
| 1990 | 28.0 | 1990 | 20.1 | 1990 | 65.2 |
| 1992 | 29.5 | 1992 | 21.8 | 1992 | 67.9 |
| 1994 | 30.1 | 1994 | 22.6 | 1994 | 68.1 |

Percent

*Source:* Office of U.S. Senator Daniel Patrick Moynihan; U.S. Bureau of the Census, *Current Population Reports,* Fertility of American Women Series, P 40, 1994.

Why has the inner city become the locus of social problems? Some observers argue that changes in the labor market from industrial goods-producing jobs to professional, financial, and technical service-producing jobs have increasingly divided the labor market into low-wage and high-wage sectors.[4] The decline in manufacturing jobs, together with a shift in remaining manufacturing jobs and commercial (sales) jobs to the suburbs, has left inner-city residents with fewer and lower-paying job opportunities. The rise in joblessness in the inner cities has in turn increased the concentration of poor people, added to the number of poor single-parent families, and increased welfare dependency.

At the same time, inner-city neighborhoods have experienced an outmigration of working-class and middle-class families. In earlier decades, most inner-city adults were employed, and they invested their income and time in their neighborhoods, patronizing local churches, stores, schools, and community organizations. Their presence in the community provided role models for youth. But their outmigration has decreased contact between the classes, leaving the poorest Americans isolated and "truly disadvantaged." Inner-city residents now lack not only nearby jobs but also access to job information and social learning through working role models. Neighborhoods that have few legitimate employment opportunities, inadequate job information networks, and poor schools not only weaken the traditional work ethic but also give rise to illegal income-producing activities in the streets—drugs, crime, prostitution. A jobless family living in a neighborhood where these ills are concentrated is influenced by the behaviors, beliefs, and perceptions of the people around them. These *concentration effects* make things worse.

## SOCIAL WELFARE POLICY

Public welfare has been a recognized responsibility of government in English-speaking countries for many centuries. As far back as the Poor Relief Act of 1601, the English Parliament provided workhouses for the "able-bodied poor" (the

# Government as the Cause of Poverty

Does the government itself create poverty by fashioning social welfare programs and policies that destroy incentives to work, encourage teenage pregnancies, and condemn the poor to social dependency? Does the current social welfare system unintentionally sentence many people to a life of poverty who would otherwise form families, take low-paying jobs, and perhaps, with hard work and perseverance, gradually pull themselves and their children into the mainstream of American life?

Poverty in the United States steadily *declined* from 1950, when about 30 percent of the population was officially poor, to 1970, when about 13 percent of the population was poor. During this period of progress toward the elimination of poverty, government welfare programs were minimal. Federal payments were available to elderly, blind, and disabled poor people. There were small Aid to Families with Dependent Children (AFDC) programs for women with children who lived alone; eligibility was restricted and welfare authorities checked to see if an employable male lived in the house. Welfare roles were modest; only about 1–2 percent of American families received AFDC payments.

Following the addition of many new Great Society welfare programs, the downward trend in poverty ended. Indeed, the number and proportion of the population living in poverty began to move upward (see Figure 17-2 in text). This was a period in which AFDC payments were significantly increased and eligibility rules were relaxed. The food stamp program, initiated in 1965, became a major welfare benefit. Medicaid, also initiated in 1965, became the costliest of all public assistance programs by the late 1970s. Federal aid to elderly, blind, and disabled people was merged into a new Supplemental Security Income program, and the number of recipients of this program quadrupled.

Why did the downward trend in poverty end in the 1970s? Discrimination did not become significantly worse during this period; on the contrary, the civil rights laws enacted in the 1960s were opening up many new opportunities for African Americans.

Poverty was reduced among elderly people due to generous increases in Social Security benefits. The greatest increases in poverty occurred in families headed by working-age persons. In short, it is difficult to find alternative explanations for the continuation of poverty. We are obliged to consider the possibility that *policy* changes—new welfare programs, expanded benefits, and relaxed eligibility requirements—contributed to maintaining poverty.

According to Charles Murray, the persons hurt most by current welfare policies are poor people themselves. In his controversial book, *Losing Ground,* he argued that current social welfare policy provides many disincentives to family life. According to Murray, generous welfare programs encourage poor young women to start families before they have sufficient job skills to support themselves; poor young men are allowed to escape their family responsibilities. Surveys show that poor people prefer work over welfare, but welfare payments may subtly affect their behavior. Persons unwilling to take minimum-wage jobs may never acquire the work habits required to move into better-paying jobs later in life. Welfare may even help create a dependent and defeatist subculture, lowering personal self-esteem and contributing further to joblessness, illegitimacy, and broken families. Murray's policy prescription was a drastic one. He recommended:

> scrapping the entire federal welfare and income-support structure for working-age persons. It would leave the working-age person with no recourse whatever except the job market, family members, friends, and public or private locally funded services—cut the knot, for there is no way to untie it.*

The result, he argued, would be less poverty and illegitimacy and more upward mobility, freedom, and hope for poor people. "The lives of large numbers of poor people would be radically changed for the better." The obstacle to this solution is not only the politicians and bureaucrats who want to keep their dependent clients but also, more important, the majority of well-meaning middle-class Americans who support welfare programs.

*Charles Murray, *Losing Ground* (New York: Basic Books, 1984), pp. 227–28.

## Homelessness in America

*A homeless camp under an interstate highway in Miami.*

The most visible social welfare problem in the United States is the nation's homeless people, who wander about in the larger cities, suffering exposure, alcoholism, drug abuse, and chronic mental illness. No one knows their total number, but the best systematic estimate is 250,000 to 350,000.*

The issue of homelessness has become so politicized that an accurate assessment of the problem and a rational strategy for dealing with it have become virtually impossible. The term "homeless" is used to describe many different situations. Many are *street people* who sleep in subways, bus stations, parks, or the streets. Some of them are temporarily traveling in search of work; some have left home for a few days or are youthful runaways; others have roamed the streets for months or years. In contrast, *sheltered homeless people* have obtained housing in shelters operated by local governments or private charities. As the number of shelters has grown in recent years, the number of sheltered homeless people has also grown. But most of the sheltered homeless people come from other housing, not the streets. These are people who have recently been evicted from rental units or have previously lived with family or friends. They often include families with children; the street people are virtually all single persons.

About half of all street people are chronic alcoholic and drug abusers; an additional one-fourth to one-third are mentally ill.** Alcohol and drug abusers, especially "crack" cocaine users, are the fastest-growing groups among homeless people. Moreover, homeless people who are alcohol and drug abusers and/or mentally ill are by far the most likely to remain on the streets for long periods of time. Among the 15–25 percent of homeless people who are neither mentally ill nor dependent on alcohol or drugs, homelessness is likely to be temporary.

The current plight of homeless people is primarily a result of various "reforms" in public policy, notably

---

**Social insurance programs:** Social welfare programs to which beneficiaries have made contributions so that they are entitled to benefits regardless of their personal wealth.

**Public assistance programs:** Those social welfare programs for which no contributions are required and only those living in poverty (by official standards) are eligible; including food stamps, Medicaid, and Aid to Families with Dependent Children.

unemployed) and poorhouses for widows and orphans, elderly and handicapped people. Today, nearly one-third of the U.S. population receives some form of government benefits: Social Security, Medicare or Medicaid, disability insurance, unemployment compensation, government employee retirement, veterans' benefits, food stamps, school lunches, job training, public housing, and cash public assistance payments (see Table 17-1). More than half of all families in the United States include at least one person who receives a government check. Thus, the "welfare state" now encompasses a very large part of our society.

The major social welfare programs can be classified as either **social insurance** or **public assistance.** This distinction is an important one that has on occasion become a major political issue. If the beneficiaries of a government program are required to have made contributions to it before claiming any of its benefits, and if they are entitled to the benefits regardless of their personal wealth—as in Social Security and Medicare—then the program is said to be

the "deinstitutionalization" of care for the mentally ill and the newly recognized rights of individuals to refuse treatment; the "decriminalization" of vagrancy and public intoxication; and urban renewal, which has eliminated many low-rent apartments and cheap hotels.

Deinstitutionalization, a policy advanced by mental health care professionals and social welfare activists in the 1960s and 1970s after the introduction of new psychotropic drug therapies, has resulted in the release of all but the most dangerous mental patients from state-run mental hospitals. Advocates of deinstitutionalization argued that aside from drugs, no psychiatric therapies have much success among the long-term mentally ill. Drug therapies can be administered on an outpatient basis; they usually do not require hospitalization. So it was argued that patients could not rightfully be kept in a mental institution against their will; people who had committed no crimes and who posed no danger to others should be released. Much of the resulting problem arose because many of these patients were unable, on their own, to maintain the schedule for their outpatient treatment.

Decriminalization of public intoxication has also added to the numbers of street people. Involuntary confinement of substance abusers is now banned unless a person is arrested while possessing an illegal substance or is found in court to be "a danger to himself or others," which means a person must commit a serious act of violence before the courts will intervene. For many homeless people—victimized by cold, exposure, and hunger, by the availability of alcohol and illegal drugs, and by the violent street crimes perpetrated against them—this means the "freedom to die with their rights on."

Community-based care has failed for many substance abusers and chronically mentally ill street people. Many are "uncooperative"; they are isolated from society; they have no family members or doctors or counselors to turn to for help. The nation's vast social welfare system provides them little help. They cannot handle forms, appointments, or interviews; the welfare bureaucracy is intimidating. Lacking a permanent address, many receive no Social Security, welfare, or disability checks. Shelters provided by private charities, such as the Salvation Army, or by city governments are more helpful to the temporarily homeless than to chronic alcohol or drug abusers or mentally ill people. Few shelters offer treatment for alcohol or drug abusers and some refuse disruptive people.

*Peter H. Rossi, *Down and Out in America* (Chicago: University of Chicago Press, 1989).
**As reported in a twenty-seven-city survey by the U.S. Conference of Mayors. See *U.S. News and World Report,* January 15, 1990, pp. 27–29.

financed on the social insurance principle. If the program is financed out of general tax revenues and if recipients are required to show that they are poor before claiming its benefits—as in Aid to Families with Dependent Children, Supplemental Security Income, and Medicaid—then the program is said to be financed on the public assistance principle. Public assistance programs are generally labeled as "welfare."

*Entitlements*   **Entitlements** are government benefits for which Congress has set eligibility criteria—age, income, retirement, disability, unemployment, and so on. Everyone who meets the criteria is "entitled" to the benefit.

Most of the nation's major entitlement programs were launched either in the New Deal years of the 1930s under President Franklin D. Roosevelt (Social Security, Unemployment Compensation, Aid to Families with Dependent Children, and Aid to Aged, Blind, and Disabled, now called Supplemental Security Income)

**Entitlements:** Any social welfare program for which there are eligibility requirements, whether financial or contributory.

TABLE 17–1  MAJOR FEDERAL SOCIAL WELFARE PROGRAMS

| Social Insurance Programs | Beneficiaries (millions) | Public Assistance Programs | Beneficiaries (millions) |
|---|---|---|---|
| *Social Security* | | *Cash Aid* | |
| Total | 42.3 | Aid to Families with Dependent | |
|   Retirement | 29.6 |     Children (AFDC) | 14.3 |
|   Survivors | 7.4 |   Supplemental Security Income (SSI) | 6.0 |
|   Disabled | 5.3 |   General assistance | 0.9 |
| | | | |
| *Unemployment Compensation* | | *Medical Care* | |
|   Total | 7.9 |   Medicaid | 33.4 |
| | |   Veterans | 0.5 |
| *Government retirement and veterans* | |   Indians | 1.2 |
|   Veterans | 3.4 |   Community health centers | 5.2 |
|   Federal | 2.8 | | |
|   State and local | 8.3 | *Food Benefits* | |
| | |   Food stamps | 27.5 |
| *Medicare* | |   School lunches | 24.9 |
|   Total | 36.2 |   Women, Infants, Children (WIC) | 5.9 |
| | | | |
| | | *Housing Benefits* | |
| | |   Total | 4.6 |
| | | | |
| | | *Education Aid* | |
| | |   Student loans | 5.6 |
| | |   Pell Grants | 3.5 |
| | |   Work study | 0.8 |
| | |   Educational opportunity grants | 0.5 |
| | |   Head Start | 0.6 |
| | | | |
| | | *Job Training* | |
| | |   Total | 1.9 |
| | | | |
| | | *Energy Assistance* | |
| | |   Total | 6.2 |

*Source:* U.S. Bureau of the Census, *Statistical Abstract of the United States, 1995,* pp. 113, 377, 378, 380, 388, 389.

or in the Great Society years of the 1960s under President Lyndon B. Johnson (food stamps, Medicare, Medicaid).

*Social Security*  Begun during the Depression, **Social Security** is now the largest of all entitlements; it comprises two distinct programs. The Old Age and Survivors Insurance program provides monthly cash benefits to retired workers and their dependents and to survivors of insured workers. The Disability Insurance program provides monthly cash benefits for disabled workers and their dependents. An automatic, annual cost-of-living adjustment (COLA) for both programs matches any increase in the annual inflation rate.

With more than 42 million beneficiaries, Social Security is the single largest spending program in the federal budget. About 96 percent of the nation's paid work force is covered by the program, which is funded by a payroll tax on employers and employees. Retirees can begin receiving full benefits at age sixty-five, regardless of their personal wealth or income (see "Senior Power," later in this chapter).

**Social Security:** A social insurance program composed of the Old Age and Survivors Insurance program, which pays benefits to retired workers who have paid into the program and their dependents and survivors, and the Disability Insurance program, which pays benefits to disabled workers and their families.

*Most of America's social welfare programs began in either the Great Depression of the 1930s or the War on Poverty in the 1960s. At the outset of the Depression, millions of unemployed Americans, like the New Yorkers in a bread line in the photo at left, had only private charities to turn to for survival. The War on Poverty of the 1960s was a reaction to the persistence of extreme poverty, like that of the rural family in the photograph at right, in the midst of the prosperity that followed World War II.*

*Unemployment Compensation* **Unemployment compensation** temporarily replaces part of the wages of workers who lose their jobs involuntarily and helps stabilize the economy during recessions. The U.S. Department of Labor oversees the system, but states administer their own programs, with latitude within federal guidelines to define weekly benefits and other program features. Benefits are funded by a combination of federal and state unemployment taxes on employers.

*Supplemental Security Income* **Supplemental Security Income (SSI)** is a means-tested, federally administered income assistance program that provides monthly cash payments to needy elderly (sixty-five or older), blind, and disabled people. A loose definition of "disability"—including alcoholism, drug abuse, and attention deficiency among children—has led to a rapid growth in the number of SSI beneficiaries.

*Aid to Families with Dependent Children* **Aid to Families with Dependent Children (AFDC)** is a means-tested, cash grant program to enable the states to assist needy children. States operate the program and define "need"; they set their own benefit levels and establish (within federal guidelines) income and resource limits. AFDC has been at the center of the welfare reform debate (see "Politics and Welfare Reform," later in this chapter).

*Medicare* **Medicare** is a two-part program that helps elderly and disabled people pay acute-care (as opposed to long-term-care) health costs. Hospital Insurance (Part A) helps pay the cost of hospital inpatient and skilled-nursing care. Anyone sixty-five or older who is eligible for Social Security is automatically eligible for Part A benefits. Also eligible are people under sixty-five who receive Social Security disability or railroad retirement disability and people who have end-stage kidney disease. Part A is financed primarily by the 1.45 percent payroll tax collected with Social Security (FICA) withholding.

Supplemental Medical Insurance (Part B) is an optional add-on taken by virtually all those covered by Part A. It pays 80 percent of covered doctor and outpa-

**Unemployment compensation:** A social insurance program that temporarily replaces part of the wages of workers who have lost their jobs.

**Supplemental Security Income (SSI):** A public assistance program that provides monthly cash payments to the needy elderly (sixty-five or older), blind, and disabled.

**Aid to Families with Dependent Children (AFDC):** A public assistance program that provides monies to the states for their use in helping needy children through payments to their parents.

**Medicare:** A social insurance program that provides health care insurance to elderly and disabled people.

tient charges. Monthly premiums deducted from Social Security benefit checks finance about 25 percent of the costs of Part B, while most of the rest comes from general taxpayer revenues.

*Medicaid*   **Medicaid** is a joint federal-state program providing health services to low-income Americans. Most Medicaid spending goes to elderly and nonelderly disabled people. However, women and children receiving benefits under AFDC automatically qualify for Medicaid, as does anyone who gets cash assistance under SSI. States can also offer Medicaid to the "medically needy"— those who face crushing medical costs but whose income or assets are too high to qualify for SSI or AFDC, including pregnant women and young children not receiving AFDC. Medicaid also pays for long-term nursing home care, but only after beneficiaries have used up virtually all of their savings and income.

*Food Stamps*   The **food stamp program** provides low-income households with coupons that they can redeem for enough food to provide a minimal, nutritious diet. The program is overseen by the federal government but is administered by the states.

## SENIOR POWER

Senior citizens are the most politically powerful age group in the population. They constitute 28 percent of the voting-age population, but, more important, because of their high voter turnout rates, they constitute more than one-third of the voters on election day. Persons over age sixty-five average a 68 percent turnout rate in presidential elections and a 61 percent rate in congressional elections. By comparison, those aged eighteen to twenty-one have a turnout rate of 36 percent in presidential elections and 19 percent in congressional elections, so the voting power of senior citizens is twice that of young people. Moreover, seniors are well represented in Washington; the American Association of Retired Persons (AARP) is the nation's largest organized interest group (see *Up Close:* "AARP: The Nation's Most Powerful Interest Group," in Chapter 9). No elected officials can afford to offend seniors, and seniors strongly support generous Social Security benefits.

*The Aged in the Future*   The "baby boom" from 1945 to 1960 produced a large generation of people who crowded schools and colleges in the 1960s and 1970s and encountered stiff competition for jobs in the 1980s. During the baby boom, women averaged 3.5 births during their lifetime. Today, the birth rate is only 1.8 births per woman, less than the 2.1 figure required to keep the population from declining. (Current U.S. population growth is a product of immigration.) The baby boom generation will be retiring beginning in 2010, and by 2030 they will constitute more than 20 percent of the population. Changes in lifestyle—less smoking, more exercise, better weight control—may increase the aged population even more. Medical advances may also extend life expectancy.

**Medicaid:** A public assistance program that provides health care to the poor.

**Food stamp program:** A public assistance program that provides low-income households with coupons redeemable for enough food to provide a minimal nutritious diet.

CHAPTER 17 • POLITICS AND SOCIAL WELFARE

*The Generational Compact*    The framers of the Social Security Act of 1935 created a "trust fund" with the expectation that a reserve would be built up from social insurance taxes paid by working persons. The reserve would earn interest, and the interest and principal would be used in later years to pay benefits. In theory, Social Security is an insurance program. (Payments are recorded by name and Social Security number.) Many people believe that they get back what they paid during their working years. Reality, however, has proven much different.

Social Security is now financed on a pay-as-you-go system, rather than a reserve system. Today, the income from all social insurance premiums (taxes) pays for current Social Security benefits. This generation of workers is paying for the benefits of the last generation, and this generation must hope that its future benefits will be financed by the next generation of workers. Taxing current workers to pay benefits to current retirees may be viewed as a compact between generations. Each generation of workers in effect agrees to pay benefits to an earlier generation of retirees and expects the next generation will pay for its retirement.

*The Rising Dependency Ratio*    Since current workers must pay for the benefits of current retirees and other beneficiaries, the **dependency ratio** becomes an important component of evaluating the future of Social Security. The dependency ratio for Social Security is the number of recipients as a percentage of the number of contributing workers. Americans are living longer and increasing the dependency ratio. A child born in 1935, when the Social Security system was created, could expect to live only to age sixty-one, four years *less* than the retirement age of sixty-five. The life expectancy of a child born in 1990 is seventy-four years, nine years *beyond* the retirement age. In the early years of Social Security, there were ten workers supporting each retiree—a dependency ratio of 10 to 1. But

**Dependency ratio:** In the Social Security system, the number of recipients as a percentage of the number of contributing workers.

today, as the U.S. population grows older—due to lower birth rates and longer life spans—there are only three workers for each retiree, and by 2010 the dependency ratio will be two workers for each retiree.

*Burdens on Generation X*   With fewer workers to support each retiree, the burdens of Social Security on the current generation of young Americans will become unsupportable. Social Security taxes alone, not including taxes for every other government function, will approach 40 percent of income if no changes are made to the current system. Members of Generation X will pay many times more into Social Security than they will ever get out of it.

*The Trust Fund Myth*   Income from the Social Security tax currently exceeds payments to beneficiaries. The "surplus" is officially used to purchase U.S. government bonds. However, Social Security taxes are lumped together with general tax revenues in the federal budget as "current revenues," which offset *all* current expenditures of the federal government. With the federal government running huge deficits each year (see "The Debt Burden" in Chapter 16), the Social Security surplus hides some of this deficit in overall federal spending, and the use of the "trust fund" to purchase government bonds aids the federal government in its deficit financing. In short, the trust fund is merely an accounting gimmick; current Social Security taxes are being used to finance current spending, and future retirement benefits will have to be paid from future revenues.

*Cost-of-Living Increases*   Currently, the annual Social Security cost-of-living adjustments **(COLAs)** are based upon the Consumer Price Index, which estimates the cost of all consumer items each year. These costs include home buying, mortgage interest, child rearing, and other costs that many retirees do not confront. Moreover, most *workers* do not have the same protection against inflation as retirees; average wage rates do not always match increases in the cost of living. Hence, over the years, COLAs have improved the economic well-being of Social Security recipients relative to all American workers.

*Wealthy Retirees*   Social Security benefits are paid to *all* eligible retirees, regardless of whatever other income they may receive. There is no means test for Social Security benefits. As a result, large numbers of affluent Americans receive government checks each month. They paid into Social Security during their working years, and they can claim these checks as an entitlement under the social insurance principle. But currently their benefits far exceed their previous payments.

Since elderly people experience less poverty than today's workers (see *Up Close:* "Who Are the Poor?" earlier in this chapter) and possess considerably more wealth, Social Security benefits constitute a "negative" redistribution of income— that is, a transfer of income from poorer to richer people. The elderly are generally better off than the people supporting them.

**COLAs:** Annual cost-of-living adjustments mandated by law in Social Security and other welfare benefits.

*The "Third Rail" of American Politics*   Social Security is the most expensive program in the federal budget, but also the most politically sacrosanct. Politicians regularly call it the "third rail of American politics"—touch it and die. Because Social Security and Medicare are entitlement programs, their spending grows automatically each year as numbers of beneficiaries increase and COLAs raise benefit levels. Because they are entitlement programs with strong political support, spending on them is sometimes called "uncontrollable."

But Congress can change or repeal any law it passes. Lawmakers can reduce entitlements, including Social Security and Medicare, in a variety of ways. They can legislate reductions in benefit levels; limit eligibility (for example, by increasing the age at which Social Security benefits begin); limit COLAs; introduce means tests to deny benefits to high-income retirees; or increase taxes on benefit payments.

## POLITICS AND WELFARE REFORM

Americans confront a clash of values in welfare policy. Americans are a generous people; they believe government should aid those who are unable to take care of themselves, especially children, disabled people, and elderly people. But Americans are worried that welfare programs encourage dependency, undermine the work ethic, and contribute to illegitimate births and the breakup of families. As Harvard sociologist David Ellwood explains:

> Welfare brings some of our most precious values—involving autonomy, responsibility, work, family, community and compassion—into conflict. We want to help those who are not making it, but in so doing, we seem to cheapen the efforts of those who are struggling hard just to get by. We want to offer financial support to those with low incomes, but if we do, we reduce the pressure on them and their incentive to work. We want to help people who are not able to help themselves, but then we worry that people will not bother to help themselves. We recognize the insecurity of single-parent families, but, in helping them, we appear to be promoting or supporting their formation.[5]

While social insurance programs (Social Security, Medicare, and Unemployment Compensation) are politically popular and enjoy the support of large numbers of active beneficiaries, public assistance programs (AFDC, SSI, Medicaid) are far less popular. A variety of controversies surround welfare policy in the United States.

*Work Disincentives*   In most states, if a recipient of public assistance takes a full-time job, the government reduces or stops assistance checks to that person. If the former recipient is then laid off, it may take some time to get back into the assistance programs. In other words, employment is uncertain, while assistance is not. In addition, the jobs available to most recipients of public assistance are very low paying and do not produce much more income than does assistance, particularly when transportation, child care, and other costs of working are counted. Finally, families receiving AFDC are generally entitled to participate in the food stamp program, to receive health care through Medicaid, to gain access to free or low-rent public housing, to receive free lunches in public schools, and to receive a variety of other social and educational benefits at little or no cost to themselves—benefits they could lose if the head of the household took a job.

*The Workfare Experiment*   In the Family Support Act of 1988, liberals and conservatives joined in an effort to reform the largest cash assistance program, Aid to Families with Dependent Children. The goal was to end long-term dependence on welfare, replacing it with a program called **workfare.** In drafting this legislation, liberals acknowledged that with most nonpoor mothers working, mothers on public assistance have no special claim to stay at home. Conservatives acknowledged that some transitional aid—education, job training, continued health care, and day care for children—might be necessary to move these mothers into the work force. The Family Support Act required states to develop a federal job training program (JOBS) for most adults receiving AFDC payments; to provide child care for JOBS participants; to furnish transitional child care and Medicaid after a participant leaves AFDC to take a job; and to strengthen its child support enforcement programs.

But welfare rolls continued to rise despite the Family Support Act. No state workfare program required all welfare recipients to take jobs or even to enroll in job training programs. Most states allowed mothers with preschool age children to opt out altogether. No state provided enough money to fund the necessary supporting services. Only about 10 percent of AFDC recipients participated in any education, job training, or job replacement programs, and even fewer actually found jobs. Workfare—moving people off welfare rolls and onto payrolls—proved to be more costly than simply providing welfare assistance.

*Time Limits on Cash Assistance*   It is argued that the availability of an unlimited entitlement to welfare payments creates disincentives to work, encourages long-term social dependency, and undermines family foundations. Most welfare recipients express a preference for work over welfare, but their preference usually does not extend to menial, low-paying, entry-level jobs, often the only jobs for which long-term welfare recipients are qualified. Over time, the work ethic is undermined; personal habits of awakening early, making arrangements for child care and transportation, arriving at the job on time, performing tasks under someone's supervision, and the like are eroded. It is argued that only the threat of a cut-off of cash payments will inspire long-term welfare recipients to seriously pursue job training and work opportunities—to break the cycle of dependency.

As a presidential candidate in 1992, Bill Clinton advocated a two-year time limit on cash assistance, "requiring those who can work to go to work, either in the private sector or in community service."[6] President Clinton and many liberals in Congress argued that time limits must be accompanied by counseling, education, and job training; continuing child care; and medical benefits after employment. Public service jobs would have to be created for people who could not find private employment. But conservatives argued that the costs of these benefits and supports would be higher than welfare payments, and they would continue to encourage people to join welfare rolls. Conservatives argued that the threatened cutoff of welfare benefits must be complete to be effective encouragement to find and keep a job. Public service, or "phony make-work" jobs, would only continue social dependency.

*Limiting Aid to Teenagers*   Yet another area of controversy surrounds the availability of cash benefits and public housing to teenage women, many of whom seek independence from parents as well as status and recognition in life as moth-

**Workfare:** Federal and state programs designed to assist welfare recipients in finding employment.

CHAPTER 17 • POLITICS AND SOCIAL WELFARE

ers. It is argued that these incentives, especially in impoverished households, encourage early unmarried motherhood. By limiting or eliminating cash payments to minors and by requiring them to live in their parental households and to continue schooling in order to receive any public assistance (reduced cash benefits, food stamps), incentives to teenage pregnancy would be removed.

*"As far as I'm concerned, they can do what they want with the minimum wage, just as long as they keep their hands off the maximum wage."*

Drawing by Mankoff. © 1989 The New Yorker Magazine.

*Family Cap*    A related controversy centers on the "family cap" proposal—denying increases in cash benefits to women already on welfare who have additional children. Liberals argue that such a denial punishes innocent children and that millions of children will face hardship under a family cap. Conservatives believe that it will discourage welfare mothers from having additional children in order to increase their monthly payments.

*Obstacles to Reform*    While nearly everyone agrees that getting people off welfare rolls and into productive jobs is the goal of reform, there are major obstacles to the achievement of this goal. First of all, a substantial portion (perhaps 25–40 percent) of long-term AFDC recipients have handicaps—physical problems, chronic illnesses, learning disabilities, alcohol or drug abuse problems—that prevent them from holding a job. Many long-term recipients have no work experience (perhaps 50 percent), and two-thirds of them have not graduated from high school. Almost half have three or more children, making child care arrangements a major obstacle. Policy makers question whether there are 5 million jobs available to these unskilled mothers, but even if there were such jobs available, they would be mostly minimum wage jobs that would not lift these women out of poverty. Cutting off aid, advocated by many conservatives, would place millions of children at risk. Orphanages are not really an economic alternative; their costs per child are many times higher than welfare payments.

*Congress and Welfare Reform*    Bill Clinton once promised "to end welfare as we know it," but it was the Republican-controlled Congress that finally did so. The GOP approach was to merge welfare reform with "devolution" of governmental responsibilities to the states (see "A Devolution Revolution?" in Chapter 4) by:

- Establishing block grants with lump sum allocations to the states for cash welfare payments.
- Granting the states broad flexibility in determining eligibility and benefit levels for persons receiving such aid.
- Allowing states to add welfare spending if they choose to do so, but penalizing states that reduce their spending for cash aid below 75 percent of the previous levels.

By transferring these programs into block grants, Congress acquires greater ability to control future costs. Indeed, the driving force behind welfare reform may have been the desire to save billions in future years and to assist in reducing federal budget deficits. Since Franklin Delano Roosevelt's New Deal in 1935, low-income mothers and children have enjoyed a legal entitlement to welfare payments through AFDC. But welfare reform, with its devolution of responsibility for determining eligibility to the states, ended this sixty-year entitlement.

However, Congress is not likely to ever give up complete control over the use of the funds it appropriates. Indeed, in the welfare block grant legislation, conservatives in Congress fought to add many strings, including a family cap denying cash benefit increases to women who have additional children while on welfare, and a denial of cash benefits to mothers under eighteen unless they live at home and go to school. After considerable debate, a compromise in Congress was reached that further strengthened federalism: states were given the option of deciding for themselves whether to impose a family cap or to deny benefits to teenage mothers. After twice vetoing earlier bills, Clinton signed the compromise bill in 1996. Some reforms have been initiated by the states themselves after obtaining "waivers" from federal regulations from the U.S. Department of Health and Human Services.

# HEALTH CARE IN AMERICA

The United States spends more of its resources on health care than any other nation (see *Compared to What?* "Health and Health Care Costs in Advanced Democracies"). Nevertheless, the United States ranks well below other advanced democracies in key measures of the health of its people such as life expectancy and infant death rate. Moreover, unlike most other advanced democracies, which make provision for health care for all citizens, Americans have no guarantee of access to medical care. In short, the American health care system is the most expensive and least universal in its coverage in the world.

*The Health of Americans*   Historically, most reductions in death rates have resulted from public health and sanitation improvements, including immunizations, clean public water supplies, sanitary sewage disposal, improved diets, and increased standards of living. Many of the leading causes of death today (see Table 17-2), including heart disease, stroke, cirrhosis of the liver, AIDS, and suicide, are closely linked to heredity, personal habits and lifestyles (smoking, eating, drinking, exercise, stress, sexual practices), and the physical environment—factors

## TABLE 17-2   LEADING CAUSES OF DEATH

|  | *Deaths per 100,000 population per year* | | | |
|---|---|---|---|---|
|  | 1960 | 1970 | 1980 | 1992 |
| All causes | 954.7 | 945.3 | 883.4 | 852.9 |
| Heart disease | 369.0 | 362.0 | 336.0 | 281.4 |
| Stroke (cerebrovascular) | 108.0 | 101.9 | 75.5 | 56.4 |
| Cancer | 149.2 | 162.8 | 183.9 | 204.1 |
| Accidents | 52.3 | 56.4 | 46.7 | 34.0 |
| Pneumonia | 37.3 | 30.9 | 24.1 | 30.9 |
| Diabetes | 16.7 | 18.9 | 15.5 | 19.6 |
| Cirrhosis | 11.3 | 15.5 | 13.5 | 10.1 |
| Suicide | 10.6 | 11.6 | 11.9 | 12.0 |
| Homicide | 4.7 | 8.3 | 10.7 | 9.9 |

*Source: Statistical Abstract of the United States, 1995, p. 96.*

# Health and Health Care Costs in Advanced Democracies

Americans spend more than any other nation in the world for health care (see figure). They spend over 50 percent more than Canadians and nearly 100 percent more than Japanese. Few people would object to heavy spending for health care if they get their money's worth. But cross-national comparisons of health statistics indicate that Americans on the average are less healthy than citizens in other advanced democracies. The United States ranks *below* most other advanced nations in life expectancy and infant death rates—two commonly used measures of national health.

The United States offers some of the most advanced and sophisticated medical care in the world, attracting patients from the countries that rank well ahead of it in various health measures. The United States is the locus of some of the most advanced medical research, attracting medical researchers from throughout the world. But the high quality of medical care available in the United States, combined with the poor health statistics of the general public, suggest that the nation's health care problems center more on *access* to care and education and prevention of health problems than on the quality of care available.

*Source: Statistical Abstract of the United States, 1995, pp. 849–50.*

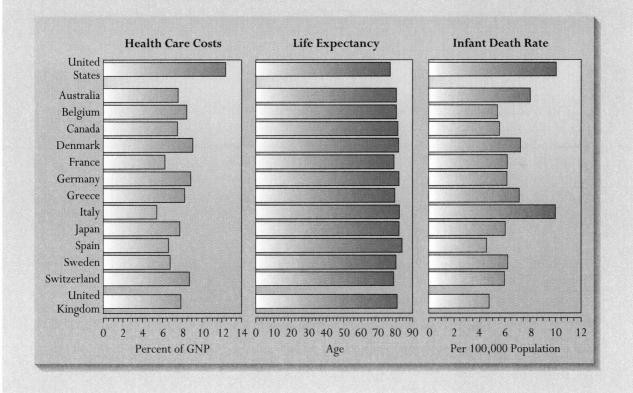

over which doctors and hospitals have no direct control. Thus the greatest contribution to better health is likely to be found in altered personal habits and lifestyles rather than in more medical care.

Thanks to improved health-care habits as well as breakthroughs in medical technology, Americans are living longer than ever before. Public awareness pro-

# Smoking: An Educational Approach

Prevention through education is often recommended as a strategy in health care, but it is difficult to point to specific successes with this approach. Smoking is a notable exception. The decrease in the percentage of adult smokers in the years since the government first labeled cigarettes a health hazard has been substantial. And yet the federal government has not banned smoking or the manufacturing of cigarettes; no federal bureaucracy has been created specifically to implement antismoking laws; and relatively few tax dollars have been spent to curtail smoking.

According to the U.S. Public Health Service, the proportion of American adults who smoke decreased from 42.5 percent in 1965 to 22.4 percent in 1995. What could account for this significant change in a health-related habit?

In 1964, the American Cancer Society persuaded President John F. Kennedy to establish a special advisory commission to the surgeon general of the United States charged with making a comprehensive review of all the data relating to smoking and health. The famous "Surgeon General's Report" concluded that cigarette smoking was a serious health hazard and that cigarette smoking was causally related to lung cancer. It also reported that cigarette smoking was associated with coronary disease, chronic bronchitis, and emphysema.* Despite tobacco industry efforts to discredit the report, cigarette sales dropped sharply. Although sales recovered after several years, increasing percentages of adults gave up smoking or never started the habit.

The Federal Cigarette Labeling and Advertising Act of 1966 required all cigarette packages (and later all cigarette advertising) to be marked with the statement: "Caution: Cigarette Smoking May Be Dangerous to Your Health." In 1970, Congress approved legislation banning all cigarette commercials on radio and television. In 1971, the Interstate Commerce Commission restricted smoking to certain sections of buses and trains, and the Civil Aeronautics Board did the same on airlines in 1973, finally banning smoking on all domestic flights in 1990. Many cities across the nation have also acted to limit smoking in public. Finally, the taxes levied on tobacco by the federal government and many state governments are designed as much to discourage use as to gain revenue. Reformers have argued that a federal tax as high as one or two dollars per pack of cigarettes would be justified to both discourage smoking and to offset the added health costs imposed upon the nation by smokers.

Note, however, that the greatest progress in reducing smoking has come about through the government's educational efforts.

*Report of the Advisory Committee to the Surgeon General of the Public Health Service, *Smoking and Health* (Washington, D.C.: Government Printing Office, 1964).

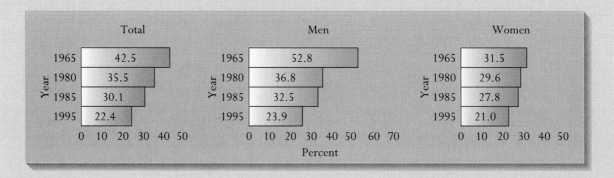

CHAPTER 17 • POLITICS AND SOCIAL WELFARE

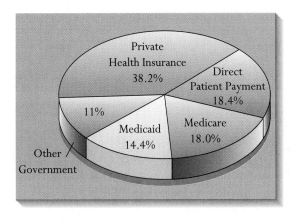

Source: Statistical Abstract of the United States, 1995, p. 109.

**FIGURE 17-5** **Who Pays the Medical Bills?**

*Critics of America's current health insurance system refer to it as a "patchwork" of different payment sources. About 43 percent of the nation's medical bills are paid by government, including 18 percent under Medicare for elderly people and 14 percent under Medicaid for poor people. Patient payments account for little more than 18 percent.*

grams concerning the risks associated with many causes of death—including heart disease, strokes, accidents, pneumonia, diabetes, and emphysema (see *Up Close:* "Smoking: An Educational Approach")—have probably contributed to declines in these causes of death. However, much of this decline has been offset by a rise in deaths by cancer, despite growth in spending for research and treatment.

*Access to Care*   A major challenge in health care is to extend coverage to all Americans. Today, about 85 percent of the nation's population is covered by either government or private health insurance. Government pays about 43 percent of all health care costs—through Medicare for the aged, Medicaid for the poor, and other government programs, including military and veterans' care. Private insurance pays for 39 percent of the nation's health costs. Direct payments by patients account for only 18 percent (see Figure 17-5).

But about 15 percent of the U.S. population—an estimated 35–40 million Americans—have *no* medical insurance. These include workers and their dependents whose employers do not offer a health insurance plan as well as unemployed people who are not eligible for Medicare or Medicaid. Another 30 million Americans suffer gaps in insurance coverage in any year owing to unemployment or shifts in jobs. People who lack health insurance may postpone or go without needed medical care or may be denied medical care by hospitals and physicians in all but emergency situations. Confronted with serious illness, they may be obliged to impoverish themselves in order to become eligible for Medicaid. Any unpaid medical bills must be absorbed by hospitals or shifted to paying patients and their insurance companies.

*Coverage Gaps*   Even people who *do* have health insurance often confront serious financial problems in obtaining medical care owing to inadequate coverage. Medicare, like most private insurance plans, requires patients to pay some *initial* charges called **deductibles.** The purpose of deductibles is to discourage unnecessary treatment. Patients must also make up any difference between doctors' actual charges and the rates allowed by their insurance plans. Indeed, it is estimated that only about half of the doctors in the nation accept Medicare rates as payment in full. In addition, Medicare and many private insurance plans do not

**Deductibles:** Initial charges in insurance plans, paid by beneficiaries.

*Lack of health insurance forces many Americans to postpone regular visits to a doctor and to rely on crowded hospital emergency rooms when they become sick.*

pay for prescription drugs, eyeglasses, hearing aids, or routine physical examinations.

More important, perhaps, Medicare does not pay for long-term care or catastrophic illness. Medicare covers only the first 60 days of hospitalization; it covers nursing home care for 100 days only if the patient is sent there from a hospital. In 1988, Congress attempted to remedy this problem by adding catastrophic health care coverage to Medicare. The program was jettisoned, however, in the face of a strong protest from seniors who opposed the tax surcharge on Medicare enrollees (elderly people) that was to have funded this coverage. Apparently senior citizens wanted their added benefits paid for by working people; if forced to pay themselves, they would rather not have the benefits.

As the number and proportion of the elderly population grows in the United States (eighty years and over is the fastest-growing age group in the nation), the need for long-term nursing-home care grows. Medicaid assistance to needy people is paid to nursing-home patients, but middle-class people cannot qualify for Medicaid without first "spending down" their savings. Long-term nursing-home care threatens their assets and their children's inheritance. Private insurance policies covering long-term care are said to be too expensive. So senior citizen groups have lobbied heavily for long-term nursing-home care to be paid for by taxpayers under Medicare.

*Health Care Cost Inflation*   No system of health care can provide as much as people will use. Anyone whose health and life may be at stake will want the most thorough diagnostic testing, the most constant care, the most advanced treatment. Sworn to preserve life, doctors, too, want the most advanced diagnostic and treatment facilities available for their patients. Under conditions of uncertainty in a medical situation—and there is always some uncertainty—physicians are trained to seek more consultations, run more tests, and try new therapeutic approaches. Any tendency for doctors to limit testing and treatment is countered by the threat of malpractice suits; it is always easier to order one more test or procedure than to risk even the tiniest chance that failing to do so will someday be cause for a court suit. So both patients and doctors push up the costs of health care, particularly when the public or private insurers foot the bill. Advances in medical technology have produced elaborate and expensive equipment. Hospitals that have made heavy financial investment in this equipment must use it as often as possible. As a result of the endless demand for, and very limited constraints on, the costs of health care in the United States, these costs have risen much faster than prices in general. Medical costs have nearly tripled over the last ten years and consume an ever-increasing percentage of the nation's total.

*Coping with Costs*   Both private and government insurers have made efforts to counter rising costs. Private insurers have negotiated discounts with groups of physicians and with hospitals—**preferred provider organizations (PPOs)**—and have implemented rules to guide physicians about when patients should and should not receive costly diagnostic and therapeutic procedures—**managed care.** Medicare no longer pays hospitals based on costs incurred; instead it pays fixed fees based on primary and secondary diagnoses at the time of admission. Both government and private insurers have encouraged the expansion of **health maintenance organizations (HMOs),** groups that promise to provide a stipulated list of services to patients for a fixed fee and that are able to provide care at lower total costs than can other providers.

Many of the efforts by both private insurers and governments to control costs have created new problems, however, including cost-control regulations and restrictions that add to administrative costs and create a mountain of paperwork for physicians and hospitals, and frustration and anger among both health care workers and patients. Doctors and hospitals argue that the *administrative* costs imposed by these cost-control measures far exceed whatever savings are achieved.

Certainly health care costs have continued to rise. Whether this trend reflects the failure of cost-control efforts or the strength of forces driving up costs is not clear. What is increasingly obvious is that payers, private and public, are finding health care costs increasingly burdensome and even insupportable.

## POLITICS AND HEALTH CARE REFORM

Health care reform centers on two central problems: controlling costs and expanding access. These problems are related: expanding access to Americans who are currently uninsured and closing gaps in coverage requires increased costs, even while the central thrust of reform is to bring down overall health care costs.

**Preferred provider organizations (PPOs):** Groups of hospitals and physicians who have joined together to offer their services to private insurers at a discount.

**Managed care:** Programs designed to keep health care costs down by the establishment of strict guidelines regarding when and what diagnostic and therapeutic procedures should be administered to patients under various circumstances.

**Health maintenance organizations (HMOs):** Health care provider groups that provide a stipulated list of services to patients for a fixed fee that is usually substantially lower than such care would otherwise cost.

*Achieving Universal Coverage*  There are three broad approaches to achieving universal coverage of health care for all Americans: (1) national health insurance paid for by tax revenues; (2) mandated private health insurance for everyone, with vouchers given to low-income families; and (3) mandated employer-sponsored health insurance for all workers and their dependents, together with expanded government insurance for nonworkers.

- *National health insurance:* Under this approach, *all* Americans would be entitled to a stipulated list of services from physicians, hospitals, and nursing homes, regardless of their employment, age, medical status, or income level. The federal government would be the "single payer" of health care costs through increased taxes. Hospitals would operate on budgets periodically negotiated with the government. Government fee schedules would dictate payments to physicians. Patients also might have to pay some share of the costs at the time of illness. This approach to health care would shift most costs from the private to the public sector.
- *Mandatory private health insurance:* Under this approach, all Americans would be required to carry health insurance (just as many states require drivers to carry automobile insurance). Low-income families would receive government vouchers to cover their costs. Though individuals and families would bear responsibility for carrying insurance, employers might still sponsor insurance plans and/or assist their employees in securing group discounts.
- *Mandatory employer-sponsored health insurance:* Under this approach, all full-time workers and their dependents would be covered by their companies, and government would extend its coverage to serve all those people who are not in the work force. Firms not currently insuring their employees might raise prices or slow growth of wages to cover their new costs. Some businesses might be excused from providing insurance if they paid a payroll tax to a government plan. This "play or pay" approach would encourage companies facing unusually high premiums or paying low average wages to choose a less costly option than sponsoring insurance. Thus the tax would have to be set high enough—roughly 10 percent of payroll—to encourage most firms to sponsor health insurance rather than pay the tax. Taxes would have to be raised to insure the currently uninsured who are not connected to a household with an insured worker.

*Controlling Costs*  Controlling health care costs is a far greater challenge than achieving universal access. Three broad approaches to controlling costs have been advanced: (1) market-based competition; (2) managed competition; and (3) government-mandated expenditure caps on health care spending.

- *Market competition:* Market-based competition relies mainly on insurance companies offering efficient services to employers and individuals. This approach may succeed in holding down some medical costs. Insurers are increasingly turning to health maintenance organizations and preferred provider (physicians and hospitals) systems. HMOs and preferred providers agree to provide medical care at predetermined discounted rates. Other cost control measures include pre-hospital-admission review and prior authorization for various procedures. But as noted earlier, these market techniques are already in widespread use, while health care costs continue to skyrocket.

- *Managed competition:* **Managed competition** is an arrangement in which **health insurance purchasing alliances** pool employers and individuals in the purchase of health insurance. Authorizing several alliances in an area would promote competition not only among insurers and providers but also among the alliances themselves. People would join together in these organizations to improve their bargaining power with insurers and providers. Alliances would be required to accept all applicants, including those with preexisting conditions, though they might receive government subsidies for members of groups expected to generate especially high costs. Alliances would negotiate prices with hospitals and physicians. Providers (health maintenance organizations, hospitals, physicians groups, as well as insurance companies) would compete for alliance business.

- *Health spending caps:* Spending caps would require the federal government to establish a ceiling on U.S. health care spending. A national budget would be parceled out among regions or states and then allocated among hospitals and other providers. No one has described in detail how such expenditure caps would be calculated, what organization would determine allocations among and within the states, and how the limits would be enforced. The objective is the imposition of budget discipline on health care providers.

*Health Care Politics*　President Bill Clinton campaigned on a promise to reform the nation's health care system by both expanding access and containing costs. The Clinton comprehensive health care plan did not include national health insurance but nevertheless shifted principal reliance for health care to the federal government. It incorporated elements of (1) mandated employer-sponsored health insurance; (2) managed competition through government health insurance purchasing alliances; and (3) national spending caps.

The Clinton plan, spearheaded by Hillary Rodham Clinton (see *People in Politics:* "Hillary Rodham Clinton and Health Care Policy Making"), failed to pass Congress for a variety of reasons. The choice of a national comprehensive plan that would have restructured one-sixth of the economy, as opposed to more modest incremental reforms, may have been the initial mistake. The complex plan caused a great deal of public confusion and enabled opponents—notably the health insurance industry, with its effective "Harry and Louise" television ads—to raise fears about the effect of the plan on consumers (see *Up Close:* "How Harry and Louise Killed Hillary's Health Plan," in Chapter 9). Indeed, for the 85 percent of Americans already covered by public and private health insurance, the plan raised more questions than it resolved. Benefits went mostly to the 15 percent of Americans who were uninsured. Cost containment, the greatest concern of the middle class, was largely ignored. Liberals in Congress, who favored a Canadian-style "single payer" governmental health care, paid for by tax increases, were only lukewarm supporters of the president's plan. Republicans and some conservative Democrats opposed employer mandates, preferring instead more modest, incremental insurance reforms, including requiring com-

**Managed competition:** An approach to health care cost control in which individuals and/or companies join health insurance purchasing organizations that negotiate with private health insurance companies, HMOs, PPOs, and private physicians and hospitals to obtain the best care possible at a low cost.

**Health insurance purchasing alliances:** Regional cooperatives that obtain the best care—lowest cost health care for individuals and businesses in a managed competition situation.

*Harry and Louise puzzle over the Clinton health care plan in one of a series of ads sponsored by the health insurance industry that helped kill the plan.*

# Hillary Rodham Clinton and Health Care Policy Making

Hillary Rodham Clinton is not the first politically powerful First Lady. That distinction belongs to Eleanor Roosevelt; however, in Roosevelt's era the power of the First Lady was exercised in a more subtle fashion. As chair of the president's health care task force, Hillary Rodham Clinton possessed official responsibility for a key area of national policy making. But her influence extends well beyond the health care field to virtually all areas of presidential responsibility, earning her the label "co-president."

Hillary Rodham grew up in suburban Chicago, the daughter of wealthy parents who sent her to the private, prestigious Wellesley College. A 1969 honors graduate with a counterculture image—horn-rimmed glasses, long, straggling hair, no makeup—she was chosen by her classmates to give a commencement speech—a rambling statement about "more immediate, ecstatic, and penetrating modes of living."

At Yale Law School Hillary met a long-haired, bearded Rhodes scholar from Arkansas, Bill Clinton, who was just as politically ambitious as she was. Both Hillary and Bill received their law degrees in 1973. Bill returned to Arkansas to build a career in state politics, while Hillary went to Washington as an attorney—first for a liberal lobbying group, the Children's Defense Fund, and later on the staff of the House Judiciary Committee seeking to impeach President Richard Nixon. But Rodham and other Yale grads traveled to Arkansas to help Clinton run unsuccessfully for Congress in 1974. Hillary decided to stay with Bill in Little Rock; they married before his next campaign, a successful run for state attorney general in 1976. Hillary remained Hillary Rodham, even as her husband went on to the governorship in 1978. She taught briefly at the University of

Arkansas Law School and eventually joined Little Rock's influential Rose Law Firm. She kept her Washington ties with the Children's Defense Fund. She also became a director of Wal-Mart Stores, TCBY Enterprises, the LaFarge Corporation, and the federal government's Legal Services Corporation.

Her husband's 1980 defeat for reelection as governor was blamed on his liberal leanings; therefore, in his 1982 comeback Bill repackaged himself as a moderate and centrist. Hillary cooperated by becoming Mrs. Bill Clinton, shedding her horn-rims for contacts, blonding her hair, and echoing her husband's more moderate line. These tactics helped propel them back into the governor's mansion. Hillary soon became a full partner in the Rose firm, regularly earning more than $200,000 a year (while Bill earned only $35,000 as Arkansas governor). She won national recognition as one of the "100 most influential lawyers in the United States," according to the *American National Law Journal*. She chaired the American Bar Association's Commission on Women and the Profession.

In January 1993, newly elected president Bill Clinton named Hillary head of the President's Task Force on National Health Reform. Once installed as the "health czar," she moved expeditiously in the corridors of power. Her task force assembled a formidable array of staff, consultants, and committees and produced a 1,342-page bill that reorganized the nation's entire health care system. The *New York Times* dubbed her "St. Hillary" because of her unyielding commitment and determination*—qualities that did not stand her in good stead with powerful interest groups such as the American Medical Association and the American Association of Retired People, or with the members of Congress in whose hands the fate of the health care plan rested.

Indeed, Hillary's uncompromising liberalism may have contributed to the defeat of the Clinton comprehensive health care plan. She blamed "the special interests" for its defeat. Later, she avoided direct policy-making responsibilities, lowering her public profile and assuming a more traditional, supporting First Lady role.

*New York Times Magazine, May 23, 1993, p. 64.

panies to accept persons with preexisting conditions and making insurance coverage "portable"—that is, carryable by employees from job to job. Republicans were able to brand the president's bill as a "government takeover" of health care. The president was unwilling to consider more modest reforms. After months of debate, public opinion polls showed a majority of Americans opposing Clinton's plan, and it failed to pass even a Democratic-controlled Congress in 1994. Finally, in 1996, a Republican Congress passed, and the Democratic president signed, a "portability" plan that guaranteed that people who lose or leave their jobs can retain their health insurance even with a preexisting condition.

*Interest-Group Battles*   Interest-group battles over the details of health care reform have been intense. Virtually everyone has a financial stake in any proposal to reorganize the nation's health care system.

- Employers, especially small businesses, are fearful of added costs.
- Physicians strongly oppose price controls and treatment guidelines, as well as programs that take away patient choice of physician or force all physicians into HMOs. Overall, support is strongest among those physicians most likely to benefit from the plan—general family practitioners—and weakest among those most likely to lose—medical specialists.
- Psychiatrists, psychologists, mental health and drug abuse counselors, physical therapists, chiropractors, optometrists, and dentists all want their own services covered. Providing such "comprehensive" services greatly increases costs.
- Drug companies want to see prescription drugs paid for, but they vigorously oppose price controls on drugs.
- Hospitals want all patients to be insured but oppose government payment schedules.
- Health maintenance organizations and preferred provider organizations expect to gain from reform, but they do not want to see government-sponsored health care alliances established to negotiate (or dictate) lower prices.
- Medical specialists fear that proposals for managed care will result in fewer consultations, and medical manufacturers fear it will limit use of high-priced equipment.
- The powerful senior citizens lobby wants added benefits—including coverage for drugs, eyeglasses, dental care, and nursing homes—but fears folding Medicare into a larger health care system.
- Veterans' groups want to retain separate VA hospitals and medical services.
- Opponents of abortion rights are prepared to do battle to keep national coverage from including such procedures, while many supporters of abortion rights will not back any plan that excludes abortion services.

While polls show that a majority of Americans are willing to pay higher taxes for comprehensive health care, many are willing to see increases only in "sin taxes" on alcohol, tobacco, and guns.

# SUMMARY NOTES

- Social welfare policy largely determines who gets what from government; over half of the federal budget is devoted to "human resources." The government is a major redistributor of income from group to group.

- The poor are not the principal beneficiaries of social welfare spending. Only about one-fifth of all federal social welfare spending is means-tested. Most social welfare spending, including the largest programs—Social Security and Medicare—goes to the middle class.

- About 13–15 percent of the U.S. population falls below the annual cash income level that the federal government sets as its official definition of poverty. But this definition includes cash income from welfare programs; without government aid, perhaps 25 percent of the population would fall below the poverty line. On the other hand, the official poverty count includes many people receiving in-kind benefits and others for whom low current incomes do not create real hardship.

- Poverty is temporary for many families, but some poverty is persistent—lasting five years to a lifetime. Prolonged poverty and welfare dependency create an "underclass" beset by many social and economic problems. Poverty is more frequent among families headed by single mothers; about one of every five children in the United States is raised in poverty.

- Nearly one-third of the population of the United States receives some form of government payments or benefits. Entitlements are government benefits for which Congress has set eligibility criteria by law. Social Security and Medicare are the largest entitlement programs. They are based on the social insurance principle: recipients made prior contributions, and they are entitled to benefits regardless of their income or wealth.

- Senior citizens are politically powerful; they vote more often than younger people and they have powerful lobbying organizations in Washington.

- Social Security is the largest single item in the federal budget. Yet proposals to modify Social Security or Medicare benefits are politically dangerous. Nevertheless, concerns over the future financing of these programs, which are now being funded out of current receipts, have led some politicians to call for reconsideration of COLAs and of payments to wealthy retirees.

- Public assistance programs, including Aid to Families with Dependent Children, Supplemental Security Income, and food stamps, do not require prior contribution, but recipients must show that they are poor in order to claim benefits.

- Social welfare policies seek to alleviate hardship; at the same time they seek to avoid creating disincentives to work. Cash welfare payments may, for example, encourage teenage pregnancies, undermine family foundations, and contribute to long-term social dependency. Workfare reforms centered on moving former welfare recipients into the work force. But doing so required increased spending on education, job training, health care, and child care, and the results were disappointing.

- Current welfare reform efforts include block grants to the states to replace federal entitlements to cash payments and time limits on welfare enrollment.

- Americans spend more on health care than citizens of any other nation, yet we fail to insure almost 15 percent of the population. And the United States ranks below many other advanced nations in common health measures.

- Health care reform centers on two related problems—extending health insurance coverage to all Americans and containing the skyrocketing costs of health care. Proposals for extending coverage include national health insurance, mandatory private health insurance, and mandatory employer-sponsored health insurance. Attempts to control costs include market-based competition, managed competition, and government-mandated expenditure caps.

# SELECTED READINGS

JENKS, CHRISTOPHER. *Rethinking Social Policy: Race, Poverty, and the Underclass.* Cambridge, Mass.: Harvard University Press, 1992. A series of essays by a leading commentator on social welfare policy, including the thesis that welfare dependency is primarily a product of the fact that low-wage jobs pay less than welfare.

JENKS, CHRISTOPHER, and PAUL E. PETERSON, eds. *The Urban Underclass.* Washington, D.C.: Brookings Institution, 1991. A collection of essays arguing that "the most important problem—the rise in the percentage of children living in poverty—is due to the increasing number of female-headed households and the decline in the earnings of young men."

KELSO, WILLIAM A. *Poverty and the Underclass.* New York: New York University Press, 1994. An excellent introduction to the debate about poverty in America, summarizing the existing research on the causes of poverty and describing how contemporary views of the poor are changing.

MARMOR, THEODORE R., JERRY L. MASHAW, and PHILIP L. HARVEY. *America's Misunderstood Welfare State.* New York: Basic Books, 1990. An argument that ideological debate over welfare overstates major criticisms of the welfare state and obscures general agreement among Americans on the structure of the "opportunity-insurance state."

MEAD, LAWRENCE M. *The New Politics of Poverty.* New York: Basic Books, 1992. A persuasive argument that the underlying problem of poverty today is one of social values—resocializing the dependent poor—rather than the provision of jobs.

MURRAY, CHARLES. *Losing Ground.* New York: Basic Books, 1984. A well-argued, yet controversial, thesis that government social welfare programs, by encouraging social dependence, have had the unintended and perverse effect of slowing and even reversing earlier progress in reducing poverty, crime, ignorance, and discrimination.

WILSON, WILLIAM JULIUS. *The Truly Disadvantaged.* Chicago: University of Chicago Press, 1987. The thesis that the growth of the underclass is primarily a result of the decline of manufacturing jobs and their shift to the suburbs, and the resulting concentration of poor, jobless, isolated people in the inner city.

# POLITICS AND NATIONAL SECURITY

## CHAPTER OUTLINE

Power among Nations
The Legacy of the Cold War
The Nuclear Threat
Post-Cold War Threats
Military Force Levels
The Use of Military Force
The Price of Peace

## FEATURES

*Up Close:* The Rise and Fall of Great Powers
*What Do You Think?* How Should We Defend against a Ballistic
  Missile Attack?
*Up Close:* The Use of Force: Operation Desert Storm
*Compared to What?* Citizens' Knowledge of the World

## POWER AMONG NATIONS

International politics, like all politics, is a struggle for power. The struggle for power is global; it involves all the nations and peoples of the world, whatever their goals or ideals. As the distinguished political scientist Hans Morgenthau once observed:

> Whatever the ultimate aims of international politics, power is always the immediate aim. Statesmen and peoples may ultimately seek freedom, security, prosperity, or power itself. They may define their goals in terms of a religious, philosophic, economic, or social ideal. . . . But whenever they strive to realize their goal by means of international politics, they are striving for power.[1]

The struggle for power among nations has led to many attempts over the centuries to bring order to the international system (see *Up Close:* "The Rise and Fall of Great Powers").

*The Balance-of-Power System*   One method of trying to bring order to international relations is the **balance-of-power** system. In the eighteenth and nineteenth centuries, nations deliberately attempted to stabilize

657

# The Rise and Fall of Great Powers

Can the United States learn from the experiences of the great powers in history? In his book *The Rise and Fall of Great Powers,* historian Paul Kennedy argues that patterns of expansion and decline in a series of great powers can be observed over the past 500 years—patterns that warn the leadership of the United States against overextension of the nation's power.

The great European powers in previous centuries—Spain, France, Great Britain, and Germany—achieved dominance when their military power, economic strength, and political skills complemented each other. But as each of these great powers expanded, their domestic economies and political wisdom were unable to match their extended military commitments. World power can only be maintained by a prudent balance between economic wealth and military expenditure.

At the beginning of the sixteenth century, Spain—Europe's first great power—developed its dominant naval forces through economic exploitation of its colonies in the New World. But soon its colonial adventures, and the wars they engendered against France and England, exhausted Spain's economic base. Spain's rulers turned to deficit financing and inflated money to support Spanish military power, but these devices only hastened Spain's decline as a great power.

France first developed formidable military forces under the Bourbon kings. After the French Revolution in 1789, Napoleon Bonaparte built the French army into the world's preeminent military force. But Napoleon overextended his empire and plundered his nation and much of Europe to support his army. This overextension made his ultimate defeat inevitable.

For more than a century, Great Britain managed to combine economic growth, military power, and political skill at managing its great empire with very small numbers of troops. But when Great Britain was finally tested by Germany's ascendancy in World War I, both powers exhausted their economies and their peoples in the prolonged and costly struggle.

At the beginning of the twentieth century, Germany's combined economic strength and military prowess might have enabled it to prevail against its European adversaries in World War I had it not provoked the United States to add its growing economic and military power to the Allied cause. In World War II, Germany's ultimate defeat was ensured when Adolf Hitler overextended his military forces, ordering them simultaneously to fight the Western powers and invade Russia.

Kennedy does not conclude from his analysis that the United States is militarily overcommitted or doomed to fall as a great power (though some liberal critics of America's power in the world have interpreted Kennedy's book in this fashion). Yet he observes that with the economic development of Western Europe and Japan and the emergence of China as a world power, the United States is not as powerful relative to the rest of the world as it was at the end of World War II. America's governmental and trade deficits resemble the problems of previous declining powers. Still, according to Kennedy, the United States can maintain both wealth and power if it recognizes the relationship between economic and military strength, uses its resources wisely, and employs its political skills to rally popular support at home and abroad.

*Source:* Paul Kennedy, *The Rise and Fall of Great Powers* (New York: Random House, 1988).

---

**Balance of power:** An attempt to bring order to international relations in the eighteenth and nineteenth centuries by creating a system of alliances among nations so that the relative strength of each alliance balanced that of the others.

international relations by creating systems of alliances designed to balance the power of one group of nations against the power of another, and thus to discourage war. For almost an entire century—from the end of the Napoleonic Wars (1815) until the outbreak of World War I (1914)—the balance-of-power system appeared to be at least partially effective in Europe. But an important defect in the balance-of-power system is that a small conflict between two nations that are members of separate alliances can draw all the member nations of both alliances into the conflict and thus can quickly turn a small conflict into a major war. This is essentially what happened in World War I, when a minor conflict in the Balkan nations resulted in a very destructive war between the Allied Powers (England, France, Russia, and eventually the United States) and the Central Powers (Germany, Austria-Hungary, and Turkey). Indeed, World War I proved so destructive (10 million men were killed on the battlefield between 1914 and 1918) that there was a worldwide demand to replace the balance-of-power system with a new arrangement—collective security.

*Collective Security*    Originally, **collective security** meant that *all* nations would join together to guarantee each other's "territorial integrity and existing political independence" against "external aggression" by any nation. This was the idea behind the League of Nations, established in 1919. However, opposition to international involvement was so great in the United States after World War I that, after a lengthy debate, the Senate refused to enroll the United States in the League of Nations. More important, the League of Nations failed to deal with acts of aggression by the Axis Powers—Germany, Japan, and Italy—in the 1930s. During that decade, Japan invaded Manchuria, Italy invaded Ethiopia, and Germany dismembered Czechoslovakia. The result was a war even more devastating than World War I: World War II cost more than 40 million lives, both civilian and military.

*Formation of the United Nations*    Even after World War II, the notion of collective security remained an ideal of the victorious Allied Powers. The Charter of the United Nations, signed in 1945, provided for:

* The Security Council, with eleven member nations, five of them being permanent members—the United States, the **Soviet Union** (whose membership is now held by Russia), Britain, France, and China—and each having the power to veto any action by the Security Council.
* The General Assembly, composed of all the member nations, each with a single vote.
* The Secretariat, headed by a Secretary General with a staff at United Nations headquarters in New York.
* Organizations to handle specialized affairs—for example, the Economic and Social Council, the Trusteeship Council, and the International Court of Justice at The Hague in the Netherlands.

The Security Council has the "primary responsibility" for maintaining "international peace and security." The General Assembly has authority over "any matter affecting the peace of the world," although it is supposed to defer to the Security Council when the council has already taken up a particular security matter. No nation has a veto in the General Assembly; every nation has one vote, regardless of its size or power. Most resolutions can be passed by a majority vote.

*The United Nations in the Cold War*    The United Nations (UN) proved largely ineffective during the long Cold War confrontation between the communist nations, led by the Soviet Union, and the Western democracies, led by the United States. The UN grew from its original 51 member nations to 185, but most of those nations were headed by authoritarian regimes of one kind or

**Collective security:** An attempt to bring order to international relations by all nations joining together to guarantee each other's "territorial integrity" and "independence" against "external aggression."

**Soviet Union:** The Union of Soviet Socialist Republics (USSR) consisting of Russia and its bordering lands and ruled by the communist regime in Moscow, officially dissolved in 1991.

*President Clinton addressing the United Nations during celebrations of its 50th anniversary. The end of the Cold War has brought new vitality and effectiveness to the U.N.*

**Superpowers:** Refers to the United States and the Soviet Union after World War II, when these two nations dominated international politics.

**Regional security:** An attempt to bring order to international relations during the Cold War by creating regional alliances between a superpower and nations of a particular region.

**North Atlantic Treaty Organization (NATO):** A mutual-security agreement and joint military command uniting the nations of Western Europe, initially formed to resist Soviet expansionism.

another. The Western democracies were outnumbered in the General Assembly, and the Soviet Union frequently used its veto to prevent action by the Security Council. Anti-Western and antidemocratic speeches became common in the General Assembly. Nevertheless, the United States, because of its wealth, paid the largest share of UN expenses.

During the Cold War, the UN was overshadowed by the confrontation of the world's two **superpowers:** the United States and the Soviet Union. Indeed, international conflicts throughout the world—in the Middle East, Africa, Latin America, Southeast Asia, and elsewhere—were usually influenced by some aspect of the superpower struggle.

*Regional Security*   The general disappointment with the United Nations as a form of collective security gave rise as early as 1949 to a different approach: **regional security.** In response to aggressive Soviet moves in Europe, the United States and the democracies of Western Europe created the **North Atlantic Treaty Organization (NATO).** In the NATO treaty, fifteen Western nations agreed to collective regional security: they agreed that "an armed attack against one or more [NATO nations] . . . shall be considered an attack against them all." The United States made a specific commitment to defend Western Europe in the event of a Soviet attack. A joint NATO military command was established (with Dwight D. Eisenhower as its first commander) to coordinate the defense of Western Europe.

After the formation of NATO, the Soviets made no further advances into Western Europe. The Soviets themselves, in response to NATO, drew up the Warsaw Pact, a comparable treaty with their own Eastern European satellite nations. But for many years the real deterrent to Warsaw Pact expansion was not the weak NATO armies but rather the pledge of the United States to use its strategic nuclear bomber force to inflict "massive retaliation" on the Soviet Union itself in the event of an attack on Western Europe.

The Warsaw Pact disintegrated following the dramatic collapse of the communist governments of Eastern Europe in 1989. Former Warsaw Pact nations—Poland, Hungary, Romania, Bulgaria, and East Germany—threw out their ruling communist regimes and demanded the withdrawal of Soviet troops from their territory. The Berlin Wall was dismantled in 1989, and Germany was formally reunified in 1990, bringing together the 61 million prosperous people of West Germany and the 17 million less affluent people of East Germany. (Unified Germany continues as a member of NATO.) The Communist Party was ousted from power in Moscow, and the Soviet Union collapsed in 1991. Its former member nations, including Russia, Ukraine, and Belarus, continue to struggle toward democratic reforms.

*NATO Today* The diminished threat to the security of Western Europe has raised a variety of questions regarding the future of NATO. Is NATO needed at all in view of the collapse of the Warsaw Pact and democratic reforms in Russia? Or should it continue, perhaps with reduced military forces, as insurance against a future renewal of a Soviet-style threat? Should NATO guarantee the security of the emerging democracies of Eastern Europe? Should NATO attempt to guarantee stability in Eastern Europe by intervening to end ethnic conflicts? Or should NATO be replaced with a new collective security arrangement, a Council on European Security that would include all European nations, including Russia, Ukraine, and other former states of the Soviet Union? What security role should the United States play in NATO, now that the principal threat to Western Europe has receded? All these questions currently confront the governments of the United States and other NATO members.

*The UN Today* The end of the Cold War has injected new vitality into the United Nations. Collective security has reemerged as a means of ordering relations among nations, even as regional security arrangements have eroded (as in the case of NATO) and collapsed (as in the case of the Warsaw Pact). Russia inherited the UN Security Council seat of the former Soviet Union, and the government of President Boris Yeltsin generally cooperated in UN efforts to bring stability to various regional conflicts. No longer are these conflicts "proxy" wars between the superpowers. Cooperation among the permanent members of the Security Council (the United States, Great Britain, France, and Russia, together with the acquiescence of China) has brought "a new world order" to international politics. But the United Nations and its Security Council must rely on "the last remaining superpower," the United States, to take the lead in enforcing its resolutions.

# THE LEGACY OF THE COLD WAR

For more than forty years following the end of World War II, the United States and the Soviet Union confronted each other in the protracted political, military, and ideological struggle known as the **Cold War.**

**Cold War:** The political, military, and ideological struggle between the United States and the Soviet Union following the end of World War II and ending with the collapse of the Soviet Union's communist government in 1991.

*Origins*    During World War II, the United States and the Soviet Union joined forces to eliminate the Nazi threat to the world. The United States dismantled its military forces at the end of the war in 1945, but the Soviet Union, under the brutal dictatorship of Josef Stalin, used the powerful Red Army to install communist governments in the nations of Eastern Europe in violation of wartime agreements to allow free elections. Stalin also ignored pledges to cooperate in a unified allied occupation of Germany; Germany was divided, and in 1948 Stalin unsuccessfully tried to oust the United States, Britain, and France from Berlin in a year-long "Berlin Blockade." Former British Prime Minister Winston Churchill warned the United States as early as 1946 that the Soviets were dividing Europe with an "Iron Curtain." When Soviet-backed communist guerrilla forces threatened Greece and Turkey in 1947, President Harry S. Truman responded with a pledge to "support free people who are resisting attempted subjugation by armed minorities or by outside pressures," a policy that became know as the **Truman Doctrine.**

*Containment*    The United States had fought two world wars to maintain democracy in Western Europe. The new threat of Soviet expansionism and communist world revolution caused America to assume world leadership on behalf of the preservation of democracy. In an influential article in the Council on Foreign Relation's journal, *Foreign Affairs,* the State Department's Russian expert, George F. Kennan, called for a policy of **containment:**

> It is clear that the main element of any United States policy toward the Soviet Union must be that of a long-term, vigilant containment of Russian expansive tendencies . . . Soviet pressure against the free institutions of the western world is something that can be contained by the adroit and vigilant application of counter-force.[2]

To implement the containment policy, the United States first initiated the **Marshall Plan,** named for Secretary of State George C. Marshall, to rebuild the economies of the Western European nations. Marshall reasoned that *economically* weak nations were more susceptible to communist subversion and Soviet intimidation. The subsequent formation of NATO provided the necessary *military* support to contain the Soviet Union.

*The Korean War*    The first military test of the containment policy came in June 1950, when communist North Korean armies invaded South Korea. President Truman assumed that the North Koreans were acting on behalf of their sponsor, the Soviet Union. The Soviets had already aided Chinese communists under the leadership of Mao Zedong in capturing control of mainland China in 1949. The United States quickly brought the Korean invasion issue to the Security Council. With the Soviets boycotting this meeting because the council had refused to seat the new communist delegation from China, the council passed a resolution calling on member nations to send troops to repel the invasion.

America's conventional (nonnuclear) military forces had been largely dismantled after World War II. Moreover, President Truman insisted on keeping most of the nation's forces in Europe, fearing that the Korean invasion was a diversion to be followed by a Soviet invasion of Western Europe. But General Douglas

**Truman Doctrine:** A U.S. foreign policy, first articulated by President Harry S. Truman, that pledged the United States to "support free peoples who are resisting attempted subjugation by armed minorities or by outside pressures."

**Containment:** A policy of preventing an enemy from expanding its boundaries and/or influence, specifically the U.S. foreign policy vis-à-vis the Soviet Union during the Cold War.

**Marshall Plan:** A U.S. program to rebuild the nations of Western Europe in the aftermath of World War II in order to render them less susceptible to communist influence and takeover.

CHAPTER 18 • POLITICS AND NATIONAL SECURITY

MacArthur, in a brilliant amphibious landing at Inchon behind North Korean lines, destroyed a much larger enemy army, captured the North Korean capital, and moved northward toward the Chinese border. Then in December 1950, disaster struck American forces as a million-strong Chinese army entered the conflict. Chinese troops surprised the Americans, inflicting heavy casualties, trapping entire units, and forcing U.S. troops to beat a hasty retreat. General MacArthur urged retaliation against China, but Truman sought to keep the war "limited." When MacArthur publicly protested political limits to military operations, Truman dismissed the popular general. The Korean War became a bloody stalemate.

Dwight Eisenhower was elected president in 1952 in large measure because of public frustration over "Korea, communism, and corruption." Eisenhower had promised to "go to Korea" to end the increasingly unpopular war. He also threatened to use nuclear weapons in the conflict but eventually agreed to a settlement along the original border between North and South Korea. Communist expansion in Korea was "contained," but at a high price: the United States lost more than 38,000 men in the war.

*The Cuban Missile Crisis*   Throughout the Cold War, the Soviet Union sought to expand its political and military presence among **Third World** nations. Many nations of Africa and Asia had recently replaced British, French, and Dutch colonial regimes, and resentment toward colonialism fueled anti-Western and anti-American politics around the world. The United States initially welcomed Fidel Castro's overthrow of the repressive Batista regime in Cuba in 1959, but when Castro allied his government with Moscow and invited Soviet military intervention into the Western Hemisphere, Washington sought his ouster. Under President Eisenhower, the Central Intelligence Agency (CIA) had planned a large "covert" operation—an invasion of Cuba by a brigade of Cuban exiles. Newly installed president John F. Kennedy approved the Bay of Pigs operation in early 1961, but when Castro's air force destroyed the makeshift invasion fleet offshore, Kennedy refused to provide U.S. air support. The surviving Cubans were forced to surrender.

The young president was tested again in 1961, when the Russians erected the Berlin Wall, physically dividing that city. Despite heated rhetoric, Kennedy did nothing. Eventually the wall would become a symbol of Soviet repression.

The most serious threat of nuclear holocaust during the entire Cold War was the Cuban Missile Crisis. In 1962, Soviet Premier Nikita Khrushchev sought to secretly install medium-range nuclear missiles in Cuba in an effort to give the Soviet Union nuclear capability against U.S. cities. In October 1962, intelligence photos showing Soviet missiles at Cuban bases touched off a thirteen-day crisis. President Kennedy rejected advice to launch an air strike to destroy the missiles before they could be activated. Instead, he publicly announced a naval blockade of Cuba, threatening to halt Soviet missile-carrying vessels at sea by force if necessary. The prospect of war appeared imminent; U.S. nuclear forces went on alert. Secretly, Kennedy proposed to withdraw U.S. nuclear missiles from Turkey in exchange for Soviet withdrawal of nuclear missiles from Cuba. Khrushchev's agreement to the deal appeared to the world as a backing down; Secretary of State Dean Rusk would boast: "We were eyeball to eyeball, and they blinked." Kennedy would be hailed for his statesmanship in the crisis; Khrushchev would soon lose his job.

**Third World:** Those nations of the world that remain economically underdeveloped.

*The Vietnam War*    United States involvement in Vietnam grew out of the policy of containment. President Eisenhower had declined to intervene in the former French colony in 1956 when communist forces led by Ho Chi Minh defeated French forces at the battle of Dien Bien Phu. The resulting Geneva Accords divided that country into North Vietnam, with a communist government, and South Vietnam, with a U.S.-backed government. When South Vietnamese communist (Viet Cong) guerrilla forces threatened the South Vietnamese government in the early 1960s, President Kennedy sent a force of more than 12,000 advisers and counterinsurgency forces to assist in every aspect of training and support for the Army of the Republic of Vietnam (ARVN). By 1964, units of the North Vietnamese Army (NVA) had begun to supplement the Viet Cong guerrilla forces in the south. Unconfirmed reports of an attack on U.S. Navy vessels by North Vietnamese torpedo boats led the U.S. Congress to pass the Gulf of Tonkin Resolution, which authorized the president to take "all necessary measures" to repel any armed attack against any U.S. forces in Southeast Asia.

In February 1965, President Lyndon B. Johnson ordered U.S. combat troops into South Vietnam and authorized a gradual increase in air strikes against North Vietnam. The fateful decision to commit U.S. ground combat forces to Vietnam was made without any significant effort to mobilize American public opinion, the government, or the economy for war. On the contrary, the president minimized the U.S. military effort, placed numerical limits on U.S. troop strength in Vietnam, limited bombing targets, and underestimated North Vietnam's military capabilities as well as expected U.S. casualties. U.S. ground troops were forbidden to cross into North Vietnam, and only once (in Cambodia in 1970) were they instructed to attack NVA forces elsewhere in Indochina.

Washington committed more than 500,000 troops to a war of attrition, a war in which U.S. firepower was expected to inflict sufficient casualties on the enemy to force a peace settlement. But over time, the failure to achieve any decisive military victories eroded popular support for the war. Official memos and documents from 1967 also show Secretary of Defense Robert McNamara and others who had initiated U.S. military actions becoming increasingly disenchanted with the military results.[3] President Johnson, seeking to rally support for the war by claiming that the United States was "winning," brought home General William Westmoreland, U.S. commander in Vietnam, to tell Congress that there was "light at the end of the tunnel." But these pronouncements only helped set the stage for the enemy's great political victory—the Tet offensive, begun on the first day of Tet, the most important holiday in Vietnam.

On January 31, 1968, Viet Cong forces blasted their way into the U.S. embassy compound in Saigon and held the courtyard for six hours. The attack was part of a massive, coordinated offensive against all major cities of South Vietnam. U.S. forces responded and inflicted very heavy casualties on the Viet Cong. By any military measure, the Tet offensive was a "defeat" for the enemy and a "victory" for U.S. forces. Yet the Tet offensive was Hanoi's greatest *political* victory. Television pictures of bloody fighting in Saigon and Hue seemed to mock the administration's reports of an early end to the war. The media, believing they had been duped by Johnson and Westmoreland, launched a long and bitter campaign against the war effort.

On March 31, 1968, President Johnson went on national television to make a dramatic announcement: he halted the bombing of North Vietnam and asked Hanoi for peace talks, concluding: "I shall not seek, and I will not accept, the nomination of my party for another term as your president." He also declined Westmoreland's request for more troops and for permission to attack North Vietnamese territory. Formal peace talks opened in Paris on May 13.

American objectives in Vietnam shifted again with the arrival in Washington of the new president, Richard Nixon, and his national security adviser, Henry Kissinger. Nixon and Kissinger knew the war must be ended, but they sought to end it "honorably." The South Vietnamese could not be abruptly abandoned without threatening the credibility of American commitments everywhere in the world. They also sought a peace settlement that would give South Vietnam a reasonable chance to survive. Toward these ends, they worked to create **detente**—relaxation of tension—with the Soviet Union and a new relationship with communist China. But even in the absence of a settlement with the communists in Vietnam, Nixon began the withdrawal of U.S. troops under the guise of "Vietnamization" of the war effort. ARVN forces were required to take up the burden of fighting as U.S. forces withdrew.

Unable to persuade Hanoi to make even the slightest concession at Paris, President Nixon sought to demonstrate American strength and resolve. In December 1972, the United States unleashed a devastating air attack directly on Hanoi for the first time. Critics at home labeled Nixon's action "the Christmas bombing," but when negotiations resumed in Paris in January, the North Vietnamese quickly agreed to peace on the terms that Kissinger and Le Duc Tho had worked out earlier.

The South Vietnamese government lasted two years after the agreement. The United States fulfilled none of its pledges, to either South or North Vietnam. Congress refused to provide significant military aid to the South Vietnamese. The Watergate scandal forced Nixon's resignation in August 1974. In early 1975, Hanoi decided that the Americans would not "jump back in" and therefore "the opportune moment" was at hand. When the NVA attacked the Central Highlands, South Vietnamese President Nguyen Van Thieu unwisely ordered a withdrawal to the coast, and the retreat quickly became a rout. President Gerald Ford never gave serious consideration to the use of U.S. military forces to repel the new invasion, and his requests to Congress for emergency military aid to the South Vietnamese fell on deaf ears. U.S. Ambassador Graham Martin, embarrassed by his government's abandonment of Vietnam, delayed implementation of escape plans until the last moment. As Saigon (now Ho Chi Minh City) fell to the North Vietnamese in April 1975, the United States abandoned hundreds of thousands of loyal Vietnamese who had fought alongside the Americans for years.[4] The spectacle of U.S. Marines using their rifle butts to keep desperate Vietnamese from boarding helicopters on the roof of the U.S. embassy "provided a tragic epitaph for twenty-five years of American involvement in Vietnam."[5]

America's humiliation in Vietnam had lasting national consequences. The United States suffered 47,378 battle deaths and missing-in-action among the 2.8 million U.S. personnel who served in Vietnam. Perhaps 1 million Vietnamese, military and civilian, in both the North and South, were killed during the war years. But the "peace" was more bloody than the war. In Cambodia, more than 2 million people were murdered by victorious communist forces in genocidal "killing fields." More than 1.5 million South Vietnamese were forcibly relocated to harsh rural areas and "reeducation camps." Nearly 500,000 "boat people" tried to flee their country; eventually the United States took in nearly 250,000 Vietnamese refugees. Unlike past wars, there were no victory parades, and no one could answer the question of the mother whose son was killed in Vietnam: "What did he die for?"

**Detente:** The relaxation of strained relations between nations, specifically used to refer to the relaxation of tensions between the United States and the Soviet Union during the Cold War.

*The Vietnam War Memorial in Washington, D.C. is inscribed with the names of the nearly 50,000 Americans who died in Vietnam. America's defeat fostered a lasting skepticism about the wisdom of foreign military intervention, leading to a new isolationism in foreign policy.*

*The Vietnam Syndrome*   A new isolationism permeated American foreign policy following defeat in Vietnam. The slogan "No more Vietnams" was used to oppose any U.S. military intervention, whether or not U.S. vital interests were at stake. Disillusionment replaced idealism. American leaders had exaggerated the importance of Vietnam; now Americans were unwilling to believe their leaders when they warned of other dangers.

In the late 1970s the Soviet Union rapidly expanded its political and military presence in Asia, Africa, the Middle East, Central America, and the Caribbean. Indeed, even as late as 1989, Soviet military forces were stationed in Asia (Vietnam, Cambodia, Laos, Mongolia), Africa (Angola, Congo, Ethiopia, Mali, Mozambique), the Middle East (Libya, Algeria, Iraq, Syria, South Yemen), the Caribbean (Cuba, Grenada), and Central and South America (Nicaragua, Peru).[6] The United States did little to respond to this wave of Soviet expansionism until the Soviet invasion of Afghanistan in 1979, when President Jimmy Carter authorized the largest covert action in CIA history—the military support of the Afghan guerrilla forces fighting Soviet occupation. The Soviets suffered a heavy drain of human and economic resources in their nine-year war in Afghanistan, which some dubbed "Russia's Vietnam."

*Rebuilding America's Defenses*   The decision to rebuild Western military forces and reassert international leadership on behalf of democratic values gained widespread support in the Western World. In 1979, President Jimmy Carter presented Congress with the first request for an increase in defense spending in more than a decade. British Prime Minister Margaret Thatcher, French President François Mitterrand, and German Chancellor Helmut Kohl all pledged to increase their defense efforts and all held fast against a "nuclear freeze" movement that would have locked in Soviet superiority in European-based nuclear weapons. When the Reagan Administration arrived in Washington in 1981, the defense buildup had already begun.

The Reagan defense buildup extended through 1985—with increases in defense spending, improvements in strategic nuclear weapons, and, perhaps more important, the rebuilding and reequipping of U.S. conventional forces. The American and NATO defense buildup, together with the promise of a new, expensive, and technologically sophisticated race for ballistic missile defenses, forecast heavy additional strains on the weak economy of the Soviet Union. (For many years the CIA had erroneously estimated Soviet defense spending at 14–15 percent of its gross national product; but recent revelations now indicate that the Soviet Union was spending more than 25 percent of its GNP on its military.) Thus, in 1985, when new Soviet President Mikhail Gorbachev came to power, the stage was set for an end to the Cold War.

*Gorbachev, Perestroika, and Glasnost*    Mikhail Gorbachev was committed to **perestroika** (restructuring)—the reform and strengthening of communism in the nation. Differing with many earlier interpretations of Marxism-Leninism, he increasingly turned to the principle of "material interest"—large rewards for better labor and management performance. He also encouraged greater decentralization in industry and less reliance on centralized state direction. At the same time, he called for **glasnost** (openness) in Soviet life and politics, removing many restrictions on speech, press, and religion and permitting free elections, with noncommunist candidates running for and winning elective office.

Gorbachev also announced reductions in the size of the Soviet military and reached agreements with the United States on the reduction of nuclear forces. More important, in 1988 he announced that the Soviet Union would no longer use its military forces to keep communist governments in power in Eastern

**Perestroika:** A Russian term meaning "restructuring," referring to Mikhail Gorbachev's policy of restructuring the Soviet system.

**Glasnost:** A Russian term meaning "openness," referring to Mikhail Gorbachev's removal of many restrictions on individual freedom in the Soviet Union.

*The destruction of the Berlin Wall in 1989 dramatically symbolized the end of the Cold War and the collapse of Soviet authority over Eastern Europe.*

European nations. This stunning announcement, for which he received the Nobel Peace Prize in 1990, encouraged opposition democratic forces in Poland (the Solidarity movement), Czechoslovakia, Hungary, Bulgaria, Romania, and East Germany. Gorbachev refused to intervene to halt the destruction of the Berlin Wall, despite pleas by the East German hard-line communist leader Erich Honecker.

*The Collapse of Communism*    Gorbachev's economic and political reforms threatened powerful interests in the Soviet Union—the Communist Party *apparatchniks* (bureaucrats) who were losing control over economic enterprises; the military leaders, who opposed the withdrawal of Soviet troops from Germany and Eastern Europe; the KGB police, whose terror tactics were increasingly restricted; and central government officials, who were afraid of losing power to the republics. These interests slowed perestroika and forced Gorbachev into many compromises that led to a rapid deterioration of the Soviet economy and the emergence of disorders and disturbances in various republics seeking independence. Democratic forces, led by Boris Yeltsin, the first elected president of the Russian Republic, were strongly critical of Gorbachev's reluctance to speed reforms. But when hard-liners in the Communist Party, the military, and the KGB attempted the forcible removal of Gorbachev in August 1991, democratic forces rallied to his support. Led by Yeltsin, thousands of demonstrators took to the streets, Soviet military forces stood aside, and the coup crumbled. Gorbachev was temporarily restored as president, but Yeltsin emerged as the most influential leader in the nation. The failed coup hastened the demise of the Communist Party. The party's offices and activities were suspended, and investigations of party complicity in the coup attempt were initiated. The party lost legitimacy with the peoples of Russia and the other republics.

*The Disintegration of the Soviet Union*    Strong independence movements in the republics of the Soviet Union emerged as the authority of the centralized Communist Party in Moscow waned. Lithuania, Estonia, and Latvia—nations that had been forcibly incorporated into the Soviet Union in 1939—led the way to independence in 1991. Soon all of the fifteen republics of the Soviet Union declared their independence, and the Union of Soviet Socialist Republics officially ceased to exist after December 31, 1991. Its president, Mikhail Gorbachev, no longer had a government to preside over. The red flag with its hammer and sickle atop the Kremlin was replaced with the flag of the Russian Republic.

## THE NUCLEAR THREAT

Nuclear weaponry has made the world infinitely more dangerous. During the Cold War, the nuclear arsenals of the United States and the Soviet Union threatened a human holocaust. Yet, paradoxically, the very destructiveness of nuclear weapons caused leaders on both sides to exercise extreme caution in their relations with each other. Scores of wars, large and small, were fought by different nations during the Cold War years, yet American and Soviet troops never engaged in direct combat against each other.

*Deterrence*    To maintain nuclear peace during the Cold War, the United States relied primarily on the policy of **deterrence.** Deterrence is based on the notion that a nation can dissuade a rational enemy from attacking by maintaining the capacity to destroy the enemy's homeland even *after* the nation has suffered a well-executed surprise attack by the enemy. Deterrence assumes that the worst may happen—a surprise first strike against a nation's nuclear forces. It emphasizes **second-strike capability**—the ability of a nation's forces to survive a surprise attack by the enemy and then to inflict an unacceptable level of destruction on the enemy's homeland. Deterrence is really a *psychological* defense against attack; no effective physical defense against a ballistic missile attack exists even today.

In the 1960s the United States deployed a "triad" of deterrent forces—land-based intercontinental ballistic missiles (ICBMs), submarine-launched ballistic missiles (SLBMs), and piloted intercontinental bombers. This combination of forces was believed to be a more effective deterrent than reliance on any single weapons system, because the diversity of these multiple forces makes it difficult for an enemy to develop a **first-strike capability**—the capability of destroying all three *retaliatory* systems simultaneously and thereby avoiding a second-strike retaliation.

*MAD Balance of Terror*    By the early 1970s, a nuclear balance existed between the superpowers. Neither side could consider launching a nuclear attack because of the terrible consequences that the other side could inflict in retaliation. If neither side could be assured of destroying the other side's retaliatory missiles in a first strike, then a mutual "balance of terror" maintained the nuclear peace. In effect, the populations of each nation were being held hostage against a nuclear attack. Commentators labeled this balance of terror as **mutual assured destruction** deterrence, or MAD.

Over time, however, the MAD balance eroded, especially after 1975, when the Soviet Union began production of a very large, accurate, multiwarhead missile, the SS-18. This missile gave the Soviets *hard target kill* capability—that is, the ability to destroy U.S. land-based ICBM forces in their silos in a first strike. The only real deterrent forces that remained—the only force capable of surviving a surprise first strike and retaliating effectively against the enemy—were U.S. SLBM forces.

Throughout the late 1970s and early 1980s, U.S. presidents and Congresses struggled over proposals to modernize the nation's strategic nuclear forces. An MX missile was developed to give the U.S. the same hard target kill capability the Soviets had achieved with their SS-18, but only 50 MXs (renamed Peacekeeper) were deployed. A new bomber designed to penetrate Soviet surface-to-air-missile (SAM) defenses, the B-1, was deployed; and research and development proceeded on the advanced technology B-2 Stealth bomber, designed to evade radar detection. The end of the Cold War halted production of B-2s at twenty, and plans to develop new mobile ICBMs were canceled.

*Limiting Nuclear Arms: SALT*    The United States and the Soviet Union engaged in negotiations over nuclear arms control for many years. The development of reconnaissance satellites in the 1960s made it possible for each nation to monitor the strategic weapons possessed by the other. Space photography made cheating on agreements more difficult and thus opened the way for both nations to seek stability through arms control.

**Deterrence:** The U.S. approach to deterring any nuclear attack from the Soviet Union by maintaining a second-strike capability.

**Second-strike capability:** The ability of a nation's forces to survive a surprise nuclear attack by the enemy and then to retaliate effectively.

**First-strike capability:** The ability of a nation's forces to completely destroy its enemy's ability to retaliate in an initial attack.

**Mutual assured destruction (MAD):** Nuclear peace maintained by the capability of each side's missile forces to survive a first strike and inflict heavy damages in retaliation against the aggressor's population.

Following the election of Richard Nixon as president in 1968, the United States, largely guided by former Harvard professor Henry Kissinger (national security adviser to the president and later secretary of state), began negotiations with the Soviet Union over strategic nuclear arms. In 1972, the two nations concluded two and one-half years of Strategic Arms Limitation Talks (SALT) about limiting the nuclear arms race. The agreement, **SALT I,** consisted of a treaty limiting antiballistic missiles (ABMs) and an agreement placing a numerical ceiling on offensive missiles. The ABM treaty reflected the MAD theory that the populations of each nation should be *un*defended in order to hold them hostage against a first strike. Under the offensive-missiles agreement, each side was frozen at the total number of offensive missiles, completed or under construction. Both sides could construct new and more destructive missiles as long as they dismantled an equal number of older missiles. Each nation agreed not to interfere in the satellite intelligence-gathering activities of the other nation. SALT I was the first step forward on the control of nuclear arms; both sides agreed to continue negotiations.

After seven years of difficult negotiations, the United States and the Soviet Union produced the lengthy and complicated **SALT II** treaty in 1979. It set an overall limit on "strategic nuclear launch vehicles"—ICBMs, SLBMs, bombers, and long-range Cruise missiles—at 2,250 for each side. It also limited the number of missiles that could have multiple warheads (MIRVs) and banned new types of ICBMs, with the exception of one new type of ICBM for each side. But the Soviets were allowed to keep their hard target kill capability SS-18 missiles, for which the United States had no equivalent. When the Soviet Union invaded Afghanistan, President Carter withdrew the SALT II treaty from Senate consideration. However, President Carter, and later President Reagan, announced that the United States would abide by the provisions of the unratified SALT II treaty as long as the Soviet Union did so.

*Reducing Nuclear Arms: START*   In negotiations with the Soviets, the Reagan Administration established three central principles of arms control—reductions, equality, and verification. The new goal was to be *reductions* in missiles and warheads, not merely limitations on future numbers and types of weapons, as in previous SALT talks. To symbolize this new direction, President Reagan renamed the negotiations the Strategic Arms *Reductions* Talks, or START. The president also emphasized that any new treaty must result in reductions of strategic arms to levels *equal* for both sides. Finally, for the first time, the United States insisted on provisions for on-site *verification* to supplement satellite intelligence. However, the Soviets objected strongly to U.S. research efforts in the field of ballistic missile defense—the Strategic Defence Initiative (SDI). In 1983, the Soviets walked out of the START talks and out of talks seeking to limit European nuclear weapons. But by 1985, after President Reagan's reelection and the selection of Mikhail Gorbachev as president of the Soviet Union, the Soviets returned to the bargaining table.

The **START I** Treaty signed in Moscow in 1991 by Presidents George Bush and Mikhail Gorbachev was the first agreement between the nuclear powers that actually resulted in the reduction of strategic nuclear weapons. Earlier, the Intermediate-Range Nuclear Forces (INF) Treaty of 1987 eliminated missiles with an intermediate range, between 300 and 3,800 miles; although the portion of each side's nuclear weapons covered by the INF Treaty was small, it set the pattern for future arms control agreements in its provisions for reductions, equality,

**SALT I:** The first arms limitation treaty between the United States and the Soviet Union, signed in 1972, limiting the total number of offensive nuclear missiles; the treaty reflected the theory that the population centers of both nations should be left undefended.

**SALT II:** A lengthy and complicated treaty between the United States and Soviet Union, agreed to in 1979 but never ratified by the U.S. Senate, that set limits on all types of strategic nuclear launch vehicles.

**START I:** The first treaty between the United States and the Soviet Union that actually reduced the strategic nuclear arms of the superpowers, signed in 1991.

and verification. The START I Treaty reduced the total number of deployed strategic nuclear delivery systems (ICBMs, SLBMs, and piloted bombers) to no more than 1,600, a 30 percent reduction from the SALT II level. The Soviet Union pledged to reduce by one-half its forces of heavy SS-18 ICBMs (leaving 154). The total number of strategic nuclear warheads was reduced to no more than 6,000, a reduction of nearly 50 percent. Verification included on-site and short-notice inspections, as well as "national technical means" (satellite surveillance).

The capstone of strategic nuclear arms control is the far-reaching **START II** agreement, signed in 1993 by U.S. President Bush and Russian President Yeltsin. This agreement caps more than twenty years of nuclear arms control negotiations by promising to eliminate the threat of a first-strike nuclear attack by either side. Its most important provision is the agreement to eliminate all multiwarhead (MIRVed) land-based missiles by the year 2003. The Russians will dismantle their powerful SS-18 missiles, the most dangerous threat to the nuclear balance of power. The United States will dismantle the MX missile and convert the three-warheaded Minuteman IIIs into single-warhead missiles. START II also calls for the reduction of overall strategic warheads to 3,500, slashing the nuclear arsenals of both nations by more than two-thirds from Cold War levels (see Figure 18-1).

*Continued Minimal Deterrence*  Democratic developments in Russia have radically changed the U.S. assessment of the intentions of Russia's leaders, but its nuclear capabilities remain awesome. More than 27,000 nuclear weapons are still stockpiled in the "nuclear republics" of the former Soviet Union—Russia, Ukraine, Belarus, and Kazakhstan. The United States has been assured that rational and responsible leaders remain in command and control of this enormous destructive force and that strategic nuclear weapons will be dismantled on schedule in accord with the START treaties. However, defense policy makers in both the Bush and the Clinton Administrations have urged the continued maintenance of sufficient strategic nuclear forces to deter nuclear attack or intimidation by any leadership groups that might someday come into control of the awesome arsenal of the former Soviet Union.

**START II:** The capstone of strategic nuclear arms control requiring the United States and Russia to reduce total nuclear warheads by more than two-thirds from Cold War levels and to eliminate all multiwarhead land-based missiles by 2003.

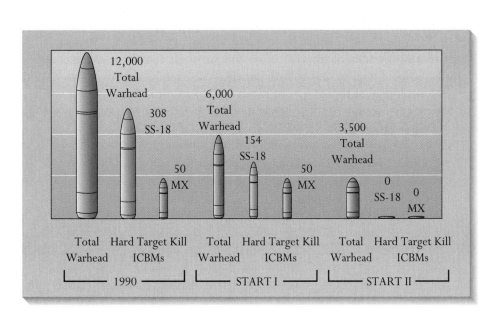

( **FIGURE 18-1** )  **Strategic Nuclear Arms under START Treaties**
*Implementation of the Start II Treaty will reduce the total number of warheads in both the United States and Russia by over two-thirds and will completely eliminate hard target kill ICBMs.*

*The USS Kentucky, a Trident class nuclear-powered ballistic missile submarine. The Trident program has survived post Cold War cuts in the U.S. strategic weapons arsenal.*

To implement minimal deterrence, the U.S. currently plans to maintain 500 single-warhead Minuteman missiles and to reconfigure most remaining long-range bombers to carry conventional (nonnuclear) weapons. Only the Trident submarine program is relatively unaffected by the cuts in strategic weaponry; a total of 18 of these ballistic-missile-carrying submarines will be built.

*Nuclear Terrorism*   Even as the threat of a large-scale nuclear attack recedes, the threats arising from "nondeterrable" sources are increasing. Today, the principal nondeterrable threats are estimated to be: (1) missiles launched by a terrorist nation; (2) unauthorized missile launches by elements within the former Soviet Union during periods of internal crisis and turmoil; and (3) accidental missile launches. Global nuclear and ballistic missile proliferation steadily increases over time the likelihood of these types of threats. Terrorist, unauthorized, and accidental launches are considered "nondeterrable" because the threat of nuclear retaliation is largely meaningless.

The threat of mass terror weapons—nuclear, chemical, or biological weapons, especially those carried by medium- or long-range missiles—is likely to increase dramatically in the next century. Iraq, Iran, and Libya, for example, are all likely to acquire mass terror weapons and long-range delivery systems in the absence of any action by the United States to prevent them from doing so. North Korea is already reported to possess nuclear weapons and to be developing long-range missiles to carry them.

Defending against terrorist, unauthorized, or accidental missile attacks requires the development and deployment of **ballistic missile defense (BMD)** systems, weapons capable of detecting, intercepting, and destroying ballistic missiles

**Ballistic missile defense (BMD):** Weapons systems capable of detecting, intercepting, and destroying missiles in flight.

while they are in flight. At present there is no defense against a ballistic missile attack on American cities. Currently, some research is under way on ballistic missile defenses, but plans to actually deploy this defense to protect the U.S. population have been postponed indefinitely (see *What Do You Think?* "How Should We Defend against a Ballistic Missile Attack?").

# POST–COLD WAR THREATS

The end of the Cold War did not eliminate all threats to America's national security. But it did force the United States to reexamine its defense policies, force levels, strategies and tactics, and budget requirements in the light of current and potential threats. For the first time in more than forty years, the United States had to design its foreign and defense policies in the absence of the dominant focus provided by the Soviet threat.

*Guarding against a Reversal of Democratic Trends*  If Russia, Ukraine, and the other new republics make a full transition to democracy and capitalism, the next century promises much more peace and prosperity for the peoples of the world than this century. But if they fail, the United States and Western nations will be confronted with many dangers, for example:

- Continuing economic deterioration in Russia may undermine the weak traditions of democracy. The specter of a "Weimar Russia," in which initial advances toward democracy fail and an authoritarian leader emerges, haunts Europeans who remember the failure of the brief Weimar democracy in Germany before the rise of Adolf Hitler.
- The collapse of the democratic movement may usher in a neo-communist, nationalistic, militarist Russian regime. Such a regime may seek to reassert its control of the new independent republics, or even reassert dominance in Poland and other Eastern European nations.
- Continuing differences between the republics of the former Soviet Union, and the rekindling of ancient hatreds among ethnic groups, may result in armed conflict. With nuclear weapons, the potential for disaster is far greater than in other regions of the world that have experienced ethnic conflicts.
- A breakdown of nuclear command and control may result in the sale of nuclear weapons to terrorists or terrorist regimes.

The Russian government is already confronted with the problem of consolidating its authority throughout the Russian Republic itself. Many non-Russian ethnic minorities remain within its borders, including the Muslims of Chechnya, who have already resorted to arms to assert their independence.

*Western Europe and the Future of NATO*  The residual threat to Western Europe posed by Russian forces, even under a hostile regime, is currently very weak. The Russian military, more than 4 million strong as late as 1990, is now down to fewer than 2 million, a number that is smaller than the forces of the European NATO countries, exclusive of U.S. forces. Moreover, Russian military morale is reported to be low and equipment in disrepair. Even if an anti-Western

# How Should We Defend against a Ballistic Missile Attack?

For a half-century, since the terrible nuclear blasts of Hiroshima and Nagasaki in Japan in 1945, the world has avoided nuclear war. Peace has been maintained by deterrence—by the threat of devastating nuclear attacks that would be launched in retaliation to an enemy first strike. But in 1983 President Ronald Reagan urged that instead of deterring war through fear of retaliation, the United States should seek a technological defense against nuclear missiles, one that would eventually render them "impotent and obsolete."

> Our nuclear retaliating forces have deterred war for forty years. The fact is, however, that we have no defense against ballistic missile attack. . . . In the event that deterrence failed, a president's only recourse would be to surrender or to retaliate. Nuclear retaliation, whether massive or limited, would result in the loss of millions of lives. . . .
>
> If we apply our great scientific and engineering talent to the problem of defending against ballistic missiles, there is a very real possibility that future presidents will be able to deter war by means other than threatening devastation to any aggressor—and by a means which threatens no one.*

*"Star Wars"* Reagan's Strategic Defense Initiative (SDI) was a research program designed to explore means of destroying enemy nuclear missiles in space before they could reach their targets. Following President Reagan's initial announcement of SDI in March 1983, the press quickly labeled the effort "Star Wars." In theory, a ballistic missile defense (BMD) system could be based in space, orbiting over enemy missile-launching sites. Should an enemy missile get through the spaced-based defense, a ground-based BMD system would attempt to intercept warheads as they reentered the atmosphere and approached their targets. SDI included research on laser beams, satellite surveillance, computerized battle-management systems, and "smart" and "brilliant" weapons systems.

*Global Protection* SDI under President Reagan was a very ambitious program with the goal of creating an "impenetrable shield" that would protect not only the population of the United States but the population of our allies as well. Reagan argued that such a shield would allow the United States to dismantle its retaliatory nuclear forces since they would no longer be necessary. Thus during the early Reagan years, SDI focused on developing space-based BMD systems. Later, more realistic goals envisioned combining deterrence with defense; BMDs would be employed to degrade a Soviet first-strike and thereby protect U.S. retaliatory forces from complete destruction.

The end of the Cold War refocused SDI away from defense against a massive Russian missile attack to more limited yet more likely threats. Today the principal nuclear threats are missiles launched by a terrorist nation, unauthorized missiles launched by elements within the former Soviet Union, and accidental missile launches. President Bush redirected SDI toward a program called GPALS—Global Protection against a Limited Strike.

*The Patriot in the Gulf War* The success of the Patriot antiballistic missile in destroying short-range Iraqi Scud missiles during the Gulf War demonstrated that enemy missiles could be intercepted in flight. The Patriot is a ground-based "tactical" weapon designed to protect specific military targets. Though developed by the army rather than by SDI, the Patriot silenced critics who had claimed that a successful intercept of an incoming missile was impossible. The Gulf War experience also demonstrated that deterrence may not protect the United States against a ballistic missile attack by a terrorist regime.

*The Future of BMDs* Despite the Gulf War experience, opposition to SDI continued in Congress. As a Reagan-era initiative, partisanship tended to cloud the debate over SDI. While Democratically controlled Congress funded most of the money requested by presidents Reagan and Bush for SDI, Congress increasingly diverted money away from research on space-based interceptors toward ground-based systems.

In 1993, President Clinton's Secretary of Defense, Les Aspin, announced the termination of the separate SDI organization, but he reassured the nation that research would continue on ground-based ballistic missile defenses. However, plans to actually deploy these defenses to protect the U.S. population were postponed indefinitely.

*President Ronald Reagan, *The President's Strategic Defense Initiative,* the White House, January 3, 1985.

*President Clinton and Russia's Boris Yeltsin at a news conference after a summit meeting in Vancouver in 1993. The United States and western European nations have supported Yeltsin as the best hope for continued democracy in Russia despite his growing unpopularity and his destructive conflict with Chechnya.*

regime were to emerge in Moscow, considerable time would be required to reconstitute a Russian force capable of threatening Western Europe.

Although the United States is likely to continue its political commitments to NATO, the key question confronting policy makers is the level of U.S. troop deployments in Europe. The total withdrawal of U.S. military forces from Europe would probably mean an end to the NATO alliance. The United States has already reduced its "forward presence" in Europe by more than half. Proponents of a continued U.S. military presence in Europe argue that it provides reassurance and stability as democracy emerges in Eastern Europe; they note that both its old allies and its new friends in Europe have urged the United States to remain involved in European security. Opponents counter that the Western European nations are now quite capable of shouldering the burden of their own security.

NATO must now decide what role it should play in the future of European security. Poland, Hungary, and the Czech Republic have petitioned for membership in NATO, hoping to acquire the protection of the alliance against any renewal of Russian expansionism. Should NATO extend its protection to these nations of Eastern Europe? Traditionally NATO forces were never deployed outside of Western Europe. Should NATO consider using its forces for peacekeeping outside of the region?

*European Ethnic Conflicts*   Religious and ethnic conflicts in Europe are as old as the recorded history of the continent. A question confronting the United States and NATO is whether such conflicts threaten the security of Western Europe, and, if so, what to do about them. Media coverage of the hardship, death, and destruction resulting from these conflicts puts added pressure on democratic governments to undertake humanitarian and "peacekeeping" roles. A combination of security and humanitarian concerns drew NATO into Bosnia in 1995 to assist in resolving war between Serbs, Croats, and Muslims. The U.S. provided about one-third of the NATO military forces deployed in Bosnia as peacekeepers.

*Regional Threats*   The most likely threats today are those posed by regional aggressors. Saddam Hussein's Iraq is the model of new regional threat. Potential regional aggressors include:

- *Iraq:* Saddam Hussein's million-strong army, with its 5,000 tanks, was reduced to one-third its size in the Gulf War. The UN-sponsored economic blockade of Iraq has hampered that nation's efforts to rebuild these conventional forces to their former size. However, Iraq continues to harbor Scud missiles and continues in its efforts to acquire weapons of mass destruction—nuclear, chemical, and biological.
- *Iran:* Iran has been rebuilding its million-strong army since the end of its war with Iraq, shopping for both conventional weapons and nuclear components in world arms markets. China and the former Soviet Union have supplied it with surface-to-surface missiles. Iran has also acquired a submarine force for operations in the Persian Gulf and a sizable air force. Iran supports terrorist groups throughout the Middle East and provides a beacon for violent Islamic fundamentalism. The Israelis consider Iran to be the principal threat to peace and stability in the region.
- *Syria:* Syria's military forces are impressive, with more than 700,000 men and 4,000 tanks. But with the collapse of the Soviet Union, its key supplier, Syria will now need to pay for weapons in hard currency—a commodity in short supply in Syria. Syria remains officially at war with Israel, and its troops occupy most of Lebanon.
- *Libya:* Muammar al-Qaddafi's military forces are not a major threat, yet Libya remains a major base for worldwide terrorist activity.
- *North Korea:* North Korea remains the most authoritarian and militarist regime in the world. It devotes a very large proportion of its economy and population to its military. It supports a million-strong army with 4,000 tanks, a large air force, and a large submarine force. North Korea's nuclear weapons program is very advanced. Its "Great Leader," Kim Il-Sung, has never renounced his intention to reunify Korea by force. His son, "Dear Leader" Kim Jong Il, is expected to replace the aged leader. In recognition of South Korea's burgeoning economy and progressive strengthening of its armed forces, the United States has undertaken a gradual reduction of American ground forces in South Korea. However, some U.S. ground forces are likely to remain in place near the border to deter invasion by North Korea. South Korea's army remains only about half as large as that of North Korea; in the event of war, the United States would need to provide immediate air combat support.
- *China:* The People's Republic of China now possesses the world's largest armed forces—more than 3 million soldiers, nearly 10,000 tanks, and more than 4,000 combat aircraft. China has ICBMs with multihead nuclear warheads capable of reaching the United States. China has always asserted that Taiwan is a province of China (as has the government of the Republic of China in Taiwan); Beijing continues to declare unification a goal. It has stated a preference for peaceful reunification, but the threat of force has always been present. The Beijing government's policies toward Hong Kong, the former British colony incorporated into the People's Republic of China in 1997, will signal China's future course. Beijing continues to voice support for market reforms of its economy, but it acted

with brutal force to suppress the democracy movement in Tiananmen Square in 1989.

*Terrorism*    The threat of terrorism creates two military requirements. The first is the ability to punish nations that sponsor terrorism and to dissuade other nations from continuing their support of terrorism. In 1986, the United States struck at Libya in a limited air attack in response to various Libyan-supported acts of terrorism around the world. In 1993, the United States struck Iraq's intelligence center in Baghdad in response to a foiled plot to assassinate former president George Bush. These types of operations are carried out by conventional military forces. The second requirement is the ability to take direct action against terrorists to capture or kill them or to free their hostages. These operations are carried out by highly trained, specially equipped Special Operations Forces.

*Unanticipated Threats*    The United States anticipated very few of the dozens of crises that required the use of military force over the past decade. Few would have forecast that U.S. troops would be engaged in combat in Grenada in 1983, or Panama in 1989, or even the Persian Gulf in 1991. General Colin Powell has tried to convince the Congress that:

> The real threat is the unknown, the uncertain. In a very real sense, the primary threat to our security is instability and unpreparedness to handle a crisis or war that no one expected or predicted. But it is difficult to convince taxpayers or their elected representatives to prepare for the unknown.[7]

## MILITARY FORCE LEVELS

Overall military force levels in the United States are threat driven—that is, determined by the size and nature of the perceived threats to national security. It is true that particular weapons systems or base openings or closings may be driven by political forces such as the influence of defense contractors in Congress or the power of a member of Congress from a district heavily affected by defense spending. And not everyone in the White House and Congress, or even in the Defense Department, agrees on the precise nature of the threats confronting the United States now or in the future. Yet defense policy planning and the "sizing" of U.S. military forces are based on an assessment of the threats confronting the nation.

For more than four decades, the Soviet threat drove defense policy, force planning, training, strategy and tactics, weapons research and procurement, troop deployments, and defense budgeting. The fundamental change in the world balance of power inspired a complete reexamination of defense policy and force sizing.

*The Base Force*    Post–Cold War military force reductions began in 1990 under Secretary of Defense Richard Cheney in the Bush Administration. A "Base Force" plan called for a reduction of total U.S. military personnel from 2.1 to 1.6 million in 1995 (see Table 18-1). This plan envisioned a continuing "forward presence" in NATO but reduced U.S. forces in Europe by more than half. Consistent

TABLE 18–1   MILITARY FORCE LEVELS

|  | End of<br>Cold War<br>1990 | Bush<br>Base<br>Force | Clinton<br>Bottom-Up<br>Review |
|---|---|---|---|
| Active duty personnel | 2.1 million | 1.6 million | 1.4 million |
| Army divisions | 18 | 12 | 10 |
| Marine expeditionary forces | 3 | 3 | 3 |
| Navy carrier battle groups | 15 | 12 | 11 |
| Air force fighter wings | 24 | 15 | 13 |

*Sources:* General Colin Powell, testimony, Committee on the Budget, U.S. Senate, February 3, 1992; Office of the Secretary of Defense, *The Bottom-Up Review: Forces for a New Era,* September 1, 1993, as revised in testimony of Secretary of Defense William J. Perry, Senate Armed Services Committee, February 9, 1995.

with the view that regional aggressors would be the most likely threats to U.S. interests in the future, forces designed principally to meet these threats suffered fewer cuts.

*The Bottom-Up Review*   While earlier serving as chair of the House Armed Services Committee and later as President Bill Clinton's first Secretary of Defense, Les Aspin argued that the end of the Cold War required a complete "bottom-up" review of the threats confronting the nation. The official **Bottom-Up Review,** which currently directs Clinton defense policy, argues that Russia is no longer a major security threat to the United States or to NATO Europe. The U.S. military contribution to NATO can be reduced to symbolic levels. Whatever military threats might arise in Europe can be treated as regional conflicts.

*Iraqi-Equivalent Regional Threats*   Military force levels are currently designed to confront major regional threats. In 1993, Secretary of Defense Les Aspin proposed structuring U.S. military force levels based on the experience of defeating Iraq speedily and decisively in the Gulf War. But current planning also envisions the possibility that a second aggressor might decide to challenge the United States somewhere else in the world while its forces were involved in an Iraqi-equivalent war. For example, if U.S. forces were involved in the Persian Gulf against Iraq or Iran, North Korea might decide to take advantage of the situation and launch an invasion of South Korea. The United States currently plans to maintain sufficient additional U.S. forces to "fight and win two nearly simultaneous major regional conflicts." The ambiguous wording—"nearly simultaneous"—recognizes that the United States may not be able to airlift and sealift sufficient forces to fight and win two regional wars at the same time. American forces would be obliged to hold one aggressor (principally with air power) while defeating the other; once one aggressor was defeated, the United States could then redeploy sufficient forces to defeat a second aggressor.

**Bottom-Up Review:** Clinton Administration's assessment of post-Cold War military force requirements focusing on regional threats.

*Future Force Levels*   The revised threat assessment in the Bottom-Up Review rationalizes deep cuts in military forces and defense budgets in the Clinton Administration. The army will field ten active combat divisions and the air force thirteen fighter wings. (A U.S. army division includes 15,000–18,000 troops; an air force fighter wing includes approximately seventy-two combat aircraft.) The Navy will deploy eleven active (one training) carrier battle groups. (A carrier battle group typically includes one aircraft carrier with 75–85 aircraft, plus defending cruisers, destroyers, frigates, attack submarines, and support ships.) The marine corps is scheduled to retain all three of its marine expeditionary forces (each includes one marine division, one marine air wing, and supporting services).

*Criticism*    The Bottom-Up Review has generated considerable controversy. While most defense experts agree on the assessment of the threat—the need to prepare to fight and win two major regional conflicts simultaneously—many believe that the projected force levels are inadequate for these tasks. Opponents contend that the reduced numbers of army and air force combat units and the limited transport and support services available to the military are inadequate for two major regional conflicts. Casualties can be kept low only when overwhelming military force is employed quickly and decisively, as it was in Operation Desert Storm. Lives are lost when minimal forces are sent into combat, when they have inadequate air combat support, or when they are extended over too broad a front. Potential regional foes—for example, Iran and North Korea—deploy modern heavy armor and artillery forces. The United States benefited from a six-month buildup of its heavy forces in the Gulf region before Operation Desert Storm began; such a period of preparation is unlikely in a future conflict. The deployment of U.S. troops for humanitarian and "peacekeeping" missions detracts from their readiness to respond to a major regional threat. More important, perhaps, the minimal force levels projected in the Bottom-Up Review would severely tax the nation's ability to respond to two conflicts simultaneously in opposite ends of the globe. Critics charge that the "bottom-up review" is really a "top-down plan" to justify budget cuts.

# THE USE OF MILITARY FORCE

All modern presidents have acknowledged that the most agonizing decisions they have made were to send U.S. military forces into combat. These decisions cost lives. The American people are willing to send their sons and daughters into danger—and even to see some of them wounded and killed—but *only* if a president convinces them that the outcome "is worth dying for." A president must be able to explain why they lost their lives and to justify their sacrifice.

*To Protect Vital Interests*    The U.S. military learned many bitter lessons in its long, bloody experience in Vietnam. Among those lessons:

- The United States should commit its military forces only in support of vital national interests.
- If military forces are committed, they must have clearly defined military objectives—the destruction of enemy forces and/or the capture of enemy-held territory.
- Any commitment of U.S. forces must be of sufficient strength to ensure overwhelming and decisive victory with the fewest possible casualties.

# The Use of Force: Operation Desert Storm

The nation's military leadership learned hard lessons from Vietnam: define clear military objectives, use overwhelming and decisive military force, move swiftly and avoid protracted stalemate, minimize casualties, and be sensitive to the image of the war projected back home. Saddam Hussein's invasion of Kuwait on August 2, 1990, was apparently designed to restore his military prestige after an indecisive war against Iran, to secure additional oil revenues to finance the continued buildup of Iraqi military power, and to intimidate (and perhaps invade) Saudi Arabia and the Gulf states, thereby securing control over a major share of the world's oil reserves. On paper, Iraq possessed the fourth largest military force in the world, with 1 million troops, battle-hardened from eight years of war with Iran. Iraqi weapons included over 5,000 tanks, 10,000 other armored vehicles, 4,000 artillery pieces, 700 combat aircraft, and surface-to-air missiles. In addition Iraq had deadly chemical weapons, which it had previously used against Iran and its own Kurdish population.*

The Iraqi invasion met with a surprisingly swift response by the United Nations, with Security Council resolutions condemning the invasion, demanding an immediate withdrawal, and imposing a trade embargo and economic sanctions. President George Bush immediately set to work to stitch together a coalition military force that would eventually include thirty nations. Early on, the president described the U.S. military deployment as "defensive," but he soon became convinced that neither diplomacy nor an economic blockade would dislodge Saddam from Kuwait and so ordered the military to prepare an "offensive" option.

The top U.S. military commanders—including the chair of the Joint Chiefs of Staff, General Colin Powell, and the commander in the field, General Norman Schwartzkopf—had been field officers in Vietnam, and they were resolved not to repeat the mistakes of that war. They were reluctant to go into battle without the full support of the American people. If ordered to fight, they wanted to employ overwhelming and decisive military force; they wanted to avoid the gradual escalation, protracted conflict, target limitations, and political inference in the conduct of the war that had characterized the U.S. military's efforts in Vietnam. Accordingly, they presented the president with a plan that called for a very large military buildup; elements of six army divisions and two marine divisions, with 1,900 tanks, 930 artillery pieces, 500 attack helicopters, and more than 1,000 combat aircraft. Coalition forces also included British and French heavy armored units, and Egyptian, Syrian, Saudi, and other Arab forces.

When President Bush announced this massive buildup of forces on November 8, however, he immediately faced a barrage of criticism at home for abandoning his earlier defensive posture. U.S. Senator Sam Nunn, respected chair of the Senate Armed Services Committee, opened hearings that urged the president to continue economic sanctions and avoid the heavy casualties a land war was expected to produce. But Bush was convinced that sanctions would not work, that Saddam would hold out for years, that eventually the political coalition backing the embargo would break up. He believed that Saddam would become an increasingly powerful opponent who would soon dominate the Arab world and Middle East oil reserves. Unless stopped quickly, Saddam would soon acquire nuclear weapons. On November 29, 1990, Secretary of State James Baker won the support of UN Security Council members, including the Soviet Union (with China abstaining), for a resolution authorizing coalition forces to "use all necessary means" against Iraq unless it withdrew from Kuwait by January 15, 1991. Following a lengthy debate in the Congress, on January 12 President Bush won a similar resolution in the House (250-183) and the Senate (52-47).

From Baghdad, CNN reporters Bernard Shaw and Peter Arnett were startled on the night of January 16 when Operation Desert Storm began with an air attack on key installations in the city. Iraqi forces were also surprised, despite the prompt timing of the attack; Saddam had assured them that the United States lacked the resolve to fight, and that even if war broke out, U.S. public opinion would force a settlement as casualties rose.

The success of the coalition air force was spectacular. More than 110,000 combat missions were flown with only 39 aircraft losses, none in air combat. Most Iraqi aircraft were compelled to stay on the ground, as runway and control facilities were destroyed; 38 Iraqi planes were shot down in combat, and 140 escaped to Iran. Strategic targets—including nuclear facilities, chemical warfare plants, command centers, and military communications—were repeatedly attacked. "Smart" weapons performed superbly. American TV audiences saw videotapes of laser-guided "smart bombs" entering the doors and air shafts of enemy bunkers. Civilian damage was lower than in any previous air war. The Patriot antiballistic missile system proved effective against Scuds; in more than eighty firings at Israel and Saudi Arabia, only one strike occurred, killing twenty-seven in a marine barracks. After five weeks of air war, intelligence estimated that nearly half the Iraqi tanks and artillery in the field had been destroyed, demoralized troops were hiding in deep shelters, and the battlefield had been isolated and "prepared" for ground operations.

General Schwartzkopf's plan for the ground war emphasized deception and maneuver. He wanted the Iraqis to believe that the main attack would come directly against Kuwait's southern border and would be supported by a marine landing on the coast. While Iraqi forces prepared for attacks from the south and the east coast, he sent heavily armed columns in a "Hail Mary" play—a wide sweep to the west, outflanking and cutting off Iraqi forces in the battle area. The Iraqi forces, blinded by air attacks and obliged to stay in their bunkers, would not be able to know about or respond to the flanking attack. On the night of February 24, the ground attack began. Marines breached ditches and mine fields and raced directly to the Kuwait airport; army helicopter air assaults lunged deep into Iraq; armored columns raced northward across the desert to outflank Iraqi forces and then attack them from the west, while a surge in air attacks kept Iraqi forces holed up in their bunkers. Iraqi troops surrendered in droves, highways from Kuwait city became a massive junkyard of Iraqi vehicles, and Iraqi forces that tried to fight were quickly destroyed. After one hundred hours of ground fighting, President George Bush ordered a cease-fire.

The United States had achieved a decisive military victory quickly and with remarkably few casualties. The president resisted calls to expand the original objectives of the war and go on to capture Baghdad, to destroy the Iraqi economy, to encourage Iraq's disintegration as a nation, or to kill Saddam, although it was expected that his defeat would lead to his ouster. Although the war left many political issues unresolved, it was the most decisive military outcome the United States had achieved since the end of World War II. President Bush chose to declare victory and celebrate the return of American troops.

The Gulf War taught the nation a number of lessons about the effective use of military power:

- The rapid employment of overwhelming forces is both politically and militarily superior to gradual escalation and employment of minimum force. The use of overwhelming force reduces total casualties and achieves an earlier and more decisive victory.
- The nation's political leadership is vastly more effective when it concentrates on developing and maintaining foreign and domestic political support for a war while leaving the planning and execution of military operations to the military leadership.
- A rapid conclusion of hostilities ensures that public support will not erode over time and that protracted combat and a steady stream of casualties will not fuel antiwar sentiments.
- Military force can capture territory and destroy enemy forces, but it cannot guarantee peace. Even a military-weakened Saddam Hussein remains a threat to stability in the Middle East.
- Perhaps the most important lesson, however, is that the end of the Cold War does *not* mean that the United States no longer requires military power.**

*International Institute for Strategic Studies, *The Military Balance 1991–92* (London: IISS, 1991).
**See Harry G. Summers Jr., *On Strategy II: A Critical Analysis of the Gulf War* (New York: Dell, 1992).

*American troops advancing against the background of burning oil fields in Kuwait during the Gulf War in 1991. President Bush argued that forcing Iraq's Saddam Hussein out of Kuwait was a clearly defined military objective and a vital interest of the United States.*

- Before committing U.S. military forces, there must be some reasonable assurances that the effort has the support of the American people and their representatives in Congress.
- The commitment of U.S. military forces should be a last resort, after political, economic, and diplomatic efforts have proven ineffective.

President George Bush argued that his decision to use military force in the Gulf War in 1990–91 met these guidelines: that preventing Iraq's Saddam Hussein from gaining control of the world's oil supply and developing nuclear and chemical weapons were vital national interests; that political and economic sanctions were not effective; and that he had defined clear military objectives—the removal of Iraqi troops from Kuwait and the destruction of Iraq's nuclear and chemical weapon capabilities (see *Up Close:* "The Use of Force: Operation Desert Storm"). And he authorized a large military commitment that led to a speedy and decisive victory.

These guidelines for the use of military force are widely supported within the U.S. military itself.[8] Contrary to Hollywood stereotypes, military leaders are extremely reluctant to go to war when no vital interest of the United States is at stake, where there are no clear-cut military objectives, without the support of Congress or the American people, or without sufficient force to achieve speedy and decisive victory with minimal casualties. They are wary of seeing their troops placed in danger merely to advance diplomatic goals, or to engage in "peacekeeping," or to "stabilize governments," or to "show the flag." They are reluctant to undertake humanitarian missions while being shot at. They do not like to risk their soldiers' lives under "rules of engagement" that limit their ability to defend themselves.

*In Support of Important Political Objectives* In contrast to military leaders, political leaders and diplomats often reflect the view that "war is a continuation of politics by other means"—a view commonly attributed to nineteenth-century German theorist of war Karl von Clausewitz. Military force may be used to protect interests that are important but not necessarily vital. Otherwise, the United States would be rendered largely impotent in world affairs. A diplomat's ability to achieve a satisfactory result often depends on the expressed or implied threat of military force. The distinguished international political theorist Hans Morgenthau wrote: "Since military strength is the obvious measure of a nation's power, its demonstration serves to impress others with that nation's power."[9]

Currently American military forces must be prepared to carry out a variety of missions in addition to the conduct of conventional war:

- Demonstrating U.S. resolve in crisis situations.
- Demonstrating U.S. support for democratic governments.
- Protecting U.S. citizens living abroad.
- Striking at terrorist targets to deter or retaliate.
- Peacemaking among warring factions or nations.
- Peacekeeping where hostile factions or nations have accepted a peace agreement.
- Providing humanitarian aid often under warlike conditions.

| TABLE 18-2 | MAJOR DEPLOYMENTS OF U.S. MILITARY FORCES SINCE WORLD WAR II | |
|---|---|---|
| *Year* | *Area* | *President* |
| 1950–53 | Korea | Truman |
| 1958 | Lebanon | Eisenhower |
| 1961–64 | Vietnam | Kennedy |
| 1962 | Cuban waters | Kennedy |
| 1965-73 | Vietnam | Johnson, Nixon |
| 1965 | Dominican Republic | Johnson |
| 1970 | Laos | Nixon |
| 1970 | Cambodia | Nixon |
| 1975 | Cambodia | Ford |
| 1980 | Iran | Carter |
| 1982–83 | Lebanon | Reagan |
| 1983 | Grenada | Reagan |
| 1989 | Panama | Bush |
| 1990–91 | Persian Gulf | Bush |
| 1992–93 | Somalia | Bush, Clinton |
| 1994–95 | Haiti | Clinton |
| 1995–96 | Bosnia | Clinton |

In pursuit of such objectives, recent U.S. presidents have sent troops to Lebanon in 1982 to stabilize the government (Reagan), to Grenada in 1983 to rescue American medical students and restore democratic government (Reagan), to Panama in 1989 to oust drug-trafficking General Manuel Antonio Noriega from power and to protect U.S. citizens (Bush), to Somalia in 1992–93 to provide emergency humanitarian aid (Bush and Clinton), to Haiti in 1994 to restore constitutional government (Clinton), and to Bosnia in 1995–96 for peacekeeping among warring ethnic factions (see Table 18-2). In addition U.S. military forces have been used in various counterterrorist actions, for example, by President Carter in Iran in 1980 in an unsuccessful attempt to rescue U.S. hostages, by President Reagan against Libya in 1986 to discourage terrorism, and by President Clinton in 1993 against Iraq in response to a plot to assassinate former President Bush.

Proponents of these more flexible uses of U.S. military forces usually deny any intent to be the "world's policeman." Rather, they argue that each situation must be judged independently on its own merits—weighing the importance of U.S. goals against expected costs. No military operation is without risk, but some risks may be worth taking to advance important political interests even though these interests may not be deemed "vital" to the United States. The media, particularly television, play an influential role in pressuring the president to use military force. Pictures of torture and killing, starvation and death, and devastation and destruction from around the world provide a powerful emotional stimulus to U.S. military intervention. Generally a president can count on an initial "rally 'round the flag" surge in popular support for a military action, despite overall poor public knowledge of international politics (see *Compared to What?* "Citizens' Knowledge of the World"). But if casualties mount during an operation, if no victory or end appears in sight, then press coverage of body bags coming home, military funeral

# Citizens' Knowledge of the World

As the sole superpower left on earth, the United States is expected to assume leadership in support of democracy around the world. But how well prepared are the American people for global leadership?

If a basic knowledge of world geography is required to understand international politics, then the American people are ill prepared for their global responsibility. Young Americans rank dead last in geographic knowledge among nine nations surveyed in 1988. On average, young Americans were able to correctly locate only seven of sixteen places on a world map. Older Americans did somewhat better.

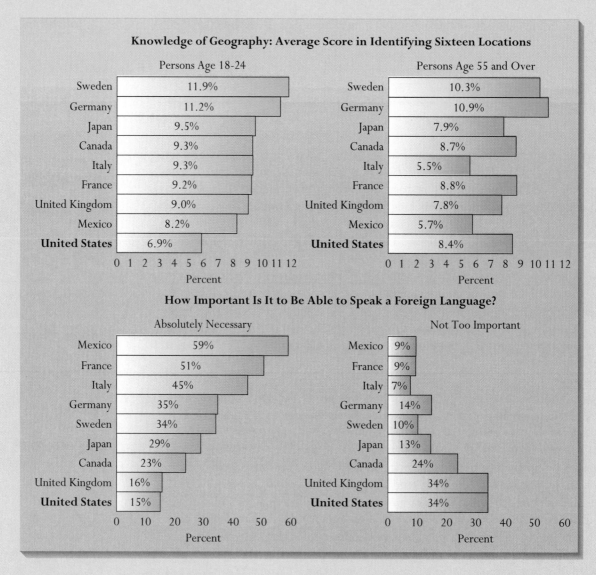

**Knowledge of Geography: Average Score in Identifying Sixteen Locations**

Persons Age 18-24

| | |
|---|---|
| Sweden | 11.9% |
| Germany | 11.2% |
| Japan | 9.5% |
| Canada | 9.3% |
| Italy | 9.3% |
| France | 9.2% |
| United Kingdom | 9.0% |
| Mexico | 8.2% |
| **United States** | 6.9% |

0 1 2 3 4 5 6 7 8 9 10 11 12
Percent

Persons Age 55 and Over

| | |
|---|---|
| Sweden | 10.3% |
| Germany | 10.9% |
| Japan | 7.9% |
| Canada | 8.7% |
| Italy | 5.5% |
| France | 8.8% |
| United Kingdom | 7.8% |
| Mexico | 5.7% |
| **United States** | 8.4% |

0 1 2 3 4 5 6 7 8 9 10 11 12
Percent

**How Important Is It to Be Able to Speak a Foreign Language?**

Absolutely Necessary

| | |
|---|---|
| Mexico | 59% |
| France | 51% |
| Italy | 45% |
| Germany | 35% |
| Sweden | 34% |
| Japan | 29% |
| Canada | 23% |
| United Kingdom | 16% |
| **United States** | 15% |

0 10 20 30 40 50 60
Percent

Not Too Important

| | |
|---|---|
| Mexico | 9% |
| France | 9% |
| Italy | 7% |
| Germany | 14% |
| Sweden | 10% |
| Japan | 13% |
| Canada | 24% |
| United Kingdom | 34% |
| **United States** | 34% |

0 10 20 30 40 50 60
Percent

*Source:* Gallup Organization international survey, 1988.

CHAPTER 18 • POLITICS AND NATIONAL SECURITY

But the ignorance of American youth is particularly worrisome; over time the map of the earth is becoming increasingly unrecognizable to the American people.

Americans have less interest in foreign language capability than other peoples. It is true that today English is widely spoken in the world and most American tourists can get by with no foreign language skills. But language skills will become essential as we move toward a global economy.

To see how well you would do, take the test below. Match the numbers on the map with the places listed.

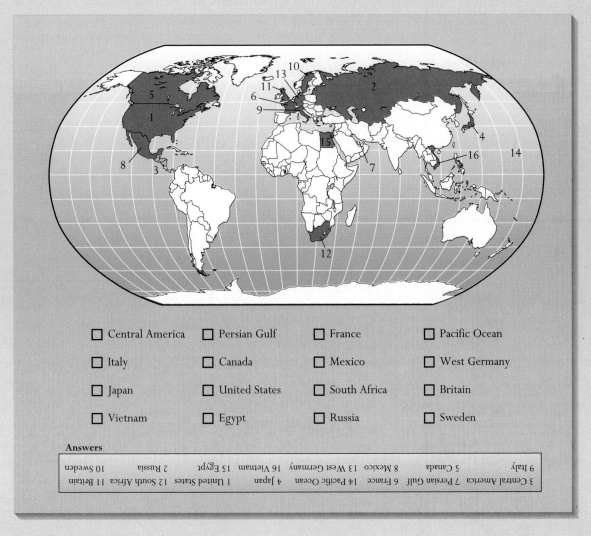

| ☐ Central America | ☐ Persian Gulf | ☐ France | ☐ Pacific Ocean |
| ☐ Italy | ☐ Canada | ☐ Mexico | ☐ West Germany |
| ☐ Japan | ☐ United States | ☐ South Africa | ☐ Britain |
| ☐ Vietnam | ☐ Egypt | ☐ Russia | ☐ Sweden |

**Answers**

10 Sweden    2 Russia    15 Egypt    16 Vietnam    13 West Germany    8 Mexico    5 Canada    9 Italy
3 Central America    7 Persian Gulf    6 France    14 Pacific Ocean    1 United States    4 Japan    12 South Africa    11 Britain

*Source:* Gallup Organization international survey, 1988.

services, and bereaved families create pressure on a president to end U.S. involvement. Unless the U.S. military can produce speedy and decisive results with few casualties, public support for military intervention wavers and critical voices in Congress arise.

## THE PRICE OF PEACE

The United States' investment in national defense over the past half-century succeeded in its most vital objectives—deterring nuclear war and maintaining the peace and security of Western Europe.

*Historical Trends in Defense Spending*  In the early Cold War years, defense spending claimed a major share of U.S. resources (see Figure 18-2). In 1955, defense spending in the United States was 58 percent of all federal expenditures and equaled 10.5 percent of the gross national product. By 1965, defense spending had shrunk to 40.1 percent of federal spending and to 7.5 percent of the GNP. The Vietnam War caused defense spending to temporarily surge upward, but following President Nixon's decision to gradually withdraw U.S. forces from that conflict, defense spending began a long decline. By 1978, defense spending was down to 23 percent of federal spending and 4.5 percent of the GNP. This was the lowest defense "effort" the United States had made since before World War II. By the end of the Carter administration, defense spending as a percentage of the GNP began to creep upward. Reagan's defense buildup brought defense spending to 6.5 percent of the GNP and 29 percent of the total federal budget by 1986. But during his second term, President Reagan and Secretary of Defense Caspar

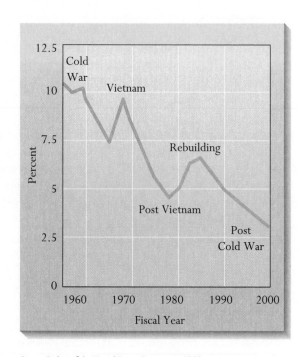

( FIGURE 18-2 )  **The Price of Peace: National Defense Outlays as a Percent of GDP**
*Current spending on defense occupies a smaller percentage of the U.S. budget (as a percentage of gross national product) than it has at any time since the start of the Cold War.*

*Source: Budget of the United States Government, 1993.*

CHAPTER 18 • POLITICS AND NATIONAL SECURITY

Weinberger fought a losing battle against a Congress determined to limit military spending.

*The Military-Industrial Complex and Other Myths*    There are many myths about military expenditures. One myth is that military expenditures are driven by "the military-industrial complex"—a network of defense contractors, military officers, and members of Congress from districts heavily reliant on defense spending. There is no question that defense industries lobby for contracts, that military officers push for more and better weapons systems, and that members of Congress look out for their districts. But there is no evidence that this jockeying for advantage affects *overall* levels of defense spending.

Actually, overall defense spending reflects fairly well the opinion of the American people regarding national security threats and the need for increases and decreases in military spending. Most Americans agreed in the late 1970s and early 1980s on the need to rebuild the nation's defenses. After the rebuilding program was well under way, most Americans believed that defense spending was "about right." The end of the Cold War convinced a broad spectrum of Americans that defense spending could be reduced.

*Post–Cold War Defense Spending*    The achievement of the Cold War objectives of the U.S. national defense policy led to a welcome result—a lessening of the threat to national security and a reduction in national defense spending. U.S. defense spending has steadily declined in real dollars since 1986; current projections indicate that U.S. military strength will be cut in half before 2000. Defense spending is projected to decline to less than 15 percent of federal spending and less than 3 percent of the nation's GNP. These are levels roughly comparable to those that prevailed before Pearl Harbor was attacked in 1941.

# SUMMARY NOTES

- The struggle for power is global. Leaders and peoples of the world protect and advance their goals and ideals through the exercise of power.
- There is no world government capable of legislating and enforcing rules of international politics. But various efforts to stabilize relations among nations have been attempted, including the balance-of-power system of alliances in the eighteenth and nineteenth centuries, the collective security arrangements of the League of Nations and the United Nations in the twentieth century, and the regional security approach of the North Atlantic Treaty Organization.
- The United Nations was largely ineffective during the Cold War, the confrontation between the Western democracies led by the United States and communist bloc nations led by the Soviet Union.

During these years, the Western nations relied principally upon the strength of the North Atlantic Treaty Organization (NATO) to deter war in Europe.
- For more than forty years, the Cold War largely directed U.S. foreign and defense policy. The United States sought to contain Soviet military expansionism and world communist revolutionary forces in all parts of the globe. U.S. involvement in the Korean and Vietnam Wars grew out of this containment policy.
- During the Cold War years, U.S. and Soviet military forces never engaged in direct combat against each other, although many "proxy" conflicts took place throughout the world. The most serious threat of nuclear war occurred during the Cuban Missile Crisis in 1962.

- To maintain nuclear peace, the U.S. relied primarily on the policy of deterrence—dissuading the Soviets from launching a nuclear attack by maintaining survivable second-strike forces capable of inflicting unacceptable levels of destruction in a retaliating attack. A "triad" of deterrent nuclear forces included land-based ICBMs, submarine-launched SLBMs, and piloted intercontinental bombers.

- In 1970, President Richard Nixon and his National Security Adviser Henry Kissenger began negotiations with the Soviet Union with a view to limiting the nuclear arms race. These Strategic Arms Limitation Talks produced the SALT I agreement in 1972, and later, under President Jimmy Carter, the SALT II agreement in 1979. Both agreements set limits on future strategic weapons development but failed to reduce existing weapons stockpiles.

- President Ronald Reagan renamed the negotiations START, emphasizing the goal of reductions in weapons rather than limitations, and stressing equality and verification. The INF Treaty in 1987 was the first agreement that actually reduced nuclear arms, although it covered only intermediate-range weapons in Europe. Later the START I (1991) and START II (1993) treaties called for reducing nuclear arsenals by two-thirds from Cold War levels.

- The end of the Cold War followed the ouster of communist governments in Eastern Europe in 1989, the unification of Germany in 1990, the collapse of the Warsaw Pact communist military alliance in 1991, and the dissolution of the Soviet Union in 1991. Russia has inherited most of the nuclear weapons and military forces of the former Soviet Union as well as its seat in the UN Security Council.

- Current threats to peace and security are likely to be posed by regional aggressors. U.S. involvement in the Gulf War in 1990–91 is representative of the type of military action most likely to be undertaken in the future. The Bottom-Up Review recommended that the U.S. be prepared to fight two "Iraqi-equivalent wars" "nearly simultaneously."

- Current political threats to national security include: a reverse of democratic trends in Russia and the emergence of a militarist and expansionist regime; European ethnic conflicts and wars; regional threats including Iraq, Iran, and North Korea; terrorism; and as-yet-unanticipated threats.

- Following the Vietnam War, many military leaders argued that U.S. forces should be used only to protect vital American interests, only in support of clearly defined military objectives, only with sufficient strength to ensure decisive victory with fewest possible casualties, only with the support of the American people and Congress, and only as a last resort.

- Recent presidents have used military forces to carry out a variety of missions in addition to conventional war, including peacekeeping, antiterrorist, and humanitarian activities. They have argued that the risks were worth taking in light of the importance of the goals.

- U.S. military force levels and defense budgets are driven by perceived threats to national security. Thus the end of the Cold War has resulted in dramatic reductions in forces and budgets.

# SELECTED READINGS

CLAUSEWITZ, KARL VON. *On War.* Edited and translated by Michael Howard and Peter Paret. Princeton, N.J.: Princeton University Press, 1984. The classic theory of war and military operations emphasizing their political character; first published in 1832.

INTERNATIONAL INSTITUTE FOR STRATEGIC STUDIES. *The Military Balance.* London: International Institute for Strategic Studies, published annually. A careful description of the military forces of more than 160 countries; this book is considered the most authoritative public information available.

KAGAN, DONALD. *On the Origins of War and the Preservation of Peace.* New York: Doubleday, 1995. Insights derived from comparative historical studies of the origins of great wars.

MAYERS, TEENA KARSA. *Understanding Nuclear Weapons and Arms Control,* 4th ed. New York: Brassey's, 1991. A well-illustrated primer on nuclear strategies and weapons,

CHAPTER 18 • POLITICS AND NATIONAL SECURITY

and a history of arms control negotiations and agreements.

NORTH, ROBERT C. *War, Peace, and Survival.* Boulder, Colo.: Westview Press, 1990. An overview of international relations, linking four levels of analysis—individual actors, nation-states, international relations, and global relations.

SNOW, DONALD M. *National Security: Enduring Problems in a Changing Defense Environment,* 2d ed. New York: St. Martin's Press, 1991. A comprehensive overview of U.S. national security issues, reflecting the changing environment at the end of the Cold War.

SUMMERS, HARRY G., JR. *On Strategy II: A Critical Analysis of the Gulf War.* New York: Dell, 1992. An analysis of the Gulf War based on Clausewitz's classic principles of war. The strategic decisions leading to victory in the Gulf contrast markedly with the decisions in Vietnam that led to defeat, a topic covered in Summers's ground-breaking first book, *On Strategy: A Critical Analysis of the Vietnam War* (New York: Dell, 1984).

# APPENDIX

## THE FEDERALIST, NO. 10, JAMES MADISON

*To the People of the State of New York:* Among the numerous advantages promised by a well-constructed union, none deserves to be more accurately developed than its tendency to break and control the violence of faction. The friend of popular governments, never finds himself so much alarmed for their character and fate, as when he contemplates their propensity to this dangerous vice. He will not fail, therefore, to set a due value on any plan which, without violating the principles to which he is attached, provides a proper cure for it. The instability, injustice, and confusion introduced into the public councils, have, in truth, been the mortal diseases under which popular governments have everywhere perished; as they continue to be the favourite and fruitful topics from which the adversaries to liberty derive their most specious declamations. The valuable improvements made by the American constitutions on the popular models, both ancient and modern, cannot certainly be too much admired; but it would be an unwarrantable partiality, to contend that they have as effectually obviated the danger on this side, as was wished and expected. Complaints are everywhere heard from our most considerate and virtuous citizens, equally the friends of public and private faith, and of public and personal liberty, that our governments are too unstable; that the public good is disregarded in the conflicts of rival parties; and that measures are too often decided, not according to the rules of justice, and the rights of the minor party, but by the superior force of an interested and overbearing majority. However anxiously we may wish that these complaints had no foundation, the evidence of known facts will not permit us to deny that they are in some degree true. It will be found, indeed, on a candid review of our situation, that some of the distresses under which we labour have been erroneously charged on the operation of our governments; but it will be found, at the same time, that other causes will not alone account for many of our heaviest misfortunes; and, particularly, for that prevailing and increasing distrust of public engagements, and alarm for private rights, which are echoed from one end of the continent to the other. These must be chiefly, if not wholly, effects of the unsteadiness and injustice, with which a factious spirit has tainted our public administrations.

By a faction, I understand a number of citizens, whether amounting to a majority or minority of the whole, who are united and actuated by some common impulse of passion, or of interest, adverse to the rights of other citizens, or to the permanent and aggregate interests of the community.

There are two methods of curing the mischiefs of faction: the one, by removing its causes; the other, by controlling its effects.

There are again two methods of removing the causes of faction: the one, by destroying the liberty which is essential to its existence; the other, by giving to every citizen the same opinions, the same passions, and the same interests.

It could never be more truly said, than of the first remedy, that it was worse than the disease. Liberty is to faction what air is to fire, an aliment without which it instantly expires. But it could not be a less folly to abolish liberty, which is essential to political life, because it nourishes faction, than it would be to wish the annihilation of air, which is essential to animal life, because it imparts to fire its destructive agency.

The second expedient is as impracticable, as the first would be unwise. As long as the reason of man continues fallible, and he is at liberty to exercise it, different opinions will be formed. As long as the connection subsists between his reason and his self-love, his opinions and his passions will have a reciprocal influence on each other; and the former will be objects to which the latter will attach themselves. The diversity in the faculties of men, from which the rights of property originate, is not less an insuperable obstacle to an uniformity of interests. The protection of these faculties is the first object of government. From the protection of different and unequal faculties of acquiring property, the possession of different degrees and kinds of property immediately results; and from the influence of these on the sentiments and views of the respective proprietors, ensues a division of the society into different interests and parties.

The latent causes of faction are thus sown in the nature of man; and we see them everywhere brought into different degrees of activity, according to the different circumstances of civil society. A zeal for different opinions concerning religion, concerning government, and many other points, as well of speculation as of practice; an attachment to different leaders ambitiously contending for preeminence and power; or to persons of other descriptions whose fortunes have been interesting to the human passions, have, in turn, divided mankind into parties, inflamed them with mutual animosity, and rendered them much more disposed to vex and oppress each other, than to cooperate for their common good. So strong is this propensity of mankind, to fall into mutual animosities, that where no substantial occasion presents itself, the most frivolous and fanciful distinctions have been sufficient to kindle their unfriendly passions and excite their most violent conflicts. But the most common and durable source of factions, has been the various and unequal distribution of property. Those who hold, and those who are without property, have ever formed distinct interests in society. Those who are creditors, and those who are debtors, fall under a like discrimination. A landed interest, a manufacturing interest, a mercantile interest, a moneyed interest, with many lesser interests, grow up of necessity in civilized nations, and divide them into different classes, actuated by different sentiments and views. The regulation of these various and interfering interests forms the principal task of modern legislation, and involves the spirit of the party and faction in the necessary and ordinary operations of the government.

No man is allowed to be a judge in his own cause; because his interest will certainly bias his judgment, and, not improbably, corrupt his integrity. With equal, nay, with greater reason, a body of men are unfit to be both judges and parties at the same time; yet what are many of the most important acts of legislation, but so many judicial determinations, not indeed concerning the right of single persons, but concerning the rights of large bodies of citizens? And what are the different classes of legislators, but advocates and parties to the causes which they determine? Is a law proposed concerning private debts? It is a question to which the creditors are parties on one side, and the debtors on the other. Justice ought to hold the balance between them. Yet the parties are, and must be, themselves the judges; and the most numerous party, or, in other words, the most powerful faction, must be expected to prevail. Shall domestic manufacturers be encouraged, and in what degree, by restrictions on foreign manufacturers are questions which would be differently decided by the landed and the manufacturing classes; and probably by neither with a sole regard to justice and the public good. The apportionment of taxes, on the various descriptions of property, is an act which seems to require the most exact impartiality; yet there is, perhaps, no legislative act, in which greater opportunity and temptation are given to a predominant party to trample on the rules of justice. Every shilling, with which they overburden the inferior number, is a shilling saved to their own pockets.

It is in vain to say, that enlightened statesmen will be able to adjust these clashing interests, and render them all subservient to the public good. Enlightened statesmen will not always be at the helm; nor, in many cases, can such an adjustment be made at all, without taking into view indirect and remote considerations, which will rarely prevail over the immediate interest which one party may find in disregarding the rights of another, or the good of the whole.

The inference to which we are brought is, that the *causes* of faction cannot be removed; and that relief is only to be sought in the means of controlling its *effects*.

If a faction consists of less than a majority, relief is supplied by the republican principle, which enables the majority to defeat its sinister views, by regular vote. It may clog the administration, it may convulse the society; but it will be unable to execute and mask its violence under the forms of the Constitution. When a majority is included in a faction, the form of popular government, on the other hand, enables it to sacrifice to its ruling passion or interest, both the public good and the rights of other citizens. To secure the public good, and private rights, against the danger of such a faction, and at the same time to preserve the spirit and the form of popular government, is then the great object to which our inquiries are directed. Let me add, that it is the great desideratum, by which alone this form of government can be rescued from the opprobrium under which it has so long laboured, and be recommended to the esteem and adoption of mankind.

By what means is this object attainable? Evidently by one of two only. Either the existence of the same passion or interest in a majority, at the same time, must be prevented; or the majority, having such coexistent passion or interest, must be rendered, by their number and local situation, unable to concert and carry into effect schemes of oppression. If the impulse and the opportunity be suffered to coincide, we well know that neither moral nor religious motives can be relied on as an adequate control. They are not found to be such on the injustice and violence of individuals, and lose their efficacy in proportion to the number combined together; that is, in proportion as their efficacy becomes needful.

From this view of the subject, it may be concluded, that a pure democracy, by which I mean a society consisting of a small number of citizens, who assemble and administer the government in person, can admit of no cure for the mischiefs of faction. A common passion or interest will, in almost every case, be felt by a majority of the whole; a communication and concert, results from the form of government itself; and there is nothing to check the inducements to sacrifice the weaker party, or an obnoxious individual. Hence, it is, that such democracies have ever been spectacles of turbulence and contention; have ever been found incompatible with personal security, or the rights of property; and have in general been as short in their lives, as they have been violent in their deaths. Theoretic politicians, who have patronized this species of government, have erroneously supposed, that by reducing mankind to a perfect equality in their political rights, they would, at the same time, be perfectly equalized and assimilated in their possessions, their opinions, and their passions.

A republic, by which I mean a government in which the scheme of representation takes place, opens a different prospect, and promises the cure for which we are seeking. Let us examine the points in which it varies from pure democracy, and we shall comprehend both the nature of the cure and the efficacy which it must derive from the union.

The two great points of difference, between a democracy and a republic, are, first, the delegation of the government, in the latter, to a small number of citizens, elected by the rest; secondly, the greater number of citizens, and greater sphere of country, over which the latter may be extended.

The effect of the first difference is, on the one hand, to refine and enlarge the public views, by passing them through the medium of a chosen body of citizens, whose wisdom may best discern the true interest of their country, and whose patriotism and love of justice, will be least likely to sacrifice it to temporary or partial considerations. Under such a regulation, it may well happen, that the public voice, pronounced by the representatives of the people, will be more consonant to the public good, than if pronounced by the people themselves, convened for the purpose. On the other hand the effect may be inverted. Men of factious tempers, of local prejudices, or of sinister designs, may by intrigue, by corruption, or by other means, first obtain the suffrages, and then betray the interest of the people. The question resulting is, whether small or extensive republics are most favourable to the election of proper guardians of the public weal; and it is clearly decided in favour of the latter by two obvious considerations.

In the first place, it is to be remarked that, however small the republic may be, the representatives must be raised to a certain number, in order to guard against the cabals of a few; and that however large it may be, they must be limited to a certain number, in order to guard against the confusion of a multitude. Hence, the number of representatives in the two cases not being in proportion to that of the constituents, and being proportionally greatest in the small republic, it follows, that if the proportion of fit characters be not less in the large than in the small republic, the former will present a greater option, and consequently a greater probability of a fit choice.

In the next place, as each representative will be chosen by a greater number of citizens in the large than in the small republic, it will be more difficult for unworthy candidates to practice with success the vicious arts, by which elections are too often carried; and the suffrages of the people being more free, will be more likely to centre in men who possess the most attractive merit, and the most diffusive and established characters.

It must be confessed, that in this, as in most other cases, there is a mean, on both sides of which inconveniences will be found to lie. By enlarging too much the number of electors, you render the representatives too little acquainted with all their local circumstances and lesser interests; as by reducing it too much, you render him unduly attached to these, and too little fit to comprehend and pursue great and national objects. The federal constitution forms a happy combination in this respect; the great and aggregate interests being referred to the national, the local and particular to the state legislatures.

The other point of difference is, the greater number of citizens, and extent of territory, which may be brought within the compass of republican, than of democratic government; and it is this circumstance principally which renders factious combinations less to be dreaded in the former, than in the latter. The smaller the society, the fewer probably will be the distinct parties and interests composing it; the fewer the distinct parties and interests, the more frequently will a majority be found of the same party; and the smaller the number of individuals composing a majority, and the smaller the compass within which they are placed, the more easily will they concert and execute their plans of oppression. Extend the sphere, and you take in a greater variety of parties and interests; you make it less probable that a majority of the whole will have a common motive to invade the rights of other citizens; or if such a common motive exists, it will be more difficult for all who feel it to discover their own strength, and to act in unison with each other. Besides other impediments, it may be remarked, that where there is a consciousness of unjust or dishonourable purposes, communication is always checked by distrust, in proportion to the number whose concurrence is necessary.

Hence, it clearly appears, that the same advantage, which a republic has over a democracy, in controlling the effects of faction, is enjoyed by a large over a small republic—is enjoyed by the union over the states composing it. Does this advantage consist in the substitution of representatives, whose enlightened views and virtuous sentiments render them superior to local prejudices, and to schemes of injustice? It will not be denied that the representation of the union will be most likely to possess these requisite endowments. Does it consist in the greater security afforded by a greater variety of parties, against the event of any one party being able to outnumber and oppress the rest? In an equal degree does the increased variety of parties, comprised within the union, increase the security? Does it, in fine, consist in the greater obstacles opposed to the concert and accomplishment of the secret wishes of an unjust and interested majority? Here, again, the extent of the union gives it the most palpable advantage.

The influence of factious leaders may kindle a flame within their particular states, but will be unable to spread a general conflagration through the other states; a religious sect may degenerate into a political faction in a part of the confederacy; but the variety of sects dispersed over the entire face of it, must secure the national councils against any danger from that source; a rage for paper money, for an abolition of debts, for an equal division of property, or for any other improper or wicked project, will be less apt to pervade the whole body of the union than a particular member of it; in the same proportion as such a malady is more likely to taint a particular county or district, than an entire state.

In the extent and proper structure of the union, therefore, we behold a republican remedy for the diseases most incident to republican government. And according to the degree of pleasure and pride we feel in being republicans, ought to be our zeal in cherishing the spirit, and supporting the character of federalists.

To what expedient, then, shall we finally resort, for maintaining in practice the necessary partition of power among the several departments as laid down in the Constitution? The only answer that can be given is that as all these exterior provisions are found to be inadequate the defect must be supplied, by so contriving the interior structure of the government as that its several constituent parts may, by their mutual relations, be the means of keeping each other in their proper places. Without presuming to undertake a full development of this important idea I will hazard a few general observations which may perhaps place it in a clearer light, and enable us to form a more correct judgment of the principles and structure of the government planned by the convention.

In order to lay a due foundation for that separate and distinct exercise of the different powers of government, which to a certain extent is admitted on all hands to be essential to the preservation of liberty, it is evident that each department should have a will of its own; and consequently should be so constituted that the members of each should have as little agency as possible in the appointment of the members of the others. Were this principle rigorously adhered to, it would require that all the appointments for the supreme executive, legislative, and judiciary magistracies should be drawn from the same fountain of authority, the people, through channels having no communication whatever with one another. Perhaps such a plan of constructing the several departments would be less difficult in practice than it may in contemplation appear. Some difficulties, however, and some additional expense would attend the execution of it. Some deviations, therefore, from the principle must be admitted. In the constitution of the judiciary department in particular, it might be inexpedient to insist rigorously on the principle: first, because peculiar qualifications being essential in the members, the primary consideration ought to be to select that mode of choice which best secures these qualifications; second, because the permanent tenure by which the appointments are held in that department must soon destroy all sense of dependence on the authority conferring them.

It is equally evident that the members of each department should be as little dependent as possible on those of the others for the emoluments annexed to their offices. Were the executive magistrate, or the judges, not independent of the legislature in this particular, their independence in every other would be merely nominal.

But the great security against a gradual concentration of the several powers in the same department consists in giving to those who administer each department the necessary constitutional means and personal motives to resist encroachments of the others. The provision for defense must in this, as in all other cases, be made commensurate to the danger of attack. Ambition must be made to counteract ambition. The interest of the man must be connected with the constitutional rights of the place. It may be a reflection on human nature that such devices should be necessary to control the abuses of government. But what is government itself but the greatest of all reflections on human nature? If men were angels, no government would be necessary. If angels were to govern men, neither external nor internal controls on government would be necessary. In framing a government which is to be administered by men over men, the great difficulty lies in this: you must first enable the government to control the governed; and in the next place oblige it to control itself. A dependence on the people is, no doubt, the primary control on the government; but experience has taught mankind the necessity of auxiliary precautions.

This policy of supplying, by opposite and rival interests, the defect of better motives, might be traced through the whole system of human affairs, private as well as public. We see it particularly displayed in all the subordinate distributions of power, where the constant aim is to divide and arrange the several offices in such a manner as that each may be a check on the other—that the private interest of every individual may be a sentinel over the public rights. These inventions of prudence cannot be less requisite in the distribution of the supreme powers of the State.

But it is not possible to give to each department an equal power of self-defense. In republican government, the legislative authority necessarily predominates. The remedy for this inconveniency is to divide the legislature into different branches; and to render them, by modes of election and different principles of action, as little connected with each other as the nature of their common functions and their common dependence on the society will admit. It may even be necessary to guard against dangerous encroachments by still further precautions. As the weight of the legislative authority requires that it should be thus divided, the weakness of the executive may require, on the other hand, that it should be fortified. An absolute negative on the legislature appears, at first view, to be the natural defense with which the executive magistrate should be armed. But perhaps it would be neither altogether safe nor alone sufficient. On ordinary occasions it might not be exerted with the requisite firmness, and on extraordinary occasions it might be perfidiously abused. May not this defect of an absolute negative be supplied by some qualified connection between this weaker department and the weaker branch of the stronger department, by which the latter may be led to support the constitutional rights of the former, without being too much detached from the rights of its own department?

If the principles on which these observations are founded be just, as I persuade myself they are, and they be applied as a criterion to the several State constitutions, and to the federal Constitution, it will be found that if the latter does not perfectly correspond with them, the former are infinitely less able to bear such a test.

There are, moreover, two considerations particularly applicable to the federal system of America, which place that system in a very interesting point of view.

*First.* In a single republic, all the power surrendered by the people is submitted to the administration of a single government; and the usurpations are guarded against by a division of the government into distinct and separate departments. In the compound republic of America, the power surrendered by the people is first divided between two distinct governments, and then the portion allotted to each subdivided among distinct and separate departments. Hence a double security arises to the rights of the people. The different governments will control each other, at the same time that each will be controlled by itself.

*Second.* It is of great importance in a republic not only to guard the society against the oppression of its rulers, but to guard one part of the society against the injustice of the other part. Different interests necessarily exist in different classes of citizens. If a majority be united by a common interest, the rights of the minority will be insecure. There are but two methods of providing against this evil: the one by creating a will in the community independent of the majority—that is, of the society itself; the other, by comprehending in the society so many separate descriptions of citizens as will render an unjust combination of a majority of the whole very improbable, if not impracticable. The first method prevails in all governments possessing an hereditary or self-appointed authority. This, at best, is but a precarious security; because a power independent of the society may as well espouse the unjust views of the major as the rightful interests of the minor party, and may possibly be turned against both parties. The second method will be exemplified in the federal republic of the United States. Whilst all authority in it will be derived from and dependent on the society, the society itself will be broken into so many parts, interests and classes of citizens, that the rights of individuals, or of the minority, will be in little danger from interested combinations of the majority. In a free government the security for civil rights must be the same as that for religious rights. It consists in the one case in the multiplicity of interests, and in the other in the multiplicity of sects. The degree of security in both cases will depend on the number of interests and sects; and this may be presumed to depend on the extent of country and number of people comprehended under the same government. This view of the subject must particularly recommend a proper federal system to all the sincere and considerate friends of republican government, since it shows that in exact proportion as the territory of the Union may be formed into more circumscribed Confederacies, or States, oppressive combinations of a majority will be facilitated; the best security, under the republican forms, for the rights of every class of citizen, will be diminished; and consequently the stability and independence of some member of the government, the only other security, must be proportionally increased. Justice is the end of government. It is the end of civil society. It ever has been and ever will be pursued until it be obtained, or until liberty be lost in the pursuit. In a society under the forms of which the stronger faction can readily unite and oppress the weaker, anarchy may as truly be said to reign as in a state of nature, where the weaker individual is not secured against the violence of the stronger; and as, in the latter state, even the stronger individuals are prompted, by the uncertainty of their condition, to submit to a government which may protect the weak as well as themselves; so, in the former state, will the more powerful factions or parties be gradually induced, by a like motive, to wish for a government which will protect all parties, the weaker as well as the more powerful. It can be little doubted that if the State of Rhode Island was separated from the Confederacy and left to itself, the insecurity of rights under the popular form of government within such narrow limits would be displayed by such reiterated oppressions of factious majorities that some power altogether independent of the people would soon be called for by the voice of the very factions whose misrule had proved the necessity of it. In the extended republic of the United States, and among the great variety of interests, parties, and sects which it embraces, a coalition of a majority of the whole society could seldom take place on any other principles than those of justice and the general good; whilst there being thus less danger to a minor from the will of a major party, there must be less pretext, also, to provide for the security of the former, by introducing into the government a will not dependent on the latter, or, in other words, a will independent of the society itself. It is no less certain that it is important, notwithstanding the contrary opinions which have been entertained that the larger the society, provided it lie within a practicable sphere, the more duly capable it will be of self-government. And happily for the *republican cause,* the practicable sphere may be carried to a very great extent by a judicious modification and mixture of the *federal principle.*

| Year | Candidates | Party | Electoral Vote | Popular Vote Percentage |
|------|-----------|-------|:--------------:|:-----------------------:|
| 1789 | **George Washington** | Federalist | 69 | — |
|      | John Adams | Federalist | 34 | |
|      | Others | | 35 | |
| 1792 | **George Washington** | Federalist | 132 | — |
|      | John Adams | Federalist | 77 | |
|      | Others | | 55 | |
| 1796 | **John Adams** | Federalist | 71 | — |
|      | Thomas Jefferson | Democratic-Republican | 68 | |
|      | Thomas Pinckney | Federalist | 59 | |
|      | Aaron Burr | Anti-Federalist | 30 | |
|      | Others | | 48 | |
| 1800 | **Thomas Jefferson** | Democratic-Republican | 73 | — |
|      | Aaron Burr | Democratic-Republican | 73 | |
|      | John Adams | Federalist | 65 | |
|      | C. C. Pinckney | Federalist | 64 | |
|      | John Jay | Federalist | 1 | |
| 1804 | **Thomas Jefferson** | Democratic-Republican | 162 | — |
|      | C. C. Pinckney | Federalist | 14 | |
| 1808 | **James Madison** | Democratic-Republican | 122 | — |
|      | C. C. Pinckney | Federalist | 47 | |
|      | George Clinton | Independent-Republican | 6 | |
| 1812 | **James Madison** | Democratic-Republican | 128 | — |
|      | De Witt Clinton | Fusion | 89 | |
| 1816 | **James Monroe** | Democratic-Republican | 183 | — |
|      | Rufus King | Federalist | 34 | |
| 1820 | **James Monroe** | Democratic-Republican | 231 | — |
|      | John Q. Adams | Independent-Republican | 1 | |
| 1824 | **John Q. Adams** | National Republican | 84 | — |
|      | Andrew Jackson | Democratic | 99 | |
|      | Henry Clay | Democratic-Republican | 37 | |
|      | W. H. Crawford | Democratic-Republican | 41 | |
| 1828 | **Andrew Jackson** | Democratic | 178 | 56.1 |
|      | John Q. Adams | National Republican | 83 | 43.6 |
| 1832 | **Andrew Jackson** | Democratic | 219 | 54.2 |
|      | Henry Clay | National Republican | 49 | 37.4 |
|      | William Wirt | Anti-Masonic | 7 | |
|      | John Floyd | Nullifiers | 11 | |

| Year | Candidates | Party | Electoral Vote | Popular Vote Percentage |
|------|-----------|-------|----------------|-------------------------|
| 1836 | **Martin Van Buren** | Democratic | 170 | 50.8 |
| | William H. Harrison | Whig | 73 | 36.6 |
| | Hugh L. White | Whig | 26 | |
| | Daniel Webster | Whig | 14 | |
| 1840 | **William H. Harrison** | Whig | 234 | 52.9 |
| | Martin Van Buren | Democratic | 60 | 46.8 |
| | (**John Tyler,** 1841) | | | |
| 1844 | **James K. Polk** | Democratic | 170 | 49.5 |
| | Henry Clay | Whig | 105 | 48.1 |
| 1848 | **Zachary Taylor** | Whig | 163 | 47.3 |
| | Lewis Cass | Democratic | 127 | 42.5 |
| | (**Millard Fillmore,** 1850) | | | |
| 1852 | **Franklin Pierce** | Democratic | 254 | 50.8 |
| | Winfield Scott | Whig | 42 | 43.9 |
| 1856 | **James Buchanan** | Democratic | 174 | 45.3 |
| | John C. Fremont | Republican | 114 | 33.1 |
| | Millard Fillmore | American | 8 | |
| 1860 | **Abraham Lincoln** | Republican | 180 | 39.8 |
| | J. C. Breckinridge | Democratic | 72 | 29.5 |
| | Stephen A. Douglas | Democratic | 12 | |
| | John Bell | Constitutional Union | 39 | |
| 1864 | **Abraham Lincoln** | Republican | 212 | 55.0 |
| | George B. McClellan | Democratic | 21 | 45.0 |
| | (**Andrew Johnson,** 1865) | | | |
| 1868 | **Ulysses S. Grant** | Republican | 214 | 52.7 |
| | Horatio Seymour | Democratic | 80 | 47.3 |
| 1872 | **Ulysses S. Grant** | Republican | 286 | 55.6 |
| | Horace Greeley | Democratic | ** | 43.8 |
| 1876 | **Rutherford B. Hayes** | Republican | 185 | 47.9 |
| | Samuel J. Tilden | Democratic | 184 | 51.0 |
| 1880 | **James A. Garfield** | Republican | 214 | 48.3 |
| | Winfield S. Hancock | Democratic | 155 | 48.2 |
| | (**Chester A. Arthur,** 1881) | | | |
| 1884 | **Grover Cleveland** | Democratic | 219 | 48.5 |
| | James G. Blaine | Republican | 182 | 48.2 |
| 1888 | **Benjamin Harrison** | Republican | 233 | 48.6 |
| | Grover Cleveland | Democratic | 168 | 47.8 |

| Year | Candidates | Party | Electoral Vote | Popular Vote Percentage |
|------|-----------|-------|----------------|------------------------|
| 1892 | **Grover Cleveland** | Democratic | 277 | 46.1 |
|  | Benjamin Harrison | Republican | 145 | 43.0 |
|  | James B. Weaver | People's | 22 |  |
| 1896 | **William McKinley** | Republican | 271 | 51.0 |
|  | William J. Bryan | Democratic | 176 | 46.7 |
| 1900 | **William McKinley** | Republican | 292 | 51.7 |
|  | William J. Bryan | Democratic | 155 | 45.5 |
|  | **(Theodore Roosevelt,** 1901) |  |  |  |
| 1904 | **Theodore Roosevelt** | Republican | 336 | 56.4 |
|  | Alton B. Parker | Democratic | 140 | 37.6 |
| 1908 | **William H. Taft** | Republican | 321 | 51.6 |
|  | William J. Bryan | Democratic | 162 | 43.0 |
| 1912 | **Woodrow Wilson** | Democratic | 435 | 41.8 |
|  | Theodore Roosevelt | Progressive | 88 | 23.2 |
|  | William H. Taft | Republican | 8 | 23.2 |
| 1916 | **Woodrow Wilson** | Democratic | 277 | 49.2 |
|  | Charles E. Hughes | Republican | 254 | 46.1 |
| 1920 | **Warren G. Harding** | Republican | 404 | 60.3 |
|  | James M. Cox | Democratic | 127 | 34.2 |
|  | **(Calvin Coolidge,** 1923) |  |  |  |
| 1924 | **Calvin Coolidge** | Republican | 382 | 54.1 |
|  | John W. Davis | Democratic | 136 | 28.8 |
|  | Robert M. LaFollette | Progressive | 13 |  |
| 1928 | **Herbert C. Hoover** | Republican | 444 | 58.2 |
|  | Alfred E. Smith | Democratic | 87 | 40.8 |
| 1932 | **Franklin D. Roosevelt** | Democratic | 472 | 57.4 |
|  | Herbert C. Hoover | Republican | 59 | 39.6 |
| 1936 | **Franklin D. Roosevelt** | Democratic | 523 | 60.8 |
|  | Alfred M. Landon | Republican | 8 | 36.5 |
| 1940 | **Franklin D. Roosevelt** | Democratic | 449 | 54.7 |
|  | Wendell L. Willkie | Republican | 82 | 44.8 |
| 1944 | **Franklin D. Roosevelt** | Democratic | 432 | 53.4 |
|  | Thomas E. Dewey | Republican | 99 | 45.9 |
|  | **(Harry S Truman,** 1945) |  |  |  |
| 1948 | **Harry S Truman** | Democratic | 303 | 49.5 |
|  | Thomas E. Dewey | Republican | 189 | 45.1 |
|  | J. Strom Thurmond | States' Rights | 39 |  |

| Year | Candidates | Party | Electoral Vote | Popular Vote Percentage |
|------|-----------|-------|----------------|-------------------------|
| 1952 | **Dwight D. Eisenhower** | Republican | 442 | 55.1 |
|      | Adlai E. Stevenson | Democratic | 89 | 44.4 |
| 1956 | **Dwight D. Eisenhower** | Republican | 457 | 57.4 |
|      | Adlai E. Stevenson | Democratic | 73 | 42.0 |
| 1960 | **John F. Kennedy** | Democratic | 303 | 49.7 |
|      | Richard M. Nixon | Republican | 219 | 49.5 |
|      | **(Lyndon B. Johnson,** 1963) | | | |
| 1964 | **Lyndon B. Johnson** | Democratic | 486 | 61.0 |
|      | Barry M. Goldwater | Republican | 52 | 38.5 |
| 1968 | **Richard M. Nixon** | Republican | 301 | 43.4 |
|      | Hubert H. Humphrey | Democratic | 191 | 42.7 |
|      | George C. Wallace | American Independent | 46 | |
| 1972 | **Richard M. Nixon** | Republican | 520 | 60.7 |
|      | George S. McGovern | Democratic | 17 | 37.5 |
|      | **(Gerald R. Ford,** 1974) | | | |
| 1976 | **Jimmy Carter** | Democratic | 297 | 50.1 |
|      | Gerald R. Ford | Republican | 240 | 48.0 |
| 1980 | **Ronald Reagan** | Republican | 489 | 50.7 |
|      | Jimmy Carter | Democratic | 49 | 41.0 |
|      | John Anderson | Independent | — | |
| 1984 | **Ronald  Reagan** | Republican | 525 | 58.8 |
|      | Walter Mondale | Democratic | 13 | 40.6 |
| 1988 | **George Bush** | Republican | 426 | 53.4 |
|      | Michael Dukakis | Democratic | 112 | 45.6 |
| 1992 | **Bill Clinton** | Democratic | 370 | 43.2 |
|      | George Bush | Republican | 168 | 37.7 |
|      | Ross Perot | Independent | 0 | 19.0 |
| 1996 | **Bill Clinton** | Democratic | 379 | 49 |
|      | Robert Dole | Republican | 159 | 41 |
|      | Ross Perot | Reform | 0 | 8 |

# PARTY CONTROL OF CONGRESS, 1901–1999

| Congress | Years | Party and President | Senate DEM. | REP. | OTHER | House DEM. | REP. | OTHER |
|---|---|---|---|---|---|---|---|---|
| 57th | 1901–03 | R  T. Roosevelt | 29 | 56 | 3 | 153 | 198 | 5 |
| 58th | 1903–05 | R  T. Roosevelt | 32 | 58 | — | 178 | 207 | — |
| 59th | 1905–07 | R  T. Roosevelt | 32 | 58 | — | 136 | 250 | — |
| 60th | 1907–09 | R  T. Roosevelt | 29 | 61 | — | 164 | 222 | — |
| 61st | 1909–11 | R  Taft | 32 | 59 | — | 172 | 219 | — |
| 62d | 1911–13 | R  Taft | 42 | 49 | — | 228 | 162 | 1 |
| 63d | 1913–15 | D  Wilson | 51 | 44 | 1 | 290 | 127 | 18 |
| 64th | 1915–17 | D  Wilson | 56 | 39 | 1 | 230 | 193 | 8 |
| 65th | 1917–19 | D  Wilson | 53 | 42 | 1 | 200 | 216 | 9 |
| 66th | 1919–21 | D  Wilson | 48 | 48 | 1 | 191 | 237 | 7 |
| 67th | 1921–23 | R  Harding | 37 | 59 | — | 132 | 300 | 1 |
| 68th | 1923–25 | R  Coolidge | 43 | 51 | 2 | 207 | 225 | 3 |
| 69th | 1925–27 | R  Coolidge | 40 | 54 | 1 | 183 | 247 | 5 |
| 70th | 1927–29 | R  Coolidge | 47 | 48 | 1 | 195 | 237 | 3 |
| 71st | 1929–31 | R  Hoover | 39 | 56 | 1 | 163 | 267 | 1 |
| 72d | 1931–33 | R  Hoover | 47 | 48 | 1 | 216 | 218 | 1 |
| 73d | 1933–35 | D  F. Roosevelt | 59 | 36 | 1 | 313 | 117 | 5 |
| 74th | 1935–37 | D  F. Roosevelt | 69 | 25 | 2 | 322 | 103 | 10 |
| 75th | 1937–39 | D  F. Roosevelt | 75 | 17 | 4 | 333 | 89 | 13 |
| 76th | 1939–41 | D  F. Roosevelt | 69 | 23 | 4 | 262 | 169 | 4 |
| 77th | 1941–43 | D  F. Roosevelt | 66 | 28 | 2 | 267 | 162 | 6 |
| 78th | 1943–45 | D  F. Roosevelt | 57 | 38 | 1 | 222 | 209 | 4 |
| 79th | 1945–47 | D  Truman | 57 | 38 | 1 | 243 | 190 | 2 |
| 80th | 1947–49 | D  Truman | 45 | 51 | — | 188 | 246 | 1 |
| 81st | 1949–51 | D  Truman | 54 | 42 | — | 263 | 171 | 1 |
| 82d | 1951–53 | D  Truman | 48 | 47 | 1 | 234 | 199 | 2 |
| 83d | 1953–55 | R  Eisenhower | 47 | 48 | 1 | 213 | 221 | 1 |
| 84th | 1955–57 | R  Eisenhower | 48 | 47 | 1 | 232 | 203 | — |
| 85th | 1957–59 | R  Eisenhower | 49 | 47 | — | 234 | 201 | — |
| 86th | 1959–61 | R  Eisenhower | 64 | 34 | — | 283 | 154 | — |
| 87th | 1961–63 | D  Kennedy | 64 | 36 | — | 263 | 174 | — |
| 88th | 1963–65 | D  { Johnson / Johnson | 67 | 33 | — | 258 | 176 | — |
| 89th | 1965–67 | D  Johnson | 68 | 32 | — | 295 | 140 | — |
| 90th | 1967–69 | D  Johnson | 64 | 36 | — | 248 | 187 | — |
| 91st | 1969–71 | R  Nixon | 58 | 42 | — | 243 | 192 | — |
| 92d | 1971–73 | R  Nixon | 55 | 45 | — | 255 | 180 | — |
| 93d | 1973–75 | R  { Nixon / Ford | 57 | 43 | — | 243 | 192 | — |
| 94th | 1975–77 | R  Ford | 61 | 38 | — | 291 | 144 | — |
| 95th | 1977–79 | D  Carter | 62 | 38 | — | 292 | 143 | — |
| 96th | 1979–81 | D  Carter | 59 | 41 | — | 277 | 158 | — |
| 97th | 1981–83 | R  Reagan | 47 | 53 | — | 243 | 192 | — |
| 98th | 1983–85 | R  Reagan | 46 | 54 | — | 269 | 166 | — |
| 99th | 1985–87 | R  Reagan | 47 | 53 | — | 253 | 182 | — |
| 100th | 1987–89 | R  Reagan | 55 | 45 | — | 258 | 177 | — |
| 101st | 1989–91 | R  Bush | 55 | 45 | — | 260 | 175 | — |
| 102d | 1991–93 | R  Bush | 57 | 43 | — | 267 | 167 | 1 |
| 103d | 1993–95 | D  Clinton | 59 | 43 | — | 258 | 176 | 1 |
| 104th | 1995–97 | D  Clinton | 46 | 54 | — | 204 | 230 | 1 |
| 105th | 1997–99 | D  Clinton | 45 | 55 | — | 208 | 225 | 2 |

# SUPREME COURT MEMBERSHIP, 1900–1996

| Justice* | Age at Nomination | President Who Nominated | Years on Court |
|---|---|---|---|
| John M. Harlan | 44 | Hayes | 1877–1911 |
| Horace Gray | 53 | Arthur | 1882–1902 |
| **Melville W. Fuller** | 55 | Cleveland | 1888–1910 |
| David J. Brewer | 52 | Harrison | 1890–1910 |
| Henry B. Brown | 54 | Harrison | 1890–1906 |
| George Shiras, Jr. | 60 | Harrison | 1892–1903 |
| Edward D. White | 48 | Cleveland | 1894–1910 |
| Rufus W. Peckham | 57 | Cleveland | 1895–1909 |
| Joseph McKenna | 54 | McKinley | 1898–1925 |
| Oliver W. Holmes | 61 | T. Roosevelt | 1902–1932 |
| William R. Day | 53 | T. Roosevelt | 1903–1922 |
| William H. Moody | 52 | T. Roosevelt | 1906–1910 |
| Horace H. Lurton | 65 | Taft | 1910–1914 |
| **Edward D. White** | 65 | Taft | 1910–1921 |
| Charles E. Hughes | 48 | Taft | 1910–1916 |
| Willis Van Devanter | 51 | Taft | 1911–1937 |
| Joseph R. Lamar | 53 | Taft | 1911–1916 |
| Mahlon Pitney | 54 | Taft | 1912–1922 |
| James C. McReynolds | 52 | Wilson | 1914–1941 |
| Louis D. Brandeis | 59 | Wilson | 1916–1939 |
| John H. Clarke | 59 | Wilson | 1916–1922 |
| **William H. Taft** | 63 | Harding | 1921–1930 |
| George Sutherland | 60 | Harding | 1922–1938 |
| Pierce Butler | 56 | Harding | 1922–1939 |
| Edward T. Sanford | 57 | Harding | 1923–1930 |
| Harlan F. Stone | 52 | Coolidge | 1925–1941 |
| **Charles E. Hughes** | 67 | Hoover | 1930–1941 |
| Owen J. Roberts | 55 | Hoover | 1930–1945 |
| Benjamin N. Cardozo | 61 | Hoover | 1932–1938 |
| Hugo L. Black | 51 | F. Roosevelt | 1937–1971 |
| Stanley F. Reed | 53 | F. Roosevelt | 1938–1957 |
| Felix Frankfurter | 56 | F. Roosevelt | 1939–1962 |
| William O. Douglas | 40 | F. Roosevelt | 1939–1975 |
| Frank Murphy | 49 | F. Roosevelt | 1940–1949 |
| **Harlan F. Stone** | 68 | F. Roosevelt | 1941–1946 |
| James F. Byrnes | 62 | F. Roosevelt | 1941–1942 |
| Robert H. Jackson | 49 | F. Roosevelt | 1941–1954 |
| Wiley B. Rutledge | 48 | F. Roosevelt | 1943–1949 |

| Justice* | Age at Nomination | President Who Nominated | Years on Court |
|---|---|---|---|
| Harold H. Burton | 57 | Truman | 1945–1958 |
| **Fred M. Vinson** | 56 | Truman | 1946–1953 |
| Tom C. Clark | 49 | Truman | 1949–1967 |
| Sherman Minton | 58 | Truman | 1949–1956 |
| **Earl Warren** | 62 | Eisenhower | 1953–1969 |
| John M. Harlan | 55 | Eisenhower | 1955–1971 |
| William J. Brennan, Jr. | 50 | Eisenhower | 1956–1990 |
| Charles E. Whittaker | 56 | Eisenhower | 1957–1962 |
| Potter Stewart | 43 | Eisenhower | 1958–1981 |
| Byron R. White | 44 | Kennedy | 1962–1993 |
| Arthur J. Goldberg | 54 | Kennedy | 1962–1965 |
| Abe Fortas | 55 | Johnson | 1965–1969 |
| Thurgood Marshall | 59 | Johnson | 1967–1991 |
| **Warren E. Burger** | 61 | Nixon | 1969–1986 |
| Harry A. Blackmun | 61 | Nixon | 1970– |
| Lewis F. Powell, Jr. | 64 | Nixon | 1971–1987 |
| William H. Rehnquist | 47 | Nixon | 1971–1986 |
| John Paul Stevens | 55 | Ford | 1975– |
| Sandra Day O'Connor | 51 | Reagan | 1981– |
| **William H. Rehnquist** | 61 | Reagan | 1986– |
| Antonin Scalia | 50 | Reagan | 1986– |
| Anthony M. Kennedy | 51 | Reagan | 1988– |
| David H. Souter | 50 | Bush | 1990– |
| Clarence Thomas | | Bush | 1991– |
| Ruth Bader Ginsburg | 60 | Clinton | 1993– |
| Stephen G. Breyer | 55 | Clinton | 1994– |

*Chief justices in boldface.

# PARTY IDENTIFICATION, 1952–1994

| | 1952 | 1954 | 1956 | 1958 | 1960 | 1962 | 1964 | 1966 | 1968 | 1970 | 1972 |
|---|---|---|---|---|---|---|---|---|---|---|---|
| Strong Democrat | 22% | 22% | 21% | 27% | 20% | 23% | 27% | 18% | 20% | 20% | 15% |
| Weak Democrat | 25 | 25 | 23 | 22 | 25 | 23 | 25 | 28 | 25 | 24 | 26 |
| Independent Democrat | 10 | 9 | 6 | 7 | 6 | 7 | 9 | 9 | 10 | 10 | 11 |
| Independent | 6 | 7 | 9 | 7 | 10 | 8 | 8 | 12 | 11 | 13 | 13 |
| Independent Republican | 7 | 6 | 8 | 5 | 7 | 6 | 6 | 7 | 9 | 8 | 10 |
| Weak Republican | 14 | 14 | 14 | 17 | 14 | 16 | 14 | 15 | 15 | 15 | 13 |
| Strong Republican | 14 | 13 | 15 | 11 | 16 | 12 | 11 | 10 | 10 | 9 | 10 |
| Apolitical | 3 | 4 | 4 | 4 | 2 | 4 | 1 | 1 | 1 | 1 | 1 |
| Total | 101 | 100 | 100 | 100 | 100 | 99 | 101 | 100 | 101 | 100 | 99 |
| Number of interviews | 1,784 | 1,130 | 1,757 | 1,808 | 1,911 | 1,287 | 1,550 | 1,278 | 1,553 | 1,501 | 2,694 |

| | 1974 | 1976 | 1978 | 1980 | 1982 | 1984 | 1986 | 1988 | 1990 | 1992 | 1994 |
|---|---|---|---|---|---|---|---|---|---|---|---|
| Strong Democrat | 17% | 15% | 15% | 18% | 20% | 17% | 18% | 17% | 20% | 17% | 15% |
| Weak Democrat | 21 | 25 | 24 | 23 | 24 | 20 | 22 | 18 | 19 | 18 | 19 |
| Independent Democrat | 13 | 12 | 14 | 11 | 11 | 11 | 10 | 12 | 12 | 14 | 13 |
| Independent | 15 | 15 | 14 | 13 | 11 | 11 | 12 | 11 | 11 | 12 | 10 |
| Independent Republican | 9 | 10 | 10 | 10 | 8 | 12 | 11 | 13 | 12 | 13 | 12 |
| Weak Republican | 14 | 14 | 13 | 14 | 14 | 15 | 15 | 14 | 15 | 15 | 15 |
| Strong Republican | 8 | 9 | 8 | 9 | 10 | 12 | 10 | 14 | 10 | 11 | 16 |
| Apolitical | 3 | 1 | 3 | 2 | 2 | 2 | 2 | 2 | 2 | 1 | 1 |
| Total | 100 | 101 | 101 | 100 | 100 | 100 | 100 | 101 | 101 | 101 | 101 |
| Number of interviews | 2,505 | 2,850 | 2,283 | 1,613 | 1,418 | 2,236 | 2,166 | 2,032 | 1,991 | 2,487 | 1,795 |

*Questions:* "Generally speaking, do you consider yourself a Republican, a Democrat, an Independent, or what?"
If Republican or Democrat: "Would you call yourself a strong (R/D) or a not very strong (R/D)?"
If Independent or other: "Do you think of yourself as closer to the Republican or Democratic party?"
*Source:* National Election Studies data, Center for Political Studies, University of Michigan.

# GOVERNMENT AND THE ECONOMY, 1960–1996

| Year | President | Gross Domestic Product ($ billion) | Total Government Spending ($ billion) | Federal Government Spending ($ billion) | Annual Federal Deficits ($ billion) | Gross Federal Debt ($ billion) |
|------|-----------|------|------|------|------|------|
| 1960 | Eisenhower | 513.4 | 135.2 | 93.4 | .5 | 290.5 |
| 1961 | Kennedy | 531.8 | 147.1 | 101.7 | −3.8 | 292.6 |
| 1962 | Kennedy | 571.6 | 158.7 | 110.6 | −5.9 | 302.9 |
| 1963 | Kennedy | 603.1 | 165.9 | 114.4 | −4.0 | 310.3 |
| 1964 | Johnson | 648.0 | 174.5 | 118.8 | −6.5 | 316.1 |
| 1965 | Johnson | 702.7 | 185.8 | 124.6 | −1.6 | 322.3 |
| 1966 | Johnson | 769.8 | 211.6 | 144.9 | −3.1 | 328.5 |
| 1967 | Johnson | 814.3 | 240.2 | 165.2 | −12.6 | 340.4 |
| 1968 | Johnson | 889.3 | 265.5 | 181.5 | −27.7 | 368.7 |
| 1969 | Nixon | 959.5 | 284.0 | 191.0 | −.5 | 365.8 |
| 1970 | Nixon | 1,010.7 | 311.2 | 208.5 | −8.7 | 380.9 |
| 1971 | Nixon | 1,097.2 | 338.1 | 224.3 | −26.1 | 408.2 |
| 1972 | Nixon | 1,207.0 | 368.1 | 249.3 | −26.4 | 435.9 |
| 1973 | Nixon | 1,349.6 | 401.6 | 270.3 | −15.4 | 466.3 |
| 1974 | Ford | 1,458.6 | 455.2 | 305.6 | −8.0 | 483.9 |
| 1975 | Ford | 1,585.9 | 530.6 | 364.2 | −55.3 | 541.9 |
| 1976 | Ford | 1,768.4 | 570.9 | 392.7 | −70.5 | 629.0 |
| 1977 | Carter | 1,974.1 | 615.2 | 426.4 | −49.8 | 706.4 |
| 1978 | Carter | 2,232.7 | 670.3 | 469.3 | −54.9 | 776.6 |
| 1979 | Carter | 2,488.6 | 745.3 | 520.3 | −38.2 | 828.9 |
| 1980 | Carter | 2,708.0 | 861.0 | 613.1 | −72.7 | 908.5 |
| 1981 | Reagan | 3,030.6 | 972.3 | 697.8 | −74.0 | 994.3 |
| 1982 | Reagan | 3,149.6 | 1,069.1 | 770.9 | −120.1 | 1,136.8 |
| 1983 | Reagan | 3,405.0 | 1,156.2 | 840.0 | −208.0 | 1,371.2 |
| 1984 | Reagan | 3,777.2 | 1,232.4 | 892.7 | −185.7 | 1,564.1 |
| 1985 | Reagan | 4,038.7 | 1,342.2 | 969.9 | −221.7 | 1,817.0 |
| 1986 | Reagan | 4,268.6 | 1,437.5 | 1,028.2 | −238.0 | 2,120.1 |
| 1987 | Reagan | 4,539.9 | 1,516.9 | 1,065.6 | −169.3 | 2,345.6 |
| 1988 | Reagan | 4,900.4 | 1,590.7 | 1,109.0 | −194.0 | 2,600.8 |
| 1989 | Bush | 5,250.8 | 1,700.1 | 1,181.6 | −205.2 | 2,867.5 |
| 1990 | Bush | 5,546.1 | 1,840.5 | 1,252.7 | −221.4 | 3,206.3 |
| 1991 | Bush | 5,724.8 | 1,940.1 | 1,323.4 | −269.2 | 3,599.0 |
| 1992 | Bush | 6,020.2 | 2,094.9 | 1,380.8 | −290.4 | 4,002.7 |
| 1993 | Clinton | 6,343.3 | 2,261.8 | 1,408.6 | −255.1 | 4,351.7 |
| 1994 | Clinton | 6,726.9 | 2,381.0 | 1,460.9 | −203.2 | 4,643.7 |
| 1995 | Clinton | 7,254.0 | 2,553.0 | 1,538.9 | −192.5 | 4,961.5 |
| 1996 (est) | Clinton | 7,621.0 | 2,705.0 | 1,572.4 | −145.6 | 5,107.0 |

| | 1952 | | 1956 | | 1960 | | 1964 | | 1968 | | 1972 | | |
|---|---|---|---|---|---|---|---|---|---|---|---|---|---|
| | D | R | D | R | D | R | D | R | D | R | I | D | R |
| **Sex** | | | | | | | | | | | | | |
| Male | 47% | 53% | 45% | 55% | 52% | 48% | 60% | 40% | 41% | 43% | 16% | 37% | 63% |
| Female | 42 | 58 | 39 | 61 | 49 | 51 | 62 | 38 | 45 | 43 | 12 | 38 | 62 |
| **Race/ethnicity** | | | | | | | | | | | | | |
| White | 43 | 57 | 41 | 59 | 49 | 51 | 59 | 41 | 38 | 47 | 15 | 32 | 68 |
| Nonwhite | 79 | 21 | 61 | 39 | 68 | 32 | 94 | 6 | 85 | 12 | 3 | 87 | 13 |
| **Education** | | | | | | | | | | | | | |
| Grade school | 52 | 48 | 50 | 50 | 55 | 45 | 66 | 34 | 52 | 33 | 15 | 49 | 51 |
| High School | 45 | 55 | 42 | 58 | 52 | 48 | 62 | 38 | 42 | 43 | 15 | 34 | 66 |
| College | 34 | 66 | 31 | 69 | 39 | 61 | 52 | 48 | 37 | 54 | 9 | 37 | 63 |
| **Age** | | | | | | | | | | | | | |
| Under 30 | 51 | 49 | 43 | 57 | 54 | 45 | 64 | 36 | 47 | 38 | 15 | 48 | 52 |
| 30–49 | 47 | 53 | 45 | 55 | 54 | 46 | 63 | 37 | 44 | 41 | 15 | 33 | 67 |
| 50 and older | 39 | 61 | 39 | 61 | 46 | 54 | 59 | 41 | 41 | 47 | 12 | 36 | 64 |
| **Religion** | | | | | | | | | | | | | |
| Protestant | 37 | 63 | 37 | 63 | 38 | 62 | 55 | 45 | 35 | 49 | 16 | 30 | 70 |
| Catholic | 56 | 44 | 51 | 49 | 78 | 22 | 76 | 24 | 59 | 33 | 8 | 48 | 52 |
| **Political affiliation** | | | | | | | | | | | | | |
| Democrat | 77 | 23 | 85 | 15 | 84 | 16 | 87 | 13 | 74 | 12 | 14 | 67 | 33 |
| Independent | 35 | 65 | 30 | 70 | 43 | 57 | 56 | 44 | 31 | 44 | 25 | 31 | 69 |
| Republican | 8 | 92 | 4 | 96 | 5 | 95 | 20 | 80 | 9 | 86 | 5 | 5 | 95 |
| **Region** | | | | | | | | | | | | | |
| East | 45 | 55 | 40 | 60 | 53 | 47 | 68 | 32 | 50 | 43 | 7 | 42 | 58 |
| Midwest | 42 | 58 | 41 | 59 | 48 | 52 | 61 | 39 | 44 | 47 | 9 | 40 | 60 |
| South | 51 | 49 | 49 | 51 | 51 | 49 | 52 | 48 | 31 | 36 | 33 | 29 | 71 |
| West | 42 | 58 | 43 | 57 | 49 | 51 | 60 | 40 | 44 | 49 | 7 | 41 | 59 |
| Union family | 61 | 39 | 57 | 43 | 65 | 35 | 73 | 27 | 56 | 29 | 15 | 46 | 54 |
| **Total** | **45** | **55** | **42** | **58** | **50** | **50** | **61** | **39** | **43** | **43** | **14** | **38** | **62** |

| | 1976 | | | 1980 | | | 1984 | | 1988 | | 1992 | | |
|---|---|---|---|---|---|---|---|---|---|---|---|---|---|
| | D | R | I | D | R | I | D | R | D | R | D | R | I |
| Sex | | | | | | | | | | | | | |
| Male | 53% | 45% | 1% | 38% | 53% | 7% | 36% | 64% | 44% | 56% | 41% | 38% | 21% |
| Female | 48 | 51 | — | 44 | 49 | 6 | 45 | 55 | 48 | 52 | 46 | 37 | 17 |
| Race/ethnicity | | | | | | | | | | | | | |
| White | 46 | 52 | 1 | 36 | 56 | 7 | 34 | 66 | 41 | 59 | 39 | 41 | 20 |
| Nonwhite | 85 | 15 | — | 86 | 10 | 2 | 87 | 13 | 82 | 18 | 82 | 11 | 7 |
| Education | | | | | | | | | | | | | |
| Grade school | 58 | 41 | 1 | 54 | 42 | 3 | 51 | 49 | 55 | 45 | 56 | 28 | 17 |
| High School | 54 | 46 | — | 43 | 51 | 5 | 43 | 57 | 46 | 54 | 43 | 36 | 20 |
| College | 42 | 55 | 2 | 35 | 53 | 10 | 39 | 61 | 42 | 58 | 44 | 39 | 18 |
| Age | | | | | | | | | | | | | |
| Under 30 | 53 | 45 | 1 | 47 | 41 | 11 | 40 | 60 | 37 | 63 | 44 | 34 | 22 |
| 30–49 | 48 | 49 | 2 | 38 | 52 | 8 | 40 | 60 | 45 | 55 | 42 | 38 | 20 |
| 50 and older | 52 | 48 | — | 41 | 54 | 4 | 41 | 59 | 49 | 51 | 50 | 38 | 12 |
| Religion | | | | | | | | | | | | | |
| Protestant | 46 | 53 | — | 39 | 54 | 6 | 39 | 61 | 42 | 58 | 33 | 46 | 21 |
| Catholic | 57 | 41 | 1 | 46 | 47 | 6 | 39 | 61 | 51 | 49 | 44 | 36 | 20 |
| Political affiliation | | | | | | | | | | | | | |
| Democrat | 82 | 18 | — | 69 | 26 | 4 | 79 | 21 | 85 | 15 | 77 | 10 | 13 |
| Independent | 38 | 57 | 4 | 29 | 55 | 14 | 33 | 67 | 43 | 57 | 38 | 32 | 30 |
| Republican | 9 | 91 | — | 8 | 86 | 5 | 4 | 96 | 7 | 93 | 10 | 73 | 17 |
| Region | | | | | | | | | | | | | |
| East | 51 | 47 | 1 | 43 | 47 | 9 | 46 | 54 | 51 | 49 | 47 | 35 | 18 |
| Midwest | 48 | 50 | 1 | 41 | 51 | 7 | 42 | 58 | 47 | 53 | 42 | 37 | 21 |
| South | 54 | 45 | — | 44 | 52 | 3 | 37 | 63 | 40 | 60 | 42 | 43 | 16 |
| West | 46 | 51 | 1 | 35 | 54 | 9 | 40 | 60 | 46 | 54 | 44 | 34 | 22 |
| Union family | 63 | 36 | 1 | 50 | 43 | 5 | 52 | 48 | 63 | 37 | 55 | 24 | 21 |
| **Total** | **50** | **48** | **1** | **41** | **51** | **7** | **41** | **59** | **46** | **54** | **43** | **39** | **19** |

# NOTES

## CHAPTER ONE

1. For a discussion of various aspects of legitimacy and its measurement in public opinion polls, see M. Stephen Weatherford, "Measuring Political Legitimacy," *American Political Science Review* 86 (March 1992): 140–55.
2. Thomas Hobbes, *Leviathan* (1651).
3. For an explanation of the worldwide growth of democracy, see John Mueller, "Democracy and Ralph's Pretty Good Grocery Store," *American Journal of Political Science* 36 (November 1992): 983–1003.
4. John Locke, *Treatise on Government* (1688).
5. James Madison, Alexander Hamilton, and John Jay, *The Federalist Papers* (New York: Mentor Books, 1961), No. 10, p. 81. Madison's *Federalist Papers,* No. 10 and No. 51, are reprinted in the Appendix.
6. E. E. Shattschneider, *Two Hundred Million Americans in Search of a Government* (New York: Holt, Rinehart, and Winston, 1969), p. 63.
7. Harold Lasswell and Daniel Lerner, *The Comparative Study of Elites* (Stanford, Calif.: Stanford University Press, 1952), p. 7.
8. C. Wright Mill's classic study, *The Power Elite* (New York: Oxford University Press, 1956), is widely cited by Marxist critics of American democracy, but it can be read profitably by anyone concerned with the effects of large bureaucracies—corporate, governmental, or military—on democratic government.

9. In *Who Rules America?* (New York: Prentice Hall, 1967) and its sequel *Who Rules America Now?* (New York: Prentice Hall, 1983), sociologist G. William Domhoff argues that America is ruled by an "upper class" who attend the same prestigious private schools, intermarry among themselves, and join the same exclusive clubs. In *Who's Running America?* (New York: Prentice Hall, 1976) and *Who's Running America? The Clinton Years* (New York: Prentice Hall, 1995), political scientist Thomas R. Dye documents the concentration of power and the control of assets in the hands of officers and directors of the nation's largest corporations, banks, law firms, networks, foundations, and so forth. Dye argues, however, that most of these "institutional elites" were not born into the upper class but instead climbed the ladder to success.
10. Yale political scientist Robert A. Dahl is an important contributor to the development of pluralist theory, beginning with his *Preface to Democratic Theory* (Chicago: University of Chicago Press, 1956). He often refers to a pluralist system as a *polyarchy*—literally, a system with many centers of power. See his *Polyarchy* (New Haven, Conn.: Yale University Press, 1971); and for a revised defense of pluralism, see his *Democracy and Its Critics* (New Haven, Conn.: Yale University Press, 1989).

## CHAPTER TWO

1. Gunnar Myrdal, *An American Dilemma* (New York: Harper, 1944).
2. See Martin Luther King, Jr., "Letter from Birmingham City Jail," April 16, 1963.
3. For a discussion of the sources and consequences of intolerance in the general public, see James L. Gibson, "The Political Consequences of Intolerance: Cultural Conformity and Political Freedom," *American Political Science Review* 86 (June 1992):338–52.
4. Quoted in *The Idea of Equality,* ed. George Abernathy (Richmond, Va.: John Knox Press, 1959), p. 185; also in Herbert McClosky and John Zaller, *The American Ethos: Public Attitudes toward Capitalism and Democracy* (Cambridge, Mass.: Harvard University Press, 1984), p. 72.
5. Quoted in Richard Hofstadter, *The American Political Tradition* (New York: Knopf, 1948), p. 45. Historian Hofstadter describes the thinking of American political leaders from Jefferson and the Founders to Franklin D. Roosevelt.
6. For a discussion of how people balance the values of individualism and opposition to big government with humanitarianism and the desire to help others, see Stanley Feldman and John Zaller, "The Political Culture of Ambivalence: Ideological Responses to the Welfare State," *American Journal of Political Science* 36 (February 1992): 268–307.
7. Robert E. Lane, "Market Justice, Political Justice," *American Political Science Review* 80 (June 1986):383–402.

8. Greg J. Duncan, *Years of Poverty, Years of Plenty* (Ann Arbor: University of Michigan Press, 1984).
9. American Security Council, *The Illegal Immigration Crisis* (Washington, D.C.: ASC, 1994).
10. *Sale v. Haitian Centers Council,* 125 L. Ed. 2d 128 (1993).
11. See Peter Brimelow, *Alien Nation* (New York: Random House, 1995).
12. For a summary of recent studies, see *America's Newcomers* (Denver: National Conference of State Legislatures, 1993).
13. See Stephen Earl Bennett, "Americans' Knowledge of Ideology, 1980–92," *American Politics Quarterly* 23 (July 1995):259–78.
14. For evidence that ideological consistency increases with educational level, see William G. Jacoby, "Ideological Identification and Issue Attitude," *American Journal of Political Science* 35 (February 1991): 178–205.
15. Richard Hofstadter, *The Paranoid Style in American Politics* (New York: Knopf, 1965).
16. Francis Fukuyama, "The End of History," *National Interest* 16 (Summer 1989).
17. See Roger Kimball, *Tenured Radicals* (New York: Harper & Row, 1990).
18. Herbert Marcuse, *One-Dimensional Man* (Boston: Beacon Press, 1964).
19. Allan Bloom, *The Closing of the American Mind* (New York: Simon & Schuster, 1987), p. 15.

## CHAPTER THREE

1. In *Federalist Papers,* No. 53, James Madison distinguishes a "constitution" from a law: a constitution is "established by the people and unalterable by the government, and a law established by the government and alterable by the government."

2. Another important decision on opening day of the Constitutional Convection was to keep the proceedings secret. James Madison made his own notes on the convention proceedings, and they were published many years later. See Max Ferrand, ed., *The Records of the Federal Convention of 1787* (New Haven, Conn.: Yale University Press, 1911).

## CHAPTER FOUR

1. The states are listed in the order in which their legislatures voted to secede. While occupied by Confederate troops, secessionist legislators in Missouri and Kentucky also voted to secede, but Unionist representatives from these states remained in Congress.

2. *Texas v. White,* 7 Wallace 700 (1869).

3. James Madison, *Federalist Papers,* No. 51, reprinted in the Appendix.

4. Ibid.

5. The arguments for "competitive federalism" are developed at length in Thomas R. Dye, *American Federalism: Competition among Governments* (Lexington, Mass.: Lexington Books, 1990).

6. David Osborne, *Laboratories of Democracy* (Cambridge, Mass.: Harvard Business School, 1988).

7. Morton Grodzins, *The American System* (Chicago: Rand McNally, 1966), pp. 8–9.

## CHAPTER FIVE

1. See James A. Stimson, Michael B. Mackuen, and Robert S. Erikson, "Dynamic Representation," *American Political Science Review* 89 (September 1995): 543–61.

2. Robert S. Erikson, Norman R. Luttbeg, and Kent L. Tedin, *American Public Opinion,* 3d ed. (New York: Macmillan, 1988).

3. For a counterargument that public opinion is more "rational," stable, and coherent than many political scientists theorized in the past, see Benjamin I. Page and Robert Y. Shapiro, *The Rational Public: Fifty Years of Trends in Americans' Policy Preferences* (Chicago: University of Chicago Press, 1992).

4. *Public Opinion* 9 (September/October 1986): 32, also cited by Erikson et al., *American Public Opinion,* p. 55.

5. For a summary of recent literature on public opinion, see James Stimson, "Opinion and Representation," *American Political Science Review* 89 (March 1995): 179–83.

6. Sandra K. Schwartz, "Preschoolers and Politics," in *New Directions in Political Socialization,* eds. David C. Schwartz and Sandra K. Schwartz (New York: Free Press, 1975), p. 242.

7. M. Kent Jennings and Richard G. Niemi, *The Political Character of Adolescence* (Princeton, N.J.: Princeton University Press, 1974), p. 41.

8. Robert D. Hess and Judith V. Torney, *The Development of Political Attitudes in Children* (Chicago: Aldine, 1977), p. 42.

9. See also Ted G. Jelen, "The Political Consequences of Religious Group Attitudes," *Journal of Politics* 55 (February 1993): 178–90.

10. See M. Kent Jennings, "Residues of a Movement: The Aging of the American Protest Generation," *American Political Science Review* 81 (June 1987): 370–72; M. Kent Jennings and Richard G. Niemi, *Generational Politics* (Princeton, N.J.: Princeton University Press, 1982).

11. See also James A. Stimson, *Public Opinion in America: Moods, Cycles, and Swings* (Boulder, Colo.: Westview Press, 1991).

12. V. O. Key, Jr., *Public Opinion and American Democracy* (New York: Knopf, 1967), p. 537.

13. *Harper v. Virginia State Board of Elections,* 383 U.S. 663 (1966).

14. Congress had earlier passed the Voting Rights Act of 1970, which (1) extended the vote to eighteen-year-olds regardless of state law; (2) abolished residency requirements in excess of thirty days; and (3) prohibited literacy tests. However, there was some constitutional

3. See Edward Millican, *One United People: The Federalist Papers and the National Idea* (Lexington, Ky: University Press of Kentucky, 1990).

4. Charles A. Beard, *An Economic Interpretation of the Constitution* (New York: Macmillan, 1913).

5. Robert E. Brown, *Charles Beard and the Constitution* (Princeton, N.J.: Princeton University Press, 1956).

6. James Madison, *Federalist Papers,* No. 10, reprinted in the Appendix.

7. Alexander Hamilton, *Federalist Papers,* No. 78.

8. Ibid., p. 265.

9. Charles Press, *State and Community Governments in the Federal System* (New York: John Wiley, 1979), p. 78.

10. *Garcia v. San Antonio Metropolitan Transit Authority,* 469 U.S. 528 (1985).

11. *McCulloch v. Maryland,* 4 Wheaton 316 (1819).

12. Civil Rights Acts of 1866, 1871, and 1875.

13. Civil Rights Acts of 1883, 100 US 3 (1883).

14. *National Labor Relations Board v. Jones and Laughlin Steel Corporation,* 301 U.S. 1 (1937).

15. *Wickard v. Filburn,* 317 U.S. 128 (1938).

16. *Massachusetts v. Mellers, Frothingham v. Mellon,* 262 U.S. 447 (1923).

17. *Federal-State-Local Relations: Federal Grants in Aid,* House Committee on Government Operations, 85th Cong., 2d sess., p. 7.

debate about the power of Congress to change state laws on voting age. While Congress can end *racial* discrimination, extending the vote to eighteen-year-olds was a different matter. All previous extensions of the vote had come by constitutional amendment. Hence Congress quickly passed the Twenty-sixth Amendment.

15. Staci L. Rhine, "Registration Reform and Turnout," *American Politics Quarterly* 23 (October 1995): 409–26: Stephen Knack, "Does 'Motor Voter' Work?" *Journal of Politics* 57 (August 1995): 796–811.

16. *General Social Survey, 1994* (Chicago: National Opinion Research Center, 1990).

17. Raymond E. Wolfinger and Steven J. Rosenstove, *Who Votes?* (New Haven, Conn.: Yale University Press, 1980).

18. John E. Filer, Lawrence W. Kenny, and Rebecca B. Morton, "Redistribution, Income, and Voting," *American Journal of Political Science* 37 (February 1993): 63–87.

19. Sidney Verba, Kay Schlozman, Henry Brady, and Norman Nie, "Citizen Activity: Who Participates? What Do They Say?" *American Political Science Review* 87 (June 1993): 303–18.

20. For a full discussion of the factors influencing black voter participation, see Katherine Tate, "Black Political Participation in the 1984 and 1988 Presidential Elections," *American Political Science Review* 85 (December 1991): 1159–76.

21. John Stuart Mill, *Considerations on Representative Government* (Chicago: Regnery, Gateway, 1962; original publication 1859), p. 144.

22. Ibid., p. 130.

23. Attributed to Arthur Hadley by Austin Ranney in "Non-Voting Is Not a Social Disease," *Public Opinion* 6 (November/December 1983): 17.

24. Quoted in ibid., p. 18.

25. Francis Fox Piven and Richard Cloward, *Why Americans Don't Vote* (New York: Pantheon, 1987).

26. Verba et al., "Citizen Activity."

27. See Michael M. Gant and William Lyons, "Democratic Theory, Nonvoting, and Public Policy," *American Politics Quarterly* 21 (April 1993): 185–204.

28. Martin Luther King, Jr., "Letter from Birmingham City Jail," April 16, 1963.

## CHAPTER SIX

1. Carl Bernstein, quoted in *Vanity Fair* (March 1989): 106.
2. E. E. Schattschneider, *The Semisovereign People* (New York: Holt, Rinehart & Winston, 1961), p. 68.
3. William A. Henry, "News as Entertainment," in *What's News,* ed. Elie Abel (San Francisco: Institute for Contemporary Studies, 1981), p. 133.
4. Shanto Iyengar, *Is Anyone Responsible? How Television Frames Political Issues* (Chicago: University of Chicago Press, 1991).
5. Michael Jay Robinson, "Just How Liberal Is the News?" *Public Opinion* 38 (February/March 1983): 55–60.
6. Ben J. Wattenberg, *The Good News Is the Bad News Is Wrong* (New York: Simon & Schuster, 1984).
7. Ted Smith, "The Watchdog's Bite," *American Enterprise* 2 (January/February 1990): 66.
8. Doris A. Graber, *Mass Media and American Politics* (Washington, D.C.: Congressional Quarterly Press, 1980), p. 49.
9. S. Robert Lichter, Stanley Rothman, and Linda S. Lichter, *The Media Elite* (Bethesda, Md.: Adler and Adler, 1986).
10. See David S. Castle, "Media Coverage of Presidential Primaries," *American Politics Quarterly* 19 (January 1991): 13–42; Christine F. Ridout, "The Role of Media Coverage of Iowa and New Hampshire," *American Politics Quarterly* 19 (January 1991): 43–58.

11. Michael Robinson and Margaret Sheehan, *Over the Wire and on TV* (New York: Sage, 1983). See also S. Robert Lichter, Daniel Amundson, and Richard Noyes, *The Video Campaign* (Washington, D.C.: American Enterprise Institute, 1988).
12. Robinson and Sheehan, *Over the Wire and on TV,* p. 138.
13. *New York Times v. U.S.,* 376 U.S. 713 (1971).
14. *New York Times v. Sullivan,* 376 U.S. 254 (1964).
15. For details, see "Anatomy of a Smear," *TV Guide,* May 1982.
16. Bernard Cohen, *The Press and Foreign Policy* (Princeton, N.J.: Princeton University Press, 1963), p. 16.
17. Austin Ranney, *Channels of Power* (New York: Basic Books, 1983), p. 81.
18. Benjamin I. Page, Robert Y. Shapiro, and Glen R. Dempsey, "What Moves Public Opinion," *American Political Science Review* 81 (March 1987): 23–43.
19. National Institute of Mental Health, *Television and Behavior* (Washington, D.C.: Government Printing Office, 1982).
20. Brandon Centerwall, "Exposure to Television as a Risk Factor for Violence," *American Journal of Epidemiology* 129 (April 1989): 643–52.

## CHAPTER SEVEN

1. Gaetano Mosca, *The Ruling Class* (New York: McGraw-Hill, 1939), p. 51.
2. James Madison, *Federalist Papers,* No. 10, reprinted in the Appendix.
3. George Washington, Farewell Address, September 17, 1796, in *Documents on American History,* 10th ed., eds. Henry Steele Commager and Milton Cantor. Englewood Cliffs, N.J.: Prentice Hall, 1988), 1: 172.
4. E. E. Schattschneider, *Party Government* (New York: Holt, Rinehart, and Winston, 1942), p. 1.
5. Conventions continue to play a modest role in nominations in some states:

   - Colorado: Parties may hold a preprimary convention to designate a candidate to be listed first on the primary ballot. All candidates receiving at least 30 percent of the delegate vote will be listed on the primary ballot.
   - Connecticut: Party conventions are held to endorse candidates. If no one challenges the endorsed candidate, no primary election is held. If a challenger receives 20 percent of the delegate vote, a primary election will be held to determine the party's nominee in the general election.
   - New York: Party conventions choose the party's "designated" candidate in primary elections. Anyone receiving 25 percent of the delegates also appears on the ballot.
   - Utah: Party conventions select party's nominees.
   - Illinois, Indiana, Michigan, and South Carolina: Party conventions nominate candidates for some minor state offices.

6. For an argument that primary elections force parties to be more responsive to voters, see John G. Geer and Mark E. Shere, "Party Competition and the Prisoner's Dilemma: An Argument for the Direct Primary," *Journal of Politics* 54 (August 1992): 365–74.

7. For an up-to-date listing of state primaries and relevant information about them, see *The Book of the States,* published biannually by the Council of State Governments, Lexington, Kentucky.
8. Louisiana is unique in its nonpartisan statewide primary and general elections. All candidates, regardless of party affiliation, run in the same primary election. If a candidate gets more than 50 percent of the vote, he or she wins the office outright; otherwise the top two vote-getters, regardless of party affiliation, face off in the second election.
9. See John M. Bruce, John A. Clark, and John H. Kessel, "Advocacy Politics in Presidential Parties," *American Political Science Review* 85 (December 1991): 1115–25.
10. For evidence that the national party conventions raise the poll standings of their presidential nominees, see James E. Campbell, Lynna L. Cherry, and Kenneth A. Wink, "The Convention Bump," *American Politics Quarterly* 20 (July 1992): 287–307.
11. *Gallup Poll Monthly,* November 1994.
12. See John A. Clark, John M. Bruce, John H. Kessel, and William G. Jacoby, "I'd Rather Switch Than Fight: Lifelong Democrats and Converts to Republicanism among Campaign Activists," *American Journal of Political Science* 35 (August 1991): 577–97.
13. For a scholarly debate over realignment, see Byron E. Schafer, ed., *The End of Realignment: Interpreting American Election Eras* (Madison: University of Wisconsin Press, 1991).
14. See Harold W. Stanley and Richard G. Niemi, "Partisanship and Group Support, 1952–1988," *American Politics Quarterly* 19 (April 1991): 189–210; Patricia Hurley, "Partisan Realignment in the 1980's," *Journal of Politics* 53 (February 1991): 55–63.
15. Yankelovich survey, reported in *American Enterprise* 6 (May/June 1995): 105.
16. Quoted in *Newsweek,* August 29, 1995, p. 37.

## CHAPTER EIGHT

1. Gerald Pomper, *Elections in America* (New York: Dodd, Mead, 1968).
2. Morris P. Fiorina, *Retrospective Voting in American National Elections* (New Haven, Conn.: Yale University Press, 1988).
3. John Stuart Mill, *Considerations on Representative Government* (1859; reprint, Chicago: Regnery Gateway, 1962), p. 144.
4. Quoted in *Congressional Quarterly Almanac, 1965* (Washington, D.C.: Congressional Quarterly, Inc., 1966), p. 267.

5. Alan Ehrenhalt, *The United States of Ambition: Politicians, Power and the Pursuit of Office* (New York: Random House, 1991), p. 22.
6. Alan I. Abramowitz, "Incumbency, Campaign Spending, and the Decline of Competition in U.S. House Elections," *Journal of Politics* 53 (February 1991): 55–70.
7. In the important U.S. Supreme Court decision in *Buckley v. Valeo* in 1976, James L. Buckley, former U.S. Senator from New York, and his

brother, William F. Buckley, the well-known conservative commentator, argued successfully that the laws limiting an individual's right to participate in political campaigns—financially or otherwise—violated First Amendment freedoms. Specifically, the U.S. Supreme Court held that no government could limit individuals' rights to spend money or publish or broadcast their own views on issues or elections. Candidates can spend as much of their own money as they wish on their own campaigns. Private individuals can spend as much as they wish to circulate their own views on an election, although their contributions to candidates and parties can still be limited. The Court, however, permitted governmental limitations on parties and campaign organizations and allowed the use of federal funds for financing campaigns. *Buckley v. Valeo,* 424 U.S. 1 (1976).

8. David J. Lanoue and Peter R. Schrott, *The Joint Press Conference: History, Impact, and Prospects of American Presidential Debates* (Westport, Conn.: Greenwood Press, 1991).

## CHAPTER NINE

1. Political scientist David Truman defined an interest group as "any group that is based on one or more shared attitudes and makes certain demands upon other groups or organizations in society." See *The Governmental Process* (New York: Knopf, 1971), p. 33.
2. Quoted in *Los Angeles Times,* January 19, 1981, and in Jay M. Shafritz, ed., *The HarperCollins Dictionary of American Politics* (New York: HarperCollins, 1992), p. 299.
3. James Madison, *Federalist Papers,* No. 10, reprinted in the Appendix.
4. Ibid.
5. Gale Research Company, *Encyclopedia of Associations,* 29th ed. (Detroit: Gale Research, 1995).
6. For both theory and survey data on the sources of interest-group mobilization, see Jack L. Walker, *Mobilizing Interest Groups in America: Patrons, Professions, and Social Movements* (Ann Arbor: University of Michigan Press, 1991).
7. Kay Lehman Scholzman, "What Accent the Heavenly Chorus? Political Equality and the American Pressure System," *Journal of Politics,* 46 (November 1984): 1006–32; see also Jeffrey M. Berry, Kent E. Portney, and Ken Thomson, *The Case for Participatory Democracy* (Washington: Brookings Institution, 1994).
8. For evidence that vote buying on congressional roll calls is rare, see Janet M. Grenzke, "Shopping in the Congressional Supermarket: The

## CHAPTER TEN

1. James Madison, *Federalist Papers,* No. 10, reprinted in the Appendix.
2. Ibid.
3. Quoted in Jay M. Schafritz, *The HarperCollins Dictionary of American Government and Politics* (New York: HarperCollins, 1992), p. 56.
4. *McGrain v. Dougherty,* 273 U.S. 13J (1927).
5. *Baker v. Carr,* 369 U.S. 186 (1962); *Wesberry v. Sanders,* 370 U.S. 1 (1964).
6. *Gray v. Sanders,* 322 U.S. 368 (1963).
7. *Gaffney v. Cummings,* 412 U.S. 763 (1973).
8. *Davis v. Bandemer,* 478 U.S. 109 (1986).
9. *Thornburg v. Gingles,* 478 U.S. 30 (1986).
10. *Shaw v. Reno* 125 L Ed 2d 511 (1993).
11. *Miller v. Johnson,* June 29, 1995.
12. For an in-depth analysis of who decides to run for Congress and who does not, see Linda L. Fowler and Robert D. McClure, *Political Ambition: Who Decides to Run for Congress* (New Haven, Conn.: Yale University Press, 1990).
13. See Robert A. Bernstein, *Elections, Representation, and Congressional Voting Behavior* (Englewood Cliffs, N.J.: Prentice Hall, 1989).
14. See Gary Jacobson, *The Politics of Congressional Elections,* 3d ed. (New York: HarperCollins, 1992).
15. See David Epstein and Peter Zemsky, "Money Talks: Deterring Qual-

9. University-based political scientists rely heavily on a series of National Election Studies, originated at the Survey Research Center at the University of Michigan, which have surveyed the voting-age population in every presidential election and most congressional elections since 1952.
10. For an assessment of gender issues in Clinton's victory, see Marian Lief Palley, "Elections 1992 and the Thomas Appointment," *P. S.: Political Science and Politics* 26 (March 1993):28–31.
11. See Martin P. Wattenberg, *The Rise of Candidate-Centered Politics* (Cambridge, Mass.: Harvard University Press, 1991).
12. For an argument that voters look ahead to the economic future and reward or punish the president based on rational expectations, see Michael B. MacKuen, Robert S. Erickson, and James A. Stimson, "Peasants or Bankers? The American Electorate and the U.S. Economy," *American Political Science Review* 86 (September 1992):680–95.

Currency Is Complex," *American Journal of Political Science* 33 (February 1989): 1–24. But for evidence that committee participation by members of Congress is influenced by political action committee money, see Richard L. Hall and Frank W. Wayman, "Buying Time: Moneyed Interests and the Mobilization of Bias in Congressional Committees," *American Political Science Review* 84 (September 1990): 797–819.
9. See, for example, Mark E. Patterson, "The Presidency and Organized Interests: White House Patterns of Interest Group Liaison," *American Political Science Review* 86 (September 1992): 612–22.
10. Paul Starobin, "Merchant Marine: Too Close to Its Clients," *National Journal,* June 11, 1988.
11. For evidence that interest groups are no more likely to win their cases than other litigants, however, see Lee Epstein and C. K. Rowland, "Debunking the Myth of Interest Group Invincibility in the Courts," *American Political Science Review* 85 (March 1991): 55–65.
12. *Brown v. Board of Education of Topeka,* 349 U.S. 294 (1955).
13. Samuel Huntington, *Political Order in Changing Societies* (New Haven, Conn.: Yale University Press, 1965), p. 28.
14. Mancur Olson, *The Rise and Decline of Nations* (New Haven, Conn.: Yale University Press, 1982).

ity Challengers in Congressional Elections," *American Political Science Review* 89 (June 1995): 295–322.
16. See Thomas E. Mann and Raymond Wolfinger, "Candidates and Parties in Congressional Elections," *American Political Science Review* 84 (September 1990): 545–64.
17. See Mary T. Hanna, "Political Science Caught Flat-Footed by Midterm Elections," *Chronicle of Higher Education,* November 30, 1994, pp. B1–2.
18. See Michael Malbin, *Unelected Representatives* (New York: Basic Books, 1980).
19. U.S. House of Representatives, Commission on Administrative Review, *Administrative Reorganization and Legislative Management,* 95th Cong., 1st sess., H. Doc. 95-232, pp. 17–19.
20. Richard F. Fenno, *Home Style* (Boston: Little Brown, 1978).
21. John R. Johannes, "Casework in the House," in *The House at Work,* ed. Joseph Cooper (Austin: University of Texas Press, 1981).
22. Glenn R. Parker, *Characteristics of Congress* (Englewood Cliffs, N.J.: Prentice Hall, 1989), p. 30.
23. See David W. Rohde, *Parties and Leaders in the Postreform House* (Chicago: University of Chicago Press, 1991).
24. Barbara Sinclair, "The Emergence of Strong Leadership in the House of Representatives," *Journal of Politics* 54 (August 1992): 657–84.

25. Roger H. Davidson and Walter J. Oleszek, *Congress and Its Members* (Washington, D.C.: Congressional Quarterly Press, 1981), p. 170.

26. John R. Hibbing, *Congressional Careers* (Chapel Hill, N.C.: University of North Carolina Press, 1991).

27. See John W. Kingdon, *Congressmen's Voting Decisions,* 3d ed. (Ann Arbor: University of Michigan Press, 1989).

28. Ibid., p. 41.

29. Larry Markinson, *The Cash Constituents of Congress* (Washington, D.C.: Congressional Quarterly Press, 1992).

30. Kingdon, *Congressmen's Voting Decisions,* pp. 31-32.

31. Donald Matthews, *U.S. Senators and Their World* (New York: Vintage Books, 1960).

32. David Rohde, Norman J. Ornstein, and Robert L. Peabody, "Political Change and Legislative Norms," in *Studies of Congress,* ed. Glenn R. Parker (Washington, D.C.: Congressional Quarterly Press, 1985), p. 175.

33. See John R. Hibbing, "Contours of the Modern Congressional Career," *American Political Science Review* 85 (June 1991): 405–28.

34. Parker, *Characteristics of Congress,* p. 12.

35. Richard Fenno, *Power of the Purse* (Boston: Little Brown, 1965), p. 620.

36. Ibid., p. 73.

## CHAPTER ELEVEN

1. For an argument that presidents encourage people to think of them as "the single head of government and moral leader of the nation who speaks for all of the people," see Barbara Hinckley, *The Symbolic Presidency: How Presidents Portray Themselves* (New York: Routledge, 1991).

2. See Theodore Lowi, *The Personal President* (Ithaca, N.Y.: Cornell University Press, 1987).

3. See Michael Less Benedict, *The Impeachment and Trial of Andrew Johnson* (New York: Norton, 1973).

4. William Howard Taft, *Our Chief Magistrate and His Powers* (New York: Columbia University Press, 1938), p. 138, reprinted in *The Presidency,* ed. John P. Roche (New York: Harcourt Brace Jovanovich, 1964), p. 23.

5. Quoted in Arthur B. Tourtellot, *Presidents on the Presidency* (New York: Doubleday, 1964), pp. 55–56.

6. Quoted in James MacGregor Burns, *John Kennedy: A Political Profile* (New York: Harcourt Brace, 1959), p. 275.

7. Quoted in Richard Neustadt, *Presidential Power* (New York: Wiley, 1960), p. 9.

8. See George C. Edwards, *The Public Presidency* (New York: St. Martin's Press, 1983). See also Richard A. Brody, *Assessing Presidents: The Media, Elite Opinion, and Public Support* (Stanford, Calif.: Stanford University Press, 1991).

9. See Paul Brace and Barbara Hinckley, "The Structure of Presidential Approval," *Journal of Politics* 53 (November 1991): 993–1017.

10. See Charles Ostrom and Dennis Simon, "The President's Public," *American Journal of Political Science* 32 (November 1988): 1096–1119; and Ostrow and Simon, "The President and the Political Use of Force," *American Political Science Review* 80 (June 1986): 541–66.

11. John Mueller, *War, Presidents, and Public Opinion* (New York: John Wiley, 1973).

12. For an irreverent description of White House reporting, see Sam Donaldson, *Hold On, Mr. President* (New York: Random House, 1987).

13. See Congressional Quarterly, *Powers of the Presidency* (Washington, D.C.: Congressional Quarterly Press, 1989), p. 87.

14. See also Jeffrey E. Cohen, *The Politics of the U.S. Cabinet* (Pittsburgh: University of Pittsburgh Press, 1988).

15. See Stanley Rothman and S. Robert Lichter, "How Liberal Are Bureaucrats?" *Regulation,* November–December 1983, pp. 16–22, for survey data on the voting behavior and political ideology of federal bureaucrats. Earlier studies asserted that the party identification of bureaucrats reflected that of the general public; see Steven Thomas Seitz, *Bureaucracy, Policy and the Public* (St. Louis: Mosby, 1978).

16. See Bradley H. Patterson, Jr., *The Ring of Power* (New York: Basic Books, 1988).

17. John Kingdon, *Agenda, Alternatives, and Public Policies* (Boston: Little, Brown, 1984), p. 25.

18. Aage Clausen, *How Congressmen Decide* (New York: St. Martin's Press, 1973).

19. See Daniel E. Ingberman and Dennis A. Yao, "Presidential Commitment and the Veto," *American Journal of Political Science* 35 (May 1991): 357–89.

20. See also Samuel B. Hoff, "Saying No," *American Politics Quarterly* 19 (July 1991): 310–23.

21. For a discussion of the factors affecting the use of the presidential veto, see John T. Woolley, "Institutions, the Election Cycle, and the Presidential Veto," *American Journal of Political Science* 35 (May 1991): 279–304.

22. G. J. A. O'Toole, *Honorable Treachery: A History of U.S. Intelligence from the American Revolution to the CIA* (New York: Atlantic Monthly Press, 1991).

23. *Mora v. McNamara,* 389 U.S. 934 (1964); *Massachusetts v. Laird,* 400 U.S. 886 (1970). The Court specifically refused to intervene in the conduct of the Vietnam War by Presidents Johnson and Nixon.

24. *In re Debs,* 158 U.S. 504 (1895).

25. Jules Witcover, *Crap Shoot: Rolling the Dice on the Vice Presidency* (New York: Crow Publishing, 1992).

## CHAPTER TWELVE

1. "Red tape" derives its meaning from the use of reddish tape by seventeenth-century English courts to bind legal documents. Unwrapping court orders entangled one in "red tape." See Herbert Kaufman, *Red Tape: Its Uses and Abuses* (Washington: Brookings Institution, 1977).

2. H. H. Gerth and C. Wright Mills, *From Max Weber* (New York: Oxford Press, 1958).

3. James Q. Wilson, *Bureaucracy: What Government Agencies Do and Why They Do It* (New York: Basic Books, 1989).

4. William Niskanen, *Bureaucracy and Representative Government* (Chicago: Aldine, 1971).

5. *The United States Government Manual 1995/96* (Washington, D.C.: Government Printing Office, 1995).

6. The constitutional question of whether Congress can establish an executive branch commission and protect its members from dismissal by the president was settled in *Humphrey's Executor v. United States* (1935). Franklin Roosevelt fired Humphrey from the Federal Trade Commission despite a fixed term set by Congress. Humphrey died shortly afterward, and when the executors of his estate sued for his back pay, the Supreme Court ruled that his firing was illegal.

7. See Nicholas Henry, *Public Administration and Public Affairs,* 6th ed. (Englewood Cliffs, NJ: Prentice Hall, 1996), ch. 11.

8. See Michael Nelson, "The Short Ironic History of American National Bureaucracy," *Journal of Politics* 44 (August 1982):747-78.

9. Quoted in U.S. Civil Service Commission, *Biography of an Ideal: A History of the Civil Service System* (Washington, D.C.: Government Printing Office, 1973), p. 16.

10. Congress sought to further protect federal employees from partisan politics in the Hatch Act of 1939, which bans federal civil servants

from partisan political activity, including running for public office, soliciting campaign funds, or campaigning for or against a party or a candidate. In the cases of *United States v. Mitchell* (1979) and *Civil Service Commission v. Letter Carriers* (1973), the Supreme Court upheld the Hatch Act against charges that it unconstitutionally denied federal employees their political rights.

11. Quoted in David Rosenbloom, "Public Personnel Reforms," *Policy Studies Journal,* November 1981, p. 1232.
12. See U.S. House of Representatives Committee on Post Office and Civil Service, *The Senior Executive Service* (Washington, D.C.: Government Printing Office, 1984).
13. See Stanley Rothman and S. Robert Lichter, "How Liberal Are the Bureaucrats?" *Regulation,* November–December 1983.
14. Aaron Wildavsky, *The New Politics of the Budgetary Process* (Glenview, Ill.: Scott, Foresman, 1988), p. 8.
15. See also Lance T. LeLoup, *Budgetary Politics,* 4th ed. (Brunswick, Ohio: Kings Court, 1988).
16. See Lawrence J. White, *Reforming Regulation* (Englewood Cliffs, N.J.: Prentice Hall, 1981).

## CHAPTER THIRTEEN

1. Alexis de Tocqueville, *Democracy in America* (1835; New York: Mentor Books, 1956), p. 75.
2. Felix Frankfurter, "The Supreme Court and the Public," *Forum* 83 (June 1930): 332.
3. Alexander Hamilton, *Federalist Papers,* No. 78 (New York: Modern Library, 1937), p. 505.
4. *Marbury v. Madison,* 1 Cranch 137 (1803).
5. *Dred Scott v. Sandford,* 19 Howard 393 (1857).
6. *National Labor Relations Board v. Jones and Laughlin Steel Corp.,* 301 U.S. 1 (1937).
7. *Buckley v. Valeo,* 424 U.S. 1 (1976).
8. *Immigration and Naturalization Service v. Chadha,* 462 U.S. 919 (1983).
9. *Ex parte Milligan,* 4 Wallace 2 (1866).
10. *Youngstown Sheet and Tube Co. v. Sawyer,* 343 U.S. 579 (1952).
11. *United States v. Nixon,* 418 U.S. 683 (1974).
12. *Brown v. Board of Education of Topeka,* 347 U.S. 483 (1954).
13. *Roe v. Wade,* 410 U.S. 113 (1973).
14. Lawrence Baum, *The Supreme Court,* 4th ed. (Washington, D.C.: Congressional Quarterly Press, 1992).
15. *West Virginia Board of Education v. Barnette,* 319 U.S. 624 (1943).
16. Quoted in Henry J. Abraham, *Justices and Presidents,* 3d ed. (New York: Oxford University Press, 1992), p. 7.
17. Quoted in Charles P. Curtis, *Lions under the Throne* (Boston: Houghton Mifflin, 1947), p. 281.
18. William O. Douglas, "Stare Decisis," *Record,* April 1947, cited in Henry J. Abraham, *The Judicial Process* (New York: Oxford University Press, 1968), p. 58.
19. *Flast v. Cohen,* 392 U.S. 83 (1968).
20. *Gideon v. Wainwright,* 372 U.S. 335 (1963).
21. *Missouri v. Jenkins,* 110 S. C.1651 (1990).
22. Robert Scigliano, *The Supreme Court and the Presidency* (New York: Free Press, 1971), pp. 147–48.
23. John R. Schmidhauser, *The Supreme Court* (New York: Holt Rinehart, Winston, 1960), p. 59.
24. At one time the U.S. Supreme Court was legally required to accept certain "writs of appeal," but today very few cases come to Court in this fashion.
25. *University of California Regents v. Bakke,* 438 U.S. 265 (1978).
26. Archibald Cox, *The Role of the Supreme Court in American Government* (New York: Oxford University Press, 1976), p. 103.
27. *Abington School District v. Schempp,* 374 U.S. 203 (1963).
28. President Andrew Jackson's comments came in response to the Court's ruling in the case of *Cherokee Nation v. Georgia* (1831) and *Worcester v. Georgia* (1832), which forbade the federal or state governments from seizing Native American lands and forcing the people to move. Refusal by Jackson, an old "Indian fighter," to enforce the Court's decisions resulted in the infamous "Trail of Tears," the forced march of the Georgia Cherokees that left one-quarter of them dead along the path west.
29. See Baum, *Supreme Court,* p. 233.
30. *Grove City College v. Bell,* 465 U.S. 555 (1984).
31. *Pollock v. Farmer's Loan,* 158 U.S. 601 (1895).

## CHAPTER FOURTEEN

1. James Madison, *Federalist Papers,* No. 10, reprinted in the Appendix.
2. *West Virginia Board of Education v. Barnette,* 319 U.S. 624 (1943).
3. *Barron v. Baltimore,* 7 Peters 243 (1833).
4. *Slaughter-House Cases,* 16 Wallace 36 (1873).
5. *Hurtado v. California,* 110 U.S. 516 (1884).
6. *Gitlow v. New York,* 268 U.S. 652 (1925).
7. For an argument that Madison and some other framers not only were concerned with lessening religious conflict but also were hostile to religion generally, see Thomas Lindsay, "James Madison on Religion and Politics," *American Political Science Review* 85 (December 1991): 1051–65.
8. *Reynolds v. United States,* 98 U.S. 145 (1879).
9. *Pierce v. Society of Sisters,* 268 U.S. 510 (1925).
10. *Cantwell v. Connecticut,* 310 U.S. 296 (1940).
11. *Employment Division v. Smith,* 494 U.S. 872 (1990).
12. *Wisconsin v. Yoder,* 406 U.S. 295 (1972).
13. *Bob Jones University v. United States,* 461 U.S. 574 (1983).
14. *Lukumi Babalu Aye v. Hialeah,* 125 L.Ed. 472 (1993).
15. *Everson v. Board of Education,* 330 U.S. 1, 15, 16 (1947).
16. Ibid.
17. *Zorach v. Clausen,* 343 U.S. 306 (1952).
18. Opening public meetings with prayer was ruled constitutional as "a tolerable acknowledgment of beliefs widely held among the people of this country." *Marsh v. Chambers,* 463 U.S. 783 (1983).
19. *Lemon v. Kurtzman,* 403 U.S. 602 (1971).
20. *Muebler v. Adams,* 463 U.S. 388 (1983).
21. *Tilton v. Richardson,* 403 U.S. 672 (1971).
22. *Walz v. Tax Commission,* 397 U.S. 664 (1970).

17. *Statistical Abstract of the United States, 1992,* p. 629.
18. For research suggesting that the appointive power is a more important instrument of political control of the bureaucracy than budgets or legislation, see B. Dan Wood and Richard W. Waterman, "The Dynamics of Political Control of the Bureaucracy," *American Political Science Review* 83 (September 1991): 801–28.
19. See Joel D. Aberbach, *Keeping a Watchful Eye: The Politics of Congressional Oversight* (Washington, D.C.: Brookings Institution, 1990).
20. Evidence of the effectiveness of interventions by members of Congress in local offices of federal agencies is provided by John T. Scholz, Jim Twombly, and Barbara Headrick, "Street-Level Political Controls over Federal Bureaucracy," *American Political Science Review* 85 (September 1991): 829–50.
21. *Immigration and Naturalization Service v. Chadha,* 462 U.S. 9191 (1983).
22. Bradley Cannon and Michael Giles, "Recurring Litigants: Federal Agencies before the Supreme Court," *Western Political Quarterly* 15 (September 1972):183–91.
23. Reginald S. Sheehan, "Federal Agencies and the Supreme Court," *American Politics Quarterly* 20 (October 1992): 478–500.

23. *Board of Education v. Mergens*, 497 U.S. 111 (1990).

24. *McGowan v. Maryland*, 366 U.S. 429 (1961), and *Braunfeld v. Brown*, 366 U.S. 599 (1961).

25. *Allegheny County v. American Civil Liberties Union, Greater Pittsburgh Chapter*, 492 U.S. 573 (1989).

26. *Engle v. Vitale*, 370 U.S. 421 (1962).

27. *Abington School District v. Schempp*, 374 U.S. 203 (1963).

28. *Wallace v. Jaffree*, 472 U.S. 38 (1985).

29. *Wisconsin v. Yoder*, 406 U.S. 295 (1972).

30. *Employment Division v. Smith*, 494 U.S. 872 (1990).

31. *Schenck v. United States*, 249 U.S. 47 (1919).

32. *Gitlow v. New York*, 268 U.S. 652 (1925).

33. *Schenck v. United States*, 249 U.S. 47, 52 (1919).

34. *Whitney v. California*, 274 U.S. 357, 377 (1927), concurring opinion.

35. *Thomas v. Collins*, 323 U.S. 516 (1945).

36. *Dennis v. United States*, 341 U.S. 494 (1951).

37. *Yates v. United States*, 354 U.S. 298 (1957).

38. *Albertson v. Subversive Activities Control Board*, 382 U.S. 70 (1965).

39. *Whitehill v. Elkins*, 389 U.S. 54 (1967).

40. *United States v. Robel*, 389 U.S. 258 (1967).

41. *Aptheker v. Secretary of State*, 378 U.S. 500 (1964).

42. *Tinker v. Des Moines Independent Community School District*, 393 U.S. 503 (1969).

43. *Brandenburg v. Ohio*, 395 U.S. 444 (1969).

44. *Texas v. Johnson*, 491 U.S. 397 (1989).

45. *United States v. O'Brien*, 391 U.S. 367 (1968).

46. *Texas v. Johnson*, 491 U.S. 397 (1989).

47. *Chaplinsky v. New Hampshire*, 315 U.S. 568 (1942).

48. *Terminiello v. Chicago*, 337 U.S. 1 (1949).

49. *Virginia State Board of Pharmacy v. Virginia Consumer Council, Inc.*, 425 U.S. 748 (1976).

50. *Bates v. Arizona State Bar*, 433 U.S. 350 (1977).

51. *Linmark Associates, Inc. v. Township of Willingboro*, 431 U.S. 85 (1977).

52. *Bigelow v. Virginia*, 421 U.S. 809 (1975).

53. *New York Times v. Sullivan*, 376 U.S. 254 (1964).

54. *Gertz v. Robert Welch, Inc.*, 418 U.S. 323 (1974).

55. *Roth v. United States*, 354 U.S. 476 (1957).

56. *Jacobellis v. Ohio*, 378 U.S. 184 (1964).

57. *Roth v. United States*, 354 U.S. 476 (1957).

58. *Jacobellis v. Ohio*, 378 U.S. 184 (1964).

59. *Roth v. United States*, 354 U.S. 476 (1957).

60. Bob Woodward and Scott Armstrong, *The Brethren* (New York: Avon, 1979), p. 233.

61. *Miller v. California*, 5413 U.S. 15 (1973).

62. Joseph F. Kobylka, *The Politics of Obscenity* (Westport, Conn.: Greenwood Press, 1991).

63. *New York v. Ferber*, 458 U.S. 747 (1982).

64. William Blackstone, *Blackstone's Commentaries on the Law*, ed. Bernard C. Gavit (Washington, D.C.: Washington Law Book Co., 1941), p. 814.

65. *Near v. Minnesota*, 283 U.S. 697 (1931).

66. *New York Times v. United States*, 403 U.S. 713 (1971).

67. *Mutual Film Corp. v. Industrial Commission*, 236 U.S. 230 (1915).

68. *Times Film Corporation v. Chicago*, 365 U.S. 43 (1961).

69. *Freedman v. Maryland*, 380 U.S. 51 (1965).

70. *Young v. American Mini Theaters, Inc.*, 427 U.S. 50 (1976).

71. *Red Lion Broadcasting Co. v. Federal Communications Commission*, 395 U.S. 367 (1969).

72. *Miami Herald Publishing Co. v. Tornillo*, 418 U.S. 241 (1974).

73. *Branzburg v. Hayes*, 408 U.S. 665 (1972).

74. *Zurcher v. Stanford Daily*, 436 U.S. 547 (1978).

75. *NAACP v. Alabama ex rel. Patterson*, 357 U.S. 449 (1958).

76. *Healy v. James*, 408 U.S. 169 (1972).

77. *National Socialist Party of America v. Skokie*, 432 U.S. 43 (1977).

78. *Frisby v. Schultz*, 487 U.S. 474 (1988).

79. James Madison, *Federalist Papers*, No. 46.

80. U.S. Department of Justice, *Criminal Victimization in the United States* (Washington, D.C.: Bureau of Justice Statistics, published annually).

81. See Wesley G. Skogan, "The Validity of Official Crime Statistics: Empirical Investigation," *Social Science Quarterly* 55 (June 1974): 25–38.

82. *Ex parte Milligan*, 4 Wallace 2 (1866).

83. *Duncan v. Kahanamosby*, 327 U.S. 304 (1946).

84. *Illinois v. Gates*, 462 U.S. 213 (1983).

85. *Arizona v. Hicks*, 480 U.S. 321 (1987).

86. *United States v. Watson*, 423 U.S. 411 (1976).

87. *Payton v. New York*, 445 U.S. 573 (1980).

88. *Spano v. New York*, 360 U.S. 315 (1959).

89. *Gideon v. Wainwright*, 372 U.S. 335 (1963).

90. *Escobedo v. Illinois*, 378 U.S. 478 (1964).

91. *Miranda v. Arizona*, 384 U.S. 436 (1966).

92. Stephen Wasby, *The Impact of the United States Supreme Court* (Homewood, Ill.: Dorsey Press, 1970).

93. *Mapp v. Ohio*, 367 U.S. 643 (1961).

94. *United States v. Leon*, 468 U.S. 897 (1984).

95. *United States v. Salerno*, 481 U.S. 739 (1987).

96. *Illinois v. Allen*, 397 U.S. 337 (1970).

97. *Maryland v. Craig*, 497 U.S. 1 (1990).

98. *Brady v. Maryland*, 373 U.S. 83 (1963).

99. *Batson v. Kentucky*, 476 U.S. 79 (1986).

100. *Sheppard v. Maxwell*, 384 U.S. 333 (1966).

101. *Williams v. Florida*, 399 U.S. 78 (1970).

102. *Johnson v. Louisiana*, 406 U.S. 356 (1972); *Apodaca v. Oregon*, 406 U.S. 404 (1972).

103. U.S. Department of Justice, *The Prevalence of Guilty Pleas* (Washington, D.C.: Government Printing Office, 1984).

104. *Furman v. Georgia*, 408 U.S. 238 (1972).

105. *Gregg v. Georgia*, 428 U.S. 153 (1976); *Proffitt v. Florida*, 428 U.S. 242 (1976); *Jurek v. Texas*, 428 U.S. 262 (1976).

106. *McCleskey v. Kemp*, 481 U.S. 279 (1987).

## CHAPTER FIFTEEN

1. See Sidney Verba and Gary R. Orren, *Equality in America* (Cambridge, Mass.: Harvard University Press, 1985).

2. *Dred Scott v. Sandford*, 19 How. 393 (1857).

3. See C. Vann Woodward, *Reunion and Reaction* (Boston: Little Brown, 1951), and Woodward, *The Strange Career of Jim Crow* (New York: Oxford University Press, 1957).

4. Civil Rights Cases, 100 U.S. 3 (1883).

5. *Plessy v. Ferguson*, 163 U.S. 537 (1896).

6. *Sweatt v. Painter*, 339 U.S. 629 (1950).

7. *Brown v. Board of Education of Topeka*, 347 U.S. 483 (1954).

8. Kenneth Clark, *Dark Ghetto* (New York: Harper & Row, 1965), p. 75.

9. The Supreme Court ruled that Congress was bound to respect the Equal Protection Clause of the Fourteenth Amendment even though the amendment is directed at states, because equal protection is a liberty guaranteed by the Fifth Amendment. *Bolling v. Sharpe*, 347 U.S. 497 (1954).

10. *Brown v. Board of Education of Topeka* (II), 349 U.S. 294 (1955).

11. *Alexander v. Holmes Board of Education*, 396 U.S. 19 (1969).

12. *Swann v. Charlotte-Mecklenburg County Board of Education*, 402 U.S. 1 (1971).

13. *Milliken v. Bradley*, 418 U.S. 717 (1974).

14. *Board of Education v. Dowell*, 498 U.S. 550 (1991).

15. Martin Luther King, Jr., "Letter from Birmingham City Jail," April 16, 1963.

16. *University of California Regents v. Bakke,* 438 U.S. 265 (1978).
17. Bakke's overall grade point average was 3.46, while the average for special admissions students was 2.62. Bakke's MCAT scores were: verbal, 96; quantitative, 94; science, 97; general information, 72. The average MCAT scores for special admissions students were: verbal, 34; quantitative, 30; science, 37; general information, 18.
18. *United Steelworkers of America v. Weber,* 443 U.S. 193 (1979).
19. *United States v. Paradise,* 480 U.S. 149 (1987).
20. *Firefighters Local Union 1784 v. Stotts,* 467 U.S. 561 (1984).
21. *City of Richmond v. Crosen Co.,* 488 U.S. 469 (1989).
22. See Justice Antonin Scalia's dissenting opinion in *Johnson v. Transportation Agency of Santa Clara County,* 480 U.S. 616 (1987).
23. *Adarand Construction v. Pena,* 132 L Ed 2d 158 (1995).
24. *Wards Cove Packing Co., Inc., v. Antonio,* 490 U.S. 642 (1989).
25. *Congressional Quarterly Weekly Report,* June 8, 1991, p. 1501.
26. Martin Luther King, Jr., "I Have a Dream" speech, August 28, 1963, in David J. Garrow, *Bearing the Cross: Martin Luther King, Jr., and the Southern Christian Leadership Conference* (New York: Viking Books, 1988), p. 284.
27. Thomas Sowell, *Preferential Treatment: An International Perspective* (New York: William Morrow, 1990).
28. Quoted in *U.S. News and World Report,* February 13, 1995, p. 35.
29. *Bradwell v. Illinois,* 16 Wall 130 (1873).
30. *Reed v. Reed,* 404 U.S. 71 (1971).
31. *Stanton v. Stanton,* 421 U.S. 7 (1975).
32. *Craig v. Boren,* 429 U.S. 190 (1976).
33. *Dothard v. Rawlinson,* 433 U.S. 321 (1977).
34. *Arizona v. Norris,* 103 S. Ct. 3492 (1983).

35. *EEOC v. Madison Community School District,* 55 U.S.L.W. 2644 (1987).
36. *Michael M. v. Superior Court of Sonoma County,* 450 U.S. 464 (1981).
37. *Rostker v. Goldberg,* 453 U.S. 57 (1981).
38. *Statistical Abstract of the United States, 1995,* p. 403.
39. National Research Council, National Academy of Sciences, *Women's Work, Men's Work* (Washington, D.C.: National Academy Press, 1985).
40. See Thomas R. Dye, *Who's Running America?* 6th ed. (Englewood Cliffs, N.J.: Prentice Hall, 1994).
41. Susan Fraker, "Why Women Aren't Getting to the Top," *Fortune,* April 16, 1984, pp. 40–45.
42. Rudolpho O. dela Garza et al., *Latino Voices: Mexican, Puerto Rican, and Cuban Perspectives on American Politics* (Boulder, Colo.: Westview Press, 1992).
43. See F. Luis Garcia, *Latinos in the Political System* (Notre Dame, Ind.: Notre Dame University Press, 1988).
44. Linda Chavez, "Tequila Sunrise: The Slow But Steady Progress of Hispanic Immigrants," *Policy Review* (Spring 1989): 64–67.
45. *Morton v. Mancari,* 417 U.S. 535 (1974).
46. See Joseph P. Shapiro, *No Pity: People with Disabilities Forging a New Civil Rights Movement* (New York: Times Books/Random House, 1993).
47. *San Antonio Independent School District v. Rodriquez,* 411 U.S. 1 (1973).
48. *Williamson v. Lee Optical of Oklahoma,* 348 U.S. 483 (1955).
49. *Gideon v. Wainright,* 372 U.S. 335 (1963).
50. *Harper v. Virginia State Board of Elections,* 383 U.S. 663 (1966).
51. *Harris v. McRae,* 448 U.S. 297 (1980).
52. *Rodriquez v. San Antonio Independent School District,* 411 U.S. 1 (1973).
53. *Serrano v. Priest,* 5 Cal. 3d 584 (1971).

## CHAPTER SIXTEEN

1. Paul Samuelson, *Economics,* 12th ed. (New York: McGraw Hill, 1985), p. 5.
2. For an insider's account of the politics of Reagan's economic program by his former budget director, see David Stockman, *The Triumph of Politics: How the Reagan Revolution Failed* (New York: Harper & Row, 1986).
3. For an argument that the money supply expands in election years in most democracies, see Edward R. Tufte, *Political Control of the Economy* (Princeton, N.J.: Princeton University Press, 1978).
4. GDP differs very little from gross national product, GNP, which is often used to compare the performance of national economies.
5. For a revealing case study of interest-group efforts to maintain tax breaks during the struggle over the Tax Reform Act of 1986, see Jeffrey H. Birnbaum and Alan S. Murray, *Showdown at Gucci Gulch* (New York: Random House, 1986).
6. Dan Rostenkowski, speech, May 28, 1985, *Congressional Quarterly Weekly Report,* June 1, 1985, p. 1077.
7. Joseph A. Pechman, *Federal Tax Policy,* 5th ed. (Washington, D.C.: Brookings Institution, 1987).
8. In response to the question, "If Congress is able to reduce spending next year, do you think the money should be used for a tax cut or should the money be used to reduce the federal budget deficit?" 25 percent of respondents chose a tax cut, and 68 percent said reduce the deficit. *Polling Report,* November 6, 1995.

## CHAPTER SEVENTEEN

1. U.S. Bureau of the Census, *Statistical Abstract of the United States, 1995,* p. 481.
2. Christopher Jenks and Paul E. Peterson, eds., *The Urban Underclass* (Washington, D.C.: Brookings Institution, 1991). See also William A. Kelso, *Poverty and the Underclass* (New York: New York University Press, 1994).
3. See Barbara Dafoe Whitehead, "Dan Quayle Was Right," *Atlantic Monthly,* April 1993, pp. 47–80.
4. See William Julius Wilson, *The Truly Disadvantaged* (Chicago: University of Chicago Press, 1987).
5. David Ellwood, *Poor Support: Poverty in the American Family* (New York: Basic Books, 1988), p. 6.
6. Bill Clinton and Al Gore, *Putting People First* (New York: Times Books, 1992), p. 165.

## CHAPTER EIGHTEEN

1. Hans Morgenthau, *Politics among Nations,* 5th ed. (New York: Knopf, 1973), p. 27.
2. George F. Kennan, writing under the pseudonym "X," "Sources of Soviet Conduct," *Foreign Affairs* 25 (July 1947): 25.
3. New York Times, *The Pentagon Papers* (New York: Bantam Books, 1971).
4. Frank Snepp, *Decent Interval* (New York: Random House, 1977).
5. George C. Herring, *America's Longest War* (New York: Random House, 1979), p. 262.
6. International Institute for Strategic Studies, *The Military Balance, 1989–90* (London: IISS, 1989).
7. General Colin Powell, testimony, Committee on the Budget, U.S. Senate, February 3, 1992.
8. See Caspar W. Weinberger, "The Uses of Military Force," *Defense* (Arlington, Va.: American Forces Information Services Survey, 1985), pp. 2–11.
9. Morgenthau, *Power Among Nations,* p. 80.

# PHOTO CREDITS

# INDEX